MONTY: THE MAKING OF A GENERAL
1887–1942

MONTY: THE MAKING OF A GENERAL
1887–1942 breaks entirely new ground. It is the
definitive, authorised biography of Field-Marshal
Viscount Montgomery of Alamein, based on his
secret diaries, private letters and vast collection of
confidential documents. For the first time we can
follow the true relationship between Montgomery
and his mother, reflected in loyal and affectionate
letters from the Western Front – letters which give
us a vivid picture of the First World War as it
shaped the destiny of one of Britain's greatest field
commanders; the true story of Monty's marriage
and the real story of Dunkirk as Monty saw it: a
shameful defeat, the avenging of which would
become the driving force behind Montgomery's
sometimes almost insane ambition to raise a new
British army at home.

MONTY: THE MAKING OF A GENERAL will
become a lasting memorial to one of the greatest
figures of the twentieth century: a general whose
decisive victory at Alamein would become the
turning point of the Second World War. After
reading this book few will doubt Montgomery's
place in the pantheon of great commanders of all
time.

D1320517

About the Author

Nigel Hamilton was born in 1944. He was educated at Westminster school and Trinity College, Cambridge, where he studied history.

In 1966 Mr Hamilton founded the Greenwich Bookshop, and two years later published his first book, ROYAL GREENWICH (written with his mother, Olive Hamilton), hailed as a 'landmark in topographical literature in this country' by *The Scotsman*.

Mr Hamilton's much acclaimed biography of the German novelists Heinrich and Thomas Mann, THE BROTHERS MANN, was published in 1978.

Mr Hamilton lives in Suffolk with his Finnish wife and four children.

MONTY: THE MAKING OF A GENERAL 1887–1942

Nigel Hamilton

CORONET BOOKS
Hodder and Stoughton

Copyright © 1981 by Nigel Hamilton

First published in Great Britain 1981
by Hamish Hamilton Ltd

Coronet edition 1984

British Library C.I.P.

Hamilton, Nigel, *1944–*
   Monty.
   1. Montgomery of Alamein, Bernard Law
   Montgomery, *Viscount* 2. Great Britain. *Army*
   – Biography 3. Generals – Great Britain –
   Biography
   I. Title
   355.3'31'0924   DA69.3.M56

   ISBN 0-340-35482-8

Printed and bound in Great Britain for
Hodder and Stoughton Paperbacks, a
division of Hodder and Stoughton Ltd,
Mill Road, Dunton Green, Sevenoaks,
Kent (Editorial Office: 47 Bedford
Square, London, WC1 3DP) by
Richard Clay (Chaucer Press) Ltd,
Bungay, Suffolk.
Photoset by Rowland Phototypesetting Ltd,
Bury St Edmunds, Suffolk

Contents

List of Maps

Author's Note

To write a life of perhaps the most celebrated Englishman, beside Churchill, of the twentieth century, is a daunting task: the more so since I am not, by profession, a military historian. Access to all Field-Marshal Montgomery's unpublished and secret papers – letters, diaries, documents – and the uninhibited help of all the members of his family and so many of his friends, colleagues and subordinates, scarcely makes it the less daunting, for I am aware that many hundreds of thousands of people the world over wish to know 'the truth' about 'Monty' now that he has passed away and the records of his life have been thrown open.

Some will wish to know more about 'the man'; others will be concerned with the military facts of his career; others still will be seeking to know where to place the Field-Marshal in the context of modern history. Some will approach this book prejudiced in favour of 'Monty'; others against him. Some – especially those of my own generation and younger – will have no bias, merely curiosity.

I have tried to keep these various – and often conflicting – expectations in mind. However, there is a further 'voice' I have listened to: that of Field-Marshal Montgomery himself. I was twelve when I first met him, thirty-two when he died. The gift of his friendship – the manner in which he took me into his house as a second son – is not something I can ever forget; and in undertaking this biography I felt I would be repaying a debt of gratitude.

This does not mean, I hope, that my aim has been to whitewash or flatter. In inscribing a copy of his *Path to Leadership* to me in 1961, Monty wrote:

To: *Nigel Hamilton*
in the hope that he will read these pages with some profit to himself, and will not disagree with everything – although I realise this is very doubtful.

Such was, indeed, the 'sparring' nature of our relationship – and he never wished or expected me to 'agree' with him over anything save the strict rules and protocol of his household. He took me to visit Churchill – to whom he introduced me as his 'socialist friend'! – to the Staff College, Camberley, to functions, institutions, rugby and tennis matches. While I was at Cambridge he sent me to India 'to see how the other half of the world lives', and he talked to me about his life – and my life – as to an intimate friend – one whom he wanted to help in every way he could. 'As you grow older you will find that unceasing work is necessary if you want to succeed – as you will most certainly do,' he wrote to me when I was sixteen, enclosing some Swiss chocolate 'to help you through your exams – and as a small token of my affection'. His affection never wavered: even on his eighty-third birthday he was writing from his mill in Hampshire that he was there 'to help you – you must lean on me. My love to you, Nigel. Ever your friend, Montgomery of Alamein.'

In repaying Monty for his years of affection and encouragement I felt I would like to produce a biography that was readable, yet which used my training as a historian and experience in biographical research to uncover the truth behind his rise as a commander. This volume is the result, and without the help of the following people, it could not have been done.

In the first place my father, Sir Denis Hamilton, has been and remains my sponsor, military adviser and counsellor. No author, no biographer could have had more unstinting help, more selfless support than I have had from him: indeed it has been one of the joys of my life to undertake this work for him and to share the delights – and vicissitudes – of 'building' this book with him.

Second, Field-Marshal Montgomery's son David, the present Viscount Montgomery of Alamein, has been intimately involved in the project since its inception, and his support – and friendship – has meant a very great deal to me – and therefore to the book. All writings by Field-Marshal Montgomery outside the Montgomery Archive remain Viscount Montgomery's copyright; he permitted me to use everything I wished, introduced me to many members of his family and friends, and has 'been at my right hand' throughout the writing of the manuscript. He has never asked me to alter a word; indeed his wish has been that I should write this book completely without interference, in my own way, expressing my own convictions – and this support has been invaluable to me – as has been the encouragement of his wife Tessa, Lady Montgomery.

Third, I should like to thank those members of the Montgomery family who have so willingly and selflessly co-operated in the research and writing of this book: the Field-Marshal's brother Lt-Colonel Brian Montgomery, the Field-Marshal's sister Winsome (Lady Michelmore), the Field-Marshal's stepsons Lt-Colonel John and Colonel Richard Carver: their contributions, I hope, are amply reflected in the book itself. To Mrs Brian Montgomery ('Bunty'), to Mrs Jocelyn Carver, and to Mrs Audrey Carver I also extend my grateful thanks.

Fourthly, there are the scores of 'friends, colleagues and subordinates' who helped me at every turn in assembling the 'evidence' of Montgomery's life up to 1942. In almost all cases I was instantly received on my research visits as an old – or new – friend, and the trust and honesty with which they imparted their recollections was very humbling – a tribute to Field-Marshal Montgomery rather than to me. In every case but one I was permitted to bring and use my tape-recorder – and the full tapes of these interviews will be deposited in the Montgomery Archive for the use of future historians. These personal reminiscences are an integral part of the modern historian's 'apparatus' in chronicling events and personalities. In this instance I have not altered or even 'polished' the extracts I have used, and some readers may be disturbed by the syntax of unrehearsed speech rather than the printed page: but I wanted to abide by my own rules of scrupulous honesty, of not tampering with, or worse still distorting, the often deeply personal nature of such recollections. Moreover I feel it is important for the historian to distinguish between oral and documentary testimony. Some personal reminiscences go back fifty years or more, and the reader must ask himself how well *he* could recall events at such a distance. By tying these personal recollections to the evidence in Monty's papers and the various military archives I hope I have come as close as possible to a balance of truth. To the following, then, my most heartfelt thanks:

The late Major G. R. H. Bailey, MBE
Brigadier A. R. ('Tochi') Barker, DSO, OBE, MC
Major-General R. F. K. Belchem, CB, CBE, DSO
Air Chief Marshal Sir Harry Broadhurst, GCB, KBE, DSO, DFC, AFC
Colonel P. B. I. O. Burge, MC
Ian Calvocoressi, MBE, MC
Field-Marshal Lord Carver, GCB, CBE, DSO, MC
Terence Coverdale
Colonel Alan Davidson, MBE
Lt-Colonel C. P. Dawnay, CBE, MVO
The late Major-General Sir Francis de Guingand, KBE, CB, DSO
Mrs Frances Denby
The late Brigadier J. P. Duke, DSO, MC
The late Colonel P. J. Gething, MC
Field-Marshal Lord Harding of Petherton, GCB, CBE, DSO, MC
J. R. ('Johnny') Henderson, MBE
Lady Gwen Herbert

Lt-General Sir Otway Herbert, KBE, CB, DSO
Professor F. H. Hinsley, OBE
Major Neil Holdich of Wadenhoe
Lt-General Sir Brian Horrocks, KCB, KBE, DSO, MC
Lt-General Sir Ian Jacob, GBE, CB
Squadron-Leader H. G. James, AFC, DFM
The late Geoffrey Keating, MC
General Sir Sidney Kirkman, GCB, KBE, MC
Ronald Lewin
Major-General R. C. Macdonald, CB, DSO, MC
Carol Mather, MC, MP
Sir William Mather, OBE, MC, TD
Major-General M. St. J. Oswald, CB, CBE, DSO, MC
Major Robert Priestley, MBE
The late Major Tom Reynolds, MBE
General Sir Charles Richardson, GCB, CBE, DSO
Major-General G. P. B. Roberts, CB, DSO, MC

General Sir Frank Simpson, GBE, KCB, DSO
Major-General Eric Sixsmith, CB, CBE
Ed Stevens
The late Field-Marshal Sir Gerald Templer, KG, GCB, GCMG, DSO
Colonel L. T. Tomes, OBE
Brigadier H. R. W. Vernon, CBE
General Sir Dudley Ward, GCB, KBE, DSO
Brigadier Sir Edgar Williams, CB, CBE, DSO
Major-General Douglas N. Wimberley, CB, DSO, MC.

In order to ensure that a just balance be obtained as well as a strict regard for factual corrections, I asked Field-Marshal Lord Harding, Field-Marshal Lord Carver, General Sir Frank Simpson, General Sir Charles Richardson, Lt-General Sir Ian Jacob, Brigadier Sir Edgar Williams, Colonels John and Richard Carver, Colonel P. B. I. O. Burge, and Lt-Colonel Brian Montgomery to read relevant sections of the manuscript before publication. For their invaluable suggestions, corrections and advice I am doubly grateful.

Fifth, I must place on record my indebtedness to the staffs of those institutions and archives whose material is so vital to a truly scholarly undertaking: to Lt-Colonel Mike Ryan, OBE, Curator of the Royal Warwickshire Regimental Museum in Warwick; to Lt-Colonel D. A. Johnson, MBE, MC, of the Ministry of Defence, Whitehall; to the Librarian and staff of the Liddell Hart Centre for Military Archives, King's College, London University; to the Director and staff of the Imperial War Museum, Lambeth; to Dr Nicholas Cox and the staff of the Public Record Office, Kew; to the Librarian, K. M. White, and the staff of the Staff College Library, Camberley; to J. W. Hunt, the Librarian, and to the staff of the Central Library, the Royal Military Academy, Sandhurst; to R. J. Kennel, Librarian of the Royal Naval College, Dartmouth; to the Librarian and staff of the Ministry of Defence Library, Whitehall; to Mr Len Fairweather, local historian of Salcombe, Devon; and to the Librarian and staff of the London Library.

My thanks also to A. D. Peters & Co Ltd for permission to reprint extracts from *Peace and War* by Frederick Morgan (Hodder & Stoughton Ltd); to Hutchinson & Co Ltd for permission to reprint extracts from J. Kennedy's *The Business of War*; to George Weidenfeld & Nicholson Ltd for permission to reprint extracts from David Irving's *The Trail of the Fox*; to Hodder & Stoughton Ltd for permission to reprint extracts from *Operation Victory* by F. de Guingand; to Cassell Ltd for permission to reprint extracts from *The Hinge of Fate* by Sir Winston Churchill and *The Alexander Memoirs* by H. Alexander; and to William Collins Sons & Co Ltd for permission to reproduce extracts from Arthur Bryant's *The Turn of the Tide*, B. Horrocks' *A Full Life*, B. Liddell Hart's *The Rommel Papers*, and B. L. Montgomery's *The Path to Leadership* and *Memoirs*.

Last but not least, I would like to thank here my father's secretary, Miss Joan Crockford, and her assistants for their help in cataloguing and obtaining the works of reference and study required for the project; Mrs Avril Westrup and her secretarial help; my indefatigable typist Miss Winifred Marshall; Patrick Leeson, who drew up the maps and designed the lay-out of the pictures; Ken White who compiled the index; my editor, Christopher Sinclair-Stevenson, Jane Everard and the staff of Hamish Hamilton; my agent Bruce Hunter; and my dear wife who has 'seen it through' to the end.

NIGEL HAMILTON
Suffolk

And so our battlefields are tending to become rather complicated. And in all these complications we tend to lose sight of those real essentials in the art of making war – which are themselves so very simple.

Every officer must be clear in his own mind about the basic fundamentals – the things that really matter if you want to win your battles in this most modern war. On this broad and solid foundation he will have to build up his military philosophy . . .

from the Address to Middle East Staff College, Haifa, given by Lt-General B. L. Montgomery, GOC-in-C, Eighth Army, 21 September 1942.

PART ONE

Genesis of a Soldier

CHAPTER ONE

A Starting-point

Bernard Law Montgomery was born on 17 November 1887 in a suburb of London: fourth child and third son of the Rev. Henry Montgomery, Vicar of St Mark's, Kennington.

Before he was two years old Bernard was aboard a steamer to Tasmania, where his father had been appointed Bishop; and it was not until he was thirteen that the family returned for good to English soil – by which time the number of children had swollen (after one death) to seven. The eighth, a boy called Brian, was born in England, where Bishop Montgomery had been appointed Secretary to the Society for the Propagation of the Gospel in Foreign Parts. In this post Henry Montgomery was to rise to great distinction, becoming Prelate of the Order of St Michael and St George – and a senior ecclesiastical Knight of the realm.

Distinction, however, was not unknown in this Anglo-Irish family – though the Bishop seems to have been a humble, saintly man, and ascribed his advancement in life to 'fair ability, common sense and industry'. 'It all comes to this:' he wrote while still in Tasmania, 'if a man will only do his very best, night and day, and be humble and live in his work, things happen.'[1] His father, Robert Montgomery, had been similarly knighted, becoming a legendary figure in the India Office; but the tradition in the family was that each generation should go its own way, without relying on family fortune or connections; a tradition that, as time went by, was to have a great influence on the Bishop's third son, Bernard.

If Bishop Montgomery owed his success to diligence and humility, he also owed much to his wife Maud, whose firmness of character and domestic authority enabled him to concentrate on his manifold pastoral duties. The Bishop had taken note of her when he was employed as a humble curate at St Margaret's Church, Westminster, for she was the daughter of his rector, Canon Frederic Farrar, a well-known preacher and prolific author. Maud was then only fourteen, the future bishop thirty-two; but undeterred he asked for her hand. They were quietly engaged; and the marriage ceremony took place two years later, on 28 July 1881, when Maud was still only sixteen.

[1] Brian Montgomery, *A Field-Marshal in the Family*, London 1973.

3

It was of course understandable that Henry Montgomery, since 1879 the Vicar of St Mark's, Kennington, should want a wife to assist him in his new responsibilities: a parish of 16,000 souls with three curates, 250 church workers, 125 Sunday school teachers, and 1500 children. Whether Maud understood what was in store for her is unclear. At St Margaret's she was the fêted daughter of a famous father, housed in the tranquil setting of the Abbey courtyards, surrounded by the milling hordes of top-hatted pupils attending Westminster School. She felt she had a right to love and affection; and the formality of life in Sir Robert and Lady Montgomery's Irish home, to which they were invited for their honeymoon, was her first taste of the adult world to come. The strict rules of conduct that governed the Montgomerys' life dismayed her – as did her husband's emotional neglect once they were plunged into vicarage life in Kennington. The Rev. Henry Mongomery, tall, shy and dedicated to his profession, was out visiting his parishioners every evening. No Gladstone, Tennyson, Browning, Lewis Carroll or Matthew Arnold came to visit them, as they had at 17 Dean's Yard, Westminster. Moreover, Henry Montgomery had now the dignity of a Vicar to uphold – a dignity easily compromised by the high spirits of a sixteen-year-old bride. Maud must have longed for the intimacy and freedom of her parents' home – a freedom, of course, largely ensured by curates such as her husband Henry who, for a virtual pittance, assumed her father's pastoral responsibilities entirely.[1]

Thus prematurely Maud bade farewell to childhood and set out on the solemn path of matrimony and parenthood. She bore five children between 1881 and 1889, when she was barely twenty-five: Sibyl, Harold, Donald, Bernard and Una. But did she want them? She later confessed she had cried bitterly in the drawing room at Kennington, she felt so lonely and had so little to do.[2] The birth of her children certainly kept her busy: but the strictness with which she brought them up betokens frustration more than love. Her dream had been the companionship of the tall, athletic curate; and, though she remained devoted to him for the rest of his life, there can be no doubt that she made him pay a price for his neglect and for the domestic and parental responsibilities with which he so soon saddled her. She was a girl of strong will and without great intellect. She began to use her domestic hegemony as a penal lever on her hard-working, missionary spouse. Within a very short time he was emasculated of all domestic authority. Maud ruled; and her rule, beside the kindly, charitable, and humorous prince of the Church, was sometimes despotic and often blind. The older children feared, but did not love, her. If they felt ill in the night they were forbidden to wake her; if they wasted their pocket money or infracted her rigid domestic rules they were almost invariably beaten.

[1] Maud Montgomery, *I Remember, I Remember*, Belfast 1945.
[2] Ibid.

4

The children, once in Tasmania, obeyed a set time-table, begin-ning at dawn, and ending with family prayers in the evening. Yet, if the Bishop was away most parts of the year visiting his vast diocese, and their mother cracking the household whip, there were com-pensations. When not supervising their duties, Maud did at least let them alone. In the affectionless, enforced islation of their own company the children found their own level of contentment and their own individual resources. Sibyl died; but Harold became a polished horseman and went to Africa in 1902, never to return. Donald went to Cambridge and then emigrated to Canada, also never to return.[1] Una married a civil servant in Egypt, where she lived for much of her life; and Bernard . . . ?

Of the first five children – for there was a five year gap in Tasmania before the sixth child came – Bernard was undoubtedly the black sheep. Whether he would have risen to the heights he did had he not resented and fought against this loveless tyranny one cannot say; but certainly his awkward, cussed and singled-minded character was moulded in the struggle of wills between them. Though he came to respect his mother, he never forgave her. Harold, Donald and Una obeyed her in everything; then emigrated. Only Bernard challenged her; and the conflict of their personalities lasted until her death in 1949. He did not attend her funeral. Throughout his later life he deprecated his Farrar blood. He even blamed his mother, in his *Memoirs,* for not having given his ailing father 'the care and nursing which might have prolonged his life' – though the Bishop had already reached the venerable age of eighty-five!

What was involved was of course more than a simple clash of wills. As Maud gradually inculcated the very formality and discipline which, as a sixteen-year-old bride, she had first found so abhorrent in the Montgomerys, so Bernard would in turn inflict the same tyrannical discipline upon others which he found so stifling in his own mother. Like her, he was not intellectually gifted; like her he had a will of steel and a fundamental inflexibility of mind. He charged his mother's lack of tenderness as cause of this; but they were by nature similar. In Maud, Bernard saw himself and, re-membering his loveless childhood, resented the affinity. All his life he would idealise his holy father, whose absence, neglect and expectations had framed his mother's adult existence; all his life he held back the bottled-up tenderness that was within him – for in the lean years of his infancy and boyhood it would have denoted surrender or ridicule to express it. As a young adult, despite his fawning devotion to Maud and even his eschewal of the company of women, it was too late. 'He would have loved my mother and often tried to show it,' his sister Winsome later recorded; 'but for some

[1] They returned, of course, on special occasions, such as their parents' Golden Wedding.

5

unknown reason she always "brushed" him off.[1] Though he lavished letters and gifts on his mother, she responded only with pride in his achievements – never with love. 'As she grew old,' Winsome related, 'he would have liked to have the image of a helpless old lady whom he could look after. But she would not have that. Then he met Betty Carver . . . and at last could pour out all the buried love that was in him; and after ten years that ended.'[2] When, as a widower, Bernard finally did become famous, he repaid his mother's long oppression with an astonishing display of embittered feeling, cutting her in public and denying her any part in his international glory.

Yet it was Maud's domestic dicatorship, so cruel and unbending, which was undoubtedly the source of Bernard's military ambition. Not only was Maud's tyranny forbidding in its austerity; its threat was to Bernard's very identity as a man. He had seen his father, the Bishop, reduced to domestic impotence: a grand old gentlemen on five shillings a week, whose word counted for nothing in the affairs of domestic state. What Bernard wanted to achieve was both freedom *and* quasi-parental approbation; and this freedom he sought not in emigration or early marriage, but in the sword. There, in the company of men and in the life-or-death arena of war, he could both vent his frustrated emotions and earn the respect he courted. As will be seen, he seemed to know no fear in battle, for death had little to make him afraid when set up against the liberation of his deeper ego and the prizes promised by success. His genius lay not so much in his natural gift for leadership – a quality not lacking in English history – as in his deliberate, almost insane pursuit of his goal; a goal he would achieve by unending pursuit of clarity and ruthless self-discipline. Without the disastrous showing of democracy against the disciplined assaults of fascism, his star, like Churchill's, would never have properly risen, and his name would probably have gone into military history, if at all, as an interesting failure, a victim of his own mental pathology. A psychologist, observing him in the North African desert, once declared Bernard to be insane. Perhaps genius is insanity; insanity turned to society's advantage. As the years went by there would be many who would seek to oppose or belittle Bernard Montgomery. Even Churchill was not initially convinced of his merits. It was said of Eisenhower that he had greatness thrust upon him. Certainly it is arguable whether Bernard Montgomery achieved the same sort of greatness: the ability to show flexibility, humanity and humility when entrusted with great power. For Montgomery's stature was of a different kind. Though he trained himself to set aside several hours a day in which to think upon current and future problems ('oases of thought', as he called them), he was a stranger to relaxation as ordinary mortals know it. Bernard

[1] Letter to the author, 20.2.78.
[2] Ibid.

6

Shaw likened him to an 'intensely compacted hank of steel wire'. Even when in the throes of marital bliss he directed the activities of the home like a sergeant-major. His ilk of greatness did not simply arrive: rather, he spent a lifetime struggling for it. Generals like Rommel might show more flair, or Patton more *élan*. But in the cold, deadly business of tactical warfare: the tempering of a half-defeated army with a legend of invincibility; the deliberate crushing of British genius for muddle; the raising of a new mood of self-respect through training, discipline and conquered fear; the waging of battle not as romance but as the cold-blooded determination to succeed in achieving laid-down objectives – here Montgomery has no equal in our century, and he rightly looked back to the days of Napoleonic war to find a peer.

He would outshine his father, the Prelate of St Michael and St George, by becoming a Knight of the Garter, and Knight Grand Cross of the Bath; would outshine his grandfather, the great proconsul of the Punjab, as well as the descendants of the Eglinton Montgomerys, merchants and clergymen, who had purchased and built up the family's 1000 acre estate in Northern Ireland. In fact he would have to look as far back as Roger of Montgomery, liege and chief army commander under William the Conquerer, for an ancestor whose achievements could stand beside his own: a cruel, Norman warrior who, like Bernard, found solace in religion and spent his last years endowing charitable institutions; ending his life a monk within his own creation, the Abbey of St Peter and St Paul, in Shrewsbury, the town of which he had been made Earl.

CHAPTER TWO

The Norman Parallel

How closely the Montgomerys of County Donegal in Ireland were related to Earl Roger of Montgomery is unclear; Earl Roger's sons were later banished from England for treason against Henry II, and only tenuous links can be established with the Montgomery families which proliferated in Scotland and ultimately sent their offspring to the nine counties of Ulster, founded by James I in 1603. Certainly Bernard's father, Bishop Montgomery, claimed direct ancestry.[1] Moreover the connection, however unprovable, must needs distract the biographer, if only because Earl Roger proved one of the ablest Norman nobles, helped Duke William of Normandy to mount the invasion of Britain in 1066; and became one of the senior administrators in the occupied territories until his death in 1094: an achievement whose inverse parallel Bernard would enact almost 900 years later.

The rise of Roger de Montgomerie, Vicomte d'Exmes to preeminence in the eleventh-century court of Duke William is one of the great success stories of Norman times. Behind this distinguished record, however, can be discerned all the hallmarks of Norman ambition, greed, and cunning. Though his contemporary biographer Ordericus Vitalis described him, after his death, as a 'wise, moderate' man, and 'a lover of justice', there can be no doubt that he achieved his success with a mixture of cruelty, deceit, and sheer force of arms. By dispossessing a number of Norman monasteries he built up his estate; by marrying the venomous Mabel, daughter of the infamous William Talvas, Lord of Belesme, he both increased his estate and acquired a confederate in crime. Together they seem to have dispossessed the larger part of William's weaker nobility. Not even Roger's dutiful biographer could exonerate him from the manner in which he did this in the years that led up to the invasion; and with some courage (for his family owed its own rise to Earl Roger) he recorded in his celebrated history of the Norman church *Historia Ecclesiastica*: 'At that period, grave dissensions arose between William, Duke of Normandy, and his barons. For one ambitious man eagerly endeavoured to supplant another, so that bitter quarrels sprang up from various causes to the great injury of the wretched

[1] Henry Montgomery, *A Generation of Montgomerys*, privately printed in 1892.

8

people. At this men of a cruel turn of mind found reason to rejoice, while all those who loved piety and tranquillity were deeply grieved. Among those who regarded these disputes with satisfaction were Roger de Montgomerie and Mabel his wife, who took the opportunity of gaining the Duke's favour by fair professions, while they exasperated him against their neighbours by their crafty manoeuvres. The Duke, naturally passionate, gave the reins to his wrath, more than justice required, disinheriting the distinguished knights, Rodolph de Toni, Hugh de Grant-mesnil, and Arnold d'Echonfour, with their barons, and compelling them to undergo a long exile without any real cause of offence.' The height of iniquity, however, was yet to come; for Mabel was not content with slanderous allegations in Duke William's ear. Inviting Arnold d'Echonfour to dine at Echonfour Castle – which she had usurped – Mabel attempted to poison him. Arnold wisely declined her refreshments, and it was Roger of Montgomery's younger brother Gislebert (who had brought Arnold under safe conduct) who fell mortally ill, dying after three miserable days of suffering. Thus 'this perfidious woman, attempting to destroy her husband's rival, caused the death of his only [surviving] brother, who was in the flower of his youth, and much distinguished for his chivalrous gallantry.' Not to be thwarted by her failure, Mabel tried again, inveigling Arnold's chamberlain: and by this ruse was successful. She herself died a gruesome death, however, in 1082, at the hands of one of her dispossessed victims – Hugh of Igé. She was decapitated as she lay in bed after a bath – an assassination that will have been greeted with relief all over Normandy.

As husband of this shrewd, politic, powerful and cruel lady, Roger of Montgomery had by then become one of the richest landowners in Normany and England: Count of Alençon and Belesme, Earl of Shrewsbury and Arundel, counsellor to the King, and feudal lord over many hundreds of thousands of officers, servants, tenants and peasants. From his earliest days when he evicted the twelve Canons of his father's monastery at Troarn for 'gluttony, debauchery, carnal delights, and worldly occupations', replacing them with monks of 'regular discipline', Roger of Montgomery had been an ardent Christian. After Mabel's death he married a gentler soul, Adeliza du Puiset, and 'prudently endeavoured to efface his former errors, by his subsequent amendment of life'. He endowed numerous monasteries and churches in England and Normandy. The Welsh territories he had conquered were named after him, and in 1094 the Earl retired to his own monastery in Shrewsbury, sending for the original habit of St Hugh of Cluni so that he might die in the simple vestments of a monk: the only Norman Earl whose title had not been revoked by William; the only one of his five brothers not to die a violent death. Moreover there was considerable irony in this last act of piety, since the lands which had first assured his family's power in Normandy had mostly been seized from monastic houses.

After William himself, Earl Roger was probably the archetypal Norman knight: ambitious, courageous, and an undoubted leader of men; both just and cruel, avaricious and yet beneficent, loyal and yet capable of treachery; in an age of personal and dynastic rivalry, he survived – the most fundamental prerequisite for history – to be scripturally embalmed by the son of one of his own counsellors.

While no one would suggest that the qualities of Earl Montgomery's warrior descendant were inherited, the parallel between them is illuminating. For there is a decidedly Norman quality about the Anglo-Irishman who commanded the combined Allied armies invading the ancient French duchy of Normandy in June 1944: an absolute singleness of purpose still considered un-British (and certainly un-American); a passion for effective administration bordering on cruelty; a Christian conviction both simple and zealous; and a temperament not above intrigue when felt appropriate. Indeed Montgomery's behaviour at the outset of the invasion of 1944 recalls that utter determination, considered by his fellow commanders to be foolhardy, demonstrated by Duke William in early September 1066. As the Deputy Supreme Commander later recorded, Montgomery showed an 'amazing willingness' to take the risk of launching the invasion prematurely without full air support, on the night of 4 June 1944.[1] Duke William was similarly thought mad to leave the harbour at Dives without a favourable wind – and was forced in fact to shelter at the mouth of the Somme until almost the end of September 1066. Prayers were offered up to Saint Valéry, and all anxiously watched the weathervane. At last the storm moderated. A south wind began to blow; and William set sail. 'Our superior confidence, repelling all the dangers, will bring us the most joyful triumph, the most brilliant honours, and the most glorious renown,' he assured his barons.[2]

On the night of 5 June 1944, after days of negative weather reports the Channel storm also abated: and Montgomery's Personal Message was read out to the hundreds of thousands of troops: 'To us is given the honour of striking a blow for freedom which will live in history; and in the better days that lie ahead men will speak with pride of our doings . . . I want every soldier to know that I have complete confidence in the successful outcome of the operations that we are now about to begin. With stout hearts, and with enthusiasm for the contest, let us go forward to victory.'

By a stroke of supreme irony both Duke William's and General Montgomery's warships became separated from the rest of their invasion fleets and both were forced to anchor in mid-Channel. Neither commander was deterred by this ill-omen. Duke William simply ordered his soldiers to eat and drink. The rest of the fleet duly caught up, and their landing at Pevensey went unopposed. Within days he had drawn King Harold to oppose him; and, despite signs of

[1] Lord Tedder, *With Prejudice*, London 1966.
[2] William of Poitiers: *Gesta Willelmi ducis Normannorum et regis Anglorum*.

failure and exhaustion in mid-battle, he persevered, inflicting a defeat so decisive it heralded the fall of the entire country. He had brought his knights across the Channel together with their steeds – a technique learned from the Norman conquest of Sicily in 1060-61 – and in the end the weight of mounted Norman armour proved victorious. By drawing Harold's own cavalry into misguided pursuit, William was able to surround and decimate the English – tactics which, on a larger scale, would determine the battle for France, under General Sir Bernard Montgomery, some eight hundred and seventy-eight years later.

CHAPTER THREE

Of Irish Ancestry

Montgomery family tradition has it that in 1623 an offshoot of the Eglinton Montgomerys (descendants of Earl Roger's son Arnold) crossed from the West coast of Scotland and, dispossessing the native Catholics, established itself in Killaghtee, County Donegal, under lease from the See of Raphoe. When the loyalists under King James II retreated from Londonderry in 1689 they unfortunately set fire to the Bishop of Raphoe's land registry, and all the records were burnt. Thus it is only in 1700 that the first mention of a Montgomery living in Killaghtee occurs; thereafter, by wills dated 1722 and 1732, the Montgomery family of Killaghtee can however be charted with some genealogical certainty. Widow Catherine Montgomery, John Montgomery and David Montgomery finally gave way to five generations of male heirs, none of whom was to die under the age of sixty-five: a line of merchants, clergymen and administrators that would contribute both the Irish home and Irish blood of the future Field-Marshal Viscount Montgomery of Alamein.

Samuel Montgomery is the first squire of whose activities we have more than last-testament knowledge: a wine merchant who was to profit by the very intoxicating beverages which his descendants – Bishop and Field-Marshal – would spurn. However, this was the heyday of Georgian wealth, of entertaining and house-building. Not only did Samuel Montgomery make a fortune from the rising vogue of social revelry, but he followed it by investing in property. His business was in Londonderry, on the river Foyle; further down the estuary, overlooking Lough Foyle, he purchased 1000 acres of farmland in 1768 which he promptly named New Park. Within five years he had built himself a country seat, of grey stone with a slate roof and designed – far from handsomely – by himself. He had married the daughter of an architect and surveyor in Greencastle, nearby, who bore him eight children; but only one son survived, educated at Foyle College, Londonderry, and Trinity College, Dublin. This son, Samuel Law Montgomery, was ordained at the age of twenty as a deacon of the Protestant Church of Ireland; and at the age of forty-four became rector of Moville, the local parish of New Park.

The Rev. Samuel Law Montgomery was very different from his merchant father (who gave orders that the business be sold on his

12

death in 1803). Samuel Law was 'obsessed' with religion, as Brian Montgomery later recorded.[1] The year his father died, he married the widow of an earlier vicar of Moville, Mrs Susan McClintock, then thirty-eight years of age (Samuel was thirty-five) and six children were born to them – the last when Susan was fifty-three.

Although Samuel Law Montgomery succeeded to the living of Moville in 1812, the church was no great benefactor to its parsons; the house at New Park had to double as rectory and Samuel Montgomery's legacy from the Londonderry business was all too soon frittered away in expensive improvements to the Moville property. By the time Samuel Law Montgomery died in 1832, his own legacies to his children had to be financed by mortgaging the property.

Samuel Law's eldest son, who succeeded his father as owner of New Park, also took holy orders, becoming Rector of Ballynascreen in County Derry. Later referred to, within the family, as 'Uncle Montgomery', this son showed even less financial wisdom than his father. An abortive engagement cost him £1200 and by the time he died, in 1874, his debts, reflected in the mortgage on the New Park property, amounted to £13,000 – a mortgage that was not paid off for another fifty years.

'Uncle Montgomery' was nothing if not eccentric. He lived alone with his two unmarried sisters, Charlotte and Mary, and was, as his nephew Henry later related, 'absolutely ignorant of the ways of the world'.[2] He lived for his faith, and spent his time reading or visiting his parishioners; yet his Christianity could not overcome his social sensitivity, and he ordered a special diminutive carriage to be built so that he would not have to give the local poor a lift. He was hump-backed, barely travelled, and withdrew more and more from 'general society', dying after long ill-health and in extreme depression. Though he had poured a fortune into improving the village of Moville – which he saw as an expanding community – he rarely stayed at New Park. After his death, ownership passed to his brother (Samuel Law's second son) Robert Montgomery.

Robert Montgomery was of a very different ilk from his weakly elder brother. Born in 1809, he was sent away to school at Foyle College before he was eight, and educated there amid much flogging and fighting between boarders and day boys. However, Robert was strong in build, and fearless by reputation – riding bareback over the Moville property, poaching and hunting with an old bell-muzzled blunderbuss. At the age of fourteen he entered Addiscombe Military College as a cadet; and his performance in the examinations there was good enough to warrant a writership in the East India Company. He left Britain at the end of May 1828, bearing £300 and a letter from his father containing 'hints for the guidance of your future conduct',

[1] Brian Montgomery, op. cit.
[2] Henry Montgomery, op. cit.

13

written 'as the time approaches which must separate us for many, many years'. Robert Montgomery never saw his father again, for the latter died four years later; but though Robert later referred to himself as having arrived in India without talent or connections he was evidently a diligent and conscientious administrator. Six years passed before he married, at twenty-four, the eighteen-year-old younger sister of the Chief Commissioner of Azamgarh (now Uttar Pradesh), Frances Thomason. Frances was shy and humble, and opposed to publicity; but she died at thirty-two, and Robert returned on furlough to England with his three children. Finally, in 1845 he remarried, this time choosing a very handsome and intelligent woman, of a strong no-nonsense character, Ellen Lambert. They returned to India, and by 1849 Montgomery was made Commissioner of Lahore, capital of the new province of Punjab, serving under his ex-Foyle schoolmates, Henry and John Lawrence.

Robert Montgomery was responsible for justice, police, roads, civil funds, and education. When the Indian Mutiny broke out he coolly arranged the disarming of the sepoy regiments, thus averting the disaster that befell Delhi, and earning for himself, some two years later, the collective thanks of the Houses of Parliament in London, written and sealed on vellum. By that time he had been promoted Lieutenant-Governor of the Punjab, a post he held until his return to England in 1865 as a Knight of the realm. 'Brave as a lion, gentle as a lamb,' Sir John Lawrence, later Lord Lawrence, called him; but Henry, his second son, felt bound to record in his *Generation of Montgomerys* the feeling of many people that Sir Robert 'never received due recognition for what he did because he was not a man to push his own claims'.

Nor was Henry – who never ceased to be amazed that his meagre talents should bring him such advancement in life: to a bishopric and also a knighthood. Sir Robert Montgomery had four sons by his second marriage; but Arthur, the eldest, died at the age of twenty, and it was his second son Henry who, first at Cambridge, then as a clergyman, culled the honours.

Henry Hutchinson Montgomery was born in India on 3 October 1847, and sent to school in England at the age of eight. He did not see his father again until he was seventeen; by which time he had been duly processed by the rigours of Victorian education for all that life might bring. At Miss Baker's evangelical preparatory school in Brighton the eight-year-old was brought up 'on almost undiluted hell fire', leaving him with 'an awful sense of the Holy Will of God,' as he later reflected.[1] It was undoubtedly this education that was to form the basis of Henry's missionary zeal as an adult.

Like his father, Henry Montgomery does not seem to have been a rebel. The principles and the aims which guided him were the same

[1] Maud Montgomery, *Bishop Montgomery*, London 1933.

that had held true for his father and grandfather: honesty, integrity, loyalty and diligence. And yet, as a devout Christian, there was of course a profound rebellion against the evangelically-revealed temptations of the world: against sinfulness. 'The Thunders of Sinai should not be forgotten by any Christian,' he wrote later;[1] and his experience at Harrow School soon gave him a vivid idea of what God intended him to avoid or surmount. 'I can still recall the misery of that first term,' he recalled,[2] and was an avid admirer of *Tom Brown's Schooldays*.[3] The Rev. John Smith – who eventually went mad and ended his life in an asylum – befriended the innocent Montgomery. 'He used to send for all the new boys and make them promise that they would not engage in evil practices,' Henry's wife Maud later wrote, quoting Henry's own account: 'I can see his tall bent figure and flowing grey hair as he went up to School, watched with reverence by all the boys. Or I can catch the tones of his voice as he pleaded with us from the chapel pulpit in the name of his master. All through my Harrow days I had this strange and penetrating influence before me . . .' According to Maud, Henry at first went about in fear and trembling of the terrible bullying, bad language and iniquities perpetrated by his elders. In Maud's somewhat jejune biography, *Bishop Montgomery*, Harrow School was reputed to have been 'in a very bad state at the time. There were many boys in Rendall's house who were as wicked as they could be–a thoroughly depraved lot. In the end twelve were expelled or asked to leave'.

Henry's response to Harrow was certainly rebelliously moral; indeed his entire career may be seen as a controlled effort to prove himself worthy of the evangelical expectations laid down by Miss Baker. Men like John Smith, and later Dr Butler and Dean Stanley, became substitute fathers for the absent pro-consul of the Punjab – John Smith even reverently keeping a photograph of Henry 'as a quiet and shy boy with turn-down collar'[4] until the day he left Harrow. Though Henry never went mad like his Harrow mentor, he was given to visions (highly popular when printed), and constantly revisited his old school. Throughout his life he reflected on the lessons of his public school upbringing. Standing well over six feet tall, he had shone at games – athletics, football and cricket – and saw in them the most valuable preparation for adult life: 'I think I learnt as much from games as from anything. They are a real education for life, helping to build up character, to endure adversity patiently, to fight uphill games, to keep one's temper, to practise unselfishness for a common object.'[5]

From terrified, sensitive new boy, Henry Montgomery became a

[1] Ibid.
[2] Ibid.
[3] Brian Montgomery, op. cit.
[4] Maud Montgomery, *Bishop Montgomery*, op. cit.
[5] Ibid.

self-confident, zealous proponent of Christian morality – of the Victorian Establishment at its best. His wife Maud claimed he was never a scholar; but he was the first Montgomery to go to Cambridge University, which he entered in 1866, the year after his father's return from India, and he ultimately took a Second Class Honours degree in Moral Sciences, being bracketed eighth with the future Prime Minister, A. J. Balfour. He was given £200 per annum by his father, and looked back on his time at Trinity College as 'another golden memory. God who kept me from the temptations of school life did not desert me at college, and who can adequately tell the blessing of looking back over a university career without pain or remorse?'[1]

Quite what the temptations of school and college life were, neither Henry nor Maud properly explained: but they were real enough to the tall, wavy-haired son of the hero of the Mutiny, and they certainly fuelled his particular brand of self-deprecating religiosity. He remained, to the end of his life, a schoolboy: charming in his innocence, humility, and grateful loyalty to the point of saintliness. It was this innocence, this ability to look back thankfully over his own childhood and with compassionate understanding rather than fervent involvement that moved the Archbishop of Canterbury to write of him, after his death: 'one of the most delightful and lovable of men . . . Like the seer of Patmos, he viewed the events of the Church and of the world with which he had to deal *sub specie aeternitatis* – as episodes in a great spiritual drama which is being unfolded in the eternal world.' The world, in a way, *was* school to Henry Montgomery; and he ascended the steps of the Church as he had once excelled at school; indeed almost as he had once jumped the steps of Old Court into the Hall of Trinity College: in one bound.

In 1869 Henry Montgomery left university, and prepared for holy orders in London, under Dr Vaughan, Master of the Temple. Here he imbibed Dr Vaughan's three Victorian doctrines: 'Personal Religion', 'Our Sinfulness', and 'Our Saviour'. These were scarcely adequate for those interested in high theology, but they appealed to Henry Montgomery's simplistic view of Faith. 'I believe,' he preached in a memorial sermon on Dr Vaughan in 1921, 'the best kind of churchman is likely to be one who began as an Evangelical and went on afterwards to the truths about the Church and the sacramental life.'[2] Henry subsequently passed first equal in his examinations, and was ordained in Chichester Cathedral in 1871. His father, Sir Robert, recognizing the importance of this moment, and mindful that little or no spiritual guidance was given before the ceremony, came down from the India Office the day before the service, having composed a special prayer for the occasion. He asked Henry to kneel with him, and read out his spiritual petition to the Almighty.

[1] Ibid.
[2] Ibid.

It was Dr Vaughan who arranged Henry's first curacy at Hurstpierpoint, Sussex – a pleasant country parish that gave Montgomery and his fellow curate, E. A. Browne, a chance to learn the stock-in-trade of such a position. In time both curates (as well as the nearby headmaster of Hurstpierpoint College) would become missionary bishops; but for the moment Henry applied himself to his post with humble determination. At the end of two and a half years he was given a curacy among some of the worst slums of London, at Christ Church, Blackfriars Road. Sir Robert, again aware of what was in store for his son, gave him £150 and told him to travel wherever he liked, and to spend the money as he wished. Henry, using a further £100 legacy from his godfather, elected to visit the biblical lands of the Middle East: Egypt, Palestine, the Levant States and Turkey; returning after four months with exactly ten shillings in his purse. His diary of the journey, *Four Months in the East*, was later published and remained in print for many years.

Immediately on his return Henry plunged into his manifold new responsibilities in Blackfriars: the spiritual care of 7000 parishioners, temperance meetings, school-teaching, men's classes, even swimming lessons given at Lambeth Baths at 6.45 every morning. It was a demanding and exhausting experience that would, he later declared, have broken his health had he not been able to relax at Moville in the summers. However, the work cannot have stopped Henry from keeping abreast of modern religious literature. A few days after the new Rector of St Margaret's, Westminster, took up his post he was approached by Henry, who told him: 'I am coming to be your curate.'[1] The new rector was the celebrated Dr Farrar, ex-Headmaster of Marlborough School – religious writer, philologist, educationalist and preacher who was to have a profound effect on Henry Montgomery and his future.

[1] Maud Montgomery, *I Remember, I Remember*, op. cit.

CHAPTER FOUR

Grandfather Farrar

Frederic William Farrar was undoubtedly one of the luminaries, if not genii, of Victorian England. Born in 1831, he was sixteen years older than his new curate at St Margaret's, Westminster; had, like Henry Montgomery, been born in India, been sent home to England to be educated, studied at Trinity College, Cambridge, and been subsequently ordained. Both men were tall, with blue eyes and sharp, prominent noses, balding early. However, there all similarity ended.

The difference between Farrar and Henry Montgomery is a vital one in understanding the lineage and background of the future Field-Marshal; for it was this difference that was to colour Bernard Montgomery's whole outlook on life in the years ahead. It was the dichotomy between Farrar's cosmopolitan, cultured approach and Henry Montgomery's practical, humble determination that was to provide both inspiration and inferiority complex to the raw youth: the confidence to succeed in life, and yet the acute awareness of a missing, inaccessible world that made him shy and often torn between humility and bigotry.

Henry Montgomery, in the words of his wife,[1] was 'a plodder'; whereas Frederic Farrar was undoubtedly one of the most intellectually gifted men of his age, a brilliant scholar, theological rebel, and educational visionary. Though born in comparative poverty – his father was a missionary curate in Bombay – Farrar early showed the makings of genius. Like Henry Montgomery, he was subjected to a strict evangelical upbringing, first at school in Aylesbury, then on the Isle of Man, at King William's College. Like Henry Montgomery, he suffered from absentee parents; but, instead of being encouraged by parental neglect to succeed in the schoolboy hierarchy and at games, Farrar privately indulged his ardent love of literature. He idealised his absent mother, and felt nothing but coldness towards his austere, strictly evangelical father – indeed, just as Bernard Montgomery would later refer to his father as a saint, so too did Farrar write of his mother: 'She passed her life in the deep valley of poverty, obscurity and trial; but she has left to her only surviving son the recollections of

<hr>

[1] Maud Montgomery, *Bishop Montgomery*, op. cit.

a saint. I may say of her with truth that she was canonised by all who looked on her . . . She was, if ever there was, a saint of God . . . I never saw her temper disturbed; I never heard her speak one word of anger, or of calumny, or of idle gossip. I never observed in her any sign of a single sentiment unbecoming to a soul which had drunk of the river of the water of life and which had fed upon manna in the barren wilderness.'[1]

Mrs Farrar had given her son, as an infant, a copy of Milton's poetical works; and, within a few years, the boy could recite much of 'Paradise Lost' by heart. His progress through school to university was marked by continuous academic distinction. When his father returned from India in 1847 and became curate-in-charge of St James, Clerkenwell, in London, Farrar moved there to live with them. He came first in the London University matriculation exams, winning both a classical and theological scholarship to King's College and a London University scholarship too. From then on he was entirely self-supporting as a student, living on his scholarships and the prizes he won. Three years later he gained a sizarship to Trinity College, Cambridge, and in 1852 a Trinity College Scholarship. There, in 1854, he took a First Class Honours degree in Classics, being bracketed fourth, and was a junior optime in the mathematical tripos. He won numerous prizes at Cambridge, including the Chancellor's Medal for English verse (in the steps of Tennyson), the Le Bas prize for an English essay and the Norrisian prize for an essay on the Atonement. In 1856 he was elected a Fellow of Trinity College; but already in 1854 he had left the university to teach first at Marlborough College, then at Harrow. From the start he was an energetic, reforming teacher, and his gift for literary expression soon found its way between book covers. His novel, *Eric, or Little by Little*, was second only to *Tom Brown's Schooldays* in popular success as a tale of school life in the nineteenth century, going into countless editions and being translated into almost every language of the world. In all Farrar was to publish some seventy-five works in his life – works on the Classics, education, philology, theology, topography, poetry, social problems and biography. At Cambridge he was known as a sort of 'Milton among students'; but as a schoolmaster he showed himself much more than a brilliant scholar and poet. He was a born educationalist, revising the Victorian rote-system of classical learning, and urging an extension of the traditional school syllabus to include the Natural Sciences. He also abhorred the fashionable English attitude that the future of Britain lay on the playing fields of its public schools.

'What fun can you see in trundling a piece of leather at three bits of stick?' he asked of a cricket fan; and, following the Royal Commission on Public Schools, he trumpeted its conclusions throughout Britain in his 'Defects in Public School Education' of 1867. 'Our

[1] Reginald Farrar, *The Life of Frederic William Farrar*, London 1904.

present system of exclusively classical education,' declared the Honorary Classical Fellow of Trinity College, Cambridge, 'is a deplorable failure.' Even of the boys who went up to university 'the larger number leave school at the age of eighteen or nineteen, not only ignorant of history, both ancient and modern, ignorant of geography and chronology; ignorant of every single modern language; ignorant of their own language and often of its mere spelling; ignorant of every single science; ignorant of the merest elements of geometry and mathematics; ignorant of music; ignorant of drawing; profoundly ignorant of that Greek and Latin to which the long, ineffectual years of their aimless teaching have been professedly devoted; and, we may add, besides all this, and perhaps worst of all, completely ignorant of – altogether content with – their own astonishing and consummate ignorance'.[1]

These were strong words; and though Farrar's reputation as author, scholar and educationalist soon spread around the kingdom – he was nominated by Charles Darwin to the Royal Society in 1866 for his work on the origins of language – he began to encounter that scourge of all British institutions: envy and a fierce resistance to change. Despite probably the best credentials and recommendations of any teacher in Britain in his time, it was to be sixteen years before he was finally given a headmastership. Undaunted, he finally took up the vacant post of Headmaster of Marlborough College in 1871 after an outbreak of scarlet fever had caused a panic exodus of pupils; and within five years had made it one of the premier educational establishments in England, famed for its academic standards and repudiation of the godliness of sport.

Farrar's religious faith had never weakened during this time. He was ordained in 1863, and his sermons were already being published in book form by 1868. It was at Marlborough College, in 1874, that Farrar wrote his *Life of Christ*, the book which, together with *Eric*, was to make him a household name in educated Victorian circles. More volumes of his sermons were published; but his defence of the 'heretic' Bishop of Natal (who said the Scriptures were not all intended to be taken literally) was not quickly forgotten, and it was not until 1875 that the Church of England made a gesture of accepting his services, when he was at last offered by Disraeli a Crown living at Halifax – something of an insult to a man whose work for the Church had not only brought him an honorary chaplaincy to the Queen, but the Hulsean lectureship at Cambridge in 1870.

The Life of Christ, though, went into eighteen editions in its first year of publication; and thereafter the Church could not long refuse him an appropriate post. He was widely tipped for the Bishopric of Calcutta that had fallen vacant; but to his chagrin (which he likened to suicidal seasickness) he was passed over. Thus, in 1876, the

[1] Ibid.

Headmaster of Marlborough College moved into 17 Dean's Yard, Westminster simply as Canon and Rector of St Margaret's – a position he was to hold for almost two decades before the Church would grant him a more senior post, as Dean of Canterbury.

Farrar's life – his reforming zeal, his desire to shake up and modernise not only the teachings of English schools but of the English church – was very different in character from that of the young curate who came, on Dr Vaughan's recommendation, to help him at St Margaret's in 1876; but it bears a remarkable, if strongly repudiated, similarity with the life of Henry Montgomery's third son, as then unborn.

'I do not care for the Farrar blood; it does not interest me,' Bernard Montgomery wrote almost a hundred years later[1]; yet the resemblance is too uncanny to go unremarked. Because he idealised his father, Bernard Montgomery would never acknowledge his Farrar genesis. Certainly in neither scholastic ability nor cultural outlook did he in any way take after his maternal grandfather. But in their ambition, their love of fame, their gift for teaching, preaching, converting; in eschewing humbug and fearlessly, even recklessly, advancing their ideas of modernism, they were surprisingly similar – and both their professional careers suffered as a result.

However, the similarity between Frederic Farrar and his grandson was not confined to such qualities. Perhaps the most striking resemblance was in their innermost natures, their very sexuality. The reason most generally given for Bernard Montgomery's rejection of his Farrar stock is the scandal caused – the blot on the family name – by two of Farrar's sons. One, a chaplain to the Queen like his father, was caught *in flagrante* with a choirboy and had to leave the country. Such behaviour was anathema to Bernard; as was the trial of another of Farrar's sons for attempting to bribe and seduce his female secretary. Even Bernard Montgomery's own son David's divorce led to bitter estrangement; yet the very fierceness of Bernard's rejection reflects the inner tumult caused by such acts. There can be no doubt that, by temperament and inclination, Bernard Montgomery was disposed towards the male sex rather than the female; and Victorian conventions being what they were, this was to cause him incalculable, if unconscious, difficulties.

Farrar was identical in this respect. From his schooldays onward his friends could not imagine his adopting the company of women. Certainly it was not until his beloved, saintly mother had died that Farrar married. In 1860, a few months after her abrupt and unexpected death, he took for a wife the nineteen-year-old daughter of a judge in India, Lucy Mary Cardew. When Farrar's companions remonstrated that as a student and young schoolmaster he had

[1] Letter to Brian Montgomery, 1961, quoted in Brian Montgomery, op. cit.

always scorned the company of women as a waste of time, he quipped from Shakespeare's *Much Ado about Nothing*: 'When I said I would die a bachelor, I did not think I should live till I were married.' Certainly the marriage was fruitful: Lucy Farrar bore him ten children, five of them girls. Yet despite his evident love for his children, there can be no doubt that Farrar was and remained a man's man. *Eric, or Little by Little* was deeply autobiographical, and its suggestion of homosexual love was only thinly veiled. His letters to his fellow students reveal his need to share more than mere companionship – a need for love and shared emotion. No impropriety ever tarnished his name; but his affection for 'his' boys and the energy he put into their education was undoubtedly homoerotic. As, later, he would publicly denounce the Church's contemporary view of eternal damnation, so, at Harrow and Marlborough, he objected to conventional forms of punishment. To teach well was to inspire the affections of his pupils – which in turn fuelled his ambition. His house was open to his boys; in 1867, on a journey to Italy, he even took one of his pupils with him, afterwards writing to his old student friend E. S. Beesly: 'The Harrow boy who came with us I had always liked, but now I love him tenfold, having been cheered by his ruddy face in perils and pleasures.'[1] Rumours did sometimes go around, in his earlier teaching days, that his particular style of teaching had resulted in lack of discipline and even violence. H. M. Butler, who became Master of Trinity College in Henry Montgomery's day, remembered that at Harrow Farrar's position 'was from the first, and throughout, original and peculiar. He was all along the companion of his boys, whether in form, or in the house, or in games or walks. He had no fears of compromising his dignity by such familiarity . . . He seemed [in his sermons] always to have before him two haunting visions, the one of boyish innocence, the other of boyish wickedness.'[2]

Nor did Farrar compromise his dignity. 'Insincerity is not one of my many faults,' he assured his friend Beesly.[3] He was not afraid to show his affection once he had gained the trust of a friend, whether man or boy; nor did he expect others to conceal theirs. Love, like the unconsummated love of Jesus, was holy, sacrosanct; sexual contact or allusion was 'lewd'. 'Do come here,' he begged Beesley in a postscript to the above letter, '– bringing a boy if you like, and whom you like – and you shall find a warm welcome from your affectionate friend.'

Farrar's friends among the most distinguished men of Victorian letters, of science and education, were legion: Tyndall, Holland, Spottiswoode, Sedgwick, Seeley, Darwin, Huxley . . . It seems that at heart, however, Farrar was actually a rather reserved man, as his Marlborough subordinate, P. E. Thompson, later recollected: 'The

---

[1] Reginald Farrar, op. cit.
[2] Ibid.
[3] Ibid.

truth is that Farrar was naturally a shy man, not at ease in all company, without the gift of small talk . . . To some he appeared stately and unapproachable . . . He may sometimes have been impatient and even hasty. He may even have been in the right or in the wrong, but a misunderstanding was impossible if you went the proper way to work. You had only to go to him, to treat him fairly, and he would at once meet you with open arms, literally so, as I once well remember.'

For Farrar the sharing of love and affection was to bridge the gap around himself, his own isolation – as was also the sometimes seemingly manic pursuit of his career, teaching all day, writing or correcting proofs all night. Far more than he ever imagined or recognised, Bernard Montgomery was to follow after this grandfather. The Farrar blood that he spurned was his own; the penchant for men and boys, Farrar's Greek ideal of platonic affection, equally so, as was the dialectic between that affection and full sexual expression. In Farrar's case the dialectic spawned an unending creative ambition. He became one of the finest pulpit preachers of his day, capable of combining his immense learning with an unusual ability to appeal to the heart. His 'peculiarity', his fearless approach to contemporary questions (such as evolution and the literalness of the Scriptures) and the florid yet penetrating style with which he expressed himself, were to make Farrar admired by many but intensely disliked by a few. That Farrar was effectively held down by the Church and denied the advancement to which his great gifts entitled him was a feature that would be repeated also in his grandson's life. In the event only longevity permitted Farrar to rise above the rank of rector and canon, for he was almost sixty-five when the Prime Minister, Lord Rosebery, finally nominated him for the Deanery of Canterbury. By then Farrar had watched many a lesser man rise to the office of Bishop which his admirers felt was his due. Among them was Henry Montgomery.

CHAPTER FIVE

Henry and Maud

Though Farrar was Rector of St Margaret's and thus responsible for a parish which contained, in his daughter's words, 'some of the wickedest streets in London, full of thieves and other evil-doers',[1] the fame of his preaching and his writing hardly suited him for common pastoral duties – as his young curate Henry Montgomery straightway recognised. He and his fellow-curate 'soon begged the rector not to trouble himself personally about the parish. He was quite new to such work; they knew all about it, and they left him to do the great work for which he was so eminently fitted.'[2] When Farrar did one day attempt a pastoral call on a drunk parishioner, he was 'dismissed with contumely,' as Henry Montgomery wryly remembered. 'It was long before the dear Canon recovered from the shock, and I suppose we young fellows laughed, and begged him all the more earnestly to reserve himself for those who called for him, while we did that rougher work for which our more brutal natures were better fitted.'[3]

Farrar was a man of mind; Henry Montgomery a man of action. While Farrar launched an appeal that would 'revolutionise' the neglected, almost derelict old church at St Margaret's, his wife and curates had to take over the accounts.

'It is still mirth-provoking to recall the subject of parish accounts during the first few months of the Rector's reign,' Henry recollected. 'It was an occasion not to be forgotten when the distinguished scholar produced a sheet of paper scored all over, and crossed with figures, which represented the accounts of numerous organisations . . . I do not think any human being ever made anything out of them.'[4]

Henry's approach to parochial duties was singularly practical. In the same way as his third son would one day refer to his own approach to war as 'scientific',[5] so Henry Montgomery looked upon

[1] Maud Montgomery, *Bishop Montgomery*, op. cit.
[2] Ibid.
[3] Quoted in Reginald Farrar, op. cit.
[4] Ibid.
[5] Bernard Montgomery: Notes on *Crusade in Europe* by Dwight D. Eisenhower. Montgomery Papers.

24

the 'science' of parish work. 'It is a science,' he wrote, 'in which growth is always possible, for it is a little world to be governed, which includes every sort of character and problem; and unless a man is ever pondering, he is likely to discover one day that he has omitted even to think of his whole classes of parishioners in any complete sense: for example, all the publicans in the parish, or the servants, or the young men lodgers, or the cabbies, or the police.'

Westminster was indeed a rough place, as Henry remembered, even after his experience of Blackfriars. 'I think it would have been difficult to have found a spot more full of crime.' Prostitution, theft, larceny, intemperance, disease and tuberculosis were a challenge indeed to the young curate. However, there were compensations. The Dean of Westminster, Dean Stanley, took a liking to Henry, and made him his secretary, with Farrar's approval. Stanley's wife had just died, and the Dean turned to Henry as to a son. He introduced him to some of the most eminent figures of the day, and even took him as travelling companion to Northern Spain in 1880.

However, it was in Farrar's own house in Dean's Yard that Henry Montgomery's domestic fate was sealed. Farrar's residence was like a home to the young curate, thronged with famous men of letters, the arts and science as well as the Church – Tennyson, Browning, Matthew Arnold, Millais, Burne-Jones, Frith, Holman Hunt, Tom Hughes, Lewis Carroll; and it is scarcely surprising that Henry, so long 'orphaned' by his absent parents and subsequently thrust into religous and social work among the slums of London, was mesmerised by the family spirit and conviviality that characterised the Farrar household. Mrs Farrar was shy, gentle, and understanding; the Rector anxious for affectionate company as a relaxation after his strenuous labours on sermons, appeals and his voluminous lectures and writings. 'What helped most to cheer and brighten my father in those early Westminster years was the society of "The Curates", who, young, ardent, bright, and intellectual, gave an atmosphere of cheerful vigour to the house, and lightened many an hour of anxiety and depression,' one of his daughters later wrote.[1] 'Chief among those he reckoned the two who afterward became members of our family . . .'

While both the Dean and the Canon warmed to the young curate, Henry Montgomery gradually fell under the spell of Farrar's third daughter Maud. In time four of Farrar's daughters would marry their father's curates; but what was singular in the case of Maud and Henry was the matter of age. Maud was twelve when Henry became a curate at St Margaret's and only fourteen when their romance began, while Henry was thirty-one. To the young schoolgirl, scarcely entering puberty, the tall, wavy-haired curate with his deep blue eyes, practical approach to life, and marked sense of humour, son of

[1] Reginald Farrar, op. cit.

the hero of the Indian Mutiny, Sir Robert Montgomery, was a prince indeed.

Far from discouraging Henry, the Farrars permitted an engagement at once – though Maud was instructed to keep it a secret even from her own sisters, and was not permitted to wear an engagement ring. Dean Stanley, too, approved the match, and insisted on marrying the couple himself in the Abbey some two years later. Stanley died a week before the wedding; but on 28 July 1881 they were married, by no less a person than Archbishop Tait, in Henry VII's Chapel.

While Farrar's career was stunted by envy and obstructionism, his new son-in-law's had already begun to flower. In 1879, the year of his engagement, Henry Montgomery was appointed Vicar of St Mark's, Kennington, one of the most important livings in South London. According to Maud, Dean Stanley burst into tears at the news, and begged him not to leave, promising him later a good Crown living and crying, 'Abraham; oh! my son, my only son!'[1]

Henry Montgomery's 'scientific' approach to his calling was destined to pay handsome dividends. He immediately imposed a system of 'government' on his new parish, dividing the territory into three smaller parishes, each under one of his three curates. Every Monday morning at breakfast a staff meeting was held. Their week's work, their visits paid, services taken and lessons given were all entered. Direct mail was tried in order to reach lodgers and students; and the traditional Jesuit principle applied: once you get hold of a person, you never let go. He amassed hundreds of church workers and Sunday school teachers. After his Sunday services – with congregations of over 1000 – he conducted 'after service meetings' in the quest for candidates for confirmation, young or old. Small wonder that, after eighteen years of such strenuous application, he was raised to episcopal rank. By then, after only seven years at St Mark's vicarage, his wife was twenty-four, and mother of five children: Sybil in 1882, Harold in 1884, Donald in 1886, Bernard in 1887 and Una in 1889.

Outwardly the marriage, like Henry's career as priest, was straightforward and successful. Maud, a vivacious girl with a cascade of dark hair, a high forehead and pronounced chin, finished her final school lesson only days before the wedding. She had only been allowed to see Henry twice a week during the engagement, and the marriage ceremony signified long-awaited freedom. They travelled, on their honeymoon, to Cambridge, York, Edinburgh, Glasgow and on to Ireland, where they stayed with Sir Robert and Lady Montgomery at Moville. In Kennington the sixteen-year-old vicar's wife then threw herself into the running of the parish as tirelessly as did her husband, anxious to share everything with him. 'No press of work

[1] Maud Montgomery, *Bishop Montgomery*, op. cit.

was allowed to interfere with his happy intercourse with his family,' she later recorded.[1] 'The children all had meals with their parents, the "baby" lying on a pillow on the floor. Their father had a great power of concentration. He could work in his study with the children playing about the room, and many of his sermons were written in the nursery overlooking the Oval cricket ground.' Every Saturday evening Henry and Maud dined with Sir Robert and Lady Montgomery at 7 Cornwall Gardens, and on Sunday night with the Farrars at Dean's Yard. 'Thus in the midst of hard work happy family intercourse was kept up'; and in the summer the Montgomerys went to Moville 'where Henry renewed his strength among his beloved hills and the children learned to love their old Irish home'.[2]

Such was Maud's idyllic record in her biography *Bishop Montgomery*. But was it so simple? In his *Memoirs* Bernard Montgomery noted that, apart from her five young children, Maud had to look after 'three small boys, distant cousins, whose parents were in India'. Thus Maud was having to mother eight small children before she was twenty-four. Moreover, whatever she might say about family intercourse and love for the old Irish home, Maud at first found her husband's parents impossibly stuffy and formal. She had not been prepared in any way for the wedding night in Cambridge, and did not exactly enjoy it, she told her son Brian many years later.[3] At Moville Lady Montgomery crushed Maud by saying 'Did your mother tell you to put on that pink dress the first morning?' The day was strictly regulated, with family prayers twice a day, social calls to be paid, and a protocol whereby Lady Montgomery solemnly escorted the bride to bed in the evening, her husband having to follow later. 'To be frank,' Maud later confided, 'I must say I was not very happy at first in our married life. My husband loved me devotedly, but he took our love too much for granted. I was young and foolish and I wanted to be told that I was loved. Also, I came from a very large family and I was often very lonely at Kennington in early days. My husband was out every evening, and I can remember sitting in the drawing room and crying bitterly because I had nothing to do and felt so lonely. But all that was changed when our first child, Sibyl, was born . . . I soon had my hands full, with so many children and parish work.'[4]

For Maud, her involvement in her husband's work and the mothering of so many children effectively disposed of her feelings of neglect and loneliness. Here was a chance to prove herself in the eyes of her parents-in-law; and the determination with which she went about this challenge certainly elicited respect from all who knew her. Possibly there were repressed feelings of anger and disappointment

[1] Ibid.
[2] Ibid.
[3] Brian Montgomery, op. cit.
[4] Maud Montgomery, *I Remember, I Remember*, op. cit.

that she should have to put aside 'childish things' so early in her life – according to her son Brian she was still at an age of children's parties and games of hide-and-seek in the garden when she married, and callers at the vicarage were often 'scandalised' to see the way she 'pelted' round the house, pursued by her brothers. At any rate the elder children, though they were allowed to eat with their parents, were soon in awe of this young, wilful mother. 'It was impossible for my mother to cope with her work as the wife of a London vicar or as a Bishop's wife, and also devote her time to her children, and to the others who lived with us,' Bernard later recorded. 'Her method of dealing with the problem was to impose rigid discipline on the family and thus have time for her duties in the parish or diocese, duties which took first place. There were definite rules for us children; these had to be obeyed; disobedience brought swift punishment . . . She made me afraid of her when I was a child and a young boy . . . I began to know fear when very young and gradually withdrew into my own shell . . . Certainly I can say that my own childhood was unhappy.'[1]

Here, then, the stage was set for a major confrontation. Harold and Donald were 'more pliable, more flexible in disposition, and they easily accepted the inevitable', as Bernard remembered.[2] The girls, too, Brian recorded, 'were never any trouble.'[3] Even Maud's husband, it seems, accepted the growing tyranny of his young wife with Christian forbearance, and, perhaps, a feeling of inevitability. How ironic it must have seemed to him, a man in his thirties, with his 'first independent command' in Kennington, as he called it,[4] that having mocked his father-in-law's inability to handle the parish accounts, he himself should in time surrender control of the domestic purse to his far from mouse-like young wife. In his *Memoirs* Bernard later quoted a German general who divided officers into four classes: the clever, the stupid, the industrious, and the lazy. Every officer possessed at least two of these qualities. Those clever and lazy were suited for the highest command; those clever and industrious for high staff appointments; but whoever was stupid *and* industrious had to be removed immediately.

It is impossible not to see in this last description the wife of the Rector of Kennington and future Bishop of Tasmania. As Maud herself related, she was not a clever woman;[5] nor had she had time to gain experience of adulthood before being tossed into the demanding rigours of married and vicarage life. Her education ceased the day she stopped her lessons on the eve of her wedding and thereafter she seems to have largely turned her back on the poetry and culture

[1] Bernard Montgomery, *Memoirs*, London 1958.
[2] Ibid.
[3] Brian Montgomery, op. cit.
[4] Ibid.
[5] Maud Montgomery, *I Remember, I Remember*, op. cit.

of her famous and scholarly father. The Farrars did not, it would seem, form any abiding friendship with Sir Robert and Lady Montgomery. Little or no correspondence between them or about them remains in the family papers; and Brian Montgomery concluded that 'all in all it seems likely that the Dean did not get on very well with Sir Robert. They would have had very little in common in the circumstances of their very different careers'. Yet despite the suffocating formality and hauteur of the Montgomery home at Moville and in Cornwall Gardens, it was this very Montgomery barrenness of culture and accent on religiosity that Maud now attempted to ape. She who had found the custom of twice-daily family prayers at Moville 'very strange'[1] would in turn impose suffocating religious and domestic discipline on her own children – even incorporating a chapel in the house at Moville and one in their London home, and insisting on twice-daily family prayers as her mother-in-law had done. Moreover, where once her Farrar home had resounded with the noise of piano practice, and talk of books and poetry, Maud's strict routine gradually expelled the children from the inner sanctum of the house, and excluded all form of cultural concern or interest, as Brian later rued.[2] From being one of the favourite daughters of one of the most celebrated intellectual homes in Britain, Maud became a wilful, cultureless wife and mother. Had she followed the example of her mother, however, the effect would not necessarily have been better. Lucy Farrar was remembered by her children and her husband's friends as a quiet, gentle, shy and affectionate woman who did everything to create a harmonious, loving and cultivated home. Yet two of her sons would cause scandal; and even Farrar's prize schoolboys, as P. E. Thompson remembered of Marlborough days, tended to be 'eccentric and – well, a bit impish', few of them reaching very distinguished positions in later life.[3] Even Bernard Montgomery, despite his lamentations about Maud's fear-invoking motherhood, learned 'to speak the truth, come what may, and so far as my knowledge goes none of her children have ever done anything which would have caused her shame . . . We have all kept on the rails. There have been no scandals in the family; none of us have appeared in the police courts or gone to prison; none of us have been in the divorce courts'.[4]

In a public sense Maud's tyranny paid dividends: no scandal attached to the family name, and one of her sons would become famous throughout the world. But privately? Six of her children emigrated from Britain, either professionally or as the result of marriage. Bernard, the third son, tried to insist that Harold's name be

---

[1] Brian Montgomery, op. cit.
[2] Interview of 18.1.78.
[3] Reginald Farrar, op. cit.
[4] Bernard Montgomery, op. cit.

put in the family bible as having 'died of drink'[1] – for Harold had come near to blows with his temperance-obsessed mother by importing a bottle of gin to New Park in 1931 when Maud and Henry Montgomery were celebrating their Golden Wedding. 'We elder ones never became a united family,' Bernard related;[2] nor did he think Maud made her husband's last few years very happy. She had bullied and bossed Henry since overcoming her first disappointment at married life; 'she ran the family,' as Bernard put it, 'and my father stood back . . . She could always make him do what she wanted. She ran all the family finances and gave my father ten shillings a week,' – even when they had returned to London and the children had all left home. 'This sum had to include his daily lunch at the Athenaeum, and he was severely cross-examined if he meekly asked for another shilling or two before the end of the week. Poor, dear Father . . .'[3]

Yet Bernard's view was expressed long after his mother's death. During her lifetime – at least until he was a national hero – Bernard would never have thought to speak of her thus. Even Sir Robert Montgomery's wife, who was considered an awesome lady – 'a very formidable woman, not to be trifled with at any time or in any circumstances,' as Bernard once told his brother Brian[4] – is recorded as having said 'she could do nothing with Henry's young bride' at the beginning of Maud's marriage, 'she was so proud and stiff'.[5] The record of Maud's parenthood suggests she became quite as formidable as her mother-in-law.

Little Bernard was not yet two years old when in the spring of 1889 the summons came to the Vicar of St Mark's, Kennington that would transform his black robes to purple. Ironically it was borne by Dr Farrar, his father-in-law – whose sermons in 1877 on the nonsense of eternal damnation had filled the Abbey at Westminster, but caused a furore within the Victorian Church and thus dashed any hopes the Canon might have of obtaining the Deanery of Westminster, let alone a bishopric.

Dr Farrar had come on behalf of the Archbishop of Canterbury to offer Henry the post of Bishop of Tasmania. Henry Montgomery was then forty-one. Although Sir Robert Montgomery had died the month after Bernard's birth, in December 1887, leaving Henry the Montgomery estates in Ireland, the young Bishop-elect was scarcely a wealthy man, for the mortgage on the Moville estate was stilll almost £13,000 – a very considerable sum in those days. Henry sold off the Ballynally farms in order to reduce the debt; but even so, Maud recorded 'there was barely enough left to keep up New Park

[1] Brian Montgomery, conversation with the author, December 1977.
[2] Bernard Montgomery, op. cit.
[3] Ibid.
[4] Brian Montgomery, op. cit.
[5] Maud Montgomery, *I Remember, I Remember*, op. cit.

and pay for the summer holiday'.[1] Thus the post of Bishop did at least promise financial improvement, even if Henry had, at that time, no idea where Tasmania was. Dr Farrar explained that too many Australian bishops were failing to stay out permanently in their sees; therefore, if Henry accepted the post, he must understand it would probably be 'for life' – as it was for the criminals and convicts who were transported there, and for whom the island was chiefly known. Henry immediately accepted, going at once to Lambeth for a short interview with the Archbishop, and then to the Athenaeum to look up where Tasmania, or Van Diemen's Land, actually was.

Henry Montgomery was consecrated Bishop on 1 May 1889, in Westminster Abbey; and on 23 October the family – the new Bishop, his wife and five children – arrived in Hobart, Tasmania. Throughout the seven-week voyage Maud imposed the same daily routine that she had established in Kennington – family prayers with guests and servants compulsorily included; then family duties and school lessons in the morning, games or exercise in the afternoon, and family prayers again in the evening. In Tasmania she built a schoolroom which the children had to keep clean and heated, chopping their own firewood and even preparing their own evening meal there. Maud's strict discipline brooked no disobedience, and she wielded the cane like a man. The beatings were 'constant',[2] and she seems to have shown little or no affection to the older children, leaving their education, once in Tasmania, to tutors imported from England, and concentrating as far as possible on her duties as wife of the Bishop.

Why Henry Montgomery allowed his young wife to 'wear the trousers'[3] as Brian Montgomery later put it, we can only guess. Most likely he too was afraid to interfere – and suppressed his qualms about the way she dominated the family. He was so often absent from Hobart, the diocesan capital, for he considered it his duty to spend nearly six months of the year travelling through the mountains and wilder parts of Tasmania, visiting each remote parish including the small offshore islands, with their indigenous population of 'Tasmanian Blacks'. From having been an athletic, gregarious, hardworking parish priest, the favourite of Dean Stanley and other senior church leaders, he gradually became a devoted, dedicated missionary Bishop, the champion of the Church Militant overseas. He was very popular and highly regarded wherever he went, for men and women instinctively trusted him. But the price he paid for this was heavy within the family – where Maud increasingly ruled. At home the Bishop gradually became a somewhat hounded, holy, if not saintly figure. As time went on Maud even imposed a further rule: that for two hours in the afternoon, whatever the weather,

[1] Maud Montgomery, *Bishop Montgomery*, op. cit.
[2] Bernard Montgomery, op. cit.
[3] Brian Montgomery, op. cit.

everybody had to leave the house so that she could rest undisturbed by noise of any kind. Only the Bishop was allowed to remain indoors, though in his study. 'She longed to organize and control both people and events,' Brian later wrote. 'She developed a passion for order and method, all governed by a strict routine and subject always to the absolute priority of religious practice and a strict morality.'[1] Apparently she was considered a handsome woman in Tasmania, with her high forehead, large wide-spaced eyes, fulsome dark hair, and a beautiful complexion. 'She looked very well in a riding habit,' Brian recalled; and she wielded her crop with alarming severity and swiftness at the slightest misdemeanour. She loved Henry 'with a fierce and passionate devotion that knew no bounds' – a frightening, often cruel, and in some respects stupid woman who, according to Bernard, mellowed with age, and was softer with her younger children.

By then, however, the seeds were sown. The Bishop had surrendered his gaiters to his wife when he took to the bush in corduroys and hob-nailed boots as a missionary, wearing a broad-rimmed prospector's hat and sporting a heavy grey beard. Sibyl, the eldest child, died; and Harold, Donald and Una gave their mother no trouble, being quite 'amenable to the regime', as Bernard put it.[2] It was to be six years before another child was born in Tasmania. In the meantime only Bernard rebelled against his mother's domestic tyranny. There followed an inevitable conflict of wills – the scars of which would last throughout Bernard's long life.

[1] Brian Montgomery, op. cit.
[2] Bernard Montgomery, op. cit.

CHAPTER SIX

Early Days

Whether the source of Bernard Montgomery's genius for command is to be found in his genealogy, his mother's tyrannical upbringing, or simply the size of his family and subsequent inter-sibling rivalry is arguable.

Brian Montgomery, the future Field-Marshal's younger brother, considered it to be the last, eschewing complex psychological explanations or even the version put out by Bernard in the *Memoirs*. 'Bernard did not grow up in an atmosphere of fear of mother, or develop any inward looking, withdrawn characteristics because of her . . . He defied his mother's authority when his wishes or actions ran contrary to her own ideas for himself, and this inevitably led to trouble. But situations of this kind are by no means unique, especially in very large families . . . The simple truth is that he inherited from her an indomitable will which frequently clashed with her own inflexible purpose.'[1] As Brian's wife later put it, all the Montgomery sons were markedly similar in both territorial assertiveness and desire to go their own way, Bernard simply more so than the others.[2]

Yet, attractive though this view may be, it is clearly insufficient to explain the complicated tensions that would drive the most successful British field commander of the twentieth century. Gentle, intelligent and loyal, Brian Montgomery was born sixteen years after Bernard and witnessed none of the childhood struggles that were to forge Bernard's wayward ambition; thereafter, too, Brian looked up to Bernard as to a hallowed elder brother who had paid for his schooling, and even dictated the essential course of his life – postponement of marriage ('You can't get married on a subaltern's pay'); rejection of the offer of a Cambridge University education and career in the Indian Civil Service ('You must return to your battalion as Adjutant, which is a great honour and crucial post to have held'); even the writing of his book *A Field-Marshal in the Family* ('I suggest you now take over [father's diaries]. You could write a book and make a lot of money'). By the time the infant Brian was old enough to take in the family personalities, Bernard was already leaving school, and had found a *modus vivendi* with his mother, based on growing

[1] Brian Montgomery, op. cit.
[2] Conversation with the author, 18.1.78.

respect and the fact that she could no longer beat and humiliate him. As Bernard wrote in his *Memoirs*: 'The time came when her authority could no longer be exercised. Fear then disappeared and respect took its place. From the time I joined the Army until my mother died, I had an immense and growing respect for her wonderful character. And it became clear to me that my early troubles were mostly my own fault.' This growing respect, however, did not entirely cover Bernard's scars, as we shall see; and when fame finally came to the third-born son, his attitude both to his mother and the other members of the family changed markedly. To the surprise of those who knew him intimately he underwent a strange metamorphosis, producing 'a streak of showmanship he never had before' as his brother Donald put it.[1] This change was attested also by his brother Brian, his sisters Winsome and Una, by Lady Gwen Herbert, Sir Basil Liddell Hart, Sir Francis de Guingand and many others. The ambitious but essentially shy and – in all but military affairs – quite humble general became boastful, vain, and anxious to gain the limelight – alone. Those who were fond of him and those who respected his outstanding military qualities were mostly prepared to overlook this embarrassing change; watched with shame the way Bernard cut his family, lorded it over his friends, and abused those to whom he owed so much. To the end of his life he would mix Christian benevolence with acts of stunning condescension or even malevolence – for fame exposed the nerve of Bernard's intimate and dutiful relationship with his home. The power to enforce his will on millions and the adulation of whole peoples was a wine headier than any that, in the long years in the 'wilderness' while he made his slow ascent within the military establishment, Bernard had rejected. Whether he was ashamed of the way his mother had kept him in dutiful loyalty for so long, or whether celebrity simply turned his head after so many years of being a figure of ridicule, it is difficult to judge. Perhaps, in a way, the two motives were complementary – for Bernard served the Army, as will be seen, with quite the same intense devotion, at once innocent and coloured with quarrels, as he served Maud, his mother. The advent of fame released him from that onerous servitude – or rather, it up-ended the relationship. The shy, determined, frustrated Bishop's son became himself the despot, able to call the tune. Bernard's at times breathtakingly mean behaviour after 1942 is probably of little consequence in itself – since there is always a darker side of genius – but it does point backwards to the severity of Maud's upbringing, his protracted emotional dependence on her, and the many years it took before he could at last cast aside his filial piety and be entirely his own man. Unless this cardinal fact be understood when reviewing the early years of Bernard's career, then the subsequent manner in which he was to treat his mother, his

[1] Alan Moorehead, *Montgomery*, London 1946.

Chief-of-Staff, members of his family, his son and many of his friends becomes simply monstrously ignoble. The truth is, as will be seen, that despite his growing experience and even distinction as a young officer, Bernard did not emotionally untie himself from his mother for a very long time.

That Bernard was the black sheep among otherwise obedient siblings is, despite Brian's later testimony, undisputed. 'He was the bad boy of the family, mischievous by nature and individualist by character,' his brother Donald told Alan Moorehead.[1] Bernard later blamed himself – 'I was a dreadful little boy. I don't suppose anybody would put up with my sort of behaviour these days';[2] but his sister Winsome blamed Maud, who simply did not love him or his nearest sister Una. One can hardly avoid the conclusion – particularly when one reflects on the six years before the next child, Winsome, was born – that both Bernard and Una were the result of unwanted pregnancies; and that Bernard's rebellious, mischievous spirit was not simply the inherited will of his mother, as Brian put it, but the protest of the unloved, attention-seeking infant.

Whatever the truth, Tasmania became the stage for a bitter trial whose unhappiness Bernard would never forget, nor quite forgive. Moreover its very freedom – an unspoilt country in which the children could ride, hunt, fish, swim and explore to their hearts' content – accentuated the difference between Maud's domestic tyranny and the open, outdoor spaces. According to Alan Moorehead, Bernard would fling himself down in the long grass of the rambling garden whispering 'What have I done? What have I done?', when he had sinned and knew that Maud's singing cane would soon be upon him. 'My early life was a series of fierce battles,' Bernard recorded, 'from which my mother invariably emerged the victor. If I could not be seen anywhere, she could say – "Go and find out what Bernard is doing and tell him to stop it." '[3]

However, the frequent beatings do not seem to have curbed the thin, wiry youngster. In a photograph taken when he was nine, Bernard stands with his cap rakishly planted on the back of his head and his fist raised in pugilistic stance. 'I never lied about my misdeeds,' he claimed. 'I took my punishment.'[4] Andrew Holden, the son of Henry Montgomery's closest friend Dr Holden, found the young Bernard a difficult, unattractive school companion, while admiring his mother, the bustling wife of the Bishop. Bernard, in Holden's eyes, had 'no charm at all'.[5] Certainly, when one reads of Bernard's pranks and outrages, one cannot disagree. Within a short while he evidently became a monstrous bully, torturing recalcitrant

[1] Alan Moorehead, op. cit.
[2] Quoted in Alun Chalfont, *Montgomery of Alamein*, London 1976.
[3] Bernard Montgomery, op. cit.
[4] Ibid.
[5] Alan Moorehead, op. cit.

colleagues and imposing his own tyrannical will as his mother did within the home. Nevertheless one cannot withhold a certain sneaking admiration for the knickerbockered, scarlet-beretted young boy who, when his mother called the children to order prior to reading out her instructions for the next event at a party, shouted: 'Silence in the pig market, the old sow speaks first!' He was led away for caning, naturally; but the episode reveals a cardinal quality that – as with Churchill – would eventually temper ambition into greatness: his sense of humour. Irreverent, often malign, it was to be a priceless asset in the years to come. If his father the Bishop, bossed and bullied by Maud, viewed the quaint antics of the world *sub specie aeternitatis* as the Archbishop of Canterbury claimed, then it was undoubtedly Bernard's great gift to focus life *sub specie ioculi*. Though he sometimes strayed into periods of vindictiveness and cruelty, he usually found his way back on to an even keel when his wit returned; and his *Memoirs*, like Churchill's *My Early Life*, abound with humour. His sharp grey-blue eyes were quick to spot the incongruities and absurdities of life, particularly his own; and, if his mother's loveless severity beat all natural tenderness out of him, this native wit at least enabled Bernard to survive and not take himself all too seriously. Indeed many witnesses – family, friends, colleagues and subordinates – attest that it was only after he became a famous figure on the strength of the battle of Alamein that Bernard finally overcame his essential diffidence and shyness, and released the floodgates of his vanity that would so worry observers like Harold Nicolson and the Members of wartime Parliament.

In the meantime, though, Bernard's childhood made its harsh passage between freedom and flagellation. He bullied other children, was beaten; he picked up an Australian accent and was forced to stand in front of the family intoning the 'correct' English pronunciation until Maud was satisfied; he sold his bicycle – a gift – to buy stamps for his collection, and had his pocket money stopped until every penny was repaid, after Maud had bought back the velocipede. He chased a girl through the house brandishing a carving knife and was flogged. He fell seriously ill with enteric fever; but survived.

In 1897 Bishop Montgomery returned to England with the whole family for the Lambeth Conference of bishops. Maud's father had at last been appointed to the Deanery of Canterbury, and he arranged for his daughter and the children to live in one of the Cathedral houses in the town. Harold, Donald and Bernard were sent to the King's School for a term. Bernard was by then nine years old; but the experience cannot have marked him unduly, for in later life he recollected nothing of his time there. It was the same year that the school's illustrious ex-pupil, William Somerset Maugham, published his first novel, *Liza of Lambeth*.

However it was only in 1901, when Bernard was thirteen, that the

Montgomerys left Tasmania for good. Inspired by his experience of missionary work among natives, miners, prospectors and settlers, the Bishop had written fulsome reports to England on the qualities and credentials needed by the Secretary of the Society for the Propagation of the Gospel in Foreign Parts, whose post had recently fallen vacant. He was somewhat surprised when a telegram arrived bearing the signatures of the two Archbishops, and the Bishops of London, Winchester, Bath and Newcastle, asking if he himself would return to England to assume the secretaryship.

At first Bishop Montgomery was inclined to reject the offer, which he felt was both below the dignity of a bishop and too clerical, too sedentary, for his own bush-roving, missionary bent. However he was by now fifty-four and after an exchange of telegrams and letters he accepted. 'To create a sort of foreign secretaryship of Anglican missions with a bishop at its head, to be a referee and guide in all Greater Britain questions. The outlook is terrifying in its possibilities. Had one the gifts one could almost transform the general ideals of the Church and make them actually embrace the world,' he wrote to his father-in-law, Dean Farrar. 'It strikes me at times as more Pauline in scope than that of any bishop in the Anglican communion, and therefore most episcopal. The last point was the greatest difficulty at first, but I am clear about it now.'[1]

In the event Henry Montgomery did not transform the 'general ideals of the Church', for he was no St Paul, and lacked the necessary arrogance for such revolutionary action. Perhaps Maud, in her self-willed way, had stolen the Bishop's thunder. At all events, the new secretaryship was not to be a stepping-stone to even higher things, and Henry Montgomery was to remain in the post until his retirement in 1921, at the age of seventy-four.

Henry Montgomery's disinclination to return home was echoed by his family. They had been in Tasmania twelve years, and their roots there were deep. If people looked askance at the way Maud conducted her home – eating rabbit, then considered vermin; travelling second class on the railways; galloping side-saddle down the Hobart beach while her husband walked – there can be no doubt she was widely respected as the Bishop's wife; and it was considered one of the sights of the Cathedral on Sunday to see Mrs Montgomery sweep in with a rustle of black taffeta skirts, trailing her six children behind her. She would never command so much attention again; and the little office in Delahay Street in London, bereft of typewriters or even shorthand clerks, must have seemed a poor substitute for the colonial residence of Bishopscourt in Hobart.

The family sailed from Melbourne in November 1901, arriving via the Suez Canal at Plymouth early in 1902. Harold, the eldest son, had already decided he was not cut out for an English career; and the

[1] Maud Montgomery, *Bishop Montgomery*, op. cit.

37

Bishop was quite content for him to enter the Army, serving abroad. 'He will dislike England,' the Bishop wrote to Dean Farrar before they sailed. 'His magnificent horsemanship will be of no use till he can enter the army in some way, and he is not brilliant at books. I think he ought to make his career in South Africa, and go there to stay. He has all the love of solitude some men gain out there, does not care much for society, is very independent, and as strong as a horse.'[1] Dean Farrar may well have pulled strings; or the name of Sir Robert Montgomery may have helped open certain doors in Whitehall, for no sooner had the Montgomerys landed in Plymouth than Harold was granted a commission in the Imperial Yeomanry, famed for their skill as marksmen and horsemen, and was off to serve in the final months of the Boer War.

Donald Montgomery, the second son, also warranted the Bishop's thoughtful consideration before the family returned. 'He is clever and ought with ease to get a scholarship at Cambridge,' the Bishop wrote to his father-in-law. What was wanted was a good school that would push the boy – 'who is strong in mathematics and has a great love for classics and literature also.'[2] In the event Donald did go to Cambridge, becoming a successful lawyer and King's Counsel in Canada.

But of Bernard the Bishop's letter said nothing save that he might go to the same school as Donald. About Bernard's talents or failings the Bishop remained silent. The future genius of North Africa and Normandy was still a thorn in his mother's side, academically of no promise, physically small, with mousy brown hair. It was eventually decided, once the family had arrived in England, to send the two boys to St Paul's, a London day school not far from the house the Montgomerys had found in Chiswick, by the Thames; and dressed in bowler hats Donald and Bernard were despatched on the first day of the following term, in January 1902. Donald had obtained a foundation scholarship, thus absolving his parents from paying his school fees; Bernard, though he also took the scholarship exam, had not.

The bowler hat, it appeared, was a mistake, and the two boys must have cursed their mother that first morning – for the wearing of a bowler hat was a privilege reserved only for the most senior members of the school. Fortunately the kindly school porter removed the offending headgear before trouble ensued; but the memory may well have stuck in Bernard's mind, for exactly forty years later he would produce the same consternation in establishment circles – risking even the censure of the King – by the adoption of the most unorthodox headwear for a serving general of the British Army.

While Donald made excellent progress at St Paul's, and won the scholarship to Cambridge which his father had foretold, Bernard's

---

[1] Quoted in Brian Montgomery, op. cit.
[2] Ibid.

school report was uniformly disappointing that first July. Life in Tasmania had obviously taught him little in the way of English composition; even in divinity his essays were 'very weak', according to Captain Bicknell, his form master. In mathematics he was positively 'backward', though improving, and in all other subjects – Latin, French, Science and Art – was marked no higher than 'fair'.[1] Considering he had joined the school's lowest echelon – the three-tiered system of 'Army' classes – this was poor indeed; and Bishop Montgomery and his wife cannot have derived much comfort from his report, especially his performance in divinity – a class in which he had already been caned by Captain Bicknell for circulating smutty doggerel.

The choice of Army class at St Paul's was apparently Bernard's, made on his first day at school in January 1902, and revealed to his parents that evening. It was not a decision that was well received.

'My father had always hoped that I would become a clergyman,' Bernard later wrote, 'and I well recall his disappointment when I told him that I wanted to be soldier.' 'But why the Army?' his parents asked.[2] Bernard had no answer, for he had apparently never shown any inclination for soldiering, except for a brief moment when a contingent of volunteers left Hobart for the Boer War in 1899 amid much local fêting and farewells. Perhaps Harold's departure to the war was the real reason; or, being lazy, he felt the Army class at St Paul's offered a soft option. At any rate, having made up his mind that day, he refused to renege. The Bishop wisely accepted it as God's will, and left the room; but Maud would not give in so easily, and there followed a fierce argument. For the first time in his life, Bernard emerged the victor. He was fourteen, and though the Army class did not commit him irrevocably to the services, it paved the way too neatly to be revoked. Together with the least talented of his school generation, Bernard could dawdle and dream his way through the school years, concentrating only on the new sports which St Paul's offered: cricket and rugby football. Within three years he was captaining both teams; within a single year he was swimming for his school under his brother Donald's captaincy. Work was considered a nuisance, and his conduct in class abysmal – or 'sometimes strange' as the Latin master put it, as gently as possible for parents' eyes.[3]

In retrospect, Bernard felt his parents were partly to blame for his behaviour and poor progress at St Paul's. 'I was thrown into a large public school without having certain facts of life explained to me; I began to learn them for myself in the rough and tumble of school life, and not finally till I went to Sandhurst at the age of nineteen.'[4] Yet,

[1] Montgomery Papers.
[2] Alan Moorehead, op. cit.
[3] Montgomery Papers.
[4] Bernard Montgomery, op. cit.

considering the way in which Bernard insisting on joining the school's Army class, and his years of bullying behaviour at home in Tasmania, it is difficult to see what the Bishop or his wife might have told Bernard that would radically have altered his career. That life at a boys' public school, even a day school, encourages a boy's most wayward, and often carnal instincts which he must guard against? As Churchill whiled his time away indolently in Harrow classrooms to the distress of his father, Lord Randolph, so in turn Bernard Montgomery ignored the real advantages of his expensive education. By 1903 the Latin master was prompted to record, in his report, that Bernard had 'brains'; and his progress in the new subjects of physics and chemistry was fair, while divinity and English were 'excellent'; but a long bout of illness in the autumn washed out such hopeful signs, and thereafter his report deteriorated until he finally reached Army Class A in the autumn of 1905, aged almost eighteen, by which time the most common criticism was that he was 'backward', and, though able to write sensible essays, he had 'no notion of style'.[1]

Outside the classroom, though, Bernard was taking full advantage of the playing fields. Though small and wiry, he had an excellent eye, and a natural sense of contest as well as leadership. If he felt his mother's lack of affection had made his childhood unhappy, he was now able to provide a substitute, and he basked in the glory which excellence at sports still fomented at a public school, notwithstanding his grandfather Dean Farrar's attempts to modernise this essentially British institution. In his own words, Bernard had arrived from Tasmania 'self-sufficient, intolerant of authority and steeled to take punishment'.[2] Life at an English public school was therefore too academically undemanding to provide more than a moral challenge to the indolent 'Colonial', and Bernard was the first to feel ashamed, later, at his idleness. Indeed his lifelong industry thereafter may partly be seen as the product of this shame – a shame heightened by the embarrassment with which he observed his self-opinionated, lazy and professionally illiterate colleagues once commissioned in the Army.

Nevertheless, Bernard could own to be content with life. Though his mother complained he was quiet and uncommunicative at home, his adolescent *joie de vivre* was given full rein at school. 'I was very happy at St Paul's,' he wrote later. 'For the first time in my life leadership and authority came my way . . . for the first time I could plan my own battles [on the football field] and there were some fierce contests.'[3] Vicious, with unflagging energy, merciless on the rugby pitch, he showed the 'exuberance' of his 'animal spirits' by assaulting his opponents, 'stamping on their heads and twisting their necks,

[1] Montgomery Papers.
[2] Bernard Montgomery, op. cit.
[3] Ibid.

and doing many other inconceivable atrocities with a view, no doubt, to proving his patriotism,' as his school magazine recorded.[1] The Bishopscourt bully had found his way beyond Maud's caning rectitude to the one arena where youth can legitimately go – 'the ruffians' sport played by gentlemen'.

Besides his shame at being so indolent, Bernard would later reflect whether he had not used this first taste of leadership and authority 'badly'. Certainly it was to take him another forty years before he was able to put his theories of leadership to their ultimate test. In the meantime, however, in July 1906, he was faced with his first challenge beyond home and school. To join the Army as an officer in peacetime he was expected to study at the Royal Military College, Sandhurst.[2] This entailed passing the entrance examination which, though hardly difficult in an academic sense, demanded certain basic skills that could not be gained on the cricket or Rugby pitches of Hammersmith. He was eighteen and a half, 'rather backward for his age', as his form-master wrote. 'To have a serious chance for Sandhurst, he must give more time to work.'[3]

This report, when sent to Bernard's parents, must have caused a certain commotion at No. 19 Bolton Road. Possibly the Bishop prayed that the Lord might enlighten his son, might wake him from the 'easy satisfaction' that marred his progress in class and make him realise that, on the meagre income provided by the Society for the Propagation of the Gospel and with so many mouths still to be fed at home, Bernard simply must take his schoolwork seriously. More likely Maud arraigned him before the rest of the family and Miss Lawrence, the governess, to make public his abysmal scholastic showing – she who had finished her schooling at sixteen.

Whatever the case, Bernard acknowledged that he was 'brought up with a jerk'[4] by the report; and though the final school verdict in the winter of 1906 was still far from rhapsodic (Chemistry: 'slow to grasp principles'; Mathematics: 'his knowledge is weak'; French: 'still backward'), all his teachers remarked on the way he had applied himself, and the High Master of St Paul's even saw fit to delete the words 'still somewhat backward' on the version sent to Bernard's parents.[5] By then, too, the matter of Bernard's school work was itself academic, for in the autumn of 1906 he had taken the Sandhurst competitive entrance exam – and had passed 72nd out of 177 successful candidates. He was in.

[1] *The Pauline*, November 1906, edited by G. D. H. Cole and A. L. Johnston.
[2] The Royal Military College Sandhurst was merged with the Royal Military Academy Woolwich in 1947, and is now the Royal Military Academy, Sandhurst.
[3] Montgomery Papers.
[4] Bernard Montgomery, op. cit.
[5] Montgomery Papers.

CHAPTER SEVEN

Sandhurst

'I was astonished to find later that a large number of my fellow cadets had found it necessary to leave school early and go to a crammer in order to ensure success in the competitive entrance examination,' Bernard Montgomery wrote later.[1] Such a cadet had been Winston Churchill, who failed twice while at Harrow – Bishop Montgomery's beloved old school – but finally got in, on his third attempt, after attending Captain James' 'poultry-farming' crammer in Cromwell Road, West London – 'the Blue Ribbon among the Crammers' as Churchill gratefully recalled in *My Early Life*.

Churchill's career was very different from that of his only rival for public adulation in the Second World War. Where Bernard Montgomery was unhappy in childhood and found fulfilment at St Paul's, Churchill hated Harrow – years that formed 'not only the least agreeable, but the only barren and unhappy period of my life,' he judged. 'I was happy as a child with my toys in my nursery. I have been happier every year since I became a man. But this interlude of school makes a sombre grey patch upon the chart of my journey. It was an unending spell of worries that did not then sound petty, and of toil uncheered by fruition; a time of discomfort, restriction, and purposeless monotony . . . I am all for the Public Schools but I do not want to go there again.' When finally he got into Sandhurst, Churchill's life flowered again. 'I had a new start,' he related, 'no longer handicapped by past neglect of Latin, French or Mathematics . . . We all started equal.'[2]

This was very far from the truth. The fact was that once selected for Sandhurst, cadets tended to divide into groups according to wealth. 'Horses were the greatest of my pleasures at Sandhurst,' Churchill wrote. 'I and the group in which I moved spent all our money on hiring horses . . . We organised point-to-points and even a steeplechase in the park of a friendly grandee, and bucketed gaily about the countryside.'

For Bernard Montgomery, entering Sandhurst some twelve years after Churchill had left, things were very different. Once again

[1] Bernard Montgomery, op. cit.
[2] W. S. Churchill, *My Early Life*, London 1930.

Maud – who signed Bernard's application forms as parent responsible for the candidate – had failed to explain certain 'facts of life' to the
boy; and it was only half-way through the cadetship that Bernard
discovered the relationship between income and regiment. Churchill
had gone into a cavalry regiment, the 4th Hussars; but a private
income of at least £300 to £400 per annum was demanded before a
cavalry regiment would consider a cadet. Even a good County
regiment required a private income of at least £100 a year.

Of this, on 30 January 1907, Bernard was unaware as he embarked
on his new military career at the age of nineteen. He stood 5 feet 7
inches tall, weighed 138 pounds, his chest girth was 34 inches and he
was considered medically fit. His mother had given him an allowance of nine shillings a week in addition to the college fees of
£150 – almost twice as much as she gave her husband, the Bishop.
While this may have seemed generous to Maud, there can be little
doubt that Bernard's behaviour problem at Sandhurst began with
her stinginess. In his *Memoirs* Bernard recorded that he was 'doubtful
if many cadets were as poor as myself . . . Outside attractions being
denied me for want of money, I plunged into games and work'.

At first Bernard's zeal produced excellent results – and after only
five weeks, on 5 March 1907, he was promoted Lance-Corporal, with
a view to being made the next Colour-Sergeant of 'B' Company. He
took up hockey for the first time in his life and was declared a
'natural'. It was not long before he found himself in the College
Rugby XV as well.

It was an auspicious moment in Bishop Montgomery's life, too; for
in April 1907 the Prince of Wales (later George V) laid the foundation
stone for a new headquarters of the Society for the Propagation of the
Gospel in Tufton Street, Westminster; and soon afterwards the
Bishop, who was organising the first world-wide Pan-Anglican
Congress, was made Prelate of the Order of St Michael and St
George, the knightly order created to honour outstanding work in
the Dominions of Great Britain.

Bernard's first term passed reasonably satisfactorily. Though he
did not work very hard and was placed 87th in the summer exams his
performance was judged 'excellent' by the Commandant. He was
learning military administration, law, history and geography, tactics, engineering, topography, Hindustani, musketry, gymnastics,
and drill. The summer was spent at New Park in Ireland with the
family, and in September he commenced what might be his final
term if he was lucky. In fact he was; for, owing to a promotion, a
vacancy had just occurred for a second lieutenancy in the County
Infantry Regiment of his selection, the Royal Warwickshire Regiment, and Bernard must have been delighted when, in early November news came that his name had been selected to fill it. The Royal
Warwickshire Regiment was not only one of the oldest English
regiments of foot, with many battle honours, but it also possessed

what in Maud Montgomery's eyes was a cardinally important asset: a battalion posted in India where with special Indian allowances an officer could virtually live on his pay.

The prospect seemed assured; all Bernard had to do was complete a meritorious second term – which no longer even included gymnastics, musketry and drill, but did encompass riding. It was at this moment in his nascent career that disaster struck.

Bernard's company at Sandhurst, 'B' Company, had already earned an unattractive reputation as 'Bloody B'. Hospitalisation in the wake of pitched battles using pokers and similar weapons was not unknown. Bernard, as a Lance-Corporal, was already by rank one of the leaders of the company; but by inclination he seems to have been the boss. Matters came to a head in December, just before the examinations. Bernard's gang broke into the rooms of a cadet who was changing into his regulation blue mess uniform, caught him in his shirt and underpants, and in Tom Brown fashion held him by hand and foot while Bernard struck a match and set fire to his shirt-tails.

Fire has many connotations in psychopathology, and all children are tempted at least once in childhood to play with it. At the age of nineteen Bernard can have had no idea of the nature of skin burns. He was evidently envious or contemptuous of the victim ('a dreadful chap'), and thought it would be a lark to singe his behind.

The consequences, however, were severe. The victim was badly burned, and conveyed at once to hospital. Though he gallantly refused to name his assailant, it was impossible to keep such a secret within the intimate confines of the College.

Rustication was not uncommon as a punishment, but Bernard's case was more serious than the usual disciplinary trespasses. The cadets went home on 18 December 1907; and between then and the first day of the following term a decision about Bernard's future had to be made. The Royal Warwicks were ready to commission him; but, in the opinion of the Commandant of the Royal Military College was Bernard actually fit to receive His Majesty's commission?

Whether Bernard at first recognised the seriousness of his crime we do not know. In the College Rugby XV photograph that Christmas he sits, brooding and sour, on a ledge of the grey building against which the team was assembled, while the rest of the back row stand. However Maud Montgomery, at any rate, realised the gravity of the situation. Telephoning the Commandant, she journeyed immediately to Camberley to stay the night with Colonel Capper and his wife.

Maud's errand of mercy was fulfilled. Colonel Capper agreed to hush up the affair, presumably to save the Bishop's name as much as for Bernard's sake. However, as a punishment Bernard was not included among fifty candidates passed out that January; and his Lance-Corporal's stripe was removed. The reversion to Gentleman

Cadet was posted among the College Orders on 29 January 1908, when the College reopened, but without explanation. He had come 74th in the order of merit in the previous term's examinations; his performance was merely marked 'Good', and no reference was made to the burning either in the College Register or in the papers sent to the War Office.

It is doubtful whether Maud saw herself as a contributing cause in Bernard's transgression. That Bernard was maladjusted must nevertheless have been evident to the discerning eye. He had blotted his copybook in the most heinous way for the son of a churchman. Perhaps his relative poverty in the college had made him anxious to avenge himself on more wealthy, but less aggressive cadets. As he wrote some fifty years later, he remembered with what envy he looked at simple wrist watches for sale in the College canteen, watches which 'most cadets acquired' at Sandhurst, yet which, until the very eve of the First World War, would remain beyond his purse.[1]

For Bernard the question was obviously whether he could come to terms with relative penury, master his envy, and make good in an adult world. But for the College Commandant the question was simpler. In an age that did not require conscription, yet in which Britain must needs produce the administrators and defenders of the largest empire ever created, the ethos of gentlemanly conduct was sacrosanct.

Bernard had sinned against this ethos; and the case under review was evidently not the first breach of conduct committed and led by the Bishop's son. Tradition had it that 'off duty' the cadets governed their own lives, without the supervision of officers. It was an arrangement of trust, and a training too for those who had led sheltered lives. Maud's error, beyond the loveless upbringing and her plainly unrealistic stinginess (she still gave the Bishop only five shillings a week spending money out of his own salary and royalties from the books he had begun to write, though her daughter Winsome claimed the family was at that time quite well off), was to have kept Bernard at home all his life under her commanding, cane-wielding, religion-obsessed stewardship. Though Bernard, as we shall see, grew to respect and even love her; though he forced himself to temper his exuberance and consider others almost to the point, in military terms, of a saintliness similar to his father's (an absolute and unremitting care for the welfare of his officers and men, even when he reached the very highest rank), he was, throughout his life, aware of his own naïveté, of the way he had been pitched into institutions like St Paul's, and then Sandhurst, without guidance, as an innocent. 'This neglect,' he wrote in his *Memoirs*, 'might have had bad results; but luckily I don't think it did. Even so I wouldn't let it happen to others.'

[1] Bernard Montgomery, op. cit.

The scandal was now forgotten; and in retrospect it was perhaps fortunate that it had occurred while he was a cadet and not – as would be the case with George S. Patton – when he was a general. Certainly Bernard seems to have turned over a new leaf. He worked hard, and by the summer examinations had improved considerably.

Moreover Bernard's new ambition – ironic in retrospect – was to join the Indian Army. Possibly, like his brothers Harold and Donald, he wanted permanent freedom from Maud's moral – and psychological – straitjacket; possibly he wanted the permanent financial independence that was assured an officer of the Indian Army. However, more likely Bernard was simply reflecting the popular esteem in which the Indian Army was then held. Later he would display a certain dislike for Indian Army officers, and fail sometimes to treat them as seriously as their military talents deserved; but, at the time Bernard was at Sandhurst, there is no doubt that the Indian Army took the cream – or at least the most industrious – of the Sandhurst cadets. Of the first thirty cadets in order of merit passing out of Sandhurst in the summer of 1908 after three terms' residence, no fewer than twenty-eight elected to join the Indian Army – though none was to achieve the distinctions of the demoted Lance-Corporal from 'B' Company.

In fact, thirty-six cadets were taken into the Indian Army that summer; and Bernard had passed out thirty-sixth in order of merit! However, eight of those selected – all of whom fared worse than Bernard in the placings – were King's Indian Cadets, cadets who for family reasons were entitled to join the Indian Army regardless of their final place.

Bernard had thus failed in his attempt. Almost fifty years later, in a speech given at the Sovereign's Parade in 1954, he wished 'happiness and success to those of you who leave the Royal Military College today; and if some of you should have thought your qualities have not received due recognition here, and that you have not received the promotion you would have liked, I can tell you that I felt the same myself when I left Sandhurst. I was reduced to the ranks in my last term. I suppose I must have deserved such a shattering blow – I didn't think so at the time. But there is hope for everyone, and there is no hurry, and your time will come'.[1]

On 19 September 1908, Bernard was gazetted into the Royal Warwickshire Regiment; and eight weeks later, on 12 December, he joined the 1st Battalion of his regiment on the North-West Frontier of India, at Peshawar. He was twenty-one and he arrived in Peshawar only months after the Royal Warwicks had taken part in the Bazar Valley and Mohmand expeditions of the spring of 1908. These punitive expeditions against mountain raiders served to enforce respect for British rule and to season British and Indian Army troops;

[1] *The Wish Stream*, Vol. 8, October 1954, No. 2.

but they involved a sometimes distasteful ruthlessness. The Regimental History of the Royal Warwicks, describing the Bazar Valley Expedition, related how the Warwicks 'made a frontal attack on [the village of Hahvai]. They were met with a smart fire, but rushed the village and scaled the hill behind, without any casualties. After the village had been destroyed the force withdrew.' Winston Churchill had himself witnessed such an expedition in the area eleven years previously as a subaltern correspondent on leave from his regiment. His account, subsequently published as the *Malakand Field Force*, created a considerable stir; but writing in 1930 in *My Early Life* Churchill was disposed to take a more ironic stance towards such punitive treatment of the tribesmen: 'We proceeded systematically, village by village, and we destroyed the houses, filled up the wells, blew down the towers, cut down the great shady trees, burned the crops and broke the reservoirs in punitive devastation . . . Whether it was worth it I cannot tell. At any rate, at the end of a fortnight the valley was a desert, and honour was satisfied.'

CHAPTER EIGHT

India

At Moville, in the summer after he passed out from Sandhurst, the Montgomerys had held a ball at which a contemporary, dancing with Bernard, found him stiff, unamusing and more interested in shooting than 'such a young girl'.[1] Certainly this antipathy towards the fairer sex – save certain sisters and trusted cousins – made it easier for Bernard than for many of his fellow-subalterns to settle down to the serious business of soldiering. His childhood in Tasmania and the summers spent in the hills above Lough Foyle in Ireland predisposed him to the mountains of North-West India; and he certainly enjoyed his time there. Fifty years later one of the officers of the regiment, Brigadier Clement Tomes, recalled:

Monty came out from Sandhurst to join the Royal Warwickshire Regiment at Peshawar on the NW Frontier of India in 1908. I was then a subaltern of seven years' service and that was when I first met him . . .

Monty was a nice young fellow but I cannot remember that there was any particular sensation over his arrival. Peshawar was a good station in those days with plenty of training, the ever present chance of a frontier expedition to keep us up to scratch and lots of games and sport to say nothing of social life. My recollection of him was that he entered into all these activities with zest and keenness. Indeed it is his keenness that seems to stand out most in my memory.

He played all games – hockey, cricket, football and so on. He bought a horse to hunt with the Peshawar Valley Hounds – an old Indian cavalry charger called 'Probyn' – and won a point-to-point with it: much, I think, to most people's astonishment for he was not outstanding as a horseman.

Training was almost exclusively in mountain warfare and was carried out mostly at a small nearby hill station called CHERAT. In 1910 it was decreed that about fifty picked men in each battalion should be trained as scouts. This was a new feature and I think it shows that Monty must have impressed the authorities, for it was

[1] Brian Montgomery, op. cit.

he who was chosen to organize it. I am sure he did it well – at any rate I have a photograph which shows him sitting in the midst of his men on a khud side, and they all look particularly fit and interested.[1]

In his *Memoirs* Bernard was to be strangely negative about this first period of his life as an infantry officer, in India. He recalled how, on arriving at Peshawar, he tasted alcohol for the first time in the ante-room of the Officers' Mess – when he was not thirsty and did not want the whisky ordered for him. But whether Bernard's later prejudice against officers of the Indian Army was really formed as a subaltern there, or was a retrospective bias, is difficult to say. There was certainly an excessive emphasis on ceremonial and ritual for a keen young officer – but probably no more so than at home in England at the time. Yet, if there was a tabu on 'talking shop' in the Officers' Mess, there was certainly no lack of challenge outside it. Where Churchill had found it impossible to communicate with his Punjabi troops except by signs, Bernard sat down and learned both Urdu and the local dialect, Pushtu. He took a specialist examination in mule transport, and studied the pages of his Field Service Regulations – his copy has survived – until he knew it by heart. In his *Memoirs* he acknowledged: 'Looking back, I would put this period as the time when it was becoming apparent to me that to succeed one must master one's profession.'

It was this ambition to succeed that now began to mark out the young Lieutenant B. L. Montgomery (as he became on 1 April 1910) from his colleagues. In October 1910 the battalion moved south to Bombay for the final two years of its foreign tour. Brigadier Tomes recalled that it was 'a bad station for soldiering with a hot humid climate which sapped one's energy. Training facilities were very limited and there was every temptation to let things go. I was now Adjutant of the battalion and I do remember that I was amazed sometimes at Monty's energy and unabated keenness – but truth to tell he was sometimes a little argumentative and did not always do as he was told'.[2]

Perhaps the best example of Bernard's self-will was given that winter, when he was made Sports Officer of the battalion. On 14 December 1910 the German battleship *Gneisenau* with the German Crown Prince aboard paid a courtesy call at Bombay. Bernard paraded among the guard of honour, but deliberately disobeyed the Adjutant's order to field a second-class football team. The Germans 'stayed about a week in the harbour and there was much interchange of courtesies,' Brigadier Tomes remembered. 'Eventually they challenged the battalion to football. Monty was told by me not to turn out

---

[1] 'Monty' – an unpublished memoir by Brigadier Clement Tomes, 1958, communicated to author by Lt-Colonel L. T. Tomes, 14.3.78.
[2] Loc. cit.

49

the full side as these Germans were not likely to give us much of a game. I watched the match. Every single man of our first team was on the field and the result was a shambles – forty to nothing I think. To my remonstrations he replied: "Oh! I was taking no risks with those bastards!"'

On 8 November 1911 Bernard sailed home to England aboard the troopship *Plassey* on six months' leave. He had not seen his family for three years; and must have wondered whether they would recognise any change in the erstwhile cadet who had almost burnt his boats at Sandhurst.

However, at Bolton Road, Chiswick and at Moville in Ireland it was still the same Montgomery clan, unchanged in the years of Bernard's absence save by the death of Desmond, the fourth son, from meningitis in 1909. Maud still ruled domestically at the family head, while the Bishop retired more and more to his study – 'trying to find out how the Israelites really did cross the Red Sea,' as one contemporary of Bernard's cynically put it;[1] or preparing for the elaborate ceremonies, such as King George V's coronation; or the services of the Order of which Bishop Montgomery was the Prelate, in St Paul's Cathedral. The Bishop 'rather enjoyed all the pomp and ceremony that was inevitable on such occasions,' his son Brian later remembered; but if, as Brian also recalled, the Bishop left 'all matters concerning the family entirely in the hands of our mother',[2] it was not only a surrender to Maud's domestic tyranny, but a true division of labour. The Bishop enjoyed ceremonial certainly; but there can be no doubt that his dedication to Christianity was sincere. Indeed his reputation within the Church and outside it was founded on his transparent sincerity. He prayed every day in turn for the five thousand members of his Order, each by name. He travelled to the USA, Canada, China, Japan, Korea, Hong Kong, Malaysia and Borneo. Perhaps it was only then, when beyond the restrictions of Maud's devout menage, that the Bishop really came into his own. 'He seldom suffered from homesickness,' Maud acknowledged in her biography *Bishop Montgomery*. 'He made friends wherever he went, and brought cheer and inspiration to countless workers on the prairie, in lonely homesteads, in crowded cities.' Everyone who met him seems to have remembered him with affection.

In such circumstances it is scarcely surprising that the returning subaltern from India, in the early months of 1912, was not thought to be particularly prodigal. Friends of Bernard who visited him at Chiswick were apparently 'astonished to see how much he was engulfed in the family and Mrs Montgomery's rule of the house,' Alan Moorehead later recorded.[3] 'They found they were obliged to push their luggage from the railway station in a wheelbarrow, and

[1] Brian Montgomery, op. cit.
[2] Ibid.
[3] Alan Moorehead, op. cit.

50

once inside the house, they too were drawn into the circle of family prayers, punctual hours for meals and early risings.' The contrast between Bernard's quietness at home and the field or military garrison was spectacular. Though his self-confidence had gained in leaps and bounds once he was emancipated from Bishopsbourne, emotionally and psychologically he remained under Maud's strict spell. His earlier struggles with his mother were replaced, as Bernard grew too old to be chastised, by loyalty, as he recorded in his *Memoirs*. But to outsiders it was strange to see this undoubted leader of men *in loco pupillari* at home.

Bernard returned to his battalion in Bombay on 3 May 1912 – where it was promptly inspected by Major-General G. F. Gorringe, Commanding Officer of the Bombay Infantry Brigade. Bernard can have had little idea that within six years he would be chosen to serve this same Major-General – as a temporary Lieutenant-Colonel, and Chief-of-Staff to his 47th Division, in the final summer of the Great War.

Bernard's star had already begun to rise. He was a full Lieutenant and when the Regimental Quartermaster went home for a year's leave, Bernard was interviewed and given the post over the heads of many more senior officers. He was the first officer in the regiment to purchase a motor cycle, and he also put himself forward as a candidate for special examination in Army Signals in October 1912 – an arduous test in all forms of army signalling from heliography to the telegraph, from cypher work to electro-magnetic telephone systems. It was an education he would never forget, and his surviving 'Army Signalling Scribbling Book' of 1912 testifies to the seriousness with which he applied himself. He kept a diary of the five-day test in helio, flag and lamp signalling conducted between Poona and Visapur Fort. His accommodation, in a bungalow on the plain, was rudimentary – with wild pigeons in profusion, 'no furniture except a few tables and chairs' and 'bugs plentiful'. Apart from morning and evening mists, the signalling went well, and in the scribbling book he added a small ditty:

I

The blinding lights on distant heights
That tell of signalling by nights
From peak to peak the message speeds
To chronicle the general's deeds

II

Swifter than the eagle's flight
The message speeds across the night
It flashes thro TA VP
The signaller reads each smallest flick

III

At morning time the heliograph
Sends messages along the path
The enemy in vain essays
To intercept the helio's rays.

IV

When the sun goes in the waving flag
Hurries the message from crag to crag . . .

The signals exam – in which Bernard passed out top with distinction – was Bernard's last success in India, for on 6 November 1912 he left the great sub-continent with the rest of his regiment, sailing via Malta, where a contingent was disembarked for garrison duty with the 2nd Battalion. He arrived home for Christmas; and on 2 January 1913 was appointed Assistant Adjutant of the 1st Battalion, the Royal Warwickshire Regiment, at its station at Shorncliffe, outside Folkestone.

These last eighteen months before the declaration of war were to be perhaps the most carefree of his entire life. At Hythe, nearby, Bernard attended the infantry officers' course at the Musketry School and passed out with distinction in rifle shooting and without difficulty in machine-gunnery. He played hockey for the Army that year, took up tennis, and showed no regret at having left India. He sold his motor bicycle and bought a Ford motor car, which he is said to have driven recklessly around the country. He was twenty-six, a keen soldier, natural sportsman, and convinced bachelor. Moreover he was fortunate in his companions – men like Captain Tomes, the Adjutant, who admired Bernard's zest for *servitude militaire*. Even more significantly, something of the *grandeur* too of his profession became clear to Bernard when he was befriended by another officer of the regiment, Captain B. P. Lefroy, who returned in January 1913 to the battalion after two years' study at the Staff College, Camberley.

In Bernard's own recollection it was Lefroy who first fired his military imagination, who first indicated to him the larger horizons of the military art – and made plain that, if he was to attain high command one day, he must study the literature of war, must attempt to draw historical lessons from the past and must base his criticisms of Britain's contemporary army on profound professional knowledge.

Together Bernard Montgomery and Lefroy would walk along the Leas cliffs, discussing books, ideas and military personalities. By the time Lefroy left the Royal Warwicks in April 1914 to go to the War Office, he had sown the seeds of a deep and lasting ambition in his young protégé.[1]

[1] Lt-Colonel Lefroy was killed at Loos in 1915.

Summer came and the Montgomerys booked their passage to Ireland, as they did each year. However, on 28 June 1914, Archduke Ferdinand was assassinated; and in the succeeding weeks the fever of war began to mount. By the end of July 1914 the War Office in London decided to act on the current scare that, in the event of a conflagration, German troops might be landed on English shores, and various regiments were warned to be ready to man the beaches of the east coast.

Such was Britain's first step towards mobilisation; and from the very start Lieutenant Bernard Montgomery was involved. All summer leave was cancelled. In an atmosphere of speculation and trepidation the Royal Warwickshire Regiment recalled absent officers and awaited orders. At 6 p.m. on 29 July 1914, they came.

PART TWO

The First World War

CHAPTER ONE

Letters Home

With the summer of 1914 and the outbreak of the Great War we come undoubtedly to the seminal period of Bernard Montgomery's career. Yet it is a period which, for lack of documentation, has gone largely uncharted in biographical accounts and which Bernard himself dismissed in five pages of his *Memoirs*.

However, among the many thousands of documents which Bernard Montgomery later deposited among his Private Papers was a large, folio-sized scrapbook, bound in red leather, containing over sixty letters written by Bernard mostly to his mother during the years 1914–18. In an Introduction to the folio, Bernard explained:

When my mother died certain of my father's papers came into the possession of my eldest brother. Among them were the letters I had written to my mother, and occasionally to my father, during the First World War – 1914 to 1918. My brother passed all these to me.

The letters are all in my own handwriting, mostly in pencil, and of tremendous interest – to me at any rate. I suppose a skilled psychologist, or handwriting expert, would be able to judge from the letters the sort of person I was during the First World War.

I was 26 in 1914 and led my platoon into battle on the 26th August at Le Cateau. When the war ended in 1918 I was rising 30, and was Chief-of-Staff of the 47th (London) Division. During those four years of war I learnt much about war and men which was to prove of very great value to me in later years.

It will be clear from the letters that in those days many of my views were not born out by events!! One thing I did learn – that uninformed criticism is valueless . . .

When war loomed ahead in July 1914, I was serving in the 1st Bn of the Royal Warwickshire Regt at Shorncliffe in Kent. Towards the end of July war with Germany appeared imminent, and the 10th Infantry B[riga]de at Shorncliffe was ordered to send a composite battalion to garrison the Isle of Sheppey – which it was considered might form an objective for an early attack on England by the Germans. I was appointed Adjutant of the battalion, which contained companies from each battalion in the Brigade.

It will be seen that I began the First World War in a Workhouse. It will also be seen that on 30th July I did not think Britain would be involved in the war!!

Until the summer of 1914 Bishop Montgomery and his wife regarded their third son with mixed feelings – certainly as second-best to the brilliant Donald, now making his career as a lawyer in Canada. However relieved they may have been that the black sheep of the family, the trouble-maker and sometime renegade Bernard, had made good in the Army, they were as yet unaware that he possessed exceptional gifts that would mark him out among his fellow men. They continued to pay him his allowance of £100 per annum, and in July 1914 set out for their annual summer holiday in Moville, expecting that Bernard would join them there with his new Ford motor car. They had never thought of the Army as more than an adjunct to the British Empire, a home for the less intellectually endowed of their offspring such as Harold and Bernard. In a past century almost unbroken by war – at least in Europe – their respect was naturally for the administrators and spiritual leaders of the Empire rather than its policing force. They seem to have kept none of Bernard's letters either from Sandhurst, India or from Shorncliffe; and it was only as the stormclouds of war began to darken the clear skies of July 1914 that their attention began to focus on their once wayward, still emotionally and intellectually immature fourth child. Sibyl, their first, had died in Tasmania; Desmond had passed away five years previously, in 1909.[1] Brian and Colin were still too young to go to St Paul's, while Harold was in South Africa, and Donald in Canada. As the eyes of the world turned first to the political situation in Europe, then to the armies that would have to enforce a declaration of war, it was thus natural that the Montgomerys should take a more concerned interest in the fortunes of Bernard. The likelihood of a civil war in Ireland had at first distracted them – in fact the Bishop was soon involved in gun-running for the secret Protestant para-military formations in Northern Ireland. But, as the holocaust poised over the Continent, Bernard's fate – and his letters – took precedence. However naïve Bernard's forecast, he would be in the front line of any eventual conflict. Through Bernard's letters in the ensuing years the Montgomerys would gain a vicarious insight into the war on the Western Front; and his letters were copied and passed round the many Montgomery relatives and friends. Moreover the letters gave –

[1] 'My favourite brother was Desmond, who was born in May 1896 in Tasmania. He died in November 1909 at our home in Chiswick from meningitis, after two serious operations; he was at that time a schoolboy at St Paul's School in London, and was 14. He is buried in Brookwood Cemetery, Woking. I was serving in my regiment in India at the time . . . Desmond was a delightful boy, and very beautiful. I was very distressed when we lost him.' Annotations to Letters, Montgomery Papers.

as they still do today – a vivid picture of a young subaltern's coming of age; his baptism under fire; and his growing confirmation as an exceptionally gifted officer. He entered the war an innocent, relatively impecunious young Lieutenant. He was to emerge from it a decorated leader of men and a staff officer of considerable repute. The boy Maud had so often despaired of – 'Go and find out what Bernard is doing and tell him to stop it' – became a man.

CHAPTER TWO

Mobilisation

Sheppey Union Minster
Kent
30.7.14

My darling Mother,
   I am sorry I haven't written to you sooner but have not had a moment to spare for the last few days. We have been expecting the order to mobilise and it came yesterday. I was out playing tennis in Folkestone and at about 6 p.m. an officer rushed down to summon us all back to barracks. I am at present in the Isle of Sheppey, right at the mouth of the Thames on the South bank, near Sheerness. While we are mobilising for war at Shorncliffe we have to furnish a battalion to guard the Sheerness defences and watch the coast in case of a hostile landing; each regiment at Shorncliffe furnishes 350 men. I have been appointed Adjutant of the battalion so am very busy. We have a great many posts out on the shore round about & have to be constantly on the lookout. I don't know how long we shall be here. I don't think the whole army is mobilising although certain brigades certainly are. I think it is just a precautionary move so as to be not caught napping. They are very frightened of a hostile landing here, as the coast is very suitable for it all round here.
   Don't be anxious about me if I don't write. I shall let you know if we are ordered abroad, but I don't think myself that the war will involve us. We may be here for a week if it does not; but if we declare war we are relieved here by Territorials and we return to Shorncliffe and go off from there.
   Best love to all at New Park from
Your loving son
Bernard

Such was Bernard's first surviving missive – which is notable, in retrospect, for its evident filial affection, and the simple, unboastful way in which he recounts his elevation to the post of Battalion Adjutant, responsible for issuing orders to over 1000 officers and men, at the age of only twenty-six.
Although Austria declared war on Serbia on 28 July, it did not at

first seem as though the dispute – fuelled by the Archduke's assassination a month before – would involve other European powers except as mediators. However Russia, as Serbia's protector, mobilised and a chain reaction began that was impossible, in the mood of the time, to halt. Fears of a German invasion of Great Britain were, however, preposterous, since Germany had neither prepared plans nor, in the last days of July 1914, had any intention of going to war with Britain. Kaiser Wilhelm hoped that Britain would remain neutral if Germany went to war with France and promised not to exact territorial penances in Europe if Germany emerged the victor. However, on 30 July, when the 10th Infantry Brigade moved to guard the Isle of Sheppey, Sir Edward Grey, the British Foreign Secretary, telegraphed to his Ambassador in Berlin that such a neutral stance 'would be a disgrace from which the good name of this country would never recover' – thus prompting Bethmann-Hollweg, the German Chancellor, to remark that Britain would be 'fighting for a scrap of paper' – Britain's guarantee to Belgium.

On 31 July Germany declared a state of war and delivered an ultimatum to Russia, demanding the cessation of mobilisation. On 1 August, denied satisfaction, Germany ordered a general mobilisation of her own navy and army and declared war on France and Russia. On Saturday, 2 August 1914, Luxembourg complained to Britain that German troops had invaded the country. It was now only a matter of hours before the Schlieffen plan would require the invasion of Belgium too.

The next day, Sunday, 3 August 1914, Bernard Montgomery again wrote to his mother. His task was the same as it would be in 1940: getting ready to repel an enemy invasion that would never come.

Minster
Sunday, 1914

My darling Mother,
I hope you have not been anxious about me. We are still here in the Isle of Sheppey and although things are still quiet we have been very busy preparing. Our battalion is split up into small detachments all over the Island; the headquarters is at Minster – the Colonel and I live in the work-house here and ride round daily to see the outposts etc. We have 550 with us here at Minster, & another 500 in various detached posts. We are preparing a position here for defence. Sheppey is an island & is only connected with the mainland of Kent by one bridge. So it would be very valuable to a hostile nation, as once they had sunk our fleet they could use the island as a base of operations against England. There is a very large naval aviation school at Eastchurch, 3 miles from us, and we have a large party there to guard it. The attempt was made by armed men last night to set fire to the aviation sheds at Chatham; they telephoned it through to us so we were on the alert. They had fired

on the Chatham sheds with rifles. I rode over to Eastchurch this morning to see if things were alright, as we only have a young subaltern in command there. An amusing thing happened while I was there. A lookout reported 2 men crawling on hands and knees through the long grass on the plain in front of the sheds; so we all rushed out with revolvers & rifles to capture them, & found they were 2 men picking up refuse from a refuse heap there.

However, as regards the general outlook, Bernard was already convinced that Britain would be forced to join in.

It is hard to know what is happening. The fleet is completely mobilised & ready for war; there are a lot of ships lying off Sheerness, in the Medway, & yesterday 4 large cruisers were anchored just off here with decks cleared for action. But the order has not yet come for the army to mobilise completely, though we expect it every hour. We have only carried out the precautionary stage, that is why we are here. I see from this mornings papers that Germany has declared war on Russia, so we are now pretty well bound to be dragged in.

This prospect, as for so many people of all ages at the time, was far from daunting.

I can't help thinking that it will be a good thing; the war is bound to come sooner or later & much better have it now & get done with it. A modern war would not last very long, & would be such an awful affair that there would be no more war for 50 years,

Bernard pronounced with confidence. Moreover Germany's strategic position, far from looking threatening, seemed to him positively bleak.

The general opinion, which I share, is that Germany will get an awful hammering. Austria will be pretty well occupied by Servia & the Balkan states who will probably come in; Italy is trying to remain neutral. So Germany will be left on her own to take on Russia & France, one on each side of her, and England. Germany couldn't possibly do this; the trouble is that she may realise this & back out of it. Then we should be as we were before, whereas it would be much better to fight it out now. [. . .] Of course it would be a splendid thing for us if Germany were to go right under; and she will if she tries to take us all on. What I expect will happen is that we will mobilise and then wait, all ready, to come in when France wants us. Our fleet is what they chiefly need, & that is ready now.

Thinking of the Bishop's problems at Moville, Bernard added:

All this has put the Irish question completely in the shade, or are they still agitating in Donegal? The people here seem quite a different race and know nothing about what is happening in the outside world. They imagine we are territorials out camping & don't in any way connect our presence with a landing of the Germans.

Neither did the Germans. However, such observations led the Bishop's son to describe for his parents the local vicar of Minster:

The old parson here looks about 96 and looks as if he had been here 50 years. He gave us a parade service this morning at 9.30 a.m. & preached to us in a whisper from a pulpit a long way off, so I don't know what it was about. He is very deaf. I spoke to him in the vestry afterwards and thanked him for the service etc. I told him England was mobilising for war but he hadn't the least idea what I meant, or what war meant. He said 'Yes, very interesting.'

The Bishop may well have chuckled over this, for it was typical of Bernard's sense of humour that he should discern so clearly the occasional comic ironies of life – a gift which was undoubtedly inherited or picked up from the Bishop himself. Having enquired whether 'all the guests' had arrived yet at Moville, Bernard finished this second letter with the reflection that being so busy looking after such a large and scattered battalion was 'good experience, & is good training, as we are on active service to all intents and purposes'.

The following day, at 11 p.m. Monday, 4 August 1914, England was at war with Germany.

Minster 5–8–14

My darling Mother,
Just time for a hurried note. The whole army is mobilising for war; we are being relieved here tomorrow morning by a Territorial Regiment & we go straight back to Shorncliffe to get ready. I suppose we shall go over to Belgium and join in there; at least it looks very much like it. Of course we may go to the north of France. We are in the 10th Brigade, 4th Division, so you will be able to follow our movements from the papers.

Anticipating such an eventuality the Montgomerys had decided to return immediately to London in the hope of seeing Bernard before he left. However, events moved too fast. The composite battalion at Minster returned to its home regiments at Shorncliffe on 6 August 1914, and on the 7th Bernard sent a card saying they were working 'night & day here to get ready', and requesting a leather purse – 'a good strong one' – and a clasp knife as they were confined to barracks. There was no time for Maud to comply, for later that same evening the battalion left Shorncliffe, in great secrecy, 'destination unknown' as Bernard cabled Moville.

CHAPTER THREE

Off to War

The destination of the 1st Battalion, Royal Warwickshire Regiment, seems to have been unclear to the War Office, too; for it was to take another three weeks of fatuous entraining and detraining before Bernard Montgomery's regiment reached French soil – weeks in which they moved from Kent to Norfolk, from Norfolk to York, from York to Harrow, and from Harrow finally to Southampton for final embarkation aboard the twin-screw steamer SS *Caledonia*. Bernard generously assumed this was designed to mislead the enemy. In fact it meant fielding a confused, hungry and exhausted army. In the meantime Maud fired off telegrams asking for a full account of what was happening if she was not permitted to come and see Bernard. To the best of his ability Bernard responded.

Sunday 9th August

My darling Mother,

I got your wire last night at about 10 p.m. I will try and describe our movements to you from when I last wrote. We left Sheerness on Friday 7th in two trains at 1.20 p.m. and 2.20 p.m. I went in the first train at 1.20 and we arrived at Shorncliffe at 3 p.m. The railways as you know have been taken over by the State so we soldiers are taken about easily, while civilians find it very hard to get about. When we arrived back the first thing I did was to start in packing up all my belongings; I had to do this in spasms as there was lots to do. I had absolutely no sleep at all on the night of the 5th (Wednesday) as I had been up all night arranging our move & going round on a bicycle telling all our outposts the arrangements I had made. Then at 2 a.m. (6th Aug) I went to the station to meet the Territorial Regt who were relieving us.

So I was pretty tired and went to bed directly after dinner on Thursday night. Our mess has been completely packed up; the colours go to the Depot at Warwick; all the silver & plate to the Goldsmith's Co; our mess pictures are stored locally in Folkestone. All this had been done when we got back from Sheerness, so the mess looked very barren, and we were having our meals off bare boards. I had a good sleep and on Friday (7th Aug) I took all the reservists of my company down to the range for some practice shooting. They shot very well on the whole. On mobilisation my job as Assistant-Adjutant ceases and I go back to my company for ordinary duty. The Company is 260 strong, and is commanded by Major Day; he used to command my company in India when I first joined. The company is divided into 4 platoons, each commanded by an officer. I command one; I have 67 men in it, they are under my sole charge and I am responsible to Major Day for it. He gives me a very free hand. My men are all very good fellows and are putting up with the present hardships & discomfort very well.

On Friday afternoon I got out my car and took it down to Folkestone to be put away. I am leaving it with a Mr and Mrs Collins, The Ingles, Castle Hill Avenue, Folkestone. They have put it away in their stables until we return. They are very nice people & I often play tennis at their house. Make a note of their address, so that in case anything should happen to me you will know where to get the car. But I hope I shall be able to return & get it myself. Meanwhile it is in safe hands and they will not use it, or let anyone else use it until they hear definite news of me. [. . .]

In the middle of dinner on Friday we suddenly got orders to move. Our destination was not told us but we left at 2.30 a.m. on Saturday (8th Aug) morning. We had a very long train journey & got in at 5 p.m. I was famished as I had had nothing to eat save a piece of cake & some of your chocolate since dinner the night before. However it is a good thing to get used to going without food as we shall often be without it before we have finished I expect. This morning early we were off again and I am writing this in the train. We slept out in a field last night and it was a bit cold but luckily there was no rain; we had no kit with us so we simply lay down in our clothes under hedges and slept. This morning at 5 a.m. I went & knocked up a waiter at a hotel, borrowed his razor and shaved. I hadn't shaved for two days so needed it badly. The people of England are all learning that they must each do their little to help. We are mobilised and a state of war exists and if you ask anyone for something & they refuse, we can take it. Of course we ask nicely first, & generally get it without going further. But twice at Sheerness I had to use force. I asked a farmer for some water to fill my men's water bottles with, he refused & said he was short of water. So I brought my men in & took it. The second time I wanted breakfast for 8 officers at a hotel; they had had a lot of work & no food for over 24 hours. It was only a small inn & they refused & said they never provided meals. I said we must have it & I would lock them all in one room while we took it, if they refused. We were willing to pay whatever they asked. We got it. That wouldn't happen now I think; it was only just starting then; now people seem to realise better.

I can't in any of my letters say where we are or what we are doing, & what our movements are. We are forbidden to do it. You have noticed that the papers have not reported the movements of any troops; they are all forbidden to. Yet troops are concentrated all over England in various places. Of course you will see from the post mark on my letters whereabouts we have been, & from my telegrams. I can give you no address but write to Shorncliffe; we shall I think go back there before we embark for abroad, & I shall get your letters there. And whenever you write put on my letters '1st Battalion Royal Warwickshire Regt.' This applies more to abroad than to here. I will let you know as soon as we are ordered abroad if I can. But it will be kept very secret and I won't know myself until we find our train along-side a ship. Even then I must not let you know, so I will send one word 'going'. You have to be very careful when crossing the sea as one German submarine could sink us all. I am afraid I won't see you; but never mind, I shall come back again alright. So cheer up dearest Mother. [. . .]

It is difficult to write well in the train, but hope you can read this. Give my love to everyone. With lots to you and Father from

yr very loving son
Bernard

This letter was posted from Cromer; but in the ensuing days the train was shunted up and down the East coast with its kitless combatants. There was no point in the Montgomerys leaving Moville to say goodbye, Bernard pointed out; 'all the other officers are in exactly the same fix and won't be able to see their parents.'

Bernard's optimism about the brevity of the forthcoming struggle evaporated, however, as news came in of Germany's successful invasion of Belgium, and the surrender of Liège. 'We are of course all looking forward very much to fighting the Germans; but this war will be no small thing & will demand all our endurance before it is over,' he wrote prophetically on 11 August 1914.

Still the War Office muddled; and for five days the train sat in a siding at York station – 'in the coal yard' as Bernard ironically related. 'I never imagined I should live in a coal yard; you can't imagine how filthy it is,' he remarked. 'It was no good washing or having a bath, you were dirty again in 5 minutes'; and by 14 August he was relieved to be out in the country, at Strensall Camp, about six miles from York.

Why we are here I haven't the least idea, nor have any of us; but we don't think it will be for long. The main idea is I think that the East Coast must be thoroughly guarded until a naval battle has taken place; we are doing it now until the Territorials are quite ready and then they will take it over from us. [. . .]

The extraordinary thing about this campaign is the way everything is kept secret and even we know nothing. Nothing is published in the papers about the movements of our troops. But I know for a fact that some of them are even now over in Belgium; and even when we go you will see nothing about it in the paper. Of course it will be when we start fighting over there, but not before. We shall probably go through the war knowing absolutely nothing, not even where the enemy is until we bump up against him. We shall be just moved about like we are being now, as a machine. This is the outcome of our experience in South Africa when the papers were allowed to publish all our plans and everything we were doing.

Asked by his mother in a letter what he required, Bernard explained that the officers were now living on the same rations as the men, with himself running the company mess. 'Of course the Government ration is not enough, so we supplement it by other things, but we don't spend more than 1/- per day each extra' – exactly the same amount that Maud gave the Bishop. All he required for the moment, wrote Bernard, was socks – and £5 which he would change into gold before they went to France.

The next day, 15 August, he wrote saying that rumour had it they would leave the following Tuesday, 21 August. There was plenty to do toughening up the soft reservists who had joined the company.

Every morning we go for a long route march to get their feet hard and finish up with some manoeuvres of sorts. Then every evening we inspect all the men's feet to see that they haven't got blisters etc., & also to see that they wash them. If you left a man alone he would never wash his feet; it is rather a smelly job inspecting feet! But it is most important, as if your men can't march they are no use.

He thanked his father and sister Winsome for their letters, promising to write to them. 'My letters are all to you but you will understand,' he pointed out, 'that they are intended for the whole family as one hasn't a great deal of time for writing.' They were still roofless, even tentless, though fortunately the weather remained 'glorious', as it would be 'very unpleasant' if it rained. 'We all have to sleep in our clothes of course which is not exactly pleasant,' he remarked, 'but you soon get used to it. We take our boots off, but nothing else.'

In fact the battalion left Strensall Camp that weekend, and from Harrow, where he had an aunt, Bernard was able to contact his father who had just returned from Moville. 'I well remember saying goodbye to him outside Victoria Station,' he later recollected.[1] Bernard himself had no doubt that he would return alive; but his parents felt quite differently – and, as circumstances would show, they were very nearly right.

[1] Bernard Montgomery, *Memoirs*, op. cit.

We sleep in tents here at Harrow. I have slept in my clothes ever since I left Shorncliffe & shall have to do so till the war is over. You must be ready to turn out at a moment's notice. We are off tonight to embark & will probably be across the other side when you get this. [. . .]

I was awfully glad to see Father yesterday. I had tea with him & Grannie: I got leave to go up to London with another fellow to get some things. I had a bath at Grannie's & had great difficulty in stopping Nurse from pressing medicines of all sorts on me to take to the war.

This was 21 August 1914. The following morning at 1 a.m. Bernard left Harrow with his battalion for Southampton, where they boarded the troopship *Caledonia*. On board Bernard wrote first to his father in London, and then to his mother in Moville.

My dear Father,
We are now off Beachy Head. We left Southampton at 11 a.m. and have kept close in to the coast all the way and are now I think going to cut across to Boulogne. I learnt a lot of interesting things from Wentworth-Shields at Southampton. He is chief engineer to the docks, and said 4 divisions have gone over, about 100,000 men. We are the last to go, at any rate for the present. We were not meant to go yet, but they suddenly decided to send one more, so it looks as if we were wanted.

The Censor will be most awfully strict on the other side; all our letters will be read by about 3 people & if there is anything they don't like they won't send them. So I shall never be able to say where we are or what we are doing, or in fact anything about us. So it will be no use asking for news of this sort when you write.
Good-bye from
yr affectionate son
Bernard

22nd August

My darling Mother
We are on the way over now. The Government have taken over this ship (and many others) as a transport; we are very lucky as she is a 1st class passenger boat while some of them are only cargo boats. I have a state room with 2 others. We left Harrow at 1 a.m. this morning; our luggage had to go off at 7 p.m. and we had to lie in the open field from 7 p.m. till 1 a.m. without coats or anything. It was awfully cold & there was a heavy dew, but I am so fit, I suppose, I didn't even get the slightest cold. We reached South-ampton at 7 a.m. & embarked at once on this boat. [. . .] The only thing you have sent me which I haven't got are the socks. But they will follow all right; and it doesn't much matter as I bought some in

London. You can't have too many socks. You have been awfully good in supplying me with things and I now have everything I could possibly want.

Good-bye. Remember me to Hubert. Best love to all the family from

yr loving son
Bernard

The SS *Caledonia* docked on 23 August in Boulogne, where Bernard posted the letters. His parents were not to hear of or from him again for a fortnight. Then, on 8 September 1914, the Montgomerys in Moville received a telegram from the War Office, London, redirected from Chiswick:

To Right Rev Bishop Montgomery New Park Moville

Regret to inform you that Lieut. B. L. Montgomery Warwickshire Regt. is reported missing this does not necessarily mean that he is killed or wounded further information when received will be telegraphed immediately.

The war was barely a month old.

CHAPTER FOUR

Into Battle

The British Expeditionary Force, admirably equipped in khaki uniforms for South African warfare, marched with two machine-guns per thousand men into a stunning right-hook with which the massed German army hoped to outflank their French counterpart. Despite some valiant cavalry charges, the British infantry divisions were outnumbered by four to one, had no motorised transport, no heavy artillery, and no radio or field telephone communications. After only token resistance, Sir John French, aware that the French armies on his right and left had fallen back, decided to withdraw; and the retreat from Mons began on 23 August – the day that the 1st Battalion, the Royal Warwickshire Regiment debouched from the staterooms and cabins of the SS *Caledonia*. What then took place was vividly described by Bernard Montgomery to his father over a month later, when the battle was beyond the Censor's concern.

My dear Father,
    It is now I think possible to give you an account of my doings since I arrived in this country. [. . .]
    The fight at Mons took place on Sunday 23rd August; we were too late for that as we only arrived in Boulogne that morning. We left Boulogne 11 p.m., 23rd August by train & detrained at Le CATEAU (near CAMBRAI) on 24th at 10 a.m. We waited there for the remainder of the Brigade to come up & at 2 a.m. on the 25th we marched to assist the British Army which was retiring from Mons. We marched all day and all night and reached a place called LIGNY at 4.30 a.m. on the 26th. We were very tired of course but there was no rest for at 6 a.m. the Germans advanced on us & began shelling us heavily. It was a curious position: the front was a very large one & stretched from CAMBRAI–LE CATEAU, many miles, but just at our point in the line we faced the Germans with a high ridge between us and them, & neither of us could hold the ridge. We were on the ridge at 6 a.m. but the fire was so heavy we had to retire as we had not had time to entrench ourselves. About 7.30 a.m. we made an effort to retake the ridge; it was terrible work as we had to advance through a hail of bullets from rifles & machine-guns & through a perfect storm of shrapnel fire. Our men

behaved very well, though they were knocked down like ninepins; we reached the top but could not stay there & had to retire. I wonder anyone came off the ridge alive; the whole air seemed full of bullets & bursting shells. I was not touched. We had 8 officers wounded, some very badly, and I should think 200 men killed & wounded; the exact numbers are not known. We retired & entrenched ourselves & the whole of the rest of the day we were heavily shelled by the Germans.

In England all the officers had had to have their swords sharpened by the armourer at Shorncliffe; but when Bernard Montgomery had asked the Commanding Officer, Lt-Colonel Elkington, if he would need money in France, Elkington had replied that money was useless in war as 'everything was provided for you.'[1] – an assurance which he fortunately ignored.

In fact, from the moment the regiment left Shorncliffe on 8 August 1914 there was an absence of proper planning; and the confusion and lack of proper provisions which resulted were only a foretaste of the military disaster that would befall the regiment. It was an experience that Montgomery would indeed never forget. 'If this was real war it struck me as most curious and did not seem to make any sense against the background of what I had been reading,' he related in his *Memoirs* over forty years later. That modern war would be 'awful' he had already acknowledged in his letters; that they would go into battle 'knowing absolutely nothing, not even where the enemy is until we bump up against him', Bernard had accurately foretold. Yet he had trusted, in his innocence, that at a higher level the staff *would* know what the regiment was doing and why; and also, at a local level, that his battalion commander would use some tactical intelligence in the disposition of his forces. In both hopes he was to be disappointed. The assistance of the British Army was characterised by both lack of communication, and, where contact was made with higher HQs, a constant countermanding of orders. From Le Cateau railway station the battalion marched north-west to Beaumont and, at 2 a.m. on 25 August 1914, to St Python. There, on high ground, they were supposed to cover the withdrawal of the 3rd Division, Cavalry Division, and 19th Brigade. In the Battalion War Diary an 'English force retiring S.' was indeed noted as having been covered, including cavalry and the 18th Brigade of their own 4th Division. The roads, however, were a mass of refugees and retreating troops. and it was difficult, if not impossible to make sense of the picture. At 6 p.m. they came under horse artillery gunfire, but without casualties; and at 7 in the evening orders were received telling them to retire 'as soon as 18th Bde had passed through'.[2]

[1] Bernard Montgomery, op. cit.
[2] War Diary, 1st Btn, Royal Warwickshire Regt, Royal Warwickshire Regimental Museum, Warwick.

Already the hot, sticky day had given way to lightning, thunder, and heavy rain. No rations arrived, and at 11 p.m. the battalion began its retreat south-westwards through Beauvois to Haucourt, about twelve miles away. Wet and exhausted they finally arrived there at 4.30 a.m., and bivouacked in a cornfield.

Aircraft observations had correctly indicated a series of German divisions, both infantry and cavalry, converging on the Le Cateau front; but according to the Official Historian (who was at the time senior General Staff Officer (GSO 1) of the 4th Division) 'this very accurate picture does not seem to have been communicated to the corps or divisions, or to the cavalry'.[1]

The Brigadier of the 10th Brigade had already the day before reconnoitred the terrain where his battalions would bivouac for the night of 25 August, namely the back slope of the ridge above the Warnelle brook. From then onwards, everything went wrong.

'The men threw themselves down and slept, hoping that, being in reserve to the division, they might have a little rest,' the Official History recorded, since the ridge was to be held by the 11th and 12th Brigades. For many of them it would be their last – as the German First Army bore down on them with relentless pressure. It had been intended that the British retreat would be continued at 7 a.m. on 26 August; but a covered withdrawal requires good rearguard positioning to delay the enemy; and, by relinquishing the high ground overlooking the line of retreat at Solesmes, the 4th Division had already surrendered this. Allenby, Commander of the Cavalry Division, urged the Corps Commander, General Smith-Dorrien, to get his divisions away before daylight, as he had insufficient forces to recapture the heights; but, assured that his units were too exhausted and too scattered to move before 9 a.m., Smith-Dorrien decided to make a stand – 'to strike the enemy hard and, after he had done so, continue the retreat.'[2]

This was pure moonshine, since troops too weary and uncoordinated to retreat were hardly likely to strike very hard at the enemy. None of them were properly entrenched, and their bivouac positions had been chosen for shelter rather than defence. There were virtually no cavalry to reconnoitre or locate the enemy, and, in the case of the 4th Division, no heavy artillery to support the infantry. Even the brigade transport columns were in confusion, so that the troops were without food or ammunition. At 3.30 a.m. on 26 August, Smith-Dorrien sent a message outlining his decision to Sir John French, the BEF Army Commander, in St Quentin. Sir John was understandably amazed. 'If you stand to fight there will be another Sédan,' his Deputy Chief-of-Staff told Smith-Dorrien on the telephone. To which Smith-Dorrien could only reply, 'It was impossible to break

[1] J. E. Edmonds, *Military Operations, France and Belgium*, 3rd Edn, London 1933.
[2] Ibid.

away now, as the action had already begun, and that he could hear the guns firing as he spoke.'[1]

Indeed he could. It was already 6 a.m., and the German assault on the 10th Brigade at Haucourt had begun three-quarters of an hour before. French's written message to Smith-Dorrien at 9 a.m. was typically convoluted:

If you can hold your ground the situation appears likely to improve. 4th Division must cooperate. French troops are taking offensive on right of 1 Corps. Although you are given a free hand as to method this telegram is not intended to convey the impression that I am not anxious for you to carry out the retirement and you must make every endeavour to do so.[2]

Such was the standard of generalship in the first month of World War One; and the result at the 'sharp end' was a massacre. The 4th Division was stretched across a five-mile front, with 15,000 unsupplied and unfed troops, without divisional artillery, signal companies, engineers, ammunition or cavalry. It was small wonder they were routed. The 12th Brigade, as Montgomery noted in his *Memoirs*, abandoned the ridge 'in great disorder' at 5.15 a.m.; and it was left to the Royal Warwickshires of the 10th Brigade to retrieve the situation.

Our battalion was deployed in two lines; my company and one other were forward, with the remaining two companies out of sight some hundred yards to the rear. The CO galloped up to us forward companies and shouted to us to attack the enemy on the forward hill at once. This was the only order; there was no reconnaissance, no plan, no covering fire.[3]

There followed the 'perfect storm of shrapnel fire' and 'hail of bullets' which Bernard Montgomery's letter described, and in which his men fell 'like ninepins'. Years later he recorded his own comic contribution to the attack: 'Waving my sword I ran forward in front of my platoon, but unfortunately I had only gone six paces when I tripped over my scabbard, the sword fell from my hand (I hadn't wound that sword strap round my wrist in the approved fashion!) and I fell flat on my face on very hard ground. By the time I had picked myself up and rushed after my men I found that most of them had been killed.'[4] The Battalion Diarist recorded at the time: 'Enemy occupied ridge & opened Maxim & gun fire. 7 a.m. The forward line in Road under Major C. Christie attacked the ridge & reached the top, but were, owing to heavy gun & Maxim fire, unable to hold the

[1] Ibid.
[2] Ibid.
[3] Bernard Montgomery, op. cit.
[4] Brian Montgomery, *A Field-Marshal in the Family*, op. cit.

position and withdrew in good order with a Company of King's Own to the road with a loss of 7 officers and 40 men killed wounded & missing. We held our position under heavy gunfire for remainder of day with further casualties, 1 officer and 14 men wounded.' In his *Memoirs* Bernard recorded the end of the engagement. 'My Company Commander was wounded and there were many casualties. Nobody knew what to do, so we returned to the original position from which we had begun the attack.' What he did not relate was that he returned up the hill later to try to bring back a wounded superior with two soldiers from C Company; without a stretcher, however, the Captain was too badly wounded to carry and was left with the village priest, together with other wounded survivors.

Nor was this suicidal charge the end of the affair; for having sent the two companies to their death, Lt-Colonel Elkington now abandoned them. As Bernard's letter went on: 'The army began to retire about 3 p.m.; we were right up in the very front firing line & somehow (through bad staffwork) we received no orders.' Only when the truth dawned on them, after dark, and they heard the Germans advance, did the remnants of the two companies, plus some lost souls from the rest of the brigade, decide to withdraw. 'About 10 p.m. we suddenly realized that we were alone & we could hear the Germans advancing in large numbers. So we hastily formed up & retired.'

Lt-Colonel Elkington, far from ascertaining the fate of his forward companies, retreated fifteen miles to St Quentin where, at the behest of the mayor, he agreed that evening to surrender to the Germans. He and the Commanding Officer of another battalion in the brigade were subsequently cashiered.[1] In such confusion it was hardly surprising that Montgomery was posted missing by the War Office, and his parents informed accordingly. For two days and nights Major Poole, the senior officer, led the group of survivors by compass to try to catch up the retreating British Army.

I shall never forget that march; we call it the 'Retreat from Moscow'. We were behind our own army and in front of the Germans; we had several very narrow escapes from being cut up and at times had to hide in woods to escape being seen by Uhlan patrols. We had no food & no sleep, and it rained most of the time. We were dead tired when we started so you can imagine what we were like when we finished it. Our men fell out by the dozens & we had to leave them; lots were probably captured by the Germans, some have since rejoined. The chocolate Mother had sent me was invaluable, as of course we had no rations all the time and there

[1] Lt-Col. Elkington joined the Foreign Legion, with whom he won the Croix de Guerre and the Médaille Militaire. He was subsequently reinstated in the British Army and awarded the DSO.

was no food in the villages. The villagers were all fleeing before the advancing Germans. All our kit was burnt to make room in the wagons for wounded etc. so we had only what we stood up in. We had passed our kit burning on the wayside; altogether the outlook was black and we were in low spirits. When we retired on the 26th we had got split up into two parties; it was a very dark night & somehow we got separated. There were 300 of us in the party I was in and about 300 in the other party. But to go on with the story. At 10 p.m. on the 28th we caught up our division & they put us on the motor lorries of a supply column; they took us to Compiegne which we reached at 3 p.m. on the 29th. We drove through some lovely forests on the way, altogether about 60 miles. We left there at 9 a.m. on Sunday 30th by train & went by train to LE MANS & had a good rest; we were far away from war there & we lunched & dined in restaurants daily. I had my last bath there on 4th September, over 3 weeks ago.

Such was Bernard Montgomery's account, written on 27 September 1914, of his first experience of battle. What he did not say – either for censorship reasons or because he was still unwilling to analyse the fiasco into which he had been pitched – was that the entire business had been characterised by a typical English mixture of confusion, gallantry, cowardice, desertion, tenacity and luck, as a result of which thousands of men died or were wounded and captured, and the battalion CO was dismissed from the Army. Smith-Dorrien's stand at Le Cateau cost the British Army more casualties than Wellington's at Waterloo: 8482 men on 26 August alone. Montgomery's performance on the 26th, and the 'Retreat from Moscow' as he called it, must however have impressed Major Poole, the officer commanding his fleeing contingent; for when Poole was subsequently made CO of the 1st Battalion he immediately promoted Montgomery to temporary Captain and put him in charge of a company of 350 men – usually a Major's appointment as Bernard informed his parents.

The débâcle at Mons had broken Sir John French's nerve. By a miracle he had evaded the claws of the German army – and, like Gort three decades later, he wanted now to separate the BEF from their seemingly doomed French allies, leaving the line altogether to 'refit'. Only Kitchener's trip to Paris on 1 September 1914 stopped him. Joffre struck back at Bülow's 2nd German Army; and Bülow appealed to Kluck, commander of the 1st German Army, which had thrown back the British, to help him. With Moltke's approval Kluck's 1st German Army now relinquished its pressure on the British and swung back south-eastwards, still to the north of Paris, instead of encircling the capital. The Military Governor of Paris, Galliéni, recognised what was happening, and launched the French 6th Army under Maunoury into Kluck's broad flank. Finally the retreating

British were told to turn about; and when after much delay they began to threaten the thinly held gap between Kluck and Bülow's Armies, Schlieffen's grand strategy came irrevocably to grief. It was the turn of the German Army now to retreat. On 4 September 1914, Montgomery's battalion moved from Le Mans to join the pursuit at Crécy, 'where the Battle of Crécy was fought', Bernard noted in his letter of 27 September. 'From 5th to the 13th September we marched hard all day, generally starting at 4 a.m. and not getting in till 7 or 8 p.m. [. . .] Every day we saw fresh signs of a retreating army, such as dead horses and men, discarded stores etc. We usually reached places in the evening which the Germans had left in the morning. [. . .] On the 13th Sept (a fortnight ago today) we came up to them & that is where we are now; I cannot name the place.' They had reached the Aisne, after hundreds of miles of gruelling marches. On the 15th Bernard related to his mother: 'We are all very hard & sleep & eat whenever possible; we sleep in the fields in all weather, & none of us have colds. We ought all to have pneumonia as it rains hard most nights, but I suppose we are all too hard. It is not pleasant being under fire, especially shrapnel fire, but you soon get used to it & treat it with indifference. I command my own company now as my major got his leg broken in our first fight; so I ride a horse, as all company commanders are mounted. I have a big beard. I have not washed my face or hands for 10 days; there is no means of washing & no time for it. The necessary things are sleep & food; washing is unnecessary. Don't forget the cigarettes, will you.'

It seems the future scourge against smoking was getting through twenty-five cigarettes in three days – Capstan Navy Cut Medium. So far the war had been a contest of manoeuvre, but as the Germans entrenched themselves by the Aisne, it began to take on its ultimate character – a far more terrible one than the skirmishing and route marching that had preceded it. On 20 September, Bernard wrote to his mother, thanking her for the first parcel from home, including some peppermint creams from his sister Winsome:

We get letters in strange situations; I eat the peppermints with a dead man beside me in the trench. I have been awfully lucky so far as I have had some very narrow shaves; on two occasions the man standing up next to me has been shot dead. The weather is perfectly vile; they say Sept is a very wet month in France. It is getting cold too and they will have to send out warm things soon for our men if they are to keep well. Any warm things you like to send out for the men of my company would be very acceptable. [. . .]

I had an awful night in the trenches last night; it poured with rain all night & the trenches became full of water. I had to go forward visiting sentries etc all night to see they kept alert. Some were very far out to the front towards the German trenches & I crawled about on my stomach in mud & slush & nearly lost myself. The advanced German trenches are only 700 yards from us, so I might easily have been captured by one of their patrols. But good luck pursues me & I am quite safe. My clothes are in an awful state of mud & of course wet through. But it doesn't seem to matter much as I haven't even a cold after it; l came straight in in my wet clothes, threw myself down and slept as I was, without taking off anything. I find that rum is a great standby; they give us some every day.

Two days later he remarked: 'I keep extraordinarily fit & well, and really believe that if I washed I should get ill!' The battalion was echeloned simply in forward and supporting trenches, each company taking it in turns to man the front line. It was 'here that

we get casualties. We have had none today so far; it is now 2 p.m. The firing on both sides is generally heaviest in the early morning from 5–9 a.m.; we can't get the wounded men away from the forward trenches as stretcher bearers coming up would at once get knocked out. So they have to lie there till it is dark, with just a field dressing on the wound. We can see the Germans coming out of their trenches at dawn, stretching themselves & rubbing their eyes; we wait until a few collect together & then fire on them. They tried a night attack the other night but we beat them off alright. What we really want is some fine weather to dry up the trenches & get all our clothes thoroughly dry. It would be fine I think but for the guns; this morning it was beautiful but as soon as the guns began it started raining. Our men are all very cheery indeed, in spite hardships and living as they are at high pressure. Of course they get very good food. They get biscuits, bully beef, bacon, jam, cheese, every day and of course we get the same. [. . .] I shall not shave again till this war is over; I wish you could see me. [. . .] I cannot write as much as I should like to as I have lots to do even when off duty, as it were. It is no small responsibility being in command of 250 men on active service & within 600 yards of the German Army; it is really a major's command and I am lucky to have it. I have 2 officers under me but the responsibility rests on me, & I am glad it does.'

As regards the general war picture on the Western Front, he still trusted there was reason in such madness. 'The two armies are sitting watching each other & have been doing so for 2 weeks,' Bernard noted in his letter of 27 September. 'Our object is I think to hold them here while the French get round behind them, or there may be some other reason; we are not told much of the strategic plans.' The German artillery was superior to the British, as they have with them the big siege guns which they had brought up to besiege Paris with. They have given us a very bad time & we have had 1 officer & a number of men killed. They are numerically much stronger than us & occasionally they attack our line, by day and by night. A night attack is not pleasant as you cannot tell what is happening; a lot of wild firing goes on & you are just as likely to be fired on by your own people as by the Germans. I am writing this under cover in a shrapnel proof shelter in our most advanced trench, as my company is on duty there. I can see the Germans in their trenches & occasionally we exchange shots; I bagged one man this morning, and one horse. The shrapnel is screaming overhead and altogether it is rather different from a Sunday at home.

Letters took just over a week to arrive. On 29 September Bernard learned of his cousin Pleasance's death – which 'upset me greatly,' he confessed. 'She was one of the few girls I have ever cared for and I liked her better than any of the others', – a sentence which his mother struck out before having it copied for other members of the family. Several of these were joining up, including his cousins Aubrey and Valentine, and his brother Donald in Canada.

I wonder if any of them will come out here or if it will all be over before they are fully trained. It looks to me as if the war will last over Xmas. I hope it won't; it is getting very cold here now and I should think a winter campaign in this country would be awful, and the troops would die like flies from the cold. I think it is too scientific a war for it to last long; Europe would not stand for it; and where is the money going to come from?

Irritated by his mother's complaint that she had not heard much from him, Bernard reiterated the 'strenuous' time his battalion had had over the past weeks; and as regards the local paragon of correspondence his mother quoted, Bernard was quite sour. 'I don't know where Paddy is but if he has found time to write long letters home he must be behind somewhere at the base or on the lines of communication. [. . .] I will write whenever I can as you know, and when you don't hear you will know it is because of duty & work which prevents me.' Though he knew by now of the War Office's telegram to his parents, it still did not occur to Bernard that his parents might be anxious lest he be killed or wounded. He had undergone his baptism of fire, and no letter of his in the long ensuing years of attrition and slaughter ever so much as hinted at fear. When he heard his sister Una's husband, Andrew Holden, was about to enlist, Bernard wrote that he was glad' 'We will want everyone before it is over and you have to take your chance with the shells and bullets. Some go through untouched, others are not so lucky.'

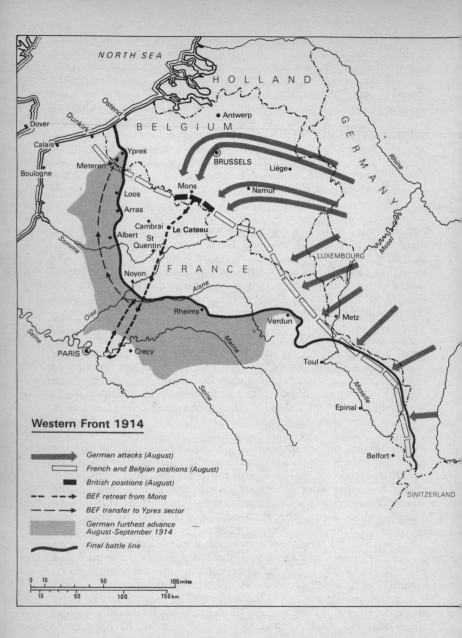

NORTH SEA

HOLLAND

BELGIUM

GERMANY

• Antwerp

● BRUSSELS   Liège •

• Namur

Ostend

Dover •

Dunkirk

Calais •

Boulogne •

Ypres

Meteren

Loos

Arras

Cambrai   Le Cateau
St
Quentin

Albert

Noyon

FRANCE

Mons

Rhine

Mosel

LUXEMBOURG

Metz •

Somme

Aisne

Rheims •

Verdun

Oise

Seine

PARIS ○   • Crecy

Marne

Toul •

Seine

Moselle

Epinal •

Belfort •

SWITZERLAND

Western Front 1914

German attacks (August)

French and Belgian positions (August)

British positions (August)

BEF retreat from Mons

BEF transfer to Ypres sector

German furthest advance
August-September 1914

Final battle line

0   10   50   100 miles

10   50   100   150 km

Bernard Montgomery was still only twenty-six, and though his letters evidenced nothing one could call style, they were remarkable for the natural clarity with which he expressed himself, and the growing authority, even paternalism that this first taste of blood and war had given him. Only two new officers had arrived from England to replace the eight lost at Le Cateau. 'I had a youngster join my company yesterday,' he recounted on 29 September; 'he only applied for a commission the day war broke out so has had no experience; but he is very keen & will do alright I think.' Such fatherly concern turned to a wry amusement in his duties as censor of his men's letters home. 'The letters are all very much the same; full of protestations of love to their sweethearts & hoping they will remain true etc. They all ask to be sent cigarettes, and some say "Thanks to our officers we are still safe." ' Occasionally a delicacy would be found with which to supplement the government rations – such as hare and vegetable stew. 'It was a tame Belgian hare which an old French woman had in a hutch in her garden, white with pink eyes, & she was only too pleased to sell it to us for 3 francs. She killed it herself in front of us!' Bernard recorded with amusement, even after all the horrors of human death he had witnessed in the past six weeks. 'The scarcity of eggs is rather interesting. There are plenty of chickens about but the French people say the sound of the guns upsets them & stops them from laying.' He even cherished the idea of bringing home some souvenirs – '2 German shell cases, in splendid condition; they will clean up & polish & look very nice on each side of the grate or fireplace.' He had formed a close friendship with 'Tin Eye' Briscoe, a twenty-four-year-old officer in his battalion who was to be killed two years later at Ypres, and together they both went walking when off duty and out of the front-line trenches. The War Office's excuse that Bernard's printed card 'I am well' of 29.9.1914 meant that he was a prisoner of war, he found 'ridiculous'. 'If I had been a prisoner I could never have got hold of the card at all,' he remarked with acid logic.

On 7 October 1914 Bernard sent his last letter from the Aisne trenches; for a few days later it was decided to withdraw the BEF, currently wedged between two French armies east of Soissons, and transfer it further north in an attempt to outflank the Germans – later misnamed the 'Race for the Sea'. Unfortunately the Germans, with copious divisions released by the fall of Antwerp, attempted to do the same. Outnumbered by fourteen to twenty, the British were thrown into battle once again.

There was the familiar confusion. 'We moved from our Aisne positions and were transferred by train round to Belgium,' Montgomery recorded in his annotation to his letters. 'We marched back for 2 days, then by train, and then forward into battle at Meteren. On the 13th October, I was again a Platoon Commander; a retired Captain had joined from England to command my Company.'

The first Battle of Ypres had begun the previous day. Bernard was more confident of success this time. 'Poole was in command, and there was a plan and there were proper orders,' he related in his *Memoirs*. '10. a.m. On reaching FLETRE enemy were reported to be holding high ground along ridge in front of METEREN,' the Battalion War Diary recorded. The Germans were driven back to Meteren itself by Major Poole, deploying all four of the battalion companies. The enemy thus withdrew from the high ground to the edge of the village; but ousting them from Meteren was to prove a costly affair. The German trenches had been dug immediately in front of houses, hedges and walls, and the earth scattered, so that the British found it almost impossible to sight the defenders. The day was wet and misty, and thus there was no artillery support available – an excuse which held good for the British at any rate; it does not seem to have stopped the Germans from using the church tower as an observation point from which to see clearly the whole of the British advance.

Despite Major Poole's more intelligent command, the battalion was once again ordered at 11 a.m. by the GOC to take the village without artillery support: and the result was almost as deadly as on 26 August at Le Cateau. 'Dash and spirit shown by all concerned,' recorded the Battalion Diarist; but not before over a hundred officers and men had fallen. The forward companies having been held up, C and D companies advanced, with Montgomery leading his platoon and brandishing his sword. This time he managed to avoid tripping over the scabbard; but no sooner had he stormed the German trench than he found a German soldier aiming a rifle up at him. Apart from ceremonial drill, no sword training had ever been given; so abandoning his weapon Bernard flung himself through the air 'and kicked him as hard as I could in the lower part of the stomach', as he related in his *Memoirs*. 'I had read much about the value of surprise in war. There is no doubt that the German was surprised and it must have seemed to him a new form of war; he fell to the ground in great pain and I took my first prisoner.'

Captain Tomes, then a company commander, was further along the line. 'I did not actually see this incident myself, but we heard about it soon afterwards,' he recorded later. 'The enemy was in some trenches just outside the village. There was a bit of a hold-up and he [Bernard] led his men to the assault with a bayonet charge and successfully carried the position. It was a very gallant affair but so far as he was concerned it was disastrous. He stood up in the pouring rain to reorganize his men and was shot in the chest and knee by Germans still in the houses.'[1]

Possibly Tomes was telescoping events, for the storming of the outer trenches had proved only the beginning. The village of Meteren was still full of Germans and at 1.30 p.m. the GOC called off

[1] Brigadier Clement Tomes, loc. cit.

the Royal Warwickshire assault. The first formal British attack of the First World War was then ordered; the entire 3 Corps was brought into action, advancing on a five-mile front, with the 12th and 10th Brigades delivering a two-pronged blow on Meteren itself. According to Bernard's own version, 'I made my platoon take up defensive positions behind a ditch and hedge about 100 yards from the village and went out myself in front to see what the positions looked like from the enemy point of view – in accordance with the book! It was then that I was shot by a sniper; the bullet entered at the back, which was towards the enemy, and came out in front, having gone through my right lung but broken no bones. I collapsed, bleeding profusely. A soldier from my platoon ran forward and plugged the wound with my field dressing: while doing so, the sniper shot him through the head and he collapsed on top of me. I managed to shout to my platoon that no more men were to come to me until it was dark. It was then 3 p.m. and raining. I lay there all the afternoon; the sniper kept firing at me and I received one more bullet in the left knee. The man lying on me took all the bullets and saved my life.'[1] It was nightfall before the Germans vacated the village, and Bernard's body could be brought in. For negligible losses the Germans had held up an entire British corps, and inflicted more than 700 casualties. The 1st Battalion of the Royal Warwickshires had alone sustained casualties of 42 killed and 85 wounded. Brave Major Christie who had led the assault at Le Cateau was killed, as well as Bernard's fellow subaltern, Lieutenant Gilliat. Bernard only seems to have escaped the same fate by a miracle. 'For three or four hours he lay in the mud before anyone could get to him,' Tomes recollected. 'When he was at last taken back to a dressing station after dark he was in a very poor state and, indeed, we heard that they had begun to dig his grave. But he survived – perhaps because he was Monty!'[2] Bernard's own account recorded: 'When dark a party from my platoon soon came to me; they had no stretcher, so four of them carried me in an overcoat to the road, and down it they met some stretcher-bearers from the RAP [Regimental Aid Post] who took me over and carried me down the road to an advance dressing station manned by RAMC [Royal Army Medical Corps] personnel. I was barely conscious. I remember being put into an ambulance, taken to a station, put into a train – and no more until I recovered full consciousness the next day in the Herbert Hospital, Woolwich.'[3]

Montgomery's gallantry did not go unnoticed or unrewarded. Major Poole promoted him to Captain in the field; and some time later, recuperating in the Royal Herbert Hospital high above the

[1] Account for Royal Warwickshire Regiment, quoted in a letter from Norman Cliff to the *Observer*, 7 April 1968.
[2] Brigadier Clement Tomes, loc. cit.
[3] Account for Royal Warwickshire Regiment, loc. cit.

Thames at Woolwich, Bernard was gratified to learn that he had been awarded the Distinguished Service Order for 'conspicuous gallant leading on 13 October, when he turned the enemy out of the trenches with the bayonet. He was severely wounded.' In an annotation to his letters of this period Bernard later commented: 'The MC had not been invented; if it had been, being only a Lieutenant I would have got that.' Doubtless this is so; but, in deprecating his own award, Bernard was ignoring the fact that, through his own gallantry, he had helped the Royal Warwickshire Regiment's 1st Battalion to retrieve its reputation after the cashiering of its CO, Lt-Colonel Elkington, in August.

Nor was this an isolated example of Bernard Montgomery's courage in those initial months of the Great War. His fearlessness under fire was already legendary in the Royal Warwickshires for, writing almost half a century later, Brigadier Tomes remembered an apocryphal tale that circulated in the regiment after Meteren. 'There was a story going round afterwards that he was arguing with a German officer in the captured trench when he was shot. Arguing about the officer's pickelhaube which he wanted as a souvenir, but which the German rather naturally refused to hand over. But I hardly think this was true.' Hardly – but quite characteristic.

Bernard's performance at Meteren was exemplary in another respect, too. Against a larger and considerably better equipped army, the BEF fought the German right flank to a standstill. Thenceforth the front of opposing troops would run, like a human river, from Switzerland to the sea at Ostend. Yet this first Battle of Ypres, which finished four weeks after Montgomery's bayonet charge, on 11 November 1914, would be responsible for the most ominous losses. By then more than half the original British Expeditionary Force were casualties – one in ten of them killed. Of the latter, three-quarters fell at Ypres.

As historians have remarked, this gigantic blood-letting signalled the death of the old British Army; but, because no break-through occurred on either side, the high command and the staff officers responsible for field operations remained intact.

'If you can't beat them, join them' was a popular cliché; and once he had recovered from his near-mortal wounds, Bernard Montgomery did. From February 1915 he would wear the bright red collar tabs of a staff officer.

CHAPTER FIVE

Brigade-Major

'There is no record of a telegram to my parents about my being wounded,' Bernard Montgomery noted in the annotations to his letters from the Western Front. 'Maybe none was sent because I was back in England on the 15th October, and spent 2 months in the Herbert Hospital, Woolwich. I recovered quickly, being very fit.'

Captain Tomes visited Bernard in hospital while on leave before Christmas: 'I saw him in Woolwich some months later, getting on well but somewhat indignant at his fate. But he was awarded the DSO for his action and this cheered him up a lot.'[1]

Bernard's recovery was indeed remarkable. According to the medical records kept at the Royal Herbert Hospital he had lain untended for three hours at Meteren (they gave the time of his wound as approximately 3 p.m.); having had his wounds bandaged at a field dressing station he was despatched to a field hospital and then sent on to a French hospital at St Omer where he remained for two days before being embarked for England. On admission at Woolwich on 18 October 1914 it was found that a rifle bullet had damaged his knee-cap, though not seriously. The critical wound was in his chest, where several rifle bullets had passed through the right thorax.

'The knee wound healed quickly,' the first medical case-sheet recorded.[2] 'The chest wound was much slower', though an exploratory puncture revealed that the internal bleeding had stopped, and the lung remained mercifully dry thereafter. The pain soon subsided, leaving the young Captain short of breath only – a disability which would dog him all his life. Within weeks even this shortness of breath disappeared, however, and by a seeming miracle Bernard Montgomery was back on his feet, getting up daily and 'except for some little stiffness of left knee he can get about fairly well. The chest is not yet quite clear,' the RAMC doctors remarked, 'and fluid not entirely absorbed.' The first Medical Board to assess his case was called on 5 November 1914. Montgomery was reported to be 'suffering from gunshot wounds of the right side of the chest with effusion

---

[1] Brigadier Clement Tomes, loc. cit.
[2] Ministry of Defence, Confidential Personnel Records.

of blood into the right pleural cavity. These wounds are now almost healed and the right lung is now beginning to expand satisfactorily.' In its opinion the Board felt the chest wound was still very severe, and its effects would be 'likely to be permanent.' It was estimated that Montgomery would be incapacitated for military duty for five months from the date of injury. A month later the Board again convened to assess Montgomery's case, for on 5 December Bernard felt well enough to leave hospital. He was given three months' leave before being reconsidered for military duty; but within two months Bernard had managed to persuade the Army Council to have him re-examined, and on 5 February 1915 at the War Office in Whitehall he was declared fit for service at home, though not for general duties. On 12 February 1915 he was posted to succeed Major J. A. Nixon as Brigade-Major of the then 112th Infantry Brigade, Western Command, at Manchester. Considering that Bernard Montgomery had been only a platoon commander and a Lieutenant when wounded at Meteren, and had only been made a temporary Captain on 14 October 1914, this says much for his reputation. The post was that of a Major; in the meantime the War Office contented itself with making his Captaincy a substantive one.

The Brigadier under whom Bernard Montgomery was deputed to serve turned out to be a retired Brigadier-General of the Royal Inniskilling Fusiliers, G. M. Mackenzie – 'a very nice person but quite useless,' Bernard later noted in the annotations to his letters, 'and it would be true to say that I really ran the Brigade and they all knew it.'

The Brigade, as formed in January 1915, was part of Kitchener's new army of volunteers, comprising four battalions of Lancashire infantrymen. Bernard insisted on a common training ground, which was impossible in the different parts of Lancashire where the battalions had been raised; so early in March the Brigade moved to North Wales where good training grounds existed. The diminutive 17th Lancashire Fusiliers were replaced by brawny troops of the 11th Battalion Border Regiment from Carlisle; but such keen preparations merely encouraged the War Office to break up the brigade and post the battalions individually to divisions preparing to leave for France. Thus, within six weeks of taking over as Brigade-Major of the 112th Infantry Brigade, Bernard Montgomery was sitting in the Brigade HQ at Chester without a brigade.

The rate of army casualties, and the build up of the German army in the west soon restored the situation, however, and by 1 May 1915, the 112th Infantry Brigade (after a few days' designation as the 105th) became the 104th Infantry Brigade, allotted to the 35th Division. It consisted of the previously ousted 17th Lancashire Fusiliers, the new 18th and 20th Lancashire Fusiliers, and the 23rd Manchesters. The Division was known as the Bantam Division, because it largely comprised 'small men, who did not want to be left out', as Bernard put it in an annotation to his letters. In June, when he was passed fit for General Service, the entire Division came together into a single tented camp at Masham in Yorkshire; and in August it moved south to Salisbury Plain 'to complete its training before proceeding to France', Bernard wrote in the Brigade History. 'This was a very pleasant spot and some real good work was put in,' he added. He was given a Staff Captain to assist him, and a Signals Officer. 'Bernard was fortunate,' his brother Brian recorded, 'as from the outset General Mackenzie, who was a wise and tolerant man, full of common sense, fully apprecitaed his Brigade-Major's worth and gave him all the support he needed, without stint of any kind.'[1]

In January 1916 orders finally came to embark for France. The Brigade had this time remained together, and would go to war with its 'old retired' Brigade Commander and his barely twenty-eight-year-old Brigade-Major, Captain B. L. Montgomery, DSO. On 29 January Brigadier-General Mackenzie wrote to Bernard's father, who had been prevented by a chill from giving the Brigade a send-off address:

> Headquarters,
> 104th Brigade
> Parkhouse Camp
> Salisbury

My dear Bishop,
   I am very sorry not to have seen you before I leave England.
   With regard to your son Bernard, I have the very highest opinion of him. He is equally good at Administration as at Training of Troops. He ought to have a brilliant future in the Army, and rise to high rank.
   Be my stay with this Brigade long or short, I shall not fail, before I leave it, to bring his admirable services to the notice of the authorities, and to do all I can to further his advancement with them.
   He has taken a great deal of routine work and drudgery off my hands, doing the work in a quiet unobtrusive way. It is, of course, his job, you may say, but it is not every Staff Officer that I have met, nor many, who have been so thorough and helpful in the work. General Pinney too knows his work and worth, and I am sure will look after his future interests.
                   With all good wishes for the future
                   Yours sincerely
                   G. M. Mackenzie

---

[1] Brian Montgomery, op. cit.

Mackenzie's appreciative letter was the first prophetic appraisal of Montgomery's 'brilliant future in the Army'; and though Mackenzie's days as Brigade Commander were not to last long, he deserves credit both for giving Bernard the freedom to develop his growing administrative talent, and for making sure that both the War Office and the Divisional Commander, Major-General Pinney, knew of Bernard's gifts.

Whatever Bernard's ability at training, the war on the Western Front to which he returned was however very different from the one he had left some fifteen months before. The Brigade HQ left Southampton on 29 January 1916 aboard the SS *Archimedes*, escorted by two destroyers, and arrived at Le Havre the next day. As part of the 35th Division it was assigned to 11 Corps under the command of Lt-General Sir R. Haking. Three days after landing Bernard wrote to his mother:

> We are in a very nicely furnished house belonging to a French lady who is away somewhere . . . We have the whole house for ourselves & servants, so are quite comfortable. It is a large house of 3 stories with about 4 rooms on each floor, and we use all their crockery & cutlery etc. I have a splendid bedroom with electric light and a dressing room. We are really much more comfortable than we were at Parkhouse Camp. Of course these conditions won't last for long. We shall be here probably for about another 10 days, then we are to move off behind the particular part of the line we are to occupy. Each battalion will then go up in turn and be shewn over the trenches and get thoroughly conversant with all the details of Trench War. Then we shall definitely take over the line.

Such luxury did not inure Bernard to the hard conditions with which the troops had already had to contend on the journey to St Omer:

> We halted at some quite obscure unpronounceable French station at 9 a.m. to water and feed the horses; and the men all got hot coffee given them. It was all ready on the platform in large cauldrons. It was a bitterly cold day with an East wind blowing; the men don't get 3rd class carriages in France but have to use cattle trucks. A cattle truck holds 8 horses or 25 men. They are very cold things to travel in as they don't give them straw, so they wanted coffee badly.

One horse actually died from pneumonia, according to the Brigade's War Diary.[1] Bernard's servant caused him wry amusement though:

[1] War Diary, 104th Infantry Brigade (WIO 95/2482), Public Record Office.

Taylor is very amusing trying to talk French. I never give him any help but just tell him what I want done. He manages somehow and has never failed me yet. He is a first class servant and I wouldn't change him for the best valet in England, for I can absolutely trust him to do what I tell him, somehow.

Preparing a virgin brigade for trench warfare was a demanding responsibility; and a week later Bernard was apologising to his mother for not having written sooner.

If my work was hard at home it is ever so much more so out here. But in one respect it is much better as I don't have to go round so much seeing the regiments do things properly. The result of all their training at home is coming out and they don't want half so much looking after as they used to.

That very morning, on 11 February 1916, the Brigade had been inspected by Lord Kitchener himself.

He is out here for a few days and we had a sudden message yesterday afternoon at 4 p.m. that he would inspect us at 10 a.m. this morning. This of course meant a lot of work for me, but we were all ready for him. It has been horribly wet all day, and the conditions could not have been worse. All the country round here is very highly cultivated and there is not a meadow or grass field anywhere. So we had to form up in a ploughed field. The mud was awful and it was raining hard. But K. got out of his motor and afterwards stood on the road while we filed past him. He was very pleased indeed with the parade and told us so.

The 1st Army Commander, Sir Charles Monro, had accompanied Kitchener – the man 'who managed the evacuation from Gallipoli . . . I expect [he] could tell some interesting tales about it,' Bernard remarked.
Such exalted inspections were certainly rare in a war in which most troops never saw or even knew who their higher commanders were. 'I went through the whole war on the Western Front, except during the period I was in England after being wounded,' Bernard wrote later in his *Memoirs*; 'I never once saw the British Commander-in-Chief, neither French nor Haig, and only twice did I see an Army Commander.'
Bernard's memory was here at fault, though his point was pitifully correct. In fact a few days before Kitchener's inspection, Bernard met Sir Douglas Haig.

We were out route marching, and he watched us march past. His military secretary, the Duke of Teck, was with him and I talked to him for about 10 minutes. He is I think a brother of the Queen; he is very deaf and you have to rather shout at him. Haig looks very worn and aged: of course he had a very harassing time at the beginning of the war in the retreat. That was when he made his great reputation. He has been out here all the time and been in all the big fights, and I suppose a man of his age (56) ages quicker and hasn't the same rebound as a younger man.

Far from decrying the conduct of the Army at the time, Bernard in fact seems to have been full of admiration at the way the panic and confusion of August 1914 had stabilised.

The organization of the Army out here is quite wonderful and one could write several books about it all. All that sort of thing has improved a lot since I was last out. We have over a million men out here now, which is not bad. Of course they are not all up at the front, but there are quite ½ a million up and we have huge reserves behind and at the bases.

His cousin Valentine was serving in the division. 'On a route march the other day I stopped and rode beside him for a short time and he said the life suited him very well.' Valentine's days, however, were numbered; while those of Bernard Montgomery's experience as a staff officer on active service were just beginning. The memory of the fierce fighting in which he had so nearly lost his life held no ghosts for him; his confidence seems to have been unbounded. On 22 February 1916 he related to his mother how he had borrowed a motor car and

went with Tomes to see the place where I was wounded, Meteren. It was most interesting going over the ground again and I remembered it all quite well. The trench I charged and captured has been used as a grave to bury the Germans we killed. I saw the exact spot where I lay for over 2 hours while they shot at me. The place is just the same except for one haystack which is not there now. All the fields about there are full of graves of our men; the graves of Major Christie and Gilliat are well kept and in quite good condition. If you have their addresses their family's might like to know that I visited the graves and that they are being well looked after.

The reality of trench warfare was sinking in, though.

A very cold snap has set in here and it is snowing hard now. We are in a very flat part of the country which is nearly all waterlogged; it is impossible to dig underground without the trenches filling with water. So all the trenches are breastworks made of sandbags.

90

The 104th Brigade had finally moved up towards its intended sector, with three of its battalions attached to the 38th (Welsh) Division 'so that all might learn the latest methods of making war before the Division was given a sector of the line to hold on its own,' as Bernard put it in his Brigade History.[1] 'Considerable difficulties were encountered when the Bantams first arrived in the trenches as firesteps were of course too low for them; it was quite a common sight at this time to see a large Welshman standing on the firestep, with the Bantam he was teaching perched on a pile of sandbags beside him. It was also reported that the enemy were heard "crowing" at "stand to" the first morning after we had arrived for instruction; the accuracy of this was never really verified, but at any rate no Bantam prisoners were captured by the enemy during this period.'

Historical hindsight has certainly distracted attention away from the organisational achievements made at this time. A new amateur army had been created; and if the tactical strategy employed by the higher commanders was barren, the courage, cohesion and discipline of the units were amazing. From 7 March 1916, when the 104th Brigade took over its first sector of the British lines near Richebourg, its four battalions would be almost constantly in action, moving up to the forward trenches for three-week spells, and then relieved for a week or ten days' rest and training. The original Bantams were only five feet to five feet three inches tall; but they stood their ground as well as bigger men, and Bernard Montgomery was justly proud of them. Yet he appears to have had a presentiment of his cousin Valentine's death from the very day the Brigade moved into its first independently held sector. On 7 March Bernard wrote to his mother that already four officers had been killed, 'two of whom are in Valentine's Regt, the 17th Battalion Lancashire Fusiliers. I hope nothing will happen to him; if anything did I couldn't telegraph to you, as they wouldn't send it. I would write at once but Aunt May would probably hear first as the War Office would telegraph to her at once. The best thing would be for him to get wounded at once, not dangerously; a broken leg would mean he would be home for a year and Aunt May would be quite happy.'

Poor Valentine was to have no such luck. 'After a few days in the line we were ordered to prepare and carry out a company raid against the enemy's trenches,' Bernard recorded in his Brigade History. 'This was entrusted to the 17th Lancs. Fus. Very complete preparations were made and the raiding party was practised continually over a model of the ground to be traversed; but in spite of very gallant leading the raid was a failure, probably owing to our inexperience in such matters.' Valentine Farrar was shot in the head during the raid and died in hospital shortly afterwards. He was 'a very nice lad', Montgomery noted in his annotation to his letters, almost fifty years later.

[1] Montgomery Papers.

By now the thick carpet of snow and the freezing cold that had kept the trenches firm had begun to thaw, turning the lines into a quagmire, sodden with rain. To his father Bernard described the situation:

Altogether the conditions for the men living in the trenches are very bad. I go out every day round the trenches and posts. The general and I start together about 9.30 or 10 a.m. After we have ridden as far as it [is] safe to do we generally separate and go to different sections of the Trench Line. We don't go back to lunch but stay out till about 4.30 p.m. when we change & have a good tea. After tea we discuss the points we have each noticed. This is I think the best way to do the work; also it is good for one to have a sandwich or biscuit lunch & come back to a good tea. Of course it means that all the office work has to be done by me before breakfast and in the evenings. There is a good deal of office work too, so I have a very strenuous life. We have to send in 3 reports a day on the situation; one at 5 a.m., one at 10 a.m., and one at 4 p.m. The first and last are sent by wire and are very brief, such as 'Situation normal' or 'Situation unchanged' or otherwise. At 5 a.m. the signaller on duty comes and wakes me up and brings me the reports from Battalions on the situation; I then write out my report. Then I go to sleep again (or rather generally lie awake) till 6 a.m. Then I get up and dress and start writing out the written report which has to be sent in at 10 a.m., all the reports for this come in about 7 a.m. I get the draft written out before breakfast. While I am having breakfast it is typed out and after breakfast the general signs it and it goes off. Then we both go out.

After tea I get through the office work; then dinner at 8 p.m. Then on again with the office work till about 11 p.m. Then bed, by which time I am very tired. Sometimes I go out at night; on these occasions I get back earlier in the afternoon, generally about 2.30 p.m. I did this yesterday; went out again at 8.30 p.m. and didn't get back till 1 a.m. this morning. Woken up at 5 a.m. for the early morning report; got up at 6 a.m.

I don't go out much at night as it makes the day too heavy. Besides you can't see anything; but the men like to see you come so one goes occasionally.

Montgomery's capacity for hard work did not go unappreciated. His keenness might be an embarrassment to superior officers in peacetime; but in a war of attrition, with the Brigade constantly being moved to different sectors, his imperturbable efficiency was a boon both to the brigade battalions and to Brigadier-General Mackenzie himself. On 2 April 1916 Bernard apologised to his mother for his recent silence.

I have hardly written a private letter of any sort for the last week or so. We came out of the trenches about 7 days ago and went into rest billets for 2 days in a very smelly straggling village. Then we moved to where we now are; that was last Tuesday. We stay on here till next Tuesday (4 April) and then we move up for another tour in the trenches. It is in a different part of the line and I have had to go all over it and get to know it before we go up. Then having got to know it I have to write out full instructions and information concerning it for the various units in the Brigade, and also draw up a scheme for its defence in case the Germans attacked it in force.

This of course is all in addition to the ordinary work, office & otherwise, of the Brigade, and arranging inspection for various Generals who have been to see us.

So altogether I have been fairly well occupied

Bernard assured his mother. It was no understatement; and, despite Bernard's age, Brigadier-General Mackenzie recommended him for promotion.

Yes he has recommended me for brevet promotion, that was about a month ago, and if they give it to me it will come out in the Honours Gazette on the King's Birthday. However I don't suppose I shall get it as there must be any number of others recommended for the same thing and we can't all get it.

Then last week they asked for a special report on me. He gave me a very good one and recommended me for a higher Staff job. So one feels that one has not done so badly, though it is of course all part of the day's work and you have to work your best whatever job you have,

he remarked with the straightforwardness and lack of vanity that was still characteristic of him at this stage of his life. He was already doing a major's job; brevet promotion would have meant that he would be entitled to a major's rank forthwith, formal promotion coming later when there was a vacancy in the army lists.

Bernard was wise to discount the probability of promotion. Though he had worked industriously and virtually ran the Brigade, the Division had not been involved in any major action, and the only attempt at raiding within the Brigade had ended in failure. 'The Brigadier did recommend me for Brevet-Major, and promotion on the staff,' Bernard noted in his annotations to his letters. 'But as he was himself given the sack and sent back to England the following week – nothing came of it!!!'

The 35th Division had been sideslipped north to relieve the 8th Division in the Fleurbaix sector; and it was there that Brigadier-General Mackenzie, Lt-Colonel McWhinnie (commanding Valentine

Farrar's old battalion of Lancashire Fusiliers) and Lt-Col Smith of the 23rd Manchesters were all relieved of their posts and replaced by younger officers. Brigadier-General J. W. Sandilands took over command of the 104th Brigade – 'a first class officer from whom I learnt a great deal,' Bernard remarked of him in his annotations.

Already on 10 April, four days before the change of command, Bernard had written to his mother about the impending transformation. He had met his old colleague from the Royal Warwicks, Clement Tomes, who was currently Brigade-Major of the 106th Brigade in the same section of the line Bernard had relieved.

I had a long talk with him. I didn't think he was looking very well; he worries over things much more than most people.

I am sorry to say that General Mackenzie is being sent back to England. They say he is too old to command a Brigade out here; I think myself they are right. He is 56 and is old-fashioned and out of date in most things he does; a younger, more modern, man is really wanted. He is a very nice man, quite charming, but that of course is nothing to do with it! I expect you remember I wrote some time back and said this would probably happen. He has been very good to me and I get on very well with him, and will be very sorry to part from him. If a younger and more modern man is sent it will mean that I shall not have so much work to do; up to date I have had to do lots of things which the general ought to do himself. Of course the above is quite private.

The confidence with which Bernard Montgomery wrote from the front is certainly amazing; and one is forced to the conclusion that war evidently suited him. His teachers at St Paul's may well have despaired of Montgomery as an essayist in class; but in the very different conditions of front-line warfare one can only marvel at the clarity and simplicity with which he described his experiences. No anxieties seem ever to have clouded his mind; and his remark about his erstwhile Adjutant in the 1st Battalion, Royal Warwickshire Regiment, Captain Tomes, is very revealing. It was Bernard's ability to concentrate on the tasks in hand without 'worrying over things' that impressed his superiors and subordinates at this time. Moreover his almost child-like mentality – this ability to see things with the simple clarity of a child – was, however unmeritorious in the classroom, a gift of the very highest value in 'the fog' of war. Others – like Captain Tomes – might be better endowed to elicit the affection of those who served under them; might – like Lt-Colonel Lefroy – have a larger vision of war, a more critical sensibility to the pros and cons of Allied tactics and strategy. But few, if any, possessed the total clarity with which Bernard viewed his own immediate world; and it was in these years of European conflict that history provided the

94

object-lessons on which to temper it. That Bernard should have written to his mother in such clear detail about military matters should not surprise. Still emotionally unattached, it was natural that Bernard should relate his activities in Flanders to the person nearest to his heart and trust at that time: in the same way that he would draw tactical exercises in the sand at Le Touquet when, years later, he courted his first serious girl-friend. Indeed, it will be seen, later, how at moments much more critical in the fortunes of his country, even of the Western world, Bernard needed to be able to correspond with someone – preferably a woman – far away from the front in a way that enabled him to exercise this unique faculty for simple exposition; and however jejune the style, each perception with its clear phrasing was a personal gesture – personal in the very discipline of mind that composed it.

We have had some rather suspicious looking aeroplanes over our trenches lately [he added in his letter of 10 April 1916].

All British aeroplanes have red, white and blue concentric rings underneath the wings so that we can distinguish them from below. The German machines have black Maltese crosses, one underneath each wing. It is quite possible that the Germans make use of machines they capture from us; to do this they must alter the marks a little otherwise they would be fired at by their own guns. So they alter the concentric rings and make them more like a square than a circle so that you can only tell the difference with a good glass. They further try to deceive us by firing at these aeroplanes themselves but of course taking good care to go very wide of the mark. They are very ingenious people and it is quite extraordinary the number of devices they have. They employ a very extensive system of listening all along our front, and by use of microphones etc. listen to our signals and conversation on the telephone. Up to date we have used what is called an 'earth return' for our wires; that is that instead of having 2 wires to a place we have one and use the earth as our return wire, as earth conducts electricity. As long as we did that the Germans could pick up our signals. So now we complete the circuit by a second wire and have what is called a 'metallic circuit', and don't use the earth at all.

Still, even then, it is extraordinary what a lot of information they do get. There are a lot of French people living quite close up behind the line, and a considerable number of Belgian Refugees. I am sure a lot of these latter are spies; they probably get their information back by means of pigeons. No one is allowed to use homing pigeons except ourselves. In our last billet we found the owner of the house kept pigeons; we we trapped them at night and made a pigeon pie! [. . .]

I wrote to Uncle Reggie a few days ago. I rather like the idea of his being on 6 weeks leave. He only went to Malta a few months ago, so that is not a bad way of 'doing the war'!

No more now. Best love from
yr loving son
Bernard

On 26 April 1916, Bernard wrote of his new Commander: 'My new General's name is Sandilands; he is only 40 years old and is in the Cameron Highlanders.' The Brigade was about to move back to its old sector. 'The day after tomorrow we go up into the Line at Neuve Chapelle. I was up there yesterday with Captain Tomes, having a preliminary look round; we are taking over from his Brigade.' The devastation appalled him.

> Neuve Chapelle is really a most extraordinary sight. At one time it must have been quite a pretty little village; now there is nothing to be seen there at all. The whole village has been razed to the ground and is nothing but a heap of rubble; not even the walls of the houses are left standing. Our line goes about 200 yards in front of what was once the village.

Bernard even wanted his father to see it – presumably as an example of the destructiveness of modern war. 'Could he not come out here with the Archbishop? He could then come and stay a few days with me. I am sure the Archbishop could easily work it. Will you see if it can be done?' he asked – a salutary request in the light of Bernard's later remark in his *Memoirs*: 'The fact that the Chief-of-Staff of the British Armies in Europe had no idea of the conditions under which the troops had to live, fight and die, will be sufficient to explain the uncertainties that were passing through my mind when the war ended.'

Bernard, at any rate, was in no doubt about the conditions. On 7 May 1916, he wrote to his mother to say how sorry he was to hear of his cousin Hugh Northcote's death – 'Uncle Jack will be very upset I expect and I have written to him about it. He is the second of the family to fall.' His father did not get permission to visit France; so Bernard described the new régime under Brigadier-General Sandilands:

> I have rather changed my habits since General Mackenzie left and since the summer began.
> I get up every day at 6.15 a.m. Breakfast at 7 a.m. Start out at 7.45 a.m.
> Sometimes I go with the General; at other times we go different ways. We come back in time for lunch at 1 p.m. In the afternoon we do the office work and after tea we go round some places near our

Headquarters or go & see the gunners or the Engineers and arrange plans.

Dinner at 8 p.m. Then more work and bed at 10 p.m. if lucky. This is a pretty lively place.

But the Censor struck out the reference to Neuve Chapelle as indiscreet.

There is always a fair amount of shelling going on by day; at night it is very lively indeed, rifle and machine-gun fire going on most of the night.

Our casualties here have been wonderfully small considering the place we are in. I have been very lucky myself in escaping the places most shelled. There are 2 ways up to the trenches and they nearly always shell the particular one which I am not using at that time,

he noted with gratitude but without a trace of apprehension for his future safety. Later on, when further promotion on the staff did come, he would miss the front-line feel of his responsibilities as Brigade-Major, and the close contacts with the battalion officers and men. General Mackenzie had given him the freedom and encouragement to create his own position in the Brigade – a position he appears to have used with indefatigable aptitude. But it was General Sandilands who began to teach him the proper nature of the Brigade Commander's job – in particular the relationship between the Brigade Commander and his artillery and engineer commanders. This was a lesson of paramount importance in young Captain B. L. Montgomery's career – a lesson he would certainly never forget. From now on he had not only the responsibility of his own job from which to learn, but also intimate daily contact with a senior commander, experienced in war and well versed in the execution of battle orders. In early March 1916 Bernard had written optimistically to his mother about the great German onslaught at Verdun:

Things are going quite well for the French at Verdun and they are not in the least anxious about it. Of course if it was really bad for them then we should help them. But as a matter of fact they have not yet used any of their reserves & they have the show well in hand. It is all part of our policy to let the Germans beat themselves to death against the stone wall. That is why we don't attack up where we are. The Germans have lost enormously and they can't afford to.

Such may have been the official attitude on the staff. But, in a laconic sentence, Montgomery later annotated this letter: 'My views on the fighting at VERDUN were not in any way in accordance with the true facts.' The truth, indeed, was the very opposite; and as the French army bled to death at Verdun the planned joint summer offensive became an all-British affair: the notorious Battle of the Somme, a battle the French demanded as a relief to their hard-pressed troops at Verdun, while discounting any real hope of a strategic breakthrough there.

The British High Command thought otherwise. Haig, who had appeared worn and tired to Bernard that February morning, actually believed that his Somme offensive would knock Germany out of the war. Full conscription to the age of forty-one had been introduced on 1 April 1916, and the one-time Expeditionary Force was growing in leaps and bounds. At New Year, 1916, there were thirty-eight British divisions in France; by the summer these had swollen to forty-seven – including Bernard Montgomery's 35th Division.

At the end of May Bernard went on leave to England for ten days. Apart from seeing his parents he arranged to visit his old Brigadier-General, Mackenzie, and meet his dead cousin Valentine's old Colonel – evidence that Bernard was in fact always personally loyal to those of his superiors and colleagues whom he liked or respected, regardless of their professional failings.

On 8 June 1916, Bernard was back at the front; and after a further spell in the front line the Brigade was relieved for a proper rest. It had become very warm, and Bernard sent home his thick winter overcoat to be put, as he punctiliously instructed his mother on 22 June, 'in the bottom drawer of the chest-of-drawers in the corner, behind the sofa, in Colin's room.' He was enjoying his respite:

It is very nice being in Rest and right out of the shell area even. We are about 15 miles behind the line. I expect next week they will make us start training again, but for this week we are having a complete rest. The men don't only want a rest from physical fatigue, they want mental rest as well. There is no doubt that they get mentally fatigued and they want to be left alone and allowed to laze about & sleep under the trees etc. They will sleep the whole 24 hours round if they are allowed to. [. . .]

We have got a Horse Show for the Brigade on Saturday afternoon next, and are giving prizes for the best turned out wagons, horses etc. The Massed Bands of the Brigade will play, and if it is fine it ought to be rather amusing.

We are living in a beautiful chateau in a small wood. It is the best place we have been in so far; my bedroom is very nice and I have beautiful sheets & pillow cases etc. The owner is away somewhere.

I am going over this afternoon to have tea with Capt Tomes.

Best love from
yr loving son
Bernard

What Bernard did not say was that the Brigade was glad not only to be in rest billets, but also profoundly relieved to be spared the veritable massacre that had awaited them in the Neuve Chapelle sector, where 11 Corps had been 'ordered to prepare a demonstration in the form of an attack to be carried out after the opening phases of the Somme Battle which was to begin on 1st July'; as Bernard put it in his Brigade History.

It was hoped this demonstration would draw enemy reserves away from the Somme area where the main attack was to be made. The Brigade was therefore ordered to prepare an attack against the BOAR'S HEAD; this was to be carried out in conjunction with an attack by the 5th Australian Division and 61st Division further to the north, towards the AUBERS Ridge. The operation never promised success; however preparations were commenced for it and enormous dumps and stores of all sorts were made in the trenches, Russian saps were commenced across NO MAN'S LAND, and altogether it must have been quite apparent to the enemy that we were preparing an offensive against him. All ranks were therefore greatly relieved when it was decided about the middle of June to withdraw the Division from the line for a rest, and the operation was handed over to the relieving Brigade of the 39th Division.

CHAPTER SIX

The Somme: 'A perfect shambles'

Bernard Montgomery's 104th Brigade had been absolved from participation in the terrible carnage of 1 July 1916, when 57,000 casualties were sustained by the British in a single day – 19,000 of them killed. Brigadier-General Sandilands had evidently made clear both to the higher staff and to Bernard that the intended demonstration against Boar's Head would, without the advantage of surprise, inevitably lead to a bloody failure. This, too, was an important lesson; but, though Bernard accepted its relevance to the operation concerned, he still failed to draw the wider, strategical inference. As he had underestimated the savagery of the German assault on Verdun, so too he misunderstood the implications of the first day's losses on the Somme. Four days after the battle began he wrote to his mother:

> We have moved since I last wrote. We were ordered to move at very short notice on Sunday evening and went off by train. We moved South and are now in Reserve behind the big offensive waiting to be used if required. Just at first the push didn't go so well as we hoped but now it has settled down more and is going on very well,

he recorded optimistically. 'We have any number of troops in Reserve and the thing should be a success.'

Not even the obvious signs of failure dimmed this optimism. Though Bernard noted that the pouring rain had postponed the offensive for two days and the conditions 'must be very unpleasant for the troops actually attacking', it did not occur to him that the offensive itself was a mistake. 'It will be very bad luck if it goes on,' he noted of the rain rather than the British attack – yet the ominous manifestations of lack of surprise were too evident not to be noted.

'We have had big casualties,' he acknowledged, 'motor ambulances with wounded go through our present village all day and night. I don't know our total losses but they must of course be very large.'

Haig had promised to call off the offensive if it met with a serious reverse; but, not unnaturally, initial failure merely strengthened his determination to succeed – a determination that was not as criminal as subsequent historians often aver, for the die-hard optimism of his subordinate officers is well represented in Bernard Montgomery's letter of 4 July 1916. It would have needed a general much greater in imagination and more willing to look beyond the enthusiasm of his own subordinates to countermand the offensive after Day One, whatever Haig had promised. Thus the suicidal 'push' went on, with staffs all-too-often concealing their casualties and reporting only the numbers of enemy troops captured; and inevitably the 104th Brigade was sucked into the disaster.

'My darling Mother,' Bernard wrote on 12 July:

I have had quite an extraordinary time since last writing; and have seen and done a great deal. We moved on Sunday morning [9 July] and got to our new place at about 12 noon. I went to bed as usual that night at 10 p.m. and at 10.30 p.m. was called to the telephone. The Brigade had to prepare to move at once. You can imagine what that meant for me; however we all got to work and at 12 midnight the first people were ready.

Indeed, so excited was Bernard by his experience of the past few days that he now committed what, in his later annotation, he referred to as 'a truly monstrous breach of security regulations'. By separate post he listed a series of village names, each one numbered, so that in his letter-proper he could describe to his mother the exact movements of his formation. 'It was lucky for me that the letters were not opened by the Censor!!' he added.

They took us in motor buses to 14 [Bouzincourt], which is about 3 miles West of 9 [La Boiselle]. I have sent a key for all the numbers separately. We all got in just before daylight and were pretty tired. From 14 we marched to 7 [Aveluy], about 1 mile West of 9. We are now at 8 [Ovillers] being heavily shelled and expecting to be ordered to advance at any moment. I have been over the whole ground and seen all the recent battlefields including 1, 2, 4, 8, 9, 10, and 11 [Beaumont Hamel, Hamel, Thiepval, Ovillers, La Boiselle, Contal-Maison, and Mametz Wood]. It was all most interesting. Of course the whole place is a perfect shambles: villages 5 and 9 [Thiepval and La Boiselle] exist no longer. When I first saw them I was on a hill, just behind them & they were pointed out to me. But I could see nothing except about a dozen tree stumps; there is nothing else to see as the whole of them has been reduced to dust. I now realise what it means for a place to be razed to the ground; but you have to see it to believe it. It will be a long time before we get all the British and German dead cleared away. They are lying about as they fell. All the wounded have I think been got back. German prisoners come in every day and all day. One dead German I saw this morning must have been at least 65. We are living in a dug-out, and a very damp one too. However one is very cheerful; the men wonderfully so. We have the upper hand of the Bosche as regards artillery and our guns must be very annoying to him. The shelling goes on all day and all night and at times is intense; the noise is perfectly deafening and at times one has to put your hands to your mouth and shout, even across the table during meals.

Albert is a very pretty little place. There is a gilt figure of the Virgin on top of the church tower there; its supports have been shot away and the figure is leaning out at right angles to the tower. The French say that when the figure falls completely down the war will end and the Germans be beaten. I expect you have seen a picture of it.

I am very well indeed. No more now from

yr loving son

Bernard

However the Virgin did not fall – and on 20 July Bernard's brigade was ordered to take part in the suicidal British advance.

'My darling Mother,' Bernard wrote three days later,

I enclose in a separate envelope a further list of places, numbered so that I can refer to them by numbers. We are at present holding the front line just east of 23 [Trones Wood]. 15 and 16 [Bazentin-le-Petit and Bazentin-le-Grand] are just to our N.W. and 25 [Delville Wood] is just to our N.

Facing us is 20 [Guillemont] with 18 [Waterlot Farm] to our left front. 21 [Maltz Horn Farm] is in no man's land.

These names would become monuments to modern slaughter – and the graveyard of Kitchener's volunteer army. Naturally one is tempted to trace back to this great exercise in senseless human destruction Bernard Montgomery's later legendary concern to avoid unnecessary casualties; but the letters he sent to his mother at this time show no such change of heart.

'The fighting here has been very fierce,' he wrote on 23 July; 'we have lost heavily in the Brigade, particularly in Officers. However you can't take part in a show of this sort without losing. We have been unlucky in losing rather a lot of officers in proportion to men,' he noted fatalistically, omitting the sense of outrage that characterised his Brigade War Diary at the way one of his battalions had been appropriated by 105th Brigade without clear directives. The entry in the Brigade War Diary ran:

23 Manchester Regt were used by the 105 Brigade to attack Maltzhorn Farm. The attack was very hurried and no clear or definite orders were given to the 23rd Manchester Regiment as to what was required. The first two companies penetrated the Ger-

man lines, and fierce hand-to-hand fighting ensued. Eventually the remnants of these two companies had to retire. A second attack took place at 11.30 a.m., for which the remaining two companies of the 23rd Manchester Regiment were used. These companies came under a very heavy artillery fire and suffered heavily. Total casualties 23rd Manchesters were 9 officers (including CO) and 162 other ranks. At 3 p.m. orders were received for the 104 Brigade to relieve the 105 Brigade in the front line.[1]

What is clear is that Bernard's growing concern was not with the conduct of war on the Western Front, but with its prosecution at a local regimental and brigade level. Only years later did the real absurdity of the Somme battle become evident to him. He became 'amazed' at the way millions of soldiers submitted to a battle of yards and inches – a battle which alone cost one million casualties for the sake of a 'wedge of muddy ground, at no point more than about nine miles deep on a front of some twenty miles or so – and of no strategic value', as he put it in his *History of Warfare*. At the time however the strategic question simply did not arise in his trusting, loyal and efficient gaze.

'We have put in 3 big attacks,' he recorded in his letter of 23 July,

and I expect one more will finish us for the time being. They will take us out to refit and collect ourselves, and will fit us up with fresh drafts.

The whole country round about here is a perfect shambles; everything absolutely shelled to bits. We have an enormous amount of artillery here and we shell the Germans all day and all night. His artillery fire is also very intense as he too has amassed a lot of guns against us.

I have come through untouched so far though I had a narrow escape this morning. I was out on an important reconnaissance with another officer and 4 big shells (8-inch) burst quite close to us; he was hit in the head and I was not touched at all.

Goodbye with best love from
Yr loving son
Bernard

Between 19 and 27 July the 104th Brigade suffered almost a thousand casualties – a truly astonishing total for a single brigade. Yet Haig drew no lessons from the disaster – and no one appears to have tried to make him do so.

Far from being encircled or even shelled into submission, the German armies put in relentless counter-attacks; and on 27 July Bernard wrote to his mother:

[1] Loc. cit.

I was returned as wounded yesterday, but am still doing duty. We have had an absolutely hellish time the last few days and yesterday morning I went up to Trones Wood to help extricate one of our Battalions which had had a particularly bad time. They were scattered about all over the place and very much shaken up. To collect them I had to run about the place in the open between Trones Wood and Guillemont,

he related, dropping the disguise of numbers now in his obvious state of exhaustion;

the latter place is strongly held by the Germans & we have so far failed to take it. Heavy shelling was going on and I was sniped at incessantly by the Bosches. However I escaped with the exception of a bit of high explosive shell which grazed the palm of my hand. It is quite alright and I am at work just the same.

No time for more.

On 31 July the 104th Brigade was finally withdrawn, decimated and exhausted, to 'Happy Valley'. 'The chief lesson to be drawn from the operations referred to,' wrote Brigadier-General Sandilands in an appreciation deposited with the War Diary the next day, 'is the time required to develop an infantry attack against prepared trenches, as apart from an immediate counter-attack which must be done at once, without wasting time over trying to get out anything approaching orthodox orders. Owing to the lack of trained officers and NCOs,' Sandilands continued, 'the slowness of thought and movement has increased to an extent which I do not believe is fully realised by all.

'It is not exaggeration to say that the recent constant change of orders involving entirely different plans, completely unhinges most of the new Army Commanding Officers, who in these days are often men quite unaccustomed to dealing with sudden and unusual situations. In my opinion, the attacks referred to [. . .] had but little chance of success owing to the lack of time for proper organization, although it is not for me to say that there were not very good reasons for attacking regardless of consequences.'[1]

This was General Sandilands' only thinly-veiled remonstrance at the way his brigade had been thrown into the futile chaos of the Somme. About the massacre of his own 23rd Manchester Regiment under the aegis of the 105th Brigade he was quite forthright: 'At 11.30 a.m. (on 20th July) the battalion was put into an attack on the Maltz Horn Ridge without an opportunity of any previous reconnaissance, and with very sketchy orders.

'It is no exaggeration to say that the majority of officers and men of the 23rd Manchester had but little idea of what they were attacking.

[1] Loc. cit.

The attack completely failed, although the officers and men went forward with great determination,' he pointed out.[1]

Bernard, as we have seen, felt great respect for his distinguished and experienced Brigade Commander; and it is unlikely that he did not share his superior officer's views as the Brigade counted the cost of its abortive efforts over the past month.

The Somme was Bernard Montgomery's first experience in the administration of large numbers of men in battle, as opposed to static trench warfare. He was still too young and too junior in the military hierarchy to question the conduct of Haig and the Army Commanders; but without doubt it was General Sandilands who helped him to recognise that without being given clear orders a largely Territorial and volunteer army could simply not be expected to penetrate well-defended trenches. This, at least, was a lesson that would become the cornerstone of Bernard's later military philosophy. He would not care whether people thought him unsubtle or unimaginative, whether they considered him self-flaunting and egocentric – but the officers and men must be given orders that were clear, as well as objectives they could identify and attain; and the holocaust of the Somme would remain the source of this determination.

A week after the Brigade was relieved Bernard recorded, in the serenity of a 'beautiful house with a charming garden' about forty miles behind the lines, his memory of the Somme:

> I don't suppose anyone can realise the awfulness of the show generally in this Somme push unless they have been in it. The French who are on our immediate right say that Verdun at its worst was as nothing compared to this.

As far as he could see the Germans were far from being defeated: 'The Germans have had time to mass a very large quantity of guns here now and use them well.

'The only consolation is that if it is bad for us it must be much worse for the Bosche, as we are far superior to him in men and especially in guns. The worst things he uses are gas shells,' he recorded – but the censor tore out the next page in which he described the 'new kind' the enemy was using.

It was small wonder, however, that in the quiet of New Park the Montgomery family waited eagerly for news of Bernard, began to copy his letters to post to other members of the family, and carefully preserved the originals.

Bernard had hoped for a month's rest and retraining. 'But I expect they will only leave us here about 10 days,' he wrote on 6 August 1916, the day after they reached the billets. Yet even ten days was more than Haig's continuing and futile offensive would allow. Four days later Bernard wrote:

[1] Ibid.

My darling Mother,
    We have left our pleasant abode away behind the line, and are
· now back in the line again in our old haunts, where I was wounded
the other day. We were of course very annoyed at only being given
4 days rest; it certainly does seem rather absurd taking us all the
way back there for 4 days. However we have to go where they
send us though it is very annoying. I hope we shall come out of it
alright this time,

he added, noting that he was suffering from severe headaches and
had asked his Aunt May to send Aspirin from England. Certainly,
when one considers his near-fatal wounds of 1914, it is extraordinary
to note the resilience with which Bernard Montgomery went through
the trials of 1916. A week later, back in the heat of battle, he was his
old self again, having recovered from his headaches, and with his
hand completely healed. It amused him to receive letters from
members of the family who had seen his name in the casualty
lists – he later wrote that he was only persuaded to report the wound
for official purposes in case it went septic[1] and he died or had to have
it amputated – and the news of his cousin Rosella's engagement he
found incredible: 'I haven't seen Rosella for many years and can't
imagine her as engaged,' he told his mother. Even his cousin Hugh,
who was a GSO 2 on the staff of Bernard's own 8 Corps had been
relieved:

    The Corps Staff which Hugh belonged to has been sent back out
    of the line and he is now right away behind training people. So I
    shall not see him again probably.
    The King has been round this way [he continued], but I did not
    see him. The Prince of Wales is on the Administrative Staff of the
    Corps we are now in; he holds a very junior appointment of course
    and I can't imagine that he does much real work.

Even within the 104th Brigade staff itself there had been some
'weeding':

    We have just turned out our old Staff Captain, the one whom
    Father met at Masham. He has been with us for a long time now
    but was really getting too old. I am now the only member of the
    Brigade Staff left who came out from England with the Brigade, as
    the Signalling Officer was wounded the other day.

[1] Gas gangrene, caused by anaerobic bacteria, was a deadly hazard; it resisted all
treatment until 1918, and surgeons were forced to amputate rather than risk fatal
further infection. See Alan Lloyd, *The War in the Trenches*, London 1976.

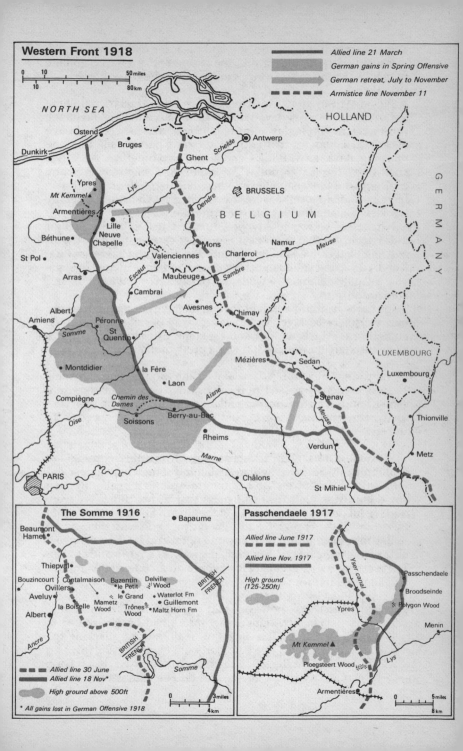

Western Front 1918

	Allied line 21 March
	German gains in Spring Offensive
	German retreat, July to November
	Armistice line November 11

0 10 50 miles
10 80 km

NORTH SEA

HOLLAND

GERMANY

Ostend
Dunkirk
Bruges
Ghent
Schelde
Antwerp

Ypres
Lys
Mt Kemmel
Armentières
Dendre
BRUSSELS
BELGIUM

Lille
Neuve
Chapelle
Mons
Namur
Meuse

Béthune
Valenciennes
Charleroi

St Pol
Escaut
Maubeuge
Sambre

Arras
Cambrai
Avesnes
Chimay

Albert
Péronne
Amiens
St Quentin
LUXEMBOURG

Somme
Montdidier
la Fère
Mézières
Sedan
Luxembourg

Compiègne
Laon
Stenay
Thionville

Chemin des Dames
Aisne
Meuse

Oise
Soissons
Berry-au-Bac
Verdun
Metz

Rheims

Marne
Châlons
St Mihiel

PARIS

The Somme 1916

Bapaume

Beaumont
Hamel

Thiepval
Contalmaison
Bazentin
le Petit
Delville
Wood

Bouzincourt
Ovillers
le Grand
Waterlot Fm
BRITISH
FRENCH

Aveluy
Mametz
Wood
Guillemont
la Boiselle
Trônes
Wood
Maltz Horn Fm

Albert

Ancre

BRITISH
FRENCH

Somme

	Allied line 30 June
	Allied line 18 Nov*
	High ground above 500ft

* All gains lost in German Offensive 1918

0 3 miles
4 km

Passchendaele 1917

	Allied line June 1917
	Allied line Nov. 1917
	High ground (125-250ft)

Yser canal
Passchendaele
Broodseinde
Polygon Wood

Ypres
Menin

Mt Kemmel
Lys

Ploegsteert Wood

Armentières

0 5 miles
8 km

Whether Bernard's valedictory foreboding at the end of his letter on 10 August was conscious or not, the sudden return to the Somme very nearly did end in his death. On 27 August he wrote home:

We have been up in the fight again and there has been no time for anything. I can give you no details about what we did as the censor is strict these days. But I had the narrowest escape I have ever had. I was up in the most forward part of our line one morning at 5 a.m. with the General and two orderlies. An 8 inch shell burst on the ground 4 *feet* from us. I was blown in one direction and the General in another. The two orderlies were also blown off their feet. We were covered in dust and surrounded by black smoke and fumes from the explosive.

Not one of us was in any way hurt or touched by the shell or pieces from it. What saved us was being so close to it. All the pieces of a high explosive shell go up into the air and descend several hundred yards away so the safest place is either very close or some way away. Of course we were all a bit shaken but we got up and went on.

On our way back about half an hour later we ran right into a very heavy artillery barrage. There was no way out of it except to go straight on, which we did and by some extraordinary manner came through it untouched. It was a pretty hot morning's work.

Bernard's narrative must have moved the Montgomerys, for this letter was evidently passed to relatives, and only a fair copy in a juvenile hand remains. In particular, though, Bernard was concerned with what his troops could and could not be expected to endure:

We came out last night and it has begun to rain this morning. We shall probably be going right away behind somewhere to rest and refit. I don't think we shall be brought up into it again: the men could hardly stand three helpings of that sort of thing. We were once again on the extreme right of the British line and fought side by side with the French. I had a good deal to do with them as we had to take over part of their line one night and I had to arrange it all with the French Staff. They could speak no English and I as you know can speak no French. However I had an interpreter and we fixed it up all right.

The Brigade War Diary, however, told a more dismal tale, uninhibited by censors. On 23 August new orders had been received to attack Falgemont Farm: 'The operation really meant attacking the German second line with one battalion on a front of 350 yards. No one was to advance on the left of the battalion used, so its left flank would be completely in the air, resting on Falgemont Farm which was a very strongly fortified strong point. The right flank of the next battalion on the left was at a point 600 yards in rear of where the left flank of the attacking battalion would finally rest. This operation appeared to be of such an unusual nature that representation was made to the GSO 1 of the 35th Division that it would be unreasonable to expect that it would be carried out successfully.

'We were informed that the operation must be carried out at all costs . . .'[1]

In the end, after various 'misfortunes', the attacking battalion was simply not ready to launch the assault on the morning of 24 August.

'The Divisional Commander came to Brigade HQ at 9.30 a.m. and these facts were pointed out to him,' the War Diary recorded.[2] As a result the suicidal attack was cancelled, and new orders were given. The 17th Lancashire Fusiliers advanced and 'only suffered about 60 casualties'. Communication was by pigeon from the front line, the messages being received at Brigade HQ in thirty-five minutes, the War Diarist noted with satisfaction.[3]

The next day Bernard apologised to his mother for the haste of his letter of 27 August. In the fierce fighting between 19 and 26 August he had forgotten her birthday; he now sent her a cheque for £5 'for you to get a birthday present for yourself with. I don't expect there is anything in Moville that you want; I personally would much prefer that you kept the money till you get back to London and used it for taxis and extra comforts etc.'

It is this letter of 28 August 1916 which bears out the contention of Bernard's sister Winsome that Bernard was forever being 'brushed off' when he attempted to show his deep affection for his mother. 'Often he would lavish a gift on her to show his feeling – a cheque with which to "buy yourself a new coat" or something like that,' Winsome remembered over sixty years later, 'and all she did was to give the money to Belgian Refugees in the First War.'[4] Bernard's stern rider to his birthday gift of August 1916 demonstrates how well aware he was of this. 'There is only one condition I make and that is that it is not to be spent on *anyone* else. I should like you to assure me on this point,' he demanded, vainly.

From Maud Montgomery's point of view the matter was not so simple. Pride in Bernard's achievements was one thing, and she had no hesitation in passing on his letters to relatives. But Bernard's presents obviously troubled her. To accept his gifts was to accept dictation by an all-too-bossy child; something which seems to have inspired in Maud the opposite emotion to that intended by Bernard. She never totally rejected him; but by deflecting his gifts and marks

[1] Loc. cit.
[2] Ibid.
[3] Ibid.
[4] Letter to the author, 20.2.78.

of filial affection she condemned him to an emotional limbo which, as Winsome pointed out, was only resolved by Bernard's tardy marriage in his fortieth year – and then for only the span of one decade. Possibly Maud felt guilty at the way she had neglected and rejected Bernard in his younger years; at any rate the insistent devotions of a grown-up un-favourite son were a constant trial which not even his military achievements could quite deflate – and she went to her grave imagining that her youngest son Brian had in fact 'done the best of all' her offspring.[1]

Brian, the Benjamin of the family, was certainly a point of reference for Maud and Bernard; and Bernard's fraternal – almost paternal – affection for Brian may well have had as its genesis the hope that in loving Brian he could share at least an emotional commitment with his mother. In the same letter in which he dictated the use of his birthday gift to Maud, Bernard requested her to give Brian £1 on his behalf 'for the repair of his bicycle; he wrote and said it wanted some new brakes etc. which would cost £1.' Not long afterwards Bernard even began to pay for Brian's schooling at St Paul's.

If Bernard was disappointed by his mother's response to his loving effusions, he certainly never showed it directly. This, indeed, was the iron determination that would single him out from a thousand more talented, more educated, more seemingly appropriate leaders of his age. He allowed nothing to show save occasional irritation; and continued to run the staff of the 104th Brigade coolly, efficiently – and with imperturbable courage; though even he was aware how the tension of front-line battle conditions inured one to the fatigue which logically the mind and body must suffer.

When one comes out of the line one gets a sort of relaxed feeling. One is of course very tired. The regiments get relieved every 2 or 3 days in the line but Headquarters have to stay in the whole time until we are due to come out. One gets no real sleep the whole time; every hour or so at night one is called to the telephone.

One is so braced up at the time one doesn't feel it, but there is of course a limit to the length of time you could go on doing it. When you come out there is nothing to keep you braced up and of course the reaction begins to set in.

At no point did Bernard ever feel that he himself, as a Staff Officer, was being asked to do too much; and those who later criticised him for his somewhat ruthlessly exacting demands on his chiefs-of-staff[2] probably had little idea of the way Bernard had unstintingly served

[1] Maud Montgomery, *I Remember, I Remember*, op. cit.
[2] Address to Egyptian Officers, Cairo, 1967: 'You've got to have a good staff. Make them do the work while you think. In the end, your Chief-of-Staff has got so much work he goes mad. It doesn't matter – get another one. The great thing is not to go mad yourself.' Reported in *The Times*, 15.5.67.

his generals between 1915 and 1918. It is probably true to say that he never later asked of any subordinate anything that he himself had not been selflessly willing to do in his own younger years.

Despite Bernard's abjuration, on behalf of the troops, of a 'third helping' in the Somme offensive, the 104th Brigade was nevertheless back in the trenches on 3 September 1916 – this time at Arras, which, by comparison with the Somme, was a 'quiet' place. There, in the relative 'peace' of static trench warfare – of shelling, mining, sniping and occasional morale-boosting raids – Bernard had at last a chance to ponder the lessons of July and August 1916 and to discuss them with his Brigade Commander, Brigadier-General Sandilands. By 18 November when Haig finally abandoned his offensive, over a million casualties had been sustained; and the Allied line had scarcely moved. It was the same story at Verdun, where a million and a quarter men were killed, wounded or gassed that year.

From September 1916 there is, however, a gap in Bernard Montgomery's correspondence with his mother. 'I must have written regularly but the letters were apparently not kept by my mother,' Bernard recorded in his annotation, 'or else they were given away. It is possible that they were pinched by members of the family,' he added, tongue-in-cheek.

Yet if Arras was a quiet sector – for the moment – this did not mean that Bernard and his Brigade Commander had been forgotten in Staff circles. General Sandilands went on leave for a fortnight that Christmas, returning on 30 December 1916; Bernard then departed for ten days to England, returning on 9 January 1917. A week later, in the absence of the Divisional Commander, Brigadier-General Sandilands assumed command of the 35th Division; and four days thereafter, on 22 January, Captain B. L. Montgomery, DSO, Brigade-Major of the 104th Infantry Brigade, left to take up his new appointment as GSO 2 on the staff of the 33rd Division. He remained, despite the promotion, a Captain, while his successor at 104th Brigade Headquarters held the rank of Major – an indication of the responsibility Bernard had carried for some two years – twelve months of them in the trenches – notwithstanding his subordinate rank.

CHAPTER SEVEN

The Battle of Arras

If 1916 had been a year bloody in fighting for British troops, the year 1917 held no respite. In April 1917 Haig ordered a new offensive with the object of capturing the Hindenburg Front – a new defensive line which the Germans had been preparing ever since September 1916, and to which they withdrew in good order in February 1917.

The spring assault on the Hindenburg Line is now known as the Battle of Arras – an offensive which, in the words of the British Official Military History, 'never enjoyed any considerable success', and whose cadenzas – Arleux, Scarpe and Bullecourt – 'were in general a failure', 'nothing less than a disaster' and 'equally calamitous'. Considering that on 6 April 1917 the United States of America declared war on Germany and joined the Allies, it is difficult to understand what made Haig so determined to fling his army against the well-prepared German line at Arras; but, whatever the reason, the result was the same as at the Battle of the Somme. In April alone the British suffered between 105,000 and 120,000 casualties.

The Battle of Arras opened on 9 April 1917. The following day Bernard wrote to his mother:

> We are at present engaged in the battle which is going on all about where I spent 4 months (Aug to Dec) last year and lived in a beautiful house with electric light & tapestries etc. The weather is appalling, alternate snow and rain, and fighting in these conditions is not easy,

he remarked. It appears he had just returned from the British Staff School in France.

> I would have liked a few days leave after the strenuous brain work at the Staff School, but with the Division moving up to fight it was out of the question to ask for it.
>
> I am glad America has finally declared war; she ought to send us large supplies of food and money.
>
> No more now.
>
> Your loving son
> Bernard

112

Four days later he elaborated on his Staff School experience.

> There was no exam at the end of the course, nor at any time
> during the course. We just went there to learn and we all helped
> each other and acquired knowledge from each other. At the end of
> the course the Commandant reports on each Officer; my report
> has not yet come in so I don't know what it is like.

Whatever the knowledge acquired, it does not seem to have
awakened Bernard to the strategic lessons to be learned from such
costly offensives, and his letter continued to describe the disastrous
Arras offensive with the same optimism that had characterised his
first letters from the Somme in 1916:

> We are in action in the Battle of Arras. So far the fight has gone
> well. I had an excellent view of the fight today and watched two
> Tanks walking down the Hindenburg Line; I was on a hill about
> 500 yards from them. The Germans shelled the Tanks hard for
> several hours but did not get a direct hit on them and nothing else
> will knock them out.
> The Hindenburg Line is very strong, too strong to attack frontal-
> ly. So we broke through at the North end of it and are rolling it up
> sideways. We had some heavy fighting before we managed to
> break through it as of course we had to do that with a frontal
> attack.

This was wishful thinking, for the Germans had not spent six months
preparing new defensive lines only to have them broken and turned.
Moreover the two tanks which Bernard described were of dubious
value, as the Divisional War Diary recorded on April 23: 'Two tanks
had been allotted to the 100th Infantry Brigade for the operation, but
owing to mechanical troubles they never arrived at the starting point,
and took no part in the operations. Their presence would probably
have enabled the 1st Queen's to gain a definite footing in the second
Hindenburg Line and given them time to consolidate their gains
effectively.'[1]
In fact the whole battle was a nightmare from the moment the
troops assembled in trenches 'knee-deep in liquid mud', as the
Official History acknowledged. Although some very limited gains
were made on the first day, by the second day Haig's objective of
Cambrai must have seemed wildly unreal to his staff. The divisions
assembled in reserve to exploit the planned break-through were one
by one sucked into local engagements as the initial offensive ground
to a halt and the front-line troops became too exhausted to face
counter-attack. Thus, from forming part of General Maxse's 18

[1] War Diary, 33rd Division, 1917 (WO 95/2406), PRO.

Corps, Bernard's Division was already requested on the evening of 11 April 1917 to help in the fierce fighting south of the Scarpe, under General Allenby of 7 Corps. After a brief lull the 33rd Division was sent in to relieve the 21st Division on the extreme right of the British 3rd Army; but the offensive had stalled, and Haig's continuation was an act of faith rather than perspicacity. The attack of the 7 Corps on 23 April 1917 was said even by the Official War History to be the 'hardest of the war so far'. After a misty dawn, cold clear sunlight illuminated the senseless bravery of tens of thousands of British troops. Despite the non-appearance of their two tanks, the 1st Queen's went forward; and even when they found their artillery had failed to smash the barbed wire, they scornfully trampled it down and captured the first trench of the Hindenburg Line. Few men, however, got any further, being decimated on the next coil of barbed wire; and by early afternoon even the initial gains were lost when the Germans counter-attacked. Elsewhere in the three brigades of Bernard's Division the story was the same. The Division advanced exactly one mile – at a cost, by 27 April 1917, of almost three thousand casualties.

Such futile slaughter seems almost inconceivable in retrospect, though given the state of arms prevailing in 1916 and 1917 it is difficult to see what alternative form the fighting on the Western Front could have taken. Certainly the courage of the troops indicated no loss of loyalty to the officers who led them on such suicidal occasions, and it was the French army, rocked by its casualties during the parallel battle of the Aisne, which began to crack, while in Russia disenchantment with the war gave way to revolution.

For Bernard Montgomery, possessed with his remarkable mental and physical resilience, the true moral of such bloodshed had still failed to become clear. Instead, immersed in the staffwork at Divisional Headquarters he was now learning techniques which were to stand him in good stead a quarter of a century later: the massing of divisional artillery under a single command; and the value of aircraft observation and intelligence reports.

On 3 May, resting after the April offensive, he wrote to his mother:

> Our glorious weather continues. Our Headquarters are at present in the middle of a large wood; all the trees and flowers are coming out and I should like to end the war here. However we won't be here much longer as we are on the move up to our second effort in the Arras battle.

Before the Division went back into action, however, he found time to visit his old 104th Brigade – a three-hour car journey to the 'south end of the line'. The 104th Brigade, once the Germans had withdrawn to their new line, was in virgin country – 'just like the country in England, not a shell hole to be seen anywhere'. However, his journey back took him through the devastated Ancre valley 'where there is not a living thing to be seen, not even a blade of grass'.

Bernard's return to his old Brigade demonstrates clearly the strangely conventional, even sentimental side to his character – his abiding loyalty to past associations and colleagues with whom he had served – a trait often forgotten in the face of his later ruthlessness in disposing of 'dead wood' among subordinates. He had in fact a remarkable memory, and could remember faces, names and places at will. To his mother he listed the villages facing which he had 'at various times sat in trenches', and recorded his pleasure at 'seeing all the old faces again in the 104th Brigade; I visited every unit and saw most people. It was a beautiful summer's day and was a real holiday for me'.

Such points may appear trivial; but in the jigsaw of Bernard Montgomery's early character they are essential pieces. Despite his avowedly unhappy childhood and the struggle of wills between himself and Maud he had found a milieu in which he could at least develop self-respect. He worked hard and conscientiously; he cared for his troops and for his colleagues. He visited those who had been sent back to England as he visited those still in action in his old Brigade; visited his Royal Warwickshire colleague Captain Tomes frequently and corresponded with his old platoon and company contemporaries from Royal Warwickshire days – even trying to get them posted to his own unit when they wrote to him that they were misplaced. He paid for his brother Brian's schooling, and even had fresh butter sent regularly from a dairy in Cornwall to his mother. His behaviour as a child and his performance at school had made him second-best in his parents' eyes; the scandal at Sandhurst had been the ultimate reflection of this. Since then, however, he had 'made good' beyond all expectation. A relentless capacity for work went hand-in-hand with conscientiousness in every direction – acknowledging gratefully letters and gifts, showing concern for the fortunes of various members of the family who had joined up, even interest in the number of birds 'bagged' by his brother Colin on the estate in Ireland. By temperament and upbringing he may have been moulded into an awkward shape; but for the moment at least he was determined to fit, both socially and professionally. Whenever he had leave to return to England he would write first to his sister Winsome, asking her to arrange a dance and to invite all her friends. He would pay for the occasion, and though his inhibition did not permit him to dance, he sat through the evening delighted to watch his sister enjoy herself, and only too pleased to converse with her many admirers. Their names he would note; and, if anything happened to them on the Western Front, he would always find out the details and inform Winsome.[1] Of his work as GSO 2 of 33rd Division there survives a revealing account written to his father:

[1] Lady Winsome Michelmore, interview of 10.4.78.

My job is a very interesting one, and not such hard work as when I was a Brigade-Major. Then I had to be an expert on every subject; not only operations but discipline, courts-martial, rations, supplies, stores, etc. as well. The latter jobs are really the Staff Captains' but Staff Captains are all New Army & have to be told everything.

A Divisional Staff is divided into 3 main branches:

A: Discipline, appointments, etc.

Q: Quartermaster-Generals branch

G: Operations etc.

Each is run by Regular officers. In addition there are Medical, Veterinary, ASC etc.

So now I have to worry about nothing except G work, operations, training etc. There is no doubt that a Brigade-Major's job is the most interesting of all Staff jobs. But it is hard work and I think I was beginning to feel the strain a bit.

There are 3 General Staff Officers in a Division, GSO 1, GSO 2, and GSO 3.

The latter does all the Intelligence work, maps, training etc. Ours is a Territorial and has to be told a good deal. The next step up from GSO 3 is Brigade-Major; then GSO 2. I have no fixed work like GSO 3; the GSO 1 and myself divide the work between us, and I am responsible that it is done and nothing is forgotten.

There is a lot to be done, but one has more time to do it than a brigade has. The GSO 1 and I take it in turn to go out and visit the trenches; he goes out one day and I the next. I use a motor car more than my horses as it is quicker. I brought my two horses with me from the 104th Brigade, with my groom. I have had them 2 years now.

We had 30 degrees of frost last night. They say there has not been such weather here for over 40 years. The snow has been on the ground now over 3 weeks and there has been never less than 30 degrees of frost every night.

Divisional Headquarters are in dugouts; there is no accommodation in this part of the country as everything was battered in as we advanced. Our dugouts are very commodious and quite warm.

No more now.

Yr affec. son
Bernard

On 6 July 1917, Bernard was promoted yet again. This time he became senior GSO 2 on the staff of an entire Corps – though still only a Captain.

CHAPTER EIGHT

Passchendaele

9 Army Corps was commanded by Lt-General Sir Alexander Gordon, and was part of Sir Herbert Plumer's 2nd Army. It was Plumer who introduced a new tactical doctrine to the conduct of British Army operations on the Western Front. Instead of attempting over-ambitious, general offensives, he limited his army to short, selected attacks on tactically important objectives only, using deep artillery barrages, and a leap-frogging replacement of forward troops by fresh units. The heart of Plumer's doctrine was training for specific tasks. Although this doctrine produced no grand victories that could wipe out the scars of the Somme and Arras, it was to provide the young GSO 2 (Operations) of 9 Corps with the deepest and most lasting lessons of the war. Plumer left the 2nd Army in November 1917 to take command of the British forces in Italy; but he left a legacy behind him which, although he himself never achieved recognition outside professional circles, would class him as the 'soldier's soldier' of the Great War. For, however much later historians – headed by Winston Churchill – might decry the blind, futile strategies employed by the generals on the Western Front, there can be no doubt that of all the campaign theatres of the First World War, it was that on the Western Front which demanded the highest morale and discipline, most efficient staffwork and closest artillery cooperation. Bernard's previous Army Commander, General Allenby, sent his 3rd Army to its doom at Arras in April 1917; but when moved to the open landscapes of Palestine in July that year he soon transformed a demoralised and half-defeated army into a legendary fighting force that captured Jerusalem before Christmas 1917, and went on not only to oust the Turks from Damascus in the following year but to force their surrender on 30 October 1918.

Thus the war on the Western Front, though it offered no scope for real break-through, was the seed-bed of modern army organisation, training for battle and cooperation between artillery and infantry. In this respect Bernard Montgomery was to prove very much a product of the 'First War' school – though hardly in a pejorative sense. The lessons he would draw from it were not so much the romantic ideals of modern, armour-clad cavalrymen, but those fundamental lessons implanted by General Plumer: namely that if offensives are planned

117

on a sound tactical understanding; if the troops are well trained and have limited, realistic and identifiable objectives; and if the full weight of modern artillery is intelligently brought to bear on a concentrated front, there is almost nothing the enemy can do except withdraw. If Bernard Montgomery was to sleep soundly and maintain complete composure throughout critical later battles, it was surely due to this conviction, born of his own experience in 1917 and again in 1918 under Monash. Like Plumer, Bernard Montgomery was at heart a 'soldier's soldier': a professional. He certainly came to abhor, in retrospect, the appalling and senseless casualties incurred in the Great War; but this was hardly the origin of his military greatness as so many historians and journalists have since averred. On the contrary, he was by his very nature and upbringing a conserver; and to the end of his life would maintain a concern not to waste – a concern so punctilious that at times it was comic, as when he sent his ADC to Switzerland immediately after the Second World War, to fetch his skiing boots from the glass case in which the proud hotelier was displaying them.[1] The wastage of human life was no more abhorrent to him than any other waste, and not really a factor bred by the Great War; nor was it a concern which he would allow to cloud his military judgment where the success of whole operations hung in the balance – as at Alamein, when he ruthlessly threatened to sack those of his commanders who complained at the high rate of casualties.

On 11 July 1917 Bernard wrote to his father from 9 Corps Headquarters:

> I like my new job very much. I am very lucky to get it. There are 3 GSOs 2 in a Corps and when the senior appointment fell vacant it would have been only natural if one of the other two had moved up. But it was given to me, although both the others are senior in rank to me, being Majors.

He had in fact gained the same appointment as his cousin Hugh in 13 Corps.

> I am easily the youngest holder of the appointment, and am also the only Captain holding such a job. In nearly all the other Corps it is held by a Staff College man.

Bernard's promotion was indeed remarkable; and if he had no time to go to Paris and meet his mother – who was staying on 'indefinitely' in the hope of seeing him – it was hardly surprising. Plumer's

---

[1] Anecdote related to the author by Carol Mather, March 1978.

grip on the Corps was very much in evidence; and its next operations were planned to begin on 31 July, as the right wing of Haig's new northern offensive, later known as the Third Battle of Ypres. General Gough's 5th Army was, however, given the decisive role in the offensive, and despite the use of 117 tanks the attack foundered in the wettest August for many years. Gough's artillery had been dispersed all along his line, and the new German technique of defence – holding the front line only thinly, with artillery and reserves of troops trained for counter-attack held back – proved too much for 5th Army. By the end of August Haig reluctantly asked Plumer to assume command of the offensive. Plumer ordered a pause of three weeks in the offensive while proper plans were drawn up and training carried out, with the object of capturing the vital high ground and thick woods west of Ypres.

Within the first days of September, 9 Corps had issued its preparatory instructions for the Autumn Offensive: a sixty-page document in the unmistakable style of its young GSO 2 (Training) – and the first of the many training manuals and notes on war which Bernard Montgomery would issue in his long career. A mind uncomplicated by subtlety and unhindered by self-consciousness transformed the complexity of command and administration to a clarity that still shocks by its absolute freshness and logical simplicity. Perhaps the very fact that Montgomery had not attended Staff College was a blessing, for it enabled him to formulate his approach without concession to anything save his own experience. What was remarkable in these preparatory instructions was not the originality of ideas, but their presentation as, point by point, Bernard Montgomery set out the doctrine that would guide the battalions, brigades and divisions of the Corps to success. The sixty pages, together with forty pages of appendices and twelve pages of maps, laid down the current Plumer principles: the creeping barrage that would precede the men; the leap-frogging of fresh units through the advancing front line (later known as 'the expanding torrent'); the preparations for German counter-attack; communications with spotter planes furnished with wireless; the training of specialist units; the use of aerial photographs and intelligence; the provision of ammunition dumps, and so forth. The ground was considered unsuitable for tanks; but otherwise the instructions would hold largely true for a further generation. Certainly once issued they provided the basis for all operational orders that succeeded them. On 3 September 1917, 9 Corps informed its constituent units that 'all plans for the offensive will be based on the instructions contained in the following publication issued by the General Staff' and gave pride of place to Bernard's 'Instructions for the training of Divisions for offensive action'. On 7 September 1917 Corps HQ ordered that 'a full dress rehearsal of the attack in every detail will be carried out by each assaulting brigade in the Berthen Training Area. The services of the GSO 2 Training, 9

Corps, are placed at the disposal of the GOC 19th Division for the purpose of assisting in the preparation of the ground'.[1]

Captain Bernard Montgomery DSO was indeed making himself known. There followed the step-by-step advances, starting in the third week of September, which proved that, properly prepared and executed, the British Army *was* capable of breaching even the most heavily manned defences: advances which helped restore morale in Britain's faltering French allies, and to which Bernard Montgomery pointed with considerable pride to Bishop Montgomery on 9 October 1917:

> My dear Father,
> Things are going very well here and we are entirely successful every time we attack. We are of course learning many very valuable lessons and there are few, if any mistakes.
> The attacks delivered on 20th Sept (Polygon Wood), 26th Sept (Menin Road), 4th Oct (Broodseinde), and today, are really masterpieces and could not have been better.
> I don't know when I shall have leave; it is impossible to say.

Plumer's three autumn attacks were indeed models of preparation and execution, the troops not only achieving all their objectives, but holding on to them despite relentless German counter-attacks. At Broodseinde 2nd Army captured 100 officers and 4000 men in a single day. Towards the end of October Bernard was officially made GSO 2 (Operations); and from 1 November all 9 Corps General Staff orders were signed by him on behalf of the Brigadier-General (GSO 1).

Still Bernard remained a Captain, despite the fact that the junior GSOs 2 were Majors. The weather had broken and Plumer was due to go to Italy, but Haig insisted on trying to extend Plumer's three limited operations into a do-or-die battle for the ill-fated Passchendaele ridge.[2] Thus the comparatively successful[3] attacks now escalated into another of Haig's bloodbaths. 'The cold weather has set in and I am collecting my winter kit together,' Bernard had noted wisely in October to his father. Soon the winter rains began to fall – 'our best ally' as Crown Prince Rupprecht of Bavaria, commanding the German Group of Armies, put it. What had been a salutary demonstration to the Germans of British offensive capacity was now squandered in the mud of Passchendaele, where so many Canadians gave their lives. Between 26 October and 11 November 1917, when Haig closed down the offensive, the Canadian Corps of four divisions

[1] War Diary, 9 Corps (WO 95/835), PRO.
[2] The decision was made at GHQ Montreuil, against the advice of the two Army Commanders, Gough and Plumer.
[3] The attacks brought some 10,000 German prisoners as well as gaining all objectives.

alone sustained 12,403 casualties. However Bernard was not impressed by the Canadians' futile gallantry – as he recorded to his mother on 8 November following a visit to his brother Donald's unit:

> I saw Donald. I went over and lunched with his Brigade. The Canadians are a queer crowd; they seem to think they are the best troops in France and that we have to get them to do our most difficult jobs. I reminded them that the Ypres Battle began on 31st July and the only part they have taken is during the last 10 days. They forget that *the whole art of war is to gain your objective with as little loss as possible.*[1]
>
> I was disappointed in them. At plain straightforward fighting they are magnificent, but they are narrow-minded and lack soldierly instincts.[2]

The Canadian effort at Passchendaele marked the finale to Haig's offensive of 1917. The past two years had provided Bernard with mounting experience of offensive warfare against a highly disciplined and determined enemy. As the last British 'push' petered out in the appalling conditions of Flanders that winter, the blind heroism of the Canadians – tinged with brotherly rivalry – had prompted Bernard to make his most concise declaration of military philosophy to date, on the eve of his thirtieth birthday.

---

[1] Author's italics.
[2] A judgement which, in the annotations to his letters, Bernard later rescinded, agreeing with Alan Brooke that the Canadian troops were magnificent soldiers, but their leadership poor.

CHAPTER NINE

The German Spring Offensive

By January 1918, with Russia out of the war and American troops still not arriving in any great quantities, it became obvious the Germans would launch their own spring offensive in an attempt to win the campaign on the Western Front while the balance of numbers favoured their forces. On 20 January, though no longer GSO 2 Training, Bernard Montgomery issued 9 Corps 'Instructions for the Defensive' – again a document of over fifty pages with copious maps. A secret 4th Army Memorandum had declared the 9 Corps sector 'probably the most important on the whole Army front and it rests with 9 Corps to make it as nearly impregnable as possible'.[1]

In the event the 9 Corps sector was taken over by another Corps, and on 30 January its constituent divisions were withdrawn into Army Reserve. The Corps Headquarters was transferred to the British 5th Army at the south of the British line, on the Somme – and for the next seven weeks its staff were detailed to study the question of British relief or intervention in the French sector in the event of a German offensive. Bernard laboriously went to reconnoitre the French lines of defence around Boure, Comin and Joncherry, and on 15 March a Staff Exercise was held. However, it was not agreed which British divisions would come under 9 Corps in such an eventuality; and when Ludendorff struck on 21 March there was pandemonium.

Ludendorff had decided to attack the British rather than the French front; and though equivalent measures had been taken for a French corps to study relief for the British sector, Pétain at first refused to help Haig, saying absurdly that his reserves were needed on the French front in Champagne. Haig declared that Pétain was 'in a funk' and was concerned only to save the integrity of the French army so that it could defend Paris; the British were to be left to retreat (as in 1940) to the Channel, 'sauve qui peut'. Bernard's 9 Corps HQ was ordered on 22 March 1918 to Mondidier 'forthwith'. On 23 March, however, as the British southern front collapsed before the German onslaught, 9 Corps HQ was ordered to prepare an English Hindenburg Line (called the GHQ Line). On 25 March, from Berna-

[1] War Diary, 9 Corps, loc. cit.

ville, Lt-General Gordon and his staff set about choosing and marking this new defensive line, about fifty miles back from the original front eight days before. The new system ran right up to the old Channel Ports' defences, and in the next weeks would consume over 23,000 tons of barbed wire and necessitate the digging of 5000 miles of new trenches. As the German 18th Army under von Hutier smashed through the Franco-British 5th Army, only Ludendorff's misguided decision to halt his southern thrust and redouble his vain efforts at Arras, further north, saved the Allies from the very split which Pétain feared would happen; and by the time Ludendorff revived von Hutier's attack, the pace of his drive was lost.

Foch was made Supreme Commander of the Allied armies. He too declined to put French troops into the battle, but for another reason: he felt the British armies would give ground but would not crack; and though Haig cursed his diagnosis, Foch was proved correct. Whenever French troops were used, they were of dubious help. The British knew the ground, and for them, after the slaughter of the preceding years, it would be considered a dishonour to give in. The Commander of the 5th Army, Sir Hubert Gough, was chosen as scapegoat and removed on 27 March 1918, together with his General Staff; Sir Henry Rawlinson, an experienced Corps Commander and Military Representative at Versailles, was put in his place. Though the German Somme offensive carried some forty miles into Allied territory and reached the suburbs of Amiens, it then ran out of steam.

By now Bernard had been made a temporary Major; and on 1 April 1918, while laying out the new GHQ line, his HQ was ordered to proceed to the 2nd Army to relieve the Australian Corps in the same sector in which 9 Corps had distinguished itself the previous autumn. On 3 April 1918 the relief took place: six days before the second great German offensive known afterwards as the Battle of the Lys, began. Having driven a forty-mile deep wedge between the British and French lines in Picardy, Ludendorff was now determined to strike further north, below the Ypres salient. He had failed at Arras to drive the British and Belgian armies north of the Somme up against the Channel ports; his new assault, code-named St George I, was a resurrected scheme devised by his strategical adviser, Major Wetzell, who did not believe that one attack on its own would break through the British front. By striking first in the south, then a hundred miles to the north, he hoped to catch the British without reserves – and had Ludendorff based his original calculations (decided at Mons on 11 November 1917 while the last British offensive floundered in the mud of Passchendaele) on Wetzell's scheme the war might well have been won by Germany. However, since the scheme was only revived after the failure at Arras, the Germans suffered from the same problem as the British – how, overnight, to move sufficient supplies and reserves so far north without the enemy knowing. It was for this reason that the Battle of the Lys followed the Somme offensive only after a ten-day pause; and though Haig ignored the intelligence reports pointing to a Flanders attack, the Germans were unable to follow up their initial break-through with sufficient arms and men to break the line. On 12 April 1918 Haig issued his historic 'Backs to the Wall' order of the day – and the line held.

The fighting, however, was savage, mustard gas mixing with the early morning fog, and an artillery barrage so intense and tactically directed that British communications were once again totally disrupted. By the morning of 10 April 1918 the Germans had put a Portuguese division at Neuve Chapelle to flight and had broken through as far as Estaires; they now extended their attack further north, in the 15 and 9 Corps sectors overlooking the Lys. By the evening of 11 April the 15 Corps Commander had been relieved of his command, with the Germans having pushed as far as Meteren on their front. 9 Corp was forced back in tandem, though holding fast to the 22 Corps at its northern boundary. Sir Herbert Plumer had returned from Italy and was again commanding the British 2nd Army, of which 9 Corps formed the southernmost boundary; when disaster after disaster befell 15 Corps it was transferred, on the morning of 12 April 1918, to 2nd Army. It was, in fact, a nightmare ten days, for 9 Corps held the all-important Kemmel ridge, overlooking the Lys basin, which, if it fell, was the key to German victory.

Unfortunately none of Bernard's letters from this period survives; but the Corps War Diaries and the Official History testify to the vital role which 9 Corps played in containing the German advance; and as soon as the Corps was relieved in line by the French on 20 April, Bernard was given special leave to return to England. Casualties had been high, and the provision and subtraction of units and divisions confusing in the extreme. Yet throughout the battle Bernard had issued – as he had since November 1917 – all Corps orders, involving some six divisions. Though the Corps front had withdrawn, it was still in possession of the Kemmel heights. The relief division of French troops subsequently lost the ridge; but by then the back of the German advance had been broken.

On 23 April 1918, while Bernard was in England, 9 Corps was transferred to the quiet of the French sector, charged with command of divisions withdrawn from the British front in the north which were on their way to reserve duty behind the French. In exchange Foch had finally agreed to send fresh French reserves to support the British in the north. Work was begun on 24 April training the 8th, 21st and 50th Divisions near Soissons, and on 3 May 1918 Sir Alexander Gordon, the Corps Commander, reported to the CIGS that a further month was required before the divisions would be once more battle-ready.

However, the same day orders were received detailing 9 Corps to take over a complete sector on the French 38 Corps front; and on 10 May 1918, 9 Corps moved into the ill-fated Chemin-des-Dames sector, from Hurtebise to the river Aisne at Berry-au-Bac. Two days later the sector was extended further south to the Marne canal: a front of some fifteen miles, disposing four tired and decimated British divisions and also French heavy artillery. One can imagine the consternation at Corps HQ when, at noon on 26 May, an intelligence report came through saying that according to an interrogated prisoner the Germans were about to launch an all-out offensive in that sector the next day.

Once again Bernard's Corps was to bear the brunt of the German spring offensive. In the Battle of the Lys the six divisions under 9 Corps had lost a staggering 27,000 casualties; indeed it was the presence of the Corps in this 'resting' sector that emboldened the Germans to strike through Soissons and thus threaten Paris – a manoeuvre which would then allow their northern armies to deliver a knock-out blow on Hazebrouck early in July, and push the British back to the sea.

Once again the Germans achieved surprise – despite the fact that from 4.30 p.m. on 26 May all units of 9 Corps were at battle stations. The French 6th Army Commander had ignored Pétain's new doctrine of elasticity, and had sited his artillery, his reserves and supply dumps far too close to the front line. Thus, when at 1 a.m. the following day the greatest artillery concentration of the war opened, the two allied Corps were instantly condemned: 3719 guns bearing down on them on a front of thirty-eight miles. By evening the Germans had penetrated some twelve miles. An entire British battalion, the 2nd Devons, was 'exterminated almost to a man' according to Sir Alexander Gordon's subsequent account.[1] By brilliant staff-work the 21st Division managed to hold arms with its neighbouring French division on the right and pull back its left through hilly, wooded country so that Reims was secure. Though the German offensive smashed through the centre junction of the French and British forces, putting German troops on the river Marne within four days, it remained a diversion, Pétain sealing off the salient with ample reserve divisions. For 9 Corps the Battle of Chemin-des-Dames, however, was a second bloodbath within six weeks; and by 30 May 1918, when German soldiers reached the Marne, 'the British fighting troops were reduced to approximately the strength of a division, and all of them had been placed under a single command, that of the 19th Division', as the Corps Commander later reported.[2] Casualties were horrendous; but the 19th Division, though technically relieved on 30 May, continued to supply units for the front, and on 6 June distinguished itself again by counter-attacking the seemingly successful German attempt to take the high ground near Épernay, overlooking the Marne valley. Finally, on 19 June 1918, the 19th

[1] War Diary, 9 Corps (WO 95/837), PRO.
[2] Ibid.

125

Division was relieved; and at the end of the month 9 Corps began to move back north to the British lines.

Meanwhile, on 3 June, immediately after the main battle, Bernard was promoted Brevet-Major (entitling him to accelerated promotion to full Major as soon as a vacancy occurred in the lists, and to hold the temporary rank of Major until such time). The Corps Commander paid tribute to the work of his staff in such 'unique, unexpected and complicated conditions . . . I can report that every member of my staff rose to the occasion,' he went on; and quoted the typically Gallic citation of the GOC Groupe des Armées du Nord:

> *Avec une tenacité, permettez-moi de dire, toute Anglaise, avec les débris de vos divisions décimées, submergées par le flot ennemi, vous avez réformé, sans vous lasser, des unites nouvelles que vous avez engagées dans la lutte, et qui nous ont enfin permis de former la ligne, où ce flot est venu se briser – cela, aucun des témoins ne l'oubliera!*[1]

[1] Ibid.

CHAPTER TEN

Chief-of-Staff

Bernard's exertions as GSO 2 (Operations) at 9 Corps were not simply rewarded by brevet-majority. As soon as 9 Corps rejoined the British Army Reserve in the north Bernard was again promoted and posted to a new formation. From 16 July 1918 he became temporary Lt-Colonel and Chief Staff Officer (or GSO 1) of the 47th (London) Division under Major-General Gorringe.

As we have seen, General Gorringe was already known to Bernard as his Brigade Commander in India in 1910. In his later annotations to his letters from the Western Front Bernard spoke very highly of his new Divisional Commander – 'a bachelor, and the senior Major-General in the Army. All the Corps Commanders under whom he served were junior to him in service. But he was very unpopular and Haig would not give him a Corps.'

Moreover to Gorringe, Bernard acknowledged a great debt: 'Gorringe made me Chief-of-Staff of the Division, and not only head of the General Staff. It was under him that I learnt the value of the Chief-of-Staff system, which I used so successfully in the Second World War.'[1]

Here was a most fortunate situation: an experienced senior commander who trusted his thirty-year-old appointee sufficiently to hand over to him wherever necessary the entire responsibility for the running of the division under his command, including administration. Gorringe laid down the policy, and made whatever major decisions were necessary; the implementation he left to his Chief-of-Staff – as was done in the German army. Moreover in Bernard he had found an ideal subordinate: a bachelor like himself, devoted to his profession and with a distinguished staff career already behind him: a young man willing to take infinite pains to get every detail right, and yet capable of the very clearest exposition of objectives, tactics and training.

Nor was Bernard slow to take over the reins. As in the desert a quarter of a century later, Bernard would not wait for the official moment when his appointment came into effect: and at 8 p.m. on the

---

[1] Annotations to letters of World War One, loc. cit.

evening before, he issued his first order as B. L. Montgomery, Lt-Colonel, General Staff, 47th Division.

The 47th (London) Division was not new to the Western Front, having been employed on active service there since 1915 and having seen much fighting in the two initial German offensives of March and April 1918, at Havrincourt, Albert and Avery Wood. It was the most northern division in Sir Henry Rawlinson's 4th Army, forming part of 3 Corps defending the vital railway network at Amiens. Having taken over the General Staff of 47th Division, however, Bernard lost no time before issuing his first divisional instructions – and four days after his official installation, on 20 July 1918, he sent out over his own name a document that would form, once again, the basis for all subsequent defensive policy in the Division: Defence Scheme, 3 Corps Northern Sector, 47th (London) Division. In Bernard's unmistakably clear style it set out the Division's frontages, their tactical features, the responsibility of the Division, general policy, and the action to be taken if attacked – including code-signs and calls he would issue from Divisional HQ to alert his brigades, disposition of reserves and, in a series of appendices, the infantry, artillery, machine-gun, tank and signals dispositions – a remarkable document to be drawn up within so short a time.

However, as the weeks went by it became increasingly apparent that Ludendorff's offensive had miscarried. The second Battle of the Marne ended in failure and the signs of tactical German withdrawal. Meanwhile the British, reinforced by hundreds of thousands of fresh troops, began to contemplate an offensive once again in Flanders; and in the utmost secrecy 4th Army swelled with Australian and Canadian divisions ready to iron out the German salient threatening Amiens. Already, by 1 August 1918, patrols reported the Germans withdrawing over the Ancre; and 47th Division was given the task of covering the northern flank of the new Allied push from Amiens. However, Haig would have done better to remain on the defensive before Amiens, for the Germans there were covered by the almost impregnable defensive lines of the Siegfried and Hermann Stellungen to the east. It was a front haunted by memories of the notorious Somme offensive; and fresh recruits could not be expected to do what trained British troops had failed to achieve in 1916. Yet Haig persisted in a frontal assault; and Rawlinson refused to use his 4th Army reserve when the Canadian Corps exceeded its objectives and threatened to break through!

Memories among troops, officers and their staffs were, in fact, the problem. 'Bite and hold' had become the conservative doctrine of the British Army on the Western Front; and though victory would eventually come, it was a victory of numbers and of attrition, not of tactics. The concept of 'holding the line' – which had spoiled Ludendorff's spring offensives of 1918 – was not easily discarded; and it was not until 18 August, several weeks after the Amiens push had begun, that the young Chief-of-Staff, 47th (London) Division, began to issue comparable instructions for offensive to those which, with such alacrity the month before, he had issued for defence.

By then 3 Corps had been in action eleven days: and its diluted, convalescent forces on the left had proved dilatory, poorly staffed, and unsuccessful compared with the magnificent performance of both Canadian and Australian divisions. Although the 47th Division was withdrawn into Corps reserve before the real battle began in that sector, Bernard cannot have been immune to the feeble showing of the 18th Division which relieved his own. The attack had quickly fizzled out, slowing down the advance of the whole 4th Army, which halted on August 11; and the offensive was not revived until the Battle of Albert began some ten days later. By then Bernard had recognised the necessity for clearly defined instructions and proper preparation. Following on the Corps directive for the coming battle he issued, on August 18, a new series of 'Instructions for the Offensive', making sure that the attack be practised on a course which he had specially taped out. By the time the final word came to launch the assault he had issued seven consecutive preparatory orders to the Division. Haig, in his telegram to the Army Commanders on the first night of the battle, insisted that 'risks which a month ago would have been criminal to incur, ought now to be incurred as a duty', for the Germans, he claimed, had not 'the means to deliver counter-attacks on an extended scale'. Bernard, however, was unwilling to prompt another Passchendaele with unseasoned troops, and none of his orders reflected Haig's optimism. He distrusted the use of tanks in such bog-ridden country, particularly as there were only ten available; and these he detailed for employment in mopping-up operations against individual strong-points that held out after the main assault had passed them. Haig hoped that cavalry would at last come into their own in the open ground behind the line; but again Bernard was cautious and scarcely mentioned them in his instructions.

Something of Bernard's later caution was thus in evidence as early as 1918 – that unwillingness to be tempted by romantic possibilities that would become the hallmark of his military doctrine, a welcome realism to most of the troops, but anathema to more imaginative officers. Haig now called for 'distant objectives', whereas Bernard was still concerned to give only those objectives that were within the compass of largely raw and untried troops – particularly after the poor showing of the sister 18th Division on 8 August. Success might thus be less striking: but it was at least assured. At 1 a.m. on 22 August 1918, the forward brigades of the 47th Division began their assault on the Happy Valley. The initial attack failed, as Bernard must have feared it might. 'Owing to bad staff work and the insufficient training of the young troops in movement in darkness, smoke and mist, the two leading battalions, 1/20th and 1/19th

London, lost count of distance and though the Germans surrendered freely, the battalions halted considerably short of the intermediate objective – as much as half a mile short on the right,' as the Official History recorded. The Germans quickly hit back, threatening the juncture with the 12th Division to the right of the 47th Division. The tanks broke down and had to be withdrawn; the lighter whippet tanks, 'without ascertaining from the Brigadier whether the road was clear', entered the Happy Valley from the South, 'and headed for the high ground on the north-east, actually behind the German front line. As soon as the leading squadron topped the rise it was confronted by a wire fence and found itself under rifle and machine-gun fire at very short range and bombing from the air. 'Retirement was at once ordered', the Official History continued – 'seen retiring at 8.55 a.m.', as the Divisional War Diary recorded laconically. At 2 p.m. the thunder of German guns heralded a massed German counter-attack; but here at least their defensive training served the Division well and the 'resistance offered was sufficient to stop the Germans, who lost heavily, fell into complete confusion and at night withdrew from their advanced and salient position'.[1] Exhausted and suffering from heavy casualties, however, the 47th Division was considered unable to continue the offensive later that evening and a right flanking advance by the 18th Division was ordered to correct the situation. On August 23 the Division rested; and on 24 August the 47th and 12th Divisions were ordered to 'capture the final objective beyond the Happy Valley, which the Corps had failed to gain on the 22nd'.[2]

This time Bernard's Division met with greater success, gaining almost all its objectives without many casualties, and with some distinguished captures of German garrisons by intelligent stalking. Yet having reached the objectives, the successful battalions did not attempt to outflank the one remaining stumbling block – a line of machine-guns and two strong-points which not even tanks could overwhelm frontally. As a result a combined 3 Corps and Australian attack planned to go off at 4 p.m., was cancelled, and only the evacuation by the Germans towards evening eased the situation.

The German history of the 120th Württemberg Regiment certainly held out no laurels to the victor – the brigades of the British 47th Division had 'rolled forward behind a mighty curtain of fire and thoroughly smothered the very mixed up combatants, who had to defend themselves simultaneously against infantry, squadrons of tanks, cavalry and aircraft. What did it matter if here and there our guns blew up a tank, if our machine-guns shot an attacking cavalry detachment to pieces, if our fighter aeroplanes shot down several hostile machines?' it recorded – and neither the War Diaries of the

[1] J. E. Edmonds, op. cit.
[2] Ibid.

47th Division nor the British Official History contradict this impression of 'force majeure'. Later on 24 August the 47th Division was relieved – and together with his Divisional Commander Bernard must have done much thinking.

On 1 September 1918, the Division once more went into the line – this time forcing the Germans to withdraw to the Canal du Nord in some particularly severe fighting. A battalion cook won the VC, and the Division managed, by intelligent exploitation later on 2 September, to discount the relative failure of its neighbouring 74th Division which had arrived hot-foot from Italy and appeared quite unprepared for the rigours – and casualties – of fighting Germans on the Western Front. By 3 September the offensive was over in Bernard's sector; and on 6 September the Division went into reserve. It had captured 1463 enemy troops as well as some 200 machine-guns and artillery pieces. On 8 September 1918 it moved to 13 Corps, 5th Army, for rest and training; and four days later Bernard Montgomery issued a pamphlet to all the divisional units: 'Lessons learnt in Operations undertaken in August and September 1918', divided into ten sections – Communications, Headquarters, Tanks, Artillery, Stokes Mortar, Mounted Troops, Machine-Guns, Employment of Royal Engineers, Supplies, and General Remarks – stressing the success of wireless communications, the need for tactical initiative rather than 'toeing the line'; the necessity for special training in order to knock out enemy strong-points and machine-gun nests; the importance of merging infantry and artillery HQs; and the advantages of varying times of attack in order to achieve surprise.

Already, though, Bernard's flair for practical training had been in evidence – with full-scale training orders issued on 11 September. 'The general principle to be borne in mind,' he stressed in these instructions for the two-week period, 'is that we must profit as much as possible by the experience gained in the recent fighting in which the Division has taken part, and that this experience must be imparted to any reinforcements which may be posted to units.'[1] In the first week there was to be brief morning drill followed by specialist training of sections; and in the afternoon recreational training involving all sports and on competitive lines. However, not only were the troops to be indoctrinated: the young temporary Lt-Colonel was adamant that all the battalion COs should also take part in brigade training exercises, together with staff officers, adjutants, and most importantly the artillery, RE, and machine-gun commanders in the brigade groups, Clear reports were to be made, and Programmes of Training were to reach Bernard 'at least 24 hours before the training is to be carried out'.[2] Week Two was to be devoted to drill and tactical exercises, using the extensive manoeuvre area that had been made

[1] War Diary, 47th Division (WO 95/2705), PRO.
[2] Ibid.

available; and a divisional signals school had been started to work on new wireless communications. The hand of Bernard L. Montgomery was certainly being felt in the Division.

On 3 September 1918 Bernard had written at length to his mother:

These are stirring times and everyone is being pushed to the limit of their endurance. We really have got the Bosche on the hop, he is thoroughly disorganized and it looks as if we might get away beyond our old battle grounds and get into country as yet untouched by shells etc. It will be splendid if we do that as we shall get into good billets again. At present I live in a tent which I have carried on my motor car; I prefer a tent pitched on clean ground rather than some bosche hut or dugout full of bosche straw, and smells and bugs.

One is gaining wonderful experience in this advance. As Chief-of-Staff I have to work out plans in detail for the operations, and see that all the branches of the Staff, and administrative arrangements are working with my plans. The day generally commences with an organized attack at dawn, after which we continue to work slowly forward all day; then another organized attack is arranged for the next morning to carry us forward again, and so on. It means little sleep and continuous work; at night guns have to be moved forward, communications arranged, food and ammunition got up, etc. etc.

The general and I work out the next day's plan and he tells me in outline what he wants. I then work out the detail and issue the orders. Then I send for all the heads of each branch of the staff, tell them the plan and explain the orders. They tell me what they propose to do to fit in with the scheme. If I think it is bad I say so and tell them what I think is a better way to do it; there is often no time to refer to the general and I take the responsibility on myself. I know his ideas and thoughts well now and so far he has always backed me up and approved of everything [he noted gratefully]. The heads of the various branches are all Lt-Colonels, older and senior in rank (but not in position as I am Chief-of-Staff) to me and one is a Brigadier-General. But we all work in very well together and they do what I tell them like lambs.

The Division has been wonderfully successful and we have never failed yet to do what we set out to do, and we have taken a lot of prisoners.

I am glad you have got Donald home on leave, but am sorry to hear he is not too fit.

Best love from

yr loving son
Bernard

CHAPTER ELEVEN

Armistice

Bernard's confidence in the achievements of his division was not necessarily mirrored elsewhere. Haig evidently disliked Gorringe; and when the moment came to decide which division should be sent to Italy that autumn, the 47th (London) Division was one of those selected – 'in exchange with a Division which is to come to France from that country,' as the 47th Division's War Diary recorded on 18 September.[1] For the next week preparations for the move to Italy were made; but every day the date was postponed until on 26 September a warning order was issued, detailing the 47th Division to move to St Pol the following day. On 30 September the Division was transferred to the 5th Army under General Birdwood. The next day the Division moved to the old Neuve Chapelle area, assigned to 11 Corps, commanded by Lt-General Sir Richard Haking.

The war had now reached its climax. Bulgaria had capitulated on 29 September 1918; and on 30 September Count Hertling, the German Chancellor, resigned. Hindenburg expected 'a catastrophe' within eight days if the Allies launched a full-scale attack. 'The proper course,' Hindenburg put in writing to the new Chancellor, 'is to break off the struggle in order to spare the German people and their Allies useless sacrifice. Every day's delay costs the lives of thousands of our brave soldiers' – and insisted that Prince Max request an armistice.

Yet neither Foch nor Haig dared risk what they had attempted to launch with comparative indifference to casualties so often before – a single, all-out break-through. Instead, the series of uncoordinated frontal pushes were, after due pause for rest and re-supply, extended. It was a broad-front policy that would be repeated a generation later with similar results. Behind a rear-guard screen of strong-points and machine-gun posts the German armies breathed again – and prepared for a fighting withdrawal towards the German border, where winter and shorter lines of defence and supply would come to their aid. By 17 October Ludendorff felt they would be able to hold the Allies in the West even without an armistice. Pershing's American army had been fought to a standstill between the Meuse

[1] Ibid.

and the Argonne forest; the French were held; and though the British breached the Hindenburg Line, they were insufficiently disposed to take advantage of their success.

Bernard's division was back in the front line on 3 October 1918; but even he had to admit the Germans were conducting a masterly retreat; for now that the British had moved out of their old areas, problems of transport and supply made it difficult to organise those concentrated efforts of artillery, tanks and troops that had first shifted the enemy. Since there was every sign that the Gremans were not prepared to stand and fight, it would have been futile to waste the lives of thousands of men in frontal attacks on the German rearguard screen. From a war of staffs, the battlefield now favoured imaginative command and tactical intelligence at the 'sharp end' – neither of which was readily forthcoming. Thus the great Allied offensive foundered on a line of machine-guns.

On 4 October 1918, the day after the 47th Division had gone into line, the 5th Army push halted; and was only resumed on 14 October, some ten days later. Gradually 11 Corps then edged its way towards Lille – which it liberated on October 17. That day the 47th Division was relieved by 57th Division and went into reserve. Eleven days later the 5th Army staged its triumphal march through the town.

My darling Mother
    We had a wonderful show yesterday in Lille,

Bernard informed his mother on 28 October:

The whole Division marched through the city making a sort of public entry. The streets were packed with people, over 200,000, who gave us a wonderful reception, and the whole place was hung with flags and bunting. All the arrangements had to be very carefully worked out and I have been busy for several days over it. The Mayor, who has been there all the time, stood on a dais in the Grande Place with all the town council, and we marched past them. I rode with the General at the head of the Division till we reached the Grande Place, then we got off our horses and stood with the Mayor while the troops marched past; it took 2½ hours for them to go by and even then we had left out most of the transport. The whole Division with all its transport etc. takes up 14 miles of road. We reduced the column to 8 miles by leaving out several units and most of the transport.

Together with Bernard Montgomery and Major-General Gorringe on the stand were Sir Richard Haking, Commander of 11 Corps, General Sir William Birdwood, the 5th Army Commander and 'some civilians' as the Divisional War Diary recorded – including 'the dignatories of Lille, and Mr Winston Churchill'.

It is strange to think of Lt-Colonel Montgomery, Chief-of-Staff, 47th (London) Division and Mr Churchill, the British Minister of Munitions, almost beside but unknown to one another at the march-past in Lille in October 1918 – two men whose names would come to symbolise Britain's military and political resistance to German fascism a generation later.

The march-past over, Bernard Montgomery retired to his quarters. He reported to his mother:

> The billets here are wonderfully good. Lille is a very rich place. I am living now in the house of a millionaire manufacturer; I have a suite of rooms, bedroom, bathroom, sitting room, all wonderfully furnished. A German staff officer had them before me; the house is full of beautiful works of art and the Germans took nothing. In other houses in the city they have taken lots of the best things away.
>
> There is a very fine theatre here and last night they had a gala performance in our honour; the show itself was bad but the enthusiasm of the audience was quite extraordinary. They had refused to go the theatre while the Germans were there although they had some quite good shows.
>
> We were quite ½ an hour singing the Marseillaise and all its encores, etc.

The future critic of luxurious living by generals and their staffs certainly made no objection to such comforts in 1918, though they did not seem to blind him to the realities – and incongruities – of war.

'I see Austria has now asked for a separate peace,' he remarked in his letter, turning to more serious things,

> and as we have got Aleppo the show in the east will be cleaned up and Turkey will make peace I suppose. I think Germany's allies will drop off one by one but that she will go on to the end, as she is going to get such rotten terms that she will fight it out unless a revolution does them in,

he prophesied – a view shared by many officers on the Western Front who were impressed by the way the Germans were staving off their pursuers.

Directly after the Lille 'show', Bernard Montgomery was back reconnoitring the front line in preparation for the 47th Division's relief of 57th Division, due to take place on 31 October.

'We are fighting under extraordinary conditions now,' he related to his mother.

There are civilians living in the houses in the front line; they go into the cellars as the line comes up to them and come up when it moves on. Sometimes the line is stationary for a week or more and they still stay on in the cellars rather than go away; this is the case with us at the moment. They get killed and wounded of course. We have a French countess, the Comtesse de Germigny, living in the cellar of her chateau which is in our front line! She has several children, and all her servants, with her. She is very pretty and extremely nice; I go and see her whenever I am up there.

It really is an extraordinary war. No more now. Best love from
yr loving son
Bernard

Despite his manifold responsibilities in getting the 47th Division back into battle, Bernard continued to issue his general notes and instructions, relating these to his previous pamphlets where necessary. On 31 October 1918 he issued his 'Instructions for Advance in the Event of an Enemy Withdrawal', and on the next day an 'Account of Operations West of Lille between 3 and 17 October 1918'. His repeated reiteration of defensive instructions 'as laid down in para 8 of "Instructions for the Defensive"'[1] indicates how cautious he was, despite the German withdrawal, lest the enemy spring a counterattack – a caution not so much the product of four years' trench warfare as a sort of professional perfectionism; a determination never to be 'caught napping' or 'off-balance' that would in time be one of his great characteristics as an Army Commander.

In the meantime, however, the German dispositions in 11 Corps sector, defending the Escaut (Scheldt) river, made progress impossible for his division without a full-scale – and expensive – assault. Thus, while Turkey and Austria sued for peace, and German revolutionaries began to push the Second Empire towards dissolution, the British 5th Army remained almost stationary. Only on 9 November did one brigade get across the river Scheldt; and on 10 November 1918 the 47th Division resumed its advance. 'No opposition was met with,' the Divisional War Diary recorded, as the Germans withdrew towards a new Mons line.

By then, however, the internal situation in Germany – as once in Russia – militated against a prolongation of the war. On 3 November the German fleet at Kiel had mutinied, and on 7 November a revolution in Munich had initiated a short-lived Republic. On the morning of 10 November, the Kaiser abdicated and fled to Holland.

'These are certainly great times,' Bernard had written to his father on 7 November, 'and the next fortnight will I think either see the Bosche accept our terms or refuse them. Personally I can't help thinking he will refuse them.'

[1] Ibid.

Despite the Allied offensive, the Germans had managed to pull back in good order, and Haig would have been content to accept an offer of withdrawal from occupied areas as the basis of peace.

History, however, had it otherwise. As the nations of Europe had gone to war without a clear idea of their aims, so now they ended it – and the way was open for the legend of the 'stab in the back'. Instead of just peace, the Allies took advantage of the young Republic and dictated terms that could only encourage German nationalism in due course.

For Bernard Montgomery it had been an extraordinary end to an extraordinary war; now aged thirty, a temporary Lt-Colonel and Chief-of-Staff of a Division, he was left to ponder its meaning and its lessons.

PART THREE

The Inter-War Years

CHAPTER ONE

The War in Ireland

While the Kaiser's empire disintegrated and Germany became torn by internal revolution, Bernard Montgomery's division was withdrawn from the front and was moved to his old training area at La Tombe. There the Brigade was put to work on the Tournai railway for a week, while COs were instructed on their duties during the armistice.

It was clear from the situation in Germany and Austria, though, that war would not be resumed; that the famed virtues of Teutonic military discipline had served to conceal an inner political confusion which must now be played out. Without an enemy to fight or even to face, the weary Allied troops thought now only of home; and within weeks the great exodus from France began. The 47th Division moved to new billets south-east of Lillers; and, though training and educational classes were begun, they were really designed to alleviate boredom and avoid riots as, one by one, different units were permitted to demobilise and return. 'World Problems after the War', 'Reconstruction', 'Alsace Lorraine', 'Industrial Peace', 'Russia' – even 'The Social Reconstruction of England' by T. Broad – were among the lectures given. By the end of January the First Army Advisory Board had visited the 47th Division HQ to assess the quality of the staff. It was obvious that almost all officers would have to accept a reduction in rank if they were to be accommodated in a peacetime army; and, while many volunteered for service abroad in whatever capacity was offered, young Bernard Montgomery must have been considered lucky to be offered at least a major's appointment at the General Headquarters of the British Army of the Rhine, as GSO 2 (Operations). Thus, when 47th Division HQ closed down at noon on 24 March 1919, it was to Cologne that its Chief-of-Staff then travelled.

Brevet-Major B. L. Montgomery was now thirty-one, and it was his first trip to the country he had been fighting against for five years. Certainly, after the devastation in Northern France, the untouched medieval streets and soaring cathedral of Cologne must have impressed and possibly puzzled him. The change-over to a republican form of government – and a socialist one at that – went remarkably smoothly. There was still grave shortage of food, and bolshevist

141

unrest; but it was handled by the Germans themselves and the British Army of the Rhine became, to all intents and purposes, a visiting delegation housed there until the peace talks at Versailles should be concluded.

Summer brought the signing of the great Treaty, and with it Bernard Montgomery's recognition that his own job at GHQ was to be axed.

'My plans will be very uncertain for a bit,' he wrote to his mother on 18 August 1919, from Cologne. 'I shall get away from here about 1st September and will not come back again; the Army is being broken up and my job (Operations) ceases to exist. So I shall bring all my kit home and will ask the War Office what they propose to do with me. I shall try and get a good long leave out of them, a month or more.'

It must have been at this moment that the tennis party took place which was to have an important influence on Bernard Montgomery's career. Despite his distinguished performance as a staff officer ever since the spring of 1915, Bernard had as yet no formal qualification to serve on the staff, since he had not passed the examinations for entry into the Army's professional college at Camberley. The Staff College had been re-started briefly in 1919; but B. L. Montgomery had not been one of the fortunate officers to gain admission on his war record without examination. Nor was he when the first lists were announced in 1919 for the one-year course beginning in January 1920. Yet it was now, in the aftermath of a war that so shattered all preconceptions, that Bernard recognised the need to make a study of what had happened and to consider the implications on the future conduct of hostilities. Invited one day by the Commander-in-Chief of the British Army of Occupation in Germany to a tennis party at his house in Cologne, Bernard therefore armed himself not only with a racket, but the determination, if the moment appeared opportune, to put his problem before his host.

Sir William ('Wully') Robertson had been CIGS from 1915 to 1918 and was the first Field-Marshal to have started in the ranks. He died in 1933, too soon to witness the meteoric rise of the young man who had never met him before, but who had the courage to solicit his help on the tennis court. Perhaps the fact that Bernard was not asking for advancement, or using social ties to press his suit, impressed Robertson. Certainly it was a strangely historic meeting, as the Commander-in-Chief of the British Army of Occupation listened to the plea of the young Brevet-Major who was to assume the identical mantle in Germany a quarter of a century later. A few weeks after the tennis party Bernard heard that his name had been added to the 1920 Camberley intake.

In the meantime Field-Marshal Robertson asked Montgomery to take charge of a friend of his, Sir Peter Fryer, who was a well-known surgeon, and conduct him on a tour of the French battlefields and military zone.

'We go by car and I will have to look after him and pilot him through the French area,' Bernard wrote to his mother in his letter of 18 August 1919, 'as being a civilian he will have difficulty otherwise. The trip will be Wiesbaden – Strasbourg – Nancy – Metz – St Mihiel – Rheims – Chemin des Dames – Soissons – Mons – Maubeuge – Louvain – Cologne. A very nice round and over 1000 miles by car altogether.' Bernard added: 'He is a rich man and I get all my expenses paid.'

Certainly neither this nor any of Bernard Montgomery's wartime letters suggest any particular ascetic bent or even disapproval of the comparative luxury in which the higher staffs lived; indeed it would appear that his indictment of the staffs and commanders began only later, in England, when the lessons of the war became etched out in a climate of growing anti-militarism.

Bernard must certainly have impressed Robertson, though, for not only did he find, on his return from touring the battlefields, that he was to go as a student to the Staff College, Camberley, but he found himself promoted once more to Lt-Colonel – Commanding Officer of the 17th Battalion, the Royal Fusiliers from 5 September 1919. This was 'a battalion of young soldiers, all under 20,' as he recalled in the annotations to his wartime letters. 'I greatly enjoyed the experience.' Strangely he did not even mention this appointment in his *Memoirs*; but in the annotations he remembered it having lasted a whole year.

In fact the appointment lasted less than three months. In November the battalion was disbanded and Bernard was given the leave he had hoped for the previous summer. Once again he stepped down in rank to Brevet-Major; and after spending Christmas with his parents he entered the Staff College on 22 January 1920.

Bernard was anxious to begin a thorough study of the military profession, past and present – and had not banked on the college returning to its pre-war preoccupation with hunting and socialising. The college had always provided a gentlemanly introduction to staff duties, helping the young regimental officer bridge the gap between battalion duties and the responsibilities of a Brigade-Major. It was not therefore surprising that Bernard quickly became disenchanted. 'I was critical and intolerant,' he wrote later.[1] Certainly he did not endear himself to the Directing Staff, who considered him a 'bloody menace', his brother Brian remembered.[2] This is borne out by an apocryphal story that circulated in the Royal Warwickshires thereafter – recalled by Colonel P. J. Gething almost sixty years later. 'I never met him during the Great War,' Gething recorded, 'but at the Staff College – this is only hearsay – one of the students was court-

[1] Bernard Montgomery, *Memoirs*, op. cit.
[2] Brian Montgomery, *A Field-Marshal in the Family*, op. cit.

martialled. His sentence was to have breakfast beside Monty for a week!'[1] Gething's memory was not at fault, for the Staff College magazine of Christmas 1920 also mocked the irrepressible student. '– If it takes ten truck-loads of 9.2 Mark V Star, Indian pattern, to stop one bath on the second floor of the Staff College from leaking, how many haynets with full echelons, and under constructional supervision by Congreve, will be required to stop Montgomery babbling at breakfast?' it asked in its conundrums column. Under the heading 'Things we want to know' it went even further, posing the question, 'If and where Monty spent two silent minutes on Armistice Day?'[2]

Like many others, Gething thought that Bernard was 'all blah' at this time – opinionated, conceited and over-talkative. Doubtless this was true, as the keyed-up self-discipline of the war years gave way to inactivity and disenchantment. He had expected too much of the college and its staff, wanted something the institution was not really designed to give: namely a chance for distinguished officers to set their experience into the context of the history of warfare and prepare a common approach to future military tasks.

The year, cannot, however, have been entirely wasted. Charles Broad – later author of 'The Purple Primer' on *Mechanized and Armoured Formations* – John Dill and Philip Neame were on the Directing Staff; Robert Haining, Bernard Paget, Richard O'Connor, Douglas Brownrigg, R. Gordon-Finlayson and George Lindsay were among his fellow-students. However intolerant, Bernard worked hard and conversed a great deal. It was a chance to debate his own views with his fellow-students, and if he found the course unsatisfactory and the instructors deficient it does not seem to have soured his belief in the institution. On the contrary, when he was offered an Instructorship himself some six years later he accepted with alacrity; and to the end of his life he preserved an affection for the college that went far beyond professional respect.

In some ways, too, the Staff College's very inadequacy encouraged Bernard: made him more vividly aware of his own talents, experience and potential. Though he was never told how well he had done during the year, Bernard must have performed creditably; for when he passed out of the college at the end of the year he found that he had been given one of the top Brigade-Majors' appointments in the British Army at that time. On 6 December 1920 the War Office wrote to offer him the post of Brigade-Major of the Kerry Infantry Brigade, stationed in southern Ireland. But on 11 December units of the 'Black and Tan' auxiliary police ran amuck in Cork and razed the centre of the town, and on 18 December the appointment was altered to the Cork Infantry Brigade – at the very centre of Republican unrest.

The Great War had intimately affected – as would its sequel – the

[1] Interview of 21.8.78.
[2] 'Owl Pie', Christmas 1920.

geography of the globe, spawning a fearsome number of individual nationalisms while upsetting the traditional balance of power among the larger nations. Thus there arose the ironic spectacle of Germany, a defeated nation with a supposedly disbanded army, being asked by the Allies to counter the threat of Bolshevism in the Baltic States while ceding part of her own eastern territories so that independent Poland could have access to the sea. In the Middle East another defeated enemy would soon be replaced on its military pedestal under Kemal Ataturk. In India General Dyer's stern measures at Amritsar paved the way for Gandhi's independence movement. School atlases became defunct within weeks as cartographers strove to keep up with the changes that followed the most expensive and bloody war ever known.

Of course the Irish 'problem', like so many other nationalisms, predated the Great War; but without the advent of that war it is doubtful whether it would have followed the same course. The Great War not only served to give military experience to a large number of Irish freedom fighters, it shifted people's perception of what was possible and impossible. War-weariness had set in; and, against the backcloth of a myriad of newly independent states within Europe (Finland, Estonia, Latvia, Lithuania, Poland, Czechoslovakia, Hungary, Yugoslavia, and others), the southern Irish decided to step up their campaign for independence. President Wilson had made Freedom and Independence the catchwords which America was prepared to guarantee in Europe – the first time the United States had become involved in European politics since its own independence a century and a half before. If ever there was a propitious moment for liberation it was now, the Irish leaders felt – a fact which the British, having ruled and settled the country since the seventeenth century, were reluctant to take into consideration.

However, the situation was complicated by the existence, in the North, of a fiercely loyal Protestant population that would have no truck with independence – in which they would be outnumbered by the Catholic majority. Lloyd George therefore had the awkward task of granting independence on the one hand while permitting the North to remain part of Great Britain on the other. That he achieved this, and secured a measure of peace between North and South for an entire generation, is largely to his credit – though it left the long-term problem unresolved.

It was Bernard Montgomery's misfortune to be cast into the Irish fray at the very worst moment, when insurrection, far from being contained by the massive increase of British troops stationed in the country, had escalated to the point of war. Although the intellectual and political centre of the revolt was Dublin, it was in the southern counties of the country that the British were hardest put to keep order. The countryside was poor in roads, and telephone and postal communications were in the pocket of the Irish Republican Army.

Loyalists were few and were isolated. The tighter the British clamped down on the rebels, the more unpopular they became. By December 1920 martial law had been declared throughout the South; the centre of Cork had been burned by irate Auxiliaries on 11 December, and Lloyd George had sent his first peace emissary (the Archbishop of Perth, Dr Clune) to Mountjoy Prison to negotiate with Arthur Griffith and Eoin MacNeill. Assassination had become commonplace.

What personal feelings Bernard must have entertained on hearing of his new appointment we can only conjecture. He was, after all, of Protestant Irish parentage; his family's estate was still at New Park (though much of the family's land was compulsorily made over to the Irish under the Government of Ireland Act in 1921), and he still went there when on leave. As New Park was outside what would become the Six Counties the Montgomerys' status and security would be bound to diminish as a result of independence or even partition. Furthermore, on 21 November 1920 the Montgomery family had been shocked to hear that Lt-Colonel Hugh Montgomery, the son of Bishop Montgomery's younger brother Ferguson, had been murdered by the IRA in Dublin. As GSO 1 on the staff of GHQ Ireland, he was responsible for Intelligence, and was one of eleven British Intelligence Officers gunned down that day – assassinations which in turn prompted a massacre among innocent civilians at Croke Park football ground that afternoon ('Bloody Sunday') by the 'Black and Tans'.

Bernard is certainly known to have been fond of his cousin Hugh, with whom he kept close contact throughout the war in France and Flanders; his name is mentioned in many of the letters he sent from the Western Front – even in Bernard's last extant letter from Cologne.

In the circumstances it would have been natural for Bernard Montgomery to feel a personal sense of mission, even vengeance, when he arrived at Cork on 5 January 1921. What he did not bargain for was the sheer size of the Brigade he was meant to run – comprising no less than seven battalions! The 17th (Cork) Infantry Brigade was in fact the largest Brigade in Ireland, commanded by Brigadier-General H. W. Higginson, DSO, who had commanded an infantry division in Flanders during the last year of the Great War. It was originally intended to split the 17th Brigade into two; but at the critical moment early in 1921 'it was considered that the situation was so complex that a new Brigadier would take several months to pick up the threads,' as Bernard wrote later.[1] Thus the 17th Infantry Brigade, based at Cork, was simply expanded, and in the ensuing months its complement would rise to some nine battalions. Higginson had been at Cork since November 1919. His new Brigade-Major,

[1] Letter to Major A. E. Percival, 14.10.23. Percival Papers, Imperial War Museum.

146

however green, was expected to cope; and he did. However even Bernard, who had never complained about the night-and-day responsibilities he bore on the Western Front, found this a tall order. 'I had 3 Staff Captains, in addition to a large "I" staff,' he recorded. 'But it was really too much . . . the work was fearfully hard.'[1]

Morale, when Bernard arrived, was not high. The Divisional Commander, in charge of the 16th, 17th, 18th and Kerry Brigades, was Major-General Sir Peter Strickland, also a Divisional Commander from the Western Front who had been brought to Ireland in 1919. He evidently hated having to put his case before politicians ('I *loathe* that sort of thing,' he recorded of a Cabinet meeting which he was asked to attend on 29 December 1920[2]), and evidently missed the time when he could hunt, shoot and fish in the beautiful countryside around his headquarters. On Saturday 1 January 1921 he lamented in his diary: 'Last year was bad enough, but nothing to this. We could move about, hunt etc. and personally I can now do neither . . . What will be the end I can't say, but I hope and trust I won't be here 1.1.22. It's been one of the worst years I've known anywhere. Murder and crime seem so deep-rooted that one wonders *how* it can be stamped out.' By February 1921 he was offering the GOC-in-C in Ireland, Sir Nevil Macready, his resignation, so weary and pessimistic did he feel. From having pursued a policy largely aimed at the local police constabulary, the IRA had responded to martial law by turning their attacks upon the military. Organising themselves on similar lines (and uniforms) as the British Army, the IRA had invented a new form of guerrilla tactics: the use of Flying Columns that could move in specially-trained units across large areas, calling upon local units to help in ambushes, concealment, re-supply and Intelligence. This was to become a model for guerrilla warfare the world over – and it certainly proved impossible for the cumbersome British formations to counter. There was little co-ordination between the Irish police, the 'Black and Tan' auxiliary forces and the uniformed British Army. As a result Intelligence was feeble, counter-productive hostility was induced by the lack of control over the 'Black and Tans', and the military was torn between those who thought it best to ride out the storm, letting politicians negotiate a settlement, and those who advocated sterner measures designed to stamp out the IRA completely.

In view of Bernard Montgomery's subsequent career, and his later attitude to great guerrilla leaders such as Tito and Mao-tse-Tung – even, indeed, the part he played first as divisional commander in Palestine in 1938 and later as CIGS in the evacuation of Palestine in 1948 – it is interesting to watch, retrospectively, his reaction to this, his first challenge in the realm of civil insurrection and struggle for national independence.

[1] Ibid.
[2] Diaries of Sir Peter Strickland, Imperial War Museum.

'In many ways this war was far worse than the Great War which had ended in 1918,' Bernard wrote in his *Memoirs*; but confined himself then to a five-line epitaph on his service in Ireland, drawing only the moral that 'such a war is thoroughly bad for officers and men; it tends to lower their standards of decency and chivalry, and I was glad when it was over'.

In truth the war in Ireland was to teach Bernard many things; and to reveal a strange dichotomy in his character, as will be seen. He appears to have thrown himself into the campaign with characteristic vigour. The Assistant-Adjutant of the Cameron Highlanders, stationed at Queenstown in 1921 as one of the Cork Brigade's eight battalions, was a certain D. N. Wimberley. Even sixty years later he could recall the Brigade-Major's 'incisiveness'. 'But it was not until a young Cameron subaltern returned to us after a short staff attachment at Cork, that I first have a vivid memory regarding Montgomery's character,' he recorded. 'This subaltern, on reporting to me on his return to regimental duty, blurted out words somewhat as follows: "Our new Brigade-Major is certainly a little tiger for work, and by Jove you have to jump when he gives you any order, and he is also a martinet as regards punctuality." ' Nor, in Wimberley's recollection, did Montgomery bow to sentiment or convention. On New Year's Day he required a 'flying column' of his best troops 'in an attempt to round up a body of rebels operating in a different part of the County of Cork'. Disregarding the Scottish tradition of Hogmanay and New Year's celebrations, Montgomery chose his Highlanders – to the consternation of the Assistant-Adjutant.[1]

Perhaps Bernard still believed, as did his CO and Divisional Commander, that the IRA could be defeated; at any rate he certainly set about organising his 9000-strong brigade on the soundest possible military lines. A special 'Cork City Intelligence' unit was set up in the city, and a stream of orders issued from Bernard's desk to the brigade battalions – so many that in June 1921 Bernard collected them together into a small booklet, printed by 6th Division HQ in Cork, entitled: '17th Infantry Brigade: Summary of Important Instructions.' It was, as its author declared in the introduction, 'intended as a reference work to assist officers, when they first arrive in Ireland, in making themselves acquainted with the various instructions laid down for dealing with the situation obtaining in that country', and was considered important enough to be issued to all 6th Division officers. It was divided into twenty-nine headings, covering fifteen pages, and signed B. L. Montgomery, Major. Although Bernard's operational and training instructions on the Western Front had demonstrated his clarity of presentation, this summary was the first printed booklet issued under his name. General Strickland evidently considered it important enough to

---

[1] ' "Monty", A Personal Memoir' by Douglas Wimberley, unpublished, 1980.

preserve among his papers,[1] since it covered every aspect of an officer's duties in the martial law area with amazing conciseness and lucidity. The headings were arranged alphabetically, so that it was, in fact, an ABC, with instructions for everything from Armoured Cars to Wireless. Arrests, ciphers, convoys, operations, patrols, pigeons, reprisals – all were set out in Bernard's compendium in simple, crystal-clear language which no subaltern, no matter how inexperienced or deficient in intelligence, could misunderstand. Despite its unprepossessing title it was in fact a model of its kind – and not least remarkable for its insistence on discretion as the better part of valour. 'The behaviour of the Army must be kept beyond reproach.'

The policy of Official Reprisals, instituted when martial law was declared in December 1920, had backfired, since the IRA merely burned the houses of loyalists in retaliation. By early June 1921 the British Government banned reprisals, and Bernard included the new edict in his booklet, adding that unofficial reprisals also were 'strictly prohibited' either by troops or police. As will be seen by Bernard's behaviour at the end of the campaign in Ireland when two of his intelligence officers were murdered, this did not only reflect official policy, but demonstrated a genuine concern that the British Army should maintain its reputation for honour and fairness despite the unending provocation by the rebels. In fact his booklet was strangely defensive for one who believed the IRA could be effectively stamped out. '"Precaution" and "cunning" are all-important,' he declared under his instructions for operations. But did he, in fact, believe the IRA could be defeated?

Here, surely, lies one of the keys to Bernard Montgomery's character – and future distinction as a commander. There were, after all, many valorous young officers who emerged from the Great War – Gort, Freyberg, de Wiart, Alexander – as well as superb staff-officers; but there were few that were both. Bernard, as Brigade-Major, became responsible for a number of large-scale manoeuvres or 'drives' in which several brigades cooperated in traversing the countryside and flushing out rebels. Meticulously planned and executed, these drives nevertheless failed to locate, let alone destroy, the IRA guerrilla columns; and were eventually discontinued. Yet while the military appealed to Churchill (Minister of War) and Lloyd George for more weapons and troops, Bernard began to recognise the futility of the struggle. He could be uncompromisingly tough, even cruel when it came to fighting. 'My whole attention was given to defeating the rebels and it never bothered me a bit how many houses were burned,' he later recorded.[2] 'Any civilian or Republican soldier or policeman who interferes with any officer or soldier *is shot*

[1] Preserved in the Imperial War Museum.
[2] Letter to Percival, loc. cit.

149

at once,' he wrote to his father after the Truce;[1] yet he was increasingly realistic about the long-term chances of success. Unlike Strickland and even Major Percival, the most ruthless of the English Intelligence Officers in the Brigade, Bernard came to see evacuation by the British as the only feasible solution to the Irish problem. 'We had a perfect organization and had "them" beat,' Strickland noted in his diary of the summer of 1921 when the Truce was declared.[2] 'At last it looked as if the Government were going to deal drastically with the gangs of murderers,' commented the 6th Division History drawn up by its General Staff, in view of the seven new battalions sent over to the division at the end of June 1921. 'The next two months were looked forward to eagerly by everyone except the IRA . . . There is no doubt that the truce of July 11, 1921, was just as unwelcome to the British Army in Ireland as the Armistice of 11th November, 1918, was welcome to the British Army in France,' the anonymous chronicler remarked sarcastically.[3] 'A short time more would have completed it [the smashing of the IRA] thoroughly. But "they" knew this and got the politicians to negotiate – with the present result,' Strickland recorded in May 1922 as Civil War loomed larger. *'Never* has the country been in such a state. No sort of order or authority in these parts. All our labour and energy have been thrown in the gutter, to say nothing of expense, and deprivation. It almost makes one wish one had never been concerned in the show at all.'[4]

Certainly the 'damned effort at peace' as Strickland called it[5] was galling to British troops who, by Government edict as part of the Truce, were confined to a role of complete passivity for some ten months pending a final settlement on Independence between Griffith and Lloyd George. During this period the British units were not permitted to challenge the IRA, which had 'never appeared until after the Truce was signed!' as the Divisional account contemptuously put it. 'As soon as all chance of immediate fighting was over, the scattered bands of desperados formed themselves into the Companies and Battalions to which they had always belonged *on paper*, and started to train, practise musketry, hold reviews, etc.'

Nevertheless, though the situation deteriorated towards winter 1921, when still no settlement was agreed and civil war between Republicans and Partitionists seemed likely, Bernard's conviction that the British should evacuate only strengthened. 'It really is most degrading for us soldiers having to stay on here,' he wrote to his father in March 1922, when the Truce was in its ninth month, 'and I shall be heartily glad to see the last of the people and the place. Our

---

[1] Quoted in Brian Montgomery, op. cit.
[2] Diary of Sir Peter Strickland, 11.7.21, IWM.
[3] History of the 6th Division in Ireland, Strickland Papers, IWM.
[4] Diary of Sir Peter Strickland 17.5.22, IWM.
[5] Diary of Sir Peter Strickland, 11.7.21, IWM.

presence here undoubtedly acts as a deterrent on the more extreme of the IRA,' he acknowledged; but he was under no illusion that the South was anything but 'entirely ruled by the Irish Republican Army, who publicly state by proclamation in the local papers that they owe no allegiance to the Provisional Government, and that they adhere to the Republic'.[1] In the months to come Bernard was to give 'a great deal of thought on the subject'; and in the autumn of the following year set down his personal opinions and conclusions for his colleague, Major A. E. Percival, who had gone as a student to the Staff College, Camberley and wished to deliver a series of lectures on guerrilla warfare in Ireland.

My own view is that to win a war of that sort you must be ruthless; Oliver Cromwell, or the Germans, would have settled it in a very short time. Nowadays public opinion precludes such methods; the nation would never allow it, and the politicians would lose their jobs if they sanctioned it. That being so I consider that Lloyd George was really right in what he did; if we had gone on we could probably have squashed the rebellion as a temporary measure, but it would have broken out again like an ulcer the moment we had removed the troops; I think the rebels would probably have refused battle, and hidden away their arms, etc. until we had gone. The only way therefore was to give them some form of self-government, and let them squash the rebellion themselves; *they* are the only people who could really stamp it out, and they are still trying to do so and as far as one can tell they seem to be having a fair amount of success. I am not however in close touch with the situation over there; but it seems to me that they have had more success than we had . . . You probably will not agree.[2]

Percival did not. He had made himself one of the most hated names to southern Irish Republicans, leading his own mobile column against the IRA, and in his opinion 'our tactics of rapid movement and surprise had had such a demoralising effect on their nerves that in another few weeks the back of the Rebellion would have been broken', had it not been for the Truce.[3] In his letter to Percival, Bernard had said he had regarded 'all civilians as "shinners" [supporters of Sinn Fein]' – an attitude which Percival, in his eventual lecture, declared was 'fundamentally wrong', for 'in conditions of this nature, you must at all costs distinguish the sheep from the wolves. If you fail to do so, you drive the whole population into the hands of the enemy'.[4] Yet it remains a fact that Percival is still

[1] Quoted in Brian Montgomery, op. cit.
[2] Letter to Percival, loc. cit.
[3] Percival lectures, loc. cit.
[4] Ibid.

remembered in Ireland as a vicious sadist, the man responsible for the 'Essex Battalion Torture Squad', the man who had personally taken 'a rifle with fixed bayonet from one of the troops and bayoneted one man ten times', as Tom Barry put it; whereas Bernard Montgomery was recognised by the IRA as an efficient staff officer who had behaved 'with great correctness'.[1] Moreover, though he was to become a respected Battalion CO, Percival was destined to undertake perhaps the most humiliating act of World War Two: the surrender of Singapore to the Japanese, while his Brigade-Major whose views he found so 'fundamentally wrong' would go on to demand in time the surrender of all the northern German armies.

There is, indeed, evidence of a distinct leap in Bernard Montgomery's stature and sagacity at this time. The ruthlessness and efficiency with which he had commanded the staff of the 17th Infantry Brigade early in 1921 gave way to a realistic acceptance of historical logic. Far from seeing the British Army's involvement in Ireland as an effort 'thrown into the gutter' as did Strickland, Bernard by 1923 conceded the inevitability of Irish independence and acknowledged that an Irish Government was the only way of effecting it. Such a *volte-face* might, in many another, have denoted weak convictions; but in Bernard's case it surely demonstrates the opposite. Though his reputation in the years to come would rest largely on his uncompromisingly iron character, it is clear that from the early 1920s Bernard had in fact learned the difficult task of reconsidering his own attitudes and revising them in the light of events – an essential feature in his quest for greatness.

Yet Bernard's service as Brigade-Major in Ireland was not to end on the note of realistic wisdom which his letter to Percival of 1923 would strike. For a long time, in the winter of 1921 and spring of 1922, it looked as if war might once more break out. 'We have to be very careful as a false step would be a match that would set the whole country ablaze again,' he wrote to his father at the beginning of March 1922. 'The situation is really impossible; we have had two officers murdered in the last fortnight . . . It is very difficult to find out how long they intend to keep us here in the south of Ireland.'[2]

Ever since January 1922 when the official Provisional Government of Ireland was established and the Treaty with Britain ratified, the British forces in the South had begun to evacuate barracks and outposts. Yet the timing of British withdrawal was naturally influenced by the explosive relations between those Irishmen who accepted the Partition Treaty, and those who demanded an all-Ireland Republic. The British Government had negotiated the Treaty, and therefore had a moral obligation to support the Provisional

[1] Col. Commandant Tom Barry to Ewan Butler, in Ewan Butler, *Barry's Flying Column*, London 1971.
[2] Quoted in Brian Montgomery, op. cit.

Government – a fact which infuriated the largely Republican-minded IRA. Thus the remaining British troops waited with considerable anxiety for their recall to Britain, while the IRA sniped and ambushed them as the last stumbling-block to a republican military coup in the South. On 26 March 1922, four weeks after Bernard's letter to his father, the IRA held a convention which formally repudiated the Provisional Government in Dublin. 'Thank God you have got to deal with it [the situation], not me,' wrote Churchill to the Chairman of the Provisional Government. On 29 March 1922, the Cork City Brigade of the IRA pulled off a spectacular coup by pirating the *Upnor*, a 700-ton British Admiralty vessel taking home arms and munitions from Ireland to Woolwich Arsenal. Armed with its contents of machine-guns, rifles, grenades, pistols and more than half a million rounds of ammunition the IRA were ready for civil war. Collins claimed it was a British trick to support the IRA – a ridiculous accusation in the circumstances, since Churchill had in fact put forward proposals for British military action to take over the centres of administration in southern Ireland if the IRA effected a *coup d'état*.

For the British troops still in the South it was a tense period indeed – and the final straw came when, on the eve of evacuation by the remaining units of 6th Division, three British officers and a private were kidnapped at Macroom, Co. Cork. One of them was a very popular Lieutenant from the Royal Warwickshire Regiment, H. D. Hendy, who was an Intelligence Officer at Bernard's Brigade HQ.

The Royal Warwickshire Regiment's 1st Battalion was stationed near Fermoy, but wisely Bernard refused to 'come and tell us because he was frightened we should go and burn the place down', as Lt-Colonel Gething remembered.[1] Montgomery 'kept us in the dark', and the next day there was a conference between the staffs of the British and Irish Brigades. Dan Donovan, the IRA Commandant, who had been responsible for pirating the *Upnor*, and Major B. L. Montgomery were detailed to represent the two sides. Evacuation was temporarily suspended. Bernard wanted to search the area with British troops, but Donovan insisted that this might only be done by the IRA – who, according to him, 'knew nothing about the missing men'. Bernard replied: 'As far as I am aware, if a tramp left Ballincollig the news of his arrival in Macroom would be heralded!'[2] Days of fruitless meetings and IRA searches finally drove Bernard to insist that he be allowed to take out a British Army search party, which he did on 30 April 1922. By the time the convoy reached the outskirts of Macroom, it was stopped by the IRA; and only last-minute intervention by the parish priest prevented bloodshed.

Bernard was evidently in a savage mood, but here was little he could do, and the convoy had to return to Cork. He offered a reward,

[1] Colonel P. J. Gething, loc. cit.
[2] Quoted in Eoin Neeson, *The Civil War in Ireland 1922–3*, Cork 1966 and 1969.

and on 2 May went out again with a detachment – although the IRA officer refused to go with him this time, fearing a shoot-out. As evacuation had ceased, the British Government became involved. 'Many wires coming and going over Hendy case,' Strickland noted in his diary. 'They are now anticipating "questions." ' By 4 May there was still no news; but Donovan declared his opinion that 'it was done by some of the IRA at Macroom who had temporarily seceded from control'. Nothing could be gained by waiting; and evacuation was recommended. Some days later the IRA announced that the bodies had been found in a bog, and Bernard went to recover them. It was a distressing finale to 'two and a half years of toil', as Strickland noted in his diary. 'Looting going on all over the place,' he recorded on 17 May, as the final barracks were vacated. On 19 May he, the Divisional and Brigade staffs left Cork to the virtual certainty of Civil War.

Though he was not decorated for his service during the Irish campaign, Bernard Montgomery's performance had not gone unnoticed at the War Office; already on 28 April 1922 the Director of Staff Duties had written to Irish Command to ask if Brevet-Major Montgomery would care for an appointment as Brigade-Major in England and whether he could be spared. The incumbent was Bernard's old Company Commander from the days of Peshawar, now Lt-Col C. R. Macdonald, who was about to take command of the 1st Battalion of the Royal Warwicks; the brigade was the 8th Infantry Brigade, belonging to the 3rd Division, stationed at Plymouth. Irish Command replied that Bernard was 'desirous' of the post; and Macdonald was asked to wait on until Bernard arrived.

Thus, after only a couple of days' leave, on 24 May Bernard travelled from Chiswick to Plymouth, little suspecting that the division to which he now belonged he would himself be leading into battle some two decades later.

CHAPTER TWO

Training the TA

How very different was Plymouth from the barbed-wire enclaves and armour-escorted travel at Cork! Though the IRA managed to assassinate Sir Henry Wilson, the CIGS, in London in June 1922, they never troubled the Cork Brigade-Major again. For the Montgomery family at New Park there was no such respite; and had Bernard's father not been a Bishop, things might have been far worse. Yet the family made no attempt to sit out the Civil War in Chiswick; the Bishop had officially retired the previous year and Mrs Montgomery even made tea for the IRA when they arrived at Moville late one night that summer, demanding arms and bedclothes.[1]

At Plymouth, meanwhile, Bernard concentrated on the facet of military service for which, over the next seventeen years, he was to become increasingly well known in army circles: training. Commanding the 8th Infantry Brigade was Brigadier-General S. E. Hollond, a distinguished staff officer during the Great War who, according to Brian Montgomery, recognised Bernard's talents vis-à-vis training and gave him his head. 'His long honeymoon with the Army was coming into its full flower', was how Bernard's first biographer, Alan Moorehead, described the period; but whether it was quite so serene is questionable. Hollond was forty-eight years old and had commanded the 8th Brigade a bare year when Bernard arrived; moreover it was Hollond's first actual command since being a company commander before the war, and he cannot have relished starting it with someone quite as energetic and independent as Bernard. At any rate the honeymoon did not last long – and within a year Bernard was moved away from his Regular Army appointment at Devonport to the 'backwaters' of a Territorial Army Division in the north of England: as GSO 2 of the 49th (West Riding) TA Division, based at York.

What Bernard felt about this transfer is not known; but even in Ireland edicts had come from the War Office to weed out inefficient and less able junior officers in consequence of the 'Geddes axe', so that there was no question of turning down the appointment. Besides, though it meant no alteration in rank, there were compensa-

---

[1] Brian Montgomery, op. cit.

tions. The Divisional Commander, Sir Charles Harington, was also new; and since no GSO 1 was ever appointed, Bernard thus became, to all intents and purposes, his Chief-of-Staff. What must have seemed, at first glance, a retrogressive step became in fact the most formative era in Bernard's career to date. He threw himself into his new job heart and soul, transforming it from a backwater into a testing ground for his ideas on training and tactical instruction – a two-year experiment that would result eventually in his appointment to an instructorship at Camberley and the rewriting of *Infantry Training Manual*, Volume II.

Even before going to York, Bernard had begun his legendary 'master classes' for young officers hoping to attend the Staff College. It was in fact one of the duties of more senior officers to help instruct their junior colleagues; but in practice most hopeful candidates prepared for the exam by correspondence courses, and senior officers merely helped when asked.

Bernard's approach was very different. Frustrated perhaps by the lowering of morale as a result of the Geddes axe, he felt that this could only be countered by a revival within the depleted army – a revival that would pivot on the Staff College, Camberley. Instead of sticking in the rut of regimental soldiering with ever-diminishing hope of promotion, young officers should be encouraged to think outside their battalion duties by preparing for the Staff College exam; and instead of doing this by faceless correspondence it ought to be done in conjunction with an officer they knew and could talk to. Thus, in 1923, Bernard began his own school for Staff College candidates at Devonport – whence he wrote to an army colleague in charge of education at the 10th Infantry Brigade, Lieutenant B. L. Hart, enclosing his notes on 'Indian Frontier Warfare' as an example of what he was trying to do.

Lieutenant Hart had come to know Bernard in 1920 through his Brigade-Major at the 10th Infantry Brigade, Major Clement Tomes:

At that time Montgomery was still a captain, with a brevet as major, and a student at the Staff College,

Liddell Hart chronicled in his *Memoirs*.

Viewing his perky manner, peaky face and small stature it seemed amusingly apt that in the Battle of the Somme he had been a staff officer in what was called 'the Bantam Division'. He did not show the natural signs of leadership, or a knack of handling men . . .

Liddell Hart was eight years Bernard's junior; but he was a restless young military theorist and, in consequence of a 1920 lecture printed in the *United Service Magazine* on tactics, had come to the notice of General Sir Ivor Maxse, then GOC Northern Command. It was

Maxse who got Liddell Hart on to the staff of 10th Infantry Brigade at Lichfield, where the Brigadier was Winston Dugan – who had been asked by the War Office that year to revise the *Infantry Training Manual* in the light of experience gained from the Great War. Dugan, finding it difficult to concentrate, gave the task to Liddell Hart; and the British Army's official training manual was thus entrusted to a twenty-four-year-old Lieutenant. The *Manual* appeared in 1921, and, although it was much doctored by the War Office, Liddell Hart's reputation was made. By the time Bernard sent a copy of his Staff College class notes from Devonport in 1923, Liddell Hart had become a prolific military essayist – a fortunate development, for in July that year a negative Medical Board report resulted in him being placed on half-pay and eventually resigning from the army. But was ill-health really the reason? Liddell Hart complained to his MP in vain; while the Chief Instructor of the Staff College, 'Boney' Fuller, was convinced it was a conspiracy by the military establishment to rid themselves of a trouble-maker.

If so, it did not stop Bernard from associating with Liddell Hart – though their 'friendship' was essentially an intellectual one, as opposed to personal. Clement Tomes had revealed to Liddell Hart that he thought Montgomery would one day reach the pinnacle of the British Army and bring great honour to his regiment – an introduction that was not lost on the lowly subaltern who depended so much on successful officers like Maxse, Dugan and Fuller. Conversely Bernard saw in Liddell Hart the sort of thinking, critical officer he had missed at Camberley, and commanding the ear of generals. Thus began their uneasy association, with its tones of subdued envy: both ambitious, vain, opinionated men. 'Montgomery's egotism was only exceeded by that of one other man I knew,' the Oxford don, Sir Edgar Williams, remarked many years later: 'Liddell Hart's.'[1]

Both men were embarrassingly conceited and self-righteous. Both had attended St Paul's School – though Liddell Hart went up to Cambridge for a year where he acquired a querulous bent that would not always serve him well. He sometimes boasted, later, that he had gone to preparatory school with Maurice Bowra, the Oxford scholar; but Liddell Hart's third-class performance at the end of his only year at Cambridge and his strident journalism did not impress Bowra. 'Liddell Hart?' queried Bowra later, when told that the Captain was coming as guest of honour to a college function. 'At school he was only Hart!'

Bernard's class notes must have impressed Liddell Hart, for he kept them to the end of his life in his archive. Though the North-West Frontier was very far from Liddell Hart's current preoccupation, Bernard's notes gave a good idea of his grasp of army organisation, dispositions, movement and battle tactics. Under the latter heading

[1] Interview of 20.12.79.

Bernard was quite dogmatic: 'Aim always to bring enemy to battle, and attack, and kill as many as possible,' he laid down as one of the major tenets of his future military philosophy. Ground as such was irrelevant, he maintained, thinking no doubt of the ultimately futile 'pushes' of the Great War. 'No good manoeuvring enemy out of his position,' he noted, for though this might look good on paper it was in fact the reverse – particularly with guerrillas. It was important, Bernard insisted, to recognise the strategic military aim, from the beginning to the end: 'Success must be followed up,' he concluded; 'inaction is useless.'[1]

The word 'useless' would become one of the cardinal terms in Montgomery's hardening military vocabulary. For Bernard Montgomery there were no shades of meaning; shades introduced complications and likely confusion, whereas it was the task of the soldier to be clear, decisive and, above all, practical. As in his 'Summary of Important Instructions' to the 17th Infantry Brigade, his Staff College class notes spelled out in characteristic brevity and clarity the salient features of the subject; Liddell Hart kept all their correspondence; every letter, every pamphlet and even scribbled notes recording his telephone conversations with Bernard. Although Bernard would, towards the end of his life, refer to Liddell Hart as 'my very great friend', their relationship was always professional; indeed they addressed each other by their surnames right up until the 1960s. It was not until 1930 that Bernard even acknowledged the Liddell in Liddell Hart's name. They were in fact opposites by nature despite their dedication to the art of war: Liddell Hart a spoiled 'mother's boy', while Bernard craved vainly his mother's affection. Over the next seventeen years they would pore over and criticise each other's views and theories as Liddell Hart became more and more widely known, yet in the Second World War it would be Bernard who would steal the limelight, and Liddell Hart who would have to be content with the role of despised prophet.

Nevertheless it was undoubtedly Liddell Hart who first diagnosed the tactical flaw in Bernard's approach to battle, as early as 1924. By then Bernard was no longer at Devonport, but had moved, in the early summer of 1923, to his new post on the staff of the 49th (West Riding) Division, at York.

For Bernard, the move to York was his first experience of the Territorial Army. Fortunately it was also the first experience of his Divisional Commander, General Sir Charles Harington, and the way was thus open for Bernard to put forward his own proposals for organisation and training. Nor was he slow to do so, for in July 1923 Bernard issued the second printed booklet of his military career: 'Tactical Notes for use in the West Riding Area and 49th (West Riding) Division TA.'

[1] Typescript preserved in Liddell Hart Papers, King's College, London.

'These notes,' Montgomery began his introduction, 'are issued in the hope that they may be of use to officers in the training of their units, and in preparing themselves for promotion examinations.' There were, of course, various existing Army training manuals and field service regulations in print (including Liddell Hart's new War Office Infantry Training Manual); but Bernard recognised the fundamental failing of such volumes: they laid down principles of warfare, but did not give methods by which officers could train their units to achieve these noble principles. Moreover there was a second reason for issuing such a booklet to the Division – namely the perception that unless the TA officers and NCO's were properly trained beforehand, the annual TA camps and manoeuvres would be a waste of valuable time. 'It appeared to us,' Bernard wrote to Liddell Hart the following year,

> that our units were trying to do what is not really possible; they went to camps in the summer and tried to do collective training without having first carried out any individual instruction of the leaders . . . Now as you know well, the underlying principle of all training is the instruction of the leaders before they in turn teach their men. It was a well-known Corps Commander in France who once said: 'Teach the teachers what to teach before they teach the Tommies'. This Corps Commander was somewhat eccentric and some people thought he was mad. He may have been (between ourselves I think he was), but he hit the nail right on the head when he said those words.
>
> So the first thing we had to do was to try and organize some form of individual training of the leaders during the winter . . . It was not easy to get this going; there was no precedent for it and the Territorial Army is very conservative. However, once we got them to realize that it was a good egg, they took it up and got down to it splendidly. Every drill hall was provided with a sand-table and evening classes were formed for officers and NCOs.[1]

It was now that Bernard enunciated his later legendary attitude to drill itself. 'Don't think that I discourage drill,' he warned Liddell Hart; 'on the contrary, I think it is most valuable. But any high standard of drill in the Territorial Army is almost impossible and it is really [a] waste of time to try and obtain it. We encourage a certain amount of drill during the annual camp, especially to start with, as it is a great assistance in getting rid of that "sloppy" look which the Territorial has when he turns out for his annual training. It is, however, quite possible to obtain a reasonably high standard in tactical training, and to my mind it is better to concentrate on that and not to devote too much time to drill.'

[1] Letter of 16.7.24, Liddell Hart Papers.

There was no hint of disappointment or dissatisfaction in Montgomery's letter; and the testimony of both Bernard's sister Winsome and his brother Brian reinforce the impression of a still young officer (he was thirty-five), a Captain and Brevet-Major, wonderfully enthused by the challenge he faced. Moreover, since the Divisional HQ had no mess of its own he sought permission to use that of the local regiment in York, the famous Prince of Wales's Own West Yorkshire Regiment. Here Bernard set up court; began, as in the 8th Infantry Brigade at Devonport, to give classes for entry by examination to the Staff College, and to get discussion groups going on every aspect of modern military organisation and warfare. When his sister Winsome married a young officer from the Royal Sussex Regiment, Bernard immediately invited him up also to stay in York. Bernard lived at the depot, and, in the words of one young subaltern who was there at the time, 'was looked upon as rather a novelty, in that he unblushingly proclaimed that soldiering was his one and only love'.[1] This subaltern, thirteen years his junior, was Lieutenant Francis de Guingand, who was also involved in training Territorials. They quickly became friends, called each other 'Freddie' and 'Monty', and played golf, tennis or squash together almost every day. 'We became great pals,' de Guingand recalled some fifty-five years later. 'We sat almost literally at his feet; he would tell us about the war, about the terrible casualties and the way the senior commanders and staffs lived in great luxury . . .'[2]

'He created a wonderfully refreshing atmosphere in the Mess,' de Guingand recorded. 'As always, he was extremely outspoken and provocative.' Bernard's brother Brian, then a cadet at Sandhurst, also came to stay at York during the summer, while waiting to hear how he had fared in the passing-out results. 'Chiefly I recall how de Guingand, although only a subaltern officer in those days, stood out from the other officers in the mess. When he was present he dominated discussion, and it was fascinating to see how he and Bernard took charge, without conscious effort, of the conversation . . . I sat silent and spellbound,' Brian remembered. When de Guingand – who had achieved distinction at the Small Arms School – required funds to help provide instruction to TA 'weapon-training cadres' it was Bernard who produced them. 'The last point I would like to emphasise is the necessity for very close touch between Regular Depots and their Territorial battalions,' wrote Bernard with some feeling to Liddell Hart the following year. 'The Depots can help enormously in the instruction of the leaders, and the Deport Training Cadre should seldom be unemployed.'[3]

What with his Divisional Staff duties, training schemes, and instruction classes for the Staff College, Bernard soon found himself

[1] Sir Francis de Guingand, *Operation Victory*, London 1947.
[2] Interview of 7.5.78.
[3] Liddell Hart Papers.

160

working as hard as or harder than he ever had in France or even Ireland. He was determined that by the summer camp of 1924 the 49th Division TA would be second to none, and during the autumn of 1923 set about the preparation of a series of lectures he would give personally 'to show officers how to teach on the sand-table' that winter. These talks, delivered in January, February and March 1924, were given in 'a series of four lectures to the officers of each battalion, and officers of units of the Divisional Troops attended at the most convenient centres . . . It was an exhausting task and I was completely done in at the end of them,' he wrote to Liddell Hart in July 1924; 'but it was well worth it.' The lectures, once again, were issued as a printed pamphlet 'solely for the purpose of rendering it unnecessary for officers to take notes at the lectures; with no notes to take officers can devote their whole attention to the lecturer and watching the sand-table, round which all the lectures were given,' Bernard noted in his Introduction. 'It is particularly important that these précis should be read in conjunction with, and not in substitution for, the official training manuals. Special attention is directed to the following War Office pamphlets . . .'

This rider was added for the simple reason that the War Office was getting increasingly perturbed by young officers – such as B. L. Montgomery – issuing their own instructions on how to train and handle troops in battle – and from the summer camp on the Isle of Man a fortnight later Bernard wrote to warn Liddell Hart: 'Please make *no reference at all* in your article to the Tactical Notes I got out for use in our Division . . . A War Office letter has just come out prohibiting the use of all unofficial pamphlets or training books . . . We now have to stop using them and must of course do what we are told.'

Evidently Sir Charles Harington had put his foot down, for it was quite out of character for Bernard to accept such edicts without a fight – especially when he had put such energy and thought into his manuals. 'Silly old bugger, he's no use anyway,' Bernard had said of an offensive brigadier who was disturbed on the green by Bernard's brassie shot while he and de Guingand were playing golf one day.[1] However, on this occasion Bernard acknowledged defeat. 'On thinking it over,' he wrote to Liddell Hart on 2 August 1924, 'I think the War Office are right. If there is need for such books they should be written by the General Staff; it would never do for each Division to have its own book. In actual fact they consider there is no need for them and so we have given up using ours.'[2] The phrase 'on thinking it over' would become a synonym in Bernard's vocabulary for 'I have been told', and no doubt Liddell Hart recognised the writing between lines, since only a week before Bernard had written him an

[1] De Guingand, op. cit.
[2] Liddell Hart Papers.

161

eight-page letter thanking him for his 'valuable criticisms on the pamphlets I sent you. I am very glad to have them,' Bernard had stated, 'though I do not agree entirely with your remarks.'

It was in this letter that Bernard acknowledged Liddell Hart's penetrating remarks about exploitation – and promised to remedy the omission:

Pages 9 and 10 of the lectures
I have not mentioned exploitation anywhere. Perhaps I should have done so, and if I ever get out a revised edition I will do so. I was anxious not to try and teach too much. The first thing to my mind is to get them to understand the elementary principles of attack and defence. But I think you are probably right, and exploitation should have been brought out.

As Liddell Hart would point out in his own *Memoirs*, this was to become a 'persisting blind spot' in Bernard Montgomery's approach to tactics.[1] Bernard never did revise his 49th Division pamphlets, nor would he amend his own version of the *Infantry Training Manual* when, six years later, Liddell Hart again pointed to the self-same omission. Clearly it was not something quite logical, for Bernard had no hesitation in pronouncing Liddell Hart correct both in 1924 and again in 1930 on the issue, and declared his intention to remedy the omission, without actually doing so. Was there, then, some obstacle in his own over-ordered mentality that hindered him from carrying out what, intellectually, he acknowledged as correct and necessary? In his letter of 24 August 1924 to Liddell Hart he strove to explain his aversion to teaching the exceptional:

You will notice that I use the word 'normal' a good deal. I am a great believer in giving people a 'normal' to work on. My methods are as follows:
a) I first enunciate the principles of the phase of war, or operation, that is to be done.
b) Then give normal methods, based on the principles.
c) Then work out a concrete case, showing how the principles are applied in practice on the ground. This may, or may not, necessitate a departure from the 'normal'. But it makes no difference.
I think 'normal' methods are a great aid as people then start on a definite basis instead of groping in the dark.[2]

The last line surely gives the most explicit key to Bernard's military philosophy and even his own psychology. Once principles and

[1] Liddell Hart, *Memoirs*, Vol. I, London 1965.
[2] Letter of 24.8.24, Liddell Hart Papers.

normal, sound methods had been established satisfactorily, he was prepared to depart from the 'normal' if necessary; but his instinct was to see the latter as a danger, a 'groping in the dark', which as a trainer he fundamentally mistrusted.

Liddell Hart could not agree; felt that this 'groping' should be encouraged, practised and studied until it became 'normal'. Each had defined his position: only war, the ultimate test, would decide who was right.

In the meantime Bernard took his Territorial Division to the Isle of Man with General Harington. Though he had worked himself to the point of exhaustion preparing the summer camp (his three clerks were so busy that his eight-page letter to Liddell Hart had to be written in longhand), he was full of wonder and respect for his amateur units. 'I find the Territorial Army most interesting,' he wrote to Liddell Hart.

The officers are very keen on the whole; they are very appreciative of assistance in improving their military knowledge . . . I often wonder why they join the Territorial Army; they get nothing out of it, in fact it costs them money. It is really the old volunteer spirit still existing; some of our units are very old and have a tremendous esprit de corps.

All this is of course excellent. The Regular Army should without doubt give of its best to the Territorial Army; unfortunately this is not always the case as service in the Territorial Army is regarded by many as a backwater. I always tell our Division that there is only one Army in England, and we all belong to it, whether we are in the Regulars, Territorials, or OTC. In that Army there are two categories:–

1. Those who devote all their time to soldiering, i.e. the Regular Army.
2. Those whose main work is some other profession, and who only soldier in their spare time.

Personally, I take my hat off to those in Category 2 every time.[1]

If anyone, in the years to come, was to ask whence Bernard's openness towards non-professional soldiers – whether on his staff or in fighting units – derived, it was surely from this period in York from 1923 to 1924. Moreover in seeking to instruct others he was himself all the time learning – particularly so in his 'astonishing "one-man" performance' (as de Guingand called it) teaching students who wanted to take the Staff College exam. Montgomery lectured on all the subjects, set the papers and corrected them. 'He can have had little sleep during this period,' de Guingand wrote in

<hr>

[1] Letter of 16.7.24, Liddell Hart Papers.

Operation Victory. 'As far as I can recollect, not so long after this, Montgomery became sick and had to take some leave.'

In fact Bernard Montgomery was not sick – though he was certainly in need of leave. On 7 January 1925 he completed his '4 year period of staff employment' as he wrote to Liddell Hart on 15 January from Moville. 'I am now on 2 months' leave and rejoin the 1st Bn of my regiment at Shorncliffe on 7th March.' That his own efforts had been extraordinary he acknowledged not boastfully, but by implication.

> My successor at York was Savile (Royal Fusiliers); he was at the Staff College with me and afterwards went to MS at the War Office.
>
> If I had been with the Division this winter I would have gone on tour again round all the units like I did last winter, lecturing on the sand table. I doubt, however, whether Savile will do so. He has been a 'Q' staff officer mostly and is not really in touch with modern training methods.
>
> I think it is awfully important to send our very best 'trainers' to the TA. The time available for training is so short that we cannot afford to waste any of it.

Yet even on leave Bernard was unable to wind down. 'I am at present engaged in a crusade that would fill you with horror!' he finished his letter to Liddell Hart.

> It is directed against our present tactical organisation which I do not consider the best one possible. It is not sufficiently elastic and it is difficult to adjust correctly the numbers required for fire and the numbers required for movement.
>
> I would prefer the Company to consist of two LG [Lewis Gun] Platoons and two Rifle Platoons. It is a big subject and I have not time to write down the various pros and cons in this letter,

he noted. For someone who had only just begun two months' leave this must have sounded curious to anyone but Liddell Hart. The latter had driven himself to a heart attack by his fanatical new devotion to military journalism. Yet side by side with his duties at York with the 49th Division and Staff College exam instruction, Bernard had also begun to command a certain attention in print. The autumn 1924 number of the *Army Quarterly* had carried a major article by Liddell Hart on the 'New Model' Army, and on 14th October 1924 Bernard had written to him:

> My dear Hart
> I have just read with interest your article on the 'New Model' Army in the *Army Quarterly*. It is quite excellent and I congratulate you on it.

George Lindsay (Comdt of the Tank Corps Central Schools) has just been staying with me; he also had read your article and was much impressed by it.

There is an article of mine in the same number. I called it 'Training in the Territorial Army' but for some unknown reason the editors thought fit to alter the title to 'Letter of Advice to a newly appointed Adjutant in the TA.'

Bernard was not even given a by-line; but it was his first published article in a military magazine, and evidently he enjoyed the medium, for in January 1925, while he rested at Moville, the Regimental Magazine of the Royal Warwickshires, the *Antelope*, carried the first of a five-part series of articles by Major B. L. Montgomery on the history of tactical warfare, entitled 'The Growth of Modern Infantry Tactics': the climax of five years of study and instruction.

I have been asked to write something for the *Antelope*. What I write is not to be humorous, or funny,

Bernard explained in his introduction;

it is to be instructive and something that will be of military value to the readers. The task is not easy, since the readers of the *Antelope* are many in number, and vary in rank from private soldiers to full generals.

I have decided, therefore, to contribute a series of articles on the growth and development of our modern infantry tactics during the last 300 years or so. This is a subject which should be of interest to everyone, whether private or general. It will also please the Editor, since it will not be possible to deal with such a large subject in one article; it will mean four, or possibly five, articles, starting with Gustavus Adolphus in 1611 and working up to 1924.

The *Antelope* – a gossipy review of Royal Warwickshire affairs designed mainly to provide regimental news and entertainment – had never known anything like it. Yet, however many deprecating remarks were exchanged that January in messes and barracks, there was no denying that young Brevet-Major Montgomery knew how to present his subject and win the reader's attention. Moreover, at the very outset of his history, he made clear his now abiding conviction about battle:

All through history, from the days of the great phalanx of the Roman Legion, the master law of tactics remains unchanged; this Law is that to achieve success you must be superior at the point where you intend to strike the decisive blow.

No clearer or more concise statement of Bernard's primary tactical belief would ever be made; moreover the articles would demonstrate that Bernard's concern with the minutiae of infantry training had not blinded him to the larger lessons of military history.

Already in October 1923 Bernard had given his view – after 'a great deal of thought on the subject' – of the lessons to be derived from the war in Ireland. In his letter to Major Percival he had declared he was 'certain that the best procedure was mobile columns mutually co-operating with each other. But they must have W/T, so that they can be operated direct from Brigade HQ if required.'[1] In his new *Antelope* articles, however, he concentrated not on guerrilla warfare but the tactics involved in major confrontations between whole armies; and after his January account of Gustavus Adolphus's seventeenth-century tactics there were many who became impatient to know what the young Major was driving towards: what views he might hold about the recent Great War; and what prophecies he might make about future military conflict.

Well aware of the 'stir' his first article had caused and shortly before returning to his regiment in the spring of 1925, Bernard went abroad to France, on what had become an annual early spring golfing holiday with Lt-Colonel Macdonald – now the CO of the 1st Battalion, the Royal Warwicks. They travelled to Dinard, on the Brittany coast – where to everyone's consternation the serious and dedicated young Major fell hopelessly in love with an English girl less than half his age: the blonde and beautiful daughter of a senior Indian Civil Servant, Betty Anderson.

Bernard had turned thirty-seven. To his disciples at York he had invariably preached that the Army, like the Catholic Church, demanded celibacy if one were serious in one's profession. 'You can't make a good soldier and a good husband', had been his constant maxim, de Guingand remembered later.[2] Bernard's sister Winsome found his lack of interest in women until this time pronounced, but unobtrusive. 'He wasn't shy with women . . . and he was a very kind, very good brother. He had me down just before the First World War to stay with him at Shorncliffe for a week, and I stayed with Captain Tomes. During the war, when on leave, he arranged parties for me. He didn't dance himself – he didn't like dancing – he'd just sit and watch.' Winsome did not see in this celibate existence the shadow of Maud, his mother. 'Oh, no, some men aren't [interested in women],' she laughed.[3] Their brother Harold, ambitious to succeed as a colonial administrator in Kenya, also married rather late.

Yet the suddenness and depth of Bernard's infatuation with Betty Anderson and his urgent desire to marry her, thus throwing over-

[1] Letter of 14.10.23, Percival Papers, IWM.
[2] De Guingand, *From Brass Hat to Bowler Hat*, London 1979.
[3] Interview of 10.4.78.

board his own dictum on the subject, suggests something more complex – and more interesting – than Winsome's rather simplistic portrait of Bernard at this period of his life. 'Something went wrong,' she acknowledged, puzzled by his later character, 'and I cannot tell you what it was, I don't know.'

Until 1925 Bernard had remained, in a personal sense, entirely under his mother's spell, not only because he so earnestly desired her affection, but because of the woman she was. 'Ooh, my word, she was strong minded!' Winsome later recalled. To herself and to the outside world Maud presented a picture of absolute fidelity and devotion to her husband, the Bishop; but Maud evidently missed a certain demonstrative affection from him which she seems to have sublimated in her energetic, even tyrannical domestic rule. Bernard's attempt to substitute for his father in this respect, to care for her and show his love had been long and unremitting. All had been rejected. 'She was too harsh with him,' Winsome felt. 'I think it was her fault. I think Bernard had an image of her she wouldn't play up to . . .'[1]

It is difficult to avoid the inference that Bernard Montgomery's sudden burst of feeling towards a beautiful seventeen-year-old blonde whom he had never met before was in some way a first bid to free himself from the hold his mother had on him. Pent up within him was, undoubtedly, a great deal of emotion which, given the framework of his military dedication, he simply had no way of expressing save within his own family. Yet the more his mother rejected his embarrassing advances, the more he must have yearned to prove his capacity for love. He had lavished attention on his sister Winsome; but she was now married. He had paid for his brother Brian's schooling and got him into his own regiment. He evidently now wanted someone close to him whom he could spoil, could cherish; and the image of the attractive blonde stirred him to a quite uncharacteristic outpouring of love and hope. 'They used to walk round the walls of St Malo, and then through the pine woods and across the dunes down to the sea shore,' Brian later recollected from the account which Betty Anderson gave him. 'There Bernard would draw pictures for her in the sand to illustrate his ideas for the employment of armoured fighting vehicles in war. He showed her how he would position his tanks (at that stage very much a novelty in the British Army) to be used in conjunction with infantry and other arms, in order to win the war which he knew, even then, was coming.'[2] The latter reference seems surprising, since in early 1925 it was much more probable there would be Civil War in England than a conflict abroad – particularly Germany, where the Rhineland had been summarily occupied by French troops when Germany defaulted on reparations. Yet the evidence of Bernard's work as a

[1] Ibid.
[2] Brian Montgomery, op. cit.

167

Company Commander in the Royal Warwickshire Regiment bears out Brian Montgomery's recollection. Moreover, despite the notoriously unreliable performance of tanks during the Great War, and his own limited experience of the use of armour, Bernard was quite willing to hold forth about them – even to veterans of Cambrai, as Major-General Wimberley later recalled with irony:

We had no tanks in those days, serving in southern Ireland, but I well remember the Bde Major giving to all the officers of the brigade a short course of lectures on the proper co-operation of infantry with tanks in battle as he envisaged it!

I thought his views were very sound, but it did cross my mind that Monty, I knew, had been badly wounded early in World War I, long before the advent of tanks, and thereafter, when recovered, served only as a staff officer. Whereas I had myself, as a regimental officer in the 51st Highland Division, taken part in the 1917 battle of Cambrai, when for the first time infantry and a great number of tanks went together into battle. Further, I expect a good number of his audience had been in that battle was well as myself, so it was clear that our Bde Major had plenty of self-confidence![1]

Though he believed in the future of tanks, Bernard still predicted a relatively modest role for them, helping to punch a gap in the enemy lines before retiring to their ' "rallying point" ', as he noted in his 49th Division Tactical Notes. 'Tanks are very blind and cannot reconnoitre for themselves,' he had written. 'In mobile war they will normally move forward by bounds in support of the advancing infantry; when their assistance is required they will be given a definite task or objective; when the task is completed, or objective captured, they will be brought back into support again until next required.'[2] The section covering tanks came, in fact, at the very tail of his résumé of army combat units, after cavalry, engineers and machine-guns!

Yet Brian Montgomery's image of the couple poring over 'pictures in the sand' is a pregnant one. Had Bernard not written in his letter of 16 July 1924 to Liddell Hart: 'We encourage the use of the sand-table and have provided one in every drill hall in the Division' – a remark which Liddell Hart had marked with a stroke of approval in the margin? Now, on the sands of Dinard and St Malo, Bernard used a real sand-table to instruct his young pupil. That she was still a girl and might not be interested in infantry tactics did not hinder Bernard, evidently; he was entranced with his young companion and 'lost no time in making this clear to her parents', as Brian later wrote, asking them whether he might hope for her hand in marriage. 'Very

[1] Loc. cit.
[2] Liddell Hart Papers.

168

wisely', Betty Anderson's parents 'left the whole matter' for her to decide.[1]

Betty gave no immediate answer. Apparently she 'particularly admired his obviously strong character and personality, including his great ambition amounting to a determination to rise to the top of his profession.' But admiration did not amount to love. Besides, young as she was, Betty seems to have recognised that she might simply not match up to the expectations of this ambitious and clearly dedicated Brevet-Major. Instead, meeting 2nd Lieutenant Brian Montgomery 'quite by accident' at a dinner party in Folkestone some weeks later, she began a flirtation with him. It was kept secret from Bernard, so as not to hurt him; but they met frequently and went dancing together.

It was some time before Bernard would countenance Betty's refusal. The letter has not been preserved, but Brian later recorded with what relief he learned from their mother at New Park that Bernard had written 'to say he knew beyond doubt that Betty did not love him. His final words were "It is all over and I have to accept it"'.[2]

It was the first time Bernard had ever directed such deep feelings outside his own family, and the attempt had not succeeded. As Brian said in his book, however, there was consolation to be drawn from the fact that Bernard could at least unburden himself to his mother.

Perhaps, too, after ten years' absence, he had wanted to return to his beloved regiment a married man, both to surprise his regimental colleagues and as a symbol of his determination to succeed *within* the sometimes stiflingly antiquated hierarchy of the British military establishment. 'You are being decapitated. I am being strangled,' J. F. C. Fuller had written to Liddell Hart on hearing the news of the latter's reduction to half-pay. Both left the army they loved – Fuller to become, in time, an impassioned fascist, Liddell Hart an increasingly tendentious newspaper correspondent. Bernard Montgomery would come very close to dismissal in the years ahead; but it says something for the moral background in which he had been raised that he recognised the danger of going too far in the advocacy of his own views. At heart he wanted to belong; and the more he felt himself to be an outsider, someone uncommon in his emotional detachment, the more he wished to be part of the 'family' that was the army. Whatever Liddell Hart may have felt about Bernard's failure to be a natural leader at this time, Bernard himself had no such qualms. He was confident that in battle he had a cooler, clearer mind than most, and in peace the ability to impart his tactical doctrine in a way that every officer and soldier could understand. He had preached celibacy to his students in an effort to make them under-

[1] Brian Montgomery, op. cit.
[2] Ibid.

stand that soldiering was a vocation, not a pastime. But in his own case he had already proved his dedication. He felt ready now to share his life with someone else and to know the pride of possession, to have a spouse.

That his first choice should have fallen on the virgin child of an Indian Civil Service official should not, therefore, surprise us – though it undoubtedly caused consternation in his family. But had his own father not fallen in love with a fourteen-year-old virgin when in his thirties? And his grandfather before him?

Yet Betty Anderson had the honesty and courage to reject him; and Bernard respected her for that. Moreover the emotional detachment that made him so different from his fellow men now came to his aid. The hopes which he had vested in Betty Anderson he repressed as quickly as he had allowed them to surface. He had hoped to return to his regiment a settled, married man – in triumph, after ten years' distinguished service on the general staff. Instead he returned the same inveterate bachelor, but with outspoken views now on tactical instruction: and a quite radical proposal for Company training.

CHAPTER THREE

Company Commander

Just how much Bernard did to prepare for his return to the 1st Battalion of the Royal Warwicks in March 1925 is evidenced by the largely handwritten 'Diary of Training' kept by Commanders of 'A' Company between 1924 and 1928, and which still survives.[1]

Romance had obviously not dulled Bernard's dedication to his profession; indeed it seems to have heightened it. No record of training had been kept by the Company since Major Tomes left it in the early autumn of 1924. Moreover, in February 1925 there had been the upheaval of the 1st Battalion's move from its Chatham barracks back to Shorncliffe – Bernard's station of pre-ways days. Far from feeling disappointed by his return to the same command he had held over a decade previously, Bernard was evidently excited at the prospect of company command after so many years serving as a staff officer; and when he reported for duty at the Napier barracks in the second week of March 1925 he had already worked out a plan for Company training covering every day from 18 March to the beginning of August. By 12 March the plan was finalised to the point where it could be printed and staple-bound. 'The idea that we aim at is that by the end of Company Training every officer, NCO and man will have a clear idea of the action of his unit in each of the various operations of war,' he declared in his preface.

There had never been anything like it in the Royal Warwicks before; and Major-General R. C. Macdonald vividly remembered, more than fifty years later, the impact that Bernard's arrival had on the battalion, commanded by his father, Colonel C. R. Macdonald.

> I can remember Monty coming to the battalion in 1925 and spending about a year with us at Shorncliffe. Even in those days everybody recognized the fact that he would probably go to the top of his profession – a rare bird in that he was a chap who was not only very astute himself – but he'd really studied the business of soldiering, which not many people did in those days – not in the dedicated sense . . .'[2]

[1] It was purloined and auctioned anonymously in 1978, when it was purchased by the Imperial War Museum.
[2] Major-General R. C. Macdonald, interview of 24.4.78.

Bernard's quasi-messianic return, armed with his four-month proposals for Company training, might well have caused uproar in such a traditional infantry regiment not desperately anxious to prepare itself for imminent hostilities. Fortunately the CO, in the words of his son, 'recognized the fact that he was himself lacking in tactical ability having spent the whole war in New Zealand. He was therefore glad to have Monty, and so handed over the training to him.[1]

Thus from the beginning Bernard's Company training was intended to provide a model for the rest of the battalion; and on 18 March 1925 at 8.45 a.m. it began. There was to be little or no drill. As soon as the elementary principles of infantry tactics had been explained, the Company was to start practising: use of ground and cover, field signals, fire orders, battle formations, platoon tactics, patrolling, night operations, withdrawal, attack, defence, co-operation with the air force, field engineering, support by tanks, etc. It was an ambitious programme that brought consternation in the officers' mess when it was revealed. At that time pains were taken only to ensure good hunting in the area; few wished to be reminded of the realities of war after the devastations of the last one. 'There was much opposition in the mess to Bernard's attitude,' Brian Montgomery later chronicled, 'and I recall witnessing some bitter slanging matches, with few holds barred.'[2]

It was not only in the mess that Bernard Montgomery encountered opposition. The preparation of such an ambitious course required a great deal of paperwork; but when Bernard approached the temporary Adjutant, Captain Gething, for a Second-in-Command to deal with this, Gething was adamant.

'We haven't got any second-in-commands, Sir. We haven't got enough officers to go round – you know that!'

'Oh – I'm tactics, I'm not in administration. I'm tactics, I can't do all this administration. I must have someone: Second-in-Command, Administration,' Monty demanded.

'I said. "A good Company Commander would do both!"

' "Um!" he said – and went out, slamming the door,' Gething recounted later.[3]

Worse still, once the programme began on 18 March, Bernard discovered that two of his four platoons had no officer to command them, so that he and his deputy, Captain Swinhoe, had to give extra help to the NCOs running Platoons 3 and 4, as well as conducting the training course.

Not that Bernard minded. He was in his element wherever there was a job to be done; and there can be little doubt, however

[1] Ibid.
[2] Brian Montgomery, op. cit.
[3] Colonel P. J. Gething, loc. cit.

unpopular he made himself in some quarters by his uncompromis-
ing professionalism in peacetime, he was sowing the seeds of his
own future greatness as a Commander. For it was now, in the spring
of 1925, that he realised how important it was for a Commander to
get himself across to his NCOs and thus his troops.

> The instructions given by the NCOs commanding No. 3 and No. 4
> Platoons left much to be desired,

he recorded at the end of the first day of Company training; and he
made his object, in himself taking command of one of the platoons,

> to teach the NCOs concerned how to impart instruction and train
> their platoons. Before returning to Barracks ¼ hours' map reading
> was done with the NCOs. They were taught how to set a map; to
> locate their own position; and how to identify distant objects on
> the ground and on the map. They displayed a great lack of
> knowledge of this subject, and much attention will have to be
> given to it in the future.[1]

Thus Gething's obstruction – 'we were like cats with our claws out
at this time,' Gething remembered[2] – served a useful purpose; and
the thirty-seven-year-old Brevet-Major Montgomery recognised that
it was not simply by autocratic rule and printed programmes that he
would achieve his military ambitions, but by learning how to put
himself across in person to his NCOs and men. It was not for nothing
he would one day be known as the 'People's General'. Ten years of
staff duties and study had given him a clear idea of the sort of army
Britain should have. Though he had congratulated Liddell Hart on
his 'Model Army' article, he did not really agree with Hart's emphasis on armour. In the end, he felt, all wars become a confrontation
between infantry – and the training of this infantry, its ability to
move with cohesion, and to co-operate with artillery, tanks, engineers and aircraft, would determine the outcome. Bernard would
never really depart from this view – though he did become converted to the idea of specialised armoured spearheads – the *corps de
chasse*. However it was only in the intimate conditions of Company
command in 1925 that Bernard recognised the cardinal importance of
putting over his vision not only to the officers below him, but to the
NCOs and men.

What had started as a model exercise in how to plan and carry out
Company tactical instruction for the whole battalion thus became a
two-way process. It was not an easy time; not would anyone pretend

---

[1] Diary of Training, 'A' Company, 1st Bn Royal Warwickshire Regt, 1924–8,
IWM.
[2] Loc. cit.

that Bernard was well suited to the miniature conditions of Company life. Even command of a battalion was, in the words of his successor as CO, too small a unit for Bernard. His sights, his horizons, were on grander things and no doubt his subordinates and regimental colleagues felt this; felt a natural unwillingness to serve as pawns in the Brevet-Major's bid for greatness.

Yet at the same time it was recognised that Bernard's zeal was not wholly egotistical. 'Underneath, as I learned, he was bloody good,' Gething later acknowledged. The over-zealous instruction might be resented at a time of hunting and enthusiasm for sports; but it would never be forgotten. One of Bernard's platoon commanders, Lieutenant G. C. Evans, was a typical example – a man who came to hate Bernard so deeply that he divorced himself entirely from the Regimental Association in later years, and would have nothing to do with Bernard's biography; yet who was to rise to great distinction in the Burmese 14th Army, eventually commanding an Army himself.

There is, thus, something moving and historic in Bernard's 'A' Company Training Diary in the spring and summer of 1925 as he stood down to the level of Platoon Commander. In the ensuing years he would come to command every unit of the British Army from a platoon to a Group of Armies involving more than two million men. It would be a slow, often laborious progress, and it would need the ultimate catalyst of war before Bernard would inspire anything approaching popularity amongst the majority of his subordinates; but no other Commander would ever follow such a linear path to greatness. If he was finally to earn a place in 'the hearts of men' it would not be from natural gifts of dignity or avuncular concern for men's welfare, but from a sheer professionalism that had had no equal in the British Army since Wellington. His doctrine of command would remain largely the same, from platoon instruction to the handling of whole armies. As his wartime Chief-of-Staff would later put it[1], he had a vision of what an Army should be that put him head and shoulders above any contemporary: an Army in which every man would know his place, his duty, and what was expected of him.

Meanwhile, already on Day 13 of Bernard's 'A' Company programme, word of this extraordinary approach to training had reached the Commander of the 10th Infantry Brigade, to which the 1st Battalion of the Royal Warwickshires belonged; and on 30 March the Brigadier came with his Brigade-Major to see for himself, as Bernard took 'A' Company on a six-mile cross-country simulation of Advanced Guard tactics, complete with Lewis Guns. 'It was a considerable test,' Bernard noted in the diary that night, 'and the men were rather exhausted after it, but they enjoyed the novelty of it. The movement was quite well carried out.'

Every evening Bernard discussed the day's performance with his

[1] De Guingand, *From Brass Hat to Bowler Hat*, op. cit.

officers, NCOs and men, before explaining what was to be undertaken the following morning. By 31 March 1925, he could write that he was 'satisfied with the results we have obtained' – as well he might. The diary alone was a model in how to chart the training of a Company.

The ripples of Bernard's programme began to spread, unbeknown to Bernard who kept his eyes firmly on the job in hand. He would allow no one to obstruct him in this; and, when Gething refused him a train ticket to Seaford to see how one of his platoons was managing in a TA camp there, he simply took his own car. When in May he took the Company out on mock defence and attack operations, he organised not only an RAF officer to be attached for a week, but a section of Pack Artillery too. 'The operation was witnessed by the Bde Comdr, Bde-Major, CO, 2nd i/c,' he noted in the Company diary on 6 May. Real artillery shells were fired, and the platoon practised closing up 'as close to possible to the artillery fire before it lifted'. He got the Commanding Officer of the local 5th Battery, Lt-Colonel Bartholomew, to give a further demonstration the next day, followed by a lecture and 'many questions' being asked by the NCOs and men. The next day No. 2 Squadron of the RAF gave a demonstration 'showing the various ways in which aircraft can cooperate with infantry in war'. Night operations followed that and, on 13 May, a 'scheme involving field entrenching, carried out in co-operation with 9th Field Company RE.'

The scenario Bernard wrote to lend realism to this latter scheme makes interesting reading today: for here, in the relative peace and security of post-war England, Bernard pictured the precise duties he himself would have to assume a decade and a half later.

Southland, an overseas power, declared war on England on 1st May 1925.

Since the Great War of 1914–1918, England has been occupied with large agricultural schemes, to the detriment of armaments. The Prime Minister was a naturalized Welshman, and under his guidance the Army & Navy had been reduced to dangerously low limits. The Army, though small, was, however, well trained.

Southland, on the other hand, possessed a large army which was well equipped with the most modern inventions. She also had a powerful fleet.

It was realized by the English C-in-C that with the forces at his disposal he would be unable to prevent hostile landings until such time as new armies could be raised and trained.

Orders were therefore issued for a network of defences to be constructed in depth in the vicinity of the most likely landing places. The role of the garrisons of these places was to offer determined resistance to enemy movement inland, and to fight stubborn rearguard actions.

In accordance with these orders, work on defensive positions was commenced early in May by the garrison of Shorncliffe . . .

By June Bernard's Company had been chosen to give an eight-day series of demonstrations to the Cambridge University Officer Training Corps; and in July Bernard arranged with the Small Arms School at Hythe for his Company to be allowed to train there in battle practice using live ammunition – a salutary lesson, since many of the 'little details learnt in section training' were forgotten, as the men seemed mesmerised by the reality of genuine fire-power.

Undoubtedly, in these Company exercises planned and commanded by Bernard himself, the foundations were laid for the wartime exercises he would conduct both before and after his return from Dunkirk.

By the beginning of August 1925, Bernard's reputation was beginning to snowball. He was asked to send a platoon of his Company to Shoreham to give another series of demonstrations – this time to the 132nd Infantry Brigade (TA). It was strange to think that Bernard was still only a Captain and Brevet-Major: but in July the War Office was at last constrained to offer Bernard promotion to full majority – in another regiment.

It appeared that from 22 April a vacancy had existed for a major in the East Lancashire Regiment, which had furnished a battalion in Bernard's 17th Infantry Brigade in Ireland. Promotion had been first offered to a senior Captain in the Somerset Light Infantry, but he declined; and the vacancy was then offered to Bernard on 16 July by the Military Secretary.

Despite his great exertions in 'A' Company, Bernard did some careful sounding.

Napier Barracks,
Shorncliffe,
Kent
18.7.25

Dear General,

It is most kind of you to offer me promotion into the East Lancashire Regt. I feel, however, that I would be acting unwisely if I accepted it. Of the majors in my own Regiment, Sydenham goes for age in September next and Filsall has just sent his papers in to retire on 1st January. His papers have not, of course, reached you yet. So I shall be promoted in my own Regiment by January next at the latest. Another point is that the youngest major in my own Regiment is 43. Therefore in 7 years time they will all have gone for age, except the two COs, and I work out that I shall come up for command in nine years, i.e. 1934, unless of course someone is brought in. I should then be 46.

In the East Lancashire Regiment the majors are much younger and I work out that I should never get command, as it would not come my way for fourteen years when I should be over age. This is of course assuming that all the majors are suitable candidates for command, and I must work on this assumption.

To sum up. Provided I keep alive and reasonably efficient I shall get promoted in my own regiment in January next and have a good chance of being considered for command in nine years time.

If I were some way down the list of Captains it would of course be quite a different matter.

So if you do not mind I will not accept your very kind offer.

Yours sincerely

B. L. Montgomery[1]

Bernard's caution proved salutary; in less than a week the War Office had Major Sydenham's retirement papers out and was offering Bernard promotion, as he predicted, within his own Regiment. Thus, on 26 July 1925, Bernard was at last promoted to the substantive rank of Major, to his own satisfaction and the delight of his family. Moreover, two days later, unaware that they had just promoted him to full major, the War Office Staff Department again had Bernard's papers out. A certain Brevet Lt-Colonel Haining was completing his tour of duty as instructor at the Staff College, Camberley at the end of the year: and at a Staff Conference on 28 July it was decided that Brevet-Major B. L. Montgomery should succeed him for a three-year term of office. Sir Charles Harington had done Bernard proud in his Confidential Report the previous October, and the War Office was evidently guided by his wise suggestion:

An officer of very marked ability. An excellent instructor and lecturer – a student of his profession – considerably above average in professional ability and knowledge – recommended for Instructor at the Staff College.

At last, after so much unstinting effort, Bernard's talents were being rewarded. At the Staff College he would be instructing alongside such officers as Alan Brooke and Bernard Paget. It would be a chance to step outside the petty jealousies and obstructionism of regimental soldiering and to put over his tactical doctrine to a large body of students. Moreover he would probably be given brevet promotion to Lt-Colonel.

Though the news must have excited Bernard he was too good a soldier to show it. On 1 August he took his Company to its demonstration at Shoreham, and thereafter, on 23 August, to Cow Down Camp, near Winchester, for the annual battalion, brigade and di-

---

[1] B. L. Montgomery, Personal File, Ministry of Defence.

visional training, followed by a special Naval Staff Course on 15 September (for which he had been selected early in July by the War Office), and Army manoeuvres from 22 to 24 September. In all these he appears to have performed with cool efficiency – as his successor as Battalion CO recollected more than half a century later. Captain Duke was then serving on the staff in Northern England, but in order to keep in touch with the regiment Duke came down to watch the manoeuvres. Hearing of this Bernard invited him to share his tent and witness a dawn attack he was going to lead early the next morning. The invitation was in increasingly typical style for Bernard – a mixture of peremptoriness and charm.

Monty said to me: Tonight we've got a night show. We're going out to do an attack at dawn. Now I've got a bivouack that takes two – so you'd better come with me!

Duke – tall, handsome and with impeccable manners – did not demur.

Whether Monty slept or not, I don't know. We got up in the middle of the night and stood to in a lane, ready to attack at dawn.
The attack took place across an open field, in which stood a number of stooks. Monty was commanding a Company and took up his headquarters behind one of the stooks; the Company was deployed behind other stooks.
To my surprise I found he had trained his Company Sergeant-Major to take down messages quickly; and runners were soon sent off very gallantly across the ground . . .
Monty was very orderly; it all worked very quietly. Of course the Army was very skeleton in those days: a platoon was four tiny sections, often with just two or three men and of course no radio.[1]

When the Battalion returned to barracks at Shorncliffe Bernard relinquished command of 'A' Company – not, as one might assume, to prepare himself for his three-year instructorship, but to inaugurate his latest innovation in the regiment: a Battalion Training Cadre, comprising the best NCOs who, after due preparation in October, would then instruct the rest of the battalion in weapon handling as well as Section Leader training.[2]
It seemed as if the indefatigable Major would not let go his grip until the day he left – an impression confirmed by the seemingly apocryphal but well-authenticated story of the Christmas tattoo at Shorncliffe.

[1] Brigadier J. P. Duke, interview of 17.8.78.
[2] The following spring Captain Ozanne, now commanding 'A' Company, paid tribute to this innovation, recording in the Company diary: 'The most marked thing was the knowledge [of] the young NCOs. This was entirely due to the good work done by them during the winter period of Section Leader Training.' Loc. cit.

'We were staging a tattoo on the Leas at Folkestone,' Lt-Colonel Gething remembered,

> before the days of the Aldershot Tattoo. We were doing an attack on a native village. I was to be in charge of the natives. Then the Army was to come in and with machine-guns see us off.
> One day in the mess Monty said to my Company Commander, Major Filsell, 'Oh, what about this tattoo?'
> 'What about the tattoo?' Filsell replied.
> 'Well, we had a meeting about 3 weeks ago and I've heard nothing more. What's happening, what are we doing?'
> Well, Monty wasn't due to take part, except in the march past. So Filsell said:
> 'We don't all talk about our work, Monty, you know.'
> 'Oh – well, anything I can do to help – I'm only too pleased to!'
> Filsell looked at him and said: 'Well, I'll tell you what you can do, Monty. When we first go on, the limelight comes on from both sides of the arena. Don't you rush in front and take the salute!'[1]

Whatever Bernard's colleagues felt about him, however, no Company Commander ever displayed the same brilliance at tactical training in the regiment, and the principles laid down during his time there were to last long after his departure to the Staff College.

The appointment at Camberley, Bernard felt, 'put a hallmark on my Army career' – so much so, in fact, that Bernard now went back on his word to his mother. To Maud he had written that he accepted Betty Anderson's verdict; but he had not. Or rather, he felt circumstances had altered since the spring. He was now a substantive Major, with a guarantee of accelerated brevet promotion to Lt-Colonel as an Instructor at the Staff College. His posting there would last three years, and he would be given a house if he wished. Without informing anyone he bought a ticket to Lenk in Switzerland, where he knew the Anderson family was staying with a party of largely Indian Civil Servants and their children. Bernard was no womaniser; but he had reached the age of thirty-eight and was at last firmly established on the ladder to success. He had, he must have felt, every right to expect an even more favourable response from the parents of Betty Anderson. And who knew? Perhaps even the eyes of the blonde young eighteen-year-old herself might now be turned, if not by his advances, then by his advancement.

[1] Colonel P. J. Gething, loc. cit.

CHAPTER FOUR

Instructor in Love

The trip to Switzerland was futile. Betty's mind was made up; and nothing that the serious, beaky-nosed Major said or did could change it.

The Andersons' party was lodged in the Wildstrubel Hotel, at which Bernard too had chosen to stay. Through the Andersons Bernard was, however, introduced to other members of the party, including Sir Edward and Lady Crowe, and the daughter of Robert Hobart, a distinguished Indian Civil Servant who had died in 1910. She was short, vivacious, far from beautiful, but popular: a widow with two children aged eleven and thirteen. Her husband had been the son of a rich Lancashire cotton mill owner, but had enlisted on the outbreak of war and was killed at Gallipoli. Bernard found her company congenial. She was the same age as he, an artist in her own right, painting in oil and watercolour, and keen on sculpture. She lived in Chiswick, not far from where the Montgomerys had once lived, came also of Irish stock, and was one of a large family. Her younger brother Stanley had attended the Staff College, Camberley with Bernard in 1920; but it was chiefly to her elder brother Percy – or Patrick as he was commonly called – that Betty was devoted: a brilliant army officer now transferred to the Royal Tank Corps and an Instructor at the Staff College, Quetta.

For the moment, Bernard's relationship with Hobart's sister, Mrs Carver, was merely friendly. Rejected by Betty Anderson, Bernard threw himself into winter sports and spent much of his time helping the various children to master their skis and skates. Then the party broke up and returned to England; the children to boarding school, Betty to Chiswick, and Bernard to his new teaching post at Camberley.

Exactly twenty years before, Bernard had attended the Royal Military College at Sandhurst. Now, from 23 January 1926, he was an Instructor at its sister institution, beyond the trees and tennis courts. He felt it was up to him to 'seize the opportunity with both hands and turn it to good advantage'. It was an 'opportunity for three years of hard study; I knew enough by then to realise that the teacher learns much more than his students'.[1]

[1] Bernard Montgomery, *Memoirs*, op. cit.

This was no idle boast. As his succession of articles on the history of tactics in the regimental magazine *Antelope* had shown, Bernard was increasingly anxious to study the past and draw lessons for the future. He was already corresponding with many of the progressive military thinkers of his day – Maxse, Lindsay, Liddell Hart – and the Staff College was to add a further field. Bernard was by no means academic, and his interest in history was never scholarly. Yet he would become perhaps the most outstanding lecturer on tactics of the inter-war period, both at Camberley and later at Quetta, so that one must ask how this could be so. He himself referred to his approach as 'one of common sense'; but it was clearly more than that. As could be seen in his letters from the Western Front, Bernard already possessed an almost child-like talent for clear and logical exposition, and there can be little doubt he would have succeeded in any profession for that gift alone.

Common sense and a gift for clarification mixed, too, with a third element: ambition. Whatever the psychological motivation for this – and there were obviously many, from infancy onwards – it was not something easily assuaged or which would ever wane. As a result he was permanently alert, tense, and inclined to be bossy. To what extent Bernard was aware of this, it is difficult to say; but what is interesting is that, unlike certain other ambitious luminaries of his age, he evidently accepted the need to temper this ambition, and to balance it. Thus while men like Gort went to the top without having truly mastered their profession; while 'Boney' Fuller, Bernard's brilliant colleague as Instructor at the Staff College, Camberley, would become a black-shirt fascist; while Liddell Hart would become a self-appointed military prophet and, for a time, a dangerously volatile *éminence grise* behind the Secretary of State for War before being dismissed by *The Times*; and while Patrick Hobart, one of the pioneers of the Royal Tank Corps, would be sacked on the eve of the war for irascible pig-headedness and insubordination, Bernard managed – just – to contain his ambition, to subordinate it always to the task in hand; to achieve success not by blindly pursuing his ultimate goal but, having identified it, by being prepared painstakingly to master every step and every facet of his profession on the tedious peacetime path towards it.

Nor was this search for balance religiously inspired – since on Brian Montgomery's testimony we know that Bernard was currently going through an almost agnostic stage in his life when he rarely went to church and could find no faith in God. Yet his faith would, in time, return; and the balance he sought was akin to religion in its self-discipline and humility. Despite the murder of his cousin and the loss of much of the Montgomery estate, he had accepted the expediency of withdrawal from Ireland. In the last of his articles on tactics for the *Antelope* in January 1926, he took very much a questioning stance over the development of tank warfare. 'The present tank is too expensive to produce in large numbers,' he acknowledged; but, if they were produced, 'it will be for consideration whether infantry can still be called the chief arm, the arm which in the end wins the battle. It seems that the time is coming when the tanks will be the assault arm of the army, the artillery will be the arm which makes the assault possible, and the infantry the arm which occupies the conquered area.

'Some hard and clear thinking will be required before we are finally settled on the right road . . . In studying a subject of this nature one naturally is influenced by one's practical experience of war, but it must always be remembered that practical experience in itself is of little use unless it forms the basis of reflection and thought.'

At Camberley Bernard devoted himself to such reflection; and it was at this turning-point in his life that he conceived a lasting admiration for one of the senior Instructors, Colonel Alan Brooke.

Brooke was an artillery officer and, like Dill and Wavell, tipped in many quarters as a future CIGS. Three years older than Bernard, he had ended the Great War as a Brevet-Colonel with two DSOs and a reputation as an expert in the technique of rolling artillery barrages. He had been brought up in France until the age of eighteen, was dedicated to the business of soldiering to the exclusion of all else, and possessed a keen, incisive mind. Hitherto, Bernard's horizons had been limited by his tasks – at least since the Great War – which had been entirely confined to infantry service. Now, at the Staff College, he found himself at the very centre of the debate over the future role of armour – a debate in which Brooke held the strongest views. Later on, Brooke would command the first Mobile Division in the British Army, as well as holding infantry and artillery commands. It would not be an exaggeration to say that Bernard stood in awe of Brooke from the moment they met – an awe that never diminished to the day Brooke died. Sternness such as Maud Montgomery had shown all Bernard's childhood and youth was something Bernard was bound to respect: and Brooke was a stern, demanding taskmaster. Moreover, Brooke's ability to take the larger view in discussions without sacrificing decisiveness made Bernard feel small by comparison – the more so since Brooke seemed so devastatingly aware of the failings and inadequacies of his subordinates. However, Brooke could be appreciative too. He had become Director of Studies the year before, in 1925; he appears to have taken Bernard under his wing, and introduced him to the wider horizons of larger-scale tactical exercises without troops. Here the lack of actual tanks or armoured units was of no consequence – indeed it was a positive benefit in instruction – since Brooke felt that modern cavalrymen or commanders of armoured units must be trained to command infantry and other arms as well as tanks, and vice versa, just as he, an artilleryman, had accepted that he must master infantry and armoured warfare in order to merit full command. When Bernard complained almost seventeen years later that his armoured generals were too specialised and did not know how to handle their infantry units, Brooke reminded him of this:

I am in entire agreement with you that Corps Commanders must be able to command both infantry and armoured Divisions,

he wrote on 22 June 1943.

I have *always* supported this, and I think if you look back in your memory you will find that I told you this was necessary at the Staff College Exercises I ran before you had ever handled any armour. It is a fundamental doctrine which I have gone for from the start, and fought against much opposition on the part of the Armoured Corps!

Whether Bernard remembered or not, his involvement in the debate on armour is demonstrated by the fact that, in the autumn number of the *Antelope* having already finished his series on tactics, he returned to the question – which, in the cheese-paring financial climate of the latter 1920s, had become very much a choice between tanks and mobile troops. 'Some Problems of Mechanicalization' was only an outline sketch of the subject – but in it Bernard managed at least to give the *coup de grâce* to horses and cavalry. 'If one thinks it out,' he wrote disarmingly, 'gas alone will completely drive the horse from the battlefield; his complete disappearance will not come just yet, probably not for many years, but it must come in the end.'

If Bernard was overawed by his Director of Studies, though, it does not seem to have affected his own performance as a lecturer. The days of 1920 when he could mock the Staff College establishment were over; with Brooke, Franklyn, Paget, Lindsell, Pownall and the other instructors[1] he approached the course with humility now and all the professionalism he could muster. Among the students he would teach in the ensuing three years were many of the most outstanding generals of the next war: from Alexander to Miles Dempsey, from Oliver Leese to Archie Nye, John Harding, Gerald Templer, Humphrey Gale, John Kennedy and Richard McCreery.[2] There is no doubt that Bernard greatly enjoyed his time there. He was already a master of the sand-table and an imaginative presenter of tactical problems. Furthermore he liked lecturing – liked the lime-light and the rapt attention of a hall full of aspiring students of

[1] Brooke left in 1927, while Lt-Colonels Giffard and O'Connor joined the staff as instructors.

[2] Other students included Sandy Galloway, Eric Dorman-Smith, 'Bubbles' Barker, D. N. Wimberley, V. C. Russell, G. C. Bucknall, J. F. Whiteley, E. H. Barker, R. Lockhart, C. Nicholson and A. F. Christison.

warfare. Other lecturers might show greater rhetoric or range of imagination; but Bernard was intent upon dispersing the fog of war, on seeing that his students master the essential techniques of command, planning and organisation before embarking on hare-brained attempts at originality. To Liddell Hart he had already explained his belief in teaching to a norm in the first instance – and he was uncompromisingly forthright with those students, like Dorman-Smith, who allowed cleverness to precede thoroughness. To another student – a future Field-Marshal – he remarked, when the latter gave his solution to a military problem Bernard had set: 'Ah, that's interesting, very interesting. It would end in only one way: a scene of intense military confusion.'[1] This determination to keep things simple would be one of his chief claims to greatness in the ensuing war; but it was not always appreciated in peacetime, when there was no fog to disperse, and Bernard probably made as many enemies as he did converts. One poor student received the sum of nought for a military paper, out of 500 possible marks. When Bernard was asked how the student could have done so badly, he answered: 'Quite simple. It says clearly that you are not to write in the margin. This student wrote in the margin. If he can't obey a simple instruction like that, he's not fit to command others.'[2]

From the beginning of his instructorship in 1926, then, Bernard's reputation grew. He had, after all, been coaching students wishing to enter the College since 1922, and his experience as Brigade-Major (for which post the College attempted in the first instance to educate its students) was distinguished, both in war and peace. The only area in which he could be said to be deficient, perhaps, was the social arena. Yet here, too, he had done his best to overcome his shyness; and towards the end of the year he made arrangements to travel once again to Lenk in Switzerland.

This second trip, in January 1927, was to have far-reaching repercussions. He had accepted Betty Anderson's implicit verdict; and, had it not been for the year's interval, one might have thought Bernard's subsequent courtship of Mrs Carver to be love on the rebound. If it was, then one can only marvel at Bernard's luck – for in Betty Carver he was to find a genuine happiness and emotional fulfilment that had eluded him for some thirty-nine years. One might well say that if the Staff College instructorship had put a hallmark on Bernard's military career, then his growing love for Betty Carver was to put a hallmark on his personal life. A certain Claude Auchinleck had married, at the age of thirty-six, a beautiful twenty-one-year-old while at the Staff College, Camberley, – a marriage that was to come to grief in the most humiliating way for Auchinleck; Gort, too, had married a twenty-year-old beauty while trying to enter the Staff

[1] Michael Carver, *Harding of Petherton*, London 1978.
[2] Colonel John Carver, interview of 3.3.78.

College – a marriage which also came apart in unseemly circumstances. It is not wholly unreasonable to ask whether, had Bernard's pursuit of Betty Anderson proved successful, he would have been able to keep her. The army, as Bernard had always reiterated to his disciples at Devonport and York, was too hard a taskmaster for the genuine devotee: marriage and military ambition did not mix.

What happened, then, on Bernard's second trip to Lenk in January 1927? According to Betty Carver's eldest son John, there was already 'something up' between Bernard and his mother. Though Bernard had never singled her out on the first trip, he had got to know her quite well, and questioned her closely on her 'chateau' in Chiswick, near his own old home. As far as John – who was in his second year at Charterhouse School – was aware, there was no meeting between Bernard and Betty in 1926; but:

> come summer of that year [1926] we came to the conclusion that there was something up, because there was always a financial crisis of one sort or another, and we never had any money, and my mother said:
> 'You liked Switzerland very much, didn't you?'
> We said: 'Yes!'
> And she said: 'Well, I think we ought to go back to Lenk again. But if we're going to afford to do this you'll have to fork out some of your savings.' (A lot of the money she had was for us, in trust, you see.)
> So we all agreed to this. In fact we thought it was tremendous. It never occurred to us that there was any ulterior motive, because we wanted to go anyway, we were very keen. But it occurred to me later there might have been an ulterior motive!

This time there was no big party: only the Crowes were there again; and Bernard. Whether it had been so arranged by correspondence between Betty and Bernard is not known. Possibly it was organised by 'mutual friends' such as the Crowes; but the inference is that Betty Carver was just as anxious to see Bernard again as Bernard was to see her. Certainly this would explain the speed of their romance after a year's separation. Moreover the legend that Bernard wooed Betty through the children is somewhat fanciful, it would seem.

> The theory is that he approached through us; but I don't think this is absolutely true . . . That year we did see much more of him,

John Carver remembered,

> but this was because the year before we had this gang of people and didn't really get involved. He certainly took some interest and said Come on, let's go and have a ski, and that sort of thing, but not more.[1]

[1] Ibid.

John's brother Dick had a similar recollection:

> At that age one thought this was a nice friend who was great fun;
> but it was a great shock when they declared they were going to get
> married![1]

Unfortunately, owing to the bombing of all Bernard's and Betty's
personal possessions in Portsmouth during the Second World War,
none of their private correspondence has survived; and a number of
fallacies have arisen about Betty and her relationship with Bernard –
such as the belief that Betty was a confirmed pacifist and that the
relationship was thus an unlikely one.

In fact Betty Carver, née Hobart, was very far from being a pacifist.
Like Bernard, her family came from Ireland, though it was believed
to be descended from the Hobarts of Blickling, Norfolk. Betty's
father, Robert Hobart, came from Southern Ireland and, like Bernard's grandfather, had entered the Indian Civil Service as a young
man. Having achieved a certain success by his forties he married a
seventeen-year-old girl from Northern Ireland, Janetta Stanley from
Dungannon, County Tyrone. It was, as Betty's son John later put it,
an almost identical family to the Montgomerys in its Irishness, its
size, the age difference of the parents, the dominance of the mother
(a strict Calvinist), and the pattern of the children entering either the
ICS or the Services. Charles, the eldest, went out to India as a Civil
Servant; Frank, the second son, went into the Navy; while Percy or
'Patrick' became a redoubtable army officer, attending the Staff
College, Camberley, the year before Bernard, in 1919, and Stanley
the same year as Bernard, in 1920.

Betty Hobart was born seven years after Patrick and, like Bernard
and his sister Una, they were very close in childhood. While Patrick
went to the RMA in Woolwich – the 'shop' – and thence to India as a
Sapper, Betty Hobart was sent to a finishing school in Lausanne,
where she made friends with Alison Carver.

Alison's father was a rich cotton magnate; he owned his own mill,
was said to be worth a quarter of a million, and kept twenty hunters
in his stables. In due course Betty was invited to stay with the
Carvers at their country seat in Cheshire. Alison's two brothers had
both entered the mill. One of these brothers was Waldo Carver: a
brilliant and handsome boy who had started rowing when at Cambridge and within four years was representing his country at the
Olympic Games. Though Betty Hobart was very far from being a
beauty, she evidently made up for this by her personality; she and
Waldo fell deeply in love.

Curiously it was not opposition from the rich Carvers which
threatened the prospect of marriage, but the prejudice then rife in

---

[1] Colonel R. O. H. Carver, interview of 17.2.78.

'professional' families about 'marrying into trade'. 'You cannot imagine the opposition there was in those days,' Betty told John, her son, later: 'the feeling that the Hobarts would thereby demean themselves.' In the end Betty's father was only persuaded to give his consent on payment of the 'most enormous marriage settlement'[1] – a fortunate agreement, since Robert Hobart, exhausted by his years in India, and only recently retired from the ICS, died only a few days before the couple were united in 1910.

From letters of Betty's that still exist it was no superficial attraction which brought them together. Betty's nature was generous and good, she had a profoundly artistic temperament, and a certain lack of emotional inhibition which endeared her to people. When Waldo was killed, her grief-stricken letter to her mother-in-law was almost incoherent; and, according to her son John, it was to take a long time before she got over it. For a while she lived with her mother-in-law in Cheshire, together with her two small children and nanny; but they did not get on well, she felt trapped and soon moved down to London where she did war work, riding her controversial motor cycle and sidecar, in which passengers travelled 'at their peril', John remembered.

After the war Betty made a number of not altogether successful attempts to achieve personal and financial independence. She took a job as an Art and English mistress at a preparatory school in Norfolk so that her two children, John and Dick, could be with her; the headmaster importuned her and she left after only a term. In the end she decided to enrol at the Slade as a student, under the famous Professor Tonks; and thus began her initiation into the artistic and bohemian world of London.

However, it was through her military brother Patrick, ironically, that Betty came to meet the Herberts, and settle down in Chiswick. Patrick was a great friend of Alan Herbert, a witty and successful young lawyer who had written one of the most moving and poignant novels about the Great War – *The Secret Battle* – a novel which Bernard Montgomery later considered 'the best story of front-line war I have ever read'.[2] The Herberts lived by the Thames at Chiswick; and Gwen Herbert took such a liking to the young widowed sister of Patrick that she offered her a house they owned in a neighbouring street, off Chiswick Mall.

Gwen Herbert still remembered this period clearly when in her eighties. Her husband Alan reckoned that Colonel Hobart was destined to achieve great things in the army, for he had a fascinating and forceful mind, and was interested in as many things outside army life as in it. Betty, by contrast, was quieter and less forceful, though gay and lively in company, trusting and loyal in friendship.

[1] Colonel John Carver, loc. cit.
[2] Letter to Sir Alan Herbert, 27.8.69.

Because the Herberts too had children, they began to spend holidays together in Cornwall where Betty started to paint seriously.

It was in the spring of 1927 that the Herberts caught the first whiff of Betty's romance. Betty called by one morning to return something. After a while, seeing that Betty was becoming nervous, if not agitated, Gwen said:

'Betty, what on earth's the matter?

'I must go,' Betty blushed. 'There's someone waiting in the car.'

'Well, for heaven's sake, bring him in!' Gwen insisted. But Betty shook her head.

'Oh, no, I couldn't do that – he's far too shy!' she answered.[1]

In the end, however, the Herberts did meet Bernard. Did they think the match a strange one? Lady Herbert recollected that they did, not for any spurious pacifism on Betty's part, since she was never that, but because they found Bernard so unremarkable. If he had achieved a certain reputation in the Army, it had not filtered through to the world outside. Besides, his tactical doctrines, so carefully thought out and incomparably presented, made little sense to an outside world that wished largely to forget about war. Patrick Hobart was an exception because he was such an outspoken personality, and held such futuristic ideas about warfare – ideas which had a certain panache and meaning to a layman; whereas Bernard's theories of tactical balance, of training and disposition, of prodding to find the enemy's weak spots and only then concentrating a local superiority in firepower, had little romantic appeal beyond the readers of the *Antelope* and the lower echelons of the Staff College. That Bernard had read widely in military literature was of scant importance in the cultured circles which the Herberts frequented; and, when Betty finally announced one day that she had become engaged, Gwen assumed that it was because she was lonely and wanted someone to help in bringing up her now teenage boys – a 'firm' hand.

Possibly there was some truth in this. Even Betty's younger son, Dick, later acknowledged that it was a 'very brave thing' for Bernard to do, taking on a widow with two children.[2] At any rate the boys took a somewhat materialistic point of view when the engagement was announced. 'Hurrah,' they shouted, 'we'll have a car at last!'[3]

When reminded of this by his wife, John Carver agreed that it was so: but his recollection of the actual car is revealing. 'Monty used to have an old *Belsize* – a wonderful thing. We thought this was marvellous. One of the greatest proofs of his love was that he allowed my mother to drive it – which was horrifying actually!'

Whatever the Herberts' feelings – and one is always protective, if

[1] Lady Herbert, interview of 1.12.77.
[2] Colonel R. O. H. Carver, interview of 17.2.78.
[3] Jocelyn Carver, interview of 3.3.78.

not envious when one's relatives or friends become attached elsewhere – there could be no denying the genuineness of Bernard and Betty's feelings for each other. For Betty, ruled in childhood by her strict, Puritan mother and deprived first of her father and then, after only five years of marriage, of her beloved Waldo, there was a certain relief in finding a man who, by his willingness to shoulder responsibility, acted as a surrogate father to her: loyal, devoted, tender, an enjoyable companion, and fatherly too towards her two sons. Moreover, if he was considered by some to be eccentric, he was far less so than her brother Patrick.

But, if Bernard was this to Betty, how much more was she to him! Approaching forty, rejected by the only girl to whom he had ever proposed, aware that he was talented and even, possibly, called upon to achieve great things in the course of time; yet lonely, often yearning to show love, to find a mother who would accept him . . . It is easy to show how, as the months went by, Bernard began to recognise that this was a much deeper and more fated relationship than ever his amour for Miss Anderson had been. To him Betty Anderson had been an ideal, a challenge, a stimulus to open up his heart and trust, with the promise of her beauty; whereas Betty Carver was undoubtedly real, a mature woman in flesh and blood, sensitive, talented artistically, a joy to be with. Had Miss Anderson said yes to his proposal, Bernard might have spent his life attempting to impress her, as he had done with his mother; whereas with Betty he was able, it seems, to attain a naturalness, a relaxed and yet excited happiness that came almost unexpectedly in his life: something God-given and which undoubtedly restored his faith in the Almighty.

So it would seem. Only Liddell Hart, in the years to come, would ever dispute the impression that Bernard and Betty formed an almost idyllic couple.

'You are a bully, Monty, a born bully. You bullied your wife unmercifully, as you bullied everyone else!' he once taunted Bernard, towards the end of his life, when staying as his guest at Bournemouth.

Bernard went pale and his face sharpened.

'Don't you ever mention Betty!' he rapped. 'Don't you ever mention her name!'

Liddell Hart was no one to talk – he who, as Sir Edgar Williams once observed, would drop his fork at a buffet meal and expect his wife to retrieve it rather than interrupt his own conversation with another man. But was there any truth in Liddell Hart's allegation? Very possibly there was – though it was a truth which Liddell Hart himself did not perceive: namely that, in falling in love with Bernard, Betty was in fact to some degree attracted by the bully in him. Such a syndrome is well known among the various patterns of human affection – and there is little doubt that Bernard's later ability to command the loyalties and affections of subordinates, particularly those young men on his more intimate personal staff, was due to this – magnified by his growing fame and rank.

In the case of Betty, however, one witnesses a much earlier and more feminine version of this. Betty, above all, was an instinctive soul – it was what endeared her to people and propelled her to paint; moreover, aged by grief and the task of bringing up two bright and relatively spoiled boys, she was maternal in a way that her friends, such as the Herberts, did not perhaps perceive. In Bernard they saw a nobody: a small, rather sharp-featured little major who was quite unread and who was shy and withdrawn in their company; whereas in Betty they saw a gifted, sensitive woman who ought by rights to be the wife of an artist. And in her brother Patrick they saw a future Army Commander: a character, a visionary about whom one might write articles and books.

It is a tribute, surely, to Betty's profundity and insight that she saw better than they: perceived in the quiet, unimposing major with the high voice and the habit of tugging his ear a genius that surpassed her own, and even her brother Patrick. Years before she had written that a woman 'is essentially the sensitive transparent globe into which man pours the riches of his originality'.[1] For Betty, any creative achievement by a woman was only a reflection, a reproduction of the creativity she absorbed from man: and in Bernard she recognised that man.

It was, to be sure, a very different love from the one she had shared with Waldo; but no less important to her for that. Indeed it was probably deeper and richer for the very experience she now had of life and of death. If her friends felt, privately, that Bernard was no match for her, it does not seem to have inhibited Betty in the least. Instinct told her she had found the right man: a man whose genius perhaps she alone, outside the army, recognised and who, despite his rather bossy ways, she could love and . . . mother? They began to meet more and more frequently in the spring of 1927, yet still he did not propose – so that, in the end, it became somewhat embarrassing, and Betty's brother Patrick pressed her to force Bernard to 'declare his intentions'.[2] This Betty was too shy to do. Meanwhile Bernard, seemingly oblivious to this, went in mid-April on a very spartan bicycling tour of the Great War battlefields, taking with him his brother Brian and three other subalterns from the 1st Battalion of the Royal Warwickshire Regiment.

The journey was planned to cover Ostend, Ypres, Tournai, Mons, Le Cateau, Lille, Armentières, and back via Ypres and Ostend: the last journey Bernard would make as a bachelor, aged thirty-nine.

[1] Quoted in a letter from Patrick to his sister Betty in K. Macksey, *Armoured Crusader*, London 1967.
[2] Colonel John Carver, loc. cit.

They sailed from Dover on 19 April 1927, armed with a 'laissez-passer' from the French and Belgian Ambassadors, their five bikes and kit. Bernard had obtained funds for the trip from the Eastern Command Army Training Grant, and at every battlefield he would stop, give a lecture on what had taken place there, and ask each subaltern how, with modern fire power, the battle could be re-fought.

What Bernard had not bargained for, however, were the bureaucratic obstacles to making such a 300-mile journey on two wheels. In the event the four young lieutenants were astonished not so much by Bernard's tactical instruction on the old battlefields, as by his bluff and bravado whenever confronted by a problem. From the day they landed at Ostend and were faced by a 'full blown Private of the Belgian Army, who appeared more or less in command of the show', Bernard demonstrated the art of surprise. 'Flourishing the "laissez-passer" in his face, Col. Montgomery shook him warmly by the hand and addressed him as "Monsieur le Colonel". This pleased him so much that he conducted us through the customs without any questions or searching of kit,' Lieutenant Poole recorded later.[1] A passing barge was prevailed upon by Bernard to give the five war historians a lift back to Mons on 21 April, and the following day Bernard brazened their way across the Franco-Belgian frontier at Malplaquet by pretending that Lieutenant Bowly's Cyclist Touring Club ticket was a Customs ticket. At Le Cateau there was more trouble in putting the bikes on the train to Lille, as they were not labelled. 'Colonel Montgomery happened to have a label on his bike, on which was written in large letters 'Southern Railway – Charing Cross to Folkestone Central'. He showed this to an official who appeared to be perfectly satisfied, and from that time onwards all was easy!'

Bernard's study tour ended on 27 April 1927; and, while the subalterns returned to Shorncliffe, Bernard put his bicycle on the train for Charing Cross and then Camberley; whence he resumed his friendship with Mrs Carver as before.

In his *Memoirs* Bernard wrote that he had fallen in love with Betty Carver already at Lenk in January 1927; why then did it take him so long to 'pop the question'? Was it shyness that prevented him? Or unwillingness to risk a second rejection? Or was he unsure whether he could take on a widow with two teenage children?

Very likely it was none of these; was simply Bernard's natural recoil from emotional 'scenes'. This utter detachment or imperturba-bility made him an ideal officer in war or action; but it did impair his performance as a suitor. In the case of Betty Anderson he had cast caution aside and immediately proposed to her, as well as asking her parents. But Miss Anderson was a girl, a child still, without the

---

[1] The *Antelope*, July and October 1927.

191

emotional and even sexual overtones implicit in a woman – particularly a woman who had been married and had two children.

Thus Bernard courted Betty – yet never discussed the possibility of marriage until the day, at Easter 1927, when Betty suggested they drive together from Hindhead to Charterhouse to look at her son John's school. John and Dick were told to busy themselves elsewhere while Bernard and Betty approached the fives courts. Betty's brother had continued to chide her, and the tension was increased by Patrick's own domestic situation. Like Bernard, Patrick Hobart had assumed for many years that he would remain a bachelor, wedded to the army. In his nephew John Carver's words, 'Uncle P – as we called him – reckoned he was going to become a Field-Marshal, and there was a tacit understanding that later on my mother would keep house for him. I mean this was seriously considered.'

According to Hobart's biographer, Kenneth Macksey, however, Hobart had in fact already begun his controversial affair with Dorothea Chater early in 1927 – controversial in that Chater had originally been a brother officer of Hobart's in the Royal Engineers; and the War Office was even prompted to promulgate an edict threatening to call for the resignation of any officer who 'disrupted' the marriage of a brother officer in the same regiment. Fortunately Hobart had transferred to the Royal Tank Corps; but knowing that Dorothea was going to divorce Chater to marry him may have made Hobart particularly concerned for his sister, who would now no longer be needed to keep house for him.

Bernard often told the story of his engagement – for his sense of humour was always stimulated by the incongruities of life: and the fives court of Charterhouse seemed to him an incongruous place to have to propose! But Betty, feeling perhaps that people were beginning to gossip about them, suggested they ought to stop seeing each other at least for a while. And Bernard, who ought to have told her this much sooner, argued with her, finally expostulating: 'Don't be silly, Betty – I love you.' Betty began to cry; and to Bernard's intense relief, it was decided. 'That finished it,' he related, 'We were engaged!'[1]

Betty's younger son took the news badly when the boys burst into the fives courts, impatient to know 'what was going on.' Dick had looked upon Montgomery as a friend – but not as a father. 'I was shocked and upset,' he confessed later. 'It had never occurred to me they might get married.'[2]

Possibly for this reason Betty asked Bernard not to rush a public announcement. The Montgomerys were informed, the Carver boys returned to school and only on 25 June 1927 did a formal announcement appear in *The Times*:

[1] Brian Montgomery op. cit. and Lady Olive Hamilton, personal recollection, May 1978.
[2] Interview of 18.9.80.

192

LIEUTENANT-COLONEL B. L. MONTGOMERY AND MRS.
CARVER
The marriage arranged between Lieutenant-Colonel B. L. Mont-
gomery, DSO, of the Staff College, Camberley, and Mrs E. A.
Carver of 2, Riverside, Chiswick Mall, London W4 will take place
very quietly in London on July 27.

Bernard and Betty were happy, the boys could boast at last of a car;
and a new chapter commenced in Bernard's life.

CHAPTER FIVE

Marriage and Authorship

The wedding was to take place in the parish church, Chiswick, a few doors from Betty's house on the Mall. Bishop Montgomery, Bernard's father, was to officiate, assisted by Colin Montgomery, Bernard's younger brother who was now a curate near Gravesend, also on the river Thames. The tidal race of life had now swept Bernard, the most difficult of the Bishop's sons, into matrimony, and the family rejoiced. Yet, if they thought that in getting married Bernard would now settle down into a more docile approach to life, they were very mistaken – a fact aptly demonstrated when, to the consternation of the family, Bernard drove Betty off after the service on 27 July 1927 with barely time for goodbyes to be said, let alone the expected reception.

It is tempting to see in this the first spark of Bernard's later rejection of his family (particularly his mother); but it is unlikely. On the contrary, Bernard's marriage brought him in many ways closer to the Montgomerys; and in the ensuing years they would spend many of their holidays in Ireland at New Park. For the moment, however, they drove to Church Stretton in Shropshire for a few days – days so etched with happiness as they played golf together and read James Stephens's *Crock of Gold* in the evenings that Bernard would insist on his stepson John doing the same when he got married some eleven years later. The happy couple then returned to London to check the boys were in good hands (they were to go to New Park in August); and continued their honeymoon where their romance had started, in Switzerland.

In marrying Betty, Bernard had promised to bring up her two boys. He was as good as his word; and from the moment he and Betty returned from their honeymoon the new Montgomery family, with its two Carver sons, came into existence.

Whatever feelings of tenderness Bernard had for Betty, love could not alter what was now ingrained in his character: a concern with order that amounted to an obsession. Thus, once the 'shock' of their parents' marriage had worn off, the two boys found themselves leading a very different life in the school holidays. Gone was the old chaos in which Betty had run domestic affairs. From now on Bernard took charge of everything. When Bernard's sister Winsome met

Betty for the first time in Ireland and asked how she was coping with being married to Bernard, Betty replied: 'It's absolute bliss after ten years battling with two small boys and bringing them up.' And she added, with a laugh: 'But I've had to give up many of my own ideas – he even engages the servants!'[1]

There was no doubt that, when he did something, Bernard did it properly. Thrilled with his new-found wife, Bernard proceeded to cosset and protect Betty from all the domestic chaos and responsibilities he thought were weighing on her, insisting she must have plenty of time to paint and to be herself – evidently an attempt to reverse the humanly-crippling role his own mother Maud had had to play in her marriage. This could have been a trial to Betty; but fortunately she saw it for what it was: an essentially lonely, pathologically over-controlled man's version of love and tenderness. In time Bernard would do the same with David, his own beloved son, around whom he cast a protective and blindly possessive net. Yet in Betty, Bernard had met his match. On the surface she appeared to give in to his militaristic rule, his passion for planning, and soon elicited the love and respect of the entire Montgomery family. 'She just fitted in with us, you see,' Winsome recorded later. 'She was a darling, and my mother adored her – we all loved her, for she made Bernard so transparently happy.'[2] However, it was not really as simple as that. Betty was actually 'a bit chary' of Bernard's mother, as Dick Carver, Betty's second son, later recalled. Though Bernard's arrival heralded 'a complete change at home . . . he took over everything . . . he couldn't bear to see anything that wasn't well run, efficiently run according to his ideas, so he ran the whole place according to military principles, on military lines', it was far from anathema to Dick's mother, 'who was terribly disorganized really and artistic, and was only too glad to let him'. Morever in matters of any real importance it was Betty's will that prevailed. Bernard might say no to her in public: but once she tackled him 'in camera', so to speak, she always had her way. 'They were indeed complete opposites in character,' Dick acknowledged, but it was 'an attraction of opposites, and there was no doubt how deeply Monty was in love with my mother'. According to Dick, neither really understood the other's world; and perhaps they respected each other so profoundly because of that, because there was and could be no rivalry, no difference of opinion in spheres so alien to each other. To which one might add that this attraction of opposites must have represented, for each of them, the attraction of areas they denied in themselves. Just as Betty's very bohemianism betrayed a certain need for order, so too Bernard's total self-discipline belied a yearning for disorder, for the unplanned, for naked emotion. 'He was at heart a romantic,' Dick Carver later declared.

[1] Lady Michelmore, interview of 10.4.78.
[2] Ibid.

195

Even the children, irritated at first by Bernard's authoritarian home-management, and his inability to admit that he was ever wrong, accepted that he was doing his best. Not only that, but accepted that this 'best' really was a product of his love for their mother. 'Everyone sympathized with my mother,' Dick remembered, 'for there was no doubt that Monty was a very difficult person, and they used to ask "How do you do it?" But we managed.'[1]

'Naturally there was a slight uphill struggle,' John Carver commented on Bernard's assumption of paternity, 'because we'd been very spoilt and hadn't had any male discipline at all. "Discipline at home" was a great cry – of which there hadn't been any, to be more or less honest. So naturally there was a certain amount of resistance to this, but it went well . . . the family existed as a unit at this period.' In fact the family existed in a more coherent way, with more opportunities for the children to be with their mother and enjoy themselves during the holidays, than ever before. 'Monty organized riding for us on the Sandhurst horses. There was also a lake on which we could take out a boat, and a swimming pool about fifty yards from the Staff College bungalow in which we lived. There were woods for bicycling and walking – compared with where we'd been before we were very well placed,' John remarked.[2]

For his part, Bernard tried hard to fit into Betty's world, just as she was doing for him. He religiously allowed himself to be introduced to her 'bohemian' friends, sat silently while they talked of art and lacerated one another's works and reputations – though he was not perhaps as shy as some have made out. If he found Alan Herbert a 'bit daunting' at first, and the atmosphere in the Chiswick salons '*un peu formidable*', he was not entirely lost for words. When asked what he made of Eric Kennington, then a rather celebrated draughtsman, he remarked with mock seriousness: 'Dreadful fella! Eats peas off his knife' – which was taken as rather a witty *bon mot* that exactly captured Kennington's genuine shyness and lack of ease.[3]

There was no doubt, too, that Betty's 'strange' assembly of friends helped to bring Bernard out of his severely military world at just the right moment in his career, when he was employed as a college instructor and was already reflecting deeply on the nature and history of war; moreover there is little question but that Bernard's later encouragement of good company in his Tactical HQ even in the midst of historic battles went back to his earlier time with Betty. However he might deprecate her friends afterwards in conversation, he enjoyed meeting them, and was certainly not blinkered as regards their talents, however little he could understand them as artists – a

[1] Colonel R. O. H. Carver, loc. cit.
[2] Colonel John Carver, loc. cit.
[3] Ibid.

fact which may go some way towards explaining his almost unique willingness, in the British Army, to employ talented 'amateur' soldiers during the ensuing war. He was, in fact, developing an 'eye' for character and ability that would stand him in good stead over the years; and the very brilliance of some of Betty's circle – such as Augustus John, A. P. Herbert, and Jack Squire – must have made Bernard doubly aware of the dullness and stupidity of many of his army colleagues. From this moment, at least, he began to develop an uncomfortably outspoken tongue, a certainly delight in flouting senseless convention, and in upsetting the complacent. His stepson Dick remembers quite clearly the pleasure with which he would walk across forbidden lawns at Sandhurst, beside the Staff College – he who laid down such strict laws about behaviour and domestic management at home. Or later, when watching a passing-out parade at the RMA at Woolwich, Betty commented that the cadet receiving the Sword of Honour would surely become a general. Bernard caused extreme embarrassment, by remarking loudly: 'What? You'll never hear of him again, never hear of him again!' – silenced only by the cadet's mother turning round in the front row and glaring at him.[1]

Bernard's rivalry with his new brother-in-law Patrick Hobart certainly knew no bounds – and did not abate until the war when, having taken all the honours, Bernard could afford to be gracious. 'Mother gave a priceless description at this period,' John Carver later recalled, 'with their horns locked. They were giving Uncle P. a lift in Monty's car, and Uncle P. was saying, "It's very stuffy in here, we want the window open, let in some air." Monty said "My car-windows stay shut!" This childish argument went on throughout the whole journey, neither giving an inch – neither at all used, in fact, to not having their wishes respected.'[2]

Nor was Bernard's rivalry confined to Betty's brother Patrick. About Frank, Betty's naval brother, Bernard was humorously cutting – delivering himself of the ridiculously amusing remark 'no good will come of wearing elastic-sided boots in Piccadilly' – a reference no doubt to naval officers' penchant for such footwear![3]

Renewed professional confidence came, it would seem, as well as happiness. This time, at Christmas 1927, instead of going out to Switzerland a lonely bachelor in search of company, 'we went out as a family,' John Carver remembered. Betty was 'desperately sick' on the way – though this time it was not just from the sea journey. Bernard fussed over her like a hen; no need went unanswered, no whim unfulfilled: for Betty was going to bear him a child. She was no longer young – she was forty – and had to be careful. The following

[1] Colonel R. O. H. Carver, loc. cit.
[2] Colonel John Carver, loc. cit.
[3] Ibid.

summer, on 18 August, Betty gave birth to a boy in their bungalow at Camberley, attended by numerous nurses and doctors. Although, as Bernard later wrote, 'she was never very strong afterwards', this was no impediment to their life together – perhaps the opposite. Bernard's mother had refused to let Bernard spoil her; had given his gifts to charity and spurned his gestures of affection – 'brushed him off,' as Winsome put it. Betty did not. 'It had never before seemed possible that such love and affection could exist,' Bernard afterwards related. 'We went everywhere, and did everything, together.' A nanny was engaged for baby David, and Bernard's pride knew no bounds.

Yet the birth of an own son does not seem to have diminished Bernard's sense of responsibility towards his stepsons. As Christmas 1928 approached, Bernard declared: ' "These boys must keep up their skiing." And so my mother was left behind with the baby, while Monty took us to Lenk. My mother agreed this was a good thing to do,' John Carver later recalled.

'We all three shared a room – and all the beds were in one line. I can remember this very clearly.'

'You see, Monty was kind to you,' remarked Mrs Carver.

'Oh, I know. In fact he was absolutely anchored to us – because there was nobody else in the hostelry! We all ploughed up the mountain every day. Funnily enough the thing I can remember him saying is: "You boys are very uncivilized. You must stand up to use a chamber-pot, you mustn't kneel down!" The thing was, we'd never been brought up with a father to tell us these things.'[1]

As always, the day was planned in advance. 'Things didn't always pan out quite as expected,' Dick Carver later recollected, 'and we did rather pull his leg about this.'[2]

'Keep to your own partums' was a constant injunction, reflecting his almost obsessive tidiness; but, equally, he was determined they should enjoy themselves. 'He was a rather cautious skier, but he fancied himself somewhat as a skater, at which he was very good, particularly waltzing on ice. He also loved music hall songs,' Dick recalled, quoting Bernard's favourite limerick:

> There was a young curate of Kidderminster
> Who very severely chid-a-spinster
> When she on the ice
> Used words far from nice
> When he quite accidentally slid-against her!

The holiday was indeed memorable for the boys. It was also a chance for Bernard to get away from England and reflect on his career

[1] Ibid.
[2] Colonel R. O. H. Carver, loc. cit.

perhaps – for at the end of 1928 his three-year term of office as a lecturer at the Staff College came to an end. The previous January Bernard had been promoted Brevet Lt-Colonel in recognition of his services; but when, in the summer, the War Office came to consider what post to offer Bernard after the Staff College, there was nothing suitable. Whether Bernard turned down any possible postings is not known – he certainly did in the ensuing years. At any rate, after four months of thought on the matter, the Military Secretary decided to send him back to his regiment. The Royal Warwicks had meanwhile moved from Shorncliffe to Woking where, at Inkerman Barracks, they were commanded by Bernard's old colleague and friend, Clement Tomes. Brevet Lt-Colonel Montgomery's appointment at the Staff College ceased, nominally, on 21 January 1929; he was granted a further month's leave, and reported for duty once again as a company commander in the 1st Battalion at the Inkerman Barracks on 21 February. Unfortunately there was no real company for him to command.

Since the war he had been holding all sorts of responsible staff appointments, teacher at the Staff College and so on,

Brigadier Tomes later recalled.

I felt a bit diffident in only being able to give him the HQ Company to command, i.e. Band and Drums, signallers, clerks and so on to look after. I need not have worried. He was just as efficient and enthusiastic over such jobs as he was over more abstruse military problems. The Band and Drums were hustled as never before and he got going a special room for the boys, a thing which was badly needed.[1]

Bernard's prediction that it would be another five years before he would be eligible for command of the regiment looked, however, like being sadly correct; so that when, in the summer of 1929, word came from the War Office that they would like Bernard to become Secretary of a committee to revise the *Infantry Training Manual*, Volume II, Bernard leaped at the opportunity.

Here, at last, was a chance to revise the pamphlets, booklets, and lectures he had given since the war in Ireland in a new form that would, if well done, become official army doctrine for the next five years at least. Thus Brevet Lt-Colonel Montgomery was temporarily removed from the regiment to become an 'attached' officer at the War Office for six months, from 15 October 1929, at the special salary of an additional five shillings per day.

[1] 'Monty' – an unpublished memoir by Brigadier Clement Tomes, 1958, communicated to author by Lt-Colonel L. T. Tomes, 14.3.78.

Bernard's revision of the *Infantry Training Manual* was to be his one and only appointment in the War Office before he became head of the British Army some seventeen years later; but in fact most of his work was done at home, in Inkerman Barracks where he lived with Betty, baby David, and his two stepsons when they came back from school.

The *Manual* had had a chequered career as regards its previous authorship. Liddell Hart had been responsible for much of the 1921 edition, and Viscount Gort had prepared the 1926 publication. However Bernard, it would seem, consulted no one in the initial preparation of his draft. He reckoned he probably possessed better experience in producing such training manuals than any other officer in the British Army. His brief, as he put it the next year to Liddell Hart, was to assembly 'a complete handbook on tactics for the regimental officer, regular and territorial', and he was determined to do precisely that. 'I decided to make the book a comprehensive treatise on war for the infantry officer,' he wrote later in his *Memoirs*. 'The book when published was considered excellent, especially by its author.'

However, it was not quite so straightforward. Bernard, rather like his father at the SPG, was nominally only the Secretary of a War Office committee which included the General Officer Commanding, Aldershot Command, Sir David Campbell. When Bernard showed his draft to the committee, there were 'heated arguments'. Numerous amendments were made, which Bernard would not accept. They went through the manual chapter by chapter; but Bernard thought their criticisms were 'nit picking' ones, and the committee 'ga-ga'. The fault was not entirely one-sided. If the *Manual* was to be 'official', it must reflect War Office rather than personal views – something Bernard was not willing to consider. The terms of reference were for a handbook on tactics; Bernard took this in its broadest sense and desired it to be a treatise on war. The twain would not meet and, when the six months were up, there was no agreement. Bernard then produced a master-stroke. He suggested the committee should be disbanded, and he would complete the manuscript in his own unpaid time, incorporating their amendments. Weary of arguing and aware of the cost-consciousness in the War Office, the committee agreed.

As Bernard wrote in his *Memoirs*, this was the signal for Nelsonian tactics: 'I produced the final draft, omitting all the amendments the committee had put forward.'

This was largely true – though fame and fortune made Bernard exaggerate, as he would over future battles of a more deadly kind. A letter addressed to Liddell Hart from the Inkerman Barracks in September 1930 gives a much more revealing idea of Bernard's essential carefulness, and plasticity. The draft Bernard produced in his own time was sent by Campbell's BGS Brigadier Bertie Fisher, to

Liddell Hart for his comments. Although Liddell Hart pretended to objectivity, he was inevitably biased, since he himself had done so much work on the 1921 edition – an edition that was heavily amended by the War Office, and much altered by Gort. Though Liddell Hart praised certain sections, his essential verdict was a 'thumbs-down'. He acknowledged that Bernard had reduced 'some of the superfluous verbiage' of the previous volume, but felt it was written for too high a level of officer – 'brigade or battalion commander' – rather than the 'company and platoon commander – who really needs its guidance'. In particular Liddell Hart bewailed the omission of exploitation in attack: 'It drops out the passages which explained exactly how reserves could exploit weak points and be passed through to "expand the torrent." '[1]

Here was the crux of their differences – both at this time and in the historical arguments that blossomed after the next war. Ever since Liddell Hart had overcome his innocent belief in the Higher Staff in 1916, he looked for a theory that would breach the stalemate of trench warfare. This, for him, was Exploitation; a theory at first based on infantry break-through, and later adapted to mean armoured break-through supported by infantry. Surprise, the exploitation of weak spots, the break-through: these were the principles which, increasingly, Liddell Hart felt would bring victory in future warfare; and which he consolidated in his unofficial primer, *The Future of Infantry*, published in 1931.

Bernard, attracted as he was by such ideas, disagreed; and the disagreement was fundamental to Bernard's personality as well as to his military philosophy. Liddell Hart and the cohorts of modern warfare enthusiasts had a vision of how future battles should be conducted and felt the army must simply be trained to suit it; whereas Bernard cautious and experienced, worked from the opposite end of the military spectrum, beginning with the common soldier, and working upwards through the NCOs to the subalterns, company commanders, battalion and brigade officers. Out of this human material one must make an army that was secure in defence and successful in attack. Since the mid-twenties Bernard had become increasingly aware of the potential of the tank, as his *Antelope* articles showed; and in the *Infantry Training Manual* he acknowledged that there would be cases where tanks would be used as the primary arm of assault, instead of serving as infantry support. This, however, was as far as he would go – and for Liddell Hart it was not far enough. Yet when Liddell Hart sent his comments to Campbell and Fisher, Bernard was the very model of tact. 'Bertie Fisher showed me some notes you had made of IT Vol II,' he wrote to Liddell Hart on 5 September 1930. 'They have been most helpful to me and I have taken on all the more important ones and made the necessary

[1] Liddell Hart Papers.

alterations in the draft. Thank you very much for the trouble you took over it.'[1] Bertie Fisher was similarly won over by Bernard, after 'a long talk', Bernard promising to incorporate Liddell Hart's points in the final proof. Thus quietened, Liddell Hart returned to his other preoccupations, and the *Manual* went to press without Liddell Hart seeing it again. Not unnaturally he was disappointed when, the following year, he received the published version. At the bottom of Brigadier Fisher's letter assuring him his suggestions would be incorporated, Liddell Hart later penned: 'But when the new manual was published it became evident that the "expanding torrent" method of exploiting a penetration had not been adequately emphasized, or grasped, by Montgomery.'[2]

By then, however, Bernard was over two thousand miles from the scene of the crime, and nothing could be done. Besides, the general reception given to the new *Training Manual* was favourable, as Liddell Hart had enviously to acknowledge. He had criticised Bernard's English in his notes; but in fact Bernard's style of presentation was remarkable for its clarity and freshness – whereas Liddell Hart's was notable for the opposite. In a 'Brief Analysis' which he wrote in 1931 of the new Manual, Liddell Hart kept his objections to a more formal level, regretting Bernard's omissions and claiming that the Manual was written from a 'divisional commander's' standpoint[3] – which was something of a back-handed compliment, since Bernard had never actually commanded anything higher than a Company in the field.

Whatever the criticisms from outside, Bernard had reason to be proud of his work – the literary seal to his three years at the Staff College, Camberley. On 10 July 1930 he was again posted back to his regiment – where within a matter of weeks he became Second-in-Command to Lt-Colonel Tomes, who was due to leave the 1st Battalion at the end of the year to take up an appointment in the War Office.

Flushed with success at getting his own way over the *Training Manual*, and confident that he would succeed Tomes as Commanding Officer of the battalion, Bernard was irrepressible. He gave a party at his house for the young officers of the regiment and their friends, which his brother Brian, a subaltern on leave from East Africa, well remembered. 'I shall always recall,' Brian wrote later, 'how some of those present found it rather disconcerting when, not infrequently, he climbed on to a table and, in ringing tones, gave everyone orders to "change partners,"'[4] – orders the poor subalterns dared not disobey.

At Moville, in the summer that year, Bernard was much the same;

[1] Ibid.
[2] Ibid.
[3] Ibid.
[4] Brian Montgomery, op. cit.

family and guests would come down to breakfast after chapel in the morning to find Bernard's 'Orders of the Day' pinned to the dining-room door. This renascent bossiness did not always find favour, however, as when Bernard ordered the gardener at New Park to cut down the ivy in front of the window. Unfortunately Lady Montgomery had given specific orders that the ivy was *not* to be cut down, and, as John Carver remembered later, there was a great row. 'You've no right to do that!' declared Lady Montgomery. 'No right at all – it's my house. 'Well, I was getting rather blinded, you see,' said Bernard, rather apologetically – though, as John recalled, he was absolutely determined to get his own way.[1]

There were similar contretemps in the regiment, too, Brigadier Tomes later recorded. Though Bernard was a 'very loyal and efficient' Second-in-Command, he could cause problems too. The trouble was that

> Aldershot Command continually demanded him for such jobs as umpire or as a staff officer on schemes. In this he did not always please. I well remember one infuriated General coming to my HQ on a scheme and demanding the blood of 'that blasted little pipsqueak – Montgomery!'[2]

However loyal Bernard was to Lt-Colonel Tomes, he was becoming so distinguished in his way that it was hard at times for him to avoid the impression that he already commanded the 1st Battalion that autumn. The Machine-Gun Company Commander was Captain G. R. H. Bailey; reminiscing at the end of his life he said he thought Bernard came straight from the *Infantry Training Manual* to command the battalion, without in fact serving as Second-in-Command at all.

Part of the reason for this was the hectic activity at the Inkerman Barracks, Woking; after many years at home the time had now come for the 1st Battalion, the Royal Warwickshire Regiment to serve overseas. Moascar was actually announced, but then altered in favour of Palestine – and Bishop Montgomery was delighted to hear his third son would be taking a battalion of his regiment to the Holy Land.

Betty, too, was delighted, though because her eldest son John was seriously ill she would have to follow later. Christmas was spent, as usual, with her sister-in-law Alison, the wife of the Dean of Canterbury, Dick Sheppard; and early in January 1931 the 1st Battalion, Royal Warwicks set sail from Southampton, bound for Port Said, whence they would travel by train to Jerusalem. Clement Tomes, Betty and baby David waved goodbye from the quay as Her Majesty's Troopship *Neuralia* drew away, and Lt-Colonel Montgomery

[1] Colonel John Carver, loc. cit.
[2] Brigadier Clement Tomes, loc. cit.

– his rank made substantive on 17 January 1931 – took formal command of a battalion for the first time since the autumn of 1919, more than a decade before.

CHAPTER SIX

Officer Commanding, the Holy Land

No man ever becomes Colonel of a regular army battalion without inculcating a certain reputation for himself that goes down in regimental history. Such a Colonel is, after all, the 'father' of an immense family, numbering almost a thousand men at full establishment; and, though the Colonel may go, the Battalion remains, with its memories and legends.

In Bernard's case, his custodianship of the 1st Battalion, the Royal Warwickshire Regiment, has not gone down in history with the same éclat or success as has his later career. Liddell Hart even went so far as to write, in his *Memoirs*: 'When he was eventually given command of a battalion, after sixteen years on the staff, he brought it to the verge of mutiny by misjudged handling.'[1] Bernard's brother Brian denied this; but, though an officer of the regiment, Brian was serving in East Africa at the time, and thus had no more personal knowledge than Liddell Hart.

To find the truth one must really go to those who served in the 1st Battalion of the regiment during this period, however distorted their evidence may have become over the passage of almost half a century. Was Bernard really such an unpopular commander? Did he really drive the battalion to the 'verge of mutiny'? And what was his 'misjudged handling'?

According to Colonel Pat Burge, who was then a platoon commander in the 1st Battalion and has since reflected on the inter-war era, there was no doubt that regimental morale and ceremonial pride suffered a great blow when Bernard took over command in January 1931; but that the fault was not entirely Bernard's.[2]

The 1st Battalion, the Royal Warwickshire Regiment, had been extremely lucky in its COs since the Great War. Colonel C. R. Macdonald, who had been Bernard's first Company Commander, was the soul of honesty and discretion – and a friend so greatly respected by Bernard that he would do everything to help and sponsor his son Ronald in the years to come. Lt-Colonel Tomes, who

---

[1] Op. cit.
[2] Colonel P. B. I. O. Burge, interview of 11.4.78.

succeeded Macdonald, was also a man of the highest principles, known as 'Old Smoulder' in the regiment owing to the eternal pipe in his mouth. Like Macdonald, Tomes drew respect by his quiet dignity and care. When junior subalterns found themselves learning drill with the lance-corporals under the RSM he would call them quietly into his office and ask them if they knew why they were doing such tedious square-bashing, having gained their first pip. 'To show *the men* you can do it,' he would point out gently.

Under Tomes the Battalion formed part of the Aldershot experimental brigade, with new company organisation and even mechanised carriers for its MG Company. Pat Burge felt it was distinctive for the courtesy and quiet efficiency of Tomes' leadership, with a strong body of warrant officers and a happy spirit throughout the Battalion, both in barracks and on exercises. 'All this was to change under Montgomery,' Burge recollected; and for a variety of reasons.

Firstly the Battalion was going abroad, after many happy years at home in an English setting, with all the social convenience this entailed, both for officers and men. Generally speaking, a tour of service overseas lasted twenty-one years for a battalion – so there was no prospect of an early return. Moreover it was traditional that the first station should last one year – and be a celibate one, without wives or families. (This did not mean that wives were not permitted – simply that the War Office would not pay for them to travel to or be lodged at a one-year station.)

Secondly, the whole composition of the Battalion was affected by the move, since the most experienced NCOs and men – those with two years or less to serve before retirement – were not sent out. However this did not apply to officers – and, in the testimony of more than one survivor, the Battalion was consequently not well enough officered for the demands and changes that were, after years of home service, now to be made. Because of the growing backlog in promotion, there were too many senior subalterns and captains who were unfitted for further promotion but who blocked the paths of junior and more energetic officers.

Thus a rather depleted Battalion containing about 400 young soldiers and a somewhat stagnant officer corps left Woking and Southampton for Palestine. Yet, to qualify for service overseas, the Battalion had to be made up to its full war establishment of about 950 officers and men. This was done at Port Said by taking a draft of young soldiers from the 2nd Battalion, returning from the Sudan after many years abroad. Not unnaturally these men had no desire to leave the 2nd Battalion or to continue to serve overseas. While the 1st Battalion had been kitted out in generally ill-fitting, standard-size brown drills, the draft from the 2nd Battalion had a very different appearance. 'Frankly we looked pretty beastly,' Burge remembered; 'whereas the draft from the Sudan arrived in tailor-made green suits and looked bloody good. At once there was a "them" and "us" atmosphere'.[1]

The task of welding these two drafts into a happy and efficient battalion was one that required great tact, understanding and firmness, Burge recalled. But before this draft had even arrived, Bernard had got off on the wrong foot, it would appear. Undistracted by wife or family, Bernard decided to use a new brush altogether in the Regiment. Instead of NCOs being promoted to Warrant Officer by long sevice, he decided to introduce a new system of promotion by merit. In this way the keener, younger NCOs would be encouraged to try harder, and the tone of the Battalion would not be levelled down. In fairness to Bernard, one must add that he began this new system with the best of motives – he firmly believed that battles would be won by the soldiers, led, trained and encouraged by the example of competent NCOs. Yet this new system backfired with unfortunate results for Battalion morale. Bernard consulted nobody in making his decision – 'and there was uproar in the Sergeants' Mess,' as a result of which 'a number of those sergeants have never been to a regimental reunion since,' Colonel Burge confided.[2]

It was this autocratic revolution – at a time when there were few promotions to be had in the regular army – which, much magnified, was evidently retailed to Liddell Hart.

Such is the memory of one impressionable young officer of the period. It is a subaltern's view, and is not supported by the testimony of Bernard's Machine-Gun Company Commander, Captain Bailey, who was stationed just outside Jaffa for the whole year in 1931. 'I just don't believe those stories that Monty was unpopular – I just don't believe there's a word of truth in it,' he protested, shortly before his death in 1978.[3] 'We had the greatest respect for Monty. Mark you, there were COs I had more affection for, let's be quite honest! But I liked Monty and I respected him and he was the finest trainer of troops I think I've ever met in my life.' Yet Bailey was, on his own admission, somewhat out on a limb in the sandy desert at Jaffa, and never went up at all to the Battalion barracks in Jerusalem. Nor were Bernard's abilities as a trainer of troops much in evidence in Palestine, owing to the dispersal of the various companies around the country, and the nature of their duties, which – as they had in Ireland in 1921 – kept the men at virtually permanent battle stations, without opportunity for battalion or even company training except in weaponry.

There is, however, a third view. Bernard never defended himself against Liddell Hart's judgement, nor did he even mention his experience of Palestine in his *Memoirs*. Yet, by the same chance that

[1] Ibid.
[2] Ibid.
[3] Major G. R. H. Bailey, interview of 8.3.78.

enabled his correspondence with his mother during the Great War to be preserved, so too a number of Bernard's letters to his mother from early 1931 were kept and have come to light in the same bound volume which he lodged with his private papers. From these letters we gain a very different picture from that of the battalion subaltern; and one that is much more in line with his previous image: namely an officer of great responsibility, with boundless self-confidence, a strong sense of humour and often surprising humility. What also emerges from these letters is that Bernard was in fact very rarely with his Battalion, and was acting as a virtual Brigadier, becoming on his arrival Officer Commanding all British troops in Palestine. Apart from his own Warwickshire battalion he had under command a battalion of the King's Own at Haifa; and, since the GOC troops in Egypt and Palestine (General Burnett-Stuart) was based in Cairo, Bernard acted as veritable Military Governor of the entire country, with the duty not only of commanding British troops in Palestine, but of meeting and maintaining contact with the foreign forces stationed in Syria, Transjordan and the Lebanon.

Owing to John Carver's illness it was arranged that Betty would join Bernard only in the summer of 1931. Thus for the first few months Bernard was a bachelor again, and the letters he wrote to his mother are couched in very much the same filial language as those from the Western Front.

'My darling Mother,' he wrote on 11 January 1931 from Mr R. Grossman's Hotel Tiberias,

> I am writing this in our hotel on the shores of the Lake of Galilee . . . Here it is quite hot and in summer must be very steamy. I was at Haifa last night, & inspected the garrison there this morning.
>
> Tomorrow I carry out inspections round here & to the north, and also see the Arab cavalry who garrison the Jordan valley. I have covered many miles by car since I have been out here & have been practically all over Palestine. It is very interesting but is hard work.
>
> Early next month I shall go up to Syria, to see the French general who commands there and discuss mutual problems with him. I shall see Beyrouth and Damascus and also want to inspect the Foreign Legion, of which they keep one Bn. in Syria.
>
> The hotel here is vile. No time for more.
>
> > Yr loving son
> > Bernard

It was evident that, right from the moment Bernard arrived in Palestine, he took his duties as Officer Commanding all troops in the country as his first priority. He had shipped out his own car for the purpose and was anxious to maintain good relations both with the French in Syria and the forces in Transjordan. One can understand that he did not in fact have much time to deal with internal Battalion affairs – and his next letter revealed that it was early February before he reached Jerusalem at all. The letter was dated 5 February 1931, and addressed from Talavera Barracks:

Life is very strenuous as I have taken over command of all the British troops in Palestine and have much work & travelling to do.

It is a wonderful place. In the new city and shopping areas outside the old walled city you have hotels that would not disgrace New York, & you can buy anything you want from a Singer sewing machine to a Rolls Royce car.

Then you go through the Jaffa Gate into the old walled city and you pass at once into an eastern city of 1000 years ago or more; little narrow streets, donkeys camels & humans all jostling each other, brilliant colours in the bazaars, & many smells. Parts of the walls are of Herod's time. I saw on Sunday the entrance gate to Pilate's hall, & the court-yard outside where the soldiers sat & played, & the paved street up which Jesus walked with his Cross. It is all underground as it has been excavated recently. But it is said to be the most authentic site in Palestine.

The Dome of the Rock (or Mosque of Omar) is really beautiful. And the view from the Mt of Olives across the garden of Gethsemane towards Jerusalem is wonderful.

I walked one evening from Jerusalem towards Bethlehem, & sat in the seat that Mrs Holman Hunt has put up in memory of her husband. It is on a little hill where you get the first view of Bethlehem as you go from Jerusalem. Rachel's tomb is just outside Bethlehem & I have visited that too . . .

All very interesting.

Yr loving son
Bernard

In some ways Palestine – especially the sea of Galilee – reminded Bernard 'very much of Ireland; the hills just now are very green & come right down to the shores of the lake,' he wrote at the end of February. 'In one month's time the whole place will be a mass of flowers.'

The style of these letters was sometimes as strangely unsophisticated – considering Bernard's rank and position – as those written when he was a Lieutenant in 1914. 'The view of Jerusalem from our camp is I think one of the finest views there is. It is even better,' he wrote to his mother, 'than the view from the Mt of Olives as you can see the Mt of Olives itself, which you cannot do if you are standing on it!' Schoolboyish but, as always, clear and unmistakable. Moreover the interest he took in his sightseeing was obviously genuine. The background of gospelling that had dominated his childhood and youth now began to make sense in a quite physical way, and there was a sense of almost childish excitement at this discovery. Relating his letter to a postcard he was sending, Bernard pointed out:

> The old Jerusalem of New Testament days was where I have shown it. The Dome of the Rock is as you see *above* it, and uphill from it, and the Temple and Holy of Holies was without question somewhere in that part. Hence you can understand the saying in the Bible 'Let us go *up* into the House of the Lord.' It was, in fact, up the hill.

This, and the long list of historic biblical names he had visited on his way to Haifa, prompted Bernard to remark that the Bible itself was really the best guide to this country.

The sight-seeing was, however, incidental to his real job; and early in March 1931 he wrote to say, 'My visit to Syria had to be postponed; things have looked rather troublesome in Palestine recently & the High Commissioner does not want me to leave the country just at present.' Nevertheless he managed to visit the great crusader castle at Acre – 'a perfect example of late 18th century fortress . . . The town has never been sacked or destroyed and is exactly the same as it was in the days of Richard Coeur de Lion in 1190 AD. I saw the place where Richard pitched his tent in 1190 and from the same place Napoleon directed operations when he besieged the town in 1799 AD.' Betty and David he hoped were now 'settled at Camberley & I hope they will stay there until they come out here'.

On 10 March Bernard gave his impressions of Bethlehem, which he had only just got to see properly. The Church of the Nativity 'is supposed to be the oldest church in the world; its date is 300 AD . . . The pathetic thing is that by the manger a policeman in uniform sits all day & night, his task being to stop fights and squabbles between the various religions when processions through the stable take place, and generally to keep order & deal with minor disturbances. It is the same wherever you go; the various religions fight over who shall have the custody of this place or that and are very jealous of their own privileges. It is the same with the Jews & Arabs,' he wrote – and gave as an example the custody of Rachel's tomb, outside Bethlehem.

> The Jews have the custody of the tomb. But the local Moslems have the right to wash their dead in the courtyard of the tomb. This they like to do just when the Jews are having some ceremony inside the tomb, out of sheer devilry of course. Result: much trouble & friction. It is all very curious.
>
> I must stop now. I am glad Father is keeping well.

Bernard's father was in fact remarkably well, considering that he was now eighty-four; and though Bernard's letters were addressed to Maud, the Bishop must have read them with pride. His relationship with Bernard was still immensely formal; but the fact that Bernard was so happily married and had returned so sincerely to the faith must have given him great satisfaction. There is no evidence that, even at this stage of his long life, he saw in Bernard a future more distinguished than his other sons'. Why should he have? Harold was doing well in Africa, Donald in Canada, Colin was now a rector, and the young Brian was adjutant of his battalion in Kenya. Yet the Bishop did, apparently, make Bernard the trustee of his will; and he left Bernard – who had, unknowingly, seen him for the last time when he embarked for Palestine – with the impression that he was watching with deep fatherly concern over his third son's progress.

As April came, the tension in Palestine rose. From Jerusalem, on 10 April, Bernard wrote to his mother:

I have been fearfully busy lately with Easter and the precautions we have to take in case riots should break out.

This is a curious place at Easter and you see a diversity of religious pageantry which you would see nowhere else in the world.

For instance on Good Friday the Christians (RCs) in enormous crowds process up the Via Dolorosa, the way Christ went with His Cross. The Jews wail all day at the Wailing Wall. The Moslems hold uproarious processions all round the town. The difficulty is to keep them from clashing. I have had troops out in the town for the last 10 days & have escaped trouble so far. After tomorrow I hope to be able to dispense with them.

This, unfortunately, was the last letter Maud kept; but four days later Bernard penned his impressions of the Miracle of the Holy Fire in an anonymous typescript which he sent to his mother, perhaps intending that she should get it published somewhere.

The ceremony, Bernard wrote, was 'the most astounding sight I have ever seen in my life', being 'the supreme ceremony of the Eastern Churches . . . in commemoration of the first victory after Calvary', and involving 'Greeks, Armenians, Copts and Syrians.'

The ceremony is conducted by the Greek Orthodox Patriarch; and a Bishop of the Armenian Churches goes with him into the Holy Sepulchre . . .

Every available piece of sitting or standing room in the church is packed with young people for several days before the event, fabulous sums are paid for balconies, and people camp out in them: babies are frequently born in the church while waiting. This is very lucky and is much sought after.

After various introductory rituals

the Shebals (young men) enter in procession, singing songs. They sing that they are happy now; as Christ who was killed is soon to rise again (the ceremony is always on the Orthodox Easter Eve), the Jews who killed Him are sorrowful at yon wall, and so on. The singing is very uproarious, and they all get worked up into a high pitch of excitement.

The Patriarch then appears, preceded by banners; is disrobed, and enters the Sepulchre where the miracle of the Holy Fire takes place.

The whole of the onlookers now get fearfully excited: everyone has a bundle of candles and they get them ready to light from the Holy Fire when it is passed out.

The Patriarch, concealed in the Sepulchre, calls upon God to produce the miraculous flame, which he then dispenses:

Runners are waiting and seize it and run up to the top galleries with it, others pass it round the people on the floor.
  In about 30 seconds every single person in the Church (about 16,000) has a lighted candle, and the effect is wonderful: as is the grease, as the people get over excited and wave the candles about. (After the ceremony my tunic was covered with grease, and also my hair.) Then suddenly the doors of the Sepulchre are opened and the Patriarch emerges holding a lighted torch in each hand . . . He then tries to get up to the Altar in the church to light the candles on it. But everyone wants to light his candle from the torch, and the crowd surged in on the old man, and he got pushed backwards and forwards, and almost trampled on. The whole crowd is shouting and singing and is worked up to a fever of excitement. Finally a squad of police picked him up and rushed him through the crowd to the altar. I bet he was glad when he got there.

Despite the changes in tense – or perhaps because of them – Bernard did manage to convey a vivid and ironic picture of the rite. Processions now started around the altar in traditional Orthodox fashion, while out in the open

the next thing was a free fight outside the Sepulchre.
  The various Orthodox Bodies are very jealous of each other, and Armenians set fire to a Coptic banner out of sheer devilry, and the two parties, Armenians and Copts, then went for each other, and the police had to draw their truncheons and charge the crowd before they could restore order. They used their truncheons really well and laid out . . .

212

Not a very Christian way to end an Easter festival – but representative, as Bernard saw it, of the problems of Palestine. In retrospect – especially when one considers the post-war occupation of Ireland by three divisions, totalling over 60,000 men – it was a miracle not that the Holy Fire was produced by the Patriarch each Easter, but that two very dispersed battalions of His Majesty's forces could cope.

For the moment, then, the pot merely simmered. Bernard's amused focus enabled him to achieve a reputation for objectivity and fairness that would stand him in good stead when he returned to the country some six years later. Besides, in June Betty arrived with David; and, in the summer holidays, John Carver. The Armstrong-Siddeley went 'magnificently', and the Montgomerys travelled as far as Petra, Jerash, Damascus and Baalbec. 'It was just his cup of tea,' John Carver recalled later. 'He was in his element; in fact I remember he got definite ideas of grandeur. He filled up a whole page of my passport. I wanted to go down to Egypt and there was something about my not having a visa, so he wrote in his own fair hand in my passport: "On duty in Egypt", signed "B. L. Montgomery". He thought that this was good enough – that you could go round the world on his signature!'[1]

Moreover, Betty enjoyed their stay in Palestine enormously. Alan Moorehead would later claim that Betty stopped painting at this time – but this was not so. Betty loved the country, and her water colour depicting Palestinians drawing water by the steps of a mosque in Jerusalem remains one of her most charming works. It was in Palestine, too, that she met the great explorer and Arabist, St John ('Jack') Philby (at whose marriage Bernard, as a distant cousin, had acted as best man in India almost a quarter of a century before), whose portrait she was to paint again in Alexandria in 1933.

At the end of 1931 arrangements were made to bring the Warwickshire Battalion by train to Port Said, and thence via the Suez Canal to their new station at Alexandria, where they were to garrison the city with a detachment of cavalry and form part of the Suez Canal Brigade, commanded by Brigadier Sir Frederick Pile. Although Bernard remained at Lt-Colonel, his later promotion to full Colonel would be backdated to 1 January 1932, in recognition of his work in Palestine. General Burnett-Stuart's 'Personal Report' which he wrote in March 1932 read:

Lt-Col B. L. Montgomery. He is clever, energetic, ambitious, and a very gifted instructor. He has character, knowledge, and a quick grasp of military problems. But if he is to do himself justice in the higher positions to which his gifts should entitle him he must cultivate tact, tolerance, and discretion. This is a friendly hint as I have a high opinion of his ability.

[1] Colonel John Carver, loc. cit.

This little sting in the tail cannot have pleased Bernard – but he evidently recognised the verity, for he copied out the report (which went to the War Office) and kept it with his private papers for the next forty years. Tact, tolerance and discretion were never qualities he would master; but to cultivate them he would at least try, as far as his ebullient character allowed. After the rigorous travelling and watchdog duties in Palestine he was once again commander of a field battalion, concentrated in one place, with straightforward duties, and above all with the chance to demonstrate his real forte: the training of troops.

CHAPTER SEVEN

Battalion Commander, Egypt

Was it Palestine, in 1931, which fuelled Bernard's ambition to get to the very top of his profession (a phrase he loved to use)? There were those, like Clement Tomes, who had already recognised his potential at the end of the Great War. Bernard had himself often spoken of running the British Army one day – an ambition wholly consonant with his gifts as a trainer, if innocent of the political and diplomatic requirements. Palestine was Bernard's first genuine experience of 'high' command, together with its responsibilities. The erstwhile Brigade-Major became a virtual Brigadier, and there can be no doubt that Bernard warmed to the experience. So much so, indeed, that when, in the next few years, he was offered various senior staff appointments, he declined them without hesitation. He had tasted power – and like so many men before him, he found it greatly to his liking.

The move to Alexandria might well have come as a disappointment therefore, since it entailed a reduction in his authority. Yet it does not appear to have done so. On the contrary, now that he was at last in sole charge of his battalion, Bernard could begin to train on the principles he had been refining for a decade and more. Palestine had been a policing operation; Egypt would be his chance to create a new sort of battalion in the regular Army: a fit, healthy body of a thousand men who, by the edge of the desert, would be trained for war – desert training that was indeed to have historic repercussions.

Captain Bailey, the MG Company Commander, was quite emphatic on this subject. '[Monty] was the finest trainer of troops I think I've ever known,' he related. 'I mean to say he behaved in a way no other CO had *ever* behaved. When it came to your Company training he'd say: "Go back to your office and make out a full programme. I want you to clear miles out of Alexandria, anywhere you like. Go and reconnoitre the place, see that there's plenty of water supply there, and everything else. Take the Quartermaster along with you if you like. Make all your own arrangements and submit to me your training programme for the next month." And there you were – you were left with that! You went out into the blue, tents and all, you know.

'And he said: "Most of the training's got to be done by night. Not less than forty-eight hours at a time away from camp."

'Well, no other CO had ever done it like that. I mean to say, the footling little Company exercises we did around Aldershot which were nothing. It was simply marvellous working under him. He said: "I'll come out and see you from time to time" – he didn't say when of course. He might turn up in the middle of the night or the daytime.

'His great thing of course was his training by night. It was really at the back of his mind more than anything else. The soldier, he'd say, *must* be trained to exercise his skills in the dark, especially with machine-guns and support guns.'

Company training led then to battalion training. 'Monty often used to surprise the troops,' Bailey remembered. 'On one occasion we carried out battalion training at Idku, a day and night march from Alexandria, among the sand hills of the Nile delta. Those were pretty strenuous days and nights, and by the time they ended the Battalion did not relish a day and night march back to barracks. Nevertheless we started the march back and unknown to all but a few Monty had arranged for a train to be waiting in a siding about half-way back, to take us the rest of the way. I can well remember how the men cheered and laughed at this well-kept secret.'[1]

Ironically, not even Bailey knew the real truth. According to Colonel Gething, Bernard's original request to take the Battalion to Idku was turned down by Brigade HQ.

Monty said he was going to take the battalion to Idku in the desert. Brigade said no, the rains are coming and we don't agree. They had a row about it – and Monty took us!

Thus the two-day march was necessitated not for training purposes but because Brigade HQ would furnish no transport, and Bernard would not take no for an answer.

He marched us all the way there – it took us two days. We bivouacked at night and marched by day.

This was the kind of thing he'd do. It was a new idea, and I think it was very useful: he made a scheme out. He got his Intelligence Officer and made him the enemy. We'd either got to go out for a couple of days and blast the enemy village, or defend some place. It was always the same layout; it didn't mean a lot of writing, except orders for the battalion. Monty was the judge. And to encourage us, when we came back every few days, he'd hold a concert party competition. Each company would have to put on a show, and the best one would be allowed two days' leave in Alexandria.

[1] 'Recollections of Monty' by Major G. R. H. Bailey, given in manuscript to the author, 8.3.78.

216

Well, Monty was right – the rains *did* hold off. But Brigade HQ was furious, and ordered Monty back. I knew this from the adjutant, Catherall. But Monty didn't let on. At the last concert party one night he got up and said to the Battalion: I've got a bit of good news for you. You've done so well while you were here that I'm taking you home tomorrow![1]

This was the background to Burnett-Stuart's report. That of the Brigadier of the Canal Brigade, 'Tim' Pile, was similarly anxious about Bernard's lack of discretion. In his confidential report the following spring he noted: 'He is definitely above the average of his rank and should attain high rank in the Army. He can only fail to do so if a certain high-handedness which occasionally overtakes him becomes too pronounced.'

Bernard's self-confidence was certainly growing in leaps and bounds. Betty was with him, and now that wives were permitted and their passage paid was found to be a very good Colonel's lady: kind and helpful to the other officers' wives, incapable of intrigue, absolutely sincere, and not in the least showy. 'I was invited often to dine,' wrote Captain Bailey later, 'and found Betty Montgomery a charming person. Though artistic – she was both a sculptress and painted – she was in no way eccentric in her dress or appearance, but wore plain sensible clothes. I found her full of fun and a lively person to talk to, with a great deal of humour. She often poked fun at Monty – I'm sure they were a devoted couple.'

The same picture emerges from all who knew Betty at this time. Her friends Alan and Gwen Herbert travelled out from Chiswick to stay with them in Alexandria. The Herberts still had no inkling that Bernard would one day be famous; he was still quiet in their presence and would apologetically absent himself from their company, saying, 'Well, I must go and command my regiment now.'[2] Certainly he still seemed to them a poor reflection of Betty's brother Patrick, then Commander of the 2nd Battalion Royal Tank Corps. The Herberts in fact were as unaware of Bernard's world as he of theirs; each tolerating the other only on account of Betty.

In the meantime the happiness of Bernard's marriage served only to encourage his ambition as a soldier, not to distract it. Whatever personal remarks his Brigadier and GOC might make in their Confidential Reports, both fell silent before Bernard the tactician – as Colonel Gething recollected later.

'This was the kind of thing that happened,' Gething recalled of army manoeuvres in Egypt:

The Battalion was attacked by tanks and we were out of action for six hours to reorganize before the tanks came and strafed us. A

[1] Colonel P. J. Gething, interview of 21.8.78.
[2] Lady Herbert, loc. cit.

conference was then held in our lines. As a matter of fact I had my Company lying down resting, just outside a mess tent in which the generals held this conference. I couldn't see anything, but I could hear.

The generals and the brigadier were holding forth about what they would do the next day. And they turned to Monty – and he was only a Lt-Colonel – and asked: What do you think of that, Monty?

Nonsense! Monty answered – and all the three brigadiers and the generals there too.

Look! he said – and he gave his plan for the next day. And they followed it – and it worked. Not often a general has his plans called 'nonsense' by a Lt-Colonel![1]

Liddell Hart's claim, in his *Memoirs*, that it was he who converted Bernard – via Tim Pile, the Brigadier – to night operations would thus appear to be specious, both on Captain Bailey's and Major Gething's evidence. Indeed the famous tactical exercise on army manoeuvres, in which Bernard first used Francis de Guingand as his Chief-of-Staff, took place at this time – a rout of their opponents that would be achieved partly by de Guingand's wise perseverance in waiting for information from an RAF spotter plane he had requisitioned, but primarily by Bernard's well-trained units which were able to move and locate the given position entirely by night.

The association between Bernard and de Guingand was certainly a salutary one; and though Bernard – the acting Brigadier for the exercise – took all the kudos for his 'victory', he never forgot de Guingand's brilliant and fertile mind, insisting he attend the Staff College without further delay.

What is interesting to note, from a military point of view, is that Bernard – who would one day be pilloried by certain historians for his excessive caution – was at this stage of his career a much more impetuous commander than he has subsequently been made out to be. 'It was on this occasion that I acted as his Brigade-Major when he was being tested in the desert on manoeuvres,' de Guingand recorded many years later, after Bernard's death. 'They used to pick a colonel of a regiment, making him command a force that the manoeuvres resolved around, and choose what they thought was a promising young officer as his Brigade-Major. I was chosen as Monty's Brigade-Major by General Burnett-Stuart, the GOC.' Far from planning a conventional desert confrontation, Montgomery was all for a pre-emptive night attack without even knowing the precise location of the enemy. 'Monty was going to make a balls of it . . . He was too eager and I was having to hold him down and hold him down, saying "Now wait, sir, we haven't got enough informa-

[1] Loc. cit.

tion. You can't say we know where the enemy forces are . . ." I got on to some friends of mine at the RAF at Cairo and I said, "Can you do a flight in a certain area, taking photographs?" They came back very rapidly showing exactly where the enemy were laagered in the desert . . . We then marched off and surrounded them by dawn. For this Monty got a very good mark,' de Guingand remembered; 'but, if he'd done what he originally wanted, it would have counted against him.'[1]

It would be a mistake to read too much into a single army manoeuvre; but the exercise is more revealing than the simple forerunner of a personal association. Encouraged by Betty's affectionate devotion, Bernard was at this stage of his life a very different commander from the cautious, iron-willed general he would become; and the very qualities which some historians have so scorned – such as the insistence on overwhelming odds before embarking on schemes – were in fact much more a mantle Bernard forced himself later to assume than is commonly believed. In fact it is only by recognising this that one can understand Bernard's wartime mistakes, such as Dieppe and Arnhem – which were not aberrations in an otherwise naturally cautious military mind but examples of the very impetuosity that Bernard had otherwise managed to control and conceal.

For the moment, however, his growing reputation was for the way he trained and the boldness with which he handled his Battalion on exercises. 'It is a positive pleasure to watch him commanding his unit on manoeuvres,' Brigadier Pile wrote in his Confidential Report of March 1933 – though he omitted to say that Bernard's exposition of his Battalion's intended operations on the sand-table was so spellbinding that Brigade HQ actually went off with the sand-table afterwards.[2]

It was, as Colonel Gething later put it, Bernard's clarity of presentation that so impressed, rather than any particular novelty of military ideas. After every scheme a conference was held; and Bernard's summings-up were so accurate and so decisive that there was often little remaining for the Brigadier or General – the actual umpires – to add, as Colonel Gething remembered:

He'd get up and hold forth about what he'd done. He'd say: I realize now that that was a mistake – I ought to have done this, that and the other. So he took the wind out of all their sails. When he'd finished there was nothing left to say!

Gething's evidence is all the more important because he had come out as a Major to Egypt in 1932 convinced it would be the end of his

[1] Interview of 7.5.78.
[2] Loc. cit.

career: 'I thought, this is where I get a bowler hat because Monty and I don't see eye to eye. He doesn't like me, and I don't like him.'

Nor was Gething far wrong, as he later found out. Having got rid of one incompetent company commander, Monty learned he was to be replaced by Major Gething; he thumped the table and said he would not have him. 'Africa isn't big enough for the two of us,' he is reported to have said of the somewhat obstinate, punctiliously correct Gething who had so often opposed his will at Chatham in 1925. 'Well, Gething, I'm giving you my worst Company,' he said, when Gething nevertheless came and reported to him in Alexandria. 'Thank you very much, Sir,' replied Gething. But, when he saw Gething's performance on exercises, Bernard soon overcame his personal antipathy. 'Men will always work well if they're well led,' he extolled Gething's company command at the first post-mortem. 'After that we made friends,' Gething recalled. 'I learned more tactics under Monty in that one winter than in all the years before: Underneath all the blah he was really good.'

In fact no one – save Liddell Hart – could fault Bernard as a tactical instructor. Burnett-Stuart, by March 1933, was writing in his Confidential Report: 'I have a very high opinion of, and a great liking for, Lt-Col Montgomery. He has been an outstanding Battalion Commander and I hope soon to see him employed in a higher capacity.'

Pile even recommended him as 'an admirable chief instructor at the Staff College' that same March – and one is left with just the slightest suspicion that both Burnett-Stuart and Pile were anxious for a quieter life.

Lieutenant Neil Holdich joined the Battalion in September 1933; and was surprised at the way Bernard, returning from a summer vacation with Betty and the boys at Moville, controlled everything himself. From a tactical point of view, the Battalion was excellent, he recalled some forty-five years later. 'Even the Lance-Corporals had begun to think tactically as they would in the field. But, when you've said that, you've said the best part about it. The Company commanders, though gentlemen and very decent people, were not particularly bright. And, with these rather average officers, Montgomery had centralized everything on himself. There was no arguing with him, he decided everything. No men could be moved from one platoon to another without Montgomery's approval. The Second-in-Command, the Adjutant, and the Quartermaster were all yes-men, his mouthpiece. Montgomery decided all the promotions himself – haphazard promotion by so-called "merit" that did nothing to help morale among the ranks. Nobody knew where they stood, and Montgomery wasn't, frankly, all that popular as a result. It was a regular, somewhat rigid pre-war army Battalion; and Montgomery's methods didn't always go down well.

'It was the same outside the Battalion. The Brigadier, Sir Frederick Pile, was really an artilleryman. Very smooth; but he didn't really get on very well with Monty. Montgomery told him what he should do – that he didn't know his infantry stuff. And he didn't tell him very tactfully.

'Nor were we popular with the Coldstream Guards, who were stationed in Cairo, and came down to Alexandria either socially, to bathe, or on manoeuvres. Monty was pretty rude to them. Except for the 12th Lancers, the cavalry was in those days still horsed – and Monty thought they were a nonsense, not serious soldiers, just there for hunting, polo, and fishing. And told them so.

'When we left, at the end of 1933, to go to Poona, in India, Brigadier Pile saw us off at Suez. He said we left with our reputation second to none. But we think he wrote differently to India; because, when we got there in January 1934, the reception we got was distinctly chilly.'[1]

Whether this was so is unknown. But both Burnett-Stuart's and Pile's Confidential Reports on Bernard when he embarked in December recommended that he be promoted. 'He is fully qualified for high rank in the Army in almost any sphere,' wrote Pile. 'Perhaps as a first step he might be employed in the Directorate of Military Training where his knowledge and advanced methods could not fail to have most beneficial results on the efficiency of the army.' Burnett-Stuart seconded Pile's recommendation. 'He has been long enough in command of a Battalion,' the General wrote, 'and it is high time he went to higher things. I should like to see him in the Directorate of Training for a year or two.'

Possibly it was this sort of suggestion which led to Bernard being offered at least two staff jobs during his time in Egypt – as Major Gething recalled:

He had his career all mapped out and allowed nothing to interfere with his plan. When he was commanding the Battalion on army manoeuvres in Egypt he was offered a staff job, I think DAQMG, which he turned down. I made the remark 'Is that wise, sir? That is the second staff job you have refused, you won't be offered another perhaps.' He replied: 'What! I'll go home and thump the table in the War Office. Look! At the end of the year I shall take this battalion to India. I shall then become a brigadier and after I shall take command of a division, ending up as CIGS.'[2]

The Battalion left on Christmas Eve, 1933, unmourned in many quarters. As Bernard's successor at Poona, the next year, would put it, the Battalion was too small a unit for Bernard's talents. Yet it would be wrong to think of him only as an impossibly self-opinionated infantryman, with a brain too active for a battalion.

---

[1] Major Neil Holdich, interview of 16.8.78.
[2] Letter to the author, 27.3.78.

Though the reception in Poona might be chilly, and morale in the Battalion somewhat bruised by the Colonel's imperious paternalism, Bernard was respected by most of the troops. 'He is really popular with his men who he regards and treats as if they were his children,' Pile wrote in his report in December 1933; and, though this may have been exaggerated, there was some truth in it. When young Lieutenant Burge was stricken with polio, Bernard summoned the top specialist from Cairo to see him, and visited him in hospital continuously with Betty until he was invalided home. He drank and smoked in moderation, betted occasionally, played bridge frequently – and well – and saw to it that there were clean brothels for the troops in Alexandria run by the garrison adjutant, an ex-RFC pilot who was an excellent administrator and a decent, honourable man. As Burge remembered:

> The ladies were inspected by our own MO. The soldiers gave only their army number, no name, and signed a chitty saying they had used the prescribed prophylactic. As a result, our VD rate was extremely low. I mean, you have to remember that Alexandria was the most remarkable place. Everything was there! Racing, tennis, duck-shooting – you name it, it was there. You couldn't stop the men getting a woman; you could ensure it was healthy. Monty encouraged it, and kept it going. In fact he regarded it as a huge joke – he used to joke with the soldiers about what he called 'horizontal refreshment'.

There were difficulties, as when a certain officer refused to buy the regimental magazine, the *Antelope*, purchase of which Bernard had made compulsory in order to help keep it alive. But in fact Bernard was very fond of the officer, and to the end of his days would tell the story of his 'emergency'. Major-General R. C. Macdonald, Bernard's successor many years later as Colonel of the Regiment, remembered it thus:

> N—— was a bachelor, an officer who liked his booze, and every so often 'fell by the wayside' over women. Eventually he began to show signs of wear and was had up before Monty. Monty, who had something of a soft spot for N——, didn't sack him, but elicited the truth and made him promise to lead a blameless life thenceforward.
>
> 'No booze. And understand, N——, no women! If you must have a woman, tell me first.'
>
> Now it happened one evening, at a dinner party, that the telephone rang at Monty's house (he always kept a telephone by his place at the head of the table).
>
> 'Who is it?' Monty asked.
>
> 'Sir, it's N——.'

'What is it, N——?'

'Sir, I've got to have a woman.'

'Hum. Well, all right – but just one, mind!'[1]

As Macdonald said, Bernard set himself very high standards, and could at times be ruthless if others did not match them. But equally, he could be understanding and even compassionate in his way. He never forgot a face or a good subordinate. The paralysed Burge, improved but not by any means fit for duty, was taken back into the Battalion; and Major Gething, at Bernard's insistence, was given the adjutancy of one of the Royal Warwickshire TA Battalions over the heads of two other contenders. He abolished compulsory church parade for the Battalion, and earned a small place in the hearts of his men by his humorous response to one Battalion concert, at which he and the RSM were brilliantly mimicked by a couple of privates. 'Can't have this from a private,' Bernard shouted, amidst uproar. 'Make him a Lance-Corporal!'

Autocratic, super-efficient, a brilliant instructor, a master at infantry tactics, he was indeed, as Sir Frederick Pile put it, 'definitely a strong character', who had his sights on the very pinnacle of the British Army. But would he get there? On 25 November 1932, his father had died at Moville, leaving Lady Monty (as she liked to call herself[2]) the titular as well as de facto head of the family. The Bishop had reached the august age of eighty-five, and had died peacefully, without pain, after three months' illness. Where Bernard later obtained the idea that better nursing by his mother might have prolonged his father's life, as he claimed in his *Memoirs*, is a mystery; but there can be little doubt that he was distressed that his father should not live to witness his rise to fame; and bitter that his mother should have taken so long to acknowledge his right to it.

For the moment, however, the presence and affection of Betty warded off such thoughts. On Christmas Eve 1933 he personally supervised the boarding of HM Troopship *Worcester* at Suez – having a line of soldiers stationed the length of the gangplank passing up babies to their waiting mothers – and he sailed off to Bombay determined that his next command should be that of a brigade.

---

[1] Loc. cit.

[2] Bishop Montgomery was made KCMG in 1928, but as a clergyman he was not permitted to receive the accolade. Strictly speaking Maud thus remained Mrs Montgomery, but no one – not even the Royal Family after Bernard Montgomery became famous – dared contradict her.

CHAPTER EIGHT

Poona: The Sloth Belt

The area to which the Royal Warwicks had been posted in India was traditionally known as 'The Sloth Belt' – an area noted for its antiquated reverence for drill, ceremonial, and the social aspects of regimental soldiering. If – as General Macdonald claimed – the 1st Battalion of the Royal Warwicks had trembled before Bernard's new broom at the end of 1930, then the Southern Command of the Indian Army may be said to have boiled with indignation at the Battalion's arrival in Poona in January 1934: for here was a battalion which ignored ceremonial church parade, was plainly incompetent at ceremonial drill, and whose Colonel was known to have supported legalised 'knocking' shops in Alexandria.

Indignation, however, mingled with a certain amount of envy, even fear. For a mere Lt-Colonel, Bernard was remarkably self-confident, if not self-opinionated. Though obviously no stickler for drill, he was known to be a fanatic for efficiency and training. He had sent home a company commander who could not ride, and he expected his orders to be obeyed instantly. He believed in promotion by merit, and he had no use for horsed cavalry. The only time he had ever paid any attention to ceremonial was when – in answer to an Italian demonstration against the presence of the British – he marched the entire 1st Battalion with Band, Drums and Antelope through the centre of Alexandria. He was openly contemptuous of idle and amateur higher commanders, and in fact trained his battalion in exercises to function entirely under its RSM and NCOs, with all officers as 'casualties'. Conversely he was known to run officers' tactical training without troops in the evening instead of cocktail parties.

Thus into an Indian station whose performance at the King's Birthday Parade was legendary marched Lieutenant-Colonel B. L. Montgomery and his thousand men.

'Poona was absolutely ghastly,' Colonel Burge related later. 'To a keen soldier I cannot think of any worse fate than to have to go there. We arrived well-trained, with a charitable description as being "adequate" in turnout and ceremonial from Headquarters, Egypt, and we fell into the clutches of the GOC Southern India Command, General Sir George Jeffreys. He was a fine, indeed wonderful man –

as Second-in-Command of a Grenadier Guards Battalion during the retreat from Mons he boasted they had not lost a single man – but he had no interest at all in training of any kind. He certainly didn't recover for a long time the first time he saw us!'[1]

There was a considerable irony in this confrontation, for General Jeffreys had written Volume I of the *Infantry Training Manual* – on drill. And if Bernard was 'mad' about tactical training, Jeffreys was equally obsessed by square-bashing. Though the story of General Jeffreys' first inspection of the Battalion – in which Bernard, having been told that he was seven paces too far to the left, simply turned round on his horse and ordered the whole Battalion to move seven paces to the right – is apocryphal, it is not far from the truth. Lieutenant Holdich, in charge of a platoon at the time, vividly remembered the occasion. It took place in January 1934 in the early morning on the race course at Poona. Jeffreys' reputation had preceded him, and Holdich made himself as inconspicuous as possible behind the large and portly figure of Captain Edlin, his Company Commander.

'Good morning, Montgomery, you should be standing whatever number of paces in front of your battalion. You are not standing the correct number of p aces,' Jeffreys said – the first thing, before Montgomery could get out 'Present Arms' or anything. After that everything went wrong. We were hopeless. It was one glorious muddle.[2]

Nor did it stop there. Jeffreys insisted on seeing the Battalion perform his favourite company drill – a complicated series of movements in which one company hinges neatly on the next.

'Monty should have given a series of orders of which he hadn't the slightest idea at all,' Colonel Burge recollected.

As a result we got into the most almighty tangle. But what Montgomery did then say – this I can swear to, because I was there – was: 'Royal Warwickshires – follow me in fours!' and steamed off on his horse. It was most unorthodox, but the soldiery disentangled themselves in some way, and followed him.[3]

If Jeffreys humiliated the Commander of the 1st Battalion, the Royal Warwickshire Regiment, on the parade ground, however, he certainly did not have things all his own way.

'Jeffreys regarded Montgomery as a bit of an upstart,' Major Holdich recalled, 'with new, advanced ideas; equally, Montgomery

[1] Loc. cit.
[2] Loc. cit.
[3] Loc. cit.

regarded Jeffreys as an out-of-date old fogey, and didn't conceal it. There was bound to be friction between them – and there was.'[1]

The rivalry between the two authors of the *Infantry Training Manual* became a veritable sparring match.

'Montgomery undoubtedly sailed very close to the wind, from the instant he went out to India,' Burge remembered.

It wasn't soldiering as we'd known it in Europe. There was a stack of 'modifications for India' which negated everything the War Office was trying to do to modernize the Army. And since the Indian Government paid for the troops that were there, and since these troops were primarily for internal security and at most to meet a threat from Afghanistan, there was no new material of any kind – transport, tanks, aeroplanes: nothing. I can well imagine that that pile of 'Modifications for India' made Montgomery see red. My impression is that he wrote off the whole hierarchy there; and there was trouble from the start.[2]

Almost immediately, HQ Southern Command queried Bernard's Sunday church parade system, insisting that, since the Indian Mutiny of 1857 had broken out on a Sunday morning when the British were at church, the Battalion must go to church collectively, armed with rifles. This, as Bernard knew, necessitated endless paperwork, as every individual rifle had to be signed for and countersigned when returned. Headquarters insisted; and in the end Bernard sent a small armed platoon to stand outside church each Sunday 'in case the second mutiny should break out again!' Jeffreys was furious – as he was over the Kirkee controversy.

'Montgomery was told to provide a Company and a half to guard the arsenal at Kirkee,' Burge related,

and he wrote back to HQ asking for instructions as to the threat against which he was to defend it. I remember there was one sentence in it – it was a most impudent letter, but it was damned funny; he had started to itemize the possible threats, and he began at the top of the page with: '*The Germans*. Presumably we would have prior notice of this . . .' He was asking for trouble. He'd written off the hierarchy there and didn't take the slightest notice of it.[3]

Bernard's attitude was tantamount to insubordination; thus it certainly seemed a good idea to all when he applied for leave to travel with his wife on the P & O Line annual six-week cruise to the Far East

---

[1] Ibid.
[2] Ibid.
[3] Ibid.

that spring, starting from Bombay and taking in Colombo, Penang, Singapore, Hong Kong and Shanghai before setting its passengers down for a fortnight in Japan. Young David Montgomery, then aged five, had been sent back to England with a nanny – the first of a long train of such abandonments – and Bernard and Betty looked forward to a complete break from regimental soldiering. Bernard had now commanded the Battalion for three years, with a single break for a month at home in August 1933. 'Nobody had any doubt that Montgomery was destined for higher things,' Lieutenant Burge – who also went on the voyage, having been granted special sick leave – was later to remember. 'But only if he didn't fall by the wayside in the meantime. One more year in Poona would have finished him, I'm sure.'[1]

The sea journey to Japan, chosen as a rest, was to be much more eventful than the Montgomerys imagined, though. For a start, General Jeffreys was also on board. Furthermore a casual perusal of the passenger list revealed an even more surprising name: the architect of the new German Army, General von Seeckt.

'Montgomery hadn't seen the passenger list for more than thirty seconds,' Burge recalled, 'before General von Seeckt found himself with his back against the wall! They used to have great talks together and the CO often used to have me up there with him, while the interpreting was done by a Colonel von Heinz.'[2]

Burge was equally surprised when, at every port of call, Bernard went ashore, taking the young lieutenant with him, 'to survey the military situation. He always seemed to know somebody, the OC Troops or a senior officer presumably from his Staff College days'.[3] Indeed it seemed as if Bernard was more an inspecting officer than a tourist. Yet the biggest surprise came at the end of March 1934, when the liner arrived in Hong Kong. Amidst the mail for Lt-Colonel Montgomery was a telegram from Army HQ Simla, offering him the post of Chief Instructor (GSO 1) at the Staff College, Quetta, in succession to his erstwhile colleague at Camberley, 1920, Colonel B. C. T. Paget.

'What always reminds me of this,' recalled Colonel Burge nearly forty-five years later, 'is that I would have thought anybody receiving such a message would have leaped overboard. Not a bit of it. "I'll brood on this," he said.'[4]

The matter was not as simple as young Lieutenant Burge imagined. Bernard had assured his Company Commander, Major Gething, that he would next command a brigade, followed by a division. He already had experience of staff college instructing; he was now forty-six and would be forty-nine when the Chief Instruc-

[1] Ibid.
[2] Ibid.
[3] Ibid.
[4] Ibid.

torship came to an end. Would this thus be a side-step, depriving him of the chance of brigade command for three vital years? The War Office in London had cabled to the C-in-C India on 19 March 1934: 'No objection to offering Montgomery. But you should tell him that failing this he will probably be selected for staff appointment at home next year'[1] and it was this rider that very likely decided Bernard.

To serve as GSO 1 at Quetta might be a three-year side-step in his military advancement; but to spend a further year at Poona under Jeffreys and his equally redundant Brigadier before being posted back to England to a staff appointment would be an even greater waste. Bernard, after consultation with Betty, cabled acceptance. It would mean he would be promoted to full Colonel on commencement of his duties in June 1934. They would have a comfortable house in the cantonment, several miles outside the picturesque city of Quetta – the gateway to Persia, perched 6000 feet above sea level in the mountains of what is now Pakistan. The Commandant had expressly asked for an infantry officer, as his British service instructors were gunners and sappers. The college was far from the Sloth Belt, and its standard of instruction was second only to Camberley's, with students nominated not only from among officers serving in India but also some from the Dominions. Within reason Bernard would be his own boss. They would be able to have David out again, and would see Betty's sons John and Dick as soon as they finished their military training as sappers at Chatham and were posted to India. Having made up his mind, Bernard thought no more about it. But at least one of his students at Quetta remembers a fatalism in the Chief Instructor's attitude: a feeling that he might have 'missed the boat' and would be too old to be given an active command when eventually war came.[2]

The trip to Japan took its course. Legend has it that, on his return to Poona in May 1934, Bernard was summoned by the Army Commander to initial his Confidential Report.

And General Jeffreys said: 'Well, you see, Montgomery, you'll have to look elsewhere for your employment in future from what I've said.' And Monty replied: 'Well, it's just as well, sir, I've got this signal from Army Headquarters this morning, appointing me as a G1 at Quetta Staff College!'
And George Jeffreys said – 'Well, I won't stand in the way of that.'
And Monty said: 'No, of course!'[3]

The story is necessarily untrue, not only because Jeffreys was aboard Bernard's boat when the signal from Simla was received, but because

[1] War Office Personal File, MOD.
[2] Colonel R. A. N. Davidson, interview of 8.3.78.
[3] Brigadier 'Tochi' Barker, interview of 25.3.80.

Bernard kept a copy of the Confidential Report – and it was far from damning:

> Lt-Colonel Montgomery is well above the average as regards knowledge, energy and power of imparting knowledge. He is very strongminded and I would advise him (and this is meant for advice, *not* adverse criticism) to bear in mind the frailties of average human nature and to remember that most others have neither the same energy, nor the same ability as himself.

In its way this was a most complimentary testimonial after the months of mutual animosity. Moreover, although Bernard did not keep his Brigadier's Report, it must also have been laudatory, for Jeffreys began his own by writing: 'I agree.' Nevertheless Bernard must have felt some pleasure at being able, on board ship, to show the War Office signal to a General with whom he was at continual loggerheads, and – as he recounted later to his brother Brian – ask for the General's advice on whether or not to accept the post.

The feeling in the Battalion itself was mixed. The regimental journal, the *Antelope*, recorded that 'all those who have served with Colonel Montgomery will regret that the Regiment is to lose an officer who has done so much to instil into all ranks the modern theory of war, and on behalf of all our readers we wish him many more steps in promotion'; but the regret did not go particularly deep. His successor, Lt-Colonel J. P. Duke, was in the great mould of Royal Warwickshire colonels: tall, elegant, sincere, without pretension. Bernard had told Duke how to plan his training course at Sandhurst in 1926 when Duke was put in charge of military training as Chief Instructor at the Royal Military College ('one term characteristics of the arms, one term larger formations, third term company tactics – a system that proved highly successful and remained the protocol for many years').[1] For Montgomery as tactics expert and instructor, Duke had the highest regard; but, though he thought Bernard would go far, he did not foresee his becoming Commander-in-Chief – 'because he could be so rude, and made himself unpopular.' Duke was intrigued, therefore, to know how Bernard had fared as Battalion Commander when he arrived to take over in June 1934.

> He was away when I arrived, although he'd left a few notes on paper.
> The younger officers were content under him; but the senior officers were in a state of revolt. They said: For God's sake take things easy, because the men are on the point of revolution. But that was balls really. They didn't like him, the senior officers. Monty thought they were a lot of dug-ins; but the mutiny story wasn't true. The senior officers were merely disgruntled.

[1] Brigadier J. P. Duke.

Well, then I was sent for by the Brigade Commander and the Army Commander, Jeffreys, and they said: Your Battalion is in a bad state. They don't drill properly and they don't turn out properly. So I had to set out to re-drill the Battalion and get that side right. But their tactics I found were good.

The truth is, there wasn't enough for Monty to do, commanding a battalion. Not in Poona – Poona was a very fashionable social place – and Monty didn't care for that much.[1]

Bernard's departure proved well timed, in fact; for no sooner had he left than a further scandal broke under his name. The Royal Warwicks had boasted, in Egypt, an exceptionally high number of first-class marksmen; but in India, range shooting was monitored by another battalion. 'It turned out they were all 3rd Class shots – and it was a first-class scandal!' Brigadier Duke remembered laughingly many years later. 'But Monty outlived that, too.' It appeared that the company commanders were so awed by his directive to do well on the range at Alexandria that they had surreptitiously altered the score-cards using a sharp pencil – though faulty Indian rifles may have been the real cause.[2]

Leaving Lt-Colonel Duke to restore the reputation of the 1st Battalion, the Royal Warwickshire Regiment, Bernard departed to the Staff College, Quetta, where on 29 June 1934 he assumed the post of Chief Instructor.

[1] Ibid.
[2] Major Neil Holdich, loc. cit.

CHAPTER NINE

Quetta

Not even the occasion of Bernard Montgomery's arrival in Quetta was to be without legendary anecdote, for on the Monday morning when Bernard made his first official appearance at the Staff College, Quetta, it was in the regalia not of Lt-Colonel, but of full Colonel – thus taking precedence over the two existing GIs – Colonels Quinan and Paget – by virtue of his brevet seniority dating back to 1 January 1932. Indeed, so vain and unbecoming was Bernard's behaviour considered in this respect that a story soon began to circulate that Lt-Colonel Montgomery must have 'changed his uniform and insignia in the train' on the way from Poona.

'That slightly riled people,' one of the students later recalled. 'It wasn't the fashion to put up your new rank quite as suddenly as that.'[1]

But though there was 'this slight umbrage about arriving on the first day as a Full Colonel and superseding the existing people'[2] it soon vanished when the new Colonel began to give his lectures.

With great wisdom the Commandant of the College decided that, although Bernard had been appointed to replace Paget, the Chief Instructor of the second-year students, this would be to waste Colonel Montgomery's skills.

'Guy Williams – now he was the most wonderful man,' Major-General Sixsmith remembered some forty-five years later.

He handled Monty in the most remarkable way. He'd been the senior Army Instructor at the Imperial Defence College before, and he was a man of the very broadest outlook. He used Monty to the full.

You learned the technique of battle in your first year and you went on to broader issues – internal security problems, Imperial problems, grand strategy, all that you went on to in your second year. So anyone who had Monty in his hands would obviously see that he was the man to teach the Junior Division [first-year students] the technique of battle command and staff duties.[3]

[1] Brigadier 'Tochi' Barker, loc. cit.
[2] Ibid.
[3] Major-General Eric Sixsmith, interview of 17.4.79.

231

Bernard was therefore made Chief Instructor of the Junior Division with a directing staff of five officers. Sixsmith entered the College the following year but Brigadier 'Tochi' Barker well remembered Montgomery's impact on the students in 1934:

> He was damn good, in my opinion, though not everyone thought so. There were a lot of old stiffs in our year – all the old stiffs of the First World War whose last chance it had been to get into the Staff College.
>
> I thought he was first-class. I remember he invented a new method of lecturing there. He'd come in with his notes, read to himself one page – taking three or four minutes reading them while one sat waiting. And then he'd walk to the front of the stage and talk splendidly, absolutely right. I used to sit there and think: that's always what I've thought, this is quite right, but I haven't got enough wit to say it, the language.
>
> Then he'd go back to his desk and study his notes for another three or four minutes. And then he'd give us another ten minutes or so, straight off, and damned good it was – in my opinion.
>
> And afterwards when I got to know Monty very well I rather ragged him, I said: 'Now, Sir, I enjoy your talks. I've always thought it, but never had the wit to put it into words as you do. My only point is: You take such frequent pauses in your progress. You go and you leave us sitting for four or five minutes while you study your notes.'
>
> And Monty said: 'I'll tell you what I'm doing. I'm training myself to think as I speak, and not read out from a script. So I like to refresh my memory with the facts, and then I like to go and give it as I think, to speak out.' And he was damned good.[1]

The new Chief Instructor was evidently out to learn new techniques of presentation, just as he was anxious to impart a new approach to the study of warfare and command. Though he was uncompromisingly forthright about those whom he considered to be 'useless' ('a great improvement – thoroughly bad,' he marked on one recalcitrant student's paper,[2]) he would take infinite pains over those who he felt showed promise. In one of the two British Army battalions stationed in the district was Captain Francis de Guingand – known as 'Wizz-Bang' for his ever fertile brain. Convinced of de Guingand's potential after their efforts together on manoeuvres in Egypt the previous year, Bernard had campaigned on his behalf for a nomination to the Staff College, Camberley. From Quetta, on 30 July 1934, he wrote to de Guingand, who had thanked him the moment he heard he had got in:

[1] Brigadier 'Tochi' Barker, loc. cit.
[2] Brian Montgomery, op. cit.

232

My dear Freddie,

Thank you for your letter. I heard from the DSD some days ago. His letter was dated 27th June and I gathered from it that as far as he was concerned all would be well. I did not tell you, as accidents sometimes happen.

I am not used to backing the wrong horse when it comes to asking favours of people in high places; it would result only in one's own undoing!! You ought to do well at Camberley. I know many of the instructors there, and some of them very well; one of them – Nye – is in my Regt. I will write and commend you to them in due course.

We are coming to your dance on 14 Aug. and are dining first with the Army Comdr.

Yrs ever

B. L. Montgomery[1]

Bernard's sponsorship of de Guingand was to be an investment that would repay him incalculably in the course of time. For the moment, however, Bernard was acting simply out of kindness and an instinctive belief that talent ought to be encouraged. De Guingand was not his only protégé at this time; that winter he arranged – and even paid for – the still incompletely cured Lieutenant Burge to come to stay with him at Quetta. The following year he would make a personal visit to the War Office in London to see that a gifted lieutenant from his first-year course be given accelerated promotion – Dudley Ward, a future Army Commander. And if Bernard could not bring himself to approve of inefficiency or shoddy work, his happy marriage nevertheless seems to have softened him. 'Don't you think you ought to give so-and-so another chance?' Betty was often heard to say. 'She was dark and vivacious, always cheerful and frequently laughing,' one young officer recalled.

Much of a height and age as Monty; she dressed soberly in the fashion of the day, but not to draw attention by being eccentric in any way; always attractively turned out. She had considerable culture and talent of her own, being a painter in oil and water-colour of high merit; besides being a sculptress of repute, and with a great sense of colour . . . Both she and Monty shared a keen sense of humour and loved pulling one another's legs. They were good and generous hosts, and I was asked to join their dinner parties on several occasions. At one of these, just before a week's spell in camp on outdoor exercises, at the end of dinner, she said: 'Ladies, do come with me and we'll discuss what we are going to do whilst Monty and the men go away to camp to play soldiers.'

---

[1] Sir Francis de Guingand, *Generals at War*, London, 1964.

Monty loved it. They were devoted to one another and didn't mind showing it.[1]

There would always be those like Liddell Hart who felt Betty had a hard time, bossed about by her egocentric spouse. But those who really knew them – Bernard's brother Brian, Betty's sons John and Dick, officers from the Royal Warwickshire Regiment in Palestine, Alexandria and Poona, students at Quetta – all testify to the opposite. Perhaps the ultimate proof lay in the artistic work Betty was able to do while married to Bernard. Previously she had made only a very erratic course towards independence after her first husband's death, teaching in a preparatory school but in the end forced to rely on her mother and mother-in-law to help cope with the children during their holidays. 'Looking back it is difficult to understand the astonishment we all felt at the marriage, an astonishment that still seems to haunt biographers,' wrote her son John many years later.[2] After Cheshire, the world of her brother Patrick, A. P. Herbert and the Café Royal literati was 'heady stuff' and she enjoyed every minute. The Herberts were unfailingly kind, Arnold Bennett told her she was a very intelligent woman and she had lots of exciting acquaintances; nevertheless – and this is the point – she was never more than half in and of this world; she was never entirely at ease with its rather lax moral standards and many of her closest friends were outside it . . . 'Monty's world was not to her such an alien one as is sometimes implied. "I am reverting to type," she would say to her astonished Chiswick friends when explaining her engagement and in a fundamental sense this was true, though she could never be a typical Army wife any more than her remarkable husband was a typical Army officer.'[3] However externally bossy, Bernard provided her with security and the freedom to paint and sculpt. And this she did, from Palestine to India, in ever increasing amounts. Young Lieutenant Burge, when staying with them at Quetta, was requested to produce various types of Indian soldier for a series of paintings she was doing. What might have been the rather stultifying Army world of regimental soldiering was transformed, by Bernard's intensity and his sense of fun, into a tremendously stimulating life. Indeed Betty produced so many canvases and figures at this time that she was able to give away a considerable number when she returned to England in 1935, and again in 1936. Brigadier 'Tochi' Barker acquired several.

Betty – she was charming, and a good artist. I've got several of her pictures still. Before she went home in 1935, in her drawing room she hung all the pictures she'd painted – quite a lot – and invited

[1] 'Monty and Betty Montgomery' – recollections prepared by Colonel Alan Davidson, 8.3.78.
[2] Colonel John Carver, loc. cit.
[3] Ibid.

her friends, including me and Mrs Barker – and said, 'Come along and pick anything you like and take it.'

So I arrived here. And Monty said: 'Ah, yes, "Tochi", I'll show you the picture you should have.' I said, 'No, no, I want to choose my own.'

Monty was insistent. 'No, no, I'll show you' – and he took me to a picture of some flowers, irises. He said: 'That's the one!' I objected. 'No, no, I shall go around and choose.' So I did. But of course I chose the one that Monty had said – it was easily the best!

Years later, after the war, I heard that Monty had lost all his pictures at Portsmouth. So I wrote to him and said, 'Now I have several of Betty's pictures,' I named them, 'and you can have them all or any one you like to pick.' And Monty wrote back straight away – he had a memory like an elephant – and said: 'I will have the "Irises"!'[1]

Bernard's admiration for Betty and her artistry was utterly and transparently genuine.

'Montgomery fussed over, looked after her devotedly,' remembered Colonel Burge of his stay there. 'She took his mind off soldiering; she made him giggle, able to laugh at himself. There was a lightness in the house, and a great deal of amusing chit-chat, gossip and talk quite apart from military discussion. Betty didn't know the difference between a Corporal and a Corps Commander – or behaved as if she didn't, which was quite superb – and very good for Monty.'[2] Certainly Bernard's brother Brian, at this time stationed in India, thought it the happiest time of Bernard's life.

Both Brian Montgomery and General Sir Dudley Ward felt in retrospect that Bernard's tactical concept of war had now fully matured. It was not spectacular for its novel ideas, but for its unity of conception and the absolute clarity with which Bernard put over this vision. Though the detailed classes were taken by the various G2 instructors, it was entirely as laid down by the Chief Instructor himself. 'At Quetta the whole of the instructing staff was under his charge,' General Ward remembered, 'and I think they learned as much from Monty as we students did. There's no doubt we all felt immensely privileged to be taught the higher aspects of our profession by someone of Monty's calibre. Indeed, any later development of one's own military ability came from Monty at Quetta, and his tactical doctrines. People like Liddell Hart I think are vastly overrated. They were obsessed by mobility – which is fine if you can have it. But it isn't often so; and the only way you can win battles is to defeat the enemy who wants to deprive you of that mobility. It was Monty who taught us how to do this. He could be very chaffing and

[1] Brigadier 'Tochi' Barker, loc. cit.
[2] Colonel P. B. I. O. Burge, loc. cit.

had a strong sense of humour. But at other times he could be deadly serious. I remember him saying the last time he addressed us: "You gentlemen must now get on with the business of making yourselves professionals in your chosen profession – because we only have the time it takes Germany to become what she considers to be sufficiently re-armed." [1] About Bernard's relations with the Commandant, General Ward felt certain they were on good terms – that Bernard left him with very little to do bar an occasional inspection. Major-General Guy Williams did indeed have a high opinion of his Chief Instructor, and within a year – in April 1935 – was recommending Bernard for 'early command of a Regular Brigade or Brigadier, General Staff'. Bernard Montgomery, he wrote in his Confidential Report, was 'a forceful personality, widely read and with practical experience in the field, he is a fine trainer and a convincing teacher. He demands a high standard of conduct and of work. I am grateful to him for his wise and constructive help in all matters connected with the College'.

Williams' report, together with Bernard's now growing file of testimonials did not go amiss at the War Office in London; and on 8 May the War Office Selection Board approved the appointment of B. L. Montgomery to command a Regular Infantry Brigade as soon as one became available.

This news, transmitted to Bernard at Quetta, must have come as a tremendous confidence-booster to the now forty-seven-year-old Chief Instructor. Yet Bernard, who was always so careful to compute in advance his chances of promotion, cannot have failed to be aware that he would be nearing fifty if no vacancy occurred before the end of his instructorship at Quetta. By the time he got the next higher command, namely that of a Division, he would be fifty-four – and still a very long way from becoming CIGS. Although he was convinced that there would eventually be war again between Britain and Germany, he began to doubt whether it would come within the period of his active career – a fact which seems to have added fuel to his exhortations to his students. Against the background of polo-playing, of regimental parties and colonial life with servants and abundant drink he warned: 'Remember it will be *your* show, and you will neglect the study of your profession at your peril.' [2]

According to Major-General Sixsmith 'there is no doubt about it that he was considered to be out on a limb in the Army, one who took his own line'. [3] Yet, if he sometimes wondered whether he would ever be given the opportunity to reach the high command to which he aspired, he never ceased preparing himself. Whatever lengths he went to in order to help talented students, he himself never relaxed his own example of command. When the new Junior Division

[1] General Sir Dudley Ward, interview of 22.2.78.
[2] Colonel R. A. N. Davidson, loc. cit.
[3] Loc. cit.

students assembled before him in February 1935 he made it quite clear what 'the form' was:

'I remember he talked to us at our first meeting with our Chief Instructor,' Major-General Sixsmith recalled many years later.

He said: 'Well, you'll all ask me to dinner. Of course I shan't come. But I shall ask all of *you* to dinner. I couldn't possibly go out with thirty of you! I couldn't possibly spare the time for that. But you'll all come to my house.'

And of course we all did.

The other thing I'll always remember about that first lecture – which showed how his mind worked – he said: 'Now after the outdoor exercises we'll all come home as we wish. Those people who've got motor cars I hope will take out those who've not got motor cars. We go in plain clothes. Once the exercise is over, we'll all go home, quick as you like – as long as no one gets in front of me!'

Then his hat – his white 'stationmaster's hat' as we called it, while we all wore Bombay bowlers.

They were all part of his outlook and technique. His outlook was a curious mixture of the cold and the warm. He wasn't a cold person as many people imagine; but he didn't easily see how other people thought . . .

But one thing he'd never allow was any sort of warm feeling or anything else to interfere with what he considered right. He was the true old Puritan in his make-up.[1]

Brigadier Barker also clearly remembered Montgomery's accent on distinctive headgear:

Monty was actually a pretty well-dressed fellow – he took pains with his attire, his suits. And he wore a white topee – an old one. This was very unfashionable, but was very popular with us students because on all the schemes – and Quetta is wide-open spaces – you could always tell where Monty was! You could see this topee, bobbing about. We were all in plain clothes, 'mufti', for exercises, but you could always spot Monty.

Later on I ragged him and I said, 'Sir, why do you wear this white topee, it's very unfashionable. We don't object of course, but it's very old-fashioned.' This was 1935. And Monty said: 'Well, people like wearing unusual hats, it stamps their personality. Winston Churchill always goes in for unusual hats – so do I!' And it's extraordinary that, because Churchill was rather in the doldrums then.[2]

[1] Ibid.
[2] Loc. cit.

Meanwhile the three-year period as Chief Instructor did not pass uneventfully. David was brought out from England by a nanny late in 1934; Dick joined his parents for the Christmas holiday; but, on the last day of May 1935, not long after Bernard heard of his future promotion, there occurred at Quetta itself one of the greatest natural disasters of the century: an earthquake which in a single night accounted for some thirty thousand deaths. The carnage was more concentrated and grotesque than anything Bernard can have witnessed in the Great War; indeed the scale of the disaster was so great and the danger of typhoid so acute that the Army Commander ordered the entire city to be ringed with barbed wire and sealed off, like an amputated limb. The College, mercifully situated on a different stratum of rock, was spared; and as long as its clock tower continued to stand it would carry on its business, the Commandant cabled in answer to the sister college at Camberley, which had offered to take the students and staff. Two days after the quake, further tremors were felt in the Quetta valley; and the college clock struck seventeen. For Bernard the earthquake entailed an eight-month separation from Betty, who, after rendering night-and-day help with the injured and homeless, returned to England with David on the P & O evacuation ship *Karanja*. David was now rising seven; more than forty years later he recollected the crumbling and shaking, followed by confusion and departure from Quetta. 'I came back to England with Mama and we went to live with the Mathers [friends of the Carver family from Cheshire] in Roehampton, on the outskirts of London. We then moved into a residential hotel on Putney Hill, not far from them, and I was sent to school there from September to December. In January 1936 I went to prep. school, and my mother returned to India. I didn't see her again until the summer of 1937.'[1]

David's memory was here at fault; for Bernard took the family to Lenk at Christmas 1936, and Betty went with David to Moville the following Easter. David, however, was talking from memory – a memory of constant separations, of stranger-nannies and the beginning of a seemingly endless succession of holidays spent in holiday homes. It is important, in view of the criticisms later levelled against Bernard Montgomery for the way he brought up his son David, to note that this began while Betty was still alive. According to her son John, Betty was never very fond of children, and did her duty by them as a responsible parent rather than as a vocation.

Meanwhile, in January 1936, after taking David to his new preparatory school at Amesbury, Bernard flew back to Quetta while Betty travelled back to India by sea. It was on this passage that she befriended a young Captain, Alan Davidson, who was about to enter the Staff College, Quetta:

[1] Viscount Montgomery, interview of 30.8.78.

I was to be one of the students in the two-year course starting there in Feb. Hearing of this, she was kind enough to ask me up to the First Class Lounge on several occasions (needless to say, as a Captain in the Fourth Gurkhas, I was saving my passage account by travelling second!), and put me into the picture of the Staff College from a wife's point of view, both socially and also partly professionally in general terms of the programme, besides mentioning individual instructors and the staff.

I remember so well when referring to Monty, she told me not to be apprehensive of him: 'he is really a very human person.' Her very sound advice to me on the whole course was: 'be natural' – words echoed by Monty himself during his opening lecture to us.[1]

Betty left behind in England a somewhat complicated tangle amongst her offspring, though. David resented being transmitted – at many thousands of miles' remove – from holiday home to holiday home: 'I was really rather miserable,' he recollected of this period. 'One was going to and from these strange places. It must have been quite obvious that I was unhappy, for towards the end of 1936 my brother Dick saved me by coming and rescuing me from one particularly unpleasant institution.'[2]

David's holiday accommodation was not the only difficulty, however; Betty's eldest son John was also something of a problem. Having trained as a sapper and gone up to Cambridge he fell in love with an Admiral's daughter aged twenty; and when it proved impossible for the girl to be invited to Lenk, John had caused uproar by refusing to go himself. From Quetta, since Betty considered that John was too young to contemplate marriage, Bernard was detailed to do battle with the girl's father, Admiral Sir Hugh Tweedie, and a bitter correspondence began, with Bernard accusing the Admiral of having no discipline over his daughter. 'Thank God I have no daughters,' he apparently wrote the Admiral; 'but if I had I'd keep them under control!'[3]

This was something of an exaggeration, and Admiral Tweedie must have put the upstart Colonel from the junior service in his place, for by summer Bernard at least had been won over. On 16 June 1936 he wrote to John at Chatham:

I've heard again from the Admiral giving me the latest situation. I've written to him again by mail to the following effect:
1) That as you are 24 and Jocelyn nearly 21 and you've fallen in love I can see no possible point in preventing you from meeting since you're both quite desirable people.

[1] Colonel R. A. N. Davidson, loc. cit.
[2] Viscount Montgomery, loc. cit.
[3] Colonel and Mrs John Carver, interview of 3.3.78.

2) The best thing is to get you to declare definitely your intentions.
3) If your intention is to become engaged now, to go to India in October and return in 2 years' time and marry Jocelyn, then I recommend him to agree and remove all restrictions as to meeting.
4) In 2 years' time you'll be 26 and Jocelyn 23 and there can be no possible objection to your getting married . . . He regards two years as important and so do I in order to make sure it is not a passing infatuation. If you approach him now, as in para 3 above, you will win.[1]

Such a letter is very revealing of Bernard's somewhat simplistic attitude towards affairs of the heart – a region he never really understood and which he sought to bring to order by an almost comic resort to military parlance and approach. Yet there is no doubt, as his other stepson Dick reflected,[2] that Bernard was at bottom a decidedly sentimental person, and that his ruthless dedication to his profession went hand in hand with an almost childlike reverence for love. To fall in love was, to him, a God-inspired thing; and if he insisted, like the Admiral, on a two-year separation, it was with the very best intentions. Nor can he be said to have been wrong. 'It was absolutely heartbreaking! Two years! They seemed like monsters, those parents, on both sides, my own as well as John's,' Jocelyn recorded later.[3] And yet her marriage to John was to prove as deep, as happy, and as devoted as that of Betty and Bernard.

Bernard continued to receive the most glowing Confidential Reports from the Commandant of the Staff College, Quetta. He had brought to the College new horizons in its training: the use of the sand-table, exercises in the field without troops, and insistence that all students learn to integrate the various branches of their profession, artillery, engineers, armour – and air. More and more Bernard was impressed by the potential of air power, and ground-to-air co-operation.[4] Years before, in his appreciation of the 1921 British campaign in Ireland for Major Percival, he had considered the use of aeroplanes futile 'except as a quick and safe means of getting from one place to another. Even the landing grounds were few and far between. The pilots and observers knew nothing whatever about the war, or the conditions under which it was being fought, and were not therefore in a position to be able to help much'.[5] Now he began to teach the importance of liaison between the two services, a policy which was at that very moment being enacted in the Spanish Civil War which had broken out on 16 July of that year.

[1] Colonel John Carver, loc. cit.
[2] Colonel R. O. C. Carver, loc. cit.
[3] Jocelyn Carver, interview of 3.8.78.
[4] Colonel R. A. N. Davidson, loc. cit.
[5] Ibid.

1936 was indeed the turning point in modern European history. On 7 March Hitler invaded the Rhineland – unopposed. In early May Mussolini conquered Abyssinia – without opposition from European nations. By summer Italian and German munitions and men were sent to Spain – and opposed only by Stalin. It proved impossible to move the British Government into a more urgent frame of mind. Besotted by the scandalous love of their young king for an American divorcée, the British public either wanted no mention of possible war, or felt the confrontation between nationalism and communism to be a Continental and entirely un-British affair. Although Liddell Hart did not feel the latter, he was adamant that the British should not get sucked into a continental military commitment beyond its means. General Burnett-Stuart – who left Egypt in 1934 to become GOC Southern Command in England – similarly felt that a Continental commitment was unwise; whereas Hobart, Martel, Lindsay and the exponents of armoured divisions thought that a war between Germany and France would be won by mobility, and saw the commitment of British infantry in a political gesture of support for France as totally misguided.

Here, despite the many thousands of miles between England and Quetta, was a controversy of the very highest importance for any thinking officer. What, then, was Bernard's attitude towards a British Expeditionary Force – in whose theoretical compass he might be commanding a brigade the following year? In his *Memoirs* Bernard was quite emphatic: 'It had for long been considered that in the event of another war with Germany the British contribution to the defence of the West should consist mainly of the naval and air forces. How any politician could imagine that, in a world war, Britain could avoid sending her Army to fight alongside the French passes all understanding.' However this was written some two decades after the event; and hindsight was coloured, as will be seen, by Bernard's total dedication to Western Union and NATO defence. For the moment, in the mid-Thirties, Bernard was not so politically conscious. He greatly admired General Burnett-Stuart, who he thought ought to have become CIGS in 1933 instead of Montgomery-Massingberd; and Burnett-Stuart caused consternation in the War Office by writing letters to *The Times* deploring the idea of a Continental commitment.[1]

Such matters, however, lay in the future, enabling Bernard to concentrate, at Quetta, on the tactical instruction of his students. He enjoyed going for long walks; and would occasionally, as Alan Davidson remembered, 'turn up at one's quarter in the afternoon, and ask one to go for a longish walk out into the Quetta countryside' where, rather than discussing European politics, he would more

[1] Letter from General Sir John Burnett-Stuart to Montgomery, and Bernard Montgomery, *Memoirs*, op. cit.

241

likely talk about 'subjects such as the then topical Simon report on future government of India and revision of the Prayer Book'.[1]

It was a time, above all, for reflection before his re-immersion in the world of military command. In November 1936 Betty's son John arrived in India to be met by his parents at Karachi; the Montgomerys were now reconciled to an informal engagement, and arrangements were made to meet young Jocelyn when they stayed in London after Christmas. But first there must be a further sentimental visit to Lenk in Switzerland. On 19 December therefore the Montgomerys left by Imperial Airways for London, collected David from Amesbury, and arrived with Dick Carver too at the Wildstrubel Hotel on Christmas Day. There they remained for almost a month, only returning to London on 19 January. Because of troubles on the North-West Frontier, the annual Quetta College tour had been cancelled, and Bernard had been given extended leave until mid-February.

In London the Montgomerys stayed in a service flat, where they were able to entertain conveniently. Both were in good form, as General Ward later remembered. 'Monty wanted to look at what I had married, so my wife and I were summoned to his service flat. Betty was absolutely charming – they complemented each other. They took us out for dinner at the Rag [Junior Army & Navy Club], then on a busman's honeymoon, then back to Piccadilly to dance. Betty was a very good dancer. It was a charming evening . . . Later on I went to Dorset to see my parents. When I got back there was a telegram from my father "Many Congratulations". As we weren't having another child this was a bit puzzling – until I got a signal from Monty. In it he said: "I've been to the War Office. You are being offered accelerated promotion into the King's Regiment. You will of course accept!"'[2]

Mrs Ward was not the only wife to be looked over. Young Jocelyn Tweedie was also summoned, with her parents, to a ceremonial introductory luncheon at the 'Rag'. Bernard and her father, mercifully, got on well; and soon the conversation developed into a name-by-name critical summary of the members of their families and mutual acquaintances. 'It was the first time I'd set eyes on either of them,' Jocelyn recollected later. 'They all went for each other hammer and tongs – discussed everyone's careers. When Betty's brother Frank came up, Monty said, "That chap's no good – useless." He was rather apt to strike people off the list in those days. But he didn't by any means get his own way with John's mother. Actually Monty was then rather being teased and being told what to do by her. He was saying no, you're not going to have the car, you're not going there this afternoon. And she said: Oh well I am actually. And she did. Monty took it very well. The whole atmosphere was very happy. She

[1] Colonel R. A. N. Davidson, loc. cit.
[2] General Sir Dudley Ward, loc. cit.

got her own way all the time.' John concurred. 'Oh, yes, we knew the form pretty well, which was that if he laid down "This or that will take place" we'd have a colloquy with Mama and she'd have a word with him. And the next day he'd say, "I've changed my mind . . ."'[1]

Betty was a shrewd and perceptive observer of people, and could even be cruel in the way she teased Bernard. 'Monty's conversation, you know, consists in asking questions,' she once said of him – which was exactly the case. Betty was, in fact, a proud and firm woman whom Bernard not only loved but deeply respected. 'She could always get her way if she felt the matter was of sufficient importance,' John Carver recollected. 'She expected a fairly high standard of everyone around her,' he also maintained.[2] Far from being the pacifist some writers have claimed, she was very much a moral realist. She utterly rejected her brother-in-law's famous Peace Pledge Movement, saying: 'It's no use crying Peace! Peace! when there is no peace in the world'; and, when Jocelyn wrote to her saying she was having second thoughts about marrying a soldier, she replied without hesitation:

War is a ghastly process, mad indeed, but inevitable for many a decade to come. We are no more civilized really than our ancestors. For us women, we can only hope that our own beloved ones remain untouched because our motives are personal. Many is the time I have thought as you do that to remain immune, untouched by love is to be outside life and one would rather have the pain than not feel it at all. We have to pay the price and be prepared to pay. Certainly nothing is actually worth having without the will to pay.[3]

Betty remained in England while Bernard returned by air to Karachi on 15 February 1937, to serve out the last few months of his appointment at Quetta. Meanwhile David was sent back to school, and Jocelyn was taken to art exhibitions, put to work in a day nursery in Notting Hill Gate and taken for trips to London's East End in an effort by Betty both to occupy her and help her confront the realities of life.

After Bernard's Junior Division instruction at Quetta, none of his students thought very highly of the Chief Instructor for their second year, T. W. Corbett. Nor did Bernard himself, as his brother Brian remembered.[4] Corbett was an Indian Army officer, and would become Auchinleck's chief staff officer in Cairo in 1942 – being sacked six months later, together with his Commander-in-Chief. Corbett was the very opposite of his fellow Chief Instructor at Quetta: an enthusiastic polo player who relished colonial military

---

[1] Colonel and Mrs John Carver, loc. cit.
[2] Colonel John Carver, loc. cit.
[3] Letter to Jocelyn Tweedie, communicated by Mrs Jocelyn Carver.
[4] Brian Montgomery, op. cit.

service and was quite unfitted to direct the staff of a modern army. In view of Corbett's later failure it is not surprising that Bernard held him in such contempt; what is more puzzling – sad, even – is that Bernard apparently met Auchinleck himself during his instructorship at Quetta, on a tour of the North-West Frontier, where Auchinleck and the Hon. H. R. L. Alexander were both brigade commanders. 'The best man,' Bernard told Lieutenant Burge who was staying with him at the time, 'was a chap called Auchinleck.'[1]

Auchinleck had similarly been Chief Instructor, Junior Division of the Staff College, Quetta from 1930–32, and was three years older than Bernard; Brigadier Alexander – whom Bernard had taught at the Staff College, Camberley – was four years his junior. Richard O'Connor, who succeeded Auchinleck as Brigadier of the Peshawar Brigade in 1936, was two years younger than Bernard. It was indeed high time Bernard re-established himself as a Commander rather than a teacher; and, throughout his period in Quetta, he appears to have been thinking about the nature of high command in a modern army. In the whole of the Great War, he told Lieutenant Burge, he had only once seen Douglas Haig, the Commander-in-Chief – and he had recognised him only because he had an escort of Lancers. 'Any future C-in-C has got to be well-known, not only to the soldiers, but to their wives and mothers,' he insisted.[2]

But did he, Bernard Montgomery, have the wherewithal – or even the opportunity – to become well known? On 20 February, a few days after his return to Quetta, the War Office cabled to offer command of the 9th Infantry Brigade at Portsmouth, due to fall vacant on 5 August that year; and on 3 March Bernard cabled back his acceptance. He would be given the temporary rank of Brigadier on commencement of his new command; meanwhile from 29 June, when his current appointment ceased, he was to be reduced to half-pay.

Such parsimony was characteristic of the Paymaster General's office; but, for the Military Secretary, Lt-General Williams prepared a final Confidential Report in March that must have amply compensated for this:

> Colonel Montgomery's work as GSO 1 and instructor at the Staff College has had a marked influence on the course, and the students who have passed through his hands have been fortunate in learning from so experienced and convincing a trainer.
>
> He has a strong personality and decided views.
>
> He is widely read and has experience both in command and on the staff in peace and war.
>
> He demands a high standard from those under him both of work and of conduct.

[1] Colonel P. B. I. O. Burge, loc. cit.
[2] Ibid.

An outstanding officer whose advancement will be in the best interests of the service.

At the bottom of this commendation was an additional note: 'He is about to take command of a Regular Infantry Brigade. Fitted now for promotion to Major-General and for employment in command and on the staff in that rank.'

As if this were not enough, General W. H. Bartholomew, the Chief of General Staff in India, added his own remarks before forwarding the Report to Whitehall: 'I agree with the opinion of the Commandant of the Staff College. Colonel Montgomery has been a great asset at the Staff College and his work invaluable.'

But the Deputy Chief of General Staff would not be drawn. 'I do not know Colonel Montgomery well enough to be able to report on him,' he wrote – and signed his name: Major-General C. J. Auchinleck.

Auchinleck's cold douche did not, fortunately, reach Bernard before he left Quetta. As he had accumulated a certain amount of leave over the past years he departed from the Staff College on 6 May and embarked on the P & O steamship *Viceroy of India* at Bombay nine days later. It was the last time he would see India before becoming head of the British Army some ten years later. The two-week passage from India was a chance to shed some of its slothful shadow and consider the realities towards which he was steaming; and while other passengers played deck-quoits, the impending Brigadier sat penning a new article, which General Williams suggested he submit to the journal of the Royal Engineers: 'The Problem of the Encounter Battle'.

CHAPTER TEN

The Death of Betty

'Viceroy of India',
Port Said
22–5–37

My dear Liddell Hart

I am on my way home to command the 9th Inf Bde at Ports-mouth. In Bombay I bought a copy of your new book *Europe in Arms* and I have been reading it during the voyage. I should like to say how much I have enjoyed it – it is a masterpiece of clear and logical reasoning and should be read by all soldiers.

Regarding the Field Force. I feel myself that the nature of our Empire demands that we should have available as a reserve a small force of say 4 divisions, properly equipped, and available to be sent anywhere at any time. It need not necessarily be kept in England; Palestine would probably be quite a good place for it, over & above the troops we shall keep in the Canal area under the new treaty. I would avoid getting this reserve committed on the continent of Europe.

I would much like to discuss this and other questions with you some time, and I hope we may meet in England.

I am at the moment engaged in writing for the next issue of the *RE Journal* an article on the problem of the encounter battle as affected by modern British establishments. The army has got to learn a new technique and this will involve a change of tactics – I feel there is a grave danger that we shall carry on with the old tactics, relying on the material solution to solve our difficulties. I shall be interested to have your views on the article when it appears in September.

Yrs sincerely
B. L. Montgomery

This letter was the first correspondence with Liddell Hart since the two men had fallen out over the *Infantry Training Manual* of 1930–1; yet it is more than likely that they met in person during the interval of seven years. Certainly Bernard gave copies of Liddell Hart's books to his stepson John to read during the latter's military training at Chatham. Moreover Bernard, as John put it, 'loved to gossip', and he cannot have been unaware, even at Quetta, that the new Secretary of State for War, Leslie Hore-Belisha, was using Liddell Hart as his personal mentor. Thus, in a very real sense, Liddell Hart had become the power behind the military throne. It was one of the strangest episodes in British politico-military history, for Liddell Hart had never seen service in the field beyond the rank of army lieutenant; he now not only had the power to influence Hore-Belisha's attitude towards army affairs in general but, more importantly, the very selection of senior officers. Liddell Hart, frustrated no doubt by his years of side-line military journalism, exercised his influence self-indulgently, achieving ultimately the very opposite of what he professed to intend. Thus the arch-exponent of modern mobile warfare argued, in his *Europe in Arms*, that Britain should not go beyond an air force commitment to the European continent in the event of war, but should concentrate on an Imperial Reserve, or Field Force, 'for the reinforcement of the overseas garrisons, the mobile defence of the overseas territories, and for such expeditions, truly so-called, as may be needed to fulfil our historic strategy under future conditions . . . Since Marlborough the British Army has rarely shone in the offensive, not through want of courage, but from lack of aptitude. It has been superb in defence, and unrivalled as an agent in maintaining order'.[1] This was so, but it ignored the renascent problem of Germany, and Liddell Hart must bear part of the blame for the unwillingness to face facts in 1937 and prepare an expeditionary force for the continent better armed and trained than its predecessor in 1914. What was even more ironic was that the crusading military correspondent of *The Times* should have persuaded Hore-Belisha to sack Deverell as CIGS – and appoint, instead, a man who had never commanded any formation larger than a skeleton brigade – the then fifty-one-year-old Lord Gort.

Possibly Liddell Hart imagined that Gort would be more malleable than his two antiquated predecessors. If so he was spectacularly mistaken, for within weeks Gort and Hore-Balisha were at loggerheads – a feud which would continue for the next, crucial three years. Gort simply lacked the experience and mentality of a Commander-in-Chief; although a serious student of military history, had he been promoted in the normal way it is doubtful whether he would have risen above divisional command.

Here indeed was the making of catastrophe, a catastrophe which only Chamberlain's policy of appeasement postponed.

In the meantime Liddell Hart's sway held – as Bernard's letter from Port Said indicated. Whether they met is unclear; but it is a matter of further irony that Liddell Hart's protégé, Lord Gort, considered that Bernard was 'only good at minor tactics',[2] and

[1] Liddell Hart, *Europe in Arms*, London 1937.
[2] Liddell Hart, *Memoirs*, Vol. II, London, 1965.

Liddell Hart did nothing at this time to dispel the impression. Gort's view was based, it would seem, on envy; his daughter Jacqueline had been impressed by Bernard, prompting Gort to write sarcastically to her, after the Quetta earthquake: 'Your friend Pandit Montgomery Karnel Sahib is once more holding forth pontifically on the rostrum while the poor students below catch an odd forty winks. He fancies himself more than ever now, I expect.'[1] Gort may well have found Bernard's perorations beyond him – General Bertie Fisher, Commandant of the RMA Sandhurst, while Gort was Commandant at Camberley, found Gort incapable of summing up a discussion, and the papers Gort presented to Hore-Belisha were generally rendered hopelessly unclear by his preoccupation with detail.

Gort's elevation to CIGS would not take place until December 1937, however; in the meantime he was made Military Secretary. Bernard arrived back in England on 31 May 1937, and decided to spend his two months' leave with Betty, motoring in the Lake District and visiting their relatives and friends in Cheshire before going to New Park on 27 July. Betty had been suffering from laryngitis of late, and wrote from Ullswater on 7 July to Jocelyn, her future daughter-in-law:

Dearest Jocelyn

Thanks so much for your letter – I am already much better & its so quiet & peaceful here that I should be quite well before I leave. I expect to be at Burnham-on-Sea with David for the last week of August and into September & perhaps you could come over & see us – it does not look far from Wraxhall . . [2]

The summer programme had been drawn up by Bernard. He was due to take over as Brigadier at Portsmouth on 5 August, but his official residence, Ravelin House, would not be decorated and furnished until September. Besides, the 9th Infantry Brigade was due to go into summer training camp near Salisbury in late August, so it was arranged that Bernard would leave his wife and son to stay at New Park with his mother until mid-August, whence they would go to a hotel at Burnham-on-Sea, near Weston-super-Mare for the rest of David's holiday. Burnham was chosen because it was the home of one of Betty's closest friends, Nancy Nicholson, who had been secretary to Dick Sheppard, and also because it was comparatively near to Bernard's camp near Salisbury, just over fifty miles away. David could play on the sands, while Betty – she was on a medical diet – would take life easy. So solicitous was Bernard about her health, in fact, that he had forbidden her to meet Jocelyn at

[1] J. R. Colville, *Man of Valour*, London 1972.
[2] Communicated by Mrs Jocelyn Carver.

Sheerness in late July 'as even if we get there I must use my voice as sparingly as possible'.[1]

Such, then, was the intended scenario for the summer of 1937, as Bernard – on War Office half-pay – prepared himself for his first command since 1934 – a command which would ultimately determine whether he was meant to become a General. The international scene moreover looked rather different in England from the way it had in Quetta. Liddell Hart's Imperial Field Force looked splendid in theory – but the war clouds were over Europe, not the Empire. In fact the situation was not so very different from what it had been on Bernard's return, as a subaltern, from India in 1913.

Bernard's task now, he felt, was to make the 9th Infantry Brigade the best-trained in the Regular Army. This time, he hoped, there would be no helter-skelter retreat from Mons. The article he had written for the *Royal Engineers Journal*[2] was at the very heart of his current preoccupation: the encounter battle. With modern transport and aircraft there would be no 'footling around' with mounted advance guards – the term itself ought to be abolished, he declared in his article. 'We have got to develop new methods, and learn a new technique,' he insisted; and the main plank of this new technique lay in the command posts of the brigade and divisional commanders themselves. It was vital, in modern warfare, that a good start be obtained. 'If the start is a bad one – either through a bad plan, or faulty dispositions, or loss of time when time is very precious, or for any cause whatsoever – then the battle can be pulled out of the fire only by the gallantry of the troops, and they are bound to suffer heavy casualties in the process . . . Although information may be lacking or incomplete, he [the Commander] must still make a plan and begin early to force his will on the enemy . . . If he has no plan he will find that he is being made to conform gradually to the enemy's plan.'

This concentration on forward planning was the new core of Bernard's military thinking. He simply did not agree that modern battle would ever revert to the static trench warfare of 1914–18; and his insistence on fighting to a definite plan went back to the days in late August 1914, when his brigade was thrown into line against the Germans without either a plan or the most elementary attempt to choose tactically advantageous ground. 'Success in the initial encounters will go to the commander who knows what he wants, has a plan to achieve it, does not allow his formation or unit to drift aimlessly into battle, but puts it into the fight on a proper plan from the beginning.' In the early stages of the encounter, the Commander must have his HQ 'well forward – he will then gain the earliest possible information, see the ground, and be able to plan ahead and

[1] Ibid.
[2] 'The problem of the Encounter Battle as affected by modern British War Establishments', *Royal Engineers Journal*, September 1937.

issue orders to subordinates before their units arrive'. Thereafter the HQ should be pulled back so as never to become 'unduly influenced by local situations on the battle front', but during the battle the commander 'must be prepared to go forward at critical periods when important decisions may be required; he must take with him the necessary means to exercise command. To remain at his HQ at such times, waiting for information that may never arrive, may be fatal'. He must have his Royal Artillery commander alongside him at his HQ and his Chief Engineer; must plan to fight at night rather than at time-honoured dawn; and be prepared to command his mobile, armoured forces himself rather than leaving it to a specialised cavalry commander.

This was a conception of modern battle more profoundly thought-out and clearly presented than the sleep-inducing rhetoric and the small-time tactics of which Gort accused Bernard. Even Liddell Hart, on his lofty perch, was moved to write: 'I have read the article with great interest and much agreement,'[1] scoring it in the margin with lines and ticks of approval. Gort himself, who boasted that he spent four hours a day reading military history and the latest articles on military development,[2] may well have seen it – though it is unlikely he agreed with it.

Bernard's 'Encounter Battle' did in fact arouse some controversy; and the following year Bernard would be asked to reply, in the *Army Quarterly*, to the most important criticisms made of it. In the mean-time, before the article had even appeared in the *RE Journal*, Bernard decided to make it the basis of his first policy document issued at 9th Infantry Brigade HQ on 14 August 1937. The Brigade was at St Giles Camp, taking part in the summer brigade exercises which Bernard's predecessor, G. T. Raikes, had arranged; but already Bernard was thinking ahead, and his Memorandum, issued through his Brigade-Major, Major F. E. W. Simpson, was intended to be the first of a series of outline proposals for winter training in 1937–8.

Major Simpson had been posted some eight months previously to the 9th Infantry Brigade from the War Office, after a period dealing with junior staff appointments. 'There was no lack of sympathetic friends to tell me that I would never stand him, or would never last,' Simpson recorded later, 'but I was immediately captured by his efficiency and dedication to training. He was among the relatively few who at that time saw clearly the certainty of war, and he intended that his command, at least, should be ready for it. His conception of training was consequently far removed from some of the "social" peacetime exercises then prevailing, and came as a distinct shock to some of the units subjected to it.'[3]

[1] Letter of 17.9.37, Liddell Hart Papers.
[2] J. R. Colville, op. cit.
[3] Recollections of General Sir Frank Simpson, recorded by Eugene Wason for Sir Denis Hamilton, 1978.

The units were in fact four battalions, most of them known to Bernard from his 17th Infantry Brigade in Ireland – the 2nd Queen's, 2nd Middlesex, 1st KOSB and, replacing the 1st Green Howards that November, the 2nd Lincolnshire Regiment. The 9th Infantry Brigade belonged to the Regular Army's 3rd Division, commanded since 1936 by Major-General D. Bernard, who still wore spurs and liked to see his men drilling in pre-war fours.[1] The GOC Southern Command was General Burnett-Stuart, who had commanded in Egypt in the early thirties, and who thought highly of Bernard.

'Raikes was a good trainer of troops, but his approach to the training was entirely different to that of Monty,' Simpson recalled. 'The 9th Infantry Brigade Camp was at Wimborne St Giles, near a place called Cranborne Chase, and we were all under tents. Monty seized hold of the training programme and said: "This won't do. I see no purpose in having several exercises lasting only one day. I will merely have four big exercises which will each last for three days and the brigade will have three nights out in the field. Troops have got to be accustomed to working by night."

'His ideas were made very clear and I had little trouble in producing a revised programme incorporating these much bigger exercises. I was quite sure that, though some of the troops of the brigade might grumble at being kept out so long, they would really fall in with Monty's plans because it was good training.

'An unexpected problem then arose. We had been told that to be included in the brigade camp was a Territorial Army regiment, the Wiltshire Yeomanry, who were horsed, and a very fine horsed cavalry regiment indeed.

'It was run like so much of the TA in those days on rather feudal lines. The officers were the bigger farmers and some landowners. The men themselves came from jobs working for the same officers, and when they heard that we were going to have those tremendous exercises – three nights out at a time – they jibbed violently.

'They said that they gave up their time and sometimes their work voluntarily to come and learn to be soldiers, but they also wanted a bit of fun while in camp. Most of them had their own cars of sorts and they had looked forward to exercises all day and then going for a bit of jollity at night to places like Bournemouth before returning about two or three in the morning.

'All this would be knocked on the head if they had to spend three nights out in the field every week. So they asked: "Please could we be excused from taking part in the lengthy exercises."

'This got Monty on the raw at once. He said: "I am not going to have these people coming back into the camp at two in the morning, probably drunk, making a noise, disturbing all my hardworking

[1] Lt-General Sir Frederick Morgan, *Peace and War*, London 1961.

troops. If they won't play over our exercises, I don't want them in the camp."

'It was no good my arguing that the War Office had directed that they should attend the camp, and there looked to be quite a problem raising its head. However, after a bit of negotiation – which gave me quite a lot of trouble – it was arranged that the Wiltshire Yeomanry could have their own camp on the other side of a small hill. This would let the War Office feel that they were in the area of the 9th Infantry Brigade Camp . . .

'This worked admirably. The infantry battalions of the 9th Infantry Brigade and their attached troops did not get disturbed at all by the Wiltshire Yeomanry, who at the same time looked on rather curiously at what the 9th Infantry Brigade was doing.

'After a bit they came to the conclusion that there was some sense in these big exercises, and they came to me and said: "Would the Brigade Commander mind if we are incorporated on the last one?" They were prepared to forego their nightly trips, away from their wives, to Bournemouth and would join wholeheartedly with the infantry of the brigade.

'This gave great pleasure to Monty, who felt that at last these soldiers had seen the light, and they were duly incorporated in the big exercise at the end of the second week.

'That exercise involved an approach march with its cavalry spearhead onto what was a prepared enemy position on a small ridge. It all went very well until the umpires stopped the cavalry – commanded by a subaltern named Brown – and told him that he could not go on because he was being fired on by an enemy machine-gun from a copse about 1200 yards to the front.

'I was there myself as assistant to the Brigade Commander, who was controlling the exercise, and it so happened that at the moment when he appeared in his car to see what was going on and while he was being told about the position – he was waiting to see what action the subaltern would take – up came the CO of the Wiltshire Yeomanry, cantering on his horse, to ask what the hell the subaltern was delaying over.

'The subaltern turned to him and said: "Sir, I am told that I am being fired on somewhat heavily by a machine-gun in yonder copse and that I cannot advance from here."

'The CO bellowed with rage and said: "Damn it, boy, you have a horse, go and catch the bloody gun!"

'All this took place immediately in front of the Brigade Commander, and Monty was horrified. He said that these people didn't understand war and could not go catching machine-guns with horses. You had to think out a way of getting round them.

' "Tell the umpires," he said, "that the whole of the cavalry troop has been slaughtered by machine-gun and let the others decide what they had best do in the circumstances."

'This was done and there seemed considerable mutterings among the Yeomanry, who shortly after that withdrew from the exercise because Monty had been so rude to them.

'Now it so happened that two nights later the Wiltshire Yeomanry were giving a guest-night in their camp – it was the big guest-night of the camping period – and they had invited quite a number of guests including the Brigade Commander and myself. We went; I was feeling slightly apprehensive considering what had happened previously. But they were the most charming hosts. Their hospitality was very fine indeed, and even Monty had a glass or two of wine. All was going very well indeed until after dinner – after the port had been brought round – and then the band changed from its usual cheerful tunes into a sort of funeral dirge and several of the officers carried in a stretcher on which was the body of the subaltern.

'They then sang "John Brown's Body" in a very mournful way and put a notice on his chest that he had been killed by order of the umpires.

'He had been made to look a ghastly corpse, his face all grey and blood coming out of his ears and mouth. It was a great success. Monty took the whole thing in wonderful heart and the party ended extremely well.

'The programme for this particular camp was due to finish with an inter-brigade battle between the 9th Infantry Brigade and the 7th Infantry Brigade, which was then stationed on Salisbury Plain. The Divisional Commander was going to control this exercise, testing out the two brigadiers and their staffs; it seemed certain to involve two nights out and perhaps two whole days as well.

'So Monty said to the Yeomanry, did they want to come on this final exercise against the 7th Infantry Brigade? They said, yes, they would like to, as that was going to be the climax of the camp.

'The task given to the 9th Infantry Brigade was the capture of a small hummock on Salisbury Plain. The 7th Infantry Brigade had the task of defending that particular area and inflicting as much damage on the attackers as they could possibly do.

'The 7th Infantry Brigade was commanded by a Brigadier William Platt, whom I had never met then, but who in much later years rose to be a four-star general. His Brigade-Major was an exact contemporary of mine at the Staff College.

'I was given the task by Monty of preparing beforehand an appreciation and plan for that particular operation, and I suppose my appreciation and plan was very much on the lines I was taught at the Staff College. It was more or less an orthodox one. We were making three feints and putting in the strongest attack behind one of them.

'Monty went through it and said: "This won't do at all. This is too orthodox. You want to do something that surprises Platt. I know him well and if you do anything too orthodox he will expect it and counter it. If you attack him from a totally unexpected direction you will get him cold."

'So he told me what he wanted to do, which was a complete flank attack in a direction I had not believed possible, and I doubted whether we would be able to get into a position to carry out that attack without the 7th Infantry Brigade discovering it, and being given plenty of time to counter it.

'Still, Monty was determined to do it, but he said: "I will do something else he does not expect. I will attack before he thinks the battle has even started."

'The exercise was planned to commence at midnight on the first day and the general assumption was that no one would really get going until daylight had come. However, Monty had said he was determined to get going at midnight as soon as the exercise had started. "All the troops will be ordered to go to sleep from teatime until 11 p.m. beforehand, and they can then be roused ready to start marching at midnight."

'So orders were issued and operations started accordingly. We certainly got into a very favourable position on the first day without being detected. There were a lot of very highly-placed senior officers taking an interest in this exercise, and I can remember being visited on that first day by the CIGS of the day [Deverell] and the Army Commander in Southern Command [Burnett-Stuart], and almost everybody else in high places in the south of England.

'The battle proceeded, very favourably from the point of view of the 9th Infantry Brigade. By the end of the second night we had got into a very advantageous position actually on Salisbury Plain in the garrison town of Tidworth. It was a dark and stormy night and Monty had taken particular pains to place road blocks manned by sentries on all the exits from our strong defensive position, just in case the 7th Infantry Brigade decided to try something surprising against us.

'I remember well having to go round in the pouring rain to see that every one of the road blocks was alerted and manned because the rain gave every excuse to sleepy troops who, after all, had been out for a couple of nights already, to get into a little shelter and have a snooze.

'Nevertheless, the atmosphere of war that Monty had instilled into the Brigade was such that I found everyone fully alert and willing to challenge me whenever I approached them. In fact, no attempt was made to infiltrate the brigade position.

'The result of all this was that by the next morning Monty was in a very good position indeed. He took advantage of the fact that the weather had improved and put in a forced march to reach his objective in the middle of Salisbury Plain. The Divisional Commander [Major-General Bernard] then called the exercise to a halt.

'Monty drove over to see his opposite number, Platt. He came back with a grin on his face and said to me: "Platt did not seem to want to see me, even to say what a good fight we had had. I think you will find he is going to sack his Brigade-Major."

'Monty took good care to see that very good reports were put up on his own staff – I know I myself was made within a few months a brevet Lt-Colonel, so he had done me very well.'

The Divisional and GOC Southern Command were equally impressed by Bernard's performance, and in their Confidential Reports that autumn both recommended Bernard for promotion. Major-General Denis Bernard wrote:

> Brigadier Montgomery has already shown himself a good Brigade Commander.
>
> He assumed command at a most awkward time – just before Bde Training – but soon took hold and trained his Bde very well. He has a quick brain and a clear head – knows what he wants to do, and does it. He is very keen and seems to have the power of conveying his keeness to his units.
>
> He showed good powers of command and leadership the only occasion when he had a chance of doing so.
>
> I have no doubt that when his turn comes he will be in every way fitted for promotion to Major-General.

General Burnett-Stuart was more urgent:

> He is most capable. He is full of ideas, can express them and pass them on. He studies his profession with vision and understanding. A rather imperious commander who at once impressed his personality on his Bde.
>
> I have known him well for some years.
>
> I have no hesitation in saying that he is fitted for promotion in any Major-General's command or employment. Especially fitted for a Regular Divisional Command.

As in Egypt and India, these were outstanding testimonials – the more so since the two Bernards – Montgomery and his Divisional Commander – were by all accounts not on the best of terms. It says much for the system of reports in those days that personal prejudice was rigorously set aside and only professional considerations taken into account.

Bernard had thus made a good start – which left him 'well placed for the next round' according to his own doctrine of tactics. Moreover, command of the 9th Infantry Brigade brought with it certain privileges which appealed to Bernard's flourishing vanity, since the senior military officer in the area became, by tradition, the Commandant of the garrison town, entitled to hold the ceremonial keys to the city, and take precedence even over more senior naval officers in the docks or aboard ships in port. Since Portsmouth was rapidly becoming the largest naval dockyard and victualling establishment in the United Kingdom, this was of no mean significance. He would have much entertaining to do at Ravelin House, and equally much ceremonial visiting of ships – so much in fact that within a few months he would soon be having to wear his own Brigadier's ceremonial dress uniform with frock coat, epaulettes, sash and sword in order to compete with the frock coats of visiting Admirals.

It was important, then, to Bernard that the redecoration of Ravelin House be completed as soon as possible after summer camp, so that he and Betty could move in. Before travelling to Ireland, Betty had chosen most of the material she wanted for curtains and the carpets they were to have. After the years of bungalow life it was going to be their first real home, decorated to their own taste; and – more importantly – a home for young David who had had to spend so many of his vacations in holiday camps since the earthquake at Quetta. John and Dick Carver, Betty's sons, would be able to stay there on leave from their stations in India. It would be Bernard's answer to New Park, his own mansion, shared with Betty; and a chance, too, perhaps to impress her Chiswick and bohemian friends who had once thought him so uninteresting.

Betty was still at New Park on 19 August, for she wrote from there to her son John – a chatty, but revealing letter that gives a vivid idea of her intelligence, her gentle snobbery, and the seriousness with which she thought about things:

Darling John. Sweet of you to remember David & send him £1 – he was so thrilled. He had a lovely birthday, lots of presents and a jolly party of 9 children for tea and then sat up for supper. His little friend Peter is a dear little chap but rather young for David as is also Gardner, the son & heir of the Montgomerys & the 'apple' of Lady M's eye – a jolly little chap but definitely above himself at times. Colin & Margaret have arrived – he looks 'prosperous' & well fed but seems to me to have developed a good deal. I always do think —— a real good sort even if definitely 'of the people'. Have been reading a good deal about India lately & suppose that now I am away from it safely I have more sense of perspective as well as the interest of having you & Dick there. 'Legacy to India' by Garratt is good & concise & also the old novel 'Passage to India'. Wonder if you can get hold of these books or if you would like me to send them . . . We (Lady M) are reading out in the evening a book about Ireland in the days of Elizabeth – most interesting as it brings in Greencastle & Rougham of the O'Neills, which was where my mother came from & the old castle was standing in the grounds which I well remember. I read an article too about officers from India who save to come home instead of spending their leave in the country & that this was to be deplored as we would thus be losing touch with native life – this is as may be. Travelling facilities will increase & so will the 'coming home' & that may be one of the reasons towards 'self government'. India is not a white man's country & inevitably to my mind, one day we shall withdraw, though whether India will ever withstand the penetration of another white nation is a surmise. I am glad to think of you & Dick together & that you have managed to meet I hope. This place is lovely as ever, but the weather has broken & now we are getting it very 'soft'. Much love, my dear, from

Mother

It was one of the last letters she would write. She and Bernard both felt that, in pursuance of the Simon report, India should be granted self-government and ultimately independence. Certainly Betty never foresaw danger at home; she had safely avoided the many diseases prevalent in India. A few days after writing this letter she left New Park with David, and made her way to Burnham-on-Sea, as planned. Almost immediately, on the beach, she was bitten on the foot by some insect. 'She could not say what sort of insect it was,' Bernard recorded ruefully in his *Memoirs*, 'and this was never known. That night her leg began to swell and became painful; a doctor was called in and he put her at once into the local Cottage Hospital and sent for me.'

This was the beginning of a terrible, lingering death, the memory of which was to scar Bernard for the rest of his own life. Yet at this stage, late in August 1937, it was treated as a mere inflammation, painful but not dangerous. Whether it derived from the insect bite, or being trodden on by a horse while in Ireland, or even from rheumatism was still unclear. Bernard however felt that these first Brigade exercises on Salisbury Plain were crucial to his career; he was loth to leave them prematurely, and so with Betty's agreement he rang young Jocelyn Tweedie's father, the Admiral, and asked if Jocelyn could come and stay in the hotel at Burnham to look after David until Betty was better. Jocelyn still remembers the telephone call:

Father: She's never stayed in a hotel by herself!
Monty: Well, it's about time that she did![1]

Thus Bernard returned to Salisbury Plain, while the innocent twenty-one-year-old fiancée of John Carver came to look after her future brother-in-law, then just nine.

Betty had been taken to the Cottage Hospital. I stayed with David in this hotel. He was an absolute terror! Actually we got on very well, but I couldn't control him at all. He was very devoted to his

[1] Mrs Jocelyn Carver, interview of 3.3.1978.

mother. He had his 'rules' . . . Every night he would read a chapter of the Bible – partly so that he would have an excuse to keep his light on, partly because his mother had told him to. He was a very bossy little boy. He used to shout and say:

'You're nothing to do with me. You're only going to get married to my brother. You can't give orders to me!'

We used to go *every day* to see John's mother. She got worse and worse. In the end she couldn't speak to David at all. He was terribly upset. He knew.[1]

Time, fortunately, would erase David's memory of this; and from the moment he returned to Amesbury School Bernard kept him well out of the way. 'Perhaps I did wrong,' Bernard wrote in his *Memoirs*, 'but I did what I thought was right.'

The little nine-year-old, however, saw more clearly than his father where all this was leading. He was, after all, on the spot, whereas Bernard, according to Jocelyn, did not appear at all in the fortnight she was there.

He never came when I was there. Yes, he came to lunch once. And he came to pack all David's things, and get his suits clean and respectable – I think it was Betty who asked for this. I don't think Monty believed it was anything much. There was nothing showing on the outside of her skin, it was inside.

By the time David took his leave of her, Betty was, however, unable to speak for pain.

Gradually she became worse, and when I took David to say goodbye before going back to school, she tossed restlessly & couldn't speak to him. He had bought her a present of a little gold sword brooch, and he just left it on her sheet, and went back to the hotel to write her a letter, which he told me to read to her after he had gone. He was only nine years old, but he seemed to know it was really goodbye.

I stayed on for a bit until Katie Hobart, her cousin, came to take over from me.

At times Betty's condition improved. Jocelyn would be made to read to her from *The Times*.

Nobody came while I was there. I remember Monty telling me on no account must Aunt Zillah [Betty's sister] know that she was ill. I thought the whole thing was rather extraordinary. I talked to Matron – she didn't know what the illness really was. There was

[1] Ibid.

certainly no specialist called down while I was there. She was very ill again when I last saw her – so ill she couldn't speak to me. That was in late September.[1]

Jocelyn had stayed on for a further week, overlapping with Katie Hobart. No one else was summoned or allowed to be there as Betty fought for her life, alternately critical and then seemingly better. On 9 October, several weeks after Jocelyn's departure, Betty asked her cousin Katie to thank Jocelyn for some flowers she had sent.

'It's difficult to say anything definite about Betty,' Katie Hobart added in her letter.

> There's no straightforward progress, it's a very up & down business, & tho' today she is ever so much better than she has been since Monday, she is not so well as she was a week ago! It's very disappointing, as she did improve a lot last weekend & one did hope the corner was turned. I think it's really the poison in her system that is retarding recovery, also all the different serum injections which she gets have strange effects . . .
>
> Poor Monty – his cut & dried plans miscarry. He had 'time-tabled' that she was to be moved to Portsmouth last week, then it was to be today. I was quite certain that she would not be fit for this & the Dr forbade it. Monty, I fear, has still to learn that in serious illness things do not work out according to plan like ordering an advance at dawn! He came over yesterday & left today, as he has some big Corporation affair with the Mayor tomorrow. David is to be there. Won't the other boys at school feel mere worms on Monday! . . .[2]

For Bernard it was a 200-mile round trip each time he visited Betty, and natural that he should want her transferred to Portsmouth, where she would also receive more expert attention. However, David's pride at being able to witness a ceremonial occasion in Portsmouth alongside his father was tainted by the knowledge that his mother still lay in the little Cottage Hospital, almost two months since they first went there. The hours of Betty's life were indeed ticking away; and on 15 October Katie Hobart was again writing to Jocelyn:

> Dear Jocelyn:
> I am terribly sorry to say that poor Betty is much worse. Her lungs are now affected by the poisoning & she has great difficulty in breathing. She is being given oxygen which eases her a little. Without hearing anything officially I thought she was terribly ill on

[1] Ibid.
[2] Communicated by Mrs Jocelyn Carver.

Wednesday & she became so bad that night that the Dr sent for Bernard who arrived yesterday. She is no worse today – in fact pulse & temperature a shade better, but she is very seriously ill & we are all very anxious & worried. One can only hope & pray she has enough strength left to pull through. I'm sorry to give such depressing news but things are very serious at present . . .[1]

They were indeed. Despite the primitive facilities of the Cottage Hospital major surgery seemed the only possible solution. 'Then came the day when the doctors decided that the only hope was to amputate the leg; I agreed and gained hope,' Bernard wrote in his *Memoirs*. He wrote immediately to David, telling him that his mother would henceforth be an invalid, but that this was not the end of the world. He must learn to do things for her, as they would all have to do. Everything, in fact, would run as before.[2]

Doubtless Bernard believed this. After all, had he not fussed over Betty since the day they married, husbanding her health and physical resources to the point of tyranny? Katie Hobart had told Jocelyn, during the week they were together at Burnham-on-Sea, that whenever she came to stay with her cousin, the time she would be allowed to be with Betty was strictly allotted by Bernard in advance, lest she overtire her.

However, there was little opportunity in which to organise Betty's new invalid life, for the amputation was a medical gesture of despair. To the very end the doctors had no idea what was really the cause of Betty's blood-poisoning, and once it had infected other parts of her body, surgery was not only futile, but a final drain on her remaining strength. She had battled for more than six weeks. Though she survived the operation itself, she quickly succumbed to pneumonia. As the end drew near Bernard read to her from the Bible: 'Yea though I walk through the valley of the shadow of death, I will fear no evil: for Thou art with me; Thy rod and Thy staff they comfort me.'

'Betty died on the 19th October 1937, in my arms,' Bernard recounted in his *Memoirs* some twenty years later. The big house at Portsmouth would never see its intended mistress; David would be motherless. Betty Montgomery was dead.

---

[1] Ibid.
[2] Viscount Montgomery, loc. cit.

CHAPTER ELEVEN

Brigadier in Mourning

There were only four mourners at the graveside in Burnham-on-Sea. The law of death required a post-mortem and an inquest – at which septicaemia was recorded – before the body could be disposed of; thereafter the matter was in Bernard's hands.

The grief-stricken Brigadier wanted no witnesses, and stood silently on a bright October day with only his Brigade-Major, Staff Captain and the driver of the staff car present as the priest – Canon Dick Sheppard – commended the departed to the mercy of Almighty God. Bernard refused to let David, his son, be present, and forbade John and Dick, his stepsons, to fly from India either. No relatives were invited, either from the Montgomerys or the Hobarts. As quietly – or even more so – as he had married the thirty-nine-year-old widow, he now took leave of her.

'It was the only time during our long friendship that I ever saw him less than in control of himself,' related General Simpson more than forty years later. 'As he faced a sixty-mile drive home alone, I urged him to come back with me in the staff car. Nothing would persuade him.'[1]

Bernard's letter to his stepson, Dick Carver, written on the day Betty died and continued after her funeral, gives the most vivid insight into his feelings at this cardinal moment of his life. On 19 October 1937 he informed Dick of her death:

I never left her for the last 24 hours and it was heart breaking to watch her slowly dying. The final end was very peaceful, just one deep sigh; and she had no pain the last few days. She knew me up to about one hour before she died, after which she never opened her eyes or spoke . . .

I think she knew she could not live. This morning when the doctor had left the room she whispered to me to go after him and ask him what he thought. And later when he came in again she gasped 'Is there any hope?' Poor darling – she had a ghastly time during the last 6 weeks and had fought most bravely to live. I used to tell her she must fight for our sakes. But it was too much for her.

[1] Wason interviews, loc. cit.

From Ravelin House two days later Bernard recorded her burial in the 'pretty little cemetery' at Burnham-on-Sea that morning:

The funeral is over and I am back at Ravelin House. It was a lovely day & brilliant sun. Dick Sheppard came and took the service most beautifully.

I sat [. . .] in the room at the hospital until they came to screw the lid on the coffin. She looked too wonderful – utterly calm and peaceful . . .

I kissed her dear face for the last time just before the lid was put on. The room was full of the most lovely flowers sent by all our friends. All my battalions in the Bde sent wreaths, and I was very touched to see one from the men of the Queens. I tried hard to bear up at the service and at the graveside. But I could not bear it and I am afraid I broke down utterly. Dick [Sheppard] was too wonderful & when everyone had gone away we knelt down together at the graveside and he said a very intimate family prayer, and we knelt there in silence. I said I could not believe it was God's will that she should have all that pain & suffering, and then die after it; surely if she had to die it should have been before all the pain. He said that God's ways of working are very mysterious, and I suppose that is true.

But, oh Dick, it is hard to bear and I am afraid I break into tears whenever I think of her. But I must try to bear up. I have come back alone to this big empty house for good now. And I get desperately lonely and sad. I suppose in time I shall get over it, but at present it seems that I never shall.

The light of his life had gone out – Betty with her slightly breathless, husky voice, who brought excitement into everything she did, no matter how trivial; Betty with her sense of fun, who alone could pull Bernard's leg, who was not irked by his eccentricities in any way, who had made an inveterate bachelor the most happily married man. They had sparked each other off; had been married for ten years and been as loving to each other as on the day of their wedding. It was not a marriage of convenience; and yet it certainly was not inconvenient either, Betty's son John and his wife would later recall. It was a marriage which suited both parties, was good for the children – for everyone. She, who was apt to get nervy, to get in a flap, was cared for by someone who had a natural if exaggerated sense of order, who loved and respected her enough to see that she had time to paint, the freedom to be happy. And in return she had looked beyond his gaucheness, his schoolboy innocence, his need to assert himself; had given the two things which Bernard's mother had always refused: her uninhibited love and her belief in his talents.

'People speculate on what might have happened if my mother had lived,' John Carver wrote later. 'To my mind a more interesting speculation concerns what would have happened if he and my mother had never met. I think there might have been real danger that those schizoid tendencies engendered by his upbringing which were always latent might have become dominant in his personality; I mean a single-mindedness progressing to narrow-mindedness, a detachment leading to lack of human feeling and suspicion of the motives of others, and that such characteristics might have developed to such an extent as to have rendered him unsuitable for high command. It may not be entirely fanciful to suggest that the country owes something at least to my mother.'[1]

This was a bold claim – namely that Betty had kept her latently schizoid spouse sane during the critical years between forty and fifty. Fanciful or not, Bernard had reached the eve of fifty without major mishap, was currently judged a 'character', but not insane – something which could certainly not be said for his brother-in-law, the irascible Patrick Hobart, who, not long later, was dismissed from his divisional command (and ultimately the Army) for being 'self-opinionated and lacking in stability'[2] nor for Liddell Hart whose work for *The Times* as Defence Correspondent became so erratic that his contract was terminated amid speculation that he was mentally unbalanced.[3]

Undoubtedly Betty Montgomery had helped Bernard to survive the gruelling ascent to power and command. The question in many minds when Betty died was: can Bernard face this tragedy? Can he overcome it – can he put it behind him and emerge a balanced individual, capable of fulfilling his manifest talents?

Letters of condolence came from all parts of the world – indeed it says something for Bernard's reputation within the Army and the impression the couple had made that news of the tragedy quickly penetrated to almost every individual and unit which had served with him.

Bernard's first instinct had been to ask in what respect he had failed – 'I began to search my mind for anything I had done wrong, that I should have been dealt such a shattering blow'; but he was too self-controlled by nature, too detached, not to sense the real question mark. 'I had duties to others,' he recalled in his *Memoirs*, 'to my Brigade and as the Commander of the Portsmouth Garrison. I realised that I must get on with my work. There was also David to be considered; we were now alone in the world, just the two of us, and he must be visited regularly at his school and well cared for in his holidays.'

Since the day Betty died, Bernard had remained alone, refusing to

[1] Colonel John Carver, 'Reflections on Bernard & Betty Montgomery, loc. cit.
[2] Lt-General Wilson, letter to General Wavell, 10.11.39, quoted in K. Macksey's *Armoured Crusader*, op. cit.
[3] *The Times* Archives.

see anyone. The decision to cease such solitary mourning was, however, dramatic.

'At 1 a.m. on the night after the funeral I was wakened in bed by the telephone. "That you, Simbo?" said the caller. "I'm afraid I've left things rather to you these last few days. Tomorrow I want all the papers on my desk at 9 a.m. and we'll get down to work,"' General Simpson recorded later. 'Happily I went to sleep. We were back in business.'[1]

[1] Wason interviews, loc. cit.

CHAPTER TWELVE

A General in Palestine

One may well question whether Bernard allowed himself time to get over Betty's death. Certainly he emerged, to the military eye, no different: energetic, conscientious, determined to prove himself as a commander; but then, Betty's influence had never shown in Bernard's profession any more than he had influenced Betty's painting or sculpture. It would be in Bernard's private life that Betty's loss showed – and in his military career only when, more than half a decade later, fame and high command swept him into circles and relationships he could not cope with alone.

Possibly, if Bernard had been less possessive over Betty's death and had allowed himself the time to adjust, emotionally, he might have emerged a deeper, richer human being. Instead he swiftly internalised Betty's memory and got on with his job. It was a time of change in the War Office. First Dill, then Wavell was tipped to be the new CIGS under Hore-Belisha, the Minister of War. Though Bernard had never served under or alongside Wavell – who was four years his senior – he had come to know him in the 1920s when Wavell was GSO 1 of the 3rd Division on Salisbury Plain, and had conceived a lasting admiration for him. Liddell Hart, however, urged that Gort be nominated; Hore-Belisha took his advice and Wavell remained Commanding Officer in the steadily worsening conditions of Palestine, while Gort became CIGS.

Gort's envy of Bernard and their mutual dislike meant that Bernard's chances of promotion to divisional command in peacetime were correspondingly small. However it was not only Gort who was opposed to Bernard's promotion – as Wavell recalled later. 'Monty's name had come up several times in front of the selection board; everyone always agreed that he ought to be promoted, but every other commander who had a vacancy for a major-general had always excellent reasons for finding someone else more suitable than Monty.'[1]

Fortunately Bernard's higher ambition was tempered, in a professional sense, by his determination to succeed at everything he undertook; and, while there were some who said Wavell was tiring,

[1] John Connell, *Wavell*, London 1964.

and had passed his peak (when, in the early 1930s, he commanded the 6th Infantry Brigade at Blackdown), the same could not be said of Bernard. Already on 14 August he had laid down the programme and policy for winter training in the 9th Infantry Brigade – and his sense of urgency was explicit:

> The introduction of new weapons, mechanisation, the increase in armoured fighting vehicles, progress in gas, air power, and scientific inventions generally, have all combined to complicate the modern battle.
>
> It will be equally obvious that as a result of these new aids to warfare we shall have to overhaul our tactics – we must in fact develop a new technique. If we enter the next war using the old methods we shall lose the first round,

he remarked in his first Individual Training Memorandum.

> All commanders, in their several grades, must have a good knowledge of the technique of staging the many and varied operations that their unit may be called on to undertake in war, whether offensive or defensive – they must understand the stage-management of the battle . . .
>
> With a view to studying some of the many problems involved the Brigade Commander will conduct a study week for officers at Portsmouth from 15th to 19th November 1937 . . .

The new GSO 1 of the 3rd Division later remembered Bernard's Officers' Study Week vividly – remembered indeed the day Montgomery marched into his office and addressed him thus:

> 'I hear you are to be GSO 1 of the 3rd Division. My name is Montgomery and I command the 9th Infantry Brigade of the 3rd Division at Portsmouth. Now I am holding an Officers' Week shortly and it would be good for you to attend. Come and stay with me at Government House for the week. You will meet my Commanding Officers and learn something of the business.'[1]

The business was war and Morgan, with whom Bernard would later quarrel over 'Overlord' and at SHAEF, was amazed by the Brigadier's *tour de force*. 'Every minute of it was of the utmost value as we were instructed in every conceivable aspect of the whole art of war. It was inspiring beyond words to meet this single-minded zealot whose enthusiasm could communicate itself even to one so far gone as myself to despondency.'[2]

[1] General Sir Frederick Morgan, *Peace and War*, op. cit.
[2] Ibid.

It was indeed a *tour de force* – for not only had Bernard prepared the Study Week in the shadow of Betty's death, but his Brigade-Major, 'Simbo' Simpson, inadvertently set fire to himself in the course of a lecture at Tidworth, so that Bernard had to conduct the entire Officers' Week himself, aided only by the Staff Captain. Not content with almost single-handedly running the week, Bernard thereafter issued a ten-page summary of tactical principles – a document not only remarkable for its clarity and imagination, but for its prophetic realism. Liddell Hart's theories of 'expanding torrent' (leap-frogging reserves through a penetrated enemy line) and 'exploitation' (not waiting to mop-up, but pressing on boldly) might appear exciting in theory – but were they realistic against a professional enemy like the Germans? Bernard thought not, remembering his experience at the end of the Great War:

> It is often assumed that once the attack has got in behind the enemy, all enemy parties on the remainder of the front will at once retire or surrender.
> This is a great fallacy. Against a good enemy there will be much hard fighting to follow.

It was Bernard's instruction in how to conduct 'the hard fighting to follow' that impressed those, like Morgan, who felt despondent about the prospect of war and the ability of the British Army to compete with an indoctrinated, trained enemy like the Germans. Attack by night, the use of reserves, organisation of defence, role of artillery, night withdrawal, river crossing: all were considered in Bernard's infectiously fresh, lucid, and wonderfully straightforward style. Liddell Hart might be stimulating in a controversial sense – but Bernard was concerned to guide his 'students' towards professional remedies for battle – and his approach was, as Morgan remarked, essentially the same in November 1937 as in the later exercises of which Monty made himself so great a master and from which so many people have benefited so greatly over the years that followed. Small wonder that Morgan recorded, 'at the end of the course even Monty began to wilt a little'.[1]

Bernard had tried to put Betty's death to the back of his mind. Despite his total dedication to his work as Brigadier he was nevertheless as considerate as always to those he liked. When Simpson was injured Bernard would not at first permit a replacement, and even had him brought home from hospital to Portsmouth to be with his wife. When the wound festered and Simpson got steadily worse in the Netley Hospital at Portsmouth, Bernard arranged for him to be 'kidnapped' – bundled through a window and taken in his car to the

[1] Ibid.

267

King Edward VII Hospital in London, where the famous plastic surgeon Archibald Macindoe operated on him.

Come Christmas, there could be no distraction, however. David duly came home from school. 'It was a dreadful Xmas, with just bereaved father and son,' David remembered, despite the new miniature railway Bernard had brought him;[1] and he went off to school with relief again in January 1938. Soon afterwards John Carver's fiancée Jocelyn came to stay, with her father Admiral Sir Hugh Tweedie. Bernard had insisted that the engagement be formally announced the week after Betty's death, and for the moment he treated Jocelyn as a daughter.

'There was a frightful atmosphere of gloom,' Jocelyn recalled. 'I remember he produced some jewellery that had belonged to Betty, and I had to choose some. We went out in the evening with the Portsmouth Admiral and Monty brought down Betty's coat and said, "You're to wear this," and I argued and there was quite a tussle in the hall. I remember I had to wear it in the end. He seemed to want to project – he was terribly lonely, and he talked quite a lot about Betty.'[2]

The Army, however, seemed to bring Bernard back to normal life. His Officers' Week had been only the start of his re-shaping of 9th Infantry Brigade; in the ensuing weeks he had considered every aspect of brigade and battalion training, the result of which was, in January 1938, the issue of a fourteen-point second Memorandum on Individual Training 'to make certain nothing has been left out'. Not content with his Officers' Study Week in November 1937, Bernard planned a second study session for officers in March 1938 'for the purpose of instruction in the making up of schemes for exercises with and without troops'. He quoted from Intelligence reports about German company training, and was insistent that battalion commanders begin to train their junior officers to take command of larger units, even the battalion itself, in preparation for the day when there would be casualties:

In the training of his officers the CO has a two-fold responsibility – to teach them the art of command, and to teach them how to teach, as they spend much of their peace time service doing this . . .

The junior officer of today is the commanding officer of tomorrow and, adequately to insure the future, some small sacrifice has to be made. Therefore the CO with the long view welcomes any opportunities of sending his more senior officers on duties away from the unit, such as umpiring, liaison, etc, during collective training. This policy kills two birds with one stone; it widens the

[1] Viscount Montgomery, loc. cit.
[2] Colonel and Mrs John Carver, loc. cit.

outlook of the more senior officer by giving him a change of environment, and it gives the junior officer the opportunity to practise command and to study his manuals carefully so as to do himself justice. When war comes senior officers may become casualties and this system repays itself ten-fold.

We must remember that if we do not trust our subordinates we will never train them.

But if they know they are trusted and that they will be judged on results the effect will be electrical.

The sniggers which Bernard's new broom had engendered both in the Brigade and outside soon ceased in the spring of 1938. By the middle of February, Lord Halifax, the Foreign Secretary, was having to deny that war was 'imminent'; and on 11 March, having dismissed his Army chiefs and made himself head of the German Reichswehr, Hitler ordered the invasion and annexation of Austria, the gateway to Czechoslovakia. It was obvious that Liddell Hart's policy of a Field Force uncommitted to Europe was bankrupt. Certainly Bernard must have realised this now, for since the previous autumn he had pressed for a divisional exercise, to be held in the summer of 1938, that would involve an amphibious assault combining all three services. Bernard's Brigade was designated for the operation – the first of its kind since Gallipoli. Together with the naval C-in-C at Portsmouth, Admiral of the Fleet Lord Cork and Orrery, Bernard organised the whole exercise. 'As one would anticipate,' the GSO 1 of the 3rd Division wrote later, 'the invasion was meticulously organised, the expenditure of foolscap paper by 9th Infantry Brigade amounting, as I recall, to 30,000 sheets for which I subsequently got the bill . . . I remember asking the Brigadier, for my own edification, for some amplification of his ideas on this business of inter-service cooperation – to which I got the simple answer, "Co-operation, my dear chap, no problem there. I tell them what to do and they do it." '[1]

Morgan may have been surprised by the immense organisation involved – Bernard's stepson Dick was even detailed, on his leave from India, to make a 15-foot model of the Slapton shoreline – but sad to say, few of the 30,000 sheets of foolscap paper relating to this visionary exercise have survived, and to all intents and purposes it was allowed to pass into utter obscurity.[2] Although dozens of books have been written about the development of the tank during the inter-war years, there was probably no more visionary exercise carried out in Britain than this combined forces assault landing. 'The object of the exercise was to investigate the tactical and technical aspects of an approach from seaward, and the landing of a force on an enemy coast; the provision and distribution of fire from ships in

[1] General Sir Frederick Morgan, op. cit.
[2] One copy of the 170-page report survives at the Staff College, Camberley.

company supporting the landing force; and the co-operation of aircraft,' Maj-General D. K. Bernard explained to the press and military observers on 5 July 1938. The naval support was significant: a battleship, two cruisers, an aircraft carrier and a flotilla of destroyers. There was joint Navy, Army and Air command – headed by Brigadier Montgomery, and his 'Eastland' army of two corps, which was represented by three battalions from 9th Infantry Brigade. The battalions were landed from the troopships *Lancashire* and *Clan MacAlister* before dawn on 6 July, ostensibly to be supported by 150 light tanks. Engineers constructed landing piers and beach tracks for the armoured vehicles, and Brigadier Montgomery, once ashore, took command of the invasion, which had taken the 'Wessex' defences totally by surprise.[1]

The Times recorded that 'the landing of an Infantry Brigade on Slapton Sands was carried out with great success this morning, under ideal weather conditions. The three regiments concerned, the KOSBS, the Lincolns and the East Yorks were brought ashore in Naval cutters and whalers and in transports' lifeboats between one-thirty and four o'clock; and when dawn broke, the guns, tanks and lorries, accompanied by numerous stores, were landed in special flat-bottomed craft. The troops will be re-embarked this evening.

Using tanks and mortars, Bernard Montgomery's brigade fought its way inland supported by twelve Fleet Air Arm Swordfish 'bombers' from the carrier *Courageous* and the heavy guns of the *Revenge*, the *Southampton* and the *Sheffield*, and five destroyers – but hopes of easy re-embarkation began to fade when the weather broke in the afternoon. The Navy, anxious about being blown on to a lee shore, decided not to wait for the end of the exercise – leaving some 1200 officers and men without tents and in driving rain.

In the end, however, cadets at the nearby Royal Naval College, Dartmouth, were ousted from their beds, and the Navy made up for its premature departure by feeding and accommodating the abandoned troops. 'All were wet through and hungry, and most of the troops had spent the previous day being seasick . . . such scenes can never have been seen here before. The quarterdeck, gunrooms, boot and changing rooms, Drake annexe and cinema rooms were all used to hold the troops who were packed like sardines in a tin,' the College magazine related. 'A pleasant change from the normal routine, it gave us a chance of seeing how the Army fare during "war time," and an opportunity to practise the very necessary organisation of inter-Service co-operation. We may well be grateful,' it concluded presciently.[2]

The CIGS, Viscount Gort, had come by car to watch the landing, and Bernard Montgomery was understandably proud of the per-

---

[1] *Kingsbridge Gazette*, 8 July 1938.
[2] *The Britannia Magazine*, Summer Term 1938.

formance, together with its manifold lessons. General Wavell was less enthusiastic. He had recently returned from Palestine and succeeded Sir John Burnett-Stuart as C-in-C Southern Command; he had watched the day's activities with a critical eye from the Naval C-in-C's yacht, and braved the storm that night at sea. The next day he landed, 'to be greeted', as Wavell's biographer John Connell recorded, 'by a Montgomery who was bubbling over with enthusiasm and full of explanations of the course of the exercise. Wavell said, "I see," and stumped on up the hill to the car'[1] and drove back to Salisbury.

Wavell had nothing against Bernard's handling of the exercise; it was the ramifications that depressed him. The situation in Czechoslovakia was critical and it was more than possible that Britain might be involved in war that year – an eventuality which, in contrast to his fellow Area Commanders, Wavell welcomed, as he thought Germany would use additional peacetime to better military advantage than would Britain. Bernard's amphibious assault was, however, a nightmarish illustration of Britain's unpreparedness – 'a pitiful exposition of our complete neglect of landing operations,' he wrote later. 'There was *one* so-called landing craft, an experimental one made many years before and dug out of some scrap-heap for this exercise, in which I rather think it sank. For the rest the troops landed in open row-boats as they had done for the last 200 years and more.'[2]

Wavell's despondency was well founded, but it reflected an attitude that was to become all too prevalent in the years ahead – the tendency to blame one's equipment to the point where one lost sight of the human factor in war. The best example of this would be Wavell's failure to hold Crete in 1941 against a German airborne landing – the operation which, with the subsequent failure of his desert offensive (Operation 'Battleaxe'), finally cost him his command in the Middle East.

Bernard, by contrast, was almost oblivious to the equipment factor. The German army had re-created itself illegally, using wooden rifles and wooden tanks. Equipment could be produced very quickly if need be; trained soldiers could not.

No sooner was the Slapton Sands exercise over than the War Office selected Bernard to conduct a series of special Gas Trials in August 1938 on Salisbury Plain, in response to the current scare over gas bombing.

Bernard's Trial Report, written and typed by 24 September, was a remarkable document. The main body of the report was a thirty-nine page answer to the detailed War Office questionnaire; but the key lay in Bernard's seven-page introduction (Part 1) in which he set out the problem, disposed of the anxiety surrounding the threat, and set

[1] John Connell, op. cit.
[2] Ibid.

forth the defensive and protective measures required to meet it. The War Office gave a sigh of relief; and Bernard's report became official policy throughout the ensuing war.

Bernard's trials revealed that, if soldiers were given certain protective clothing – eye-shields and sleeve detectors – and carried anti-gas ointment, there was no danger from contamination. Moreover, if the troops were well trained and deployed themselves intelligently, there was little likelihood of their becoming contaminated at all. 'Spray attacks against deployed troops will not produce results commensurate with the risks involved to the aircraft, since to get appreciable results aircraft must fly fairly low,' he argued. Where troops were locked in combat the danger was even smaller, while in the more vulnerable rear areas protective clothing could be at hand without impairing operational efficiency.

'The menace of gas must not be allowed to throw the Army off its balance. The tendency is to over-estimate the danger, whereas the problem is quite simple,' Bernard concluded. 'It is necessary to have a sense of proportion, and in war legitimate risks will have to be accepted. It is probably better to be sprayed with gas than to be shelled or bombed with high explosive.' He recommended the setting up of a central gas school, and ensuring that every Army division had its own Gas Officer. Beyond that, it was merely a matter of good training and the provision of the necessary ointment, eye-shields and sleeve detectors.

The War Office was quick to congratulate Bernard on 'a most excellent and clear report', as the Army Council put it; and the Director of Military Training was equally appreciative. 'I myself am just finishing reading it now,' wrote one senior War Office general on 7 October, 'and I would like to congratulate you on it very much indeed. What is so good about your report, and is so unusual in most reports, is that you give an absolutely definite answer to each question.' Wavell was slower in commenting; and, when he did, it was to ask Bernard for his views on the suitability of the kilt as battle dress in Highland Regiments. 'I meant to ask you, when you were doing your gas experiments this summer, to consider what advantages and disadvantages the kilt would have over other battle dress from the point of view of contamination and decontamination,' he wrote on 11 November.[1] To which Bernard replied: 'I have never considered the kilt to be a good battle dress, suitable for all weathers and climates; I have of course never worn one and possibly my opinion on the subject is not of any great value . . . It is the vapour which is the real danger. I dealt with this in my report, and if you will look at the top of page 16 you will see what I said . . . The damage occurs chiefly in places where perspiration is most marked. I understand that the best Scotchmen do not wear drawers under the kilt;

[1] John Connell, *Wavell* op. cit.

the results, therefore, might be very unpleasant,' he added, tongue in cheek.[1]

Meanwhile, by a great irony, the campaign Bernard had selected for winter study by all officers of the 9th Infantry Brigade was the 'Campaign in Egypt and Palestine from the outbreak of war with Germany to June 1917'.

Probably the most interesting operation during the period, Bernard wrote in his Instruction No. 4 of 7 October 1938,

is the 1st Battle of Gaza in March 1917, for the following reasons:
a) It was fought by just such a force as might be employed during the early stages of a future war in Europe or the Middle East.
b) It is prolific in lessons in command, staff duties, and organization.
   The personality of the commanders played an interesting part in the battle.
   The fog of war was more than usually a deciding factor in the conduct of the battle by the commanders of both sides.
c) The plan for battle was sound.
   The execution of the plan by a large part of the troops was faultless.
   The battle was at one time to all intents and purposes won.
   And yet it was a failure.
   There are many advantages in studying an operation which was a failure. The 1st Battle of Gaza failed, among other things, owing to a number of accidents and to the almost incredible lack of information available.

When writing this, Bernard had no inkling that within a month he would himself be a Divisional Commander in Palestine. Nor was the study of this campaign a mere bookish affair: each battalion was to furnish a specialist six-man study syndicate under a major, and the lessons of every step in the campaign were to be clarified and demonstrated on the brigade model. COs were to form 'a Criticism Syndicate for the purpose of deducing lessons for our future guidance; they will also consider the effect present day armament and organization would have on the operations, and how the same problem would be tackled in 1939'.

Four days after issuing these Training Instructions Bernard received the offer of command of the 8th Division in Palestine – one of two new divisional formations being set up to quell the growing Arab insurrection. A Royal Commission under Lord Peel had recommended partition in 1937; but the Partition Commission of 1938 found this to be unworkable. Pending a solution – namely a ban on

[1] Letter of 26.11.38, Montgomery Papers.

further Jewish immigration – the British Army was called upon to maintain order.

Bernard can have had no illusions about what the job entailed. He had spent a year and a half in Ireland during the 'Troubles', and he had already acted as OC British Troops in Palestine in 1931. Moreover it meant leaving the 9th Infantry Brigade at a time when negotiations were going on in earnest with the French over a British Expeditionary Force – a force in which the 9th Infantry Brigade would be bound to take a prominent part.

However, there were disadvantages in staying in England. For one thing, Bernard was anxious to take command of a division and become, at last, a Major-General; for another, despite his brilliant testimonials from Wavell and Major-General Bernard, he had in August 1938 caused an unholy row in higher quarters by arranging direct with the Mayor of Portsmouth the leasing of government property for a Bank Holiday fairground. This deal had brought £1000 into the married families' Welfare Fund of the Portsmouth Garrison, and £500 to the Mayor for a 'pet scheme'. 'The fur then began to fly,' Bernard recorded in his *Memoirs*. 'I produced all the receipts. The Major-General i/c Administration Southern Command, Salisbury, came to see me and said that this incident had ruined my chances of promotion in the Army.'

The War Office offer of 8th Division in Palestine thus came as a god-send. Wavell had managed to keep the fairground case fluid by passing the relevant file backwards and forwards between Whitehall and Salisbury; but it was, as Bernard recognised, 'growing rather large'. Arranging to leave David in the care of the Carthew-Yorstoun family in Havant – Major Carthew had worked on Bernard's staff as Garrison Adjutant and had two younger boys – Bernard therefore accepted the appointment and left England on 28 October bound for Haifa. No sooner had he arrived in Palestine, though, than he received a further communication from the Military Secretary – namely that, at a Selection Board held on 8 November 1938, he had been selected to succeed Major-General Denis Bernard on his retirement in December 1939, in command of the 3rd (Iron) Division.

This appointment was entirely Wavell's doing. In his Confidential Report of October 1938 Wavell had written:

I have known Brigadier Montgomery for a number of years. He is one of the clearest brains we have in the higher ranks, an excellent trainer of troops, and an enthusiast in all he does. His work this year in the Combined Operation Exercise and Gas Trials was of a very high order. He has some of the defects of the enthusiast, in an occasional impatience and intolerance when things cannot be done as quickly as he would like or when he meets brains less quick & clear than his own.

Days later, Wavell was asked by the Selection Board 'whom I wanted to succeed Bernard in the 3rd Division. I replied at once – "Monty". There was something like a sigh of relief from the other Army Commanders and instant acquiescence.'[1]

For Bernard these were glad tidings: a year's command of a division in the field in Palestine, followed by a command of one of the traditional component divisions of a British Expeditionary Force.

Wavell himself had been GOC in Palestine from 1937–8, but had failed to crush the Arab rising. 'Dealing with the rebellion was a very unsatisfactory and intangible business,' was all he would commit himself to say in retrospect, 'and I don't think I produced any better answers than anyone else. But I think I kept it within bounds and did as much as I could with the troops available.'[2]

Bernard Montgomery, by contrast, went out determined to achieve positive results. Wavell's successor as GOC in Palestine was General 'Bob' Haining, the former Director of Military Operations and Intelligence at the War Office, and Bernard's predecessor at the Staff College, Camberley; the commander of the 7th Division in the south of Palestine was Major-General 'Dick' O'Connor who had been an instructor with Bernard.

Instead of the 9th Infantry Brigade model or sand-table Bernard now had the actual terrain of Palestine at hand and there can be no doubt that, despite the essentially policing nature of the 1938–9 campaign, Bernard was out to learn every lesson he could in the handling of a regular army division in quasi-war conditions. Moreover, he was fortunate to have one important friend in the War Office – Lt-General Sir Ronald ('Bill') Adam, the Deputy CIGS. On 8 November, while still en route to Palestine, Bernard had written to Adam to give his views on army training; Adam had thanked him and indicated he would be grateful for Bernard's observations on the situation in Palestine. Although, sadly, the War Office later destroyed Bernard's views on training, his letters from Palestine were considered important enough to be preserved – and are today perhaps the most vivid depiction of this, one of the least known campaigns conducted by the British Army in the twentieth century. Bernard's first letter was dated 4 December 1938, and was sent from the 'Headquarters 8th Division, Haifa, Palestine':

My dear Bill,
    You asked me for my views on the situation out here. I have been terribly busy since I arrived and have not been able to write earlier, but I will try and set out the situation as I see it.
    1.   When I arrived in Palestine I decided that I did not want to

[1] John Connell, *Wavell*, op. cit.
[2] Ibid.

take over operational and administrative control of the 8th Div until I had toured the whole Divl area and studied the situation and the problem.

Force HQ agreed to this; so I sent my 'Q' staff to Haifa to get our HQ ready, and I set out with my 'G1' to tour the 8 Div area. This area includes Samaria, Galilee, and the whole of the frontier district. During my tour I visited every single military garrison, detachment and post in the area; interviewed every civil servant; and talked to every single British policeman. It was an immense task and it took me one week; I got up at 5.0 a.m. each morning and went to bed at midnight. My division is in 35 garrisons and detachments, but it was well worth while, and enabled me to take over operational control with a definite and formed policy.

2. Before leaving Jerusalem I said to Force HQ that I wanted the answer to the following question:

Is the campaign that is being waged against us a National movement, or is it a campaign that is being carried on by gangs of professional bandits? Obviously the policy to be adopted must depend on the answer to this question. Force HQ was quite clear that the campaign was definitely a national movement.

3. When I had got about halfway on my tour it began to be clear to me that the campaign was *not* a national movement. I am certain now that this view is correct.

The campaign against us is being waged by gangs of professional bandits; these constitute an Army, with a definite though somewhat crude organisation. There are three 'Army' Commanders and they take their orders from Damascus; there is little cohesion in the rebel forces and the esprit-de-corps is a 'gang' one.

A gang is anything from 50 to 150 men, and each 'Army' commander controls the gangs in his area by means of sub-area commanders. There is no higher organisation than the gang as far as is known.

The 'Army' commanders are very elusive and it will be difficult to catch them; we know where they keep their women, and that is about all. The gangs operate in the country and live in the hill areas. They move about from place to place and conscript the local peasants – against their will – and force them to take up arms against us; the peasants have to comply, since refusal means death and the destruction of their houses. The gang leaders also have agents in the towns, and by means of them they carry out assassinations and commit other acts of terrorism; this is very difficult to combat, especially in a large place like Haifa with a population of over 100,000.

4. The net result is that the British Army in Palestine is at war with a rebel army which is one hundred per cent Arab.

If you now examine the feelings of the general public, including the peasantry, you find it is as follows:

The bulk of the Arab population of the country are 'fed up' with the whole thing; they are very short of food and are hustled about by both sides i.e. the British and rebel armies; they would like to see law and order restored; they would be quite content to live under the British mandate so long as Jewish immigration is limited to a fixed total (say of 500,000).

The Jewish population go on with their work as if there was no war on but they defend their own colonies stoutly with arms which we allow them to have for the purpose; the colonies are all protected by wire obstacles, powerful search-lights operate all night long, and there is a regular system of sentries and patrols in each colony by day and night.

5. The above gives a brief picture of the situation and having read so far I think it is important to realize that we are definitely at war. British soldiers are being killed and wounded in battle with the rebels every day. The enemy army wears uniform when operating by gangs and for movement about the country it resorts to civilian dress. The normal uniform in the North is a high neck polo sweater of a saffron colour, with riding boots and khaki trousers or breeches.

6. I think that what has been lacking out here has been any clear cut statement, defining the situation and saying what was to be done about it. I decided that I must issue such a statement of policy at once in my division so that all efforts would be directed along the same lines. Having briefly defined the situation as it appeared to me, I went on to give the tasks on which we would concentrate. They were as follows, in order of importance:

a) To hunt down and destroy the rebel armed gangs. They must be hunted relentlessly; when engaged in battle with them we must shoot to kill. We must not be on the defensive and act only when attacked; *we* must take the offensive and impose our will on the rebels. The next few weeks, before the winter rains set in, is an opportunity and during them we may well smash the rebel movement given a little luck. We must put forward our maximum effort *now* and concentrate on killing armed rebels in battle; this is the surest way to end the war.

b) To get the dwellers in urban areas, and the peasantry, on our side. To do this we must be scrupulously fair in our dealings with them. We want them to realize that they will always get a fair deal from the British army; but if they

277

assist the rebels in any way they must expect to be treated as rebels; and anyone who takes up arms against us will certainly lose his life.

c) To prepare the police force to take over from us when the rebellion is crushed.

The police are working as soldiers. Large reinforcements are coming in and these are practically all ex-soldiers; they are fitted out in Jerusalem and then drafted straight out to their districts (I am referring to the British police, of whom there are to be some 3000).

It is the British police who will form the backbone of the future Palestine Police Force. They are now being used like soldiers, but we cannot stay here for ever and when we have restored law and order we shall want to hand over control to the police; we have therefore got to help them to get back gradually to their duties as 'police'. They are under our orders and so we have a definite responsibility in the matter. In order to do this they must receive training; they require instruction in police duties and they must be able to speak Arabic.

The British police are now concentrated in the larger towns and on the Northern frontier; as their numbers increase we must aim at getting them out into the country areas working with our military detachments; it is the British police who will form the backbone of the mounted gendarmerie that will eventually be organized for the control of rural areas, and we must begin to fit them for this role.

7. I started off with this policy in the North and Dick O'Connor is doing much the same in the South. He and I are great personal friends and we are keeping in the closest touch. During the last week in my area the rebels have been brought to battle twice and dealt two smashing blows. On 28th November we cornered a gang of about 60 in the Carmel Range and killed fifty of them; they fought like wild beasts, knowing that they were 'for it' and in one case there was a hand-to-hand conflict between a Corporal of the Irish Fusiliers and an Arab in which the Arab was finally killed. All the killed men were armed and dressed in uniform. Present with the gang was ABU DORRAH, the 'Rebel Army' Commander in the North; it is reported he was killed but we cannot definitely confirm this; the action took place in the afternoon and in the broadcast from Beyrouth that night it was stated he had been killed.

This is the real way to end the war, i.e. to kill the rebels and particularly their leaders. To do this we must take the offensive and hunt them relentlessly.

8. Now for a few comments on things in general. I think there have been 3 main troubles out here.

The first one has been the very high degree of centralisation of everything at Force HQ. Nothing could be done without asking permission; no operation could take place until it had been approved by Force HQ; forecasts of operations a week ahead had to be sent in, thus prejudicing secrecy. In fact Force HQ tried to run the whole country in detail; the result was that they had no time for anything let alone to think, and the staff was fearfully hard worked.

Dick and I had to make it very clear that all this was to cease now that there were two divisional commanders to deal with instead of five infantry brigadiers. I had to do some very plain speaking on the subject!!

The second trouble has been the lack of a really good senior 'Q' staff officer. One sees it on every side. I'm afraid the present occupier of the post is no good; I am told that his successor (Hutchinson) is a good man; I certainly hope so.

The third trouble has been this. Bob [Haining] is really a C-in-C; he is fighting the war, and has an immense amount of political affairs to contend with as well. In such a situation your senior staff officers must be 'the cat's whiskers', otherwise the C-in-C gets involved in all sorts of details which he shouldn't have to bother about. I have no hesitation in saying that Simmons and Brunskill do not come in this category. The former is, I am told, a very good commander; he is not a good senior General Staff officer, and I do not think it is his line of country; possibly he would do better in a brigade command.

9. The young regimental officer out here is quite splendid. Of course it is magnificent training; it is a wonderful thing to visit a post of 50 men commanded by a 2/Lieut of one year's service; he will tell you all about his post, his role, and how he carries it out; he has a wireless set and on receiving his orders to act suddenly on some intelligence received, he leaves a defensive garrison in the post and sallies forth with the remainder by day or night to play his part in the operation that is being staged.

It makes a man of him; officers who are supposed to be not much good develop surprisingly good qualities when forced to act on their own in this way.

To my mind it shows that the type of officer we are now taking into the army through our military colleges is of the right type, and just what we want. You could not have a better test than this one out here, and they are coming through it without blemish.

Similarly, with the soldier. The British soldier out here is magnificent; there is nothing really curious about this as he

279

always is magnificent anywhere, but this is rather a curious sort of war; you don't often see your enemy but all the time you are exposed to the risk of being murdered or blown up.

It is amazing what a difference it makes to a company or a battalion after it has had a good battle with the rebels in open fight. All the men are on their toes after such a battle and that unit is never likely after that to be caught at a disadvantage by the rebels.

10. The Bren-gun is superb; it is far-and-away superior to the Lewis gun and never stops or becomes clogged up. The rebels dislike it intensely because of its power of maintaining fire. All officers and men speak of it in terms of the greatest admiration.

11. I am strongly of the opinion that the troops out here should be given a medal for Palestine. They are engaged in fighting a rebel army which wears uniform and has a definite organisation. Soldiers are killed and wounded in battle with the rebels, the troops having a very hard time; the work is very hard and arduous, and many of my men get only one night in bed out of two; they are frequently out in the field in operations against the rebels for 72 hours at a stretch.

A medal does not I imagine cost very much and the resulting uplift among the troops would be wonderful.

12. Bob has had a very difficult and trying time out here and he has come through it very well. His position vis-à-vis the civil officials is very difficult, and the atmosphere is often rather tense. He has no confidence in his senior staff officers; personally of course I would get rid of a staff officer in whom I had no confidence, but I suppose we are all different. He has been dealing with a number of inf[antry] brigade commanders who have been running large areas; they have been doing it very well but he has obviously felt at times that they required a bit of holding and possibly lacked a balanced judgement in difficult situations. I think he is immensely relieved to have two divisional headquarters in charge now, and he has taken quite a new lease of life lately.

13. For the future I am full of hope. The situation is definitely in hand and there are very distinct signs that the rebel movement is crumbling. The surest way to complete this crumbling process is to direct all our energies *now* on killing the armed rebels.

I have taken off my brigadiers all the administrative details with which they were cluttered up and have loosed them on the task of killing rebels.

'Dreadnought' Harrison and Jack Evetts require no urging in this respect! During the ten days ending today we have killed a hundred in my divisional areas; there are probably more but I take account only of dead bodies actually collected.

14. There will be some very difficult problems ahead of us when the actual rebellion is crushed. But one thing at a time; for the present I am concentrating on killing the rebels.

15. This letter is private and personal and I know you will treat it as such. I have made certain observations which I would not normally make but you asked me for my views and I have given them at some length.[1]

From this and other evidence, it is clear that it was not Haining but Major-General B. L. Montgomery who took over responsibility for crushing the rebellion – an assumption of command he would repeat in Egypt less than four years later, at the critical juncture of World War Two. In London, in the meantime, despite the loss of British soldiers' lives, the Palestinian war was completely overshadowed by events in Europe. The Deputy Chief of the Imperial General Staff, at least, was grateful for Bernard's 'clear account of the situation as you see it'. He had reservations, however: 'I am not certain that you are correct that there is not a national spirit among the Arabs,' he remarked in his reply of 19 December 1938, suggesting that 'certain Arabs are fighting the campaign by the employment of professional bandits', but he was astute enough to recognise that, with a European war on the horizon, it was imperative to act decisively in Palestine. Congratulating Bernard on his appointment to command the 3rd Division in due course, he added: 'I hope you will have completed the war in Palestine before you are due to move on. Again, many thanks for your letter which does give one a most admirable idea of the situation.'[2]

Headquarters
8th Division, Haifa
1st Jan 1939

My dear Bill,
You may be interested to hear further news of our doings. I have at last persuaded Force HQ to put the Jordan Valley, and the squadron of the Trans-Jordan Frontier Force in it, under my command. Up to date it has been a separate area under the AOC, who in turn is under Force HQ. The Air Force were very jealous of it and no British troops were allowed in the Jordan Valley area; there was no co-ordination of operations; the valley was becoming a safe harbourage for the rebels who were being chased out of the 8 Div area. The men of the Frontier Force live mostly in Palestine; they have friends amongst the rebels and it is really wonderful

[1] Miscellaneous War Office file (WO 216/111), PRO.
[2] Ibid.

how they have remained loyal. The Jordan Valley Command was the last hold of the Air Force and Bob has been very reluctant to take it from them, and possibly hurt their feelings. I spent one month in arguing about it, with no result. Finally I wrote a letter, and gave it as my opinion that we should not win this war until the whole of the North of Palestine was treated operationally as one entity; to continue as at present could result only in failure; and the judgement of historians in the future that we deserved to fail. That finished it and I now have the Jordan Valley under me!!

2.   I have borrowed the Greys from the 7th Division for 3 weeks.

My own Div Cav Regt is the Royals. I am moving these two regiments up North.

Together with the squadrons of the Frontier Force now in the Jordan Valley, these two British Cavalry Regiments will constitute what amounts to a Cavalry Brigade. This Cavalry force will operate in the plain ESDRELON – the JEZREEL VALLEY–JORDAN VALLEY, in co-operation with the mechanised infantry units.

It will be interesting to see how the horsed cavalry compares with infantry transported in MT. It will in fact be a very good test for the horsed cavalry.

I hope to get good operational results from the above. Operations begin on the 4th January and will continue in that area for some three weeks, by which time it should all be cleaned up.

I am then going to move the cavalry force slowly southwards through Samaria, and clean that area up also; this movement will start about 21st January.

So January is going to be a month of really intensive operations and I only hope that the rains will not interfere too much. The black cotton soil makes movement very difficult after heavy and continuous rain.

It is interesting that the Royals and their move North will follow almost exactly Allenby's route through the Mus-Mus Pass.

3.   We are now entering on a very difficult stage of the war. The rebel army as such has had almost enough; our intensive operations have split up the large gangs; there are a few gangs of 30 men or so still about; but for the most part the rebels are in small bodies of 6 or 7, trying to avoid contact with our forces. These small parties get together at intervals and carry out what sabotage they can, and snipe at barracks, etc.

The enemy is thus much more difficult to deal with than when he operated in large gangs and would meet us in battle.

But until we have collected in the last remnants the rebellion cannot be said to have been stamped out. We have therefore got to keep at it and not relax the pressure. Any slackening off on our part now would put new encouragement into the rebel leaders and they would begin to exert their influence again. At present their influence is rather on the wane.

4. To carry us successfully through this last phase we require very good intelligence, and, in particular, good agents who know the rebels and can pick them out.

    We have some good agents and are slowly but surely roping in the gangsters.

5. But there is another difficulty.

    This process of collecting in the rebels and putting them into detention camps, has filled all the available detention camps to their full capacity.

    For some reason the powers that be are reluctant to erect more hutted accommodation for detainees.

    The problem of overcrowding was solved by releasing 300 detainees in order to make room for those that we keep putting in!!

    The 300 to be released were to be persons of minor value.

    It is an amazing picture.

    We rope in all rebels and enemies and lock them up; the detention camps then get full; we then have to start letting them out; if I put in 50 I must let out 50.

    I have no doubt that as the time for the London conference approaches we shall be ordered to let out a good many, in order to create a good 'atmosphere' for the talks. We adopted this policy during the Shinn Fein war in Ireland in 1920/1; it produced the most dreadful repercussions and prolonged the war for many months.

    There is no doubt that we British are an amazing people. We never seem to learn from past mistakes. I went up to Beyrouth last week to liaise with the French and had lunch with the French C-in-C, General Cailloux.

    The French of course think we are quite mad as regards our conduct of the war in Palestine. They are expecting trouble themselves in Syria and have everything ready to stamp it out in one day; and they will be quite ruthless; they have 28,000 troops in the country and can cope with any situation.

6. However, we seem to win our wars in the end and one must, I suppose, preserve a sense of humour. But this letting out of rebels to make room for other rebels may not be so funny in the end, and may be the cause of British soldiers losing their lives.

7. But there is no doubt about one thing. The war out here is the most magnificent training for the army and the RAF and we are producing seasoned fighting men second to none.

8. No time for more now.

It was kind of you to give me the 3rd Division: it was exactly what I wanted.

Yours ever

Monty[1]

Six days later Bernard was again writing – this time to protest at the way the future policing of Palestine would be jeopardised by the retention of 'useless' senior police officers at a moment when the force was to be expanded by 3000 new recruits. It was an uncompromisingly frank letter; but it indicates better than any other witness or evidence of the time Bernard's intense and sincere belief in the responsibility of senior officers towards the men they command.

Headquarters,
8th Division, Haifa
6 Jan 1939

My dear Bill

Anything you can do to make known to the Colonial Office the true situation regarding the Palestine Police will be well worth while. It is no use passing the information merely to subordinates. The Secretary of State *himself* should know the facts and he should know them at once. He should also be told that when we hand over to the police and the civilian government finds that they (the police) are no use, they must never say that we soldiers did not tell them that their police force was useless or that we never gave them our advice as to how to remedy this state of affairs. I give below an outline of the situation.

2. A large British police force is being recruited for Palestine; it will be nearly 3000 strong. This will form the backbone of the Palestine police force, which will have to contain Arabs and Jew personnel as well.

3. Recruits for the British police are coming in fast. They are nearly all ex-soldiers.

   They are magnificent material and from it a really fine police force could be formed. I have spoken personally to nearly every British constable in the North of Palestine and I see a lot of their work, and I am not speaking without knowledge.

4. This magnificent material is slowly sliding down the hill. The men are badly looked after and badly housed. Their officers take no interest in them. They (the men) are drinking very heavily.

5. The real trouble is that the senior officers in the Palestine police are utterly and completely useless. Furthermore the

[1] Ibid.

organisation is basically unsound; there is no proper chain of command which enables responsibility to be fixed when things go wrong; everyone is imbued with the spirit of 'passing the baby' to someone else. The organisation could of course be put right if the senior officers were any good.

6. The basic root of the whole trouble is the senior officers. If the Colonial Office want to have a proper and efficient police force in Palestine they will have to make a clean sweep of the present senior officers and bring some really good men.

Nothing else will be of any use.

If they do not do so the Police Force will continue to deteriorate, and there will always be rows and troubles in Palestine.

7. The matter is urgent. Strong action requires to be taken *at once*. There is therefore in my opinion, only one solution to the problem. The present Inspector General of Police should be removed, and Sir Charles Tegart should be made Inspector General in his place.

The latter is a really good man and he must be given a free hand, and a mandate to push out any officers he likes.

8. I gave my views as above, with Bob's full agreement, to the High Commissioner when he was last in Haifa. In fact Bob suggested I should do so in order to reinforce his own repeated statements about the inefficiency of the police senior officers.

9. To sum up two things are really important:
   a) action as in para 7 above.
   b) make it quite clear to the Secretary of State for the Colonies what is the matter with the Palestine Force and give the remedy.

10. I regard 9(b) as fearfully important. The police are at the moment under our orders, though we cannot interfere in their internal affairs or push out officers. But the fact that they are under our orders gives us a definite responsibility to help them; we must also point out to the Civil Government what is wrong with them.

We do not want it said later that when we had the police under our orders we never told the Civil Government what was wrong with its Police Force.

11. I give you all the above privately, but if you agree in principle with para 10 you can get full details from Force HQ and they will tell exactly what I have said above.

12. I have given my views frequently to Bob, and I know he agrees very definitely.

I feel that a strong man as Secretary of State for the Colonies would soon take action if he knew the true facts.

Our own Secretary of State, Hore-Belisha, would get a move on at once and would soon put it right.[1]

General Adam acted, and Bernard's letter was immediately sent over to the Secretary of State at the Colonial Office. 'Curiously enough,' Adam related in his letter of thanks on 12 January 1939, 'they rather like getting material in this manner,'[2] and he was certain that, even though the Colonial Office did not 'like to admit there is a war in Palestine',[3] Bernard's remarks would 'get to the proper quarter . . . Your letters are most valuable,' he added, 'and go behind the normal official stuff that we get.'

Bernard's letters from Palestine were also shown to Lord Gort, the CIGS, and as Gort was due to go on tour of the Middle East that spring, Bernard drew up, in February 1939, a series of 'Notes' on the 'Past', 'Present' and 'Future' of Palestine from the British military point of view. The continued Jewish immigration had impelled Arab insurgency, particularly when Lebanese landowners sold off property in Northern Palestine to the Jews. Eventually this had led to the disintegration of the mixed Arab-Jewish police force and the breakdown of law and order. However 'the arrival of additional troops' in the country had enabled the rebel forces to be hunted down and subdued. Intensive operations were undertaken in November, December and January, and by 1 February 1939 the military situation was well in hand.

C The Present

4   The backbone of the armed opposition has been smashed.

The rebel activities are no longer organised and controlled as they were some weeks ago.

The leaders are being so harried that they are losing their prestige; they are ceasing to be public heroes and are becoming hunted outlaws; the 3 chief leaders have left the country and are in Damascus.

5   There are no longer any large armed bands of the rebel army left in the divisional area. There are still some small bands who are endeavouring to keep the pot boiling, and there are a number of bandits who are working purely for self-gain. Until these persons are killed or captured we shall have difficulty in obtaining the complete support of the peasantry, as they still continue to exercise a certain measure of terrorism over the villages and townspeople.

6   The main bulk of the active members of the rebel army, and a good proportion of active rebel organisers, have been

[1] Ibid.
[2] Ibid.
[3] Letter of 19.12.38. Ibid.

captured. Including ACRE detention camp I have 2500 in prisoner cages in my area . . .

7   From a military point of view we are definitely on top, and our military activities are maintaining a good degree of law and order. But the present time is a critical one.

There are definite signs that certain sections of Arabs are becoming weary of the rebellion and are anxious to return to more peaceful ways.

On the other hand there is no doubt that below the surface, Arab feeling generally is seething with discontent on account of the propaganda of the Mufti; the atmosphere is still charged with electricity.

If we weaken at all now, or relax our military pressure it will put new heart into the rebel cause; the chief leaders would return from DAMASCUS and the whole rebellion would be liable to flare up again.

D   *The Future*

8   We must continue our present activities which aim at the pursuit and destruction of the remnants of the dying [rebel] population, and must at once nip in the bud any attempts to form new gangs. We must concentrate still more on the destruction of the bandits and their leaders, who are terrorizing the decent people.

Until our task is completed the police will not be able to take over responsibility for law and order, and the Civil Government will be unable to exercise its functions of governing the country.

9   It must be realised that the Civil Government exercises its function only in the towns; control in the rural areas is exercised by the army. There is a complete gap between the two; the civil officials never visit the country districts and know nothing about what is going on in the villages. Civil control in rural areas has thus broken down completely. The Mukhtras and other notables look to the army, for the soldiers are the only signs of government that they see. They have lost faith in the Civil Administration and ask always that the Army should not go away.

10   The degree of lawlessness that has obtained in PALESTINE during the last 6 months will take some time to settle down and we must not expect to go from a state of complete lawlessness to one of complete peace in a few weeks.

Furthermore when the detainees begin to be released the lawlessness may be expected to flare up again in certain areas.

11   During the transition from lawlessness to peace the country must be controlled with a very firm hand and *there must be*

sufficient force available to crush instantly any recrudescence of lawlessness.

The Police Force is in no condition to carry out this task. It is making a brave attempt now to put its house in order to regain its morale; but any success it is obtaining in its reorganisation is due almost entirely to the endeavours of the army on its behalf.

The material in the rank and file of the Police Force is magnificent, but the senior officers are useless, and once the 'drive' and energy at present supplied by the army is removed the police will fall back into their old ways.

The Police Force must have an Inspector General who is a man of character and 'drive'; he must be a man of action who knows what he wants and how to set about doing it. I consider that the Police Force will make no real headway until the present Inspector General is removed and replaced by a first-class man. The present Inspector General is a very nice person but he is quite unfit for his present appointment and so long as he retains it the PALESTINE police will never become an efficient force.

12 The Police Force at present exercise control only in the towns, where they have the backing of the army.

At present control in the rural areas is exercised entirely by the Army.

The Police have got to regain control in the rural areas.

13 All this will take time.

It will be fatal to remove the Army before the police are firmly in the saddle.

14 I consider that the strength of the 8th Division in North PALESTINE must not fall below 8 battalions and a Cavalry Regiment until the rebellion is finally crushed, the police are re-established in full control, and civil government is functioning effectively.

I estimate that to attain this end will take about another 6 months.

If there is any undue haste in reducing the present strength of the 8th Division, it will take much longer.

The above strength is based on a division of 9 units. These fit over the civil administration boundaries; the strength is the minimum which is necessary to clean up the dying rebellion and exercise effective military control.

15 The size of the future garrison of PALESTINE will depend largely on the efficiency of the road communications. The essential roads for public security purposes in rural areas are being built by the army; these must be made into first-class all weather roads without delay.

Providing this is done I consider that the garrison of PALES-

TINE could be reduced to one division of 9 battalions in 6 months time.

But this division must not be tied to PALESTINE; it should be available for operations anywhere in the Middle East.

There should, therefore, be one additional infantry brigade over and above the division; this brigade would always remain in Palestine for internal security duties.

It must be realised that if the Army goes, then all work on the security roads will cease and they will be sabotaged and cut up by the rebels.[1]

This memorandum, dated 8 February 1939, became the basis for the War Office's stance over Palestine in 1939, pre-empting even General Haining's official report to the War Office in April 1939. However, by then events in Europe were gathering pace: for on 15 March 1939 Hitler's troops marched into Prague and annexed the remainder of the once independent state of Czechoslovakia.

[1] Ibid.

CHAPTER THIRTEEN

Ready for War

Exactly one month after the fall of Czechoslovakia, the Military Secretary at the War Office, Lt-General Brownrigg, wrote to Bernard telling him that he would be required to take command of the 3rd Division earlier than anticipated, as Major-General 'Podge' Bernard had been appointed Governor-elect of Bermuda and was expected to take up his post early that autumn. Four days later Bernard Montgomery wrote back from HQ, 8th Division, Haifa:

My dear Brownie,
Thank you for your letter of 15 April. I had seen that Bernard was to go to Bermuda. I shall be quite ready to come home at any time that you order me; the rebellion out here as an organized movement is *smashed*; you can go from one end of Palestine to the other looking for a fight and you can't get one; it is very difficult to find Arabs to kill; they have had the stuffing knocked right out of them.

I shall be sorry to leave Palestine in many ways as I have enjoyed the 'war' out here.

But I feel there is a sterner task awaiting me at home.

Next winter's individual training season in England will be a fearfully important time; it will have to be carefully organized on a sound plan. Quite confidentially, between ourselves, I do not think Podge will bother about it; the programme for the winter has to be issued to the troops in August so that all can think ahead and make their plans.

Possibly Podge will take 2 months leave in July. *I should like to come home in July* and take over the 3rd Division then, so that I can organize and launch the winter training. I could be on leave from here and my successor need not take over here till September. I do not want any leave myself. I am very fit and well and thrive on plenty of work.[1]

These were famous last words – for a week later Bernard began to suffer sudden nausea and vomiting, followed by slight gastric symp-

---

[1] Personal File for B. L. Montgomery, MOD.

toms. He ignored them for the moment, and on 19 May Brownrigg sent him official War Office orders to assume command of 3rd Division at home 'on or about 1st October. It is not possible to state the exact date of the vacancy as that depends on the date that [Denis] Bernard leaves the United Kingdom for Bermuda.' However, Brownrigg had taken the Commander-elect's point about winter training, and in the most tactful way he suggested how Montgomery might effect it:

> [Denis] Bernard will probably go on leave for about 2 months before he embarks, and during this period the Division will be commanded by his senior Brigadier. Perhaps if you wish to interest yourself in the affairs of the Division before you take over, you will arrange it unofficially with [Denis] Bernard.
> Yours ever
> W. D. S. Brownrigg, Lt-General.[1]

From now on, however, things began to go wrong. On 24 May after two days of 'dull persistent headache, rising fever and growing weakness in the legs' Bernard Montgomery was admitted to the Military Hospital in Haifa. For eleven days he lay there with fever and slight lung congestion while various blood culture tests were done. There was then a lull for about a week, and he wrote to his sister Winsome at Moascar, suggesting he come to spend a week with her and her husband in absolute quiet to recuperate. Then the fever recurred, with pain in the chest on 14 June, and definite signs of pleurisy on the 18th. He was treated with M & B for thirty-six hours and a series of X-rays were now taken of his chest. On 19 June, the radiologist tendered his report, maintaining that there was 'evidence of tubercular infiltration in the mid-zone of the left lung, with minimal pleural effusion at the base'. At a Medical Board meeting summoned the next day the senior consultant physician to the British Forces in Palestine was called upon to diagnose the case. Despite his fever and the difficulty he had in breathing – he found it impossible even to bring up enough sputum to be analysed for TB – Bernard now pulled rank on the Lt-Colonel. Talk of tuberculosis was ridiculous, he said, it was very likely his old war wound that was playing up in the hot, humid climate of Haifa. It was imperative that he get home to England to take over the 3rd Division's training programme; he was certain that the sea passage would restore his health.

If Lt-Colonel Marsh was won over it was not on medical grounds – for Bernard's war wound had been in his right not his left lung. Marsh acknowledged, in his report, that the 'general clinical picture of the case, coupled with X-ray results, are strongly suspicious of the

---

[1] Ibid.

causal organism of the whole illness being the tubercular bacillus, but unless TB are found in the sputum I do not consider tuberculosis should be diagnosed'. He recommended that the General be invalided home to the UK at once, declaring that he was fit to travel as a stretcher case, accompanied by two sisters, and two male orderlies.

The War Office was informed, a bed was reserved at the Queen Alexandra Military Hospital, Millbank, London, and permission given for Bernard to travel home aboard the next available ship, the SS *Ranchi*, due to sail from Port Said on 3 July. Bernard had got his way.

How sick Benard really was is difficult to say. He had clearly lost a lot of weight, looked pale, and was too ill to move from his bed or cough up sputum; yet the doctors in their reports would not commit themselves beyond a prognosis of three months' sick leave. Certainly Bernard was considered too ill to travel by rail to Egypt, and was thus transported by air with his nursing entourage on 2 July from Haifa direct to Port Said. Bernard's sister Winsome was by chance due to travel home on the same ship; she saw him in the Military Hospital at Port Said, where she found him 'very white and ill and in bed, unable to walk', and Bernard explained the arrangements that had been made for his passage. He was to have a large cabin, and would admit no one during the voyage save Winsome, every morning at 10 a.m.

'The next day, aboard ship, we watched him being put in a carrying chair from the stretcher, and I remember the other passengers saying "Wonder who that is? Some General, I believe, who's been ill." '[1]

It would have been most out of character for Bernard to have exaggerated his condition – he could just as easily have taken several months' leave, as he had suggested to Brownrigg, to return and make preparations for the 3rd Division's winter training. Yet the fact remains that Bernard was carried on board the SS *Ranchi* a 'stretcher case' at Port Said, and walked off, a few weeks later, 'fit as a fiddle'. It was indeed a miraculous recovery, the like of which the ship's doctor had never seen before.

Winsome, who saw Bernard every day during the voyage, thought it quite simply an act of supreme will. 'I watched Bernard every day with the greatest interest being carried up on deck, unable to walk; then he'd get out of the chair and he'd walk. He'd walk say the length of this room, and the next day the length of the deck, and in no time at all he was walking around it. But the ship's doctor came up to me one day and said: "Mrs Holderness, I believe you're the General's sister?" I said, "Yes." "Well, may I have a few words with you?" We walked up and down the deck. He said: "I'm terribly worried about that brother of yours. His lung is in a very bad state. Now, do you

---

[1] Lady Michelmore, loc. cit.

mind me asking if anyone in your family has had TB?" And I said, "Yes, I have, very badly indeed and I'm completely cured now. And an aunt – that's all." Anyway, he said, "Well, he hasn't got TB, but his lung's in a very bad state and he thinks he's going to serve in the war that's coming. Well, he's not – he'll never see action." And that was July 1939.

'Well, Bernard got better and better. He wouldn't mix with anyone – wouldn't let anyone come near his cabin.

'But I think he was beginning to get known, because when we stopped at Malta a launch came out to meet us, and some high official came aboard. When I asked Bernard the next day, he said, "Yes, that was the Governor." It was the same at Gibraltar.

'He wouldn't leave the ship, not even when we got to Casablanca. We just used to sit and chat.

'It was just sheer guts, will power. He wasn't going to give in. There was the sea air, rest, good food. He had Betty's photographs in the cabin, and two very nice male nurses.

'And then when we got to Tilbury I packed my things and went up to the First Class and asked him, "What are you going to do now, Bernard?"

' "Well, I've got to attend a medical board – but that'll be all right," he said confidently. "I feel as fit as a fiddle."

'I've often wondered what the ship's doctor thought . . .'[1]

The authorities at the Military Hospital, Millbank were equally mystified. They had received papers from Egypt telling them to expect a stretcher case; instead on 14 July in walked a sprightly Major-General who 'looks fairly well, says he feels very fit, has no pain in the chest. Temperature normal. Tongue clean. Heart normal. Liver not enlarged . . .'[2]

Bernard was kept at the hospital for five days while more tests were made; but on 19 July, as no sign of any disability had been found, he was discharged. The pleurisy had vanished and there was no evidence of tubercular infection. In their records the hospital could only state that he had suffered from an 'infection – causal organism unknown'.[3] He was told to take another three weeks' sick leave, and to report for a final medical board on 10 August 1939. Delighted, Bernard went off to stay with his old Commandant while at Quetta, Sir Guy Williams, who lived near Sevenoaks, Kent, and from there he kept urging that he be given immediate command of the 3rd Division in the absence of General Bernard.

Unfortunately, the Military Secretary, General Brownrigg, had just been promoted to Director of the Territorial Army, and Bernard had no influence with his successor, Lt-General Giffard. Bernard

[1] Ibid.
[2] Personal File for B. L. Montgomery, MOD.
[3] Ibid.

therefore decided to appeal directly to the CIGS, Lord Gort, asking in a letter of 21 July to be allowed to take informal command of the 3rd Division, and enclosing his final verdict on the situation in Palestine. He was positive that the Arab rebellion was now 'definitely and finally smashed; we have such a strong hold on the country that it is not possible for the rebellion to raise its head again on the scale we previously experienced'. However this was not to say that the future should be seen as rosy. The 'Jew versus Arab problem' was another matter: it was 'going on in Palestine *now*' and, in Bernard's view it would 'go on for the next 50 years in all probability. The Jew murders the Arab, and the Arabs murder the Jew' – but for the moment at least 'the campaign of murder and assassination' was 'in no way anti-British', and should not therefore be looked upon as a military matter – 'their solution,' Bernard declared, 'is really a police matter.' What concerned him, therefore, was to make quite clear within the War Office that, given the storm-clouds in Europe, 'there are far more troops in Palestine at the moment than are required to assist the police to maintain law and order'. One of the two divisions should, he felt, be closed down, and at least one infantry brigade 'could be transferred to Egypt if required in that country'. However this was not all: it was imperative, Bernard stated, to ensure that those troops remaining in Palestine should be trained for professional war rather than anti-bandit operations:

> The essential thing at the moment for all troops in Palestine is training in the methods of first-class, or even second-class, war.
> The troops are experts in fighting a savage and mobile enemy, who is armed only with the rifle and the knife – they know nothing about other forms of war,

he warned with remarkable prescience.

> Battalions are organized in mobile columns, and not in the latest British War Establishments. Such things as Pioneer platoons, Carrier platoons, AA platoons, etc. are unknown – the situation regarding specialists is very bad.[1]

Gort did not reply personally, but instructed his MA, Major Gordon, to acknowledge the letter and to tell Montgomery that his paragraph 8 would be passed to the Director of Military Training – a euphemism for doing nothing. However Gort did instruct his MA to inform the new Military Secretary about Montgomery 'being available for duty' in the 3rd Division. General Giffard, therefore, wrote on 27 July to the new GOC Southern Command, Lt-General A. F. Brooke, who was that very day taking over from General Sir Archibald Wavell:

[1] Miscellaneous War Office file (WO 216/46), PRO.

The CIGS has had a letter from Montgomery, who, as you may know, is home on sick leave from Palestine. He is due for a medical board shortly to find out whether he is fit or not by the 26th August, which is the date on which he completes his 91 days' leave.

It is not proposed, even if he is passed fit, to send him back to Palestine for what would amount to only a few weeks in that country, and he will be placed on the unemployed list until the 1st October, the date on which he is due to succeed [General] Bernard. He is very anxious, provided that you agree, to act in Command of the 3rd Division while Bernard is on leave. I am not quite sure when Bernard is going on leave, but I suggest that the necessary arrangements might be made between them and you. Will you let me know your ideas about the proposal?[1]

Brooke must have acquiesced, for on 4 August 1939 Bernard Montgomery made his way to the Queen's Hotel, Southsea, near Portsmouth, where he set up his unofficial HQ – and began his training programme for the 3rd Division.

F. W. Simpson, who had returned to the War Office as assistant to the Military Secretary, remembered this time well:

D. K. Bernard had been selected to be Governor of Bermuda, where he was due to go in September, 1939; and to get himself fit for what he thought was going to be an arduous post he went off in July, 1939, to Ireland on a two months fishing holiday. So the 3rd Division with HQ at Portsmouth was left without a commander on the spot, and the war clouds were building up fast.[2]

Having integrated Austria and Czechoslovakia, Hitler had now turned his attention to Poland, which held the contentious corridor to Danzig and East Prussia.

The situation worried Monty, who went down to Portsmouth, took up his quarters in a hotel, and started to run the Division although he was not in any position to do so.

I used to get very humorous messages from my predecessor at the War Office, Colonel Morgan, as to how the Divisional Commander-to-be was going to upset all the orders given by the Divisional Commander of the day who was not present to argue about them.

Monty, too, used to ring me up to say: 'This is a monstrous situation. Here we are, getting ready for war, and the man who ought to be getting the Division ready is quietly fishing in Ireland. Can't you get him out?'

[1] Ibid.
[2] Wason interviews, loc. cit.

There was nothing I could do about getting him out. All I could do was to report Monty's wails to my general, the Military Secretary.

It was a tragi-comedy in which, before war was actually declared, little or nothing could be done. General Haining was signalling from Jerusalem to ask whether he could appoint a successor to Montgomery, still technically the GOC 8th Division; Montgomery was busy preparing to re-train the 3rd Division, of which he was still not legally the Commander, so as to be able to take it abroad the moment war broke out; Brownrigg had gone to take command of the TA; and General Bernard fished on in Ireland!

At 11 a.m. on 10 August, at a medical board at the Queen Alexandra Military Hospital, Millbank, Major-General B. L. Montgomery was finally declared fit for General Duties; but as August drew on the question of mobilisation loomed larger. Chamberlain refused full mobilisation for political reasons; unofficial part-mobilisation was, however, initiated by Hore-Belisha.

Paradoxically this was to Bernard's disadvantage, for it was a War Office rule that on mobilisation all appointments were frozen. On 23 August Germany and Russia concluded a 'non-aggression' pact, and on the 25th Britain confirmed its mutual assistance treaty with Poland. Hitler cancelled his military invasion planned for 25 August, and summoned a Polish plenipotentiary to Berlin.

European war now hung in the balance; but at Portsmouth there was great embarrassment. A successor – Brigadier A. R. Godwin-Austen – had been appointed on 23 August to take over the 8th Division in Palestine; meanwhile General Bernard was due to return from his fishing holiday and would find a usurper commanding his Division. Frantically Montgomery telephoned the War Office.

'Monty rang me up in a state of great perturbation from Portsmouth,' Simpson recalled,

to ask what was going on. I had no difficulty about explaining the rule about cancellation of appointments, and he then asked what was to happen to himself. I replied that he would be put into the pool of Major-Generals for a future appointment, and I was certain a very good one would be found for him in due course.

Monty was incensed at this and said: 'Here is a Division getting ready for battle and it has no Divisional Commander at all. It is just drifting aimlessly at the moment. It has got a good staff but the Divisional Commander is enjoying himself in Ireland. I will get on to the GOC Southern Command [who was by now Lt-General Sir Alan Brooke] and tell him it is all nonsense.'

I went and reported all this at once to the new Military Secretary, who just grinned and said nothing – he felt he could do nothing about this particular appointment.

I discovered afterwards that Monty had got on to Alan Brooke. However, although Alan Brooke said that he would see what he could do, Monty was told to go away somewhere and stay in the pool.

Monty then got into his car and drove to stay with an old friend, General Sir Guy Williams, at Sevenoaks, in Kent.[1]

However, all was not lost. Brooke liked and respected Montgomery, whom he had got to know well as a fellow instructor at the Staff College, Camberley in the 1920s. Brooke rang Simpson, and was eventually put on to the new Military Secretary, Sir George Giffard. Brooke was as concerned as Montgomery at the poor state of readiness for war of the 3rd Division, which had had neither divisional nor even brigade training. General Bernard 'was on leave and had taken little interest in the training of the Division in those dark days prior to the War,' Brooke later recalled.[2] It seemed the height of idiocy for the War Office to cancel Montgomery's appointment and recall Major-General Bernard. 'Giffard took Brooke's strictures very calmly and then said he wanted to sit down quietly and think for a period,' Simpson remembered:

He had a mischievous grin on his face and I wondered what he was thinking. I very soon discovered. He was, of course, well known in the Colonial Office (he had spent most of his military career serving in East and West Africa) and he decided he would go over and see them.

He saw one or two of the very senior civil servants and I think the Colonial Secretary. He came back with a written request to the Secretary of State for War from the Colonial Secretary to say that they understood the reasons of the War Office for wanting General Bernard to take the 3rd Division to France; but the Colonial Secretary would like to feel that the interests of the Empire were more important than those of the British Army and that the Empire was unlikely to play its full part in the war unless this distinguished soldier, General Bernard, was allowed by the War Office to go to take up his post as Governor of Bermuda. General Giffard showed this to the Secretary of State for War, who said, 'Of course we must allow that. Get someone else to command the 3rd Division at once.'

I then had the great joy of ringing up Monty, who had just arrived at Sevenoaks, and ordering him on behalf of the Military Secretary to return to Portsmouth at once and take command of the 3rd Division.[3]

[1] Ibid.
[2] Alanbrooke, 'Notes on my Life', partly published in A. Bryant, *The Turn of the Tide*, London 1957. MS preserved in the Liddell Hart Centre for Military Archives, King's College, University of London.
[3] Loc. cit.

Brooke had got what he wanted. Telegrams were despatched from the War Office ordering Montgomery to take command of the 3rd Division with effect from 28 August 1939.

'My dear Charles,' the new Commander wrote from the Queen's Hotel, Southsea on 27 August, 'I have your telegram and take over Command of 3rd Division tomorrow morning. Podge leaves here today; he is in great form and is I think quite pleased at your decision . . .'[1]

It had been a near-run thing. Several days later, on 1 September, Hitler invaded Poland. The British Army mobilised officially at 2 p.m. that day. After two further days of hesitation, the British Government declared war on Germany at 11 a.m. on 3 September 1939, to be followed, at 5 p.m., by France. The Second World War had begun.

[1] Personal File for B. L. Montgomery, MOD.

PART FOUR

Dunkirk

CHAPTER ONE

A Real Job to Do

Lieutenant-General Brooke's intervention had ensured that Bernard Montgomery would, after all, command the 3rd, or 'Iron', Division in 2 Corps, as part of the British Expeditionary Force. Despite the assurances given to Poland, though, there was never any intention of sending the force to the Baltic. As in 1914, the BEF was destined to cross the Channel to form part of a Franco-British army defending Western, not Eastern, Europe. It was also expected that, as in 1914, the Inspector-General of the Forces (General Ironside) would automatically become C-in-C of the BEF. Failing this, it was hoped in most serious military quarters that Lt-General Sir John Dill – undoubtedly the ablest administrator and keenest mind in the senior military hierarchy – would take command.

As in 1937, however, Hore-Belisha was determined to do the unorthodox; and command of the BEF passed on 3 September 1939 to his protégé, the Chief of the Imperial General Staff, Lord Gort: a man who had never commanded any formation above a brigade. In an equally disastrous decision, the unhappy General Ironside was made CIGS. Sir John Dill was appointed commander of 1 Corps, and Brooke, as expected, assumed command of 2 Corps. Poland was allowed to perish without a single British shot being fired to defend the very ally Britain had declared war to protect, and the BEF was put in the hands of arguably the bravest but most incompetent British army commander of the twentieth century – a general whose limitations were only to be exceeded by those of his French and Belgian counterparts.

It is unlikely that Bernard Montgomery foresaw in September 1939 the utter débâcle that was to befall the BEF; yet there can be no doubt that his future greatness as a field commander was to rest primarily on his experiences over the following eight months as a divisional commander in France and Belgium. In his *Memoirs* Bernard attempted to give due credit to Gort for ensuring the evacuation of the BEF at Dunkirk; but privately he believed Gort's performance to have been a mockery of High Command. Gort's pitiful display became for Bernard the most pungent object-lesson in how *not* to command a modern army. To the very last days of the Second World War, the memory of Dunkirk would rankle, and there can be little doubt that, together with his personal misfortune in losing his beloved Betty, it was the desire to avenge Dunkirk that made Bernard such a ruthless army commander. The twenty-two days of fighting between 10 May and 1 June 1940 would not only drive home every tenet of his own existing military philosophy; they would demonstrate a great deal more. In order to face troops as resourceful and efficient as the Germans, neither the doggedness of World War One soldiery nor the well-intentioned camaraderie of the English officer corps was sufficient. A modern army must be run with dictatorial efficiency; officers who could not stand the pressure of war must be removed; units must not be squandered piecemeal but be put into battle properly trained – divisions as divisions, brigades as brigades, complete with the modern appurtenances of war, from tanks to artillery; communications must form the very lifeblood of command, and good staffwork its heart.

For Bernard there would be no easy scapegoats, such as the weight of German armour, or the paucity or inappropriateness of British arms. What he witnessed would be engraved on his memory always: poor allies, bad generalship, lack of communication, loss of faith. At the same time he was privileged to serve under a model Corps Commander, whose impeccable generalship during critical moments he would likewise never forget. Dunkirk was, for the British Army, a disaster; but for Bernard Montgomery it would be the turning-point in his higher military career. Three of his finest army and corps commanders would emerge with distinction from the débâcle – Dempsey, Leese, and Horrocks. It was, Bernard came to see, the end of the road for British amateurism, the final catastrophe for a nation that had been unwilling to take modern warfare seriously. The lessons were self-evident; yet the catastrophe would repeat itself in Norway, Greece, Crete, Burma, Malaya, Libya, Cyrenaica and in Egypt before a general emerged with the iron determination to put those lessons into effect. Many hundreds of thousands of British and Empire soldiers would have to be killed, wounded or taken into captivity before a commander would be appointed who was capable of forging a British army that could face, let alone challenge, its German counterpart in battle.

Without Dunkirk it is questionable whether Bernard Montgomery would have become that commander; without the subsequent two years of military defeat it is equally uncertain whether officers and men would have rallied to Montgomery's dictatorial leadership in the way they did – for Bernard Montgomery's Norman ruthlessness, Cromwellian piety, and Nelsonian bravado were not qualities to evoke acclaim in either British military or domestic circles save in war. Not even Alan Brooke, his guiding spirit, foresaw the name Bernard would make for himself in British and world history when the BEF left for France in September 1939; in fact Brooke probably thought Bernard would never rise above divisional or at most corps command – for Bernard was, as Wavell had found before him, an unpopular officer among his seniors and even his contemporaries, with little notion of strategy, uncultured, and seemingly blindly devoted to soldiering; awkward as a subordinate and, though blessed with a crystal-clear brain, inclined to rash behaviour beyond his conventional military prerogatives. In fact, as Wavell had saved Bernard's career over the fairground incident in the summer of 1938, so, in late 1939, it would fall to Brooke to hush up a similar *faux pas* which might otherwise have ended Bernard's chances of further promotion.

Bernard Montgomery was, *tout court*, a peacetime misfit; talented but unpredictable, a still relatively junior Major-General of only one year's standing; a useful soldier in a tight spot, as in Palestine; a brilliant teacher but uncongenial as a colleague or subordinate; rather tense and, outside military matters, unimaginative. Brooke's other divisional commander was Major-General D. G. Johnson, VC – a charming, amiable officer commanding the 4th Division, without Montgomery's flair for training, but well liked by his subordinate officers and capable of evoking great loyalty among them. With these two divisions, whose training and equipment 'left much to be desired',[1] Lt-General Brooke went to war in September 1939 – little imagining that the GOC 3rd Division would become a field commander of world historical dimensions, destined for far greater fame than himself.

For the officers and men of the 3rd Division, the picture was very different; and there were few, as in the past, who served under Montgomery who did not feel he was fated for higher things. To an outsider he might appear blinkered and shallow; but to his own subordinates he was a revelation: a general who welcomed the war as a chance to get down to 'real' soldiering. His confidence was infectious, his personal abstemiousness salutary, and his views on command, training and morale, clear and cogent. Above all he had firm convictions about the conduct of modern war which differed both from the World War One diehards and the visionary thinkers who saw in air power and the tank the two principal arms of future combat. He had gone on record in 1937, in his 'Encounter Battle' article in the RE *Journal*, as to the tactics a successful commander must adopt in modern continental warfare: namely a reversal of the accepted British doctrine whereby the divisional commander sat behind a phalanx of his main battalions with an 'advance guard' to scout out the enemy. A modern divisional commander, he had declared, must be willing to command the front-line units himself: to gauge for himself the intentions of the enemy and to adopt his own clear-cut plan for meeting or attacking that enemy, disposing his own forces in well-trained mobile formations ready to adopt a

[1] Alanbrooke, *Notes on My Life*, King's College, London.

303

genuine tactical plan. Liddell Hart had objected that the crushing impact of modern armoured thrusts would make such encounter doctrines superfluous – that battle would be joined from the moment of collision: *l'attaque brusquée*. But in the *Army Quarterly* of August 1938, Bernard pointed out the fallacy behind such thinking. He acknowledged that the main enemy attack might be by armoured divisions; but he made clear that, in order to succeed, such thrusts would have to be concentrated, leaving normal infantry divisions to follow up or hold flanking sectors, thus becoming vulnerable to 'encounter battle' tactics: tactics in which choice of ground, mobility of troops, central control of artillery, trained co-ordination and adequate communication were the vital factors. Above all, the divisional commander's battle orders should follow a 'general plan' previously made known to all commanders, at every echelon. Circumstances might require an amendment to that plan; but at least officers would know what was being attempted and why, thus being enabled to think for themselves.

In many ways, Bernard's article was a blue-print for what would happen in May 1940. He gave the seven most important elements in a corps commander's instructions, and indicated the fundamental method of modern command which a divisional commander must adopt: namely the co-ordination of his forward troops with both divisional artillery and his main body of troops. Once in contact with the enemy on a wide front, the commander must 'take the control of the battle into his own hands', looking ahead to decide the ground on which he would choose to fight, giving out a general plan, and making sure that his command was in depth, without relying completely on telephone or radio contact which was 'unlikely' to be '100 per cent reliable' in battle.

But if Bernard Montgomery was ready for war as a divisional commander, was he ready as a human being, less than two years since his wife's tragic death? Following his collapse in the spring of 1939 Bernard had vowed not to touch alcohol or tobacco again – a vow to which he stuck with iron determination. Moreover he doggedly refused to surrender charge of his son David to the relatives who offered to care for him: for David was his hostage to the memory of Betty, and thus was 'not for sale'. Care of David thus became – and would remain until 1942 – a strangely arbitrary, disordered affair; indeed David would find it impossible, casting his mind back in later years, to remember clearly the sequence, reason, places or people with whom he spent his holidays away from school. In 1937 he had been sent as a boarder to Amesbury Preparatory School about forty miles from Portsmouth, run by a retired army major called Tom Reynolds, who had commanded the Small Arms School at Hythe when Bernard was a company commander with the 1st Battalion, the Royal Warwickshire Regiment, at Shorncliffe. In the holidays, when not sent to a holiday home, David lodged with the Carthews. This arrangement was to stretch over the following years; except, that as the Carthews became posted to successive distant locations, David began to go more frequently to Jocelyn Carver, his half-brother's young wife, in Berkshire. From 1939 David was sent in the summer holidays to a home in Devon, Near Barnstaple, run by a Miss Charlotte Hogg – an arrangement which Bernard was instantly to terminate in 1941 when he heard David was happily recuperating there from a broken leg and therefore missing school. To David this was another nail in his often coffin-like childhood, administered by a somewhat ruthless, distant father embittered by death,[1] but in Bernard's own complex psychology it was probably an attempt to maintain his own absolute emotional and domestic independence – to be beholden to no one save those whom he had himself appointed. Thus David would never, in these years, be allowed to see his grandmother, Lady Montgomery, or any other member of the Montgomery family save his sister-in-law Jocelyn – and even this relationship would be later aborted at Bernard's orders.

Bernard had insisted that Jocelyn's engagement to John Carver be formally announced in *The Times* only a fortnight after Betty's death in 1937; but the marriage in 1938 he did not attend. 'I will not bend my knee in your Catholic church,' he had given as his reason – though it is more likely he wanted no public occasion at which members of the Montgomery family might have to be invited and Betty's absence be rubbed in, for privately he insisted the couple must stay at the same hotels in the same places which he and Betty had frequented on their own honeymoon over a decade before – even the same books they must read.[2]

Betty's death cannot be said to have affected Bernard's single-minded pursuit of his military career, any more than their marriage had; but it did certainly affect his personality. The friends he had made through Betty were largely dropped and, as in his attitude towards David, his erstwhile patriarchal instincts turned to a Balzacian possessiveness which served as the outlet for much deeper psychological woes. As Bernard's younger brother Brian has written, there was much in Bernard's post-marital behaviour that recalled an earlier, pre-marital Bernard: awkward, egocentric, sometimes vindictive, often vain. Undoubtedly Betty's death opened up the wound from which Bernard had always suffered: namely the iron, excluding will of his mother, which he had sought so hard both to escape and to appease. The list of macabre actions towards his own family in the ensuing years would grow, and scarcely any close friend or colleague would not, at one time or another, find himself at extreme loggerheads with Bernard; for there could be no pretending that the psychological demon which at times motivated his behaviour was an

[1] Viscount Montgomery, interview of 30.8.78.
[2] Colonel John Carver, interview of 3.3.78.

easy one to placate. Yet this was essentially but the reverse side of that ambition to succeed as a general, as a leader of men, which those who served with him recognised as genius – and thus forgave. As Gwen Herbert remembered saying to her husband in September 1939 *à propos* Bernard: 'Well, perhaps it's a good thing this war's begun. Horrible – but it's a chance for Monty to recover. At last he's got a real job to do.'[1]

---

[1] Interview of January 1978.

CHAPTER TWO

The BEF in France

Bernard's job was indeed a challenge. General Wavell had not taken Bernard's Combined Operations assault landing seriously the year before because it was performed with similar rowboats to those with which Wolfe had stormed Quebec almost two centuries before; and in some respects the 3rd Division of the BEF was to go to war with the same ridiculous equipment in 1939. The Division's road party, for instance, would be held up at Falmouth for days because the Movement Control authorities did not believe a regular British Army division could be setting off to a continental war with impressed laundry vehicles.

Yet neither now nor in the previous year had Bernard been daunted by appearances. As far back as 1925 he had himself argued for such an arrangement whereby commercial vehicles might be subsidised by the government in order to have a cheap transport reserve in case of war.[1] By the spring of 1940 English Territorial soldiers with spades, and even cooks, clerks and craftsmen, would be fighting German troops; it was irrelevant to Bernard how soldiers were turned out; the question was only whether they would fight. Time was required to furnish the British Army with full war equipment, but in the meantime the Division must be welded together into an efficient, mobile body of men, capable of operating intelligently on foreign soil, irrespective of appearances, he felt. Almost half the men were reservists who would anyway take time to re-acclimatise themselves to army life; and so, from the day he took command of 3rd Division, Bernard concentrated primarily on the problems of organisation and command.

Most senior soldiers agree that, after command of a battalion, command of a division is the most rewarding post a man can hold – 'the smallest formation', as Field-Marshal Slim once put it, 'that is a completed orchestra of war and the largest in which every man can know you.'[2] The 3rd Division comprised three infantry brigades, the 7th, 8th and 9th; three field regiments of Royal Artillery, one anti-tank company, and three field companies of Royal

---

[1] Cf. 'Mechanicalization' articles in the *Antelope*, loc. cit.
[2] W. Slim, *Defeat into Victory*, London 1956.

307

Engineers. It soon took under its wing a machine-gun battalion. Together with its signals unit it was indeed a complete infantry orchestra, with three élite Guards battalions as its outstanding performers – the 1st and 2nd Battalions of the Grenadier Guards, and the 1st Battalion Coldstream Guards. By 8 September, when the Division began to assemble at Crewkerne in south Somerset, it numbered over 10,000 men.

Initially, only one corps was to represent the BEF in France – Dill's 1 Corps; but political and military considerations, as well as the deteriorating situation in Poland, quickly made it necessary for Hore-Belisha to send 2 Corps as well. Thus, no sooner had the 3rd Division assembled for training and equipping in Crewkerne, than word came through that it would have to travel east again, to embark at Southampton.

For Bernard this was no new occurrence – the first weeks in August 1914 had been spent in similar bunglings. Besides, the initial move from Portsmouth to Crewkerne was useful practice in moving a division from scratch. As far as the Divisional HQ was concerned, Bernard had already by 9 September listed seven lessons for future moves, including the proper complement for an advance party, the ideal location (the Red Lion Hotel was most comfortable but offered no experience to the HQ catering staff!), and proper medical and sanitary arrangements. He had also sent out reconnaissance officers to requisition suitable land at Crewkerne for brigade digging schemes, weapon training and the like; and despite the growing likelihood of a move to France these went ahead in the following days. A signals exercise without troops on the 13th, and, after King George VI had inspected the division at Misterton on the 19th, Advance Divisional HQ and Divisional Intelligence exercises were held the next day. Finally on 21 September an advance party of five officers left for France, whilst the Division's road transport set off for Falmouth the following day. Meanwhile the date for troop embarkation was set for 29 September, with embarkation at Southampton as in August 1914, but with Cherbourg as landing-point in order to discourage the Germans from bombing the nearer Channel ports.

On 26 September, Bernard addressed all brigade and battalion commanders of the Division, laying down his offensive and defensive policies, as well as his views on mobile warfare. One hundred thousand rounds of rifle ammunition had been used in an effort to ensure that every reservist in the Division had had an opportunity to fire a gun; but before the Division sailed Bernard also insisted that each man throw at least three grenades. On the morning of 29 September a series of trains bore the Division and its officers to Southampton. Embarkation began at 10.30 a.m., and just before midnight the fleet sailed, arriving at Cherbourg the next morning. Meanwhile hundreds of miles away the Division's road transport was still being unloaded at Brest where it was found that the French dockers had managed to pilfer every officer's locked car boot, as well as forcing many of the doors on the laundry vans.

It was not an auspicious beginning. There were no vehicles to be impressed or even hired at Cherbourg, but by pooling the advance party's transport the Division somehow managed to set off, by train and car, for Everon, the designated assembly area near Laval. On 1 October, without road transport, equipped with only what they carried, the 3rd Division took over the billets recently vacated by 1st Division. The Corps Commander, Lt-General Brooke, had been assured that a period of intensive training would now be possible before the Corps would be required to man the French frontier defences; but to his chagrin this was countermanded when Brooke visited Gort, the Commander-in-Chief, at Arras on 2 October. On the 3rd orders were given out for the 3rd Division to move forthwith to a defensive area south of Lille, around Lesquin, again taking over from 1st Division – a highly pregnable stretch of ground offering a single anti-tank ditch as its sole obstacle to enemy penetration. Had the Germans invaded then, as Brooke noted in his diary, it would have been a walk-over.[1]

Hitler, as it happened, had similar thoughts. In a conversation with the German Army's Chief-of-Staff General Halder on 27 September (the last day of Polish resistance), Hitler urged an immediate assault on Northern France, through Holland and Belgium. Not only would this act as a pre-emptive strike, lest the French do the opposite and invade the Ruhr; but even if, as in 1914, it led to stalemate it would ensure North Sea and Channel bases for German U-boats as well as aerodromes for the Luftwaffe. 'Necessary to prepare an *immediate* invasion of France,' Halder recorded in his diary that day.[2] Hitler's views were intuitive: 'The French will not have the stuff of the Poles . . . [They have] no training in mobile warfare . . . The decisive element will be the English.'[3]

The British Official History skates over the 'phoney war' in France, devoting only a handful of pages to the eight-month war of waiting. Equally, many historians such as Lord Gort's biographer have assumed that, in the absence of British armoured divisions, the BEF was doomed from the start. Gort himself is reported as having said, when informed in the winter of 1939 that the Germans had ten armoured divisions poised for attack in the West: 'In that case we haven't an earthly chance.'

Yet, for the officers and men who were seriously engaged in preparing the BEF for war, the result was by no means a foregone conclusion, and the war was by no means 'phoney'. Given trained and resourceful defence, tanks were not unstoppable; given skilful

[1] Arthur Bryant, *Turn of the Tide*, London 1957.
[2] F. Halder, *Kriegstagebuch 1*, Stuttgart, 1962.
[3] Ibid.

generalship the Germans could be lured on to unfavourable ground and exposed to a long campaign for which, as Hitler himself acknowledged, Germany was neither materially nor politically well suited. If the BEF could be trained to face both infantry and armoured assault, and be commanded by officers of adequate calibre, the chances of swift success for the Germans were not beyond question.

It was this vital respite (Hitler quoted a maximum number of ten months to Halder) before German invasion which gave the Allies a chance to prepare for war in the West – a chance they had not had in 1914. Yet, having virtually emptied the War Office of senior officers to serve with him at GHQ in the BEF, Gort permitted himself to be given a subordinate role in the French military hierarchy not much superior to that of a junior Corps Commander. Moreover he approved a scheme whereby, in the event of German invasion of Belgium, the entire British Expeditionary Force should relinquish its prepared defences on the French border and meet the Germans on unreconnoitred ground of the latter's choosing. In his anxiety over possible German aerial attack, Gort split his Headquarters at Arras into an untidy and uncohesive bureaucracy with disparate messes, and in separate villages covering an area of more than twenty-five miles. Gort was incapable of discussing with either Dill or Brooke the military policies he would pursue in any likely contingency – indeed he was said to be basically afraid of having to overrule two such distinguished subordinates – and during the entire eight months he had to prepare his HQ for the campaign he never once conducted an administrative, signals, Intelligence or even movement exercise. His eventual performance in May 1940 would be excused by successive government and even independent historians who blamed Britain's allies, her deficient arms, and the brilliance of German strategic and tactical generalship; but these excuses only serve, as they did in 1940, to obfuscate the simple truth – a truth which Bernard Montgomery would subsequently triumphantly demonstrate: namely that an army is the creation of its commander, not the sum of its units. The indignities suffered by the BEF in May 1940 were amply presaged in the winter of 1939–40; or as Bernard informed the CIGS in a private interview on 2 June 1940: 'I gave it as my opinion: that the BEF had never been really "commanded" since it was formed, and that for the next encounter we must have a new GHQ and a new C-in-C. I said that the only man to be C-in-C was Brooke.'[1]

Brooke was indeed the sole Corps Commander to emerge from the Dunkirk campaign with any laurels, for only Brooke prepared himself in mind and deed for the campaign that must come. Poor Dill, rendered despondent by Gort's brave but inadequate performance in the winter of 1939–40, was exchanged with the Deputy CIGS on the eve of battle in April 1940, while the hapless Lt-General Barker was

[1] Montgomery Papers.

appointed to command 1 Corps and Sir Ronald Adam took over the mythical extra 3 Corps.

Brooke towered above his colleagues; it was his ability to see the larger issues of a problem, to weigh them, and to make iron-cast decisions which provided an inspiration to Bernard Montgomery – as well as his sheer professional acumen. Brooke, first British master of the creeping artillery barrage in World War One, was the least romantic of English soldiers, and he approached higher military command as scientifically as if he were directing the fire of a co-ordinated brigade of artillery batteries. He correctly foresaw that within months the BEF would be 'hanging on by our eyelids';[1] but the task of getting Gort to run a pukka HQ or even sand-table exercises was not within his competence. Hore-Belisha, in a bid to rid himself of the very CIGS he had himself appointed, had doomed the BEF. 'He was unfitted for the job – and we senior officers all knew it,' Bernard wrote of Gort later in *The Path to Leadership*, 'he loved detail and couldn't see the wood for the trees.' Brooke was even more caustic at the time. 'Gort's brain has lately been compared with that of a glorified boy-scout!' he noted in his diary on 21 November 1939. 'Perhaps unkind, but there is a great deal of truth in it.'[2]

By contrast Brooke had a magisterial capacity for seeing both wood and trees; and Bernard was undoubtedly immensely privileged to have him as his Corps Commander. Indeed Brooke's example would in many ways be the model for his own conduct as a Corps and as an Army Commander for the rest of the war: a man constantly planning ahead, but firm and decisive in the present. Moreover for Bernard, driven from childhood to 'prove' himself and thus win approval, it was essential to have a mentor whose judgement he could respect, and whose professional *imprimatur* he could earn. For Bernard, such a man was Brooke.

In the meantime, in the autumn of 1939, the cares of Brooke as a Corps Commander were very different from those of his divisional lieutenants. However much Gort bungled the future of the BEF, Brooke was determined that 2 Corps would acquit itself as the most efficient in the British army; and in Bernard he began to recognise a brilliant divisional trainer and organiser. The two men conferred about the move into the line on 1 October; thereafter he left Bernard largely to fend for himself. On 9 October Bernard issued his Division-al Operation Instruction No. 1, and four days later the 3rd Division took up its positions. Priority was given to anti-tank obstacles and emplacements, with minefields being laid to 'shepherd enemy tanks into areas covered by AT weapons', and 'all positions, defences, Observation Posts, etc. will be examined from the enemy point of

[1] Entry of 30.1.40, Alanbrooke Diaries, Liddell Hart Centre for Military Archives. *See also* A. Bryant, op. cit.
[2] Ibid.

view'. The instruction was signed by Bernard himself. A continuous trench system was also to be dug, together with tank-proof reserve positions, and artillery units sited both to cover the front and provide additional anti-tank support. Digging began immediately; and within several days, on 18 October, there came news of German troops concentrating on the Belgian border.

In fact the first German operational plans for an invasion in the West were not issued until the next day, 19 October; Hitler did not like them, and they were impracticable before November.

The French Commander-in-Chief, General Gamelin, proposed that, in the event of a German violation of Belgian neutrality, the Allied forces in North-West France should move into Belgium to meet the Germans there – a strategy which, as already stated, Gort accepted without demur, much to Dill's and Brooke's disgust, for the Belgians would have nothing to do with such a proposal, clinging to the idea that if they observed the strictest neutrality Germany might by-pass their country. The Belgians therefore refused to allow a single Allied observer even to reconnoitre the ground; whereas Gamelin, bearing in mind the terrible destruction Northern France had suffered in the Great War, conversely insisted that the encounter battle take place in Belgium, not France. Gort's strategic blindness and stubborn discipline in loyally supporting his French Commander-in-Chief's proposals thus meant the BEF was committed from the start to folly. And yet it was the BEF who would have to bear the brunt of such an encounter battle (the French 16 Corps which would be on the BEF's left was still not even in line in October); moreover, though the BEF only comprised as yet four divisions, Hitler himself had calculated them to be worth twelve French counterparts, and feared that the longer he delayed an invasion, the more the BEF would put heart into the defeatist French.[1]

Bernard himself seems to have been undismayed by the proposals for a headlong dash into an unreconnoitred Belgium. For him, this was a challenge to train his division in mobile, delaying warfare. Europe might wait impatiently for a climax to the 'phoney' war, but for Bernard every extra week of peace meant more time to teach his 10,000 men the art of manoeuvre; the ability to move forward as a cohesive unit, to cross bombed or demolished obstacles, the art of digging in and organising defence in depth; and the highest art of all: the fighting withdrawal.

There was no question in Bernard's mind about the latter – for no four English infantry divisions would be able to hold a concerted German attack, particularly if armoured. However, by bounding forward to one of the series of Belgian water obstacles – the Scheldt, Escaut or Dyle – the BEF would have all the more opportunity to slow down the German advance, harrying, counter-attacking, de-

---

[1] David Irving, *Hitler's War*, London, 1977.

molishing: a Wellingtonian retreat that would preserve the intiative in defence, luring the Germans further from their own bases and nearer those of the Allies. Such a prospect was actually exciting – if the BEF could train itself accordingly. Brooke agreed: although the more he saw of his French allies the less prospect of success he saw. Gort was quite simply out of his depth. As Bernard wrote in *The Path to Leadership*, Gort merely perorated on his obsession, the last war, citing Foch's clichés instead of giving his subordinates an idea of the future campaign.

By 15 October Bernard had issued three divisional operational instructions on the defence of their allotted sector; but with the outline plan for a move into Belgium, and the alarm about imminent invasion on the 18th, Bernard decided that the Division must start exercises in mobility and battle manoeuvre. In the ensuing months of the 'phoney' war he would personally devise and mount some five full-scale divisional exercises that would make the 3rd Division the most highly trained mobile division in the British army.

The first of these field exercises took place on 30 October, and lasted four days. It was called 'Manning the Defences' and included motorised movement by night, marches by day, setting up road blocks for civilian traffic, and a 'telephone battle' simulating at Battalion, Brigade and Divisional HQs the transmission of reports and orders. The exercise was watched by officers from Gort's headquarters, and Brooke took a keen interest in the proceedings. 'It was a matter of the greatest interest watching Monty improving every day as he began to find his feet as a Divisional Commander,' wrote Brooke of that period[1] though he was not satisfied that Bernard's artillery dispositions were right, and on 2 November he called on Bernard to have them improved and also to ensure that his parties visiting Lille were 'better turned out and more of a credit to our Corps than they are at present,' he noted in his diary that night.[2] Bernard however was more concerned with his divisional exercise than troop turn-out, and there is no record in the War Diary that he issued any formal instructions on the latter.[3] Instead he concentrated on his divisional conferences of all unit commanders of the 3rd Division both before and after the exercise. Apart from traffic control points such as the use of headlamps, the most important lesson to emerge was in communication. On 1 November Bernard had ordered the Divisional Advance HQ itself to move, and at least four units had failed to receive notification of this – thus bearing out Bernard's contention in his 'Encounter Battle' articles that W/T and R/T transmission could not be relied upon to function one hundred per cent efficiently in

[1] *Notes on My Life*, loc. cit. *See also* A. Bryant, op. cit.
[2] Loc. cit.
[3] War Diary, HQ 3rd Division, September 1939–June 1940 (WO 167/218), PRO.

battle. Liaison officers and messengers, as of old, would also be required in modern battle.

Already Bernard's reputation within the 3rd Division was improving by leaps and bounds as officers and men began to witness his sheer professionalism. This was more than could be said of Gort and his Headquarters. Bernard's erstwhile Brigade-Major at 9th Infantry Brigade, Colonel Simpson, was transferred from London to the Military Secretary's office at GHQ Arras at this time – an appointment insisted upon by General Giffard at the War Office after a visit to Gort's HQ where he found the most amateur arrangements conceivable. The Military Secretary apparently followed Gort like a page-boy, while his deputy concentrated entirely on the wines and food for the mess of the Quartermaster-General at Noyelles Vion, a village some miles west of Arras. How, in such circumstances, the BEF was supposed to swell itself into an eventual formation of two armies, with nearly half a million men, was incredible – the more so since Gort's policy of dispersal at Arras meant that those communications that did penetrate from the War Office had to make a tortuous round of GHQ before they could ever hope to be received by the unit concerned.

For Bernard, 'Simbo' Simpson's arrival at GHQ was a godsend; and no sooner had 'Simbo' settled into his new office than Bernard began to ask him to get rid of 'useless' officers – particularly captains and majors who were obstructing the promotion of younger men.

'I used to get frequent letters from Monty,' Simpson later recollected, 'saying that he wished to get rid of some inefficient officer who was somewhere in the division under him, and would I please find this individual another job. As far as I could I did,' Simpson recalled – for it seemed to him better to find the victim alternative employment before his whole army future was doomed by a scathing report from the Divisional Commander; and within a short time a large number of Montgomery-outcasts were standing on French platforms directing troop trains – 'telling the CO on the train where the halts were going to be, where the men would have to get out and cook their meals, where the latrines would be en route, and all that sort of thing.'[1] Whether Bernard realised that such dismissed officers would eventually form a distinct critical groundswell in the British army which would resent his gradual rise to fame, is unlikely, but, even if he had, he would not have cared. His task as he saw it was to create a highly efficient weapon of war, in which there was no room for backsliders. Nevertheless, Simpson's train-conducting discards did not always fare so badly, as one hilarious episode was to prove.

'It was decided to send out a party of new students from the Staff College,' Simpson recounted, 'which was taking in a lot of temporary officers in those days to train to be staff officers. They were to go to

---

[1] Wason interviews, loc. cit.

France to look over the way the BEF was behaving and, of course, several of these parties went to Monty's division.

'Just at that time two of Monty's rather unsatisfactory officers were ordered off to be train-conducting officers and the temporary camp into which they went for the night also contained a party of Staff College students. Where the confusion occurred I never knew, but when the Staff College students left after their two or three days, they [the discarded officers from 3rd Division] went with them, and were duly taken into a class at the Staff College.

'It took the directing staff at the Staff College about a week or two to discover that they had two most unsuitable students under them. Further investigation took place and the wretched officers were turned out.

'It took me a long time to live that down although I really had no responsibility for the confusion. It delighted Monty to be told that his two discarded officers eventually finished up at the Staff College! He said he wished I had been able to add that they were the two most brilliant students they had ever had!'

Such mix-ups were the stuff of Evelyn Waugh; yet that November Bernard was himself to be entrapped in a similarly unfortunate episode: the 'VD affair'.

Encouraged by the success of his first four-day divisional exercise, Bernard turned his attention to the welfare of the troops. Since October 1939 parties of men had been permitted to go on weekend leave to Lille. Here the brothels were clean and regularly inspected; but by 15 November more than forty cases of VD had been reported – and the figure was expected to rise sharply. On making enquiries Bernard found that men were subsidising the local country girls for favours 'in the beetroot fields'; he therefore sat down and promulgated a Divisional Order on the subject.

'My view is that if a man wants to have a woman, let him do so by all means: but he must use his common sense and take the necessary precautions against infection – otherwise he becomes a casualty by his own neglect, and this is helping the enemy.'

Bernard's solution was straightforward. The battalion COs must address the men frankly, condoms must be on sale in the NAAFI shop, and sexual hygiene promoted. The cleaner brothels in Lille must be extolled, and the men taught the French for 'French Letter' in case they wished to buy one in a French shop. 'We must face up to the problem, be perfectly frank about it, and do all we can to help the soldier in this very difficult matter,' Bernard concluded his order.[1]

As Bernard later confessed, he was rather proud of his effort:[2] in a time of traditional sexual hypocrisy it struck a refreshingly sensible and candid note. Moreover there was no suggestion the Commander

---

[1] Quoted in Brian Montgomery, *A Field-Marshal in the Family*, op. cit.
[2] Bernard Montgomery, *The Path to Leadership*, op. cit.

was arguing from personal experience, since he was known to be in all respects an abstemious and strictly moral person. Bernard's mistake was in issuing the five-point document as an order under his own name, for within a very short time a copy had been passed to the senior chaplain at GHQ in Arras, who demanded that Gort take action.

Gort, as has been seen, was clearly envious of Bernard. His immediate response was to insist, via the Adjutant General, that Bernard publicly withdraw the document, and Brooke, as Bernard's superior officer, was duly informed of this. As Brooke was aware, however, to make him withdraw an order would have meant making Bernard's position in the Division impossible. 'I should have been forced to withdraw Monty from his Division and to send him home.'[1]

Fortunately for Bernard, Brooke was well disposed towards him. Brooke had fought to have Bernard re-appointed to the 3rd Division in September 1939; he was not particularly willing to surrender him two months later, especially after witnessing the astonishing aplomb with which Bernard had organised his first divisional exercise. Moreover the time was hardly appropriate for a change of commander. For three days from 12 November the Corps had been at three or even two hours' notice to move into Belgium, on whose borders German troops were again massing. This time the alarm had been genuine: dissident elements in the German military hierarchy had leaked to the Dutch Hitler's plan for an invasion beginning on 12 November, including the occupation of both Holland and Belgium. 'The violation of Belgian and Dutch neutrality is unimportant,' Hitler had told his assembled generals *in camera*. 'Nobody will ask about such things after we have won.'[2] On 5 November Hitler had postponed the German invasion to 15 November; on 9 November, after missing assassination in the Munich Bürgerbräu cellar by only twenty minutes, he postponed the attack to 22 November. Autumn had meanwhile broken, contradicting the weather experts, so that on 16 November – the day Gort was informed of Montgomery's infamous order on VD – Hitler was forced to postpone the date to 26 November; and on the 20th he shifted it to 3 December.

Given the seriousness of the military situation, Brooke felt Gort was fiddling while Rome burned, and rejected Bernard's inevitable dismissal on the eve of battle. Brooke instead insisted that as Corps Commander he should be permitted to deal with the problem himself; and on the morning of 23 November he telephoned to 3rd Division HQ asking Bernard not to go out visiting units before he arrived.

'I did not know about the storm which was blowing up,' Bernard later wrote, 'and when I received a message that the Corps Comman-

---

[1] A. Bryant, op. cit.
[2] David Irving, op. cit.

der was coming to see me, and I was to remain in until he arrived, I thought in my innocence that some urgent tactical problem was to be discussed. I was mistaken! He arrived, and I could tell by the look on his face and his abrupt manner that I was "for it" – and I was right. He let drive for about ten minutes, and I listened.'[1] Brooke did not mince his words: 'I pointed out to Monty that his position as Commander of a Division had been seriously affected by the issue of such a document and could certainly not withstand any further errors of this kind,'[2] he recorded in his diary on the night of 23 November.

Bernard however could scarcely believe the Corps Commander was being serious; as he later remembered: 'When he had run out of words he became calmer, and even smiled. I then plucked up courage and said I reckoned my circular letter was rather a good one, and extremely clear. That finished it; he began again and I received a further blasting!'[3]

Brooke was perfectly serious. 'I informed him that I had a very high opinion of his military capabilities and an equally low one of his literary ones!' Brooke recorded in his published diary;[4] the unpublished version reveals that he thought Bernard's efforts downright 'obscene', and in his *Notes on My Life* written a decade later he still maintained that 'the language in which this document had been written had to be seen to be believed'.[5]

From Brooke's point of view as a Corps Commander he could not understand how a promising and dedicated general could put at risk his military career for the sake of a matter that was the prerogative of the medical or even religious staff; whereas for Bernard the order demonstrated his very devotion to the welfare of his men – just as his brothel in Alexandria had done. Nevertheless Bernard recognised from Brooke's tone that the matter was far more serious that he imagined; possibly Brooke told him how close it had come to dismissal, and Bernard piped down. As he wrote in retrospect: 'I have since come to the conclusion that it is better to remain silent on such occasions and take all that comes to you.'[6]

In the event Bernard's reputation did not suffer, though one or two rude ditties circulated in the Division, referring to him as the 'General of Love' and suchlike – one of them written by a young signaller who was destined to become a High Court judge. The incidence of venereal disease diminished, so that Bernard felt quietly vindicated, while Brooke, casting his mind back to the occasion in his later *Notes*

[1] Bernard Montgomery, *The Path to Leadership*, op. cit.
[2] A. Bryant, op. cit. and Alanbrooke Diaries, loc. cit.
[3] *The Path to Leadership*, op. cit.
[4] 23.11.39, A. Bryant, op. cit.
[5] Loc. cit.
[6] *The Path to Leadership*, op. cit.

on My Life, was equally pleased at the conclusion: 'I never ceased to thank Heaven that I saved Monty at this danger point in his career . . . I should never have had the opportunities that I had in 1940 to estimate his true value, and should probably have remained ignorant of them and consequently failed to recommend him for command of the 8th Army in the Middle East.'[1]

One further reason for Gort's dislike of the Commander of 3rd Division may have been his recent visit there with the Secretary of State, Hore-Belisha, on 18 November. The Deputy Director of Military Operations, John Kennedy, accompanied Hore-Belisha, together with the War Minister's Military Assistant, Major de Guingand, and in his Memoirs Kennedy recorded: 'We went next to the front of the 2nd Corps, commanded by Brooke, and saw Montgomery's and Johnson's 3rd and 4th Divisions. Gort had sent out orders that the men were not to parade, but to continue their work. Montgomery's men, nevertheless, were drawn up in lines on the roadside. Gort was angry when he saw them, and said, "Just like Monty – I will take it out of him for this." '[2]

Gort, who by now detested Hore-Belisha and was being treated like a schoolboy by Ironside, was determined to play just such a schoolboy prank on Hore-Belisha – namely by subjecting the latter to a physical tour of defences which no sedentary politician or civilian could withstand. Bernard, for all his political naïveté, was a surprising realist in many ways; he knew that Hore-Belisha would be pleased by some acknowledgment of his position as political head of the army and thus ignored the GHQ order not to parade the division. Probably it reflected also Bernard's determination always to hold the reins and initiative as a Commander. Had Hore-Belisha expressed a desire to see the men at work, Bernard would have then ordered it, demonstrating his authority. It was a foretaste of the manner in which Bernard would treat Churchill; as it was, as Bernard informed Ironside on 1 December, 'Belisha had thanked him for showing him round the men and not the fortifications, which did not interest him'.[3]

In fact this was not quite the case. Upset by Gort's spartan programme and sensing that all was not well with the BEF, but not being able to identify the cause, Hore-Belisha complained at home that the BEF was not showing the correct sense of urgency in building concrete pill-boxes, whereas the French were building them in three days flat. This, however, was the very reverse of the truth – the French pill-boxes he saw had been built by the British, and French construction schedules were fictions of the French Commander-in-Chief. Gort and Ironside therefore decided to pool their

[1] A. Bryant, op. cit. and Alanbrooke Papers, loc. cit.
[2] *The Business of War*, London 1957.
[3] R. Macleod (Ed), *The Ironside Diaries 1937–40*, London 1962.

dislike of Hore-Belisha and have him hounded out of office for the slur. Thus, five weeks later, Hore-Belisha was forced to resign by the very two generals he himself had appointed to the top posts in the British Army.

The change of political direction did no good, though. Ironside was bold and had many brilliant insights – for instance his premonition that Hitler would attack through the Ardennes – but he did not possess the consistent wisdom of a War Office chief that the Cabinet needed. By July 1940 all three men – Hore-Belisha, Gort and Ironside – would be sacked and it would be up to new men to prove their worth.

Bernard Montgomery, fortunately, was uninvolved in such machinations. Brooke had saved him from Gort's wrath, and he must prove himself worthy of Brooke's faith. The weather served to postpone the German invasion, but it also made conditions in the divisional defence area reminiscent of the Great War: the banks of the river Marcq began to fall in, the trenches so painstakingly dug by the troops filled with water, and the mechanical diggers bogged down. Despite the appalling conditions, though, Bernard's policy of training exercises went ahead: a signals exercise with the RAF on 21 November, and a divisional R/T exercise again on 26 November. With the certainty of an advance into Belgium in the event of German invasion, though, Bernard felt certain he must now concentrate on mobility. The second full-scale divisional exercise was thus planned to take place in December, shortly before Christmas 1939.

CHAPTER THREE

Training the 3rd Division

If Bernard Montgomery lacked imagination in non-military matters, the same could not be said of his work as a divisional commander. As his future Chief-of-Staff would write, Montgomery was such a thorough professional that he virtually made imagination redundant.[1] While Gort spent sleepless nights worrying about whether the British soldier should carry his helmet on his left or right shoulder, and while Hore-Belisha came to grief over his vision of a Belisha line of pill-boxes to match the Maginot line, Bernard set out exercises for his 3rd Division that were the very blue-print of what would be required in May of the following year. The object of his December exercise was: 'a) To practise rapid movement in M/T to seize and hold a river line, pending the arrival of additional troops and b) To practise the staging and delivering of a counter-attack, supported by infantry tanks and air and artillery to drive an enemy back over an obstacle over which he may have succeeded in establishing a bridgehead,' as the Divisional War Diary recorded.[2]

The exercise took place, despite bitterly cold weather, between 13 and 15 December for the majority of the Division; it was then repeated on 19 to 21 December by the mechanised corps cavalry, the divisional machine-gun battalion and the 9th Infantry Brigade which had meanwhile manned the front.

However, Bernard's second divisional exercise did more than practise mobility and counter-attack. By directing the Division westwards to defend a line on the river Canche above Amiens, Bernard was enabling it to practise movement of the Division into Belgium, but in reverse (since Belgium would still not permit Allied troops across her borders); moreover Bernard even set the future German break-through there, predicting the dire straits of a British Expeditionary Force of an Allied army which had been outflanked by the Germans east of Amiens. Bernard's 'Opening situation' narrative ran:

'As it is possible that Jumboland [Allied] frontier defences of the Somme will be outflanked by a hostile move East of Amiens, BEF is,

[1] De Guingand, *From Brass Hat to Bowler Hat*, op. cit.
[2] Entry for 13 December 1939, loc. cit.

320

as a first step, to seize and hold the line of the R. CANCHE from incl. WAIL to excl. REBREUVIETTE.

'A defensive position has been prepared and extends from RE-BREUVIETTE to ARRAS. ARRAS itself is strongly fortified. Jumbo-land Army is to withdraw to this position, if it finds itself unable to hold the line of the Somme . . .'

This was accurate to within several miles of what was actually to take place in May 1940; and had Gort called for similar exercises with his other corps and divisions the unholy confusion that eventually reigned on the east flank of the BEF might well have been avoided. (In the event 5th Division, which joined 2 Corps on 5 December 1939, was asked five months later during the battle for France to make this very move to Arras including a squadron of the 15th/19th Royal Hussars which took part in Bernard's repeat exercise of 19–21 December 1939.)

Fortunately Bernard's handwritten notes for his pre-exercise conference survive. It is clear from these that he had made a thorough study of the tactics he would adopt in modern mobile warfare. The creation of a firm anti-tank front was given higher priority than securing designated map-references. The leading divisional mechanised cavalry (with carriers and light tanks) were to be held very much under control of Divisional HQ, and not squandered in local engagements: it was therefore the task of follow-up machine-gunners and artillery to free the cavalry as soon as possible 'without waiting for any further orders', themselves in turn being relieved by the infantry. Moreover, for the purpose of the exercise, phases 1 and 2 were to be consecutive – i.e. officers, clerks, signallers, NCOs and troops must for three days and nights practise a 'proper system of adequate reliefs for rest and sleep'.[1] Of all the reasons that would emerge for the chaotic performance by much of the BEF in May 1940, lack of proper sleep would probably contribute the most.

The repeat exercise from 19 to 21 December went well. Certainly the dates chosen were fortunate for, by the time the units had returned to their sector, fog had descended on Northern France, and it was not until 27 December that Bernard could hold his by now customary post mortem.

At this conference – the handwritten notes of which also survive – Bernard was not content simply to criticise the Division's perform-ance; as in later years the conference was designed to be an educa-tional exercise in itself. By describing how and why he himself had acted as Commander, Bernard hoped that the unit commanders and other officers would be able to see the battle retrospectively from *his* point of view, thus not only helping them to understand what had taken place, but encouraging them in the exercise of their own commands.

[1] Montgomery Papers.

1. *The objects of the exercise*. Describe the two roads.
2. *A difficult operation* when opposed by an enemy with a strong air force.
   Will you do it by day or by night?
   Some say you must do it by night.
   I don't agree. Confusion at night is hopeless.
   By day you can see what is happening.
   Best to spread the movement over the 24 hours; low density by day – high density by night.
   If by night – the light problem – no lights or all lights?
3. *Formation to adopt*. In any problem, will vary with conditions.
   Front may crack.
   Must be so disposed that you can move forward covered by mobile troops and present a strong anti-tank front to the enemy as you progress.
   Must be able to grip on to, and hold, ground secured by the cavalry as the movement progresses; other troops required for this, so as to free cavalry for other recce tasks.
   Must have close touch between these other troops and the cavalry, to save delay.
   Must have infantry handy to take over at dark.
   Applying these principles I decided to move the Division as shewn in the general diagrammatic layout in the diagram.

   Describe layout; explain the reasons.

The Main Lessons

1. *Pre-vision* is essential when thinking out dispositions.
   Advantages of being able to foresee your battle.
   Can't always do this accurately.
   But can use imagination and think out what is likely to happen; you then adopt such layout as will ensure you can do something about it whatever the enemy may do.

   I have explained my layout – and why.
   The principles I worked on must be carried down to the unit.

   Suitable dispositions are the first essential on the road to victory – because you have no time to recover from bad ones.
2. *Traffic control & road discipline*
   Not good – room for much improvement.
   Telescoping on roads – big blocks of vehicles nose to crop – officers sitting complacently and doing nothing. They allow vehicles they are in to close up on vehicle in front.
   Traffic jams, and too many troops, in villages.
   Must get the 'idea' – traffic blocks and concentrations of troops and transport in villages will lead to loss of life – safety lies in dispersion. *The senior officer present must take charge*. How? Give examples.

3. *Security – ground and air*

Local protection not instinctive.

In mobile operations and fluid fighting cannot take security for granted because other units are in front; every unit at all times must be certain it cannot be surprised; may be over-run but don't let it come as a surprise and you may then be able to do something about it – if it comes as a surprise you are lost.

In the air we have got to learn to tighten up on our R/T and W/T discipline.

If you speak or send out signals on the ether the enemy will locate you by DF, and, knowing the type of set used, will soon get the signal layout opposite him.

There are 3 points to note particularly:

(a) Keep conversations short – 30 secs and then close down. This avoids risk of DF.

(b) Don't give away your own position to the enemy by map references etc. when ordering moves or reporting locations.

(c) Don't give away to the enemy what we know about him.

A really vital message must be sent by more than one means.

4. *The problem on arrival at the river.*

Secure the crossings; recce beyond them; reach out with your fire and keep the enemy at a distance if you can.

Prepare for other dispositions when enemy is in close contact; must be able to move after dark to new positions from which you can do your task properly; unit do recce for this before it gets light.

All recce parties well forward during the forward move; main bodies of units can then be kept back.

The traffic problem will become acute when the Division begins to pile up on its head.[1]

Bernard's exercises and simulation of battle went back more than a decade and a half. It is difficult to understand how, in a supposedly advanced nation, such exercises were so rare and considered so revolutionary; yet even to Brooke, the Corps Commander himself, they were an 'eye-opener' as he later wrote.[2] In fact, of all the innovations Bernard would make as a general of the British army (and later in NATO) it was perhaps his concept of the modern, co-ordinated exercise which would have the most fundamental and lasting impact. Many an officer outside the division would be astonished how, after twenty-one days of fighting, on the eve of evacuation at Dunkirk, Bernard showed no signs of demoralisation or confusion; but the answer was quite simple. In Brooke's retrospec-

---

[1] Montgomery Papers.
[2] A. Bryant, op. cit.

tive words, the value of Bernard's exercises was triumphantly proved in the battle for Belgium and Flanders when 'his 3rd Division worked like clockwork.'[1] Generals, officers, troops and later historians might blame inadequate weaponry; but Bernard's contention was that there was no weapon that could defeat a properly trained and commanded army.

For Brooke, Bernard's exercises were an 'eye-opener'; but to Bernard himself the exercises were the culmination of sixteen years of study, reflection and practice. He had endured the envious irritation of his battalion colleagues, the horror of his superiors in India, and the indifference of Wavell to his Combined Exercise assault landing in the constant attempt to find the best ways to teach tactics and command. Bernard was never an intellectual – and yet his approach to military tasks reflected the triumph of mind over matter. Brooke had found his VD pamphlet not only pornographic but totally lacking in literary ability. This was unfair. Perhaps more than any other British soldier, perhaps more than any soldier of any country in the twentieth century, Bernard Montgomery mastered the art of simple, unmistakable communication: the ability to impart clear and logical thought in a vibrant way to his officers and men. Those who took part in the 3rd Division exercises in the winter of 1939 were, to use Slim's analogy, the privileged players at a concert conducted by a musician of genius. For them, the rise of Bernard Montgomery to eventual fame could only be a matter of time; and it was to him, in the coming months, that so many of them would owe their lives.

In much of the BEF and beyond, however, an atmosphere of boredom and disbelief reigned. On 16 December, during a visit to the 3rd Division, the British Prime Minister Neville Chamberlain had murmured quietly to Bernard: 'I don't think the Germans have any intention of attacking us, do you?'[2] – hardly an inspiring remark to a general trying to prepare his division for imminent battle.

'In my view,' Bernard told Chamberlain, 'the attack would come at the time of their [the Germans'] own choosing; it was now winter and we must get ready for trouble when the cold weather was over.'[3]

Two days after his divisional conference on the December exercise, Bernard collapsed with 'flu – and not even the visit of Lord Sankey and the Lord Privy Seal Sir Samuel Hoare (both members of the War Ministry) could raise him. He was exhausted and was content to recuperate for a few days in bed, whence he could reflect on the affairs of man. As he later recorded in his *Memoirs*: 'France and Britain stood still while Germany swallowed Poland; we stood still while the German armies moved over to the West, obviously to attack *us* later on; we waited patiently to be attacked; and during all

[1] Ibid.
[2] Bernard Montgomery, *Memoirs*, op. cit.
[3] Ibid.

this time we occasionally bombed Germany *with leaflets*. If this was war I did not understand it . . . My soul revolted at what was happening.'

So far, since September 1939, Bernard had not left the 3rd Division save to attend conferences at 2 Corps. Now, in January 1940, he decided to visit the Maginot Line in Western France to see how one of his units was doing in its brief period of duty there – and the truth finally dawned on Bernard that the French were not going to fight.

CHAPTER FOUR

Rehearsal for Retreat

'During the winter GHQ arranged for divisions to send infantry
brigades in turn down to the active front in the Saar, holding
positions in front of the Maginot Line in contact with the German
positions in the Siegfried Line. I went down there in January 1940 to
visit one of my brigades and spent a few days having a look around.
That was my first experience in the war of the French Army in action;
I was seriously alarmed and on my return I went to see my Corps
Commander, and told him of my fears about the French Army and
what we might have to expect from that quarter in the future. Brooke
had been down there himself and had formed the same opinion . . .
Brooke and I agreed not to talk about it to our subordinates; I believe
he discussed the matter with Gort.'

Brooke had indeed attempted to discuss the matter with Gort, but
to little avail. Gort seems to have known the facts but, either to
preserve British morale or because he was powerless to influence the
French, he ignored the dilemma. Every day his HQ grew larger but,
beyond singing the virtues of 'fighting patrols', Gort did nothing to
prepare the BEF for a French demise. The advance to the Dyle in
Belgium was planned in detail (though often without adequate
consideration of road-tolerances or realistic boundaries); what the
BEF would do once it had reached the Dyle was a mystery Gort did
nothing to dispel. The French would tell him nothing about the likely
disposal of strategic reserves. There was no contingency planning,
and the prospect of a helter-skelter retreat through Belgium if the
French or Belgians – or both – cracked was not considered. Gort
complained that the Territorial divisions he was now being sent were
untrained; but he himself failed the army by failing to train his own
administration for the battle he knew must come.

For Bernard, however, there was no let-up. His ever-vigilant eye
was as ruthless with his own staff as with his fighting units; and,
while GHQ at Arras swelled like an inoperable cancer, Bernard cut
down his own Headquarters to a size that would at all times be
mobile. In England he had been thinking of an Advanced and Main
HQ; but his exercises demonstrated the need for a single and
cohesive communications base. By upgrading his GSO 1 to the role of
Chief-of-Staff (as Gorringe had taught him in the Great War), he was

able to leave a deputy at HQ capable and authorised to take major decisions in his absence while he visited units. Moreover, the commanders of Divisional Artillery, Engineers and Signals were brought in as an integral part of the mobile Divisional HQ, thus ensuring centralised operational planning and command.

By 1 January 1940 Bernard was on his feet again. The next day he gave orders for Divisional Signals HQ to be reduced in size, and began planning a third full-scale divisional exercise to be held again in the St Pol area at the end of the month. The cold weather had, however, hardened the ground, and by mid-January the division was once again put at four hours' notice to move, pending a possible German attack. Hitler had in fact ordered the invasion to begin on 17 January; but, as two million German troops prepared to attack, a Luftwaffe major was shot down on 11 January carrying full details and maps of the intended German operations. This and the weather report forecasting an imminent thaw that would reduce the Low Countries to a bog convinced Hitler he must postpone his assault until the spring; and on 18 January Bernard's 3rd Division received a message cancelling the alert. The danger had passed.

Unfortunately it was this last-minute cancellation of 'Operation Yellow' that caused Hitler finally to alter the original thrust laid down by his Army Commander. If the British and élite units of the French army were to race into Belgium to meet his invasion, why not cut them off in the north by a flank attack through the Ardennes, aimed at Arras, Amiens and the sea? Von Rundstedt's erstwhile Chief-of-Staff, Erich von Manstein, was known to be urging the same idea. Manstein was asked to prepare a detailed plan; and the fate of the Allies was sealed. By loyally agreeing to the French plan for an advance to the Dyle, Gort had thus unwittingly committed the entire BEF to destruction.

Owing to the late January thaw and the disruption caused first by the general alert and then by an abortive exchange of sectors with General Franklyn's 5th Division, Bernard's Divisional Exercise No. 3 was now postponed until March – though sand-table, signals and divisional Intelligence exercises were in the meantime conducted. The latter (on 23 February) were so realistic that GHQ actually believed the practice message sent to it concerning a German parachute drop. Dissatisfied with his Divisional Intelligence Officer, however, Bernard sacked him and asked his Guards Brigade Commander, Brigadier Whitaker, for a replacement. 'Who's your best young officer?' Bernard asked. Not wishing to lose his best Intelligence man, Whitaker sent a young merchant banker, a Territorial temporary captain in the Coldstream Guards by the name of Christopher ('Kit') Dawnay. No one was more surprised than Dawnay by the reception he was given by the Divisional Commander.

'Well, Dawnay, if you're going to be my Intelligence Officer you've got to know how I think and I've got to know how you think. From now on you'll live in my mess, and take all your meals with me,' Bernard ordered.[1] Dawnay would go on to command Montgomery's Tactical Headquarters at the surrender of the German armed forces in northern Europe some five years later; at that time, early in 1940, he was aware of the BEF's gross deficiencies in transport, mortars, ammunition, anti-tank guns and shells, so that the prospect of defeating Germany seemed somewhat remote, if not impossible. Nevertheless he was deeply impressed by Montgomery, who seemed quite unlike the typical senior British officer in the very sharpness of his intellect – 'the rapier as compared with the bludgeon,' as Dawnay later put it.[2] Dawnay had never expected to be included in the Commander's mess, and he was equally surprised by Montgomery's absolute impartiality over whether an officer was a Regular or a non-Regular. 'His sole criterion – and this was at the very start of the war – was: is he any good at his job? He collected around him a number of men who became known as "Monty men", and he went to great lengths to push them up the ladder. Equally there were others whom he considered useless and whom he pushed down.'[3] Bernard's Chief-of-Staff was highly respected in the division – a Royal Marine Colonel known therefore as 'Marino' Brown who was to distinguish himself in the coming battle, but to lose his life on a special mission for the Commander shortly before the final evacuation at Dunkirk.

Having postponed the invasion of the West until spring, the Germans now concentrated on psychological warfare, dropping leaflets that chided the French for believing in anything so ridiculous as a German attack, and encouraging the French to see their British allies as mischievous warmongers.

February turned to March, completing the thaw, and the weeks before likely invasion began to tick away all too fast.

'We had our hands tied behind our backs from an Intelligence point of view,' Dawnay remembered, 'Because we could not even send air patrols over Belgium. The only information we had was what we could get from our Military Attaché in Brussels. We assumed that German tanks would be involved, and our own anti-tank rifle was hopeless. Nevertheless Monty was quite confident we could use our artillery in an anti-tank role, and that mobility was the key to the future . . . He certainly foresaw that we would have to withdraw, and apart from practising the art of limited counter-attack to push an enemy back behind a defensive obstacle, we did nothing in the way of training for offensive action. Although Monty made no predictions about the course of the battle, it followed almost exactly the way he had anticipated in his exercises.'[4]

[1] Lt-Colonel C. P. Dawnay, interview of 23.8.78.
[2] Ibid.
[3] Ibid.
[4] Ibid.

These exercises now became more and more intense as spring approached. Bernard's experience at Le Cateau, in the retreat from Mons, had not been in vain and Divisional Exercise No. 3 took place on 7 and 8 March 1940. It was to be a forty-eight hour continuous operation, but in two definite phases:

(a) A night advance from the divisional area to secure before day-light the next day a river obstacle some sixty miles distant.

(b) A disengagement by night from close contact and a withdrawal to a position in rear, the enemy being delayed in following up the next day by the action of mobile troops, artillery and aircraft.

In essence, these were the very movements that were to be asked of the 3rd Division some seven weeks later; and without Bernard's rehearsals it is difficult to imagine how the 3rd Division could have made its celebrated night move in the middle of the northern break-through battle, on the night of 27 May, which saved 2 Corps and the BEF from being outflanked. Brooke would refer to the latter as 'accomplishing the impossible'; but it is evident from Bernard's hand-written notes for both the preliminary Conference of Commanders and the post mortem on the exercise on 11 March that his aim from the very beginning was to train the Division to achieve the impossible. The exercise, he declared afterwards, had been 'a very delicate operation', involving a night movement of an entire division advancing sixty miles and taking up positions 'in a strange area which could not be recced by day', working only from maps and against a simulated enemy air force watching its movement.[1]

'Some said it was impossible to move a division sixty miles by night, deploying it in the dark and be ready to fight at dawn,' Bernard said in his address to the commanding officers and their staffs. 'I maintained that the 3rd Division could do it, and it did.'

The exercise had been 'a great strain on our MT drivers and motor cyclists; some drivers were at the wheel for 10 hours; when the head had reached the river the tail had not started.

'We owe it to our drivers and MT personnel that we did it; I think it is clear that they are now trained up to a high standard; and they are physically fit.

'Plenty of things went wrong and I am glad they did; it has given me food for thought and points on which to concentrate in our further training; but in the main the movement was well carried out by the Division.'

About the second phase of the operation, Bernard stated:

'On the early morning of Thursday the Div was on a front of 8000 yds and extended back to a depth of 20 miles.

'It was my intention to lie concealed all that day and move up 7 Gds Bde after dark to take over the front.

'But at 6 a.m. in the morning a situation arose which involved an

[1] Montgomery Papers.

329

immediate change of plan; our Allies in front had been driven in, our flanks were in danger of being turned, and GHQ ordered a withdrawal to the St Pol line on which the Allied armies would stand and fight . . .

'*The problem involved*. To disengage, and withdraw the Division back some 17 miles to a rear position. To get that rear position organised. To give the enemy no inkling that a withdrawal was to be carried out . . .' This change of plan in the middle of the 'battle' meant that a rearguard had to be created to mask the division's withdrawal. For this Bernard deployed the divisional cavalry, machine-gun battalion, anti-tank regiment and supporting heavy and field artillery, but such was the preparedness of British Army doctrine for modern war that there was no clear guidance in any army manuals for the command, let alone organisation of such a 'delaying' rearguard force. In the event Bernard had created an Advance HQ, separate from his main HQ, and from this he had taken command of the mobile rearguard himself – which was 'not really right', as he himself acknowledged.

The withdrawal of the main infantry bodies had been conducted admirably. The transport lorries had driven without lights, while the men had marched on average some twenty miles in the dark without a single man falling out. Observer aircraft had spotted nothing during either phase of the exercise. Only the preparations for blowing the bridges by the engineers left room for criticism – 'in many cases bridges would not have been demolished.'

Demolition was, as Bernard saw it, one of the keys to a successful fighting withdrawal – and the exercise had taught him that it must be further studied: blowing not only bridges over water obstacles, but cratering roads as well. 'The first thing to do,' he felt, 'is to get all units to realise the value of demolitions and how they may save their lives; at present they regard them as some curious black magic the sappers play with and which is a great nuisance to everyone.'

The Division had however proved that, given further practice, the impossible could be achieved. But, as Bernard pointed out, it would not be feasible to keep this up over any length of time unless the administration of the Division was well conceived and executed, ensuring that the troops were properly fed (a good breakfast before dawn, haversack rations for the day, and another meal after dark). Moreover 'rest and sleep for commanders, staffs, clerks and troops must be organised'.[1]

Brooke, who had moved with the 3rd Division, despite Gort's summons that he should go to GHQ to discuss a matter of relative unimportance, was amazed at the confidence with which Bernard carried out the exercise – 'a great success' as he noted in his diary – followed by Bernard's equally impressive conference: an 'excellent'

[1] Ibid.

affair, 'very well run' by the 3rd Division's Commander, he was moved to record.[1]

By contrast the 4th Division had fallen far behind in their training. Since October 1939 they had failed to mount a single full-scale exercise; their 'movement exercise' of 12 March 1940 Brooke considered 'not up to the standard of the 3rd Division', and the artillery movement so weak that Brooke wished to remove the artillery commander. The full-scale exercise on 18 March was no better – 'not a very good exercise,' Brooke noted in his diary, 'but the first that the 4th Division had yet done. A lot that wants putting right.'[2]

Would there be time enough? Gort's ineffective performance as C-in-C was not helped by Ironside or the British Government, who were incapable of deciding what priorty to give the BEF in France. At one moment Brooke found his 2 Corps swollen to some five divisions, since the 'Finnish wild goose enterprise' (as Brooke privately called it[3]) messed up plans for the formation of 3 Corps. However on 20 March 1940 Brooke heard that the BEF was to be split into two 1st and 2nd Armies, of which Dill was to command the 2nd. 2 Corps would, to Brooke's delight and relief, be under Dill.

Such tidings, unhappily, were short-lived. 'What will be the next venture?' Brooke had asked his diary,[4] after the Finish assignment had been cancelled. The answer was Norway – and the idea of two British armies in France, one of them under Dill, was consequently abandoned. Auchinleck who, in anticipation of forming 4 Corps, visited Brooke and the 3rd Division on 30 March, was instead designated C-in-C of the Northern Norway campaign; worse still, on 18 April 1940 'the BEF sustained the most serious loss since the beginning of the war,' as Brooke recorded solemnly in his diary.[5] Sir John Dill was removed from 1 Corps on the eve of German invasion and made Deputy CIGS to Ironside in London. What no one in Whitehall seemed to grasp was that although numbers were irrelevant, training of the existing BEF was crucial. Ironically, it was the French who put up a first-rate performance in the fiords of Norway, while the British troops, according to Auchinleck, seemed lacking in 'self-reliance and manliness generally. They give an impression of being callow and undeveloped, which is not reassuring for the future, unless our methods of man-mastership and training for war can be made more realistic and less effeminate'.[6]

The man who would produce such methods, sadly, would never take a liking to Auchinleck personally or even respect the latter's undoubted vocation for high command. For the moment, in the

[1] Alanbrooke Diary, loc. cit.
[2] Ibid.
[3] Ibid.
[4] Ibid.
[5] Ibid and A. Bryant, op. cit.
[6] John Connell, *Auchinleck*, op. cit.

spring of 1940, Bernard concentrated on his beloved 3rd Division, running it as intimately and paternally as he had his 1st Battalion of the Royal Warwickshire Regiment in Egypt. As in Egypt, his training exercises were not always well liked, and the French authorities tried hard to stop the manoeuvres of an entire British division across the plains of Northern France, with all the consequent expropriation of roads, bridges, rivers and even air-space; and it was only at Brooke's insistence that Bernard was able to get his way.[1]

The 3rd Division had meanwhile become Brooke's principal formation in 2 Corps, and it was intended it should lead the 2 Corps advance into Belgium on the outbreak of war, spearheaded by the Corps allotment of mechanised cavalry (infantry tanks and carriers).

Brooke's evident satisfaction with Bernard's Divisional Exercise No. 3 must have encouraged Bernard greatly; but it did not cause him to sit back. Bernard was particularly dissatisfied with the performance of his cavalry regiment, the 15th/19th Royal Hussars, who to his mind attached more importance to billets and messes than to organised rehearsal for battle. Within days of his final conference, therefore, he was issuing warning orders about Exercise No. 4, enabling his third remaining infantry brigade to practise the same two manoeuvres as the 7th and 9th Brigades had done, but making his cavalry screen rehearse its movements a second time. The exercise was mounted between 29 and 31 March 1940; by which time the German invasion was just five weeks away.

Bunching of vehicles, stray lights, lost units, noisy loading and unloading of lorries, guns not limbered into position, HQs not reporting their positions, and a 'scene of intense military confusion in the main square of Frévent' as a result of 'blocked' bridges, all denied Bernard a sense of perfection and he continued to ram home the lessons by personal visits, conferences and memos. Brooke meanwhile wisely took ten days' leave, knowing he would need every bit of physical and mental strength for the days ahead. With the plans for two British BEF armies aborted in April, and Auchinleck's 4 Corps abandoned, Brooke was now left with three divisions: the 3rd, 4th and 50th – the latter a Territorial Northumbrian division commanded by Major-General Giffard le Q. Martel.

Martel, born in 1889, was quite as pugnacious as Bernard, having been Army and Inter-Services Welter-weight Boxing Champion both before and after the Great War; Like Bernard he also claimed Norman descent, was a sapper and tank enthusiast who had served with the Tank Corps from 1916 to 1918, and had gone on after the First World War to design and build his own experimental machine-gun carrier. He was a keen horseman and had even had his two hunters transported to the Cotswolds when the Division left Northumberland early in 1940. Despite having only a Territorial division, Martel was

[1] General Sir Frank Simpson, Wason interviews, loc. cit.

anxious to do more than advance to river obstacles and withdraw. 'I had set my heart on being part of a highly mobile force working with armoured brigades,' he wrote in his Memoirs.[1] 'But now it looked as though my division was to be put in to hold the line defensively and that no mobile forces would be kept in hand for such tasks as striking at the enemy communications. I raised this point several times but there was no response.'[2]

Brooke was not impressed by Martel as a Divisional Commander, particularly his inability to be ruthless in dismissing inadequate subordinates. On 14 April, only three weeks before the German invasion, Brooke had to persuade him of the 'need to change one or two of his brigadiers'[3] if the Division was to face an enemy as tough as the German army had already proved itself to be. Yet, despite the amateur nature of the Division, it was Martel who would be selected by Gort to perform, under General Franklyn, the only British counter-attack, with tanks, of the Battle of France.

Fortunately Bernard would not witness Martel's moment of glory – for such futile gestures were anathema to him. Gort had been wont to quote Foch's famous dictum: 'My flanks are turned; my centre gives way; I attack!'; but to Bernard this was romanticism. Modern warfare, Bernard felt, was a science: and victory would go ultimately to those who were best able to organise themselves for victory. Leadership for Bernard was not blind bravado, but the fearless application of reason and intelligence: this had been the lesson of the Great War for Bernard, the development of the British Army from the suicidal bungling of Le Cateau to the unbreakable organization of 1918 – a development which no amount of post-war legend of blind sacrifice could confuse, since Bernard had been there, and had made his own mind, heart and promotion the long journey from sword-waving heroics to the deadly art of operational tactics, the science of military organisation, the controlled use of firepower and trained, disciplined infantry.

Martel and Bernard were opposites, yet serving in the same Corps. It was a situation that would repeat itself in another form later in the war, when Bernard served alongside the distinguished fire-eating proponent of American armour, George S. Patton; and the fateful days of May 1940 must go a certain way towards explaining Bernard's essential mistrust of such people. In the eyes of the contemporary world and even subsequent historians, Dunkirk would be the triumph of German armour; whereas for Bernard German armour was a myth. In the whole of the BEF campaign he would never see a German tank; at the end of three weeks of battle the 3rd Division still numbered over 13,000 men, the largest and most coherent division

[1] *An Outspoken Soldier*, London 1949.
[2] Ibid.
[3] Alanbrooke Diaries, loc. cit.

left in the British Expeditionary Force. For Bernard this would be the vindication of his beliefs, and the confirmation of that occasional sense of divinely-inspired vocation he had felt since his days as an instructor at the Staff College, Camberley. No amount of tanks could magically reverse Britain's military fortunes – the French possessed them in large numbers and yet failed. The terror tanks could inspire was largely a matter of morale, for at the end of the day tanks were merely weapons, armour-protected artillery that was mobile and used by the Germans to pierce enemy defences at a particular point. But if the defending troops were well trained, were themselves mobile, were adept at Peninsular War tactics of withdrawal – why then, even the most spectacular Panzer was in itself powerless; and the training of at least one division of such an army, a skilful, cohesive body of men, had become Bernard's great challenge within the BEF.

For the moment, in April 1940, the tactics, timing, even the very likelihood of a German invasion were all conjecture. However, on 9 April German troops invaded Denmark and Norway: the final overture to Operation Yellow, Hitler's invasion of the West.

For the 3rd Division this was to be the most trying month of the 'phoney war' for on 11 April the entire Allied army came under a general *alerte*, and all units had to be at six hours' notice to move. For over a week the *alerte* remained in force, thus spiking Bernard's plans for a fifth divisional exercise, which this time was to be a four-day affair to practise not only the holding and evacuating of a given defensive line, but a full-scale initial assault to attain the desired river obstacle. Because of the false alarm it became impossible to conduct serious exercises on a divisional or even brigade level; and as the warm, sunny days went by Bernard became disturbed lest all the intensive rehearsals be forgotten. Indeed by 29 April he was moved to write a memorandum to his brigadiers and commanding officers, instructing them that 'work on the defences is to be relegated entirely to a second place' and to concentrate on 'essentials': namely 'to bring the troops to that state of physical, mental and military fitness which will enable them to take on the Germans (or anyone else) with complete confidence'. During the *alerte*, driving exercises by day and night which Bernard had instigated on 5 April had also to be abandoned; but on 22 April Bernard now ordered them to begin again, as well as operational night training by all units, and a minimum of twenty miles' marching per week per man by all infantry soldiers. Across the file copy of this personal memorandum to his commanders Bernard later wrote: 'Issued because I felt sure a German attack was imminent.'[1]

Already the tenor of the German propaganda leaflets being showered upon the Allied lines was altering. Previously the aim had

[1] Montgomery Papers.

been to sow discord between French and British troops by representing the British as well-fed, war-obsessed 'milords', and Germany as
an innocent friend who desired only peaceful co-existence. Now, as
April gave way to the early summer, the propaganda began to sound
a note of dread. War, from the French point of view, it was suggested, would be suicide – one only had to look at the example of
German military success in Poland to see that. Was it actually worth
fighting?

Surprisingly no general alert was sounded in May. GHQ warning
orders for a new planned move into Belgium (Plan D) were however
issued, and confirmed on 8 May. On the 9th Bernard's HQ at Lesquin
issued orders for the move, which was to take place the moment
Germany violated Belgian neutrality. The BEF would move to the
river Dyle, east of Brussels, on a two-Corps front: Brooke's 2 Corps
on the left, 1 Corps on the right, with 3 Corps behind, covering the
Escaut. The French 7th Army would be on the immediate left of the
BEF, and would join forces with the Belgians there, thus closing the
Allied front from the Dyle to the Scheldt and the sea. The British
Official History by Major L. F. Ellis records that 'a lovely spring had
succeeded the bitter winter, leave was open in the British Expeditionary Force, and the troops were in good heart'.[1]

The troops may have been, and Lord Gort certainly was; but
Brooke was not. The removal of Sir John Dill on 18 April had left him
feeling sadly isolated in the echelons of high command. Moreover
Dill had been replaced, without objection from Gort, by Lieutenant-
General Michael Barker who was to prove a disaster and even
cracked under the strain of battle. Finally the Commander of the 2nd
Division, which belonged to Barker's 1 Corps, was Major-General H.
C. Loyd, who visited Bernard on 4 May, but did not inspire confi-
dence; he also would break down under the stress of battle and have
to be removed.

It is in the context of these and similar cases that Bernard's
ruthlessness in sacking subordinates must be judged. 'When the real
test comes,' Bernard wrote in his last memorandum of 29 April 1940,
'it is leadership that is going to pull us through. Our British soldiers
are capable of anything if they are well led. We have got to see to it
that our officers and NCOs are fit to lead, and are instructed in the
essential details of training as affecting their commands. No officer is
of any use as a leader unless he is mentally robust, and has that
character and personality which will inspire confidence in his men.
All officers who fail in this respect must be removed from the
Division at once; if their names are reported to me I will do the rest.'
In the Military Secretary's office at GHQ Colonel Simpson had cause
to know that Bernard was not joking, and that the Commander of the
3rd (Iron) Division spared neither subalterns nor COs, particularly of

---

[1] *The War in France and Flanders*, London 1953.

the Territorial battalions he had been sent in the spring of 1940. When Bernard dismissed one particular Territorial Lt-Colonel, the officer remonstrated:

'Sir, I think this is unreasonable. I am very highly trained. For the last ten years I have spent two or three evenings a week, practically every week-end, and every year a full summer camp with my battalion learning how to do my job.'

Monty said: 'I fully appreciate that, but within a month or two you are going to meet in battle a German Lt-Colonel who for the last thirty years has given all his time every day in every week in every month learning his job and you will not be able to take him on. You have got magnificent soldiers under you, but I think they must be given a chance under a better commanding officer.'

That Lt-Colonel himself told me that story and he said: 'I could not but agree that Monty was right. I had not thought of it in that way.'

He was sent back to England, given another command there, and as far as I know trained himself into a very good professional soldier in the following year or so.[1]

Bernard was taking no chances. Within a short time the BEF would be ranged against the most proficient and highly indoctrinated army in modern times. Whichever way the battle swung Bernard was determined that the 3rd Division should prove itself the premier fighting division in the British Expeditionary Force.

Within the BEF the 3rd Division had been selected by Brooke to spearhead the possible advance into Belgium of 2 Corps, with 4th and 50th Divisions following. It would seize a defensive line, as it had been trained to do, on the banks of the Dyle from Wavre to Louvain; but beyond Brussels no formal plans for advance were given in the orders of 9 May for an eventual Plan D, as 'such moves will depend entirely on how the tactical situation develops' – a prescient rider in view of the unexpected obstacle the 3rd Division was destined to meet.

The above orders were issued at 1045 hours on 9 May 1940. At 2200 hours, according to the War Diary, 'hostile aircraft flew over'. All previous German invasion plans had been leaked or interpreted in advance; this time Operation Yellow was watertight. Neither French High Command nor GHQ of the BEF at Arras (despite warnings from London[2]) issued a formal or informal alert; but at 0400 hours on 10 May further hostile aircraft appeared, and officers and men of the 3rd Division were awakened by a furious anti-aircraft fusillade. As dawn began to break, 2 Corps passed on an immediate *alerte*, putting all

[1] General Sir Frank Simpson, Wason interviews, loc. cit.
[2] GHQ War Diary, 7 May 1940 (WO 167/4), PRO.

units at six hours' notice; and at 0500 hours a message came through that Belgium and Holland had been invaded. At 1100 hours Bernard assembled his commanding officers and told them that Plan D would come into immediate effect, with 1430 hours as the Divisional zero hour – the moment at which forward units of the 3rd Division would cross the frontier into Belgium.

Twenty-six years had passed since the last German invasion of the West. The erstwhile Lieutenant of the 1st Battalion, the Royal Warwickshire Regiment was now a Major-General. Strange to say, he issued no Order of the Day: there was a great deal to do in order to launch an entire division across the frontier within the space of a few hours and without any previous alert. He did, however, ask his commanders to 'impress on the troops that this is the real thing and not an exercise'.[1]

The sun blazed in a cloudless sky as the advance units of the 3rd Division made their way into friendly territory (the King of the Belgians had formally requested Allied assistance at 0400 hours), but which the Belgians had never permitted the BEF to reconnoitre or even photograph from the air. In one case the Belgian frontier guards demanded that the leading 3rd Division cavalry regiment stop and show its formal authority to enter Belgium; a last tragic gesture of democratic niceties, while in the North-West a Blitzkrieg was already in full progress.

The 3rd Division swept away such frontier obstacles. As news of the German invasion of Luxembourg, Belgium and Holland became more widespread, the British units were cheered, and found the Belgian civilians so helpful they hardly needed to map-read. Only at Alost was there any bombing; otherwise it was deceptively easy – so much so that Bernard's seemingly endless training in day and night movement, with disciplined spacing to reduce susceptibility to air attack, appeared, as it often had to GHQ, over-fussy, even obsessive. Crowds lined the streets to watch and cheer. The virtual absence of German air attacks was uncanny – yet no one, even Brooke, seems to have smelled the proverbial rat: namely that the BEF and the French 7th Army were being lured northwards into a trap.

Until now Bernard had kept no diary, nor did Maud Montgomery keep his letters as she had done during the Great War; but on 10 May as the shooting began, Bernard commenced a pencil-written 'Itinerary of Events'. Twenty-three years later he recorded:

Note

I found this diary in an old locked box in my attic box room. It is a day-to-day diary of events from 10 May 1940, when the BEF advanced in Belgium, until I withdrew 2 Corps on night 31 May/1 June.

[1] War Diary, 3rd Division RA HQ, 10 May 1940 (WO 167/220), PRO.

It was written each night in my own handwriting and shows how I handled my Division (3rd Div) . . .

It is of very great value.

M of A/August 1963[1]

The climax of the diary would be his entries concerning Gort and the evacuation of the BEF from Dunkirk, followed by Bernard's personal interview with the CIGS, Sir John Dill. But the diary began modestly enough and without emotion. While Brooke noted 'less interference from bombing than I had anticipated', and reflected that this was the 'first step towards one of the greatest battles of history',[2] Bernard confined himself to a terse, three-line summary:

10 May   Enemy aircraft over Lesquin
             Belgium and Holland invaded
             Plan D put into force – zero 1400 hrs.

[1] Montgomery Papers.
[2] A. Bryant, op. cit.

CHAPTER FIVE

Dunkirk

At half-past two on the afternoon of 10 May 1940, the first units of the 3rd Division had crossed the Belgian border; at four o'clock Bernard's Command Group left Lesquin: destination Louvain. At Alost, west of Brussels, the Commander was seen 'eating a large banana' as his column halted;[1] by 1 a.m. on the 11th he had moved into his new Divisional HQ at Éverberg Château – home of a princess – and the headquarters vehicles were camouflaged in the park outside. Everything had gone like 'clockwork', as Brooke noted in his diary.

However, the clockwork abruptly stopped when the advanced units of the division arrived in the early hours of the morning of the 11th at their pre-ordained sector of the river Dyle, several miles east of Louvain – for a Belgian infantry division was *in situ*; and when dawn broke the Belgians began firing on the 3rd Division's machine-gun battalion.

This was an unexpected rebuff to the eight-month-old 'Plan D'. Just as Hitler intended to trap the BEF and French 7th Army in the Low Countries, so Allied strategy devolved on confronting the Germans on the line of the Dyle and the Scheldt with a phalanx of French, Belgian and British troops, systematically disposed behind a natural water obstacle and in considerable depth.

The Commander of the 10th Belgian Division, however, was unconcerned with Allied strategy when Bernard contacted him. 'There was practically war between Britain and Belgium when dawn broke that morning,' 'Kit' Dawnay remembered;[2] taking Dawnay as interpreter Bernard made his way immediately to the Belgian Divisional Headquarters to make clear that, by agreement of the Allied High Command, Louvain was to be defended by the BEF, so that British troops could be 'blooded', as Bernard put it.

The Belgian general, white-haired and distraught, refused to budge, maintaining that 'his King had entrusted him with the defence of Louvain and that he would never leave his post without orders from his King',[3] despite the agreed 'Gamelin-line', which

[1] War Diary, 3rd Division Signals (WO 167/222), PRO.
[2] Lt-Colonel C. P. Dawnay, interview of 23.8.78.
[3] A. Bryant, op. cit.

allotted a sector north of Brussels and Louvain to the Belgians. Messages now began to fly between headquarters, arguing over the proposed boundary lines of the BEF while German troops methodically seized the Belgian bridges over the Albert canal. Brooke went personally to see King Leopold the next day; but Gort was not similarly disposed. As so often in the past and in future weeks, Gort was incapable of standing up to his Allied colleagues and superiors. At 6 o'clock in the evening of the 11th, without bothering to ascertain the morale or genuine fighting power of the Belgians in Louvain, Gort ordered 2 Corps to squeeze the 3rd Division into the left flank of 1 Corps, rather than risk dissension with the Belgians.

Bernard, however, had other ideas. Louvain was the key to Brussels, he felt, and the city and its high ground were too vital to be defended by a weak Belgian division with only horse-drawn transport. He therefore withdrew the 3rd Division west of Louvain, echeloned as a second line of defence behind the Belgians rather than moving into the 1 Corps sector, and informed the Belgian commander of this at 10 a.m. on 12 May. At lunch Bernard told Brooke – who had found the Belgian King immovable under the evil influence of his ADC Major-General van Overstraeten – that all was now well.

'I expressed surprise,' Brooke recorded, 'and asked him how he had settled the matter. He then told me: "Well, I went to the Belgian Divisional Commander and said to him: '*Mon général*, I place myself and my Division unreservedly under your orders, and I propose to reinforce your front.' " He said that the Belgian Commander was delighted with this arrangement. I then asked Monty what he proposed to do if the Germans started attacking. He replied: "Oh! I then place the Divisional Commander under strict arrest and I take command." '[1]

Brooke and Bernard then went to reconnoitre the Louvain front. Meanwhile Gort had visited HQ 2 Corps and given instructions that his suggestion that the 3rd Division move into 1 Corps boundary, leaving the Belgians to defend Louvain on their own, was now an order. When Bernard returned to his own HQ he heard this news, and in a tart, written reply, sent by liaison officer to Brooke, he reiterated his determination to remain in Louvain.

'Before my troops went into the line,' he wrote, 'the morale of the Belgian troops was very low. I go so far as to say that they would have retreated without fighting if attacked. Once my division began to move up to the line Belgians recovered.

'I am informed by liaison officer just arrived from Belgian GHQ (Needham Mission) that enemy armoured forces were reported this afternoon moving west . . . General Needham is worried about this and considers the Belgians will not stand and fight.

'In view of the poor state of morale of the Belgian troops as known

[1] Ibid.

to me and the possibility of a danger to the left flank of the BEF or to the right flank of the Belgian Army I consider that to move my division south from the high ground running west from Louvain is most inadvisable and might have very serious consequences. I discussed the whole problem with you this afternoon so you are in full possession of the facts.

'Will you please send further instructions. I will delay any move until I hear from you. I consider the best action would be for the 3rd Division to be in depth behind the 10th Belgian Division . . .'[1]

This was insubordination. The entire episode is absent from the British Official History of the campaign, *The War in France and Flanders*, yet there can be no doubt that the 3rd Division's successful defence of Louvain in the days ahead avoided what General Needham, in his telephone message to Gort on 12 May, predicted might become 'a rout';[2] for on 13 May came the moment of truth, as the Germans chased the retiring French and Belgian forces up to the river Dyle. Gort issued a message 'to all ranks', congratulating the BEF on its admirable advance to the Dyle. 'We are now on the eve of one of the great moments of our history,' he declared. 'The struggle will be hard and long, but we can be confident of final victory.'[3]

The struggle, however, was to be all too brief. As German pressure built up on Louvain, the Belgian 10th Division decided, after all, not to fight – thus relieving Bernard of the necessity of arresting its Commander. The latter maintained that he was moving out so that his 'tired troops could rally, rest and support our defence', as he put it to the signals officer of the 3rd Division who was taking over his HQ.[4] Brooke found Bernard 'quite happy and in great form',[5] and it was arranged that that night (13 May) the 3rd Division assume command of the whole Louvain sector. The following night the battle for Louvain seemed to have begun in earnest. According to German Army Group B the front between Louvain and Namur had to be smashed quickly before the French and Belgians could dig in; the Germans thus received a rude shock when they found two British corps barring their assault towards Brussels. On the night of 14 May German patrols appeared to have penetrated into Louvain and were savagely counter-attacked by a battalion of the Grenadier Guards. Bernard rang through to 2 Corps after midnight to give the glad tidings – but sadly it was found by daylight that the enemy patrols had in fact been fleeing Belgians of the 10th Division who had got left behind and had now heard the ever-nearing bursts of German gunfire. By mid-morning of 15 May, however, the Germans were

[1] War Diary, 2 Corps, G. Ops (WO 167/148).
[2] War Diary, GHQ BEF, loc cit.
[3] Ibid.
[4] Loc. cit.
[5] A. Bryant, op. cit.

indeed pushing their way into the outskirts of Louvain – and a series of vicious local engagements followed.

Bernard's assessment of the Belgian troops proved all too accurate, while Gort, according to Brooke, simply failed to recognise their 'poor fighting quality'.[1] Panic had spread throughout the Low Countries since the capitulation of the Dutch on 14 May – so much so that the British Ambassador in Brussels packed precipitately that night, and fled secretly west without word to Brooke or the BEF, only to be captured a few days later by German armoured forces that had broken through at Sedan. Brooke worried about his left flank ('I would not trust the Belgians a yard,' he confided to his diary on 15 May[2]); but poor Gort's days of field command were numbered. He had failed to rehearse his headquarters in either movement or communication in battle; divided into three echelons, command of the BEF began to disintegrate at the very moment when inter-allied communication and co-operation were of paramount importance. Rumours fed rumours and Gort was summoned by his corps commanders to make decisions like a helpless captain whose ship is sinking. On 15 May the Belgians claimed that Louvain was in German hands; and since GHQ had no contact with 2 Corps it was impossible for them to know that Montgomery was still in firm possession of the town. Moreover news from the French front to the right of the BEF was also frightening, for it appeared that German armoured columns had broken through the French lines. In his diary that night Brooke noted that the BEF 'is likely to have both flanks turned, and will have a very unpleasant time extricating itself out of its present position';[3] yet Gort failed to see the consequences. In the ensuing, critical days as the German Army Group A smashed its way through to the English Channel, an *ad hoc* collection of Macforces, Polforces, Petreforces, Woodforces, Frankforces and Usherforces[4] would be independently and locally organised to protect the southern flank of the BEF – and only Rundstedt and Hitler's decision to halt their armoured forces at Calais saved the BEF from total piecemeal destruction.

Gort's 'boy-scout' brain, his lack of forward planning, his inability to train an army for modern warfare, his chaotic command structure and his deference to his French superiors were the death-seal of the BEF. As Brooke noted later, reflecting on the first day of the German assault on 10 May, 'I had by now few illusions as to the fighting efficiency of the French. The Belgians still remained to be seen, but what I had heard about them was not promising. On top of all I had no confidence in Gort's leadership when it came to handling a large

[1] Ibid.
[2] Loc. cit. and A. Bryant, op. cit.
[3] A. Bryant, op. cit.
[4] Named after the senior officer responsible.

342

force. From all that I had seen of him during the last seven months he seemed at most times incapable of seeing the wood for the trees . . .'[1] Gort's three HQs were constantly out of touch with one another, and Gort's policy of taking his Chief-of-Staff with him everywhere meant that in the end Gort merely rubber-stamped local commanders' initiatives when his command posts finally informed him of them. Despite the lack of proper, concrete information from his Allies, Gort permitted his Chief of Military Intelligence to become a Force Commander on 17 May, and was thereafter without proper Intelligence. What would have been one of the biggest scandals in British military history was only veiled by the incredible cowardice and incompetence of Gort's Allies – 'nowhere was any resistance attempted,' Rommel recorded in his account of the campaign.[2] Gort's biographer, J. R. Colville, acknowledged the 'administrative disaster' that befell the BEF in consequence of Gort's command set-up; yet the administrative chaos of the French headquarters was even worse. 'Incredible though it might be,' commented Colville, 'the professional staff of one of Europe's most professional armies was totally unorganised for war.'[3] Though some Belgian units eventually put up a fight, the majority surrendered their country to the Germans without a shot being fired.

Yet for Bernard Montgomery the picture was very different from that of GHQ. He had insisted that the 3rd Division defend the ancient city of Louvain, the gateway to Brussels: and all day on 15 May he 'bloodied the Germans' noses' as the latter unsuccessfully tried to enter the town:

15 May   Enemy attacked on left of RUR [Royal Ulster Rifles] front and got into Louvain station. Counter-attacked & pushed out (1000 hrs). At 1330 hrs attack developed on Coldstream front; heavy shelling all afternoon; Coldstream suffered severe casualties but front intact. No attack on our front during night 15/16 May,

Bernard recorded in his diary. Whatever happened elsewhere, the 3rd Division would prove its mettle. 'It was during this campaign that I developed the habit of going to bed early, soon after dinner. I was out and about on the front all day long, saw all my subordinate commanders, and heard their problems and gave decisions and verbal orders,' Bernard related later. 'I was always back at my divisional HQ about tea-time, and would see my staff and give orders for the night and next day. I would then have dinner and go to bed, and was never to be disturbed except in a crisis. I well remember

[1] A. Bryant, op. cit. and Alanbrooke, *Notes on My Life*, loc. cit.
[2] B. Liddell Hart (Ed.), *The Rommel Papers*, 1953.
[3] J. R. Colville, *Man of Valour*, 1972.

how angry I was when I was woken up one night and told the Germans had got into Louvain. The staff officer was amazed when I said: "Go away and don't bother me. Tell the brigadier in Louvain to throw them out." I then went to sleep again.'[1]

This ability to rest and wake refreshed would be the counterpart to Churchill's famous cat-naps; moreover, having trained his 3rd Division to a pitch of enthusiasm and proficiency, he was beginning to enjoy one of the prerogatives of a senior commander: the confidence to delegate responsibility. 'There were no weak links,' he wrote of his division. 'All the doubtful commanders had been eliminated during the previous six months of training.' Some – like the divisional Artillery Commander – had been sacked within ten days. 'The division was like a piece of fine steel,' Bernard wrote. 'I was immensely proud of it.'[2]

One new CO was Lt-Colonel Brian Horrocks, who on 13 May had arrived from the Staff College to take command of the divisional machine-gun battalion, the 2nd Middlesex Regiment. Horrocks was pleasantly surprised by the standard of his new unit: 'The period of the phoney war had obviously been used for some hard, intensive training. I doubt whether this country has ever been represented at the outset of a war by a more efficient army that this BEF of 1940.'[3]

The standard of the 3rd Division, however, was not necessarily that of the BEF; and, as their Belgian and French allies began to crack, the pressure on British commanders became acute. Brooke proved a tower of strength – 'a dim and distant figure', as 'Kit' Dawnay remembered,[4] but a model commander as far as Bernard was concerned. Dill's successor at 1 Corps, Michael Barker, was unfortunately not made of such stern stuff. There, as news of the German penetration on their right flank became hourly more alarming, Barker began to suffer virtual hallucinations from lack of sleep. Eventually on 16 May he was persuaded to relieve his Commander of the 2nd Division – six days after the latter had shown symptoms of a nervous collapse. It was Barker who had first put pressure on Gort to bring the 3rd Division into his 1 Corps sector south of Louvain on 12 May; and by the 15th Gort had given him no less than four divisions (1st, 2nd, 5th and 48th) to defend his sector, reducing Brooke to two. Still Barker grew more rattled. German pressure on both 1 and 2 Corps' fronts increased, and the 3rd Division's Coldstream Guards again suffered heavily on 16 May. With Belgians and French caving in on both BEF flanks Gort finally called a conference of his corps commanders at 11 a.m. that day at the headquarters of 1 Corps, at which it was decided to withdraw the two corps that night in two stages to the Escaut canal line, lest they be surrounded. When

[1] *Memoirs*, op. cit.
[2] Ibid.
[3] Sir Brian Horrocks, *A Full Life*, London 1960.
[4] Lt-Colonel C. P. Dawnay, loc. cit.

344

Brooke went to Bernard's HQ at Everberg, they were burying a sapper officer killed by shelling. Bernard was not in the least perturbed by Brooke's news – 'Completely unaffected by the seriousness of the situation and brimfull of efficiency and cheerfulness. It was indeed easy work settling the details of his retirement with him,' wrote Brooke. 'I left him full of confidence that he would bring off this rather difficult move with complete success.'[1]

This was scarcely surprising, since all Bernard's full-scale divisional exercises had been to this very end: the withdrawal of the Division by night or day from a defended line under enemy attack. Indeed the 'narrative' notes Bernard used for his commanders' conference after Exercise No. 3 in March 1940 ran: 'Phase 2: *Situation necessitating withdrawal* . . . At 6 a.m. in the morning a situation arose which involved an immediate change of plan; our Allies in front had been driven in, our flanks were in danger of being turned, and GHQ ordered a withdrawal to the St Pol line . . .'[2] Small wonder that, eight weeks later, Bernard was unperturbed by the Allied collapse. Moreover this was not merely a matter of personal mental preparation as in, say, Gort's ascetic régime, based on bare plank work-tables and great physical fitness. Bernard's concern throughout his divisional exercises had been to rehearse the troops in their likely roles, and to make sure his commanders and COs were self-critical in the way they made their various dispositions. 'I would like every commander to think back,' Bernard had said in his summing up of Exercise No. 3, 'and consider his dispositions at every stage of the operations, and the degree of control he exercised. Were my dispositions always such that I could not be surprised? Whatever happened could I always do something about it? The fighting was fluid; was I all right if some enemy AFV [Armoured Fighting Vehicle] had suddenly appeared round my flank and got in to my HQ area where my forward transport was – and so on. Were there any moments I had not got control?'[3]

Having failed to break into Louvain by 16 May, General Bock had meanwhile ordered a coordinated German assault to begin on the 17th. By then, of course, the bird had flown. Bernard issued his orders for the withdrawal at 2 p.m. on the 16th, the entire division to be on its way to the Dendre by nightfall.

Used two cav regts on left flank to cover withdrawal; later cavalry covered rear. Used artillery to effect a clean breakaway.
8 Inf Bde covered withdrawal of forward Bdes & then acted as rearguard.
DIV HQ to CRAINHAM and later to AYGEM

[1] A. Bryant, op. cit.
[2] Montgomery Papers.
[3] Ibid.

> Whole Division on R. Dendre by dusk except 8 Inf Bde
> 4 DIV in front on R. Senne,

Bernard noted coolly in his diary.

The 4th Division, standing on the Senne, was designed to act as a defensive screen through which the 3rd Division should pass on its way to the Dendre. In turn the 4th Division would itself retire to the Dendre on the 17th. But its withdrawal was less practised than that of the 3rd Division; its retirement was messy and it allowed one of the corps cavalry regiments – the 15th/19th Hussars whose performance in Bernard's exercises had caused concern – to be outflanked and almost totally destroyed by the Germans, only one squadron of tanks and carriers escaping to tell the tale. This misfortune was to have a profound effect on Bernard's attitude towards his own British armoured units, reinforcing his existing prejudices about English cavalry commanders – namely that they were essentially blind Anglo-Saxon Don Quixotes whose dream was to tilt lyrically against windmills, without properly educating themselves in the essentials of modern warfare: good staff-work, adequate communications, trained discipline, and above all co-operation with other arms – artillery, engineers, air force and infantry. Indeed, had Britain possessed the greater number of tanks which contemporary prophets and later historians claimed were essential, it is very likely they would have been as wastefully squandered as those of the French. Thus while Bernard's 3rd Division waited intact behind the Dendre for the next phase in the defensive battle on 18 May, it was forced to watch impotently as its vital armoured mobile cavalry screen was thrown away.

At that time such misfortunes were still unusual in the BEF; among Britain's Belgian and French allies they were commonplace, as the planned withdrawal turned into General Needham's feared rout. Indeed it was the sudden disappearance of its flanking Belgian forces which led to the 4th Division's loss of its cavalry regiment. However, General Barker's 1 Corps was faring no better, and, had it not been for Brooke's stern resolution, 1 Corps might well have disintegrated. On the night of 16 May Barker sent a despatch-rider to Brooke saying 2 Corps was now outflanked by German Panzers – which turned out later to be motor-cyclists. When Brooke visited Barker early on 17 May he found him 'in a difficult state to deal with. He is so over-wrought with work and the present situation that he sees dangers where they don't exist and cannot make up his mind on any points,' Brooke recorded in his diary.[1] The following day Barker was even worse. 'He has been worse than ever today,' Brooke noted, 'and whenever anything is fixed he changes his mind shortly afterwards.'[2] In fact so tired was Barker that he insisted he must stay

[1] Loc. cit.
[2] Ibid.

346

where he was 'and fight it out' like Smith-Dorrien at Le Cateau in 1914.[1] Brooke persuaded him that he must move to conform with the BEF withdrawal; Barker agreed, but asked for twenty-four hours to rest. Reluctantly Brooke agreed; but on return to his HQ found that Barker – who had panicked and claimed he was 'surrounded by German tanks'[2] – had given orders to 1 Corps to withdraw at dawn on 19 May instead of midday as had been agreed. 'This put 2 Corps in a serious position,' as Brooke noted, for it threatened to leave 2 Corps' right flank in the air, behind which the Germans could penetrate and thus cut the route of withdrawal. Major-General Alexander, commanding the 1st Division that now abutted 2 Corps' right flank, quickly ordered the 1 Corps cavalry regiment in to cover him there; Bernard did the same with the 5th Inniskilling Dragoon Guards (the only 2 Corps cavalry left). Bernard was undisturbed.

'Disengaged in daylight,' he recorded in his diary,

and withdrew back to L'Escaut.
Took out two centre Bdes at 0800 hrs. Covered this gap with cav Regt. Put 2 Mx and 1/8 Mx (under Horrocks) on left flank . . .
Withdrew flank Bdes and cav at 1000 hrs, Bdes being covered by rearguards of carriers and Bde Anti-tank Companies.
Used artillery to effect a break-away.
Sent all guns back at 0500 hrs keeping one troop, a battery of DIV Artillery, and whole of 2 Royal Horse Artillery.
Used a lot of shells.
Had two Bus Companies.
Whole DIV back on L'Escaut line by dark. A very tricky operation.

It was indeed: and the picture of the two divisional Generals, Montgomery and Alexander, calmly shepherding their forces of over 20,000 men back to the Escaut (the original line the BEF was intended to hold) was one which was not lost on Brooke in retrospect:

'It was intensely interesting watching him [Alexander] and Monty during those trying days, both of them completely imperturbable and efficiency itself, and yet two totally different characters. Monty with his quick brain for appreciating military situations was well aware of the very critical situation that he was in, and the very dangers and difficulties that faced us acted as a stimulus on him; they thrilled him and put the sharpest of edges on his military ability. Alex, on the other hand, gave me the impression of never fully realising all the unpleasant potentialities of our predicament. He remained entirely unaffected by it, completely composed and appeared never to have the slightest doubt that all would come right in the end . . .'[3]

[1] Ibid.
[2] Ibid.
[3] A. Bryant, op. cit.

Whether it would or not became daily more doubtful; and poor Gort became, as a very consequence of the BEF's intact front line, the whipping-boy. Both Churchill – who was now British Prime Minister – and the French demanded that Gort use the BEF to sever the ugly German head which had pierced the French 1st and 7th Armies. Unfortunately the head was armoured, and the forces at hand inadequate for such an offensive task. Marrying the 5th Division to the 50th Division and the 1st Royal Tank Regiment, Gort attempted to do his best. The effort was doomed to failure; but Martel's plucky attack from Arras certainly unnerved the senior German commanders, and Martel proudly bore 400 German prisoners back to England with him, like the 'bag' from a Northumbrian shoot. Whether the units would have been better employed organising a sound defence of the BEF's exposed right flank and lines of communication is debatable; certainly, in the relatively confined area occupied by British troops, a more flexible use of Gort's forces would have been possible if he had been able to exercise better command. As it was he was torn in all directions – Paris and London urging him to attack southwards and cut off the German salient, Barker exhausted and fearful on the right front flank of the BEF, Brooke anxious lest the Belgians collapse on the left. It is not surprising, therefore, that Gort attempted at first to answer all demands, thereby satisfying none.

Perhaps the most astonishing fact to emerge from a study of the BEF campaign is that the chaotic, last-minute miracle evacuation of the Expeditionary Force at the end of May 1940 was not only foreseen by certain members of Gort's headquarters some ten days before it took place, but outline plans were prepared for the eventuality by Gort's Deputy Chief of the General Staff, Brigadier Sir Oliver Leese. Already on 18 May Leese – who, when Gort and Pownall were out of touch at their advanced command post or visiting units, had to take vital decisions on behalf of his superiors – had drawn his own conclusions from the darkening situation reports, and had prepared a contingency plan for withdrawal of the BEF to Dunkirk. This plan was read out to Gort, Pownall, the QMG, and Engineer-in-Chief, at Wahagnies Command Post shortly after midnight on 18–19 May, when General Billotte, co-ordinator of the Nothern Allied Armies, had arrived to tell the unhappy story of French disintegration on the right of the BEF – fleeing madly to avoid bombing, mistaking their own tanks for Germans, even shooting one another. Leese's plan, according to the GHQ War Diary, was 'to move the BEF in the form of a hollow square with 50th Div providing a flank guard along the La Bassée Canal. It was then estimated that the reserves of one division would be sufficient to mount guard on every bridge from Raches to the sea'.[1] In this way the integrity of the BEF would be maintained, and with proper planning much of its material and most of its

---

[1] War Diary, GHQ BEF, May 1940 (WO 167/27, 28, 29 and 31), PRO.

personnel be saved. Had Gort been able to act unequivocally on Leese's outline plan, an orderly, well-administered evacuation could have been effected instead of the near débâcle that actually followed.

Everything, however, militated against such logic. Above all, Gort had accepted a subordinate position in the Allied military hierarchy which precluded him from making independent decisions. He was thus anchored to catastrophe; and, though he did allow Leese on 19 May to explore with the Admiralty the likely naval requirements for an eventual evacuation, it was kept as quiet as possible, and few if any military provision made for the sea-lift of such a huge army. Instead Gort propagated a fiction, namely that the BEF was being forced by enemy pressure to withdraw north-westwards owing to the collapse of the French 1st and 7th Armies – but not saying where it was heading for. Thus, at a GHQ Conference of Corps Commanders on 19 May, a strategy of withdrawal to Dunkirk was privately agreed (Brooke, interestingly, favoured evacuation through the Belgian ports of Ostend and Zeebrugge, but was overruled on the grounds that the Belgians might collapse completely – which is what eventually happened); yet neither the French nor the Belgians were ever informed of this, and as late as 28 May, as the final evacuation of British troops began in earnest, the Commander of the Allied Northern Army Group claimed to have no idea that the British intended to leave French soil.

Nor were the French and Belgians the only people to be deceived by Gort's proposals. Neither the War Office in London nor Churchill's War Cabinet was willing to countenance defeat; thus until 26 May the British Government did nothing to sanction the policy (or the end-result of such a policy) being pursued by its own Commander-in-Chief in the field. Gort was made to pretend, and the question of evacuation was concealed in phrases such as 'contingency plans in the event of failure of French operations to the south'.[1]

Gort cannot be blamed for the culpable anarchy and lack of courage of his Allies; but his command of the BEF and the chaotic communications between his own units, his French and Belgian allies, and the Government at home were the inevitable result of his own failings as a higher commander. His pride revolted at the idea that the French might accuse him of absconding from the field of battle; therefore he espoused a public policy of waiting on events, of pretending ultimately to be forced into an inescapable choice of last-minute evacuation – when in fact such a policy was the only possible strategy once Billotte, co-ordinator of the Northern Allied Armies, had acknowledged French defeat on the night of 18–19 May. Moreover, by declining to make his real strategy clear even to his own formations, Gort was led into a seemingly endless succession of stop-gap measures on his western flank which demoralised both

[1] Ibid.

men and officers in the BEF. Even today many participants cannot remember in what division, sometimes even in what brigade, they served, so incoherent was command there.

Fortunately this was not the case on the original front, now the eastern flank of the BEF. There the British were able to present a solid phalanx to the enemy. Divisions fought as divisions and, thanks largely to Brooke, a sense of unity and order prevailed and rippled back through the BEF, giving courage to many who would have otherwise despaired.

Gort and Pownall believed that only a small proportion of the BEF could be safely evacuated through Dunkirk, and no material. Moreover, having permitted Leese to ask the Admiralty to draw up contingency evacuation plans on 19 May, neither of them paid further attention to the naval and military requirements of such an evacuation. Gort believed his task was to show firm moral fibre; Pownall actually began to think things might not be so bad when, on 19 May, the 1st French Army 'reappeared from somewhere. They would occupy a line – it fitted in with our arrangements. And the evening ended tranquilly,' he noted obtusely in his own diary.[1] Nothing was done to examine the defences of Dunkirk port, or prepare the beaches for the emergence of more than 300,000 British troops, not to speak of Allied units. No naval beach personnel were brought over from England, no piers erected, no AA guns sited or HQ positions prepared, ready with proper communications. Had the Germans not halted their Panzers outside Dunkirk on 24 May Gort might have lost the entire BEF.

As it was, the Germans had successfully trapped the Northern Allied Armies; they had only to tighten the pincers of their two Army Groups A and B, and Allied surrender would be inevitable, they believed.

The King of the Belgians certainly saw matters this way, and was only persuaded to continue his country's struggle by the orderliness of the British 1 and 2 Corps' retirement alongside the Belgian army's flight. As this retirement moved inexorably back towards the frontier of France, though, the argument for prolonged Belgian resistance became weaker and weaker. More Belgian troops would be killed, more Belgian roads, bridges, towns, villages, ports and property shelled, bombed and damaged. And for what? So that a Belgian army could fight a doomed battle on French soil? Given the influence of that *éminence grise* van Overstraaten, and the domino logic of events, it is altogether remarkable that the Belgians remained technically at war until 28 May 1940. The word 'technically' must be used, since very few Belgians could be persuaded to fight; they either deserted or joined an ill-assorted mass fleeing northwards, while the BEF withdrew west. Inevitably the two Armies would split apart – and it was

[1] B. Bond (Ed.), *Chief-of-Staff*. The Diaries of Lt-General Sir Henry Pownall, London 1972.

through this gap that the Germans hoped to drive a wedge of their 4 Corps, which would then cut off the eastern flank of the BEF from the sea. Gort's attention, meanwhile, had shifted to his southern and western flank, and instead of planning the inevitable evacuation of the BEF he committed himself to a second offensive against the German salient in order to appease both the French and the British War Cabinets.

This attack was not merely a gesture, as historians have traditionally assumed; it was to be the spearhead of a new plan to withdraw the *entire* BEF southwards now, through the German salient and into the 'safety' of the main body of the French army beyond the Somme. It entailed abandoning the Belgians to their own fate, and it was revealed to Brooke on the morning of 25 May. Brooke was not sorry. He felt the Belgians had put up a miserable fight, and that they could not last another twenty-four hours; he felt, too, that the idea of being crushed up against the coast with only a single port by which to evacuate or be reinforced was equally, if not more, hazardous than a break-out to the south.

'I was then informed that the "rush for the sea" plan was abandoned,' Brooke wrote in his diary that night. 'I have always hated this plan. The new plan is to try to break through to the French forces south of the German penetration. It might be possible, but I should doubt it. I then went round 4 & 3 Divs to discuss our breakthrough plans with them.'[1]

Strangely this change of plan by Gort has never been publicly revealed. Gort did not mention it in his despatches, Sir Arthur Bryant omitted the passage in Brooke's diary in his edited version *The Turn of the Tide*, and even the British Official History of the campaign did not disclose it. Yet, not only is the change of plan documented in Brooke's unpublished diary entry, it is also confirmed in Bernard Montgomery's diary of 3rd Division events on 25 May:

Had DIV Conference 1030 hrs to co-ordinate all work and plans.
General situation appeared worse; Belgians on left giving way.
Corps Comdr visited me 1600 hrs with outline idea on how the BEF might abandon the Belgians and fight its way through to join the French.
Assembled my Brigadiers at 1800 hrs and ordered certain moves and recces as precaution; all B Echelon to join up with units.

Would such a break-through have succeeded? Brooke evidently doubted it, but felt it would be more valiant than defeat on the coasts of Northern France. Bernard gave no indication in his diary of his own feelings on the subject, nor did he ever reveal the plan in later years. However, he did refer to it obliquely in his *Memoirs* when, at

[1] Loc. cit.

351

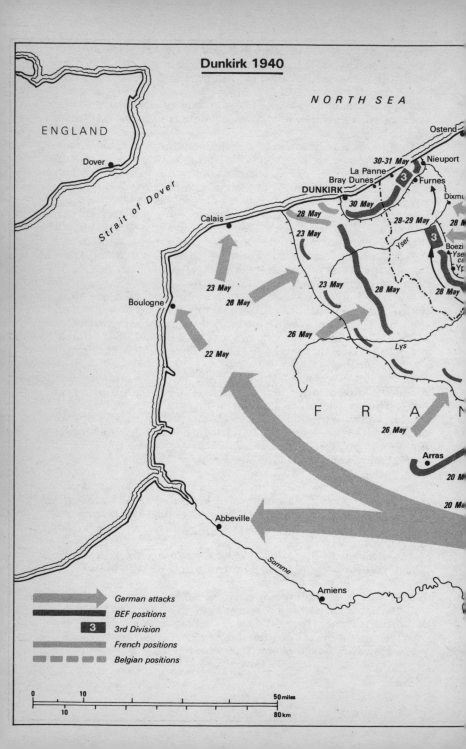

Dunkirk 1940

NORTH SEA

ENGLAND

Dover

Ostend

Strait of Dover

Calais

Boulogne

Abbeville

Amiens

Arras

DUNKIRK

La Panne
Bray Dunes

Nieuport
30-31 May
Furnes
Dixmu

Boezi
Yse
ca
Yp

30 May
28 May
23 May
23 May
23 May
28 May
28-29 May
28 May
28 May
28 M
23 May
26 May
22 May
26 May
26 May
20 M
20 Ma

Yser
Lys
Somme

F   R   A   N

German attacks
BEF positions
3 3rd Division
French positions
Belgian positions

| 0 | 10 | | 50 miles |
| 10 | | | 80 km |

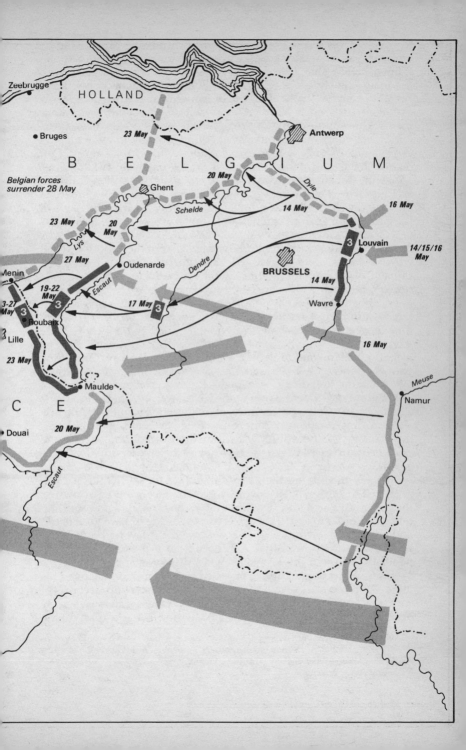

Zeebrugge

HOLLAND

● Bruges

B E L G I U M

Antwerp

23 May

20 May

*Belgian forces
surrender 28 May*

Ghent

Schelde

Dyle

14 May

16 May

23 May

20 May

Lys

27 May

Oudenarde

Dendre

3 Louvain

*14/15/16
May*

Menin

*19-22
May*

3

Escaut

BRUSSELS

Wavre

14 May

*3-27
May*

3

17 May

3

Roubaix

Lille

23 May

Maulde

16 May

C   E

Namur

Meuse

● Douai

20 May

Escaut

the end of his assessment of the BEF campaign and of Gort's performance, he remarked: 'A cleverer man might have done something different [than evacuating the BEF],' and regained touch with the main French forces beyond the Somme. 'If he had done this,' Bernard went on, 'the men of the BEF might have found themselves eventually in French North Africa – without weapons and equipment.' This supposes that a break-through would have been possible, if well commanded; but a study of the general situation map on the evening of 24 May lends no confidence to such a supposition. Although the neck of the German salient was barely thirty kilometres wide, the salient itself contained by then no less than fourteen armoured or motorised German divisions, as well as numerous infantry divisions. To have detached itself cleanly from the jaws of the German pincer movement and fought its way southwards across this German salient was, as Brooke acknowledged, a very dubious proposition; some units might have made it, but the majority would inevitably have been destroyed or captured. Capitulation by the British Government might thereafter have been inevitable.

Plans for such a BEF break-through were however short-lived. Bernard had laid down a policy of offensive patrolling on his front which, although it resulted in a nasty encounter on 24 May when nine officers and almost a hundred men in the 8th Infantry Brigade were wounded (a 'raid' severely criticised in the British Official History), paid off suddenly in the most spectacular way. One of the patrols pounced on a German staff car. the German car driver was killed, but the staff officer[1] escaped – leaving a wallet containing not only the entire Order of Battle of the German army, but tactical plans for a German 6 Corps pincer movement designed to outflank the BEF at its northern extremity where the Belgians could be detached – thus rolling up the entire BEF from the north. Brooke took the documents from 3rd Division HQ to GHQ that afternoon – and once again Gort was forced to re-think his strategy. He had been 'a slave to events', as his Chief-of-Staff Pownall put it,[2] for seven critical days, anchored to allies whose cowardly performance would go down as the nadir of French and Belgian military history. Hitler's confirmation of the order to stop the Panzer assault on the BEF western flank, and the general lull in the fighting on 24 and 25 May, had led Gort to believe the BEF might still extricate itself from its precarious northern peninsula and join the French beyond the Somme; but, when the captured VI Corps plans were revealed by Brooke, Gort changed his mind. A French attack from the south had – despite initial reports of success – failed completely. Boulogne had fallen, Calais was in its death throes, and reports from the 4th Division on the left flank of the

[1] Ironically it was this very officer – then Lt-Colonel Kinzel – who would surrender to Field-Marshal Sir Bernard Montgomery on behalf of the German Northern Armed Forces on 4 May 1945 at Lüneburg Heath.
[2] B. Bond (Ed.), op. cit.

BEF suggested that Belgian resistance had crumbled already. If the German two-corps attack towards Ypres succeeded, then the BEF would be severed from the coast and entirely surrounded. The likelihood of a successful break-through to the south plummeted as the odds against it were counted. Ammunition was already so low it was having to be parachuted in from England, rations had had to be reduced by half, and were only expected to last two and a half days outside the coastal area. If the Belgians surrendered in the next hours, the entire German western army could be turned against a surrounded pocket of twelve battered English infantry divisions, some of which, having been brought over to dig trenches and prepare airstrips, were only armed with shovels.

Within twelve hours of his earlier decision to break out south-wards, then, Gort was forced to rescind it. Hitler's strategy of luring the BEF into a trap had succeeded, and the question now was simply, how to parry the German *coup de grâce*. Without consulting his Government or his allies, Gort made the fateful decision to postpone the southward move of the BEF. It was undoubtedly the greatest decision of his life, and however tardy it was one which would secure him a place in history as the saviour of the British Army. He called off his intended 3 Corps spearhead attack and gave the divisions instead to Brooke's 2 Corps. 'The penetration scheme is now temporarily abandoned,' Brooke noted in his diary that night.[1] The security of the north-eastern flank of the BEF became the first priority; and by the following morning Gort finally realised he could never hope to reach the Somme. The ultimate decision to evacuate the BEF via Dunkirk was thus made.

However much Bernard deplored his performance as an Army Commander, Gort's decision on 25 May to rescind his order to attack in the south and his instruction the next day to evacuate the BEF, were ones which in the years that followed came to seem more courageous to Bernard. That Gort made such decisions so late in the campaign seemed less important than the fact that he did finally make them. 'For this I give him full marks,' wrote Bernard with complete honesty in his *Memoirs*, 'and I hope history will do the same. He saved the men of the BEF. And, being saved, they were able to fight again another day . . .' In his *Path to Leadership* Bernard summarised: 'But when all said and done, it must never be forgotten that in the supreme crisis of his military life, in May 1940, he acted with courage and decision – doing the right thing for Britain. If he had failed at that moment, disaster might well have overtaken British arms. He did not fail.'

Having made his first decision at GHQ on the evening of 25 May, the question in Gort's mind was only: was it too late? Could sufficient troops be sent to block the German attack towards Ypres, whilst also

[1] Loc. cit.

ensuring a stop-line to the sea if the Belgians capitulated? Everything now depended on Brooke. If Gort's unilateral decision, the following morning, to evacuate via Dunkirk was the high-point of his military career, it was Brooke's generalship in those forty-eight hours which mark his greatness as a field commander. Using the 5th and 50th Divisions, Brooke blocked the German attack on the Ypres-Comines canal; then extracted Bernard's 3rd Division from the line and in the middle of the night of 27 May transferred it north of Ypres to the junction with the river Yser – which would then be the cornerstone of the BEF withdrawal, allowing all the British and allied forces in the peninsula to pivot backwards on and subsequently behind it.

To begin with, Bernard was unaware just what critical decisions his Corps Commander must make in order to save the BEF; in fact it was not until the late afternoon of 26 May that Bernard was formally told by Brooke that the BEF would not go south, but would evacuate, according to Bernard's diary:

> Corps Commander arrived 1600 hrs & said BEF was to be with-drawn to the coast and embarked; all guns, vehicles, stores, etc. would be abandoned.
> Had conference at 1730 hrs and gave our preliminary orders.

In fact, until Brooke arrived to give Bernard his new orders in person, Bernard was singularly unhelpful. Although night patrols on 25 May did not gain contact with the enemy, Bernard refused to extend his divisional sector northwards by a single battalion frontage when Neil Ritchie, Brooke's BGS, requested him to do so on the morning of 26 May in order that the 4th Divison could in its turn sidestep and help 5th Division defend the vital Ypres–Comines canal. According to the 3rd Division War Diary, the Commander of the 3rd Division told Ritchie 'that in view of the close nature of the country and the number of houses on his front such action would make it difficult for him to hold his present front securely'.[1]

This was fiddling while Rome burned, for the German attack towards Ypres had already begun and the documents captured by Bernard's own patrol indicated that the Germans now intended the 3rd Division front to be a holding one while they struck hard to the north. In fact Bernard would never have tolerated such 'belly-aching' on the part of one of his own subordinates, and certainly demanded total obedience by brigade commanders to his own Chief-of-Staff, Colonel Brown. Fortunately Brooke was alive to Bernard's intractable character, and recognised that Bernard's very professionalism made it difficult for him to accept advice unless it was given either as a direct order, or in such a way that Bernard recognised the logic of what was required of him. Ritchie, although an excellent staff officer,

[1] Loc. cit.

simply lacked the necessary firmness to deal with a capricious commander who was in rank his senior.

Brooke was forced therefore to make a visit himself to Bernard's HQ on the afternoon of 26 May. Brooke had undertaken a thorough personal reconnaissance of the Ypres sector that morning – during which he was very nearly stranded in no-man's-land by a British bridge demolition party – and found that both Belgians and the 1st French Motorised Division had flown, the latter leaving only their postal service *in situ*. If the 5th and 50th Divisions could hold the new sector, Brooke must find reserves to send north beyond them – hence the choice of 3rd Division. At 6 o'clock that evening Bernard passed on Brooke's information to his brigade commanders: 'The French had failed to make headway in the south and so could not join up with us,' he explained. 'In the North-East the Belgians were giving way. Therefore the BEF would retire on the channel ports of Dunkirk and Nieuport. Units of the Division were ordered to be ready at 2100 hrs.'[1]

Because the various units of the 5th and 50th Division were not all in line till late that night, however, Brooke decided to delay the 3rd Division's flank movement so as not to entangle the two axes, a decision which would afford Barker's 1 Corps more time to prepare for its own withdrawal towards the Dunkirk 'perimeter', as it was to be called. Thus it was only on the night of 27th May that the 3rd Division was withdrawn from the line and sidestepped behind the 4th, 5th and 50th Divisions to take up its northern sector about three miles north of Ypres. By then, as Ritchie had predicted, the German assault on the Ypres–Comines Canal had grown so savage that it had become imperative for 3rd Division to give help, and at 2 o'clock on the afternoon of 27 May Bernard had been ordered to relieve the right flank of 4th Division 'immediately'[2] – which he did with the 9th Infantry Brigade.

If Bernard had been cussed in not acting sooner to help the 4th Division, however, he certainly made up for it that night. The side-step movement he was asked to perform was perhaps the most difficult manoeuvre a division can make in war. Not only had he to disengage the entire division from contact with the enemy, but to cross the lines of communication of no fewer than three fellow divisions in total darkness, a few miles behind a fluctuating front line, and take up an unreconnoitred position before dawn. 'It was a task,' Brooke later acknowledged, 'that might well have shaken the stoutest of hearts, but for Monty it might just have been a glorious picnic! He told me exactly how he was going to do it, and was as usual exuberant in confidence. There is no doubt that one of Monty's strong points is his boundless confidence in himself. He was price-

[1] Ibid.
[2] Ibid.

357

less on this occasion, and I thanked Heaven to have a Commander of his calibre to undertake this march.'[1]

There was every reason, however, for Bernard to feel his 3rd Division could perform such a night withdrawal. Had the Division not already rehearsed the movement time after time on exercises, and again and again in battle, withdrawing successfully from the Dyle to the Dendre, from the Dendre to the Escaut, and from the Escaut to the French frontier defences from which they had first sallied forth on 10 May? Bernard's Intelligence officer, 'Kit' Dawnay, still remembered the occasion nearly forty years later. Ever since news of the German break-through in the south Dawnay had known the BEF would have to evacuate 'from the beaches somewhere' or be forced to surrender. 'Monty, however, was completely calm,' he recalled, 'and gave no indication that he was at all worried. At one moment we had a very complicated night march, a retirement where we marched across the face of the enemy to take up positions further to the left. Monty treated it exactly the same as if it had been an Exercise. The route was carefully marked, guides were put out all the way. Monty had studied movement to a very big extent, we were a very mobile Division, we had wireless, he exercised very close control and it went extremely well.'[2]

Brooke was delighted. 'Found he had, as usual, accomplished almost the impossible,' Brooke entered in his diary on the 28th.[3] But, having made his fateful decision to evacuate, Gort now lost control of the BEF. Between the morning of 27 May and his final hours at La Panne beach near Dunkirk, Brooke never once saw Gort or a senior member of GHQ, and for long periods he was not even informed where GHQ was situated. The decision he made – commandeering 1 Corps artillery and units of Alexander's 1st Division as they withdrew under 1 Corps – was entirely on his own initiative. GHQ had estimated that no more than twenty-five per cent of the BEF would ever get away; that it managed to evacuate its entire personnel in the few days between 26 May and 2 June can largely be ascribed to Brooke's generalship – a fact which no officer involved in those critical days and hours has ever disputed – though Brooke himself ascribed it to the unbelievable resilience of the British soldier who, as in Rudyard Kipling's poem, kept his head while all about him were losing theirs. Having been brought up in France and having admired the way France held firm in the Great War, he was inevitably saddened by the sheer cowardice and disintegration of French morale – epitomised at his HQ on 29 May when élite French cavalrymen began killing their horses and throwing away their guns although the Germans were more than twenty miles away.

However, it was the final surrender of the Belgians which was to

[1] A. Bryant, op. cit.
[2] Lt-Colonel C. P. Dawnay, loc. cit.
[3] A. Bryant, op. cit.

cause Brooke his biggest headache, for, as Bernard rushed his 3rd Division north of Ypres, the Belgians had begun to sue for an armistice. Thus no sooner had Bernard arrived to take up his new sector at 7 a.m. on 28 May than he found there would be no allied troops between him and the sea at Nieuport – a gap of some fifteen miles.

'Here was a pretty pickle!' Bernard chronicled in his *Memoirs*. In his *History of Warfare* he wrote: 'At dawn on 28th May I learned that the King of the Belgians had surrendered the whole of his army to the Germans. I decided in my own mind that it is not suitable in the mid-twentieth century for kings to command their national armies in battle. One thing was fortunate – there were so many Belgian soldiers between my division and the sea that the Germans would have some difficulty in getting through, thus giving me a little time to think about it!'[1]

The position of 3rd Division was awkward, for it was intended that it should dig in on the water-line running north from Ypres, and like a mantled arm shield the 4th Division as, in its turn, it retreated to the safety of the Dunkirk perimeter. In the event the missing flank was protected by an ad hoc collection of French troops and 3rd Division artillerymen and engineers who were, where necessary, hastily given rifles and told to hold the Loon canal until the night of 28–29 May, when the 4th Division could get back to stop the gap; but, already during the afternoon of 28 May, Bernard's Signals HQ had picked up wireless reports that German units, advancing down the Belgian coast, had got into Nieuport, where only a single regiment of cavalry was ready to stop them. Fortunately, heavy rain and low cloud kept the German air force from the scene, and this undoubtedly saved the day, since the roads were crammed with Allied troops and transport running nose to tail. Bernard had immediately sent a messenger to Brooke's HQ when he heard news of the German penetration in Nieuport – 'he knew enough about my plans to realise at once the importance of this new and unexpected development,' as Brooke wrote later.[2] That night Bernard again sent a message to Brooke, to give him the latest information on the 'gap'; but this time he felt it so important that he sent his own Chief-of-Staff, 'Marino' Brown. While Bernard slept at the Trappist monastery he had selected as his HQ, Brown made his way through the darkness to 2 Corps HQ. 'On his way there he was held up by a bad traffic block. He got out of his car to investigate and immediately afterwards he was shot, probably by a sentry,' the 3rd Division's War Diary recorded the next day. Brooke was convinced that there was more to it that that – namely that Brown had been murdered by French deserters he had upbraided: 'he was known to have a hottish

[1] *A History of Warfare*, London 1946.
[2] A. Bryant, op. cit.

temper, and he may well have used the rough of his tongue on some of this rabble . . . It was a real tragedy as he had a brilliant future in front of him,' Brooke noted.[1] What Bernard felt is unknown. He had trained Brown to be not only the head of his staff, but his veritable deputy, and there was no time now to find a replacement. For the final days of Dunkirk his GSO 2, Charles Bullen-Smith, acted as his Chief-of-Staff. In his diary Bernard confined himself to three words: 'GSO 1 (Marino) killed.'

After the comparative orderliness of the 3rd Division's operations hitherto, the last days of Dunkirk were a nightmare; and 'Marino' Brown's death was like a first salvo. Even for Brian Horrocks, by now temporarily in command of the 3rd Division's two machine-gun battalions, it was 'a far more nerve-shattering experience than the vast battle in Normandy' in 1944.[2] On 29 May the 3rd Division again withdrew, this time to be the central stop-gap at Furnes on the eastern perimeter of the Dunkirk bridgehead. With four enemy divisions now concentrated upon it, and the withdrawal routes choked with abandoned lorries, equipment and troops, this was far from simple and there were severe casualties as the Germans infiltrated and exploited every small gap that could be forced between retreating units. However, by dawn on 30 May the 3rd Division was in position, with its HQ in La Panne, overlooking the sea. Tirelessly Bernard inspected his front, the left flank of which was manned mainly by the artillerymen and engineers he had converted into infantry now that their equipment had had to be abandoned.

'8 and 9 Inf Bdes got in very late, and all very tired. Spent morning organising front,' he recorded in his diary. The campaign was now twenty-one days old and it was natural that exhaustion should have set in. 'This lack of sleep affected everyone,' Horrocks later described, 'high and low, with one exception – General Montgomery. During the whole of the withdrawal he insisted on having meals at regular hours and never missed his normal night's sleep. Consequently when we arrived at Dunkirk he was as fresh as when he started. And he was about the only one who was . . .

'I saw him every day, sometimes several times a day, and he was always the same; confident, almost cocky you might say, cheerful and apparently quite fresh. He was convinced that he was the best divisional commander in the British Army and that we were the best division. By the time we had reached Dunkirk I had come to the same conclusion!'[3]

Certainly the 3rd Division, numbering still some 13,000 men, was the largest of Brooke's four divisions when he toured their sectors on 30 May. 'Our casualties were not heavy compared with others,'

[1] Ibid.
[2] Sir Brian Horrocks, with Eversley Belfield & Major-General H. Essame, *Corps Commander*, London 1977.
[3] B. Horrocks, *A Full Life*, op. cit.

Dawnay recorded. 'The division felt itself quite confident about seeing the Germans off as far as it was concerned; it was a question of whether other people had let us down, put us in an impossible situation.'[1]

Retiring to Dunkirk, however, was one thing; whether the Division would be able to evacuate by sea was another – though Bernard gave no hint of anxiety on that score either. 'I don't think I had any great worries,' Dawnay recollected. 'I was supremely confident in Monty. He gave one a tremendous feeling of confidence. He made a great joke of it, actually – "extraordinary sort of party these people have put us in," he'd say, and gave everyone else around him a tremendous feeling of confidence too.'[2]

That morning Lt-General Brooke arrived at Bernard's HQ at La Panne. It was a scene that would haunt Bernard for the rest of the war, and beyond. Although Brooke had known since the previous day that he had been ordered home by the War Office to help 'reforming new armies', he had told no one. 'After having struggled with the Corps through all its vicissitudes, and having guarded it to the sea, I felt like a deserter not remaining with it till the last,' Brooke later wrote.[3] He had used every minute of his final twenty-four hours trying to see that the left flank of the BEF was secure, and to force Gort to agree that 2 Corps should embark first – the latter not for reasons of loyalty to 2 Corps, but because the western flank around the port of Dunkirk, currently held by 1 Corps, must obviously be defended to the bitter end.

The meeting with Bernard was unexpectedly emotional. Brooke had managed almost single-handed – as far as higher command was concerned – to foil the German pincer movement from 25 to 30 May when he saw Gort once again. Whether it was the tragedy of the BEF or the accumulated tension after so many days of unremittingly distinguished generalship, Brooke now gave way to tears.

'He arrived at my headquarters to say goodbye and I saw at once that he was struggling to hold himself in check,' wrote Bernard later in his *Path to Leadership*; 'so I took him a little way into the sand hills and then he broke down and wept.'

Brian Horrocks was a surprised witness. He had been summoned to 3rd Division HQ and 'as I approached I saw two figures standing in the sand-dunes. I recognised our corps commander, General Brooke, and my divisional commander, General Montgomery. The former was under a considerable emotional strain. His shoulders were bowed and it looked as though he were weeping. Monty was patting him on the back. Then they shook hands and General Brooke walked slowly to his car and drove away'.[4]

[1] Lt-Colonel C. P. Dawnay, loc. cit.
[2] Ibid.
[3] *Notes on My Life*, loc. cit.
[4] *A Full Life*, op. cit.

That Brooke, so reserved, so austere and deliberate, should break down in front of the commander of his 3rd Division amazed Horrocks. To Bernard, however, Brooke's breakdown signified something much deeper than a momentary lapse of self-control. 'When the reserve of the English heart is broken through, most of us like to be alone,' Bernard wrote in his *Path to Leadership*. 'And so when Alanbrooke broke down and wept on my shoulder, I knew it meant his friendship was all mine – and I was glad to have it that way. That scene in the sand-dunes on the Belgian coast is one that will remain with me all my life.'

Brooke had decided to make Bernard his successor as Commander of 2 Corps. Whether Brooke's lowering of his impassive mask was quite the symbol of friendship that Bernard took it to mean is doubtful. If anything it tells us more about Bernard than about Brooke. Lonely, limited by the single-mindedness of his military obsession, jealous, suspicious or contemptuous of his contemporaries and seniors, unable to show tenderness now that Betty was no longer alive, Bernard was moved beyond words by Brooke's gesture of trust. One day Churchill too would burst into tears in front of him, and thus cement a friendship for life – for such tears represented the very acceptance Bernard had craved from his mother, and received only from his beloved Betty.

'I remained a silent and interested spectator of this astonishing scene,' wrote Horrocks. 'Monty beckoned me over and said, "General Brooke has just received orders to hand over the 2nd Corps to me and go back to England."'[1] Brigadier Kenneth Anderson from the 4th Division was to succeed Bernard at 3rd Division, and Horrocks was to take over Anderson's Brigade.

In his diary Bernard recorded:

Corps Comdr visited me 1100 hrs and said he had to go home to UK to help in organizing the armies at home. I was to take over command of 2 Corps; very awkward as I am the junior Div Comdr in the Corps, and the youngest.

Actually Major-General Martel of 50th Division was younger still than Bernard; moreover there was no question but that Bernard should be chosen. Franklyn had tirelessly switched his 5th Division from one BEF front to another, and his stand on the Ypres–Comines canal had undoubtedly saved the BEF from being outflanked; but his division was down to two weak brigades, numbering about 1200 men in all, and Martel's 50th Division was similarly decimated. Major-General Johnson had also performed bravely, but he was the first to acknowledge afterwards that he was too old to command a division in modern war – in fact he was so wearied and upset by the

[1] Ibid.

Dunkirk campaign that he found it impossible to draw up a list of officers and men for decoration in England.[1] Brooke at any rate had 'no hesitation' in choosing Bernard to succeed him.

More awkward than the question of seniority or merit was the problem of successfully extricating the Corps from beneath the noses of the German army and evacuating it during the next forty-eight hours. Bernard had comforted Brooke 'saying that we would all get back to England somehow and join up with him again,' Bernard recalled, 'but I must confess that at that moment it wasn't clear to me how it would be done, but it became clearer later that day when I had time to study the problem at Corps HQ.'[2]

Bernard's promotion was to be effective from 5 p.m. on 30 May. At 2 p.m. Bernard held his last divisional conference for unit commanders, at which he took stock of his remaining forces and discussed plans for continuing the defence of the perimeter. Fortunately the Division had managed to bring back most of its field artillery, with plenty of ammunition; moreover the very narrowness of the now contracted perimeter meant that units could cover one another in the event of German infiltration. Though the higher German commanders boasted that encirclement and destruction of the BEF were almost complete, there was no real effort by local German commanders to breach the perimeter – something which could only be done at suicidal cost in casualties. Thus the German infantry sniped, patrolled, and relied on their artillery to do the rest – without realising that the majority of artillery shells were relatively ineffective in the sandy coastal dunes and soil. Provided the perimeter defences were manned with resolution and intelligent use of local reserves was made, the BEF had every chance of evacuating the larger part of its remaining troops. That afternoon Bernard wrote out his first Order of the Day – the first of perhaps the most historic series of such orders in British twentieth-century military history.

3rd Division

SPECIAL ORDER OF THE DAY

30 MAY 40.

1. I have been ordered to hand over command of 3rd Division and to take over command of 2 Corps.
2. We have been through much together since mobilization last September, and I had hoped to be able to lead the 3rd Division safely through the present difficulties. But one has to do one's duty and I have now to take over command of the Corps; the 3rd Division is in the 2nd Corps and I shall make it my special task to

---

[1] Wason interviews with General Sir Frank Simpson, loc. cit.
[2] *Path to Leadership*, op. cit.

watch over its welfare. I have asked that on return to England I may be allowed to return to the 3rd Division if I am no longer required as a Corps Commander.

3.   I would like to thank all ranks in the 3rd Division for the good work they have done since the outbreak of war. The 3rd Division has never failed to carry out well any task given to it; I feel that this has been due mainly to the whole-hearted co-operation of officers and men and not to anything I may have been able to achieve myself.

4.   We have not quite finished our task yet, and the next two or three days may see some hard fighting. Provided we maintain our present positions, all will be well; if we fail to maintain them our difficulties will become enormous.

During the next few days we shall need stout hearts and cool heads, and all must be prepared to uphold the good name of the 3rd Division by hard fighting.

To our task, then, with determination and good British tenacity. The 3rd Division will stand firm and show the way; I have complete confidence in its ability to hold its own and prevent any enemy penetration of its front.

> B. L. Montgomery
> Major-General,
> Commander,
> 3rd Division.

Bernard's Chief-of-Staff, inherited from Brooke, was Neil Ritchie, who sent Bernard a message offering to pick him up in his car and take him to the Commander-in-Chief's conference at GHQ at 6 p.m. Instead, since the 3rd Division's HQ was only a short walk from GHQ in La Panne, Bernard walked there early. According to Bernard it was the first time he had seen his Commander-in-Chief since the campaign began on 10 May. Gort was 'alone in the dining room of the house and looked a pathetic sight, though outwardly cheerful as always,' Bernard recalled in his *Memoirs*. 'His first remark to me was typical of the man: "Be sure to have your front well covered with fighting patrols tonight."'

Accounts of this final conference vary, and the British Official History of the campaign skates over the evacuation period with little attention to truth in detail or in atmosphere, claiming for instance that Lord Gort appointed Major-General Alexander as Commander of 1 Corps when Churchill requested him to nominate a rearguard commander for the final evacuation. By contrast Bernard claimed in his *Memoirs* that Gort actually appointed Michael Barker the rearguard commander – a fact which is borne out by the GHQ War Diary for 30 May 1940, written by Lord Bridgeman: 'C-in-C saw General

Barker and told him he would be nominated as the Commander.'[1]
Moreover Bernard's own diary for 30 May records:

> Attended Conference of Corps Commanders at GHQ 1800 hrs.
> C-in-C read out telegram from War Office ordering one Corps to be
> surrendered to enemy with the French at Dunkirk; Barker selected
> and 1 Corps; 2 Corps to be evacuated; gave it as my opinion we
> could not hold present sector after night 31 May/1 June.
> Plan made to disengage and evacuate whole Corps at two
> beaches – La Panne and Bray.
> This was a very fateful conference, of GHQ.
> The atmosphere was tense and those members of GHQ who were
> present were obviously out of touch with realities and lacked any
> sense of proportion. The C-in-C could make no constructive
> proposals and could give no quick and definite decisions. Barker
> (1st Corps) was excited and rattled; his BGS was frightened and
> out of touch.
> I gave my definite opinion as to what was, and was not, possible.
> Brooke (who had handed over 2 Corps to me) was present for the
> first ¼ hour & then left for England; he was first class and must
> play a big part in the future schemes of re-organization.

Gort's biographer, J. R. Colville, also skimmed over the last days of
the evacuation – despite the fact that in a long letter in 1952 Bernard
had given Colville an eye-witness account of the 'fateful' GHQ
conference:

> I was present as Commander 2 Corps; I had taken over from
> Brooke, who was to return to UK that evening.
> The Commander 1 Corps was Michael Barker, an utterly useless
> commander, who had lost his nerve by 30 May.
> Alexander was not present; he was GOC 1st Division, in 1 Corps,
> under Barker . . .
> It was obvious that the evacuation plan would have to be based on
> withdrawing 2 Corps through 1 Corps, leaving 1 Corps to get away
> last.
> I arrived early at the conference as my HQ were on the outskirts of
> La Panne. Gort was in a house on the sea front.
> He was alone when I arrived.
> I don't think I have ever seen a more pathetic sight; the great and
> supposedly famous C-in-C of the British Army on the Continent,
> alone; the staff of GHQ was scattered to the four winds of Heaven;
> he had in La Panne two staff officers; one was first class (Oliver
> Leese); the other was useless . . .
> Gort, in my opinion, was finished. He was incapable of grasping

[1] Loc. cit.

the military situation firmly, and issuing clear orders. He was incapable of instilling confidence or morale. He had 'had it' and I remember saying as much to Brooke, who was at the Conference and left for England from the beach immediately it was over.

Gort had a telegram in his hand.

He told us the gist of what he had been ordered to do; he finished by telling Barker he did not think the 1 Corps would be able to get away and that he (Barker) must stay with it and surrender to the Germans.

The effect on Barker was catastrophic; he was incoherent at first and then relapsed into silence.

I knew Gort very well, personally.

After we had broken up I got him alone and told him that we could not yet say it was impossible to get 1 Corps away; but that it would *never* get away if Barker was in control, and that the only sound course was to get Barker out of it as soon as possible and give 1 Corps to Alexander. Gort agreed and Barker was sent away; he was never employed again and I have never heard anything of him, or seen him, since that Conference at La Panne on the evening of 30 May 1940.[1]

Barker, in fact, was retired from the Army after Dunkirk and died in obscurity in 1946. But did Gort really intend to surrender the rearguard Corps of the BEF? Churchill's telegram had been sent at 2 p.m. in the afternoon of 30 May. Its final lines read:

The Corps Commander chosen by you should be ordered to carry on the defence in conjunction with the French and evacuation whether from Dunkirk or the beaches, but when in his judgement no further organized evacuation is possible and no further proportionate damage can be inflicted on the enemy he is authorized in consultation with the senior French Commander to capitulate formally to avoid useless slaughter.[2]

Whether Gort read the telegram or gave a précis of it is disputed; however, in an atmosphere in which he could no longer himself give firm direction and did not even know in what order to evacuate his remaining corps and divisions ('I found Gort undecided as to how to continue evacuation,' Brooke noted in his diary[3]), the very mention of capitulation was unwise. Certainly Bernard's diary entries are, like Brooke's, consistent in their image of Gort as a broken reed. Immediately Bernard left the GHQ Conference he summoned his divisional commanders to his new 2 Corps HQ and told them they

[1] Letter of 25 August 1952, Montgomery Papers.
[2] L. F. Ellis, op. cit.
[3] A. Bryant, op. cit.

were to be embarked on the following evening. On 31 May he recorded:

> Continued plans for embarking 2 Corps. Enemy attacked almost continuously but was held.
> C-in-C very pathetic sight, a defeated and disappointed man. He was to leave by destroyer at 1800 hrs.

Moreover, according to the GHQ War Diary for 31 May kept by Oliver Leese, there can be no doubt but that Gort believed the rearguard would have to capitulate, for at 8.30 a.m. Major-General Alexander called on the C-in-C: 'He was told to thin out his division as it appeared probable that he would have to surrender the majority alongside the French in accordance with War Office instructions.'[1]

During the morning, however, Barker 'made certain difficulties as to the take-over' according to the GHQ War Diary, and in the end not Gort but Bernard seems to have dealt with them, for they 'were settled by direct negotiations with 2 Corps'.[2] Bernard's diary records that he 'visited Gort a good deal' and it is more than likely that it was Bernard who finally convinced Gort he must sack Barker and appoint Alexander instead to finish the evacuation.

Certainly Lord Bridgeman, Gort's DCGS, thought so. In a letter to Bernard after publication of his *Memoirs*, Bridgeman wrote: 'What you have said about Lord Gort is to my mind absolutely fair, which some previous comment was not. And what you have said about his running no GHQ exercise strikes at the root of the whole of his relationship with Dill and Brooke. To have run such an exercise would have inevitably resulted in Gort's having to give his casting vote on some difference of opinion between those two Commanders and that, as I was well aware at the time, he did not want to do.

'Lastly, those who were in 1 Corps in the final scenes at Dunkirk have good reason to thank you for what you did in putting Alex there. Some of us in G branch at GHQ had for some days been calling attention to the state of affairs in 1 Corps but did not think the penny had dropped and, later on, wondered what had made it do so!'[3]

At 1 p.m. on 31 May 1940 Alexander was summoned to lunch at La Panne with Gort, who at last told him 'he was to command 1 Corps'.[4] After lunch Alexander was given 'written orders by the C-in-C. He [Alexander] stated his intentions at all costs to extricate his command and not to surrender any part of it. Lt-General Barker was told to hand over 1 Corps to Major-General Alexander and to go back to England,' GHQ War Diary recorded.[5]

[1] Loc. cit.
[2] Ibid.
[3] Letter of 30.11.58, Montgomery Papers.
[4] War Diary, GHQ BEF, 31 May 1940, loc. cit.
[5] Ibid.

The fate of the BEF now lay in the hands of its two remaining Corps Commanders, Montgomery and Alexander. Bernard's plan for the evacuation of 2 Corps was straightforward. The Germans were to be viciously counter-attacked whenever they attempted to cross the Nieuport-Furnes Canal, with as much artillery fire as possible and air attack; then, under cover of darkness, the 3rd and 4th Divisions were to thin out and make for the beaches of La Panne and Bray Dunes, where they were to embark using jetties made from transport vehicles that were being run out into the sea. At 9 a.m. that morning Bernard summoned all RE troops in his three divisions to help build up such piers at La Panne beach. While Gort lunched with Alexander, Bernard messed with Brigadier Anderson, his successor at 3rd Division. 'General Montgomery came to lunch and informed GOC on work being done on the piers on the La Panne beach,' the 3rd Division's War Diary recorded.[1]

Despite the squally weather that had brought beach evacuation almost to a standstill that morning, Bernard exuded confidence. At 2.30 p.m. he gave his final conference of commanders and issued his last written orders. He had already moved Corps HQ down to La Panne beach in the morning 'to control the evacuation'[2] as well as the perimeter defences – a move necessary not only from an administrative point of view, but to ensure that morale did not ebb. Brooke's Chief Administrative Officer at 2 Corps was Brigadier Geoffrey Mansergh who, as Brooke recorded, had exhausted himself preparing for the 2 Corps final withdrawal.[3] Mansergh's last letter, written in his own hand at 11.15 a.m. on 31 May, only hours before he was killed aboard an evacuation craft, gives a vivid idea how even the most senior officers, from Gort downwards, were pessimistic about the chances of success. His letter was addressed to Bernard's Chief-of-Staff at 2 Corps, Brigadier Ritchie:

Dear Neil,
     The situation here at La Panne is poor. There is the same lack of power boats and other facilities for embarking as there always has been. The loading of Corps troops is going very slowly and is not nearly finished.
     As soon as I heard the situation I went in to see the C-in-C to ask if the situation was realized. I find that it is and that every authority in London has already been phoned to speed up arrival of proper craft. This being so we can do nothing but continue to do our best to get things away and hope for the best . . .
     Frankly the position seems somewhat gloomy at present. Un-

---

[1] Loc. cit.
[2] War Diary, 2 Corps, 31 May 1940, loc. cit.
[3] A. Bryant, op. cit.

less conditions improve greatly it looks somewhat doubtful that the proposed programme can be adhered to . . .'[1]

'Landing beaches were a sight worth seeing,' ran the 2 Corps War Diary. 'Thousands of troops, many ships large and small and numerous aircraft patrolling. Embarkation was difficult owing to the choppy seas and piers were built over the top of lorries. There were numerous air battles and bombing raids.'[2]

Bernard had arranged that reception camps be set up in the dunes and soldiers were only sent down on to the beach for embarkation when the beach commander called them – a system that worked admirably thanks to the redoubtable 3rd Division's signallers who managed during the retreat to bring back enough cable to link not only the perimeter with Divisional HQ but reception camps with the beach commander. Despite Mansergh's gloomy forecast, embarkation in the afternoon and evening went surprisingly well, with very few casualties despite the heavy German shelling. At 9 p.m., after dark, the great exodus was stepped up. At 8.30 p.m. Bernard had seen Alexander – 'We were both confident that all would be well in the end,' Bernard later recalled.[3] Gort had embarked at 7 p.m. and there was now an air of calm and complete authority. The two commanders agreed that if La Panne became unusable, 2 Corps would withdraw entirely via the beaches at Bray Dunes; if that became untenable the port of Dunkirk itself would be closed to 1 Corps personnel until 2 Corps was safely evacuated.

This was a fortunate agreement, for the Navy had still not provided adequate beach liaison parties and after 11 p.m. on 31 May evacuation from the beaches became impossible. In his diary Bernard ascribed this to German shelling which 'smashed the piers and caused a great many casualties to the troops'; but from the HQ War Diaries it is evident that the other culprit was the tide. Between 11 p.m. and 3 a.m. the next morning it was simply too low for the piers to be usable – a factor the army beach staff had failed to take into account. Remaining troops were thus forced to march from La Panne to Bray Dunes from 11 p.m. onwards; but at Bray Dunes Bernard directed them on to Dunkirk itself – a march of over fifteen miles for the troops of 4th Division. As Bernard described in his diary:

It was clearly impossible to continue embarkation at the beaches and I ordered the troops to move on to Dunkirk and embark there; this they were loath to do as they saw the ships lying off and hoped boats would come to the shore; but no boats came.

[1] Attached to 2 Corps War Diary, loc. cit.
[2] Loc. cit.
[3] *Memoirs*, op. cit.

With the last of 2 Corps perimeter defences withdrawing in the early hours of 1 June, it was imperative that the whole Corps be within the Dunkirk port perimeter by dawn; therefore Bernard remained at Bray Dunes until 3.30 a.m., personally directing all traffic 'straight on down the beach towards Dunkirk'. At one point a shell landed in the sand nearby, wounding his ADC. Bernard told him he was a fool not to be wearing a helmet – at which the ADC remonstrated that his Corps Commander was not wearing one either!

Fortunately Brooke had warned Admiral Ramsay at Dover that the greatest effort would be needed on the night of 31 May–1 June, and the weary 2 Corps, as they reached Dunkirk, were not disappointed. Altogether some 68,000 troops were evacuated on 31 May – almost 23,000 of these from the beaches, the remainder from the great mole at Dunkirk.

Having decided to leave Bray Dunes at 3.30 a.m. on 1 June, Bernard walked with his Chief-of-Staff Ritchie and his wounded ADC.

Left Bray at 0330 hrs and walked down the beach towards Dunkirk.

Enemy was shelling the beach but caused no casualties. After one hour we struck inland and picked up a lorry which took us in to Dunkirk; the town was being shelled and bombed and was in a complete shambles.

Found the naval shore station on the Mole and got sent off to a destroyer (HMS *Codrington* – Capt. Stevens-Guille, DSO, OBE)

Heavy bombing attacks while lying at the Mole and on the journey to Dover.

Arrived London 1500 hrs and reported to CIGS at War Office.

Such was Bernard's diary entry for 1 June 1940. His 3rd Division Artillery Commander, Brigadier R. H. Towell, was more descriptive. He also had to walk the beaches until a cutter from HMS *Niger* found him and Brigadier Robb of the 9th Infantry Brigade. For seven hours they stood to, off Bray, until the destroyer was full; then they steamed back to Dover.

'The last view of Dunkirk was a blazing town over which hung a dense pall of black smoke. The sea all around was dotted with life jackets and masts and funnels of sunken ships,' he recorded.[1]

By the following evening Alexander had managed to evacuate the entire rearguard of the BEF. From the British Army's point of view the 'Dunkirk' campaign was over. A quarter of a million British troops had been saved. They were sent to reception camps throughout Britain, from Aldershot to Lancashire, from wales to Yorkshire, regardless of the units to which they belonged. Churchill warned,

[1] War Diary, CRA, 3rd Division, 1 June 1940 (WO 167/220), PRO.

when the House of Commons reassembled on 4 June, that 'wars are not won by evacuation. We must be very careful not to assign to this deliverance the attribute of a victory'. But to the nation Dunkirk *had* been a victory, and the returning troops were treated as heroes. The true lessons of Dunkirk foundered amid the general rejoicing; and, instead of leading to a complete rethinking of British Army command and organisation, it heralded two long years of bungling, from the débâcle of Norway to the loss of Greece, Crete, the Far East and the shores of North Africa to the very gates of Cairo.

Whatever Bernard Montgomery's failings as a human being and as a commander, it would be his mission to reform the British Army – to avenge Dunkirk, and prove that under intelligent and inspired leadership, democracies *could* defend themselves, and could reverse the chain of defeat into a march of victories unseen since the days of Wellington.

CHAPTER SIX

'Mad, is he?'

On the morning of 2 June 1940, Bernard went back to Whitehall. 'I had had a good night's sleep in a hotel and was feeling very full of beans,' he recalled later.[1] In his diary that night he entered:

> Visited War Office and demanded a private interview with CIGS. Informed him as to the condition of Gort and Barker at the final conference at La Panne on evening 30 May; said that the events of the past few weeks had proved that certain officers were unfit to be employed again and should be retired.
> I gave it as my opinion that the BEF had never been 'commanded' since it was formed, and that for the next encounter we must have a new GHQ and a new C-in-C. I said that the only man to be C-in-C was Brooke.

Sir John Dill had succeeded Ironside as CIGS on 25 May; although he agreed with much of what Bernard said, he was anxious not to lower morale by critical talk and cautioned Bernard not to repeat such things outside the four walls of his office. Bernard promised; but he was far too angry at the way the BEF had been mishandled to keep quiet. By 5 June Dill was constrained to write to all divisional commanders:

> I learn that there is a certain amount of rather loose criticism going on among commanders of the BEF regarding the manner in which their seniors, their equals and their juniors conducted the recent operations in France and Belgium. Such criticism is calculated to shake the confidence of the Army in its leaders of all ranks, and I need not emphasize its dangers, particularly at a time like the present.
> I look to you to put a stop to all this. Any failings of commanders or staff officers should be submitted confidentially through the proper channels but on no account must they be discussed unofficially.[2]

[1] *Memoirs*, op. cit.
[2] Montgomery Papers.

On the same day Gort's Chief-of-Staff, Henry Pownall, wrote personally to Bernard:

> My dear Monty,
> Among the flood of stories and rumours that are being spread is one which has come to me, and to the C-in-C, that you have yourself been telling exaggerated stories! I don't think this is in the least likely but I am writing to say that this *is* being said of you, so I thought I'd pass you the word. After the strain & tension that we've all been through, and nobody more than yourself, there is certainly a tendency for tongues to wag (I've found it myself) but it's a dangerous business and more likely to bring discredit than honour to the BEF. This would be a pity after the magnificent showing the BEF have made. Of all the divisional commanders the C-in-C reckons you have come out either a good second or equal first, so I do hope that if there's any truth in the story I've heard you won't do anything to upset the tremendous opinion the C-in-C has formed of you.
> Yours ever
> Henry Pownall[1]

Pownall's letter was sent from Gort's new headquarters in Buckingham Palace Road where Gort had been given an office, and was busy writing his despatches, unperturbed by the fate of France. In his famous speech to the House of Commons Churchill had not only exhorted his countrymen to fight on the beaches, but assured the House that 'we have to reconstitute and build up the BEF under its gallant Commander, Lord Gort'. Yet, if Pownall hoped to silence Bernard by his veiled threat that Gort might not recommend him for an honour or future command, it was an empty gesture. Dill had already agreed that Bernard could return to command the 3rd Division – to whose new HQ at Frome, Somerset, he travelled on 6 June – and in due course Bernard was awarded the CB, together with Franklyn, Martel, Anderson and others. Pownall himself was knighted. At the bottom of Pownall's warning letter Bernard later pencilled: 'Lieut-General Sir Henry Pownall, Chief of the General Staff of BEF, under Gort. He was completely useless' – a view seconded later by Field-Marshal Templer who was largely responsible for the successful defence of the BEF's western flank, under General Mason-Macfarlane.[2]

Pownall sat in Buckingham Palace Road helping Lord Gort write up his despatches, aided also by Lord Bridgeman. Hard though they might try to concoct a convincing tale of wondrous feats of arms and

---

[1] Ibid.
[2] Field-Marshal Sir Gerald Templer, interview of 27.4.79.

leadership, their hour of glory was over, however, and Churchill's reference to Lord Gort was rhetorical. Though Gort continued to call himself C-in-C, British Expeditionary Force, he was in fact quietly dropped from active command. Bernard's 3rd Division was 'selected to be the first Division of the BEF to be re-fitted, and was to return to France for the second time,' Bernard noted in his diary on 3 June. When he heard that not Gort but Brooke was to be his Commander-in-Chief, he was delighted and wrote immediately both to congratulate Brooke and to say how much he looked forward to joining him again in France. On 10 June Brooke replied – though without disclosing his feelings on the futility of such an expedition so soon after the disaster at Dunkirk:

My dear Monty
Very many thanks for your letter & for all you said in it. I thank heaven for the fact that you & the 3rd Div were with the 2 Corps throughout our trip to Louvain & back. I don't know what I should have done without you.
I only wish you were with me now when we start, but delighted that you won't be long in following on behind. I did my best to have 3 & 4 Divs made up at once for what they had [lost] & sent out instead of what they are doing. But I was told that political reasons made it essential to produce something at once.
I have had a very busy time getting 2 Corps HQ plus additions together & am practically ready now.
I am off in a very short time now, and shall welcome you with open arms when you turn up.
Best of luck to you Monty, & again a thousand thanks for all your help and assistance since the war started.
Yours
Brookie[1]

Two days later Brooke was in France again; nine days later he was back in England having ensured the embarkation of more than 200,000 Allied troops in spite of Pétain's sudden and secret armistice. Again Bernard congratulated him, and again, on 24 June, Brooke replied:

Yes, I am back and it is a relief to be out of it! I did not enjoy this last trip. From my first interview with Weygand & Georges I saw it was quite hopeless and that the only thing to do was to extricate the remainder of the BEF as quick as possible if we wanted to avoid another Dunkirk.
But it was not easy to get the Government to appreciate what the situation was, & I had some anxious moments.[2]

[1] Montgomery Papers.
[2] Ibid.

In fact, when the Prime Minister insisted by telephone on 14 June that Brooke should sacrifice his 52nd Division in order to 'make the French feel that we were supporting them', Brooke replied angrily that it was impossible to make a corpse feel.

With the final disbandment of the BEF Brooke was now made Commander-in-Chief, Southern Command – the post he had held when war first broke out.

> I do wish you were in the Southern Command. I should give a lot to have the old 3rd Div back with me. I have a very great affection for it,

Brooke finished his letter to Bernard.[1]

Just what Command 3rd Division did belong to was a moot question once the second BEF was closed down. Nominally it belonged to Southern Command, and had been intended to join Brooke's BEF in France on 20 June; yet on 15 June, before Pétain had even capitulated, the War Office cancelled the move. Instead the 3rd Division moved on 19 June to the Sussex coast between Brighton and Bognor, with its HQ at Pulborough, in 12 Corps area; but on 21 June it was withdrawn from 12 Corps into War Office reserve, although still made responsible for the area in the event of a German invasion. For the next ten days it then became the subject of a succession of War Office fantasies. Two naval officers and an extra GSO 2 arrived to help the Division become Britain's mobile Combined Operations unit, and overnight plans were prepared for the division to seize the Azores. The destination was then changed to the Cape Verde islands. Finally this plan was dropped and Bernard was told to be ready by Friday 28 June to seize Cork and Queenstown in the Irish Republic! 'I had already fought the Southern Irish once, in 1921 and 1922,' Bernard later recalled, 'and it looked as if this renewed contest might be quite a party – with only one division.'[2] At 9 a.m. on 28 June Bernard held his final commanders' conference on the invasion of Ireland. 'At the close of the Conference,' the Divisional War Diary recorded, 'a telephone message was received from the War Office saying that the Division would not after all move abroad. GOC and GSO 1 went to London to elucidate the matter.'

To Bernard this continual change of mind was anathema; no doubt, being the character he was, it added to his sense of frustration at the way the British Army was failing both to decide on its priorities, and to draw the lessons of Dunkirk. On 27 June he met Lt-General Auchinleck, Commander of the neighbouring 5 Corps – a command Bernard was himself to assume in barely a month's time. They discussed how, if the 3rd Division went abroad, Auchinleck could cover the coastal sector; it was their second meeting since

[1] Ibid.
[2] *Memoirs*, op. cit.

India in 1936, and Bernard did not warm to the 'blue-eyed boy' of the Indian Army.

That Bernard should have found Gort an incompetent Army Commander is understandable; that he should have conceived, from the beginning, such a dislike of Auchinleck is less so. Although Auchinleck had been defeated in Norway, he had in the course of the campaign captured Narvik and proven himself a clear-minded, authoritative general – a commodity which, as Bernard well knew, was extremely rare in Britain in the summer of 1940. Moreover Auchinleck's views on the defence of Britain, morale, training, and even his attitude towards Dunkirk, seemed on the surface remarkably similar to Bernard's – so much so that Barnard's remark in his *Memoirs* that he could not 'recall that we ever agreed on anything' would appear far from generous. Certainly they agreed about Dunkirk. Bernard was appalled when he saw 'British soldiers walking about in London and elsewhere with a coloured embroidered flash on their sleeve with the title "Dunkirk," ' as he later recalled. 'They thought they were heroes, and the civilian public thought so too. It was not understood that the British Army had suffered a crushing defeat at Dunkirk and that our island home was now in grave danger,' he wrote in his *Memoirs*. In his letter to the VCIGS on 29 June 1940 Auchinleck expressed very similar sentiments: 'By the way, there is some bizaar "gupp" about a "Dunkirk Medal"! which is causing some alarm amongst level-headed people. I hope it isn't true, and I can't believe it is. We do not want to perpetuate the memory of that episode, surely?'[1]

Similarly on 25 June Auchinleck had issued a most stirring Order of the Day, dictating that henceforth the area would become a 'War Zone', abolishing all ceremonial guards and ordering all commanders to run their units as they would in a 'forward theatre of war'. To the VCIGS he lamented the distinction between Regulars and Territorials – 'We shall not win this war so long as we cling to worn out shibboleths and snobberies. I am sure of this. Cobwebs want removing at once.'[2]

Surely these were sentiments after Bernard's own heart? Yet, much as Bernard revered Brooke, so he would withhold respect and even obedience from Auchinleck – a personal repudiation he would pursue to the end of his life. Though Auchinleck was the first, in August 1942, to recommend that Bernard take over 8th Army in North Africa; though Auchinleck would write in all humility in 1958 to Sir Francis de Guingand: 'Of course you have a high regard for Monty. So have I – for his great achievements and great qualities,'[3] Bernard would never be reconciled – writing back to de Guingand: 'I

[1] Quoted in J. Connell, *Auchinleck*, op. cit.
[2] Ibid.
[3] Letter of 6.12.1958, de Guingand Papers.

note you say the Auk admires *me*. But I don't admire him – and never have from the day I first served under him in the Southern Command after Dunkirk. That experience was enough for me.'[1]

Neither 'Kit' Dawnay, who became Bernard's ADC at Frome, nor 'Simbo' Simpson who became Bernard's Chief-of-Staff at 5 Corps, nor Gerald Templer who became commander of a beach brigade under Bernard, could ever explain this antipathy, for all of them conceived a great admiration for 'the Auk', and thought that beyond any doubt he was one of the strongest leaders of the Second World War, one of the few commanders of undeniably great stature. In Templer's phrase, Bernard was 'a cocksparrow beside this great, handsome man'. Bernard's brother Brian wondered whether it was not something to do with Auchinleck's Indian Army background – an inverted jealousy after Bernard's failure to pass into the Indian Army on leaving Sandhurst in 1907. Certainly Auchinleck's Indian Army background was a matter of general surprise in the British Army at the time – and when, a few weeks later, Auchinleck was promoted from 5 Corps to Southern Command in place of Brooke (who became C-in-C Home Forces on 19 July) one of his staff wrote: 'It is a great achievement for a man from the Indian Army to get Southern Command, as such plums are usually the preserve of the British Service.'[2]

If this was the cause of Bernard's dislike it does him no credit. Even Bernard's contempt for Gort caused his own admirers to wince. 'Monty despised Gort,' Field-Marshal Templer once declared when asked about the Montgomery-Gort relationship. 'And I despised Montgomery – for despising Gort!'[3]

But were Bernard's feelings towards Auchinleck really inspired only by envy, and was his contempt for Gort so despicable? It is important both to remember the context in which these feelings were engendered – the triumph of Hitler over the allied forces of democracy – and Bernard's own state of mind at the time: for it was undoubtedly Bernard's experience in the Dunkirk campaign which set the seal on his views about army command. The problem of relying on an ally, the necessity for clear leadership, training by rehearsal, ruthless choice of commanders, adequate communications, mobile headquarters – all had been spelled out in the campaign. Indeed, just how deeply the events and lessons of those fateful May days had affected him is illustrated by the testimony of 'Kit' Dawnay, who made his way straight to Frome as soon as he had returned from Dunkirk – only to find that Montgomery had no intention of allowing anyone leave to see their families before returning to the battle in France:

[1] De Guingand, *From Brass Hat to Bowler Hat*, op. cit.
[2] John Connell, *Auchinleck*, op. cit.
[3] Told to the author. 19.2.79.

Within a few days Monty arrived. His ADC had been slightly wounded in the final evacuation, so he took me round as his ADC and saw all the troops. The Division was to be immediately re-equipped, and was intended to go back into France via Brest.

Monty decided that nobody was to have any leave. He went round the Division and saw practically everybody. He made the same speech to them all: the 3rd Division had done magnificently, had been chosen to go back into the fight, was instantly to be re-equipped, what a great honour, etc.

It was received extremely badly.

In fact the Coldstreams even went so far as to barrack him! Everybody, having got through the Dunkirk party, wanted at any rate just to *show* themselves to their families. To have no leave whatsoever was, to say the least, very frustrating.

Bernard's miscalculation, his misreading of the minds of his own men, was so pronounced in this instance that one is tempted to ask whether his stepson John Carver's fears of a growing schizoid personality, ameliorated only by the love and understanding and humour of Betty, might not be true. Bernard's own son David does not remember a visit from his father after Dunkirk; indeed it would seem that Bernard's obsessional desire to prove himself in war now blinded him to other more human considerations. It was from this moment, at any rate, that people began to refer to Montgomery as the 'mad General'.

'Oh! He is mad, is he? Then I wish he would bite some other of my Generals!' George II is reported to have said to the Prime Minister when doubts were raised as to whether General James Wolfe was a suitable choice for the capture of Quebec. Perhaps madness is a prerequisite of military genius – at least a determination and self-discipline bordering on insanity. One is reminded of Bernard's own tale, in his *Memoirs*, of his interview with the CIGS, General Sir John Dill, on 2 June 1940 at the War Office. Dill had looked despondent, had asked Bernard if he realised that for the first time in a thousand years of history Britain was in serious danger of being invaded. Bernard had laughed. Surprised, Dill had asked what Bernard found so funny. And Bernard had replied that no one would believe Britain was in serious danger of invasion when it had such incompetent fools in home commands – and had listed their names.

Bernard's 'mad' laugh; his conviction that his entire 3rd Division should go back into battle from England without being allowed to see their families; the iron discipline which now ruled his personal life – his abstinence from drink or tobacco, his rigid mealtimes, his ordinance about regular sleep . . . It is impossible to say that Bernard's character changed in the course of the early summer of 1940, since such features of his personality had been in evidence long before. Moreover madness is often indefinable except as abnormality – and abnormality, the unwillingness of English people from Churchill to the Home Guard to accept defeat, was undoubtedly what saved Britain in 1940 and 1941. Yet there can be little doubt that there was, in the early summer of 1940, a definite intensification of those areas of his character which distinguished Bernard from other men and other commanders. War – the command of human lives in conditions of crisis, of death and devastation – acted as an incitement to disciplined violence of character: the power to take life or to save life. And within that violence raged also the intensity of his parents' Christian morality: the shame of having done wrong at Sandhurst, the shame of having been inconsiderate, even vindictive, in the futile attempt to compel his mother's attention.

In a very real sense one may say that in the summer of 1940 Bernard was waging a struggle not only with Nazi Germany, not only with an anachronistic British military hierarchy, but with himself. It was a struggle which would go on throughout the war, and would continue thereafter as fame rocketed him into spheres of responsibility and society which very few mortals can handle with humility; a struggle which, however, badly, he may be said to have won, as he won it in Frome in early June 1940:

> He came back to his HQ at Frome that evening. He sent for his Chief-of-Staff and his head of Divisional administration and asked the latter about the likely schedule for re-equipment. The head of administration said the tap had been turned on, but that the stuff wouldn't come in for another 48 hours by the time it was unloaded, checked, etc. After considerable discussion Monty suddenly said: 'Right, everyone in the Division must go on leave for 48 hours from tonight!' We were stunned. It meant that he was completely reversing the command he had given verbally to practically every officer, NCO and soldier in the Division that day. The order was sent out immediately – it was already between 7 and 8 p.m. 'There we are,' he explained to his commanders, 'supplies are not coming through as quickly as we thought. Therefore you must all go on 48 hours leave from midnight tonight!'
>
> He got a very high feeling of admiration from the Division for being able to reverse his own decision like that. It showed his stature, the realism that underlay his absolute professionalism. The Division dispersed overnight; the supplies came through; and with fresh determination we prepared to go back to France.

Such was 'Kit' Dawnay's account of a seemingly trivial but salutary test of Bernard's stature as a commander – a test that would be made again and again as the war continued: moments when obsessive,

379

excessive determination, the iron hallmarks of his command, gave way to sudden, total realism, even humility – thus earning forever the loyalty and admiration of his staff and of his troops.

CHAPTER SEVEN

Churchill's Leopards

There is one other account which bears out the quasi-insane determination of Bernard Montgomery on his return from Dunkirk: and that is given by 'Simbo' Simpson, whose own gallantry in the defence of Arras earned him the DSO. Simpson had returned to the Military Secretary's office at the War Office, and one of his first acts was to get the AA and QMG (Assistant Adjutant and Quartermaster-General) of the 3rd Division promoted to Brigadier i/c Administration in a Corps. On the strength of this, Colonel Lorie invited Simpson to lunch with him at the Army and Navy Club:

> Not being very hard pressed with work I accepted and we went to the club and had a couple of gins before lunch, then walked into the dining room. There, sitting all alone at a table not far from the door, was Major-General Montgomery. I went up to him straight away and said: 'Sir, I am sorry to tell you that we are removing your AA & QMG from you at once. He has been appointed Brigadier "Q" of the 1st Corps.'
>
> Monty replied: 'Capital. He's just the right man for that sort of appointment and I'm delighted he should get it. Now, we're going back to France next week and I have to fill his place. I want somebody I can trust to take on the job.'
>
> There was a pause.
>
> 'I know!' he said. 'You, Simpson, will take it on. I don't think you'll be doing anything useful in the Military Secretary's branch from now on, and you'll find plenty to do as AA & QMG of my division. I'll fix this. Please be on the 4.30 train from Waterloo this afternoon.'
>
> I protested in somewhat light-hearted fashion, saying that I really did not know much just then about the administrative side of affairs and that I would almost certainly let him down: for instance the troops in brigades going back into battle would probably get no rations, ammunition, petrol or anything like that. I wouldn't know exactly how to do it and I could hardly learn in a week.

Simpson therefore refused to take the matter seriously. However when he arrived back in his office that afternoon it was to find that

Bernard had indeed 'fixed it'; he was expected on the 4.30 train from Waterloo. Simpson protested to his chief, who sympathised and proposed he go instead to the 4th Division, where he would get at least three weeks to learn his job before the division sailed again for France.

> While the discussion was going on the telephone rang. The Military Secretary motioned me to answer it and I found Monty at the other end, seeking confirmation from the Military Secretary that I would be on the train at 4.30. I again made my protest to him, perhaps in rather stronger terms than earlier.
>
> He was obviously nettled and said: 'I see. You obviously don't want to come and serve under me. If you don't want to, I don't want you. I will easily get someone else' – and he slammed the receiver down.

Bernard was obviously in a towering rage and must have re-telephoned the Military Secretary personally that afternoon, for about two hours later Simpson was summoned to the latter's office. There he was informed

> that I was in deep disgrace, having refused so highly prized an appointment as AA & QMG and the opportunity of going into battle the following week.
>
> He told me that I must realise that for the rest of the war I would remain an assistant military secretary at the War Office and would receive no promotion thereafter.
>
> I could not argue and I went away feeling even more sad than I had felt before.[1]

Bernard's tryanny obviously knew no bounds now, and he was prepared – through the Military Secretary – to freeze Simpson's entire military career because of it. Could this, by any stretch of the imagination, be considered normal behaviour?

It is important, however, to stress that such bouts of inconsideration, of vindictiveness and caprice that began more and more to mar Bernard's character from 1940 were not, so to speak, unknown to their author. Brian Montgomery tells the story how, in later years, when he presented his brother with a copy of his book *A Field-Marshal in the Family*, Bernard asked what sort of a book it was. 'I'm afraid it isn't always a nice portrait of you,' Brian answered sheepishly. 'Nice? But I'm not a "nice" person, Brian,' the bed-ridden Field-Marshal remonstrated.[2] Moreover, it is important not to take Bernard's more extreme behaviour out of context, but to see it within

---

[1] Wason interviews, loc. cit.
[2] Told to Lady Olive Hamilton.

The Rev. Henry Montgomery and his wife Maud, with their first child Sibyl, in Kennington, 1883. (*Private collection*)

Bernard Montgomery aged four. (*Private collection*)

New Park, Moville, built in
1773 and the Irish home of
the Montgomerys for almost
two centuries. (*Private
collection*)

Bernard Montgomery at
King's School, Canterbury,
summer of 1897, age ten.
(*Private collection*)

'Rather backward for his age', B. L. Montgomery performed poorly as a pupil, but represented St. Paul's School in swimming (in 1904, above), cricket and rugby football (in 1906, above right and right). (*By courtesy of St. Paul's School*)

The Victory Parade in Lille, 1918. Behind Lt-Col. Montgomery sits the Minister of Munitions, Mr Churchill. (*Imperial War Museum*)

The last family Christmas at Lenk, 1936, before Betty's tragic death in 1937.

Betty with son Dick. (*By courtesy of Col. Richard Carver*)

Bernard with the 'boys'. (*By courtesy of Col. Richard Carver*)

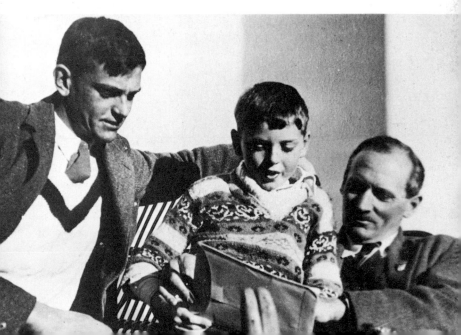

Brigadier in mourning: Brig. B. L. Montgomery, Commander of 9th Infantry Brigade and the Portsmouth Garrison, in dress uniform, with sword, March 1938. (*By courtesy of Col. Richard Carver*)

Palestine 1939: 'The rebellion out here as an organised movement is *smashed.*' Major-Gen. Montgomery confers with Gen. Haining, the C-in-C, during the visit of Lord Gort, CIGS (in background), Jerusalem, March 1939. (*By courtesy of Col. Richard Carver*)

Lt-General A. F. Brooke, GOC2 Corps, with his Commander 3rd
Division Maj-General B. L. Montgomery, in France, 6 December 1939.
(*Imperial War Museum*)

The Prime Minister, Mr. Churchill – resembling an American gangster – brings King Peter of Yugoslavia to visit the Commander of 12 Corps, Lt-Gen. B. L. Montgomery, 4 July 1941. (*Imperial War Museum*)

the framework of his extreme professionalism and the extreme urgency of the time. Dunkirk, under Gort, had been a disaster; under Brooke the new BEF might even avenge its defeat, but only if the divisions under his command were better equipped and led than their German counterparts. The 3rd Division, Bernard was adamant, would at least be better led.

He really felt that the 3rd Division, in the Dunkirk campaign, had proved his general methods of training. The division could stand up to the test of war – that the thing had worked. He wasn't going to re-open that sort of issue,

'Kit' Dawnay remembered almost forty years later.

Therefore his attitude was: We've seen off the Germans. There was no major disaster on the 3rd Division front during that period. It was a question, for him, of continuity. 'You know how to do it, and we're off again. The only thing to do now is to get reorganized with the right equipment – and with the right leaders.'[1]

Provision of new equipment rested with the War Office; provision of the right commanders, according to Bernard, did not.

Monty held a conference about the second day after he'd got back. He assembled his staff, his brigadiers, and the senior officers of every unit of the division, and announced who was to take command in each case. He did this unilaterally – without waiting for War Office approval he put in the men he wanted – like for instance making his GSO 2, Charles Bullen-Smith, CO of the 1st Battalion, KOSB. The appointments were all later rather unwillingly and crossly confirmed, but Monty said: 'We've no time. If we're going to go back and fight again I must get the right people in the right places *at once*, down to battalion commander level'. And it was the same story with his staff.[2]

As will be seen, not all Bernard's appointments were successful, and he would be the first to dismiss his own candidate if the choice proved unwise in battle; but his essential drive to get the 'right man for the right job' was for him the first lesson of Dunkirk, and would become, together with his unique ability to abstract the essentials of any problem, the touchstone of his genius as a commander. The conduct of battle had borne out how dependent a commander is on his subordinate officers; moreover the strains of modern war – particularly the almost hallucinatory effect of aerial attack – very

---

[1] Lt-Colonel C. P. Dawnay, loc. cit.
[2] Ibid.

quickly sorted the goats from the sheep. The most capable-seeming peacetime officers were not necessarily those who stood up best to the strain of battle. As Dawnay remembered, Bernard refused to indulge in recriminations: 'I'm not going to question anything you've done in the past,' he declared at his conference, 'I am simply going to re-organise the division on the best lines for the coming battle.'[1]

However deplorable, it is therefore understandable that Bernard should be upset when Simpson declined his appointment: for Bernard's choices, however necessary in the exigencies of war, were also gestures of faith. It will be seen that, once Bernard had identified a talented officer, he would leave no stone unturned in his efforts to guide his protégé upwards. This characteristic had long been in evidence – had been demonstrated from the 1920s, and was as pronounced when he was a company commander as when a battalion commander or staff college instructor. Now, however, in the changed atmosphere of war, without a wife or an abundance of close friends to whom he could 'unburden' himself, Bernard's choice of the officers who should lead his troops, the men who should comprise his staff, and the staff who should comprise his daily company, became matters of more than military logic. Having made his choice he rewarded loyalty with loyalty; and loyal company with love. As Galsworthy wrote in *The Apple Tree*, the British as a people are afraid to show real sentiment or feeling and are therefore interested only in lust; whereas Bernard Montgomery, however iron and ascetic his public image, was quite unafraid to show his private feelings. There is evidence that Bernard's concept of sexuality was primitive, to say the least: that the 'horizontal refreshment' he thought a natural outlet for his troops was not a powerful drive in his own life and had featured only as a very minor part of his relationship with Betty. This absence of sexuality suggests that from childhood onwards Bernard's normal drives were sublimated in his violent ambition to be a successful soldier; but, whatever the case, Bernard's sentimental self seems to have occupied a quite distinct part in his character. His feelings for his staff were feelings: feelings of which Bernard had no need to be ashamed. To Bernard the word love had an almost naïvely pure connotation. Deprived of the only woman to whom he had willingly surrendered his ego, charged by a growing sense of historic vocation, Bernard collected about him young officers whose intelligence he could respect and whose youth helped to keep him young himself. No one could ever say Bernard was happy in the years after Betty's death; but the company of his devoted staff came more and more to substitute for that lost relationship; and the very fact of their youth dispelled the nightmare of Betty's death. Perhaps this goes some way towards explaining Bernard's apparent fetish about the length of his subordinates'

[1] Ibid.

384

hair – as is movingly demonstrated in a letter which Bernard wrote to 'Kit' Dawnay in September of 1940. He had seen his brilliant ex-CRA (Commander, Royal Artillery) Roland Towell the day before, and was strangely worried:

> He looked to me to have aged somewhat, but this can hardly be the result of his marriage 5 days ago. Possibly it was because he wanted his hair cutting! Don't let him get old and mossy.[1]

To the last days of his life death frightened Bernard – 'going over Jordan' as he called it. This fear was ironic in someone so utterly fearless on the battlefield; but it was so and helps further to explain his need of and interest in young people.

As much as Bernard feared death, so he was fearless in acknowledging the good things in life. He looked upon his young ADC in the 3rd Division, Charles Sweeny, as a father might on his favourite son; and, when Sweeny was posted back to the Royal Ulster Rifles in the autumn of 1940, Bernard was desolate:

> I have lost my Charles; I really do miss him terribly and life seems quite different without him. We have been through a good deal together and I have a very great and real affection for him; I had to let him go though. He is a dear lad and I hope and pray no harm will come to him in this war . . .[2]

Alas, harm would come, as it did later to another of Bernard's chosen young companions on his staff, John Poston. How little the charge of homosexuality comes near to the essence of these relationships! Nor is the matter one of confidentiality or privacy. In his *Memoirs* Bernard openly confessed of Sweeny: 'He was a delightful Irish boy and I loved him dearly.' For Bernard there was no shame in love; moreover it was this quasi-paternal affection for his young staff which would become an essential component in Bernard's mystique as a Commander. Allied to Norman ruthlessness there was visible to the lowliest soldier in Bernard's army a paternal affection, a regard for the conditions of service, a concern with casualties, an awareness of the importance of family that would distinguish him from almost every other commander of his time and earn him perhaps his greatest epithet: 'the people's General'.

Such things were, however, scarcely predictable in June 1940 as Bernard's almost messianic fervour threatened to turn the 3rd Division against him and destroy the future career of a recalcitrant assistant to the Military Secretary in Whitehall. Although Bernard regained the loyalty of his division, as has been seen, and even saw

[1] Letter of 20.9.40, Dawnay Papers.
[2] Ibid.

fit to forgive Colonel Simpson his *faux pas*, to others he often seemed on the borderline of insanity – dictatorial, aggressive and insubordinate. Yet the record of his work in the 3rd Division after his return from Dunkirk is phenomenal, and demonstrates clearly Bernard was driving himself harder than anyone. The day he arrived at the 3rd Division's Frome HQ on 6 June, he began by reconsidering his formula for the organisation of a modern mobile divisional HQ – subsequently laying down the protocol for movement in battle, and giving also signal, transport and defence requirements. On 8, 10, 11, 12, 14, 15 and 17 June Bernard held GOCs conferences, covering everything from billets to training, from grants to movement plans back to France. By 10 June all commanders were to give Bernard written views on the lessons learnt during the Dunkirk campaign, and on 14 June Bernard issued a five-page memorandum: 'Important lessons from the operation of the BEF in France and Belgium May 1940', together with some twenty-two pages of appendices. He was the first to acknowledge the superiority of German tactics:

> When gaining contact with the Germans it will be found that they come very quickly into action against troops in position, and in doing so they will seldom expose themselves.
>
> They are experts at concealment.
>
> Within a short time of gaining contact the Germans establish an extremely efficient observation and sniping organisation, and this is quickly followed by heavy mortar fire on our forward positions in order to shake the morale of our infantry.
>
> They then begin to tap all along the front and finally make attempts to break through at certain places; once they have gained a footing in our defences they are very good at exploiting success by infiltration. Artillery is quickly into action and shelling of rear areas starts very soon, and is very accurate.
>
> His methods of wireless DF [Direction Finding] are quite excellent; accurate fire is brought to bear in a very short time on any wireless set which opens up, and sets have to be well away from HQ; use remote control, and move frequently if they open up.
>
> The Germans carried out all their operations by day, and at night merely had defensive patrols on the front.
>
> It may be said at once that the German technique was first class.
>
> It was extremely difficult to locate any German positions; one very seldom saw a German except an occasional one dodging among the houses.
>
> As a contrast, the British soldier was very careless in exposing himself; he would dig in the open daylight with NCOs standing about supervising the work; officers would visit posts with no attempt at concealment till fired at.
>
> It all had to be paid for in blood; positions were given away, and

the inevitable and accurate mortar fire soon followed.

The lesson was soon learned, and after one or two encounters the Germans never got much change out of the 3rd Division.

What the Germans most disliked, Bernard claimed, was concentrated artillery fire – an observation which, more than any other, was to influence Bernard's approach to warfare from this moment onwards. On 17 June at 9.50 a.m. Bernard addressed all 466 officers of the 3rd Division – the first of his great wartime addresses to large audiences, and prefaced by a new rule: namely that there must be no coughing or throat-clearing once he began to speak. It was the first sign of Bernard's realisation that, to command a large body of men successfully, he must become known to them all, not only by sight as in unit inspections, but by his ideas and their presentation. Several officers have maintained, thinking back to Bernard's addresses in 1940, that he was a poor speaker: that he had a high-pitched voice and attempted to say too much in his talks. Yet reference to Bernard's actual pencilled notes for the address on 17 June – probably written on the train from London to Somerset – suggests that he was much more anxious about the nature of his address as a performance than with details. For instance he deliberately divided this first address into two parts, separated by an interval. In the first part he referred back to the Dunkirk campaign, and the actions both of the 3rd Division and its German opponents. At the end of this he mentioned the distinguished performance of Brigadier Robb – and presented him publicly with the DSO. Only after the interval did he map out the areas which he wanted the 3rd Division to concentrate upon in its future training – culminating in the instillation in its soldiers of such a high level of morale 'that they will have complete confidence in their ability to take on any enemy at any time'.

By the evening of 17 June, however, the Division began to move to a new area. Not only was it to prepare for possible Combined Operations abroad, but to take responsibilty for the defences of the Brighton-Bognor sector of the south-east coast of England, nominally under the aegis of 12 Corps. Secret War Office information suggested the Germans would invade between 2 and 9 July. In view of the imminence of such an assault, Bernard called on 30 June a commanders' conference at which he outlined draconian new proposals: all training for special War Office operations would cease and the division would dispose itself to meet an enemy landing. In doing so it would, however, be hampered by the local population. It was difficult to get the troops to realise that Britain might be invaded within forty-eight hours, Bernard declared, and for this he blamed 'the presence of women, children and evacuees in the beach area. Many schools were still open. It was necessary to tighten up everything,' Bernard told his commanders. He therefore ordered 'that the following action be taken':

a) All beaches, esplanades and amusement parks on sea fronts were to be cleared of all civilians by 1700 hrs daily (beginning 1 July), and that no civilians would be allowed on them until 0500 hrs next morning. Troops would be used to help the police.
b) Wives and families of officers and men were to leave the Div area on Monday 1 July and were not to return.
c) An endeavour was to be made to get all women and children and schools etc. to be sent away. He expected that the Duke of Norfolk would be able to help in this.[1]

This new policy created consternation not only in the 3rd Division, but in the Brighton-Bognor area.

The Divisional Commander said we had now got to the stage where we must do what we like as regards upsetting private property. If a house was required as an HQ it must be taken. Any material required to improve the defences should be taken. On matters of this nature unit commanders must decide for themselves and must not decentralise. Kindness, firmness and politeness was all that was required.[2]

It is easy to see how unpopular Bernard became as a result. After all, he was a single man, and did not possess a home that could be expropriated as an HQ, or even be demolished for purposes of defence. Brian Horrocks had been appointed by Bernard to command the 9th Infantry Brigade on 17 June; even he was surprised. 'Monty used to pay constant visits,' Horrocks recalled. ' "Who lives in that house?" he would say pointing to some building which partly masked the fire from one of our machine-gun positions. "Have them out, Horrocks. Blow up the house. Defence must come first."'[3]

It was from this moment, as Bernard's reputation as the 'mad' General began to grow, that apocryphal stories also began to abound. Wives were forced to adopt assumed names, and ingenuity was put to great test in order to avoid the harsh effects of Bernard's ruthless policy. Many who suffered would never forgive him, and his later fame in battle only served to inflame their prejudice. More and more he became a general one either admired or detested.

To what extent Bernard deliberately sought such a reputation is debatable. While his actions were militarily correct there was nevertheless an occasional indisputable, almost impish, delight in dictatorship, as will be seen. Yet side by side with this exercise of power went a continual concern for the welfare of his men – as illustrated by a confidential memorandum on 'Present Conditions of Service', which Bernard issued to all his unit commanders on 6 July, in which

[1] War Diary, HQ 3rd Division, loc. cit.
[2] Ibid.
[3] B. Horrocks, *A Full Life*, op. cit.

he drew attention to the fact that many of the privileges of active service abroad – better rations, free postage, free cigarettes, cheap cinema and entertainment, etc. – were no longer available to the soldier in England. 'It is essential to keep the troops happy and contented,' Bernard emphasised. 'Every Unit Commander must hold the balance evenly between the work to be done and keeping his men happy and contented'[1] – particularly during the daytime when there was no danger of an invasion without prior warning.

In fact Bernard disliked Ironside's policy of beach defence, and when on 2 July Winston Churchill visited the 3rd Division, Bernard challenged it. It was the first time Bernard had ever spoken to Churchill, and he made sure the 3rd Division was at its most impressive by arranging a mobile counter-attack on an aerodrome near Lancing that was supposed to have been captured by the Germans. Churchill then invited Bernard to dine with him in Brighton – a fateful meal at which Churchill displayed his wit, and Bernard his military ideas.

'He asked me what I would drink at dinner and I replied – water,' Bernard remembered in his *Memoirs*. 'This astonished him. I added that I neither drank or smoked and was 100 per cent fit; he replied in a flash that he both drank and smoked and was 200 per cent fit.' Of all the stories told about Churchill and Montgomery, this would become the most quoted; yet the meeting itself was to have important ramifications for the defence of Britain in the days, months and even years ahead.

'The 3rd Division . . . was deployed in an anti-invasion role,' Bernard recalled elsewhere, 'on the South Coast to the west of Brighton. In those days I was not impressed by politicians; indeed I knew little about them. But I was keen to see this politician who for many years before the war had been telling a series of governments what would happen. They had not listened and now it had happened. He impressed me enormously on this our first meeting and not only because he approved wholeheartedly of my dispositions. I refused to string my divisions out as you spread butter on bread, being weak everywhere and strong nowhere. I deployed a minimum in the front line to break up and disorganise any invasion and kept the maximum in reserve for counter-attack. He was delighted with these mobile reserves and kept referring to them as "leopards, waiting to pounce on the enemy."'[2]

Having sought Churchill's approval of his tactical strategy, Bernard then asked Churchill why his division – the only division to emerge virtually intact from Dunkirk, and the only one highly trained as a motorised division – could not at least 'be given buses, and be held in mobile reserve with a counter-attack role.'[3] Churchill

[1] Montgomery Papers.
[2] Draft article by Field-Marshal Montgomery for the *Sunday Times*, 7.6.63.
[3] *Memoirs*, op. cit.

agreed to take the matter up. He was as good as his word, and the next day sent a memorandum to the Secretary of State for War, appropriating Bernard's views as his own:

I was disturbed to find the 3rd Division spread along thirty miles of coast, instead of being as I had imagined held back concentrated in reserve, ready to move against any serious head of invasion.

Moreover Churchill declared himself 'astonished' that the division had not been provided with buses when there were at that moment 'a large number of buses even now plying for pleasure traffic up and down the sea-front at Brighton'.[1] Enquiries were made; not unnaturally GHQ Home Forces resented the way a mere divisional commander should voice objection to GHQ policy and practice. 'General Montgomery did not give you quite the whole picture,' General Ismay, the Military Secretary to the War Cabinet, replied to the Prime Minister on 4 July: if necessary a divisional commander had authority to hire transport 'for the conveyance of one brigade'. Churchill was not appeased. In red ink he scrawled across Ismay's letter: 'The 3rd Division *above all* should be fully mobile in every brigade. Has this been done? When is it going to be withdrawn into reserve?'

In the face of such badgering GHQ gave in. The 3rd Division would, its Chief-of-Staff wrote on 9 July, be withdrawn into reserve 'within the next few days' and be made one hundred per cent mobile.

There is evidence, however, that Bernard's complaint to Churchill had a more far-reaching effect than even Bernard knew at the time, for Churchill took the 3rd Division Commander's other remarks about meeting a German invasion very much to heart – and it may not be exaggerating to say that it contributed to the imminent downfall of the C-in-C Home Forces, General Ironside. For, enthused by Bernard's views on mobile defence, Churchill fired a new broadside on 8 July, this time addressed to Ismay, Ironside and Dill: 'Knowing that we are in complete agreement on the main principles of defence against invasion,' he began,

I think it necessary to press most strongly for the carrying out of those principles in action. A division in reserve is worth 6 divisions on the beaches. Since only one in seven will in all probability be present at the points of impact we have at the present time only a sixth of our divisions in reserve, where the aim must be to have at least a third. It would seem therefore that during the next few days we should add at least two divisions, presumably the 3rd and 1st, to the Mobile Reserve, which can certainly be applied to the battle. It would be well if another two divisions could be pulled out next week.

[1] W. S. Churchill, *Their Finest Hour*, London 1949.

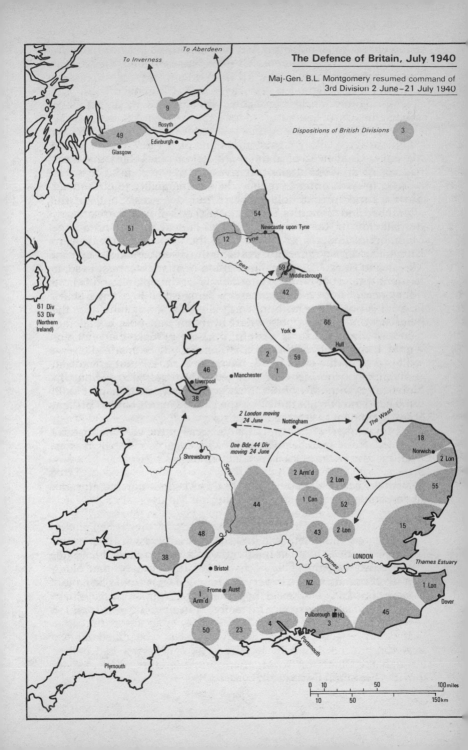

The Defence of Britain, July 1940

Maj-Gen. B.L. Montgomery resumed command of
3rd Division 2 June – 21 July 1940

To Inverness

To Aberdeen

9

Rosyth

49

Edinburgh ●

Glasgow

Dispositions of British Divisions 3

5

51

54

Newcastle upon Tyne

12 *Tyne*

Tees

59

Middlesbrough ●

42

66

York ● 59

Hull

2

59

61 Div
53 Div
(Northern
Ireland)

46

● Liverpool

● Manchester

1

38

*2 London moving
24 June*

● Nottingham

The Wash

18

Norwich ●

2 Lon

*One Bde 44 Div
moving 24 June*

● Shrewsbury

Severn

2 Arm'd

2 Lon

55

44

1 Can

52

15

43

2 Lon

48

Thames

LONDON

Thames Estuary

38

● Bristol

NZ

1 Lon

1
Arm'd

Frome ●

● Aust

Dover

Pulborough ■ HD

3

45

50

23

4

Portsmouth

Plymouth

0 10   50   100 miles

10   50   150 km

The next day Ironside replied that he was 'completely in agreement with you' that GHQ reserves should be strengthened, and that he was proposing to 'pull out the 3rd Division and move it into reserve in the Southern Command'. However, as to Churchill's 'main principles of defence against invasion', Ironside was by no means in agreement:

I do not agree with your statement that only 1 in 7 of the forward divisions is likely to be at the points of contact. I think that if the Germans decide to attempt an invasion, they will do so on a very broad front in order to reduce their vulnerability to air and sea attack, and to find 'soft spots' in our defences. South of the Humber and along the South Coast they will use a great many small craft for this purpose and will endeavour to land a large number of troops over a wide area; they will also endeavour to capture a certain number of ports for the disembarkation of tanks, guns and stores. To meet this method of attack we must to some extent spread our forces to guard likely landing places and to hold the enemy whilst mobile forces are being called to counter-attack . . . It is possible to withdraw any division at any time from the beaches and to move it elsewhere by motor transport, but I do not consider it would serve a useful purpose to make plans for this until I know where the enemy's effort will be made. Reserve divisions, on the other hand, have plans worked out to move in any direction in which they are likely to be required to operate. If a division is withdrawn from the beaches I have no transport to fill the gap, and I do not think that the Home Guards have at present the equipment to fit them for this role.

I am so short of troops that large areas of the coast and inland which I feel should be protected, have no garrisons; to be reasonably secure I need at least another 6 divisions . . .

Churchill would have no truck with this Maginot-minded attitude. He applauded Ironside's proposal to pull Montgomery's 3rd Division into reserve, but deplored Ironside's views on invasion:

I find it very difficult to visualize the kind of invasion all along the coast by troops carried in small craft, and even in boats. I have not seen any evidence of large masses of this class of craft being assembled, and except in very narrow waters it would be a most hazardous and even suicidal operation to commit a large army to the accidents of the sea in the teeth of our very numerous armed patrolling forces . . .

According to the Admiralty no large German vessels had passed through the Straits of Dover; there was therefore no immediate threat to the South Coast at all:

Even more unlikely is it that the South Coast would be attacked. We know that no great mass of shipping exists in the French ports, and that the number of small boats there is not great. The Dover barrage is being replenished and extended to the French shore . . . Therefore I find it difficult to believe that the South Coast is in serious danger at the present time . . .

In Churchill's view, the only possible threat would be from 'the Dutch and German harbours', aimed at the East Coast: and even this he was inclined to discount – a 'fishing boat invasion', as he called it, that seemed far too hazardous for the Germans to risk.

I hope, therefore, relying on the above reasoning to be checked with the Admiralty, that you will be able to bring an even larger proportion of your forward divisions back from the coast into support or reserve so that their training may proceed in the highest forms of offensive warfare and counter-attack, and that the coast, as it becomes fortified, will be increasingly confided to troops other than those of the forward divisions, and also the Home Guard. I am sure you will be in agreement with this view in principle, and the only question will be the speed of the transformation.

Bernard cannot have known the ripples his remarks to Churchill had caused – though the above letters were subsequently filed by the Cabinet Office under the heading 'Home Forces: the 3rd Division';[1] however, he was delighted to be informed by GHQ Home Forces that his division was to be given a 'mobile offensive role', leaving a thin screen of non-divisional troops to man the beach defences. The 3rd Division 'may be required to operate at short notice in South Wales, in relief of a threat to Bristol, or on the Dorset coast', as Bernard pointed out in operation instructions on 13 July, and his detailed notes on the conduct of such a counter-attack role shows how much he was now following the example set by the Germans in the Dunkirk campaign:

The drill and technique of recce parties must be overhauled, and be thoroughly understood by every officer, WO and NCO. They must realise that time is best saved by thinking and working ahead; to rush units into battle without giving them time to reconnoitre and make preparations merely tends to increase casualties.

The organisation for observation must be such that it is 'in being', and working well, *before* contact is gained.

The sniping organisation must be capable of putting forward its

[1] CAB 120/237, 239 and 438, PRO.

maximum effort the moment that the first enemy soldier is seen.

On gaining contact the enemy infantry must be at once sub-jected to mortar and artillery fire; this will shake its morale and prepare the way for attacks by our own troops . . .

With wide fronts it will not be possible to attack the enemy all along his front.

Attacks by one or two companies at selected points, supported by concentrated artillery fire, will often give better results; and having broken into the enemy front at a number of points, success should be exploited by infiltration through these points.[1]

The first divisional exercise to be held since the return from Dunkirk was arranged for 25 and 26 July, and although training had to be considerably revised owing to the absence of any infantry tanks, divisional cavalry or even specialised reconnaissance units, the exercise was planned very much on the lines of its forerunners in France during the 'phoney' war: movement by the entire division, gaining contact with an enemy force, halting enemy movement on a chosen line; followed this time by attack rather than withdrawal. Bernard's mastery of such exercises was now at last acknowledged, and there is no doubt that they were to become the inspiration and model for all large-scale exercises held in Britain over the next two years. Moreover, if Bernard was incorporating the lessons of German success at Dunkirk in his training policies, he never lost sight of his own deep-seated doctrine: namely that an army must be trained and commanded as a cohesive whole, with paramount emphasis on communications, and a deliberate refusal to allow units to decentral-ise and split up.

However, even before Bernard's first divisional exercise on Eng-lish soil could take place, he received news of his promotion. On 21 July he issued his second Special Order of the Day:

1. It is with great regret that I have to announce my departure from the 3rd Division.

On 30 May I issued a farewell order to the Division in France, when I left to take over command of 2nd Corps.

But I managed to return to the Division on arrival back in England, in order to help in its re-equipping.

This time there is no escape; I have been promoted to command 5th Corps and leave the Division tomorrow.

2. I cannot express adequately my feelings on leaving the Divi-sion.

I have always tried to give of my best in order that the Division should fight with every advantage in the battle; it has been my

[1] 3rd Div Operation Instruction No. 6, 14 July 1940, Montgomery Papers.

constant hope that the officers and men of the Division would have confidence in my leadership.

All ranks have responded magnificently, and the 3rd Division has a reputation in the Army which fills me with pride.

I would like to thank all officers and men for the way in which they have striven to increase the fighting efficiency of the Division; it is their efforts, and not mine, which enabled the Division to 'see off' the Germans so successfully.

3.   And so I say good-bye to the 3rd Division, in which I have so many friends among the officers and also among the rank and file.

We shall meet again, I hope often. And I shall always follow the fortunes of the 3rd Division with great interest.

Good-bye to you all.

B. L. Montgomery
Major-General[1]

It was the last document he would sign as a Major-General. On 22 July 1940 Bernard became a Lieutenant-General, and Commander of 5 Corps.

---

[1] Montgomery Papers.

CHAPTER EIGHT

Corps Commander

Bernard's promotion to Corps Commander resulted directly from the dismissal of Sir Edmund Ironside as C-in-C Home Forces – a post Ironside had held for scarcely seven weeks since his deputy Sir John Dill became CIGS. On 19 July Ironside was sacked, made a Field-Marshal, and placed on the retired list. Sir Alan Brooke became C-in-C Home Forces, and Lt-General Auchinleck took over Brooke's post as GOC Southern Command. Major-General Eastwood, the new commander of the 4th Division, temporarily assumed command of 5 Corps; but on 21 July, presumably at the instigation of Alan Brooke, Bernard Montgomery was given the command.

The manner in which Alan Brooke took charge of the defence of Great Britain in the summer of 1940 is well known. Ironside declined to hand over command in person, nor did he leave a single word as to the dispositions, state of readiness or policy of the Home Forces – only a piece of paper regarding his privately owned Rolls-Royce at his disposal as Commander-in-Chief. Yet within months Brooke made himself master of the situation in an endless tour by road, rail and air of all the units under his command, and showed his determination to provide vigorous leadership 'from the top'.

Auchinleck, too, was an obvious choice for promotion, being a natural leader of men and the soul of integrity. After his experience in Norway, Auchinleck was determined to repel a German invasion by denying the Germans use of the southern coast beaches and then, if there was time, raising a special armoured reserve to deal with any German pockets which did manage to penetrate the beach defences. From the moment he had formed 5 Corps HQ in June 1940 Auchinleck had pursued this policy. 'Throughout this planning period,' the 5 Corps War Diary recorded at the end of June, 'the policy laid down was that the enemy is to be defeated on the beaches.'[1] On 25 June Auchinleck instructed Major-General Martel, the Commander of 50th Division, 'to have, in the first stage, field defences sited well forward on the beaches',[2] and in a letter to the VCIGS on 29 June he wrote, 'I am sure that we should make every effort to prevent the

---

[1] War Diary, HQ 5 Corps (WO 166/249), PRO.
[2] John Connell, *Auchinleck*, op. cit.

enemy landing on the beach. I still believe that this is the most difficult task, and my recent small experience confirms me in this opinion . . . Until he can get his heavy stuff ashore the enemy cannot do much. Therefore he must be prevented by all possible means from getting it ashore . . . Once he does establish himself at all securely it won't be possible to get him out, if experience goes for anything.'[1] Auchinleck was convinced that 'lack of equipment and transport does not make it possible for us to fight a mobile battle in the interior' and that it was therefore the 'right policy' to 'have all our goods in the front window'.[2] Nevertheless he hoped that when the equipment did come through it would be possible to stage inland counter-attacks, and on 23 June he had specified to Southern Command the composition of such a counter-attack force, amounting to a full armoured division. It was to include one armoured brigade, one infantry brigade, one tank regiment, one light anti-aircraft regiment, two companies of Engineers, two machine-gun battalions and a Field Ambulance unit. Not unnaturally, in the context of June and July 1940, Southern Command held out no hope of providing such a mobile reserve.

It was in this context, however, that Bernard Montgomery took over 5 Corps from Auchinleck: and the stage was set for that unfortunate quarrel that would never be resolved in their lifetime.

Bernard was now one of Britain's six home Corps Commanders, a Lieutenant-General, and the recipient, in the King's July Birthday Honours, of the Companion of the Order of the Bath (CB) for his services in the BEF campaign. He drove over to Melchett Court on 21 July to meet Auchinleck at his HQ and arrange the take-over; and he left with Auchinleck's Brigadier General Staff a list of the officers he wished to see the next day, and at what times. His drilling blue eyes and brisk manner left no doubt there was to be a shake-up; and within hours, on 22 July, the first explosions came.

It is difficult not to sympathise with Auchinleck. It was his fate in Norway, at 5 Corps, at Southern Command, and subsequently in the North African desert to be given tasks beyond his resources: and to be followed, both at 5 Corps and in the desert, by a difficult if not mad general who did everything possible to disparage his predecessor's efforts. From Bernard's point of view, however, the matter was not so straightforward. If Bernard despised Gort for his boy-scout brain, the same could not be said of Auchinleck, who was a soldier of undoubted intellect. Yet it would seem that Bernard, in taking over 5 Corps from Auchinleck, was determined not only to erase his predecessor in the minds of the Corps, but to diminish him to insignificance now that General Auchinleck was GOC Southern Command and Bernard's own boss. Bernard arrived early on 22 July

[1] Ibid.
[2] Ibid.

at Melchett Court and immediately gave out a new policy, without reference to the C-in-C. Work on the beach defences was to be stopped. Auchinleck's request for an armoured division to provide a mobile counter-offensive reserve was to be scrapped: 5 Corps would instantly be re-organised so that it could provide its *own* mobile reserves. At 1.30 p.m. the first orders to this effect left 5 Corps HQ:

Now that great progress has been made all along the front in the making of defences and obstacles against an enemy landing, steps must be taken to reduce the number of troops in the forward areas, so far as may be possible, in order to increase the strength of the mobile reserves.[1]

This done, Bernard turned his attention to the heads of the services at Corps HQ and the HQ staff itself. By late afternoon the first dismissals had been made; at the same time no less than seven motor contact officers were requested from the War Office – the forerunners of Bernard's famous band of liaison officers that he would build up in the North African desert and thereafter. The number of Intelligence officers was also increased.

5 Corps comprised, in July 1940, only two divisions: the 4th and the 50th, both of which Bernard had already commanded in the Dunkirk perimeter at the end of May. 5 Corps area included, however, the entire south coast sector from Bognor to Lyme Regis, including the Isle of Wight, so that for instance the garrison of Portsmouth which Bernard had commanded in the 9th Infantry Brigade in 1937 also came under his operational jurisdiction. No sooner had Bernard swept into 5 Corps HQ with his new broom than he swept out again on a personal inspection of his new domain. On 23 July he visited the 4th Division; and forthwith issued the first of his confidential but little-concealed reports that were to bring him into collision with his C-in-C, to whom they were submitted.[2]

This first document was so uncompromisingly frank it must have taken Auchinleck's breath away. Not only had the new Commander of 5 Corps overturned his beach-defence policy on the first day of his command, not only had he 'reformed' the corps HQ but he was now tendering a devastating report on the operational efficiency of the prime division in the Corps whose command Auchinleck had relinquished only days before.

Although Bernard complimented 4th Division on the work it had done on sector defences, the 'general condition of the division' was very far from satisfactory, he stated in the report.

The artillery is definitely below standard; at Div HQ there is a lack of knowledge of artillery and how it should be handled, and the

[1] War Diary, HQ 5 Corps, loc. cit.
[2] Montgomery Papers.

power of artillery as a battle winning factor is not understood.

The Division lacks all those finer points which make for battle efficiency and which save casualties:

a) no organisation within the unit for observation and sniping
b) no adjustments on vehicles for making it possible to bring into action every Bren gun against enemy aircraft
c) no arrangements for using mortars from the carriers
d) no proper lighting system on vehicles to enable big scale night movements to take place without being seen from the air
e) no motor contact officers
f) no night driving practice without lights etc. etc.

Without all these things the Division is at a disadvantage from the start.

The reason for this was not lack of enthusiasm, but the quality of leadership and direction at the top, Bernard felt:

There is a lack of knowledge at Div HQ as to what is wanted.

There is no one there who knows. G2 *should* know, but he is quite useless.

Bernard's remedy was straightforward:

There is a lot of 'dead wood' which must be cut out.
The following should be removed at once:
   CRA [Commander, Royal Artillery]
   Two Field Regiment Commanders
   CRASC [Commander, Royal Army Service Corps]
   GSO 2
The Division requires a really high class GSO 2 who has had recent experience in France and Belgium.

I have discussed the removal of the above with the Div Commander: he agrees and is taking action; he should have done so before.

As for the defence of the Isle of Wight, under 4th Division, Bernard was equally surgical:

In the Isle of Wight the CO of the 50th (Holding) Battalion, Hampshire Regiment, is far too old and quite unfit to command a battle with an operational role, or in fact any battle.

He must be removed at once. I have told the Divisional Commander to take action.

Nor was the Divisional Commander himself spared:

Generally the 4th Division has gone back somewhat. It lacks that sure and firm guidance from the top; it lacks a strong commander, who knows exactly what is wanted and exactly how to set about getting it.

This somewhat brazen analysis was tempered by a final note of optimism – an increasingly characteristic Montgomery technique whereby salvation was assured if left in Bernard's willing hands:

> The Division will need a lot of help. It must be done kindly and tactfully, through the Divisional Commander and his GSO 1; the latter is out of his depth somewhat but will train.
>   They are both delightful people to deal with and there will be no difficulty. Every point I have suggested so far has been seized on at once with delight, and noted for action.

If not entrusted to Bernard 'there was no doubt' that the Division 'would have a lot of unnecessary casualties', he declared.

The 'delightful' GSO 1 of the 4th Division was in fact none other than 'Simbo' Simpson who, several days after Bernard's damning forecast of his career, had been appointed to the post by the Military Secretary. Fortunately Simpson had written to congratulate his erstwhile commander on the award of the CB when the King's Honours were published; and by return of post Bernard had thanked him, adding:

> I am sorry you did not feel able to come and serve under me, but thinking it over I now quite agree with you. You said that you would have let me down. You are quite right. In those circumstances you would have let me down. But don't worry; another opportunity will surely arise soon and I will then get hold of you again for a job under me.[1]

Simpson was therefore all the more relieved that he had been 're-accepted into Monty's fold, as it were' when Bernard suddenly appeared on 23 July as the new Corps Commander.[2]

By comparison with his report on the 4th Division, Bernard's assessment of the Portsmouth Area of 5 Corps was, if anything, even more damning. Bernard had spent the following days of 24 and 25 July visiting the sector – which included the Isle of Wight, the garrison at Portsmouth, and the surrounding area – and his report began by insisting on the dismissal of the Area Commander and a number of his staff:

[1] Wason interviews, loc. cit.
[2] Ibid.

After a whole day spent in close investigation of the situation in the Portsmouth Area I have no hesitation in saying that the Area Commander, and certain members of his staff, should be at once removed.

The situation in Portsmouth itself is particularly bad. There are some 8000 armed men in the garrison,

Bernard pointed out,

which is ample for defence needs as there are a large number of armed sailors in addition. But the organisation and administration has been very sketchy; reserve supplies are all held centrally instead of each unit having two or three days of its own; medical arrangements are practically nil; the late Garrison Commander seems to have done nothing. The Area Commander has exercised no supervision and taken no steps to see that things were put on a proper basis.

The new Garrison Commander was, in Bernard's view, 'a first-class chap and a very live wire; he is doing his best to put things right'. He had sacked his Adjutant as being 'unfit for his job and actively disloyal'; but the Area Commander had then recommended this erstwhile Adjutant for employment on the Provost's staff – to Bernard's indignation:

This of course is complete nonsense; having failed and proved himself disloyal, his services should be dispensed with. His age is 46.

As for the defenders of the Isle of Wight, the 8th Battalion, the Hampshire Regiment, Bernard was almost disbelieving:

The CO is 63.
The 2nd i/c is 59.
I interviewed several platoon commanders of 55.

Originally recruited as officers in the Home Guard, these men now commanded companies of young recruits:

The battalion has been ordered to form coys of young soldiers, boys of 18 years old.
I saw one of these companies at Stubbington.
It is absurd to allow these companies of boys to be commanded by old men of between 50 and 60, and this matter should be taken in hand urgently,

the fifty-two-year-old Corps Commander demanded.

401

The CO is a really pathetic sight. He served in South Africa in 1899; he is very old, frail, and looks very ill. He should be removed from command at once, and sent away to end his life in peace somewhere.

The 2nd i/c is old and decrepit, and should go at once.

All the officers should be checked over, and the worst cases replaced by younger men.

For this to happen, though, a new area commander was necessary. Although a 'nice person', the existing Commander was 'quite unable to stand up to exacting cross-examination' by Bernard.

He is ineffective, lacks initiative, energy and drive and is obviously extremely idle.

He is quite unfit to be a Major-General, and should be relieved of his command at once and placed on retired pay.

The AA & QMG was similarly disparaged:

An old retired officer of the 60th Rifles. Is idle and has taken to drink. He should never have been made the senior administrative staff officer of an important area. He is a director of a brewery, and farms his own estate. His services should be dispensed with at once and he should go back to his farm.

The Commander of the Royal Engineers brought up the rear in this catalogue of senility and alcoholic indolence:

Completely and utterly useless. He has served many years in India and is prematurely aged; has also taken to drink. He is unable to explain anything clearly and gives the impression of being mentally deficient. He is a serving regular soldier and should be retired at once.

Bernard signed this report on his return from the Portsmouth Area on 25 July and certainly forwarded it, with his notes on the 4th Division, to Auchinleck, for he ended by saying:

The Portsmouth Area is only under 5 Corps operationally. I presume that if it is intended to take action as recommended by me, then such action will be initiated by Command HQ.

On the other hand if the GOC-in-C would prefer that I should put the matter forward officially, and initiate the necessary adverse reports, I am quite prepared to do so.

What Auchinleck felt when he received this we do not know; but, if he hoped that by ignoring Bernard's recommendations – and the suggestion at the end of the report that Bernard should go direct to the War Office in the matter – the problem would disappear, Auchinleck was sadly mistaken; for three days later, on 28 July, Bernard produced yet another report. This time it concerned the other division in the Corps, Major-General Martel's 50th Division. Although couched in more discreet language, complimenting the Division on its high morale and 'amazing' work on beach defences, it was if anything an even more direct attack on Auchinleck's defensive strategy:

The standard of training in the Division is low. All energies have been directed to work on the defences . . . The nett result is that all the finer arts of how to compete with the Germans in battle have been put in the background. There are men who have never in their lives fired more than 5 rounds with the rifle; there are men who have never fired the Bren gun; the use of carriers is not practised; the Headquarters of formations and units are untrained; the technique of observation and sniping as learnt from the Germans is untouched; and so on . . .

The result of concentrating entirely on defensive works and neglecting other matters is going to reflect adversely on the battle efficiency of the Division unless we are careful. I met companies who had been in the same place for one month, doing nothing but dig and work on defences. The men had done no drill, no PT, no training. The men did not seem to be on their toes; I did not see the light of battle in their eyes.

'The best defences in the world are in themselves of little value unless the troops in them are full of beans and mentally alert,' Bernard warned, no doubt remembering the BEF campaign and the fatal French belief in the Maginot Line. 'The Division would fight well defensively, and would put up a dogged resistance,' he acknowledged, recollecting their plucky performance before Dunkirk.

But it is on a front of over 80 miles; fluid fighting would develop and in its present state the Division has no hope of competing with the Germans in mobile war with any reasonable chance of success. I have discussed the matter with the Divisional Commander, and he agrees.[1]

Bernard then promised that he could put the matter right in 'two months' if Auchinleck let him have his way: namely by allowing Bernard to reverse the defensive policy of facing the enemy on the beaches; refusing to allow any further removal of trained officers or NCOs from the Division; and by reducing the Division's eighty-mile front.

[1] Montgomery Papers.

403

Auchinleck was furious, perhaps understandably. By return of messenger he thanked Bernard for his notes and agreed with 'much of what you say'; but insisted that the work on beach defences continue:

> I want to make it quite clear, however, that I wish the instructions as to the urgent need for the completion of the defences so as to admit of the withdrawal of men for training, which I issued to the Corps just before I left (Operation Instruction No. 14) carried out. I intend to issue a Command Instruction to the same effect.

Nor did he agree with Bernard's estimate of two months as the time that it would take to bring the 50th Division back to offensive operational ability, judging himself that a minimum of six months was required. Furthermore, although he agreed that it was wrong of the War Office to withdraw trained personnel from the Division at this critical moment, he emphasised that 'orders are orders and will, of course, be obeyed'.[1]

The two Commanders were thus at loggerheads – at the very moment when, across the Channel, German divisions were carrying out intensive training for 'Operation Sea Lion' – the invasion of Southern England. This was unfortunate – certainly one cannot imagine that, Churchill's defiant speeches notwithstanding, the Germans would have had much difficulty in conquering Britain in the aftermath of Dunkirk, had they been able to subdue Britain's air defences. History would prove, on the coast of Normandy, that not even the best defended beaches can withstand a concentrated assault, and Auchinleck was probably wrong to sacrifice divisional training and battle efficiency for beach protection. In fact the disagreement between Bernard and Auchinleck provides a clear illustration not only of their different styles of leadership, but a distinct preview of their differences at Alamein. Historians would later argue that, if Auchinleck had not been relieved in the North African desert, he would have pursued the same course as Montgomery and with equal success. Even Auckinleck's BGS, Brigadier A. A. B. Dowler, recorded in the War Diary of 5 Corps at the end of July 1940 that Bernard's new doctrine was but the 'natural development' of his predecessor's:

> At the end of July certain changes were made in defence policy in 5 Corps area. In general these changes consisted in holding more battalions in reserve areas than previously. This was the natural development from the fact that the beach defences were now more fully constructed and allowed troops thus held in reserve to obtain more training in offensive action.[2]

[1] John Connell, *Auchinleck*, op. cit.
[2] Loc. cit.

This was certainly a loyal valediction to Auchinleck; but was it really true? Not only did Auchinleck try to stop Bernard from carrying out his reversal of policy, he seems not to have understood the fallacy behind his own beach-defence thinking: namely the impossibility of holding such a long front and the vulnerability of over-extended defences to concentrated German attack at selected points. It was this fundamental military mistake which Bernard abhorred. Ever since the latter years of World War One, Bernard had made himself an enemy of dispersion, and an advocate of strength through concentration and mobility – techniques he had practised in the closing stages of the Great War on the Western Front, in Southern Ireland thereafter, in his battalion, brigade, and divisional commands. At every level, from a company to a corps, Bernard insisted on centralised control, and in the ruthless selection of subordinates to ensure the cohesive force of the unit. He had been happy to revert to divisional command after Dunkirk because, in Slim's words, it permitted him to remain sole conductor of his own orchestra. Now, less than two months later, he was charged with command of divisions that were dispersed into a thin line of beach guards, with area troops under command of elderly retired officers, much as in the second, expansionist phase of the British Army in the winter of 1914–15. To Bernard this was anathema – and Auchinleck's hope that such defences would be made secure simply by War Office provision of an armoured division seemed to him quite unreal. The 4th and 50th Divisions were battle-experienced and had proved themselves capable of mobile action equal to any German attack. To squander them in static defence was to Bernard a criminal waste at a most critical moment.

It is clear, then, that, in the aftermath of the BEF campaign, Bernard was given to a kind of visionary over-zealousness, a determination to avenge the BEF's defeat by the Germans and the faulty command structure which had accompanied its downfall. Added to this he had now to serve under a commander whose views on defensive strategy and on tactics Bernard felt to be at fundamental variance with his own. Brooke's mastery of artillery matters and acid eye for weaknesses in organisation inspired Bernard's genuine respect; but, in the context of the summer of 1940, as the German air fleets began to drone across the Channel and invasion barges to assemble in the French ports, Bernard found Auchinleck a commander he could not serve: a commander who tolerated 'useless' subordinates, who had no vision in the training of an army because he had no idea how to fight an enemy like the Germans. Auchinleck's distinguished performance as a Brigade Commander – which had won him the DSO in 1934 – was against tribesmen; while the campaign in Norway had been utterly abortive. Though Auchinleck dreamed of armoured divisions, there was little chance of their being effective without prolonged training even if they could be created;

whereas the answer was, in Bernard's eyes, quite simple. As early as 1926, in his *Antelope* articles on infantry tactics, Bernard had declared that in modern warfare there were two cardinal rules when preparing defence, namely to:

a) Ensure the development of sufficient fire power to stop him [the enemy] in front of this line
b) Have reserves available to drive him out should he gain a footing in it.[1]

The Great War, Bernard knew from his own experience, had been won not by guns, tanks, aircraft, trenches or barbed wire – but by the manipulation of reserves. Every break-through on the Western Front, German or Allied, had eventually come to grief by the timely use of defending reserves; and only in 1918 when the German High Command recognised they had no further reserves did they instruct their political counterparts to šue for peace and recognise defeat – despite their defensive lines remaining for the most part intact.

A commander's task, therefore, was not only to train and direct his forces competently in battle: it was to understand the art of creating or marshalling those reserves. Bernard had written in 1925: 'As few troops as possible are used to beat off the enemy's attack with fire, i.e. the purely passive defence. As many as can be spared are kept in hand for counter-attack purposes, or for use as a reserve by means of which the commander may influence the fight as it develops.'[2] Bernard's future success in his three great defensive battles – at Alam Halfa, Medenine and the Ardennes – would prove the simplicity and straightforwardness of this doctrine, just as the 3rd Division's seemingly effortless performance in Belgium and Flanders had done. Bernard called it 'active defence', and it is easy to see how Auchinleck's Maginot-minded defence policy in 1940 aroused a distaste in him that he could not conceal, and which, together with his personal antipathy or jealousy, led him then to underestimate Auchinleck's considerable powers of leadership.

Not that it can have been easy for Auchinleck to command a subordinate as brilliant as Bernard. Wavell and Alexander would manage by simply leaving Bernard to run his own show; and had Auchinleck done this he might well have earned Bernard's loyalty. He couldn't however; and for the next three critical months there was a continual battle between Southern Command HQ and HQ 5 Corps. While Auchinleck impressed his superiors as one of the very few army commanders of natural stature, Bernard's remarkable training programme and the chain of exercises he would mount were to establish him beyond doubt as the most professional field comman-

[1] The Growth of Modern Infantry Tactics, Chapter V: Present Day Infantry Tactics, the *Antelope*, 5 January 1926.
[2] Ibid.

der in Britain – so much so that Auchinleck later confessed to feeling a 'bit inadequate'[1] in Bernard's presence.

In fact what happened to Bernard in the summer of 1940 was a transformation, and one may legitimately describe it as a turning-point in his career. Professionally, his tactical concept of modern warfare was already formed in the early 1920s, while his approach to training went even further back to his service in the Great War. The years since then had seen a refinement of those views: above all, the art of communicating his beliefs to his subordinates. However, it was the experience of the BEF campaign, of Dunkirk, the threat of German invasion and the struggle to get his views on 'active defence' accepted which turned Bernard from an enthusiastic and efficient officer into a visionary and, to some, insane genius – and which inculcated a new urgency into his life, a tension which would last for another twenty years before age mellowed him. It was not that Bernard's character suddenly altered in its component parts, but that circumstances caused those components all to be exaggerated to quite abnormal intensities as he recognised his probable destiny. The contradictions in his character, which had always been unusual, even eccentric, now became alarmingly stretched; and, the greater his military achievement, the stranger sometimes became his be-haviour. For instance, just as he had ordered the return of the 3rd Division to battle without leave after Dunkirk, so now, on assuming command of 5 Corps at the end of July, in the midst of a most impressive display of military acumen, he dazed his assembled subordinate commanders by an almost paranoid performance that, again, would not have been out of place in a Waugh novel. General Sir Frank Simpson remembered it well, nearly forty years later. It happened on 25 July 'on the flat roof of the roadhouse overlooking the causeway leading on to Portsmouth Island'.[2] Present were Bernard; Major-General Eastwood, the Commander of the 4th Divi-sion; and the Portsmouth Garrison commander, each with their principal staff officers.

'Monty seemed satisfied generally with the dispositions which existed,' Simpson recalled.

> He then proceeded to ask the Brigadier, who was the Portsmouth Garrison commander, how the Garrison funds were getting on.
> The Brigadier clearly had never heard of there being garrison funds. He was concerned merely with operational matters and he had left the garrison funds – if indeed there were any – to the Garrison Adjutant. This excited Monty at once.
> Monty had a great personal interest in the garrison funds. It will be remembered that he got into big trouble in 1938 over those very funds – he had let out a piece of War Department land in Ports-

[1] John Connell, *Auchinleck*, op. cit.
[2] Wason interviews, loc. cit.

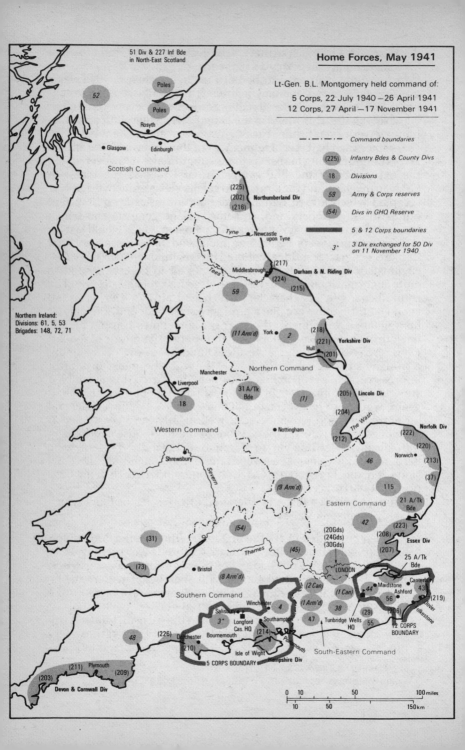

Home Forces, May 1941

51 Div & 227 Inf Bde
in North-East Scotland

Lt-Gen. B.L. Montgomery held command of:

5 Corps, 22 July 1940 – 26 April 1941
12 Corps, 27 April – 17 November 1941

— · — · — *Command boundaries*

(225) *Infantry Bdes & County Divs*

18 *Divisions*

59 *Army & Corps reserves*

(54) *Divs in GHQ Reserve*

▬▬▬ *5 & 12 Corps boundaries*

3· *3 Div exchanged for 50 Div on 11 November 1940*

52

Poles

Poles

Rosyth

Glasgow   Edinburgh

Scottish Command

Northern Ireland:
Divisions: 61, 5, 53
Brigades: 148, 72, 71

(225)
(202)   Northumberland Div
(216)

Tyne   Newcastle upon Tyne

Tees   Middlesbrough   (217)
(224)   Durham & N. Riding Div
59   (215)

(11 Arm'd)   York   2   (218)
(221)   Yorkshire Div
Hull   (201)

Manchester   Northern Command

Liverpool   31 A/Tk Bde   (1)   (205)   Lincoln Div
18   (204)

Western Command   Nottingham   (212)   The Wash

Shrewsbury   Severn   Norfolk Div
(222)
(220)
46   Norwich   (213)
(9 Arm'd)   (37)

115   21 A/Tk Bde

(54)   Eastern Command   42   (223)

(31)   Thames   (45)   (20Gds)   (208)   Essex Div
(24Gds)   (207)
(30Gds)
(73)   Bristol   LONDON   25 A/Tk Bde

(8 Arm'd)   (2 Can)   (1 Can)   44   Maidstone   Canterbury   43
Ashford   56   (219)
Southern Command   Winchester   4   (1 Arm'd)   38   (29)   (206)   Dover
Salisbury   3·   47   Tunbridge Wells   55   12 CORPS
Longford   Southampton   HQ   BOUNDARY
Cas. HQ   (214)
48   (226)   Dorchester   Bournemouth   South-Eastern Command
(210)   Isle of Wight   Hampshire Div
(211)   Plymouth   5 CORPS BOUNDARY
(203)   (209)
Devon & Cornwall Div

0   10   50   100 miles
10   50   150 km

mouth to a fun-fair operator, who paid him a large sum of money which he proceeded to put into the garrison funds, which were meant to provide amenities for the troops. The War Office having discovered this, Monty was very nearly sacked.

Well the whole tenor of the conference changed from operational matters to what had happened to the garrison funds, and Monty cross-examined the Garrison Brigadier on the Adjutant's qualities.

It transpired that the Garrison Adjutant was a reserve officer who had been called up from a job in the dog-racing world. This was too much for Monty. He connected dog-racing with every form of crookery and demanded to know the name of the officer.

Not only did the Brigadier tell him the name, but he announced that he had not been a very satisfactory Garrison Adjutant and was in fact leaving the job that very day. He was due to get on a train at any moment.

There now followed an amazing pantomime:

Monty then got very excited and asked that the military police should be sent down to the station to stop the Garrison Adjutant from getting on the train until he could give a proper account of the garrison funds. We all dispersed from the conference in some confusion, the Brigadier in a very worried state going off to his office to interview the ex-Garrison Adjutant.

It transpired that the garrison funds were exactly as they had been when Monty deposited them in the bank in 1938 – they had not been touched by anybody and had in fact drawn some considerable interest since 1938.

So the Garrison Adjutant went off to whatever appointment he was going to. My good General Eastwood never quite understood this episode. He said nothing like that had ever happened to him.

Whether Auchinleck ever heard of this drama is not known; yet it was Auchinleck as GOC Southern Command, who had to deal with Bernard's recommendation, in his report, that the Garrison Adjutant be dismissed entirely from the army, so that one cannot help but sympathise with him. Indeed it is sometimes difficult to imagine that, without the exigencies of war, Bernard's prospects of higher command could ever have been realised. As it was, Auchinleck and others must have complained to the new C-in-C Home Forces, General Sir Alan Brooke, for among Bernard's papers is this letter, hand-written and dated 5 August 1940, from Brooke himself:

GHQ Home Forces

My dear Monty,
    I have been wanting to write to you for some time to tell you how *delighted* I am that you have got command of a Corps.

I know your qualities well after our time together in France, and I have complete confidence that the 5 Corps will give the Germans the right reception if they set foot in this country.

I know you well enough also Monty to give you a word of warning against doing wild things. You have got a name for annoying people at times with your ways, and I have found difficulties in backing you at times against this reputation.

I have backed you strongly and shall go on doing so, and only ask you not to let me down by doing anything silly.

With *very* best of luck to you,

Yours ever,

Brookie

Brookie's rebuke was obviously intended to clear the air a little; but it cannot have achieved its object, for the following day, 6 August, Bernard travelled up to London to receive his CB at an investiture at Buckingham Palace – and to interview the Adjutant-General at the War Office in defiance of Auchinleck's 'orders are orders' instruction. Bernard made it abundantly clear that he could not train his constituent divisions into first-rate fighting units if men with BEF experience were siphoned off by the War Office. When Auchinleck heard of Bernard's direct appeal to the Adjutant-General he was understandably annoyed:

'I am quite aware that it is a common practice in the Army for officers of all ranks to visit the War Office,' he wrote to Bernard,

but in this case it appears that you interviewed the Adjutant-General on a matter which directly concerned my Headquarters, in that they had issued orders for certain transfers to take place. I do not consider this is the proper manner in which this, or any other matter of this nature, should be handled. When orders are issued from these Headquarters, whether they come from the War Office or direct from these Headquarters, and you wish to make a protest, from whatever point of view, against these orders, I wish such protests to be made to these Headquarters and not to War Office officials over my head.[1]

Auchinleck insisted that Bernard withdraw his 5 Corps Memorandum on the subject and desist from engaging in such 'short-cut' tactics; but Bernard took little, if any, notice. He reorganised his sector as he had indicated he would, by giving the 4th Division a larger share of the coastline in order to relieve 50th Division and he laid down that no unit was to provide more than fifty per cent of its forces for defence work, the remainder of the troops being made to train or be sent on leave. On 10 August he gave the first of his great

[1] John Connell, *Auchinleck*, op. cit.

wartime lectures, entitled 'Tactics in the light of Recent Experience in France and Belgium', at the Eastney Barracks; and he thereafter indulged not only in a policy of the utmost resistance to Southern Command/War Office transfers of experienced personnel, but a constant endeavour to get back his own chosen favourites from his previous command. On 20 August he was writing to 'Kit' Dawnay, still GSO 3 (Intelligence) at 3rd Division:

> I have hopes I may get you posted here as my G2 (I); I have asked MS [Military Secretary] for you and it is now being considered.
> As you know (or perhaps you don't) I have a high opinion of your abilities and am trying to take you along with me wherever I go.
> Please keep this ENTIRELY to yourself for the present.
> I am afraid I haven't asked you if you want to come with me, and it may be that you would sooner stay with the 3rd Division. Let me know. Charles [Sweeny] and I would like to have you with us; if they let you come you will become a Major and Charles will have to call you 'Sir'.
>> Yours ever,
>> B. L. Montgomery

Five days later, acknowledging failure, Bernard informed Dawnay exactly to what lengths he had gone to obtain his services:

> I regret to say that the Military Secretary will not agree to your coming here as G2 (I) . . .
> I fought hard to get you but have been defeated; I even sent a motor contact officer who left here at 0600 hrs and arrived in London at the MS house with a personal note from me at 0800 hrs – much to his amazement.
> I am not accustomed to being defeated and shall think over my next step.
> I may 'push out' the fellow they send me, and ask for you again; and go on doing this with each succeeding G2 until the MS is exhausted.
> However I shall have to have a look at him first. He arrives tomorrow.
>> Yrs ever
>> B. L. Montgomery

To Auchinleck this manipulation of the military machine to Bernard's personal advantage was a constant sore, particularly since he, as Commander-in-Chief had to deal with irate unit commanders from whom Bernard 'pinched' staff (3rd Division was still not in 5 Corps). And yet, however wrong in a logical sense, Bernard's

411

methods can be excused to some degree in that he was, by and large, such a brilliant selector of personnel.

Moreover it is to Bernard's credit that, however much he was inclined to become a law unto himself, he always retained a saving sense of reality, even humour. His 5 Corps Intelligence officers in fact served him very well, and were kept. Yet his faith in the talents of Captain Dawnay were not thereby forgotten; Bernard still asked Dawnay privately for a regular intelligence appreciation of German intentions, visited the Dawnays' home on several occasions, stood godfather to their first son, and not only got Dawnay a Brigade-Major's appointment that winter, but personally ensured his acceptance on the shortened Staff College course the following spring.

What may have added to Auchinleck's vexation was the un-pleasant truth that not only was Bernard intent upon a reversal of defence policy in 5 Corps area, but was carrying out the reversal without GOC approval and with such manifest success. Already on 5 August, the day that Brooke was writing to caution him, Bernard had issued an operation instruction laying down his new proposals. In future, Bernard maintained, Home Guard beach brigades would man the beach defences, while corps troops and the two constituent infantry divisions would withdraw behind them, concentrating on a winter training programme that would involve exercises at every level from section leading to divisional and even corps manoeuvres. Troops would be billeted either in or near towns, and the accent would be on offence, not defence. Thus, even before the great German air fleets began to pound the naval, military and air force installations of the south coast, Bernard was planning his winter training schemes – thereby effectively snubbing Auchinleck, who impotently called for the battle to be fought on the beaches, who 'really did think invasion was coming' as he put it later, and who was mortified when, on 10 August, the CIGS made the decision to send virtually the whole of Britain's armoured reserves out to Egypt.

Overnight Auchinleck's strategy – based on fighting the enemy on the beaches and using armoured reserves to finish him off – was in ruins, while Bernard's policy was triumphantly vindicated. Auchinleck's biographer, John Connell, describes this armoured ex-odus – insisted upon by Churchill – as a geographical transference of Auchinleck's essential vision 'of the Army of the future, which he expounded to Haining [the VCIGS] in June 1940' and which 'was in large measure fulfilled in the Western Desert, in Burma and in North-West Europe'.[1] This is absurd, and Auchinleck's performance in the Western Desert in 1941–2 would demonstrate that, until the very final weeks of his command, Auchinleck had little notion of how successfully to integrate the use of armour into battlefield operations. Liddell Hart, 'Patrick' Hobart, Auchinleck and many

[1] John Connell, *Auchinleck*, op. cit.

other well-known theorists and commanders would all make this elementary mistake, blinded by their excitement at discovering a modern version of the age-old romance of cavalry. Indeed Brooke and Montgomery would both be pilloried by the arch-proponents of the tank for their 'backward thinking' on armoured formations – the point thus being entirely missed. For, if Brooke resisted Churchill's and Martel's dream of a 'tank army', it was not because he was old-fashioned, but because his experience had taught him that tanks were but the spearhead of a highly trained body of infantry and artillery; and that without the latter tanks were only of use against demoralised and poorly trained troops. The war, he knew, would never be won by tank production; it would be won by abandoning Churchillian romance and by training a modern British and Dominions army in which infantry, tanks, support aircraft and artillery were successfully merged into an unbeatable team. It was this vision, first as C-in-C Home Forces, and later as CIGS, that Brooke pursued with relentless determination – and which his protégé, the gauche, short, reputedly mad Lt-General Montgomery would enact. Yet strangely it was to take a further two years and the unpredictable death of the 8th Army Commander-Designate, before Bernard was once more given battlefield command – two years during which the catalogue of bungled British efforts grew and grew until Churchill's very future as Prime Minister and Minister of Defence was put in doubt.

What is so moving – and hitherto largely unchronicled – is to recognise in the War Diaries of the period, in contemporary letters and documents, and in the recollections of those who were involved, how inevitable was Bernard's success as a field commander: how, in the two years from the summer of 1940 to that of 1942, Bernard Montgomery schooled himself and the forces under his command to become superior as a team even to the Germans in the mortal business of war – so that in his eventual take-over from General Auchinleck in August 1942 one has the impression almost of *déjà-vu*. Historians may carp at Montgomery's failure to exploit some of his later victories, his excessive belief in military 'tidiness' and his reluctance to stand down as Allied Land Forces Commander after the crushing victory in Normandy in August 1944: but the measure of Bernard's greatness as a commander, the unchallengeable evidence that his success in battle was neither accidental nor simply – as envious tongues would have it – the product of superior arms and numbers, must be sought in his performance long before he ever flew out to Cairo to face Rommel's last bid to conquer Egypt. Whatever his personal motives in crossing Auchinleck as GOC Southern Command, Bernard's vision of British offensive military renascence after Dunkirk was both genuine and obstinately undeterred or deflected by the threat of German invasion. From the beginning of August 1940 Bernard laid down the objectives, methods and timetable of 5 Corps training that would take it through to the spring of 1941.[1] Though part of this training was to deal with a possible German invasion, Bernard does not seem to have believed, like Auchinleck, that it would materialise in 1940. Bernard's letters to 'Kit' Dawnay, thanking him for his forecasts of likely dates of invasion, indicate just how lightly he took the threat. On 20 August he wrote mockingly:

> I notice in your successive appreciations you keep putting off the date – of invasion.
> If I remember right, No. 1 said it *must* come by 15 August or not at all.
> Now it is to be in September.
> I will ask you again in September – what the real date is!!

Bernard himself had 'certain ideas on what is likely to happen'; and exactly a month later, when Dawnay had sent his third appreciation, Bernard confided:

> My own view is that they [the Germans] are not coming over just at present; I think there may well be some dirty work in the Middle East this winter.

Whether Bernard foresaw that he would be one day called to serve in the Middle East is not known; but there are a number of indications that he did – in particular, as will be seen, his decision that some of his winter corps exercises should be devoted to manoeuvres in mock-desert terrain, complete with mock-Arab place names. He certainly never faltered in his belief that the Germans would eventually be defeated, as his letter of 16 October 1940 to Dawnay illustrates:

> Headquarters,
> 5th Corps,
> Home Forces

> My dear Kit,
> Thank you for the appreciation, which I found waiting for me when I got back from your [3rd Division] exercise today.
> You must not get too pessimistic about the war. It is high time you came and stayed with me for 48 hrs leave, and got 'binged' up; I should love to have you, so do come. I will place a ducal bedroom at your disposal.
> We have got to keep our morale high; we have plenty of resources and, provided we can keep our ports working and our ships at sea, can go on for ever.

[1] cf. 5 Corps Training Instruction No. 3, 5 Aug. 1940, et seq. War Diary, 5 Corps (WO 166/249), PRO.

414

This is not so in Germany. She has a certain amount of stuff at the moment but is having great difficulty in getting it distributed. The transport problem can only be solved satisfactorily if, by securing uninterrupted use of the eastern Mediterranean, Germany can get oil and produce round by sea. Neither the railways, nor the Danube and inland waterways, afford a solution; the produce of the Danube basin has always reached Germany by sea.

You cannot suddenly change a system of distribution which has been built up over centuries; the economic life of Europe is built up on stuff coming in by sea, & going out by sea; the ports in western Europe are destroyed; the Dardanelles is closed.

Last winter distributional difficulties caused great discontent in Germany; this winter they will be worse, & discontent will grow. The German population is bound to lose keenness when it is discovered that the new ration cards will not provide the promised overcoat; she has no wool, and cannot make synthetic wool that is waterproof. They will discover that the summer increase in the butter ration was due to the looting of Denmark, and that the fat ration this winter is going to be less than last. And so on.

Our great hopes are Yugo-Slavia and Turkey, especially the latter. If Turkey will stand firm we are all right; and she *will* stand firm so long as we hang on to Egypt.

The cause of the German downfall in the last war was morale and as a result Hitler has given great thought to it. But curiously enough civilian morale in Germany has not been improved by all the recent victories; they have the haunting fear of another winter on short rations and short coal, with a great deal of bombing chucked in as well; there is an uneasy feeling over the nonreporting of casualties, and over the delay, and this is making the population disquieted.

Nevertheless there is still a blind faith in the leaders, and no sign at all of any collapse. So we must just keep at it, and keep our own morale high . . .

Do come and stay. You will have a very warm welcome from the 3 Div contingent here – now growing in size. We will binge you up and provide inspiration for the future.

Yrs ever
Monty

There is a certain irony in a Commander having to lecture a Divisional Intelligence Officer on the economic-geographical reasons why Hitler's Reich would fail; but this was typical of Bernard and his unshakable confidence. Moreover in Dawnay's 'pessimism' Bernard saw the evil influence of Southern Command's defensive outlook; for to wait upon Hitler's initiative throughout the summer and early autumn was bound to sap the confidence of the troops, particularly the younger ones. Training, especially winter training when there was no question of invasion, thus possessed for Bernard a double merit – that of inspiring morale as well as competence. Strangely, there was at this time no guidance on training from above – as Bernard made clear in a second lecture to the shortened Senior Staff College course at Minley Manor, Camberley, on 25 October: *Training in War Time* – of which Bernard's pencilled notes still exist:

> Anything I say is my own personal view & has no official significance.
> Will tell you what I do myself and how I train my Corps . . .
> 2. Influence of battle experience on training:
>   The object of all training is success in battle; obviously the lessons of recent battling must be checked up.
>   Had no guidance from above on a high level on the subject.
>   Made out my own lessons – 12 lessons – these represent my own military philosophy.
>   Nothing new in them – but it is sound occasionally to collect your ideas and put down in concrete form what are the things that really matter in battle. No one does it. It is these points that will colour your whole training.

Bernard had then run over the most important of his '12 lessons' – which he had enunciated both in his first 5 Corps lecture, and as the basis for his own Corps Study Week starting on 7 October. In particular he blamed the Staff College for British military disasters in the past:

> People to blame have been psc [Passed Staff College] officers. Bad initial plan, mistakes in the staff work, the operation started badly, and never got right.
> It has become increasingly difficult to rectify initial mistakes – in fact you can't. If you start on the wrong leg you are done.
> Defensively – layout must be good, artillery properly deployed, everything so balanced that you can always do something about it.
> Offensively – recce echelons properly positioned, technique of battle drill perfect, HQ in the right places, good arrangements for inter-communication, and so on.

However, good staff work and organised command were only half the battle:

> No good trying to fight a first class enemy unless the soldiers are absolutely on their toes.
> They must have a 'stomach for the fight'. They must have the light of battle in their eyes.
> They must look forward to a good fight.

They must be full of 'binge'.

Cannot be full of binge if you are not fit; must have that exhilaration that comes from physical well being; optomistic [sic] outlook on life; no good being pessimistic with a face like a piece of cheese.

Physical fitness and powers of endurance are essentials for victory.

PT drill & highest standards of smartness in the execution of all duties; great aids. Cross country runs – get rid of all the smoke and gin.

Cannot be full of 'binge' if you are always 'belly-aching'.

Too much of it in the Army. Stop it.

Must have 100% binge – No belly-aching.

Military fit – mentally fit – physically fit.

Thereupon Bernard instanced the German battle technique – and the way to confront it, using centralised artillery, defence in depth, and reserves.

4. Bearing in mind these lessons, how are we to organise our training in wartime?
5. The pre-war training seasons.

    Their disadvantages.

    Their repercussion on readiness for battle at any time – never ready till July.

    The system did not meet the requirements of modern world conditions even in peace-time; in war time definitely dangerous.

    A formation or unit in war has to be able to operate against the enemy any time – as a complete unit.

    Often stated it cannot do this as it has not yet done platoon training; that to make it do battalion exercises before it has done platoon training is to ask it to run before it can walk – and that this is absurd.

    The real points are these:

    a) A situation may arise when it has got to do it – this may be tomorrow.
    b) Therefore the unit must go out 'as a unit'; the stage-management of the battle must be practised & the machinery of the unit exercised; the unit comdr. must have practice in handling his command.
    c) An untrained unit may do badly [in exercises]. That does not matter – it will all be experience which will save casualties when the operation has to be done in battle – possibly next week.
    d) After an exercise of this sort the unit can return to its individual or sub-unit training.

By working in this way it will be found that minor training will assume an added interest, as officer and OR [Other Rank] will learn how everything fits in to the final picture; they will learn by trial and error that if the machine as a whole is to run smoothly at all times, a very high standard of individual and sub-unit efficiency is necessary.

Therefore individual training must be sandwiched in with collective training, it being remembered that the enemy may have to be met at any time.

There followed what was, by now, Bernard's classic formula for the organisation of army training, comprising:

Individual or sub-unit training
The model
Brigade Signal Exercises
Collecting training – in which at least once a week battalion and brigade exercises are practised, with the complete Division moving out on exercise at least once a month.[1]

Nor was this – as Major Gething had discovered in the 1920s – 'all blah'. Within 5 Corps, after a four-day visit at the end of September to the War Office and to Sir Alan Brooke at GHQ Home Forces, Bernard's strategy had been approved. By the middle of October Bernard was able to withdraw his two divisions entirely from beach defence work, which was now handed over to specialist beach-defence battalions raised for that purpose; and on 15 October the first small-scale 5 Corps Exercise began.

As Bernard indicated to the Senior Staff College course, all minor training was undertaken in order that units be able to carry out large-scale operations, while large-scale operational exercises made the constituent units aware of their roles and their current state of individual and unit efficiency, or otherwise. By the beginning of October all battalions, brigades and the two divisions of 5 Corps had been out on exercise. Between 7 and 12 October all unit commanders down to battalion COs assembled at Longford Castle (5 Corps' new HQ since 13 September), and took part in Bernard's 5 Corps Study Week.

Based on the study weeks Bernard had devised in 9th Infantry Brigade at Portsmouth, this Study Week sought to get commanders to think out the requirements of various operations of war on a cloth model and in discussion, before having to enact them either in full-scale exercises or in battle. Bernard introduced the week, laid down the programme and even devised the questions that would be shot at the assembled commanders. Both Sir Alan Brooke and

[1] Montgomery Papers.

418

Auchinleck came to 'listen in'. 'I used to go and listen in to his lectures,' Auchinleck later recalled, '– no coughing, no smoking, runs before breakfast – all very inspiring and made me feel a bit inadequate.'[1]

Small wonder that Auchinleck felt inadequate in the face of such virtuosity by a subordinate commander. Moreover, sensing perhaps that he had captive souls among his audience, Bernard insisted on turning the screw yet tighter. The first problem he put to the assembled commanders was this: Assume a German invasion of the south coast had taken place; assume it had been driven back into the sea by 5 Corps; but had been successful further west, in the rest of Southern Command territory, and 5 Corps had to come to the rescue: how, when allotted certain roads by the corps commander, would divisional commanders use them? How would brigadiers dispose their brigades during movement 'in order to present a fighting front without delay'? What would be a 'suitable layout for the leading battalion'?[2]

Bernard's inference was unmistakable – only 5 Corps was trained and commanded in such a way that it could meet a German threat successfully. Movement, first contact, attack, night attack, and now the art of close support bombing with the RAF, were the major topics covered during the week. Above all, commanders must aim at fitness for battle, Bernard insisted. Troops must be able to march a minimum of twenty-five miles and go in to fight at the end of such a march; the art, organisation and administration required for attack must be studied, involving rapid movement and rapid exploitation. Training was to be undertaken as far as possible in brigade groups, with artillery regiments directly involved and quartered with them . . .

Each evening there was a lecture, by an expert, on the world and European military political and economic scene – no doubt the latter being the source of Bernard's retort to Dawnay's 'pessimistic' letter.

Auchinleck later questioned whether 'runs before breakfast really produce battle winners, of necessity';[3] but the doubt – written in relation to Bernard's Study Week – was unworthy of him. Physical and mental fitness were so obviously but a part of what Bernard was attempting to achieve – something amply evidenced when a few weeks later Bernard launched his first full-scale corps exercise.

By now Bernard was – as he wrote to Dawnay – convinced the Germans would not invade before the summer of 1941; indeed so certain was he, that when news came through his naval liaison officer, on 19 October, that the Royal Navy was 'standing to' (the new code word for an expected German invasion) around Portsmouth, Bernard simply ignored it and continued his inspection of

[1] John Connell, *Auchinleck*, op. cit.
[2] War Diary, 5 Corps, loc. cit.
[3] John Connell, *Auchinleck*, op. cit.

the new Hampshire Area Command that had assumed responsibility for beach and non-divisional defence.

It is difficult in fact to understand where Bernard got the tireless energy with which he devised, planned and ran the training of 5 Corps. Auchinleck had said in August 1940 that it would take six months to train the divisions to real fighting efficiency; Bernard had said two; and he pursued this aim with almost messianic fervour. Moreover there seems to have been no area or echelon of activity within the Corps which Bernard left out. He lectured to the Home Guard; he introduced a new 5 Corps school with a four-week training programme for junior officers, and a special wing for training MT personnel. He made it an axiom of his command that he should – like Sir Alan Brooke – spend at least half of every working day visiting units and talking to everyone, from Commanding Officer to the NCOs and troops themselves. Often, where he did not know the CO, he would insist on inspecting the men at work without the CO being present. Finally, on 23 October, he formally instituted 'weekly cross-country runs for personnel of Corps HQ: Those taking part to be:

a) All officers up to the rank of Captain
b) All Majors up to the age of 40
c) All Other Ranks.'[1]

Together with his implacable order that no wives or families be allowed in his area, this was to be, strangely, the most controversial, even legendary decision Bernard made in these years in Home Command. Long after his unique contribution to the retraining of the British Army after Dunkirk had been forgotten, the memory of these cross-country runs for sedentary officers would survive and provoke bitter discussion.

Gradually the image of a Corps Commander called Montgomery was forming – not the 'dim and distant figure' that Brooke had cut, for all his intelligence and decisiveness, but the image of a professional commander the like of whom had not been known in living memory.

[1] War Diary, 5 Corps, loc. cit.

CHAPTER NINE

The Offensive Spirit

And all the time Bernard was meeting and getting to know, for good or ill, the commanders who, in later years, would serve under him – or be removed! The Canadian Commander, Lt-General McNaughton, the Australian troops under Brigadier L. J. Morshead, 10th Brigade under Brigadier 'Bubbles' Barker, 210th Brigade under Brigadier Gerald Templer, and many others whose names Bernard carefully noted in a little black book he kept. Moreover, he rarely lost contact with those officers whose future he judged to be starred: they were sure to receive invitations to lectures Bernard was giving or exercises he was conducting, regardless where they had since been posted.

In November 1940 Bernard pursued this latter policy to its logical conclusion. He had remained in close touch with the 3rd Division ever since leaving it in July; in October, as has been seen, he even managed to get it to cooperate in his small-scale corps exercise. Finally, on 2 November, he visited Lt-General Franklyn, the Commander of 8 Corps, and asked whether he might exchange 3rd Division for the 50th. Franklyn liked the idea – he had had 50th Division under command in the counter-attack at Arras on 21 May, and the two divisions had fought side by side in the perimeter defences of Dunkirk. By 8 November Bernard was writing to Dawnay a little coyly: 'I think the 3rd Division will probably come under my Corps in due course'; and on the 11th the Commander of 50th Division, Major-General Martel, was informed of the decision at 5 Corps HQ. Ten days later the change-over had taken place: Bernard now commanded the 3rd and 4th Divisions of the British Army, just as Brooke had done in the BEF.

However, Bernard's willingness to lose Martel, with his hare-brained visions of tank armies, did not imply that Bernard was uninterested in armoured mobile warfare – as his first full-scale corps exercise at the beginning of December was to show. It was undoubtedly the largest and most important exercise held in Britain since Dunkirk. It took almost the whole of November to plan, and the initial cloth-model demonstration, attended by some 150 commanding officers and guests, took place at Longford Castle on 25 November. It was, in almost every respect, a pioneering achievement. The object of the exercise, Bernard declared, 'is to study the employment and handling of a Corps consisting of an Armoured Division, a mobile Infantry Division, an army Tank Brigade, parachute troops, close-support aircraft (dive-bombers), taking part in an offensive against enemy forces in a desert area'.

The exercise, though it promised – when Sir Alan Brooke said a few words at the preliminary cloth-model demonstration – to be 'very interesting',[1] turned out to be something of a disappointment. Neither energy nor imagination had been spared in planning the exercise. The sandy areas of Salisbury and Marlborough had been designated limestone deserts, and the river Kennet had even been given an Arab name, Nahr-el-Kennet. A special half-inch map had been printed instead of the usual Ordnance Survey maps used, marked with areas of soft-going ground usable only by lighter vehicles and infantry, and lava outcrops that were impassable. There was little cover from air attack, with only infrequent plantations and date palms that could be used. However, it was perhaps in Bernard's detailed instructions to the umpires that one can gauge the sheer professionalism of the undertaking. They were to mark and report on: troops on the move, speed, spacing and correction of VTM, concealment from air attack, flank protection, bridging diversions owing to demolitions; choice of assembly areas and hide-outs, concealment from air and ground observation and protection against air and tank attack; reconnaissance for attack, concealment and control of recce parties, the obtaining at HQs of information from troops holding the line, and drill for issuing of orders; the attack fire-plan, use of ground, arrangements for timing and intended effect of close-support bombing, operation of SAS parachutists, energetic exploitation of success, keeping in touch with flank formations . . .

Even the preparation of mock Intelligence information on the enemy was carefully thought out. Against the forces of 5 Corps – consisting of the 4th Division, an army tank brigade under command, and the 1st Armoured Division – was a supposed German Motorised Infantry Division, represented by the 11th Hussars under Lt-Colonel J. Galbraith, transformed into General-Major Johann Galbraidt, with a full German military biography. The 1st Armoured Division was intended to reach the Nahr-el-Kennet; the 4th Division would, during a thirty-mile night march, close up behind it, relieve it, and put in a dawn river-crossing attack. 'Simbo' Simpson, then GSO 1 of the 4th Division, well remembered the difficulties:

It involved a very big move right across Salisbury Plain and it was so designed that there were few roads to guide us. Certainly my 4th Division, which was then commanded by Major-General

[1] Alanbrooke Diary, 25 November 1940, loc. cit.

Swayne, was in some very considerable difficulty at one time in the middle of the night. We tried to cross the Plain with our prismatic compasses, but inevitably when we reached a road it tended to divert us to make the going easier.

It was, of course, the beginning of December, and the Plain was very muddy in places. I know that as the GSO 1 I ought to have managed things a bit better, but we did get into a considerable amount of traffic trouble in the early hours of the morning. These things always seemed worse in the dark. Certainly the 4th Division came to a complete standstill while some of us sorted out the mess into which we had put the division.

We did get it sorted out, but Monty was very caustic afterwards.

If Bernard was caustic, it was not because he had expected the exercise to go like clockwork. On the contrary, the skeleton exercises held by Auchinleck during the summer had little value other than as signals drill, for it was only in full-scale battle manoeuvres that the true conditions of war were rehearsed. Similarly, those later historians who were to criticise Bernard for his failure to exploit to the maximum effect the fruits of his victories over Rommel at Alam Halfa and El Alamein ignored the realities of the battlefield, the state of training and the genuine capabilities of army units totalling almost 16,000 men per division. No one, charting the course of Bernard Montgomery's career after the First World War, could ever claim that he was hidebound or even unduly cautious. Liddell Hart criticised Bernard retrospectively for having failed to emphasise the importance of exploitation in his teaching: but this was very far from the case. Not only had Bernard himself shown brilliant powers of exploitation as a battalion commander in manoeuvres in Egypt in 1932–3 and as a Brigadier commanding the 9th Infantry Brigade; it was a factor much stressed to his umpires when conducting exercises as a Divisional and Corps Commander. But if, as in Corps Exercise No. 1, it proved a major difficulty just to bring a subordinate infantry division into battle, then the cart obviously must not precede the horse. It was better, Bernard felt, first to ensure that one's forces were sound in defence, cohesive in movement, and co-ordinated in offence before rehearsing the question of how best to exploit victory once won. History would prove this a wise decision: and the only flagrant risk he allowed his forces to take in the course of World War Two – the parachute assault on Arnhem – proved an expensive failure. Against opponents as professional and unyielding as the Germans, Bernard had learned in the Great War and again in Belgium and Flanders in May 1940, the answer was not romantic dreams of 'exploitation', but the creation of an army that was simply more professional and implacable than the enemy. It was this object which drove Bernard after Dunkirk, and which marked the transformation of his character from talented but still junior Major-

General to a Commander of almost despotic vision, long before he ever came to make his reputation in the North African desert.

At the end of 5 Corps Exercise No. 1, on 7 December, Bernard held his by now traditional post mortem. Alan Brooke had been 'very much impressed' by the exercise, particularly by the use of parachutists – an innovation which made Brooke 'feel certain that we must develop an Airborne Brigade with the least possible delay, probably in Canada'.[1] Brooke had felt sorry for the poor 4th Division 'who had had a hard night . . . stuck in the mud' on the mock-desert ranges; but Bernard's recapitulation and critical review of the whole exercise elicited this accolade from the usually testy Brooke in his diary for the 7th December:

> Went to Winchester where I attended Monty's 5 Corps Conference on the big exercise he had just concluded.
>
> The Conference was in the Odeon Cinema and absolutely packed, at least 800 officers!
>
> Monty gave a first-class discourse & I said a few words after him.[2]

Brooke was genuinely surprised – as he had been in France in the winter of 1940 – by the sheer professionalism with which Bernard planned, executed, and drew lessons from an exercise involving over 30,000 troops and which sought not only to rehearse the various arms in battle manoeuvre, but to experiment with new battle techniques. The difference between this exercise and Bernard's 3rd Division exercises in France only a year before was heartening. In France Bernard's rehearsals had been devoted to motorised movement by night, the seizure of defensive lines, and the art of planned withdrawal – whereas the accent now was on attack, using the potential resources of a modern army. Parachutists were to be dropped ahead of 5 Corps' armoured spearhead; the tanks were to be rapidly relieved at night by infantry; and by the following dawn the enemy's river obstacle was to be vaulted, using divisional sappers, massed artillery – and close-support bombers.

It was use of the last which interested Bernard most of all. As Brooke found at GHQ, the Royal Air Force was too busy defending Britain from the Luftwaffe to commit itself to a firm policy of army support. Bernard's efforts at 5 Corps were largely locally-inspired, and involved a certain amount of horse-trading. In return for aggressive army provision to counter-attack German parachute landings on British airfields in 5 Corps area, Bernard asked for – and got – agreement on tactical liaison with RAF light bomber squadrons. The RAF loaned liaison officers to serve in Bernard's 'tentacles' – small

[1] Op. cit.
[2] Loc. cit.

424

wireless-operating units attached to brigade or alternatively Corps headquarters. 'The object of the exercise is to experiment in the best method of controlling close-support aircraft,' Bernard laid down in advance, 'and the two different systems shown above will therefore be tried.'

Finally, the 4th Division had been given an army tank brigade for the exercise, so that in essence the format of Bernard's famous 8th Army desert combination was already being rehearsed in the winter of 1940: an armoured division working hand-in-glove with a tank-reinforced motorised infantry division, intimate co-operation by RAF close-support bombers, the Special Air Services who provided the parachutists for the exercise, and, as always, the integrated firepower of the complete Corps artillery and constant assistance of the Royal Engineers. Against a combination of this kind, Bernard felt, not even the Germans could resist, and he was therefore justly confident. From hopeless beach-bound defence in the summer of 1940 Bernard felt he was beginning to change the whole outlook and posture of the army on the central southern coast of England. On 17 December, the exercise was repeated, this time with the 3rd Division taking the place of 4th Division.

The strain of Bernard's visionary army metamorphosis naturally fell hardest on Bernard's Chief-of-Staff, so that it was not altogether surprising when, for Exercise No. 2, Bernard decided to replace Brigadier Dowler.

'I was suddenly told that I had to leave the 4th Division,' its GSO 1 Lt-Colonel Simpson, recalled.

As I had been with the division for only six months or so I was surprised and asked General Swayne where I was going. He said that although he had been told not to tell me immediately because one or two procedural formalities had to be completed, he could whisper to me that I was not going very far away but merely being promoted upstairs to be the Brigadier GS to Monty himself at his Corps HQ. So Monty was faithful to his promise to me at the end of June 1940 that one day he would get me to serve him again. Of course I went with every pleasure.[1]

This time, as even Simpson acknowledged, the 3rd Division acquit-ted itself considerably better than the 4th Division. Once again, in the great Odeon Cinema at Dorchester, Bernard assembled the partici-pating officers and addressed them after the exercise, on 20 Decem-ber. Some 250 parachutists had taken part in the two exercises; every soldier in the Corps had been out, the infantry had marched between twenty and thirty miles at night before being launched into 'battle' proper; and the whole question of desert warfare had been success-

[1] Wason interviews, loc. cit.

fully sown in the minds of both troops and staff officers. Bernard knew, presumably from Brooke, that certain reinforcements were to be sent out imminently to the Middle East; he must have hoped that he would be selected to accompany them. By 11 December the first stage of Lt-General O'Connor's desert victories was over, and Sidi Barrani had been captured. By 22 January 1941, Tobruk would be in British hands; and at Beda Fomm, on 7 February 1941, virtually the entire Italian army in Libya would surrender to O'Connor.

Two years younger than Bernard, O'Connor had lectured at the Staff College, Camberley, alongside Bernard in the 1920s, and had commanded the 7th Division in Palestine when Bernard had commanded the 8th. 'Boldness, mobility, and above all the generalship of O'Connor together with inter-service co-operation were the elements in this success,' Bernard was to write almost thirty years later, in his *History of Warfare*. For those in Britain, the battles of the Western Desert Force were a welcome tonic; and, to the enthusiastic Commander of 5 Corps in particular, a measure of what a trained, mobile British corps could achieve under a good general, backed by an able C-in-C – Bernard's erstwhile C-in-C from the summer of 1938, General Sir Archibald Wavell. Alongside cuttings from *The Times* referring to his corps exercises in December 1940, Bernard filed the advertisement for Wavell's new book on *Generals and Generalship*, the preface for which the CIGS had himself written. 'I am confident that if the victorious General of today had to give his own reasons for his victory,' Sir John Dill declared, 'he would repeat word for word the principles enunciated by the General so little known to the public two years ago.' Bernard admired the book (the printed version of Wavell's Lees Knowles lectures at Cambridge in 1939) as much as did Dill, and in his *Path to Leadership* maintained 'the lectures were the best treatise on that subject which I have ever read'. Moreover Bernard was also an admirer of Wavell's biography of Allenby – *Allenby, A Study of Greatness*, which was published in September 1940 – 'the best book he wrote,' Bernard felt; and in the autumn of 1938 had recommended Wavell's *The Palestine Campaigns* as essential reading for his 9th Infantry Brigade officers' winter study project.

Wavell's name was suddenly on everyone's lips; O'Connor was knighted and Churchill jubilant. Demoralised by the fate of their colleagues at Beda Fomm, the Italians in East Africa collapsed; the British seemed masters of the Middle East.

Paradoxically, of course, it was the very success of the British against the Italians which goaded Hitler into action. The Air Battle of Britain had failed; and week by week 5 Corps War Diary recorded in its Intelligence summaries the movement of German air squadrons and troops towards the Mediterranean – and Russia. It must have been clear to Bernard that, however easy the British victories over the Italians, a confrontation with the German army would be a very different affair. As Bernard later wrote: 'It is interesting to reflect that

426

Wavell's only major victories were against the Italians in Africa – in Abyssinia, and in Egypt and Cyrenaica . . . Is it possible that he underestimated the Germans?'[1]

It was here, perhaps, that Bernard's Dunkirk experience stood him in good stead. He had no illusions about the modern German army, and while Wavell first made his reputation, then shattered it in an uninterrupted series of miscalculations, Bernard indefatigably pursued his vision of a 'New British Army' as *The Times* called it on 6 December 1940:

Forty Thousand Men in a Field Exercise

The new British Army that has largely been created since Dunkirk has just carried out the most ambitious exercise in the field that has ever taken place in this country. Certainly nothing like it has ever been seen before in wartime conditions . . . What I saw – would that the whole story could be told – gave vital meaning to current references to the future offensive of a new and enlightened BEF . . .

Moreover, while Wavell refused offers of more divisions from England on the grounds that he wished primarily to replenish the ranks of his Regular forces, Bernard had no such inhibitions about Regular and Territorial or even conscript forces. As will be seen, no sooner had he satisfied himself about the battle-worthiness of 5 Corps after five full-scale exercises, than he turned to the task of achieving the same standard among his area defence units. If Hitler was to be defeated, Bernard felt, it would require the combined efforts of the entire uniformed services, not just a pre-war trained élite in North-East Africa. As General Jackson put it in *The Battle for North Africa 1940–43*, 'Beda Fomm was the last battle fought by Britain's pre-war professional army'.[2]

When Brooke assumed the post of C-in-C Home Forces in July 1940 he had been appalled by the state of Britain's military defences, and above all by the lack of training in Britain during the previous ten months. In January 1941 Brooke was still insisting, at an exercise at the Staff College, Camberley, on 'instilling a more offensive spirit into the army', and also 'expressing my views as to the present stagnation of higher training'.[3] The disasters that were to befall Britain in the following eighteen months were to bear out the folly of British strategy, the failure of her higher commanders, the poor state of training of troops sent out from Britain and the Dominions; and the sheer professionalism of her enemies. If Bernard Montgomery was able, within weeks of his arrival in Egypt in 1942, to stem this

[1] *The Path to Leadership*, op. cit.
[2] W. G. F. Jackson, London 1975.
[3] Alanbrooke Diary, 8 January 1941, loc. cit.

tide of maldirection, of incompetence and fatalism, it would be because for two long years after Dunkirk he had so utterly dedicated himself to the task of army-building. Just as he rejected Auchinleck's beach-defence policy as bad for morale, inducive of defensive-mindedness, and likely to lead to piecemeal defeat, so in the late summer of 1942 he would likewise reverse the policies of his predecessor, reconstructing his new army on the same principles he had followed since Dunkirk.

Whether Auchinleck witnessed either of Bernard's great corps exercises in December 1940 is doubtful. Certainly Auchinleck was still in England until Boxing Day; he had, however, been officially informed in October 1940 that he was to be the new Commander-in-Chief in India, and was succeeded on 2 December by Lt-General the Hon. H. R. L. G. Alexander from 1 Corps – instead of Montgomery, Auchinleck's logical successor.

If Bernard was disappointed by Dill's decision, however, he did not show it; certainly Alexander's pragmatic approach to war was paradoxically more amenable to Bernard than the misguided firmness of Auchinleck. Alexander at least recognised the futility of fixed defences from his experiences in the BEF, and though incapable of organising large-scale exercises himself, he was genuinely delighted that Bernard – his erstwhile teacher at Camberley – should do so with such aplomb.

Seen historically, the relationship between Alexander and Montgomery from December 1940 to April 1941 was an important one. Bernard genuinely respected Alexander for his imperturbability, his refusal to concede invincibility to the Germans, and his innate charm, which made for easy relations between Corps HQ and Command HQ – 'The only man, yes, the *only* man under whom any admiral, general or air marshal would gladly serve in a subordinate position,' Bernard once remarked.[1] Alexander, conversely, had now a ringside seat at the spectacle of Bernard's 'New British Army', as *The Times* called it. His own fame, as a higher Commander, would largely rest on the achievements of this one subordinate and, like a sensitive painter who recognises a good subject, he made sure that he remained on the very best terms possible with Bernard.

The year 1940, meanwhile, drew to a close. Though Bernard scarcely ever saw his son David, he refused suggestions within the Montgomery family that his relatives should visit the boy, let alone look after him or even send him, for safety's sake, to Canada. The Carthews continued to look after David in the holidays or arrange to which camp or hostel he should be sent – for Bernard himself adhered rigidly to the doctrine he had laid down in 5 Corps about wives and families.

Besides, he had no home to which, say at Christmas time or on

[1] Goronwy Rees, *A Bundle of Sensations*, London 1960.

leave, he could have repaired with David. Even his belongings –
furniture, books, silver, documents, pictures and mementoes –
were in store in one of the depositories of Messrs Curtiss & Sons Ltd
in Gunwharf Road, Portsmouth, where Bernard had consigned them
on his departure from Ravelin House in 1938. But on the night of 10
January 1941, German bombers once again raided Portsmouth. The
depository in Gunwharf Road was hit by an incendiary bomb and
totally destroyed. The Board of Trade later assessed the value of
Bernard's possessions at £1000, less £7 'in lieu of insurance pre-
mium'; but locked away as the accumulated memory of his beloved
Betty, they could never be replaced.

Bernard, however, took the loss philosophically. The BEF had
survived at Dunkirk without its equipment; he himself would survive without chattels. On Boxing Day, as Auchinleck left Bournemouth for India, Bernard compiled his list of officers to go on the next
Staff College course in April 1941. The future lay not in equipment,
Bernard felt, but in the men who would use it.

CHAPTER TEN

The Stage-Management of Battle

Not everyone took to Bernard's style of 'army-building'. There was the case – which later became celebrated as an archetypal 'Monty' story – of the portly colonel who protested he would die if made to run the weekly seven-mile course. 'I then said,' Bernard recounted in his *Memoirs*, 'that if he was thinking of dying it would be better to do it now, as he could be replaced easily and smoothly; it is always a nuisance if officers die when the battle starts and things are inclined to be hectic. His state of health was clearly not very good, and I preferred him to do the run and die.'

The colonel – who did the run and lived to tell the tale – was one of many officers who resented the 5 Corps Commander's methods; and there were some, even in those days, who thought Montgomery a sight too showy for a mere infantryman. There were others, again, who felt Montgomery was wrong to engage the Corps in such strenuous winter exercises when they had endured such a nerve-racking summer preparing for likely invasion. Yet others felt – particularly after the successes in North Africa – that a political accommodation with the Germans might eventually be made, and that in the meantime the war was shifting irrevocably eastwards.

Bernard himself harboured no such illusions. His Intelligence officer was required to give, each week, a summary of the world military situation, together with forecasts of likely developments, and this was forwarded to all unit commanders. Political and military 'experts' were asked to speak at the 'study weeks' conducted within the Corps. As Bernard had written to his old GSO 3, 'Kit' Dawnay, German morale had not shown any real sign of falling; moreover it looked as if German policy towards Britain was becoming one of blockade, with the German Air Force acting under strategic naval command, mining the Western Approaches and blitzing the Atlantic-coast cities. If so, there was little likelihood of invasion before such a blockade could prove successful; and in the meantime Bernard felt it his duty to train his Corps for the battles he knew were ahead. He was determined that 5 Corps should become the premier fighting corps in the British Isles, and first War Office choice should such a corps be required for operations abroad. On 7 February 1941 he went to London to see Sir Alan Brooke and Sir John Dill, to whom

Lt-General Montgomery photographed on arrival in Cairo, 12 August 1942, having been summoned to take command of 8th Army. (*Imperial War Museum*)

General Sir Claude Auchinleck: 'A man of very great personal stature and integrity . . . but a defeated man.' Having personally assumed command of 8th Army after the fall of Tobruk, Auchinleck confers with his Director of Middle East Intelligence, Brig. de Guingand, 27 June 1942. (*Imperial War Museum*)

General Auchinleck outside 8th Army HQ after the disasters of 21–22 July 1942. (*Imperial War Museum*)

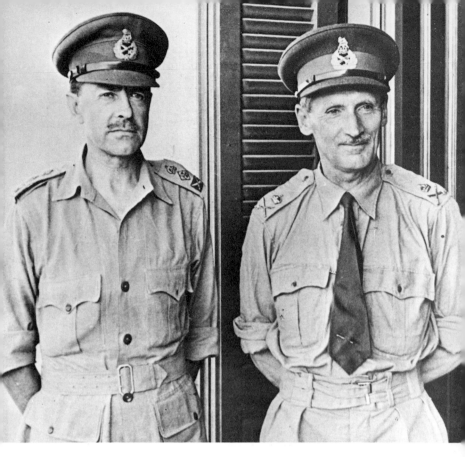

'Fit and fresh – new brains on an old problem' – the new C-in-C, Middle East, General Alexander, and the new 8th Army Commander, Lt-General Montgomery, evening of 12 August 1942. (*Imperial War Museum*)

'May the anniversary of Blenheim . . . bring to the Commander-in-Chief of the 8th Army and his troops the fame they will surely deserve.' A delighted Churchill with Lt-Gen. Montgomery, followed by Brooke. (*Imperial War Museum*)

(Opposite top) 'Everybody knew that we were not moving back, we were fighting here! That is that!' Brig. 'Pip' Roberts (in beret), Commander of 8th Army's only surviving Grant tanks, listens to the Army Commander's instructions, 20 August 1942. John Poston, ADC, and Lt-Gen. Horrocks on left. (*Imperial War Museum*)

(Opposite below) 'Every officer must be clear in his mind about the basic fundamentals – the things that really matter if you want to win your battles in this most modern war' – flying to the Middle East Staff College, Haifa, 21 September 1942. (*Imperial War Museum*)

Alamein: 'The enemy will not surrender . . . determined leadership will be very vital in this battle.' Inspecting officers of 1st Armoured Division, 10 October 1942. Lt.-Gen. Lumsden behind Montgomery's left shoulder. (*Imperial War Museum*)

Portrait of Rommel by Willrich which Lt-Gen. Montgomery hung in his caravan. (*Imperial War Museum*)

At the climax of the Battle of Alamein, Lt-Gen. Montgomery surveys the battlefield from his Grant tank. (*Imperial War Museum*)

Victory at Alamein: Gen. von Thoma, Commander of the famed Afrika
Korps, surrenders to Montgomery at 8th Army Tac. HQ, 4 November
1942. (*Imperial War Museum*)

no doubt he made his views on the subject clear; for six days later 'Orders were received from the War Office through Southern Command that HQ 5 Corps and 5 Corps troops were to mobilise with a view to becoming an overseas reserve'.[1]

In the event the orders were illusory; it was decided, much to Bernard's disgust, that a striking force be built up in the north of Scotland, to be titled Force 110 – under the command of Lt-General Alexander. History would prove that, despite the imagination and ingenuity of such contingents in the European theatre of operations, their value was almost invariably disproportionate to the energies, equipment and administration required to back them. The course of disasters in 1941 and 1942 would show that, until Britain recognised the importance of reconstructing her armies so that they could take on the Germans in the field, she was doomed to lose the war – and Churchill's Expeditionary Force schemes for the capture of the Canary Islands, Sicily, etc. were at best distractions, at worst a culpable misdirection of resources.

More and more it became Bernard Montgomery's historical mission to correct this disastrous British slide towards romanticism and parochialism in war – a mission which, as he would note with exasperation after Alamein, was itself much more gruelling than the comparatively straightforward task of defeating Germans in battle.

The responsibility of such a mission, together with the power – and, later, celebrity – that it brought, was bound to test Bernard's mental as well as physical health. That he managed to preserve a semblance of sanity is perhaps more surprising than his occasional quasi-schizoid 'turns'. Brigadier Simpson, as the new 5 Corps Chief of General Staff was, for instance, alarmed by Bernard's strict adherence to his own Corps rules, though fortunately he was not afraid to speak up before his new master. At the 4th Division Major-General Swayne had wisely 'tempered' the Corps instructions about weekly exercise: 'General Swayne said he could see no point in himself, aged about fifty, running round a seven-mile course, but he walked round the course at a pretty brisk pace and he usually invited me to walk with him,' Simpson recalled. Although some ten years younger, Simpson declared, 'I would certainly have been incapable of running seven miles at a stretch.'[2] Swayne's tempering 'seemed to satisfy everyone.'

> To my horror, however, when I got to Corps HQ I found that Monty himself, then into his middle 50s, was jogging round the course, and I was very strongly of the opinion that this was not good for him. So I put the argument to him as General Swayne had put it to me, that we slightly older people should not stretch ourselves to an intolerable extent.

[1] War Diary, HQ 5 Corps, loc. cit.
[2] Wason Interviews, loc. cit.

I told Monty that I certainly wouldn't run seven miles at a stretch but that I would walk briskly around the course. To my relief he saw my point at once and said: 'You and I will walk together.' And every week we did walk together very briskly round the course. I like to think that by this I saved Monty for his triumphs later on in the war!

Simpson also encountered proverbial ice in 5 Corps HQ mess, where the senior brigadiers and colonels – Artillery, Engineers, Signals – ate with the Corps Commander. Because Bernard had turned teetotal after his illness in 1939, and knowing his propensity to see in every sundowner-drinker a possible alcoholic, no one dared to drink openly before the meal. Instead a

> surreptitious sort of alcove, rather like a cupboard, was installed in the passage outside the mess and they used to slip in there for a quick one or two before dinner.
> Whether Monty realised what was going on or not I never knew, but I thought it was something quite undesirable. So on my first evening in the mess I went up to the Corps Commander and said: 'Sir, you know my habits. I like a drink or two before dinner. Do you mind if I set up a table in the ante-room for drinks?'
> He looked at me and said: 'Of course, Simbo – I have no objection. So do what you want – but don't ask me to join you.'
> The other faces round about lightened up at once and in no time at all a table was installed in the ante-room. After that everything was fair and above board.
> I tell this little story to show that Monty was not the inhuman man he has sometimes been made out to be . . .

Meanwhile, Bernard's relentless programme of training was continued. On 28 January 1941, 5 Corps Exercise No. 3 began: a night operation carried out by the 3rd Division and Corps troops to see whether it could achieve the same success as an armoured division assaulting by day. 'The object,' as the Tactical Instruction No. 1 announced on 3 January, 'is to study the handling of a Corps

a) Brought up from the reserve area some 70 miles behind the battle-front
b) Being then passed by night through a front broken by other troops
c) And being given the task of continuing relentless pressure on the retreating enemy

'The Corps will in fact be used by night to carry out a task which would be carried out by day by an armoured division if one was available.

'Bridging problems will play a large part in the exercise and the R. Thames will be bridged by the Corps and divisional troops.'

432

Parachutists and close-support bombers were also involved, and the exercise followed Bernard's now familiar technique of a cloth-model demonstration in advance, on 18 January, at which Bernard gave
a) The General Setting
b) The Problem confronting 5 Corps
c) The Intention and Plan of the Corps Commander
d) Verbal orders by Corps Commander
e) Description of support to be provided by the RAF, parachutists, close-support and tactical recce aircraft
f) Arrangements for inter-communication
g) Administrative arrangements[1]

After the exercise, on 3 February, the umpires, participating officers and guests attended the by-now traditional Bernard post mortem conference at the Plaza Cinema, Dorchester.

The same exercise was then repeated by the other field division in 5 Corps, the 4th Division, beginning on 11 February. This time Bernard's address, at the Odeon Cinema, Bournemouth on 17 February, was issued as a typescript record – a ten-page review which not only gives a valuable insight into Bernard's growing confidence in the art of addressing large numbers of officers, but also the tactical concepts to which, early in 1941, he attached most importance.

In the winter of 1939–40, Bernard's BEF exercises had rehearsed the technique of mechanised movement (especially by night) of a complete infantry division with all its arms, headquarters and attached troops. Now, early in 1941, he was satisfied that large-scale movement by MT was thoroughly understood, to the point where commanders could count on bringing a reinforcing division *in toto* a distance of seventy miles by night and into action without fear of muddle or confusion: 'As a result of the experience we have gained I am prepared to state definitely that large-scale movement by MT such as was done at this exercise is possible [in battle] and I am also prepared to say that a speed of 15 MPH can be maintained throughout.'

In Bernard's first 5 Corps exercises he had experimented in the additional use of an armoured division and infantry support tanks. The new exercises, early in 1941, had now involved the RAF in a closer support role (as the Luftwaffe operated), had experimented further in the use of parachutists (four drops had taken place) and had provided an opportunity to study the techniques of exploitation, once enemy defences were breached.

Far from being too cautious or uninterested in exploitation, as Liddell Hart later claimed, Bernard was, from the moment he felt his Corps was properly trained in the basic techniques of cohesive movement, of sound defence and organised attack, its ardent cham-

[1] War Diary, HQ 5 Corps, loc. cit.

pion. No one was more aware than Bernard how the final months of 1918 on the Western Front had involved quite different techniques of warfare than the preceding years; and before the 800-odd assembled officers Bernard now re-examined the very precepts which, until this moment, had characterised his own training doctrine. For instance, Bernard had always insisted on the paramount importance of centralised artillery control, and the need to command a division as a division, lest it fragment into units that were used piecemeal, thus dissipating the division's greatest collective asset. However, once the corps had punctured the enemy defence and had moved into the realm of mobile operations different techniques were called for:

Offensive Operations in Mobile War
23.   When the battle is fluid, centralized control of supporting arms and weapons will not produce successful action. Resources such as artillery, tanks and so on, must be decentralized and placed under command of infantry brigades and when necessary infantry battalions. In fluid operations and generally when moving against unarmoured resistance, general progress will depend on the skilful grouping of the various arms. The more fluid the fighting, the greater should be the degree of decentralization, the aim being to have *available immediately* those weapons which are necessary for cracking the nut involved at the moment.
    For example the forward companies of a battalion should have available the immediate support of artillery, tanks, etc. for quick action where needed. There will be periods when light forces – i.e. carriers and motorcyclists, will be used forward; when this is the case the heavy forces – i.e. tanks, etc. – must be kept handy in reserve. When the light forces encounter resistance which is too strong for them the heavy forces (the infantry tanks) move up and deal with the problem, the light forces watching the flanks or taking other appropriate action.

To illustrate this policy in the minds of the assembled officers Bernard used one of those similes which gave his subordinates the feeling that battles, like most things in life, were quite straightforward matters if one only applied logic and common sense. Decentralisation, Bernard declared, could be

compared to a carpenter going to work and carrying his bag of tools. The bag contains every tool likely to be required during the day's work; he uses for each job the particular tool essential for that job, taking it from the bag as and when needed.

This state of affairs, however, could only last so long:

25.   There will come a time when further progress by those means will not be possible. Extreme decentralisation of resources is not suitable in dealing with resistance which is in any way organized. The decentralised resources will have therefore to be gathered in, so that a good blow can be delivered at the selected point.

The speed with which this could be done depended largely on the relations between infantry and artillery:

26.   The time that it will take to stage this blow will depend on what is required from the artillery. Generally the success of the attack will depend on the concentrated fire of artillery on certain areas from which comes the fire that is holding up the advance. It will be necessary for the infantry to locate those areas and point them out to the artillery.
        It will be for the artillery to register them, and take such action as is necessary to ensure that accurate fire can be brought to bear at the required moment.
        All this will not be done within any reasonable time,

Bernard warned,

unless the infantry and artillery thoroughly understand the technique involved, and are highly trained in its application. Artillery resources are allotted from above – but the detailed fire-plan is built up from below, and the infantry company commanders and gunner FOOs [Forward Observation Officers] have got to be very active and in very close touch, and both have got to know what is involved.

There had been a time when such things were part and parcel of regular army training; now with the urgency of war and the increasing number of officers without previous experience, it was important to clarify the problem and teach the techniques of dealing with it.

They must make sure that they seize and hold securely all necessary viewpoints on the front so that the future attack can be prepared. This must be their main pre-occupation as soon as it becomes apparent that the advance is going to come to a standstill.

The young infantry officer must be taught co-operation with the other arms; conversely

the gunner for his part has got to ensure that he can profit immediately from the results of good action by the infantry.
        Firstly OP [Observation Post] parties must be so organized that

they can deal with any situation that may develop. Usually one officer with R/T in an armoured carrier is provided.

The FOO is on a mission of great importance. He must carry through his task in the face of casualties to personnel or equipment or when faced with difficulties on ground. A proper OP party should consist of armoured OP with an officer, one truck carrying a good WO [Warrant Officer] or Sergeant, one or two signallers with reserve signalling equipment and 2 or 3 miles of cable with two telephones, and one motorcycle DR [Despatch Rider]. Such a party, suitably disposed and concealed, could deal with any situation; and artillery support would not cease if the armoured OP was put out of action or the R/T failed to work.

Secondly in cases where artillery has to move, single guns must be sent forward early to register from the new position. There must never be any question of artillery, which has had to move forward, being unable to shoot until batteries have got shot in from new positions. Constant pre-vision must be exercised so that artillery support will be continuous.

One by one Bernard drew the lessons of the exercise and gave the clearest indication of what was required in order to deal with the problems that arose. His message was always one of common sense. For instance it was idle to assume that because of the danger of interception one ought to observe W/T or R/T silence – as had happened in the BEF before the Germans launched their attack on 10 May 1940. The subsequent chaos in communications was ridiculous and unnecessary. All that was needed was to study 'what the interceptor organisation can do' and 'learn to employ any and every artifice which will help to defeat the interceptor organisation'. Given brevity, jargon, and care not to reveal one's own dispositions or too much about the enemy's, there was no reason why, with constant practice, R/T and W/T communication should not be characteristic of modern mobile warfare.

It was time now, Bernard felt, for the various units of the Corps to concentrate on individual training and a thorough review of the lessons learned in the past six months. Fifty percent of the Corps transport was to be withdrawn from the roads for maintenance, repair and fresh training of MT craftsmen. There would be a six-week pause before the next corps exercise – in which the two field divisions would fight each other – and in this time training was to be aimed at the handling of mortars, fieldcraft, weapons, unit and sub-unit training, night training, and junior leader training.

Bernard certainly had good reason to be proud of his work over the past six months, and in his own hand he drew up a summary which he sent to Alexander at Southern Command – and doubtless also to Sir Alan Brooke at GHQ Home Forces. It was, and would remain, a model of how a defeated army can be rebuilt – and makes Auchinleck's remark about Bernard's efforts being 'mostly rubbish' a strangely self-revealing one.[1]

Bernard's 5 Corps Training Report October 1940–March 1941 covered some six foolscap pages, and provides ample proof, if proof were needed, of his outstanding impact as a Corps Commander. What Bernard was anxious to show was that he was not simply hardening soldiers for eventual battle, or ensuring their efficiency at their various jobs, as Brooke had done in command of 2 Corps. The object of 5 Corps' winter training was no less than the creation of a modern army: an army such as Britain had not fielded for more than a century, trained in England, but capable of meeting a modern enemy force anywhere in the world.

This object had been achieved by a logical and coherent approach to training. First, a Corps Study Week had enabled unit commanders to meet and discuss on the cloth-model the various operations of war they would be likely to conduct. Unit training had then been geared to train the Corps up to a standard at which such operations could be mounted successfully; and, from platoon to full corps level, 5 Corps had prepared itself for and rehearsed the various operations. Each field division had 'gone out, like a ship in full sail, and remained out for 48 hours, and in later exercises for 4 days,' Bernard recorded. 'The machinery of command has been exercised, Commanders of all grades have got practice in facing up to difficult situations under realistic conditions and in the hurly-burly of the battle. Unit commanders have been given the opportunity of commanding their units under battle conditions. Administration, services supply, the recovery of vehicles, etc. have been well stretched and tested out. Staffs have got really good practical training.' Moreover, 'in between the large-scale formation exercises have been smaller exercises for brigades, and minor sub-unit training. Each battalion has been "out" once a week. In these exercises the junior leader has been taught his trade, and has been practised in the handling of his sub-unit (the platoon, the mortar platoon, the artillery troop, and so on).' Finally the 'individual training of the man and the use of his weapons or his specialised job, has been carried out throughout the whole winter. Great emphasis has been paid to the improvement of mental fitness and the training has been directed to bringing officers and men to that state of mental and physical fitness which will give them complete confidence in their ability to take on an enemy at any time.'

As a result, Bernard declared, 'I am satisfied that the 3rd and 4th divisions can be classified as 1st Class Divisions, and fit in every way to engage in battle with the Germans'.

Could this be said of other divisions, and of other commanders, in Britain in February 1941?

'We have today,' Bernard noted in his report, 'divisional comman-

---

[1] Roger Parkinson, *The Auk*, London 1977.

ders and divisional staffs who have never handled a division under "full sail" at any time, not even on the training area. Administration is weak and co-ordination of staff at Divisional HQ is inclined to be sketchy. These large-scale Corps exercises were very necessary,' Bernard argued. 'It is essential that all administrative echelons should be tested out and be well stretched. An exercise lasting 48 hours hardly does this. I have therefore in my last 2 exercises had divisions out for 4 days, and it has proved well worth while.'[1]

Bernard had reversed the pre-war convention that winter training be confined to indoor instruction. The weather had limited his ambitious use of tactical air support, but in view of the winter campaigns in Tunisia in 1942, in Italy in 1943, and in North-West Europe in 1944, Bernard's relentless approach was salutary. Moreover, in training British troops to smash an enemy invasion, Bernard was able to rehearse the very scenario that would apply to his German opponents on the shores of France in 1944. If Bernard was able to radiate confidence in the success of a cross-Channel assault in 1944, and welcomed Rommel's doctrine of meeting the Allied invasion on the beaches, it was because he had already fought this battle with his own commanding officer, General Auchinleck, in the summer and autumn of 1940. In other words, Bernard's great corps exercises in the winter of 1940–41 not only served to train the various echelons under his command: they were the nearest equivalent to battle-experience for the Commander of 5 Corps too. Where Gort had squandered every opportunity to train his army and himself in the long months of the 'phoney war' the previous winter, Bernard was determined not to waste a moment in command; and what was an education in modern warfare and training to his subordinates became for him too an invaluable preparation for high command.

The climax of Bernard Montgomery's efforts to train 5 Corps for operations abroad was Exercise No. 5: a sort of Cup Final in which he would set his two infantry divisions against one another. Once again it was to be a four-day affair, lasting from 24 to 27 March. This time, however, there were no pre-ordained or circumscribed tactical features to seize or cross. 'The object of the exercise,' Bernard declared in his first secret instructions on 1 March, 'is to study certain aspects of mobile operations between two forces where opposing commanders have freedom of action and manoeuvre.' The 4th Division, representing Hampshire, was instructed to invade Dorset, defended by the 3rd Division, and given as its object the Tank Centre at Bovington.

The two divisional commanders were left free to plan, prepare and execute their own operations. Four weeks later, on 31 March, Bernard addressed all five hundred or so officers who had taken part in the 'battle for Bovington' at the Odeon Cinema, Bournemouth. His

[1] War Diary, HQ 5 Corps, loc. cit.

address, once again, lasted for several hours as he first set the scene of the exercise, then chronicled the course of the battle, depicting how the commander of the assaulting 4th Division had swung with his right, while the commander of the 3rd Division had expected a thrust on the enemy left. By means of a brilliantly clean break-away on the first night the 3rd Division withdrew its forces intact: luring the fumbling enemy the following day on to a belt of prepared demolitions which cut off the leading troops from the main echelons of the 4th Division and forced Bernard to intervene in order to keep the exercise going. The exercise had ended with a head-on dawn collision between attacking and counter-attacking brigades of the two divisions, followed by a parachute landing near Bovington and a break-through assisted by tanks.

Few officers present at the Odeon Cinema would ever forget the ease and clarity with which Lt-General Montgomery recounted the saga of the exercise. Here was no distant, austere commander known only by edicts from HQ. Short in stature, smartly turned out but not yet distinctive, in modern battle-blouse and trousers, with balding small head, wispy grey hair, sharp cheekbones and a long, beaky nose, he spoke in a high voice with a pronounced lisp in his Rs; and he held his audience spellbound.

No one has ever satisfactorily explained the secret of Bernard Montgomery's unique impact as a military orator, but doubtless his ability to command the attention of the officers of an entire Corps assembled in an English cinema lay partly in the interaction between his ruthless, ego-orientated character (epitomised in the 'No smoking or coughing' order during his address) and the strange humility intrinsic in his exposition: namely the patent ingenuousness of his interest in the 'art' of war, and his transcending confidence that, if properly put over, it would interest others. Here in fact, to those sensitive to the shades of history, was a presentation by perhaps the greatest educator in the art of war that Britain had ever produced. His students, whether in the Royal Warwickshire Regiment or the Staff Colleges at Camberley and Quetta, had always been convinced of his outstanding talents as a tactical instructor. But here now was a somewhat different Montgomery: an active Corps Commander anxious to impart to every officer in his constituent field divisions not only a clear retrospective picture of the 'battle' in which they had just been engaged, but to use that battle to illustrate and help examine the very principles and tactics a modern British army must employ in order to be successful in the field. In a single winter he had transformed 5 Corps from a collection of divisions 'defending' Britain's southern coast into a modern army trained to fight anywhere in the world: trained in movement, the co-operation of all arms – infantry, artillery, engineers, air support, tanks, and parachutists – and the paramount virtue of being able to bring to bear the cohesive might of an entire fighting division:

General Lessons of the Exercise
This exercise brought out very clearly certain basic points in the art of fighting a mobile battle. With wide fronts and speed of movement that is possible today, experience in this war has pointed to the fact that operations are likely to be very mobile.

I would like to give you my views on certain aspects of the mobile battle against an enemy like the Germans,

Bernard declared.

I will deal with 5 main points.

First: The Art of Night Movement
I am convinced that we have got to cultivate the art of moving by night and this night movement must have as its object the gaining of such ground or positions as will enable the battle to be pursued with advantage when daylight comes. The Germans do not move by night. This then is our opportunity to gain tactical advantages and defeat him.

Move by night, fight by day.

I am not prepared to admit that in 5 Corps we cannot do anything we like by night. In all our exercises this winter we have done things by night which some people would say were not possible.

It is all a matter of training. A higher commander must know how to plan and stage-manage the night movement of an operation; after that what he can do will depend on the standard of training of his troops in operating by night. If A can move and operate any hour of the 24 and B can move and operate only by day, then A will always beat B. And this is very applicable to the mobile battle.

But this philosophy of battle has certain repercussions and the technique has got to be studied. Unless the main points are clearly understood, you will not get successful results. Two of these points affect the handling of artillery and the traffic problem.

Second: The Handling of Artillery
In mobile operations it is undesirable to commit to action all the artillery until it is clear as to the area in which the main artillery effort is required. In this exercise in the 4th Division a group of two Field Regiments was placed under command of each leading infantry brigade when the advance started at midnight on the night 25–26 March.

In 3rd Division all the artillery was deployed in action before the direction of the enemy's main effort became clear.

The handling of the two Field Regiments as a group by one Lt-Colonel is quite simple once stabilization sets in. But it is much

440

more complicated in mobile operations and is generally inadvisable.

It is mainly a matter of ammunition and how many tubes are required to fire the available shells. It is also a matter of congestion on the roads and, in mobile operations with an enemy with a strong air force, it is essential not to have on the roads more vehicles than are absolutely necessary to fight the battle. One Field Regiment, less its B echelon to transport, has 109 vehicles and at 15 VTM covers 7 miles of road.

I consider that normally, in mobile operations, it would be best to commit to action in support of an infantry brigade only one Field Regiment in the first instance. The remainder is best kept in reserve under divisional control, moving forward by bounds along such routes as will render it as simple as possible to reinforce the front or to a flank. The regimental commanders of reserve units, with their staff, should be well forward, keeping in constant touch with the CRA [Commander, Royal Artillery] and carrying out reconnaissances as directed by him.

Third: The Traffic Problem
It is vital for the successful conduct of operations in mobile war that the roads should be free for movement and that the congestion of traffic should not occur. This will necessitate a thorough understanding of the problem by every commander and in this connection there are two points that are very important.

First, we must arrive at what is the minimum number of vehicles that are required to carry the unit into battle. I have already referred to road space of 7 miles taken by a Field Regiment. An infantry battalion must study how to split its A echelon transport into A1 and A2 groups and should be able to manage with about 18 vehicles, the A2 group moving by bounds in the rear. Similarly for other units.

Second, there must be a good traffic plan covering the divisional area. This must include a combined RE plan to deal with demolitions, craters and other blocks on essential routes. Generally it happens that brigade transport, other than that with units, is scattered about over a large area in small packets. This does not facilitate control, movement or the rapid execution of orders, and creates difficulties in so far as protection is concerned. Infantry brigades must keep a tight hold over their transport and move it forward by bounds. In a rapid advance or withdrawal it may sometimes be necessary for the divisional staff to assume some measure of control; this may be particularly necessary where bridges, communications, etc. are limited. Unless this is done there can be no proper traffic control plan, nor can reinforcing units be brought forward with certainty on time . . .

Finally the staff must make such arrangements as will enable a

441

demolition or cratering plan by the enemy to be dealt with energetically.

There must be a combined G, Q and RE plan. The essentials will be early information, reconnaissance, provision of tools, and labour.

Fourth: Demolitions

I am convinced that in mobile operations we can get good value from delaying demolitions.

In this exercise we had a good example of a force withdrawing deliberately in order to draw the enemy on; when the enemy was astride the concealed demolitions they went off and caused great delay and confusion.

It may not always be advisable to leave firing parties to fire charges in accordance with traffic conditions. It will be more normal to produce a belt of craters with delayed action explosives timed to go off at set hours.

Alternatively we must learn how to deal effectively with a demolition scheme laid on by a retreating enemy. There is no doubt that a cunningly prepared scheme of demolitions is one of the greatest delaying factors there is. If these form a deep belt over a wide front they can stop all movement.

We must therefore study the demolition problem in 2 ways: A) How to use them. B) How to overcome them when used by the enemy.

Fifth: Man Management

In prolonged mobile operations a great strain is imposed on commanders and staff and troops – particularly on infantry who have to move everywhere on foot.

It is essential that the standard of physical fitness should be high and the powers of endurance great. This is just as necessary in the case of commanders and staff as it is in the case of troops. The more senior the greater the need for him to attend to his own fitness.

Many senior officers exhort others to be fit, and neglect to become so themselves. It is very necessary that the soldiers be given a good breakfast, however early this may be. He is then given a haversack ration and a full water bottle, and he must be trained to last on this till after dark, when he must be given a good meal.

Every commander must understand that the infantry soldier cannot move and fight all day and all night, continuously. A fit soldier will carry on continuously for 24 hours without sleep or rest. He will go on longer, but after that period he cannot be expected to have the same energy or 'binge'.

The aim must be to confront the enemy always with soldiers who are 'on their toes'. Therefore a nice balance must be held between operational requirements and the need to keep the infantry units fresh. The answer lies in reliefs and in ensuring that units in reserve do take advantage of every opportunity to get the troops rested.

In Field Army units we have now got this subject well understood. This exercise lasted five days for all units, and seven days for some units. I was much impressed by the fitness of the infantry, as was shown by the fine bearing of those units I saw marching home after the exercise . . .

It is interesting to note how the daily sick rate drops as the troops become fit and hard. The average daily admission to hospital in divisions of 5 Corps during the past winter has been 10 per day per division of 16,000 men.

On this exercise which lasted five days the sick rate dropped to 5 per day per division. It was wet and cold, and the troops had no billets.

It seems therefore that our troops thrive on continuous operations in unpleasant weather. All through this winter and in fact always, it has been a basic principle in 5 Corps that no exercises are stopped because of the weather conditions. We carry on under any conditions and I am sure that this is right.

These 'lessons' are quoted at length because they so clearly show the reasons for Bernard's growing reputation as a trainer of troops at this time. What was involved was not simply the provision of minor battle schools (as Lt-General Alexander pressed for) nor the preparation of troops for certain specific manoeuvres. Field-Marshal Templer, then a Brigade Commander in 5 Corps, would later reflect that 'it was Monty's achievement to re-build the British Army in England after Dunkirk. There is no doubt that, however much he was mocked outside 5 Corps, his methods were copied and in time became the accepted doctrine throughout the Army, particularly in Southern England'.[1]

What concerned Bernard was not simply 'training' in the normal sense, but a re-education in the art of modern warfare as understandable to a 2nd Lieutenant as to a Divisional Commander. He had the ability, as no other general in the British Army had demonstrated since Napoleonic times, to marry the disparate and often competing elements of modern warfare into an understandable, meaningful whole, conveying a vision in which he was able to address himself in the same breath to a commander's conduct of battle and to the nutritional requirements of a fit infantry soldier. All were woven together into a uniquely clear picture of the requirements of modern warfare.

Moreover the addresses Bernard gave to his officers in 5 Corps in

---

[1] Field-Marshal Sir Gerald Templer, loc. cit.

1940–41 provide a fascinating glimpse into certain tactical views held by a commander still largely unknown within, let alone outside the British Army, shortly before some of the seminal battles in military history. Few of his exercises had been strictly related to the repulse of a mythical invasion: Bernard was educating himself and the many thousands of officers and men under his command for future battles abroad, and was therefore not disheartened by RAF indifference to his vision of an air striking force working hand-in-glove with the army – it was enough for the moment, he felt, that he had managed to educate the formation HQs in the skeletal use of air 'tentacles' in battle exercises. Another example, in the light of the battles of Normandy and Arnhem fought some three years later, was the role of parachute troops – on which subject, in his address on 30 March 1941, he had this to say:

The Employment of Parachute Troops
We have studied this problem for some time in 5 Corps and have certain practical experience on exercises. I will now deal with certain lessons we have learnt.

A basic principle of their employment is that there should be a good and reasonable chance that after they have completed their mission they will be picked up again by our own troops. I regard this of the first importance. Any violation of this principle is bound to affect morale adversely. It follows therefore that they will not generally be suitable for example as part of a defensive plan, unless good facilities exist for getting them back by some round-about means, or possibly by sea.

Next: Harassing tasks Harassing operations against enemy headquarters, signals or columns, communications and adminis-trative areas is probably the most suitable employment for para-chute troops. Their sub-unit organization caters for this type of operations – a troop consisting of 50 men carried in six aircraft. The limit to the size of party which can be dropped depends on the number of aircraft available.

Seizing key points This is another very suitable role. When our own troops are advancing, parachute troops can be dropped behind enemy lines in order to secure vital points such as bridges. The main problem in connection with this type of operation is recognition . . . Experiments are going on with the dropping of a small wireless set of very limited range. This set will probably be dropped on the men. Provided that the necessary arrangements for tuning in to the proper frequencies are made beforehand, the use of these sets will greatly assist in overcoming the problem of recognition. When parachute troops are used in this role it is essential that they shall not be employed too deep into the enemy's country in order that the time before relief by the advance of our own forces or troops shall be as short as possible . . .

This was a salutary rider. Moreover, among the requirements Bernard gave for parachute operations was a 'dropping zone clear of enemy parachute troops' and 'absolutely up to date information about enemy troops in the area in which they are to operate' – requirements tragically neglected in the drop of the British 1st Airborne Division at Arnhem in 1944.

Nevertheless Bernard's interest in the whole question of parachute operations was pioneering in the winter of 1940–41, and much more than gimmickry.

'In a modern army,' he declared to the assembled officers of all ranks,

the employment of parachute troops must have a very definite place in any plan of battle. For this reason I wish greater attention paid to the subject and in 5 Corps we will work on the general principles outlined above.

Again, this was a preoccupation by the Corps Commander that did not readily convince officers and men outside 5 Corps of its immediate relevance – until, to the consternation of the world, the Germans launched an airborne invasion of Crete some seven weeks later.

It is certainly likely that Bernard hoped he would be called upon to take the field divisions of 5 Corps abroad in the spring of 1941. Throughout his relentless training programme during the winter he had always kept a sharp eye on developments on the Continent. The weekly Intelligence summaries which his Corps Intelligence had to produce were usually between five and ten pages long, with compulsory forecasts; and Bernard's interest did not stop there, for he was constantly seeking out verbal or written 'appreciations' from Operations and Intelligence officers – such as 'Kit' Dawnay – outside the Corps. His Corps Intelligence correctly predicted the German attack on Russia, the assault on Greece, and Rommel's build-up of forces in Libya. We know that General Sir Alan Brooke visited Bernard at Longford Castle the day after Bernard's final conference on Exercise No. 5, and it is more than likely that Bernard informed Brooke that he felt his field divisions were now ready for battle – so much so, in fact, that he had decided to dispense with further exercises and follow a new policy: that of training, in the next weeks and months, his non-field forces to the point where they could relieve the 3rd and 4th Divisions for active service abroad.

Already in January 1941 Bernard had pushed through a reorganisation of his non-field forces, whereby they were to be formed into proper divisions – a Hants Division and a Dorset Division. From the end of March they were to abandon work on defences and – in the same way that the field forces of 5 Corps were told by Bernard to drop the work ordered on defences by General Auchinleck in July 1940 – to start intensive training as cohesive, modern infantry divisions. In

445

his Training Instruction No. 20 issued on 21 March, Bernard had announced this new policy – which hinged on his field divisions providing both the equipment and the instructors.

'We have a great chance to produce a really first class army in England,' Bernard declared.

To do so the County Divisions must be helped by the Field Army. The material is excellent and progress will be rapid once the help is provided. 3 and 4 Divisions have been training hard all winter and are now in a position to help others.

The change in work and outlook will be good for all concerned.

By raising County Divisions to a high standard we shall be making it more possible for Field Army troops to leave this country should they be needed elsewhere.

The tendency in the past in County Divisions has been to concentrate on defences and to neglect the training of the men. But the defences are now getting very good. We must therefore now concentrate on the men who are to hold them. Good and well-trained men who are mentally alert, offensively minded and skilled in fieldcraft are just as essential as good defences. They are in fact more essential.

This instruction was spelled out by Bernard at the end of his address on 31 March to the officers of 3rd and 4th Divisions. Just as he had, in 1923, decried the division of the British Army into Regular and Territorial forces, he now called for the final abandonment of the term 'beach-defence' – a term of contempt now among his highly-trained field forces:

We do not want two categories of troops and I am quite certain that we do not want two armies in England. As far as I am concerned the 5 Corps consists of four divisions: 3 Div, 4 Div, Hants Div, Dorset Div. All must consist of first class troops, trained up to a high standard. All belong to the 5 Corps with all that that implies; that does imply a good deal, because our standards are high.

I do not want to hear any more talk of Beach Divisions or Beach Battalions. 5 Corps is responsible for some 215 miles of English beaches, but I have never heard anyone refer to 5 Corps as a Beach Corps.

Units of County Divisions will in future be referred to as County Battalions. The expression Beach Battalion can result only in defensive beach-bound mentality, and is forbidden . . .

I have given orders that as from 1st April all work on coastal defences will be cut down to what is necessary to maintain existing works in proper repair. In place of work the County Battalions will devote their energies to training in their present sectors. In addition each battalion in turn will come off the coast for a month's training, and during this month it will be concentrated in a camp inland where it can have a central officer's mess, sergeant's mess and be out of sight of the beaches . . .

The assistance that will be given by battalions of 3 and 4 Divisions will be up to 100% of what is asked for, even if their own training thereby suffers. In order to get County Battalions off the coast and concentrated for training they will have to be relieved by Battalions of 3 and 4 Divisions. While they are out of the line they will have to take part in any large-scale exercises there may be, taking their place in the brigade concerned, and being lent the transport of that battalion. That is going to be the policy as regards our County Divisions.

Conclusion

Finally I would like to remind you as to what are the basic principles which govern all our training in 5 Corps. They are three: *First*: The large-scale formation exercise to teach the stage-management and technique of battle. The whole formation goes out like a ship in full sail and everyone knows his own particular part in the battle and it is brought home to everyone that if the machine as a whole is to run smoothly and efficiently, a very high degree of unit and sub-unit efficiency is essential.
Second: The minor tactical training, and the specialist training of the individual. Once battle is joined, the final result is going to depend on the junior leader and his sub-unit. If the standard of the sub-unit efficiency is low, then you fail, however good your higher leading.
Third: The training of physical and mental fitness, to which we pay so much attention in 5 Corps. What is the use of being militarily perfect if the soldiers haven't got the will to kill Germans, and haven't got the light of battle in their eyes? It is no use.

Certain Germans and Germanophile historians would take exception to this exhortation to 'kill Germans', maintaining that this was somehow unchivalrous.[1] It is however obvious to anyone who either served under Montgomery or has studied his career that the phrase 'killing Germans' denoted no great blood-lust or even hatred of Germans. On the contrary, all Bernard's addresses and memoranda after Dunkirk had extolled the professional expertise of the German soldier and his well-mannered discipline. It was Bernard's belief that English morale could be best raised not by Hitlerian rhetoric or propaganda but by a new attitude, a new professionalism, in the British Army: a pride in doing things efficiently. Yet, having trained the field divisions of 5 Corps to modern battle-worthiness, he was at

[1] Cf. David Irving, *The Trail of the Fox*, op. cit.

pains to remind his officers that faultless technique would not, in itself, bring success. War was not a game; and to this new professionalism must be allied a fundamental determination to kill or be killed.

We know from Brooke's diary that Brooke had conferred with Sir John Dill on 4 February 1941, about the 'promotion of Corps Commanders'. Evidently this did not include Bernard; nor was Bernard now sent abroad, as he had hoped. In the time-honoured British fashion, catastrophe must follow catastrophe and failure be heaped upon failure before a leader be appointed capable of reversing the tide of German victory. Alexander, Brooke, even Churchill would owe their survival and varying measures of their fame to Bernard's eventual success in battle; yet in 1941 Alexander largely took the credit for the new professionalism sweeping through Southern Command; Brooke failed to put Bernard forward as a candidate for active command abroad until the summer of 1942, when the capital of Egypt was threatened; and even then allowed Churchill and his South African adviser Smuts to overrule him, and appoint instead a general ten years younger to command of 8th Army.

It is to Bernard's credit that he never once voiced, on this issue, the slightest dissatisfaction with the decisions of his superiors. However egotistical he would later be accused of being, he was at this time a soldier entirely dedicated to the cause of his country, and never allowed his confidence to weaken that one day he would be 'called'.

In the meantime, on 7 April 1941 Bernard was summoned to GHQ Home Forces, where Sir Alan Brooke informed him of a change of command. If Bernard hoped he might be offered an area or army command (such as Auchinleck had assumed on leaving 5 Corps the previous summer, or Alexander on leaving 1 Corps the previous December) he was sadly mistaken. Instead he was merely sidestepped to 12 Corps, which was responsible for the defence of the south-east coast, covering Kent and Sussex. This was, of course, the primary target of a potential German invasion; but as Bernard's Chief-of-Staff, Brigadier Simpson, later recalled, Bernard did not believe such an invasion would come – not at least until Hitler had disposed of Russia and the Balkans, which could not happen overnight.

On 10 April Bernard departed for a few days' leave. No doubt he also wished to think over his move to 12 Corps, and how to present this to his staff and subordinates at 5 Corps. He was anxious to take his Chief-of-Staff with him; he had recommended the Commander of 4th Division, 'Teddy' Schreiber, to succeed him as Corps Commander, and the Brigadier of 210th Brigade, Gerald Templer, to succeed Simpson as Chief-of-Staff at 5 Corps. He thus ensured that the tactical and training doctrines he had introduced to 5 Corps would be carried on – so successfully, in fact, that when interviewed in his eighties, Field-Marshal Templer was sure he had moved to 5 Corps as Chief-of-Staff to Montgomery himself at this time.[1]

On 21 April Bernard again travelled to London 'to be put in the picture of the new Corps he takes over from "Bulgy" [Thorne]', Brooke noted in his diary; and on the 24th Lt-General Montgomery issued a Special Order of the Day:

1. I have been ordered to leave 5 Corps and take over another command elsewhere.
    It is with regret that I leave.
2. I would like to thank commanders of all ranks and all those serving under them, for their enthusiastic co-operation during the time I have commanded the Corps.
    Our standards have been high and we have aimed at nothing but the best.
    We have made great progress during the past winter in the Corps – containing the same divisions as the old 2 Corps in the BEF in France. It is a first class fighting Corps ready and fit to fight any enemy anywhere.
    It can be said, and with pride, that the name of 5 Corps stands for a good deal throughout the army in England.
3. I am very conscious of the fact that the results we have obtained together have been due to the wholehearted co-operation and hard work on the part of every individual in the Corps, and not to anything I may have been able to achieve myself.
    I wish this fact to be made known throughout the Corps, my grateful thanks conveyed to every officer and man.
4. The best of luck, and good fighting to you all.

The same day he bade farewell to all his brigadiers in person. On 25 April, he travelled to Portsmouth to say goodbye to the Naval C-in-C, Admiral James, and to Lt-General Alexander at Wilton House, the headquarters of Southern Command. The following day he assembled the entire staff and field officers of 5 Corps at Bournemouth for a last personal address, and to those he could not see before leaving, he said goodbye in writing – such as to 'Kit' Dawnay, Brigade-Major in a nearby unit.

Headquarters, 5 Corps

My dear Kit,
    This is to tell you that I am leaving 5 Corps. Various changes are in progress, and the C-in-C has decided that he wants me to be in command of the Kent danger area and to take the first shock of invasion. So I am being switched over to command 12 Corps which

[1] Loc. cit.

holds Kent; I believe my HQ are just out of range of the German cannons on the French coast! I suppose these changes are good for one and I have always said it is a mistake to get too dug in anywhere.

One reason why I dislike going is that I shall not see so much of you. I have a very great affection for you Kit, and I count you as a real friend . . .

I am glad that I have been able, before going, to get you to the Staff College. And when you leave that place I shall try and rope you in to 12 Corps.

Yrs ever
Monty

On 27 April 1941 Bernard Montgomery moved to Tunbridge Wells and took command of 12 Corps.

CHAPTER ELEVEN

Transfer to 12 Corps

The speed of events in the spring of 1941 took the world off-guard, just as it had in May 1940. Within three weeks Greece was conquered by the Germans, the Balkans cleared of British troops, and Cyrenaica overrun by Rommel. In eleven days an inferior number of German parachutists succeeded in capturing Crete, defended by almost 30,000 British and Commonwealth troops as well as two Greek divisions. Twenty-two days later the Germans invaded Russia. Again, with inferior forces they nevertheless managed to reach a line from Leningrad to the Crimea in six weeks, and by winter were on the outskirts of Moscow.

It was against this background that Bernard Montgomery took command of 12 Corps – and the ruthlessness with which he introduced his doctrine of command and training must be seen in that light.

Brian Horrocks later likened Montgomery's arrival at 12 Corps to a series of atomic bombs 'exploding all over this rural corner of Britain'. Before his arrival a 'distinctly peacetime atmosphere had prevailed; officers and warrant officers were in many cases living with their families and, according to Monty, commanders and staff were spending too much time in their offices to the detriment of active training.

'All this changed almost overnight, and the first bomb exploded among the wives and families, who were summarily packed off, out of the Command . . .'[1]

Horrocks in fact only arrived in the Corps in June 1941, but Bernard's Chief-of-Staff, 'Simbo' Simpson, confirms Horrocks' impression:

> I moved to Tunbridge Wells at 12 hours' notice and found it a very pleasant place for a headquarters. Monty had one look round and decided that it was too pleasant and must be toughened up. He said to me:
>
> 'I want you to go through the Corps HQ staff and report to me on anyone who you think is not up to his job because I have a

[1] B. Horrocks, op. cit.

strong suspicion that most of them here in Tunbridge Wells have been leading somewhat soft lives. Also, get them out on a weekly run at once.'

On 7 May 1941, Bernard himself wrote to Dawnay:

I have been very busy since my arrival here. I rather fancy I burst in Kent like a 15" shell, and it was needed!!
Wives are being evacuated by train loads; it is just a matter as to whether the railways will stand the traffic.
A number of heads are being chopped off – the bag to date is 3 Brigadiers and 6 COs. The standard here was very low.

The peremptory way in which Bernard dismissed such officers – within a week of arrival – naturally caused something of a scandal, compounded perhaps by the way in which he boasted of his indecent surgery. Yet no one, looking at Bernard's career, could accuse him of hidden motives. On the contrary, the manner in which Bernard took command of 12 Corps in April 1941 was in many respects a blue-print for his take-over of 8th Army some fifteen months later. The whole 'feel' of the Corps – which comprised three field divisions – was wrong, and he was determined to shake it up, and recreate it upon 'sound' lines without delay. Moreover this was not simply a matter of personalities and wives – as Simpson later recalled: 'Monty had long felt that the dispositions of the 12th Corps were unsound. The three divisions had been set to see that every inch of the coast line of Kent was strongly defended with pill-boxes and entrenchments on a linear basis all along the coast line.

'He had felt that this meant there was no depth in the defensive lay-out and that there were no reserves, or very little reserve, available for a counter attack. He also found that in rear there were all sorts of stop-lines being built – quite elaborate affairs – and he had wondered what troops were going to be available to man those stop-lines. It eventually transpired that there were hardly any troops for the purpose, so Monty was quite pleased to be ordered to go to command the 12th Corps.'[1]

Bernard certainly wasted no time in making his views felt. General Thorne might have been promoted to full army command (in Scotland); but his dispositions, tactical views and training were anathema to Bernard. There was, in Bernard's mind, no likelihood of a German invasion that year; but the threat would at least be an excuse to explore the problems both of staging such an invasion, and of meeting it – lessons which were to be of immense importance in the coming years.

Alan Brooke had never confided any dissatisfaction with General

---

[1] Testimony of General Sir Frank Simpson (Wason interviews) and others.

Thorne or his dispositions in his diary, and had actually been responsible for his promotion to Scottish Command; yet there can be no doubt that Bernard transformed 12 Corps virtually overnight. Already on 2 May 1941 – less than a week after arriving at Tunbridge Wells – Bernard had issued his first Corps Instruction, reversing the tactical doctrine of his predecessor:

'The very long frontages which have to be held,' he informed unit commanders,

have led to a desire to defend every possible yard of the beach or coast; this has led to undue dispersion, and the principle of locality defence has been entirely disregarded.

It must be realised, however, that isolated section posts have no possible hope of survival in the modern battle. Risks must be accepted in order to concentrate platoons, and where necessary companies, in strong, well-wired localities, capable of all-round defence and capable of holding out until our reserves get into action.

There may often be gaps between platoon localities; that cannot be avoided when holding long fronts. The enemy may penetrate between platoon localities; that will not matter providing the localities themselves are mutually supporting, and are so strong that they can hold out . . .

Bernard concluded:

It is vital that the principles of true locality defence should be adhered to in our dispositions on the coast, and in fact anywhere. To ignore them is to lose the battle before it has even begun . . .

All defences on the coast, and elsewhere in the Corps Area, will be based on these principles. In cases where the existing defensive layout is at variance with these principles, the necessary steps will be taken at once to re-group sub-units conforming to the principles of locality defence outlined above. [1]

This, however, was just the beginning. Three days later Bernard gathered the entire staff of 12 Corps to elaborate on his ideas – in particular his desire to get rid, once and for all, of the 'beach defence' mentality.

Just how deep this mentality prevailed is evidenced by a mock Liaison Officer's Report to 44th Division's commander in Exercise 'Divex', a 12 Corps exercise mounted by General Thorne two weeks before Bernard took over command of the Corps. The report ran:

---

[1] Operation Instruction No. 25 dated 2 May 1941, War Diary, HQ 12 Corps (WO 166/344), PRO.

> 18 April: I left 43 Div HQ at 1100 hours. The situation on the Div front then was as follows: The last packets of enemy in the Deal-Sandwich area had surrendered by 1000 hrs. We had got about 4000 prisoners, including wounded, and I gather the sight on the beaches beggars description. Boche dead are just lying there in heaps.

Such mock reports were not only ridiculous – they were positively dangerous in Bernard's eyes: for it was obvious to anyone with the remotest knowledge of German military methods that they would hardly impale their primary invading army so conveniently on the pill-box machine-guns of 12 Corps beaches. On 12 May, Bernard therefore assembled the entire serving officers of the 43rd and 56th Divisions at Folkestone to instil some common sense; the next day he did the same before the officers of the 44th Division at Maidstone; and on 16 May he formally issued his '12 Corps Plans to Defeat Invasion'.

It was clear to Bernard that any German invasion would involve both airborne and seaborne assault – the latter supported by armour. The answer was therefore to concentrate coastal defences into localities that could hold out until reserves got into action; to identify the main harbours, airfields and communications centres vital for a successful German bridgehead – and hold them at all costs; and to marshal sufficient trained, mobile reserves to deal with enemy penetrations, employing such concentrations of infantry and armour that no enemy could withstand the onslaught.

The pivots of such a plan would be the vital garrison towns of Dover, Folkestone, Ashford and Canterbury – 'The importance of these places is immense,' Bernard declared. 'As long as they hold out and remain intact, then East Kent cannot be lost. They must therefore hold out – and will do so.'

The other essential was to preserve the concentrated power of divisions – both those 'in the line', and in reserve. By intelligent use of the garrison towns, there was no reason why these divisions should ever allow themselves to become dispersed. Territory as such was unimportant: 'Reserves will *not* be used to occupy defensive positions or to hold extended stop lines; they will be kept assembled so that they can act offensively and strike blows, and will be trained accordingly.'

> The underlying principle of the Corps Plan is to fight the invasion battle with troops who are mentally alert, who are skilled in fieldcraft, and offensively minded,

Bernard went on.

The troops will be imbued with that state of infectious optimism which comes from physical well-being; they must have in their mental make-up that spirit which will make them want to kill Germans . . .

The powers of endurance of all ranks will be brought to the highest pitch. Every officer and other rank must be able and mentally wishful, to take part in a real rough-house, lasting for weeks. If they are to do this they must be 100% fit. They must in fact be more than fit, they must be hard. They must be 100% enthusiastic for battle and must possess 100% 'binge'.

Attention will be paid to developing the initiative and resourcefulness and mental robustness of all troops and junior leaders. They will be made to understand that the only thing that is certain in battle is that everything will be uncertain. They will be taught to grasp rapidly the essentials of a military situation, and how to do something about it quickly. They will be taught how to act quickly on verbal orders.

All training will be based on the above principles.

Bernard's four-day June exercise – in the wake of the fall of Crete – was in fact called 'Binge'; and if there were those who felt the new Corps Commander's ideas were all 'flannel' they were brought up with a rude start. The object of the exercise has been 'to study the use of Corps reserves in defeating invasion', and on 30 June Bernard addressed almost two thousand officers of the Corps with his verdict: an almost unmitigated castigation of the Corps' performance:

A great deal went wrong on this exercise. The army is not a mutual congratulation society; great issues are at stake; if we lose the battles in Kent we may lose the war.

We have the very great honour of being in the front row of the stalls in the forthcoming fight. We cannot afford to be complacent about our mistakes. Let us be quite frank about it, and see what went wrong. Let us put it right; and we can be thankful we have time to do it. This is the way to approach the lessons of this exercise.

The problem, as Bernard went on to explain, was not that the troops lacked enthusiasm or even fitness: the problem was that commanders simply had no notion how to put a modern army into battle.

'There is a great need today for clear thinking,' Bernard declared. 'If our thinking is wrong, our doing will be wrong.' There were 'three essentials for success in battle,' he maintained: first, proper launching; second, the courage, initiative and skill of junior leaders once battle was joined; and third, the fighting spirit of the troops. 'If any one of these three is missing then you lose the battle.

'Let us now examine the battle in the fierce light of these three points,' he exorted: and proceeded to demonstrate, stage by stage, how the battle had been lost almost before it had begun. In particular the use made of Royal Engineer units, and the staff-work needed for large-scale movement of combined arms was virtually non-existent. Yet if troops and artillery could not be properly launched into battle 'then you start the battle on the wrong leg; you are then easily thrown off balance by a good enemy'. It was essential that the 'dispositions of the fighting troops, employment and positioning of supporting arms, the arrangements for keeping communications open, the organisation of supply services and so on – all must be good initially . . . If they *are* good, then the forward troops will have every chance to seize the tactical advantage early in the battle.'

Unfortunately there seemed no understanding of the simplest problems of modern battlefield command: not only the marshalling and movement of large-scale formations, but countering the most elementary obstacles such as demolitions. Bernard's diagnosis is historically important: for in it he recognised the primary fault of the British Army in the early years of the Second World War. This was not weaponry – the commonest excuse for any defeated army – but the inevitable decline of military knowledge and expertise as the army was expanded to meet its wartime commitments. The same dilution and fragmentation that accompanied such expansion seemed then to characterise the way such armies fought: so that one witnessed the spectacle, in North Africa, of a pre-war trained British army exhibiting the greatest feats of daring, courage and administrative intelligence in 1940–41 when faced by Italians; yet declining into an erratic, polyglot collection of disparate units when confronted by German troops thereafter.

It was to be perhaps Bernard's greatest contribution to military history that, at a time when almost every nation in Europe had succumbed to German military aggression, he virtually single-handedly changed the course of British military technique. Almost alone among senior British field generals he produced a vision of a trained, modern, largely conscript army in which mind triumphed over matter. Bernard was utterly confident that not even the most daring of German army commanders could vanquish a British army, if only certain fundamental principles of modern war were recognised and observed. One of these was the basic doctrine of fighting in divisions.

'And so we see,' Bernard addressed his 2000 officer audience on 30 June – at the very moment when General Sir Claude Auchinleck was arriving in Cairo to take over British military forces in the Middle East from Wavell, whose counter-offensive against Rommel (operation 'Battleaxe') had come to grief,

that the first essential – the proper launching of the formation – does not stand up to very close investigation. I consider that this is due to fighting in brigade groups on all occasions.

Here was a cardinal point which, despite his undoubted moral authority and intelligence as a commander, General Auchinleck singularly failed to put right in Egypt in the following fourteen months. Given superior intelligence (particularly from Ultra), superiority in numbers of tanks, artillery, vehicles, fighters, bombers, and supplies, Auchinleck and his lieutenants frittered away every advantage and happily permitted subsequent historians to invent every conceivable excuse in order to distract attention from the real problem: the inability to ensure that the 8th Army fought with the cohesive, crushing weight of modern fighting divisions.

Bernard acknowledged that there would be moments in war when to fight in brigade groups *was* the correct procedure: but Exercise 'Binge' in which the fictional flower of the German invasion army was ensconced in various parts of Kent, was not one of them:

The division is a fighting formation of all arms, and the way you fight it will vary with the problem,

Bernard allowed. But from his own experience in the BEF he emphasised his message:

I commanded a division in battle against the Germans in this war. I never fought it in brigade groups once; I was never embarrassed by the Germans – nor do I propose to be in the future.

This was no idle boast, nor simple self-confidence, as his two-hour address revealed. There was no military problem, he maintained, which could not be solved, given thought and determination. Discussions on the cloth-model, signal communication exercises, training by battalion commanders – all had been found wanting, and the result was evident in the Corps exercise, where the troops had not even been fed properly.

'Every commander will know in his heart what is wrong with his unit,' Bernard declared, 'and what is wrong with himself. We must put these issues right, knowing that the fate of England is involved.'[1]

It is in this context that Bernard's desire to bring in some of his 'own' men to the Corps, both on the staff and as commanders, must be understood. He had spent the best part of nine months making 5 Corps the most battleworthy corps in England; if he was to raise 12 Corps to the same standard in the minimum time possible, it was essential to introduce men who would help spread the new profes-

[1] War Diary, HQ 12 Corps, loc. cit.

sionalism. The manner in which he absconded with 5 Corps officers and pressed the Military Secretary to obtain yet more of them for 12 Corps may have smacked at times of impudence and even something of the *enfant terrible* vis-à-vis higher authority – but his purpose was constructive, not vain; moreover he was the first to admit, with a sense of humour, when he was 'beaten'. To 'Kit' Dawnay he wrote bullishly on 6 June:

> I have a great many 5th Corps people over here now; my latest Brigadiers in Kent are
>
> | Knox (RUR) | 130 Bde |
> | Bullen-Smith (KOSB) | 219 Bde |
> | Pike (G3 5 Corps) | B-M, 219 Bde |
> | Boxshall (1 Surreys in 4 Div) | 206 Bde |
> | Butler (CRASC 3 Div) | DDST 12 Corps |
>
> and my latest triumph is that I have managed to get Birch switched from 226 Bde to command a Field Army Bde in Kent.
>
> I just failed over Desmond Harrison. The Chief Engineer at Home Forces pinched him before I could get going.
>
> I have also failed (temporarily!!) over Jerry Feilden.
>
> I am told that 5 Corps are very angry.
> > Yrs ever
> > Monty

This acceptance of occasional defeat over certain talented officers he had earmarked was reflected in other ways too, and reveals something of the realism that lurked behind the iron mask – as his stepson John Carver later recalled.

> If he did have to retreat on some occasions he was prepared to do so. I remember he said: 5th Corps will occupy some castle in Wiltshire when he was commanding 5 Corps, and when I went to see them they were somewhere else. I said 'what happened about that castle?'
>
> 'Well, it was a good place,' he answered, 'but in fact I found that the artillery was too strong!'
>
> The owner was a big friend of Winston Churchill and had plenty of strings to pull. So rather than commit himself to a fight he reckoned he'd lose. Monty forgot about the place. He was far more of a realist than he's been made out to be.[1]

The forty-five-year-old Commander Royal Artillery of 56th Division recalled not only the new Corps Commander's realism, but also his constant preparedness to cast his net wider in the search for talented officers to serve him:

'Monty'd just taken over the Corps,' he recounted forty years later

[1] Colonel John Carver, loc. cit.

and we had a cloth-model exercise in our division. Halfway through Monty turned up – we were having a coffee break. Then Monty got up and made a small speech about gunners. Afterwards he came up to me and said: 'You're the CRA, aren't you?' I said, 'Yes, sir.' Mind you I didn't know Monty, knew nothing about him at all. He said: 'What did you think of my speech?' And I said, roughly, 'Well the speech was all right but you missed out the two most important points: A and B.' And he said, 'All right.'

Well, we went back and did a bit more of the exercise, and then just before Monty left he stopped, got up again and said:

'Gentlemen, there are just two things I forgot to mention: A, B.'!!
Now that was my introduction to Monty! He took no offence.

Far from taking offence, Bernard would take Brigadier Kirkman with him wherever he went, and soon promoted him to be Commander of his 12 Corps Artillery – CCRA.

He said: 'You'll come in two days' time, and I'll give you 2 hours to take over from the chap who's there now . . .'
When I went to 12 Corps I discussed the problems we had in the defence of England with my predecessor who was about to get the sack. And he said, 'As a matter of fact I've suggested three changes to the Corps Commander, and he's said they're nonsense.' I said, 'What are the changes?' I've forgotten what they were – moving some regiments, that sort of thing.

Anyway a week later I went to Monty and I said: 'I've got three changes to suggest.' He accepted them straight away – the ones he'd turned down with my predecessor, when he wouldn't listen to them. He was prepared with me to accept them straight away – which gives you an aspect of the man. If he had faith in you, then he was prepared to accept practically anything. If he hadn't any faith in you, then he wasn't interested – it wasn't an opinion worth having . . . From then on, by and large, I had no trouble working with him – he was the most easy person to work with.[1]

Moreover, once Bernard's 'faith' had been won, it was for life. He would write regularly to members of his regiment – such as Major Patrick Burge – in captivity, and his seemingly omniscient eye never missed a name. When he heard that Roger Taverner, his erstwhile Brigade-Major at 9th Infantry Brigade in 1938 and Chief-of-Staff at 3rd Division after Dunkirk, had also been captured he wrote immediately to 'Kit' Dawnay:

What a dreadful affair about Roger Taverner. He will hate being a prisoner. I am particularly upset as he was one of my 'chaps', that I

[1] General Sir Sidney Kirkman, interview of 16.4.80.

took a special interest in and pushed up the ladder. Will you send me the address of Mrs Taverner, so that I can write to her.

As a postscript he squeezed in at the very bottom of the page:

I have got Horrocks here now, as a Major-General commanding 44 Div. This took a lot of doing and is a great triumph. He arrived yesterday.

Perhaps no one who did not come within the Montgomery aura can quite comprehend the awe and devotion this strange soldier inspired. Those who met Churchill recognised a radiance of greatness much as Dr Johnson cast around him. There were men like Alan Brooke, whose very unapproachability belied a coolness of judgement which people in wartime admired. Similarly with Wavell. Auchinleck, too, had a presence which automatically evoked respect – and there were few men, if any, who did not, having met or worked with him, ascribe a bigness of character, of spirit, to him which might pass for greatness.

With Bernard this was not so. There was no sense of divine selection, of a human being naturally gifted with a largeness of presence that instilled respect. In fact it was the very opposite: namely his very unnaturalness, the very abnormality of his beak-like nose and steel-blue eyes which arrested attention. The respect he engendered was a mixture of awe – for there was a frightening, ruthlessly penetrating coldness in those eyes – and this curious, self-imbued sense of destiny which either repelled or attracted. To be 'chosen' by Montgomery was to feel both pride and anxiety – indeed Johnny Henderson, his only wartime ADC to survive, at first asked to be released after a week's 'trial' in the North African desert rather than serve under him.

Yet, however frightening he could be, he was generally acknowledged to be by far the most professional trainer of officers and troops in anyone's memory. The standard he had set at 5 Corps became, in General Sir Dudley Ward's later words, 'the standard of training of the British army at home'.[1] His exercises were not only brilliant rehearsals for specific operations of war; they were, for many officers, a veritable military education in themselves. Bernard's use of the Chief-of-Staff system was immediately adopted in other commands – 'everybody saw the merit of it in freeing the commander from matters of detail,' General Ward recalled, 'and wondered why it hadn't been introduced before. Yet in every staff on which I had served till then, the chief administrative officer had in fact been senior to the senior operations staff officer.' People might mock or cajole at Bernard's edicts on wives and families living in the Corps

---

[1] General Sir Dudley Ward, interview of 22.2.78.

area – 'but goodness, wasn't one really grateful for that! You were working so hard, you'd have brought no joy to anybody. And it was a much greater refreshment that every few months you got away for a week, with perhaps an occasional weekend in between, with your family.'[1]

Moreover, although Bernard was to become renowned for his ability to pick out talented specialists, the majority of his appointments were made with a view to providing all-round experience for future promotion – a concept not always recognised at the Military Secretary's office in Whitehall. Few of Montgomery's selections did not prosper either in war or in later life. Ward himself was brought in as G2 (Ops) at 5 Corps for the last three of Bernard's great corps exercises. He was then brought on to the staff of 12 Corps at the end of 1941 and became a brilliant brigade and then divisional commander in the field in Italy from 1943 to 1945. Perhaps the best illustration of Bernard's unique ability at 'talent-spotting' is given by General Sir Frank Simpson – an officer all too well versed in the bureaucratic machinery of officer-promotion at the Military Secretary's office both at Whitehall and with the BEF under Lord Gort:

Having spent some time weeding out those officers whom he considered unsuitable from field command, Monty had to replace them with people who did know their job, and that wasn't always easy.

Monty's system was that he would look out for somebody of Lieut-Colonel rank who might make a brigade commander and then try him out in a situation where he would have command, however temporarily.

This led to some curious incidents. There was a particular Lieut-Colonel commanding a battalion of the Cheshire Regiment who looked a likely candidate for brigade command, and I was told by Monty to order him to appear on a particular exercise and put him into command of a brigade in the middle of a rather troublesome battle . . .

The trial-Brigadier arrived in due course in his battle kit.

We then drove in my car to the HQ of a certain brigade, commanded by Manley James, a man who'd emerged from the First World War with a VC and an MC. He was quite a serious soldier and we hit his brigade HQ at a moment when he was giving out his operational orders for a counter-attack.

I went up to him in the middle of his orders and said (he was a very old friend of mine): 'Jimmy, I'm afraid a shell has landed very

---

[1] Loc. cit.

461

near to where you are now and you've been killed. I have a substitute to take your place.'

This upset James very much and he said: 'Really, Simbo, you can't do this to me! Just let me finish my orders and tidy up the situation and then you can have me killed.'

I told him that was out of the question and he must get out of the way at once. The Lieut-Colonel had a quick talk with the Brigade-Major, sized up the position, went on with the orders, and acquitted himself extremely well. The counter-attack was a complete success in the opinion of the umpires.

When I recounted that tale to Monty the same evening he had no hesitation in ordering the Lieut-Colonel to become a Brigadier within the next few days – and right through the rest of the actual war the Brigadier, whose name was Geoffrey Harding, did extremely good and valuable service in battle command, especially in North-Eastern Italy.[1]

It is strange to think that only a year before this the BEF had not known the meaning of the word 'exercise', and Bernard's exercises in 3rd Division had been an 'eye-opener' even to Brooke. Thereafter, since Dunkirk, Bernard had not only overturned the tactical doctrines of his two predecessors at 5 and 12 Corps, but had begun to propagate an entirely new vision in the leadership and training of a modern British army. His dictum about conducting conferences in the midst of battle ('They must be short and snappy. All "belly-aching" must be stamped on at once. An officer must be trained to give and take verbal orders. If not, the sooner he is removed the better')[2] might smack of authoritarianism: but the very fact that this advice was given to some 2000 officers of every rank from subaltern to Major-General is proof of the far deeper democratic element that Montgomery introduced to Britain's conscript army. This time, Bernard felt, a British Expeditionary Force would move abroad as an army, a team trained to fight in modern warfare, with proper communications, the men knowing who their leaders were, and what was expected of them.

Not even Sir Alan Brooke, the brilliant commander of 2 Corps in the BEF up to Dunkirk, could compete with Bernard at this. As John Carver remembered of the final Conference on Exercise No. 1 at 5 Corps, at which Brooke spoke:

Alan Brooke came down and arrangements were very carefully made that Monty would sum up. And he was terribly good at this, there's absolutely no doubt, he very much upstaged Alan Brooke.

[1] Wason interviews, loc. cit.
[2] Summing up after Exercise 'Binge', Montgomery Papers.

He made no doubt that he, Monty, was the big person – which he was.[1]

Brian Horrocks wrote of Bernard's performance at these conferences as being hypnotic, even when lasting over two hours. 'By now Monty had perfected his famous conference technique', Horrocks later described in *A Full Life*,

> when the lessons learned during the exercise were rammed home to all concerned. It was a superbly staged performance. All the officers and, if there was room, warrant officers as well, were concentrated in some immense cinema. On the stage were large maps and diagrams, while the walls were covered with 'No Smoking' notices. Suddenly the audience would be called to attention, as the well-known figure of the army commander wearing battle-dress advanced to the centre of the stage.
> 'Sit down, gentlemen,' he would say in a sharp, nasal voice. 'Thirty seconds for coughing – then no more coughing at all.' And the curious thing is that we didn't cough.

Bernard's Chief Gunner agreed.

> Was he influential in creating a more professional approach? Oh, tremendously. He was terribly good at these exercises. He used to have strenuous exercises with troops all over Kent, and he was terribly good at summing them up afterwards. He always saw the essentials and he was a gifted speaker. He very often wrote out in his own hand the whole speech he was going to make. Made the speech without reference to it. And at the end would chuck it at his Chief-of-Staff and say: 'Type that out – have it circulated down to Lt-Colonels.'
> And of course he started this theatrical business – No smoking, no coughing, and all the rest. We used to have these in cinemas. And he at once established a great reputation as a trainer – there's no question about that.[2]

Gerald Templer later claimed that, as Bernard mastered his technique and repeated it, so it became 'excruciating to watch' and caused Templer to 'writhe in agony' – so much so that he once asked Bernard:

> 'How can you go on repeating the same thing all the time? All that acting! Last night was – well, the end.'
> And Monty said: 'I rehearse it. I take immense trouble over what

[1] Colonel John Carter, loc. cit.
[2] General Sir Sidney Kirkman, loc. cit.

I say. I write it down beforehand, I practise it in front of the mirror when I'm shaving.'[1]

No other member of Bernard's staff has ever confirmed the story of the shaving mirror, but he certainly did take great pains over such addresses – just as Churchill did. Both were showmen – yet their ability to spellbind their listeners lay in the man, not the rhetoric. To millions of Britons, Churchill embodied a sense of dogged purpose, a pride in history and a sense, a most powerful awareness of historical moment; while to the officers and men of 5 and 12 Corps Montgomery heralded a new, meritocratic approach to command; an all-embracing, comprehensive, team-work approach to battle; and a radiating, infectious optimism – an assurance that if they only pulled themselves together and acted resolutely and in unison, there was nothing they could not achieve. Both Churchill and Montgomery would make mistakes in the conduct of the war and perhaps claim more than their due in retrospect, belittling or ignoring the contribution of others – but neither could ever overestimate his effect on the morale and spirit of his people or his men.

Meanwhile, on 4 August 1941, Bernard's second great 12 Corps exercise began – Exercise 'Morebinge'. Its object was the study of forward infantry brigades in dealing with airborne and seaborne landings, and the action of corps reserves. Bernard was determined to get rid, finally, of all ideas of, linear advance and withdrawal. At the end of Exercise 'Binge' he had warned:

> in mobile operations enemy resistance must be met with quick deployment, rapid manoeuvre to outflank the opposition, pressing on where progress is possible, and not worrying about flanks. Tanks must be well forward and used at once to stamp on enemy resistance quickly. All these things were conspicuous by their absence.

At his final conference on Exercise 'Morebinge' at the Granada Cinema, Maidstone on 12 August Bernard now paid tribute to the way the reserve division – the 43rd – had 'progressed beyond all recognition since it came out of the line for training at the end of May'. Together with the 25th Army Tank Brigade their task had been to recapture the Isle of Oxney and Rye area and to move in *'behind* the German forces advancing on London', while the 44th and 56th divisions, by remaining concentrated around their 'nodal points', made it impossible for the enemy to reinforce his strikeforce.

Yet, despite a performance which had involved more than a hundred miles of marching for some units, Bernard was still not satisfied that commanders were sufficiently air- or engineer-minded.

[1] Field-Marshal Sir Gerald Templer, loc. cit.

The Chief Engineer *must* be fully in the picture as to the divisional commander's battle plan, Bernard emphasised – only then could he marshal men and materials swiftly to the vital bridge or demolition point. As regards the air,

> The leading troops of 43rd Division were storming the island [of Oxney] from the North. The enemy must withdraw from the island or be wiped out. Actually he was withdrawing and his withdrawal was across a river obstacle which was unfordable and crossed by only two bridges.
>
> Obviously here was a good use for air power, to bomb relentlessly the enemy columns on the two roads off the island. Yet it was not done, nor was any request for air support ever made.

There was the question, too, of the correct use of tanks; and, once again, Bernard sought to emphasise the difference between mobile operations and the requirements when enemy resistance stiffened. Each situation, each moment in war would be different: communications. They must also train their reconnaissance, tank and infantry units to co-operate fully when enemy resistance was stiff, but to open up and exploit relentlessly when the battle was fluid. Apart from the big corps exercises, therefore, each division must go out 'under full sail', at least once a month, on its own exercises; and, while sub-units concentrated on their own training, skeletal communications exercises must constantly be taking place to rehearse the flow of information and command.

Finally, Bernard declared, there must be no relaxation.

> There is a great deal of talk these days about the war being over: the Germans being finished off in the East by the Russians and so on. Anyone who thinks that the Russians, or the Americans, are going to win this war for us, is making a very grave error. *We* have got to win this war ourselves, and we shall not do so without a very great deal of hard fighting,

he prophesied.

> We are fighting a ruthless and very efficient enemy who is prepared to do anything at any time,

Bernard warned. Meanwhile he exhorted each one of the two thousand officers to make a personal commitment:

> Each one of us will prepare himself militarily, physically, and mentally so that when the test comes we shall one and all do our duty – and not fail.

The officers rose; Lt-General Montgomery left the platform. The war was very far from over, and many of the assembled officers would be killed or be wounded in battle before it was. Many others would feel, afterwards, that they owed their lives to a commander who had forced them to consider the art of war, and the need to prepare for battle now, long before they were to see action.

CHAPTER TWELVE

Exercise 'Bumper'

General Sir Alan Brooke, C-in-C Home Forces, had been deeply impressed by Bernard's stage-management of field exercises in 5 and 12 Corps; he therefore felt in the summer of 1941 that full-scale army manoeuvres would set a seal upon the intensive training of the army since Dunkirk. Accordingly he planned Exercise 'Bumper' in which an invasion force commanded by the GOC Eastern Command would 'bump up' against home forces commanded by Lt-General Alexander.

Bernard Montgomery was made Chief Umpire – and it would seem that, from the start, Bernard took control. Already in August, some five weeks before the exercise began, Bernard was making his preparations. He wrote to 'Kit' Dawnay, then at the Staff College, on 21 August:

> All the Staff College students are coming out on Army manoeuvres.
>
> I have earmarked you to come to me as my personal assistant. You will find it very interesting . . .
>
> The manoeuvres actually begin on 29 Sept and end of 3 October . . .

The manoeuvres were indeed 'very interesting'. It had been one of Brooke's primary ambitions, on promotion to the job of C-in-C Home Forces, to build up armoured forces capable of the same mobility and penetration as the German Panzer divisions. There were a number of English Galahads such as General Martel who were obsessed with the raising of an élite tank cavalry, acting almost independently of infantry. Brooke and Montgomery both resisted this vision, insisting on a higher ratio of infantry in the composition of armoured divisions, and a greater degree of co-operation between armoured and infantry forces, arguing that the Germans were far too professional an adversary to be defeated as the French had been in 1940.

How then should the new British armoured divisions be employed? For Exercise 'Bumper' some four armoured divisions and nine infantry divisions were involved. The exercise followed very much the pattern of Bernard Montgomery's own pioneering efforts, and he evidently took considerable delight in refereeing a match between Alexander, his somewhat idle GOC at 5 Corps, and General Carr, the GOC Eastern Command.

At the Final Conference at the Staff College on 10 October, Bernard stole the show by narrating the various phases of the exercise before the 270 senior officers – 'He did this admirably,' even Brooke acknowledged later, 'and produced a masterly picture.'[1]

Both Brooke and Bernard felt that the armoured divisions had been poorly disposed by Alexander and Carr, who had obviously done little thinking on the interaction between armour and infantry.

Alexander later claimed that, in his final Lessons of the Exercise, Brooke had unfairly criticised him, on the grounds that he had been constrained by certain deadlines in the movement of his armour. Yet this objection begged the issue, for Brooke's strictures applied to his handling of his armour throughout the exercise. Faced with an inland thrust by superior enemy forces, Alexander had allowed his own armoured reserves to be 'steadily drawn off piecemeal' to his left by the course of operations; 'throughout these days,' Brooke summarised to the audience of senior commanders, 'there was a steady drag of the British reserves from the right to the left flank' – a drag 'dictated by the enemy . . . against the wishes of the British Commander.' By failing to position his armour correctly at the outset, Alexander had lost all hope of carrying out the offensive on his right flank which he had originally intended; moreover when finally Alexander did attempt to carry out his offensive move, he failed to realise, 'in spite of an intercepted message', that Carr was withdrawing his forces, and altered his plan to a thrust from his left flank pivoting on his right, now exposing himself unwisely to an enemy counter-attack on his 'left wing' and 'without achieving any decisive result.' The 'laborious' move of Alexander's 2nd Canadian Division in the rear of the 25th Army Tank Brigade had robbed him of all chance of striking 'at the enemy's flank and rear', and his – as well as Carr's – command had been characterised by faulty location of headquarters, inability to summon air support quickly or accurately, failure to ensure the speedy passing of information forwards, backwards and laterally, and 'failure to press forward ruthlessly.'[2]

Alexander, often pragmatic and trusting in his ability to react coolly to a given situation, had no more than a very basic tactical understanding, and was never really aware of his own failings in this respect. Leadership for him was the ability to give decisive judgments when they were required of him: he had no real constructive or creative military brain. He had not used his brief experience as

---

[1] Alanbrooke Diary, loc. cit.
[2] 'Exercise Bumper', 27 Sept.–3 Oct. 1941. Comments by the Commander-in-Chief Home Forces to be read in conjunction with the Narrative of events. Military Headquarters Papers, Home Forces (WO 199/727), PRO.

GOC of a corps to develop the skills of such a Commander in modern war, nor had he been appreciably more constructive as an Army Commander in charge of Southern Command. Yet he had been appointed, simultaneously, Commander-elect of Britain's only expeditionary force, training in Scotland, and would in time, as Britain's 'finest' fighting general, be sent personally by Churchill to conduct operations in Burma, which had been invaded by the Japanese. His later Chief Staff Officer, Sir Ian Jacob, once asked Field-Marshal Slim, Commander of the retreating Burcorps in 1942, what Alexander had been like as C-in-C in Burma. Slim smiled. 'I don't believe he had the faintest idea of what was going on,' he confided.[1]

Bernard would also later have profound reservations about Alexander as a Field Commander – reservations he would confide to his diary but never state publicly in his lifetime. In the meantime he returned to command of 12 Corps and began planning his own next exercise – the final corps exercise he would mount. Entitled Exercise 'Greatbinge', it mirrored his final exercise at 5 Corps the previous spring, in which 'maximum freedom of movement' was permitted, and the objective – the capture of the Tank Centre at Harrietsham – got right away from the restrictive focus of invasion and counter-invasion. The exercise began on 24 November, and ended when Horrocks' 44th Division captured its objective on 27 November. There remained the by now traditional final conference; but already the 12 Corps War Diary had recorded, on 17 November, the temporary assumption of command by Major-General J. A. H. Gammell, from 3rd Division, 'in the absence of Lt-General B. L. Montgomery'; and though Bernard attended, it was not as Corps Commander now, but as Commander-elect of South-Eastern Command, embracing both 12 Corps and Canadian Corps.

[1] Lt-General Sir Ian Jacob, loc. cit.

CHAPTER THIRTEEN

Army Commander

Quite when Bernard must have heard the news – confirmed by the War Cabinet at its meeting on 17 November – that he was to become GOC-in-C South-Eastern Command in succession to Lt-General Paget we do not know. Paget was promoted to C-in-C, Home Forces, while Brooke was to succeed the now ailing Dill as CIGS. The appointments were to be made official from Christmas Day 1941; but Paget left on 17 November 1941, and according to its War Diary Bernard took over the same day at the Reigate headquarters of South-Eastern Command.

Bernard must have been delighted. He would now be on a par with Alexander at Southern Command; moreover, although Alexander had been made Commander Designate of Force 110 – the new BEF – there was every hope that when one day a Second Front was opened on the continent of Europe – possibly in 1942 – Bernard would be given command of an army.

In order to prepare for that moment Bernard Montgomery decided now to re-title his new command 'South-Eastern Army' and to style himself 'Army Commander'. In this way he would not only accustom his officers and men to the notion of an army command with an unmistakable commander at its head, but it would also, Bernard hoped, help to ease the introduction of a 'common doctrine' not only in the two constituent field corps but the rest of South-Eastern Command troops.

Having first visited all his senior subordinate commanders Bernard therefore issued his first 'Army Commander's Personal Memorandum' on 28 November, setting out his training policy for the winter. As in his previous commands, this embraced the individual training of the soldier, field exercises with troops, and skeleton exercises without troops 'designed to exercise commanders and their HQs in the handling of their formation in battle. 'Five of these exercises are being organised and directed by Army HQ in December, January and February, and dates have already been notified'. Moreover, 'every Home Guard unit must be affiliated to an Army unit for training, assistance and co-operation', since the defeat of a German invasion in 1942 would not be possible by the Field Army alone; 'the efficient co-operation of the Home Guard is essential; we must therefore train the Home Guard up to a very high standard'.

However, the central concern of this first Personal Memorandum was the training of officers:

I consider that we must make a special effort this winter to train our officers to a high standard of professional knowledge. This can be done indoors on the model, without in any way interfering with our main objects set out in para. 1a).

The following are 3 points which I would like to emphasize as requiring special study:

a) *The divisional battle*

When advancing to gain contact with some unknown threat it will be necessary to decentralize supporting arms so that infantry brigades can fight quickly and with effect on the main axes of advance.

But where definite and co-ordinated resistance is met it will be necessary to centralize control in order to strike a hard blow at the selected point. This is not easy to do quickly and it requires study and practice in the drill required.

b) *The art of resolute fighting in small self-contained groups, or packets, of all arms.*

We have got to learn how, at the right moment, to break down the large-scale divisional battle and continue the fight by means of very hard-hitting smaller packets.

The Germans are extremely good at this; and in the mobile and fluid operations on the modern battlefield it is this type of fighting that completes the success gained in the divisional battle.

It requires skilful grouping, and resolute leadership. A very high standard of battle drill and operational discipline is necessary.

Success in such fighting lies in the hands of our company commanders; the technique must be taught at Army, Corps and Divisional Schools.

c) *Operations by night*

Night operations are not peculiar to the infantry; every unit of every arm must be able to operate by night with complete confidence.

Practice is required in all the varying types of night conditions, i.e. bright moonlight or complete darkness or the many variations that lie between these two extremes.

The technique to be employed will vary with the night conditions.

471

Within the unit, Bernard felt, it was the responsibility of the CO to train his officers. 'Well-trained officers soon produce a good unit; if the officers are not well trained, nothing happens.' The answer was for each CO to 'have his officers to himself one day a week all through the winter, i.e. an Officers Day once a week . . . The important point is that the CO uses these "days" to get across to his officers his views on all subjects, not haphazardly but in accordance with a definite and systematic programme over a definite period, i.e. during the next four months.'

Officers of 'supporting arms and services' were to meet at 'regular intervals to exchange ideas and discussion of their problems' – 'it is only by this way that we shall train on the Lt-Colonels, and fit them to hold high appointments'.

At the heart of Bernard's winter training programme, however, was the Corps Study Week, which he had introduced the previous autumn in 5 Corps, and had already prepared for 12 Corps prior to his promotion:

Corps Study Week
12 Corps Week is taking place between 15 and 20 December, and I know that a warm invitation is being sent to the Canadian Corps to send representatives to the discussions. The Commander Canadian Corps and myself are going to attend the discussions on 16, 17 and 18 December.
Canadian Corps Week is to take place some time in January and I hope that Commanders from 12 Corps will be invited to attend.
I regard these Corps Study Weeks as being vitally important; they require much careful preparation and very hard work for those who are responsible for the instruction, but it will be time well spent and the mutual exchange of ideas between 12 and Canadian Corps will be of the greatest value to each Corps, and in fact to all of us.[1]

The 12 Corps Study Week took place in due course at the Spa Hotel, Tunbridge Wells. Although this study week followed the pattern that Bernard had first set in 1937 at 9th Infantry Brigade, it is interesting to note the subjects for discussion. Already on 12 November Bernard had issued a pamphlet on 'Lessons learned during the first two years of war'; co-operation with the RAF and the use of tanks now filled an even larger part of the study week agenda than the previous year, as well as the conduct of operations by night, and co-operation between tanks, artillery, and infantry in attack. On 19 December there was a discussion on 'Defence: with particular reference to anti-Panzer tactics.'

However, most intriguing of all to the subsequent historian was

[1] Military Headquarters Papers, Home Forces, South-Eastern Command (WO 199/2623), PRO.

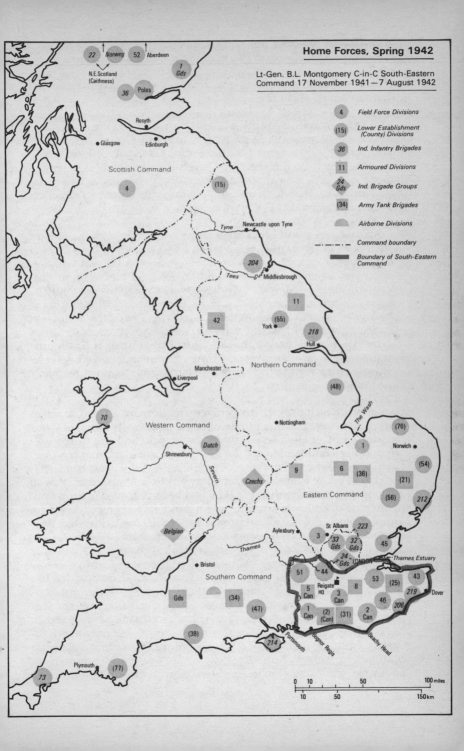

Home Forces, Spring 1942

Lt-Gen. B.L. Montgomery C-in-C South-Eastern
Command 17 November 1941 — 7 August 1942

4	*Field Force Divisions*
(15)	*Lower Establishment (County) Divisions*
36	*Ind. Infantry Brigades*
11	*Armoured Divisions*
24 Gds	*Ind. Brigade Groups*
(34)	*Army Tank Brigades*
	Airborne Divisions
— · · — · · —	*Command boundary*
▬▬▬	*Boundary of South-Eastern Command*

22 Norweg   *52* Aberdeen

N.E.Scotland (Caithness)

1 Gds

36 Poles

Rosyth

Glasgow   Edinburgh

Scottish Command

4

(15)

Tyne   Newcastle upon Tyne

204

Tees   Middlesbrough

11

42   York **(55)**

218

Hull

Manchester

Liverpool   Northern Command

(48)

The Wash

70   Nottingham

Western Command

Dutch

Shrewsbury   **1**   Norwich **(76)**

Severn   **9**   **6** **(36)**   **(54)**

Czechs   **(21)**

Eastern Command   **(56)**   *212*

Belgian   St Albans *223*

Aylesbury   **3**   *33 Gds*   *32 Gds*   **45**

Thames   *24 Gds* · LONDON   Thames Estuary

51   **44**   **53** **(25)**   **43**

Bristol   **5 Can**   Reigate HQ   **8**   **206**   Dover

Southern Command   **3 Can**   *219*

Gds   **(34)**   **1 Can**   **(2) (Can)**   **(31)**   **2 Can**   **46**

(47)

(38)   *214*   Portsmouth   Bognor Regis   Beachy Head

Plymouth   **77**

73

0   10   50   100 miles
10   50   150 km

the discussion agenda for 17 December: 'The Problem of Cross-Channel Raiding'. Beneath this heading ran the lines:

> The whole procedure for laying on a raid will be investigated and demonstrated. Training for raiding operations.

This was an imaginative and salutary command; yet the evidence is that Bernard Montgomery's promotion to South-Eastern Army Command was bitterly resented by the senior Canadian officers. At 12 Corps there was no difficulty, for Bernard's successor – Lt-General James Gammell – was almost embarrassingly anxious to satisfy the new Army Commander – as 'Simbo' Simpson, Bernard's Chief-of-Staff, who remained at 12 Corps, recalled.

> James Gammell and I had known one another because he was an instructor at the Staff College when I was a student, and I found him a very easy man to work with. His only trouble was wondering whether any action he would take would please Monty because he felt that Monty's standards were so high that he might be found wanting. So he was always asking me what I felt about some order or manoeuvre he was doing. Actually, I had little doubt that everything he did would have satisfied Monty because James Gammell himself had high standards. But at times it was a little unnerving to have to advise my Corps Commander on whether he was right or wrong in the light of what the army commander might be thinking.

Gammell in fact proved no problem to Bernard. The Canadian Corps, however, was an entirely different matter. Its nominal Commander – Lt-General McNaughton – was sick, and the Corps was temporarily commanded by the GOC 1st Canadian Infantry Division, Major-General Pearkes, VC, DSO, MC. However, the Canadian Chief of the General Staff at Ottawa, Lt-General Crerar, was so anxious for active command that he had been prepared to drop rank to Major-General; on arriving in England in December 1941, he found himself the senior divisional general in the Corps and thus displaced Pearkes as temporary Corps Commander.

For Bernard this game of Canadian musical chairs was anathema; worse still Crerar, having held such a vital post in Canada, considered himself not only temporary Canadian Corps Commander, but guardian of the Canadian national military interest – an attitude that was to bring him more than once on to a collision course with Bernard. Right into the spring of 1942 the Canadians declined to address correspondence to South-Eastern Army, but only to South-Eastern Command; moreover, when Bernard attempted to draw up contingency plans in February 1942 for the use of GHQ reserves in South-Eastern Army area in the event of an actual invasion, Crerar protested that Canadian reserves could only be allocated with the express consent of the Canadian government or its authorised representative. To Bernard – who within months would be commanding Polish, French, Indian, Australian, New Zealand and South African forces as well as British – Crerar's pedantry was a form of 'belly-aching' more likely to lose wars than win them; and his relations with Crerar (and McNaughton, who became 1st Canadian Army Commander on 6 April 1942) suffered for the rest of the war.

Nevertheless, the outlook – given Bernard's determination to forge a new Army in the South-East of England – was not entirely bleak. The Canadian troops were volunteers, and came from the same stock as the heroes of Passchendaele about whom Bernard had written to his mother in 1917. They were tough and self-reliant, and wanted only good leadership – something Bernard was determined to see they got. The Corps BGS, Guy Simonds, was an officer of exceptional ability and, as 'Simbo' Simpson later recalled, Bernard soon had the three Chiefs-of-Staff – of SE Army, 12 Corps and Canadian Corps – closetted together in the evenings to co-ordinate their staffwork.

The first two priorities, as regards the new Canadian Corps, were training and planning. A Corps Study Week, on identical lines to the one Bernard had organised for 12 Corps, was arranged to take place in January 1942; meanwhile already in November 1941 he insisted that the Canadians adopt a systematic approach to training, starting with unit and sub-unit training, moving on to mobile HQ exercises at the end of December 1941, and full-scale corps exercises the following spring.

In the same way as he had in 12 Corps, Bernard simultaneously defined the role and tactical doctrine which he wished the Canadian Corps to adopt. However unlikely a German invasion, the prospect provided at least the framework for planning and training. As with 12 Corps, Bernard's first intention was to put paid in the Canadian Corps sector to the 'defensive mentality'. On 2 December 1941 Bernard therefore issued his official Army Instructions on 'Locality Defence', beginning:

1. A system of linear defence based on isolated selection of posts is useless in modern war and will in all cases be avoided. The principle of LOCALITY DEFENCE will be applied throughout South-Eastern Army.
2. LOCALITY DEFENCE implies the concentration of platoon and in some cases companies in strong, well-wired localities designed for all-round defence.
3. When holding long frontages considerable gaps between localities cannot be avoided. Enemy penetration through these gaps is of no great importance so long as the localities can hold out till our counter-attacks can be launched . . .

Having clarified the sort of defences he wanted, Bernard concentrated on this counter-attack role; and on 2 January 1942 he addressed all officers of Canadian Corps on their first exercise, code-named 'Beaver'. The object had been 'to practise the staffs and HQs of Canadian Corps in handling operations in the full-scale invasion battle', and in implementing the 'plan to defeat invasion'. What was this plan?

Without realising it, the officers of Canadian Corps were being drawn into General Montgomery's web: a web designed not only to give them a clearly defined role to play in South-Eastern Army over the coming months, but to educate them in such a way that they would one day be able to apply the same logical approach to different operations. Once again, there would be those – like General George S. Patton later – who found the Montgomery method too disciplined, too much like 'school' for grown men to submit to. For others, however, Bernard's approach was a revelation in the exercise of high command, setting entirely new standards by which, over the ensuing months, they would come to judge themselves. Finally, for a few there was an awareness of a historic moment having arrived both in their lives, and perhaps for the 'free world' – that despite the disaster of Pearl Harbour on 7 December, the subsequent fall of Hong Kong on 25 December 1941, and the currently poor Allied performance in North Africa, the Western democracies were not so much failing because of inferior forces or equipment, but in their mental approach to modern war.

Would that those two thousand Canadians who arrived in Hong Kong on 16 November 1941 had received the same lucid exposition on defence as was given by Lt-General Montgomery to the assembled officers of the Canadian Corps in England on 2 January 1942. First he enunciated the eight principal features of his South-Eastern Army 'Plan to Defeat Invasion'. Next he chose to 'examine certain points which affect the general conduct of the invasion battle', under the heading 'The Correct Mentality'.

12. In the invasion battle the enemy has the initiative. Therefore initially our operations tend to have a defensive bias. In the general layout of our dispositions is a defensive layout.

But the successful defeat of invasion will never be achieved by defensive action.

Successful defeat of invasion will be achieved by offensive action.

This being the case our worst enemy is 'defensive mentality'. We have got to develop the offensive spirit in our officers and men. As the enemy has the initiative and we may have to meet a great avalanche at any moment, we want to be clear as to what is meant by the 'offensive spirit'.

It does not mean that we will knock our heads up against

every snag that the enemy likes to prepare for us, regardless of the situation.

It means that we are offensively minded.

It means that although initially we may be forced to act on the defensive, we are on the watch all the time for opportunities to take *offensive action*, and when those opportunities occur we will be ready to seize them with both hands and get on with it.

The opportunity when it does come may be fleeting; immediate advantage must be taken of it before the chance passes; any relapse to a purely defensive mentality, even when everything seems hopeless, must never be allowed.

Nothing is ever hopeless so long as hearts are stout, and men have the weapons with which to fight.

I therefore say that the first requirement in the successful defeat of invasion is proven, well-trained soldiery, who are mentally alert, skilled in field-craft, expert in the use of their weapons, and are offensively minded.

Given such a soldiery, if put into battle properly, and well led in the battle by their junior leaders, then all will be well.

13. There is a tendency to think that the only way to defeat invasion is to have good defences, with plenty of pill-boxes.

Such defences will be of no avail if the men inside them are dull, with no fighting spirit and are defensively minded.

If I were to choose between good defences and good men I am quite definite that I would sooner have the men described in para 12 and *no* defences rather than have the best defences in the world manned by a soldiery with no fighting spirit.

Good soldiers will be greatly helped in their task by good defences. The second requirement therefore is that our soldiery who are to fight this invasion battle against superior numbers should have the best defences that are possible; this will enable improved areas to be held with fewer numbers and will set free the maximum numbers for offensive action at the right moment.

14. I suggest that in preparing your schemes and plans, you should not use the nomenclature or words 'defence schemes'. These words tend to give the impression of defence only. But the successful defeat of invasion is based on offensive action.

I therefore recommend that your written schemes should be entitled 'Plan to Defeat Invasion'.

Bernard then proceeded to define the lessons of the exercise: the proper positioning and defence of headquarters 'so that the divisional or brigade commander can give his whole attention to the battle going on in his area or sector'; the proper organisation of command, with a clearly-known hierarchy in which Home Guard and reserves would know the chain of command; the correct dispositions for units, following the principles of 'locality defence', avoiding 'undue dispersion which is strong nowhere'; and in the light of the exercise, assessing those major features which must be held 'at all costs'. In this case, the exercise had brought out the imperative need to hold the Downs of Sussex: had shown these to be poorly defended because their defences were thin and too dispersed. 'The problems need to be examined so that you hold *very strongly* the really good approaches on to the Downs and ignore the rest,' Bernard declared. Moreover there was the question of road communications and demolitions.

It was no good, Bernard felt, simply blowing all bridges. Only in the front line, on the coast, was such a policy defensible; behind that line it was important that the Chief Engineer of the corps be in firm control, together with his Corps Commander. Certain bridges might be needed for counter-attack; and besides, to send out all the engineers in the corps in demolition parties was once again to invite defeat through undue dispersion, leaving the CRE empty-handed just when he might require his forces.

There was the important matter of signals ('if there is any lack of co-operation between staff and signals, then you're done'); the need to fight to kill, 'without quarter asked or given', if the Germans dared set foot on English soil; and lastly the paramount importance of air support.

I mention this last not because it is least important – but because it is the most important of all the points I've touched on. I mention it last so that you are more likely to remember it.

The exercise had shown how little 'air-minded' was the Canadian Corps still – how hours after the original report of a 'German invasion' the RAF support squadrons had still not been alerted, nor were they subsequently used in operations. 'It is very necessary that you should cultivate an "air"-sense,' Bernard emphasised. 'You must become air-support minded. The Germans have a system which gives extraordinary quick support . . . We must be satisfied with nothing less.'

All this had emerged, as Bernard pointed out, without a single soldier having been mobilised for the exercise. Training, Bernard reiterated, was not play: it was the intellectual and physical preparation for success in battle. If the commanding officers ensured they put their troops into battle on the right footing, if the junior leaders led with intelligence and resolution, and if the soldiery was hardened for 'a real rough house lasting for weeks', then success would be inevitable. 'Canadian officers and men have always been renowned for these qualities,' Bernard concluded and they possess that very great quality of being able to rise to the top of their form when all is not going well.

A soldiery with these sterling qualities will always excel in battle.

43. So for you the outlook is bright.

If you officers ensure you put properly into the fight the magnificent material you possess, then there is no Corps taking part in this world-wide war – of any nation – that will be able to compete with you.

Such an address had become by now one of the hallmarks of Bernard's growing reputation in the British Army, and there is evidence from witnesses, from the Canadian War Histories and the Canadian War Diaries, that Bernard's influence on the Canadian Corps was revolutionary – indeed subsequent Canadian Corps Instructions for Training and Operations would come to reflect, word for word, the edicts of the new Army Commander.

Yet the transformation of Canadian Corps from being a jealously-guarded contribution by the Canadian Government into a battle-worthy, integral component of Montgomery's new South-Eastern Army was not quite as straightforward as such sources maintain. In hitherto unpublished letters from General Brooke, the CIGS, there is also evidence of the resentment caused by Bernard's radical form of generalship and Army command. In fact it would seem that the Canadian senior generals were incapable of the same adherence to the normal command-structures as, say, their Australian counter-parts; and McNaughton's and Crerar's wish to play military politics as well as holding field command was to bedevil the performance of Canadian forces throughout the war.

Crerar, for example, took great exception to Bernard's address at the Final Conference on Exercise 'Beaver', and made noises direct to Brooke, who invited him to lunch to sort things out. To McNaught-on – still technically the Canadian Corps Commander – Brooke wrote on 7 January 1942 to suggest the formation of a Canadian Army Headquarters that would free the Corps Commander from the administration work involved in 'rear services, workshops, base organization, etc.' for the 'job of commanding and training the fighting formations. That in itself is a full-time job!'[1] It was, in fact, Brooke's way of trying to kick McNaughton upstairs.

However to Bernard, the next day, Brooke wrote in a very different vein. He was 'delighted that things are going so well with the Canadian Corps', as Bernard had informed him in a recent letter. Yet he felt he had to warn Bernard not to underestimate what he was up against.

[1] C. P. Stacey, *Official History of the Canadian Army in the Second World War*, Vol. I, op. cit.

They are grand soldiers, that I fully realized after spending 1½ years with them in the last war.

But they are very touchy and childlike in many ways. You will therefore have to watch your steps with them *far* more than you would with British troops. I had Crerar to lunch, and he is delighted with all your help, and all out to play to the utmost.

But he warned me of three dangers which I had not thought of:–

a) The possibility that the umpires sent to assist formations [Bernard had offered to send junior umpires to help] may be looked on as 'spies' to report on efficiency and state of training. This will want watching by careful selection of umpires.

b) The danger of the impression being created that you were trying to 'drive' the Canadian Corps!

c) The danger, in large conferences of all ranks, of criticizing the senior officers in front of the juniors. As Canadians they are only too ready to criticize their own seniors, but they resent having their Brig & Div Commanders criticized by a British officer! Their tendency as Canadians will at once be to take [sic] pacts against the British officer & to resent his remarks.

I pass these points on to you for what they are worth.

This was in fact the first time in Bernard's career that he had had seriously to consider the extreme sensibilities of an Allied partner in war – save for the moment, in May 1940, when he had found a Belgian Division occupying his proposed sector of front at Louvain. On that occasion he had been outwardly diplomatic, but inwardly determined to arrest and remove the Belgian commander the moment the Germans appeared.

Now, however, he was faced with a less transigent problem – and one that would haunt him for the rest of his military career. What he felt about one of his corps commanders complaining direct to the CIGS we can only guess; it certainly did not raise his estimation of Crerar. In an annotation relating to his letter to his mother of 8 November 1917, about Canadian shortcomings, Bernard later wrote:

I give my views on the Canadian Army: wrongly. In point of fact the soldiers were far better than their senior officers! It was those senior officers who were the trouble.

I had great troubles with Crerar, the Commander of the Canadian Army in North-West Europe in 1944–45. He was utterly unfit to command an Army, and some of his Divisional Commanders were very poor. I complained to Alanbrooke (the CIGS) about it and he replied that I must somehow pull them along. He said he had the same trouble in the First World War, when it was found necessary to replace Byng by Currie. However, Alanbrooke did

manage to get McNaughton kicked out; he was a useless commander, and was really a scientist.

The Canadian Army produced only one general fit to hold high
command in the Second World War – Guy Simonds.

The extreme touchiness of Crerar and some senior Canadian officers
may help explain the fiasco of the Dieppe raid, planned in the spring
of 1942; for the moment, however, Bernard was under instructions to
tread warily, and only the extreme professionalism of the chief
Canadian staff officer, Guy Simonds, ensured that Bernard's new
South-East Army doctrine was adopted throughout the Canadian
Corps. Simonds' staffwork was, as is evidenced by the Canadian
Corps War Diaries for 1942, second to none – and the Canadian
Corps was soon issuing its own 'Corps Plan to Defeat Invasion',
modelled on that drawn up for 12 Corps by Bernard.

Did Crerar really object to Bernard's 'driving'? Brooke had put an
exclamation mark after the quote: for both he and Bernard would
come to feel that fighting Germans was easier than co-operating with
and commanding one's own allies. Brooke's task was, in this respect,
infinitely the more difficult – and Bernard must have thanked
Heaven he had not the direction of a world-wide war on his hands,
but the comparatively simple role of commanding an army at home.

Even this was complicated enough, given Bernard's determination
to enact his vision of modern field command in the rather trying
circumstances of almost peacetime conditions in England. Somehow
he had to convince the tens of thousands of troops under his
command that, while the threat of invasion might have receded, the
Axis powers would never be beaten by standing guard on Britain's
beaches. Somehow an army must be trained at home that was
capable of beating the enemy on foreign soil, by offensive action: and
sadly this became more and more of a problem as the first months of
1942 passed. The Japanese were proving every bit as thrusting as the
Germans. Having crippled the American fleet at Pearl Harbour they
invaded the Philippines, took Hong Kong, and landed on 8 February
1942 in Malaya. Within a single week they had forced Arthur
Percival, Bernard's erstwhile colleague in Southern Ireland but now
the GOC in command of some 70,000 troops defending Singapore, to
surrender in what would become known as 'the most ignominious
capitulation in British history'. On 27 February the Japanese navy
won the Battle of the Java Sea, and the following day the Japanese
invaded Java, taking this and Sumatra by early March. Worse still, in
Burma the Japanese began an advance that would take the capital,
Rangoon, and bring them to the very gates of India. At Sittang on 23
February 1942 the only bridge was disastrously blown, leaving the
17th Division cut off – a tragic example of one of the very dangers
Bernard had warned of to the Canadian Corps on 4 January.

Churchill had already begun to feel the cold hand of ill-fate; on 15

February 1942 he broadcast to the nation an appeal for national unity. On 18 February Brooke noted in his diary: 'Burma news bad. If the Army cannot fight better than it is doing at present we shall deserve to lose our Empire.'[1] The following day it was finally decided that a new Army Commander be sent out to Burma: a commander capable of arresting the tide of Japanese victory, of inculcating in the forces under his command a determination to halt the enemy by intelligent, cohesive defence and, in time, to counter-attack. Bernard Montgomery, Commander of the South-Eastern Army, might well have felt himself to be the logical choice. However, the name quoted in the cables that went out to Wavell, C-in-C Far East, was not Montgomery but Alexander.

[1] Alanbrooke Diary, loc. cit.

CHAPTER FOURTEEN

War or Opéra Bouffe

Whether or not Brooke was right in his assessment of the army's performance in Burma (most historical commentators have excused it by giving high praise to the training and élan of the Japanese), there remains the question of why Alexander was chosen. Field-Marshal Slim's retrospective verdict on Alexander has been quoted; the American General Joe 'Vinegar' Stilwell when he heard a BBC radio broadcast after the fall of Burma, extolling Alexander as a 'bold and resourceful commander who has fought one of the great defensive battles of the war', gave his own laconic opinion in his diary: 'Crap!'

As at Dunkirk, Alexander was imperturbable: but even his British Corps Commander, Lt-General Slim, acknowledged that the British had, at heart, been outgeneralled. Alexander, unlike Bernard, had no tactical 'vision' and it was only the disastrous British performance against the Japanese which caused Slim himself to recognise the need to impart such a vision, both in training and in operational command. For Slim, the fall of Burma was his own personal Dunkirk.

Some historians have assumed that it was Churchill who chose Alexander to replace General Hutton in Burma; but reference to Brooke's diaries reveals that it was in fact Brooke as CIGS who first put Alexander forward: a suggestion with which Churchill readily concurred. On 19 February 1942 Brooke's diary runs: 'After lunch was sent for by PM who said he agreed to Alexander being sent out. Only hope Alexander arrives in time as the situation in Burma is becoming critical. Troops don't seem to be fighting well there either [as well as N. Africa] which is most depressing.'

In the event it was Slim[1] who brought Burcorps safely back to India, rather than Alexander. However, the question must be asked why Bernard Montgomery was not considered for the post in Burma. It was true that Alexander had commanded a brigade on the North-West Frontier – but the Japanese were not to be equated with hill-tribes, and in the end one must conclude that Brooke, however much he admired Bernard's talents in battle and in re-training, still hesitated to give him field command of an army lest – particularly where allied units were concerned – he 'do something silly'.

Yet if Bernard felt 'passed over' once again, he did not show it. Not

[1] Alanbrooke Diary, loc. cit.

only did he foresee a prolonged war in which, one day, his talents must finally be employed in the field, but he was well aware that his methods and style of military leadership made him unpopular, if not suspect, among his political and military superiors. In the meantime, therefore, he did the only thing he could: he concentrated on the men whose loyalty he could command – the officers and men of South-Eastern Army. It might not be command of troops engaged in battle, but Bernard was determined to treat it as a field army, and to learn the vital lessons of higher army command while there was still time. In Bernard's view his first mission was to lay down a coherent policy for his Army, which he did by ensuring that both his Corps Commanders – however disgruntled Crerar might be – followed his 'Plan to Defeat Invasion'. His next task was to bring both Corps, by hard training, to a state of military proficiency where they could answer to the Army Commander's tactical orders immediately and with a will to win. Thirdly, there was the more personal question of his own leadership as an Army Commander: how, at one and the same time, to imprint himself and his 'vision' of a modern British army on his subordinates, and yet delegate sufficient power and authority in order to maintain his own clarity of mind and purpose.

This was a problem no British army commander had resolved since war began. Gort's generalship in France had borne all the hallmarks of traditional British rectitude and obtuseness. Not only had Gort no tactical vision to impart or impose as an army commander, but he was, at heart, afraid to have to intervene between his two Corps Commanders. In the Middle East Wavell had launched – with pre-war trained British forces – a brilliant campaign in the field, but in the end had succumbed to dispersion, to political pressure, and had failed – as in the example of Crete – to train and prepare his forces for known eventualities, and to ensure that his commanders had positive plans to deal with them. In the Far East, the British performance against the Japanese – as Slim acknowledged – had been shameful. 'In preparation, in execution, in strategy, and in tactics we had been worsted, and we had paid the penalty – defeat,' Slim wrote later. 'Defeat is bitter. Bitter to the common soldier, but trebly to his general.'[1] Finally, Wavell's successor in the Middle East, General Auchinleck, was already tasting in North Africa the same fruit. His first act on assuming Wavell's mantle had been to form an 8th Army out of the Western Desert Force: but his choice of commander – though no worse than Churchill's preferred general, Lt-General Maitland Wilson – revealed Auchinleck's greatest flaw: his inability to choose good subordinates, which is the essential part of delegation. Auchinleck chose Alan Cunningham as 8th Army Commander: the same age as Bernard, an artilleryman, and younger brother of Admiral Cunningham. The appointment was made on 16 August 1941. Auchinleck had never met Cunningham before appointing

[1] W. Slim, *Defeat into Victory*, op. cit.

him, and admitted to Dill in a letter that day that he was 'handicapped by my lack of personal knowledge of most of those concerned [nominated to commands], but I am convinced that I am right, and have now no further doubts in the matter'.[1] Three months later, at the height of his ill-starred 'Crusader' offensive, Auchinleck wrote to Cunningham: 'I have formed the opinion, however, that you are now thinking of defence rather than of offensive and I have lost confidence in your ability to press to the bitter end the offensive which I have ordered to continue.' He therefore relieved Cunningham of 8th Army Command; asking him in a more personal letter, which he attached, to go into hospital – not because he was ill, but 'in the public interest'. Accordingly Cunningham entered No. 64 General Hospital at Alexandria on 26 November 1941 under an assumed name. Though exhausted, he was perfectly fit within three days, and the consultant physician – insisted upon by Admiral Cunningham – reported there was no question of a 'nervous breakdown'. Auchinleck wrote to him at hospital on 27 November to thank him for 'the way in which you accepted my decision, and for your very great loyalty and public spirit in agreeing to go into hospital secretly and against your will. I ask your forgiveness in having inflicted this indignity on you, and I know very well how you disliked having to pretend that you are sick, when you are not'.[2]

Bernard Montgomery may well have heard mess-gossip about Cunningham's removal, and certainly the affair fascinated him, as he seems to have purloined the War Office file (or a copy of it) when he himself later became CIGS – a file he titled, in his private papers, 'The true story of how Auchinleck removed Alan Cunningham from command of the Eighth Army in November 1941'.

In point of fact Bernard agreed with Auchinleck's 'true' assessment of Cunningham; he would himself, as will be seen, have very similar problems over Cunningham's 'defensive' mentality in the final evacuation of Palestine in 1948. Moreover he felt Auchinleck was absolutely correct in removing, at a critical moment in a critical battle, a commander whose judgement he did not trust – just as he, Bernard, would temporarily remove even his most successful Corps Commander, Brian Horrocks, at a critical moment in the Battle of the Ardennes in December 1944. Even the concoction of a medical story to explain the removal was, in Bernard's view, a reasonable method – it would, in fact, be his own chosen manner of removing Crerar in the autumn of 1944 from command of 1st Canadian Army.

For Bernard the matter of selection of subordinates was of paramount importance, and would become in time one of his most important contributions to British generalship in the twentieth century. However unseemly Bernard Montgomery's vanity, it was matched by a veritable genius both for smelling out inefficiency and

[1] John Connell, *Auchinleck*, op. cit.
[2] Montgomery Papers.

for discovering and nurturing young talent. Far from losing or discarding this curiosity when promoted to Army command, Bernard felt it to be one of the first priorities of an Army Commander: to know the men under his command; to weed out the inefficient and to promote carefully the proficient.

The War Diary for South-Eastern Army thus records, from 17 November 1941, an endless progression of 'visits' made by the new Army Commander – and few of the many tens of thousands who served in that Army will forget them. Brian Horrocks later remarked that Bernard Montgomery would have made a 'first class talent spotter for any football club':

> Army Commanders with many thousands of troops under their command tend to become remote God-like characters whom few know even by sight, yet in some extraordinary way Monty's influence permeated all strata of SE Command and his knowledge of the personalities under his command was uncanny. Often he would ring me in the evening and make the most searching inquiries about some young second-lieutenant whom he had noticed on training . . . The only way I could deal with these inquiries was to have a book containing details of every officer in the division handy beside the telephone.[1]

Often this curiosity about people and their performance at their jobs put his informants in an embarrassing situation – as Sir Frank Simpson, who remained BGS at 12 Corps, recalled:

> Monty frequently used to ring me up from his Army HQ to ask an opinion on somebody or something – an opinion he ought to have got from the Corps Commander. He could not get out of the habit of getting in personal touch with me as somebody he knew very well indeed.[2]

It was in fact this loyalty to the competent and constant interest in locating, assessing and promoting lesser-known talent that was to characterise Bernard's command. It was not long, for instance, before he had brought Brigadier Kirkman to South-Eastern Army as his Chief Gunner. Moreover, though he could appear selfish or self-centred – as in his fury when 'Simbo' Simpson declined to go to 3rd Division – he was at heart altruistic, and was genuinely pleased when his protégés did well, even if promotion took them to other commands. For instance, on 21 February 1942 he wrote to his erstwhile GSO 2 (Intelligence) at 12 Corps, 'Kit' Dawnay:

---

[1] B. Horrocks, op. cit.
[2] Wason interviews, loc. cit.

My dear Kit,

I am planning to bring you into Army HQ as my GSO 1 (Intelligence). When I left 12 Corps I was determined to get you back to me again as head of my intelligence as soon as I could do so.

The opportunity has now arrived, and I have asked for you to succeed Oulton . . .

It will be delightful to have you back with me again. You should keep this to yourself until it is through officially – but I do not anticipate any snags.

Snags, however, there were, as Bernard's letter some six weeks later shows:

My dear Kit,

I am quite delighted that you are going as GSO 1 (I) to the Expeditionary Force. But I am desolated at losing you from my Army. The whole thing is really a complete foul, as they would not let you come to me as GSO 1 (I) – saying you were too junior. I gave you such a 'write-up' when trying to get you on my staff that they have now bagged you for something else. However, you will find it intensely interesting, and perhaps we may yet fight the Bosche together again. I hope so.

Nor was this concern with talented personnel confined to his staff. Bernard was adamant that soldiers as well as officers should feel the measure of his indefatigable interest. Stephen Grenfell, serving under Montgomery in 12 Corps, later wondered

whether he got any sleep in those days, but he seemed to be everywhere. His appearances weren't visits; they were visitations. A couple of staff cars would erupt into your line of vision. A tough, stringy, bird-like little man would jump out; there'd be a fluttering of salutes and the General would be right amongst the pigeons. Striding on ahead, with his staff stumbling behind in the sand dunes, he'd make straight for the nearest private soldier. 'Who are you? Where do you come from? What are you doing? Do you know what's going on? Are you in the picture? Can you see the coast of France today? Good; that's where the enemy is . . .'[1]

Certainly these 'visitations' did not diminish once he became Army Commander. The War Diary for HQ Southern Command at the beginning of January 1942 runs:

Jan 2: Army Commander lectured to all officers of Canadian Corps on Exercise 'Beaver'. Commander visited 43 Div area

[1] 'Montgomery of Alamein', BBC recording of 24.9.58.

Jan 8:   Army Commander visited 44 Div area
Jan 9:   Army Commander visited 46 Div area
Jan 10: Army Commander visited Canadian Corps HQ
Jan 11: Army Commander visited West Sussex Home Guard
Jan 13: Army Commander lectured to Senior Officers' School
Jan 14: Army Commander lectured to Staff College, Camberley

and continues in an unceasing record of activity, attending exercises, tactical discussions, the Canadian Corps Study Week, demonstrations of new weapons, setting out the roles of GHQ reserve formations in the event of invasion, issuing instructions regarding air support, and – in March 1942 – visiting every single aerodrome in the South-Eastern Army area, from Redhill to Gatwick, Gravesend and Detling. He called for an end to any further work on defences, stressing on 1 April in capital letters that 'NO NEW PILL-BOXES WILL BE CONSTRUCTED'; simultaneously he badgered Paget's Home Forces GHQ with his insistence that there be a definite, all-embracing Home Forces plan for resisting invasion should it come – a plan that would at least train staff officers at every echelon of command to prepare themselves in advance for the possible roles they might be called upon to play, and to rehearse them in the issuing of operational instructions.

Such ceaseless activity might suggest an atmosphere of frenzied endeavour at South-Eastern Army HQ at Reigate. Strangely however, this was not the case. On the contrary, in comparison with Paget's Home Forces GHQ in London, the atmosphere in Reigate seems to have been positively tranquil – as is evidenced by a young Intelligence major who was transferred from Paget's Home Forces GHQ to Montgomery's staff on 3 March 1942:

At GHQ Home Forces, at its higher levels, something of the same air of tension and strain prevailed as at Combined Operations Headquarters.

Goronwy Rees later recalled in *A Bundle of Sensations*:

At GHQ Home Forces, staff officers at the higher level always seemed to be overworked, harassed, pressed for time and as a result irritable . . . In the case of the Commander-in-Chief [Paget], however, I knew that his brusque manner, that seemed to combine rudeness and bad temper, was the result of the almost continuous pain in which he lived as a result of an old wound suffered in the First World War. But I began to understand a little why Monty liked to have about him men who were physically well and whose nerves were relaxed by the sedative of physical exercise.

And indeed how different things seemed when at regular intervals I went down to Reigate to report to the Army Commander. It was never difficult to see him; when an appointment was made, he was always punctually available, and he always gave the impression that he had nothing in the world to do except the business which was in hand. There were never any papers on his desk, there were never any interruptions; one almost had the feeling that here was an idle man, and that but for one's own visit he would have been at a loss to fill up his time. Most remarkable of all, to myself, was that he actually listened to what I said, gravely and politely, though very often I felt it was not worth listening to; and when he made any comments, or issued any instructions, one felt that they had already been considered, calmly and dispassionately, in the cool of the evening, in the garden, when he had given himself just the right amount of time required for reflection. I began to think that the difference between him and other commanders I had come to know was that he actually *thought*, in the same sense that a scientist or a scholar thinks. His subject matter happened to be war, but the mental processes, of definition and analysis, of coming to conclusions on demonstrable evidence, were the same . . . When he was thinking about war, which he did with wonderful lucidity and concentration, he seemed to me to come as near as any could to exemplifying the dictum of my old tutor, H. W. B. Joseph, that the will is reason acting.

Anyone who ever served under or worked with Montgomery will testify to the accuracy of this portrait. Yet, if it was true that Montgomery's HQ radiated such calm, and that Bernard himself managed – in contrast to his continual daily round of visits and lectures – to find the necessary peace and tranquillity in the evening in which to reflect, one must ask whence came this facility, a determination never to be the pawn of events, but, almost as a scholar, to examine them in quiet and thus to dominate them – as 'reason acting'.

One clue is to be found in Rees' account of his first interview with the Army Commander, late in March 1942. Summoned one evening after dinner to meet Montgomery, Rees searched his memory for any 'omission or commission' he might have made since his arrival that might have merited such a summons:

The Army Commander occupied a comfortable villa on the hill overlooking Reigate . . . Through the open french-windows I could see a small, rather unimpressive figure walking on the lawn, head slightly bent and hands clasped behind its back . . . When he had received his ADC's message, the little figure turned and came into the study.

One saw a narrow foxy face, long-nosed, sharp and intelligent and tenacious, with very bright and clear blue eyes, and a small, light, spare body. The effect was not at all imposing, except for his eyes and an indefinable look in his face of extreme cleverness and sagacity, like a very alert Parson Jack Russell terrier. But what was impressive was an air he had of extraordinary quietness and calm, as if nothing in the world could disturb his peace of mind . . .

The air of calm and peace which he carried with him was so strong that after a moment my panic and alarm began to die away; it was something which one felt to be almost incongruous in a soldier. He made me sit in a window seat with my back to the garden, so that my face was in shadow and the evening light streamed in on his and I had the opportunity to see how very finely it was moulded, with the fineness one sees in some animals that are very highly bred and trained for the particular purpose they have to fulfil. And as one talked to him, one was aware all the time of the stillness and quietness that reigned all around him, in the study itself, in the entire household, in the garden outside, as if even the birds were under a spell of silence; it was a kind of stillness one might associate more easily with an interview with a priest than a general . . .

Rees' insight is remarkable – for there is no doubt that it was at this stage of his life that the posthumous figure of Bishop Montgomery came more and more to influence Bernard in the conduct of high command – an influence Bernard himself was the first to acknowledge, as 'Simbo' Simpson remembered from the time Bernard commanded 12 Corps:

There was a battery of artillery put out to defend the Dungeness marshes down in the South of Kent, and it so happened that they went and dug two or three gun-pits in the cemetery of the local church.

Complaints were made to the Bishop, who took the matter up with GHQ Home Forces, who referred it to 12 Corps. Eventually Simpson felt the matter was getting volatile enough to merit a letter to the Bishop from the Corps Commander himself, at least apologising for digging the gun-pits without prior consultation with the parson. Simpson therefore dictated a letter.

It was typed and all Monty needed to do was to sign it. He read it through, signed it. Then he added a postscript in his own hand-writing: 'I wonder if you knew my father, the former Bishop of Tasmania. He had a great influence on my life, and I am sure he would have taken the same line as you have over this unfortunate incident . . .'[1]

[1] Wason interviews, loc. cit.

Was it then the memory of his father which gave Bernard this increasingly spiritual, thoughtful dimension? Bishop Montgomery had made it a matter of episcopal duty to visit his missionaries wherever they were; had organised conferences both for his clergy and fellow bishops in Australia to consider their objectives and organisation, and in time he had become the mainstay of the Anglican missionary movement throughout the world.

The parallel with Bernard's own life is certainly an interesting one. Bernard had now, finally, reached 'episcopal' rank within the army as C-in-C South-Eastern Command though his missionary vigour and his unorthodox ways had earned him in some quarters the reputation of a madman ('Of course there's nothing wrong with Monty really. He's just a bit mad,' Rees' Brigadier at GHQ had told him[1]); and in certain respects this was undoubtedly true, as the strain of his own evangelical military vocation expressed itself in improbable suspicions or wild impetuosities. He had provoked a Prime Minister's directive, requiring Prime Minister's personal permission before firing the great coastal guns at Dover – the result of a mishap at 12 Corps when Bernard ordered the guns to be fired indiscriminately at Calais, giving rise to a full retaliatory raid by the Luftwaffe on Dover which killed or injured some twenty civilians. He once rejected a letter from his own stepson, John Carver, who was in hospital suffering from measles. 'Your letter has been received here,' Bernard replied. 'I ordered it to be burned immediately and I haven't read it.'[2] He sacked a perfectly good Intelligence officer at 12 Corps because he was fat and had German connections about which GHQ had become anxious – 'Can't have that here,' Bernard told his Chief-of-Staff. 'Get rid of him at once. He must leave the Corps area in three hours from now.'[3]

'Every day new rumours would circulate about his latest eccentricities,' Rees recorded. 'At that time the name of the Army Commander, however awful in Whitehall, had not earned the fame which belonged to it later; soldiers who cared for the dignity of their profession were often scandalised by the pretensions of the GOC-in-C, South-Eastern Army, while those who suffered from them directly, like his staff and his formation commanders, sometimes wondered, with a mixture of alarm and scepticism, whether they were playing a part in war or *opéra bouffe*. Sometimes, in Reigate, one had the feeling that the Army Commander might at any moment lead his army directly across the Channel in a personal campaign to liberate Europe.'[4]

Within two years this would be exactly what Bernard Montgomery

[1] Goronwy Rees, op. cit.
[2] Colonel John Carver, loc. cit.
[3] General Sir Frank Simpson, Wason interviews, loc. cit.
[4] Goronwy Rees, op. cit.

would do; but in the spring of 1942, as the tide of Axis victories rose once more as it had done in 1940 and 1941, this did, in fact, seem insane. Brooke's diary for the first seven months of 1942 makes sorry reading, and he must often have rued the day he was made CIGS. The Chairman of the Chiefs-of-Staff Committee, Admiral Pound, was in the last months of his life and senile; Churchill, brilliant though he could be, insisted on personally directing the war effort, aided by his equally brilliant but flighty protégé Mountbatten (promoted to Adviser and then Director of Combined Operations Headquarters and given in March 1942, at Churchill's behest, a seat on the Chiefs-of-Staff Committee); de Gaulle was proving an impossibly over-sensitive leader of the Free French, while Britain's once-reluctant Allies, the Americans, were now hot to wage war in Europe, yet without the remotest strategical conception of how to do so or the problems involved.

Such disadvantages could, however, have been overcome if, by 1942, the British armed services had shown themselves competent in the field of battle against Germans or Japanese. But this, sadly, was very far from being the case. Rangoon fell, and Alexander's forces were pushed relentlessly out of Burma. Japan established naval supremacy as far as the Indian Ocean, even bombing Ceylon; in the Mediterranean it was becoming impossible to get convoys through to Malta, and even in the English Channel the Germans were able to bring home the battlecruisers *Scharnhorst* and *Gneisenau* from Brest with impunity. The RAF was now obsessed with night raids on German cities, and showed barely the vaguest interest in developing army-air support. Moreover it was against this background that Brooke's own vision of a gradual Allied 'come-back' in Europe, beginning in the Middle East with simultaneous offensives in Libya and seaborne landings in French North-West Africa, was rudely shattered by the defeat of 8th Army by Rommel.

More than anything, it was the poor British showing in the desert which brought Brooke to despair in the spring and early summer of 1942 – for it was the one area, he felt, in which the British could and ought to taste victory. Without such victory it would, Brooke recognised, be very difficult to get the Americans to endorse British strategy in the Mediterranean, since it was elementary that they would reinforce progress, but highly dubious whether they would reinforce defeat. Knowing from his Intelligence sources – including Ultra – how reluctant was the German High Command to back Rommel at a moment when they were fully preoccupied with their second great summer offensive in Russia, Brooke railed in his diary against the hapless Auchinleck: identified, prophetically, Auchinleck's failings and yet, strangely, remained stubbornly loyal to him when Churchill strove to dismiss his C-in-C Middle East.

One has only to look at Brooke's diary to see how far back went the dissatisfaction in Whitehall at Auchinleck's handling of British forces in the Middle East. By 29 January 1942, reading some long letters on 'proposed reorganisation', Brooke had begun – as he subsequently explained in his *Notes on My Life* – to be 'upset by the many messages that emanated from Auchinleck's office. I was beginning to suspect that 'Chink' Dorman-Smith, one of his staff officers, was beginning to exercise far too much influence on him. Dorman-Smith had a most fertile brain, continually producing new ideas, some of which (not many) were good, and the rest useless. Archie Wavell had made use of him, but was wise enough to discard all the bad and only retain the good. Auchinleck was incapable of doing so and allowed himself to fall too deeply under Chink's influence.'

The next day was, in Brooke's words, 'one of the dark days of the war'. In his diary he recorded: 'The Benghazi business is bad.' Benghazi was captured in a lightning offensive by Rommel on 29 January, and even Churchill was forced to concede, in a speech in Parliament: 'We have a very daring and skilful opponent against us, and, may I say across the havoc of war, a great general . . .' Brooke was less chivalrous. It was 'nothing less than bad generalship on the part of Auchinleck,' he went on to note in his diary. 'He has been overconfident, and has believed everything his optimistic Shearer [Director of Military Intelligence] has told him. As a result he was not in a position to meet a counter-blow.' Shearer had based his Intelligence advice on Ultra, rather than the 'Y' services on the front, and had 'lulled Auchinleck into a sense of false security', as Brooke recalled. 'Auchinleck to my mind had most of the qualifications to make him one of the finest of commanders,' Brooke continued, 'but unfortunately he lacked the one most important of all – the ability to select the men to serve him.'[1]

By 3 February Brooke was recording: 'After lunch I had a long talk with [Bob Haining] on the situation in the Middle East. The more I find out from various quarters, the more disturbed I am at the situation out there. I do not like the combination of Arthur Smith [Chief of the General Staff, GHQ], Shearer and Auchinleck. It is not a good combination.'[2] Auchinleck was prevailed upon to replace the exhausted Smith, who had served there 'since the start of the war and had seen our forces going backwards and forwards across the desert without achieving decisive results', as Brooke later noted.[3] But the Chief-of-Staff with whom Auchinleck replaced him was, to Brooke, the most extraordinary choice of all. 'Unfortunately when I brought Arthur Smith home to command London District,' Brooke noted, 'and offered the Auk the whole of the Army to choose from for his Chief-of-Staff, he chose Corbett. I did not know Corbett, nor did anybody I asked about him. Had I had at that time any idea of his

[1] *Notes on My Life*, loc. cit.
[2] Diary, loc. cit.
[3] *Notes on My Life*, loc. cit.

unsuitability for the appointment, I might have advised the Auk to choose someone of higher calibre.'[1]

Brooke did, however, manage to get rid of Shearer after much badgering and protestations from Auchinleck – who eventually replaced him by Colonel Francis de Guingand in the post of DMI.

The rot, however, did not stop. Worried about the 8th Army's handling of its armoured forces, Brooke decided at the beginning of March 1942 to send out his own 'expert' to advise Auchinleck.

I had been worried for some time by Auchinleck's handling of armoured formations, mainly due to his listening to the advice of Chink Dorman-Smith. I therefore informed him that I was sending him out one of our best armoured divisional commanders to act as his adviser at headquarters on the use of armoured forces. I knew that Dick McCreery might have a difficult time with the Auk and I warned him frankly that he might have a difficult furrow to plough. I must say I had not expected that he would be practically ignored and never referred to by the Auk on the employment of armoured forces.[2]

Not only would Auchinleck not use McCreery and continue to rely on the erratic Dorman-Smith as his adviser, but he refused Churchill's summons to come back to England to discuss the Middle East problem, in particular the plight of Malta. Churchill was irate; on 5 March Churchill had been almost on the brink of resignation over India, and he was soon threatening to dismiss Auchinleck for insubordination – 'I shudder to think what he may put in it,' Brooke reflected on Churchill's threatened telegram on 13 March.[3] On 24 March, however, Churchill's frustration reached even more demonic proportions:

'Called by PM before the COS meeting,' Brooke's diary ran that night.

Found him in bed with the dragon dressing gown on. Evidently still unhappy about delays of Auchinleck's attack. Even suggesting replacing Auchinleck by Archie Nye. I've ridden him off trying to replace him by Gort! It is very exhausting, this continual protecting of Auchinleck, especially as I have not got the highest opinion of him![4]

That Churchill should seriously have contemplated putting Gort in command of the Middle East is surely the ultimate vindication of Brooke's qualms about Churchill – qualms which, when Arthur

[1] Ibid.
[2] Ibid.
[3] Diary, loc. cit.
[4] Ibid.

494

Bryant published a selection of them, were considered an impudent slur on a great national hero. But, though Brooke sometimes attributed his testy diary entries to 'liverishness', his assessment of Churchill in this respect was not a fleeting misjudgement. On 31 March Brooke recorded:

The last day in the first quarter of 1942, fateful years in which we have already lost a large proportion of the British Empire, and are on the high road to losing a great deal more of it! During the last fortnight I have had for the first time since the war started a growing conviction that we are going to lose this war unless we control it very differently and fight it with more determination.

To begin with a democracy is at a great handicap when up against a dictatorship when it comes to war. Secondly a government with one big man in it, and that one a grave danger in many respects, is in a parlous way. Party politics and party interests still override larger war issues. Petty jealousies colour decisions and influence destinies. Politicians still suffer from that little knowledge of military matters which gives them unwarranted confidence that they are born strategists. As a result they confuse issues, affect decisions, and convert simple problems and plans into confused tangles and hopeless muddles. It is all desperately depressing. Furthermore it is made worse by the lack of good military commanders. Half our Corps and Divisional Commanders are totally unfit for their appointments; and yet if I were to sack them I could find no better. They lack clarity, imagination, drive, and power of leadership.[1]

This was a grave diagnosis indeed, and helps to explain why, far from Auchinleck being kept as C-in-C in the Middle East by virtue of his talents, he was retained for so long for want of anyone better. The appointment of Gort would have been a calamity, as Brooke knew all too well from Dunkirk; the appointment of Nye – who, like Gort before his BEF post, had never commanded anything above a brigade – 'would have been gambling with fate,' as Brooke later put it.[2] Indeed, when Churchill sent Nye out to draw up a personal report from the Middle East once Auchinleck declined to come back to Britain, Nye voiced no damning criticism of Auchinleck. To Nye, Auchinleck quoted the strategic worries and shortages of men and equipment which made offensive action against Rommel impossible – and Nye concurred, to Churchill's chagrin, much as Stafford Cripps had done on his way out to India. Yet it was obvious to more perceptive officers on the spot that the 8th Army had, in equipment and men, more than a two to one superiority over its German

[1] Ibid.
[2] *Notes on My Life*, loc. cit.

opponents, and equality with the Italians. What it lacked was not so much equipment, but a commander.

Several times in the spring of 1942 Brooke attempted to get Auchinleck to replace Ritchie at the head of 8th Army, urging him to discard Corbett and take Ritchie as his Chief-of-Staff; but Auchinleck declined, and the stage was set for yet another rout. On 7 May came the first mention in Brooke's diary of the possible replacement of Auchinleck by Alexander (then still in Burma); but the die was cast, and on 26 May Rommel launched the offensive that would win Gazala, capture Tobruk, send the British forces in North Africa reeling back towards Cairo, cause most of the British fleet to evacuate Alexandria and the British embassy in the capital to burn its secret documents.

That Auchinleck, in his fourteen months as C-in-C Middle East, had every opportunity to fashion, equip and even personally lead (as he was urged by Churchill to do) the primary British field army ranged against Axis forces is undeniable. What is less easy to understand is why it took defeat in North Africa – and, even then, the death of the commander-designate of 8th Army – for Montgomery to be appointed to battlefield command. Yet one may search Brooke's diary between January and July 1942 in vain for the name of Montgomery. The names of Alexander, Adam, Paget and other senior generals would crop up repeatedly – as has been seen, Churchill even proposed Lord Gort and the inexperienced VCIGS Archie Nye – but never, it seems, was Montgomery's name so much as mentioned. In the light of subsequent history this was perhaps the strangest omission of the war, so that any historian must ask how it could be. Until the day it was decided to send Alexander to replace Auchinleck, there was no question even of Bernard assuming the mantle of army commander-designate for the landings in North-West Africa – a mantle hitherto accorded to Bernard's successor at 5 Corps, Lt-General Schreiber, when Alexander temporarily went out to Burma. And, even when Alexander returned, it was Schreiber who was then made commander-designate of future Allied landings in France.

Yet at the same time it was widely acknowledged that, in retraining the British army at home to repel a potential German invasion, no man had done more than Lt-General Montgomery. Montgomery's doctrines not of linear but of aggressive, tactical defence had become the accepted military philosophy throughout southern England, and his reputation in military circles was one of frightening professionalism. As Rees remembered, when appointed to South-Eastern Army in March 1942, even GHQ Home Forces was in awe of Montgomery. Rees' Intelligence brigadier at GHQ shot him 'a sympathetic look as if he were sentencing me to immediate execution'.

'You'd better be on your toes, or he'll have you back here in no time and then there'll be hell to pay. He'll be up here himself before you know.' He spoke as if this were to be avoided at all costs. I had the feeling that I had been selected, for no very good reason, for a specially dangerous mission, with the particular objective of protecting GHQ Home Forces from this unknown but mysteriously terrifying general.[1]

Gort, Gott, Nye, Cunningham, Ritchie, Alexander, Beresford-Peirse, Auchinleck himself: all were given or proposed for the role of Commander 8th Army between the summers of 1941 and 1942 – months in which Bernard Montgomery revolutionised the whole concept of command and tactical approach to battle at home in England. Yet the 'terrifying general' seems not to have entered the lists at this critical period of his country's history; moreover, the very people whose own careers were most to benefit – after the seemingly never-ending succession of military reverses – from Bernard's eventual victories in the field, namely Brooke and Churchill, seemed through the first seven months of 1942 to be oblivious to Bernard's promise as an army commander in the field of battle.

Strangely – considering his later reputation for vanity – Bernard does not appear to have pressed his own claim for command in the field, whatever his feelings about the prosecution of the war in the Far East or Middle East. As his stepson John Carver remarked, Bernard was not ambitious in the usual sense of one who pushes unremittingly for greater power. Since quite early days the compass of his military thinking and tactical philosophy – as an Instructor at the Staff College, Camberley, or when writing the Infantry Training Manual in 1929–30 – embraced the proper exercise of high command: divisional, corps, Army. Yet, successfully or unsuccessfully, he had personally always concentrated his day-to-day energies not on the ideal of advancement, but on the best possible exercise of the immediate command with which he had been entrusted. He seems therefore to have ignored the more spectacular promotion of his fellow divisional commander at Dunkirk, Alexander, and concentrated his energies on what he himself had to offer – and learn – as a Corps Commander. Whether Bernard's style of Army Command at Reigate was 'war or *opéra bouffe*', he was probably unique in modern British history in being able to simulate at home in Britain the tasks and training requirements of battlefield command. Brooke might warn Bernard to be wary of 'driving' his Canadian Corps: yet it was this very quality which, in his diary entry for 31 March 1942, Brooke complained was lacking in British higher commanders.[2]

While the 'dark days' of spring and summer 1942 added catas-

[1] Goronwy Rees, op. cit.
[2] Loc. cit.

trophe to failure and surrender to defeat, Bernard thus pursued with relentless energy his programme for eventual victory in the field – a programme which, although virtually ignored by biographers and historians alike, must surely be one of the clearest object lessons in all history of the way in which a commander can prepare himself for greatness. As Bernard himself acknowledged, 'what happened in the various commands I held in England during the years after Dunkirk was the basis of success in all that happened in the long journey from Alamein to Berlin'. The doctrine he developed in Britain between 1940 and 1942 was, he claimed, 'the same which I carried with me to Africa in 1942, to Sicily and Italy in 1943 and to Normandy in 1944'[1] – and this was no more than the truth.

By late January 1942 both 12 and Canadian Corps had held their Corps Study Weeks and, in spite of the winter weather, a period of intensive battalion, brigade, divisional and corps exercises began, in order to rehearse in the field what had been discussed on the cloth model. Step by step Bernard was determined to train an army that would not only be able to defend itself in depth, but be able to mount a successful counter-offensive reflected in 12 Corps exercises such as 'Galahad', 'Conqueror', 'Victor', 'Lancelot'. By April 1942, following divisional exercises, the Canadian Corps was also able to mount full-scale five-day corps exercises in the field: Exercise 'Beaver III' from 22 to 27 April, and 'Beaver IV' from 10 to 15 May – 'the first in which the Canadians participated on a large scale as an offensive force' as the Canadian War Historian recorded.[2] Operational staff-work, administration, movement, integration of artillery, infantry and air support, mobile operations – as each aspect was mastered, so the exercises became more demanding – and longer.

Finally on 19 May 1942 Bernard mounted what he called – in a note twenty years later penned across the file copy of his Final Conference remarks – 'the most strenuous exercise ever held in England. It is still talked about in Canada!'[3]: Exercise 'Tiger'.

[1] *Memoirs*, op. cit.
[2] C. P. Stacey, *Six Years of War*, Ottawa, 1955.
[3] Montgomery Papers.

CHAPTER FIFTEEN

Exercise 'Tiger'

Exercise 'Tiger' had nothing to do with invasion. It was 'the last exercise I directed in England before leaving to take command of the Eighth Army', as Bernard also noted,[1] and in many ways it was a dress-rehearsal for what would be called the turning-point of the Second World War – for the exercise was designed to bear out Bernard's growing belief that Allied armies, in order to seize the initiative and inflict defeat on highly professional enemies such as the Japanese or the Germans, must be trained to fight in 'a real rough-house lasting at least ten days'. There would therefore be nothing accidental about the battle of El Alamein, nor fortuitous: it would be a decisive battle executed by a commander who had decided in his own mind, earlier that year, that nothing less than a ten-day 'rough-house' could reverse the tide of Axis victories.

Exercise 'Tiger', lasting from 19 to 30 May 1942 was thus an historic performance five months before its desert counterpart, and the climax of Bernard Montgomery's training programme in England in the years that followed Dunkirk. As in his previous exercises, Bernard set one half of his forces against the other, with complete freedom of manoeuvre. 12 Corps was pitted against 1 Canadian Corps (a second Canadian Corps was in the process of being raised) with more than 100,000 troops in the field. Streams of important visitors came to view the exercise – including a senior American staff officer, sent from Washington to see why Allied preparations for a cross-Channel assault were not progressing faster: General D. D. Eisenhower. In his notes on his mission Eisenhower logged on 27 May 1942: 'Spent the day with a large field exercise in the Kent-Sussex area . . . General Montgomery is a decisive type who appears to be extremely energetic and professionally able.'[2]

One particular object of the exercise – and the reason given by the War Office to Eisenhower for its taking place – was to 'test out the new divisional organisation of the British'.[3] In fact, as we know from a later letter from Bernard to Brooke, the 'new divisional organisa-

---

[1] Ibid.
[2] *The Papers of Dwight David Eisenhower, The War Years: 1*, Baltimore 1970.
[3] Ibid.

tion' was the brainchild of the irascible Bernard Paget, C-in-C Home Forces – proposals which Bernard was to repudiate after experience in real battle. On 12 January 1943 he would write that 'the reorganisation was entirely a GHQ production in England, as far as I know, no Army Commander was consulted and I certainly was not; we were presented with a copy of the GHQ letter to the War Office. We all accepted it loyally as being the decision of the C-in-C. Personally I never liked it; but I backed it 100% and publicly, in loyalty to my C-in-C.'[1]

Paget, Eisenhower and the War Office might be interested in testing out the new 'divisional organisation', but Bernard Montgomery was concerned, in Exercise 'Tiger' with a great deal more. On 4 June 1942 Bernard held his final conference, in the Odeon Cinema, Tonbridge, at the start of which he congratulated all concerned 'on a really fine performance'.

The exercise lasted eleven days. Throughout, all troops had only the scale of rations; mobile canteens were forbidden to operate; troops were forbidden to purchase supplies of food or drink from civil stores. Administration under war conditions was thoroughly tested.

No MT was allowed to be used for the carriage of infantry or other dismounted personnel, and most infantry units marched over 150 miles during the course of the exercise. When the operations ceased many infantry soldiers had no soles on their boots. Some infantry units had marched and fought over 250 miles of country when they got back to their normal locations.

The powers of endurance of the troops were stretched to the limit, and two very tired Corps faced each other when operations ceased.

A great many lessons emerged from the exercise. These could not have been learnt unless the powers of endurance of the troops had stood up to demands made on them.

As for the new divisional organisation,

All commanders must understand clearly that the new model division, whether armoured or infantry, is an entirely different instrument to the old type. A new technique is involved and it is this we must study. The principles remain the same, but the old methods are no longer suitable with the new instrument.

Obviously, much practice will be necessary before we reach a final doctrine; and it will probably require the practical experience of battle to prove the right use of the new instrument.

But meanwhile we must have some basis on which to work, and on which to base our future training.

[1] Letter to Alan Brooke, 12.1.43, Montgomery Papers.

> I will now lay down the principles on which we will work in our
> future exploratory study of the subject,

Bernard began. For the next two hours he both adumbrated his new
Army doctrine and reminded the two thousand officers present of
the enduring rules of military command. There were intervals for
coughing; pencils scratched as the slight, sharp-nosed figure on the
rostrum systematically laid down his principles of waging modern
war and examined the course of the exercise in the light of those
principles.

The new Army Corps was to consist of a new-style armoured
division and two new infantry divisions. The new Armoured Division would consist of an armoured brigade, an infantry brigade, and
divisional troops. The new Infantry Divisions would each contain
only two infantry brigades, an Army tank brigade, and divisional
troops. The role of the Armoured Division, with its complete mobility, might be different from the infantry but, Bernard warned, it was
not an independent one. Its task was certainly to destroy enemy
armoured formations and smash through the enemy rear; but above
all it was a tactical instrument whereby the army commander could
'keep the battle fluid' and 'create favourable opportunities for the
action of infantry divisions to complete the victory.' The addition of
lorry-borne infantry gave the new armoured divisions increased
power to hold ground once taken. Meanwhile the non-motorised
infantry divisions were still the main weapon with which to 'crush
the enemy's main forces', and, acting in tandem with the armoured
divisions, were to enable the latter to drive 'either round the enemy
flank or through his front' and then capitalise on their break-
through. The inclusion now of a heavy tank brigade in each infantry
division meanwhile gave the new infantry division itself not only
greater defensive but also offensive power.

> *NOTE*
> The important point to note,

Bernard cautioned,

> is that the roles of the two types of Divisions are inter-related, and
> we shall get the best results when their action is co-ordinated.

Although a corps was now nominally to consist of two new infantry
and one new armoured division it would be a mistake, Bernard
pointed out, to think that the corps would retain this combination in
actual battle. Tactics was a competitive art and 'as the battle proceeds
an Army Commander may often re-group his divisions, forming a
Corps of two, or even three, armoured divisions for operations
further afield.'

This principle of flexibility was, to Bernard, of the most vital importance; and the ability of an Army Commander to beat an enemy as professional as the Germans would ultimately depend on the equivalent ability of his corps commanders to translate such orders into action. A modern corps commander must be able not only to handle his nominal tally of divisions, but if necessary be capable of handling 'any combination' of divisions – armoured or unarmoured.

> We do not want special Corps HQ to handle armoured divisions; any Corps HQ must be able to handle any type of division, and any combination of armoured and infantry divisions . . .
>
> Every commander has therefore got to understand fully the handling of armoured formations, and how to get the best value from the combined action of armoured and unarmoured units.

It is salutary to think that, at the moment Bernard was delivering these words, his erstwhile BGS at 2 Corps on the sands of Dunkirk, Neil Ritchie, was himself trying vainly to establish this new concept of the combination of armour and infantry – vainly because by 10 June Rommell had won the 'Battle of the Cauldron', thus initiating 'a cumulative progression of avoidable disasters' as General Sir William Jackson put it in his *Battle for North Africa 1940-3* – a progression of fiasco, and of fool's paradises in which 'the full extent of the Cauldron defeat was never really appreciated by the British higher commanders . . . because other disasters followed in bewildering succession'.

Bernard Montgomery was adamant that, whatever disasters currently befell British forces in the field, he himself would be ready for command in battle if chosen. Rarely has there been a case in British military annals of an army commander propounding, rehearsing and constantly re-examining before vast audiences of senior and junior officers the doctrines of command and tactical expertise that he would use in battle – and which would bring such a march of victories. Wavell had studied military history and had lectured sagely on the lessons of high command; even Gort, by repute, was a better lecturer on military history than was Bernard. This, however, was a very different matter. What Bernard was concerned to put over were not the abstract lessons of history, but a blueprint of command and tactics for the day: a prescription which, if followed intelligently, *guaranteed* success in modern battle. Hence the picture, in May 1942, of an Army Commander rehearsing some 100,000 troops in an eleven day 'rough-house' and subsequently declaring in a two-hour address – later circulated to all commanders in typescript – the very doctrine which, within a matter of months, would bring him victory over arguably the finest German field commander of the Second World War.

Whatever Field-Marshal Templer might later feel about the 'excruciating stage-performance' aspect of Bernard's great addresses, there is no doubt that they were electric in effect because, however 'managed', their clarity and penetration were so obviously a true reflection of the man. Cold widower though he might be, this man spoke from his military heart and withheld nothing. His address on 4 June was the culmination of two years of radical, if not revolutionary military re-education of those under his command – from the 15,000 officers and men of the 3rd Division to the 100,000 officers and men of South-Eastern Army.

Before Dunkirk Bernard had rehearsed his division in mobility and the tactical integration of infantry, artillery and engineers in defence; since Dunkirk Bernard had systematically studied the problems of offence. However dismal the story of British defeat from 1940 onwards – in Greece, Crete, North Africa and the Far East – Bernard was utterly determined that the army being raised and re-trained in England should concentrate on certain essential principles of modern war. He had been the first senior commander in Britain to develop the use of RAF support aircraft; he had followed closely and taken an intimate part in Staff College exercises and discussions on the role and use of tanks. Like Brooke, he thoroughly resisted the notion of armour being nurtured in élite cavalry formations – at least against an enemy as professional as the German army. He therefore strongly supported Brooke in ensuring that armoured divisions be composed of at least one lorry-borne infantry brigade, working in close co-operation with the armour; like Brooke – who wrote after Exercise 'Tiger' on 10 June to say he had been through 'the whole paper with the greatest interest, and am in complete agreement with the doctrines you propounded'[1] – he felt the key to success lay in the army commander's ability, however, to re-group his divisions in battle in order to apply overwhelming force at chosen points. To do this required corps commanders capable of managing both armoured and unarmoured divisions as necessary in the heat of battle; also divisional commanders capable of the same flexibility if they were to command the new model divisions with their additional Army Tank Brigades, and which also might require regrouping in battle:

A Div HQ must be able to command a number of Army Tank Brigades, or a number of infantry brigades, or any combination of the two types. And, as the battle proceeds, re-grouping within divisions may frequently be necessary, being organized by the Corps Commander to suit the changing tactical plan.

[1] Montgomery Papers.

The danger of dispersion and dissipation was not, however, forgotten, and in contrast to Auchinleck's desert policy of thinking in terms of brigades Bernard insisted that:

> Any grouping of Army Tank and/or infantry brigades that involves a break-up of the normal divisional organisation should be for a definite object and be temporary. When that object is achieved, and conditions allow, Army Tank and/or infantry brigades should rejoin their own Divisions.
>
> It will be clear, therefore, that our divisional organisation must be very flexible, so that grouping and re-grouping can be carried out entirely in accordance with the requirements of the tactical battle.

This led to the question of how, in modern warfare, ought the new British armoured divisions to fulfil their purpose.

We can now pass on to consider the general principles of the handling of the armoured division,

Bernard continued.

The importance of ground
Whatever may be the task or role of an Armoured Division, the first stage towards achieving success will nearly always be to secure ground which dominates the battle area.

The destruction of enemy armoured formations can most easily be brought about,

Bernard declared in what was to become a classic theme of his success in battle,

> by forcing him to attack our own armour on previously selected and occupied ground. To ensure he attacks, possession of the ground selected must be vital to the enemy.

Moreover, to achieve success, there must also be sufficient concentration of armour, which was not to be wasted by allotting it in 'penny packets':

> The strength of the armoured division in the attack lies in the use of this armoured brigade *concentrated*, and supported by the action of the other arms.
>
> Tanks are most effective when used in large numbers in the decisive area; failure to use tanks in sufficient mass may result in high casualties.

However, such concentration was not simply a matter of numbers: the tank regiments must not be 'caught by the enemy too dispersed. As contact becomes imminent, therefore, the tendency should be for the armoured brigade to come on to a narrower front'. An entire brigade might well have to attack 'on a front of one regiment', and it had to think in terms of a cohesive, irresistible combination of tanks, artillery, air support, and infantry:

> The Armoured Division is a relatively small formation of all arms; it is mobile, hard-hitting, and can develop great fire power.
> The successful action of the Division will depend on the intimate co-operation of all arms, and on the close co-operation of air forces.
> Tanks alone are never the answer,

Bernard warned.

> The attack of the armoured brigade must be supported by the maximum effort of all other arms; armoured OPs from the artillery must accompany the tanks so as to be able to engage by observed fire any localities holding up the attack; infantry must follow closely to take over the ground gained and to hold the battlefield.

All this, too, must be done according to a definite plan. The divisional commander must not allow his division to 'drift aimlessly into the battle, or become involved in the fight piecemeal and without a definite plan'. Armoured car regiments, with fighting infantry, were to probe in advance of the main elements so that the plan of attack followed not only the dictates of topography but the weak spots in enemy dispositions; the divisional commander's task was to react decisively on the information given by his forward bodies.

By co-operating closely with the infantry, and if necessary attaching an infantry battalion to the leading armoured brigade, the 'ragged ends' of a gap created in the enemy front could be cleared up so that the armour might pass through cleanly. By bringing up infantry brigades behind the armour, complete with anti-tank guns, the armour would then be well-placed 'with a view to drawing the enemy armoured units on to the infantry anti-tank defence' – the central theme that would inform the battle of Alamein four months later.

Exercise 'Tiger' had shown up the tendency for the 12 Corps Commander to rob the Armoured Division either of armour or motorised infantry 'for specific tasks'. In one case this had produced an admirable feint; but it was important, Bernard reminded his audience, to preserve as much as possible the 'integrity' of the new formations, to remember that their strength lay in trained co-operation of arms, and therefore to ensure that they quickly re-grouped. He summarised:

It will be seen that the whole conception of the offensive employment of an armoured division is based on:

a) keeping it intact, and ready to operate as a complete division . . .
b) using the armoured brigade concentrated
c) not allowing the division to drift with the battle piece-meal, but ensuring that it is committed to the co-ordinated plan of the divisional commander
d) mounting a co-ordinated attack on a comparatively narrow front, using all the resources of the division
e) holding the objective, or battlefield, with infantry and anti-tank guns and freeing the armoured brigade for a further mobile role.

As regards defensive operations, Bernard insisted that the armoured division must not be wasted by making it a part of the defensive layout. Instead it should be held by the corps commander ready for counter-attack as a complete division, acting always offensively. If it was necessary to withdraw, then the armoured division provided a useful weapon with which to savage the enemy if he strove to attain vital ground. Once again, however, it was not to be squandered in infantry-style defence. Within the armoured division the armoured brigade could be used to extricate the infantry brigade; it would then be able, by means of its mobility and fire-power, to break off the engagement unassisted.

Finally there was the matter of surprise:

The division must be expert at concealing itself from air observation so that its blow, when delivered, will come as a complete surprise.

If there is any reason to believe that the division has been observed from the air, it should be capable of moving after dark to a new area and being completely concealed by dawn.

So much for the Armoured Division. The new Infantry Division also required tactical re-thinking.

The new model infantry division is a very different instrument to the old type. The inclusion of an Army Tank Brigade has definitely added hitting power and 'punch' to the Division,

Bernard began.

But the Division now requires to be handled in a different way; all commanders must realise this and must study the new methods

506

– methods which were much more demanding than they appeared. Because the heavy tanks were slow, they would hamper an advance if put out in front; however, where strong resistance was met, their 'punch' would be required to 'maintain the momentum of an advance'.

> There will generally *not be time to re-group* between these two phases; to do so would involve halting and this might well lead to a loss of tactical advantage and of the initiative.
> The main problem confronting the Div Commander in the early phases will therefore be whether:
> i) he should advance strong in front, with his reconnaissance regiment stiffened up with other arms and possibly with tanks, or
> ii) he should advance weak in front, only the reconnaissance regiment being in front and unsupported by other arms.

Each case had to be considered on its merits:

> There are many disadvantages in advancing strong in front; it drives in the enemy reconnaissance troops, and throws him on the defensive as a result of the initial clash.
> But commanders must bear in mind that the capacity of a regimental HQ to command a mixed force of all arms is limited; it is definitely unsound to place a number of units under command of a reconnaissance regiment; this unit operates normally on a wide front, and it cannot at the same time take command of a number of other units.
> Therefore, in cases where it is decided to advance strong in front there must be a proper organisation for command in the forward area.

Bernard gave several possibilities as to the grouping of forward units in the advance of a new infantry division, encouraging commanders to think out for themselves not only the requirements of a vanguard – in artillery, engineers, etc. – but the question of the best positioning of HQs, and the inherent limits to that which could be asked, for instance, of the commander of a reconnaissance regiment who, in light mobile operations, would be 'fully occupied in commanding his own unit, and is usually unable properly to control other arms under his command'.
All this led back inexorably to the role and tasks of the divisional commander himself:

> The main preoccupation of the divisional commander will be to ensure that his division does not drift aimlessly into the battle, but is put into the fight on a co-ordinated plan of his own making.

Therefore, although possibly not in contact with the enemy, he must have a definite plan.

Initially this will be one of ground. His aim will be to secure that ground which will assist the development and conduct of his further operations, which may be offensive or defensive. Such ground may include dominating high ground, centres of road communication, close country to assist concealment, obstacle lines, etc.

In his advance to secure this ground he may be moving on a broad front. His aim will be to drive in the enemy covering troops and to gain contact with his main position.

Subsequently, if his role involves offensive action, his aim will be to stage an attack in force against that portion of the front which has been found will produce the most promising results. The full 'punch' of the Division can be developed only by moving the tank brigade in close co-operation with one of the infantry brigades.

Step-by step Bernard took his assembled officers through the principles of offensive organisation and command. The divisional commander must regroup, must concentrate his attack, and be 'supported by the full weight of divisional artillery'; moreover, once penetration has been achieved, the commander must guard against counter-attack. He must therefore again regroup, to ensure that there was at least 'some infantry, anti-tank guns, and artillery' well forward 'to break up and disorganise any enemy counter-attack while the tanks are held in readiness to counter an enemy move'.

Above all, the commander must study the topography of his battlefield:

It must always be remembered that suitable ground is necessary for the tank brigade to develop its full power. The choice of ground from this point of view must play a large part in the planning of an operation.

A hard blow by a mass of tanks, supported by infantry and artillery, may alter the whole run of the battle.

The aim must always be to use the tanks in large numbers; the tendency to employ tanks in small packets as adjuncts to small-scale infantry attacks must be resisted to the utmost.

Those historians who later criticised Montgomery for his excessive caution, and who saw in him an unimaginative proponent of superiority of *matériel* were all too often guilty of confusing ends with means. Mastery of the battlefield, Bernard maintained, would not be gained by the largest army or the best equipment: it would go to that army which was most supple, an army in which there was clarity of purpose, flexibility in re-grouping, and a firm belief in the concentration of overwhelming force at certain points. This was the very opposite of First World War tactics – and, as will be seen, the opposite of most American and Russian army tactics in the Second World War. Because Bernard's approach was to lead to such crushing victories in the field, there was a tendency among soured contemporaries and jealous historians to attribute success to numbers. However no one, examining the record of Bernard Montgomery's self-preparation in the years after Dunkirk, can fail to be impressed by the range and tactical imagination shown in his great addresses. As in 1924, he believed initially in training to a basic, easily understandable doctrine, or 'normal'; having reached that he gradually encouraged his officers to recognise the challenges involved in modern war – challenges which could only be met, when fighting a good enemy, by the study and practice of tactical flexibility:

Flexibility

It will thus be clear that in handling the new model infantry divisions, stereotyped methods, and methods which ignore the use of ground, will be quite useless.

The divisional commander must be prepared to re-group his division as is dictated by the changing tactical plan.

Necessarily this re-grouping should permit the commander to attack in strength – or defend in depth – by narrowing his front:

Whether in attack or in defence the division cannot operate on a wide front.

The whole essence of modern tactical methods is:

Concentration

Control

Simplicity

Commanders must be trained to stage a number of strong attacks on relatively narrow fronts; this is the 'Schwerpunkt.'

From the penetrations thus made, troops must work outwards and attack the intervening enemy positions from the flanks and rear; this is the 'aufrollen'.

It is by these tactics that we shall achieve success with the new model divisions, and they must be closely studied.

This was all very well in theory; but the extra 'punch' of the new tank brigades would not be achieved unless such tank brigades were absorbed as integral parts of the new infantry divisions rather than being viewed as strangers.

There is no doubt that the infantry have got a tremendous 'kick' out of at last having their own tanks in the Division, and being able to work in close co-operation with them.

This must be exploited and followed up. The Army Tank Brigades must be taken into the Divisional 'fold' completely, and a system worked out which will produce the closest co-operation between the tanks and the infantry, artillery, and other arms.

Great use was made in this exercise of infantry being carried up to the battle riding on tanks. This subject must be further studied and practised; it is very suitable in the earlier phases of the contact battle, or in the pursuit battle.

Commanders were exhorted to determine who would command where tanks were operating – ideally both infantry and tank battalion commanders working from the same tank when fighting together. Moreover, as the tanks gave extra 'punch' to the infantry in attack, so the infantry must work for the tank units by providing close reconnaissance and Intelligence.

Conversely, the tactical concept of defence would have to undergo a radical change under the new divisional format. The linear principle was now dead: 'Static defence must now disappear. The main function of the defence will be *counter-attack* and everything will be designed to this end. *The object of the defence will be to destroy the enemy and not merely to stop him.*'

From the corps commander's point of view this would necessitate the choosing of smaller fronts to hold, and the holding of these 'in great depth, with strong battalion localities on a "staggered" layout'.

If the enemy penetrates between battalion localities, he will be disorganized and shot up by the infantry and anti-tank guns holding the localities. He will then be attacked and destroyed by tanks under conditions favourable to the defenders and on ground of their own choosing.

Localities will be designed not only to produce fire to break up the enemy attack and to separate his armour from the supporting infantry, but also to support the counter-attack.

Ingenuity was necessary, too: for the idea was no longer 'to keep the enemy out', but, by careful choice of obstacles and the siting of minefields, to shepherd the enemy 'into the areas where he is wanted', and where he could be 'shot up' and counter-attacked.

Paradoxically, the new mobility of battle, and the reduction of infantry brigades in the division to make way for tank brigades, meant that the infantry soldier would be required to footslog more, further, and harder than ever before. A modern commander therefore not only had to work out new techniques of co-operation with tanks, with attendant tactical developments: he must also be concerned with 'man management', as Bernard called it. There was, for instance, the basic but vital question: how much weight could a modern infantry soldier carry in battle and 'yet develop his full fighting form' – and on the answer to this would hinge further questions of what arms could be left to be brought up by battalion transport, or carriers. Once again a new technique was required that would allow for the evolving format of the new Infantry Division: a technique which would give the infantry soldier greater mobility by lightening his load and making up his fire power by the intelligent use of carrier-borne mortars and guns.

Such, then, was Bernard's blueprint for the new model divisions in the British army. He then passed to the major lessons learned from the eleven-day exercise in which 12 Corps had operated in the new divisional format, the Canadian Corps in the old. Undoubtedly the outstanding lesson was the need for better integration of Army and Air Force staffs. The air operations of the Canadians, and to some extent of 12 Corps, 'often appeared "scrappy" and hastily improvised,' Bernard remarked. Yet

> without the closest touch between Army and RAF Staffs the co-ordination of the Air Plan with that of the Army cannot be as effective as it should be, and in emergency may well fail. It involves the whole of the Air action – the employment of the fighter force for air superiority and protection at the right time and place; the employment of the heavy bomber force and careful selection of bombing objectives best calculated to assist the military aim; and not least the careful planning of air reconnaissance without which the close support squadrons for the attack of ground targets cannot operate with maximum efficiency.

The Air Force must therefore be involved not just in response to army requests for support, but at the highest staff levels from the very beginning, when the army plans were actually formulated. The Air Staff at headquarters of Army formations 'should be regarded as part of the General Staff and not as something separate dealing in black magic'.

The Canadian Corps had been given a 'strong' air force – seven fighter and two bomber squadrons. 'Yet never at any time were their demands for close support sufficient to employ fully four fighter squadrons, and the bomber squadrons were less than half fully employed' – a recipe for doom against a good enemy. New techniques must be evolved in order that the new 'mission' fighters giving ground support remained in touch both with ground observation tenders and with their originating aerodrome, while this aerodrome in turn kept in contact with the commanding RAF officer who must be alongside his army counterpart at a combined HQ.

Similarly the use of artillery in the exercise had again shown up the current inflexibility of command. The challenge was to evolve a battlefield technique permitting local command of artillery support in 'fluid' operations, but centralised control by the CRA at divisional headquarters whenever a selected front of attack was in need of

511

maximum artillery support. In Exercise 'Tiger' one 'attack' had actually failed because of the absence of such centralisation of artillery command, and other attacks had faltered. Conversely 'several attacks, including two divisional attacks, were planned during the exercise in which fire plans by concentration were made entirely from a 1" map. Little if any detailed information of enemy dispositions was available, or sought for, and any reconnaissance made was of a casual nature. Certainly in one case no reconnaissance was made at all. In many cases the areas were not occupied by the enemy'. In other words, centralisation of divisional firepower was a weapon of tremendous importance in mounting an attack, or meeting an enemy offensive: but such centralisation would only be effective if the CRA was in intimate touch with the realities of the battlefield, by air and ground observation, signals, Intelligence, and so on – 'Casual methods can only lead to one result,' Bernard summarised, 'a costly failure.'

Signals technique, administration and movement control were also criticised by the Army Commander, as well as certain words which were henceforth to be banned in South-Eastern Army. 'Consolidate' was one, which 'often produces inaction, and even a defensive mentality'; a 'Force' or special body of troops was another – and one which 'merely makes everything more complicated'.

By and large Bernard had been satisfied, however, that the 'soldiery' would rise to the challenge of modern battle, involving prolonged fighting and many hundreds of miles of marching. The question was: could the commanding officers 'put them into battle properly and with a good chance of success? Every officer should search his own conscience and answer that question himself,' Bernard exhorted. For good or ill, the new organisation of armoured and infantry divisions had been decided, 'and it has come to stay. It is quite useless for commanders to say they want more infantry, or more something else. Such statements really mean that the commander does not know how to make the best use of what he has got'.

He will get no more infantry and it is no use asking.
He must train the infantry he *has* got to:
> live hard,
> move light,
> fight simply,
and to have very great powers of endurance.
The new model organization will be accepted with enthusiasm, and all commanders will learn how to make the best use of it.

There would be cloth-model discussions and signal exercises henceforth 'in order to work out the stage-management of the battle, and the technique and procedure involved', and July, August and

September 1942 would be devoted to training, using live ammunition and the rehearsal of 'co-operation of all arms in battle together with the co-operation of air forces'.[1]

The two thousand or so Army, Corps, Divisional and Battalion officers of South-Eastern Army rose as the Army Commander replaced his notes in his wallet and left the stage. Those who had expected greater congratulation on their eleven-day 'Tiger' endeavours were muted by the realisation that, in the art of war, time never stood still and every improvement in training and efficiency revealed further challenges.

If there were those who, over-confident or indolent, doubted the need for such large-scale exercises, and the constant re-examination of battlefield techniques, the next few days were to prove Bernard's point that to 'adopt a complacent attitude' would be 'fatal', and that there was 'much to be done in order to fit ourselves for the hard fighting that lies in front of us'. For by 12 June the Battle of the Cauldron was over – a British military disaster which opened the way for Rommel to seize Tobruk. The British had no master plan and, without one, large armies of the size operating in the desert in 1942 could not be controlled. As General Jackson summarised: 'There has to be a unifying force to steer all the many strong-willed men in an agreed direction. That force is the commander's will, but it cannot make any impact without a policy and plan which all can understand.'[2]

At dawn on 21 June, Tobruk was surrendered, with more than 32,000 troops. Churchill, in Washington, was told by Roosevelt. Churchill winced; 'Defeat is one thing,' he would write, 'disgrace is another'. Within a fortnight, back in England, Churchill was facing his first formal vote of No Confidence in the House of Commons, and considering the evacuation of Egypt in the Chiefs-of-Staff Committee.

The situation in Cyrenaica and Egypt was now critical. On 25 June, after a long tête-à-tête with Air-Marshal Tedder, the RAF C-in-C, Auchinleck finally sacked Ritchie. In Ritchie's place Auchinleck wished to put Corbett, his loyal but incompetent Chief Staff Officer, as 8th Army Commander – a folly as incredible as Churchill's momentary espousal of Lord Gort. Fortunately, however, Auchinleck was dissuaded, and that evening he took command of the 8th Army himself.

To his credit Auchinleck, having reluctantly assumed the mantle of 8th Army Commander himself, now made a last-ditch attempt to restore morale as his forces fell back in disorder and sometimes panic to the last defensive positions before Cairo: El Alamein. Moving into a desert caravan, sleeping in the open, eating under cage netting

[1] Remarks of Army Commander, SE Army: Exercise 'Tiger', Montgomery Papers.
[2] General Sir William Jackson, op. cit.

which only bottled in the flies of Egypt, Auchinleck strove belatedly to set a personal example of steadfast, ascetic courage. Edicts and orders flowed from his pen, prompted and supported by the ubiquitous Dorman-Smith, now acting as his Chief-of-Staff in the field. Luck favours the brave: and although even Auchinleck later acknowledged that he had no confidence, in the last days of June, that Rommel could in fact be held, a series of German miscalculations – based on mistaken reconnaissance and intelligence reports – wrested the prize of Cairo from their hands in the moment of victory. Although Auchinleck issued no 'Backs to the Wall' message to the troops, and although Lt-General Gott was apparently quite defeatist at this point, the RAF managed to delay the approaching German columns, and the effects of good artillery fire from the South African, New Zealand and 1st Armoured Divisions compounded the Germans' mistake. Recognising – particularly from 'Ultra' sources – how tenuous was Rommel's long line of communication, Auchinleck now attempted a counter-offensive.

Though Bernard would never – or only very grudgingly after protests over his *Memoirs* – give Auchinleck any credit for what he achieved in July 1942, there can be no doubt that Auchinleck's heart was in the right place and that, by his very insistence on counterattack, he temporarily wrested the initiative from Rommel, forcing him to halt and bring up further supplies, equipment and men for a final assault on Cairo and Alexandria. None of Montgomery's subordinates who had served under 'the Auk' were later prepared to disparage Auchinleck as Bernard did: all were embarrassed by Bernard's absence of magnanimity, and some – like General de Guingand and Brigadier Williams – sought vainly to get Bernard to relent, as will be seen. Nevertheless, though Auchinleck's five piecemeal counter-attacks stalled Rommel in his original intention to press on and take Cairo, there could be no pretending that they were victories in any real sense of the word. All five 'heaves' failed, and the British Government had to face up to the fact that, by the summer of 1942, the British Army had failed to win a single battle against either the German or Japanese armies in the field since the beginning of the war. It was indeed, as Churchill put it, a national 'disgrace'; and the failure of Auchinleck's five 'heaves' proffered no hope that, if Auchinleck were left in command, the future would be any different.

What Bernard Montgomery made of events in the Middle and Far East we unfortunately do not know. It was now fully two years since he had seen a shot fired in battle against the Germans, and reports emanating both from Burma and North Africa made painful reading. Worse still, there was the same tendency – as after Dunkirk – to blame inferior equipment, armour, numbers, anything but the true reasons for British failure: namely the inability to provide first-rate generalship.

At South-Eastern Army Bernard had at least gone all out to show the sort of generalship the Allied armies required. He had impressed Eisenhower, as he had once impressed Churchill at Brighton in 1940, but he had not aroused their faith in him as, say, the debonair, brave but inexperienced Mountbatten had done. Churchill had promoted Mountbatten to the Chiefs-of-Staff Committee; Eisenhower progressed to be made commander of the cross-Channel invasion that year or the next. Once again, Bernard's name never even entered the list of 'possibles' for field command at the time.

Unabashed, Bernard continued, in July 1942, his seemingly endless programme of visits to units, the pioneering of an RAF army-support course at Old Sarum, further lectures to the Staff College and Senior Officers' School and the overseeing of formation exercises.

The need for secrecy meant that there was no reference in the various HQ or unit War Diaries to the great raid that was planned that month across the Channel, as Bernard waited for the call that never came. On 7 July, however, the assault on Dieppe was cancelled and Bernard burned all documents relating to it; yet its tragic resurrection in August 1942, after Bernard had finally been sent out to 8th Army in the North African desert, bears too many of the critical fingerprints of the Commander South-Eastern Army for Bernard Montgomery to be completely exonerated.

CHAPTER SIXTEEN

Dieppe

The story of the Dieppe raid of 1942 is still surrounded by prejudice, myth and inadequate documentation. Whether for reasons of secrecy or the chaotic mismanagement for which it was renowned, Combined Operations Headquarters maintained little in the way of War Diaries, which were in any case largely put together retrospectively.

Like Arnhem, the Dieppe operation bears traces of hasty planning, of obtuse enthusiasm on the part of those units desperate to see 'action', and of amateur, even tragic, over-ambitiousness. And at the centre of the fiasco was a young acting Commodore – soon to be promoted Vice-Admiral – whose only experience of shore operations was shelling Cherbourg, harrying Rommel's lines of communication and supporting the New Zealand division in its doomed attempt to save Crete. As Bernard Montgomery remarked of Mountbatten: 'A very gallant sailor. Had three ships sunk under him. *Three* ships sunk under him. [Pause] Doesn't know how to fight a battle.'

Once again, as with Alexander, it was Mountbatten's personification of the young medieval and courageous knight[1] that nevertheless charmed Churchill, rather than any genuine qualifications for the post of Chief of Combined Operations. Thus on 27 October 1941 Admiral Roger Keyes was dismissed by Churchill from the post, and acting Commodore Mountbatten made Adviser to the Chiefs-of-Staff on the subject of Combined Operations – a title which was soon raised to Chief of Combined Operations, accompanied by a Vice-Admiralcy, and even accorded a seat on the Chiefs-of-Staff Committee, the veritable War Executive Cabinet of the armed forces, by 5 March 1942.

Such miraculous elevation was, however, to prove fatal in the most literal sense of the word – at least to the thousand Allied soldiers and sailors who lost their lives in nine hours on a single day in August 1942, having done nothing more than knock out a single enemy coastal battery and alerted the Germans to Allied intentions. The prize at Arnhem was at least the cutting off of Holland with its V-bomb sites and a 'bouncing' of the Rhine; but the raid on Dieppe

---

[1] Mountbatten was the son of a Prince; Alexander the son of an Earl.

never promised anything more than a graphic illustration to the Germans of the current state of Allied amphibious operations. Instead of frightening Hitler into drawing reserves from the East or Middle East, it simply served to make the British doubly unwilling to undertake a cross-Channel Second Front at all – thus introducing far greater strains in the Anglo-American alliance than those it was apparently intended to dispel.

Dieppe was to be Mountbatten's greatest defeat; later on, when elevated yet higher to the post of Supreme Allied Commander with – like Alexander – a fundamentally diplomatic role to play, he would shine; but as Chief of Combined Operations he was a master of intrigue, jealousy, and ineptitude. Like a spoilt child he toyed with men's lives with an indifference to casualties that can only be explained by his insatiable, even psychopathic ambition. Where Bernard Montgomery evolved a doctrine of professional organisation and warfare which could only finally be tested and proved by high command, Louis Mountbatten's vanity stemmed directly from his character – a man whose mind was an abundance of brilliant and insane ideas often without coherence or consistent 'doctrine'. Allied to the equally undisciplined, wildly imaginative Churchill – with whom Mountbatten would often stay for weekends -- the two made a formidable and dangerous pair. Indeed the historian may well wonder that so few of their dramatic concoctions ever saw action. For this it is Alan Brooke who must surely be commended – the only Chief-of-Staff with the courage, integrity, and unimpeachable authority to curb Churchill in his wildest excesses. By dint of hard, relentless military logic Brooke forced Churchill, Roosevelt and Marshall to abandon all ideas of a 'lodgement' bridgehead in France in 1942, let alone a full-scale invasion: but, before the insidious appeals of the brave young Chief of Combined Operations, Brooke was finally persuaded to agree to a limited cross-Channel raid that would give heart to the sorely-tried Russians, and provide invaluable experience for the mounting of Allied amphibious assaults later in the war. With Brooke's agreement, therefore, Mountbatten was permitted to draw up plans in the spring of 1942 for a Combined Operations raid in which tragically little combined. As Brooke noted later, Mountbatten's job was 'to evolve the technique, policy and equipment for the employment of the three services in combined operations to effect a landing against opposition'. Instead of this, by virtue of his seat on the COS Committee, Mountbatten was accorded an official place in the formulation of war strategy. Tersely, Brooke remarked of the period at the beginning of March 1942, when Mountbatten's appointment to the Committee was made: 'There was no reason for his inclusion in the COS Committee where he frequently wasted his own time and ours.'[1]

[1] *Notes on My Life*, loc. cit.

The insight into higher strategy may well have been valuable experience for Mountbatten in his future posts; but undoubtedly it caused him to lose sight of his real job at this time. Not only was his headquarters – as many, including Goronwy Rees, have testified – often chaotically ill-ordered, but there was little or no real attempt to develop the very doctrine for which Mountbatten had been appointed. Instead there was a mad hunt for suitable targets for 'hit and run' raids, an endless dispersion of brains and intelligence, and a total sense of unreality. At times it seemed as if Combined Operations Headquarters was more concerned with dreaming up exploits to win medals (which, Mountbatten urged, were to be given within days of a raid and with maximum publicity, according to the Combined Operations War Diary) than developing the technique of landing whole armies on hostile shores.

The entire philosophy of Combined Operations Headquarters was diametrically opposed to Bernard's policy in South-Eastern Army. For two years Bernard had attempted to put over a doctrine of command based on first-class staffwork; the tactical education of every officer in the division, corps or army; the increasing integration of infantry, artillery, sappers, tanks and support aircraft; and finally a revival of professional morale through systematic study, cloth-model discussion, and rehearsal in the field at every echelon from platoon to a complete army. One can imagine that when, on a certain day late in April 1942, Bernard was informed of Mountbatten's latest brainchild, he was far from pleased. The recent Combined Operations raid on St Nazaire on 28 March had been a model of heroism; but its toll in casualties was frightening: almost a quarter of the hand-picked force were killed, and more than half the remainder captured.

The Dieppe raid is commonly supposed to have been conceived thereafter, in early April. However, evidence in contemporary War Diaries suggests that Dieppe was selected as a possible target by Mountbatten already in February 1942. By 3 March intelligence about enemy batteries in the Dieppe area had been requested and received from Paget's HQ Home Forces, and by 18 March Naval Intelligence had reported on the feasibility of blocking Dieppe harbour. On 21 March Mountbatten – no doubt eager for aggrandisement – agreed a *quid pro quo* with Paget whereby, in return for taking charge of all raids on the enemy, Combined Operations Headquarters would 'include a fair proportion of Home Force in raids', and would receive representations from Paget's HQ about possible targets.

It was in this perhaps nefarious way that the Dieppe raid was born – the most tragic and, in ratio to participating forces, the most costly Allied offensive assault of the war. Paget seems to have been keen. He had inherited from Sir Alan Brooke, his predecessor at GHQ Home Forces, a directive or authorisation concerning raids which, though it commenced with minor projects, envisaged operations of a far greater magnitude in the future. As the GHQ War Diary for 18 October 1941 recorded:

C-in-C Home Forces has been authorised to carry out raids on the French, Belgian and Dutch coasts
a) Small informative raids
b) Large informative and destructive raids, up to 2 nights and a day
c) Establishing a limited bridgehead
d) Major operations on the continent.

Why then did General Paget surrender this authorisation to Mountbatten – a substantive Captain at the time, acting Commodore? Perhaps the only explanation can be found in Mountbatten's personality and his high connections, both with the Royal Family and with Churchill. Certainly Admiral Keyes was astonished at the powers granted to his successor. No doubt Mountbatten argued forcibly for an intelligent, modern combined approach to amphibious assault landings; but his own seat on the Chiefs-of-Staff Committee, as we have seen, encouraged delusions of grandeur as a strategist that made it impossible for him to carry out his real task. Operations 'Rutter', 'Sledgehammer', 'Clawhammer' and a dozen other projects vied for Chiefs-of-Staff approval while the true challenge of developing modern combined operations was accorded second place.

One by one the alternative propositions put up by Combined Operations Headquarters were shot down, until only 'Rutter' – a 'butcher and run' raid on Dieppe as Churchill called it – remained. Every military consideration argued against this expensive form of exercise, and it is noticeable that the Germans declined utterly to indulge in such operations on the British coast. Even Mountbatten later claimed to have disliked the idea of a frontal assault on Dieppe, preferring the idea of a pincered flank assault. By then, however, the die was cast and tactical subtlety of no value. The Americans were arguing for a Second Front, and the hard-pressed Russians demanding one. Logistically such a front was impossible either to mount or to maintain in 1942, and perhaps not even in 1943: but it was felt that a hard, punishing blow might be delivered with full army and air support which would force the Germans to take a Second Front seriously, and thus possibly divert material and manpower from the Russian front. Mountbatten's original Commando-style raid he now sold to Churchill and the Chiefs-of-Staff as major demonstration of British cross-Channel intent.

Having, by virtue of his seat on the COS Committee, insidiously 'sold' his plan for a major raid on Dieppe, Mountbatten lost no time, and planning thereafter moved in leaps and bounds. The first official Combined Operations meeting to discuss it took place on 3 April 1942. By the 25th an Outline Plan had been agreed to the satisfaction both of Combined Operations Staff and Paget's representative, involving a frontal assault at Dieppe, the use of tanks, and a heavy preliminary aerial bombardment. On 13 May Mountbatten formally submitted the plan to the Chiefs-of-Staff Committee; and it was accepted.

Diplomatically Mountbatten had done wonders. The RAF were anxious to lure the Luftwaffe into an inescapable air battle on favourable terms; the Navy and Army administration services were anxious to explore the whole problem of capturing a Channel port in the event of a full-scale Allied invasion. The use of tanks gave the operation an aura of savage modernity – the reverse side of the Dunkirk coin.

Yet who on the military side would carry out this ambitious programme? Paget's 'pact' with Mountbatten envisaged Home Forces troops rather than commandos or marines; and, since the port selected was directly opposite South-Eastern Army, Paget had the choice either of detailing troops from his GHQ Reserve or South-Eastern Army. He chose the latter.

Quite when Bernard Montgomery became informed is difficult to know, owing to the secrecy of the operation. According to the South-Eastern Army War Diary Bernard visited GHQ on 20 April and was possibly told then; certainly no one has ever claimed that he played any part in the original selection or planning of the operation, which 'would be carried out by Combined Operations Headquarters,' as he told Major Goronwy Rees, the Intelligence officer he selected to be his representative, and who attended the first official meeting of the Planning Committee for the raid on 25 April.

Several historians have later asked why Montgomery chose a Canadian division, without battle experience, for such an ambitious frontal-assault role – particularly when it is known that he was not yet satisfied with the standard of Canadian training in South-Eastern Army. That the decision was very much Montgomery's own is reflected in the 1951 interim official account, published pending a British Official History which never came. Written by Christopher Buckley, this version[1] recorded:

> Lieut-General B. L. Montgomery, GOC-in-C South-Eastern Command, had acted as chief representative of the Army at some of the preliminary discussions. It was his influence which made the raid on Dieppe so largely a Canadian affair. At the end of April he confided the outline of the plan to Lieut-General A. G. L. McNaughton, commanding the Canadian Army in England. The 1st Canadian Corps was in the South-Eastern Command and its commander, Lieut-General H. D. G. Crerar, selected the 2nd Canadian Division to provide the troops. The points of attack –

[1] C. Buckley, *Norway – The Commandos – Dieppe*, London 1951.

the four flank landings and the frontal assault by tanks and infantry upon Dieppe – were already settled: henceforward Canadian commanders and staffs bore their full share in hammering out the details of the plan.

This version was in several respects inaccurate. The only Combined Operations meeting which Bernard formally attended was on 5 June 1942, almost three months after the operation was first conceived. Moreover he did not go first to Lt-General McNaughton, Commander of the newly established but skeletal Canadian Army Headquarters, but made arrangements first with his own subordinate Corps Commander Crerar – even selecting which division would participate – and only then went to McNaughton, on 30 April. According to Canadian sources, Bernard claimed he had been 'pressed to agree' to a composite Anglo-Canadian force, but had himself insisted upon a homogeneous entity, stating that in his opinion the Canadians were the 'best suited' to the task. McNaughton gave his grudging *post factum* consent – but asked Paget in future to inform him *before* any outline scheme involving Canadian forces was mooted.

Here indeed was the nub of the affair. A Canadian division had been selected as the major participating force in the first large-scale demonstration landing on the Continent since the débâcle of June 1940. It was indeed an honour, and there is little doubt that Bernard intended it to appear as such – a gesture of appeasement to the over-sensitive charges who seemed to find his 'driving' too fierce and his criticism of Canadian commanders after exercises too humiliating. Neither Crerar nor McNaughton could decline – and yet they were being asked to undertake a mission about which even Montgomery (as he confessed to Goronwy Rees at the time[1]) had only the sketchiest notion.

If Bernard's decision to use Canadian troops is understandable, his approval of the outline plan is less so. Bernard was, after all, a veteran of Dunkirk – a port which had resisted the combined assaults of two German army groups and permitted an entire Allied army to embark before surrendering. Did Bernard seriously believe a Combined Operation, using untried soldiers, could successfully smash its way into the heart of Dieppe and beyond – to the airfield of Arques – in a matter of hours, and then be successfully re-embarked on the following tide? Furthermore, Bernard's own instructions relating to the defence of South-East Army's coastline, with clear-cut orders on states of readiness of coastal batteries, the manning of radiolocation units, all-round wiring-in of strong points, and constant rehearsal of counter-attack operations, could hardly have left him in any doubt that his equally professional counterparts across

[1] Goronwy Rees, op. cit.

the Channel would be similarly trained to repulse enemy raids.

Bernard certainly never offered any genuine clues as to how he came to approve such a suicidal plan – in fact the two causes of misfortune he gave in his *Memoirs* (the replacement of parachutists by commandos on the flanks, and the cancellation of heavy initial aerial bombardment) were either irrelevant or, in the case of the latter, the result of the very meeting of 5 June at which he himself presided as Chairman.

Any answer must therefore be speculative. If it intrigues us, however, it is not from morbid desire to apportion blame for the death, injury and years of captivity of so many brave Canadians, but simply because an analysis of Bernard's involvement in the Dieppe episode may provide another of the unwritten keys to his character and his particular brand of generalship. Moreover, the parallel with Arnhem is too acute to be overlooked: for in both cases a man who would become renowned as one of the most thorough and professional military commanders of the century allowed himself, willingly, to be sold a plan which was both beyond the abilities of his limited forces to fulfil, and which grievously underrated enemy resistance.

Some months before he died, Bernard's Chief-of-Staff Sir Francis de Guingand discussed this aspect of his Commander's character. Montgomery was, de Guingand felt, a far more impetuous personality at heart than was commonly supposed. Since childhood his character had been marked by boldness, rashness, and athleticism. What had distinguished Bernard as an army officer were, however, the self-imposed qualities of total professional discipline and the will to master all aspects of his profession. Thus, when innate character acted in conjunction with self-conscious vocation, there arose a combination that would not only take him to the 'top of his profession' but bring him world-wide acclaim; but when such a conjunction did not occur – when rashness overtook studious mastery of tactical possibilities and impossibilities, or when iron discipline caused him insufficiently to value boldness and risk – then the result was often failure or mediocrity.[1] It was for this reason that a first-class chief-of-staff was so essential to Montgomery: a subordinate who could not only carry out the detailed staffwork involved in his commander's plans, nor simply give decisions in the absence of the commander, but a man who had the constructive ability to help keep Bernard's two great virtues in tandem.

It was unfortunate, in this respect, that the vital decisions over the Dieppe raid were made at a time of flux in the staff at Headquarters, South-Eastern Army. Bernard's preferred Chief-of-Staff, 'Simbo' Simpson, had remained as BGS 12 Corps when Bernard assumed Army Command; in April 1942 Simpson was brought into the higher directorate of the War Office as Deputy Director of Military Opera-

[1] Interview with Sir Francis de Guingand, May 1978.

522

tions and, as will be seen, was so highly valued there by Sir Alan Brooke that he was not permitted to go out to the Middle East when requested in August.

Bernard's Chief of the General Staff at South-Eastern Command, Brigadier John Sinclair, was also moved, on 7 March 1942, to become CRA, being superseded by Brigadier Chilton, who was new to Bernard's command. The War Office had turned down Bernard's request that 'Kit' Dawnay come as G1 (Intelligence), and even the G2 (Intelligence) – Major Rees – only arrived on March 3, as has been seen. There was, therefore, a fatal vacuum at this critical moment: and Bernard, as the one soldier – apart from Brooke – who possessed the undisputed prestige and authority to scrap the project, tragically agreed to undertake the raid.

Although the actual raid on Dieppe was to take place after Bernard Montgomery left England to take command of 8th Army, it was in most essentials the same operation conceived and planned in March and April 1942, and approved by Montgomery. What then was the real flaw in the Dieppe plan which allowed generals as senior as Brooke, Paget, Montgomery, McNaughton, and Crerar to give it their blessing while – in retrospect – making it so suicidal? This cannot have been the preliminary air bombardment, which was cancelled for the quite logical reasons that it would destroy surprise and make speedy movement of the tanks in Dieppe town difficult, quite apart from political repercussions. Nor was it the replacement of parachutists by commandos in the landings on the flank beaches and cliffs. It was the most basic flaw of all, obvious to the Canadians cut down in their thousands on Dieppe beach as to the historian who cares to examine the Combined Operations plan for the raid: namely Mountbatten's promise of naval support artillery that never came. Mountbatten's first operational plans envisaged the use of old battleships as floating artillery, but Churchill and the senior naval staff rejected the proposal. Thereafter Mountbatten stressed again and again that it was the primary duty of the naval destroyers to provide amphibious artillery support for the troops and tanks as they landed – an emphasis which, tragically, was taken at face value by Brooke, Montgomery and the senior army commanders. Only Mountbatten and his naval advisers could know that, in the face of hostile coastal batteries and attacked by a Luftwaffe air fleet deliberately enticed into battle above Dieppe, his destroyers had no possible hope of providing effective artillery support. Not only were they unlikely, in the reality of battle, to be able to provide it, but there was almost no attempt, between March and August 1942, to assess, rehearse, or improve such support as could be given.

Like a classical tragedy, however, the Dieppe operation continued to unfold, despite considerable murmurings and objections. Characteristically, Bernard would have nothing to do with such 'belly-aching': the important thing was to see that the troops involved were given the very best training and staffwork possible. When the first rehearsal (Exercise Yukon on 11–12 June) turned out to be a shambles, he refused to lose heart; the operation was postponed in order to give the participants the chance for a second rehearsal which Bernard attended with Mountbatten and Paget on 22–23 June. This time the various units were landed on the correct beaches and on 1 July Bernard wrote to Paget that he was satisfied the operation – now due to take place on 4 July or a succeeding day – 'as planned is a possible one and has a good chance of success, given:–

a) favourable weather
b) average luck
c) that the Navy put us ashore roughly in the right places, and at the right time.'[1]

The weather was not favourable: and by 7 July the operation had to be called off. Since Mountbatten and Major-General Roberts had personally briefed the participants on the object of the raid, Bernard was adamant that for security reasons it should be cancelled 'for all time', and put this in writing to Paget.

For Bernard the Dieppe raid had always been a peripheral if not actually distracting operation. He had supported it wholeheartedly because there was, in his own nature, a love of boldness that caused him to neglect the inherent impossibility of success in the plan; however, as Rees recorded, it remained of marginal importance in his self-appointed mission of raising a new army in South-Eastern Command.[2] He refused to allow a single exercise to be cancelled as a result of preparations for the raid, and for his mammoth eleven-day Exercise 'Tiger' he got his old 3rd Division to move down from Eastern Command and deputise for 2nd Canadian Division. Thus when bad weather put a stop to the Dieppe raid early in July 1942, Bernard shed no tears in recommending it should be completely abandoned, and the 2nd Canadian Division duly returned to its 'proper' role in South-Eastern Army. Indeed so vehement was Bernard in his insistence that the operation now be dropped 'for all time' that one suspects he had begun to entertain doubts himself as to its feasibility – doubts which he had hitherto refused to voice or acknowledge lest he affect morale among the Canadians, morale which, in his letter of 1 July to Paget, Bernard noted was not always firm: 'There was a moment when certain senior officers began to waver about lack of confidence on the part of the troops – which statements were quite untrue. They really lacked confidence in themselves.'[3] Certainly General Montgomery's total opposition to resurrection of the raid was taken so seriously by Mountbatten and Paget that, when ten days later they began to press for its revival,

[1] C. P. Stacey, op. cit.
[2] Goronwy Rees, op. cit.
[3] C. P. Stacey, op. cit.

they proposed a new chain of command by which Montgomery would be excluded altogether! This new system, with the Canadians being responsible for the raid under Crerar and McNaughton, who in turn were directly responsible to Paget, was militarily indefensible, and it is most unlikely that Bernard would have permitted such a circuitous system of command unless, in his heart of hearts, he had 'written off' the raid and wanted no part in responsibility for it.

For Mountbatten, Paget, McNaughton and Crerar it was a very different situation. With Brooke's veto on large-scale operations on the continent of Europe before and unless the Allies were prepared for the ultimate conquest of Germany, Mountbatten's role on the Chiefs-of-Staff Committee was reduced to one of current irrelevance. Instead of accepting this and quietly concentrating on the development of future combined assault operations, Mountbatten now allowed himself to be driven by the timeless forces of hunger for power and prestige. By manipulating the similar motives (and national pride) of Crerar and McNaughton – as well as Paget – Mountbatten achieved the seeming impossible. Still acutely sensitive to Russian demands for a Second Front, not to speak of American pressure and even a growing movement in Britain, Churchill – who at the fall of Tobruk had become deeply anxious whether the Dieppe operation was not too risky – first refused then gave his assent – as did Brooke, who felt that the techniques of landing an army, including tanks, rather than mere commando 'spoiling' raids *had* to be tried out in battle in miniature before committing a full Allied spearhead. Moreover, by re-mounting the Dieppe raid, the Chiefs-of-Staff would prove to the Americans that, despite their strategy of further landings in North Africa and the gradual conquest of the Axis forces in the Mediterranean, the British were nevertheless genuinely committed to a cross-Channel Second Front in due course.

The raid on Dieppe thus became a pawn in a political charade and personal power-game. As Lord Lovat (the only commanding officer to be able to claim success on 19 August) wrote later, this was disastrous because, at a military level, it was a case of amateurs taking on professionals. It was an operation which called for a 'split-second standard of excellence' – a standard which, at that stage of the war, the Allies simply did not possess. Moreover Lovat squarely blamed Mountbatten for being 'over-bold and prepared to take unjustifiable risks' in staging the operation.[1]

Lovat's account appeared after Montgomery's death, but Bernard would have been much troubled by the accusation of amateurs versus professionals, however justified. Professionalism was the very core of Bernard's military creed; he had set his heart on ensuring that every formation under his command reflected it. He had no high opinion of Major-General Roberts, the commanding officer of 2nd

[1] Lord Lovat, *March Past*, London 1978.

Canadian Division, but he did feel that the GSO 1, Colonel Mann, was a brilliant staff officer who would ensure a professional performance at least by the Canadians.

Yet, as Lovat wrote, there was a failure to assess the likely enemy response to such a raid: a failure to take into account the German commanders (among them Generals Rundstedt and Haase), and the futility of asking conventional infantry troops to undertake such a specialist, split-second operation relying on total surprise and with the inbuilt need to re-embark tanks and combatants within only a few hours of landing. As a professional soldier, Bernard should have recognised what the Allies were up against and rejected the outline plan from the beginning. Certainly he should have had nothing to do with Combined Operations Headquarters at this stage of the war when it had developed none of the elaborate fire-support techniques necessary in landing any but highly-trained, self-sufficient commando units. There is certainly no doubt that, had the raid taken place as intended in July 1942, it would have been as disastrous as the revived raid which was actually carried out on 19 August, nine days after Bernard's departure from England. Moreover there is evidence – from a letter to Brooke the following year – that Bernard still did not take seriously the immense problems involved in cross-Channel assault until he was himself appointed to lead the great Allied undertaking of 1944.

By then, of course, he had won his spurs in battle – had proved himself the equal if not the superior of any German field commander, including Rommel. He would, as well, have the assault landings on Sicily and the toe of Italy under his belt. Yet, if he had been amateur in his support of the original Dieppe raid, the two years from the summer of 1942 to that of 1944 were to bear out his deeper professionalism; indeed it is ironic that it would be the 'larger' version of Dieppe that would represent probably the greatest military performance of Bernard's life, perhaps the boldest and most professional military undertaking in modern history.

What Bernard wanted was not a raid, then, but a campaign. He had inculcated a new doctrine and a new professionalism in the army in southern England, had revolutionised the army's approach to training, in fact to the very education of the modern soldier for war. Both Bernard and his subordinates had learned a great deal in the mounting of Exercise 'Tiger'; but only the test of battle could tell whether Bernard's methods would actually be successful in the field against opponents as professional, hardy, and ideologically indoctrinated as the Germans.

The Dieppe raid was cancelled on 7 July. By then Auchinleck had offered to resign as C-in-C in the Middle East, and had even suggested Alexander to take his place, on his way back from Burma; yet still no one suggested Montgomery for command of 8th Army, for C-in-C Middle East or in relation to the possible landings in North-

West Africa (Operation 'Gymnast'). From 11 to 12 July, Bernard attended Exercise 'Freehold' at the Staff College, Camberley; from 14 to 18 July he watched 46th Division training, attending the final conference on their exercise on the 20th. Again from 26 to 29 July he attended 12 Corps' Exercise 'Harold', as well as its final conference. He had been distressed, in June, to find 'when talking to many senior officers that the study and practice of modern tactical methods seem to be making little progress,' and he tirelessly sought to ensure that his tactical ideas of concentrated attack, and integrated and flexible use of the different arms was incorporated in South-Eastern Army training. 'German methods are well worth a study so that we can take from them what is good, and turn it to our own advantage,' he exhorted, even quoting 'Rommell's' [sic] use of thrust-line codes as a superlative example of a drill for axis of advance which 'gives nothing away, and is impossible to discover since he changes the thrust-line as necessary . . . This code has the great merit of being very simple; for this reason alone it is worth studying'.[1]

Possibly, in the atmosphere then prevailing in England, Bernard Montgomery's approach to command was considered almost esoteric; Rees certainly remembered the attitude of the doomed commander of 2nd Canadian Division 'who was as rough and ready as Monty was fine and calculating, [and who] commented that no doubt General Montgomery was an admirable trainer of troops but perhaps he was getting a little old to lead them into battle'.[2]

It is conceivable that, had Auchinleck's operations in the Middle East proved more successful, Bernard Montgomery might have gone down in history – like General Paget – simply as a fine trainer of troops.

Bernard's own faith, however, never diminished – that the hour would one day come when he would be called – and he continued zealously to prepare himself, and his formations, for the moment of truth. At last, early in August 1942, more than two long years since Dunkirk, it came.

[1] War Diary, South-Eastern Command: Army Commander's Personal Memorandum No. 3, 22 June 1942 (WO 199/2623), PRO.
[2] Goronwy Rees, op. cit.

CHAPTER SEVENTEEN

The Call to the Desert

'Early in August 1942 a large-scale exercise was to be held in Scotland and General Paget, then C-in-C Home Forces, suggested I should go up with him to see it. I was delighted to have an opportunity to see what other troops were doing and travelled north with Paget in 'Rapier', the C-in-C's special train,' Bernard recalled in his *Memoirs*. He had hoped to see his stepson John Carver who was currently serving with a unit in Scotland, but the exercise had barely begun when, on 7 August 1942, Bernard received a telephone call from the War Office appointing him to command the Northern Task Force in the Anglo-American landings due to take place in North Africa in October (Operation 'Torch'). He would replace General Sir Harold Alexander, who was now to be C-in-C Middle East in Cairo, and he would be under the overall command of an American, General D. D. Eisenhower.

'It was explained to me,' Bernard recounted in his *Memoirs*,

> that Alexander had already gone to Egypt to become C-in-C, Middle East . . . I returned to London at once . . . and then went to the War Office. I was there given more details and was told that the first thing I must do was to get Eisenhower to make a plan for the operation; time was getting on and the Chiefs-of-Staff could not get Eisenhower to produce his plan. The whole thing did not sound good to me; a big invasion operation in North Africa in three months' time, and no plan yet . . . I returned to my Headquarters at Reigate hoping for the best.

Eisenhower had in fact only been appointed Supreme Commander of 'Torch' eleven days previously, on 26 July – and this was not made official until 14 August. Moreover Marshall refused to give Eisenhower the Chief-of-Staff – Walter Bedell Smith – whom he wanted until 10 September.

Ironically the other Army Commander beside whom Bernard was to serve under Eisenhower was none other than General George S. Patton. At the American Desert Training Centre, Patton had impressed all by his energy and ambition, as well as his flair for tactical exercises. In many ways Patton's self-preparation for war was the counterpart of Montgomery's, and from this flowed a similar conviction of the rightness of his own military tenets and beliefs. Just as Bernard insisted on changing the name of South-Eastern Command into South-Eastern Army, so Patton had bullied colleagues and seniors into seeing that standardisation and material were but half the battle, and that there was a need for proper insignia and markings on all 'trucks and vehicles showing the company, regiment, and division to which they pertain . . . To die willingly, as many of us must,' Patton warned the head of American Army Training, 'we must have tremendous pride not only in our nation and in ourselves but in the unit in which we serve.'[1] He was certain he would one day be given the chance to fight against the Desert Fox and 'just to keep my hand in for Marshal Rommel', he was in the habit of shooting at least a hare a day with his ivory-handled revolver.[2]

Certainly there were many points of similarity between the two Allied Army Commanders – both considered brilliant by many, mad by some, and intolerable by others. Yet there was, also, an intriguing difference in their military philosophy already at this stage of the war, as they both prepared to serve under Eisenhower on 'Torch' – a difference that made them, despite all other similarities, as variant as chalk from cheese. For Patton believed that the exercise of command in battle was an art and 'he who tries to define it closely is a fool' – whereas it was Bernard Montgomery's great belief that command *could* be defined, and ought to be; ought to be something so clear, so widely known among his subordinates, and so rehearsed that victory over 'any enemy anywhere' was assured.

Both generals had now proved themselves as trainers and potential commanders to the point where they had been simultaneously selected to lead their national forces in Operation 'Torch'. Patton was to command the Western Task Force landing on the coast of Morocco, Montgomery the Northern Task Force landing inside the Mediterranean. On 7 August Patton reported to Eisenhower in London. Montgomery and Patton were due to meet the next day for a conference at which a basic plan for 'Torch' was to be agreed. Patton was naturally afraid that Montgomery was to be given the lion's share of the fighting – indeed his diary for 8 August records that he 'said that Northern Task Force was being favoured at expense of Western Task Force. Finally got some change . . .'

The concession, however, was not at Bernard's expense. Fate had thrown both men almost together – but not quite. For, as Bernard shaved at his villa at Reigate at about 7 a.m. on 8 August, there was an urgent telephone call from the War Office. His orders regarding 'Torch' were cancelled. He was to fly immediately to the Middle East and assume command of 8th Army.

[1] *The Patton Papers*, Vol. II, edited by Martin Blumenson, New York 1972.
[2] Ibid.

Bernard's relief is evident from his *Memoirs*: 'Instead of carrying out an invasion of North Africa under a C-in-C whom I barely knew, I was now to serve under a C-in-C I knew well and to take command of an Army which was at grips with a German and Italian Army under the command of Rommel – of whom I had heard great things. This was much more to my liking and I felt I could handle that business, and Rommel. So it was with a light heart and great confidence that I made preparations for going to Africa,' he recorded – adding that his only anxiety concerned his son David.

By good fortune, in an old tin trunk in Yorkshire, Bernard's letters to Mr and Mrs Reynolds, the headmaster of David's preparatory school at Amesbury, were recently found to have survived, and these letters give a unique insight into Bernard Montgomery's personality on the eve of the greatest challenge of his life.

Already at the beginning of May 1942, David had left Amesbury to go to Winchester College. Bernard had taken him there by car, reporting to the Reynolds afterwards: 'We all had tea together with the Housemaster & Miss Robertson, and David seemed quite happy and not in the least upset or nervous.'

Handing David over at the ancient public school – which Reynolds had recommended in preference to Bernard's old school St Paul's – had made Bernard reflect on how much he already owed the Reynolds:

I cannot thank you and Tom enough for what you have done for him. It has been the greatest relief to me to know that you were watching over him, and you have brought him on in a way that no one else could have done.

Indeed, perhaps recognising the extent of his neglect of David since 1937, Bernard was prepared to see in the firm custodianship of the Amesbury Preparatory School headmaster and his wife a cause for excessive gratitude:

He lost his Mother when he [was] 8 and the fact that he is now *what he is*, is due entirely to you and Tom. I am truly grateful to you both.

In turn this led Bernard to see in Tom and Phyllis Reynolds a future home for David.

I discussed future plans with David in the car.

We would both very much like that you should be a base to which he can return for all matters in connection with his clothes, etc. while he is at Winchester. That is to say he would like to come to you direct from school at the end of term, bringing his trunk, etc. and staying for 2 or 3 days. Then he would go off to the Carvers for the holidays. Then return to you 2 or 3 days before returning to school, and go back to school direct from you.[1]

Written on 2 May, this was certainly prescient: for Bernard's next letter, written on the morning of 8 August, was of necessity more urgent. It was addressed to Tom Reynolds:

My dear Tom,
    I have to leave England at very short notice to take charge in a very important place. My destination will appear in the papers in due course.
    I have been given 8 hours in which to hand over, pack some clothes, and be off. I have not time to see David. He is with

Mrs John Carver
Corner Cottage
Littlewick Green
Berkshire
Tel: Littlewick Green 83

    John Carver is on the Staff in Scotland, and may go anywhere.
    She (his wife) is not really capable of looking after David's affairs, though it is a very good place for him to go in the holidays whenever he likes.

This was somewhat patronising, considering that Bernard had left his dying wife in young Jocelyn's care, and that David now went to stay with Jocelyn every holiday. However, as will be seen, this was as yet a mild form of the almost pathological urge to reject his family – or see in them a potentially virulent threat.

Bernard therefore looked to the Reynolds rather than to any member of his own family as the natural guardians of David:

Will you and your lady wife take charge of David for me until I return.
    I would sooner leave him with you than with anyone I know.
    I am anticipating your acceptance of this task. There is really no one else who could do it.
    I am sure you will do this. I can never really repay you, but will do my best.

He enclosed a copy of his will – leaving 'everything I possess' to David – and £200 on account.

I would like you to pay his school bills, buy his clothes, and in fact be his guardian so long as I am out of England.

[1] Montgomery Papers.

531

Give him whatever pocket money you think right. Last term I sent him to Winchester with £2 and gave him another £1 halfway through the term.

He also enclosed David's school reports – a half-term report from June, as well as the end of term report for July – which, in his haste, Bernard wrote as 'Xmas'.

'There is one thing I want you to watch,'

Bernard warned,

His Grandmother is Lady Montgomery, New Park, Moville, Co. Donegal
    She is an old lady and quite unable to take charge of anyone. She will want David to go and stay in Ireland for his holidays.
    On no account is he to go.
    She is a menace with the young.
    He can have very happy holidays with you, or the Blacklocks, or at Littlewick Green with Mrs John Carver – this is 3 miles from Maidenhead on the Bath road.

The vehemence with which Bernard referred to his mother raises many questions about Bernard's state of mind, just as had a number of his actions since Dunkirk. Whether it was the pressure of war, or his dedication to what he increasingly saw as his historic vocation, that drove him to this, he now saw his mother as a direct threat – and would increasingly do so as time went on. The tension which seemed to grip him after Dunkirk never relaxed – or not until Maud Montgomery was dead and old age began to mellow him. By then Bernard had quarrelled savagely at least once with almost everybody who had ever come to mean anything to him, had scandalised his family by his pretensions and his treatment of his mother, had 'insulted and injured' colleagues, seniors, subordinates, friends – and, in a final irony, turned against the very son David whose custodianship he had, in the summer of 1942 and afterwards, so jealously guarded and apportioned.
    In the meantime, on 8 August, he begged the Reynolds to 'write and welcome' David as 'a No. 2 son'. He had himself written to David, who might be 'rather upset when he gets my letter'. David was 'all I have left now', and he left him to the Reynolds.
    Bernard signed himself 'Monty'. Below this signature he added, somewhat indiscreetly:

For your special information and not to be spoken about for a day or two, my address will be:
            HQ 8th Army,
            Middle East Forces

In fact Bernard's flight was cancelled that day; the following day, 9 August, Bernard wrote again from Reigate to reiterate his almost manic determination that no member of his family be allowed power or even the right to advise over David:

> My dear Tom,
>   I am just off.
>   In case my letter (the long one) of yesterday did not make it clear, I want to say again that I put David in your *complete* and *absolute* charge. If any members of my family chip in and want to advise, see them right off. The sole authority in EVERYTHING connected with David is yourself; I want you in fact to be his official guardian as long as I am out of England.
>   If I am killed his legal guardian is then John Carver. But I shall not be killed.
>   Good-bye to you.
>   Yrs ever
>   B. L. Montgomery

At Lyneham, weather conditions again delayed Bernard's journey. That day Lt-General James Gammell once more took over Bernard's vacant role as acting Commander of South-Eastern Army. (A month later, however, Lt-General J. G. des R. Swayne was officially appointed to the post.)

At last, on the evening of 10 August, Bernard was able to leave England. He landed the next morning in Gibraltar, taking off in the evening for Cairo.

'During the journey I pondered over the problems which lay ahead,' he recalled later, 'and reached some idea, at least in outline, of how I would set about the business.'[1]

The question of his son, in so far as Bernard was concerned (he had deliberately not telephoned), was now resolved. Once again he was taking over a military command which he hoped to imprint with his own distinctive authority, to make his own. This time, however, it was an historic undertaking, at what could become a turning-point in the war.

When asked to become CIGS, Brooke later recounted, though he was not an exceptionally religious person his first impulse had been to 'kneel down to God for guidance and support in the task I had undertaken'.

Now it was Bernard's turn to request heavenly guidance. A 'proper sense of religious truth' was the final quality Bernard recorded as necessary to successful leadership in summarising his 'doctrine of command' in his *Memoirs*, as he conceived this doctrine to be on his flight to Egypt in August 1942.

[1] *Memoirs*, op. cit.

For all leadership, I believe, is based on the spiritual quality, the power to inspire others to follow; this spiritual quality may be for good, or evil. In many cases in the past this quality has been devoted towards personal ends, and was partly or wholly evil; whenever this was so, in the end it failed. Leadership which is evil, while it may temporarily succeed, always carries within itself the seeds of its own destruction.

There can be no doubt that, against the forces of fascism, democracy had hitherto put up a very feeble performance. Whether Bernard realised, on his way out to Cairo, that it would be his historic task not only to show the British and Allied armies how to fight opponents as professional as the Germans, but also to inspire the peoples of so many democratic nations and provide a national cause is doubtful. Indeed there is every evidence that Bernard was totally surprised by the fame and myth that grew around his name in the ensuing months, and made it household the world over. But certainly it was this moral inspiration that Field-Marshal Templer considered Bernard Montgomery's greatest contribution to modern history, not his tactical technique; and certainly Bernard's inspiration to so many millions of people – not only soldiers but civilians of all creeds, professions and status – was something no other Allied general would ever evoke.

Somehow, despite his own eccentric, if not pathological, character, Bernard Montgomery bore in him a spiritual power that accorded with the historical moment at which he was given a great military command – a power of inspiration vital to the Allied nations. Since 1940 Churchill had embodied the indomitable determination to survive, despite constant defeat; yet it was not until Bernard Montgomery took command of 8th Army in Egypt in 1942 that Britain – and the Allies – produced a leader capable of arousing a spirit of unyielding offensive self-sacrifice: the determination not only to survive, but to win for a just cause; a spirit which would ripple through 8th Army as it would, in the following months, throughout the Allied world.

PART FIVE

Alamein

CHAPTER ONE

Decisions and Revisions

One would like to think that Churchill's decision, summoning Lt-General B. L. Montgomery to take command of 8th Army in August 1942, was the logical outcome of British failure in the Middle East and Montgomery's matchless reputation as an army commander in England. Unfortunately this was not so; and the decision to appoint Montgomery came not only as the culmination of a veritable farrago of Churchill alternatives, but also as the result of a complete Churchillian misconception – and a strange desert tragedy.

The CIGS, General Sir Alan Brooke, had been given permission from Churchill to go out to the Middle East late in July and was due to fly via Malta on 31 July. However, on 30 July, Churchill decided that he must also go – a trip that would enable him both to assess in person the changes necessary in the Middle East, and then to fly on to Moscow in order to 'soften the blow' about the Allied decision not to open a cross-Channel Second Front in 1942, despite the critical German offensive in the Caucasus.

The Prime Ministerial party duly left England by air in the early hours of the morning of 2 August 1942 from Lyneham in Wiltshire. They arrived at Gibraltar at 8.30 a.m. and took off again that evening, flying south by west across Algeria and then following the 28th parallel until striking the Nile at Fayum, when they bore north for the Pyramids, landing outside Cairo on the morning of 3 August. There they were joined by Brooke, who had flown via Malta, and by Field-Marshal Smuts, who had travelled specially from Capetown; the following day General Sir Archibald Wavell flew in from India for the 'council of war'.

Some historians, intent on rectifying what they saw as an injustice to a proud and noble commander, have claimed that Churchill left London intent on sacking Auchinleck. This is fanciful. Churchill, having persuaded Roosevelt to drop the idea of a cross-Channel Second Front in 1942 and concentrate instead on a pincer-movement in the Mediterranean, was naturally anxious to shake up command of the British forces in Egypt after a year and a half of failure. Auchinleck had refused to come to London to discuss the situation in March 1942 and had offered his resignation in June; when Auchinleck failed to remove the Axis threat to Egypt in July it was therefore natural that Churchill should wish to go out to the desert to decide for himself what was wrong and what was required. Had he already made up his mind he would scarcely have invited Smuts and the previous incumbent as C-in-C Middle East, General Wavell. Moreover his series of wild cast lists for the new Middle East theatre in the days that followed illustrate Churchill's essentially intuitive and impetuous method of working. He wanted a shake-up; but who should go, who should come in, he left to his flair for creative improvisation as he had so often done before – not always with conspicuous success for British arms. However necessary at a political level the Norwegian fiasco, the near-suicidal effort to force Gort into the German net before Dunkirk, to sacrifice Brooke on the Somme, the decision shared with Eden, Dill and Wavell to denude the Middle East and reinforce Greece, the insistence on holding Tobruk a second time had almost wrought Churchill's downfall, and were counterbalanced only by the tremendous awe in which he was held by the American President: an awe which had produced Lease-Lend before Pearl Harbor; a commitment thereafter to concentrate on the defeat of Germany before Japan; the immediate gift of 300 Sherman tanks following the humiliating fall of Tobruk; and the decision to mount 'Torch'. Given such mighty gestures of American faith and support, it was utterly understandable that Churchill should seek to put his own military house in order; to ensure that at this most critical juncture of the war, when the USA had elected to follow British strategy in the Mediterranean, his plans should not be rendered worthless by continued British failure on the field of battle. 'Torch' was valueless in isolation: its success depended on British victory in Egypt – as did the very survival of Malta, which could not be re-supplied unless the Martuba airfields were taken. Yet in his haste to ensure the success of his overall strategy, Churchill came close to wrecking his own chances of victory. Impatient for offence, and with inadequate understanding of the facts of modern military life, he sought a new commander of the 8th Army and resolutely refused to listen to Sir Alan Brooke's considered recommendations. Between 3 August and 6 August 1942, a veritable circus of alternatives was discussed, proposed, countermanded and redrafted.

To Churchill's consternation he found on arrival in Cairo that Auchinleck's Chief-of-Staff, Lt-General T. Corbett, was himself preparing to go up to Alamein as the new Commander of 8th Army. To the Prime Minister Corbett announced that when Auchinleck came back to Cairo to resume his post as C-in-C Middle East, 'I am to succeed him in command of the Army. In fact I have been living with my kit packed for the last week.'[1]

This was news to Churchill, who was not impressed by Corbett. 'Bill' Williams, who had worked in GHQ Intelligence that summer

[1] W. S. Churchill, *The Hinge of Fate*, op. cit.

under the overall direction of Corbett, later referred to him as 'uniquely stupid'[1] an epithet with which Bernard Montgomery, Corbett's erstwhile co-instructor at the Staff College, Quetta, concurred, as will be seen. Corbett was an Indian Army cavalry officer, possibly the most ill-chosen Chief Staff Officer ever to serve in Cairo, 'a complete fathead' in the words of General de Guingand;[2] and how Auchinleck imagined Corbett could face Rommel in the field is exceedingly difficult for the historian to understand. Once already Brooke had dissuaded him from such a decision, when Ritchie was sacked and Auchinleck proposed to replace him by Corbett. That Auchinleck should have revived this idea at the beginning of August 1942 suggests either a total dearth of imagination, a grossly inappropriate loyalty to fellow Indian Army officers, or – as seems more likely – an obstinate intent, as with Ritchie, to control the battlefield himself by means of a puppet commander of 8th Army.[3]

Churchill must have straightaway disabused Auchinleck of any such idea, for Auchinleck immediately agreed not only to drop any suggestion that Corbett might command 8th Army, but ultimately to Corbett's dismissal as CGS in Cairo. No doubt Churchill – in his first interview with Auchinleck since 1941 – made clear the vital importance of success in the desert, now that the Americans had agreed to 'Torch'. Auchinleck himself could not continue both as 8th Army Commander and C-in-C Middle East; it was important therefore to choose a new 8th Army Commander with the right credentials for success. Churchill had already sounded a number of officers at GHQ and had been impressed by the reputation of the Commander of 13 Corps in 8th Army, the forty-three-year-old Lt-General 'Strafer' Gott – a man whom he had never met. Churchill's first inclination, then, was to appoint Gott to take over 8th Army, allowing Auchinleck to return to Cairo to prepare the next offensive; and on the night of 3 August he put this proposal to Brooke – who did not concur.

Brooke had been making his own investigations. He had heard a different story, namely that Gott was past his peak and was suffering from exhaustion after two years of desert fighting. Brooke also had formed a dismal opinion of Corbett – and was relieved to find, in conversation with Auchinleck on 4 August, that they both favoured the same man for 8th Army: Lt-General B. L. Montgomery. In their view, Montgomery should be summoned from England, Gott should take command of troops in the Delta, and Corbett be sacked entirely, as should the Commander of 9th Army in Palestine, Lt-General Maitland Wilson.

By 4 August, however, the seeds of Auchinleck's own downfall

[1] Sir Edgar Williams, interview of 20.12.79.
[2] Sir Francis de Guingand, interview of 7.5.78.
[3] Later Auchinleck acknowledged that Corbett had not 'been a success' – a fact which he attributed though to Corbett's marital problems, Major-General E. F. Sixsmith recalled, interview of 17.4.79.

had been sown, for in the early evening, cross-examined by Churchill on his intentions for launching an attack to pave the way for 'Torch' at the other end of the Mediterranean, Auchinleck poured cold water on any hopes of an immediate British offensive. The Germans were only sixty miles from Alexandria, and were building up not only powerful defences, but considerable resources with which to mount their own Axis offensive. The 8th Army needed time to re-equip, re-group, re-train: and this simply could not be achieved overnight if there was to be any prospect of long-term victory.

At this point Churchill seems to have lost interest in 'explanations'. He had heard them from Wavell in 1941, he had heard them again and again in telegrams from Auchinleck over the past twelve months. The Prime Minister's strategy demanded offence, not procrastination. Later on the evening of the 4th he again asked the CIGS for his views. Brooke said that he and Auchinleck agreed on Montgomery as the new 8th Army Commander, and on the dismissal of Corbett and Wilson.

Churchill was livid. He had met neither Gott nor Wilson, but Anthony Eden had recommended them,[1] and Churchill insisted they were the 'two best men' in the Middle East. There was no time to send out a new man from England; Rommel must be smashed *before* he began to hammer on the very gates of Cairo. Brooke replied that no one could be got sooner than Montgomery; that Gott was widely acknowledged to be both exhausted and insufficiently experienced to conduct a major, critical army campaign. The argument continued into the night; but there could be no doubt that, in exasperation, Churchill was moving towards a more radical change in command. Already the previous night he had suggested wildly that Brooke himself should take over as C-in-C Middle East; and the next day, Churchill made a personal visit with Brooke to the front. They were given breakfast by Auchinleck at 8th Army Headquarters behind the Ruweisat Ridge 'in a wire-netted cube, full of flies and important military personages'.[2] Churchill, delighted by the 'princely hospitality' at the British Embassy in Cairo, was not impressed by this boy-scout reception – rather like the one Gort had given Hore-Belisha on the Western Front in 1939. Sir Charles Wilson, Churchill's doctor, seconded the impression in his diary: 'There were flies everywhere. When they were disturbed they rose in a cloud with a buzzing sound.'[3] It seemed a very inconsiderate way to show a Prime Minister in precarious health how tough and spartan was the staff of 8th Army HQ. Moreover, Auchinleck's briefing of Churchill in his Operations caravan was a sad performance, even to his own staff who were listening outside. 'Bill' Williams remembered the moment vividly:

[1] Both Gott and Wilson were Riflemen, as Eden had been.
[2] W. S. Churchill, *The Hinge of Fate*, op. cit.
[3] Lord Moran, *Churchill, The Struggle for Survival*, London 1966.

Hugh Mainwaring [G1(Ops)] and I virtually heard Winston Churchill sack the Auk because we stood outside the caravan waiting to be summoned if wanted on the Ops side or the Intelligence side – and Winston gave this astonishing description of what Rommel was doing and said to the Auk: 'Well, what are you going to do about that? What's your plan?' I mean he was incredibly well-briefed, of course he'd got his Ultra,[1] he'd sort of thought it out: Rommel's doing this, what are we going to do?

And knowing the Auk . . . the Auk, he wasn't very articulate then. I walked away and I remember Joe Ewart was up there from GHQ and I remember saying to Joe: 'Well, we'll get a new Army Commander now. Who the hell will it be?'[2]

Churchill was all for Gott. He had Gott sit beside him in the car when he left Army Headquarters and sounded him on promotion: possibly even suggesting he take command of the Army. 'Gott said that no doubt he was tired . . . but he declared himself quite capable of further immediate efforts and of taking any responsibilities confided to him.'[3] Sir Charles Wilson claimed also to be impressed by Gott's 'air of authority. Those near him appeared to listen very attentively whenever he spoke . . . I fancy that the PM must have decided that he is not too tired to take over the Eighth Army'.[4]

This was just what Brooke feared, as he confided in his diary that afternoon: 'I do not know what opinion the PM formed of [Gott] and how much he will press for him instead of Monty.'[5] Brooke drove to 13 Corps Headquarters himself to have a private interview with Gott. 'There is no doubt that a rest home would do him a lot of good, and I do not feel that he would be ready to take over the Eighth Army,' he noted in his diary that night.[6] Later, in his *Notes on my Life*, Brooke remembered Gott's confession at tea: 'I think that what is required out here is some new blood. I have tried most of my ideas on the *boche*. We want someone with new ideas and plenty of confidence in them.'[7]

That night the arguments over 8th Army command flared up for the third time, and it was 1 a.m. before Brooke was allowed to go to bed. Faced with this *impasse*, Churchill – who had been told by senior RAF officers that the army had been poorly commanded under Ritchie and Auchinleck and that army-air cooperation had virtually closed down in all but name – woke on 6 August with his latest brainchild. He would split the Middle East Command into two sectors. Auchinleck would have one, a new Persia-Iraq command;

[1] Decrypts of high-grade German coded signals.
[2] Sir Edgar Williams, loc. cit.
[3] W. S. Churchill, *The Hinge of Fate*, op. cit.
[4] Lord Moran, op. cit.
[5] A. Bryant, *Turn of the Tide*, op. cit.
[6] Ibid.
[7] Ibid. Verified by Field-Marshal Lord Carver, interview of 14.1.81.

Brooke himself would take over in Cairo – and could have Montgomery as his 8th Army Commander.

Here was a tantalising offer. There can be little doubt in retrospect that Brooke and Montgomery would have formed an historic team. Both were out-and-out professionals; moreover Bernard revered Brooke, and the increasing strains in the higher direction of the North African campaign during the next year, over the conquest of Sicily and then the invasion of Italy, might have been greatly lessened.

Yet this is to view the smaller picture. As with the fateful decision by Roosevelt to appoint Eisenhower as overall C-in-C for the launching of the Second Front in 1944 instead of General Marshall, the Chief-of-Staff, US Army, there was a more important consideration at stake. Brooke rightly judged that he had become indispensable in his position as CIGS – the only senior general capable of standing up to Churchill's impetuosities, and of ensuring that a considered strategy based on modern military reality was pursued. No previous CIGS – not even Sir John Dill – had been able to supervise the modernisation of the British army to the point where it could successfully fight indoctrinated professional armies such as those of Germany and Japan, and also to ensure that the Minister of Defence – in this case also the Prime Minister – follow a cohesive strategy within the capabilities of British forces. It was Brooke's historic role to achieve this, and the historian can only admire his courage in rejecting Churchill's proposal.

Yet, if Brooke felt he alone had the authority to temper Churchill's military romanticism, he curiously failed to exert his influence at this cardinal moment of decision. Certainly he confessed later in his *Notes on My Life* that he had been weak.[1] Having rejected Churchill's offer, repeated on the afternoon of 5 August by Field-Marshal Smuts ('It had been hard to resist Winston's pressure, but it was doubly difficult to resist that of Smuts . . . He painted a wonderful picture of the great field that lay open to me if I accepted: I had an opportunity of turning the tide of the war and of my name going down to posterity as the man who played the major part in leading our Forces towards final victory'),[2] Brooke now approved a disastrous alternative. Churchill would promote Gott to command 8th Army; would remove Auchinleck, offering him instead the Iraq-Persia command; and would summon instead General Sir Harold Alexander – commander of the British contingent of 'Torch' – to be C-in-C Middle East. This was a typical politician's compromise, and it is amazing that Brooke, despite his 'bitter despair'[3] at having to turn down the appointment of C-in-C himself, consented. To anyone who knew

[1] *Notes on My Life*, in A. Bryant, op. cit.
[2] A. Bryant, op. cit.
[3] Ibid.

Auchinleck, it was unlikely that this proud man would accept demotion to the Persia–Iraq command. Moreover, when looked at closely, the 'team' of Gott and Alexander did not bode well: the one exhausted and the other a general without ideas. Churchill later confessed he chose Gott partly as a sop to the feelings of 8th Army personnel who might take it 'as a reproach upon them and all their commanders of every grade if two men were sent from England to supersede all those who had fought in the desert'.[1] Yet Brooke knew from Gott's own mouth that a fresh mind was required, and that Gott was not the right choice – 'I knew that Gott, although first class, was much too tired for the job, but they would not listen to me,' as he later confessed to Bernard.[2] As for Alexander, Churchill later wrote that he and Brooke 'both greatly admired Alexander's magnificent conduct in the hopeless campaign to which he had been committed in Burma',[3] but Brooke had seen how little Alexander understood of the true nature of the Dunkirk withdrawal and, had he troubled to make confidential enquiries, would have discovered that Alexander, though wonderfully imperturbable, was equally borne by the tide of events during the Burma campaign.[4] In any case, both campaigns had been retreats – hardly the most encouraging experience for a man expected to reverse the tide of military failure in the Middle East. Finally, in the one major exercise in England in which Alexander had held command of armoured divisions, he had committed them piecemeal, and been condemned by Brooke himself at the summing-up.

The question thus remains: why, having rejected the notion of a partnership with Montgomery in the Middle East, did Brooke give way to Churchill's suggestion of Alexander for C-in-C Middle East, and reversion to Gott as commander of 8th Army? The only clue we have is in Brooke's later testimony, namely that his conviction that Montgomery was the right man for 8th Army was 'not strong enough'[5] to stand up to the combined forces of Churchill and Smuts. 'I had long arguments with [Churchill] and Smuts pressing for you to take over 8th Army,' Brooke confided after the war to Bernard. 'However, Gott made such a name for himself, and was so strongly backed by the general opinion in the ME that Smuts convinced Winston to select him.'[6] However much he admired Montgomery, Brooke evidently felt that without his own firm hand to guide him, Montgomery was not necessarily better than Gott – and might be worse.

[1] W. S. Churchill, *The Hinge of Fate*, op. cit.
[2] Letter of 23.1.48, Montgomery Papers.
[3] W. S. Churchill, op. cit.
[4] Cf. testimony of Brian Montgomery, Intelligence officer, Burcorps 1942, and others.
[5] *Notes on My Life*, loc. cit.
[6] Letter of 23.1.48, Montgomery Papers.

Thus the fateful decision was taken, and at 8.15 p.m. on 6 August 1942 Colonel Ian Jacob handed over for encyphering the historic proposals of his political and military masters for transmission to Attlee (acting Prime Minister) and the War Cabinet at home. With their agreement General Alexander would become C-in-C Cairo, with Lt-General Gott the new Commander of 8th Army. General Auchinleck would be offered the New Persia–Iraq command, and Lt-General Montgomery would take Alexander's place in command of the Northern Task Force in 'Torch'.

CHAPTER TWO

The Death of Gott

As Churchill, Brooke and Smuts wrestled over the changes in command, Colonel Jacob set down in his diary his own review of the situation in the Middle East. Although he felt Churchill was right to remove Auchinleck, he was unhappy about the choice of Lt-General Gott. Jacob himself was only two years younger than Gott, and they had attended the Staff College, Camberley, together; many others of Jacob's contemporaries and friends held posts and commands in 8th Army and the Middle East – including the Commander of the Suez Canal troops, Major-General P. Rees (whom Gott had dismissed as Commander of 10th Indian Division in a fit of temper after the fall of Tobruk) and Noel Martin, BRA of 8th Army.

As a result of my own conversations with the various people of my own standing whom I have met in the Middle East, I have gathered a number of interesting impressions,

Jacob noted on Friday, 6 August 1942.

As a result of events of the last three months, the Army in the Middle East is in a rather bewildered state. They have just lost a big battle, which they felt they ought to have won. They are disturbed by various happenings in the Desert, and nearly everyone you talk to has a different explanation of why there was a failure. There are certain things, however, on which all agree. I can perhaps best summarise what I have learned as follows:

a) There is universal respect for General Auchinleck as a big man, and a strong personality. No one openly criticises him. Nevertheless, he has not created a coherent Army, and most of the criticisms and explanations which people give are directed to matters which are his immediate concern.

b) Everyone groans over General Corbett as CGS. His shortcomings have been particularly apparent since General Auchinleck went up to command the 8th Army. GHQ has been a rudderless ship since then. General Corbett can perhaps best be described in the words of the Prime Minister, 'a very small, agreeable man, of no personality and little experience'. This is the man General Auchinleck chose above all others for CGS, and had designated as Commander of the 8th Army.

c) Everyone regards General Dorman-Smith as a menace of the first order, and responsible for many of the evil theories which have led to such mistakes in the handling of the Army. General Auchinleck thought Dorman-Smith had a brilliant brain, and also thought he could keep him under control. In this he was quite mistaken.

d) Our misfortunes in the Western Desert are not universally attributed to inferior equipment. In fact, one officer of the Armoured Corps of considerable experience went so far as to say that equipment had nothing to do with the outcome of the battle. All are agreed, however, that faulty leadership and bad tactics were the principal causes of our defeat. It seems that General Auchinleck and General Ritchie, perhaps influenced by Dorman-Smith, came to the conclusion that one of the main lessons of the previous campaign (Crusader) was that warfare in the desert demands great flexibility. The theory was that the Division was too unwieldy a formation, and that operations should be carried out by the Brigade Group, or the 'Battle Group' – an even smaller detachment. This theory was put into effect on a grand scale, with the result that no formation ever fought for long under the Commander and Staff who had been training it. Brigades were taken from their Divisions and pushed into the battle piecemeal. Some Cavalry Regiments were even broken up, squadron by squadron, and sent up to join other regiments. The well-tried principle that the best results from artillery are obtained by its centralised control was forgotten. A good example is offered by the 10th Indian Division, which was thrust into the fight, and suffered severely, without even being commanded by its own Divisional Commander. The Army was broken into a thousand fragments. Whether or not this flexibility-run-wild was responsible, it is undoubtedly true that we showed ourselves incapable of concentrating superior force, and of utilizing the whole of our resources simultaneously. This showed itself in the dismal recurrence of the same event, namely, the overrunning of brigade after brigade by an enemy in superior force, while the rest of the Army appeared powerless to assist.

For example, the 1st South African Division and the 50th Division took no effective part in the battle of Gazala, while Bir Hacheim, and later a brigade of the 50th Division itself in an isolated locality, were overwhelmed. Throughout the battle the

Germans were always in superior force where the fighting was taking place.

e) In the later stages of the battle, the co-operation between the Infantry and the armoured formations deteriorated. The Infantry had had heavy losses in attacks in which they had not been properly supported by the tanks. The Armour had lost confidence through having been engaged on many occasions against superior enemy tanks, and through being outranged by the enemy's guns. The result of all this was that in the battles fought during July on the El Alamein front, at a time when the Italians were at the end of their tether, and the Germans were hard put to it to stop the gaps with their much reduced Panzer Divisions, our Army was unable to seize its opportunities and complete the local successes gained. The fundamental causes can undoubtedly be traced back to the faulty tactics already referred to.

f) The effectiveness of the 8th Army was much reduced by its heterogeneous composition. Nevertheless, even making allowances for the patchy composition of the Army, there were far-too many cases of units surrendering in circumstances in which in the last war they would have fought it out. Three main causes may have accounted for this. First, the great expansion of the Army meant that formations arriving in the Middle East were very inexperienced, and there was no method by which they could be introduced gradually to the battle. In the last war, new Divisions could be placed first in quiet sectors, and thus gradually worked up till they found their feet. There were no means of doing that this time, and these new formations found themselves plunged straight into a big battle. Secondly, the discipline of the Army is no longer what it used to be, and in the last resort it is discipline which counts. Thirdly, there is lacking in this war the strong incentive of a national cause. Nothing concrete has replaced the old motto, 'For King and Country'. The aims set before the people in this war are negative, and [it] still does not seem to have been brought home to people that it is a war for their own existence.

Finally, there is the need for new blood, and a more rapid interchange between the Middle East and home, and particularly among the Commanders. All spoke in the highest terms of 'Strafer' Gott, but he had been two years in the desert without a break, and had gone through the hardest fighting from beginning to end. His experience would have been invaluable at home, but everyone said that he would not last much longer unless he had relief from the strain. The same is true of many lesser men. As Noel Martin said to me: 'If only we had Monty out here, and some of the other fresh leaders who abound in Home Forces!'

The Prime Minister's visit will have been worth while, if only for the stimulus which he has given to the Army, and for the new blood which he has introduced.[1]

As it happened, there was to be more new blood than intended – for having discussed with Churchill his possible assumption of command of 8th Army the exhausted Gott sought permission to take a few days' leave in Cairo, and Auchinleck agreed that, after the 13 Corps tactical discussion on 7 August, Gott could go. What then happened has been told many times, though never correctly. Almost forty years later the pilot of a certain Bristol Bombay aircraft from 216 Air Transport Squadron, RAF, recalled the sequence of events.[2] The squadron ran a daily service between Heliopolis and the front line as part of its 'maid of all work' army-cooperation duties. On this occasion, on the afternoon of 7 August 1942, the Bombay was detailed to pick up some fourteen severely wounded soldiers from Burg-el-Arab, where there was a small landing strip. At 4 p.m. Sgt-Pilot H. G. James, aged only eighteen and with 410 flying hours already to his credit, touched down. The Bombay was armed only with two Vickers machine-guns at the front – its rear guns being wooden dummies owing to the poor balance of the aircraft when carrying a tail-gunner.

The wounded men were all waiting with their medical orderly in the fierce heat of the afternoon; because of the exposed nature of the airstrip it was considered important to load the wounded and despatch the aircraft within as short a time as possible. However, no sooner had the Bombay come to a halt than the RAF Liaison Officer rushed up to say the aircraft must wait as a 'high-ranking general on a very special mission to Cairo' was expected. The wounded men were lifted back into the ambulances, and nervously the crew waited. Finally, some thirty minutes later General Gott arrived. He apologised for the delay, and at 4.45 p.m. the aircraft climbed slowly off the ground on its journey back to Heliopolis, the pilot flying the virtually unarmed plane only fifty feet above ground in order not to attract enemy attention – for which same reason no fighter escort was provided.

After only a few minutes, disaster struck. A flight of ME 109 Fs,

[1] Colonel Ian Jacob, 'Operation Bracelet', unpublished diary of August/September 1942. Some veterans, such as Field-Marshal Lord Carver (interview of 14.8.80) later felt that Jacob's criticisms were unfair, and did not take account of the difficulties of holding extended positions at the end of long lines of communication, with ill-equipped, immobile infantry that could easily be outflanked by Rommel. Jacob's diary, however, reflected the views of some of the most sensible and intelligent soldiers in the Middle East at the time; moreover they revealed the imperative used to re-think 8th Army's approach to command and tactics now that it had withdrawn to defensible positions close to its base.
[2] Squadron-Leader H. G. James, interview of 3.11.80.

firing tracer shells through the nose of their propellors, pounced on the Bombay. Within seconds the two engines of the Bombay were alight. The young pilot ordered that the rear door be lifted off its hinges into the back of the plane and with great skill landed the burning plane safely on a treacherous sand plateau – its brakes shot away, and the plane running on for about eight miles. Meanwhile, despite the fact that the aeroplane had been shot down and was on fire the six German fighters attacked again and again, in pairs. The pilot ordered that the passengers must start baling out of the open door even before the aircraft came to a stop. The pilot, the second-pilot, the wireless operator, the medical orderly, and one wounded soldier – all badly wounded – managed to get out through the cockpit floor hatch: but to their chagrin they found, once outside, that the rear door had not been lifted off its hinges, and had subsequently jerked closed. The aircraft was engulfed in flames, and there was no way of getting at General Gott, the two RAF fitters, a senior member of the Palestine Control Commission and the thirteen severely wounded soldiers who were inside.

Sgt-Pilot James, severely burned and wounded, nevertheless marched some five miles back across the desert. As he collapsed he was seen by an Arab camel-driver who gave him water, mounted him upon one of his fifty beasts, and rode with him a further ten miles to an army post. Sgt-Pilot James then personally led the rescue-team to the scene of the incident, reaching it just before nightfall, and in time to save the other four survivors.[1] The fuselage, however, had burned like a funeral pyre, and regretfully the Major in charge radioed back that General Gott had definitely perished.

It was 11 p.m. before the news was relayed by GHQ Cairo to the British Embassy where Churchill and Brooke were staying. It fell to Colonel Jacob to inform Churchill, meeting him on the stairs. Having told Churchill of the tragedy, Jacob added: 'It may be a blessing in disguise', aware that Gott was by no means as highly-regarded in the desert as Churchill imagined, and assuming that Montgomery would now be sent for.[2]

Churchill, however, frowned. 'All my plans were dislocated,' Churchill later recalled. 'The removal of Auchinleck from the Supreme Command was to have been balanced by the appointment to the Eighth Army of Gott, with all his Desert experience and prestige, and the whole covered by Alexander's assumption of the Middle East. What was to happen now?'[3]

Brooke was consulted. According to Churchill's later account,

[1] For his gallantry and devotion to duty, Sgt-Pilot James was subsequently awarded the DFM.
[2] Interview of 23.9.80. Later, on return to England on 24 August 1942, Churchill turned the tables on Jacob. 'You were right!' he suddenly announced to the nonplussed Jacob. After a pause he explained: 'It *was* a blessing in disguise.'
[3] W. S. Churchill, op. cit.

'There could be no doubt who his [Gott's] successor should be.' But Brooke, in his diary, recorded a different version: 'I pressed for Montgomery to replace Gott. Had some difficulty; PM rather in favour of Wilson. However Smuts assisted me, and telegram has now been sent off to Cabinet ordering Montgomery out to take command of Eighth Army.'[1]

The cable finally went off around midnight, much to Brooke's relief, and at dawn on 8 August the VCIGS Lt-General 'Archie' Nye detailed a staff captain to inform Montgomery immediately. The unfortunate Colonel Jacob meanwhile spent the entire night of 7–8 August trying to get confirmation by telephone that the Cabinet agreed to Churchill's proposals; then early on the morning of 8 August, Churchill wrote out his fateful letter relieving Auchinleck of command of 8th Army and the Middle East, and handed it to Jacob to take to Auchinleck at HQ 8th Army, 'having learned from past experience that that kind of thing is better done by writing than orally'.[2]

Sir Ian Jacob, looking back on the unhappy task he had to undertake, was absolutely certain that for Auchinleck 'it was the first intimation that he was being relieved',[3] though Auchinleck himself claimed later to have guessed what was contained in the letter. 'He opened it and read it through two or three times in silence. He did not move a muscle and remained outwardly calm, and in complete control of himself . . . I could not have admired more the way General Auchinleck received me, and his attitude throughout. A great man and fighter,' Jacob noted in his diary.

The stage was now set for Generals Alexander and Montgomery to take command in the Middle East, as C-in-C and 8th Army Commander respectively. Yet, even now, having made the fateful decision and obtained approval from the War Cabinet, Churchill still failed to recognise what he had done – believed that it was the substitution of General Alexander in Cairo that would alter the complexion of British military performance in the Middle East – while Brooke vainly sought to tell him it would be Montgomery, not Alexander, who would be in sole charge of the forthcoming battles.

'Churchill thought Alex was the great fighting soldier of the British army,' Sir Ian Jacob recalled almost forty years later, '– quite the wrong impression. CIGS kept telling him, it won't be Alex at all, it'll be 8th Army Commander who'll fight the battle!' But Winston had this picture of Napoleon sitting in Paris preparing to attack Austria and when the moment arrives he takes to the field. Winston thought Alex would do likewise in the Middle East, you see. It never occurred

[1] Alanbrooke Diary, loc. cit.
[2] W. S. Churchill, op. cit.
[3] Lt-General Sir Ian Jacob, interview of 18.5.79.

to him that the C-in-C would sit in Cairo and let 8th Army Commander fight the battle.'[1]

As to why Churchill held such an exaggerated opinion of Alexander, Jacob had no illusions. 'My dear chap – Alex took part in Fowler's Match at Harrow' – the historic cricket match between Harrow and Eton, when Fowler, captain of Eton, retrieved the game from an impossible position. 'On top of that he had been one of the youngest battalion commanders in the First World War. Then the last commander at Dunkirk. Then he had conducted the retreat in Burma. He had the qualities that appealed to Churchill – namely he had terrific courage, he liked to be under fire – and he looked the part.

'Winston wasn't a good judge of character, you know. Being so unpredictable himself, he liked dependability and loyalty on the part of others. It never really sank in – even in the latter stages of his political career, when he appointed Alex Minister of Defence. When I went to see Monty a few years ago, I asked him about Alex, and he said: "Well you know I taught him at the Staff College and we, the directing staff, came to the conclusion then that he had no brains – and we were right." They jolly well were. CIGS agreed, and I've talked to a lot of people who were in a position to judge.'[2]

This view is seconded by Major-General E. F. Sixsmith, at Staff Duties in the War Office when Alexander was appointed; later he served under both Alexander and Montgomery. 'There's no question about it. Alexander was an aristocrat and carried an air of complete confidence in himself. But what, if anything, went on inside his head, is a complete mystery.'[3] Few people ever found out. To Lt-General Jacob, who later served as Alexander's Chief-of-Staff at the Ministry of Defence for much of 1952, Alexander remained as much an enigma at the end of the year as at the beginning. 'He never once produced a single idea, or suggestion during the entire time I served as his Chief Staff Officer.'[4] Alexander's biographer, Nigel Nicolson, drew a similar blank after years of research and interviewing – as did the writers assigned to escort Alexander round his old battlefields in Italy in an attempt to ghost Alexander's *Memoirs* in 1961–2. A member of his Intelligence staff wrote his *Despatches* and later even tried to invent a portrait of 'genius. He had a fantastically active mind which was interested in everything under the sun from the sciences to the arts but which at the same time could also focus with blinding concentration on the problem before it,' wrote Sir David Hunt in *A Don at War*.[5] Though he certainly inspired great and lasting loyalty as a leader, no one else has ever alluded to the activity

[1] Lt-General Sir Ian Jacob, loc. cit.
[2] Ibid.
[3] Loc. cit.
[4] Lt-General Sir Ian Jacob, loc. cit.
[5] London, 1966.

of Alexander's mind; indeed, as will be seen, Patton regarded Alexander as a 'straw man', and even attributed his small brain to the 'exceptional' smallness of his head.[1]

The irony behind Alexander's appointment as C-in-C Middle East was therefore twofold: not only was Churchill misguided in thinking he had appointed a fighting commander who would be responsible for the forthcoming battle, but he had not replaced Auchinleck by a man of superior military ability.[2]

Despite Jacob's and de Guingand's pleadings, Auchinleck turned down the Near East Command. He had always held that dismissed officers such as Generals Gort and Loyd should not be re-employed;[3] he therefore intended to retire into obscurity. He left his 8th Army Headquarters on 10 August and according to Richard Casey, the Minister of State in Cairo, he intended at that time 'to go straight off to India' before Churchill and the CIGS returned from Moscow, whence they had departed the same day.

Whether it was Casey who made Auchinleck change his mind is difficult to say. Churchill's letter of dismissal was delivered on Saturday, 8 August, and ran: 'Alexander will arrive almost immediately, and I hope that early next week, subject of course to the movements of the enemy, it may be possible to effect the transfer of responsibility on the western battlefront with the utmost smoothness and efficiency.' The enemy made no movement; but Auchinleck suddenly told Alexander in Cairo that he did not wish to hand over command until 15 August, a full week after his supercession. Alexander, loth to be ungentlemanly, agreed. Thus Montgomery, whose appointment Churchill had first vetoed on the grounds that he 'could not possibly arrive in time to hurry on the date of the 8th Army offensive', was put in the invidious position of arriving nevertheless three days too early.

[1] *The Patton Papers*, ed. Martin Blumenson, Boston 1972.
[2] This is not to say that Alexander did not possess, as will be seen, a veritable genius for inspiring those under his command to serve a common cause. 'The word "enigma" is rightly used,' wrote General Sir Charles Richardson of Alexander. 'I saw quite a lot of him when I was the British Deputy Chief-of-Staff to Mark Clark in Italy. He was not an intellectual, he had not studied deeply the art of war, he was not a skilled strategist or tactician, and he was intellectually lazy.' However, as Richardson recalled, 'he chose good subordinates and he was a leader. He got people to work for him enthusiastically, and they admired him, whether they were US, British, French, Indian, New Zealanders or whatever.' (Letter to the author 24.9.80.) Field-Marshal Lord Harding, who later became Alexander's Chief-of-Staff, felt that the trust Alexander inspired in Churchill was a vital factor in the prosecution of the war, but that his tactical and strategic ability was almost wholly dependent on his subordinates. That Gott might well have lost the battle of Alam Halfa, Harding was quite clear; moreover he felt that Alexander could never have rectified such a disaster, unless possibly his Chief-of-Staff, McCreery, had found a way. (Interview of 20.11.80.)
[3] Lt-General Sir Ian Jacob, 'Operation Bracelet', op. cit.

CHAPTER THREE

Arrival in Cairo

Fortunately for him, Montgomery never knew – until publication of Brooke's diaries in 1957 – quite what machinations had lain behind his appointment to command 8th Army. To Bernard, as has been seen, his promotion to command 8th Army in the field came as a godsend, and he travelled out to Egypt knowing that he had been given at last the chance he had cherished: command of a modern army in battle.

In the eyes of many officers who were in the Middle East and who watched Montgomery's subsequent rise to fame, it was his assumption of command of 8th Army in Egypt that was to be his 'finest hour'; certainly it must go down in history as one of the great single-handed reversals of military fortune. Although, in the light of the Normandy landings, the desert campaign was a relatively small affair, it nevertheless – perhaps because of this – possesses a clarity of outline and perspective in which it is far easier to delineate Bernard Montgomery's contribution. For, from the moment his aircraft touched down outside Cairo, the Middle Eastern campaign became – at least in his own mind – Montgomery's 'show'. Lt-General Sir Harold Alexander, his erstwhile student, would for the most part act as Gentleman-in-Waiting; no American land forces were involved. As Commander, 8th Army, Montgomery would be his own master: and to him must the historian pay tribute for the salutary manner in which he transformed the tide of history. Before Alamein, as Churchill later remarked, it might almost be said that the British failed to win a single battle against the German armies; after Alamein they were never again to taste defeat.

Lt-General Montgomery arrived in Cairo early on the morning of 12 August 1942: the day Churchill had informed London that Alexander and Montgomery were to take over their commands. However, Churchill himself had left on the night of 10 August and Auchinleck was thus able to conceal from him the delay in transfer of command to the end of the week.

If General Alexander acquiesced in the postponement of the take-over without demur, not so Montgomery, who had come to Egypt with a vengeance. Bernard had already demonstrated his ability to take over an existing formation and to infuse it with his own doctrine of command, ever since his appointment to 9th Infantry Brigade in 1937. His experience in the BEF had furthermore given him proof that this doctrine of command was effective in modern battle. Thereafter he had worked single-mindedly to re-train the 3rd Division, the 5 Corps, the 12 Corps, and finally South-Eastern Army to undertake offensive action. He thus arrived in Cairo on 12 August 1942 determined to launch the very offensive which, ironically, Churchill had been so reluctant to appoint him to command; and it was this offensive eagerness which brought him into direct collision with the outgoing commander, Auchinleck. Having bathed, breakfasted and sent his ADC, Captain Spooner, to buy some desert clothes for him, Bernard was driven to GHQ to meet the outgoing C-in-C and 8th Army Commander in person.

The resulting interview at 11 a.m. on 12 August 1942 was to be, for Bernard, as 'fateful' as the GHQ conference held by General Gort outside Dunkirk on 30 May 1940. Just as Bernard bore away from the Dunkirk conference the impression of a defeated man, so now his piercing grey-blue eyes studied the face of the soldier he was to replace as Commander, 8th Army. He remembered how he had succeeded him once already, as Commander of 5 Corps, and how on that occasion he had instantly reversed Auchinleck's policy of static beach defence; remembered the subsequent quarrels between them while Auchinleck remained GOC Southern Command. In his *Memoirs* Bernard later confessed he had not looked forward to the meeting at GHQ Cairo. Auchinleck also, despite his initial recommendation of Montgomery, must have felt embarrassed at now having to hand over command when he himself had been sacked. As a result, instead of speaking to Bernard simply as outgoing Commander, 8th Army, he seems to have addressed him with all the stern gravitas of C-in-C Middle East which, he began by announcing, he would remain until the end of the week. The 8th Army was re-fitting; it had suffered enormous casualties over the past months, and there could be no question of an immediate British offensive. On the contrary, it was known that Rommel was building up supplies for another attack; if he was successful, it was imperative that the 8th Army should not be allowed to become fragmented and destroyed. It was the only coherent, battle-worthy army in the Middle East, and contingency plans had been made for part of the army to withdraw up the Nile and part into Sinai. These plans were being prepared personally by one of his subordinates, the deputy Chief of the General Staff, Major-General John Harding.

'I listened in amazement,' Bernard recounted in his *Memoirs*, 'but I quickly saw that he resented any question directed to immediate changes in policy about which he had made up his mind.'

Did Bernard exaggerate Auchinleck's pessimistic briefing? There can be no doubt, as will be seen, that exaggeration was one of Bernard's techniques in dealing with both human and military problems. He was, one might say, a born caricaturist, with a genuine love of that art. He filled his house in later years with the originals of newspaper cartoons, and relished the prose of Bernard Levin, the latter-day Swift of English journalism. Certainly Montgomery had the caricaturist's gift for over-simplification and exaggeration for effect. As a caricaturist does, he observed intently, sketched an outline in his mind containing all the essentials of the matter under review, and then brought forth an impression brilliantly clear to all. Often that impression was distorted – even grotesquely so; but in the main it was frank, sincere and arrestingly simple. To him, the picture of Gort at La Panne was, and would remain for the rest of his life, that of a defeated man, a broken soldier – and Gort's contingency order to Lt-General Barker to surrender would be the ultimate proof of this image. Similarly, his impression of Auchinleck on 12 August 1942 was of a toppled general, resentful of his fall and bankrupt of hope: an image typified by the plans for withdrawal. Some weeks later, on the eve of the battle of Alamein, Bernard set down a chronicle of events as he had seen them on his arrival in Egypt:

Situation in August 1942

Early in August 1942 the Eighth Army was in a bad state; the troops had their tails right down and there was no confidence in the higher command. It was clear that Rommel was preparing further attacks and the troops were looking over their shoulders for rear lines to which to withdraw. The Army plan of battle was that, if Rommel attacked, a withdrawal to rear lines *would* take place, and orders to this effect had been issued.

The whole 'atmosphere' was wrong. The troops knew that they were worthy of far better things than had ever come to them; they also knew that the higher command was to blame for the reverses that had been suffered.

It was in this 'setting' that General ALEXANDER and myself arrived in Cairo in the second week in August 1942; General ALEXANDER had arrived about three days before me. General AUCHINLECK was very difficult to deal with, and he resented any questions which were directed towards immediate changes of policy.

The CGS (CORBETT) was quite useless.

The VCGS (DORMAN-SMITH) was a menace.

Both AUCHINLECK and CORBETT had been told they were to go; so had DORMAN-SMITH.

But I found in the DCGS a first-class officer who had been a student under me at the Staff College – Major-General HARDING. HARDING seemed to me to be the only officer at GHQ who talked sense, and who obviously knew what he was talking about. The DMO and DMI were, in my opinion, quite unfit for their jobs.

During the journey out by air I had considered the problem very carefully. It was clear to me that what was wanted in Eighth Army was a reserve Corps, very powerful, very well equipped, and very well trained. This Corps must be an armoured Corps;[1] it must never hold static fronts; it would be the spearhead of all our offensives.

The Germans had always had such a reserve formation – the Panzer Army – which was always in reserve and was highly trained.

We had never had one;[2] consequently we were never properly 'balanced' and we had never been able to do any lasting good. I came to the conclusion that the formation, equipping, and training of such a reserve Corps must be begun at once and must be a priority commitment.

Immediately on arrival in Cairo on the morning of 12 August, I put the project to General ALEXANDER. He agreed, but we had to be very careful as he was not yet C-in-C. It was obviously useless to discuss the matter with General AUCHINLECK or the CGS, so I put the question, quietly and unofficially, to the DCGS (Gen. HARDING) and asked him to prepare a paper on the subject and to say definitely whether such a reserve Corps could be formed from existing resources. There were 300 new Sherman tanks due at Suez on 3 September, and these would provide the equipment for the Armoured Divisions.[3]

Harding certainly remembered the interview well. He knew Churchill and the CIGS had been in Cairo, but had met neither of them. By 12 August rumours had begun to circulate about a change in command, so that when, that afternoon, he was sent for by the C-in-C, he asked, 'Who is the C-in-C?' No one seemed sure: he was merely told that General Alexander was in the C-in-C's office.

So I went to the Commander-in-Chief's office and there I found Monty sitting in the C-in-C's chair at the desk, and Alex sitting on the desk drumming his heels. Monty greeted me, introduced me to Alex and explained the posts they had been appointed to.

'Now you've been out here for some time, John,' Monty went on. 'You know all the people in these parts; I want you to tell me something about them, who's good and who's no good.' And for about an hour he put me through a long questionnaire about all the

[1] There seems little doubt that Montgomery's concept of an armoured corps was based on the success of Rommel's Afrika Korps, as well as the Experimental Armoured Corps Montgomery had tried to fashion in his Exercise 'Tiger' in England in May 1942.
[2] An armoured corps had, of course, been formed in the desert in November 1941 (30 Corps), but it had never been used in a reserve role owing to the nature of the positions held and the battles that were fought.
[3] Montgomery Papers.

commanders and formations in the desert at that time down to the brigade level.[1]

During the entire interview Alexander said nothing: there was no question but that Montgomery was now master. How much Montgomery had already made up his mind as to what he would do, and was prejudiced about the current state of affairs before even going out to 8th Army, is a moot point.

> I think I got the impression that he had probably made up his mind that the army was in a mess and that it had got to be sorted out and revitalized. He'd probably made up his mind too that he would have to fight a major battle with Rommel in order to gain the initiative. You see, one of Monty's great points in his teaching at the Staff College, Camberley, when I was a student there was that the critical thing in war was to gain and keep the initiative. And I guessed he'd already made up his mind before he arrived on the scene that he would have to fight a major battle in order to get the initiative and keep it. And in order to do that he would have to reorganize and revitalize the 8th Army. Those were the things he'd probably made up his mind about; how to do it, he probably kept an open mind about. And this is why he wanted to hear from me personally about the state of the army, the confidence of the various commanders and how he could reorganize the army.

Concerning the state of 8th Army, Harding was quite forthright.

> I remember going through all the formations and telling him about them and about their commanders – that at brigade and divisional level they were very good and efficient and morale was very good. But as a total, no, they were disorganized and they were rattled. They had lost their confidence. And he then asked me, 'Well I want to form a Corps de Chasse in order to be able to carry out a major offensive and drive the German/Italian forces out of Egypt and Cyrenaica.' And he asked me, he'd got in mind having two armoured divisions and a mobile infantry division and how could this be organized? I said: 'And I presume to hold the front at the same time?' And then I said, yes, I thought I could produce a plan to do this.
>   'Well, I've got to go now with the C-in-C, General Alexander, to see the Ambassador. Can you get on with it for me?' Monty asked. I said yes, if you don't mind it being in my own handwriting I can have it ready in an hour or so. So Monty went off with Alex and I went to my office, where I locked the door and got down to produce those two armoured divisions and mobile infantry divi-

[1] Field-Marshal Lord Harding, interview of 23.5.79.

sion as a main striking force to drive the Axis army out of the desert.

The irony of the situation was that Harding was now serving two masters. Montgomery had asked him to draw up plans for a British armoured striking force, while Auchinleck had asked him to draw up plans for the withdrawal of 8th Army:

> The situation at that time was that 8th Army was bewildered. It had been taken by surprise, and they realized they had fought a disjointed sort of battle and had lost it: that they'd been run back to Alamein. Cunningham had been replaced by Ritchie, and then Ritchie had been replaced: the Auk had come up and taken command himself, and nobody knew whether they were standing on their arse or their elbow. The army had got completely mucked up: I think the word bewildered describes it better than any other word I can think of.
>
> The front had certainly been stabilised by the end of July. But the army was in a disorganized, bewildered state. What the Auk had done was, he'd stabilised the position at Alamein but only, as far as the army could see, temporarily. The army was really only where it had come to rest after the retreat; or to put it the other way, the German advance had run out of steam. The 8th Army had come to rest where it had come to, and was in a defensive position – more or less on the Alamein position, but it was really more where it had come back to than any organisation of the defensive position as such. Very little had been done to fortify it, as far as I remember . . .[1]
>
> I don't agree with those who now talk of a 'First Alamein' – they were far too disjointed as operations. Rommel was halted, but his was really only a probing operation, particularly on the south side.
>
> As far as the atmosphere in Cairo was concerned, it had changed in that the position had been stabilised at Alamein: the 8th Army was in position there: on paper it was a cohesive position, and the Axis advance had stopped, they'd run out of steam. But nobody was at all sure – I mean nobody was in any doubt that sooner or later Rommel would resume the offensive, and then it was a matter of conjecture whether the Alamein position would be held or not. And so the Auk decided to have plans prepared for a withdrawal. And these plans were duly prepared. I myself was involved, as DCGS, because I was given the job, in the event of

[1] 'There had been a plan – the trouble was, it envisaged more troops than were available . . . The first plan was that Mersa Matruh was going to be the lay-back position. So 30 Corps was sent back to that; then they realised that that wasn't going to be held for long, and we were sent back to Alamein where we found that it stuck out much too far to the south-west.' – Field Marshal Lord Carver, interview of 14.1.81.

withdrawal taking place, of trying to delay the German advance into the Delta by holding a series of canal lines and so on. I had a temporary staff, a small number of staff officers and DRs, on a very temporary and sketchy basis. The plan was that part of the army should withdraw into the delta and should make its escape into Sinai, and the other lot would go down south into the Sudan. This was rather a sketchy plan for a withdrawal from the Alamein position, and how far it was widely known I wouldn't like to say – but certainly I knew about it, and took it seriously, because personally I was quite uncertain that the 8th Army on the Alamein position could hold its own against a further offensive by Rommel.

To what extent, in the Auk's mind, it was only a contingency plan is difficult to say: but my instructions to prepare such plans at that time indicates a doubt in the commander's mind as to the ability of the army to hold its position. There was also a potential threat from the Caucasus, in the north, and contingency plans were drawn up to deal with this; but I personally was much more concerned with a renewed offensive by Rommel penetrating into the Delta. My responsibility was to impose the maximum amount of delay on the German forces when they came into the delta, between Alamein and the Nile. I was just drawing up my proposals when Monty arrived. How likely did the Auk think such an evacuation would be necessary? I suppose about 40/60, I'd say.

Certainly Auchinleck never denied having informed Montgomery of his intentions to withdraw 8th Army 'in being' in the event of Rommel's offensive proving *successful*; w... he objected to was Montgomery's later statements that this was anything more than a contingency plan which any responsible C-in-C Middle East was bound to prepare.

Bernard may well have exaggerated this part of his 'fateful' interview with Auchinleck; but he was certainly not inventing the possibility of or even preparations for a withdrawal. When Auchinleck protested at Bernard's version of these events in his *Memoirs* in 1958 and threatened to take legal action, Bernard wrote privately to the editor of the *Daily Telegraph*, Sir Colin Coote:

23 October 1958

My dear Colin,
    Your letter of the 19th October. The answer to your question is as follows:
1. Auchinleck's philosophy was that the Eighth Army must not be destroyed by Rommel; in his view it was the only decent army we had; it must be kept in being.
2. Therefore, if Rommel attacked and his offensive could not be held, the Army would withdraw to the Delta – which area was being reconnoitred for defence, and positions prepared. If

the Delta could not be held, the Army would withdraw up the Nile towards Khartoum.

3. If these withdrawal movements were to be carried out smoothly, the staffs must work it all out. This was being done. At Eighth Army HQ certain officers were working on it.

4. There is no possible doubt that the withdrawal plans were ordered to be worked out, and held in readiness. This was, of course, very right and proper, if that was the philosophy of the C-in-C – who was also in command of the Eighth Army.

    But officers and soldiers in the Eighth Army knew this was going on. Morale was low – very low. And there was much uncertainty about what was, in fact, needed.[1]

Bernard also claimed that he had made notes of his interview with Auchinleck at the British Embassy and there could be 'no possible doubt whatever about what he said, about what he had in mind about the essential need to preserve 8th Army in being, and about the absolute fact that staffs were working out the withdrawal moves in case they had to be implemented'. On 27 October 1958 he added: 'Of course, no orders for any further withdrawals had been issued; but the plans were being worked out and it was that which caused uncertainty and a lowering of morale.'[2]

Field-Marshal Harding's testimony certainly bears this out; and the picture of the 8th Army Commander-elect switching Harding from planning for withdrawal to planning for offensive was the first example of Montgomery's 'electric' impact in the Middle East.

In fact the story of Bernard Montgomery's arrival in Egypt in August 1942 has distinct parallels with his assumption of command of Auchinleck's 5 Corps in July 1940. In both cases Bernard felt the need to restore aggressive morale; in both cases he abhorred the notion of awaiting an enemy initiative, of digging in and yet preparing rearward defence lines that were, in Bernard's opinion, not defensible. 'Harding was put in charge of organising the defence of the Delta,' Bernard wrote in his letter to Coote, 'which is of course indefensible'[3] – and Harding later agreed.[4] The secret of successful defence, Bernard had maintained in England after Dunkirk, was to regain the initiative; to pick out those areas of the south coast of England which lent themselves to defence, and to concentrate on giving them depth while meanwhile re-grouping his units to create a powerful counter-offensive force that would drive the German invaders into the sea. Auchinleck's Chief-of-Staff loyally maintained, as has been seen, that this was but the logical continuation of Auchinleck's own policy of beach defence – just as Auchinleck's

[1] Montgomery Papers.
[2] Ibid.
[3] Ibid.
[4] Loc. cit.

Deputy Chief of the General Staff in the desert, Dorman-Smith, would later claim that at the end of 'First Alamein' in July 1942, there were plans to put into operation both a defensive scheme against a likely German outflanking sortie to the south of Alamein, as well as preparations for a British offensive in late September. Certainly the precedent of 5 Corps in Southern Command in 1940 lends no credence to such a view, since we know that Auchinleck bitterly resented the way Bernard cancelled his orders for beach defence in July 1940, proved an unwilling GOC when Bernard nevertheless set the style of British coastal defence in Southern England, and dismissed Bernard's training programme as 'mostly rubbish'.[1] Similarly in Egypt, his negative interview with Bernard and the fact that no staff officer or field commander was aware of a clearly defined policy that would have led to German defeat, belies such claims. As one senior staff officer at 8th Army HQ under Auchinleck recalled:

To me Auk seemed a defeated man. A man of very great personal stature and integrity who had carried an enormous load, but a defeated man. We used to meet the Auk every night in his caravan about 9 o'clock – just about six of us – to review the day's operations, and to plan the future. Now this was very depressing: there seemed to be very little inspiration and certainly no optimism. Perhaps I was expected to provide it, but I think Winston Churchill talked of 8th Army at that time as 'Brave but baffled'. I was certainly baffled.

This was General Sir Charles Richardson, then a Colonel at 8th Army HQ in charge of plans for operations five to seven days in advance. To him, the latter-day references by devotees of Auchinleck to a 'First Alamein' were as specious as they were to Harding. Richardson went on to relate:

At the time [July 1942] I certainly was quite aware that we were 'stabilising'. All I was aware of was a chaotic series of attacks scraped together, which to my mind at the time could scarcely have been said to have succeeded.
My feeling at that time was that we were improvising reactions, and that this would continue until finally Rommel would put in a proper attack and that would be the end of it. I was particularly aware of one attack where a friend of mine in the Green Howards, down in the South, was involved. They were flung into an attack which was preceded by hardly any reconnaissance whatever, and they suffered appalling casualties. This seemed to me at the time typical of the sort of attack which has since been heralded a feat of stabilisation. Well I suppose historically it may be true that if we

[1] Roger Parkinson, *The Auk*, op. cit.

hadn't attacked, Rommel might have been able to push us further off more quickly. But at the time – co-ordinated? Absolutely not. The word 'stabilising' has become a post-war cliché – but it didn't apply *at all* at the time.

Dorman-Smith's idea initially was that the Germans would attack us frontally at Alamein. Later, possibly due to Ultra, it was felt Rommel would attack in the South. But as G1 Plans I was not aware that we were heavily reinforcing the Ruweisat and Alam Halfa ridges. In fact I know we were not. I think the Auk did have a plan to hold fast in the North, let Rommel penetrate in the South and then come in on Rommel's flank, but it was very vague, and based on Dorman-Smith's obsession with mobility. We were to keep mobile, and to keep 'in being'. So when Monty came there was enormous relief. No one had any real faith in the existing plan, there was so much that might go wrong – hence the plans also for withdrawal. I myself had to draw up plans for a withdrawal to Khartoum, and there were others. If you'd spoken to the front-line soldier you'd have got the answer: 'there's no question of retreat'; but, the higher up you got, the more the idea of a strategic withdrawal seemed probable.[1]

In the meantime Bernard had cause to be satisfied with his first day's unofficial work in Egypt. He had arrived after forty-eight hours' uncomfortable flying from England; the precipitate flight had given him no time to bring suitable clothes for the August heat of Cairo, which made his interview with Auchinleck doubly uncomfortable. Undaunted by Auchinleck's attitude he had then sought out Alexander and 'got his general agreement to the course of action I would pursue in the Eighth Army', as Bernard himself recorded later. After seeing Harding and the British Ambassador 'I spent the afternoon buying clothes suitable for the desert in August', and at 6 p.m. he and Alexander returned to GHQ to see Harding.

'Harding produced a plan that looked good and we decided to adopt it,' Bernard wrote in his diary. Harding's British Afrika Korps was not a three- but a four-divisional affair, later called 10 Corps, but originally intended to be formed from 13 Corps, which would be withdrawn from the line:

1 Armoured Div ⎫	each to consist of: One Armoured Brigade
8 Armoured Div ⎬	One Infantry Bridge
10 Armoured Div ⎭	Div Troops

New Zealand Div (Two Infantry Brigades and one Armoured Brigade)

[1] General Sir Charles Richardson, interview of 7.11.79.

Of this intended Corps one division and two armoured brigades were currently in line at Alamein – the 2nd New Zealand Division and the 22nd and 23rd Armoured Brigades.

However, to plan such a re-organisation and to put it into practice were two different things. Auchinleck had obtained Alexander's agreement that the hand-over of command was not to take place before the end of the week, a Saturday, and had told Montgomery that, although he might visit 8th Army, he was also to wait until that day before assuming command.

It was then only Wednesday. It seems, in retrospect, an amazing state of affairs that the two incoming Middle East and Army Commanders should not only have been shackled in this way, in defiance of Churchill's orders, but also driven to feel that they could not openly suggest any change of plans or army organisation to the outgoing commander; yet such was the case. Harding was told to wait until Saturday 15 August before issuing any instructions relating to the formation of the new armoured Corps. Meanwhile, Bernard had asked Alexander's Military Assistant if he could recommend a second ADC. The MA recommended Captain John Poston who had been ADC to Lt-General Gott. Bernard interviewed him immediately, took him on, and set off to dine with the British Ambassador, Sir Miles Lampson, together with Alexander, telling Poston to have a car ready at 5 a.m. for an early start the next day.

That night, in the wake of Churchill and Brooke, Bernard slept at the British Embassy by the banks of the Nile. Was he, as Ian Jacob later remarked, already relatively old at fifty-four for battlefield command?[1] Cunningham, the first Commander of 8th Army, had been the same age, but had succumbed to nervous tension and over-anxiety in the field; Ritchie, Cunningham's successor, had been only forty-four, but was palpably too young and inexperienced to command full obedience from his corps commanders. Auchinleck, on relieving Ritchie in the field, was already fifty-eight; but he too, though he had commanded much loyalty among his subordinates, was ultimately unable to instil optimism among his HQ staff or commanders. Churchill's nominee, Lt-General Gott, had been the same age as Ritchie; but by most accounts was not yet experienced enough, let alone sufficiently fresh to become an army commander. Finally, Field-Marshal Rommel – promoted to that rank after his brilliant capture of Tobruk – was four years younger than Bernard, immensely experienced, but tired and often unwell.

If Bernard felt daunted by the proposition of succeeding in a command where so many had failed, he did not show it. His age gave him a distinct authority; mentally he was fresh and undoubtedly

[1] Interview of 18.5.79.

excited by the prospect of battle-field command. Moreover, although he had had no experience of battle since Dunkirk, he had taken full advantage of his promotion in Home Forces to develop his ideas and techniques as a field commander. It was a very different style from Rommel's, who employed the dashing opportunism of the old-fashioned cavalry commander. To Bernard pragmatic command was quite foreign – and wholly inappropriate in the commander of an army. As Goronwy Rees has noted, there was something almost ascetic in Bernard's approach. The truth was, he saw his profession, if not life itself, as a panorama of problems urging a solution – and solutions were not to be found by muddling through or improvising. If clear priorities were drawn up in one's mind, Bernard felt, then each problem could be addressed in turn and would admit of a solution. As Harding recalled, Montgomery came to the desert wishing to restore the initiative to 8th Army, and to reconstruct the army into an instrument capable of being wielded offensively. How this was to be achieved would be dependent on the state of 8th Army, and his own ability to imprint – as he had done at 3rd Division, 5 Corps, 12 Corps and South-Eastern Army – his special style of command.

Despite the gloom of General Auchinleck, Bernard had some cause to be optimistic. The situation, after all, was familiar: Auchinleck ceding, as in December 1940, to General Alexander, Bernard's erstwhile student at the Staff College, Camberley, who could be counted on to do everything Bernard wished. Within twelve hours of his arrival, Bernard had laid down the composition of an armoured Corps for 8th Army. Moreover he had obtained Alexander's agreement over some six senior officers he wanted sent out from Britain (Major-General Horrocks, Brigadiers Arkwright, Kirkman, Simpson, and two others), and a signal had been sent that afternoon to the War Office.

Yet, if in this respect Bernard had cause to be optimistic, Auchinleck's deliberate delay in handing over command had produced perhaps the most confused situation as regards field command in the entire war – a situation in which Bernard was asked to visit but not take command of an Army whose two existing Corps were both led by acting commanders, under command of an Acting Army Commander whom Churchill intended to sack, responsible to an outgoing C-in-C in Cairo whom Churchill *had* sacked, and an outgoing Chief-of-Staff and Deputy Chief-of-Staff, GHQ, both of whom Churchill had also dismissed! To Bernard's tidy mind this was a situation of fantastic inconsistency at a critical moment in history, as the *Panzerarmee Afrika* steadily built up its forces for a renewed advance on Cairo. Moreover Auchinleck had even told Bernard that if the Germans attacked before the end of the week he, Auchinleck, would resume command of 8th Army in the field.

Whether therefore Bernard made up his mind in the British

Embassy in Cairo to defy Auchinleck is not known; but it was hardly a situation he could be expected to condone as incoming Army Commander. If Wednesday, 12 August 1942 had been a fateful day in Cairo, Thursday, 13 August would be even more momentous.

CHAPTER FOUR

The 'Meat-Safe'

At 5 a.m., 13 August 1942, Lt-General B. L. Montgomery, CB, DSO, left the British Embassy, Cairo, by car for his first visit to 8th Army. From Cairo he took the road to Alexandria and, at the crossroads outside the city where the road branched left to the desert, he was met by Brigadier 'Freddie' de Guingand, BGS of 8th Army, who had been detailed to take him to 8th Army Headquarters, just behind the Ruweisat Ridge.

It was now 7.30 a.m. De Guingand had prepared a paper to show the new Commander-elect, but Bernard, having asked de Guingand to join him in his car, characteristically pushed away the paper and insisted on a verbal précis.

The two men's paths had crossed often before: in Southern Ireland in 1922, in York in 1924, and more importantly when de Guingand served as Bernard's Brigade-Major during Brigade Exercises near Suez in 1932. Bernard had been instrumental in getting de Guingand nominated for the Staff College, Camberley in 1935, but they had not met since de Guingand visited the 3rd Division as MA to Hore-Belisha in December 1939.

Since then both men had made their mark. While Bernard had risen to Corps and then Army Command, de Guingand had served as an instructor at the Middle East Staff College at Haifa, had acted as a planner in Greece under Wavell, had been made Director of Middle East Intelligence under Auchinleck, and finally BGS of 8th Army also under Auchinleck at the end of operations around Alamein in July 1942. He was a man few could dislike, with a warm sense of humour, natural charm, tremendous *joie de vivre* and an immensely fertile mind. Auchinleck, not usually a good picker of men, had recognised de Guingand's merits – though whether or not he could have used them to advantage is debatable. De Guingand later confessed that his promotion to DMI, Middle East, was an act of rashness, considering he had no experience whatsoever of Intelligence work; similarly his promotion to be the Brigadier General Staff (Operations) at 8th Army when he had never served on the field staff of a single unit during the entire war – indeed since he left his battalion in 1935 – smacked somewhat of naïveté on Auchinleck's part.[1] The truth, de Guingand

[1] Interview of 7.5.78.

566

felt, was that Auchinleck was a lonely figure by virtue of his Indian Army background. He liked to have men around him he could trust, and it was his desperate need of such loyal courtiers that led him to such a series of unwise appointments – such as the choice of two of his senior staff officers in Cairo, first Major-General Ritchie and then Lt-General Corbett, to be 8th Army commanders when neither could really be expected to evince the loyalty or obedience of the field commanders of 8th Army. In the same way, he had permitted Dorman-Smith, a planning assistant of Wavell's, to assume the role of unofficial Chief-of-Staff in the field, leading to great confusion and ill-will with the existing BGS of 8th Army, 'Jock' Whiteley. According to many witnesses, field commanders often had no idea who Auchinleck's chief staff officer in the field really was, Dorman-Smith or Whiteley; and it had been one of de Guingand's first requests on becoming BGS 8th Army that Dorman-Smith be despatched back to Cairo to resume his post as Deputy Chief of the General Staff there.

It cannot therefore be wondered at that Montgomery was at first unsure whether he would keep on de Guingand as his BGS – the more so since Bernard, in the same style as the German army, always insisted on making his senior operational staff officer his chief-of-staff, responsible not only for *all* staffwork, both operational and administrative, but his absolute deputy in his absence. Undoubtedly the best Chief-of-Staff he had had, Bernard felt, was 'Simbo' Simpson, his Chief-of-Staff at 9th Infantry Brigade, 5 Corps and 12 Corps. If the War Office would release him, Bernard hoped to have Simpson sent out to Egypt; in the meantime he listened to de Guingand's 'situation report' on 8th Army as he had listened to Harding's the day before: 'a first-class review of the present situation and the causes of it – with nothing held back,' as Bernard recalled.[1] 'We sat close together with a map on our knees and he told me the story; the operational situation, the latest intelligence about the enemy, the generals commanding in the various sectors, the existing orders of Auchinleck about future action, his own views about things. I let him talk on. Occasionally I asked a question but only to clarify some point. When he had done there was silence for a moment or two.'

This was undoubtedly one of Bernard's greatest gifts, as Goronwy Rees so well described at South-Eastern Army: the ability to listen.

On the Intelligence front, it seemed that Rommel was definitely building up supplies and reinforcements for another thrust towards Alexandria and Cairo – in fact the period of the next full moon was considered a likely date. Originally it had been thought he would attack in the north, along the coastal road, but the strength of the British minefields and prepared positions now made this less likely – suggested instead an outflanking move to the south with a very mobile force while feinting in the north: this would be characteristic'

[1] *Memoirs*, op. cit.

of Rommel, and give him tactical surprise, since he could assemble his force in the centre-rear of his positions and withhold the direction of his attack until the very last moment.[1]

Auchinleck's answer had been to prepare a re-hash of 8th Army's defences at Gazala: a system of lightly-held Forward Defence Localities and behind them a string of 'boxes' into which the Army would retreat if heavily attacked; behind these there were further proposed lines of defence at Wadi Natrun and the Delta; if these could not be held 8th Army would split into two, part retreating north into Palestine, part going south to Khartoum. If however 8th Army was successful in countering Rommel's thrust, it was then proposed to mount an offensive in late September, and a training area had already been established where divisions could begin to practise minefield clearance and the like.

Asked what were his personal views on the state of 8th Army, de Guingand expressed his qualms about the current policy of fighting in mobile brigades and battle groups, the lack of co-ordination between army and air force, and the worrying tendency of staff and commanders to 'look over their shoulders'.[1]

When later Bernard's *Memoirs* triggered bitter controversy over this subject, de Guingand would claim that it was 'quite possible' that he had been at fault in 'stressing the "withdrawal" plan too forcibly when making my report to my new Commander'.[2] Certainly anyone who knew Montgomery would agree that when he set himself to listen, and invited one to 'open one's heart', there was a temptation to streamline one's account and present it in the sort of outspoken terms he himself used. Bernard hated diffusion or dissimulation; moreover the way his mind worked was to create a scenario, or plot – he had in this sense the mind of a dramatist, capable of reducing situations to bare essentials and peopling his stage with clear, colourful characters even at the risk of distorting their more complex natures. On 8 August, the day Auchinleck received news of his dismissal, de Guingand had written that it was a 'victory for the old and privileged school' – thinking no doubt of Auchinleck's Indian Army background and the way Grigg, Gort and Ironside had conspired to oust the Jewish Hore-Belisha.[3] But, sitting beside a new Army Commander whom he knew to be probably the most professional field commander in the British Army, he cannot have believed this to be the case. In fact he had himself suggested Montgomery or Slim to Auchinleck as potential new commanders for 8th Army when asked, earlier in the month.[4] Bernard's studious quiet, and the respect it implied for de Guingand's judgement, will

[1] De Guingand, *Operation Victory*, op. cit.
[2] Draft letter for publication, to the Editor of the *Sunday Times*, 15.2.68. Montgomery Papers.
[3] John Connell, *Auchinleck*, op. cit.
[4] De Guingand, *Operation Victory*, op. cit.

undoubtedly have encouraged de Guingand to be doubly forthright, even to oversimplify – for this knack which Montgomery had of taking one into his complete confidence, of breaking the ice with a schoolboy expression ('Put that bumf away and unburden your soul') and listening with rapt, almost priest-like attention, was hard to resist. Only on the subject of army command and morale did de Guingand decline to say too much, for fear of maligning Auchinleck, whom he greatly respected and who had promoted him to his current position.

It was undoubtedly the uninhibited accounts given by Harding and de Guingand, though, which set the seal on Bernard's intention to 'stir things up' at HQ, 8th Army. 'In due course we left the coast road and turned south along a track into the open desert. We were quiet now and I was thinking: chiefly about de Guingand,' Bernard later related.[1] De Guingand was well aware his own future now hung in the balance.

At 11 a.m. the car drew up at Tactical Headquarters, 8th Army, where the acting commander, Lt-General Ramsden, was waiting. It was, in the words of one staff officer there, an 'absurd' headquarters, far too far forward, so that it was both within German artillery range and regularly being attacked by the German air force, as well as being set up at 'a not very attractive place: an intersection of camel tracks just behind the Ruweisat Ridge, with a liberal supply of camel dung all around, on which Winston Churchill commented when he came there'.[2] More important, it was more than forty miles from Desert Air Force HQ.

'The sight that met me,' Bernard recalled, 'was enough to lower anyone's morale. It was a desolate scene; a few trucks, no mess tents, work done mostly in trucks or in the open air in the hot sun, flies everywhere. I asked where Auchinleck used to sleep; I was told that he slept on the ground outside his caravan. Tents were forbidden in the Eighth Army; everyone was to be as uncomfortable as possible, so that they wouldn't be more comfortable than the men. All officers' messes were in the open air where, of course, they attracted the flies of Egypt.'[3] The senior officers' mess at the Headquarters was in fact the construct of the Chief Engineer: an aviary-type frame, over which mosquito netting had been drawn, thus entrapping the very flies it was meant to keep out. Here Churchill had breakfasted; here Bernard was expected to take lunch. 'What's this?' Bernard turned to de Guingand, however. 'A meat-safe? Take it down at once and let the poor flies out.'[4]

As Bernard observed, Auchinleck's spartan life at Army Head-

[1] *Memoirs*, op. cit.
[2] General Sir Charles Richardson, loc. cit.
[3] *Memoirs*, op. cit.
[4] De Guingand, *Operation Victory*, op. cit.

quarters was designed to show officers, men and visitors that 8th Army high command was not immune to the ordeal the army had been through in its flight from Gazala; perhaps unconsciously it was Auchinleck's way of compensating for the very failure of command that had led to the British defeats, and to an extent, judging by the personal loyalty Auchinleck inspired, 'it worked', as Auchinleck's biographer John Connell put it.

Bernard's attitude was not the same. He had no personal reason to feel ashamed at the way 8th Army had been commanded or miscommanded. He himself had a reputation for the austerity of his life, the insistence on physical as well as mental fitness which even Auchinleck mocked in 1940. Now the tables were turned, with Bernard mocking the Auchinleck régime for the lack of physical comfort at headquarters. John Connell remarked that 'Rommel fought and worked under the same conditions',[1] as though this might excuse Auchinleck for imitating him. Yet the fact is that Rommel was in poor health as a result. It was not Rommel's mess conditions that required adoption by 8th Army, but certain of his techniques, such as the organisation of an armoured corps, Bernard felt. Besides, the staff should cease feeling guilty at their reverses, which no tentless headquarters would mitigate; they should concentrate on the best way of now defeating Rommel and fulfilling the Prime Minister's directive to clear Egypt and Cyrenaica of enemy forces. This would not be effected from a 'meat-safe'; it would require an uplift of morale. Moreover there was no point in making mock-gestures of sharing the same conditions as the common soldier. What the soldier wanted was success in battle; he only complained at the comforts enjoyed by his superiors when denied that success.

Bernard's interview with General Ramsden confirmed the accounts of de Guingand and Harding. De Guingand had referred, in his appreciation in the car, to Ramsden as 'bloody useless', he later recalled,[2] a verdict shared by most officers at Army Headquarters at that time. Moreover Ramsden has been a mere battalion commander under Bernard in Palestine in 1938–9; it was inconceivable to Bernard that he should continue as Acting Commander for a further two days while Bernard 'waited in the wings'. Both 30 and 13 Corps lacked a proper commander, and Ramsden himself was, in the view of both Churchill and Brooke, already above his ceiling as a Corps Commander let alone an acting Army Commander. It is a mark of Bernard's authority that, when he told Ramsden to return to 30 Corps, Ramsden did not 'belly-ache', but accepted Bernard's decision to take over command of 8th Army immediately without hesitation or even checking this with GHQ. 'He seemed surprised . . . but he went,' Bernard recalled.[3]

[1] John Connell, *Auchinleck*, op. cit.
[2] De Guingand, loc. cit.
[3] *Memoirs*, op. cit.

Having given his demolition order for the 'meat-safe', Bernard sat down to lunch in the open, beneath the hot sun. He was now *de facto* Commander of the 8th Army; he had to inform GHQ of this, and to start revitalising 8th Army from top to bottom. 'During lunch I did some savage thinking,' Bernard related.[1] After lunch he issued the first of his historic edicts. The first was for a servant:

To Mideast from Main A 8th Army
Army Commander requires best available soldier servant in Middle East to be sent to Main A Eighth Army at once.[2]

His second explained the first:

To Mideast from Main Eighth Army
For CGS Lieut-Gen. MONTGOMERY assumed command of Eighth Army at 1400 hrs today.[3]

Bernard claimed in his diary: 'I learnt later that the arrival of this telegram made Auchinleck very angry.' There was however nothing Auchinleck could do: he had already drafted his farewell message to 8th Army – in fact it had been enciphered at 12.30 that same day, and was deciphered at Army Headquarters on the Ruweisat Ridge at 4.45 p.m., ending 'I know you will continue in same fine spirit and determination to win under your new Commander. I wish you luck and speedy and complete victory'.[4] A copy of the signal had gone to both 13 and 30 Corps, and it was too late to cancel it. Thinking back to Bernard's devastating reports on assuming command of 5 Corps in July 1940, Auchinleck must have felt it was merely typical of Montgomery to 'jump the gun'.

Not yet knowing of Auchinleck's signal, however, Bernard decided to make himself scarce, and to visit the Acting Commander of 13 Corps – Lt-General Freyberg of the 2nd New Zealand Division. However there were two more orders he wished to give. Having assumed command of 8th Army, he told de Guingand to send out a message to every unit cancelling all plans and orders for possible withdrawal. The 8th Army would stand and fight on its existing positions – alive or dead. He then told de Guingand to summon the whole staff of Army Headquarters for a conference.

'When, sir?' asked de Guingand.

'Why, this evening of course,' Montgomery replied[5] – and left to see Freyberg.

---

[1] Ibid.
[2] War Diary, HQ 8th Army, August 1942 (WO 169/3910/3915/3916), PRO.
[3] Ibid.
[4] Ibid.
[5] De Guingand, *Operation Victory*, op. cit.

CHAPTER FIVE

No Withdrawal

The story of Montgomery's take-over in the desert has become enshrined in legend and counter-legend. A 'brave but baffled' army parried Rommel's final lunge towards Cairo and Alexandria in the battle of Alam Halfa, and prepared itself for one of the decisive battles of history: a battle that would reverse the tide of German success, would ensure the outcome of Allied landings in North Africa, and open one of the most famous campaigns in British military annals.

But who was responsible for this reversal in British fortune? Was it inevitable, given the growing superiority in British arms and troops in Egypt? Could any other British army commander have achieved the same – even improved upon the performance? Such questions are bound to arise in victory, as in defeat – the more so since Montgomery was wont to blow his own trumpet, and showed little magnanimity towards his valiant but ill-fated predecessor. Moreover Bernard, for reasons we shall investigate, developed a quasi-paranoid streak of subsequent self-justification, a noxious insistence that his battles and campaigns were fought exactly according to plan – claims so obviously untrue that some historians and critical contemporaries were bound to see him as a boastful and profoundly suspect figure, and seized every opportunity to denigrate him. Bernard himself remained unrepentant, and went to his grave declaring that, in more ways than one, 'the rats will get at me'.[1]

Is it possible, in such circumstances, to navigate an objective path between myth and counter-myth, claim and counter-claim? To get behind Bernard Montgomery's own often distasteful boastfulness and conceit, and chronicle not only the true story of the man, but the historic battles and campaigns he fought? Certainly the sincere biographer steps with caution, aware of the many pitfalls; proceeds nevertheless in the hope not only that 'truth will out' but that justice can be done: for, however vain and ego-orientated Bernard Montgomery's bearing, there is evidence that he was in this respect his own worst enemy, that his achievements as a commander were more profound, more subtle and of greater historic dimension than he,

---

[1] To author.

single-minded, possessed with the ideal of clear leadership – and thus clear history – could ever really appreciate. He liked later to see himself as heir to Marlborough and Wellington; yet in many ways he was much closer to egotistical Nelson who, had he not fallen at Trafalgar, might also have become noted for insufferable vanity and arrogant over-simplification. By one of the quirks of history both men attained fame in Egypt; mixed loyalty and insubordination in equal measure; possessed a genius for tactics in war; were professionals to their fingertips, trainers of distinction, leaders of inspiration, commanders with an unsurpassed eye for selecting subordinates, and a driving ambition to mould their own *own* navy and army. England was an afterthought to Nelson, as much as it was to Montgomery: for first and foremost came the loyalty they earned and then expected from their men as successful battle commanders. Moreover, had Nelson not been the ambitious, faintly ridiculous character who bequeathed his mistress to the nation (which cared nothing for her, not unsurprisingly), it is difficult to imagine that he could have inspired the same child-like following among officers and men. Wellington was a man of privacy, cold in marriage, cool in war; by contrast both Nelson and Montgomery were schoolboys in mentality, in impudence, vanity, ambition and human relationships. Both gloried in their fame, as well they might. But both knew it would desert them in defeat, and therefore pulled out every stop to fight wisely: to attack in strength, plan in advance, weigh intelligence, put themselves in the minds and hearts of their opponents. No other commanders in modern British history have matched their success in battle, or their popularity both with their men and with the public at home.

Yet, in the summer of 1942, Lieutenant-General B. L. Montgomery was quite unknown to the general public, indeed to the larger part of the British Army. He had been passed over for promotion to command in the field since Dunkirk; and only the fortuitous gunning-down of a man ten years younger than himself gave Montgomery the chance to make such decisive history.

Without doubt the battle of Alamein was for Britain the turning-point of the war: the vindication of Churchill's strategy, of Alan Brooke's wearisome struggle to postpone a doomed American-fostered Second Front in 1942; of the War Office's patient work to re-equip and prepare for modern battle unseasoned forces; of the years of labour by men and women in beleaguered Britain to manufacture arms and materials; and of the generosity of the United States President in providing tanks, guns and aircraft. All depended on the ability of the commander in the field to marshal his forces, to inspire, and so put his men into battle that they could face and defeat a highly disciplined indoctrinated enemy. That Bernard Montgomery managed to do this was no accident. But the manner in which he was selected; the false notions entertained by Churchill; and the problems in creating a military machine equal and then superior to the Panzer army: these were by no means so straightforward. What later appeared to be inevitable – according to Montgomery *was* inevitable – was in fact one of the most fortunate reversals of historical momentum in modern history. Had Montgomery not taken command of 8th Army; had the battle of El Alamein, so precariously balanced, not swung Montgomery's way, the configuration of World War Two might have been very different. One can only speculate on the consequence of such a failure: the loss of Malta; the possible cancellation of the 'Torch' landings in North Africa or their defeat in detail by the Germans, aided by the Vichy French; a radical change in American policy, switching priority to the Pacific theatre; or, worse still for Europe's sake, a premature landing on the Continent meeting the same end as the raid on Dieppe. Certainly the war would have been much prolonged and millions more lives – the lives of Jews, political prisoners and peoples of Eastern Europe – would have been sacrificed to the German mania for a mythical racial purity and for *'Lebensraum'*. What is certain is that Bernard Montgomery was not exaggerating when he declared, in his Personal Message to all troops of 8th Army on 23 October 1942: 'The battle that is now about to begin will be one of the decisive battles of history. It will be the turning-point of the war. The eyes of the whole world will be on us, watching anxiously which way the battle will swing. We can give them their answer at once, it will swing our way.' It did – but only just.

The 'myth' of Auchinleck's plans for evacuating Egypt was, in the eyes of Auchinleck's admirers, the worst dishonour done to 'the Auk'; Auchinleck himself complained, in a letter to the *Sunday Times* when it was serialising Montgomery's *Memoirs*, that 'such a plan had ceased to be seriously considered since early in July 1942, when Rommel had been forced back on the defensive and the English Army had regained the power of attack'.[1] Sadly, the evidence shows that this was not the case: that not only were plans of retreat taken seriously at GHQ Cairo until the very day Auchinleck officially handed over command to Alexander, on 15 August 1942, but that they were very much a 'part of life' within the formation headquarters of 8th Army – from 8th Army Headquarters down to brigade and even regimental level. John Connell, writing on behalf of Auchinleck in 1959, denied that 'there was any intention to retreat eastwards into the Delta in the face of heavy attack', and decried the 'ritual smearing of the scapegoat'.[2] His eloquent plea was taken up the following year by a young historian, Correlli Barnett, who collected all the sad tales of the sacked generals of the desert;[3] but

[1] John Connell, *Auchinleck*, op. cit.
[2] Ibid.
[3] Correlli Barnett, *The Desert Generals*, London 1960.

neither Connell nor Barnett had access to the still secret War Diaries of 8th Army units. Instead, they made great play on an 'Appreciation' drawn up on 27 July 1942 by Auchinleck's Deputy Chief-of-Staff, 'Chink' Dorman-Smith – an appreciation which correctly predicted a German break-through south of Alamein that would give rise to a 'modern defensive battle' before the end of August 1942, followed by an offensive battle mounted by 8th Army in September that year. On the basis of this document, Connell and Barnett attempted to persuade the world to disregard any allegations of intended 8th Army retreat, and even to consider the battle of Alam Halfa, as fought under Lt-General Montgomery, as a victory stolen from Auchinleck – accusing Montgomery, in Barnett's words of 'wearing a second-hand coat of glory'.[1] Even the Official Historian of British Intelligence in the Second World War, writing in 1980, became infected with this view – a view which accorded the July operations the title of 'First Alamein', ascribed their failure only to the 'brilliance' of Rommel, and made Dorman-Smith's appreciation of 27 July the 'blue-print' for Montgomery's success at Alam Halfa.[2]

The secret War Diaries do not bear out this interpretation; nor does the witness of those staff officers responsible for operations, planning, administration and intelligence in 8th Army. All through the minor 'pushes' of July 1942 there had been what the G1 (Plans) at 8th Army HQ called 'a confusion of purpose endemic' in Auchinleck's battle plans and orders[3] – and this is borne out by the records now freely available to historians in the Public Record Office. On 6 July 1942, 30 Corps issued its Order No. 60, which was to set the tone of its orders for the next month:

> This order is ONLY issued in case it becomes necessary to withdraw from EL ALAMEIN position quickly. It cancels all other orders re withdrawal from above position . . .
> EIGHTH ARMY, when it withdraws, is to cover the approaches to ALEXANDRIA and CAIRO from the WEST, delaying enemy's advance by all means in its power . . . INTENTION: The intention is definitely to stand and fight on our present position, but, if it is considered essential to withdraw EIGHTH ARMY from the EL ALAMEIN position, 30 Corps will withdraw EAST of the main road CAIRO–ALEXANDRIA.[4]

Thereafter, as Auchinleck rallied his forces, his orders swung like a great pendulum between fantasies of success and disaster. On 10 July 30 Corps' Operation Order No. 63 ran:

[1] Ibid.
[2] F. H. Hinsley, *British Intelligence in the Second World War*, Vol. 2, London 1981, and interview of 28.11.80.
[3] General Sir Charles Richardson, loc. cit.
[4] War Diary, HQ 30 Corps (WO 169/4034), PRO.

The enemy's advance has been checked in the EL ALAMEIN position where our forces are being reorganized and reinforced in preparation for striking a decisive blow.

The Army Commander's policy is therefore offensive, but a situation may arise requiring EIGHTH ARMY to act on the defensive. Measures to insure against this eventuality are therefore necessary.[1]

These measures were an extension of Dorman-Smith's 'cow-pat theory' – a series of 'defended positions in rear of EL ALAMEIN position'. Between these positions the divisions of 8th Army were to furnish 'battle-groups' that would 'operate against the enemy attacking our localities or attempting to by-pass them'. Each division was told to furnish up to nine such battle-groups – consisting of artillery, an anti-tank troop, infantry, machine-gun platoon, engineers, ambulances, anti-aircraft platoon and mortar platoon – while sending all excess infantry back to the Delta. The accent was on mobility. By 14 July the importance of the Alam Halfa ridge had been appreciated in Gott's 13 Corps; in fact the strategy of 8th Army was becoming one of lightly held FDLs (forward defence localities), behind which were Dorman-Smith's 'cow-pat' Alamein positions, which would now include Alam Halfa.

13 Corps will make preparations for a withdrawal eastwards pivoting on the ALAM EL HALFA feature 4388 which will be placed in a state of defence at once . . . New Zealand Division will be responsible for preparation of the ALAM EL HALFA position and occupation if required . . . The ALAM EL HALFA position will be prepared for two brigade groups operating as Battle Groups.[2]

In fact little was done to fortify Alam Halfa for the next month, save the erection of some wire and the laying of some minefields. Every few days, as the pendulum of Auchinleck's morale rose and fell, operational orders veered from fantastic optimism to ominous preparedness for retreat. In fact every 13 Corps operation order was prefaced with the words: 'Nothing in this order is to be interpreted as a weakening in our intention to hold the present position or as an indication that our efforts have or are likely to fail.'[3] It is easy to see why Churchill's phrase 'baffled and bewildered' is considered by veterans to be so apt. On 19 July 13 Corps were ordering 7th Armoured Division to be prepared 'to move on FUKA', even to 'pursue and harass enemy forces as far west as inclusive CHARING

---

[1] Ibid.
[2] War Diary, HQ 13 Corps (WO 169/4006), PRO.
[3] Ibid.

CROSS', and to 'be prepared to continue pursuit as far as the frontier without pause';[1] and on 21 July 30 Corps' Operation Instruction No. 67 outlined the pursuit of the mythically retreating Axis army, adding that:

> our ability to pursue the enemy relentlessly and inflict the maximum destruction will depend largely on our operating on a hard scale with only those units which are fully equipped and mobile as possible, and on our leaving behind all non-essential personnel and equipment to lessen the strain on maintenance and transport.

The pursuit would be carried out by both Corps, 'without awaiting further orders, with all available armoured and mobile forces. Divisions will pursue with Battle Groups organized as shown in Appendix "A". This organization is forwarded for information and guidance as it has already proved very successful in the most recent fighting'.[2]

In fact the obsession with Battle Groups had proved 8th Army's undoing; but, despite failure after failure, Auchinleck and Dorman-Smith stuck to their doctrine. On 25 July another 30 Corps attack envisaged an advance upon Fuka and Daba:

> The enemy has suffered considerable casualties to personnel and equipment. It is essential to strike hard before he has time to build up his strength . . . 7 Armoured Division will be prepared to exploit to FUKA or DABA, 5 Indian Division will be prepared to secure DABA with a brigade of Battle Groups while the remainder of the division mop up in own area and prepare to come into reserve.[3]

There was little mopping up to do save of blood, however. Almost forty years later one staff officer of 8th Army Headquarters could remember Dorman-Smith coming to the Operations caravan in the morning, tapping the map with his long fingers and declaring with frighteningly unreal afflatus: 'I think we'll attack here – tonight!'[4] 'He really was as near being a lunatic as you can get,' Major-General Oswald, another staff officer at divisional and then army level at the time, remarked.[5]

In the final 30 Corps attack on 27 July, the 9th Australian Division – heroes of the siege of Tobruk – was thrown into yet another ultimately unco-ordinated assault that decimated the attackers and

[1] Ibid.
[2] War Diary, HQ 30 Corps, loc. cit.
[3] Ibid.
[4] Brigadier H. R. W. Vernon, interview of 11.4.80.
[5] Major-General M. St. J. Oswald, interview of 22.4.80.

brought casualties in the Australian Division for the single month of July to no less than 146 officers and 3070 men.[1]

By 30 July Auchinleck had given up hope of reaching Fuka or Daba, and all orders thenceforth related to the likely Axis offensive. Yet even now Auchinleck could not make up his mind where Rommel would aim his blow, and his plans for the defence of Alamein were far from convincing – as Churchill intuitively appreciated. Auchinleck reverted to the defensive policy he had espoused at the beginning of July, based on 'boxes' and 'battle-groups': but with a much depleted 8th Army. His GHQ *Monthly Review of Operations in the Western Desert* recorded no less than 13,250 casualties for July 1942,[2] apart from frightening losses of armour, vehicles and equipment – and on top of some 90,000 casualties sustained in battle since Auchinleck launched his 'Crusader' offensive in November 1941. Already on 19 July 8th Army Intelligence had drawn up an analysis of Rommel's tactical methods, noting his preference for 'concentration of force at the decisive point', using an anti-tank screen of highly-mobile artillery and 88-mm guns against 8th Army's counter-attacks, and clearly depicting Rommel's method of 'concentrating on defended localities in turn – another example of the given application of the principle of concentration'.[3]

Despite this, Auchinleck, Dorman-Smith and Gott clung to their policy of 'boxes' – though, as Major Oswald, then a G2 Staff Officer at 10th Indian Division and subsequently 8th Army HQ, recorded in his diary, the idea of 'boxes' was now modified into 'Defended OP Areas':

Owing to the wide area that had to be held during the GAZALA battle and during the subsequent retreat, these 'boxes' had frequently been out of supporting distance of each other. Once our armour was defeated they fell an easy prey to the GERMAN armour and infantry.

A compromise was then adopted of 'Defended OP Areas' and 'Battle Groups'. The underlying theory was that 'Jock Columns' (which had so successfully covered the Frontier of EGYPT during the summer of 1941 and had harried ROMMEL's retreat to AGHEILA) were too weak to attack effectively, while 'boxes' were not sufficiently offensive. The latter moreover proved very costly and had too frequently been over-run. The idea was that certain key points, generally those giving good observation, should be held by infantry and anti-tank guns. A division was expected to establish three or four such defended OP areas which were not to be more than 10,000 yards apart. Within this framework the rest of

[1] War Diary, HQ 30 Corps, loc. cit.
[2] War Diary, GHQ Middle East, August 1942 (WO 169/3800), PRO.
[3] War Diary, 8th Army HQ, 'I' Section, July–December 1942 (WO 169/3937), PRO.

the division was expected to operate as battle groups. The basic battle group was one 25-pdr battery, one or two infantry companies, anti-tank guns, RE detachments, and, wherever possible, some tanks. These battle groups of which a division could produce up to 9, were to operate offensively against the enemy, falling back when necessary into the defended OP area. Any surplus infantry was to be sent back to base as being only a liability to the Divisional Commander. This system was an indifferent compromise between the offensive tactics of the 'Jock Columns' and the defensive tactics of the 'box'.[1]

Looking back, Major-General Oswald thought these ideas 'lunatic', not only because they entailed a disastrous fragmentation of divisions – the traditional strength of the British Army – but also because they split up the one arm which, in his view, had stopped Rommel from penetrating beyond Alamein: the artillery. 'I don't mention Dorman-Smith by name here,' he tapped the copy of his desert diary, 'but this lunatic sort of tactical doctrine was an absolute recipe for defeat.'[2]

The 'recipe' was indeed a strange spectacle. The front line, Dorman-Smith persuaded Auchinleck, should be seen solely as a screen. If Rommel attacked in strength, the whole of 8th Army was to withdraw into the 'Defended OP Areas' and fragment into battle groups, sending all surplus infantry back to even more rearward defence lines being dug between Alamein and the Nile.

Plans had been made for the evacuation of the forward positions of the ALAMEIN line in the event of a German attack in force.

Oswald's diary of August 1942 ran.

The positions selected and dug further in rear were no more formidable than those already occupied, and merely shortened the line by closing up to the NORTH. This allowed the enemy free access to the barrel track which strikes the CAIRO–ALEXANDRIA road some 40 kilometres from CAIRO.

Defensive positions based on the tactical doctrine outlined above were dug at WADI NATRUN, midway between CAIRO and ALEXANDRIA to cover the barrel track, or to delay the enemy should he advance on CAIRO from the direction of ALEXANDRIA. Defences were also dug on the outskirts of ALEXANDRIA and of CAIRO.

Plans were also made for the evacuation of EGYPT, partly to PALESTINE, and partly up the Nile valley. The Fleet had long

[1] Major-General M. St. J. Oswald, 'From Alamein To Tunis', unpublished diary.
[2] Interview of 11.4.80.

since left ALEXANDRIA. In short there was 'much looking over the shoulder'.[1]

The secret War Diaries of GHQ Middle East and the formations involved in Egypt all confirm Oswald's record. In its Operation Order No. 144 of 29 July 1942, 13 Corps had given its units the following 'information'; that defensive positions were being prepared in the Wadi Natrun area, between Alamein and Cairo; that 'the defences covering ALEXANDRIA are being strengthened and are under DELTA force'; and 'the MENA defences are being prepared by BTE' (British Troops in Egypt).[2] Already on 22 July, in Operation Instruction No. 7, this so-called Delta force had issued orders that ran:

> Our positions at EL ALAMEIN are being rapidly strengthened and EIGHTH ARMY intends to give battle there should the enemy take the offensive. If, however, the enemy's superiority makes it necessary to break off the engagement, the EIGHTH ARMY, less two infantry divisions, will withdraw on CAIRO, and two infantry divisions will withdraw on ALEXANDRIA, coming under the command of DELTAFORCE . . .[3]

This instruction remained in force into August 1942, the commanders of both Delta force and British troops in Egypt being exhorted by Auchinleck's Chief-of-Staff in Cairo on 4 August that GHQ 8th Army 'should be kept fully in the picture as regards the arrangements made for tactical demolitions in your area'.[4] The 44th Infantry Division which had arrived from England in mid-July had been given to Delta force and was detailed to reconnoitre the 'Barrage' sector; yet the scare of a German break-through was still so strong on 10 August that one of its brigades was held back east of the river Nile.[5] On the same day Corbett issued Operation Instruction No. 137 for the possible evacuation of GHQ to Sarafand in Palestine, adding next day the latest baggage allowances – Lt-Colonels and above: 75 lbs; Majors and below: 60 lbs.[6] Even on 14 August 1942 – the day *after* Bernard Montgomery prematurely assumed command of 8th Army – General Corbett was writing to the Commander of British Troops in Egypt that the Arab population living in the rearward areas between 8th Army and Alexandria/Cairo 'should be moved EAST of the NILE in order to avoid the possibility of subsequent moves, should the battle of the DELTA have to be fought'.

[1] Major-General M. St. J. Oswald, op. cit.
[2] War Diary, HQ 13 Corps, July 1942, loc. cit.
[3] War Diary, HQ 10 Corps, August 1942 (WO 169/3987), PRO.
[4] War Diary, GHQ Middle East, August 1942, loc. cit.
[5] Ibid.
[6] Ibid.

Small wonder, then, that a distinct atmosphere of 'looking over one's shoulder' existed in the headquarters of almost all 8th Army formation headquarters. The Afrika Korps was known to have taken up a position 'in the centre of the ridge which governs Alamein' as the 8th Army Intelligence Summary for 28 July pointed out.[1] From tactical air reconnaissance, Y intercepts and Ultra, a pretty complete picture was obtained of Rommel's dispositions and alarmingly rising tank strength. By 2 August it was estimated that Rommel could field as many as 140 Mark III and IV Panzer tanks; and 'the total is expected to rise greatly once the expected delivery of tank engines has been made'.[2] The Italians could provide a hundred tanks: 'Thus the enemy's armoured strength is once more formidable,' the Summary acknowledged – only days after the July 'battles' which in Auchinleck's later view had put paid to Axis hopes of driving on Cairo.

8th Army's response remained the same mixture of fantasy and uncertainty. The initiative lay with Rommel. A series of possible German thrusts was envisaged by 30 Corps, the most likely of which would be 'towards BIR EL THEMID or via DEIR EL HIMA to ALAM HALFA' in 13 Corps area.[3] In its Operation Order No. 144 of 29 July, 13 Corps also appreciated the likelihood of an attack towards Alam Halfa.[4] Despite its orders of 14 July, 'no permanent garrison' had been allotted either to Alam Halfa or Gebel bein Gabr, the other threatened ridge, nor was one to be allocated.[5] The idea, as in early July, was simply to 'reconnoitre' these positions, some fifteen miles to the rear of 13 Corps' front line. When Rommel attacked, the entire front line defence would then be withdrawn 'on the codeword "GRATUITY"'.[6] In such case the whole area of ground south of the Ruweisat Ridge currently occupied by 5th Indian Division and 2nd New Zealand Division would be surrendered to Rommel. These two infantry divisions would stream back – the Indian Division into 'Army Reserve in the area Ruweisat station', the 2nd New Zealand Division to 'ALAM HALFA defended locality', covered by armour. Having reached the Alam Halfa ridge, the New Zealanders would be split up into 'mobile battle groups'.[7] At a conference of corps commanders the following day (30 July) General Auchinleck confirmed this policy, insisting that 'the essence of the defensive plan was fluidity and mobility'.[8] 1st Armoured Division's orders on 30 July outlined the manner in which it would 'cover the withdrawal of the

[1] War Diary, 8th Army, 'I' Section, July–December 1942, loc. cit.
[2] Ibid.
[3] War Diary, HQ 30 Corps, July 1942, loc. cit.
[4] War Diary, HQ 13 Corps, July 1942, loc. cit.
[5] Ibid.
[6] Ibid.
[7] War Diary, HQ 13 Corps, July 1942, loc. cit.
[8] Auchinleck's Despatch, the London Gazette, 15 January 1948.

forward infantry to the ALAM HALFA ridge.'[1] Once again nothing in the order was to be 'interpreted as a weakening in our intention to hold the present position or as an indication that our efforts have or are likely to fail'.[2] The New Zealand 5th Brigade Commander, Brigadier Kippenberger, later summed up the orders: 'A series of reserve positions was prepared twelve or fifteen miles to the east. We were allocated sectors and took our officers back to look at them. Our transport was kept well forward and we did not know whether we would fight where we stood, or in the reserve positions, or run away.'[3]

While the New Zealand and Indian infantry of 13 Corps withdrew to Ruweisat Station and Alam Halfa, 30 Corps in the North would also 'thin out' the 'forward zone' and occupy rear 'defensive localities', composed each of 'two infantry battalions, one field battery and one anti-tank battery'. Between these defended localities 'battle groups will counter-attack any enemy who may attempt to attack or outflank our positions'. Moreover 'Battle Groups will be controlled by brigade and divisional HQs. Arrangements will be made and recces carried out to enable them to operate rapidly in support of neighbouring Divisions or of 13 Corps'. This strategy was laid down in Operation Order No. 71, dated 10 August, confirming the original instructions made in 30 Corps Operation Order No. 70 of 31 July.[4] The Battle Groups were to be 'organized and trained to act in the above way'. 'In this situation the maximum number of Battle Groups will also be used to pin the enemy down and harry his columns,' the order ran, if Rommel outflanked or broke through – assisted by an unspecified 'armoured reserve under the command of EIGHTH ARMY'.[5]

It was this plethora of orders, instructions and contingency plans, not Dorman-Smith's general appreciation of 27 July, which greeted Bernard Montgomery when he arrived at 8th Army on 13 August. His professional pride revolted at such confusion and make-believe. Apart from a 'discussion' on the morning of 7 August no rehearsal or training exercise for such complicated manoeuvres was ever held by the infantry divisions who were supposed to withdraw to the rear-defended OP areas; yet Auchinleck simultaneously ordered his Rear Army HQ to prepare a special training ground 'on lines similar to localities at present occupied by German troops in the EL ALAMEIN area. The general purpose of the scheme will be to enable formations and units to carry out exercises in breaking through the enemy defences with special attention to the clearing of a gap for armoured forces through the enemy minefield'.[6] This order was

[1] War Diary, 1st Armoured Division HQ, July 1942 (WO 169/4054), PRO.
[2] Ibid.
[3] Sir Howard Kippenberger, *Infantry Brigadier*, London 1949.
[4] War Diary, HQ 30 Corps, July and August 1942, loc. cit.
[5] Ibid.
[6] War Diary, Rear 8th Army HQ, August 1942 (WO 169/3926), PRO.

given on 6 August – but on the 13th recces were still being carried out for the new site. How seriously the 8th Army took its training for the forthcoming battle is illustrated by the fact that the day 13 Corps did finally carry out its Exercise No. 1, attended by General Auchinleck, the Corps Commander departed on leave in the afternoon – to his death. Brigadier Kippenberger, recalling the conference seven years later, remembered Gott being in a 'brand new uniform', and the news that he was to succeed Auchinleck as Commander, 8th Army; but the 'exercise' itself made no impression at all. 'When the conference, which did not seem to be about anything in particular,' he wrote in *Infantry Brigadier*, 'had ended, Gott went straight off to fly to Cairo in an old troopcarrier. Almost as soon as the machine left the ground it was shot down, and he and fourteen others were killed.'[1]

The so-called exercise Gott conducted was in fact a brief 'discussion'[2] by divisional and brigade commanders of possible enemy moves, and 13 Corps' reactions. No signal exercises, let alone exercises in the field, were ever conducted to practise the supposed formation, command or debouching of Battle Groups. 'The situation when I arrived was really unbelievable; I would never have thought it could have been so bad. Auchinleck should never be employed again in any capacity,' Bernard wrote to "Simbo" Simpson at the War Office some weeks later.[3] The uncertainty caused by widely-known contingency plans for retreat to Palestine and the Nile, the current lack of army/air co-operation, and the profusion of ill-considered plans for a mass withdrawal from the front line to rear defensive boxes, with the 8th Army split up into a host of untrained Battle Groups, and vague references to armoured army reserves, were indeed a serious indictment of General Auchinleck. That Bernard was genuinely appalled is confirmed by his Diary, drawn up on the eve of the battle of Alamein, in which he was similarly emphatic:

I arrived at Army HQ at about 1100 hours on 13 August. The atmosphere was dismal and dreary; the HQ has had AUCHINLECK and DORMAN-SMITH living there for some weeks and was obviously suffering from this. The battle situation was explained to me by the acting Army Commander, Gen. RAMSDEN, the Comd of 30 Corps.

I cross-examined him, and the BGS about the Army plan for a withdrawal if ROMMEL attacked.

Certain orders had been issued about the withdrawal, but they were very indefinite and no one seemed clear as to exactly what was to be done. There was an air of uncertainty and a lack of 'grip'.

[1] Kippenberger, op. cit.
[2] War Diary, HQ 13 Corps, August 1942, loc. cit.
[3] Letter of 12.10.42.

583

Army HQ was completely out of touch with Air HQ Western Desert.

It was clear to me that the situation was quite impossible, and, in fact, dangerous, and I decided at once that I must take instant action. I also decided that it was useless to consult GHQ and that I would take responsibility myself.

At 1400 hours on 13 August I telegraphed to GHQ that I had assumed command of Eighth Army; I learnt later that the arrival of this telegram made AUCHINLECK very angry as he had told me not to take over till 15 August.

I then cancelled the orders about a further withdrawal. I issued orders that if ROMMEL attacked we would fight him on the ground where we now stood; there would be NO WITHDRAWAL and NO SURRENDER.

Having sent off this telegram to GHQ, I then set out to see my Corps Commanders, so as to be away if any protest came. My order of 'no withdrawal' involved a complete change of policy. If we were to fight where we stood, the defences must have depth, and ammunition, water, rations, etc. must be stored in the forward areas. I wanted more troops brought forward from the DELTA. Once General ALEXANDER became C-in-C all would be well as he would get a real move on; but he was not to take over till 15 August; the existing régime at GHQ regarded me as an unpleasant new broom, so I had to be careful.

The 'unpleasant new broom' had indeed begun to sweep – and not a moment too soon. 8th Army intelligence estimated that by 15 August Rommel would have 200 serviceable Mk III and IV Panzer tanks, 80 guns, and 100 anti-tank guns alone in Afrika Korps, which would boast 15,000 men; '90 Light Division should muster 5000 men with possibly 100 anti-tank guns by the same date. Should the enemy then decide to live by "hunt and peck" supply methods during operations there can be little else to delay the beginning of his offensive save our own action.'[1] 164th (German) Division would furnish a further 10,000 men, 48 guns, and 50 anti-tank guns. Even on 10 August, the day Auchinleck left 8th Army Headquarters, it was estimated that Rommel already had a field force of some 37,000 German soldiers, 185 medium German tanks, 203 guns, and 295 anti-tank guns including '88s'; his Italian contingent was smaller, numbering 28,700 men and 110 second-class tanks, but a disturbing 240 guns and 270 anti-tank guns: a fighting army of 65,700 men, 295 tanks, 443 guns and 565 anti-tank guns. Given such strength there seemed every likelihood that an immediate offensive might be launched. One German prisoner, on regaining consciousness after an abortive raid,

[1] War Diary, 8th Army HQ, 'I' Section, August 1942, loc. cit.

had even been heard to say, 'Has Rommel broken through in the South yet?'[1]

Bernard's premature assumption of command, then, was not simply the deliberate insubordination of a man intent on snubbing Auchinleck while adopting his defensive plans, as some writers have claimed.[2] To Bernard the situation was both incredible and critical; and, having issued his orders to rescind all plans for withdrawal, Bernard made straight for the vital area of 8th Army's defences, manned by 13 Corps. Having lost its Corps Commander on 7 August, 13 Corps had been temporarily commanded by Major-General 'Callum' Renton, GOC 7th Armoured Division until the evening of 11 August – when the redoubtable Lt-General Freyberg, GOC 2nd New Zealand Division, took over as Acting Corps Commander. Freyberg, still recovering from wounds received in July, was much opposed to the splitting up of his division into Auchinleck's mobile Battle Groups. Thus, when the new 8th Army Commander arrived at 13 Corps Headquarters in the early afternoon of 13 August 1942, Freyberg was the first to welcome his new approach. Two years younger than Montgomery, they shared the same Christian name and experience on the Western Front in World War One. Freyberg's defence of Crete had demonstrated his failings as a higher commander – but as a Divisional Commander he probably had no equal in the Allied armies. It was said that there was no task which, once given, the 2nd New Zealand Division would not carry out; and, when Bernard Montgomery announced that he was cancelling Auchinleck's planned withdrawal from the front line to the rear 'defended OP areas', Freyberg was delighted. The New Zealanders, Montgomery instructed, were to 'stay put'. There would be no mass evacuation to Alam Halfa, and *no* fragmentation into Battle Groups. The front line from the Ruweisat Ridge to Alam Nayil would no longer be an FDL: it would be *the* defence line, to be held dead or alive. When Freyberg asked who would then man the Alam Halfa area, Bernard told him not to worry: there were plenty of units wasting in the Delta – they would be brought up. The important thing, he stressed, was to look to the front, not backwards: to see that his defences were prepared in depth, with proper attention paid to minefields and to artillery so as to enable the chief gunner, if necessary, to bring the combined weight of divisional, even corps artillery, on any one spot. Auchinleck's policy of 'mobility and fluidity' was henceforth redundant. In this battle the New Zealanders would simply stand firm. They would be provided with a further brigade of infantry from the Delta. All unnecessary transport was meanwhile to be sent back; stores of ammunition and supplies

[1] Ibid.
[2] Cf. Correlli Barnett, John Connell, Roger Parkinson, R. W. Thompson, inter alia.

must be well forward. Moreover, once the coming German offensive had been brought to a standstill, then the New Zealanders could begin preparing for a more aggressive mobile battle-role in conjunction with the new corps de chasse – a role equivalent to that of the German famous 90th Light Division.

As for the Corps perspective, Bernard stated, there was every possibility that Rommel might launch an armoured thrust to outflank 8th Army; however, if the front line of 30 Corps and the New Zealanders held firm, Rommel would be unable to press on towards Cairo and Alexandria for fear of becoming entirely cut off; he must therefore wheel and try to roll up 8th Army from the rear. Provided Alam Halfa was properly garrisoned, there was nothing to fear. 8th Army would be meeting Rommel on ground of its own choosing. Given well-sited, cohesively-controlled artillery and anti-tank guns, and judicious husbanding of 8th Army's own armour, Rommel could achieve nothing. Thereafter it would be 8th Army's turn to take the offensive. 30 Corps would become responsible for the whole front; 13 Corps would be withdrawn to train as a highly mobile, armoured break-in Corps, in which the New Zealanders themselves would be re-equipped as a motorised Infantry Division, similar to Bernard's erstwhile 3rd Division, but with its own brigade of support tanks.

Leaving Freyberg to draw up orders embodying his instructions, Bernard left 13 Corps HQ and returned to his own unsatisfactory headquarters on the Ruweisat Ridge. He had ordered de Guingand to arrange fighter cover by the Desert Air Force at 1800 hours, so that he might address the Army Headquarters staff without interruption from enemy air attack. To one waiting officer this 'Air Umbrella' seemed quite risible:

> We thought this was a very comic thing – because we didn't think we were very precious. And, what is more, before Monty actually arrived the 'Air Umbrella' had disappeared – because he was late. They'd gone before he arrived, which made the 'Air Umbrella' an even more hilariously enjoyable concept.[1]

This was Major 'Bill' Williams, G2 Intelligence, who little anticipated the effect Montgomery was to have, not only on 8th Army, but on his own meteoric military career. For if the headquarters staff was baffled by the succession of defeat and failure – drummed home by the very vulnerability of the headquarters site to German shelling and air attacks – it was doubly sceptical about a new Commander sent from England. He would be the fourth Army Commander within a year: He did not have 'sand in his shoes', and had probably no idea of the extent to which Rommel had transformed operations in the desert. Moreover, when Montgomery did finally appear half

---

[1] Sir Edgar Williams, loc. cit.

an hour late at 6.30 p.m. he looked, in his new desert shirt and slacks, absurdly thin and small: a foxy, pointed face with high cheekbones and long, sharp nose beneath the peaked hat.

It was a large gathering of between fifty and sixty officers, for although it was so far forward it was not a tactical HQ but represented all the branches of 8th Army Headquarters from operations to artillery, engineers to administration, Intelligence to plans, signals to staff duties.

The talk Bernard was to give was undoubtedly historic, for it exemplified the manner in which a great general, by sheer force of personality and military intellect, can re-create the morale of a broken Army. 'It was one of his greatest efforts,' de Guingand was to chronicle some years later. 'The effect of the address was electric – it was terrific! And we all went to bed that night with new hope in our hearts, and a great confidence in the future of our Army. I wish someone had taken it down in shorthand, for it would have become a classic of its kind.'[1]

By good fortune Bernard's address *was* taken down in shorthand, and found its way into a thin manilla file in the War Office in London, where it was preserved. Entitled 'Address to Officers of HQ Eighth Army by General Montgomery, On taking over command of the army 13 August 1942,' it gives the authentic wording of one of the seminal military addresses in British history, as intimately revealing of the general on the verge of greatness as of the man only weeks away from world acclaim. The officers stood to attention and saluted. Bernard returned the salute, stood on the steps of his predecessor's caravan, bade the gathering to sit in the sand, and addressed them thus:

1. I want first of all to introduce myself to you. You do not know me. I do not know you. But we have got to work together; therefore we must understand each other and we must have confidence in each other. I have only been here a few hours. But from what I have seen and heard since I arrived I am prepared to say, here and now, that I have confidence in you. We will then work together as a team; and together we will gain the confidence of this great Army and go forward to final victory in Africa.

2. I believe that one of the first duties of a commander is to create what I call 'atmosphere', and in that atmosphere his staff, subordinate commanders, and troops will live and work and fight.

   I do not like the general atmosphere I find here. It is an atmosphere of doubt, of looking back to select the next place to which to withdraw, of loss of confidence in our ability to

[1] *Operation Victory*, op. cit.

defeat Rommel, of desperate defence measures by reserves in preparing positions in Cairo and the Delta.

All that must cease.

Let us have a new atmosphere.

3. The defence of Egypt lies here at Alamein and on the Ruweisat Ridge. What is the use of digging trenches in the Delta? It is quite useless; if we lose this position we lose Egypt; all the fighting troops now in the Delta must come here at once, and will. *Here* we will stand and fight; there will be no further withdrawal. I have ordered that all plans and instructions dealing with further withdrawal are to be burnt, and at once. We will stand and fight *here*.

    If we can't stay here, then let us stay here dead.

4. I want to impress on everyone that the bad times are over. Fresh Divisions from the UK are now arriving in Egypt, together with ample reinforcements for our present Divisions. We have 300 to 400 Sherman new tanks coming and these are actually being unloaded at Suez *now*.[1] Our mandate from the Prime Minister is to destroy the Axis forces in North Africa; I have seen it, written on half a sheet of notepaper. And it will be done. If anyone here thinks it can't be done, let him go at once; I don't want any doubters in this party. It can be done, and it will be done: beyond any possibility of doubt.

5. Now I understand that Rommel is expected to attack at any moment. Excellent. Let him attack.

    I would sooner it didn't come for a week, just give me time to sort things out. If we have two weeks to prepare we will be sitting pretty; Rommel can attack as soon as he likes, after that, and I hope he does.

6. Meanwhile, we ourselves will start to plan a great offensive; it will be the beginning of a campaign which will hit Rommel and his Army for six right out of Africa.

    But first we must create a reserve Corps, mobile and strong in armour, which we will train *out of the line*. Rommel has always had such a force in his Africa Corps, which is never used to hold the line but which is always in reserve, available for striking blows. Therein has been his great strength. We will create such a Corps ourselves, a British Panzer Corps; it will consist of two armoured Divisions and one motorized Division; I gave orders yesterday for it to begin to form, back in the Delta.

    I have no intention of launching our great attack until we are completely ready; there will be pressure from many quarters

---

[1] This was a deliberate exaggeration. The Shermans were not due to arrive until early September 1942.

to attack soon; *I will not attack until we are ready*, and you can rest assured on that point.

Meanwhile, if Rommel attacks while we are preparing, let him do so with pleasure; we will merely continue with our own preparations and *we* will attack when *we* are ready, and not before.

7. I want to tell you that I always work on the Chief-of-Staff system. I have nominated Brigadier de Guingand as Chief-of-Staff Eighth Army. I will issue orders through him. Whatever he says will be taken as coming from me and will be acted on *at once*. I understand there has been a great deal of 'belly-aching' out here. By 'belly-aching' I mean inventing poor reasons for *not* doing what one has been told to do.

All this is to stop at once.

I will tolerate no belly-aching.

If anyone objects to doing what he is told, then he can get out of it; and at once. I want that made very clear right down through the Eighth Army.

8. I have little more to say just at present. And some of you may think it is quite enough and may wonder if I am mad.

I assure you I am quite sane.

I understand there are people who often think I am slightly mad; so often that I now regard it as rather a compliment.

All I have to say to that is that if I am slightly mad, there are a large number of people I could name who are raving lunatics!!

What I have done is to get over to you the 'atmosphere' in which we will now work and fight; you must see that atmosphere permeates right down through the Eighth Army to the most junior private soldier. All the soldiers must know what is wanted; when they see it coming to pass there will be a surge of confidence throughout the Army.

I ask you to give me your confidence and to have faith that what I have said will come to pass.

There is much work to be done.

The orders I have given about no further withdrawal will mean a complete change in the layout of our dispositions; also that we must begin to prepare for our great offensive.

The first thing to do is to move our HQ to a decent place where we can live in reasonable comfort and where the Army Staff can all be together and side by side with the HQ of the Desert Air Force. This is a frightful place here, depressing, unhealthy and a rendez-vous for every fly in Africa; we shall do no good work here. Let us get over there by the sea where it is fresh and healthy. If Officers are to do good work they must have decent messes, and be comfortable. So off we go on the new line.

The Chief-of-Staff will be issuing orders on many points

very shortly, and I am always available to be consulted by the senior officer of the staff. The great point to remember is that we are going to finish with this chap Rommel once and for all. It will be quite easy. There is no doubt about it.

He is definitely a nuisance. Therefore we will hit him a crack and finish with him.[1]

Bernard stepped down, the assembled officers rose and stood to attention. 'One could have heard a pin drop if such a thing were possible in the sand of the desert,' Bernard recollected in his *Memoirs*. 'But it certainly had a profound effect and a spirit of hope, anyway of clarity, was born that evening.'

[1] Cabinet Papers (CAB 106/654), PRO.

CHAPTER SIX

The Formula for Victory

Even in the final years of his life de Guingand remembered Mont-gomery's first address as 'brilliant, absolutely brilliant';[1] even the sceptical Oxford don 'Bill' Williams found his impression of ridicu-lous hilarity over the Air Umbrella altering to one of reluctant admiration. He had been in Intelligence at GHQ Cairo until June, when at de Guingand's prompting he was posted to 8th Army. In both positions he had been primarily responsible for interpreting and relaying Ultra – and had become frustrated and testy over the pathetic use to which this unique intelligence had been put.

'I can remember the address,' he confided almost forty years later;

> I think the interesting thing was the astonishing removal of dubiety, the feeling that, well, thank God this chap has got a grip. He talks the most astonishing sort of stuff, but he has the meat of the gospel as it were. There was very much a feeling of 'Well, we'll give it a go'. I think we had this rather arrogant view that we'd had rather a lot of generals through our hands, in our day. And this was a new one – but he was talking sense, although in a very sort of strange way: the manner, the phraseology. You've got to remember that the sort of people I'd talk to would be the intel-ligentsia so to speak and this sort of stuff was straight out of school speech-day. And yet . . . I remember it was, it was a feeling of great exhilaration: a feeling that here was somebody who was really going to use his staff. And I remember relating it purely personally to this sort of feeling: well, God, he's the sort of chap who's going to be able to *use* Ultra, you see. You had this feeling that we kept producing stuff that was out of this world in terms of the amount of information we were getting about the enemy and somehow it never seemed to get put to any purpose.[2]

Williams's feelings were mirrored through the staff. Lt-Colonel Belchem, who had been in charge of Staff Duties at 8th Army since it was formed in September 1941, was also 'rather surprised' by the

---

[1] De Guingand, loc. cit.
[2] Sir Edgar Williams, loc. cit.

new Army Commander's confidence. Churchill's phrase, 'a brave but baffled Army', was to Belchem

> a polite way of saying we were all fed up. I liked the Auk, but had lost confidence in his generalship.
>
> We were fed up because we didn't think the Germans were really better than we were, except that they had better equipment as regards tanks, and therefore what had really happened: we had lost the confidence of the troops in our leadership – in the leadership. Because we didn't see why we were being pushed around and had been pushed around so much by Rommel – 'the bogey-man'.[1]

Belchem had been nonplussed by Auchinleck's edict that Rommel was not to be mentioned by name in 8th Army: 'Even if he were a superman, it would still be highly undesirable that our men should credit him with supernatural powers . . . We must refer to 'the Germans' or 'the Axis powers' or 'the enemy' and not always keep harping on Rommel.'[2] In fact, Belchem considered this 'the most extraordinary cable that's ever been sent in the annals of the British Army',[3] and thought it typical of Auchinleck's strangely weak grasp of reality – particularly its curious postscript: 'PS. I am *not* jealous of Rommel'. The reality was that Rommel, as the personification of German drive and efficiency, was there to stay; and Montgomery was, after eleven months of often bitter fighting, the first British general to recognise, instinctively and within hours of his arrival in the desert, that the way to overcome the 'bogey-man' image of Rommel was to supplant it with his own.

Major Williams also noted the way the new Army Commander was prepared to use the personality cult of Rommel to his own advantage; as did young Captain Keating, of the Army Film and Photographic Unit, who despite his age was probably the most seasoned campaigner in the desert, having served in Norway, France, Dunkirk, France again, the desert, Greece, Crete, Tobruk, Syria, Iraq, Persia, and the retreat to Alamein. He had photographed the first 88-mm gun, had seen de Gaulle in action; become the confidant of generals from Wavell to Auchinleck, whom he admired, personally, as a man and soldier of the highest integrity and natural leadership. As Freddie de Guingand's escort in the desert he had eaten regularly in the 'meat-safe', and found that by and large it was successful as fly-protection, but highly vulnerable to enemy air raid; indeed he remembered seeing Auchinleck – 'who was a very big man' – throwing himself not only upon his ADC but a third un-

---

[1] Major-General David Belchem, interview of 28.9.79.
[2] Quoted in Desmond Young, *Rommel*, London, 1950.
[3] Loc. cit.

fortunate soul in a slit trench one morning when attacked by Messerschmitts. Keating was one of the few officers who had met Montgomery before – had been made to sit beside Bernard at table when escorting a visiting journalist to the 3rd Division in France early in 1940.

> I do know that when I heard Montgomery was coming, I was very excited. Excited because I knew his attitude to me personally, and the press.
> I knew too that he'd taken on the defence of England because he was the only commander in France who brought his formation back intact from the débâcle. And he had been ready – I think someone had told me his 3rd Division was ready to fight within 2 weeks of Dunkirk.[1]

Looking back many years later, Keating blessed the sense of professionalism which Montgomery brought with him that first day in the desert, and the 'electrifying effect' of his first 'harangue'.

> Monty knew all the rules of the conduct of war and the fighting of battles. He was like a surgeon, you know: he could take your tummy out and put it back. And I was, by this time, the time of his arrival, I had already personally experienced endless defeats. I'd been wounded five times; and here I was, sure that this was the man who had victory. And if you ask me to explain why I was sure – it was something he exuded, it was professionalism.[2]

In the days to come Keating would virtually become Bernard's 'PR' man, a 'colossal protagonist for Monty because I remembered him from France, and his marvellous personality when at table he seated me on his right; and here I was preaching the Monty doctrine in a very big way. I was regarded by the old hands – who were not to be neglected – as slightly disloyal in throwing my hat in so much with him. Monty of course was regarded as rather a vulgar chap . . . But I knew in my heart of hearts that here was a man who had the formula for victory.'[3]

For Colonel Richardson, G1 in charge of Plans, Bernard's address was a turning point of the war. He too had a high opinion of Auchinleck as a man and a leader, but thought him a 'terribly bad judge of men. I mean there is no question of the Auk's moral and physical courage. All else had failed,' he remembered of the moment when he joined Auchinleck on 25 June 1942 after the fall of Tobruk.

[1] Geoffrey Keating, interview of 30.11.79.
[2] Ibid.
[3] Ibid.

593

Ritchie had failed, everything else had failed, he was being tormented by Churchill and so forth. He didn't lose his head, but at the end he was a defeated man. There was no prospect in my mind of him ever – even if he'd been given thousands of new tanks and new divisions and so on – there was no possibility in my mind of that brain ever being able to produce a new élan.[1]

It was Montgomery's unique achievement to produce this élan from the moment he arrived: to restore leadership, purpose and morale to an exhausted army. As one of his staff, who joined him before the Battle of Alamein, put it: 'He made you better than you thought you were;'[2] or another: 'Monty absolutely deserved all the credit he could get for the way he changed us. I mean, we were different people. We suddenly had a spring in our step.'[3]

The seeds of a new army had indeed been sown. It was as though, in their hearts, the staff of 8th Army had been waiting for this moment, knew they were capable of better things. The chief administrative officer, Brigadier Sir Brian Robertson, was forty-seven years old, his deputy, Colonel Miles Graham, was forty-eight, and Brigadier White, the Signals CO, was forty-five, but the actual operations staff were still in their thirties: Colonel Mainwaring G1 (Ops) was thirty-six, Colonel Richardson G1 (plans) was thirty-four, Colonel Belchem, G1 (Staff Duties) was thirty-one; and Major Williams, the G2 Intelligence, a mere twenty-nine. As Williams remarked many years later, the two years of desert fighting, culminating in the catastrophe at Gazala, had sloughed off most of the excess 'flesh' from the staff. Geoffrey Keating noted the same thing happening within the fighting units: a skeleton of brave young officers and NCOs who were the backbone of the army – and who only lacked generals capable of giving them the leadership they deserved.

To these young men, baffled by the reverses of the summer of 1942, it was leadership from above that was lacking. In his eve-of-Alamein diary entry, Bernard concluded:

The condition of Eighth Army as described above is not over-painted; it was almost unbelievable. From what I know now it was quite clear that the reverses we had suffered at GAZALA and East of it, which finally forced us back to within 60 miles of ALEXANDRIA, should never have happened.

Gross mis-management, faulty command, and bad staff work, had been the cause of the whole thing.

But the final blame must rest on General AUCHINLECK for allowing an inexperienced General like RITCHIE to mishandle

[1] General Sir Charles Richardson, loc. cit.
[2] Sir William Mather, interview of 23.1.80.
[3] Robert Priestley, interview of 18.2.80.

grossly a fine fighting Army, and for allowing a policy of dispersion to rule.

Divisions were split up into bits and pieces all over the desert; the armour was not concentrated; the gunners had forgotten the art of employing artillery in a concentrated form.

If changes in the higher command had not been made early in August, we would have lost EGYPT.

Actually, they were made only just in time.

A clean sweep was required in the Middle East, and new Commanders had to be brought in; Commanders who would NOT be influenced by past events, but who would take each situation on its merits and decide on a method suitable to the occasion and to local conditions.

When Churchill came to read a copy of this part of the diary later that year, his heart must have swelled; it had taken courage and ruthlessness to make such changes of command at a critical moment in the war. However, Churchill's pleasure will have been tempered by the succeeding remarks:

GOTT was to have commanded Eighth Army. I am convinced that this appointment was not sound and might have led to disaster. GOTT was one of the old regime and had been in EGYPT all the war; his tactical ideas were influenced by past events; his plan in 13 Corps for fighting ROMMEL if he attacked in August was very bad and if it had been put into effect I consider the Eighth Army would have been defeated.

On the evidence now freely available to the public, there is little doubt Bernard was right. The chaos produced by the mass exodus of divisions from their forward defence lines, the lingering obsession with mobility, the lack of a proper garrison at Alam Halfa, the dispersion of armour, and the fragmentation of the infantry into Battle Groups might well have resulted in the greatest British military disaster of the war. As the G2 (Ops) at 8th Army Headquarters noted in a later footnote to his own diary of the time: 'Fortunately this tactical doctrine was never put into practice.'[1]

That Bernard's new directive, two days before he was due to take over command of 8th Army, altered the whole concept of 13 Corps and 30 Corps defence is amply proven by the records kept in the unpublished War Diaries of the formations. Among the incoming signals logged at HQ 8th Army after the Army Commander's visit to 13 Corps on 13 August was the following from Lt-General Freyberg, dictated at 2120 hours:

---

[1] Major-General M. St. J. Oswald, op. cit.

Consequent on decisions given by Army Commander today. Request immediate despatch arriving if possible tomorrow one Bde Gp complete with A/Tk and Fd Arty for Garrison locality F rpt F [Alam Halfa ridge] followed by remainder Div. On arrival 21 Ind Bde will be concentrated locality E rpt E [the other end of the Alam Halfa ridge]. Further request approval dump three days water and ammunition 8th Army rates plus sufficient 25 pdr ammunition to make 150 rds per gun in addition first line. On completion above requests satisfied N Z Div fwd position and localities E and F will be sufficiently strongly garrisoned and furnished carry out Army Commander's immediate policy. Consider present absence of adequate garrison E and F most dangerous and prejudicial to carrying out fresh policy.[1]

There was no doubt at least in Freyberg's eyes that Montgomery had laid down a 'fresh policy'. Those later historians who claimed that Bernard had merely adopted Auchinleck's plans while reserving the credit for himself were standing up for a great man but a deeply flawed commander. Without access to the documents in the War Office they remained naïve, even in some cases deceitful. All were duped by the dismissed *bête noire* of 8th Army, 'Chink' Dorman-Smith; Montgomery's unofficial biographer, Alun Chalfont, even declared in 1976, when all the 1942 War Diaries were long since available, that 'Montgomery adopted this plan [the Auchinleck–Dorman-Smith appreciation] with one or two minor variations and changes in emphasis. Yet, characteristically, in his memoirs he seems to deny credit to anyone but himself'.[2] What was characteristic was in fact the wilful ignorance of certain English historians and journalists who were disturbed by the ' "Monty" myth' and sought retrospectively both to denigrate him and replace it by an Auchinleck mythology. General Sir Charles Richardson, reflecting on this in 1979, remarked: 'I think it's a strange paradox really, because Corelli Barnett/"Chink" Dorman-Smith (I bracket them together) gave the Auk a brief period of undeserved success as it were; but the pendulum may swing too far because of that phoney "success".'[3]

To Richardson and the other members of the operations and planning staff in 8th Army who had all served under Auchinleck, there was not the smallest doubt but that Montgomery entirely re-cast the approaching battle in defence of Egypt.

In 1962, when annotating his volume of First World War letters together with some from World War Two, Bernard himself wrote:

Much controversy has arisen over the question of who made the plan for the Battle of Alam Halfa, and later for the battle of

[1] War Diary, 8th Army HQ, August 1942 (WO 169/3911), PRO.
[2] A. Chalfont, *Montgomery of Alamein*, op. cit.
[3] Loc. cit.

Alamein. Alexander's war memoirs have merely confused the issue. The plain truth is that I had only one order from Alexander: to defeat Rommel. The plans for the defensive battle of Alam Halfa, and the offensive battle of Alamein, were made by me and my staff at Eighth Army HQ and Alexander was merely told by me what I was planning to do; he himself has given the impression that the plan for Alam Halfa was 'accepted' by me. This is utterly untrue. I took over *no* plans from Auchinleck, and was given *no* instructions by Alexander. Alam Halfa was never in the picture at all until I took over. I have, of course, never said this. It is far better to let the controversy die down. There is quite enough trouble in the world already without making more trouble by arguing 'who did what' in Hitler's war.

This statement, made by a man who in other circumstances enjoyed causing controversy, may seem strange; but it is founded on fact. In his *Memoirs*, Bernard did not relate the truly disastrous state of 8th Army planning and command when he arrived in the desert; but the little he did reveal of Auchinleck's contingency plans for withdrawal – in order to explain his own orders for no retreat – was enough to create great bitterness between Auchinleck and himself. Thereafter he never referred to the subject again.

As to Bernard's remark that 'Alam Halfa was never in the picture at all' until he took over, this was – if taken literally – an exaggeration, for the importance of the heights had been acknowledged since early July 1942; but Auchinleck's contingency plan to evacuate the front line and withdraw the entire New Zealand Division some fifteen miles in the midst of battle, to a series of ridges held only by a few battalions of British and Indian infantry with a single regiment of artillery – the move being covered by British armour that would be unable to react to enemy moves until the New Zealanders reached Alam Halfa – was in Bernard's eyes so ridiculous as to be unthinkable: which was why he issued his orders for 'no withdrawal' before even setting off to see Freyberg on 13 August. Moreover, when he did reach Freyberg at 13 Corps HQ, it was to discover that the ten-mile ridge of Alam Halfa was occupied by a single battalion of Scottish infantry, and one and a half battalions of Indian troops[1] – who had only been stationed there a week and had not done much more than dig holes and stretch small lengths of wire.

Moreover, although Auchinleck had troops in the Delta, there is no suggestion in any of the surviving documents or in anyone's recollection that Auchinleck ever intended to bring them forward to reinforce his positions at Alamein. As the G2 (Ops) at Army Headquarters later recalled, Dorman-Smith's attitude to infantry had become one of fear of encumbrance in the event of withdrawal.

[1] War Diary, HQ 13 Corps, 2 August 1942, loc. cit.

Demoralised by the superiority of the German tanks, and the poor performance of the 2-pounder British anti-tank gun, Dorman-Smith 'thought infantry were a liability. All that was required was for our own armour to be defeated, and the luckless infantry had no future – they had nothing but 25-pounders to protect them. "The sooner we have just tanks and anti-tank guns and artillery, and send the bulk of the infantry back to the Delta where they may be able to hold something . . ." – that was the sort of feeling,' Major-General Oswald later recalled.[1]

For Bernard, unshadowed by the failures and defeats since Gazala, the picture looked very different. Instead of sending infantry back, troops must be brought forward to help create a bastion so strong Rommel would have no chance of storming it – and for this he required three brigades: one to reinforce the New Zealanders in the front line, and two to man the Alam Halfa heights.

The question now was how quickly Bernard could procure the three brigades of 44th Division from the Delta – one of which, as we have seen, Auchinleck had ordered to be kept *east* of the Nile in case of a successful Axis break-through. In his *Memoirs*, Bernard recalled that 'on de Guingand's advice I decided to make no demands on GHQ as a result of the change in policy till evening of the 14th August', but his memory was here at fault, and such diplomacy out of character. In fact de Guingand was told to telephone GHQ and ask for the *immediate* despatch of 44th Division on the evening of 13 August. De Guingand claimed he spoke direct to Major-General McCreery, Alexander's new Chief-of-Staff;[2] in Field-Marshal Harding's later recollection it was he, as existing DCGS, who took the call.[3] Either way, de Guingand's request was refused, on the grounds that the 44th Division had only been in Egypt three weeks, was not yet properly equipped for desert warfare and after the disasters of July was in any case considered too green to be put straight into line. According to de Guingand this was reported to the new Army Commander, who angrily snatched the telephone and insisted on being put through direct to Alexander. To de Guingand's astonishment, Bernard 'then convinced Alex in about two or three minutes to send the division. You see,' de Guingand explained at the end of his life, 'Alex looked on Monty as his military superior. Monty had taught Alex at the staff college and the relationship remained basically the same.'[4] Harding's memory was different in detail, though not in substance. He was still unsure who *was* C-in-C. Auchinleck was consulted. 'Have you asked Alexander? See what he says,' Auchinleck told Harding.[5] Alexander was found talking to the

[1] Major-General M. St. J. Oswald, loc. cit.
[2] De Guingand, loc. cit.
[3] Field-Marshal Lord Harding, loc. cit.
[4] De Guingand, loc. cit.
[5] Field-Marshal Lord Harding, interview of 20.11.80.

British Ambassador and told of Bernard's urgent request. 'Is that what Monty wants?' he asked. 'Yes,' Harding replied. 'Well, do it.'[1]

A call was put straight through to the Commander of 44th Division in the Delta. In its War Diary for 13 August 1942 is recorded the simple entry:

> 2200 hours: Orders received for 44 Division to move into 8 Army Area.

Whatever the confusion over who was in command in Cairo, within 8th Army there could be no doubt about who was the new Army Commander or what was the 'fresh policy'. The BGS of 13 Corps for instance sent out a signal that night to all 'heads of branches' of 13 Corps, ordering them to appear for a conference at 13 Corps Headquarters at 0900 hours the next morning, 14 August 1942[2] – a conference at which 'the following new policy' was underlined:

> A. *Immediate Policy*: to consider our present positions as the main line of defence involving the strengthening of the New Zealand position by an all-round minefield and the addition of a Brigade group of 44 Division.
> 2. Occupying the Alam Halfa and Khadim defended localities by the remaining two Brigade groups of 44 Div.
> 3. Placing under command 13 Corps 1 battalion 23 Armoured Brigade in area 890 280 to prevent the enemy establishing an anti/tank screen to the south of this area.
> 4. Enlarging and strengthening of the minefields in 7 Armoured Div front. At the same time keeping our forces in the south in the highest state of mobility.
>
> B. *Long-term Policy*
> 1. 30 Corps to assume control of the whole front.
> 2. 13 Corps HQ to be withdrawn to an area suitable for the organization of a highly mobile force consisting of 2 armoured divisions and 1 infantry division.
> 3. Infantry divisions in defended localities to have their transports reduced to the number necessary for providing necessary mobility for reserves only.[3]

Orders in 30 Corps would mirror these. Thus already, on 13 August, Bernard Montgomery may be said to have laid the foundation stone of his victories at Alam Halfa and Alamein. That evening he had a long talk with de Guingand. Finally Bernard retired to bed in one of

---

[1] Field-Marshal Lord Harding, interview of 23.5.1979.
[2] War Diary, 8th Army HQ, August 1942, loc. cit.
[3] War Diary, HQ 13 Corps, August 1942, loc. cit.

Auchinleck's caravans. 'By the time I went to bed that night I was tired . . . I'm afraid it was with an insubordinate smile that I fell asleep: I was issuing orders to an Army which someone else reckoned he commanded!' he recalled impishly in his *Memoirs*. For Brigadier de Guingand, now the Army Commander's deputy in the literal sense of the word, there was little sleep, though. The great tide of re-organisation and redeployment was just beginning. At 2320 hours de Guingand sent a signal to Rear Army HQ and to 13 Corps:

> Warning order. Plan will be made immediate for routing major formation ex DELTA for 13 Corps. Possible equivalent Brigade Group may leave DELTA 14 August. Rear Army arrange diversion columns to C track. 13 Corps arrange guides to meet on C track at P due south of HAMMAM station. Traffic reps will be ordered ahead to grids 152 and Ops reps to Main 13 Corps. New formation will relieve 21 Ind Inf Bde Gp on arrival . . .[1]

In Cairo, meanwhile, some of Auchinleck's staff seemed still to be obsessed by preparations for GHQ withdrawal to Jerusalem. Lt-General Corbett, Auchinleck's chief staff officer, had that day signed his latest orders to the head of the 'Q' administrative staff following the general evacuation plan laid down by Dorman-Smith on 10 August:

> *13 August 1942 G(Op) 3052 to Col Q (B)*
> As a result of the appointment of an additional DCGS to GHQ, air passages will now be required for 4 officers, viz
>   Generals Corbett, Dorman-Smith, Harding and Brig. Davy [DMO][2]

The days of British evacuation to Palestine, however, were over and the only air passages Corbett and Dorman-Smith would be making would be to obscurity.

[1] War Diary, 8th Army HQ, August 1942, loc. cit.
[2] War Diary, GHQ Middle East (G Ops), August 1942 (WO 169/3800), PRO.

CHAPTER SEVEN

Preparations for Alam Halfa

'I was woken up soon after dawn the next morning by an officer with the morning situation report. I was extremely angry and told him no one was ever to come near me with situation reports; I did not want to be bothered with details of patrol actions and things of that sort. He apologized profusely and said that Auchinleck was always woken early and given the dawn reports.

'I said I was not Auchinleck and that if anything was wrong the Chief-of-Staff would tell me; if nothing was wrong I didn't want to be told,' Bernard recalled in his *Memoirs*.

The duty officer was not the only one to be surprised. Immediately after breakfast on 14 August 1942 Bernard left his headquarters to visit 30 Corps area – where he would acquire his first distinctive desert hat, an Australian bush hat on which he would gradually pin the badges of all the regiments he inspected – and to check defences of the vital Ruweisat Ridge in the centre of the British front line. Brigadier de Guingand meanwhile departed in the opposite direction. When Auchinleck's GHQ Liaison Officer arrived at 1230 hours from Cairo, he therefore found the Army Commander's cupboard bare; moreover his staff now flatly refused to co-operate with Auchinleck's proposed 'Deltaforce War Game' for which 8th Army had been requested to provide two staff officers. 'In view of 8th Army's signal U453 timed 0904/14,' the officer reported, 'it is confirmed that no, repeat no, staff officers will be available.' Similarly Auchinleck's request for a 'Plan of Wadi Natrun defences to be given to staff officer who was organizing it' was treated with contempt. Colonel Mainwaring, the G1 (Ops) 'stated that in view of 8th Army Commander's new order for "no looking over your shoulder" and "fighting on present position" there is no need for a Wadi Natrun defensive position, therefore there is no action required.'[1]

Bernard's edicts and his address to his staff had evidently done the trick: the staff was behind him. The Liaison Officer concluded his report with a note about 'Future Moves'. Neither Army Commander nor BGS were seen, 'latter being on a recce in the Burg-el-Arab area,

---

[1] LO Reports from 8th Army, War Diary, GHQ Middle East (G Ops), August 1942, loc. cit.

neighbourhood of HQ RAF, Western Desert Force. This recce was with a view to moving HQ 8th Army to a site in this locality. The present hope is to move on Sunday 16/8'.[1]

It was the end of the disastrous separation of RAF and Army which Auchinleck had permitted. As Bernard wrote in his diary:

> When I took over command, Army HQ was right forward, and Air HQ Western Desert was right back near the landing grounds. The Army was fighting *its* battle and the RAF was fighting *its* battle. There was no combined HQ, with the two Commanders and the two staffs completely in each other's pockets. I gather there had been very close touch in the past. But the arrival of AUCHINLECK and DORMAN-SMITH at Army HQ seems to have altered that; the RAF had no use for either of these two, and Army HQ and the two staffs seem gradually to have drifted apart.
>
> I decided to remedy this at once and moved Army HQ back to Air HQ, and brought the AOC and his senior staff officers into my mess. This was a good move, and from that moment we never looked back.

Whether the RAF had 'no use' for Auchinleck and Dorman-Smith is debatable; there was certainly a feeling within the Desert Air Force that the RAF had saved 8th Army after Gazala, and that the Army was suffering a crisis of generalship. The Commanding Officer of the Desert Air Force was 'Mary' Coningham; as 'Bill' Williams remembered, Coningham considered himself very much the 'king of the desert' at this time.[2] He welcomed this sudden move for closer collaboration, as did Tedder, the Air C-in-C of the Middle East; but neither had any idea of the comeback the Army was about to stage, or the manner in which the new Army Commander would usurp the role of *roi du désert*.

While de Guingand reconnoitred the site for the new Army headquarters, by the sea, Bernard continued his blitz on the front. 30 Corps' instructions about the 'organisation of battle groups and the disposal of troops and equipment which are not essential for mobile operations'[3] was to be cancelled immediately: there would be no such mobile operations. Orders for a possible retreat to 'rear defended OP areas' were also cancelled. More mines were to be laid in the front line, anti-tank guns brought forward, together with an interwoven network of defences, covered by a comprehensive corps artillery plan. There would be no withdrawal from these forward positions: 8th Army would stay where it was, dead or alive. Having

[1] Ibid.
[2] Sir Edgar Williams, loc. cit.
[3] Operation Instruction No. 67 of 21.7.42, War Diary, HQ 30 Corps, July 1942, loc. cit.

successfully defended Alamein, it would then be 8th Army's turn to attack.

By 2 o'clock Bernard had reached 5th Indian Division on the Ruweisat Ridge; cover was difficult in the rocky, bare ground, but the ridge was obviously the key position in the front line, therefore it would have to be strengthened by further mines, more dug-in and blasted positions, and the siting of an armoured brigade of Valentine tanks behind the front, Bernard ordered.

South of the Ruweisat Ridge were the New Zealanders, whom Bernard had visited with Freyberg the previous afternoon. Bernard was satisfied that, reinforced by a brigade of 44th Division, the New Zealanders would hold firm. The New Zealanders, equally, were impressed by the new Army Commander – as Brigadier Kippenberger, Commander of 5th New Zealand Brigade, later recalled:

> The new Army Commander made himself felt at once . . . He talked sharply and curtly, without any soft words, asked some searching questions, met the battalion commanders, and left me feeling much stimulated. For a long time we had heard little from Army except querulous grumbles that the men should not go about without their shirts on, that staff officers must always wear the appropriate arm-bands, or things of that sort. Now we were told that we were going to fight, there was no question of retirement to any reserve positions or anywhere else, and to get ahead with our preparations. To make the intention clear our troop-carrying transport was sent a long way back so that we could not run away if we wanted to! There was no more talk of the alternative positions in the rear. We were delighted and the morale of the whole Army went up incredibly.[1]

The important thing was to make sure the 44th Division got up without delay from the Delta – and Bernard ordered that this be given top priority. Alan Moorehead, then a War Correspondent in North Africa, later reconstructed the scene around Alamein:

> Insistently and steadily, hour after hour, the orders went out, and a great commotion spread across the desert. Thousands of men and vehicles on the backward trek were suddenly halted and turned round. Tens of thousands of men, new guns, new tanks and new vehicles began to pour down towards the front from the Nile Delta. Liaison officers in jeeps were dashing about from unit to unit; *Cancel the previous orders, here are the new – for immediate action*. Headquarters abruptly began to pack their trucks, strike their encampments and set off across the open sand. Huge columns were preparing to move, some going south, some north,

[1] Sir Howard Kippenberger, op. cit.

some towards the front and others away from it. Isolated convoys carrying landmines and signals, tanks workshops and camouflage gear, hospitals and petrol, barbed wire and food, ammunition and tentage, water and clothing, artillery and spare parts – all the paraphernalia of this strange expedition in the sand – began to chart their courses and drive off through the dust. Everywhere men were digging or on the march.[1]

The transformation of 8th Army went indeed with alacrity. Moreover there could be no doubt about Army Command's 'grip'. A 'fed-up', humiliated headquarters now came back to life. Corps commanders were summoned to a conference at 8th Army Headquarters at 0900 hours on 15 August to 'discuss future policy' – and were required to bring 'tracings of minefields laid and projected' for inspection.[2]

Bernard began the conference by giving an address very similar to his talk to his staff on 13 August. Freyberg was impressed and noted in his diary that he agreed with everything the Army Commander said.[3] The GHQ Liaison Officer reported back to Cairo that evening:

8th Army's defence policy is to stand and fight on present positions, and no withdrawal is to be made. The words 'Army Reserve Position' are being deleted from printed maps.

Defended localities are being considerably strengthened, in both personnel and e.g. fresh minefields.

The new Army Commander attaches particular importance to the holding of the Ruweisat Ridge.[4]

30 Corps reflected the Army Commander's new directive in its Operation Order No. 72:

Introduction
1.   All orders and instructions which refer to withdrawal from or thinning out of our present positions are hereby cancelled.

Intention
2.   30 Corps will defend the present FDLs at all costs. There will be no withdrawal . . .

[1] Alan Moorehead, *Montgomery*, op. cit.
[2] War Diary, 8th Army HQ, August 1942, PRO.
[3] R. Walker, *Alam Halfa and Alamein*, Official History of New Zealand in the Second World War, Wellington 1967.
[4] LO Report from 8th Army in War Diary, GHQ Middle East (G Ops), August 1942, loc. cit.

Defence Schemes
8. Brief defence schemes will be submitted . . . to include a trace showing
   a) Battery and Coy areas
   b) A/Tank layout
   c) MMG layout
   d) Primary defensive fire tasks
   e) Mined areas and density of mines.[1]

The influence of the Army Commander was unmistakable. Later that afternoon the new commander of 13 Corps arrived: Lt-General Brian Horrocks. He had left his division in Northumberland on the evening of 12 August; on arrival in Cairo on the morning of 15 August General Alexander had indicated that Horrocks would be required to command the new Corps de Chasse as soon as the September convoy with its cargo of 300 Shermans arrived; in the meantime he was wanted at the headquarters of 8th Army.

'I arrived in Egypt three days after General Montgomery,' Horrocks related in an account for the Official British Historian in 1945.

He had wired for me to come out. On arrival I motored up to his Headquarters in the desert, where I spent the first night and where he gave me his appreciation.

Although he had only been a very short time in Egypt his appreciation was remarkably accurate. I will not go into details except to emphasize the following points:

a) He anticipated that Rommel would make one all-out effort to capture the Delta, and that this attack would be made on the frontage of my Corps, 13 Corps, which was holding the left sector of the Alamein position. He ordered me to defeat the Germans, *but not under any condition to become mauled in the process*, because he was then thinking of his offensive operations. He continually stressed this point afterwards and it is important to consider this when remembering how we fought the battle.

b) In his appreciation he even showed me on a map the area in which he proposed to launch the main attack during the battle of Alamein. Looking back on this conversation the interesting point is that the plan, as outlined by General Montgomery, was adhered to in almost every detail.

c) On his arrival he'd given orders that the 8th Army was to fight in its present position and this had a most excellent effect on morale.

d) I was instructed to go up to 13 Corps and to examine the existing plan in considerable detail, as General Montgomery

[1] War Diary, 30 Corps HQ, August 1942, loc. cit.

was not very happy about it. He emphasized that the ground vital to the defence was the Alam Halfa ridge, where two brigades of the 44th Division were constructing a defensive position.[1]

Looking back, in 1960, Horrocks called it 'the most remarkable military appreciation I ever heard',[2] for it seemed incredible that the Army Commander should be more interested in the future 8th Army offensive than in Rommel's immediate thrust. However, it was only in his mid-eighties that Horrocks revealed the real truth behind his summons to Egypt. Alexander had been charming but vague, almost out of touch: 'All he said was: "Monty has some great plan for driving the Germans out of Egypt. I don't know what it is, but you are to take part in it, and I'm letting him get on with it" – that's all he said.'[3] Thus when Horrocks arrived at 8th Army Headquarters he still had no idea what his appointment was to be, and when Montgomery, having outlined his plan for the British offensive at Alamein, announced that Horrocks would command the armoured Corps de Chasse to be formed out of 13 Corps, he was horrified.

I said, no, Sir, it's no good you know. He said why not? I said, well look: I've already commanded an armoured division in England – the 9th Armoured – and I know they'll resent it. You see, I came from a very humble regiment, the old diehard Middlesex Regiment, and I knew at once that the reaction of the cavalry to me being put in charge of them would be bad. I said No! For God's sake don't do that! Put Lumsden in – because Lumsden was the great hero, he'd won the Grand National, God knows what else, you know what I mean? *He* was the man. And Monty eventually said yes, I think you're right. I will. So he said Well, you take command of 13 Corps . . .[4]

Was this the origin, then, of a third 10 Corps as the Corps de Chasse, instead of 13 Corps?

Yet, if Horrocks hoped that his appointment meanwhile to command 13 Corps as a conventional Corps in the forthcoming defensive battle would be any easier, he was mistaken. Montgomery warned him:

The point was, he said to me, that our armoured formations are too brave. They always attack. And all the Germans do is withdraw their 88s behind the line and then knock out all our tanks. What's

---

[1] Cabinet Papers (CAB 106/654), PRO.
[2] Sir Brian Horrocks, *A Full Life*, op. cit.
[3] Sir Brian Horrocks, loc. cit.
[4] Ibid.

more their 88s have a far better range and the Germans have far better tanks than we've got.

So the cavalry really are hunting the whole time. They're after the fox. They'll go, they'll always attack. That's their one element.

Now, he said, I'm not going to have that. I want you to go up there, to go up on to the Alam Halfa ridge, and I want you to arrange to lure the Germans on. And when we've really got them into a trap, then we'll go for them. In other words all our anti-tank guns must be dug in, and all our tanks dug in. Everything dug in. And let Rommel come on. Let him come on down the side of the ridge . . . And then when the moment comes, we come in at his soft stuff – because he's getting a bit short of fuel and one thing and another. In fact, he said, it's a case of dog eat rabbit. That was his phrase: 'dog eat rabbit' . . .[1]

For Horrocks there followed 'about the most difficult time I had in the whole war'.[2] Freyberg, resentful at having yet another junior British general promoted above him, did everything he could to make Horrocks' life hell. 'Every order I issued was queried,' Horrocks recalled, 'and it was a very nasty, difficult time.'[3] In his diary Freyberg recorded Horrocks' arrival at 13 Corps HQ on 16 August 'full of optimism and ready to consider changes in the plans',[4] but Freyberg never did settle under Horrocks' command, and after the New Zealand Division's unfortunate performance in the forthcoming battle Bernard was careful to deal with Freyberg as far as possible himself. But Freyberg was not the only thorn in Horrocks' side. The Army Commander's directives for the battle meant a complete reversal of the Auchinleck–Gott plan for the use of armour, and the armour – as Horrocks had foretold – jibbed both at the new Corps Commander and the task.

The 13 Corps plan for a mobile, armoured battle in the South was to be scrapped. The dozens of variations of plan – with codewords like 'Pheasant', 'Snipe', 'Snippet', 'Grouse', 'Cheeper', 'Gamebirds', 'Hamla', 'Woodcock', 'Lobster' – were to be torn up. There would be one plan, and one plan only, as Bernard had outlined to Horrocks on 15 August. Rommel would be lured through the defences in the south and on to Alam Halfa. He would not be counter-attacked; here would be no battle of manoeuvre. The British armour would be positioned on the Alam Halfa ridge: *and would stay there*.

It is difficult, almost four decades later, to realise both the extent of Bernard's reversal of 8th Army doctrine, and the opposition which he encountered. If the battle of Alam Halfa was won so convincingly

---

[1] Ibid.
[2] Ibid.
[3] Ibid.
[4] R. Walker, op. cit.

at the end of August, and with so few casualties, it was not only because Bernard's new plan of battle proved successful, but because the real battle – the battle to overcome the prejudices and obstructions put up by his own forces – was fought and won before the shooting ever began.

Even in his eighties Sir Brian Horrocks remembered this bitter and fateful struggle. Freyberg resented him; the Commander of the 7th Armoured Division, Major-General Renton, was equally recalcitrant – 'Renton – that's the man,' he recalled: 'he was the man who caused all the trouble.'[1] Michael Carver, G1 at Headquarters, 7th Armoured Division later remembered General Renton well: 'He was an attractive character in lots of ways, but by this time he had seen a great many Riflemen either go "in the bag", or gallant attacks which then achieved nothing . . . He was imbued with a feeling that it was important to preserve his forces "in being", rather than to hold any specific bit of ground' – such as Alam Halfa. 'Well, there was a tendency to keep your forces "in being" in order to take them backwards! That was Horrock's real criticism of Renton.'[2] Sensing the difficulties Horrocks would have to face, Bernard suggested a meeting of senior 13 Corps commanders on the Alam Halfa ridge that day, 16 August. Brigadier 'Pip' Roberts, who commanded 22nd Armoured Brigade, the only unit in 8th Army equipped with Grant tanks capable of meeting German Panzer Mark III and IVs in battle, remembered the meeting well:

We all knew he was coming. I'd never met him before and all I knew about him was he was quite a fire-eater and that he was very keen on physical fitness and everybody in his division in England was on PT. And I said, God if this man comes and tries to put us on PT I shall go bolshie. Because of course we were under tremendous air dispersion whenever we rested – vehicles at least 100 yards from one another – and it was a very tiring business going round your regiment, brigade or whatever, and when we came out of the battle the last thing we wanted to do really was PT. And I thought, if this man is obsessed with PT, we're not going to get on awfully well together![3]

Roberts need not have worried on that score.

The first day I met him he was coming to see the front – or rather, we weren't in the front then, we were in the area of Alam Halfa itself. That's where we were sitting, or not far away. I was told to meet the new Army Commander on Point 110 at Alam Halfa. And

[1] Sir Brian Horrocks, loc. cit.
[2] Field-Marshal Lord Carver, loc. cit.
[3] Major-General G. P. B. Roberts, interview of 8.1.80.

I arrived a little bit early, naturally. One or two other cars drove up, and as so often in the desert you go to one place and you say you're on the spot and somebody else goes to another place and *they* say they're on the right spot. Well I arrived first and I put myself in one spot and two armoured cars arrived up and they went to another spot. So I joined them and we agreed it must be the point where we were going to meet. And various other people came up, including General Horrocks – he arrived next – one or two more armoured cars came and I wondered when the Army Commander was coming. And then a man got out of a car with very white knees, clearly he'd not been in the desert long, and wearing an Australian hat with not many badges on it at that time because he'd only just arrived, and I thought it was one of the journalists, you see. So I didn't take a great deal of notice, and then he came up to me and said: 'Do you know who I am?' So of course I knew at once who he was! Without any further ado, I said, 'Yes, sir,' and that's how I first met Monty – on this place where the battle of Alam Halfa was fought.[1]

As commander of an armoured brigade, Roberts had not been concerned with the new orders for the infantry to stay put. The merit of the new Army Commander, in Roberts' view, was that, whereas in the past there had been a plethora of plans for the use of British armour, when Montgomery arrived there was *one* plan:

Before Monty arrived we had a number of different plans. Plan A was this, Plan B was this, Plan C was that, you see. Now when Monty came we had one plan. As far as I was concerned, as far as 22nd Armoured Brigade was concerned, there had been various tasks in various possible situations. Now when Monty came, there was only one task; to stay on Alam Halfa. All our job was, was to stay there.

Immediately the air was cleared, as it were. Everybody knew that we were not moving back, we were fighting here! That is that! Certainly a different atmosphere pervaded, at once. Liddell Hart doesn't agree with me quite on this, but he wasn't there, so he doesn't know. I mean, we all had a very high opinion of Auchinleck, we also had a very high opinion of 'Strafer' Gott. But Monty gave as it were a new light on the whole thing: a simple, clear, firm light. And there's not the slightest doubt that if it made a difference to me, naturally it made a difference to the people under me. There's not the remotest doubt about the effect his arrival had.[2]

[1] Ibid.
[2] Ibid.

Moreover, Roberts was delighted to have a role he *knew* he could fulfil, rather than a series of highly dubious possible tasks, from covering the withdrawal of the New Zealand Division to a flank attack on the combined Afrika Korps.

> You see, the defence is much more powerful than the attack, and to be effective in the attack you have to have a preponderance of 3 to 1 or thereabouts – something like that. No, if we were going to stay put like that, fine, we'd stay put. I didn't mind at all. It was a simple plan. I knew that if we could hold our fire and we stayed put, then we would inflict more casualties than were inflicted on us.[1]

There was, also, the preciousness of 22nd Armoured Brigade's tanks to consider. These were the only serviceable Grant tanks left in 8th Army after the disasters of June and July.

> We had all the Grant tanks that were left – all the leftovers from all the other units that had gone back to re-equip. Ours was really the only armoured brigade left in the desert – there was another brigade that was left up, called the 23rd Armoured Brigade and they had a few Valentine tanks – these were armed with only a 2-pounder gun so they were not at all effective against the German tanks. So I was in the enviable – you might think rather nervous – situation of being in command of virtually the only armoured brigade we had in the desert at that time: a rather responsible command, and one which was referred to by General Horrocks as 'Egypt's Last Hope'.[2]

Roberts became, to Horrocks, a tower of strength. 'The man who backed me up was "Pip" Roberts, completely,' he recalled.[3] Renton, by contrast, disagreed – as even Bernard vividly recalled in his *Memoirs*:

> During the day I met on the southern flank the general commanding the 7th Armoured Division, the famous Desert Rats. We discussed the expected attack by Rommel and he said there was only one question to be decided: who would loose the armour against Rommel? He thought he himself should give the word for that to happen. I replied that no one would loose the armour; it would not be loosed and we would let Rommel bump into it for a change. This was a new idea to him and he argued about it a good deal.

[1] Ibid.
[2] Ibid.
[3] Sir Brian Horrocks, loc. cit.

Horrocks wrote later that 'there were one or two distressing scenes before I could get things done'.[1] This was an understatement, for Renton, as commander of 8th Army's only armoured division, was considered so moody and unreliable that, with Montgomery's backing, his armoured brigade was taken from him that evening and put directly under 13 Corps – leaving Renton with only light armoured forces in the far south. Renton was furious, but Roberts – who felt Renton, who a year ago had been commanding the Rifle Brigade, to be an amateur in the use of armour – was delighted. As Horrocks confessed to the Official Historian, 'this was an untidy picture, as a Brigade should not operate directly under Corps Headquarters, but I did not want there to be any risk of the Grant tanks being launched into battle by 7th Armoured Division without my order'.[2] Had Renton been allowed to control the 'vital Grant tanks' of 22nd Armoured Brigade, and had he used them as envisaged under the Auchinleck–Gott plans, Horrocks felt the whole battle would have been in jeopardy: 'As we were outnumbered and out-tanked, if this Brigade was launched head-on at the Germans there was every chance that it would be completely written off; in which case we should really have lost the battle.'[3] This was to simplify, since, if anything, Renton had become *excessively* cautious about casualties – but it indicates clearly the scepticism felt by Horrocks and 'Pip' Roberts as to Renton's ability to use tanks well in a battle of manoeuvre.

Brigadier Roberts set to work with a will. The tell-tale hunting code-words were cancelled; engineers were brought in to blast and bulldoze a series of hull-down positions for the tanks on the slopes of Alam Halfa, while a screen of anti-tank gun positions was set up in front of them. On 19 August Roberts confirmed the orders to his 22nd Armoured Brigade in writing:

22 Armoured Brigade is to take up an impenetrable position which it is hoped the enemy will attack and from which, if he bypasses it, the Brigade can debouch and attack his rear. This position by the area south of Point 102 has already been recced in detail by units. It should be appreciated in all ranks informed that

a) The position is a strong one and will resist any enemy tank or other attack, the rear of the position being protected by Fortress 'E' [Alam Halfa, garrisoned by 44 Division].
b) The battle positions for armoured regiments are good, give considerable scope for troop commanders' initiative, enable tanks to remain concealed until fire is required and provide good hull-down positions.
c) Anti-tank guns are so sited that not only do they cover their

[1] Op. cit.
[2] Sir Brian Horrocks, Letter to British Official Historian, 1945 (CAB 44/992), PRO.
[3] Ibid.

own front but can cover the front of armoured Regiments thereby enabling them to remain concealed until a severe threat develops.

d) Although apparently static positions are being taken up the Brigade must retain its power of mobility and be at instant readiness to benefit by any opportunity the enemy may give to attack him.

In conclusion Roberts added the prescient words: 'By taking up these positions it is hoped that for once the enemy may have to attack us in good positions of our own choosing.'[1]

Meanwhile, aware that there was considerable resistance in some quarters to his 'new broom', Bernard's first reaction was to assume that his no-nonsense Chief-of-Staff in England, Brigadier Simpson, was the man he needed to help stamp out the 'belly-aching' within 8th Army rather than the more affable de Guingand. On 16 August, three days after the arrival of the new Army Commander, the headquarters on the Ruweisat Ridge was closed down and re-opened simultaneously at Burg-el-Arab, alongside the headquarters of the Desert Air Force by the sea.

'Several days after Montgomery's arrival,' de Guingand recalled in *Generals at War*,

I was crossing the area between my caravan and the operations' vehicle, when he stuck out his head and in that rather shrill staccato voice, which later I got to know always prefaced something important, cried:

'Freddie, come along here. I want to have a word with you.'

Bernard's purpose was to tell de Guingand that he was to be replaced.

As was his custom, he got straight to the point. 'Now I don't want you to be hurt by what I have to stay, but I feel I must tell you that I had a Chief of Staff in England, whom I trained myself and who knows my ways. Before leaving England I told him I would probably get him out here as it would save me a lot of trouble. So if this does happen, please don't get upset for it's no reflection on you personally and I will certainly see that you get any job you would like to have.'

General Sir Sidney Kirkman, Bernard's artillery brigadier at 12 Corps, certainly remembered seeing Simpson's name beside 'half a dozen people Monty wanted' when summoned to the War Office. As far as Kirkman could recall, Bernard 'got three of them. He didn't get

[1] War Diary, 22nd Armoured Brigade HQ, August 1942 (WO 169/4251), PRO.

the other three'.[1] But was it to be his own Chief-of-Staff that Bernard requested Simpson? If it was, Bernard was not willing to admit it when he wrote to Simpson some weeks later:

I also tried to get you here as DCGS [to Alexander, in Cairo] a Major-General's job but the War Office have said you cannot be spared. I think Steele is coming. I advised Alex to accept Steele when we knew we could not get you. You ought to come out here, and we will have another try later on.[2]

'Bill' Williams later discredited any idea that Bernard could have been dissatisfied with de Guingand; whereas the idea of getting Simpson in to 'clean up' the 'enormously overstaffed' and 'most incoherent bunch of characters'[3] at GHQ Cairo, whose chief preoccupation for the past six weeks had been their baggage allowance in their retreat to Palestine, was all too understandable:

I can imagine him [Montgomery] saying it would be a good idea to have Simbo out because he'd be very good in GHQ Cairo, and I can imagine he would well have thought of Simpson as frightfully good at that. 'Have a friend at court, Middle East' in Simbo, that sort of thing.[4]

Williams disbelieved that Bernard could ever have seriously intended to replace de Guingand, 'because I think he must have recognized terribly quickly how astonishingly well-briefed he'd been by Freddie on arrival.'[5]

Williams did remember de Guingand wondering whether he would be kept on, however:

He didn't tell me that Monty had said to him he might not last, but he did tell me his *own* opinion was that he might not continue because he said, in a sort of wry, chuckling way,

'Well, I'm on appro – in fact we're all on appro, and I know there are going to be some changes.'[6]

In William's retrospective view, any doubts in Montgomery's mind must have very quickly been dispelled by de Guingand's performance in his new role as Chief-of-Staff, not merely BGS:

In a *very* short time it became obvious that Freddie had ceased to be on appro because he was so clearly in command of the conference

---

[1] General Sir Sidney Kirkman, interview of 16.4.80.
[2] Letter of 12.10.1942. Copy in Montgomery Archive.
[3] Sir Edgar Williams, loc. cit.
[4] Ibid.
[5] Ibid.
[6] Ibid.

situation – it couldn't emerge before because BGS wasn't Chief-of-Staff. It was that which made the difference – and it was a very great difference, you see. You've got to remember that Brian Robertson was really a very senior sort of chap, he had come back into the army and was the DAQMG; Fred Kisch was CRE – another very senior chap.

These two were, as it were, old 8th Army hands. And Freddie'd only just come up to succeed Jock Whiteley not very long before. And that he should be Chief-of-Staff, that they had now to defer to him – that it happened so quickly and agreeably was a tribute to Freddie.[1]

De Guingand's chairmanship of the morning conference when, with his characteristic 'sort of bill-board', he would tick off the items on the agenda, stuck in Williams' memory as a superb example of a 'directing mind'.

Once he'd been told he was Chief-of-Staff – and also he was getting these very clear directives from Monty – I think that gave him the power of command by transfer.[2]

Certainly de Guingand's metamorphosis into one of the most brilliant war-time Chiefs-of-Staff in the British Army was, like Bernard's own assumption of complete command, one of the miracles of the desert campaign. If Bernard exacted lasting loyalty from a staff which had previously given their allegiance to Auchinleck, it was because he commanded such loyalty by his supreme professionalism. In the case of de Guingand, however, what was evoked was not only respect for his evolving stature as a Chief-of-Staff, but also an affection bordering on love. As his friend Geoffrey Keating recalled, 'Freddie didn't have an unworthy ingredient in his character. I mean he was above it all – he belonged to a different dimension – an adorable man. And yet marvellously civilised.'[3] Comparing de Guingand and Montgomery on the occasion of the former's death in 1979, Brigadier Sir Edgar ('Bill') Williams declared:

De Guingand was essentially and loyally subordinate, he admired the Army Commander deeply and with a most genuine affection, but he had a far wider range of human qualities than his master's, a more intuitive understanding of sensitive spots, an instinctive gift for friendship and great good humour.[4]

---

[1] Ibid.
[2] Ibid.
[3] Geoffrey Keating, loc. cit.
[4] Sir Edgar Williams, Memorial Service. Address on the death of Sir Francis de Guingand, 21.9.79.

To those who admired and loved 'Freddie' de Guingand it seemed inconceivable that Montgomery should even consider replacing him as Chief-of-Staff; yet the truth is that within four months, in December 1942, Bernard would be requesting permission from Brooke to send de Guingand home – a fact which, when revealed to 'Bill' Williams nearly forty years afterwards, produced utter bafflement.

Certainly Bernard was capable of surprising even those who thought they knew him best; and it seems more than likely that de Guingand's version of impending transfer in August 1942 was the truth. Whether Simpson or any other Chief-of-Staff could have served Bernard as well as de Guingand can only be conjecture; yet it is important to stress that de Guingand was never the inspiration behind Montgomery. As General Sir Charles Richardson later explained to the historian, Anthony Brett-James:

> He wasn't a crutch. Freddie had the complete confidence of Monty, and I am sure that Monty made it very clear to him very early on that he, the Army Commander, was going to have plenty of time to think out the battle and personally control it, discuss it with his subordinate Commanders, and visit them and so on, and leave all the detail to his Chief-of-Staff. And so by this means Monty was free for the really important issues and it was quite clear to all of us that it was his brain and his decisions that were dominating the scene the whole time. Of course these decisions, once made, were very, very rarely changed and so the staff were able to get going, in a very informal sort of atmosphere, to do all their business without having chopping and changing brought in and so on – getting on with the detail . . . So I would say that he [de Guingand] wasn't a crutch, he was a superb complement to Monty.[1]

The same may be said of Major Williams, whom many outsiders would later consider the 'brain' behind Montgomery, not only because of his background as an Oxford don, but because of his special concern with Ultra, the decrypted German secret signals. Yet Williams had been supplying the same Intelligence and Ultra material all July to Auchinleck, without any sign that it was properly appreciated or put to good use. He had been surprised, despite himself, at the address given by the new Army Commander on 13 August; he was staggered by his first interview.

> I was summoned pretty early on, 15th or 16th August, 1942, perhaps. The new Army Commander had uncomfortably piercing eyes, which also seemed hooded: a disconcerting combination,[2]

[1] Sir Charles Richardson, in Ministry of Defence film 'Montgomery and his Staff'.
[2] 'Face to Face with Montgomery', 3 April, 1976, Montgomery Papers.

he recalled almost forty years later.

> I can remember his very, very searching questions. You know, at
> the time one was glad to have good questions because there had
> been this curious incoherence because of Dorman-Smith and Jock
> Whitely, well nobody had been quite certain who was in charge as
> it were.[1]

Frustrated by constantly producing 'stuff that was out of this world'
but which 'never seemed to get put to any purpose,'[2] Williams both
welcomed Montgomery's incisive interest and was tantalised by the
difference between the new Army Commander and his predecessors:

> I remember that morning I spent with Montgomery trying to
> explain how the enemy was positioned, being tremendously
> aware that the questions being put to me were the sort of questions
> I *wanted* to hear put to me. This was something quite different from
> my previous encounters with generals.[3]

To Williams in retrospect 'what was so interesting about the Alam
Halfa business was – and I think this is where Ultra played its
part – that he believed right away these items of information we
supplied him with. It was rather staggering. You see never before
had we gone to a general with cold, hard information which they'd
seen the point of, and seen how to deal with. Because all "the Auk",
who was not foolish at all – but somehow or other you never got
from him a feeling that although he'd taken the point, he was going
to do *that* as a result of it. And the strange thing with the Auk was
this: that twice he'd stopped the rot when other nerves were failing –
and he didn't know what to do immediately after. He was a prey to
bright ideas I think, particularly from chaps like "Chink" Dorman-
Smith . . .'[4]

Williams was amazed and at first assumed that Montgomery's
receptivity to 'the cold hard intelligence estimate' was determined by
his respect for Ultra; but as time went by he came to see that it went
much deeper. Ultra's unique insight into enemy plans, dispositions
and forces meant so much to the new Army Commander because, as
Williams came to realise, 'he was so very professional. Sometimes [in
interpreting the Ultra material], you'd say to him, "well I think it
means this, er, but what would you do, sir, in the [enemy] situation?" And he was very good about that because he was a very good
soldier and he could therefore see – because the Germans were also

[1] Sir Edgar Williams, loc. cit.
[2] Ibid.
[3] Ibid.
[4] Ibid.

616

very good soldiers – what a good soldier would do – and so much better than I could do because I wasn't a good soldier'.[1]

In his caravan, Bernard had hung an artist's drawing of Rommel; from the moment he began to think over his task as Commander of 8th Army on the flight from England, Bernard had attempted to 'put himself in the enemy's shoes'. As Williams came to see, this was not so much a feat of imagination as the logical transposition of one supremely professional military mind into that of another. His instinct, on arrival at 8th Army and after being briefed by de Guingand on the alternatives open to the enemy, was to see the Ruweisat Ridge as the key to Alamein.[2] Rommel would *have* to have it. Far from abandoning it, as Auchinleck had planned, and retreating eastwards to various 'boxes' including the ill-defended Alam Halfa position it was obvious to Bernard that 8th Army *must* hold fast on the Ruweisat Ridge and force Rommel to attempt to outflank it on the south. Instead of dashing itself to pieces on Rommel's anti-tank screens, moreover, the British armour must be kept concentrated on the Alam Halfa ridge, well dug in. If Rommel attacked Alam Halfa he would be stopped in his tracks; if he tried to by-pass it his only lines of communication would be at the mercy of British armour. Provided 8th Army could produce concentrated artillery fire and co-operation from the RAF, Rommel's Panzer Army could be given a drubbing without in any way prejudicing 8th Army's own intended offensive.

Thus, in summoning Williams, the new Army Commander was not – as Williams had first supposed – seeking Ultra-based Intelligence on which to build a battle-plan: his plan of battle had already been made the day he assumed premature command of 8th Army, on 13 August. His questions were so 'surprisingly good' because, having formulated this plan, he now wanted confirmation; indeed, as Williams would find, the only problems that would arise would come later, when Intelligence contradicted the Army Commander's genius for tactical decision-making – as at the height of the battle of Alamein, and two years afterwards, at Arnhem.

In the meantime, however, the 'cold hard Intelligence estimate' simply reinforced Bernard's conviction about Rommel; and, as if to demonstrate this, Bernard then changed the subject. Like General Horrocks, Williams was astonished by the way Montgomery 'spent most time that first morning I ever spent with him – I had barely become a major – interrogating me about the enemy defences at Alamein. The new General was already one battle ahead of me'.[3]

'He'd only just arrived and why should be believe me?' Williams reflected many years later. 'Well, he did. And this established a relationship.'[4]

[1] Ibid.
[2] Confirmed by General Sir Charles Richardson to author, 24.9.80.
[3] Sir Edgar Williams, in *The Times*, loc. cit.
[4] Ibid.

If Bernard's manner towards those he disliked or thought incompetent was often scandalously peremptory and contemptuous, this trust in the talents of those whom he respected was the reverse: and earned the lasting loyalty of his staff. At Burg-el-Arab the Headquarters of 8th Army was now transfigured, becoming overnight perhaps the most professional field operation team of its kind in any theatre of war at the time. Almost without exception it was the same staff that had served Auchinleck; yet when Churchill arrived a few days later on his way back from Moscow he could barely credit the change. Gone was the 'meat-safe' and the 'liberal supply of camel-dung'. A sea breeze blew in off the shimmering Mediterranean. Colonel Mainwaring, the G1 (Ops) had ensured that the caravans were laid out in such a way as to provide an operations courtyard, with maps both inside the lorries and draped outside, Army and Air Force officers worked side-by-side, sharing Intelligence – Intelligence which, on the night of 17 August had, via Ultra, confirmed Rommel's intention to strike in the south and given a target date of 26 August for the battle.[1]

Churchill's visit was paid on 19 August – the same day as the Allied raid on Dieppe. Yet if Dieppe was a catastrophe only thinly concealed by Mountbatten (who reported that the naval losses had been extremely light), the atmosphere at 8th Army Headquarters and within the units Churchill visited entranced the Prime Minister. Churchill's cable home the next day stated he was 'sure we were heading for disaster under the former regime' and applauded the 'complete change of atmosphere' he had found. 'The highest alacrity and activity prevails. Positions are everywhere being strengthened, and extended forces are being sorted out and regrouped in solid units. The 44th and 10th Armoured Divisions have already arrived in the forward zone. The roads are busy with the forward movement of troops, tanks, and guns,' Churchill signalled.[2] Auchinleck's biographer, John Connell, would write in 1959: 'About this disagreeable, inaccurate and offensive document the less said the better';[3] yet the following year Correlli Barnett said more, repeating the assertion that Montgomery had merely mouthed the same appreciation of the situation and tactical plans as Auchinleck had done before Churchill on 5 August 1942.[4]

Such assertions evince loyalty to a fallen idol, but are profoundly misleading. No one more than Churchill had resisted the appointment of Montgomery to command 8th Army. Had fate not taken a hand, Churchill would, on 19 August, have been listening not to Lt-General Montgomery's plans of holding fast from the sea to Alam

[1] F. H. Hinsley, op. cit.
[2] W. S. Churchill, *The Hinge of Fate*, op. cit.
[3] John Connell, *Auchinleck*, op. cit.
[4] Correlli Barnett, op. cit.

Nayil and of refusing a battle of manoeuvre by remaining *in situ*, heavily defended, on the Alam Halfa ridge, but to Lt-General Gott, with very different plans of mass withdrawal from the front line and the fragmentation of 8th Army into mobile Battle Groups. 'This re-grouping, planned to take place during a forced withdrawal, would have been utterly beyond the capabilities of 8th Army and have given Rommel ample opportunity to exploit,' the G1 (Plans) himself later wrote.[1] No doubt Churchill's nineteenth-century feel for cavalry manoeuvre would have warmed to Gott's plans, and it is all the more credit to Bernard's masterly exposition that he was able to convince Churchill of the rightness of his logical, simple and unfolding design. Nor was it simply a matter of presenting new fruits of Ultra, for Churchill was himself the most avid of Ultra readers – and knew that Montgomery could not have altered the whole tactical stance of 8th Army in a single day, since receiving the Ultra decrypt of Rommel's intentions only the previous morning.

What astounded Churchill, as it astounded the normally dour Brooke, was the speed with which Montgomery, arriving in the desert some eight days after the Prime Minister and CIGS, had imposed his own vision not only of the tactical strategy he intended to adopt but the kind of professional army he wished 8th Army to become.

'I knew my Monty pretty well by then, but I must confess I was dumbfounded by the situation facing him, the rapidity with which he had grasped the essentials, the clarity of his plans, and, above all, his unbounded self-confidence – a self-confidence with which he inspired all those that he came into contact with,' wrote Brooke later.[2]

There could be no doubt about Churchill's genuine submission to the 'Montgomery-magic' that evening: indeed Connell's distaste for Churchill's telegram reflects an intuitive recognition that the language Churchill used (phrases such as 'heading for disaster under the former regime', divisions being 'reduced to bits and pieces') was much more characteristic of Montgomery than Churchill – and the phrasing of Bernard's diary confirms this. Like an old but obdurate hunting dog, Churchill had finally picked up the scent that had eluded him for two long and wearisome years of war. It was the smell of victory. It now pervaded everything and everyone Churchill met. It had nothing intrinsically to do with equipment or numbers of troops – indeed in the six days he had been in command of 8th Army Bernard had scarcely a tank or gun that had not been available to Auchinleck. And yet everything was different. It was a revelation, beside which the Combined Operations fiasco at Dieppe paled into insignificance. Moreover Churchill's response was not merely a

[1] General Sir Charles Richardson to author, 24.9.80.
[2] *Notes on My Life* in A. Bryant, op. cit.

warming to the prospect of military success at last in Egypt; it was, too the awareness of an historian.

In Montgomery's visitors' book Churchill searched for a parallel – and found it in his own ancestor the Duke of Marlborough. 'May the anniversary of Blenheim which marks the opening of the new Command bring to the Commander in Chief of the Eighth Army and his troops the fame & fortune they will surely deserve,' he wrote the day he left Burg-el-Arab, 20 August 1942.[1] Three days later Brooke echoed the sentiment in a final letter before 'the great enterprise' began.

> British Embassy
> Cairo
> Aug 23/42

My dear Monty,

Before leaving Egypt I must just send you a short line to tell you how happy I am to feel that the 8th Army is in your care.

I have had a difficult time out here trying to get things in better shape, and am leaving with a great feeling of satisfaction at the thought of Alex & you at the helm out here.

You have wonderful prospects out here and I have the fullest confidence that you will make the most of them.

You can rest assured that if there is anything I can do from my end to help it will be done if it is possible.

Look after yourself, don't work too hard, and may God give you all the help and assistance you may require.

God bless you, and the *best* of luck to you in your great enterprise.

> Yours ever
> Brookie[2]

In a matter of hours Bernard had convinced Churchill that the strategy of meeting an enemy attack while planning a great British offensive for the autumn was correct – and Churchill faithfully conveyed this to the War Cabinet at home. Ironically, Auchinleck's plans for a battle of manoeuvre would have been much more to Churchill's taste, but Auchinleck's muddled presentation and the lack of faith in the 8th Army carrying it out had given Churchill no confidence. In selecting Gott to command 8th Army, Churchill had hoped to inspire a more aggressive spirit; yet Bernard Montgomery's exposition 'uplifted' Churchill[3] without promising any of the tactics which Churchill desired.

[1] W. S. Churchill, op. cit.
[2] Original in Montgomery Papers. Quoted by A. Bryant, op. cit.
[3] W. S. Churchill, op. cit.

Winston Churchill had in fact met his match. It was not, as one fanciful historian would later claim, a matter of mere 'public relations', a question of Montgomery giving up his 'own caravan for the Prime Minister to sleep in . . . near the sea for ease of bathing', nor of 'wine and brandy at dinner in the mess'.[1] As Geoffrey Keating later remembered, though the meat-safe came down and tents went up, the standard of cuisine remained more or less the same. Corporal Wells, the Mess Corporal, was later instructed to 'chambrer' the port,

and he boiled it! Exploded it! And I think it was Monty who said to Churchill, 'Do you like it boiling hot?' You see, a Mess Corporal had never handled port in the desert before.[2]

It was not the quality of spirits offered which therefore impressed Churchill, but the new spirit of the Army. Auchinleck's austerity had been ineffective in the long run because, however genuine, it was so inappropriate, convincing neither the 'soldiery' nor visitors to the 'meat-safe'.

By contrast Montgomery's personal austerity – no smoking, no drinking, going early to bed – did not offend Churchill but intrigued him. When Churchill went to lunch with his erstwhile comrade-in-arms from the trenches of World War One, Lt-General Freyberg, he was surprised to see Montgomery pull out outside yet refuse to join them in a meal at the New Zealand Divisional HQ. Instead the new Army Commander 'sat outside in his car eating sandwiches, and drinking his lemonade with all formalities,' Churchill recorded with wry amusement, explaining that Montgomery had made it a rule not to 'accept hospitality from any of his subordinate commanders'. Napoleon would at least have had roast chicken from his travelling *fourgon*, Churchill commented, and was led to compare Montgomery's eccentricities with those of Napoleon, Marlborough and Cromwell.[3]

The day Churchill left 8th Army, Bernard issued a 'Special Message to Officers and Men of Eighth Army'; the first of his famous Orders of the Day to 8th Army.

1. The enemy is now attempting to break through our positions in order to reach CAIRO, SUEZ and ALEXANDRIA, and to drive us from EGYPT.
2. The Eighth Army bars the way. It carries a great responsibility and the whole future of the war will depend on how we carry out our task.
3. We will fight the enemy where we now stand; there will be NO WITHDRAWAL and NO SURRENDER.

[1] Correlli Barnett, op. cit.
[2] Goeffrey Keating, loc. cit.
[3] W. S. Churchill, op. cit.

Every officer and man must continue to do his duty as long as he has breath in his body.

If each one of us does his duty, we cannot fail; the opportunity will then occur to take the offensive ourselves and to destroy once and for all the enemy forces now in EGYPT.

4. Into battle then, with stout hearts and with the determination to do our duty.

And may God give us the victory.

B. L. Montgomery
Lieutenant-General[1]

According to Sir Ian Jacob's diary, Churchill was so 'particularly pleased' with this and one other Special Message by Bernard that on his arrival at Cairo that night 'he gave instructions that they should be circulated to the Cabinet on his return. They certainly are the most inspiriting documents,' Jacob added, 'and it is quite clear who means to be master in the desert.'[2]

While Bernard's special message went out to the troops, Churchill cabled back to Attlee, his Deputy at home: 'I am satisfied that we have lively, confident, resolute men in command, working together as an admirable team under leaders of the highest military quality' – and added (no doubt reflecting the influence of General Brooke), 'It is now my duty to return home as I have no part to play in the battle, which must be left to those in whom we place our trust.'[3]

But did Churchill really trust the new Army Commander, despite his dazzling 'grip' of the situation? In truth, Churchill was acquiescing in the very opposite of what he had intended to happen in the desert. In appointing Alexander to replace Auchinleck as C-in-C Middle East he had hoped to install a fresh, fighting general who would take the offensive without delay. Equally, in appointing Gott to take command of 8th Army, Churchill had intended perhaps to highlight what he approved in Auchinleck's plans: namely the accent on offensive mobility and manoeuvre. Certainly Churchill's original intention, as told to Brooke on the flight back from Moscow, was to stay in Egypt for the coming battle, which intelligence sources now predicted would take place in a few days' time, at full moon. Moreover two other of the Prime Minister's statements on 20 August suggest that, though he applauded the new spirit in 8th Army, he either misunderstood or disagreed with Montgomery's plans: namely his 'unfavourable opinion' of Horrocks' new defensive plans as 13 Corps Commander at Alam Halfa ('Trouble with you generals is that you are defensive minded. Why don't you attack? That's the way to win battles, not by sitting down in defence,' he barracked,[4] and his

[1] R. Walker, op. cit.
[2] Sir Ian Jacob, Diary loc. cit.
[3] W. S. Churchill, op. cit.
[4] Sir Brian Horrocks, op. cit.

cable to Attlee in which he reported that the 'strong line of defence' being developed across the Delta from Alexandria to Cairo was 'to give the fullest manoeuvring power to the Eighth Army in the event of its being attacked next week'.[1] In fact the Delta defence scheme was being undertaken by 51st Highland Division for the very opposite purpose – namely in order that 8th Army might remain dug in on Alam Halfa, leaving 51st Division to meet any over-ambitious German columns that attempted to by-pass the ridge.[2]

The extent to which Churchill misunderstood his new 8th Army Commander is of the highest interest: for it was a misunderstanding that would be mirrored in an identical manner in Eisenhower's headquarters two years later, at the height of the battle for Normandy. In both cases Bernard held his superiors in a state of awe by the utter clarity and simplicity of his tactical forecast; yet somehow, the moment Churchill or Eisenhower left him, they became a prey to their own deeper fears and convictions. Indeed it is impossible to resist the impression that Churchill tolerated Montgomery, a soldier so unlike his romantic ideal, only as long as Bernard produced victories – and was the first to round on ' "your" Monty', as Brooke recalled, whenever victory took longer to achieve than the impatient Prime Minister was prepared to wait.[3] Brooke, however, would be as good as his farewell word from Cairo; and in the fateful months, even years, ahead it was Brooke who watched over and where necessary shielded the fortunes of 'his' Monty.

Obsessed with his own picture of British amateurishness, meanwhile, Rommel paid no attention either to the British announcement of changes in command on 19 August, or to the changes going on within the British lines – indeed his lack of reconnaissance by air or patrol in the southern sector of the British front, though intended to lull the British into a sense of false security there, was also a sign of contempt for his opponents. Trusting to the superior professionalism of his armoured forces, Rommel had based his plan on a 'decisive battle . . . to be fought out behind the British front in a form in which the great aptitude of our troops for mobile warfare and the high tactical skill of our commanders could compensate for our lack of material strength'.[4] His only major concern was the arms race – a race to build up the maximum number of Axis tanks, ammunition and petrol before the British could be reinforced . . . 'The situation is changing daily to my advantage,' Rommel wrote to his wife on 10 August.[5] From German agents in Cairo he knew that a large convoy 'laden with a cargo of the very latest weapons and war material for

[1] W. S. Churchill, op. cit.
[2] War Diary, 51st (Highland) Division, August 1942 (WO 169/4163), PRO.
[3] A. Bryant, op. cit.
[4] B. Liddell Hart (Ed.), *The Rommel Papers*, London 1953.
[5] Ibid.

the Eighth Army would arrive in Suez at the beginning of September'.[1] He therefore delayed his attack to the very final moment in August, unaware that every day's grace was manna to the 8th Army under its new Commander.

'By the end of August,' Brigadier Kippenberger recalled, 'our positions were so solidly dug, the spirit of the men so high, and our preparations so promising that I was almost sorry that the expected blow [a frontal attack] was never delivered.'[2]

Bernard's new spirit of optimism had indeed gone right through 8th Army. Whether Rommel was right in referring to the Axis 'lack of material strength' is debatable: it would appear that both sides over-estimated each other's strength and underestimated their own. To the British, the German Panzer Mark IIIs and IVs were weapons of ominous power, and the knowledge that, already by 15 August, the enemy possessed over 200 of them was a matter of considerable disquiet, dominating all 8th Army Intelligence reports for the period. The motley array of British Valentine tanks, the single Brigade of already ancient Grants – 'Egypt's last hope' – and the knowledge that none of the new Sherman tanks would be in line before mid-September was equally worrying. Fortunately Rommel, in his turn, considerably exaggerated the British forces confronting him. He credited the British 30 Corps with a division still held back in the Delta under Alexander (50th Division), and assumed there were two British armoured divisions in reserve behind 7th Armoured Division ('The Desert Rats'), south of the New Zealanders – whereas until 27 August there were only two armoured brigades, one of which was in the north, armed only with Valentines, the other on the Alam Halfa ridge.

In fact probably at no other time in the war had two opposing Armies been so evenly matched; and, despite – or because of – Rommel's urgent appeals for more troops, ammunition and petrol, the Axis build-up far exceeded that of 8th Army. The insight provided by Ultra was ominously revelatory. By 19 August Major Williams was reporting in his 8th Army Intelligence summary that 'Enemy strength is still growing', and now included 5000 élite parachute troops from Crete.[3] By 21 August he reported there had been a 'significant change in the last week'. The enemy's 'mobile forces have been released from their temporary positional role. He is trying to deny our observation; and he has moved his artillery concentrations further south. His positional infantry, both German and Italian, are now bedded down and anti-tank guns have begun to come up for 164 Div. A definite acceleration of shipping programme is noticeable. There is no reason to believe his supply situation is any

[1] Ibid.
[2] Sir Howard Kippenberger, op. cit.
[3] War Diary, 8th Army HQ, 'I' Section, August 1942, loc. cit.

longer a strain. The parallel to mid-May begins to be pointed . . . Further information from German parachutes makes it evident that the stage is almost set'.[1] In Cairo Churchill sat down with McCreery and Lindsell (Chief of Administration) to 'spend a happy couple of hours at the good old pastime of whittling away the enemy's strength on paper,' Ian Jacob recorded in his diary. 'In the end the Prime Minister was satisfied that he had got a fair comparison of men, vehicles, weapons, etc. and it was generally agreed that taking one thing and another into account, we were about fifty-fifty with the enemy in the desert.'[2]

Nevertheless, by 24 August the Afrika Korps was understood to field at least 230 tanks, together with a screen of 90th Light Division boasting 'at least 100 guns fully mobile'. The purely German mobile strength was estimated as 'at least 29,000 men, over 100 guns, 200 anti-tank guns and perhaps fifty 88s,' Major Williams recorded in his 8th Army Intelligence summary.

The build-up was even more ominous than Major Williams could convey, for over a hundred and seventy of the German tanks now sported a long-barrelled 50-mm gun and extra frontal armour ('Specials') as well as twenty-six Panzer Mark IV Specials armed with 75-mm guns.[3] Together with the 281 tanks of the Italian armoured divisions Rommel was expected to possess over 500 (234 of them German) tanks, compared with an 8th Army strength of 478. Of the latter only 71 were Grants; the rest were obsolescent (117 Valentines, 15 Matildas, 139 Stuarts, 136 Crusaders) and with their unreliability and 2-pounder or 37-mm guns of limited account against German Panzers. 'At any moment Rommel might attack with a devastating surge of armour,' Churchill recalled the period in *The Hinge of Fate*, recording with disarming honesty how he had hinted to the British Ambassador's wife that she might be safer, with her baby son, in the Lebanon. Lady Lampson refused to go; but at Churchill's insistence the defence of the Delta was reviewed, new orders issued, and General Maitland Wilson appointed GOC-elect of the Cairo defences in case Rommel did succeed in penetrating.

Churchill, having returned to England, soon became embroiled in the arrangements for the British-American landings in North-West Africa; but he need not have grown anxious. The confidence inspired by the new 8th Army Commander radiated through its formations and units and, as Kippenberger remembered, the men worked themselves up to a pitch of excitement waiting for the coming battle. Moreover, as he had in the BEF, Bernard insisted that all formations should rehearse their likely rôles in properly umpired exercises. 30 Corps carried out its first exercise on 22 August; but it was in 13 Corps

[1] Ibid.
[2] Sir Ian Jacob, Diary, loc. cit.
[3] F. H. Hinsley, op. cit.

area that the enemy was expected to make his main thrust and there that Bernard Montgomery's most lasting contribution to the British Army was enacted in identical fashion to the exercises of 3rd Division, 5 and 12 Corps, and South-Eastern Army. The War Diary of 13 Corps records how on 19 August the new Corps Commander 'held conference for senior officers and explained his plans for meeting any enemy offensive'; and 20 August there came 'practice moves of 22nd Armoured Brigade ['Egypt's last hope'] to battle positions on Alam Halfa ridge'; on 21 August 'BGS held conference of umpires discussing plans for exercise on August 22'; and on 22 August Exercise 'Gala' began at five o'clock in the morning, ending at four in the afternoon, and attended by the Army Commander himself.

Tasks: To practise
  i) Move of 22nd Armoured Brigade into battle positions
  ii) Control throughout the Corps
  iii) Actions of commanders in certain situations[1]

Each possibility was rehearsed. If Rommel, having penetrated the lightly-held southern minefields, wheeled left to roll up the front line, he would be met by Roberts' 22nd Armoured Brigade, hull-down on high ground, leavened by medium artillery, anti-tank guns and with 23rd Armoured Brigade available to back it up if need be. This would be the ideal situation. If however Rommel attempted to press on towards El Hamman, 22nd Armoured Brigade would then threaten his rear, with 23rd Armoured Brigade in turn assuming the hull-down positions on the Alam Halfa ridge behind them.

Numerically, 8th Army was now only one-third as strong in medium-gunned tanks as it had been at Gazala – where it had boasted almost 170 Grant tanks alone. At Gazala, Rommel had turned the cumbersome generalship of 8th Army to magnificent advantage, and he hoped to do so again. However, the days of panic were over at 8th Army. Horrocks' 13 Corps exercise was mounted and conducted on the same lines which he had been taught in England by Montgomery, and his directions were almost word-for-word those used in Bernard's exercises in England. He warned the umpires that

The exercise will be of no value unless each umpire takes considerable trouble in preparing the picture he's going to paint and gives it realistically to his formation. This will entail an amount of hard work and the preparation of a number of information messages such as would actually be received from units.[2]

[1] War Diary, HQ 13 Corps, August 1942, loc. cit.
[2] Ibid.

626

They were to 'produce situations based on our experience of enemy methods within the recent fighting, e.g.

a) Minelifting under the cover of Stuka raids and smoke
b) an anti-tank screen always protecting the flank of an armoured advance
c) his preference for avoiding an armoured action initially if possible
d) the rapid advance of 90 Light side-stepping operation – this will become strung out along his thrust-line
e) guns got quickly into action in depressions and tanks working forward under cover
f) use of mist or dust . . .

The day after the exercise Horrocks held a conference of formation commanders to go through 'the lessons of the Exercise Gala and adjustments of plans found necessary'. He also issued a Personal Memorandum in writing for all commanders down to Brigadier. He noted that 'this is likely to be a decisive battle because if we can cause the enemy heavy casualties the subsequent operations to round him up will be much facilitated'.[1]

2. *Conduct of the Battle*
I have explained to all commanders how I intend to fight the battle and our plans are all ready. Provided therefore that all ranks of 13 Corps fight with the same guts that they have shown on previous occasions, I have complete confidence in the result. In fact if the enemy really knew our strength, I'm certain he would hesitate before attacking us . . .

3. *Preparations for the Battle*
Prior to the opening of the battle I want attention paid to the following points:
A. Confidence
The importance of this battle and the way we propose to fight it should be explained to all ranks throughout the Corps. This is vital. We have a good plan with every chance of success and provided the men realise this they will fight with confidence and intelligence. Inspiration comes from the officers, and officers must assemble their men and talk to them. During these talks officers will impress on the men the fact that there is no withdrawal from this area – we fight it out here. So no plans will be prepared for the destruction of water points or dumps of material . . .[2]

[1] Ibid.
[2] Ibid.

To ridicule Horrocks as a mouthpiece of the new Army Commander, as envious tongues did to certain later historians, was to miss the historic significance of what took place in the desert in August 1942. Rommel was unwell, and highly nervous about his supplies – but no more so than he had been before his amazing attack at Gazala. It was perhaps the nervous anxiety of the ambitious performer, mesmerised by the prize of Alexandria and Cairo, and propelled also by the intuitive feeling that, unless either he or the German army in the Caucasus broke through, the greater material output of the Allies would doom Germany to eventual defeat. Even if he failed to get through to the Nile, Rommel hoped at least to 'give the enemy a pretty thorough beating' before the arrival of the September convoy, as he wrote to his wife on the day his offensive was to begin. Indeed, he claimed to be 'feeling quite on top of my form. There are such big things at stake. If our blow succeeds, it might go some way towards deciding the whole course of the war'.[1] Across the minefields his adversary was equally confident, however – and equally aware of the importance of the impending battle:

'It is a man's job if ever there was one and a great deal will depend on what results we can achieve here,' Bernard wrote to Brigadier Tomes in England on 25 August. 'I am wonderfully fit, as are all the Troops. You could not have a more healthy life,' he declared – adding in almost the same terms as he used to write to his mother from the Western Front:

The difficulty is Water: every man has one gallon a day but that is to do for drinking and for the radiator of his vehicle; the net result is that in bad times he has to do on a full water bottle for drinking and washing.

A man soon becomes an expert in performing his complete ablutions in one mess tin of water; it is important to get the right sequence in which to do things, i.e. Shave, Teeth, then Wash.[2]

This concern of the new 8th Army Commander for the niceties of his troops' toilet on the day Rommel was expected by Intelligence to launch his much-vaunted attack was yet another facet of Bernard's strange psychology – though Tomes knew Montgomery well enough not to be in the least surprised.

Rommel, however, did not attack that night, nor the next; and by 27 August 8th Army Intelligence was suggesting from Ultra evidence that the German attack would take place 'not tonight but two nights later'.

It was in fact this delay by Rommel that removed in the minds of most senior officers of 8th Army the last vestiges of doubt whether 13

[1] *The Rommel Papers*, op. cit.
[2] The Royal Warwickshire Regimental Museum, Warwick.

Corps could contain a blitz attack by the Afrika Korps with 230 Panzer Mark IIIs and IVs; for on 27 August the 8th Armoured Brigade rejoined 8th Army with a further sixty to seventy Grants. The two Grant-armoured brigades were now put under command of Major-General A. H. Gatehouse who set up his 10th Armoured Division Headquarters alongside Horrocks; and, by placing 8th Armoured Brigade squarely on the track leading towards El Hamman, Rommel's only exit from the Alam Halfa trap was sealed.

The arrival of the 8th Armoured Brigade, Horrocks later wrote, 'was a godsend to me and it altered the whole picture'.[1] The next day, 28 August, Horrocks held another training exercise so that Gatehouse could practise not only communication with his two armoured Grant brigades, but also the summoning of the third Valentine-armoured brigade from the North in the event that it might be required in the South. By 29 August there was 'still no conclusive evidence re timing,' and Intelligence put this down as 'temporary delay perhaps due to supplies'.[2]

In London Churchill – reading the same Ultra decrypts, but also with benefit of Intelligence from agents, began to have doubts whether the Axis offensive would, after all, take place that month. Full moon had passed, and the moon had begun to wane. 'What do you now think of the probabilities of "Zip" coming this moon?' Churchill cabled to Alexander on the 28th. 'Military Intelligence opinion now does not regard it as imminent.'[3] To which Alexander replied: ' "Zip" now equal money every day from now onwards. Odds against increasing till September 2, when it can be considered unlikely.'[4]

According to the *Official New Zealand History* of the war, both Montgomery and Horrocks were certain, by the morning of 30 August, that 'the danger of an immediate attack was passing, if it had not already passed', and the time had come for the New Zealand Division to be withdrawn from the front line in order to start retraining as a motorised division – equivalent to the German 90th Light Division – to accompany the Army Commander's new Corps de Chasse. Whether Montgomery and Horrocks did feel the danger was over is difficult to say; according to Army records a general 'Stand To' was definitely ordered on 30 August in expectation of an attack, and Brigadier Williams could afterwards recall no change in the Army Commander's policy[5] – a recollection confirmed by recent publication of the Ultra decrypts, which even on 29 August recorded no change in the enemy's intention to attack as soon as his fuel

---

[1] Sir Brian Horrocks, Letter to the British Official Historian, loc. cit.
[2] War Diary, 8th Army HQ, 'I' section, August 1942, loc. cit.
[3] W. S. Churchill, op. cit.
[4] Ibid.
[5] Interview of 6.11.80.

situation was satisfactory.[1] Y Intelligence reported moreover, on 30 August that 15th Panzer Division was moving south. On the other hand Bernard seems to have spent the day writing out his general training policy for the future 8th Army offensive battle at Alamein, which was issued the following day.

Whatever the truth, the two New Zealand brigades were just commencing their phased departure from the front line that night when there were reports of an enemy attack against 5th Indian Division on the Ruweisat Ridge. At Burg-el-Arab the Army/Air headquarters was alerted, and shortly after midnight came the first indications of an enemy advance in the south. Brigadier de Guingand waited until there was enough evidence of an enemy offensive rather than a series of raids, then made his way excitedly to the Army Commander's caravan. The General's response he would remember to his dying day; the Army Commander merely murmured 'Excellent, excellent' – turned over, and went back to sleep.[2]

[1] F. H. Hinsley, op. cit.
[2] De Guingand, loc. cit.

CHAPTER EIGHT

Alam Halfa – The Beginning

Perhaps the most remarkable aspect of the battle which became known as Alam Halfa was its relative importance in the minds of the two opposing Army Commanders: Field-Marshal Erwin Rommel and Lieutenant-General Bernard Montgomery.

For Rommel, Alam Halfa was his last bid for victory in the Middle East. 'Today,' he announced on 30 August in a special message to his troops, 'our army sets out once more to attack and destroy the enemy, this time for keeps. I expect every soldier in my army to do his utmost in these decisive days!'[1]

For Bernard Montgomery, by contrast, the battle promised to be merely a holding operation: a prelude to his own autumn offensive. All 8th Army had to do, therefore, was to sit tight and block Rommel's thrust without incurring heavy casualties. Thus, while Rommel made himself ill with anxiety, Montgomery appeared quite unruffled at breakfast on 31 August. He was not relaxed – as General Sir Charles Richardson later made clear:

I don't think relaxed is the right word because his style in fact was very taut. Of course there was never any hurry, no flap and that sort of thing, and this was really due to his iron self-discipline – his professional approach to the art of command – rather than to a relaxed style.

His philosophy really went like this: that a Commander must radiate confidence at all times – that was his great expression: radiate confidence. And if he couldn't control his emotions and conceal his fears, then he shouldn't be a Commander at all. So in order to preserve the nervous energy to carry out that bit of self-discipline, he would have a very orderly regime of sleep and rest and diet and so on.

Now secondly, a Commander must personally control the battle throughout; and in order to be able to do that he must plan it so that he remains in balance – what he called 'poise' ('always retain poise'), and he would personally encourage his subordinates – visit them, and control the battle by word of mouth personally.[2]

[1] David Irving, *The Trail of the Fox*, op. cit.
[2] Sir Charles Richardson, loc. cit.

Rommel had hoped, by keeping his armour behind the centre of his line, to conceal the axis of his impending thrust. In the event he himself was deceived. 8th Army had sown much deeper minefields that Rommel expected in the south – almost 200,000 – and had dug in mortar, artillery and machine-gun posts which gave the Panzer Army a rude shock when it reached the sector around midnight on 30 August. Moreover, the moment the first reports of an enemy attack were relayed by 13 Corps to Army headquarters, the new 8th Army partnership with the Desert Air Force came into operation. Already on 14 August, the day after Bernard assumed command of 8th Army, 13 Corps had issued an Operation Instruction relating to the action of the Desert Air Force, outlining its new policy of holding the front line as far south as Alam Nayil and Alam Halfa 'at all costs', and predicting an enemy attack south of the New Zealanders as the most likely. The task of the Desert Air Force was therefore stated as:

a) to give early warning of enemy offensive
b) to break up enemy formations before his attack develops
c) to attack the enemy's forces during his advance
d) to prevent hostile air action against our positions and L of C.[1]

It is a tribute to Bernard Montgomery's 'new broom' that these tasks, laid down on 14 August, were so successfully carried out when Rommel's offensive opened some sixteen days later. The initial picture nevertheless was not as clear as subsequent historians have depicted, and if the Army/Air headquarters had not been merged at Burg-el-Arab it is unlikely that the Desert Air Force could have made Rommel's main thrust so uncomfortable. The Axis Air Force, with 758 aircraft, considerably outnumbered the 565 Allied planes of the Desert Air Force, and it was therefore imperative not to squander Allied bombers and fighter escorts attacking secondary or diversionary attacks. By the evening of 30 August the move of the German-Italian tanks south-east had been spotted, so when shortly before midnight the first diversionary raids began in the north, the Desert Air Force was told to wait. The 9th Australian Division easily repulsed the raid in its sector; the 5th Indian Division on the Ruweisat Ridge – which Bernard had visited that very afternoon – gave way a little, and had to mount a dawn counter-attack.

While Bernard slept, however, de Guingand sifted the incoming reports, concentrating on those from 13 Corps in the south. As soon as the Axis columns were tied down in the British minefields de Guingand authorised the first air force bombing attacks. At 2.40 a.m. on 31 August the area in the south was lit up by parachute flares and soon became an inferno. German casualties began to mount quickly; the Commander of the German Afrika Korps, General Nehring, was

[1] War Diary, HQ 13 Corps, August 1942, loc. cit.

wounded by a fighter-bomber, while the Commander of the 15th Panzer Division, Major-General von Bismarck, was killed by a mortar bomb. It was an ominous beginning to an offensive designed to smash the 8th Army and capture Cairo and Alexandria. In his memoirs Rommel recalled:

> Shortly after passing the eastern boundary of our own minefields, our troops came up against an extremely strong and hitherto unsuspected British mine belt, which was stubbornly defended . . . Before long, relay bombing attacks by the RAF began on the area occupied by our attacking force. With parachute flares turning night into day, large formations of aircraft unloosed sticks of HE bombs among the troops.
>
> The Army staff spent most of the night on the telephone, with reports pouring in in a continual stream. Even so there remained considerable uncertainty about the situation, although it gradually became clear that things could not have gone altogether as planned.[1]

This was an untypical understatement, for Rommel had given orders that his motorised forces were to advance no less than thirty miles east by moonlight and then strike north at dawn.

Such optimism, based on such poor reconnaissance either by air or foot patrols, was a major error for a newly-created Field-Marshal (though Bernard would commit a comparable error at Arnhem, seventeen days after himself becoming a Field-Marshal), and it is difficult to understand why Nehring, von Bismarck and von Vaerst (Commander of 21st Panzer Division) subscribed to such a bold plan without more accurate information. As Bernard had warned in his 1937 'Encounter Battle' article which Liddell Hart found so largely unconvincing, the development of modern warfare demanded that an army or formation *must* be put into battle according to a well-conceived plan; if the plan was poor it would, in modern conditions, become increasingly difficult to rectify one's mistake.

Rommel's plan for the final conquest of Egypt fell into this category. The success with which, though vastly outnumbered, he had thrown back 8th Army at Gazala, snatched Tobruk, and held on to his gains in July 1942 had blinded Rommel to almost all problems save those of supply. He alienated his air force by his derision of their efforts and allowed himself to become almost megalomaniac in his assumptions about the enemy. He had banked on surprise and speed, and when he found his plan had not worked by dawn on 31 August, his heart sank, and his famed *Fingerspitzengefühl* or military sixth-sense warned him not to go on.

Ironically, such was the legendary effect of Rommel's command,

---

[1] *The Rommel Papers*, op. cit.

that he became now a prisoner of his own reputation. The DAK Chief-of-Staff, Colonel Bayerlein, met him at 8.15 a.m. on the battle-field, having become the acting Commander of the Afrika Korps when Nehring was wounded; Bayerlein urged that they be allowed to continue, since both 15th and 21st Panzer Divisions were at last emerging on the far side of the minefields. Rommel hesitated, telling the Panzer divisions to halt and wait for new orders. In his memoirs he claimed that the long delay in the minefields 'had given the enemy units in the threatened sectors time to send alarm messages and situation reports back to British Headquarters, and had enabled the British commander to take the necessary counter-measures'.[1] Forced to commit suicide in 1944, Rommel never did learn that 'the British commander' had made up his mind how he would fight the battle as early as 13 August 1942, had ensured that 8th Army rehearse its movements in proper exercises in the intervening weeks, and had simply gone back to sleep when told the battle had begun.

The specially jewelled Field-Marshal's baton being held for Rom-mel in Berlin was now of no use; he had lost the opening round of the battle and his instinct was to pull back. Bayerlein, however, reflected the magnificent courage and ardour of the Afrika Korps, which would have felt betrayed if recalled from the far side of the minefields it had so painfully crossed. Still unaware that the area *beyond* the minefield was a trap, Rommel now committed his second error. 'We no longer had the advantage of the time the British would have needed, in the event of a quick break-through in the south, to reconnoitre the situation, make their decisions and put them into effect,' Rommel afterwards summarised.[2] He therefore decided to abandon his over-optimistic objective of Hamman (to the rear of Burg-el-Arab), and proposed instead to make straight for Alam Halfa, from which ridge he could then dominate the rear of 8th Army's front line and the centre of the battlefield, much as he had done by capturing 'Knightsbridge' in the Gazala Battle. He knew it had recently been fortified and expected a 'very severe' battle to take it: but as at Gazala he recognised it was 'the key to the whole El Alamein position'.[3]

Three weeks before, such a tactical decision might well have brought Rommel victory, given the fantastic confusion that would have resulted from the Auchinleck-Gott proposal to withdraw the front-line infantry from their prepared positions and divide up into mobile Battle Groups centring on an Alam Halfa ridge held by two and a half decimated battalions of 21st Indian Brigade. That moment, however, had passed. Knowing that Rommel's intention would be to push as far as possible towards Hamman and the coast road to Cairo and Alexandria, Bernard had made Rommel's supply lines his chief

[1] Ibid.
[2] Ibid.
[3] Ibid.

offensive target, while ensuring that Alam Halfa became an impregnable stronghold if in fact Rommel swung north. Churchill, when told by Horrocks that he had been ordered to attack not Rommel's tanks but his 'soft-skinned' vehicles, had recommended to Montgomery that he sack him. 'Look here, sir, you stick to your sphere and I'll stick to mine,' Bernard is said to have replied.[1]

That Rommel should so soon have fallen into the 8th Army trap by deciding to swing north was a tribute, among other things, to Bernard's grasp of the air weapon. Four years before, in August 1938, in the *Army Quarterly*, Bernard had defended his 'Encounter Battle' theories against Liddell Hart, while reiterating his vision of the proper tactical use of air power in battle. Reflecting on the great German spring offensive of 1918, he remarked that the Allies had done nothing to attack the German concentration of forces from the air. The spring offensive had 'very nearly won the war for Germany,' he recalled, 'whereas, if the entire Allied Air Forces had been used to attack the concentration, it was possible that the offensive might never have taken place at all.

'The lesson seems to be that full advantage must be taken of the flexibility of air forces to direct every ounce of power when the decisive moment arrives on to what is then the decisive target. Thus the moment may come for switching off the attacks on the enemy's economic centres and concentrating everything in an overwhelming attack on his assembling armies. The speed at which ground forces can now move suggests that plans for this "switching over" of air effort must be formulated in advance, so that they can be implemented within a few hours.'[2]

The preliminary bombardment of the Axis forming-up positions and depots, and then the great Desert Air Force blitz on Rommel's mobile forces as they tried to force their way through the British minefields in the southern sector at Alamein on the night of 30–31 August, was Bernard's first opportunity as an Army Commander to put his air-power theory into effect. While it is true that the sinking of Rommel's petrol-supply ships sealed the fate of the Panzer Army, there can be no doubt that Rommel's decision to abandon his first plan and to drive up against Alam Halfa was not the immediate product of those sinkings, but the direct result of Bernard's two-point plan for the opening phase of the battle: concealed depths of defended minefields and a punitive British air bombardment.

Rommel's hesitation at dawn on 31 August did credit to his military intuition. Both Kesselring, the German C-in-C South, who arrived on the scene at 9.45 a.m., and later Hitler himself failed to understand this pause. Kesselring considered that, since the Axis forces managed to continue in battle for another week, lack of petrol

[1] Sir Brian Horrocks, op. cit.
[2] Loc. cit.

supplies could not be blamed. 'The defeat may be attributed to causes of a more psychological nature,' he wrote later. 'I had at the time the conviction that this battle would have presented no problem to the "old" Rommel. Had he not been suffering in health from the long strain of uninterrupted campaigning in Africa, he would never have pulled out when he had already completely encircled the enemy – the British "Last Hope" position, as it was called, had already been outmanoeuvred. I know today that his troops were unable to understand the order to retire.'[1]

Kesselring, with his airman's view of strategy, saw the vital importance of taking both Alexandria and then Malta before the Allies rebuilt their tattered strength in the Mediterranean – as did Hitler. Neither appreciated however the extent to which the Panzer Army had been outwitted; in fact only Rommel seems to have recognised, in his bones, that his plans had been misconceived: that by relying so heavily on tactical surprise he had failed to do the necessary reconnaissance for such an ambitious thrust, and that to continue would be to take a massive gamble with his men's lives.

In fact, as events were to show, Rommel's intuition was proved right. The Italian divisions were still stuck in the minefields, and though the Afrika Korps refuelled, took on more ammunition and set off at 1300 hours in a merciful dust-storm that precluded air bombardment, the assault on Alam Halfa was doomed.

For the first time since he returned from Dunkirk, Bernard now began to keep a battle diary, as he had in May 1940:

Night 30/31 August [1942]

Enemy carried out two big raids

One against Australians, to capture prisoners. This failed and Australians captured 12 German prisoners.

Other against South Africans. This lost direction and hit right company of West Yorks, the right battalion of 5 Indian Division. It was a battalion raid and Coy W. Yorks was stamped on and disappeared. The enemy remained on the Ruweisat Ridge for some hours and was finally ejected by a counterattack by Essex Regiment. Line restored, minefields re-laid and all positions re-occupied by 0700 hours 31 August.

Eighth Army raided as follows:

South Africans – three raids which secured 51 Italian prisoners.
New Zealanders – one raid which secured 30 Italian prisoners.

Such was Bernard's first entry, and he allowed it to stand as such in the secret 'Notes on Alam Halfa' which he drew up the day the battle ended – and which were immediately flown back to the War Office

---

[1] Field-Marshal Kesselring, *Memoirs*, London 1953.

for the Secretary of State and CIGS.[1] Yet the style of the entry and its vantage point are those of a Divisional Commander, not an Army Commander. Perhaps sensing this, Bernard began his next entry – for 31 August – in a quite different and more analytical manner. He ignored the raid on the Australians, and regarded the night's events in terms of the gathering enemy offensive:

Monday 31 August

0100 Rommel attacked. *Two thrusts.*
       One against the RUWEISAT RIDGE; some initial success against W. Yorks; situation restored and at 0730 hours the Ridge was intact. This thrust was proved later to be a Battalion raid.
       Other against minefields between New Zealand left flank and HIMEIMAT. Two gaps made.
0600 Enemy being held on second minefield
0700 Enemy tanks and infantry through second minefield
0930 Two large concentrations east of second minefield
1000 Large movement eastward of strong tank columns between GABALLA and RAGIL depression.
       Possibly 15 Panzer Division, possibly 15 *and* 21 Panzer Divisions.
1030 Not clear yet whether this movement, when it has cleared the gap between GABALLA and RAGIL depression, will continue East or turn North-East towards locality 'E' [Alam Halfa]. Latter course most likely.
       4 Lt Armoured Brigade holding at GABALLA and operating from that place. 13 Corps ordered to keep this Brigade 'in being' and not to get it lost or surrounded in GABALLA.
       7 Motor Brigade still holding on second minefield South of New Zealand area and between that area and Point 102 (22 Armoured Brigade).
1100 No big concentration opposite RUWEISAT Ridge. Appeared certain that main enemy armoured movement was on southern flank.
       Placed 23 Armoured Brigade from 30 Corps under command 13 Corps. 13 Corps moved this brigade southwards towards Point 102.
       One squadron left with each of Australian, 5 Indian and New Zealand Divisions.
       Whole of armour now concentrated under 13 Corps.

Bernard's hour-by-hour chronicle indicates the ruthlessly logical manner in which he now exercised his first battlefield Army Command. Until he was sure – from prisoner identification and recon-

---

[1] Cabinet Papers (CAB 106/2247), PRO.

naissance – that *both* Divisions of the Afrika Korps were committed to the southern thrust, he held on to the 108 Valentine tanks of 23rd Armoured Brigade in 30 Corps. Once it was clear that no serious threat was likely on the Ruweisat Ridge, he released the Valentines to Horrocks, as per 13 Corps exercises – though in the event he retained a squadron each for the division of 30 Corps, 'just in case'.

Was this the 'slow reaction of the British command and troops' upon which Rommel had based his plan? What was certain was that two very different Army Commanders now faced each other – both professional soldiers to their fingertips, both destined to become the most legendary generals of the Second World War. Historians have all too often concentrated on the secondary factors involved in the battle, particularly the various 'Official' historians anxious to fit all the formation War Diaries into a cohesive jig-saw. Such accounts may do justice to the nationalities and units – to the men who risked or often gave their lives in the struggle of opposing forces; but they tell us little of the real nature of command. The fact remains that the encounter that became known by the British as 'Alam Halfa', and by the Germans as 'The Six-Day Race', was decided by the respective Army Commanders, Field-Marshal Rommel and Lt-General Montgomery. Long after the war was over Rommel would still be accused – especially by Afrika Korps veterans – of losing his nerve, while Montgomery would be criticised for his excessive caution. What such criticisms and such 'Official' accounts ignore is something that would become clearer in the ensuing battle of Alamein: namely the battle of wills between opposing Commanders. Those who criticised Rommel – Kesselring, Hitler and certain officers of the Afrika Korps – offended the deeper understanding of the battle which Rommel had. The battle of Alam Halfa, as fought by the *Panzerarmee Afrika*, was Rommel's own battle: the culmination of the desert offensive he had begun at Tripoli in 1941 – and nobody knew better than Rommel what was at stake. He had proved by his North African campaign that his belief in concentration and in the exploitation of enemy weakness could turn numerical inferiority into superiority; that with his flair for improvisation he could run rings round his brave but amateur opponents. Alam Halfa was designed to be the climax, his crowning achievement – after which, as he informed the German High Command, he deserved a good rest, and someone else could assume the reins of Panzer Army Afrika. It was his plan, his battle – he had himself sketched the units and thrusts which would go on to take Alexandria, Cairo, and the airfields at Fayum – and nobody understood better than he the omens of success or failure. If he hesitated on the minefields between Alam Nayil and Himeimat it was not for lack of courage or from exhaustion, but because he recognised that his plan had gone awry. He had failed to achieve surprise; he had himself been surprised by the 'unsuspected mine barriers' secretly laid by 8th Army; and far from being supported by the terrifying Stukas which had once been the hall-mark of German offensives, he was being bombed and strafed unmercifully by the RAF.

In deciding to go on he wished to keep faith with the Afrika Korps he had created; but with loss of surprise and limited by his lack of petrol, his original plan of racing to El Hamman could never work unless the British armour on his left flank was brought to battle and destroyed. To do this he *must* take the key Alam Halfa ridge, which German air reconnaissance now declared to be 'heavily fortified'. He therefore authorised the Afrika Korps to continue, but to aim now for Alam Halfa, not Hamman.[1]

It took hours, literally, to refuel and re-arm the Afrika Korps, as well as the Italian Littorio Armoured Division; but at 1300 hours the new assault began. As if in answer to a prayer, a desert sandstorm blew up, grounding the RAF, and eventually in the late afternoon the Alam Halfa ridge became visible.

It was now imperative that the Afrika Korps take the ridge, 'the key to the whole El Alamein position'. From Alam Halfa, Rommel could dominate 8th Army's rear; the British would be forced to contest this move, and so brought to battle that the superior Panzer Mark IIIs and IVs could then deal with each British attack in turn. Morale in the Korps was second to none: they had after all fought their way some 1360 miles along the shores of North Africa, and felt themselves within striking distance at last of the capital of Egypt and the port of Alexandria.

To the officers and men waiting on the Alam Halfa ridge, meanwhile, the emergence of the Afrika Korps resembled an armada issuing from a sea mist – hundreds upon hundreds of German tanks like ships filling the desert.

What then took place was, from Bernard Montgomery's point of view, the vindication in battle of his theories both of defence and of command.

For Rommel it was the end of his belief in the independent power of armour. It seemed inconceivable that, having altered his plan of battle to take Alam Halfa only a few hours before, the normally 'slow reaction' of the British command could take up impregnable positions on the ridge and bring the combined assault of the Desert Afrika Korps to a complete standstill. Yet this was what happened.

Bernard's diary recorded the end of German aspirations in the Mediterranean in the simplest terms possible. Like the rest of 8th Army he still had no way of knowing Rommel's morning order for the Afrika Korps to wheel on Alam Halfa.

1300   Clear that 15 and 21 Panzer Divisions were collecting in RAGIL depression. Not yet clear what direction these would take.

[1] *The Rommel Papers*, op. cit.

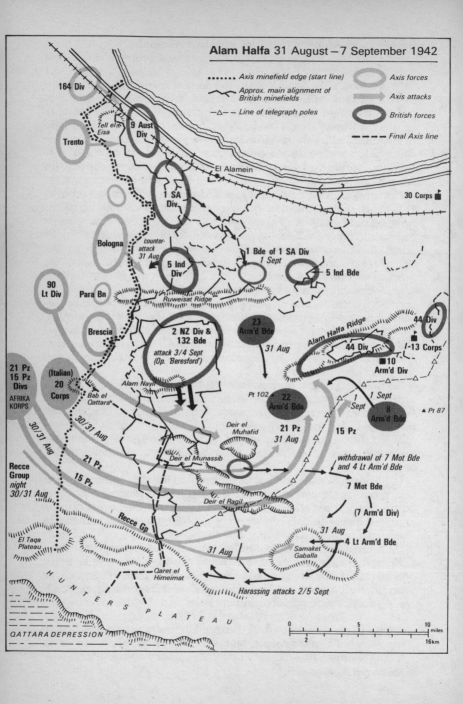

Alam Halfa 31 August – 7 September 1942

······· Axis minefield edge (start line)
~~~~ Approx. main alignment of British minefields
–△– Line of telegraph poles

⬭ Axis forces
⟹ Axis attacks
⬭ British forces
– – – Final Axis line

164 Div

Tell el Eisa

Trento

9 Aust Div

El Alamein

30 Corps

1 SA Div

Bologna

counter-attack 31 Aug

1 Bde of 1 SA Div
1 Sept

5 Ind Div

5 Ind Bde

90 Lt Div

Para Bn

Ruweisat Ridge

23 Arm'd Bde
31 Aug

Alam Halfa Ridge

44 Div

Brescia

2 NZ Div & 132 Bde

attack 3/4 Sept
(Op. Beresford)

44 Div

I–13 Corps

10 Arm'd Div

21 Pz
15 Pz
Divs

AFRIKA KORPS

(Italian) 20 Corps

Bab el Qattara

Alam Nayil

Pt 102

22 Arm'd Bde

1 Sept
1 Sept

8 Arm'd Bde

▲ Pt 87

30/31 Aug

30/31 Aug

21 Pz

15 Pz

Deir el Muhafid

21 Pz
31 Aug

15 Pz

Recce Group
night 30/31 Aug

Deir el Munassib

withdrawal of 7 Mot Bde and 4 Lt Arm'd Bde

7 Mot Bde

(7 Arm'd Div)

Deir el Ragil

Recce Gp

El Taqa Plateau

31 Aug

4 Lt Arm'd Bde

31 Aug

Samaket Gaballa

Qaret el Himeimat

31 Aug

Harassing attacks 2/5 Sept

H U N T E R S   P L A T E A U

0   5   10 miles
2   16km

QATTARA DEPRESSION

1330   Left Army HQ to visit Corps Commanders.
1503   Panzer Divisions began to move. Direction was NE and
        slightly N of NE. They were in fact moving into area for
        which 8th Army layout was designed.
        Strong wind was now blowing and the dust was such that
        the RAF squadrons were unable to take off. This was a
        tragedy. From 1200 hours to about 1600 hours two enemy
        armoured divisions were in and about the RAGIL depress-
        ion and could not be touched.
1700   Enemy Panzer movement hit 22nd Armoured Brigade in
        position on 102 feature. This was a heavy armoured attack.
        It was met by 22 Armoured Brigade on ground of its own
        choosing and was driven off, heavy casualties being in-
        flicted on the enemy.

Rommel was dumbfounded. Not only could he not believe the
manner in which the British armour and artillery had dug itself in, he
could not understand why, on past experience, the enemy did not
come out and attack him. In order to conserve petrol and to tempt out
the British he closed down both Panzer Divisions' offensive operations that evening, hoping that by jabbing attacks the next morning
he might entice out the reluctant enemy tanks. But, as the German
88-mm Flak War Diarist recorded, Rommel was to be disappointed.
'The swine isn't attacking,' he complained bitterly to Kesselring the
next day, 1 September.[1]

To the Germans, in the front line, the picture was by no means so
clear. Pounded by air-strafing, shelling and mortar fire the German
reconnaissance had been abysmal, and its map-reading equally
poor – so that at last light the Commander of 15th Panzer Division
actually believed he was on the brink of capturing the Alam Halfa
feature, and only 21st Panzer Division's feebleness was holding him
up.

To the British units the picture was the reverse – though by no
means without anxiety. There had been some consternation when
the first long-barrelled Panzer 'specials' became visible – 'the devil of
a gun' as Brigadier 'Pip' Roberts of the 22nd Armoured Brigade put it:

On they come, a most impressive array . . . And now they all turn
left and face us and begin to advance slowly . . . I warn all units
over the air not to fire until the enemy are within 1000 yards; it
can't be long now and then in a few seconds the tanks of CLY
[County of London Yeomanry] open fire and the battle is on. Once
one is in the middle of a battle time is difficult to judge, but it seems
only a few minutes before nearly all the tanks of the Grant
squadron of the CLY were on fire. The new German 75-mm is
taking heavy toll. The enemy tanks have halted and they have had

[1] Quoted in R. Walker, op. cit.

their own casualties, but the situation is serious; there is a complete hole in our defence. I hurriedly warn the Greys [the reserve tank regiment] that they must move at all speed from their defensive positions and plug the gap. Meanwhile the enemy tanks are edging forward again and they have got close to the Rifle Brigade's anti-tank guns, who have held their fire marvellously to a few hundred yards. When they open up they inflict heavy casualties on the enemy, but through sheer weight of numbers some guns are overrun. The SOS artillery fire is called for; it comes down almost at once right on top of the enemy tanks. This, together with the casualties they have received, checks them . . .[1]

Roberts' account illustrates the intimate co-operation of hull-down tanks, anti-tank guns and artillery required to halt a full Panzer advance. But how near the Germans came to luring 22nd Armoured Brigade from their positions emerges from an interview Brigadier Roberts gave almost forty years later, using tableware to describe the positions:

As a matter of fact, although Monty says in his *Memoirs* that the instructions were that the tanks were to stay put in their position on the Alam Halfa position, we did come very near to moving.
You see, the Germans advanced and came up towards Alam Halfa. Now here were we sitting; the Germans came up the [line of] telegraph poles, and when they got there – instead of coming up here they swung away like that.
Well my divisional commander was then a man called Alec Gatehouse. And he was sitting further back . . . he could see what was happening too. And here were our forces with all the German Panzers going along like that past our position. And in fact although Monty says he gave instructions that on no account was the 22nd Armoured Brigade to move its position, at that time Alec Gatehouse said to me, over the air:
'I don't want you to think we're peeing in our bags here, but you may have to come out of your position and attack him from the rear.'
Now whether he had got Horrocks' permission to make such a statement, whether he'd been told by Horrocks that that might happen, and whether Horrocks had referred it to Monty I've not the slighest idea. However that is what he said to me. So I issued preliminary instructions to people that they'd got to be prepared to move out of their defensive positions – just thinking about it.
However at that moment the German tanks stopped and they all turned towards us – just turned, individual tanks, like that, so the situation never arose. But that is a fact – and I shall always wonder

[1] B. Liddell Hart, *The Tanks*, Vol. II, London 1959.

whether the idea of leaving our positions at all had been sanctioned by Montgomery. I don't know. In fact we stayed put and it was very effective even though they, the Germans, produced for the first time a long-barrelled 75-mm gun in their Mark IV tank – which was much more effective than our 75-mm gun and it knocked out one squadron of our Grants very efficiently, before we could do anything about it.[1]

The importance of remaining in position was to be illustrated the next morning, when Gatehouse ordered the 8th Armoured Brigade, with all the remaining Grant tanks in 8th Army, to work its way round north-west – now that there was little chance of the Afrika Korps making for El Hamman – to join up with 22nd Armoured Brigade: for despite its seventy-two Grants and twelve Crusaders 8th Armoured Brigade failed utterly to penetrate the gun line put out by 15th Panzer Division.

As Bernard had noted in his diary, it was by meeting the enemy on 'ground of its own choosing' that 8th Army had so successfully halted Rommel's attack. At 8 p.m. he noted: '2000 hours: enemy Panzer Division drew off and went into harbour for the night.' On the southern flank the harrying tactics of 4th Light Armoured Brigade had caused the enemy to show his teeth, and Bernard wisely ordered that it should be withdrawn 'to avoid destruction'.

By imposing his implacable will on 8th Army, Bernard had so far outwitted his adversary. Ironically, however, it was only Rommel himself who really understood this: his own commanders were all for continuing the battle, while Montgomery's subordinates too became more and more frustrated by the 8th Army Commander's directive that no heavy armour was to leave its hull-down position, even in pursuit – 'it was difficult to restrain the commanders from launching attacks on the Germans,' as General Horrocks later wrote.[2]

For Rommel it was the British refusal to attack which was most galling – the more so since he had neither the petrol nor command of the air which would have enabled him to entice out the British armour by imaginative manoeuvre. His remark to Kesselring that the 'swine' wasn't attacking the following day was a cry of despair; and, though he would authorise limited attacks on Alam Halfa it was – as long as the British refused to leave the ridge – a policy of despair.

All night long the Panzer Army was bombed. As Bernard recorded in his diary for the night 31 August–1 September: '2100. Dust now better and the RAF began night bombing. The Albacores found two large concentrations – one of 2000 tanks and MT, and one of about 1000. These were bombed all night.

[1] Maj-General G. P. B. Roberts, loc. cit.
[2] Sir Brian Horrocks, Account for the British Official Historian, loc. cit.

One enemy harbour area of about a hundred tanks within range of artillery of 13 Corps was shelled all night,' Bernard noted with satisfaction. In his war memoirs Rommel had cause to remember it painfully well:

> After nightfall our forces became the target for heavy RAF attacks, mainly on the reconnaissance group, but also – though less severe – on other units. With one aircraft flying circles and dropping a continuous succession of flares, bombs from the other machines – some of which dived low for the attack – crashed down among the flare-lit vehicles of the reconnaissance units. All movement was instantly pinned down by low-flying attacks. Soon many of our vehicles were alight and burning furiously. The reconnaissance group suffered heavy casualties . . .

Bernard had gone the first step towards avenging Dunkirk. As the British artillery and Desert Air Force pounded the German positions unmercifully, Bernard slept. For Rommel, however, there was little sleep. His famed Afrika Korps was stalled beneath the ridge of Alam Halfa, before the hull-down tanks, anti-tank guns, and supporting artillery of 22nd Armoured Brigade. Alongside them was a further Brigade of more than a hundred Valentines, to the east another Armoured Brigade with Grant tanks, and on the ridge itself the 44th Division, dug-in with minefields, barbed wire and endless artillery. Rommel's hopes of overrunning British petrol dumps had been dashed, and, though the Panzer Army was still a composite force with tremendous fire-power, it was like a bull in a ring. There was no way out to the north, for Alam Halfa was impregnable; there was no way out east for, even if the Afrika Korps could smash its way through the seventy-two Grants of the 8th Armoured Brigade, it could not leave its entire lines of communication at the mercy of Montgomery's forces on its northern flank. And to the south there was merely the impenetrable expanse of the Quattara depression. The Panzer Army could only hope to retreat the way it had come. On the morning of 1 September Rommel permitted his Panzer divisions a few limited attacks; but in his heart he knew the battle was lost – knew also that he would be tarred a defeatist for withdrawing, but that there was no option. To Berlin he signalled that the offensive should be played down in the press and on the radio. By denying Rommel the opportunity of a mobile battle, Montgomery had put paid to his last hope of reaching Cairo and Alexandria. 'Shortage of petrol' would be the official reason given to the bewildered German troops – though, as Kesselring later commented with the suggestion of a sneer, there was enough to bring all the units back. 'It was this cast iron determination to follow through that was lacking,' Kesselring concluded.[1] To Hitler Kesselring complained: 'It was a mystery

[1] Field-Marshal Kesselring, op. cit.

why he didn't go on with it. We had the British on the run again, we only had to pursue them and knock the daylights out of them.'[1]

Whether Rommel would admit defeat or throw everything he had into a last ditch attempt to push past the 22nd Armoured Brigade and reach the Ruweisat Ridge by thrusting west of Alam Halfa, Bernard however had no way of knowing. Certainly he was taking no chances: and his diary reveals the almost mathematical precision with which he balanced his own forces, and counted those of the enemy, as the battle for the Alam Halfa heights continued.

[1 September]

0500   It had become clear during the night that the enemy *Schwerpunkt*, or axis of advance (after he had broken through astride and West of Himeimat) was directed on locality E (44 Division) and hence northwards onto RUWEISAT Ridge.

Decided to concentrate the heavy armour in the area between 44 Division and New Zealand Division. Whole of [10] Armoured Division concentrated in this area:

    23 Armoured Brigade on right (western flank)
    22 Armoured Brigade in centre
     8 Armoured Brigade south of eastern end of locality E
       (eastern flank)

South African front re-organized, and one brigade pulled into reserve and positioned on the Ruweisat Ridge and to North of 8 Armoured Brigade.

0700   Enemy armoured units attacked 22 Armoured Brigade in position and tried to work round each flank of 22 Armoured Brigade.

Enemy suffered casualties, achieved no results, and drew off to the south.

At 10 a.m. Bernard noted the enemy tank strength, derived from Ultra intercepts:

1000   Enemy tank strength appeared (from interceptions) as follows:

5 Panzer Div (8 Tank Regt): Started on 31 August 110 runners: Situation on 1 September 94 runners
21 Panzer Div (5 Tank Regt): Started on 31 August 124 runners: Situation on 1 September 72 runners

Thus, on the first day of battle, 8th Army and the Desert Air Force had knocked out – quite apart from 'soft' vehicles and guns – no less than fifty-two Panzers: a figure which caused some commentators later to question why Montgomery was so cautious in preparing an 8th Army counter-attack. Bernard, however, was jumping to no false

[1] D. Irving, *The Trail of the Fox*, op. cit.

conclusions. As he added to the diary entry relating to 21 Panzer Division: 'Of the 52 casualties 42 are repairable' – a wise rider, since later records showed German losses as probably 22 tanks in all that day.[1]

To Bernard it was still imperative to hold fast, concentrating his armour still further, and wisely conjuring reserves from 30 Corps in the north just in case the British armour gave way, or allowed itself to be lured into mobile battle. In fact a number of Grants of 22nd Armoured Brigade *did* leave their positions during the day, and some five Grants were destroyed before Roberts restrained them.[2]

In analysing the situation at 10 a.m. on the morning of 1 September Bernard therefore saw the area between the New Zealand Division and Alam Halfa as the only sector in which Rommel might seek a 'showdown'. The Afrika Korps could, he reckoned, field 166 Mark III and IV Panzer 'runners'; against this, 8th Army had only 149 Grants – although these were backed by 100 Valentines, 76 Crusaders and 53 Honcys in the sector. Provided the regiments refused to be drawn, there was little likelihood of a German break-through. Therefore – though he expected the engagement around Alam Halfa to last several more days – he began at midday, 1 September, to consider possible 8th Army offensive action.

No serious military historian has ever questioned the manner in which, only two and a half weeks after assuming command of 8th Army, Bernard Montgomery fought the defensive battle of Alam Halfa. Whether he ought to have done more to discomfort Rommel – whether indeed he might have made Alam Halfa, and not Alamein, the deciding Battle of Egypt – is a different question. Correlli Barnett, in his round-up of the views of the sacked generals of the desert – Dorman-Smith, Gatehouse, Ramsden, Renton, even went so far as to declare:

> This was the moment for an annihilating counter-stroke in the grand style, driving across Rommel's communications to the Quattara Depression, sealing his armour in a cauldron of bombardment, and achieving a complete and historic victory by Rommel's surrender *en rase campagne*.[3]

Even the New Zealand *Official History* – so uninhibitedly critical of Auchinleck's command – felt that an 'opportunity to strike really hard at the *Panzer Army*' was missed.[4] Before he died, General de Guingand also spoke frankly about a 'missed opportunity'. He remembered Montgomery summoning him to his caravan on 1 September 1942 – recalled indeed that it was his own plan that Montgomery adopted:

[1] Michael Carver, *El Alamein*, London 1962.
[2] R. Walker, op. cit.
[3] Correlli Barnett, op. cit.
[4] R. Walker, op. cit.

I felt he ought to [deliver a counter-attack] and I persuaded him. He said: 'What shall we do now?' – he had me into the caravan. 'Rommel's had a hell of a smacking, he's lost a lot of armour, some of his supplies have been blown up by our Air Force.' And I said: 'There's a gap here – the New Zealand Division was there – why don't you get the New Zealand Division to have a crack south, try to cut him off?'

If the New Zealand Division had really been more robust I think we could have achieved big things there, there's no doubt about it.[1]

Time and again, at the climax of Alamein, at Falaise, in the Ardennes – the same criticism would be levelled: that Bernard, despite his ruthless style of command, somehow lacked the verve to risk a *coup de grâce*. No doubt the question will be asked as long as military history is debated; yet it is clear that the answer cannot have lain, as the New Zealand military historian supposed, in Montgomery's innate cautiousness as a Commander. To anyone who knew Bernard, such an attribute is misleading. Certainly he could be stubborn to the point of exasperation; certainly he was not one to get involved in anything which promised confusion, or a 'dog's breakfast'; yet he was certainly capable of extreme recklessness, in actions or in relationships – a recklessness that had marked his character from childhood. Moreover in battlefield tactics he was the last to teach or practise excessive caution – as his subordinate company commander, Captain Gething, had found in Egypt in 1932, as Major de Guingand had found in the Canal Brigade manoeuvres the following year, and as Major Simpson witnessed in the brigade manoeuvres on Salisbury Plain in 1937. Bernard's initial willingness to undertake the gamble of the Dieppe raid, his later adoption of the Arnhem airborne offensive – indeed the very concept of a single-thrust offensive in 1944 to take Berlin: these were not the hall-marks of an obsessively cautious commander. It was Bernard's implacable will that would transform 8th Army and would bring victory at Alamein; moreover it was Bernard's fundamental belief in concentration of offensive effort that would produce the copy-book armoured victories at El Hamma, at Wadi Akarit, and the final capture of Tunis. It was this same belief in the inexorable success of concentrated force applied at the decisive point that would characterise the Allied landings in Sicily and Normandy, as well as the 'dash to the Seine' in August 1944. If, therefore, Bernard allowed the 'Desert Fox' to escape the net which 8th Army had thrown around the Panzer offensive on Cairo and Alexandria, it is unlikely that the explanation will be found in excessive cautiousness as a Commander. Rather we must look for an answer to the two great protagonists themselves – to Field-Marshal

---

[1] De Guingand, loc. cit.

Rommel and Lt-General Montgomery: for they alone ultimately controlled this battle. Both were regularly visited by their C-in-Cs – Kesselring and Alexander – but in neither case did the C-in-C make any decisions affecting the conduct of the battle. The battle of Alam Halfa was planned and commanded by Rommel and Montgomery alone: and it is in their respective responses to their adversary that the key to the strange development of the battle must lie. Far from lacking nerve, Rommel's very professionalism and instinct as a soldier told him what his own corps and divisional commanders could not know: that to pursue the assault on Alam Halfa would lead to a battle of attrition and armoured annihilation – for this time 8th Army was not going to be panicked into premature withdrawal or a battle of manoeuvre, was instead going to stand and fight. Moreover if the Afrika Korps, with its temporary superiority in tanks, were to be destroyed, then it would be the end of the Axis campaign in North Africa – for Rommel had pinned his strategy on tactical aggression and had hoped that Malta, the key to Mediterranean supply, would fall 'inevitably' if the enemy was kept constantly in check: a single-thrust strategy which was remarkably analogous to the Allied controversy in North-West Europe in the autumn of 1944.

From the first night, however, Rommel had known intuitively that his luck had run out. His tactical intellect nevertheless told him to maintain an offensive posture – to bear his teeth – but neither to look for a genuine showdown, nor to lose the cohesion of his two Panzer Divisions; meanwhile the path of his retreat must be secured by carefully corseted German-Italian artillery, anti-tank weapons and mobile infantry.

As in a game of chess, Rommel's opponent was equally unwilling to 'exchange Queens' in an all-out battle of armour. Rommel had shown his hand; it was now time for 8th Army to make its own move. In doing so, however, it was vital not to give Rommel the chance for an armoured riposte by initiating the sort of rash, often ill-coordinated and ill-executed tank manoeuvring that had characterised the use of British armour over the past year. The British armour was well positioned, on high ground, dug-in and protected by artillery and anti-tank guns. To surrender that advantage would have been insane.[1] The obvious weak link in the enemy chain was at the neck of his salient, to the south of the New Zelanders, as de Guingand pointed out. If the New Zealanders attacked southwards, they would at the very least frighten Rommel into withdrawing his armour from Alam Halfa for fear of being cut off. If well planned and conducted, there was even a chance that Rommel's armour *could* be cut off; without further petrol it would be obliged to surrender or to try to break out. Providing 8th Army was methodical, however, and

[1] As it was, some 18 Grants and 3 Crusader tanks were lost in the inconclusive skirmishing by 22nd and 8th Armoured Brigades on 1 September.

took no risks, there would be nowhere where the Panzer divisions *could* break out.

Liddell Hart, writing in his famous history of *The Thanks*,[1] found the battle of Alam Halfa dull and flat. 'Rarely has any vital battle been as uneventful as that which is now engraved in history as the "Battle of Alam Halfa," ' he declared, but the contention was unjust. In the first thirty-six hours the battle undoubtedly conformed to Montgomery's design. But from the moment the Afrika Korps had been brought to a halt below the Alam Halfa heights the battle did *not* go according to Montgomery's plan: and in the uneasy manoeuvring to pinch out Rommel's salient there would be an illuminating insight into the still disastrous lack of offensive skills in the 8th Army.

[1] Op. cit.

CHAPTER NINE

Alam Halfa – The Middle

'At 1200 hours on 1 September decided to re-group so as to form reserves and make troops available for closing gap between New Zealand area and Himeimat, and seizing the initiative,' Bernard noted in his diary.

The aim was laudable: but in the execution, in the middle of a critical battle to halt the German attempt to take Cairo and Alexandria, Bernard was to discover something of the dilatoriness, mistrust and lack of co-operation which the failures of the past year had bred in 8th Army. Moreover the omens – as they had been for Rommel – were negative from the start: for early that morning (1 September), the 9th Australian Division had carried out a diversionary raid in the northern sector of the Alamein line, code-named BULIMBA. Undertaken by a battalion of Australian infantry, it was supported by a squadron of tanks, and although its aim remains obscure to this day, one of its purposes was undoubtedly to be a 'test' attack prior to Bernard's autumn offensive – for it was planned to take place in exactly the same sector as Bernard had, on 15 August, revealed to Lt-General Horrocks that the main 8th Army thrust would later be launched. The Australian raid would give valuable information not only about enemy dispositions and defensive tactics around Tell el Eisa, but provide important experience in the stage-management of an operation in which the infantry would clear the enemy minefields and allow tanks to follow up immediately and exploit the gaps made. The raiding battalion was withdrawn into reserve as early as 20 August, and its plans were ordered to be complete by 25 August, prior to Rommel's expected attack. The final order for the raid to take place was given by 30 Corps on 31 August; and the troops moved across their start-line at 5.35 a.m. on 1 September.

Naturally the full lessons of 'Bulimba' cannot have been clear to Bernard when, just over six hours after its launching, he made his plans for 'seizing the initiative'. That it had failed to dent the German line, however, was apparent from 9 a.m. when the battalion survivors were recalled. Bernard's diary entry was laconic:

Australians. Before dawn on 1 September attacked and made a gap in enemy lines. 100 German prisoners taken. A raiding force was to pass through the gap after dawn. Enemy counter-attack after dawn. This counter-attack was heavy and the Australians suffered heavily and could not pass the raiding force through. Total casualties 15 killed, 120 wounded. Six tanks lost.

The lack of co-operation between tanks and infantry had been total, and though the lesson would have to be studied Bernard cannot be blamed for doubting, in his heart of hearts, whether an unrehearsed operation to cut off all Rommel's forces in the southern salient would achieve significantly better results. The very principle of his defence at Alamein and Alam Halfa was the disbanding of Battle Groups, the fighting of divisions as divisions, and the inculcation of a spirit of 'stand or die'. Churchill, while applauding Bernard's new atmosphere in 8th Army, had taken Alexander to task for not doing more to prepare for a possible German break-through – 'in the fullest accord with General Alexander and the CIGS, I set on foot a series of extreme measures for the defence of Cairo and the water-lines running northwards to the sea . . . all the office population of Cairo, numbering thousands of staff officers and uniformed clerks, were armed with rifles and ordered to take their station, if need be, along the fortified water line,' Churchill recorded. 'The 51st Highland Division was not yet regarded as "desert-worthy", but these magnificent troops were now ordered to man the new Nile front', under the potential command of General 'Jumbo' Wilson. There was therefore no infantry reserve capable of taking the mythical *rase campagne* measures which some subsequent historians would have liked to see. As for the heavy armour, Bernard was adamant that it should stay put on ground of its own choosing. If he was to 'seize the initiative', then the troops would have to come from Alexander, notwithstanding Churchill's waterways-edict. Alexander, however, would only agree to provide a single infantry brigade – the 151st Brigade of the erstwhile 50th Division, currently defending the Ameiriya landing grounds. Even this brigade would first have to be relieved by a brigade from the Highland Division.

While the Afrika Korps beat up against the defences of Alam Halfa, therefore, Bernard could only hope to dispose of two reserve infantry brigades: the reserve South African Brigade on the Ruweisat Ridge behind Alam Halfa and the 151st Brigade in Amiriya. Of these he wanted to keep one temporarily in the north-east as a 'long-stop' in case 8th Armoured Brigade was by-passed. This left only a single brigade free to reinforce the front line – the South African Brigade.

As soundly as the defence of Alam Halfa had gone, the preparations for Bernard's 'initiative' now ran into difficulties. The Commander of the South African Division – understandably after the disasters of the early summer – objected to the removal of one of his brigades, and, though he was overruled, Bernard had to agree to a complicated system of side-stepping as a result.

On paper the plan looked simple enough. The area of 8th Army's southern defences which Rommel had breached on the night of 30 August was covered by parallel minefields running north-south. The New Zealand Division had been *in situ* for over a month and knew the area well. Of all the units of 8th Army the New Zealanders were probably most feared by the Germans and Italians, and stories of Maori ferocity abounded. Bernard noted in his diary that he would transfer a full medium regiment of artillery and an anti-tank gun regiment from 30 Corps to reinforce the New Zealanders, who would attack on the night of 2 September, in a southward direction to close the neck of Rommel's salient.

On night 2/3 September 13 Corps to begin to re-establish minefield, working south from New Zealand area.

11 Hussars to work armoured car patrols round south flank and to tap in at Himeimat.

Task of 13 Corps: gradually to close gap

Task of 30 Corps: to thin out and form reserves

Task of 10 Corps [a Corps Headquarters staff recently formed in Cairo]: to be prepared to take command of all reserves available and push through to DABA. 9 Australian Division coming possibly under 10 Corps. Issued orders re above to commanders 13 and 30 Corps verbally on afternoon 1 September, and to commander 10 Corps at 1100 hours on 2 September.

Given the failure of the Australian 'Bulimba' raid, it is unlikely that Bernard genuinely imagined it would be possible to pass a pursuit force through the Axis line in the northern sector of Alamein unless Rommel's nerve broke and he ordered a general Axis retreat. But whatever the subsequent views of Kesselring and Hitler, Rommel's nerve did not break; despite the dreadful hammering he was receiving from the Desert Air Force and 8th Army artillery, tanks and anti-tank guns, he still hoped that the new 8th Army Commander might commit an error that would give him the chance to turn defeat into victory. Thus, while his Panzer divisions searched vainly for weak spots in the Alam Halfa defences, Rommel nervously watched for signs of an enemy counter-offensive he might turn to his advantage.

The position on 1 September was therefore one of stalemate as Rommel and Montgomery each attempted to read the other's mind. That few staff officers seriously believed 8th Army had the necessary forces to cut off the enemy is reflected in the War Diary of 13 Corps that night:

As a result of the day's fighting it was determined that in order to threaten enemy columns:

a) 7 Armoured Division would operate offensively NW and W from its present positions
b) 2 New Zealand Division would extend their position southwards along the line of our minefields
c) 10 Division would remain in battle positions already held and would not attack the enemy.

Each Army Commander therefore hoped the other would now make a mistake: if Rommel became inextricably engaged at Alam Halfa or even tried to break out to the east, the 8th Army pincers would shut off his supply route; whereas Rommel hoped that, if he marked time for long enough around Alam Halfa, he might persuade 8th Army into a *sottise* which would give him the chance to administer the 'thorough beating' he had promised the British in his letter to Frau Rommel on 30 August.

The clearer it became that Rommel was sitting out the battle, however, the more imperative it became that the New Zealand attack should be well conducted, and give Rommel no opportunity to swing back and punch too hard with his armour, either cutting off the New Zealand extension, or even smashing its way through on to the Ruweisat ridge. Freyberg, at any rate, believed this to be possible. Thus when the New Zealanders were asked by Horrocks, the Corps Commander, to prepare a full-scale attack southwards, there was some considerable 'belly-aching', and Horrocks was pressured into offering a brigade of 5th Indian Division, not in order to free New Zealanders for the attack, but as the attacking force itself. When Montgomery heard this he rejected the proposal immediately: the New Zealanders knew the ground and the minefields, and they, not the Indian Brigade, should undertake the attack, he ordered.

Although Freyberg had been requested to investigate the possibility of a southward attack as early as 30 August, there now followed a series of arguments reminiscent of the worst days of June and July under Ritchie and Auchinleck. Freyberg's brigadiers were, from the start, unwilling to leave the defensive positions they had so strenuously fortified, and their original plan on 30 August was to furnish merely a mobile column consisting of a single battalion. When Horrocks told Freyberg on 1 September that the Army Commander wanted the New Zealanders, not the brigade from 5th Indian Division, to carry out the attack, Freyberg protested that even an entire New Zealand brigade would be insufficient: it ought to be two. Moreover he was unwilling to commit the security of his defensive position to two 'outside' brigades, leaving the two-brigades-strong New Zealand Division to do all the attacking; he therefore suggested that 132nd Brigade of 44th Division should take part, alongside 5th New Zealand Brigade.

Once again Montgomery resisted this compromise. He had promised Alexander, in order to get the 44th Division released to 8th Army at all for the battle, that its units would be used solely for defence, and even after the war was over Horrocks was pierced with remorse over the use of its 132nd Brigade. The Division had been Horrocks' first divisional command the previous year in Kent, and despite its rigorous training in England he was loth to put it so early into a critical desert attack at night on ground which it did not know. Horrocks took the blame – 'my only regret,' he wrote to the Official Historian in 1945, 'is the comparatively severe losses incurred by 132nd Infantry Brigade when they carried out their attack under the orders of the 2nd New Zealand Division. I feel now, looking back, that this was rather an ambitious attack for a brigade which had just arrived in the desert. On the other hand they were the only troops available and they had to be used. As you will read from the official narrative, everything went wrong.'[1]

This was no understatement. Whether Montgomery should have dealt personally with Freyberg is a moot point, for there is no question but that Freyberg – a Lieutenant-General senior even to Montgomery in the Army Lists – resented having to take orders from Horrocks, who had only been a Lieutenant-General for a fortnight. Freyberg, soured by the vulnerability of his infantry, the chaotic command and miserable communications during the Gazala retreat, added to his own disastrous defeat in Crete the previous year, was a man who needed careful handling, and it would be a tribute to Bernard Montgomery's generalship that within so short a time he was able to allocate a major part of the Alamein offensive to the 2nd New Zealand Division.

For the moment, however, Bernard worked through his Corps Commander, General Horrocks. By promising to bring a full divisional headquarters in with 151st Brigade to take over the New Zealand defensive position, Bernard hoped to placate Freyberg, and encourage him to agree to an all-New Zealand attack; but the headquarters (50th Division) was not forthcoming and Freyberg was subsequently told he would have to be responsible both for the defensive position and the attack: a task that was beyond him. Insisting that if this was the case he should be allowed to choose what units took part in the attack, Freyberg reverted to his original scheme for using the virgin 132nd Brigade – and a débâcle ensued.

Freyberg cannot be entirely blamed. He was the senior officer of New Zealand's only expeditionary force, and had a personal responsibility direct to the New Zealand Government for the lives of his New Zealand soldiers. The 9th Australian Division's 'Bulimba' attack

[1] Loc. cit.

on the morning of 1 September had been a failure; the South African Division's commander had initially refused to provide his reserve brigade as an 8th Army reserve, and on the southern flank the Commander of 7th Armoured Division was eventually to declare it would be impossible to 'tap in' at Himeimat in order to help the New Zealanders. Montgomery himself refused to transfer any heavy Grant tanks from Alam Halfa either for the attack, or to cover the original New Zealand defensive position. Moreover Rommel was on the look-out for a break in 8th Army ranks; and the moment he received German Air Force reports of extensive movement in the New Zealand sector, he ordered both air attacks and a strengthening of the threatened 'neck' of his own salient.

While Horrocks and Freyberg argued over the size and composition of the New Zealand attack, as well as the covering forces Freyberg wanted in his sector, all the signs began to point to an abandonment of the Axis offensive, if not a withdrawal. By the morning of 2 September, Bernard Montgomery recorded in his diary: 'Clear from the front that Panzer Army was not going to take the offensive. Possibly short of petrol, supplies, and so on. Adopting a defensive attitude.[1] Proceeded with plans for regaining initiative'.

By 4 p.m. it was 'clear from reports from ground and air that whole area south of our positions was one mass of vehicles – tanks and MET. This was bombed and shot at by artillery all day. On East, South-East and South, the enemy forces consisting of Panzer Army, and a mass of Italian troops was ringed in by armoured car patrols'. Nevertheless, as Bernard also noted, his own heavy tank strength was already down to 120 Grants, with 52 of the light Crusaders, 68 of the even lighter Honeys, and 100 of the obsolete Valentines, armed only with 2-pounder guns. It was, as he recorded in his diary that evening, still 'important not to rush into the attack', and waste armour and crews in wild assaults on the German anti-tank screens. With only 120 Grants available he could not hope to achieve decisive success in a concentrated heavy-armoured attack on the enemy: the time for that would come in due course when the promised Sherman tanks arrived and 8th Army was in a position to mount its own planned and rehearsed offensive. For the moment 8th Army had everything to gain by teasing Rommel without giving him anything solid to hit back at; to punish him with artillery and air bombardment, day and night, concentrating particularly on his soft-skinned vehicles. With the New Zealanders threatening the neck of his salient and 7th Armoured Division squeezing Himeimat in the south, Rommel would then be forced to pull out.

'13 Corps given two main tasks,' Bernard therefore wrote that evening, 2 September:

[1] This was confirmed that morning by an Ultra decrypt of Rommel's announcement to Berlin at noon, 1 September, that he was going temporarily on to the defensive – cf. F. H. Hinsley, op. cit.

i) To shoot up and harry and destroy enemy MET. To tear the guts out of the enemy by destroying his vehicles and soft stuff. Savage 'rabbit' tactics against all enemy MET by everyone.
ii) To gradually and methodically close the gap, working southwards from NZ area; at same time mobile forces to operate northwards from Himeimat.

Because the South Africans were so dilatory in moving their reserve brigade, the New Zealand attack had to be postponed for twenty-four hours, however; but the extra time in which Freyberg was able to plan the attack was more than offset by the gathering retreat of the Panzer Army which brought the Afrika Korps itself within striking distance of Freyberg's 'extension'.

Here indeed was the critical moment of the battle, so often overlooked or ignored by historians. The defence of Alam Halfa was the first large-scale defensive battle to be fought successfully by the Western Allies in World War Two; it would become, as General Sir Oliver Leese later remarked, the model for the defensive battle of Medenine, and to some extent the battle of the Ardennes. With the very minimum of casualties it put paid to the German dream of hegemony in the Middle East, demonstrated the fallibility of armour as an independent weapon and proved decisively that future battles and indeed the war itself would have to be won by co-operation between all arms, and between all three services. In this sense it was a classic engagement, a copybook exercise in command and execution – up to the moment when late on the evening of 3 September the New Zealand attack finally began to close the neck of Rommel's salient. The casualties sustained in this operation – codenamed 'Beresford' – amounted to almost three-quarters of the recorded casualties suffered by 8th Army in the entire battle, and more than ten per cent of the total casualties later sustained in the battle of Alamein itself. No less than 1140 men were killed, wounded or captured in the thirty-six hours of the operation; without it 8th Army would have finished the battle with fewer than 500 casualties – a negligible amount for such a cardinal action.

CHAPTER TEN

Alam Halfa – The End

Ironically, operation 'Beresford' proved to be quite superfluous, for by the night of 1 September Rommel had given his corps commanders orders to retreat to the erstwhile front line in a series of bounds, and on the 2nd this movement began to take shape. It was therefore too late to cut off the Afrika Korps, and unnecessary in terms of persuading Rommel to withdraw – the co-ordinated tank and artillery reception beneath the Alam Halfa ridge, the incessant pounding from the air, and the paucity of petrol supplies from the rear had convinced Rommel he must pull back. However, until Rommel did withdraw this could not be known for certain within 8th Army. On the contrary it was estimated that up to 150 of the Afrika Korps Panzer Mark III and IVs were still runners; moreover on 2 September two German parachutists carrying a white flag had come into the 8th Army front line on the Ruweisat Ridge, demanding the surrender of the British troops. 'They'd come, the officers said, to avoid bloodshed as the enemy commander was in the back of our positions,' 8th Army Intelligence summarised that evening, 'and it was proposed to take over Ruweisat forthwith. Thus we were provided with a valuable insight into the enemy information service, together with a nice legal problem [whether to return the 'parlementaires']. When the Germans make a plan and it fails, they have shown a tendency not to blame the plan itself but rather the way it has taken shape in action and they return to it in their own time. It is obvious,' the Summary concluded, 'from enemy movements, the continued attention of Stukas to Alam el Halfa, and from the captured maps showing German compass readings that Point 103 [102] is to the enemy the vital spot. To this,' the Intelligence Summary warned, 'he will return.' Neither Ultra nor the 8th Army's Y service gave any indication of Rommel's intention to retreat.[1]

When, the next day, all signs pointed to a withdrawal rather than a resumption of the attack on Alam Halfa, there was still much speculation at 13 Corps and 8th Army Headquarters about Rommel's next move. As the GHQ Liaison Officer reported to Cairo that night, it first looked suspiciously as though Rommel was going to attempt a

---

[1] War Diary, 8th Army HQ 'I' Section, September 1942 (WO 169/3937), PRO.

new attack on the rearward side of the New Zealand defensive position just as the German parachutist 'parlementaires' fore-warned.

Enemy intentions It was believed that earlier in the day the enemy's intentions were to attack Northwards with the object of squeezing out 6 New Zealand Brigade and the 5 Indian Division [which had sidestepped into the NZ area to cover Operation 'Beresford']. About 1600 hours reports began to come in giving the impression that the enemy was beginning withdrawal; probably as a result of the basting he had received from the RAF during the night and from our guns during the day. It does not now seem likely that he has any intention of carrying out the attack to the North tonight and he appears to be withdrawing behind the line of our old minefields.

The 13 Corps War Diarist was similarly uncertain: 'By the end of the afternoon,' he recorded, 'it appeared that the enemy was with-drawing, but it was as yet too early to assume this true.'[1] In Bernard's own diary he had noted on the night of 2 September: 'Learnt from prisoners' statements that Rommel visited the forward area on 29 August and told the troops that they would be in ALEXANDRIA in a few days.' Would Rommel really risk the humiliation of having to retreat? On the morning of 3 September Bernard continued:

0700   Reports at dawn that enemy had withdrawn from contact and moved south, and that his main force seemed to have moved West slightly.

Bernard was therefore taking no chances.

Issued orders:
a) There will be no forward movement from our main fortified positions except by patrols.
b) Armoured car ring to close in on enemy and picket him.
c) Attack on enemy MET to continue. Strong patrols to operate and to contain artillery and RE. All derelict MET to be blown up.
d) 13 Corps to proceed vigorously with their operations to close the gap, working carefully and methodically from present NZ area towards Himeimat.

Whether he credited the possibility which his own Army Head-quarters feared – namely that Rommel might strike northwards into the rear of the New Zealand position – is not known. He did not

[1] War Diary, HQ 13 Corps, September 1942 (WO 169/4007), PRO.

mention it in his diary, and to Freyberg's nervous appeals for heavy tanks he gave a flat refusal. There were now no fewer than four infantry brigades in the New Zealand area, together with the New Zealand artillery and cavalry, plus an extra regiment of medium artillery, a regiment of anti-tank guns, and two squadrons of Valentines to back up the infantry. Provided Freyberg worked his way south 'methodically', Bernard felt, Freyberg need have no fear of a Panzer penetration.

a) At 2230 hours New Zealand Division began an attack southwards

he noted in his diary for the 'Night of 3/4 September,

as the first stage towards closing the gap over minefields N of HIMEIMAT: 5 NZ, 132 and 6 NZ Brigades were used, in that order from east to west.
b) Attack met strong resistance from 90 Light Division. Fierce fighting took place. The Maoris went up to and beyond their object (of 5 NZ Brigade).
c) 132 Brigade were successful on east with Buffs. But on West the 2 RW Kents battalion suffered severe casualties. Brig. Robertson was severely wounded. CO of Buffs (Nicholson) wounded.
d) On extreme West, battalion of 6 NZ had very severe casualties. Brigadier Clifton was missing.
e) Final situation: objective reached on the east flank but not on the west.

Casualties were still not known in detail, but were thought to be heavy; moreover this was only Stage One of the operation, designed to clear an easy path for 151st Brigade to exploit. 'Quite clear that enemy extremely sensitive to attempts to close the gap,' Bernard concluded.

Everything, as Horrocks recalled, had gone wrong. Clifton's men, intending only a diversionary New Zealand raid, ran into the crack Italian parachutists of the Folgore Division, together with German parachutists of the Ramcke Brigade from Crete. According to Volkmar Kuhn's *German Paratroops in World War II* the Ramcke Force was visited personally on the morning of 2 September by Rommel, who 'expressed his satisfaction with its location and the paratroopers' defences. Turning to Ramcke he asked, "Well, Ramcke, how do you think the situation will develop now?"

'"In my view, Feldmarschall," Ramcke replied, "the enemy would be stupid *not* to counter-attack in this sector. Their artillery has already started ranging on our dummy positions, and I am expecting them to attack any time now."

'"I think you're right, Ramcke," said Rommel, as he got into the car which was to take him to his command post, "and I am relying on you to hold on here . . . otherwise the Afrika Korps is going to be in real trouble." [1]

Possibly this story, like so many, has been embellished: but if true it is a useful instance of Rommel's style of command. The Ramcke Force proved far tougher than either Freyberg or Horrocks anticipated, and Bernard's conclusion about the enemy's sensitivity was correct. Ironically, however, neither Montgomery nor Rommel was capable of influencing the battle now. Having been counter-attacked continuously all day on Friday 4 September, Freyberg decided towards evening to withdraw his battered brigades from the 'gap' without Horrocks' or Montgomery's permission. Meanwhile Rommel, fearing that the New Zealand attack had been successful, ordered 21st Panzer Division into the battle and 15th Panzer Division to stand by – thus halting – on paper – the withdrawal of the Afrika Korps. However the Italian divisions were by this time in full flight, the Panzer divisions had no wish to be left behind in exposed positions and so they too ignored their Army Commander's orders, leaving Ramcke and the other 'locals' to restore the situation!

Operation 'Beresford' had therefore failed: it had not closed the 'gap', had not even caused the Afrika Korps' withdrawal (though it may well have hastened it); moreover it had come to grief simply on the local German-Italian defences set up during the Panzer Army's advance through the British minefields.

Any disappointment in 8th Army, however, was quickly overshadowed by the growing realisation that the battle as such had been won – the Afrika Korps was in full retreat, leaving a field littered with spoils: tanks, artillery, vehicles, burned-out aircraft. By midday on 4 September Bernard recorded his certainty 'that enemy was going to withdraw'; not unnaturally he disliked Freyberg's unilateral decision to pull back from the Munassib area; but, given the casualties suffered and the apparent confusion, there was little to be gained by insisting. That night he recorded 'NZ Division withdrew infantry to original positions and left mobile troops to work southwards'.

At 8th Army Headquarters there was now a sense of great excitement: and for Bernard this was capped by the arrival of President Roosevelt's personal emissary, Mr Wendell Willkie, who stayed the night at Burg-el-Arab, and was taken round the 'forward area' by Bernard the following day. After the disasters and defeats of Norway, France, Greece, Crete, Tobruk, Cyrenaica and in the Far East, it was a proud moment to be able, as 8th Army Commander, to show the American President's adviser a German army in full retreat.

Willkie's world tour on behalf of the American President had put the wind up the Foreign Office in London, for Willkie was known to be somewhat anti-British in the manner of old-fashioned Americans

[1] Volkmar Kuhn, *German Paratroops in World War II*, London 1978.

who, recalling the War of Independence, deeply mistrusted the British Empire. On 5 September Churchill wired anxiously to the British Ambassador in Cairo: 'I hope you are taking trouble with Wendell Willkie who is a good friend of our country. He should be given every chance to see the front and anything else of interest that he desires. It is most important he should be warmly welcomed. You might mention him to Alexander if the latter is not too busy.'[1]

As the war progressed Bernard would often arouse ill-feeling by his refusal to allow VIPs to visit his headquarters – indeed one of his first edicts at 8th Army Headquarters was to ban all visits without his own personal permission. However in this instance he needed no pressure by Churchill to recognise the importance of Willkie's mission, and Churchill's cable arrived in Cairo twenty-four hours *after* Willkie had left for Burg-el-Arab. Willkie himself was bowled over by the new 8th Army Commander. 'On the way to Cairo at the end of August bad news came to meet us,' Willkie wrote in his famous chronicle of the journey *One World*.[2]

At Kano, Nigeria, there was open speculation as to how many days it might take General Rommel to cover the few miles which lay between his advanced scouts and Alexandria. By the time we reached Khartoum, this speculation had become hard reports of what is known in Egypt as a 'flap' – a mild form of panic . . . I recalled the President's warning just before I left Washington that before I reached Cairo it might be in German hands. We heard tales of Nazi parachutists dropped in the Nile Valley to disorganize its last defences. The British 8th Army was widely believed to be preparing to evacuate Egypt altogether, retiring to Palestine and southward into the Sudan and Kenya.

Cairo he found

full of rumours and alarms . . . In a half hour at Shepheard's Hotel you could pick up a dozen different versions of what was taking place in the desert not much more than a hundred miles away.

So I accepted eagerly an invitation from General Bernard Montgomery to see the front myself, at El Alamein . . .

General Montgomery met me at his headquarters, hidden among the sand dunes on the Mediterranean. In fact, it was so near the beach that he and General Alexander and I took our next morning's bath in those marvellous blue-green waters. Headquarters consisted of four American automobile trailers, spaced a few dozen yards apart against the dunes for concealment purposes. In one of these, the General had his maps and battle plans. He gave

[1] Prime Minister's files, re Wendell Willkie (PREM 4 – 26/6), PRO.
[2] Wendell Willkie, *One World*, London 1943.

me one for sleeping-quarters. In another his aide put up, and in the fourth the General himself lived, when he was not at the front.

This was not often. The wiry, scholarly, intense, almost fanatical personality of General Montgomery made a deep impression on me when I was in Egypt, but no part of his character was more remarkable than his passionate addiction to work . . .

Almost before we were out of our cars, General Montgomery launched into a detailed description of a battle which was in its last phases, and which for the first time in months had stopped Rommel dead. No real news of this battle had reached Cairo or been given to the press. The General repeated the details for us, step by step, telling us exactly what had happened and why he felt it was a major victory even though his forces had not advanced any great distance. It had been a testing of strength on a heavy scale. Had the British lost, Rommel would have been in Cairo in a few days . . .

At first it was hard for me to understand why the General kept repeating in a quiet way: 'Egypt has been saved.' The enemy was deep in Egypt and had not retreated. I remembered the scepticism I had found in Cairo, born of earlier British claims. But before I left the trailer in which General Montgomery had rigged up his map-room, I had learned more about desert warfare, and he had convinced me that something more than the ubiquitous self-confidence of the British officer and gentleman lay behind his assurance that the threat to Egypt had been liquidated.

General Montgomery spoke with great enthusiasm of the American-manufactured General Sherman tanks which were just then beginning to arrive in important numbers on the docks at Alexandria and Port Said . . . Almost his central thesis was his belief that earlier British reverses on the desert front had resulted from inadequate co-ordination of tank forces, artillery forces, and air power. General Montgomery told me that he had his air officer living with him at his headquarters, and that complete co-ordination of planes, tanks and artillery had been chiefly responsible for the decisive check to Rommel of the past few days.

Bernard invited Willkie to dine with him that evening; but, though Willkie accepted gratefully, Burg-el-Arab was soon alight with jealousy. The American Air Force had begun to provide both bomber and fighter-escort squadrons in the desert, under the overall command of Major-General Brereton. Bernard had no idea who Brereton was when introduced together with Willkie, and did not include him in his invitation to dinner. Brereton took lasting umbrage at this, and only the timely intervention of Alexander averted a row. Although dinner was given in Montgomery's mess, Alexander took over as host, invited Brereton to come, and to Brereton's delight General Montgomery was placed 'down by the salt'.

Bernard later accompanied Willkie to his caravan.

He made sure my sleeping bunk was in order, and then we sat on the steps of the trailer, from which we could see the whitecaps breaking on the sea under the moon and hear at our backs in the distance the pounding of his artillery against Rommel's retreating forces. He was in a reminiscent and reflective mood and talked of his boyhood days in County Donegal, of his long years in the British Army, with service in many parts of the world, of his continuous struggle since the war began to infuse both public officials and Army officers with the necessity for an affirmative instead of a defensive attitude. 'I tell you, Willkie, it's the only way to defeat the Boches' – he always spoke of the Germans as the Boches. 'Give them no rest, give them no rest. These Boches are good soldiers. They are professionals.'

When I asked him about Rommel he said: 'He's a trained, skilled general, but he has one weakness. He repeats his tactics – and that's the way I'm going to get him.'

The following day Bernard personally took Willkie round the front, visiting a group of Americans training with a British tank regiment, and inspecting 'the dozens of German tanks scattered over the desert. They had been captured by the British and blown up at Montgomery's orders. As we would climb up on these wrecked tanks, he would open the food boxes and hand to me the charred remnants of British provisions and supplies which the Germans had taken when they captured Tobruk. "You see, Willkie, the devils have been living on us. But they are not going to do it again. At least they are never going to use these tanks against us again." '

For Willkie, after Roosevelt's ominous warning and the rumours he had heard all the way from Washington to Cairo, the picture of this small, beak-nosed Army Commander, who personalised everything and yet who had such a mastery of military detail, clambering up a wrecked German tank and opening its food boxes, was mesmerising. 'Again I was enormously impressed by the depth and thoroughness of General Montgomery's knowledge of his business. Whether it was Corps or Division, brigade, regiment or battalion headquarters he knew more in detail of the deployment of the troops and location of the tanks than did the officer in charge. This may sound extravagant but it was literally true . . . On the way back to General Montgomery's headquarters he summed up what I had seen and heard. He minced no words at all in describing his situation as excellent, and the battle just concluded as a victory of decisive significance. "With the superiority in tanks and planes that I have established as a result of this battle, and with Rommel's inability to get reinforcements of matériel across the eastern Mediterranean – for our air forces are destroying 4 out of every 5 of his matériel transports – it is now mathematically certain that I will eventually destroy Rommel. This battle was the critical test.'' '

Even Brereton noted in his diary – though he muddled the date of Willkie's visit – that 'Rommel's bid for Egypt had failed. It was one of the major turning points of the war'.[1]

Bernard's diary entry that evening – 5 September – recorded: 'By 1900 hours enemy was right back in the minefield area, covered only by rearguards.'

What he did not record was a conference he had had with Alexander after Wendell Willkie had gone to bed the previous night at 9.30. Rommel had been beaten – but should the British trumpet it as a major victory? The first ships of the great Allied convoy with new tanks and weapons had begun to dock on 2 September – with no less than 194 Sherman tanks aboard. If Rommel learned of this – which he must, inevitably, since there were so many spies operating in Cairo, quite apart from aerial reconnaissance – would he remain in strength at El Alamein, at the end of such long lines of communication, and having suffered in the past days such grievous losses in men, vehicles, guns and tanks? Would he not be tempted to withdraw to less extended positions at Fuka, Sollum, or even as far as Agheila? Not only would such a withdrawal affect the whole supply and communication basis on which 8th Army's autumn offensive was being planned, but it could also prejudice the outcome of 'Torch', of which both Alexander and Montgomery had in turn been Commander-elect, and by which the Prime Minister set such store.

'Looking back, I see it was a mistake to remain there,' the German C-in-C South Field-Marshal Kesselring wrote after the war. 'All things considered,' he reflected, 'it would have been better to have retired behind a rearguard to a more easily defended position, for which the Halfaya Pass would have been suitable; or else, under pretence of offering the main resistance from the El Alamein line, to have accepted the decisive battle some twenty miles further west in an area – the so-called Fuka position – which had all the advantages of the El Alamein zone and was better protected on the left wing by the terrain.'[2] Moreover Kesselring did not believe the decision to remain at Alamein was a political one; Rommel's prestige with Hitler was such, he felt, that 'neither the OKW nor the Commando Supremo would have strongly opposed any serious intention of Rommel to retire to a rear line. Rommel had hitherto always found means to get what he wanted. But he believed in the strength of the Alamein line'.[3]

Bernard's prescience in this instance was truly remarkable – and has never been acknowledged by historians. That night Alexander's

[1] General Lewis H. Brereton, *The Brereton Diaries*, New York 1976.
[2] Field-Marshal Kesselring, op. cit.
[3] Ibid.

War Diary ran: 'C-in-C had a conference with Army Commander and reached various decisions.' Undoubtedly the major one was the decision to tone down publicity of Rommel's defeat in the interests of the next battle. The next morning Alexander cabled the War Office in London. The text was unmistakably Bernard's:

> Consider it most desirable to forestall publicity. Please arrange press publicity on following lines:
> Enemy attacked our southern flank with whole Panzer Army. After five days' heavy fighting, at times intense, enemy has been driven back by combined efforts all arms, armoured and un-armoured, magnificently assisted throughout by RAF. In spite of every effort, enemy failed to penetrate our main defensive system at any point.
> Enemy losses in personnel and material have been severe, our own comparatively light.[1]

To Wendell Willkie, before he left 8th Army on 5 September, Bernard said the same thing:

> He had stopped Rommel, but he was anxious for him not to begin to retreat into the desert before some 300 American General Sherman tanks that had just landed at Port Said could get into action. He estimated that this would take about 3 weeks. He figured that if he made a formal public announcement of the result of the battle, Rommel's withdrawal might be hastened.[2]

Willkie, having been the only civilian outsider to witness the British victory, therefore agreed to help Bernard by making a personal statement to the press 'which would not be regarded by Rommel as a sign of aggressive action on his part, while at the same time it would have an even greater effect than a formal British communiqué in stiffening the morale of Egypt, Africa, and the Middle East'.[3]

Ironically, it proved simpler to trick Rommel than to convince either the British press reporters, or even Bernard's own subordinates – some of whom were aghast at the way the Army Commander now allowed Rommel not only to occupy the old British minefield positions in the south, but the commanding heights of Himeimat.

'He accordingly called the representatives of the press to his headquarters,' Willkie recalled,

> and I told them the results of the battle in the language which he and I had agreed upon in advance; 'Egypt is saved, Rommel is stopped; and a beginning has been made on the task of throwing the Nazis out of Africa.'

[1] Cabinet Papers. Telegrams 26 August 1942–30 January 1943 (CAB 105/19), PRO.
[2] Wendell Willkie, op. cit.
[3] Ibid.

The press reporters were sceptical.

It was the first good news from the British side that these British newspapermen had had in a long time. They'd been fooled many times and were wary. The battle line, to their eyes, had hardly sagged, Rommel was still only a few miles from the Nile, while the road to Tripoli, from where we were. seemed long and a little fanciful and the road to Cairo painfully short.[1]

Similarly, Horrocks was at first chagrined to learn, that day, that the Army Commander was not going to fight for Himeimat. Horrocks had had much 'belly-aching' before being able to ensure that his subordinates fought the battle according to the new Army Commander's tactical strategy. At Alam Halfa these tactics had proved triumphantly successful: so successful that the 'whole Panzer Army' was in full flight. To allow the Germans not only to appropriate the British minefield area but also Himeimat seemed to them sheer madness, a sign of ridiculous caution. Even 'Pip' Roberts, the Commander of 22nd Armoured Brigade and almost the sole wholehearted backer of the new Corps Commander, baulked at this refusal to contend possession of Himeimat – an opinion he still held almost forty years later.

I do know that the fact that the Germans had Himeimat was a very severe handicap to us when we came to the main battle of Alamein. And I'm thinking of myself because 7th Armoured Division was in the south and had this bloody Himeimat looking right down on us all the time. If we'd taken Himeimat then it would have eased that. From there one saw a very large amount of the battlefield. It was a tremendously useful position – and very difficult to get people off it . . . I think personally it would have been worthwhile having a try, and if it seemed difficult, then give it up. I don't know how much Monty appreciated that it was a tremendous vantage point, looking up the whole of the Alamein line.[2]

The 8th Army G1 (Plans), Charles Richardson, later remembered the sense of frustration at being told that heavy armour was not going to be risked in following up the Axis retreat, nor was possession of Himeimat to be contended – though the passage of time caused Richardson to see the issue as more equivocal:

We were all rather maddened – when I say 'we', I mean the Lt-Colonels – we were all rather maddened that Monty would *not*

[1] Ibid.
[2] Maj-General G. P. B. Roberts, loc. cit.

do more in pursuing Rommel when he started to pull out and so on – at Alam Halfa – and I can see Freddie [de Guingand] coming back – because I think Freddie was of the same mind – coming back saying: 'No, no, he won't have it. He won't have it. He may be right' – something like that.

But in retrospect he *was* right. I meant he . . . the argument, Monty's argument, was that the troops who would have done this aggressive follow-up if they had been ordered to, were not trained sufficiently not to be tripped up again by Rommel – because Rommel could react so quickly, with better trained troops, and he could have turned the tables. And although some casualties might have been inflicted, it would have upset his longer-term plans for Alamein.[1]

Field-Marshal Lord Harding, reflecting on his long experience in the desert before Montgomery's arrival, as well as command of the 7th Armoured Division during and after the battle of Alamein, felt that the Army Commander had been 'absolutely right.'[2] Possibly in order to forestall criticism within 8th Army, however, Bernard issued his own special message to his troops on 5 September:

The battle of Alamein has now lasted six days, and the enemy has slowly but surely been driven from 8th Army area. Tonight, 5th September, his rearguards are being driven west, through the Minefield area north of Himeimat. All formations and units, both armoured and unarmoured, have contributed towards this striking victory, and have been magnificently supported by the RAF. I congratulate all ranks of 8th Army on the devotion to duty and good fighting qualities which have resulted in such a heavy defeat of the enemy and which will have far-reaching results. I have sent a message to the AOC Western Desert expressing our thanks to the RAF for their splendid effort.[3]

Though the press might remain sceptical and some of the armoured commanders feel frustrated, a definite air of jubilation now permeated 8th Army Headquarters and the whole of the Army. Almost four decades later one of the G2s recalled the amazement felt by Montgomery's staff:

Before the battle it didn't seem at all certain that we were going to win. I mean there was a perfectly good plan and Intelligence was good and all the rest of it – we knew where Rommel was going to come, it was a certainty, you didn't even have to have Intelligence: he was going to cross in the south. He always did that because it

[1] Sir Charles Richardson, loc. cit.
[2] Interview of 20.11.80.
[3] War Diary, 8th Army HQ, September 1942 (WO 169/3917), PRO.

was the only way round. And yet it didn't seem a certainty that we were going to win.[1]

The fact that Rommel had been halted without moving the main positions of 8th Army, after the endless crises of the past campaign, seemed somehow unbelievable as the battle drew to a close.

Almost nobody moved. Now that was a thing that staggered everybody because in every other battle once Rommel was on the loose, people tended to go haywire in all directions trying to pin him down. But here he'd done absolutely everything we wished him to, and run his head against a brick wall. And of course he'd lost 50-odd tanks, vehicles, soldiers – a lot of casualties, all in plain daylight, shelled unmercifully the whole time, bombed from the air and everybody up on the Ruweisat Ridge or at Alam Halfa or in 7th Armoured Division could see this going on: and that was about the biggest morale booster that everybody had – it did everybody a power of good.[2]

Robert Priestley, a staff officer in 8th Armoured Brigade, also recalled this quite new sensation:

It was a *fascinating* battle. For the first time since the Germans came into operations in North Africa we were told to do a job we really felt we could do . . . The actual battle went, as far as I could tell, absolutely according to plan. I remember on the second day of the battle visibility was superb – and it very rarely was in the desert. You could see 5 miles or more quite easily. And we could see the whole of the German army laid out in front of us. I got on a tank with Derrick Mullins, a regimental CO, and we sat there watching the German army being shelled and bombed. And I remember writing home after that battle saying, 'All right, this battle's changed the war. Now we shall win. No two ways about it. We shall win.' And that confidence never left really.[3]

Certainly Sir Charles Richardson later felt – as did almost all veterans of Alam Halfa – that neither Gott nor Auchinleck could have achieved more in this respect; in fact, on the contrary, Richardson actually doubted whether Auchinleck would have stopped the Panzer offensive.

I doubt it extremely because my impression of the battle plans and the orders and so on during those several weeks when I was close

[1] General M. St. J. Oswald, loc. cit.
[2] Ibid.
[3] Robert Priestley, loc. cit.

to the Auk were that there was a confusion of purpose endemic in them; that the units themselves were not wholeheartedly in what they were going to do, because they felt there was doubt and chaos and so on, and only after Monty arrived and instilled this idea of certainty and stage-management could that battle have been won. I mean it was a complete psychological change – a complete change of technique.[1]

Perhaps the most attuned judge of Bernard's tactics – as he had been throughout the battle – was Rommel. In his memoirs Rommel summarised the reasons for the 'failure' of the Axis offensive and noted that

> British ground forces, as has been shown, had hardly put in an appearance during the offensive. Montgomery had attempted no large-scale attack to retake the southern part of his line; and would probably have failed if he had. He had relied instead on the effect of his enormously powerful artillery and air force. Added to this, our lines of communication had been subjected to continual harassing attacks by the 7th Armoured Division. There is no doubt that the British commander's handling of this action had been absolutely right and well suited to the occasion, for it had enabled him to inflict very heavy damage on us in relation to his own losses, and to retain the striking power of his own force.[2]

But, if the two Army Commanders understood the significance of the battle, their two political chiefs did not. Hitler, worried by the way the German armies were bogged down at Stalingrad and in the Caucasus, treated Rommel almost with superciliousness when he asked for urgent strengthening of the Luftwaffe in Egypt and more field weaponry, from tanks to rocket launchers. Apart from promises, all that Hitler gave him on 30 September was the ceremonial Field-Marshal's baton to wave before Goebbels' news reporters.

As for Churchill, he seems to have lost, in London, the confidence which Montgomery had inspired in him in the desert. There were critical wrangles with the Americans over the size and date of the 'Torch' operation. On 2 September Churchill summoned his Director of Military Operations, Major-General Kennedy.

'He did not seem to be in very good form,' Kennedy later recalled.[3]

> At that moment it appeared to us that Rommel might wish to develop the battle as he had at Gazala. He had got inside our lines, and his most probable course of action seemed to be to attack

[1] Sir Charles Richardson, loc. cit.
[2] *The Rommel Papers*, op. cit.
[3] Sir John Kennedy, *The Business of War*, London 1957.

northwards, in an attempt to destroy our forces piecemeal . . .

The Prime Minister was obviously on tenterhooks, and no wonder. It was a critical moment in the war, and I suspected he was having difficulties with some of his colleagues.[1]

With a map of Alamein before them Churchill swept 'his hand over the German positions, said that he hoped our whole line might eventually swing round, pivoting on our left, and so close Rommel in against the Depression'.[2]

Clearly Churchill understood little, despite his visit to 8th Army, of the problem of holding a defensive line and providing the reserves for a well-mounted counter-offensive – a misunderstanding that would come to a head several weeks later when he attempted to insist on an 8th Army offensive in September 1942, not October.

For the moment, however, Bernard was pleased with the way the battle had developed. He attended a thanksgiving service with General Alexander in the sands of Burg-el-Arab on Sunday 6 September, and the following day he called off the battle, 'at HQ 13 Corps 0900 hours. Plans for formation of 10 Corps set in motion'.[3] In his Summary of the battle the same day, Bernard added: 'Having called off the battle all energies were then directed to continuing the plans for our own offensive and knock-out blow.'

The battle of Alam Halfa was over. The battle of El Alamein – the battle of Egypt – was yet to begin.

[1] Ibid.
[2] Ibid.
[3] Diary, loc. cit.

CHAPTER ELEVEN

Training the Eighth Army

To Bernard's 'tidy' mind there was one further task associated with
Alam Halfa to be carried out on 7 September: namely to set out the
lessons.

Main Lessons of the Battle

he headed the final entry in his diary that day: and with customary
clarity he listed them:

1. The proper stage-management of the battle is vital. The
    general lay-out of dispositions must be sound initially, so
    that the troops can fight with advantage from the start.
      This was an Army battle; the general plan of battle had to
    be made at Army HQ and a firm grip kept on the battle
    throughout *by* Army HQ.
2. Dominating ground must be held strongly by infantry forma-
    tions with a strong anti-tank defence, and with plenty of
    artillery.
3. The armour must be kept concentrated. It must be so posi-
    tioned on important ground that the enemy will be forced to
    attack it, i.e. he will have to attack our armour on ground of
    its own choosing.
4. Armoured units in position in hull-down positions must be
    covered by a good screen of anti-tank guns, and concentrated
    artillery fire must be able to be brought down quickly against
    any enemy attack.
5. Infantry 'pivots' (para 2) must be so strong that they will hold
    out against any attack. Infantry garrisons must not rely on
    armoured units to help them beat off attacks.
      The armour will then be free to choose its own battlefield
    and will be able to base its manoeuvre on securely held
    pivots.
6. Divisions must fight as divisions, with definite tasks and
    clear-cut objectives.
7. The concentrated fire of artillery is a battle-winning factor of
    the first importance. Artillery command must be concen-

trated under the CRA of the Division so that he can use the Div Artillery as a 72-gun battery when necessary.

8. Once the enemy shows signs of giving way, he must be shot up by artillery fire from all sides. Strong patrols of artillery and tanks must be used boldly and well forward so that the enemy is given no peace and no rest.

Such 'lessons' related to the tactical command of an army in defence; but Bernard was well aware that even the best tactical dispositions and methods in the world would never, of themselves, win battles. Alam Halfa, he felt, had been a trial not only of tactical technique between himself and Rommel, but of character. He therefore added to his lessons two further paragraphs:

9. Never react to enemy moves or thrusts. The great point is to pursue your object and to work continuously on your own plan; once you have to react to the enemy thrusts you will begin to react to the enemy's tune, and once this happens you are done.

10. Grasp the initiative as soon as you can and, having done so, keep it. Once you have the initiative it is essential to pursue your own object relentlessly, you must never be drawn away from it by having to react to enemy thrusts.

The layout of dispositions must be such that enemy thrusts can be dealt with without difficulty, and will have no repercussions on your own plans.[1]

The importance Bernard ascribed to 'the initiative' was not rhetorical. As will be seen, not all Bernard's battles would go 'according to plan', and in retrospect there would be gross discrepancies between his own version of events and local reality. However to Bernard, as caricaturist *par excellence*, such niceties were of lesser importance than the need for the Commander to have a clear picture of what was happening at the time, and to be master of it. His lessons of Alam Halfa were not carefully concocted post-war Despatches: they were the immediate expression of Bernard's thinking on the day he 'called off' the battle. The attempt, within 13 Corps, to 'seize the initiative' in the battle by closing Rommel's salient at its neck had palpably failed, as had the Australian attempt to breach the German-Italian front line in the north; moreover, despite the pounding of the RAF and 8th Army artillery, Rommel had been permitted to withdraw in comparatively good order, and the initial 8th Army estimates of German tank losses soon turned out to be wildly optimistic when an actual count was made on the battlefield.

And yet, in the wider sense, Bernard *had* wrested the initiative

[1] 'Notes on Alam Halfa', loc. cit.

from Rommel. By his re-casting of 8th Army plans for Alam Halfa he had cramped tight the parameters within which Rommel could conduct his offensive, and had borne out Rommel's worst fears. The brave British amateurishness which, that summer, Rommel had so brilliantly exploited was over, and Rommel's deeper anxiety about an enemy which made few mistakes and had all the advantages of time behind it were confirmed. By refusing to attack Rommel's concentrated armour with his own medium tanks, Bernard had imposed his will upon the battlefield, and denied Rommel his only hope of success. Despite the New Zealand Division's failure in 'Beresford' Bernard felt the principle – of thinning out in the North and forming reserves for an 8th Army counter-attack – had been validated. He had not squandered the heavy armour he would need for a full-scale offensive in September or October, but had 'relentlessly' pursued his object of pushing Rommel's forces back. 'There was never any reaction to Rommel's thrusts,' Bernard wrote, somewhat exaggeratedly, in his 'Conclusion'; 'the 8th Army worked calmly at its own plan; and on the third day of the battle Rommel was beginning to have to react to British thrusts.' If this was clearly untrue at a local level – for instance the abortive move of 8th Armoured Brigade to stop 21st Panzer Division from working its way round the flank of 22nd Armoured Brigade, or the way in which the Italian retreat became such a rout by 4 September that the Afrika Korps had to ignore Rommel's orders to counter-attack the New Zealand thrust – it was true at a deeper level. Moreover it was important that Bernard should believe it to be true: for on his will to achieve victory would depend the will of 8th Army.

Sir William Mather later recalled how, at Alamein, someone had asked Bernard whether he was going to switch the 9th Australian Division to meet a German attack. 'Monty said: "I won't react to Rommel. Rommel will react to me." This went through the whole of 8th Army after that: "*Rommel will react to me.*" '[1] Some might laugh; historians might subsequently question the extent to which Bernard actually held the initiative at certain moments: but the fact was that for the first time in the war of will, Montgomery had clearly and indisputably defeated Rommel.

Here indeed was the nub. Rommel's Alam Halfa gamble had failed, and with the loss of initiative he was doomed. From now on, save at Kassarine and the abortive attack at Medenine, the rest of his life would be spent in defence: in trying to predict enemy intentions, trying to meet enemy attacks, looking over his shoulder for lines of retreat. Psychologically the battle of Alam Halfa broke Rommel. Within twelve days of its end a deputy would arrive to take over *Panzerarmee Afrika* in order that Rommel could convalesce in Germany; but no rest could restore to him the initiative he had surren-

---

[1] Sir William Mather, loc. cit.

dered at Alam Halfa. By the time Montgomery launched his massive October offensive, Panzer Army had only just regained the tank strength it had possessed prior to the 'Six-Day Race'.

For Bernard the situation was the opposite. He had abhorred Auchinleck's beach-defence policy in 1940 because it entailed total compliance to the enemy's initiative. Such static defence, even involving a forward movement as in the defence of Belgium in May 1940, merely gave the enemy the freedom to concentrate and strike as he wished: meant abdicating the moral advantage. The defence of Alam Halfa was for Bernard only the 'first round' in the struggle to gain and retain initiative – as his letters home to England testify. While the sick Rommel made his arrangements to fly back to Germany for his 'cure', Bernard found the desert and his struggle against Rommel so bracing he declared he felt better than 'for years'. To his son's guardian, Tom Reynolds, he wrote for the first time since leaving England:

> HQ 8th Army
> Middle East Forces
> 21–9–42

My dear Tom

I have just received today the Airgraph letters of 12th, 19th, and 23rd August sent off by you and your lady wife. I was delighted to get them as it was the first communication I had received from you since I left England. I was given 8 hours to pack up and leave England, and in my desperate situation I just handed David to you. I could not even ask you if you would accept the trust. But I felt in my heart that you would do so. And there is no one in the whole world that I would sooner give David over to, than you and your wife. It is a great comfort to me to have confirmation that you have accepted the trust and have taken him on.

You need never worry about money. Spend as much as you like on anything you like. He is all I have, and he can be given anything you think good for him. As he gets into things at Winchester he may want to do more things, and have bigger school bills. If you think it suitable let him do them; the money need not enter into it.

I took over command of this Army on 13 August. And there was at that time a very definite, and very considerable, threat to Egypt.

On 31 August I was heavily attacked by Rommell [sic] with all the forces he could muster; he wanted to reach Cairo, Alexandria, and Suez, and drive the British out of Egypt.

At no time did he penetrate my prepared positions. He moved the whole Panzer Army, plus two Italian Army Corps, round my southern flank and attempted to destroy my Army; if he had done so, then Egypt was his for the taking.

To begin with he had the initiative. But on the 3rd day of the battle the initiative began to slip from him; I started to wrest it from him on 2nd September and by 6 September I had driven him right back to where he came from, having inflicted heavy losses on him.

His losses were such that he is incapable now of staging any offensive that could do me any harm or even cause me any embarrassment. The threat to Egypt has been removed.

I have never before faced up in battle to a Field-Marshal, but there is no doubt that I won the first round – or won the first game when it was his service.

I enjoyed every minute of the battle. And I fought it in accordance with the doctrine I have been teaching and preaching in England since the Dunkirk days; which makes the victory all the more satisfactory.

I am extremely well in health; better than I have been for years. There is no doubt the desert is a very healthy place. I have not had a bath for 4 weeks; I am convinced we all wash and bath far too much!!

I wonder if David ever got the message I sent him when I broadcast for the BBC from here about 2 weeks ago.

I had Winston Churchill and the CIGS staying with me on 20 August and I asked the CIGS to telephone you when he got back and enquire about David . . .

Tell David that I am very flourishing and enjoyed fighting Rommel! – and that I saw him right off.

Goodbye to both of you; and thank you both from the bottom of my heart.

I shall regard Amesbury as my home also when I come back to England on leave.

Yrs ever
Monty[1]

Written after his first victory in battle as an Army Commander, this letter illustrates perhaps better than any other evidence the enormous self-confidence with which Bernard infected 8th Army. The world at large might not be aware of the change that had been wrought in the desert, but the men of 8th Army were. A tide of optimism and pride swept through the units. The first Sherman tanks began to arrive – already by 20 September there were ninety-five ready for action. The lighter Crusader tanks were being fitted with 6-pounder guns, and large numbers of the new 6-pounder anti-tank guns were being issued. A new flail tank had been converted from the old Matildas to clear gaps in minefields. The army had proved itself in a defensive battle against concentrated armour: now it must train itself for the task ahead – an all-out offensive battle.

'I soon realised that although the Eighth Army was composed of magnificent material,' Bernard recorded in his *Memoirs*

[1] Montgomery Papers.

it was untrained; it had done much fighting, but little training. We had just won a decisive victory, but it had been a static battle; I was not prepared to launch the troops into an all-out offensive without intensive training.

It was now that Bernard's impact as Army Commander began to be felt as something more than that of a new general with sound ideas in an old army. For Alam Halfa Bernard had only made a single change in command or staff – the summoning of Horrocks to replace Gott in 13 Corps. But now heads began to roll. Ramsden, Commander of 30 Corps, was sacked, and one of Bernard's Camberley Staff College students appointed in his place: Lt-General Sir Oliver Leese, who arrived in the desert from England on 15 September 1942. Renton, Commander of 7th Armoured Division, was replaced by another of Bernard's ex-Camberley students, Major-General Harding from GHQ Cairo on 17 September. The 51st Highland Division, under another ex-Camberley student, Douglas Wimberley, also came into the line. Meanwhile Horrocks' reluctance to take on the new Corps de Chasse, and the difficulty Horrocks had had with some of his armoured commanders at Alam Halfa persuaded Bernard to take Lt-General Lumsden, to whom Churchill had promised a corps command, for his new third Corps, 10 Corps. This would be the 8th Army's armoured spearhead. 'After long consultation with Alexander I agreed to give 10 Corps, my *Corps d'élite* which was to resemble Rommel's Panzer Army, to Lumsden; he had commanded the 1st Armoured Division in the desert and was highly spoken of in Middle East circles,' Bernard wrote later. 'I hardly knew him and so could not agree with complete confidence; but I accepted him on the advice of others.'[1] One of these was Alexander's Chief-of-Staff, Lt-General McCreery, who recalled in 1959: 'Monty wanted Horrocks to command the Corps de Chasse rather than Herbert Lumsden. [. . .] I did venture to say that it would surely be very difficult for an officer straight out from home, no matter how capable, to command an armoured corps in the desert, whereas General Lumsden had had to control at least three armoured brigades and he was the one armoured commander in whom everyone had great confidence. Monty made no direct reply, but later on he mentioned Herbert Lumsden as the commander, 10 Corps.'[2] A host of brigadiers and colonels vanished – such as the CO of a certain unit who, when asked by Bernard who trained the officers, answered that this was done by the Second-in-Command. 'I came across the second-in-command later in the day,' Bernard recalled in his *Memoirs*. 'The poor man denied that he was responsible for training the officers and said that it was done by the CO. I ordered that a new CO be found for the unit at once; it was clear that nobody trained the officers.'

[1] *Memoirs*, op. cit.
[2] 'Recollections of a Chief-of-Staff', in the 12 Royal Lancers *Journal*, April 1959.

What is not generally known is that Bernard himself assumed responsibility for training in 8th Army – he had no officer on his staff to do it, nor probably could have found one. He therefore issued his own training instructions ('8th Army Training Memorandum No. 1'), and saw personally that all three Corps of 8th Army acted upon them. The training instructions of all units in 8th Army – infantry, armour and artillery – now reflected almost word for word those of the Army Commander – and were almost identical to those Bernard had issued in Home Forces. On 10 September, only three days after the battle of Alam Halfa was over, General Gatehouse's 10th Armoured Division headquarters issued a new training instruction to the constituent armoured brigades as they moved to become part of the Corps de Chasse for the Battle of Egypt:

General
8th Army Training Memorandum No. 1, recently issued by the Army Commander, lays down that training will be directed to ensure that we can fight the battle in accordance with certain fundamental principles which are enumerated below:

4 Basic Points:
a) The stage-management of battle operations.
    It is difficult for a formation or unit to recover if it is put into battle badly in the first instance. The stage-management of the battle must be good from the very first start; the general layout of dispositions must be sound initially. If formations are launched badly into battle, and dispositions are not balanced, then the fighting troops are beset with difficulties from the start and fight at a disadvantage.
    A good kick-off is essential. Whether acting offensively or defensively, it is becoming increasingly difficult to rectify initial errors.
    All officers must understand the stage-management of battle and the conduct of battle operations on their own level.
b) Individual and sub-unit efficiency.
    Once battle is joined the issue passes to the junior commander and his sub-unit. Success will now depend on a high standard of initiative and skill on the part of the junior leaders and on the tactical efficiency of units and sub-units. It is essential that the standard of junior leadership, sub-unit efficiency, and individual efficiency of the soldier in fieldcraft and skill and the use of his weapons, should be very high; if it is NOT, then we fail no matter how good the higher leading.
c) The fighting spirit.
    All cmdrs from general down to junior leaders, and all soldiers in the ranks, must possess determination, enthusiasm, and stout hearts. In the end it is the initiative and fighting spirit

of the junior leader and the soldier in the ranks, that wins the battle.

Morale is the big factor in war. Officers and other ranks have got to be imbued with that infectious optimism which comes from physical well-being; they must be brought to that stage of physical and mental fitness which will enable them to take on Germans (or anyone else) with complete confidence; they must be full of offensive eagerness and have the light of battle in their eyes.

d) Battle drill

1. Battle drill must be highly developed. By means of this battle drill we ensure a common line of approach to the sub-unit battle problem, and a common procedure within the sub-unit.

   The fact that every offr & NCO & man is taught this common procedure ensures full co-operation in the battlefield area, even when casualties necessitate changes in junior cmdrs & reinforcements to replace wastage.

2. Battle drill must be our servant and NOT our master. A good system of battle drill wisely used will enable deployment to be speeded up and the sub-unit to develop its maximum battle power quickly.

3. Battle drill must not be regarded as peculiar to the infantry, or as applicable only to the sub-unit. Every unit of every arm must develop a battle drill suitable to its own special needs. In units and formations the main points about battle drill will be the correct positioning of commanders, the composition and disposition of recce parties and so on.

Battle operations generally

2. a) No good results will ever be obtained by splitting up formations and using isolated groups away from the parent formation and scattered over wide areas, as a permanent measure.

   Divisions must be fought *as* divisions and under their own commander with clear-cut tasks and definite objectives; only in this way will full value be got from the great fighting power of the division, and only in this way will concentration of effort and co-operation of all arms be really effective.

   It must be realized that the artillery of a division will be most effective when centralized under the CRA; that the engineers of a division work best under their own CRE and so on.

b) The whole essence of modern tactical methods is: concentration of effort, the co-operation of all arms, control, simplicity, speed of action.

c) In fluid fighting on ground giving scope for manoeuvre, certain important areas of dominating ground must be held as 'pivots'. These areas must be strongly held by infantry, artillery, anti-tank guns and mines; they must be able to hold out against attack by armoured or unarmoured forces. Such areas form bases or pivots for offensive action by armoured and mobile forces and artillery, supported by air striking forces. They must be able to hold out unaided.

d) It is armoured forces and artillery, together with air power, that wins the battle in wide open spaces.

But they must have freedom of action and they must not be hampered by calls from the infantry to assist in beating off armoured attack on infantry localities; such localities must be made so strong that they can look after themselves. The armour must be free to choose its own battlefield and will then operate so as to gain armoured superiority in the whole battle area; only in this way will the enemy be destroyed. The available armour must be used concentrated; on no account must it be so dispersed that it can be dealt with piecemeal by the enemy.

e) The garrison of infantry 'pivots' must be active in assisting armoured and mobile forces operating independently.

A definite force must be held available for offensive action outside the locality, especially at night.

f) Whatever may be the task of unarmoured formations its first step towards achieving success will be to secure ground which dominates the battle area. This ground is required as a firm base from which to operate offensively & upon which subsequently to re-organize. It must be so important to the enemy that he will be forced to attack our armour on it, i.e. on ground of our own choosing.

On approaching such ground the enemy may attempt to establish strong anti-tank fronts in order to hold off the armoured formation while he deals first with some other threats; he must be prevented from establishing such an anti-tank front, by means of artillery and machine-gun fire, & by troops moved forward for the purpose. In this way the armoured formation will retain its power to manoeuvre as may be necessary.

3. Training in general will be designed to inculcate the above principles in all ranks with particular reference to the task that 10 Army Div is likely to be called upon to carry out, as communicated verbally by the Div Cmdr.[1]

The Training Instruction went on to cover particular items, such as formation of Tactical Headquarters, the co-operation of all arms, night movement, passage through gaps in minefields, gunnery, use of anti-tank guns, co-operation of motorised infantry, wireless security, passing of vital information and physical and mental fitness. The

[1] War Diary, 10th Armoured Division HQ, September 1942, PRO.

following day General Lumsden, the new Commander of 10 Corps, issued the first Corps Training Instruction. It laid down that '8th Army Training Memorandum No. 1 be read once a week and carefully studied by all commanders'; that Training Programmes 'will be prepared by all commanders down to Commanders of troops, platoons or equivalent sub-units'; and that skeleton exercises 'down to Division and Brigade HQ will be held by the Army Commander during the month'.[1] Although signed by the BGS the Instruction came almost straight from Bernard's pen.

Part I *General*
This war cannot end in our favour until we have killed sufficient Germans. It is the duty of every one of us to fit himself to the fullest degree to take his place in 10 Corps so that we can kill the maximum number of Germans with the minimum loss to ourselves.

It will depend on us how soon the war in North Africa is finished.

  2. 10 Corps will be an armoured Corps. Its operations will be mobile and essentially offensive even when 8th Army is fighting a defensive battle. Mobility means speed in action, and has little to do with m.p.h. and has less to do with haste. Speed in action is achieved by:
      a) Immediate decision by commanders at each level
      b) Rapid issue of orders or instructions
      c) Instant and intelligent obedience on the part of subordinates

Immediate decisions are only possible if commanders' minds are *continually* appreciating the situation. The ability to issue and, more important, to act on brief verbal orders or instructions is a matter of training. Alertness of mind, brevity and lucidity in orders, and instant and loyal obedience will be insisted upon by all commanders during training and operations . . .

Part II *General Training Policy*
  5. Training will be devoted to the study and practice of the approach phase and the attack. In particular the following will be studied:
      a) Movement by night through restricted routes to an assembly area, concealment in that area, and forward movement under similar conditions to a deployment area.
      b) The passage of enemy minefields, through which lanes will have been previously cleared, by day and night.
      c) Rapid occupation of an area vital to the enemy.

[1] War Diary, HQ 10 Corps September 1942 (WO 169/3988), PRO.

d) The operation of an armoured or motorized division with special reference to the artillery fire-plan against:
  1. A hastily prepared a/tank gun and infantry screen.
  2. An enemy infantry and a/tank gun position which has had 3 or more hours in which to be organized and prepared.
e) How to remain in position on the field of battle.
6. Special attention will be paid during all exercises to the urgent necessity for passing back information rapidly and accurately. Without accurate and 'hot' information, commanders of mobile units and formations cannot make the rapid plans and decisions which are the essence of speed in operations.
7. The importance of troop (platoon) training cannot be over-emphasized. It is the foundation of success. If troops are well trained and in complete control of commanders, if signals are efficient, and if officers know their jobs and are experienced in handling not only units or sub-units of their own arm, but also forces of all arms appropriate to their rank, the unit or formation may have every confidence of success on the battlefield. In armoured units the troops' battle practice is the climax of troop training.

Grouping of Arms
8. Practice is required in rapid assembly and movement of regimental and brigade groups, and in the handling of such groups so that each arm produces its maximum efforts.

  For one week during their training period, armoured brigades will be organized into regimental groups and will work and live together. By this means each arm will get to know the other arm and how they function.

  Brigades and regiments will require to study the handling of the administrative echelons of regimental groups.

Flexibility and Organization
9. There will be periods when regimental groups will operate by themselves, and periods when each arm will have to be concentrated under the control of the brigade or divisional commander. Therefore at all times junior groups must be ready to revert to the control of their senior commanders. For example, a battle may begin with regimental groups, the artillery fire-plan of which may be subsequently co-ordinated by the RHA regimental commander. In these circumstances the regimental commander should be able to concentrate the fire of one or more batteries on one target, from mutually supporting group localities. At a later stage it may be necessary to concentrate the fire of artillery regiments under the

681

CRA. It must be remembered that armour should never be divorced from its guns.

Commanders
10.   In mobile operations the actions of the junior leaders and commanders win the battles. They must therefore be taught above all things and at all times to be OBSERVANT: They will then learn to be good soldiers as well as good fighters and as a Corps we shall be invincible.
11.   To win the battle a commander must first produce his force on the field of battle and subsequently fight the enemy with all arms.

To ensure this, his force must be well trained in driving, maintenance, and march discipline, in order to reach the battle. They must also be well trained in the handling of their weapons so as to ensure that they kill when they shoot.

Man Mastership
12.   A trainer, whether of animals or human beings, aims at producing his charge at its highest pitch of energy and efficiency on the day of the event for which he is training. This is identical with the military conduct of war . . . All commanders must study the problems of the correct ratio of food, rest and training in order to produce their commands at their highest pitch on the day of the battle and throughout the battle. This proportioning of food, rest and training must be practised on exercises. Rest will be compulsory if necessary.

Such were the objectives of training in 10 Corps, the Corps de Chasse. But to achieve them the officers must know *how* to train:

Sequence of Training
15.   Training should be progressive and should be in the following sequence:
      Discussion
      Sand-table or cloth-model exercise
      TEWT [Training Exercise without troops]
      Skeleton exercise
      Exercise with troops
      Some of these may be omitted, though even in some small sub-units such as troops etc. it is a waste of time and training mileage to train with vehicles until all ranks understand exactly what is being done. This is taught on TEWTs & demonstrated on cloth models.

Practice in Crossing Minefields
16. Training is required in the lifting of enemy mines and in the marking & crossing of minefields. The lifting of mines is primarily the task of RE who will be protected by infantry and artillery barrage or smoke-screen. Passages through minefields may be made by day or night. It is impossible to lay down a drill to cover all circumstances under which minelifting may have to be carried out; but it is essential that RE and the infantry are practised in the technique on this subject.

   8th Army has constructed a model minefield for training purposes in the rear area 440868, 445868, 445860, 440860. This area will be allotted to formations on a roster issued by this HQ.

Guidelines were laid down for training of headquarters staff and the officers of all arms:

Formation and unit headquarters
17. Responsibility for efficient stage-management rests with headquarters in their several grades.

   All HQs will bring their battle drill up to date and carry out at least one skeleton practice each week, which may be included in divisional and brigade exercises. Special attention will be paid to:
   a) Method of issuing orders (written, verbal & RT)
   b) Form & brevity of signal messages
   c) Use of RT & map reference codes
   d) Organisation of work and periods of rest
   e) Control and vehicle discipline on the move
   f) Layout & marking of internal communications at the halt
   g) Local protection at all times (including recces)
   h) Individual weapon training for all personnel
   j) Camouflage & track discipline

RAC
18. Armoured regiments will study:
   a) The action of the recce troop and the co-ordination of recce troop, action of armoured cars and light squadrons
   b) The recce role of light squadrons
   c) The drill for bringing medium squadrons (Grants, Shermans) into action rapidly & effectively
   d) Co-operation with RA in the fire-fight against enemy armour or infantry & a/tank guns
   e) Taking over a front from the armoured car regiment
   f) Use of ground to mystify and mislead the enemy

g) The tactical use of close support tanks including the use of their own smoke dischargers (to be tried out in battle practices)

RA

19. RHA & Field Regiments: special points for Training:
    a) The economic layout and co-ordination of OPs
    b) The neutralisation of enemy a/tank guns, especially the enemy 88 gun.
    c) The co-ordination of fireplans between 25-pdrs and 75-mm guns of the medium squadrons of armoured regiments
    d) The replenishment of ammunition during mobile operations. All ranks must be trained to consider economic use of ammunition
    e) The centralization of fire-control within the regiment and division and the building up of the highest possible concentration without necessarily concentrating the guns in space
    f) The selection of positions suitable for carrying out the allotted fire tasks but which cannot be overlooked by hull-down tanks at ranges between 1000 and 2500 yards.
20. Medium regiments will study the employment of medium artillery in support of armoured operations.
21. A/Tank regiments will study:
    a) The rapid formation in company with tanks, forward artillery and infantry of an anti-tank screen
    b) The offensive use of anti-tank artillery in close co-operation with armoured formations. Particular consideration will be given to the employment of a/tank guns on the flanks of the armour.
    c) The siting and firing of a/tank guns at night
    d) The passing of information to individual a/tank guns in position

RE

22. RE will be required to practise
    a) Methods for rapid clearance and making of passages in an enemy minefield day and night either undisturbed or in the face of enemy opposition
    b) Methods of destroying disabled enemy tanks on the field of battle by day and night
    c) The rapid destruction of enemy equipment and dumps
    d) The recce and clearance of enemy booby traps
    e) The repair or operation of ALG's [Advanced Landing Grounds] in emergency

Signals, signals security, and the tasks of the infantry brigade in the armoured divisions were all carefully itemised:

Infantry
25.   Motor, lorried and MMG battalions will study and practise the following:
   a) The use of MMGs with Mark 72 ammunition for the destruction of enemy a/tank guns.
   b) Fighting patrols at night against enemy tank harbours
   c) Offensive handling of infantry and a/tank guns, and mortars
   d) Operations with RE in minelifting and tank destruction
   e) The prevention of the formation of an enemy a/tank front
   f) The attack and clearance of hastily organized enemy a/tank front by day, or more probably, by night
   g) The attack, in co-operation with tanks and artillery on enemy a/tank front which has had time to organize its fire-plan and dig in.
   h) The rapid formation of an a/tank front for the protection of the front or flanks of armoured forces
   j) The rapid formation of a defended locality organized for all-round defence.

Administration, replenishment, medical and even personal hygiene instructions were given:

i.e. proposals for drinking, cooking and washing, and in the straining of washing water for use afterwards for washing clothes . . .[1]

Nothing was left to chance.

These training instructions have been quoted at length because they demonstrate the exemplary manner in which Bernard attempted to re-train 8th Army after the battle of Alam Halfa, and why he would come to consider it to be 'his' Army. Moreover they clearly reveal the 'knowledge of his business' which so impressed Wendell Willkie. Those later historians who came to resent the 'myth' of Montgomery all too easily overlooked the professional foundations on which Bernard's success as a commander lay, and in countering this myth by that of the material superiority of 8th Army over its opponents, they did historical truth a great disservice. Certainly no successful British field commander had ever evinced the genius for training that Montgomery did; and the victory of Alamein would result not from simple superiority of arms, but from an army which was capable of using them. Every detail of the Training Instructions

[1] Ibid.

would play its part in preparing 8th Army for the battle of Alamein only six weeks away; and every technique ignored would be paid for in blood.

This professionalism and the iron grip with which Bernard Montgomery transformed 8th Army is vividly reflected by the later testimony of one of his staff officers, Sir William Mather, who had been in the desert since 1940, and was wounded in the summer of 1942:

I got wounded in the Gazala battles and I was in the General Hospital at Kantara, recovering. I was there about three months. And one of the things you do in hospital is to try and fix yourself up with a good job when you come out. I got myself fixed up with what I thought was the best job in the army, which was to be Brigade-Major of the 1st Armoured Brigade – which was a very good armoured brigade, and I was only a Territorial. I thought it was a tremendous feather in my hat and I was cock-a-hoop. I was just about to be released from hospital when Monty arrived to take command in the desert.

And you know, I was rather surprised because I knew he was quite a good soldier, of course, but it didn't mean very much to me. And I thought, how odd, he wasn't desert-worthy, as we used to say, in any way. One of those . . . sort of 'Ingleezis' coming out to control the desert sweats who really thought we knew the ways of the desert backwards. So I was really rather surprised – even though we'd been pushed back to Alamein . . .

I was congratulating myself on getting the job when a new posting came out to me just as I was about to leave hospital. I was to go as a Liaison Officer to 8th Army Headquarters!

Well I regarded a Liaison Officer, even a G2 Liaison Officer as a Major, as a pretty low form of life compared with being Brigade-Major of the 1st Armoured Brigade. So I went to see the Commandant of the hospital and told him – asked him: Can you keep me for another few days until this thing blows over? So he said, Oh yes, fine; and I stayed there for about ten days, thinking that they'd be too impatient, they'd post somebody else to this job.

The Battle of Alam Halfa was fought; but Major Mather's hopes that 8th Army Headquarters would tire of waiting for him were rudely dashed.

Not a bit of it! An order came out for my arrest! And I realized times had changed!! So I shot off post-haste to 8th Army Headquarters, Burg-el-Arab, and I was straightway summoned to Monty. He said:
    'Mather, you were malingering!'
I thought, how do you know? And – it was the most extraordin-

ary thing about Monty that he *always* knew what you'd been up to! He was such a rogue himself in many ways that he could see through anybody. *Nobody* could pull a fast one over him, at all. And this was so absolutely apparent that no one bothered after it'd been tried once or twice. Anyway, he said:

'Why?'

So I thought the best thing was to come clean – which people soon realized with Monty. So I said what the position was, that I didn't fancy being a G2 Liaison Officer instead of being Brigade-Major at 1st Armoured Brigade. And he retorted:

'So you think being Brigade-Major at 1st Armoured Brigade is better than a job being one of my Liaison Officers?' I said, 'Frankly, yes, sir.' He said:

'Well may I tell you that I'm destroying the desert trades union. And the 1st Armoured Brigade's going to become a Tank Delivery Regiment!' Similarly with the Bays, the 10th Hussars and the 9th Lancers – he also broke their brigade up![1]

Faced with such a prospect, Mather accepted the job of Liaison Officer, but within days was made G2 (Plans) under Colonel Mainwaring, whom he considered one of the best operations staff chiefs ever – the founder of the system of monitoring signals sent by 8th Army's own units ('J'), and the architect of 8th Army's new Operations set-up, based on a group of caravans, bringing intelligence, air, staff duties, and plans together.

It was fascinating because we all used to go down and bathe on the beach before breakfast, all wearing our nothings, and when we were all set the atmosphere was tremendous because Monty had got a complete grip of the Army at once,

Mather recalled.

He moved into what was a very tight trades union operation which was governed by the 'cavalry', the Guards and the Greenjackets, and all the old sweats who thought they were very superior people. They thought they could lick the hides off the Germans if they had the right equipment and the right generals – which was in fact true. We all loved the desert and we thought we were very desert-worthy and so forth. We were very disapproving if people came out from England – Monty in particular.

Of course he broke their trades union at once – which was not an easy thing to do. He found – I think it was either the 16th or 12th Lancers had something like 20 brigadiers in the desert, for

[1] Sir William Mather, loc. cit.

example! Which wasn't very efficient. And he broke the whole thing up.

I mean he was a *professional*, much more professional – I mean we all thought *we* were professionals, but by Jove he was in a different class!

And the two things were: that without any effort he virtually knew everybody by name, down to the rank certainly of second-in-command of regiments and brigade-majors. I mean he knew everybody above major certainly – all senior majors he knew by name – and usually their Christian name and knew all about them. In the whole of the Army! It was absolutely fantastic – and without any apparent effort. He would discuss the merits of different people: and he always used to get it right! It was absolutely extraordinary, the way he could sum people up. We called him 'The Oracle'. Because when you had a problem, you asked Monty. And he knew what the answer was – inevitably he got it right. It was absolutely extraordinary! He was always known as 'Master', but he was also called 'The Oracle'.[1]

Colonel Charles Richardson, as G1 (Plans), also found the Army Commander's oracular ability amazing.

At Alamein I was asked, as the Planner, to give a figure for the casualties at Alamein, about a fortnight before the battle. And I had to say to Freddie [de Guingand], 'I've got no experience on which to base this estimate and there's nothing in the books.' So he said, 'All right, I'll ask the Army Commander.' And he came back the next day, and he said, '13,000.' Well now that was precisely, within a matter of hundreds, the figure for killed, wounded and missing at the end of the battle.[2]

Having laid down the principles for training 8th Army in the coming weeks, Bernard had meanwhile to draw up in writing his plan of battle for the great offensive. Sir William Mather remembered the moment vividly. It was 13 September 1942 – six days after the end of the battle of Alam Halfa:

You see, when he wrote the Operation Order for the battle of Alamein it was like a hen giving birth. He walked backwards and forwards on the sands of Burg-el-Arab all day, backwards and forwards, like Napoleon with his head down, his hands behind his back. And we all said: 'Master is giving birth.'

And he came back into his caravan and in about 4 hours – I remember now it was on 14 sheets of paper – he wrote the whole

[1] Ibid.
[2] Sir Charles Richardson, loc. cit.

Operation Order for Alamein. That was it. It wasn't changed, or very few variations were made to it.[1]

The plan was called 'Lightfoot', and the document Bernard wrote out was historic, for it marked the beginning of a series of offensive battles that would take the Western Allies from Alamein to the heart of Germany over the next two and a half years.

[1] Sir William Mather, loc. cit.

CHAPTER TWELVE

The 'Mutiny'

14 September, 1942

LIGHTFOOT

General Plan of Eighth Army

OBJECT

1. To destroy the enemy forces now opposing Eighth Army. The operations will be designed to 'trap' the enemy in his present area and to destroy him there. Should small elements escape to the West, they will be pursued and dealt with later.

PLAN IN OUTLINE

2. The enemy will be attacked simultaneously on his North and South flanks.

3. The attack on the North flank will be carried out by 30 Corps with the object of breaking in to the enemy defences between the sea and inclusive the MITEIRIYA Ridge, and forming a bridgehead which will include all the enemy main defended positions and his main gun areas. The whole of this bridgehead will be thoroughly cleared of all enemy troops and guns. 10 Corps will be passed through this bridgehead to exploit success and complete the victory.

4. On the South flank, 13 Corps will:
   a) Capture HIMEIMAT.
   b) Conduct operations from HIMEIMAT designed to draw enemy armour away from the main battle in the North.
   c) Launch 4 Lt Armd Bde round the Southern flank to secure DABA and the enemy supply and maintenance organization at that place, and to deny to the enemy air the use of the air landing grounds in that area.

30 CORPS OPERATIONS

5. The break-in attack will be carried out in the moonlight and will be supported by a great weight of artillery fire. Zero hour will be after moonrise on D1 i.e. probably about 2200 hours. See para. 12.

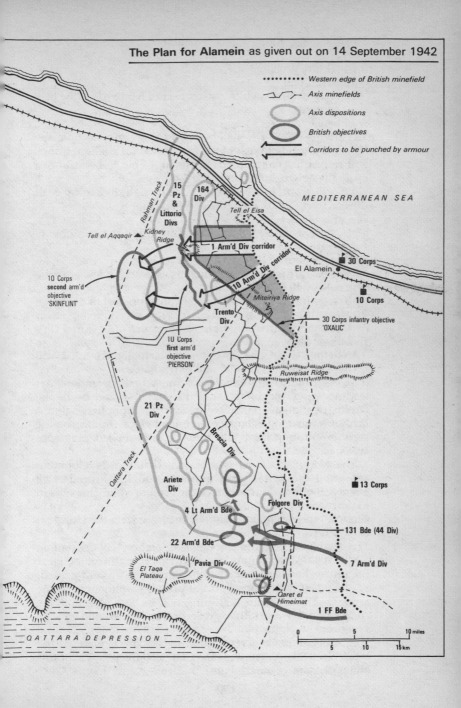

The Plan for Alamein as given out on 14 September 1942

•••••••• Western edge of British minefield

Axis minefields

Axis dispositions

British objectives

Corridors to be punched by armour

15 Pz & Littorio Divs

164 Div

Rahman Track

Tell el Eisa

MEDITERRANEAN SEA

Tell el Aqqaqir

Kidney Ridge

1 Arm'd Div corridor

30 Corps

El Alamein

10 Arm'd Div corridor

10 Corps

10 Corps second arm'd objective 'SKINFLINT'

Miteiriya Ridge

Trento Div

30 Corps infantry objective 'OXALIC'

1U Corps first arm'd objective 'PIERSON'

Ruweisat Ridge

21 Pz Div

Brescia Div

Qattara Track

Ariete Div

13 Corps

4 Lt Arm'd Bde

Folgore Div

22 Arm'd Bde

131 Bde (44 Div)

El Taqa Plateau

Pavia Div

7 Arm'd Div

Qaret el Himeimat

1 FF Bde

QATTARA DEPRESSION

0   5   10 miles

5   10   15 km

6. The following troops will be available:
    9 Aust Div.
    51 (Highland) Div.
    23 Armd Bde.
    2 NZ Div (less such troops as are not required for the task allotted).
    1 SA Div.
7. The troops of NZ Div will be used to capture and hold the MITEIRIYA Ridge West of the QATARA track. These troops will return to command 10 Corps at a time to be arranged mutually between 10 Corps and 30 Corps.

    1 SA Division will swing forward its right to join up with the NZ troops on the MITEIRIYA Ridge.
8. The attached tracing shows:
    a) Objectives of 30 Corps. These include the main enemy gun areas.
    b) Assembly area 10 Corps.
    c) The two areas where gaps in the enemy minefield are to be made by 10 Corps.
    d) Routes from 10 Corps assembly area forward to the battle area.
    e) Deployment areas of armoured brigades of 10 Corps.
    f) Subsequent areas to be occupied by 10 Corps. As to whether these precise areas are actually occupied will depend on the development of the battle.
9. It is essential to the success of the whole operation that leading armoured brigades of 10 Corps should be in the deployment areas (para. 8(e)) ready to fight at first light on D2. They must not become embroiled in local fighting on the early morning of D2 whilst moving in to their deployment areas.

    Therefore, 30 Corps will ensure that the development areas and the routes to them are thoroughly cleared of all enemy troops and guns before the armoured brigades begin to move in to them.
10. Gaps in our own minefields will be cleared, marked, and lit, by 30 Corps.
11. The successful result of the whole operation will depend on whether 30 Corps achieve success in the break-in attack, clear the bridge-head area, and hold securely the ground gained. A great deal will depend on the proper employment of the artillery. Up to about 400 guns will be available and the concentrated use of this great fire power should ensure success.

    In order to make certain that the best use is made of the available artillery resources the CCRA 30 Corps will, for this attack, assume command of all the artillery in 30 Corps. Once

692

the bridgehead area has been secured, artillery must reach out to deal with targets further afield and to assist in beating off counter-attacks.

12.   30 Corps will report the desired zero hour for the attack, consulting with 10 Corps. The ruling factor is as given in para. 9 above. A full moon will be assumed.

10 CORPS OPERATIONS

13.   See attached tracing, referred to in para 8 above.
14.   The operations of 30 Corps are so designed that 10 Corps can pass unopposed through gaps in the enemy minefields and be launched into territory West of these main minefields. 10 Corps will then pivot on the MITEIRIYA Ridge, held by its own NZ Division, and will swing right round till the Corps is positioned on ground of its own choosing astride the enemy supply routes.

   Further operations will depend on how the enemy re-acts to this initial thrust.

   The aim in the development of the further operations will be based on:
   a) The enemy being forced to attack 10 Corps on ground of its own choice.
   b) 10 Corps being able to attack the enemy armoured forces in flank.
   c) The fact that once the enemy armoured and mobile forces have been destroyed, or put out of action, the whole of the enemy army could be rounded up without any difficulty.

15.   The move of 10 Corps to its assembly area will take place by night, the Corps being assembled by dawn on D1 day. Several nights will be used as may be decided by 10 Corps. See para 25 (a).

   The move forward from the assembly area to deployment areas will begin after dark on D1 day; see paras 9 and 12.

16.   10 Corps will be responsible for:
   a) Marking and policing of its routes from the assembly area up to the gaps in the enemy minefields.
   b) Clearing its own gaps in the enemy minefields. See para 8 (c). CE Eighth Army will arrange for any additional RE assistance that may be required.

17.   30 Corps will be responsible for:
   a) Construction of routes forward from 10 Corps assembly area up to the present forward positions.
   b) AA protection for all gaps in minefields, including 10 Corps gaps in the enemy minefields.

13 CORPS OPERATIONS

18. The task of 13 Corps is twofold:

    First. To assist the main armoured battle in the North by drawing off enemy armour to the South.

    Second. To launch a mobile and armoured force round the enemy Southern flank to secure and hold the enemy supply base, maintenance organizations, and air landing grounds, in the DABA area.

19. For both tasks, and especially for the successful conduct of the first task, a secure base is essential. 13 Corps will therefore begin its operations by breaking into the enemy positions at or about HIMEIMAT. This attack will begin at the same time as the attack of 30 Corps; see para. 12.

20. Operations can be so developed that 4 Light Armd Bde can be launched at first light on D2 to secure DABA vide para 18.

    It will be particularly important to destroy all enemy aircraft found on the ground at DABA; also to deny the enemy the use of the landing grounds; holding them for our own use later on.

    On arrival at the DABA area 4 Light Armd Bde will come directly under Army HQ.

21. Having launched 4 Light Armd Bde to Daba, 13 Corps will operate with 22 Armd Bde with the object of drawing enemy armour down to the South and away from the main battle area in the North.

    All enemy MET, and transport generally in rear of the enemy positions in the South will be destroyed; enemy armoured divisions attacking 10 Corps from the South will themselves be attacked from the rear by 22 Armd Bde.

    The operations of 22 Armd Bde will be conducted with the greatest vigour and determination. But in order to ensure that Eighth Army is at all times properly balanced, and has no need to re-act to enemy thrusts, it is essential that 22 Armd Bde should not be destroyed by superior armoured forces; it must remain 'in being' on the Southern flank, operating as indicated above, until it is clear how the battle is going to swing; at the appropriate moment everything will be thrown in to the fight by the Army HQ in order to finish off the enemy.

SEA LANDING

22. A combined operation is being planned and organized with the object of landing a small force of tanks, artillery and infantry on the coast about RAS ABU EL GURUF.

    This force, having landed, will operate Eastwards towards SIDI ABD EL RAHMAN and assist the operations of 30 Corps and 10 Corps.

The time of landing will be synchronized carefully with the main operations of Eighth Army.

This force will come directly under Army HQ.

AIR OPERATIONS
23. These are being developed on the following lines:
   a) Heavy bombing of the enemy main aerodromes during the September full moon period. No attack by our land forces will follow.
   b) Heavy bombing of the enemy main aerodromes during the October full moon period.
   c) At zero hour on D1 day heavy bombing attacks of the enemy armoured formations. These will continue all night on a very heavy scale.

DECEPTION MEASURES
24. Every endeavour will be made to deceive the enemy as to our intentions to attack at all and, if this fails, as to the direction of our main attack.
25. Offensive intentions are usually given away by concentrations of transport, thereby implying concentration of troops and force for an attack. It is therefore essential that a certain normal density of vehicles should be decided for any area and that density be stabilised on 1 October and not altered after that date. This is vitally important in the following areas:

   a) *Assembly area of 10 Corps*
   This area must be made a general living area *now*, and arrangements made so that the number of vehicles in it by 1 October will be approximately the same as when 10 Corps is in the area during daylight hours on D1.

   Furthermore, the positions of the vehicles should be approximately those the tanks and vehicles of 10 Corps will occupy on D1.

   On the nights before D1 the units of 10 Corps will move into the area, and the appropriate transport echelons now there will move out.

   For this scheme to be a success the most careful plans must be made by 30 Corps, and the most complete co-operation arranged between 10 Corps and 30 Corps.

   b) *Area of 9 Australian Division*
   This Division will require a certain amount of transport for use during exploitation towards SIDI RAHMAN. All other transport should be sent back.

   c) *Area of 51 (Highland) Division*
   This Division will require practically no transport, or very little. 30 Corps must ensure that when the Division moves

in to its concentration area for attack, the density of transport remains unchanged.

d) *Area of NZ Division (see para. 7)*

This Division, with tanks co-operating, will capture and hold the MITEIRIYA Ridge, and later may be required for further mobile operations Westwards. A good deal of transport will be necessary.

30 Corps will have to watch carefully the density of transport in this area.

e) *Area of 1 SA Division*

This Division will require practically no transport.

26. Orders will be issued by Army HQ regarding the camouflage, and formation, of dumps in the assembly areas and further forward. The camouflage will be erected first, before the dumps begin to form.

27. Orders regarding the movements, positioning, and handling of artillery in 30 Corps area will require very careful organization, in order not to give away our intentions to the enemy, but rather to deceive him. Further detailed orders on this subject will be issued by Army HQ.

28. Work on tracks and routes forward from 10 Corps assembly area will be started now, work being confined to those places which take a long time to complete. See para. 17 (a).

The remaining portions of the tracks will be finished off on the last two nights before D1 day.

It is not possible to camouflage long lengths of track, but much can be done by careful organization of work.

CE Eighth Army will co-ordinate all work in connection with the construction of tracks and routes forward.

It is important that tracks forward should start at the Eastern end of 10 Corps assembly area.

SECRECY

29. It is impossible to over-stress the need for secrecy regarding operation 'LIGHTFOOT'.

Details of the operation will not be communicated below Div HQ, and at Div HQ no officer will be told anything about the operation except the CRA and GSO 1. All work in connection with preparations for the attack will be given to officers as part of their normal work, and they will not be told the reason for the work. Nothing will be written about the operation; all orders will be verbal for the present.

TRAINING

30. All formations and units will at once begin to train for the part they will play in this battle. Time is short and we must so

direct our training that we shall be successful *in this particular battle*, neglecting other forms of training.

31.   This battle will take place during the period of the full moon.

The initial break-in attack by 30 Corps, and the initial operations by 13 Corps, and the move forward of 10 Corps to deployment areas, will all be carried out by night with a full moon.

Therefore full advantage must be taken of the September full moon period to practise operating on a moonlit night and actually to rehearse the operations concerned, using similar bits of ground.

32.   There will be a great weight of artillery fire available for the break-in battle. During the training period infantry and other arms must be accustomed to advancing under the close protection of artillery fire and mortar fire.

We must have realism in our training and use live ammunition in our exercises with troops, even if this should result in a few casualties. I will accept full responsibility for any casualties that may occur in this way.

33.   The accurate fire of mortars will be of the greatest value in the break-in battle. No troops can stand up to sustained heavy and accurate artillery and mortar fire without suffering a certain loss of morale; low category troops will be definitely shaken by such fire, and can then be dealt with easily by our own attacking troops.

34.   Tanks that are to work in close co-operation with infantry in this battle must actually train with that infantry from now onwards.

35.   The individual soldier must be given practice so that he will reach a high degree of skill with the weapons he will use in battle.

There is plenty of ammunition available for this purpose.

36.   Full use will be made of the model in preparation for this battle. Every formation headquarters and every unit should have a model of the ground over which it is to operate, and on this model all officers will be instructed in the stage-management of the battle.

Finally all NCOs and men will be shown on the model the part they will play in the battle.

As far as officers and NCOs are concerned the model will be any ordinary piece of ground; the actual place names must not be shown. As the day of attack approaches more information can be disclosed.

No information about our offensive intentions will be disclosed to any officer or other rank who has even the slightest chance of being taken prisoner in a raid; this order will not be relaxed until the morning of D1 day.

37. I direct the attention of Corps and Divisional Commanders to Eighth Army Training Memorandum No. 1 issued on 31 August 1942. The fundamentals outlined in that memorandum will govern the conduct of our battle operations, and will therefore form the basic background for all our training.

Battle drill must be highly developed and a good system organized in every formation and unit.

Unless our standard of battle drill and operational discipline is on a very high level, we shall fight at a disadvantage.

MORALE

38. This battle for which we are preparing will be a real rough house and will involve a very great deal of hard fighting. If we are successful it will mean the end of the war in North Africa, apart from general 'clearing-up' operations; it will be the turning point of the whole war. Therefore we can take no chances.

39. Morale is the big thing in war. We must raise the morale of our soldiery to the highest pitch; they must be made enthusiastic, and must enter this battle with their tails high in the air and with the will to win.

There must in fact be no weak links in our mental fitness.

40. But mental fitness will not stand up to the stress and strain of battle unless troops are also physically fit.

This battle may go on for many days and the final issue may well depend on which side can best last out and stand up to the buffeting, and ups and downs, and the continuous strain, of hard battle fighting.

There will be no tip and run tactics in this battle; it will be a killing match; the German is a good soldier and the only way to beat him is to kill him in battle.

41. I am not convinced that our soldiery are really tough and hard. They are sunburnt and brown, and look very well; but they seldom move anywhere on foot and they have led a static life for many weeks.

During the next month, therefore, it is essential to make our officers and men really fit; ordinary fitness is not enough, they must be made tough and hard.

42. This memorandum will not be reproduced or copied. It will form the basis of all our plans and preparations for operation 'LIGHTFOOT'

B. L. Montgomery
Lt. Gen.
G.O.C.-in-C.
Eighth Army.

This was the 'Masterplan' which was delivered personally to each of the thirteen corps and divisional commanders of 8th Army on 14 September 1942 and given to the staff of 8th Army Headquarters 'to work out the details.' David Irving, in a recent biography of Rommel,[1] claimed that 'Rommel relies on his own wits; Montgomery uses the brains of others,' but his comparison was specious, and like so much latter-day criticism of Montgomery, ignorant of the reality of Bernard's method of command. The 'Masterplan' of Alamein was the product of Bernard's mind alone, as was confirmed by Colonel Richardson, the G1 (Plans) at Burg el Arab, to whom de Guingand indicated the Army Commander's plan for Alamein within a week of Montgomery's arrival in Egypt. 'Freddie told me to make an appreciation. There was no question of my putting up any recommendations as the planner. I think the appreciation was more as a sort of safety measure, to make certain that the whole ground was covered,' he recalled quite clearly.[2]

Bernard's plan was original in a number of ways. Unlike Rommel, Bernard intended this time to feint in the south, while making his main effort in the north. Moreover the attack in the north would be a leap-frogging affair in which one Corps would break open the 'enemy's front line and allow another Corps – the Corps de Chasse – to pass through into the enemy rear. However, like Rommel, Bernard planned to attack by moonlight and to have broken right through 'at first light' on the first morning of the battle. Like Rommel's Alam Halfa plan, this was ambitious in the extreme, the more so since Bernard was intending to attack the strongest, key area of the enemy's defences, not simply a lightly-held front as at Alam Halfa. However, as Rommel's prestige brooked no objections to the German plans for Alam Halfa, so too Bernard's iron-willed authority brooked no objections to his plan for Alamein. Instead, Richardson pointed out in his appreciation how important it would be to train the various Corps in their respective roles to raise morale, and to ensure by adequate deception measures that the enemy could not concentrate his forces against the attack before it had broken through.[3] Richardson himself was put in charge of the deception measures, while de Guingand and the operations staff worked out and co-ordinated details of the attack.

It was at this juncture that Lt-General Sir Oliver Leese arrived from England to replace Ramsden.

'I went out to command 30 Corps on September 15th, on which date General Montgomery gave us his original conception for the battle of Alamein,' he informed the Official Historian in 1949. 'I had therefore not been in any of the previous fighting and so had no

[1] David Irving, *The Trail of the Fox*, op. cit.
[2] General Sir Charles Richardson, MOD Filmscript, loc. cit.
[3] Ibid.

preconceived ideas about the previous fighting in the desert. General Montgomery made it quite clear to me that I was to attack with 30 Corps on the night of the 23rd October, with four divisions. My task was to breach the enemy defences and minefields in order that the head of 10 Corps might pass the forward troops at daylight on the 24th.'[1]

In his unpublished memoirs, Leese also recalled the manner in which the Army Commander received him at Burg-el-Arab. He had waited a day before leaving the Guards Armoured Division in England, and then been delayed a further day by engine trouble at Gibraltar. Having arrived in Cairo early on 15 September he had breakfasted with McCreery, Alexander's Chief-of-Staff, had bought some desert clothes, and finally motored in a leisurely fashion to Burg-el-Arab.

'I soon came down to earth as the Army Commander greeted me warmly and then quickly asked me why on earth I had taken so long to get to him! I found him in his caravan on the sea shore in a tiny encampment with the few caravans and signal vehicles of his Tac Headquarters [sic]. He told me that I was just in time for his first conference for his forthcoming offensive. He gave me the plan and he told me that at this conference next morning I would meet my divisional Commanders. I was to spend the night with him at his Headquarters.'[2]

At the conference of corps and divisional commanders on 16 September Bernard unveiled his plan. No one dissented. All three corps commanders were 'new', having all been divisional commanders only four weeks previously. Some of the Commonwealth divisional commanders – such as Pienaar, Morshead and Freyberg – resented the way they were constantly passed over for promotion, which always went to more junior British officers, but for the moment all were impressed by the Army Commander's authority, determination and zeal. The armoured divisional commanders were still pleased by the prospect of forming a British equivalent to the Afrika Korps, which would in fact be the equivalent of a full division stronger and be equipped with the new and mighty Sherman tanks. The infantry, so often the poor Cinderella of the desert, vulnerable owing to lack of cover and ungainly because of their lack of mobility, here had a tremendous challenge in effecting the 'break-in' by night. In the South, although their operations were primarily intended as a feint, 13 Corps – victors of Alam Halfa – were to draw off the enemy armour, and to get light armour through the defences and across the enemy supply lines, even capturing his forward airfields. As at Alam Halfa these were clear objectives, clearly stated by an Army Com-

[1] Sir Oliver Leese, letter of 23.3.49, Cabinet Papers (CAB 106/672), PRO.
[2] Unpublished Memoirs, Papers of Sir Oliver Leese, communicated to author by the Literary Executor of Sir Oliver Leese, Ian Calvocoressi.

mander who had just proven himself in battle against the 'bogey-man' Rommel. It was only after the senior commanders returned to their formations that the true enormity of the undertaking began to sink in and the problems began. Indeed, given the objections raised within 8th Army and the pressures outside, it is altogether remarkable that Bernard was able to launch his offensive five weeks later substantially as he laid it down in the 'Masterplan' of 14 September.

Almost the first objection came from Churchill. Never a patient man, the Prime Minister had already cajoled and harried two Commanders-in-Chief to their professional doom in the Middle East. In appointing Alexander to replace Auchinleck, moreover, Churchill had hoped to install a loyal and obedient soldier who would do what he was told. It never occurred to Churchill – who knew a lot about regiments but nothing about the Staff College – that Alexander would obey not his political master but his erstwhile teacher. Churchill cabled Alexander on 17 September, 'anxiously awaiting some account of your intentions. My understanding,' he said, 'with you was the fourth week in September'.[1] Alexander went straight to Burg-el-Arab where he showed Bernard the telegram. In his diary, written up on the eve of the battle of Alamein, Bernard noted tersely: 'About the middle of September my C-in-C was pressed by the Prime Minister to start the Eighth Army offensive at an early date. A reply was sent that this was not possible.' De Guingand later recalled the incident in more detail:

Alex came up with this signal from Churchill: 'You must do it in September.' Monty called me in. I was the only other person there. He said:
'Now, Alex, I won't do it in September. But if I do it in October it'll be a victory.'
And Alex said:
'Well what shall I say to him?'
Monty said:
'Freddie, give me the pad' – I always carried a note pad – and he wrote out the message himself for Alex to send. I quote it in my book [*Operation Victory*]. And Alex said:
'Thank you very much, Monty, I'll do that' – and he sent off the signal which was not his but Monty's.[2]

The signal was very simple. If 8th Army attacked in September, the troops would be insufficiently trained, and the new equipment that had come with the September convoy would be wasted: 'If the September date were taken, failure would probably result, but if the attack took place in October, then complete victory was assured.'[3]

[1] W. S. Churchill, op. cit.
[2] Sir Francis de Guingand, loc. cit.
[3] De Guingand, *Operation Victory*, op. cit.

'Monty said very few Prime Ministers would face the record if it were known they had been warned, but had insisted on premature attack,' de Guingand remembered.[1] Nevertheless, the signal went out in Alexander's name, and it was against Alexander that Churchill railed when he received it. There followed the well-known telephone call to the CIGS who had gone grouse shooting on the Durham moors near Catterick. A furious interchange took place on the 'scrambler', Churchill accusing Brooke of being 'out of touch with the strategic situation', and Brooke replying that he had 'not yet solved how I am to remain in touch with the strategic situation whilst in a grouse-butt'.[2] Montgomery's cable was sent to Catterick by Contact Officer. Brooke thought 'Alexander's reasons . . . were excellent. I told him [Churchill] so on telephone and thought he said that he agreed with me'.[3] In this Brooke was mistaken. Whilst Brooke continued his brief holiday, Churchill bombarded Alexander with signals, stressing the need to draw German forces away from 'Torch', which was due to begin on 4 November. To each signal Bernard had to formulate a reply, and in his diary he candidly recorded: 'After some protesting and "belly-aching", the Prime Minister accepted the inevitable, and agreed; when the true facts were put to him clearly he saw the point at once.'

Again, Bernard was mistaken. Churchill was under great strain – as he professed to his doctor later, September and October 1942 were for him the most anxious months of the entire war. He had promised Stalin 'Torch'; and only after tremendous and sustained pressure had he got the Americans to back the operation whole-heartedly, on 5 September. Then Stafford Cripps, Leader of the House of Commons, announced on 21 September that he wished to resign – in protest at the way Churchill was running the war. Cripps gave voice to a 'widespread sense of frustration and discontent' in Britain[4] – a feeling that, despite the great exertions of the people, the conduct of the war left much to be desired. What was wanted was a victory, a tangible sign of success. Alam Halfa, owing to Bernard Montgomery's strategic intentions, was not popularly regarded as a victory. By begging Cripps to delay his resignation until the outcome of 8th Army's desert offensive, Churchill won himself a breathing space: but he was well aware, as he recalled in his history of the war, that Cripps' resignation would precipitate a 'political crisis' that might well bring him down.[5] He had won one vote of confidence in the Commons; whether he would survive another was less certain. As Brendan Bracken, Minister of Information, said to Churchill's

[1] De Guingand, loc. cit.
[2] A. Bryant, op. cit.
[3] Ibid.
[4] W. S. Churchill, op. cit.
[5] Ibid.

physician at this time: 'There may be trouble ahead. The Prime Minister must win his battle in the desert or get out.'[1] Lord Trenchard, legendary 'father' of the RAF, was adamant that the crippling casualties involved in land warfare could only be avoided by air offensive – a 'bomber "blitz"' , as he put it in a widely-read paper at the end of August 1942.[2] Germany's greatest asset, Trenchard argued, was the German Army – and direct confrontation on land, either on the continent or elsewhere would mean a return to the stalemate trench warfare of the First World War.

Little wonder, then, that Churchill 'belly-ached'. Although he gave in on 23 September – at Brooke's behest – and promised Alexander 'we shall back you up and see you through', he was far from satisfied. He had forced Alexander to divulge Montgomery's 'Lightfoot' battle-plan; moreover he had, through Ultra, his own accurate picture of Rommel's dispositions and measures for meeting an 8th Army offensive. He therefore knew of the ever-deepening belt of Axis minefields at Alamein. Doubtless in conversation with his military advisers Churchill began seriously to doubt whether, having postponed his offensive, Montgomery could possibly now 'blow a hole in the enemy's front', as he signalled yet again to Alexander:

> There is a point about the fortifications which the enemy will make in the interval which I should like to put to you. Instead of a crust through which a way can be cleared in a night, may you not find twenty-five miles of fortifications, with blasted rock, gunpits, and machine-gun posts? The tank was originally invented to clear a way for the infantry in the teeth of machine-gun fire. Now it is the infantry who will have to clear a way for the tanks, and it seems to me their task will be a very hard one now that fire-power is so great. No doubt you are thinking about all this and how so to broaden your front of attack as to make your superior numbers felt.[3]

As one of Churchill's secretaries once said to the Director of Military Operations, John Kennedy: 'The mistake you people make is that you think what the PM wants is a logical, reasoned argument. There is nothing he dislikes more.'[4] In his illogical, intuitive way, Churchill had put his finger on the nub of the problem – for the wrong reasons, with the wrong solution, and addressed to the wrong man!

For the moment Bernard would countenance no changes in his 'Masterplan', however. The Prime Minister had the most amateur notion about the modern use of armour, and Bernard certainly had

[1] Lord Moran, op. cit.
[2] W. S. Churchill, op. cit.
[3] Ibid.
[4] Sir John Kennedy, op. cit.

no intention of using it in the initial breaching of the enemy defences, which could be better done by infantry at night. Moreover the idea of 'broadening the front of the attack' flew against the cardinal principle of concentration that characterised modern military thought – most particularly Bernard's. In fact, in his memoirs, the Corps Commander responsible for the 'break-in', Sir Oliver Leese, later remarked that the frontage of his actual attack was, if anything, too wide for the troops at his disposal. Of his five infantry divisions, one was incapable of offensive action (4th Indian), two were a brigade short and therefore only 'good' for a single attack in the battle (2nd New Zealand and 1st South African), one had never been in battle before (51st Highland, reconstituted after the surrender of the original division at St Valéry in 1940), and only one, the 9th Australian, was up to strength and capable of sustained operations.

After the Conference [15 September] my first decision was to see for myself the ground over which I was to do the attack . . .

We were obviously up against a tough proposition. The whole area was quite flat, except for the Miteiriya Ridge which was some 300 ft high and which was mostly in German hands. And it stuck out a mile that it was going to be very difficult to conceal our guns, ammunition, tanks and infantry during the concentration prior to the battle . . .

I spent three days in reconnaissance and then I had to decide on the actual point of attack. I had too few Divisions and also too few guns to attack all along my front. I found a certain defilade to cover my right flank about Tel-el-Eisa and I rested my left as best I could on the Miteiriya Ridge. It gave me an initial frontage of 12,000 yards on the first objective, unfortunately extending to 16,000 yards on the second. I have often thought that if I had to do the attack again, I would somehow have shortened it still more.[1]

Contrary to popular legend, Leese was acutely aware that, for a ten-mile wide break-in, he was short of artillery – 'In point of fact I only had 452 field guns and what was more worrying only 48 medium guns to cover the 30 Corps break-in attack.'[2]

If Leese worried whether he had sufficient infantry and artillery to achieve success, he was even more alarmed by the realisation not only that the Corps de Chasse had little confidence of being able to break out on the first morning of the battle, but that the infantry divisional commanders also doubted whether the armour was up to such an ambitious role.

'On arrival in the desert,' Leese recalled,

[1] Sir Oliver Leese, unpublished memoirs, op. cit.
[2] Ibid.

I had been horrified at the state of ill-feeling that existed between Infantry and Armour. Neither had confidence in the other. All mutual trust seemed to have been drained out in the previous battles.

When I held my first Corps conference my divisional Commanders listened politely to what I had to say, and then said quite quietly that the Armour would not pass through their gaps in the minefields. I replied that they would of course do so as the Army Commander had issued the order to that effect. The divisional Commanders just repeated again quite quietly their previous opinion that the Armour would not do so.[1]

Indeed, when Freyberg was shown a draft of the British Official History relating these 'doubts', he commented tartly in his large, child-like hand: 'It was not that we doubted. We did not feel it was possible. And it wasn't.'[2]

Whether at this stage Bernard realised that he had so many doubters, from the Prime Minister to his own corps and divisional commanders, is unknown; he made no mention of the problem either in his diary or his *Memoirs*, mentioning only that GHQ Cairo disliked the idea of a northern thrust and would have preferred to see the conventional inland hook around the south. Yet it seems unlikely that Bernard – who as Mather discovered 'knew everything' – was unaware of such dissension, even though no one dared voice his misgivings openly before the Army Commander. Preparations went ahead inexorably, and the morale of the troops rose steadily higher. The deception plan, under Colonel Richardson, became a classic of its kind – and, to make sure none of the commanders or senior officers obstructed Richardson, Bernard wrote out an imprimatur that became law:

I produced some proposals which I took along to Freddie who accepted them, and then we both went along to see Monty. I said my piece, and the Deception Plan was agreed there and then; and very soon after, I think the same day, he wrote a letter to the Corps Commanders saying that Colonel Richardson was in charge of the Deception Plan and they must do exactly what he says – I think those were his very words.[3]

The Deception Plan would, it was hoped, guarantee tactical surprise. The artillery plan was to Bernard even more important. The artillery must pave the way for the infantry, protect it once it had reached its

[1] Ibid.
[2] Sir Bernard Freyberg, Letter to Sir Howard Kippenberger, quoted by latter to British Official Historian 24.5.49, Cabinet Papers (CAB 106/723), PRO.
[3] Sir Charles Richardson, MOD Filmscript, loc. cit.

objectives, and co-ordinate the complicated leap-frog of the Armoured Corps from an artillery point of view. In order to be absolutely sure that the full, concentrated weight of 8th Army artillery could be brought to bear on the two break-in points, Bernard entrusted the artillery plan to his erstwhile Chief Gunner at South-Eastern Command – Brigadier Sidney Kirkman – whom he had summoned with Horrocks, but who had had to come out the long way from England.

Like Leese, Kirkman stayed his first night in the desert in Bernard's guest-caravan; after dinner Bernard took him to his map-lorry, explained his plan of battle and instructed Kirkman to see that 'the gunner plan is absolutely as good as it can be – it's one of the most important factors,' Kirkman recalled many years later.

> And I said, 'Yes, sir, I understand.' So that was that.
> The important thing was, he never referred to that again to me. He never said, 'Are you satisfied? Have you see this?' Never, never. He told me I was responsible. As far as he was concerned there was no more to be said. He was satisfied that I would do the job – why therefore waste time discussing it?

Recalling the incident almost four decades later, Kirkman felt this to be remarkable.

> I mean if one looks back, almost any other Commander in history, having attached importance to an event of that sort would probably have said 'Is everything all right – are you happy?' Not a bit of it. He never mentioned it again. I mean I had plenty of interviews with him, mostly at my request but between that moment and the Alamein offensive he never again referred to the gunnery plan. He was satisfied that since I was there it would be as good as it could be. There are very few people who have that faith! Quite extraordinary from my point of view . . .[1]

Bernard's faith was not misplaced. Indeed he was quite satisfied that the infantry, by the last week in October, would be trained and ready for their role, as would the artillery. The 'nigger in the woodpile', in his view, was the armour. Would it really penetrate beyond the Axis minefields in the North by the first morning of the battle; and if it did, was it to be trusted to remain concentrated and destroy the German armour on ground of its own choosing? Could one hope to create a cohesive Corps de Chasse, akin to the Afrika Korps, with new tanks about which the crews and maintenance teams knew nothing, in a bare five weeks? Moreover, Churchill's fears of a twenty-five-mile-deep system of fortifications, although exaggerated, were in essence

[1] Sir Sidney Kirkman, loc. cit.

well-founded. On 27 September 8th Army Intelligence reported that the Italian Trento division had been 'sandwiched between German units' and that Ramcke's parachutists were forming 'iron lungs for Italian infantrymen' by being peppered in battalion strengths within the Italian defensive lay-out.[1] To test the strength of Rommel's defences two brigades of the 44th Division carried out an attack on the last day of September in the ill-fated Munassib Depression area where the 132nd Brigade had come to grief during the battle of Alam Halfa. Once again they ran into both Ramcke and Folgore parachutists, sustaining heavy casualties, and failing to achieve their object.

Finally, on 5 October, 8th Army Intelligence drew up its latest and most accurate analysis of Rommel's defensive lay-out, instituted before he left for his cure on 21 September. Using up to half a million mines he had ordered the sowing not only of a series of conventional mine belts, but also a system of 'dividing walls' formed by defensive positions . . . connecting the two main north to south belts at intervals of 4 to 5 kilometres thus forming a series of hollow areas'. These 'hollow areas' were intended as 'traps for penetrating troops' who breached the first minefield belt, since they would be forced to move either right or left of the 'dividing wall', thus 'dissipating the force of the attack.'[2]

For Bernard Montgomery this new intelligence at last forced him to reconsider his whole tactical plan of operations. 'D' day was fixed as 23 October – only two and a half weeks away. Not only were the Commonwealth divisional commanders still sceptical whether the British armour would break out beyond the minefields, but the commanders of the British armoured formations were now to be heard openly announcing they had no intention of so doing.

'About a fortnight before the battle,' Leese recalled for the Official Historian,

> my Chief-of-Staff attended a conference at 10 Corps and came back to me and said he now agreed with the divisional commanders and he did not think that 10 Corps really meant to try and break out during the night.
>
> I therefore went to General Montgomery . . . and told him that I was doubtful if 10 Corps really meant to break out and he issued absolute definite orders to 10 Corps that they were to do so.[3]

In his published memoirs Leese repeats this:

> I heard some disquieting rumours, possibly exaggerated, as to the attitude of some of the Armoured Commanders towards the Army plan. Accordingly I told the Army Commander about it and he

[1] War Diary, 8th Army HQ, 'I' Section, September 1942, loc. cit.
[2] Ibid.
[3] Sir Oliver Leese, Letter to British Official Historian, loc. cit.

assured me that he would again impress on the Armour that they must fight their way through the minefields into the open even if the Infantry had not completed the lanes for them. It was a difficult situation, as right up to the start of the battle my divisional Commanders stuck to their original views . . .[1]

This was hardly an encouraging situation for an Army Commander about to launch the most critical Allied offensive of the war, upon whose success the outcome of 'Torch' depended, the saving of Malta, as well as the entire American commitment to the war in the Mediterranean. For failure at Alamein would probably lead to French refusal to support the 'Torch' landings in North-West Africa, as well as giving Hitler ample reason to reinforce his German armies in North Africa, concentrating then on the capture of Malta – which was due to be re-supplied by a convoy that could only enjoy air protection if 8th Army recaptured the Martuba airfields by 16 November 1942. It has become usual for present-day historians to record the relevant balance of forces at Alamein and to assume that the relative superiority of arms and men enjoyed by 8th Army somehow guaranteed Montgomery success. Yet the truth is that 8th Army had enjoyed relatively greater superiority over Rommel in the 'Crusader' operations of November 1941, and at Gazala in May 1942. Lumsden, supposedly the most experienced armoured commander in the desert, had now been given the first truly armoured reserve Corps in Allied battle history – yet his diffidence over the chances of breaking out beyond the Axis minefields was known to all the senior commanders of 8th Army and their staff. 'Armour is a very brittle thing,' he had reputedly declared at a 10 Corps conference, 'it can break very easily;'[2] and he went on to say that he did not propose to 'break' his armoured weapon – which was designed to be a Corps de Chasse – on minefields which the infantry ought first to clear.

De Guingand recalled the incident very well:

Monty had been called away to give a lecture at the Staff College, Haifa.[3] Lumsden was commander of 10 Corps, and I thought I'd better go over and listen to what he'd got to say. And he got up:

'Monty's plan – there's one point I don't agree with: that tanks should be used to force their way out of the minefields. Tanks must be used as cavalry: they must exploit the situation and not be kept as supporters of infantry. So I don't propose to do that.'

So after the conference I went up to Herbert and I said: 'Look here, my dear boy, you can't do this, you know Monty. You must

[1] Sir Oliver Leese, unpublished memoirs, loc. cit.
[2] Sir Francis De Guingand, loc. cit.
[3] Address to Senior Officers' School, Haifa, 21 September 1942. Text in Montgomery Papers.

know him well enough – he won't permit disobedience to his orders.' And he said: 'Oh, leave that to me.' 'Well, I warn you,' I made clear. Monty came back the next day and I repeated to him this conference. He said: 'Whistle in Lumsden . . .'[1]

This was tantamount to mutiny, and it illustrates how little the so-called 'superiority' in arms and men enjoyed by 8th Army really meant to the generals of 8th Army at the time. Moreover, it demonstrates better than any other evidence how deeply the defeats and failures of 8th Army under Cunningham, Ritchie and Auchinleck had affected the senior commanders, compounded by the inferiority of British anti-tank guns and tanks relative to German. Although many hundreds of new 6-pounder anti-tank guns and Sherman tanks had arrived after Alam Halfa, the 'old hands' of the desert – Pienaar, Freyberg, Morshead, Tuker, Gatehouse, Lumsden and Briggs – still bore the indelible scars of the past.

With only two and a half weeks to go, the situation was critical. There could be no question of postponing the offensive. Equally it was too late for wholesale changes of commanders: Bernard had already brought in his own two new Corps Commanders, a new Chief Gunner and a new Chief Armoured Adviser, Brigadier Arkwright. In fact the creation of the Corps de Chasse had probably been a mistake, for rather than promoting a really professional armoured formation of the calibre of the Afrika Korps it had encouraged the amateur independence that characterised British armoured units. As Sir Sidney Kirkman reflected long after the war, the idea of a Corps de Chasse which, for the purposes of the battle at Alamein would have to be superimposed on an infantry Corps in the same area to achieve a break-through was, in the circumstances which then existed, impractical. 'I think Monty would admit it if he were here now, I think he would have done far better if he'd allotted, as was done later on, armour to each division and not had Herbert Lumsden at all. Not because of Herbert, but because two corps commanders can't operate in the same area. There was terrible confusion . . .'[2]

In Kirkman's view 'the armour was never very good in the desert . . . They didn't understand the gunners – they used to charge about by themselves, whilst the Boche was much more cunning, would have his anti-tank guns put out, and would then retire and our people would charge in on the anti-tank guns. There was nothing like that on our side at all'. This view is seconded by Major-General Belchem, then G1 Staff Duties at 8th Army Headquarters, who felt that Montgomery was disappointed by the Corps de Chasse he had created. 'He saw them [1st and 10th Armoured Divisions] in opera-

[1] De Guingand, loc. cit.
[2] Sir Sidney Kirkman, loc. cit.

tion and I think instinctively he realized that the handling of these divisions as a Corps was not up to the standard that had been exhibited in the past by 15th and 21st Panzer Divisions.'[1] It is clear from the Training Instructions issued by the 8th Army Commander, and from Brigade Training Instructions based on them – such as those of Brigadier 'Pip' Roberts in 22nd Armoured Brigade – that the concept of the armour working hand in glove with its own infantry, with anti-tank gunners, with the artillery, and with the air was appreciated and was the aim laid down by Montgomery. Yet to create a new Armoured Corps, equipped with new tanks, and instructed to do battle according to new tactical principles all in five to six weeks, at a time when the break-in divisions were for the most part in line and unable to train with the armour except in small formations when temporarily withdrawn: all pointed to an ambitiousness that was simply beyond the capability of 8th Army in the autumn of 1942.

It was impossible to ask for more time; postponement from September to October had only been permitted by Churchill after considerable opposition. The 'Torch' landings and the survival of Malta were at stake. Therefore, reluctantly, Bernard took the only course open to him: he altered the plan.

[1] Major-General R. F. Belchem, loc. cit.

CHAPTER THIRTEEN

A Killing Match

The more Bernard thought about the problem, the more he realised that, despite the lessons of the victory of Alam Halfa, despite the arrival of so many new anti-tank guns and the imposition of Corps artillery programmes under Kirkman, the infantry themselves were at heart frightened of making such a deep penetration into the Axis lines, without tank support. Conversely, the armour was still terrified of being caught in a 'trap', unable to manoeuvre and becoming the subject of artillery attention from the dreaded German 88-mm guns. Lumsden's personal bravery was unquestioned, but his experience at Gazala had made him reluctant to risk heavy casualties: and this was reflected in his subordinate commanders.

It was too late now, however to replace Lumsden or even close down the Corps de Chasse and allot its armoured divisions to 30 Corps; therefore the only answer, Bernard felt, was to alter the plan so that 10 Corps fought *with* 30 Corps, giving the infantry the security they so lacked, while the armour would receive the full benefit of a corps of infantry, replete with artillery and anti-tank guns. There need be no interruption or alteration in the planning: the attacks would go in as arranged. Only, instead of breaking out into the open beyond the minefields, the armour would simply settle itself on good ground of its own choosing and 'shield' the infantry whilst it now undertook the major role; that of methodically eating away or 'crumbling' the defending Axis troops. The German armour could not possibly watch its defending infantry being so destroyed; would be forced therefore to attack the armoured shield of 10 Corps on ground of the latter's own choosing – with the same result as at Alam Halfa.

How this idea came to Bernard at this critical moment is a mystery which none of his staff could ever explain. It transformed an imaginative but over-ambitious 'Masterplan' into a much more basic proposition, a battle of attrition – and for this romantic historians would never forgive him. Yet in retrospect the genuine historical observer can only marvel at the way Bernard turned an ominous situation to advantage. It was a superlative example of his underlying realism; yet, because it implied that his original concept of a corps de chasse was wrong, Bernard never took the credit he deserved. In his diary he put it thus – making no mention of the 'mutiny':

> By the first week in October I was satisfied with the leadership.
>   The equipment situation was also good; we had a good heavy tank and it contained a good gun; we had a great weight of artillery and plenty of ammunition; I could concentrate some 400 guns for the operation of blowing the hole in the enemy positions in the North.
>   *But the training was not good* and it was beginning to become clear to me that I would have to be very careful, and that I must ensure that formations and units were not given tasks which were likely to end in failure because of their low standard of training.
>   The army had suffered 80,000 casualties, and the re-born Eighth Army was full of untrained units.
>   The troops had fought a successful defensive battle on 31 August and following days. But this next battle was to be an *offensive battle*, which is a very different proposition. I was determined to have no more failures. The troops in the Middle East had a hard life and few pleasures; they put up with it willingly. All they asked for was success – and I was determined to see that they got it. It was clear that I must so stage-manage the battle that my troops would be able to do what was demanded of them, and I must not be too ambitious in my demands.
>   And so, on 6 October, I issued a Memorandum of how I intended to fight the battle. This Memorandum is interesting; it will be attached as an Appendix to my notes on the battle.

The Memorandum was five typescript pages long. Although the original plan of 'Lightfoot' envisaged very tough fighting, the accent had been – just like Rommel's at Alam Halfa – on speed and surprise. Now, seventeen days from 'D' day, the Army Commander's new tactical policy for the battle signified a long drawn-out killing match: 'This battle will involve hard and prolonged fighting,' Bernard's Memorandum ran. 'Our troops must not think that, because we have a good tank and very powerful artillery support, the enemy will all surrender. The enemy will not surrender, and there will be bitter fighting.

'The infantry must be prepared to fight and kill, and to continue doing so over a prolonged period.

'It is essential to impress on all officers that determined leadership will be very vital in this battle, as in any battle. There have been far too many unwounded prisoners taken in this war. We must impress on our Officers, NCOs and men that when they are cut off or surrounded, and there appears no hope of survival, they must organise themselves into a defensive locality and hold out where they are. By so doing they will add enormously to the enemy's difficulties; they will greatly assist the development of our own operations; and they will save themselves from spending the rest of the war in a prison camp.

'Nothing is ever hopeless so long as troops have stout hearts, and have weapons and ammunition.'

The change of tactical policy therefore entailed 8th Army preparing itself for a longer, harder and more deadly infantry battle than was first assumed – and this in turn threw a new responsibility upon the Army Commander himself. By altering the tactics to be employed in the battle, Bernard was ensuring that infantry and armour would fight together in 'combined' operations that precluded the sort of failures which had become endemic in 8th Army's previous campaign, with infantry and armour fighting separate battles. Once out beyond the 30 Corps objectives there would be no way in which the armour of 10 Corps could retreat; they would *have* to shield the infantry. Equally the infantry would have no reason, given so much armour and artillery, as well as air support, for failing to 'eat the guts' out of the enemy. 'When we have succeeded in destroying the enemy holding troops, the eventual fate of the Panzer Army is certain – it will not be able to avoid destruction,' Bernard's Memorandum claimed. This policy, however, meant training and bringing 8th Army's infantry and armour to such a pitch of determination and enthusiasm that it would be able to sustain its offensive for perhaps ten days or more.

It is doubtful whether any other field commander could have carried out these two changes at such a critical moment of the war, and in the time available: to acknowledge, implicitly, his mistake in grouping a corps de chasse that could not be asked to carry out such an ambitious plan as the original 'Lightfoot' operation; and to retrain 8th Army instead to embark on a battle of attrition, a prolonged killing match previously unknown either in the desert or anywhere else in Western Europe. Yet this is what Bernard did, and though many bewailed the use of armour in such a 'shielding' role, no veteran of Alamein would ever deny Montgomery the credit for inspiring an Army capable, once and for all, of sustaining a full-scale offensive battle involving the combined forces of air, artillery, infantry and over a thousand tanks. If Alam Halfa was a turning-point in so far as it proved that, under a good general, an Allied army could defend itself quite adequately against a highly professional Panzer army, then the battle of Alamein was to be an even more auspicious event in that it became the proving ground of the Allied offensive spirit: its determination to strike back and to regain the initiative. The tide had begun to turn at Alam Halfa – and Bernard was adamant that this time there would be no going back, no let-up until the armies of the Allied cause had completely conquered Germany. As he had written in a special Memorandum to corps and divisional commanders on 29 September 1942:

713

We cannot go on with this business of going backwards and forwards to Benghazi.

This time we will hit the Germans for 6 right out of Egypt and Libya, and will go ourselves to Tripoli and Tunis.

If every officer and every soldier goes into this battle with the determination to win and to kill the enemy, then only one result is possible – and that is complete success![1]

That Bernard managed to inspire 8th Army with the will and determination to undertake such a decisive 'killing-match' was, in the end, what raised him head and shoulders above any other Allied general in the war so far – indeed Field-Marshal Templer would later remark that it was this quality, far more than any tactical ability, which was Bernard's true genius, and the reason why he would go down as one of the greatest captains of history – just as Churchill would for his moral leadership of a beleaguered nation in 1940 and 1941.[2]

Churchill's courage was born of an indomitable spirit, of a lifetime's political struggle, and a deep awareness of the epic nature of history. Bernard Montgomery's courage also derived from an unrelenting spirit that would never admit defeat, and a conviction, formed by a lifetime's soldiering and study of the art of command, that if properly led, victory must come in time to the Allies. Churchill's confidence, however, was subject to moods of profound depression – his 'dark fears' as his doctor called them – and his night sleep was only guaranteed by a 'red tablet'.[3] Perhaps the most extraordinary facet of Bernard's whole character was his infectious and unshakable self-confidence; and if he was mad, as many thought, then it was a strange madness that excluded doubt and guaranteed his sleep. This gift of self-confidence Bernard now brought to bear in a tireless bid to enthuse and prepare his army for the coming battle. He made it his business to visit virtually every unit of 8th Army, formally and informally: like his father before him in Tasmania he took his gospel out to the troops – 'it was a great achievement,' Sir Oliver Leese recorded in his unpublished memoirs, 'as day by day his own personality was spreading through the Army, and in the end the battle plan became the personal affair and interest of each man.'[4]

Churchill had inspired the free world by a rich rhetoric that did justice to the cause of humanity and civilisation; even on his brief visit to selected units of 13 Corps on 20 August, Churchill had not failed to evoke images that would remain in the minds of the men of his old regiment – the 4th Hussars – on the eve of the battle of Alam

[1] Montgomery Papers.
[2] Field-Marshal Sir Gerald Templer, loc. cit.
[3] Lord Moran, op. cit.
[4] Sir Oliver Leese, loc. cit.

Halfa: 'Gentlemen, you will strike – ah – an unforgettable blow – ah – against the enemy. The corn will be ripe – ah – for the sickle – ah – and you will be the reapers. May God bless you all.'[1]

Bernard's style was undoubtedly less rich, but equally, if not more, effective. His orders had always born the unmistakable imprint of his mind – that talent for clarifying and simplifying problems and tasks until they appeared to be quite straightforward. Yet, as if to mirror the contradictions of his character, an impish vanity revealed itself in tandem with his awesome professionalism and struck a bond with ordinary soldiers that would be unique in the history of his country. Churchill was admired, but as his wife Clemmie once said: 'He knows nothing of the life of ordinary people. He's never been in a bus, and only once on the underground';[2] whereas Bernard's mischievous, schoolboy humour and his evident concern for his men turned respect into loyalty of a new kind. His phrases and sayings circulated 8th Army like a mass transfusion. Moreover the situation was quite different from the previous campaigns of the war, as Brian Horrocks later emphasised, and was ripe for the sort of leadership which Bernard gave. Indeed the confrontation of the two armies, in bare desert, without the complicating factors of civilians or property, had a classical military quality not unlike the battles of ancient Greece and Rome. As Bernard noted in a letter to the Reynolds on 6 October – the day he issued his revised plan for Alamein – there was little to do in the desert but prepare for battle:

> I have been very busy since I last wrote. In fact one has no spare time at all; this is probably just as well as there is not a great deal to do in the desert – you cannot for instance go and play golf!! What I miss most is books; I read a great deal . . .
>
> I have my stepson, Dick Carver, joining me this week from the Staff College out here – where he is a student. I am devoted to him and it will be delightful to have him with me. John Carver is still in Scotland.
>
> It will be very interesting when I begin to get the Times. I take it by the year but the copies all come by sea and I suppose I shall get about 80 back copies on one day!! I shall be able to read what the Press said about my appointment,

he remarked with characteristic, almost unconscious egoism. He added that he was instructing his bank in London to transfer some £500 to Reynolds, 'and to keep you always on that mark or thereabouts. Then if anything *should* happen to me David would be all right for about a year or so; this would tide over the time they always take

---

[1] From an anonymous contemporary letter from the Western Desert, August 1942, Cabinet Papers (CAB 106/783), PRO.
[2] Lord Moran, op. cit.

to wind up one's affairs. Actually,' he assured Reynolds, 'I haven't the least intention of letting anything happen to me, and I know it will NOT. But I would like you to have the money and then I needn't bother.'[1]

Despite the enormous responsibility he carried, Bernard's interest in the military situation at home never waned. Six days later he was writing to Brigadier Simpson for the first time since he left England:

My dear Simbo,
   I hope all goes well with you.
   I am enjoying life out here and have seldom felt better in my life. My first encounter with Rommel was of great interest; luckily I had had time to tidy up the mess (and it was 'some' mess I can tell you) and to get my plans laid, so there was no difficulty in seeing him right off. I feel that I have won the first game, when it was his service. Next time it will be my service, the score being one –love . . .
   Good senior officers out here are scarce. I have already had out Horrocks, Leese, Kirkman, Arkwright, Sugden; I tried to get Dudley Ward for the ME Staff College but failed. I also tried to get you here as DCGS, a Major-General's job but the War Office have said you cannot be spared. I think Steele is coming. I advised Alex to accept Steele when we knew we could not get you. You ought to come out here, and we will have another try later on.
   Write and tell me the news from home, one is rather cut off here. What have they done with Ritchie?
                    Yours ever
                    B. L. Montgomery[2]

On the same day he wrote again to the Reynolds:

My dear Tom
   All well here. I have my stepson Dick Carver with me now and he is a GSO 2 on my staff; I am devoted to him and very glad to have him here. He is a Sapper, like John . . .
   I have not heard from David since he has returned to Winchester, but will hear soon. I shall be interested to know how he likes his new form, and what games he is playing this term.
   The coal ration will hit people pretty hard in England this winter, and a good many will be cold and have not too much light.[3]

This was the last letter he would write to David's guardians before the battle of Alamein began. As early as 28 September Bernard had laid down the system and timing by which 8th Army would be

[1] Montgomery Papers.
[2] Simpson Papers.
[3] Montgomery Papers.

informed of the plan of battle. Except for those units furnishing patrols, every man in 8th Army would eventually be told, at least in outline, what the plan was: brigadiers and CREs immediately, battalion and regimental commanders on 10 October, company and battery commanders on 17 October, and all remaining officers on 21 October – commanders whose duty was to see that *'all troops'* were properly informed: 'Wed 21 October and Thurs 22 October will be devoted to the most intensive propaganda as regards educating the attacking troops about the battle, and to getting them enthusiastic.

'All ranks must be told that this battle is probably the decisive battle of the war; if we win this battle and destroy the Panzer Army it will be the turning point of the war.

'Therefore we will make no mistake about it. We have great superiority over the Germans in artillery and tanks, and the Germans have no conception of what is coming to them in this respect . . .

'If every tank crew, and every 6-pdr A.Tk. gun team, will hit and disable one enemy tank, then we must win.

'If every disabled enemy tank is destroyed at once by the RE before it can be towed away, our win becomes all the easier.

'These, and other, facts must be got across to the troops in no uncertain voice. They must be worked up to that state which will make them *want* to go into battle and kill Germans.'[1]

Having altered his tactical policy for the battle, Bernard himself seems to have had no doubt about the outcome. As he summarised in his diary relating to the eve of the battle:

As the days passed, it became clear to me that if 30 Corps was successful in blowing the hole, and if 10 Corps could get its leading armoured Brigades out through the gaps unopposed before day-light on D plus 1, then we would have no difficulty in winning the battle. It would merely be a question of time.

There would be much hard fighting, and I was prepared for a real dog-fight to go on for at least a week; but our resources were such that we must win.

I could see that great determination and willpower would be necessary; the enemy would fight hard and there might be many awkward periods; if we wavered at these times we might lose the battle.

The critical essentials would be:
   To keep the initiative
   To maintain the pressure and proceed relentlessly with the Army plan
   To preserve balanced dispositions so that we need never re-act to enemy thrusts . . .
   An essential feature of my plan was that every Commander in

---

[1] 'Lightfoot' Memorandum No. 1, 28.9.1942, Montgomery Papers.

the Army, right down to the Lt-Col level, should know my whole plan, how I meant to fight the battle, what issues depended on it, and the chief difficulties the enemy was up against.

I was also determined that the soldiers should go into battle having been worked up to a great state of enthusiasm.

This was essentially an Army battle, fought on an Army plan, and controlled carefully from Army HQ. Therefore, everyone must know how this part fitted in to the whole plan; only in this way could perfect co-operation be assured.

Thus, apart from his daily visits and inspections of units, Bernard also repeated the technique he had developed in Home Forces of addressing his officers at a large gathering, down to Lt-Colonel level. In England he had done this at post mortem conferences following an exercise; now he began doing it *before* the battle. As one of his staff officers later acknowledged, it was this willingness of the Army Commander to announce openly to his troops what he intended to do in the coming battle that astonished even those who admired the way Alam Halfa had been won. After Alam Halfa

people paid more and more attention. But when he really stuck his neck out before Alamein and said 'This is how it's going to go, and what is more, see that every single soldier knows this' – now that's taking a hell of a chance. Because if you're wrong, there's nothing for you to do but remove yourself from the scene.[1]

Major – later Major-General – Oswald had been in the Middle East since 1940 and had campaigned as far as Tobruk under Auchinleck.

Most people had been up on at least one 'up and down' and the local Arabs used to say: 'You're like the swallows: you come in the autumn and in the spring you go away again . . .'

I can't recall any senior officer, even a corps or divisional commander – they might give a sort of pep talk, but certainly none had opened their mouths as wide as Monty, particularly just before Alamein when he gave these talks at different levels. And you know, you could see from the faces of the people who were there, some of whom had long experience of the desert: they said, 'By golly, he must be pretty sure – he fairly stuck his neck out.

'We've never heard anybody say in such detail exactly what's going to happen in the ensuing battle. We've heard generals explaining why we didn't quite manage to win the last one. But here he stuck his head out and he must be jolly certain of himself.' Now that had made a very profound impression . . .[2]

[1] Maj-General M. St. J. Oswald, loc. cit.
[2] Ibid.

Major Mather was given the task of organising one of the briefings at Amiriya.

> He had everybody down to Lt-Colonel there and he told them how the battle was going to go. I don't know if there's any reprint of the lecture he gave – but he'd got it right. It was absolutely amazing. We were there for two hours – I was a Major organizing it. All the rest were Lt-Colonels or above and he went through it, day by day, and told us how we'd be feeling; how we'd come to a point where we might start to lose hope – and saying but we would carry on. And so it transpired.[1]

Bernard kept no transcript of the briefings, only his pencil-written notes, for he spoke extempore. He recapitulated what had taken place since August, his first plan for 'Lightfoot', and his re-casting of the battle early in October. He gave the 'new plan', explained the 'crumbling' operations that would take place, reversing 'accepted methods'. The battle would have three phases: the 'break-in', the 'dog-fight', and the 'final "break" of the enemy'. He warned officers not to 'expect spectacular results too soon'; it would be a steady, methodical battle which the enemy could not withstand, but which 8th Army could. He predicted it would last twelve days. Providing they operated 'from firm bases' re-organised quickly on gaining their objectives, kept balanced, and kept up pressure, then there was no way in which the Panzer Army could succeed in holding 8th Army. 'If we do all this, victory is assured.'[2]

He drummed in the need never to lose the initiative, de Guingand recalled in *Operation Victory*,

> and how everyone – *everyone* must be imbued with the burning desire to 'kill Germans'. 'Even the padres – one per weekday and two on Sundays!' This produced a roar . . .
> The men were let into the secret on October 21st and 22nd, from which date no leave was granted. And, as a result of everything, a tremendous state of enthusiasm was produced. I have never felt anything like it. Those soldiers just knew they were going to succeed.

On the morning of 23 October Bernard addressed the war correspondents at a special press conference. 'Many of the war correspondents were rather shaken by the confidence – this bombastic confidence he displayed,' de Guingand recorded. 'They felt there must be a catch in it – how can he be so sure?'[3]

The same doubts had pervaded the gathering of reporters at the

[1] Sir William Mather, loc. cit.
[2] Montgomery Papers.
[3] De Guingand, *Operation Victory*, op. cit.

end of the battle of Alam Halfa, and reflected the mood of those outside 8th Army, about which Bernard was – largely thanks to Alexander – quite ignorant. Indeed the way Bernard treated Alexander was, to Alexander's staff, a matter of great indignation. Far from sitting in GHQ Cairo, Alexander – who hated 'desk-soldiering' and was, in Field-Marshal Templer's words, 'constitutionally lazy'[1] – liked to be 'up at the front'. He had stayed almost every night at Burg-el-Arab during the battle of Alam Halfa and was regularly in evidence thereafter. 'I often used to sit in the Army Commander's caravan when Alexander paid his visits to Eighth Army before the battle of Alamein,' de Guingand wrote: 'Monty would rattle out his requests – troops, commanders, equipment, whatever it might be. His Commander-in-Chief took Mshort notes, and with the greatest rapidity these requirements became accomplished facts.'[2]

'I think he [Alexander] was . . . my memory is he seemed to be about a lot of the time,' Sir Edgar ('Bill') Williams later recalled.

I remember also the curious feeling I had – I remember one evening having to brief both of them on Ultra and other stuff – and Monty had completely seized every point which one had made – immediately. And I came away with a sort of wonder whether Alex had really quite taken it, and then persuaded myself that of course Monty had taken it because it was his immediate enemy, whereas Alex didn't have that same immediacy, because he wasn't personally coping with it and therefore his slowness to react, his slowness had that possible explanation that he wasn't as close to the thing as Monty was. I have a feeling that my first reaction was the righter of the two – and it wasn't that Monty was closer and Alex further away, but that Monty was in fact much swifter in perception anyway. I remember years afterwards Archie Nye was staying with us and I can remember him saying at breakfast: 'Of course Alex was terribly nice, wasn't he? He wasn't very awfully strong up here, you know.' [Indicating forehead.]

I always remember this terrific stuff about Alex as a strategist was really tosh. He wasn't a strategist. He had some extremely able chaps working for him, but his real gift was his personal appearance on a battlefield, seeing what was necessary and getting it sorted out. After all he'd done that at Dunkirk, he'd done it in Burma, he did it at Salerno and then Anzio. But his reputation as being the great Generalissimo may have been really that he's been praised for the wrong thing.

But as for the situation at Alam Halfa and so on . . . Monty was really rather rude to him because I was only a very junior officer, but in front of me he almost said, you know, this is the thing, and,

[1] Nigel Nicolson, *Alex*, London 1973.
[2] De Guingand, op. cit.

not exactly shut up, but that sort of feeling. He wasn't – you got the impression in a way – Monty had taught Alex at the Staff College, that was it, there was this sort of atmosphere that, you know, 'I'm telling you,' and I think it rubbed off on oneself in a sense that you talked to Monty on – you didn't spell it all out because he knew it, you didn't have to make it in rounded sentences, you could do it sort of quickly and then in a sense you had to turn to Alex and elaborate somehow, because he didn't have the context quite so much at his fingertips.[1]

General Sir Sidney Kirkman was more forthright.

Alexander's deputy Chief-of-Staff was James Steele, who was a great friend of mine, and since the war we've often discussed those days and there's no doubt, according to what Jas Steele said to me, that Monty was incredibly off-hand with Alex – in fact damned rude! Alex came to see him one time and Monty said: 'I'm sorry, Alex, I can't stop now, I'm going off to . . .'
Monty was, after all, the most difficult subordinate to anyone.
The great thing about Alex was: he was a very sensible man, very charming, very sensible and he saw that Monty was likely to win this battle. He saw that he was saddled with Monty, so he – well, you'll put up with any insubordination in war from a subordinate if he'll win battles – and Alex was sufficiently astute to see that Monty would win the battle. There was no object in having a row, so there it was . . . But there's no doubt that Monty was damned insubordinate to Alex. To the end they remained amiable, and laughing together. But in point of fact Monty had no great respect for Alex, and Alex disliked Monty.[2]

The rest of Alexander's staff, Kirkman recalled, were both less sure that Bernard would win the battle, and more offended by Bernard's rude and peremptory manner with his Commander-in-Chief – particularly when Bernard indulged in what Kirkman called Monty's passion for 'interfering in things that had nothing to do with him':

Another case: This is fact. There was a local Staff College at Haifa. And a friend of mine called Smith – now General Sir Cecil Smith – was appointed Commandant. Now the school at Haifa was nothing to do with Monty – Monty was commanding the Eighth Army. Nonetheless Monty rang up Alex and said: 'This chap's no good – it's no good having Smith as Commandant at Haifa. He was in the RASC [Royal Army Service Corps]. He doesn't know the stuff. I suggest so-and-so.' And Smith's appointment was

[1] Sir Edgar Williams, loc. cit.
[2] Sir Sidney Kirkman, loc. cit.

cancelled, and somebody else was appointed. Didn't affect Smith – he said to me recently: 'If I'd gone there I doubt if I'd ever have got promoted. I'd have ended up as a Brigadier.' But my point is: here's Monty interfering again in something that has *nothing* to do with him.

Moreover the 8th Army Commander was not altogether unaware of this awkward trait:

He did it – this again is Monty's own story, told to us in the mess – when he was a Major in the Royal Warwickshire Regiment. There was to be a new CO, and there were two possible candidates, A and B. And Monty wrote to the Military Secretary of the day and said, 'I know it's nothing to do with me, but I have been serving with this regiment for so-many years and I really think I must tell you that A is the chap who should get command and not B.'
And he got a letter back two or three days later: Dear Montgomery
As you say it has nothing to do with you.
Yours sincerely

                    *   *   *

Monty told us this story. I can quite believe it! I don't doubt it for a moment! He could not confine himself to his own affairs. He always wanted to put everyone right, whether it was his business or not – it was part of his character.
Now this interference of course caused bitter relations between Monty and the Middle East staff. They knew quite well that Monty was always interfering in things that did not concern him and they also knew that Alex usually gave in. Well that caused a lot of bitterness between McCreery and – between all of the staff and Monty. They resented this interference into what they considered their function. Alex didn't, but they did.[1]

From Kirkman's point of view, it was the same Monty operating in the desert as he had known in 12 Corps and South-Eastern Command – exuding clarity and self-confidence, but with less 'opportunity for clashes' with his superiors. The desert suited him, was one area of the world where he could introduce his vision of how an army should be created without the constraints of civilians, political considerations, or a difficult Commander-in-Chief. The preparations for the battle were legion, and it seemed scarcely possible that an army of such magnitude could be assembled and launched into battle with complete tactical surprise: and yet, by brilliant staff work and a common effort as yet unseen among the Western Allies, the stage

[1] Ibid.

722

was set. Rommel was in Austria, recuperating near Wiener-Neustadt where he had, in 1938, been Commandant of the Kriegsschule. To an old colleague he was boasting that with three shiploads of fuel for his tanks he would be in Cairo within forty-eight hours. His old Panzer Army subordinates, though less sanguine, were equally confident that they could hold the line at Alamein. The acting Panzer Army Commander, General Stumme, the C-in-C South, Field-Marshal Kesselring, and Colonel Westphal, the Chief-of-Operations-Staff at Panzer Army HQ, all predicted defeat for the 8th Army if they attacked. Stumme had even written to Rommel that the British 'are none too happy about it [the impending offensive]. We're going to wipe the floor with the British'.[1] The complacency of the senior German commanders was mirrored in the visit of Colonel Liss – Chief of Western Intelligence in Berlin – to the Alamein line on 23 October, and his report to Berlin that no attack was expected before November.

Whatever the feelings of the Panzer Army commanders or of GHQ Cairo, the mood within 8th Army was a tribute to the planning and inspiration that had gone into the preparations for the battle. That 8th Army Headquarters had done all it could and in good time was well demonstrated by the fact that the Chief-of-Staff, Brigadier de Guingand, was able to take thirty-six hours' leave immediately before the offensive began.

De Guingand returned on 23 October for the Army Commander's press conference, and in the afternoon he motored with Montgomery to the new 8th Army Tactical Headquarters, which had been set up alongside 30 and 10 Corps Headquarters by the sea, arriving at 4.15 p.m. From here Bernard would control the forthcoming battle, and, in order that he might continue to visit both commanders and units during the operations, a special Grant tank was provided. Sir Oliver Leese remembered the afternoon:

On the last afternoon before the battle started, I motored slowly round the battlefield talking to as many platoons, gun and tank teams, sapper parties as I could. One went very slowly to keep down the tell-tale dust and as usual one had no windscreen to catch the rays of the sun. The men were quiet and thoughtful – many were writing letters and you often found the Padres giving a last service to their men. Everywhere there was a feeling of expectancy and of high confidence, but a realisation of the magnitude of the task that lay ahead. Everyone knew what they had to do and I think that somehow we all realised the terrific issues at stake. The morale of the army was tremendously high and the will to succeed and confidence in their preparedness was evident everywhere . . .

[1] David Irving, *The Trail of the Fox*, op. cit.

I dined with the Army Commander on the eve of the battle. After dinner he asked me what I was going to do. I said I was going to look at the [artillery] barrage. He asked what I'd see and what good I'd do; and he then went on to say that there was now nothing further that I could do to influence the battle. My job, he said, was to go to bed early so as to appear fresh in the morning and be able by my appearance to give confidence to the troops. I had then to be on top of my form so as to accept the inevitable shocks of battle; and be able to plan quickly and soundly the next night's attacks. He could not have been more right.[1]

Eighth Army Intelligence reported on the telephone to the Army Commander that they did not think 'the enemy expect an attack tonight';[2] however in the daily Intelligence Summary Williams had noted with anxiety that 'the enemy adds to his 600 tanks an impressive number of anti-tank guns'.[3]

This was an ominous warning – though whether the armoured units were really prepared for the anti-tank gun duels of the coming days is arguable. The Army Commander's training policy had emphasised the importance of intimate co-operation between the armour and artillery, and this policy was repeated as early as 15 September in the armoured brigade training instructions – such as those of 'Pip' Roberts' 22nd Armoured Brigade: 'Armoured regiments must be able rapidly to select good hull-down positions and anti-tank gunners must be able rapidly to select suitable positions from which to co-operate with the armour. RA regiments must get into action quickly, sited not only for their normal supporting role, but also to undertake anti-tank gun shoots if necessary.'[4]

Instructions were one thing, however; reality was another. As the 8th Army's Chief Gunner later recalled, this was partly the fault of the artillery officers who, after the long saga of 'Jock' Columns and 'Battle Groups' under Auchinleck, had lost cohesion, confidence, and identity. One of Kirkman's first tasks, on arriving in Egypt in September, had been 'getting regiments back under the command of the CRA . . . Even after Alam Halfa there was still what I call administrative disorganization. And to such an extent had the Auk got this "group" mania into his head that RA Commanders – commanding three regiments of artillery – were not allowed to fly pennants on their cars. I went straight away to 8th Army staff and said: This is absolute nonsense, that they must at once issue orders that C's RA will fly pennants like any other Brigadier in command of troops. There was some opposition, but it was clear that if it wasn't

[1] Sir Oliver Leese, unpublished memoirs, op. cit.
[2] War Diary, 8th Army HQ, October 1942 (WO 169/3918), PRO.
[3] War Diary, 8th Army HQ, 'I' Section, October 1942 (WO 169/3937), PRO.
[4] War Diary, 22nd Armoured Brigade HQ, September 1942, loc. cit.

done the next day I was going to Monty – and it was done. I didn't fly a flag – I didn't care two hoots one way or the other. What I wanted to do was re-establish the position of the C's RA and the artillery.' To reverse the dogma of a whole year of desert fighting, however, was not really possible in the few weeks at hand. 'I think to some extent the gunners had failed to impress on the armour what they could do, what their task was,' Kirkman acknowledged – though he blamed, too, the amateurishness of many of the armoured commanders who 'never realized the value of artillery – and particularly concentrated artillery'.[1] The worst offenders, he felt, were the old-fashioned yeomanry armoured cavalry regiments.

> The worst of all were some of these Yeomanry Regiments. There was a certain Yeomanry Regiment during the battle of Alamein, and on someone's instructions a field artillery regiment was sent to support them. This chap went up and said: 'I've been sent to support you.' And the Yeomanry CO said: 'No, you're not wanted here. I'm only supported by 2 RHA' – or whatever the unit was! – That was the attitude you see.[2]

Whether or not the training was all that it could be, there was now nothing more that Bernard could do. He had already written a Personal Message to 'be read to the troops on the morning of D day'. Of all his famous messages, this one would be his most memorable – as historic, in its way, as the signal sent by Vice-Admiral Nelson at the commencement of the battle of Trafalgar.

> When I assumed command of the Eighth Army I said that the mandate was to destroy ROMMEL and his Army, and that it would be done as soon as we were ready.
> We are ready NOW.
> The battle which is now about to begin will be one of the decisive battles of history. It will be the turning point of the war. The eyes of the whole world will be on us, watching anxiously which way the battle will swing.
> We can give them their answer at once, 'It will swing our way' . . .

In his diary Bernard noted:

> And so we come to D day, and everything is set for a great struggle.
> The enemy knows we intend to attack, and has been strengthen-

[1] Sir Sidney Kirkman, loc. cit.
[2] Ibid.

ing his defences. On our side we have the initiative and a great superiority in men, tanks, artillery and other material.

We also have an Army in which the morale is right up on the top line; and every officer and every man knows the issues at stake, knows what is wanted, and knows how the battle will be fought and won.

The leadership is all right, and the equipment is all right.

The training is NOT all right and that is why we have got to be very careful. Having made a successful 'break-in', we must not rush madly into the mobile battle with wide encircling movements and so on; the troops would all get lost.

We must finish up the 'break-in' battle so positioned that we have the tactical advantage, and will be well positioned to begin the 'crumbling' operations which are designed to destroy all his holding troops.

His armour cannot stand back and look on; it will have to counter-attack, and then we can destroy that too.

The 'break-in' battle has been planned accordingly.

He ended gravely:

The battle will be expensive as it will really become a killing match. I consider that the dog fight of the 'crumbling' operations may last for a week, during which time we shall never let go our stranglehold. I have estimated for 10,000 casualties in this week's fighting.

All we need now is average luck and good weather.

However, Bernard Montgomery would not have been true to himself had he been contented with this. While de Guingand nervously phoned Main Headquarters for the latest news and Leese – unable to resist the temptation – went up to a promontory to watch the great artillery barrage, Bernard retired to his caravan and before going to sleep considered the future. He had eleven divisions, as well as five brigade-size independent units, such as the Free French and Greek brigades. 'It is becoming increasingly difficult to keep this large Army up to strength in men and material; in fact, we cannot do so; we shall be able to do so far less when this coming battle is over.' He had 832 25-pounder guns and 753 6-pounders; 267 Sherman tanks, 205 Grants, and 105 Crusaders mounting the larger 6-pounder guns. In a battle of attrition the losses would be necessarily severe: 'I have no reserves of equipment, and I am bound to have losses,' he noted in some 'Reflections on the Future'.

'My great difficulty, therefore, is to keep formations and units up to strength in men and equipment. When casualties occur we have to combine two units into one; this system of linked units is not satisfactory.

'I would far rather have a less number of formations, with strong reserves in the depots so that they can be kept up to strength in men and equipment. At present, I have many formations below strength in men and some with only 50 per cent strength in transport; every one is short of something.

'What will the situation be when I have had 10,000 or 20,000 casualties in the forthcoming operations, and have also lost a lot of tanks?

'When we have cleared the Germans from North Africa we shall have to re-organize our forces.

'The plan for it should be considered *now*.'

He felt the War Office should send out the Director of Staff Duties 'and get right down to working out the forces we can keep going in the Middle East'.

8th Army, Bernard felt, should consist of only two corps – an armoured corps, and an infantry corps, together with various 'Army Troops'. This would entail using the third existing Corps HQ to look after the lines of communication after the battle, and 'doing away with' some four divisions – two armoured and two infantry. 'By doing this,' Bernard reflected, 'we shall save in overheads . . . A reduction of four Divisions will mean a saving in staffs; it will enable reductions to be made in schools and training establishments; in fact, reductions could be made all along the line right down to base units.

'We want the formations we keep to have proper reserves of men and material; it is quite useless to have a large number of formations with no reserves.

'We also want reserves of leaders, right down to non-commissioned ranks.'

Bernard also went on to forecast 'some rude shocks later on' unless the gulf between England and the 'active front' in Egypt were bridged.

'The point is this:

We have coming to the fore in England a generation of Commanders who have commanded nothing in battle in this war, and many of whom have seen no fighting in this war.

When new formations arrive out here from England they generally have no one in them who has seen a shot fired in this war; this is very bad, and as a result these formations do not do well initially and they suffer avoidable casualties.

I consider that we should cater very carefully for the education and experience of our senior Commanders. Officers like EASTWOOD, GAMMELL, and SWAYNE are not really fit to command Armies, because they have commanded nothing in battle in this war and lack battle experience.

They are young and virile and in good health. GAMMELL and

727

SWAYNE should be sent out here to an active front and learn their battle stuff.

EASTWOOD is no good and his ceiling is a Divisional Command.

All appointments to command of field Army Divisions in England might well be officers from the active front in the Middle East.

We have had so many failures on the part of our Generals in this war that we should try them out in an active theatre before they are given high commands.

As regards the more junior officers. I consider that we should send home from Eighth Army about four *good* officers from each unit and should take in exchange an equal number of good officers of the same ranks from England.

The real point is that we have an active front and we make no use of it in order to fit our *Army as a whole* for battle . . .

EGYPT is our only practical and active front. EGYPT is the only front where intimate co-operation between Army and Air Forces in battle is actually practised; in England this subject is not on the map at all, and the RAF cannot be got to play in this matter; in EGYPT they play 100 per cent.

As the troops of 8th Army counted the minutes before the beginning of the battle, Bernard assumed it to be won save for the actual fighting, and now looked ahead. 'We must make more use of our one active front,' he reiterated. 'If we do NOT, then we shall have some rude shocks later on.' As always, he was searching for a larger policy. It is a measure of his greatness as a Commander in the field of battle that, on the eve of a seminal offensive that would inexorably reverse the tide against the Axis armies, he should have turned his attention to the future needs of his army.

I consider that our great need today in this war is a long-term policy on which we can plan and work.

Having got this, we must decide on the size of Army we need. And I have seen enough fighting in this war to be able to state quite definitely that it is quality and not merely quantity that we should go for.

The Army we have must be one which can always be kept at full strength *in men and material*, and it must be no larger than this. This means a *relatively* small army; and we should use that small Army in the right place – and the right place is NOT Western Europe at present.

The four things that matter in this war at the moment are:
The Battle of the Atlantic.
The defence of Britain.
The North African coast.
The bombing of Germany.

728

Therefore, the right place for our Army is in North Africa, from where we can invade Europe via Italy.

He read a few pages from a novel, and some time after nine o'clock he went to sleep. At 9.40 p.m. the artillery barrage opened. The ground shook, the cloudless black of the night was lit by the flashing of over eight hundred guns, and twenty minutes later the first infantry crossed the starting line. The battle of El Alamein, the turning point of the Second World War, had begun.

CHAPTER FOURTEEN

El Alamein – 1: The 'Break-in'

The confusion of the first night – the mines, mortar, dust, break-down in communications, casualties – had cleared miraculously by the time the 8th Army Commander awoke, at dawn on 24 October 1942.

First it was clear that the attack had achieved complete surprise – General Stumme's last situation report to OKW shortly before the thunderous outbreak of the battle, ran: 'Enemy situation unchanged.'[1] For at least an hour there had been virtually no response by the German or Italian artillery. Moreover the series of simultaneous 8th Army raids, from the sea to the Quattara Depression, meant that Stumme – who believed the eventual 8th Army attack would be delivered just south of the centre of his line – had no means of knowing which thrust he should concentrate upon. Indeed for the Panzer Army it was a disastrous opening to the battle. It was by no means lost, but Rommel's fire-fighting doctrine, by which he had hoped to smother any attack before it could break out of the minefields, invited disaster, and by failing to garrison adequately the Miteiriya Ridge Rommel had given Montgomery a lever by which 8th Army could prise open his whole defensive lay-out. Stumme's temporary responsibility for the *Panzerarmee Afrika* was thus fatal and, although he would become for many the scapegoat for the eventual defeat at Alamein, he was much wronged. He was an experienced armoured commander, well-liked, and had seen much action on the Russian front. Nevertheless Rommel refused to entrust the battle to him, except on a temporary basis, as Rommel confessed quite blandly in his Memoirs: 'General Stumme was to deputize for me as Army Commander during my absence . . . He was rather put out when he heard that I proposed to cut short my cure and return to North Africa if the British opened a major offensive. He supposed that I had no confidence in him . . .'[2] Stumme faithfully 'executed' Rommel's defensive plans for Alamein, and considerably improved relations between the Germans and Italians, as well as the Army and the Luftwaffe: but Rommel's iron conviction about the way the battle should be fought doomed the Axis forces to defeat, and Stumme to

[1] R. Walker, op. cit.
[2] *The Rommel Papers*, op. cit.

death, for Rommel completely misread his opponent. He felt certain that Montgomery would try a series of probing attacks, reinforcing any breach that prospered in order to pass out his mobile armour. Besotted by his fuel and supply problems, Rommel eschewed his normal policy of holding the Afrika Korps as a concentrated mobile reserve. Instead it was corseted with the Italian armour in an additional, reserve artillery role to the rear of the Axis infantry defences, from the sea to Quattara, and held ready in groups that could clamp down upon any likely breaching of the minefields. Rommel thus failed to recognise Montgomery's *coup d'oeil militaire*, the likelihood that he would choose as objectives areas of high ground on which to consolidate and dominate the battlefield.

Similarly Rommel clung to his appreciation of British tactics under Auchinleck – namely their failure to conceive a plan and to stick to it relentlessly. The July operations had convinced Rommel that 8th Army, despite the stamina of its Commonwealth troops, was incapable of well-conceived operations, ruthlessly carried out. Rommel had been permitted to remain at Alamein in July 1942 with only a handful of fit tanks, until reinforcements arrived with which to make his bid for Cairo. To the end of his days Rommel therefore clung to the notion that he had been defeated at Alamein not by the tactical astuteness of his adversary, but by the British superiority in numbers – just as he blamed Alam Halfa on the lack of supplies rather than the tactical positioning of the enemy. Yet at Alamein, as at Alam Halfa, it was the first twelve hours of battle that were crucial.

Rommel correctly appreciated that the advantage lay with the defender: 'The defence was here at a certain advantage because it could dig in and protect itself with mines, while the enemy had to make his attack exposed to the fire of the dug-in defence.' All calculations made after the First World War indicated that, against stoutly defended lines, an attacker must have a preponderance of at least three to one in order to guarantee success. On paper, therefore, the Axis line was impregnable, for in no department did the British enjoy as much as a two-to-one superiority in numbers, let alone quality. Moreover the 'British' were in fact a hotch-potch of Australians, New Zealanders, South Africans, Poles, Free French, and Indians as well as UK troops. The Sherman tank was reputedly powerful, but was being tried out in battle only for the first time. Against some 250 well-tried German medium Panzer tanks, apart from 280 medium Italian tanks, the British could muster only a total of 500 Shermans, Grants and 6-pounder Crusaders – which must first penetrate half a million mines, almost a hundred 88-mm guns, a further hundred 76.2-mm guns, and a network of defensive posts held by over 100,000 troops[1] before getting to grips with the German-

[1] There were 49,000 German troops and 54,000 Italians in the forward Alamein area, while 8th Army, forward of the Nile Delta, is reckoned to have contained up to 195,000 men.

Italian armour. That 8th Army, in a single night, could breach the most thickly-held part of the line in the north and position itself on the relative security of the Miteiriya Ridge with infantry, armour, artillery and anti-tank guns was inconceivable to Rommel – who believed he would have at least two days' warning of the move of enemy armour and main bodies of supporting infantry.

The situation at dawn on 24 October was therefore an encouraging one for the 8th Army Commander, and a shattering one for his opposite number, General Stumme. In eight and a half hours 30 Corps had smashed its way on to the Miteiriya Ridge on its left and, although it was held up short of its objective on the Highland Division's front in the middle, it was right through the enemy minefields on its right, at the northern, Australian end of the assault perimeter. Casualties varied, and were still not accurately known, but they did not look exorbitant for such a magnificent infantry performance. Moreover, for the first time in the history of the desert campaign, dawn had broken with the British armour out in battle positions alongside the foremost infantry on the left of the salient. It had not yet penetrated beyond the Miteiriya Ridge in order to form the outer 'shield' for 30 Corps' 'crumbling' operations – but it was at least through the minefields on the Ridge and in considerable strength.

To General Stumme the situation was by no means so clear. The combined weight of the 8th Army artillery barrage and air force bombing had knocked out most normal Axis communications, with aircraft 'jamming' the radio frequencies. News of enemy attacks, however, was coming in by messengers from all parts of the line. Instead of waiting for the position to be clarified by reports at first light, Stumme did what Rommel would also have done – he set out to see for himself. The depth of the Australian penetration north of the Miteiriya Ridge must have been completely unknown, for it was there, on Minefield 'J', that his staff car was shelled and he died of a heart-attack. As Kesselring later wrote: 'Anyone who knows how decisive are the first orders in a defensive engagement will have no difficulty in understanding what the loss of General Stumme meant for the whole battle.'[1] Command passed temporarily to General von Thoma, Commander of the Afrika Korps, at midday; but since there were no signs of enemy armour breaking out of the 'Devil's Gardens' – or defended minefield areas – von Thoma stayed his hand.

Would Rommel have reacted differently? In his Memoirs Rommel wrote: 'I was convinced that even the most skilful Panzer General would be unable to take the right decisions in an emergency on the Alamein front unless he were familiar with the British. Words alone cannot impart one's experience to a deputy . . .'[2] This, however,

[1] Field-Marshal Kesselring, op. cit.
[2] *The Rommel Papers*, op. cit.

was written with hindsight; moreover, almost two years after Alamein, Rommel would face the same General on the beaches of Normandy, and employ the same 'firefighting' technique as he had laid down for Alamein. Moreover, it is inconceivable that he would have ordered a full-scale armoured counter-attack with artillery and infantry during the first eight hours of battle had he been present: yet in failing to garrison the Miteiriya Ridge properly this was the only way in which the first phase of the battle could have been turned to Axis advantage. If the British 30 Corps attack had immediately been driven back it is very doubtful whether 8th Army could have mounted a second 'break-in' operation – indeed in all previous cases where attacks had failed to start off on the right foot ('Bulimba' on the night of 1 September 1942, 'Beresford' on the night of 3 September, and at Munassib again on the morning of 30 September) the new 8th Army Commander had authorised withdrawal rather than further expenditure of life. Moreover the battle of Mareth some six hours later would demonstrate conclusively Montgomery's disinclination to develop a thrust if it was soundly beaten back.

The situation at dawn on 24 October was therefore very largely of Rommel's own making – though he would not be recalled until 3 p.m. that afternoon, and would not arrive until the evening of the following day. He had made no plans for an imaginative defence, as the British had done at Alam Halfa, allowing the enemy armour to penetrate the minefields and luring it on to concealed garrisons; indeed, given Montgomery's change of tactical policy on 6 October, this would not have worked, but would only have made the 'break-in' easier than it was – for Rommel could not have watched his infantry being 'crumbled' methodically to the left and right of the 'break-in' without reacting. All that von Thoma could do, then, was to carry out the policy which Rommel had laid down before leaving – and hope that the enemy's nerve would fail in the bitter fighting that must come. After all, Auchinleck had failed to press his advantage in July, and the Axis positions and strengths were inestimably greater now. Thus the Panzer Army accepted battle on Montgomery's terms: and the 'dog-fight' began.

In his diary Bernard recorded the salient moments and features of the battle; but his entries were written retrospectively each evening. Fortunately, although 8th Army's HQ War Diary was burned in an accidental conflagration at the end of the North African campaign, the log-book of messages between Tactical and Main Headquarters has survived, and from this it is possible to reconstruct the battle-picture at Bernard's Tactical Headquarters minute by minute. For instance on 24 October Bernard recorded in his diary that 30 Corps was almost everywhere through to its final objective:

Aust Div on second objective throughout.
51 Div had two Coys of right Bn up on second objective in touch

with Aust Div. But a strong enemy locality in the centre of the Northern 'funnel' was holding up the progress of 2 Armd Bde of 1 Armd Div.

NZ Div on second objective, and held MITERIYA [sic] Ridge securely.

SA Div on second objective except on right, where troops were held up 500 yards from objective. The Eastern end of MITERIYA Ridge was securely held.

The real trouble was that 1 Armd Div could not get out through the Northern funnel because of the enemy resistance still holding up 51 Div.

The enemy minefields were extensive and deep, and they caused great delay. The whole area was one enormous mine-field.

However this picture had not been so clear at dawn that morning. For instance the first incoming reports suggested the very opposite of the truth as it would emerge: suggested that the New Zealanders had got on to the Miteiriya Ridge 'with no a/tk guns or tanks. The minefield behind is not yet clear and no vehicles can pass through'; whereas first reports were so optimistic about the progress of the Australians on the right that the Chief Operations Officer, Colonel Mainwaring, was warned 'that if Aust Div had only slight casualties the Army Commander may decide to attack on coastal sector to clear up that while the going is good. Heavy bomber support will be required . . .'[1] This was at 0550 hours. At 9.15 a.m. the picture had reversed; no armour was through on the right and instead of the Australians being ordered to start crumbling operations to the north of the salient, it was the New Zealanders who were intended to exploit south of the Miteiriya Ridge.

0915   Army Commander's Intention:
       30 Corps: Tasks in order of priority
       1. Clear the Northern Lane
       2. Exploit success in South. 152 Brigade to take over from NZ Div on Miteiriya Ridge. NZ Div to exploit South . . .
       5. Exploitation by 9 Aust Div North not to start yet. Possibility of exploiting North tonight if armour is through gap is being explored . . .[2]

However, until 10 Corps could get out beyond the infantry divisions of 30 Corps, *no* 'crumbling' would be possible: and it was soon clear to Bernard that the armour was dragging its feet. 1st Armoured Division in the right-hand (northern) funnel of the salient was at a

[1] War Diary, 8th Army HQ, October 1942, loc. cit.
[2] Ibid.

standstill with much of its forces still not having reached the minefields at all; while, in the left-hand (southern) funnel, 10th Armoured Division had got one brigade of tanks on to the Miteiriya Ridge where, after severe shelling, they retired and dispersed, drawing tremendous artillery bombardment on to the hapless New Zealander infantry sheltering there. This was not what Bernard had envisaged for the strongest armoured corps fielded by the Allies in the war so far. In his diary he noted:

> On the right, 1 Armd Div could not get out into the open because of the resistance still not overcome by 51 Div.
> On the left 10 Armd Div could not cross the MITERIYA Ridge without heavy casualties owing to heavy fire from enemy artillery and A.Tk guns to the South-West.
> I began to form the impression at about 1100 hours that there was a lack of 'drive' and pep in the action of 10 Corps. I saw Herbert LUMSDEN and impressed on him the urgent need to get his armoured divisions out into the open where they could man-oeuvre, and that they must get clear of the minefield area. He left me about 1130 hours to visit his Divisions. So far he has not impressed me by his showing in battle; perhaps he has been out here too long; he has been wounded twice. I can see that he will have to be bolstered up and handled firmly.
> Possibly he will be better when the battle gets more mobile.
> This 'sticky' fighting seems beyond him.

This was the first reference in Bernard's battle diary to his disappointment over the British armour. It can have come as no surprise to him, for it had been the armour's lack of faith in the original 'Lightfoot' plan which had caused Bernard to re-cast their role. 'All the infantry Brigadiers were a little maliciously pleased when he said that he had altered his plan after seeing that the armour was not trained,' Kippenberger wrote retrospectively of the change;[1] and, yet, despite their less ambitious task, the armour had still failed to achieve their object.

> 1200 In the North we had successfully broken in to the enemy positions and had secured a good bridgehead,

Bernard recorded in his diary.

> But we had so far not been able to pass Armoured Divisions of 10 Corps out in to the open.
> My plan now was:
> 1. To get 1 Armd Div and 10 Armd Div out into the open as *soon as*

[1] Sir Howard Kippenberger, op. cit.

possible. This to take priority of everything else. The whole artillery resources of 30 Corps to be used to assist . . .

Thereafter the New Zealand division could begin its crumbling operation, while down near Himeimat – where Horrocks' 13 Corps had penetrated the first enemy minefield but not the second – there should be another determined effort 'to break through the second enemy minefield and into open country on night 24/25 October. Verbal orders to above effect were issued to Corps Commanders on morning 24 October at 1200 hours,' he recorded – adding a further censure of the armour's performance so far:

> I gained the impression during the morning that the Armoured Divisions were pursuing a policy of inactivity; they required galvanising into action, and wanted determined leadership. There was not that eagerness to break out into the open on the part of Commanders; there was a fear of casualties; every gun was reported as an 88 mm.

To Sir Oliver Leese, writing after the war, this was the lost opportunity of the battle. 'The armour now had a great opportunity,' he declared. '. . . Rommel had not yet returned from Italy [sic]. There was no controlling head and for once the Panzer Corps was fighting piecemeal. General von Stumme had been killed by shell fire . . . and if we could only have broken out during the early morning of the first day, we would have had a good chance to destroy the German armour piecemeal. But by midday on that day it was obvious that the armour had not broken through and to me it was very doubtful whether they could now do so.'[1]

Whether these strictures were entirely fair is not easy to say after almost forty years. Some veterans and military historians blame Montgomery, saying that even the revised 'Lightfoot' plan was too ambitious, and that there was never any chance of getting the armour 'out' on the first night, just as Rommel failed to get *his* armour 'out' before dawn at Alam Halfa – where the defences were much thinner – on 31 August. Yet both Rommel and Montgomery appreciated the 'art' of war better than any critic – knew that in modern warfare one must unbalance the enemy, and that an attack which relied on penetrating enemy minefields on the *second* night was psychologically and militarily wrong-footed. Such an approach gave the enemy ample time to gauge intentions and to counter them, if not pre-empt them. Looking back almost forty years later. Major-General Oswald felt the Panzer Army had done well to breach the British minefields at Alam Halfa in a single night with only mobile infantry and sappers to help the tanks; yet, as has been seen,

---

[1] Sir Oliver Leese, unpublished memoirs, loc. cit.

Rommel still faltered for over an hour, not knowing whether to call off the whole Axis offensive because of the delay and thus loss of surprise.

At Alamein Bernard Montgomery seems to have had no such doubts; but his disappointment was as marked, for with his armour well out beyond the minefields engaging its German counterparts he could have begun his 'crumbling' operations immediately, thus forcing on the Panzer Army Commander an insoluble dilemma: how to protect his forward infantry without first clearing a superior number of enemy tanks shielding its 'crumbling' forces. By contrast the failure of the armour to break out beyond the minefields meant that the enemy now had a chance of roping in the British salient, and bringing such artillery, tank, anti-tank and machine-gun fire to bear on the congested, mine-ridden peninsula as to make withdrawal advisable. Whether or not his revised 'Lightfoot' plan had been an over-ambitious proposition, Bernard knew he had been right to aim for success on the first night; recognised the magnificence of Oliver Leese's infantry corps in breaking into the northern sector, despite heavy casualties, and was maddened by the reluctance of the armoured units to advance further – for which, he knew, they would pay dearly in the coming days. 1st Armoured Division had not even got through its 'funnel' to the forward infantry line on the right; 10th Armoured Division had got its entire 8th Armoured Brigade on to the Miteiriya Ridge on the left by 5 a.m., but had pulled back behind it on encountering enemy anti-tank guns at dawn. Freyberg had then called for an armoured advance; but neither Lumsden – who was with 1st Armoured Division further north – nor Gatehouse – who was establishing a 10th Armoured Division Tactical Headquarters somewhere else – could be contacted. A Tactical Reconnaissance report from the RAF at 0900 hours recorded 'General impression: no movement in any direction'.[1] General Gatehouse, Commander of 10 Armoured Division, had reported to Lumsden at 0910 hours;

10 Armd Div Cmdr just returned from recce to Miteiriya. Situation as follows:
a) Few of our infantry on South of Ridge
b) Ridge held by armoured regiments of 8 Armd Bde. Movement down forward slopes draws heavy anti-tank and gun fire.
c) One regiment of 24 Armoured Brigade has been placed in right rear to guard against several small parties reported to be moving East towards 51 Div area.
d) Much congestion of transport, guns and tanks in NZ area.[2]

[1] War Diary, 8th Army Tactical HQ, October 1942 (WO 169/3911), PRO.
[2] War Diary, 10 Corps HQ, October 1942, PRO.

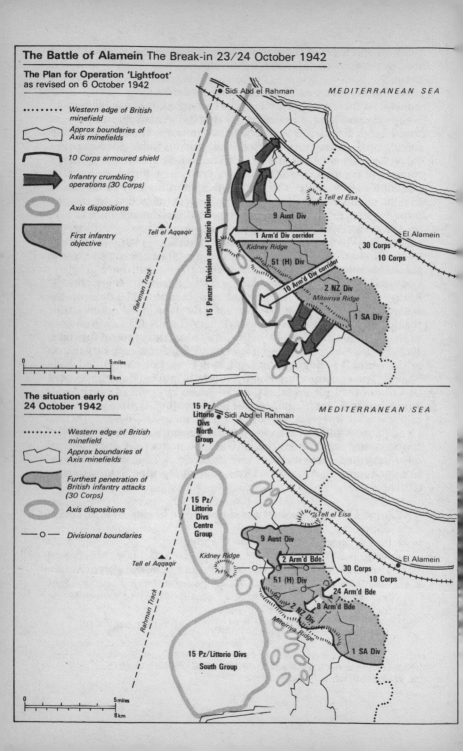

The Battle of Alamein The Break-in 23/24 October 1942

The Plan for Operation 'Lightfoot'
as revised on 6 October 1942

.... Western edge of British minefield

Approx boundaries of Axis minefields

10 Corps armoured shield

Infantry crumbling operations (30 Corps)

Axis dispositions

First infantry objective

MEDITERRANEAN SEA

Sidi Abd el Rahman

Tell el Eisa

9 Aust Div

1 Arm'd Div corridor

Kidney Ridge

El Alamein

51 (H) Div

30 Corps

10 Corps

15 Panzer Division and Littorio Division

Tell el Aqqaqir

Rahman Track

10 Arm'd Div corridor

2 NZ Div

Miteiriya Ridge

1 SA Div

0   5 miles
0   8 km

The situation early on 24 October 1942

.... Western edge of British minefield

Approx boundaries of Axis minefields

Furthest penetration of British infantry attacks (30 Corps)

Axis dispositions

—O— Divisional boundaries

15 Pz/ Littorio Divs North Group

MEDITERRANEAN SEA

Sidi Abd el Rahman

15 Pz/ Littorio Divs Centre Group

Tell el Eisa

9 Aust Div

Kidney Ridge

Tell el Aqqaqir

2 Arm'd Bde

30 Corps

El Alamein

10 Corps

51 (H) Div

24 Arm'd Bde

8 Arm'd Bde

2 NZ Div

Rahman Track

Miteiriya Ridge

15 Pz/Littorio Divs South Group

1 SA Div

0   5 miles
0   8 km

To Bernard this was monstrous. The New Zealanders held the Miteiriya Ridge securely with infantry and anti-tank guns, and had no need of 10th Armoured Division in their midst; moreover Leese, who toured the area that morning, reported remarkably little congestion.[1] Worse still, the Germans spent the entire day laying *new* minefields to the west and south of the Miteiriya Ridge, under the protection of their artillery and anti-tank guns. Leese even suggested as early as 8 a.m. that Lumsden use the Miteiriya Ridge 'funnel' to get his right division (1st Armoured) through the minefields, thus by-passing the hold-up, but Lumsden was out of touch and his BGS would take no decision without referring it to him. By 10 o'clock it was obvious that all value of surprise had gone. At 10.40 a.m. Lumsden's BGS spoke to Montgomery about the left thrust:

> BGS explained the situation to Army Commander who agrees that to cross the Miteiriya Ridge would require full artillery support.[2]

This was easier said than done since, according to the Chief Gunner, Lumsden had no understanding whatsoever of artillery co-operation and did not even have his CCRA with him.[3] Leese, who was at the New Zealand Headquarters behind the Miteiriya Ridge, now telephoned Montgomery. Leese had finally found Gatehouse but was infuriated by his unwillingness to exploit the success of the infantry, as he told the Army Commander. Freyberg was personally offering to take his own armoured support brigade (9th Armoured Brigade) 'over the top' providing Gatehouse gave him some support from 10th Armoured Division. This Gatehouse refused to do:

> Gatehouse says . . . anything that puts its nose over the ridge gets shot up. G's main preoccupation at moment is to get 10 Armoured Div into position to receive attack from someone else . . . He keeps saying he is trained for a static role. I think that is getting above him. I have told Bernard [Freyberg] to hold a meeting with Gatehouse and Brigadiers. I am placing whole Corps artillery at his disposal and am suggesting that under smoke they try and do something later in day . . . Now there is hardly anything happening.[4]

At 12.25 hours the Army Commander signalled urgently to Lumsden:

---

[1] Sir Oliver Leese, Letter to British Official Historian, loc. cit.
[2] War Diary, 10 Corps HQ, October 1942 (WO 169/3990), PRO.
[3] Sir Sidney Kirkman, loc. cit. This was strange, as Lumsden had started his military career in the Royal Artillery, but his failure to co-operate with and exploit the advantages of his – and Leese's – Corps artillery, is well attested.
[4] R. Walker, op. cit.

From Army Commander: It is necessary to get the two armoured divisions out through the 30 Corps final objective before the enemy can ring them in still further. Steps are already being taken to get 1st Armoured Div forward with 51 Div. Gen. Lumsden should meet Gen. Leese at NZ Div HQ and arrange support of 30 Corps artillery to get 10 Armoured Div out through the NZ Div front. The plan must be really properly teed-up with adequate artillery support, hence the necessity of starting early, if the operation is to be brought off this afternoon.[1]

Leese and Lumsden met, but Freyberg's brigadiers (it is said that Freyberg would never make a decision without the advice of his brigadiers, especially Kippenberger) counselled a night attack – even though it was to be an armoured operation without infantry, who were needed for the forthcoming 'crumbling' operations. As this would be primarily a 10 Corps operation under command of General Lumsden, aided by the New Zealand cavalry and its supporting armoured brigade, Leese could only protest, being painfully aware that the longer the Germans were given to re-organize, the more difficult would be the task of Lumsden's armour. When the Army Commander heard of Lumsden's proposal – a night attack rather than an afternoon assault – he telephoned Lumsden's BGS at 1305 hours and told him to:

Inform Corps Commander that Army Commander considers it essential to get 10 Armoured Div out this afternoon.[2]

Forty-five minutes later, Leese's BGS reported to the Army Commander that 'at approx. 1600 hours 10 Armd Div supported by Corps Artillery attack to cross Miteiriya Ridge'.[3] At 2.05 p.m. Bernard signalled to Lumsden's BGS, to emphasise that 'one more effort to get through bridgehead must be made. He is prepared to accept casualties provided armoured divisions get out into open so he can continue NZ operation. Corps Commander to be informed of this'.[4] Unfortunately 1st Armoured Division in the northern 'funnel' was achieving even less than 10th Armoured Division. At 1.50 p.m. the Chief Engineer, Brigadier Kisch, had signalled to Bernard that the forward brigade of 1st Armoured Division 'appears to be making no progress'.[5] Had Lumsden diverted the rest of the division via the New Zealand bridgehead early that morning as Leese had suggested, there would have been no problem; as it was Bernard now had to intervene directly.

[1] War Diary, HQ 10 Corps, October 1942, loc. cit.
[2] Ibid.
[3] Ibid.
[4] Ibid.
[5] War Diary, 8th Army Tactical HQ, October 1942, loc. cit.

I was beginning to be disappointed somewhat in LUMSDEN,
BRIGGS (1 Armd Div) and FISHER (2 Armd Bde), and also in
GATEHOUSE,

Bernard noted in his diary.

> But the main lack of offensive eagerness was in the North; both 9
> Aust Div and 51 Div were quite clear that 1 Armd Div could have
> got out without difficulty in the morning.
> LUMSDEN was not displaying that drive and determination
> that is so necessary when things begin to go wrong; there was a
> general lack of offensive eagerness in 10 Corps.
> I therefore spoke to LUMSDEN in no uncertain voice, and told
> him he must 'drive' his Divisional Commanders, and that if
> BRIGGS and FISHER hung back any more I would at once remove
> them from command and replace them by better men.
> This produced good results and plans were made in conjunction
> with 30 Corps for Armoured Divisions to break-out.

An infantry attack by 51st Division was launched at 3 p.m. to clear a
passage for 1st Armoured Division, and at 3.45 p.m. it was reported
that 'in the North 1st Armoured Division is being pressed to push on
by Army Commander'.[1] Within half an hour news came that the
forward armoured brigade had at last 'found a gap and will go
through when they have finished mopping up'.[2] By early evening 1st
Armoured Division was finally 'out' beyond the forward infantry.
'My application of "ginger" had worked,' Bernard noted with relief
in his diary. By 5.20 p.m. one brigade of 1st Armoured Division
reported itself to be on 'Pierson', the original 'Lightfoot' objective of
the Armoured Corps, bounded on the northern extremity by a mild,
kidney-shaped elevation[3] known as 'Kidney Ridge'.
In fact 1st Armoured Division was being unduly optimistic:
according to artillery observers the brigade was still far short of its
target. For the moment, however, Bernard could only go according
to the reports, and he now turned his attention to the 'left' division,
under Gatehouse, which was intended to cross the Miteiriya Ridge,
link up with 1st Armoured Division on 'Pierson' and thus form the
armoured shield essential to the infantry's 'crumbling' operations.
8th Armoured Brigade had begun a reconnaissance attack across the
Miteiriya Ridge at 4 p.m., but it was very half-hearted, and at
6.45 p.m. Lumsden's 10 Corps reported to the Army Commander:

> Situation on 8 Armoured Brigade front: 8 Armd Bde are on
> Northern side of Miteiriya Ridge in hull-down positions. They've

[1] War Diary, 8th Army Tactical HQ, October 1942, loc. cit.
[2] Ibid.
[3] Actually a depression.

been held up by minefields South of Miteiriya Ridge on the 289 grid. This minefield was laid today. The minefield is covered by guns and M.G's and a force of tanks – probably 21 Panzer. Littorio Group has been operating South of this minefield and has been engaged with 8 and 9 Armoured Brigades. Up to 17 tanks have been claimed, with small loss to ourselves. An operation is being staged tonight to get 10 Armoured Division into the open. Location of 24 Armoured Brigade not known.[1]

The operation to get 10th Armoured Division 'out' beyond the Miteiriya Ridge had thus been postponed till nightfall – 'zero' hour being 10 p.m. This was galling to Bernard – particularly in view of the fact that Lumsden had 'lost' his entire 24th Armoured Brigade.

Happy at least that 1st Armoured Division was on 'Pierson' – which was confirmed by 10 Corps at 9 p.m. ('General Lumsden is satisfied that 2nd Armoured Brigade is on kidney-shaped feature')[2] Bernard retired to bed. It had been a frustrating day, but the surprise and violence of the initial infantry assault had served to outweigh the subsequent failure of the British armour. Armoured operations were now running almost twenty-four hours behind schedule, but once Gatehouse's 10th Armoured Division was 'out' alongside Briggs' 1st Armoured Division Bernard could begin 'crumbling'. He still held the initiative, he felt: and he was determined not to surrender it.

---

[1] War Diary, 8th Army Tactical HQ, October 1942, loc. cit.
[2] Ibid.

CHAPTER FIFTEEN

El Alamein – 2: The Crisis

When Bernard Montgomery awoke in the early hours of Sunday, 25 October, it was to see the pale and anxious face of his Chief-of-Staff, Brigadier de Guingand. It was 2 a.m. De Guingand apologised for waking him, but explained that there was something of a crisis brewing. He had spent the hours since 10 p.m. in the Armoured Command Vehicle listening to reports of the armoured attack, and had grown alarmed when, after three hours of moonlight, 10th Armoured Division had not even set forth across the Miteiriya Ridge.[1] He had gone then to see General Leese – who had a sad story to tell. To the Official Historian Leese later described the events of that night:

> Soon after nightfall General Freyberg spoke to me on the telephone and said that he was not at all confident that 10th Armoured Division were properly set up for the attack.
> General Lumsden's HQ was fairly close to mine and he came round to see me. He told me in as many words that he did not feel confident in the decision to break out with the armour during the night, and though I told him that if he really felt this he should go at once to see General Montgomery, he left me.[2]

Lumsden had no intention of going to Montgomery, for he resented the new Army Commander and disliked him intensely. As the Staff Officer who was to act as Liaison Officer between Lumsden and Montgomery later in the battle recalled:

> Herbert Lumsden was a most polished gentleman, tall, always in immaculate dress. He had his own tank which was painted white and which he drove by himself, because he had the most remarkable sense of location. What he did was quite wrong: he'd swan all over the place by himself in his white tank. He had beautifully pressed cavalry trousers, immaculate bush shirt and white silk scarf and everything else – and he was very morale-raising, be-

[1] Sir Francis de Guingand, loc. cit.
[2] Sir Oliver Leese, Letter to British Official Historian, loc. cit.

743

cause he'd suddenly appear, this immaculate creature, like somebody from the Gods. We were all sweating while he was completely relaxed – very much the gentleman and the complete antithesis of Monty.

Herbert Lumsden had very great abilities, there's no question about it – but the effect on Herbert Lumsden of Monty was like a stoat on a rabbit. He'd freeze up, become . . . not himself: and Monty saw him in this frozen-up state. Herbert was scared stiff of Monty.

First of all Monty saw right through him – this tremendous sort of surface glaze on Herbert Lumsden. He wasn't as good as he was made out to be, but he had such tremendous polish, always had the answer to everything, always had such charming manners. And Monty saw right through this – and it made Herbert collapse.[1]

'Bill' Williams was also aware of the tension between Montgomery and Lumsden.

I can remember in the days when he was coming back at odd times to Army Headquarters for consultations with Monty about training for the plan. I had a sort of feeling that whereas Horrocks and Leese were *clearly* subordinate – they just were, Horrocks almost going out of his way to be subordinate, sort of saying 'isn't he wonderful?', this sort of stuff – and Lumsden not having that sort of business at all. Arriving rather elegant – you know, his scarf was always silk, bush shirt – always bandboxy as it were and having an *insouciance* about it. All this stuff – Monty's comic hats – he obviously didn't go for that sort of stuff at all.

It was almost a social difference between them. It was this old-fashioned sort of cavalry approach to this funny little man who was arsing about in these comic hats. I'm making it up, I'm only giving you the impression it left on me. But this was his poise and attitude . . .

I think Lumsden had a jealousy of Monty, plus a sort of contempt: it was partly Monty's manner of walking, the way he carried his head – 'arrogant bastard' – that sort of thing.[2]

Freyberg's part in the crisis has been confused because he afterwards took the attitude that one should be understanding 'in dealing with men who fail. We should "look upon them as the good comrades who fall in the first wave of an attack that paves the way for ultimate success"'.[3] (Lumsden was killed in 1945). Freyberg later felt

[1] Sir William Mather, loc. cit.
[2] Sir Edgar Williams, loc. cit.
[3] Sir Bernard Freyberg, Letter to Sir Howard Kippenberger, loc. cit.

that Lumsden was right to question an armoured assault on positions 'held in depth with 88-mm guns', without infantry support. 'I felt it could not be done until a hole was made,' Freyberg wrote to Kippenberger in 1949. 'I do not think General Lumsden was wrong in his appreciation, either before or during the battle. It must be conceded to him that he was the most experienced tank Commander in the Western Desert at the time, and he had seen what had happened to our tanks at Knightsbridge [during the Battle of Gazala] in a few minutes. He, I know, did not believe in the plan for armour to break out unless there was a hole in the defences. In my opinion General Lumsden was right; but he was quite wrong not to have made his case clear to the Army Commander.'[1]

This, however, was written in hindsight. At the time Freyberg was incensed at the diffidence of the armoured formations: for his own New Zealand Cavalry had led the way across the Ridge at 10 p.m. on 24 October, were followed by his supporting armoured brigade – but then let down by the armour of 10th Armoured Division which, having sustained minor casualties, had held back. The Germans, puzzled by the failure of the British to press their advantage either that morning or that afternoon, had correctly predicted a night attack – but with infantry. A Stuka attack was arranged; this set light to a column of supply vehicles which rapidly became a beacon for enemy shelling. Instead of urging his armour over the Ridge away from this, the Commander of 8th Armoured Brigade appealed to the Divisional Commander to cancel the attack, and allowed his regiments meanwhile to disperse. Freyberg's units thus sat alone beyond the Ridge waiting for support from the heavy armour that did not come. At 1.40 a.m. on 25 October Gatehouse referred the decision to Lumsden – who prevaricated.

It was at this moment in the battle that de Guingand decided, notwithstanding the Army Commander's edict about not being woken, that this was a crisis which only the Army Commander could resolve. He therefore convened a conference of corps commanders for 3.30 a.m. at 8th Army Tactical HQ in the Army Commander's map lorry, and went to Montgomery's caravan to wake him.

'I told him the situation,' de Guingand recalled many years later,

and he said, 'They're coming along at 3.30? I agree with you – quite right. I'll be there.'

Shortly before the appointed time I went to his map lorry and there he was, sitting on a stool facing his maps, pencil chalks, you know . . .[2]

Whether it was de Guingand's briefing that misled Montgomery is

[1] Ibid.
[2] Sir Francis de Guingand, loc. cit.

difficult to say, but Bernard certainly began the conference, according to his diary, believing that all was going well save on the Miteiriya Ridge front. At 2.30 a.m., he recorded, 1st Armoured Division was 'out in the open' on the right of the salient; that on the left of the salient '9 Armd Bde of NZ Div was through the minefield and was planning to move SW in accordance with the ['crumbling'] plan'; while Horrocks's 13 Corps in the far South, near Himeimat, had reported that '7 Armd Div had cleared gaps in the minefield and that the leading Armd Bde was moving West to pass through into the open'.

In fact 1st Armoured Brigade, though in the open on the right of the salient, was still far from its objective 'Pierson'; the New Zealanders' 9th Armoured Brigade had barely moved out a mile from the Miteiriya Ridge; and 7th Armoured Division in 13 Corps was nowhere near passing through into the open – having failed utterly to breach the second 'February' minefield confronting it. Unaware of this, Bernard felt that only the failure of 10th Armoured Division was now hindering the 'Lightfoot' plan from proceeding:

> 10 Corps reported that the break-out of 10 Armd Div was not proceeding well and that minefields and other difficulties were delaying progress. GATEHOUSE had said he did not care about the operation and that if he did get out he would be in a very unpleasant position on the forward slopes of the MITERIYA Ridge; his Division was untrained and not fit for such difficult operations; he wanted to stay where he was. LUMSDEN was inclined to agree with GATEHOUSE.

At 0300, Bernard's diary entry continued:

> It was clear to me that my orders about the armour getting out into the open were in danger of being compromised by the disinclination of GATEHOUSE to leave his hull-down positions on the MITERIYA Ridge. LUMSDEN was agreeing with GATEHOUSE and some quick and firm action was necessary.

Bernard must have rued the day he appointed Lumsden to command the Corps de Chasse instead of Horrocks – but it is by no means certain that Horrocks could have altered the situation. In the southern thrust near Himeimat Horrocks had evidently misjudged the enormity of the task of penetrating the Axis minefields, as 'Pip' Roberts later recalled:

> There were two minefields to be got through – 'January' and 'February' – and clearly one needed infantry to co-operate to get through. We had infantry from the 44th Brigade and we had our own infantry; but instead there was a little plan – I think it was

hatched up by Horrocks – in which we tried for the first time to use what were called 'Scorpions' – they were flails being used on what were old Matilda tanks, and they were very unreliable. They were going to clear a gap through the minefield.

Well, to follow them Horrocks collected together an enormous number, almost a battalion of carriers, which were then going to rush through the gaps and bug the area with carriers, you see, taking everybody off the ground. It was nothing to do with me. I honestly didn't have much faith in what the carriers could do, because it was very vulnerable, a carrier. I mean it's got very thin armour and so forth, and I never put much faith in what their armour could do. The carriers were to precede us – 22nd Armoured Brigade.

Oh yes, they would have been under fire from artillery, etcetera. I never thought they had a hope in hell myself. But they weren't under me, they were directly under the [7th Armoured] Divisional Commander, so O.K., let them have a shot. But then, as our main effort to make gaps in the minefields was to be done by these Scorpions, and the Scorpions broke down and got in the way and then the Sappers had to come up and do it by hand – there was a great deal of delay. And after the first night all we'd got through was the first minefield. And then we sat between the minefields – and the two minefields were here, like that, and Himeimat was there – I mean within 2000 yards – absolutely looking down on us. It was the most uncomfortable situation.

And then we tried again the next night. And then we didn't have Scorpions working, we only had Sappers and the Queen's Regiment, and somehow or other – I couldn't quite tell you how, the Queen's Regiment – who were going to form the bridgehead in front of the gap that had been made by the Sappers, they went one way and some people went another and we went where the gap was, and there were no other infantry there, and then we got – there was only one gap, like that – every tank knocked out, either by mines or by anti-tank fire. We struggled all night and made no progress. We came back. And so we called it off . . .

I know that Horrocks was disappointed that we didn't get through. I think he felt we ought to have exerted more push, but that was it: tanks going through this one gap which was made, knocked out one after the other. John Harding [Commander of 7th Armoured Division] came up and saw the situation too; but I'm sure Horrocks felt we ought to have dashed through. But it was a very, very narrow funnel, with anti-tank guns covering it . . .[1]

---

[1] Maj-General G. P. B. Roberts, loc. cit. For a fuller account of 7th Armoured Division's difficulties, see Michael Carver, El Alamein, op. cit.

In the light of this, Roberts afterwards had great sympathy for Lumsden and Gatehouse in the north: 'Oh, I do think he [Monty] expected much more than they could possibly achieve – *much* more. I mean whenever you attack with tanks – and this was on a really detailed, pre-conceived plan – you get heavy casualties – very heavy casualties. When you *give* the enemy heavy casualties is when he attacks you. Now whenever the Germans attacked during Alamein – which they did, because they put in counter-attacks – *they* had heavy casualties. And what did he [Monty] do, but he ordered Currie's [9th Armoured] Brigade to go forward and they were *all* written off. It was terrible. I do think he didn't fully appreciate how the tanks could be handled to their best advantage – and the best advantage was to get on a piece of ground which was the only ground on which to counter-attack you, and then you inflict heavy casualties.'[1] Field-Marshal Lord Harding later agreed with Roberts – 'the best armoured Commander we had in the desert.' Harding felt that the Army Commander had not allowed for the enormous difficulties in crossing such deep minefields under enemy fire, or the accumulated psychological effect of a year and a half of German superiority in equipment and skill in the combined use of armour, artillery, infantry and air power.[2]

Disregarding the rights or wrongs of Montgomery's expectations, Roberts nevertheless felt – as did Freyberg – that Lumsden and Gatehouse were quite wrong to disobey orders in the midst of a critical battle. This was in fact the root of the crisis. As the New Zealand Official Historian remarked: 'The armour was perpetuating the tradition, established by General Gott (under whom both Lumsden and Gatehouse had served) of giving lip service to the plans but holding to a determination to run the armoured battle its own way.'[3] Lumsden had warned Freyberg, when setting up the attack, that playing with armour was 'like playing with fire . . . It is like a duel. If you don't take your time you will get run through the guts. It is not for tanks to take on guns'.[4]

Almost two years later, having gained a bridgehead in Normandy, Bernard would be faced with the same problem – a problem which many subsequent historians could never understand. Churchill might 'sweep his hand over the German positions' on a map and suggest some grand manoeuvre – as at Alam Halfa – but what if the British armour refused to obey?

That the Commander of 10th Armoured Division *did* decline to obey the Army Commander's orders at Alamein is revealed in a letter which Gatehouse wrote to Montgomery in 1958, when he took issue

[1] Ibid.
[2] Field-Marshal Lord Harding, interview of 20.11.80.
[3] R. Walker, op. cit.
[4] Ibid.

with Montgomery's *Memoirs*. Acknowledging that he had been told
to take his whole division over the Miteiriya Ridge, he recalled how
he had 'refused to obey, and therefore had no other course but to
report to you why I had done so'.

In his diary and later in his *Memoirs* Bernard considered this
disobedience to be the 'real crisis in the battle' – a crisis of confidence
by the armoured commanders both in themselves and in their Army
Commander. In his diary Bernard recorded the fateful conference at
3.30 a.m., attended by Leese, Lumsden and de Guingand:

> Each Corps Commander explained his situation. In 30 Corps the
> NZ movement SW from the MITERIYA Ridge was beginning to
> develop; its success depended on 10 Armd Div breaking through.
> In 10 Armd Div, one Regt of 8 Armd Bde was through into the
> open; GATEHOUSE wanted to withdraw this Regt back on to the
> Ridge. 24 Armd Bde was not yet through but the Brigadier re-
> ported he hoped to be through by dawn.
>   GATEHOUSE wanted to withdraw both these Armd Bdes back
> behind the minefields and to give up all the advantages he had
> gained; his reason was that his situation out in the open would be
> very unpleasant and he might suffer heavy casualties.
>   LUMSDEN agreed with GATEHOUSE.

According to Bernard's *Memoirs* Lumsden begged him to speak
personally to Gatehouse on the telephone – 'the real trouble is that
LUMSDEN is frightened of GATEHOUSE and won't give him firm
orders,' Bernard remarked in his diary – adding that Gatehouse's
divisional headquarters were eleven miles from the front: 'right back
on SPRINGBOK Road, some 16,000 yds behind his leading Armd
Bdes.' In his *Memoirs* Bernard claimed then to have spoken to
Gatehouse on the telephone 'in no uncertain voice, and ordered him
to go forward at once and take charge of his battle; he was to fight
his way out, and lead his division from in front and not from
behind'.

Not unnaturally Gatehouse resented this slur, for as he put in his
letter of 5 December 1958, if Montgomery 'cared to make some
enquiries' of the various formations Gatehouse had commanded,
'you will, I think, learn that I normally commanded my armd
formations from a point either level with or slightly in advance of the
leading armd regt.'[1] He had in fact come back to his headquarters on
the Springbok Road in the early morning of 25 October because, as
his divisional War Diary recorded, he could get no firm decision from
his Corps Commander, Lt-General Lumsden:

---

[1] Maj-General A. F. Gatehouse, Letter to Field-Marshal Viscount Montgomery of
Alamein, 5.12.58. Montgomery Papers.

0350 Neither brigade has made any progress through the minefield. The situation was most unsatisfactory as it seemed that both brigades were likely to be caught in a disorganized state just emerging from the minefields. Corps Commander's decision had been sought as to whether it was not advisable to withdraw to the original position, but although this had been asked for some 3 hours previously no decision was yet forthcoming. A telephone conversation between GOC [10th Armoured Division] and Corps Commander was now in progress, GOC strongly advising withdrawal to former positions.[1]

To be castigated, on the telephone, by the Army Commander for 'leading from behind' – even though the divisional headquarters was ridiculously far back – seemed therefore most unfair to Gatehouse. What the armoured commanders failed to recognise was that unless a deeper penetration was made by the armour, not only could the 'crumbling' operations not begin, but the enemy would not be obliged to counter-attack at all.

Meanwhile, having berated Gatehouse and insisted he 'fight his way out' Bernard

spoke very plainly to LUMSDEN and said I would have no departure of any sort from my original plan and orders; I was determined that the armour would get out from the minefield area and out into the open where it could manoeuvre; any wavering or lack of firmness now might be fatal; if GATEHOUSE, or any other Commander, was not 'for it' and began to weaken, then I would replace him in command at once.

I then issued definite orders to 10 Corps and to 30 Corps.

Four hours later, Bernard noted,

Information received that 24 Armd Bde had broken through into the open and was in position, two-up, about 2000 yds West of the minefield area; its right Regt was in touch with IOH, the left Regt of 2 Armd Bde.

To the SW the whole of 9 Armd Bde was now through the minefield.

In the centre 8 Armd Bde had one Regt 'out'.

And so all was now working out well, and we were in the positions we had hoped to have been in at 0800 hours on 24 October. It is a good thing I was firm with LUMSDEN and GATEHOUSE last night.

The great lesson of the battle so far is the need for firmness of the Commander in charge of the battle, and the need to have to apply

[1] War Diary, 10th Armoured Division HQ, October 1942, PRO.

ginger almost continually to weak Commanders. It is amazing how many weak Commanders we have. At one stage in the battle yesterday the whole of 10 Corps was inactive and doing nothing, waiting for other people to do things. There was no 'drive' to get things done, and to get a move on; the whole show had to be galvanized into action, and I had to do this myself. However, all is now well-placed for us to crack along and to keep the initiative; there was a danger yesterday that we might lose the initiative.

De Guingand, both in his post-war account *Operation Victory* and to the end of his life, maintained that this firmness of the Army Commander was a crucial affirmation without which the British offensive might well have foundered: 'Unless it had been made I am firmly convinced that the attack might well have fizzled out, and the full measure of success we achieved might never have been possible. The meeting broke up with no one in any doubt as to what was in the Commander's mind.' Sir Oliver Leese felt the same: 'There is no doubt in my mind that this Conference cleared any shadow of doubt from anyone's mind as to the Army Commander's intention.'[1]

This may well have been true at a psychological level – de Guingand called the Army Commander's conference a 'tonic';[2] and it certainly bore out Bernard's declaration before the offensive about command – 'The Army Commander has decided that this will be an Army battle controlled by him, and not three Corps battles' as the G3 at Tactical Headquarters, Captain Vernon, recorded in his diary.[3] But was it true at an operational level? Gatehouse was adamant after reading Montgomery's *Memoirs*: 'I think it fair to you,' he wrote, 'that if you repeat your version of the action of 10 Armoured Division on Oct 25th 1942, which you must, by now, be aware is quite untrue, I shall have to consider what action lies open to me.

'As you must remember, I received orders from my Corps Commander to take my whole Div. (2 Armd Bdes = 6 armd Regts) over the MATERIA [sic] RIDGE, at night, through an un-lifted minefield, and be 800 yards down the forward slope of that ridge by dawn the next morning. This order I refused to obey, and therefore had no other course but to report to you why I had done so.

'This I did, in the telephone conversation, which you mention, and you immediately saw my point or so I believed, and you agreed to my doing this operation with one armd Regt. viz: – with one-sixth of the force originally envisaged.

'This attack by the Staffs Yeomanry was a complete failure.

'Your statement that on the next morning my Div was through and out in the open is quite untrue, which is more or less borne out by

---

[1] De Guingand, *Operation Victory*, op. cit. and interview of 7.5.1978.
[2] Ibid.
[3] Brigadier H. R. W. Vernon, handwritten diary of preparations for the battle of El Alamein.

751

your statement on, I think, the following page, where you say that further progress on this part of the front proved too costly, and that you therefore abandoned it.'[1]

Gatehouse's stricture was quite correct in relation to the Miteiriya Ridge, as is proved by the 10th Armoured Division's War Diary which, in the early morning of 25 October, continued:

0420 GOC's telephone conversation with Corps Cmdr finished, having lasted for over an hour, and orders were given for 8 Armoured Brigade to maintain one Regiment forward (the Staffs Yeomanry) with role protection and contact with flank of 9 Armd Bde [2nd New Zealand Division's support brigade]. Meanwhile to improve the gap in the minefields behind them so as to allow movement backwards and forwards.[2]

Unfortunately Gatehouse's HQ was so many miles from the front line that it proved impossible to relay these orders to 8th Armoured Brigade, and Freyberg, out with his own 9th Armoured Brigade, had meanwhile had to act himself as armoured GOC in the area in Gatehouse's absence. Whatever Freyberg later maintained, he was at this time even more adamant than the Army Commander that the armour break out beyond the Miteiriya Ridge, and managed to persuade 8th Armoured Brigade to pass out all three of its regiments. When Gatehouse's orders finally got through at dawn, calling for only one regiment to remain in front of the ridge, the *entire* brigade rushed back behind the Ridge, leaving the New Zealanders' armoured brigade under Brigadier Currie completely unsupported. Finally at 7.15 a.m. Gatehouse moved up his Main HQ, as ordered by the Army Commander, but it was too late to reverse the flight, and for the rest of the morning Currie's 9th Armoured Brigade was left out on its own beyond the Ridge, abandoned by 10th Armoured Division.

With Gatehouse so out of touch with his own brigadiers, there was a grave danger of the battle reverting to the confusion and incoherence that had characterised the 8th Army's performance of old. In correcting Montgomery's version in his *Memoirs* Gatehouse revealed how little he himself had been in control; moreover he ignored the operations of his other armoured brigade – 24th Armoured. For here Bernard's determination seems to have borne fruit, for after a night of hesitation and wariness shortly before dawn, at 5.20 a.m. one regiment finally broke out of the minefields, with the task of joining up 10th Armoured Division with its sister division, 1st Armoured Division, on the right of the salient. Forty minutes later a second

[1] Maj-General A. F. Gatehouse, Letter, loc. cit.
[2] War Diary, 10th Armoured Division HQ, October 1942 (WO 169/4117) PRO.

regiment was 'out', and by 6.15 a.m. the three regiments of the Brigade were reported to be on 'Pierson', having established contact with 2nd Armoured Brigade of the 1st Armoured Division. Thus by the time the Army Commander re-awoke, early on 25 October, he had reason to believe that – albeit twenty-four hours later – his Armoured Corps was on its final objective on its right, threatening the Panzer Army's lines of communication and in good position to shield Leese's 30 Corps, which could now begin simultaneous 'crumbling' operations to left and right as soon as 8th Armoured Brigade also got 'out' in brigade strength beyond the Miteiriya Ridge. At 7.15 a.m., under the illusion that Gatehouse had one regiment of tanks well out beyond the Miteiriya Ridge, and had cleared up the minefields behind it so that he could pass through the remaining regiments of the armoured brigade, Bernard confirmed his orders to Lumsden – as recorded by Lumsden's HQ.

0715 *Instructions to 10 Corps by Commander 8th Army, early 25 October.*
10 Corps will:
a) Get out West of minefield where it can manoeuvre
b) Locate and destroy enemy armoured Battle Groups
c) Ensure that operations of 2 New Zealand Division South-West from Miteiriya Ridge are not interfered with by enemy armoured forces in the West.[1]

Even at 10 a.m. Bernard firmly believed he could carry out 'Operation Lightfoot' as planned, and his 'Intention' was passed to Main Headquarters, 8th Army. This was to get out Gatehouse's 'remaining' regiment (Notts Yeomanry) beyond the Miteiriya Ridge in order to form an armoured 'hinge', behind which the New Zealanders could begin to 'crumble' south-westwards, using their 9th Armoured Brigade as support. In anticipation of this the New Zealanders' place on the Miteiriya Ridge had already been taken by Gatehouse's 133rd Lorried Infantry Brigade. Meanwhile the right-hand 'hinge' of the armoured salient would be formed by General Briggs' 1st Armoured Division, which would take Gatehouse's 24th Armoured Brigade under command.

Bernard's confidence in this assessment must have been upset half an hour later, when 10 Corps finally informed him that 1st Armoured Division was *not* on its objective, 'Pierson', and that 2nd Armoured Brigade held 'only Eastern end of kidney-shaped feature', the majority of which was occupied by German 88-mm guns. Moreover down in the South 13 Corps now confessed that they were not, after all, 'in the open', and that the Corps Commander, General Horrocks, had in fact ordered 7th Armoured Division to give up its assault on the 'February' minefield. Shaken, but not revealing any signs of a crisis,

[1] War Diary, HQ 10 Corps, October 1942, loc. cit.

Bernard left at 11.30 a.m. for the Headquarters of 2nd New Zealand Division to ensure its first 'crumbling' operation was properly set up – and it was there that the bitter truth was at last revealed to him. Gatehouse's 'Sitreps' from 10th Armoured Division had been utterly misleading. Neither the move of all three regiments of 8th Armoured Brigade beyond the Miteiriya Ridge, nor their prompt withdrawal *en masse* after dawn, had been mentioned. All Gatehouse had hitherto reported was that the Staffs Yeomanry, supposedly beyond the Ridge, had been 'forced to retire a little'.[1] When Bernard reached Freyberg's headquarters, however, he found, to his consternation, that Gatehouse had in fact no armour whatsoever out in front of the Miteiriya Ridge. Bernard's left-hand 'hinge' therefore did not exist. There would be no armoured shield to protect the New Zealanders' 'crumbling' operation. Far from having 'galvanised the whole show into action', his early morning conference and his obsession with keeping to his battle-script had only served to obfuscate the truth, frightening Lumsden into resentful silence, Gatehouse into a suppression of the true facts, and Briggs into wildly over-optimistic reports of progress on 1st Armoured Division's front.

Far from being in a position both to threaten the Panzer Army's lines of communication and to shield the 'crumbling' operations of 30 Corps, the British Armoured Corps was stuck – glued to both 2nd New Zealand Division and 133rd Lorried Infantry Brigade on the Miteiriya Ridge, and clinging to the eastern extremity of the Kidney Ridge beyond the 51st Highland Division's sector. Further south, Horrocks' 13 Corps had stalled too. The 'Masterplan' had failed.

---

[1] War Diary, 10th Armoured Division HQ, October 1942, loc. cit.

CHAPTER SIXTEEN

El Alamein – 3: Surprising the Enemy

Bernard Montgomery's later insistence that everything went according to plan was not only untrue, but unfortunate. In so insisting, Bernard intended to point up the importance of *having* a plan, of not 'drifting aimlessly into battle'. Yet from a historian's view he thereby concealed a vital aspect of his own military stature: namely his ability to *alter* his plan when tactically necessary, and to impart confidence to all around him when his original plan of battle failed. Certainly one of his senior staff officers, Colonel (later General Sir Charles) Richardson felt this:

> The scene of chaos [on 25 October 1942] was absolutely unbelievable. Monty had planned for 30 Corps to clear the minefields for the armour. Well this never happened at all. They became inextricably mixed. It was a fundamental difference between the plan and the actual battle that the armour was stopped in the dog-fight area.
>
> I think terrific credit goes to Monty at that early stage and from then onwards that he was able to impose his will on his commanders – who were very mulish, Gatehouse in particular – and say: we will do this. We will not sit down and call it a day – that's his greatness I think. But of course that's never come out, perhaps because he liked to deceive himself that Alamein went according to plan – you know, 'every good commander in battle gives out a plan . . .' But it didn't go according to plan – and we at his Tactical Headquarters, we thought the battle was going bloody badly for a time.[1]

At the New Zealand Division Headquarters shortly before midday on 25 October, Bernard assessed the local situation with Freyberg and then spoke to Leese and Lumsden, who had once again been summoned for a conference. Freyberg, angered by the excessive caution of Gatehouse's armoured brigades, considered it impossible to go ahead now with the intended 'crumbling' operations. Equally he had no faith that Gatehouse would ever break out beyond the Miteiriya Ridge; he therefore advised the Army Commander to

---

[1] Sir Charles Richardson, loc. cit.

postpone further operations until the evening, and then allow the New Zealand infantry to mount an artillery-supported attack to gain the 'Pierson' line for the armour, about 4000 yards beyond the ridge. The armour could then follow up.

Lumsden agreed. General Montgomery did not. In his diary he recorded the conference in the very briefest essentials, and made no mention of the Freyberg-Lumsden proposal, not only because he disliked admitting to failure, but because his rejection of Freyberg's and Lumsden's suggestion was intuitive, and came from his heart as well as the head. Although Bernard liked to refer to his military approach as 'scientific' – reducible to principles and systematic knowledge – his own genius for command had a deeper, more personal, more competitive core. From the moment of his arrival in the desert he had reversed Auchinleck's edict about reference to the enemy, and had personified the German-Italian Panzer Army as 'Rommel'. Bernard's plan for the battle of Alamein had rested on the cardinal element of surprise – and in this it had worked, catching the Panzer Army without its Commander and driving a wedge into his defensive line where least expected. The British armour had failed by its diffidence to exploit this early advantage. Some thirty-eight hours of battle had passed, and von Thoma – to judge by the fierce counter-attacks, with tanks, that had begun to build up that morning – was now well aware that the thrust from the Miteiriya Ridge was the principal effort by 8th Army. Even a night attack with infantry would be likely to sustain heavy casualties – casualties which would blunt the infantry weapon Bernard wished to preserve for the real dog-fight or 'crumbling' operations of the coming week. The South African Division, as Leese later recalled, was already 'fought to a standstill and its two brigades were now too weak for further offensive operations'.[1] The New Zealanders also possessed only two brigades and had had heavy casualties – as had 51st Highland Division in this, its first battle since reconstitution. Only the Australians were up to full strength, their losses made good by reserves.

Although he wished to keep to his outline tactical strategy, Bernard nonetheless felt in his bones that he must continue to surprise the enemy, must reinforce strength not weakness. If the New Zealanders failed in their infantry assault, or if Lumsden's armoured commanders found further pretexts for refusing to obey, the battle would be, to all intents and purposes, lost. Bernard therefore said no. There would be no further operations either to advance the left-hand armoured shield beyond the Miteiriya Ridge, or to 'crumble' the enemy infantry and guns south-westwards, for the moment.

'The Army Commander sized up the situation very quickly,' wrote Sir Oliver Leese later,

[1] Sir Oliver Leese, loc. cit.

and made one of his characteristic quick tactical decisions which he so often did in the midst of the heat of a battle and which enabled him to pull an awkward situation out of the fire, without appearing in any way to alter the shape of his original battle plan.[1]

Gatehouse's armoured division was to be withdrawn, Freyberg's infantry rested. Everything would now be thrown into the right-hand sector, pushing out the 1st Armoured Division shield and starting crumbling operations northwards by the infantry of the 9th Australian Division. 'This really meant a new thrust line or axis of operations, from South to North, a switch of 180 degrees. I hoped that this completely new direction of attack might catch the enemy unawares,' Bernard noted in his diary. The decision, duly recorded and signed by Bernard, is to be found in the Tactical HQ War Diary for 8th Army:

Decisions given by Army Commander at Conference held at HQ NZ Div at 1200 hrs 25 October 1942. Present: Army Commander, Commander 10 Corps, Commander 30 Corps.
1. Direction of 'crumbling' operations being undertaken by 30 Corps to be changed. 30 Corps to hold Miteiriya Ridge strongly and not operate SW from it.
2. Instead 30 Corps to undertake crumbling operations Northwards towards the coast using 9 Aust Div.
3. 10 Corps to operate Westwards and NW from bridgehead gained by 1 Armd Div.
4. 10 Armd Div (less 24 Armd Bde) to be withdrawn from the NZ Div area for use 10 Corps vide para 3.
                    B. L. Montgomery
                    Lt-General[2]

The Conference at the New Zealand Division HQ at 12 noon on 25 October thus marked the first real turning point in the battle. Far more than Bernard's insistence, in the early hours of the morning, on the armour getting out beyond the Miteiriya Ridge it was this Conference which set the tone of the rest of the battle: Montgomery's battle.

Some historians have attempted to belittle Montgomery's stature as a general by referring to the battle of Alamein as a battle conceived in the mould of World War One; but such claims are specious. It was as a result of the mutinous murmurs of his armoured commanders that Bernard was forced to redesign his original plan of battle on 6 October – and even the more limited role given to the armour had now proved over-ambitious. Far from insisting on the gain of ground as an object in itself, the essence of Bernard's plan was to bring

[1] Ibid.
[2] War Diary, 8th Army Tactical HQ, October 1942, loc. cit.

Rommel's armour to battle on ground of 8th Army's choosing, to destroy it, and then round up the unarmoured mass of his Panzer Army. In rejecting the Freyberg-Lumsden proposal Bernard was demonstrating the very opposite of World War One tactics. Lives would not be squandered simply in order to gain ground. Indeed it was his very reluctance to do the orthodox which characterised Bernard Montgomery's generalship at this moment, in contradistinction to his corps commanders and to Freyberg's proposal. In the evening a number of German counter-attacks were put in, with tanks. 'The attacks were piecemeal and isolated,' Bernard noted in his diary, 'and varied in strength from 20 to 40 tanks . . . So long as the enemy will attack us, that is excellent; and especially if his attacks are isolated and piecemeal.' On the right of the salient a single Australian sergeant knocked out five enemy tanks with his 2-pounder anti-tank gun – a fine example of how even inferior equipment, given courage and good leadership, could be used to hold its own against Panzer attacks.

The Australian infantry, in fact fought with exemplary determination, despite mounting casualties. At midnight that night the Australians successfully carried out the first 'crumbling' attack ordered by the Army Commander, advancing 3000 yards, taking the vital 'Point 29' and overrunning a German battalion whose orders showed that no large-scale German counter-attack by the Afrika Korps was envisaged. Bernard's switch of 'crumbling' axis had proved a complete surprise to the enemy, and the courage of the Australian infantry had been salutary. By the morning of 26 October 30 Corps had sustained 4643 casualties, whereas Lumsden's 10 Corps had suffered only 455 – less than half the casualties even of 13 Corps in its infantry-and-armoured feint operation in the South.

This lack of determination was reflected in the failure of 10 Corps' armoured operations on the night of 25 October, for, despite the urging of the Australians, 1st Armoured Division failed to push the armoured 'shield' right on to the kidney feature in order to help screen the Australian 'crumbling' attacks and entice Axis armoured counter-attack. In his diary Bernard recorded the situation as it was reported to him on the morning of 26 October.

0600   The attack Northwards by 9 Aust Div was completely successful . . .
0800   1 Armd Div had failed to progress Westwards and North-Westwards.

The armour – both Gatehouse's 10th Armoured Division and now Briggs' 1st Armoured Division – had proved a broken reed. Their navigation was so poor that they refused at first to admit they did not possess the whole of the kidney feature, and would not co-operate with the Royal Engineers in surveying-in their positions as the

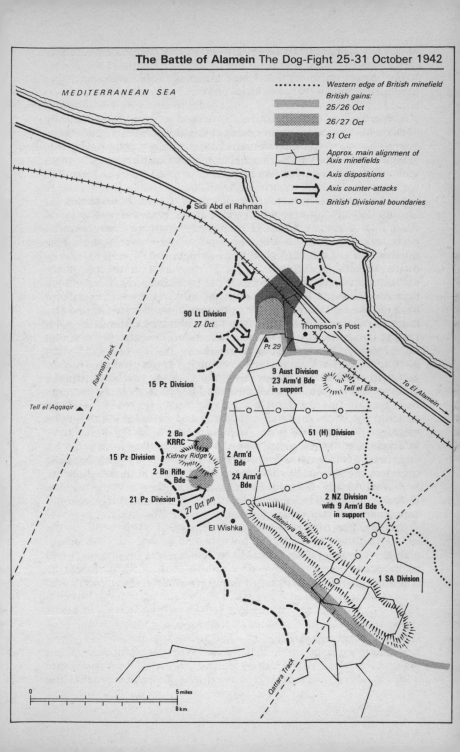

The Battle of Alamein The Dog-Fight 25-31 October 1942

MEDITERRANEAN SEA

Western edge of British minefield

British gains:
- 25/26 Oct
- 26/27 Oct
- 31 Oct

Approx. main alignment of Axis minefields

Axis dispositions

Axis counter-attacks

British Divisional boundaries

Sidi Abd el Rahman

Rahman Track

90 Lt Division
27 Oct

Thompson's Post

Pt 29

15 Pz Division

Tell el Aqqaqir

9 Aust Division
23 Arm'd Bde
in support

Tell el Eisa

To El Alamein

51 (H) Division

2 Bn
KRRC

Kidney Ridge

15 Pz Division

2 Bn Rifle
Bde

2 Arm'd
Bde

21 Pz Division

24 Arm'd
Bde

27 Oct pm

El Wishka

2 NZ Division
with 9 Arm'd Bde
in support

Miteiriya Ridge

1 SA Division

0   5 miles
8 km

Qattara Track

infantry did. Worse still, they had insufficient grasp of corps artillery co-operation.

The situation, once more, was alarming. 'Bill' Williams' daily Intelligence Summary for 26 October ran:

> The battle has so far assumed a pattern of its own, the armour by day seeking elbow room for manoeuvre, the infantry widening the breach and mopping up by night. The enemy response has been to wear down our attack piecemeal without committing his main mobile forces for a decisive blow.[1]

26 October was, in fact, to be the fateful day for both armies. At 11 p.m. the previous evening, Field-Marshal Rommel had assumed command of the re-named 'German-Italian African Panzer Army'. Early on 26 October Rommel made a personal reconnaissance of the northern salient, particularly the new bridgehead – Point 29 – taken by the Australians during the night. There were a number of courses open to him. As he later wrote: 'What we should really have done now was to assemble all our motorized units in the north in order to fling the British back to the main defence line in a concentrated and planned counter-attack;'[2] however he had himself ordered the splitting of the Afrika Korps so that half its units were in the south; moreover the British had already moved so much artillery into their salient that it was doubtful whether such a concentration could be achieved without unacceptable losses 'from air and artillery bombardment'.[3] Alternatively he 'could have made the action more fluid by withdrawing a few miles to the west and could then have attacked the British in an all-out charge and defeated them in open country. The British artillery and air force could not easily have intervened with their usual weight in a tank battle of this kind, for their own forces would have been endangered,' as Rommel reflected.[4] However, to encourage mobile battle in the north meant withdrawing the German-Italian armour from the south – where the British 13 Corps were already through the first minefield belt and threatening to break out.

Rommel was thus presented with no option but to continue the fireman's policy he had laid down before he left Africa a month earlier. Moreover he could not but react in the way Montgomery had intended, for despite the relative failure of the British armour he could not stand and watch 8th Army 'crumbling' his infantry and artillery defences. As at Alam Halfa he was forced to fight the battle in the way which Montgomery dictated, launching attack after attack

---

[1] War Diary, 8th Army HQ, 'I' Section, October 1942, loc. cit.
[2] *The Rommel Papers*, op. cit.
[3] Ibid.
[4] Ibid.

at 'Point 29'. 'Rivers of blood were poured out over miserable strips of land which, in normal times, not even the poorest Arab would have bothered his head about,' he acknowledged sadly.[1] He had failed to train his infantry for night attacks with co-ordinated air, artillery and tank support and – providing the determination of 8th Army did not weaken – the situation was critical.

For Bernard the position was both encouraging and disappointing. He had estimated for a minimum of 10,000 casualties. Already, after two days' fighting, he had reached two-thirds of that figure. The armour had so far proved a failure, lacking in determination and professionalism. It was important now, he felt, not to squander the magnificent achievements of the infantry, nor to overtax them with casualties so early in the battle. The infantry must now be given a chance to rest before undertaking further 'crumbling' operations, and the armour *must* begin to fight. At 9 a.m., 26 October 1942, therefore, Bernard issued a general policy document which he then gave out at a conference of corps commanders held at the head-quarters of Morshead's 9th Australian Division at 11.30 a.m.[2] 'After thinking the problem over, I came to the conclusion that 30 Corps needed a short period with no major operations,' Bernard noted in his diary at 9 a.m. 'Divisions had been fighting hard since 2200 hours 23 October, and were somewhat disorganized; a period was wanted in which Div areas could be tidied up, and things sorted out.' Leese was told that, although 30 Corps was to be responsible for the bridgehead, it would carry out no major offensive operations for the moment – 'Divisions of that Corps are to be so re-organized and rested that they can conduct major operations in the near future'[3] In Horrocks' 13 Corps the armour of 7th Armoured Division was also to be relieved of offensive tasks. The only offensive action would be conducted by Lumsden's 10 Corps – whose task was 'to make progress to the West and North-West from the Kidney Hill area'. Lumsden was to concentrate on this 'one hundred per cent', and to stop worrying about the 'security of the bridgehead' – which was Leese's responsibility.

Lumsden returned to his headquarters to prepare a 10 Corps plan for a night advance from the British toehold on the Kidney Ridge – and this plan was relayed to the Army Commander at 7.15 p.m. By then, however, Bernard's faith in his armour had reached its nadir. At noon he had examined the tank casualty figures – which showed a loss of 239 tanks of all types, mostly on minefields and easily repairable. Together with the very light casualties in officers and men in 10 Corps it was difficult, therefore, to understand the ineffective-ness of the armoured performance. The success of Bernard's 'crumb-

[1] Ibid.
[2] War Diary, 8th Army Tactical HQ, October 1942, loc. cit.
[3] Ibid.

ling' concept had already been reflected in the number of piecemeal counter-attacks put in by Rommel's armour; but it was the infantry of 8th Army that was having to take the brunt of the casualties, and there was a limit to the number of 'crumbling' operations they could conduct. One half of the Afrika Korps had still not been engaged; yet it seemed impossible to make Lumsden understand that the armour must play its part in the battle and not simply sit back doing the job of 30 Corps' own anti-tank guns.

At 4 p.m. on 26 October Brigadier Kirkman had reported the artillery ammunition situation. Kirkman was worried by the current rate of expenditure.

> I said to him, 'I've been going into the ammunition situation and it's very difficult to find out how much ammunition there is in the Middle East. But as far as I can find out we can go on with this battle for ten days at the present rate – but we can't go on indefinitely.'
>
> And Monty replied: 'Oh, it's quite all right, absolutely all right, don't worry about ammunition. This battle will be over in a week's time. There'll be no problem.'
>
> We argued a bit. I said, 'Well it wouldn't be a bad thing if we cut 13 Corps down to 40 rounds per gun per day anyway.' And he said, 'All right, we'll do that.'
>
> The point is this: When I saw Monty he was relaxed, he was by himself, quite amiable, talkative; and – there's no question – full of confidence.[1]

Indeed Bernard was not worried about the *eventual* outcome of the battle. 'If we fire 150 rounds a gun per day, we can continue the battle for three weeks,' he remarked confidently in his diary.[2] What worried him more was the amateurishness of his commanders – for Kirkman also reported that Lumsden was failing to keep in touch with his Chief Gunner:

> I said, 'The next time you see Herbert Lumsden, I wish you would point out to him that he must keep his CCRA in the picture. He wanders about the country by himself and the CCRA doesn't know what's going on.'[3]

To Bernard this was exasperating. In his diary he noted at 5 p.m. that day:

> I have just discovered that LUMSDEN has been fighting his battle

[1] Sir Sidney Kirkman, loc. cit.
[2] Entry at 1600 hours, Monday 26 October 1942. Montgomery Papers.
[3] Sir Sidney Kirkman, loc. cit.

without having his CCRA with him. I have ordered him up at once.

There is no doubt these RAC [Royal Armoured Corps] Generals do not understand the co-operation of all arms in battle. I have had many examples of this since the battle started.

LUMSDEN is not a really high-class soldier.

The failure of Lumsden to push out an armoured shield in front of the New Zealanders or the Australians, together with Kirkman's revelation that Lumsden was not fighting with his chief gunner alongside him, finally forced Bernard to re-consider the way he would fight the remainder of the battle. It was imperative not to allow the offensive to peter out; switching the axis of his crumbling operations would not in itself win victory – as the futile 'pushes' of 8th Army in July had shown. It was vital now, while retaining the initiative, to start re-grouping his forces in order to assemble 'a new infantry-cum-tank assault force', as Leese described it later. An hour before even seeing Lumsden's plan for taking the Kidney Ridge, therefore, Bernard summoned Leese: and gave the orders which, six days later, were to lead not only to the victory of Alamein, but the almost complete annihilation of the German-Italian Panzer Army.

CHAPTER SEVENTEEN

El Alamein – 4: Planning the Break-through

In his diary at 6 p.m. on 26 October 1942 Bernard recorded his new decision:

> After careful thought, I decided to regroup, and re-position, with a view to creating fresh reserves for further offensive action.
>
> By holding longer fronts in the Southern and Central areas, I could pull the NZ Div into reserve.
>
> I had already decided that the next offensive operation would be by 9 Aust Div Northwards to the coast, so as to write off all the enemy in his original positions in the coastal sector by getting in behind them.
>
> I gave the necessary orders at a Conference at 1900 hrs.

The Conference was attended by Leese, Leese's 30 Corps BGS, de Guingand and the Army Commander. 'In order to produce a reserve the following moves would take place,' the Minutes began – and recorded in detail the wider frontages and side-stepping required to bring the New Zealanders and possibly 10th Armoured Division into reserve, while enabling the Australians to renew their 'crumbling' operations northwards from the salient towards the sea:

> a) SA Div to take over from NZ Div. NZ Div to come into 30 Corps reserve.
> b) 4 Ind. Div to take over present SA Div front.
> c) Reserve brigade of 51 Div to take over sector of 9 Aust Div as far North as 299 Northing grid.
> d) 13 Corps to take over from 30 Corps up to 277 Northing grid.
> e) 7 Armd Div (less 4 Lt Armd Bde) to be prepared to move to Northern sector. This move to be dependent on move of 21 Pz Division and other factors.
> *Timings* All major moves with exception of NZ artillery to be completed by dawn 28 October.
> *Future plans* On night 28/29 October 9 Aust Div to continue attack northwards.[1]

---

[1] War Diary, 8th Army Tactical HQ, October 1942, loc. cit.

Simultaneously, as the War Diary of the Tactical HQ 8th Army recorded at 8 p.m. on 26 October, 10 Corps would also produce plans for an armoured assault reserve, consisting of 'the New Zealand Division and 9th Armoured Brigade, 10 Armoured Division and possibly 7 Armoured Division.'[1]

Leese was enormously impressed by the Army Commander's refusal to be put out by the current failure of the armour. Far from being allowed to feel that the offensive was 'fizzling out', Leese had a new and quite clear challenge. 'The Australians on the right were already in the midst of desperate fighting with the Panzer Divisions,' he recalled.

> Their job was by offensive action to contain the Panzer Corps on their front. He [Montgomery] told me to reorganise the remainder of the line – to pull out the New Zealand Division and to form a new striking force under General Freyberg . . . He was making use of the magnetic leadership and personality of General Freyberg, with his most efficient Headquarters, to drive the final wedge into the enemy front. The line was to be held very thinly by the South African and Highland and Indian Divisions. There appeared little chance, if any, of enemy counter-attacks. The Australian Division was to continue its attacks with the object of drawing the Africa Corps on to its front . . . The Armour was to be re-fitted and with the exception of the 9th and 23rd Armoured Brigades was to be held in reserve ready for the break through . . .
>
> Directly I received my orders verbally from the Army Commander I held a conference in a tiny corrugated dug-out by the sea to arrange the take-over and reliefs in the line. I have never had such willing co-operation and help. Everyone realised the urgency and the importance of the situation; and very soon Divisional Commanders were vying with each other to find ways and means by which they could help each other to speed up the necessary moves. It was a wonderful tonic to me. Speed was the essence of the plan and when the Army Commander gave me my orders, I fully realised that it could never be done without a superhuman effort by all Divisional Commanders. That they did it so willingly is a great tribute to the spirit and efficiency of their Divisions and of themselves. Moreover, it was a particularly fine effort on the part of a Division like the South African Division who had been over-run more than once in the past, and who now willingly took over a very long front with complete faith in our future.[2]

Leese's confidence that there would be no concentrated armoured counter-attack by the enemy was partly based on his experience of the battle so far, and partly on an appreciation given by the Army GI

[1] Ibid.
[2] Sir Oliver Leese, loc. cit.

Intelligence, Colonel 'Spud' Murphy. Shortly after the Army Commander's evening Conference on 26 October, Murphy reported the capture and translation of the 'Defensive Policy Plans' of the Italian Triest Division – which were to 'wear down' the attack with all means in their power, 'without using concentrated armoured division counter-attacks'.

> It looks as if this is in fact happening and I do not expect concentrated counterattacks from DAK [German Afrika Korps] until either our armour has completely broken through or until the infantry have been so weakened that they cannot continue to resist in the Northern sector,[1]

Murphy gave as his opinion. In fact Murphy was spectacularly mistaken, as the next day's fighting would reveal. During the afternoon of 26 October Rommel grew more and more anxious about the Australian salient; he brought in 90th Light Division from his northern reserve to try to retake 'Hill 28' (Point 29), from the Australians, and finally made the irrevocable decision to risk a further British armoured offensive in the far south by bringing up 21st Panzer Division to the north.

Montgomery's insistence that Lumsden push out beyond the kidney feature in order to shield the Australian 'crumbling' operations was now bearing fruit: for on the night of 26 October, 1st Armoured Division, at its second attempt, finally got its Motor Brigade forward almost onto its objectives, 'Woodcock' and 'Snipe', thus forming a flanking shield for the Australians – and forcing Rommel to react, which he did the next day. In his memoirs, Rommel remarked on the brilliance of 8th Army's 'crumbling' attacks by infantry at night – 'particular skill was shown in carrying out this manoeuvre at night and a great deal of hard training must have been done before the offensive,' he acknowledged.[2]

The sight of the British armour at last exploiting the successful progress of the Australian infantry caused Rommel to blunder. Mistakenly assuming that 8th Army was already seeking to break out of its salient, he hurled his entire armoured forces into battle. The front on 27 October became an inferno of shelling, bombing, dive-bombing, infantry and tank engagements. 'No one can conceive the burden that lies on me,' Rommel wrote in his daily letter to his wife. 'Everything is at stake and we're fighting under the greatest possible handicap. However, I hope we'll pull through. You know I'll put all I've got into it.'[3]

He did. Time and again the Germans and Italians attacked to try to prevent the presumed British break-out: 'Every artillery and anti-

[1] War Diary, 8th Army HQ, 'I' Section, October 1942, loc. cit.
[2] *The Rommel Papers*, op. cit.
[3] Ibid.

aircraft gun which we had in the northern sector concentrated a violent fire on the point of the intended attack. Then the armour moved forward,' Rommel recalled in his memoirs.[1] 'A murderous British fire struck into our ranks and our attack was soon brought to a halt by an immensely powerful anti-tank defence, mainly from dug-in anti-tank guns and a large number of tanks. We suffered considerable losses and were obliged to withdraw. There is, in general, little chance of success in a tank attack over country where the enemy has been able to take up defensive positions; but there was nothing else we could do.'[2]

Captain Vernon, G3 on Montgomery's staff at Tactical Headquarters 8th Army noted in his own diary:

> 27 October: This was a heavy day's fighting. The whole of 15 Pz Div and Littorio attacked all day on the front of 2 Armd Bde, 7 Motor Bde and 24 Armd Bde. The brunt of the attack all day was borne by 2 RB [2nd Battalion Rifle Brigade], who stood firm all day in the face of as many as 100 Tanks. 1 Armd Div, after the day's fighting, claimed over 60 enemy Tanks destroyed. Of these 2 RB claim 37 burning and a further 20 hit. 2 Armd Bde lost no Tanks.
>
> It was undoubtedly a very successful day. The enemy attacked Armour and Anti-Tank guns in hull down positions and 15 Pz Div undoubtedly lost severely.
>
> 24 Armd Bde lost a number of Tanks on mines. After dark, 2 RB was overrun, as they had run out of ammunition . . .[3]

Even at 12.30 p.m. on 27 October Colonel Murphy considered 'evidence is against 21 Pz being in the North'.[4] However later in the afternoon the headquarters of 21st Panzer Division was pin-pointed, and the violence of the assault on the northern salient thereby explained.

Bernard Montgomery meanwhile had begun the day by studying the casualty figures. The 9th Australian Division had lost over a thousand officers and men, the 51st Highland Division some two thousand. Compared with this the losses sustained by the Armour appeared minimal, and Bernard's frustration, in his diary entry at 8 a.m. had been marked. He had hoped to 'drive' his infantry north to the sea from the salient then 'Westwards along the axis of the road and railway.' To shield the infantry drive he had intended to push out an armoured shield westwards along the left flank of the infantry – 'During these operations I shall plan to move the armour on my Southern flank, holding off the enemy armour and outflanking resistance met frontally.' The lack of offensive zeal in the armoured

[1] Ibid.
[2] Ibid.
[3] Brigadier H. R. W. Vernon, Diary, loc cit.
[4] War Diary, 8th Army Tactical HQ, October 1942, loc. cit.

formations, and their inability to work closely with artillery, how-ever, belied such hopes:

> My own armour is at present breaking out through the Northern 'funnel'; it is actually out, but its progress Westwards and North-Westwards is very slow.
> It is a 'sticky' fight and artillery plays a great part in it.
> But the Armoured Div Commanders do not know anything about artillery; they are used to having it decentralised by batter-ies; there is no CRA of an Armoured Division who understands how to handle a Div artillery; they have never been trained by their Div Commanders or by the CCRAs of Corps.
> Of seven British Divisions in Eighth Army, four of the CRAs are unfit to hold the job of CRA. They have never been trained. There is no CRA in Egypt who is fit to be CCRA of a Corps.
> The Commanders of Armoured Divs are quite unfit to train anything in their Divisions except the armour; they are therefore not really fit to command Armoured Divs.
> All this makes it very difficult. The best soldier out here is Oliver LEESE. HORROCKS is next. LUMSDEN is a good Div General but he is not very good as a higher Commander. He is very excitable, at one moment elated, at another depressed; he does not give clear orders to subordinates and I doubt if they really know what he wants; he does not know how to handle infantry, or artillery, or RE. He is lost when it comes to hard solid fighting.

The bravery of the tank and anti-tank gun crews during the day, however, heartened the Army Commander. 'All day the enemy has been attacking the 1st Armd Div which is in the open to the West of the "funnel"'; all attacks have been beaten off and there seems no doubt that we have destroyed about 40 tanks,' he recorded in his diary late in the afternoon of 27 October. In the evening he added: 'The one thing we want is that the enemy should attack us. 1st Armd Div have today destroyed 50 enemy tanks (all burning) without loss to themselves.'

It was the stalwart defence of Kidney Ridge by 1st Armoured Division on 27 October which to some extend restored Bernard Montgomery's faith in the guts of his armoured formations. How-ever, the following morning he heard that the 2nd Battalion of the Rifle Brigade had been overrun after the most valient effort by their anti-tank gunners, unsupported by either 2nd or 24th Armoured Brigade; moreover 24th Armoured Brigade had run into a minefield, causing considerable losses to their tanks – '24 Armed Bde had suffered considerable casualties owing to mishandling by KEN-CHINGTON' as Bernard noted testily at 7 a.m. on 28 October.

The fury of Rommel's counter-attacks in the Kidney Ridge area convinced Bernard that the 'infantry-cum-tank asault' force he was amassing in reserve would never be able to breakout via the Kidney Ridge, any more than it had beyond the Miteiriya Ridge.

> It is also clear that we now have the whole of Panzer Army opposite the Northern funnel and that we shall never get the armoured divisions out that way. I therefore decided to make this a defensive front, to be taken over by 30 Corps. 1 Armd Div and 24 Armd Bde to be withdrawn into reserve.

An hour later, at 8 a.m. Bernard recorded his conference with Lumsden and Leese, at which he ordered the virtual complete withdrawal of Lumsden's 10 Corps from the current battle, and the handing over to Leese of all offensive operations:

> I explained that after 9 Aust Div operation tonight, the next operation would be a 'drive' NW to 30 Corps to get SIDI RAH-MAN; I then wanted to launch armoured cars South-West from that place, to get across the enemy supply routes and to prevent rations, petrol, water, etc. from reaching the forward troops.
>
> The NZ Div would be used for this operation, but it was now very weak.

Although not usually appreciated by historians, this was Bernard's most pronounced departure from his 'Lightfoot' Masterplan; moreover it remains one of the clearest illustrations of Bernard's tactical 'feel' of battle. He had insisted on his armoured forces pushing out towards their original objective since the beginning of the battle, despite the unwillingness and even disobedience of their commanders. Accepting the failure of the armour to proceed beyond the Miteiriya Ridge he had shifted the full weight of his attack to the north of the break-in salient, while adhering to his original tactical policy. Rommel had reacted exactly as Bernard had predicted, being unable to 'stand back and look on' as 8th Army 'crumbled' the Axis holding troops. But having finally drawn Rommel's armour into costly and abortive counter-attacks, Bernard now withdrew his entire armour into reserve, and proposed that Leese take over the battle of Alamein as an infantry battle, with armoured cars instead of tanks for the break out. The only question in Bernard's mind was where he could obtain sufficient reserves of infantry to back up a New Zealand Division thrust through the Australian bridgehead. Summoning Horrocks from 13 Corps at 11 a.m. he told him his intention, and together they agreed on the infantry formations which could be spared in the south if 13 Corps sector now became a defensive front.

13 Corps to hand one Inf Bde of 50 Div at once to 30 Corps; this Brigade was to go into the NZ div.
151 Inf Bde was selected.

A second Inf Bde was earmarked by 13 Corps; this Bde to be held ready in reserve to join NZ Div when required.

Finally, the Greek Brigade would be sent to the NZ Div.

About his commanders, Bernard was quite emphatic: 'It was clear to me by now,' he wrote in his diary at noon, 28 October, 1942,

> that my best Corps Commander was Oliver LEESE; LUMSDEN was very poor.
> Easily my best fighting Divisional Commander is FREYBERG, and then MORSHEAD.
> I am therefore going to fight the battle for the present

Bernard noted with resignation

> with 30 Corps, and have placed one armoured div under command of 30 Corps.
> The NZ Div will be used to 'drive' along the coast towards SIDI RAHMAN and beyond. To keep the NZ Div up to strength and to enable it to operate offensively, British Inf Bdes in turn will be put into it:
> First   151 Bde (DLI)
> Second   131 Bde (Queens)
> Third   Greek Bde
> This will enable 2 NZ Div to keep going. As each Inf Bde in turn becomes exhausted, so it will rejoin its own Division in 13 Corps and the next Bde will come up.

If Leese could do this, the battle would be won; the enemy's unmotorised infantry could not get away, while 8th Army's armoured cars could harry Rommel's supply route. He would still have his three armoured divisions – 1st, 10th and 7th – which could then be passed out to 'finish off' any pockets of enemy resistance; a task he hoped would not, this time, be beyond them.

Such was the plan at midday on 28 October, Bernard Montgomery had not, however, reckoned on the political repercussions: the fickleness of Churchill and Eden.

CHAPTER EIGHTEEN

El Alamein – 5: Political Pressure

It was the withdrawal of 8th Army's armour which, more than anything else, was to cause consternation in Cairo and London, for there had been no mention of such an eventuality in the 'Lightfoot' plan, which assumed that the armour would remain 'out' until it had destroyed the Axis armour. Now Bernard was withdrawing the whole of 10 Corps (even Gatehouse's 8th Armoured Brigade was due to be pulled out 'on night of 29/30 October if the situation permits'). Quite who began to spread the rumour that all was not well in 8th Army is unknown – but from Brooke's diary it is clear that the culprit in London was none other than Anthony Eden, Churchill's Foreign Secretary. That night – 28 October – Eden went round to 10 Downing Street 'to have a drink with him [Churchill] and had shaken his confidence in Montgomery and Alexander and had given him the impression that the Middle East offensive was petering out!!' Brooke learned the following morning.[1] 'Before I got up this morning I was presented with a telegram which PM wanted to send Alexander. Not a pleasant one!' Brooke then recorded.[2] He managed to scotch the telegram, but at Eden's insistence the British Minister of State in Cairo, Richard Casey, was cabled to go up to the Alamein Front and report back – a sad reflection of Eden's conspiratorial and meddling faithlessness. When Brooke heard about it a little later he was furious. 'During COS [Chiefs-of-Staff meeting] while we were having final intervals with Eisenhower and I was sent for by PM and had to tell him fairly plainly what I thought of Anthony Eden and [his] ability to judge a tactical situation at this distance,' he noted in his diary.[3] In his *Notes on My Life*, Brooke later elaborated: 'What, he [Churchill] asked, was MY Monty doing now, allowing the battle to peter out? . . . he had done nothing now for the last three days, and now he was withdrawing troops from the front. Why had he told us he would be through in seven days if all he intended to do was to fight a half-hearted battle? Had we not got a single general who could even win a single battle, etc. etc. When he stopped to regain his

---

[1] Alanbrooke Diary, loc. cit.
[2] A. Bryant, *The Turn of the Tide*, op. cit.
[3] Alanbrooke Diary, loc. cit.

breath I asked him what had suddenly influenced him to arrive at these conclusions.'[1] On hearing that the nigger in the woodpile was Anthony Eden, architect of the British catastrophe in Greece the previous year and thus the whole train of disasters in North Africa, Brooke lost his temper. 'The strain of battle had had its effect on me,' Brooke acknowledged in retrospect, 'the anxiety was growing more intense every day and my temper was on edge.'[2] Churchill retorted that he was entitled to consult whomsoever he pleased. 'He continued by stating that he was dissatisfied with the course of the battle and would hold a Chiefs-of-Staff meeting under his chairmanship at 12.30 to be attended by some of his colleagues.'[3] In front of Smuts and the Chiefs-of-Staff Churchill produced the infamous telegram again, criticising Alexander and Montgomery. All Churchill's fears about the depth of the Axis minefields at Alamein and the peril of delaying the British offensive beyond September seemed to him to have been borne out. Once again Churchill's own political position was at stake, not only in terms of possible Parliamentary rejection of his premiership, but in relation to the Prime Ministers of the Commonwealth, whose troops were so deeply committed in the Alamein battle. On top of the losses suffered by New Zealand, Australian, South African, Canadian and Indian forces in Greece, North Africa, the Far East and at Dieppe, the heavy casualties sustained already at Alamein promised – if Montgomery failed to achieve decisive victory – to cost Churchill his head.

Brooke, however, was in the same critical situation, and his diary records quite unequivocally how much he felt his position as CIGS hung on the successful outcome of the battle of Alamein – 'if we had failed again I should have had little else to suggest beyond my relief by someone with fresh and new ideas!' he confessed at the end of the battle.[4] Yet it was precisely the critical importance of the battle to his military strategy and to his personal position that now made Brooke stand up to Churchill in a way that he had failed to do in August, when Churchill appointed Gott to 8th Army. Brooke had not heard from Montgomery directly, but he felt sure Bernard was withdrawing formations in order to create new striking reserves. 'I then went on to say that I was satisfied with the course of the battle up to the present and that everything I saw convinced me that Monty was preparing for his next blow.'[5] Churchill climbed down, and lied to Smuts, pretending he had not previously discussed the matter with Brooke, and that he agreed with the CIGS entirely. The telegram was scrapped. Brooke, however, was far from convinced by his own military logic. 'On returning to my office,' he later recalled, 'I paced

[1] A. Bryant, *The Turn of the Tide*, op. cit.
[2] Ibid.
[3] Ibid.
[4] Ibid.
[5] Ibid.

up and down, suffering from a desperate feeling of loneliness. I had during the morning's discussion tried to maintain an exterior of complete confidence. It had worked; confidence had been restored. I had told them what I thought Monty must be doing, and I knew him well, but there was just that possibility that I was wrong, and that Monty was beat. The loneliness of those moments of anxiety, when there is no one one can turn to, have to be lived through to realize their intense bitterness.'[1]

Were Brooke's fears groundless? Brooke confused the issue, in his *Notes on My Life*, by remarking that it was 'fortunate that on that day I had not yet received a letter from Monty which arrived a few days later telling me what his feelings were at this juncture of the battle'.[2]

This letter from Montgomery was written on 1 November, when Bernard had made up his mind about the use of the armoured striking reserves he had collected – but there is nothing in the letter to indicate that Bernard at any time feared his offensive was 'petering' out. On the contrary, Bernard insisted that he had 'managed to keep the initiative throughout and so far Rommel has had to dance entirely to my tune; his counter-attack and thrusts have been handled without difficulty up to date'.[3] Where Bernard was less sanguine was in his record of the artillery direction (Brooke himself was a gunner and claimed to have taught Bernard the value of artillery control and co-operation), and of Lumsden's performance as Commander of the Corps de Chasse. The letter will be quoted in its proper place; but, in order to ascertain Bernard's true appreciation of the progress of the battle on 28 October, one has to look carefully at his diary and the documents kept by his headquarters. To his staff Bernard showed nothing but confidence – retired to bed at the same time each night and exuded optimism by day. Yet from his diary and his bitter disappointment in Lumsden it is evident that he was far from satisfied with the way the battle had gone since the break-in on the first night; moreover in withdrawing the armour of 10 Corps he was in fact bowing to the inevitable. From the very beginning Lumsden and the Armoured Commanders had been unwilling to fight 'up front' in closely contested country. The years of ultimate failure since Beda Fomm, of being out-gunned and outmanoeuvred, had bred a fatal lack of confidence which could not be dispelled overnight; moreover there was as yet no Patton-like Corps or even divisional armoured commander capable of instilling the necessary resolution within the formations, nor the co-operation with other arms – air, artillery, and infantry – which Bernard expected. In withdrawing his armour Bernard was abandoning the policy he had laid down for the battle – that of the armoured shield which would

---

[1] Ibid.
[2] Ibid.
[3] Letter of 1.11.42. Copy in Montgomery Papers.

protect the infantry's crumbling attacks and draw upon itself the German armoured counter-attacks – and instead reverting to an infantry-style battle that would entail further heavy casualties. That Bernard considered his armour to be more of a liability than a help is demonstrated by the fact that, within hours of Rommel having thrown in the combined weight of his Afrika Korps, Bernard was planning to send his entire armoured Corps to the rear and allow Leese to undertake the protection of his own bridgehead. The armour had indeed been instrumental in forcing Rommel into costly armoured counter-attacks – but in such a limited area that, as Bernard recorded in his diary, he would 'never get the armoured divisions out that way'.

For the moment, then, Bernard decided to fight the battle of Alamein as an infantry battle, keeping his armour entirely in reserve. That night, 28 October, the Australians delivered their next 'crumbling' attack northwards from the bridgehead. Through this Australian 'thumb' as it was called at 8th Army headquarters, Bernard hoped to pass the infantry reserve he was assembling under Freyberg; however, since the British armour had failed to push out the intended broad armoured shield ahead of the infantry, it was now increasingly difficult for the intrepid Australians to make headway in such a narrow area. For Rommel the battle had already become, quite literally, a matter of life or death. He had written to his wife on the morning of 28 October – at the same time that Churchill was ranting against his generals in the field – 'Whether I would survive a defeat lies in God's hands. The lot of the vanquished is heavy . . . My last thought is of you. After I am gone, you must bear the mourning proudly.'[1] The capture of a British map showing Montgomery's intended drive north-west from the Australian salient confirmed Rommel's feeling that the critical moment of the battle had arrived – thought he mistakenly thought Montgomery was about to launch an all-out armoured break-through. Accordingly 'the whole of the Afrika Korps had to be put into the line,' he recorded in his Memoirs, and he 'again informed all commanders that this was a battle for life or death and that every officer and man had to give of his best'.[2] That evening his day report to OKW for 28 October was decrypted, describing the situation as 'grave in the extreme'.[3] Churchill summoned Brooke at 11.30 p.m. – an hour and a half after the Australian attack began – and showed him Rommel's decrypted message, obtained from Ultra: 'He had a specially good intercept he wanted me to see and was specially nice,' Brooke recorded in his diary.[4] Referring to the Middle East he said, 'Would

[1] *The Rommel Papers*, op. cit.
[2] Ibid.
[3] F. H. Hinsley, op. cit.
[4] Alanbrooke Diary, loc. cit.

you not like to have accepted the offer of Command I made to you and be out there now?'[1]

After Churchill's tirade that morning this *volte-face* astonished Brooke – especially when Churchill went on to say how grateful he was that Brooke had elected to stay and serve the Prime Minister in London.

The courageous resistance put up by the Germans in the north blunted the Australian attack, which reached the coastal railway line, but not the sea. For Rommel, however, it was quite obviously but the tip of the iceberg. 'No one can conceive the extent of our anxiety during this period,' he wrote afterwards.

That night I hardly slept and by 03.00 hours was pacing up and down turning over in my mind the likely course of the battle, and the decisions I might have to take. It seemed doubtful whether we would be able to stand up much longer to attacks of the weight which the British were now making, and which they were in any case still able to increase. It was obvious to me that I dared not await the decisive break-through but would have to pull out to the West before it came. Such a decision, however, could not fail to lead to the loss of a large proportion of my non-motorized infantry, partly because of the low fighting power of my motorised formations and partly because the infantry units themselves were too closely involved in the fighting. We were, therefore, going to make one more attempt, by the tenacity and stubbornness of our defence, to persuade the enemy to call off his attack. It was a slim hope, but the petrol situation alone made a retreat which would inevitably lead to mobile warfare, out of the question.[2]

The RAF and the Royal Navy had kept up their pressure on Rommel's petrol supply routes – as at Alam Halfa – and by the morning of 29 October Rommel was clear that he must prepare for withdrawal to Fuka 'before the battle reached its climax'.[3] To his wife he confessed in his daily letter: 'I haven't much hope left. At night I lie with my eyes open, unable to sleep for the load that lies on my shoulders.'[4] He was certain that this was the decisive battle of the war. At 2.45 p.m. his aide noted in a diary: 'C-in-C enlarges over lunch on his plan to prepare a line for the army to fall back on at Fuka when the time comes, now that the northern part of the Alamein line is no longer in our hands.'[5]

For Bernard Montgomery there was no such problem over sleep;

[1] A. Bryant, *The Turn of the Tide*, op. cit.
[2] *The Rommel Papers*, op. cit.
[3] Ibid.
[4] Ibid.
[5] David Irving, *The Trail of the Fox*, op. cit.

nevertheless the responsiblity for ensuring victory was equally heavy. The battle had raged for eight nights and seven days. From the tally kept of enemy tanks and guns destroyed, as well as mounting numbers of prisoners and his Ultra decrypts, he knew how desperate the situation must look to Rommel. At 11.15 p.m. the previous night, 28 October, his Intelligence staff had identified 90th Light Division fighting in the extreme north, to the West of the Australians – an indication that Rommel was throwing everything he had into that sector in order to prevent 8th Army breaking out. In fact the heavy casualties sustained by the Australians and the damage done to their support tanks on minefields forced Bernard now to postpone their follow-up attack:

Thursday, 29 October
0600 Attack of 9 Aust Div made good progress and some 200 prisoners were taken. The Australians got hampered by minefields and did not reach the railway as I had hoped.

The new front is being reorganized and the attack will be resumed tomorrow night, i.e. Friday, 30 October, when I hope the Australians will reach the sea and clean up the whole area.

The Army Commander was therefore in no hurry, but was prepared relentlessly to pursue his plan for an infantry coastal offensive when, for the first time in the battle, he was made aware of the political pressure being brought to bear from London. At 11.50 a.m. on 29 October he was informed that Churchill's son-in-law, Duncan Sandys, would visit him the next day; meanwhile, Alexander himself suddenly appeared with the Minister of State in Egypt, Richard Casey, bearing Churchill's revised telegram. In this the Prime Minister pointed to the imminent Allied landings in North-West Africa and painted a rosy (though illusory) picture of the prospects – namely that the French would assist the Allies in Tunisia and perhaps rise up in Vichy France. 'Events may therefore move more quickly, perhaps considerably more quickly, than had been planned,' Churchill signalled, urging that everything now be done to expedite a victory by 8th Army.[1] De Guingand recalled the deputation in his book *Operation Victory*:

The Army Commander described the situation and his plans, and radiated confidence. There had been a signal or two which suggested that some people were a bit worried that things had not gone faster,

he recalled coyly.

[1] W. S. Churchill, op. cit.

776

Montgomery's reply to such suggestions was that he had always predicted a ten-day 'dog-fight' and he was perfectly confident that he would win the battle. I was taken aside by Casey, who asked me whether I was quite happy about the way things were going.[1]

In fact Casey was so alarmed by the apparent stalemate and the withdrawal of the entire Corps de Chasse, that he showed de Guingand a draft signal to London preparing Churchill for a possible reverse. Brigadier Williams remembered the moment quite clearly.

> I remember I had a curious sort of truck which had a shelf-cum-bench in it, and Freddie brought Casey into it and we sat on this bench. I talked to Casey and told him the enemy point of view – and then suddenly there was this business of Casey mumbling away that he ought to go and prepare a signal to warn Winston that things weren't going well, and Freddie having this incredible burst of temper, saying: 'For God's sake don't! If you do, I'll see you're drummed out of political life' –

a threat which greatly amused Williams at the time since de Guingand clearly had 'no appreciation that he [Casey] wasn't in political life anyway!'[2]

In his *Memoirs* Bernard claimed to have been too busy to bother about what signal Casey eventually sent. However the evidence of his diary confirms that he certainly took seriously the pressure from Casey and Churchill. Churchill's telegram stated that 'Torch' was going ahead on the date planned – now only ten days away.

' "Torch" is on 8 November' Bernard recorded in his diary.

> It is becoming essential to break through somewhere, and to bring the enemy armour to battle, and to get armoured cars astride the enemy supply routes.
>
> We must make a great effort to defeat the enemy, and break up his Army, so as to help 'Torch'.
>
> I have therefore decided to modify my plan,

he concluded: and set down his new intention. Rather than driving the New Zealanders in a self-replenishing infantry offensive through the Australian 'thumb' and along the coast road to Sidi Rahman, he would allow the Australians to continue their assault towards the sea in the far north; however, instead of exploiting it, he would then put all his reserve forces into an infantry and armoured attack westwards from the Kidney Ridge area. This 'hole' would be 'blown' by Freyberg, and would be some three miles deep; through it Bernard

[1] De Guingand, *Operation Victory*, op. cit.
[2] Sir Edgar Williams, loc. cit.

would then pass his entire armoured Corps and two armoured car regiments.

> The Armd Car Regts will be launched right into open country to operate for four days against the enemy supply routes.
> The two Armoured Divisions will engage and destroy the DAK.
> This, in effect, is a hard blow with my right, followed the next night with a knock-out blow with my left. The blow on night 31 Oct/1 Nov will be supported by some 350 guns firing about 400 rounds a gun.
> I have given the name 'SUPERCHARGE' to the operation.

From being held back in reserve until Leese had gradually smashed an infantry path through the Axis forces along the coast, Lumsden's 10 Corps was being asked once again to take part in an offensive capacity – a 'knock-out blow'. Whether the armour would co-operate any better than it had in the battle so far, remained however to be seen.

CHAPTER NINETEEN

El Alamein – 6: 'Supercharge'

The decision not to pursue a coastal thrust, but to strike further inland has gone down in history as the death-blow to any hopes that Rommel might be able to stave off defeat at Alamein; moreover historians have often argued over its true provenance. Alexander's Chief-of-Staff, Lt-General Richard McCreery, afterwards claimed that it was he who had pressed Montgomery to alter his intended coastal thrust, and Alexander seconded this claim in his *Memoirs*.

> On this morning of 29 October Eighth Army had reserve strength enough for only one last big push. Hence the vital nature of the decision that was about to be taken at the meeting attended by, apart from Monty, Dick McCreery and myself, Freddie de Guingand, Montgomery's Chief-of-Staff and Oliver Leese, commanding 30 Corps.
> The Eighth Army Commander appeared to favour an attack as far north as possible. But Dick McCreery, as an experienced armoured commander, was emphatic that it should go in just north of the existing northern corridor. There is no doubt at all in my mind that this was the key decision of the Alamein battle, nor have I any doubt that Monty was suitably grateful to my Chief-of-Staff.[1]

Bernard disliked McCreery and was by no means 'suitably grateful'; moreover it was quite clear to members of Montgomery's staff that it was not McCreery but de Guingand, if anybody, who persuaded the Army Commander to alter the axis of his thrust. According to the G1 Plans, Colonel Richardson, de Guingand went to brief Montgomery before breakfast on 29 October and presented the new Intelligence reports indicating that 90th Light Division was definitely committed in the coastal sector. De Guingand, Mainwaring, Richardson and Williams all felt that, with so many Germans committed by the sea, and abandoning their erstwhile policy of corseting

---

[1] Field-Marshal Earl Alexander of Tunis, *The Alexander Memoirs*, ed. John North, London 1962.

the Italian units all the way down the line, it would be wiser to strike further inland, against weaker, largely Italian opposition.

'It wasn't a specially brilliant idea,' Williams recalled,

> because I mean it was a fairly obvious thing to do, and I can remember it was mainly a matter of one's chinagraph – there was this great map hanging on the side of the operations truck; I can remember my own sort of feeling that you'd leave the Panzers the wrong side of the track so to speak if you did it down there rather than across here. We had the chance to leave the Germans the wrong side of it, stranded as it were, while they were virtually cut from below and by-passed.[1]

According to Sir Charles Richardson, de Guingand did try to persuade the Army Commander to alter the axis of his thrust-line at his early morning briefing, without avail.

> The sequence of events really was the Ultra – showing 90th Light having been moved north – Bill Williams appreciating the significance of the Ultra, discussing it with Freddie and Freddie deciding, coming to the conclusion that instead of going, absolutely charging straight at 90th Light, wouldn't it be better to move further south and to attack on the German-Italian boundary and then get round behind? Now that, I'm quite certain, was Freddie's idea, perhaps prompted by Bill Williams. But it took some persuasion, because he went to discuss it with Monty and came back saying, 'No, he won't have it.'[2]

De Guingand discussed the matter with McCreery when he came up with Alexander and Casey. 'McCreery also felt that "Supercharge" might work better further south,' de Guingand recalled in *Operation Victory*, but Williams remembered quite clearly de Guingand's injunction against McCreery mentioning it to the Army Commander.

> I can remember Freddie tried to say to Dick McCreery: 'Look I will go and talk to Monty about it again – don't you, for goodness sake, because if you do there'll be – he won't do it. But if one can persuade him it's his own idea, so to speak, then I'm sure it's the right thing to do.' I can remember the atmosphere: 'for God's sake don't go and muck about now' because it'll only cloud the issue.[3]

[1] Sir Edgar Williams, loc. cit.
[2] Sir Charles Richardson, loc. cit.
[3] Ibid.

Richardson recalled de Guingand's success on his second attempt, after Alexander's visitation was over: 'He [de Guingand] went back and had another go; and the second, final time Monty did accept it.'[1]

A sigh of relief went through the staff. In his diary Bernard mentioned nothing of de Guingand's suggestion. Instead he ascribed his change of plan some days later in his diary to new Intelligence: 'At 1100 hours on 29 October I changed my plan and decided to attack further to the south, because I had learnt that 90 Light Div was in that area, also that the enemy is very short of petrol';[2] – ignoring the fact that this intelligence was received by his Tactical HQ staff at 11.45 p.m. on 28 October and must have been in his hands at dawn the following day.

Montgomery's staff considered de Guingand the decisive influence in changing the Army Commander's mind, while Alexander congratulated McCreery when he heard about the new plan that afternoon on his return to Cairo. Whether the matter was quite so straightforward is questionable, however, for it is clear from Bernard's first diary entry on 29 October that it was the political pressure to help 'Torch' which really forced Bernard to change both the composition and axis of his 'Supercharge' thrust. His soldierly instinct was to smash his way with infantry on to the coast road, despite the heavy casualties this would entail; as he noted, successive infantry brigades under Freyberg would be put into the attack and the remnants returned to 13 Corps when exhausted. The armour would be held right back, for Bernard had lost faith in it entirely. Moreover by exploiting the Australian success by the sea, he need only guard one flank, could call on help from the Royal Navy, and would ultimately ensure that almost nothing of Rommel's army got away, for he would then control the only road access to Fuka. Certainly this was what Rommel feared. In his memoirs Rommel recalled that his army 'had been so badly battered by the British air force and artillery that we could not now hope to stand up for long to the British break-through attempt, which was daily or even hourly expected'.[3]

Whether Bernard was right or wrong to favour an infantry assault along the coast road, the necessity for speeding up the final phase of the battle in order to help 'Torch' was in fact what caused him to alter both his plan and the axis of the 'Supercharge' thrust-line. Instead of conceiving it as a relentless infantry operation, he had now to re-introduce the Armoured Corps that had proved so disappointing to him, in a repeat of the first night of the battle. Given the narrowness of the Australian bridgehead there was, however, no possibility of launching a full-scale armoured attack that way; therefore Bernard

[1] Ibid.
[2] Entry at 0800 hours Sunday, 1 November 1942. Montgomery Papers.
[3] *The Rommel Papers*, op. cit.

had no option but to redirect his thrust further inland – with the compensating advantage that it would be driven home through a predominantly Italian-held sector.

Although hailed by Alexander and McCreery as the 'key' decision of the battle, then, this misunderstanding inflated their own moment of involvement and veiled the disappointing performance of the British armour, which was now summoned solely to expedite the climax to the battle.

In fact, as will be seen, Bernard's disinclination to use the armour again before the infantry had won the battle was not mistaken – indeed, far from speeding up the victory of 8th Army, the armour very nearly squandered it.

By first breaking in to the Axis position between Miteiriya and Tell el Eisa; by then cancelling the New Zealand 'crumbling' operations from the Miteiriya Ridge and instead reinforcing success in the northern, Australian sector of the salient; and in thereafter creating fresh infantry reserves by thinning out his front and taking formations from 13 Corps in the south, Bernard had put 8th Army into a position where victory was within grasp. Bernard himself had never lost his nerve or his grip on the battle; indeed his optimism, his constant faith in the eventual outcome, had astonished even his own staff. Colonel Richardson never forgot the anxiety felt at Tactical Headquarters when the Army Commander continued to fight the battle solely from the Australian bridgehead, with only Valentine infantry tanks and 30 Corps artillery to support the Australians.

'Could I just add,' he insisted, in describing the course of the battle,

that when the Germans counter-attacked the Australians, I should think it was about D plus 4 or 5, that sort of time, we thought – certainly I thought, and Freddie thought, and I think Bill Williams thought – that this looked terribly dangerous. Because we could see Rommel – if this here was the coast road – exploiting his penetration of the Australian position, getting round, going south, and getting right behind 30 Corps with Panzers. And I can remember Freddie coming back, having seen Monty – who had been to see Morshead – and Freddie had a sort of tentative smile on his face, saying, 'Oh yes, Master's quite happy about it. He's seen the Australians and he's quite happy about it.' And of course the Australians destroyed the German counter-attack . . .[1]

The battle of Alamein had been brought to a winning position by the resolution of the infantry troops and the work of the anti-tank

[1] Sir Charles Richardson, loc. cit.

782

and Royal Artillery gunners – about whom Bernard would be particularly complimentary in his letter to Brooke.

Meanwhile at twelve noon on 29 October Bernard held his first conference 'to decide on preliminary arrangements for "Supercharge" '; the following day he wrote out his orders for the operation (quoted in full in his *Memoirs*). Freyberg was to take under command both the 151st Brigade Bernard had ordered up from 13 Corps, and a brigade of the Highland Division. With this, his New Zealanders, and his newly re-equipped 9th Armoured Brigade in support, he was now to smash a passage westwards to Tel el Aqqaqir on the Rahman track – the original objective of 10 Corps in Operation 'Lightfoot'. From there 10 Corps would launch armoured cars into the rear Axis areas while the armoured divisions cut off all Rommel's tanks in the north by driving north-west to the coast. Following so soon after the next Australian attack, which was to be delivered that night (30 October), there was every hope that 'Supercharge' would, if mounted with determination, hasten the end of the battle. 'This operation if successful will result in the complete disintegration of the enemy and will lead to his final destruction,' Bernard maintained in his Army Commander's Directive.

It will therefore be successful.

Determined leadership will be vital; complete faith in the plan, and its success, will be vital; there must be no doubters; risks must be accepted freely; there must be no 'belly-aching'.

I call on every commander to carry through this operation with determination, to fight their formations bravely, and to instil optimism and offensive eagerness into all ranks.

SUPERCHARGE will win us the victory.[2]

Freyberg was delighted with the plan – indeed he told Leese it was what he had wanted to do earlier in the battle – but soon after the Australians launched their attack on the night of 30 October he suddenly informed Leese that he needed more time to set up his attack. 10 Corps had refused to move out of their rear positions in order to allow the New Zealanders to assemble their forces, until de Guingand overruled Lumsden; moreover Freyberg found many of the infantry tired and the artillery bewildered by the need first to support the Australians in the north, then the New Zealanders to the west. The situation on the ground was indeed fantastically confused – so confused in fact that the GSO 1 of the New Zealand Division and the G1 (Plans), 8th Army, were told to go and identify all units on the ground and, by authority of the Army Commander, order those not involved in "Supercharge" to withdraw to the rear

[1] Quoted in *The Memoirs of Field-Marshal Montgomery* but misdated (should be 30 October 1942), op. cit.

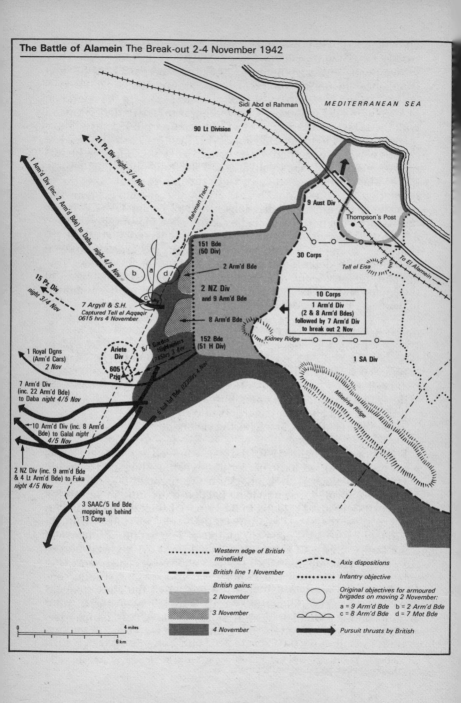

The Battle of Alamein The Break-out 2–4 November 1942

MEDITERRANEAN SEA

Sidi Abd el Rahman

90 Lt Division

21 Pz. Div night 3/4 Nov

1 Arm'd Div (inc. 2 Arm'd Bde) to Daba night 4/5 Nov

15 Pz Div
night 3/4 Nov

Rahman Track

9 Aust Div

Thompson's Post

151 Bde
(50 Div)

2 Arm'd Bde

30 Corps

To El Alamein

Tell el Eisa

2 NZ Div
and 9 Arm'd Bde

8 Arm'd Bde

Kidney Ridge

10 Corps
1 Arm'd Div
(2 & 8 Arm'd Bdes)
followed by 7 Arm'd Div
to break out 2 Nov

7 Argyll & S.H.
Captured Tell el Aqqaqir
0615 hrs 4 November

b   a   d
c

5/7 Gordon
Highlanders
145hrs 3 Nov

152 Bde
(51 H Div)

1 SA Div

1 Royal Dgns
(Arm'd Cars)
2 Nov

Ariete
Div

605
Pzjg

7 Arm'd Div
(inc. 22 Arm'd Bde)
to Daba night 4/5 Nov

5 6 Ind Inf Bde 0220hrs 4 Nov

10 Arm'd Div (inc. 8 Arm'd
Bde) to Galal night
4/5 Nov

2 NZ Div (inc. 9 arm'd Bde
& 4 Lt Arm'd Bde) to Fuka
night 4/5 Nov

Miteiriya Ridge

3 SAAC/5 Ind Bde
mopping up behind
13 Corps

.... Western edge of British
minefield

– – – – British line 1 November

British gains:

2 November

3 November

4 November

– – – Axis dispositions

.... Infantry objective

Original objectives for armoured
brigades on moving 2 November:

a = 9 Arm'd Bde   b = 2 Arm'd Bde
c = 8 Arm'd Bde   d = 7 Mot Bde

➡ Pursuit thrusts by British

0   4 miles

0   6 km

immediately. Freyberg begged permission to postpone the attack by twenty-four hours – a request Leese could only pass on to the Army Commander. Since so much depended on Freyberg's leadership, Bernard could hardly refuse. Therefore early on 31 October he authorised the postponement.

'It became clear to me,' Bernard noted at 5 a.m. that morning,

that the stage-management problems in connection with 'SUPER-CHARGE' were such that the operation could not be launched really thoroughly tonight; by trying to get it launched tonight there was a risk of failure.

An hour later, at 6 a.m. on 31 October, he recorded that the Australian assault in the north had been 'a great success. By dawn over 400 prisoners had been taken, all Germans, and the attack had reached the coast. The rest of 164th German Division were trapped and will not be able to escape'.

If Bernard began to wish he had held to his intention to break out from the Australian sector, given the apparent success of the Australian attack, such thoughts must have been quickly dispelled by the fierceness of the German counter-attacks. Far from reaching the coast the Australians were only able to take the road and railway – to which they clung tenaciously despite everything Rommel did to dislodge them in the next thirty-six hours before 'Supercharge'. Some of the most savage fighting of the battle now occurred, as ground was taken, lost and retaken on both sides. Leese recalled the bravery of the Australians with enduring admiration:

The Australians . . . established a very difficult salient beyond Point 29 which they held against continuous Panzer counter-attack. If the front of that Division had been penetrated during their four-days' ordeal, the whole success of the 8th Army plan could have been prejudiced. As it was, they suffered over 5000 casualties, but they beat off all enemy attacks, withstood intense hostile shelling and maintained a firm base for subsequent operations by 8th Army. They drew on their front most of the Panzer Corps of which they destroyed a great part with their anti-tank guns. It was a magnificent piece of fighting by a great Division, led by an indomitable character, Leslie Morshead.[1]

Rommel himself directed the Panzer and infantry counter-attacks against 'Point 29', summoning the Afrika Korps commander to his side. The next day, 1 November, he wrote to his wife: 'It's a week since I left home – a week of very, very hard fighting. It was often doubtful whether we'd be able to hold out. Yet we managed it each

[1] Sir Oliver Leese, unpublished memoirs, loc. cit.

time, though with sad losses. I'm on the move a lot in order to step in wherever we're in trouble. Things were very bad in the north yesterday morning, although it was all more or less cleared up by the evening. The struggle makes very heavy demands on one's nervous energy, though physically I'm quite well . . .'[1]

Rommel was obsessed still by his understanding of Auchinleck and his experience that July, when the Panzer Army had maintained its position despite being pitifully outnumbered. He still seemed to have no idea that the British were now operating according to carefully conceived plans, and assumed that, as in July, they were simply attacking in haphazard directions with the intention of breaking through wherever they could find a weak link – hence his own indefatigable stepping-in 'wherever we're in trouble'. Although he had ordered two days before that the Fuka line be reconnoitred, for the moment he put all his faith in his original fire-fighting policy, hoping against hope that the British determination to break through would wilt. Accordingly he refused permission for 90th Light Division to extricate their remaining troops bottled up by the Australian 'thumb', but instead instructed a battle-group of 21st Panzer Division to break through into the German pocket around 'Thompson's Post' – which they did that evening. Rommel's latest English biographer, David Irving, accuses him of deviousness in having reconnoitred the Fuka position at all – permitting himself "the fatal "backward glances" that no commander should ever allow himself in battle'[2] but there can be no doubt that, in these last days of the struggle, the Axis troops fought with undiminished courage and that Rommel remained an inspiration to them. Bernard Montgomery, certainly, had no such criticisms of his foe. To Major-General Godwin-Austen of the Staff College he wrote on 1 November:

> I am in the middle of a terrific battle with Rommell. I would like to lecture to the Staff College about it!! I hope to defeat him in a few days time. So far it has been a complete slogging match, carried on in an enormous mined area.[3]

To Alan Brooke, he wrote on the same day, shortly before 'Supercharge' began:

> My dear General,
>   You may like a few notes on this battle. I obtained complete surprise and broke into the enemy positions in the north; he was expecting the attack in the south and our deception measures

[1] *The Rommel Papers*, op. cit.
[2] David Irving, *The Trail of the Fox*, op. cit.
[3] The Royal Warwickshire Regimental Museum, Warwick.

worked well. A real hard and very bloody fight then began, and has gone on now for 8 days. It has been a terrific party and a complete slogging match, made all the more difficult in that the whole area is just one enormous minefield. The artillery fire has been superb and such a concentrated use of artillery has not been seen before in N. Africa; we could not have done what we have done without the artillery, and that arm has been wonderful. A great trouble has been that most of the C's RA knew very little about how to handle this artillery when concentrated; the policy of dispersion, and of Bde Groups, had been the rule and they had not been properly taught.

I have managed to keep the initiative throughout and so far Rommel has had to dance entirely to my tune; his counter-attack and thrusts have been handled without difficulty up to date. I think he is now ripe for a real hard blow which may topple him off his perch. It is going in tonight and I am putting everything I can into it; I think we have bluffed him into where it is coming. I hope to loose two regiments of Armd Cars into open country where they can manoeuvre. If everything goes *really well* there is quite a good chance we may put 90 Light Div and 21 Panzer Div both in the bag. But battles do not go as one plans, and it may be that we shall not do this. We have got all the Germans up in the north in the Sidi Rahman area, and I am attacking well south of that place. There will be hard and bitter fighting as the enemy is resisting desperately and has no intention of retiring.

I am enjoying the battle, and I have kept very fit and well. It is getting chilly now, especially at night, and I have taken to 4 blankets at nights. Tonight's battle I have called 'Supercharge' and I enclose a copy of my orders for it. If we succeed it will be the end of Rommel's army.

Oliver Leese has been quite first class; so has Horrocks, but he is away in the south and has little to do.

Lumsden has been very disappointing; he may be better when we get out into the open. But my own view is that he is not suited for high command, but is a good fighting Div Commander. He is excitable, highly strung, and is easily depressed. He is considerably at sea in charge of a Corps and I have to watch over him very carefully. The best of the lot is Oliver Leese, who is quite first class. Freyberg is superb, and is the best fighting Div Comd I have ever known. He has no great brain power and could never command a Corps. But he *leads* his Division into battle, going himself in front in a Honey tank with two other Honies in attendance. The only way to find him during a battle is to look for a group of 3 Honey tanks in the NZ area; that will be Freyberg!!

My great task is to keep morale high and spirits up.

I believe that the attack we launch tonight may just do the trick. I am placing great reliance on the Armd Cars, and if I can launch them into enemy rear areas the morale and material damage they will do will be immense.

I hope you are keeping fit.

Yours ever

Monty[1]

It was clear from this that, though he expected to make a successful infantry break-in and to get his armoured cars 'out' behind the enemy front line, Bernard was sceptical of the likelihood of his armoured commanders actually cutting off 21 Panzer and 90th Light Divisions, after their performance in the battle so far. Years later, in his *Memoirs*, Rommel wondered why Montgomery had not thrown in 'the 900 or so tanks, which they could safely have committed on the northern front, in order to gain a quick decision with the minimum of effort and casualties. In fact, only half that number of tanks, acting under cover of their artillery and air force, would have sufficed to destroy my forces, which frequently stood immobile on the battlefield . . . In all probability their command wanted to hold back its armour for the pursuit, as their assault formations could not apparently be re-grouped quickly enough to follow up.'[2] To the end of his life, evidently, Rommel failed to appreciate the amateurism and diffidence of the armour which had forced his opponent to withdraw 10 Corps from the fighting; nor that Operation 'Supercharge' involved every fit tank in 8th Army, including the whole of 7th Armoured Division which had been brought up from the south. It was this failure of the British armour that had led to the 'slogging match' to which Bernard referred in his correspondence. In a third letter sent on the eve of Operation 'Supercharge', Bernard wrote to the Reynolds:

I am fighting a terrific battle with Rommel. It began on 23 October and he is resisting desperately. I hold the initiative. But it has become a real solid and bloody killing match. I do not think he can go on much longer. I am dealing him a terrific blow in the very early hours of tomorrow 2nd Nov and it may well be that that will knock him off his perch. I hope so. You will follow in the papers the events and if you keep 2nd Nov in your mind, and study events from that date, it may help you.[3]

At 0105 hours on 2 November the combined artillery of two British Corps thundered: a shattering and ominous herald of the major British attack most Axis troops in the north of Alamein knew must come.

[1] Letter of 1 November 1942. Copy in Montgomery Papers.
[2] *The Rommel Papers*, op. cit.
[3] Montgomery Papers.

CHAPTER TWENTY

El Alamein – 7: Victory

0100   Attack went in under a creeping barrage on a front of 4000 yds fired by over 300 25-pdrs. It was probably the first creeping barrage ever used in EGYPT. The attack was a complete success,

Bernard recorded in his diary on 2 November 1942. Once more however, as on the first night of the battle, the performance of the British armour failed to exploit the magnificent feat of the infantry in reaching their objectives. In many respects it was a carbon copy of the opening phase of 'Lightfoot', with Rommel quite certain that the thrust was coming on the front further north, through the Australian 'thumb'. So certain was Rommel that this was so, he did not order the Afrika Korps to concentrate on the actual break-through to Tell el Aqqaqir until well after dawn on 2 November – by which time Bernard Montgomery hoped to have many hundreds of tanks debouching beyond the Rahman track, thrusting north-east to put 21st Panzer and 90th Light Divisions 'in the bag'.

It was not to be. Once again Lumsden's armour was too slow to follow-up, and when it did – as on the night of 24–25 October – it sheltered behind the New Zealanders' support brigade under Brigadier Currie, rather than driving forward. At 6 a.m. Bernard noted in his diary:

1 Armd Div was late and did not get up before daylight.
    The enemy launched heavy counter-attacks against the North flank of the area of penetration.
    Very heavy fighting developed and went on all day.
    1 Armd Div slowly gained ground and took heavy toll of the enemy tanks and anti-tank guns, while not suffering too much themselves.

Currie's brigade, in the forefront of the advance, had 'suffered heavily', he recorded sadly. Nevertheless at 5 p.m., with the Afrika Korps having decimated itself in vain counter-attacks, Bernard felt the 'situation good, and our pressure being kept up. About 1500 prisoners taken'.

Oliver Leese was more caustic about the failure of the British armour. 'The attack [by 30 Corps] exceeded all expectations,' he wrote in his unpublished memoirs.

The effect of the tanks of the 9th Armoured Brigade [the NZ support brigade] moving along the lanes in rear of the infantry was devastating to the enemy morale; and neither infantry brigade had even to mop-up. By dawn all objectives were captured and the 9th Armoured Brigade were on the Tell el Aqqaqir feature.

Once again there seemed to be a chance for the Armour to break out. Two Armoured Car Squadrons of the Royals had got out but the armour was again unable to get beyond our FDLs. The 9th Armoured Brigade themselves had had a great success but they had had many casualties and were forced to withdraw.

Once again it was up to the infantry soldier. I almost said: 'as usual.'[1]

The records of the units bear out Leese's contention, for the only Axis anti-tank guns facing 9th Armoured Brigade at that time were 47- and 50-mm calibre which could only halt Shermans or Grants at short range. Had 1st Armoured Division pressed on behind the self-sacrificing Brigadier Currie, the battle might then have been won. Again and again Freyberg signalled to Leese to urge on 1st Armoured Division, but without avail. As Bernard had warned Brooke, 'battles do not go as one plans'. By 7 a.m. wireless intercepts made it clear that the chance had been missed, and that Rommel was now ordering the whole of the Afrika Korps to counter-attack. The opportunity to get behind Rommel and cut off his armour had been lost, but, providing Leese and Lumsden brought up plenty of anti-tank guns and concentrated their artillery fire, there was at least the likelihood of destroying the bulk of Rommel's remaining armour – which to the credit of the British armour, artillery and anti-tank gunners they now did, 8th Army's Y service having intercepted at 0911 hours Rommel's order to 21st Panzer Division to counter-attack and having immediately passed it to both Leese and Lumsden. By evening the Afrika Korps' tally of fit tanks had been halved, with only thirty-five German tanks and twenty Italian still in battle order. Freyberg was understandably distressed by the failure of the intended break-out, but the Army Commander was more sanguine. He had a further two armoured Divisions – 10th and 7th – ready for action, and all day he and Leese had been assembling infantry reserves. If 1st Armoured Division could hold the Afrika Korps to the north and west, Bernard felt certain he could follow up the success of his armoured cars in breaking out to the south-west of the salient, thus completely by-passing the Afrika Korps. Planned

[1] Sir Oliver Leese, unpublished memoirs, loc. cit.

originally for 4 p.m. on 2 November, the first stage of this operation – an infantry attack supported by tanks – took place at 6.15 p.m., and was completely successful.

Although the battle was by no means over, Rommel himself had admitted defeat. At 4.30 p.m. on 2 November he announced to his staff that the cordon around the enemy salient was only to be a rearguard: the retreat of the Panzer Army to Fuka was to begin. He delayed a final decision on this until he had spoken to the Commander of the Afrika Korps, General von Thoma. Von Thoma confirmed that it was now impossible to hold back the British, he had lost so many tanks during the day.

German and Italian infantry began marching that night. To his wife Rommel wrote of 'the end'[1] and to OKW he radioed at 7.50 p.m. on 2 November his famous admission of defeat:

> After ten days of extremely hard fighting against overwhelming British superiority on the ground and in the air the strength of the Army is exhausted in spite of today's successful defence. It will, therefore, no longer be in a position to prevent a new attempt to break through with strong enemy armoured formations which is expected to take place tonight or tomorrow. An orderly withdrawal of the six Italian and two German non-motorized divisions and brigades is impossible for lack of MT. A large part of these formations will probably fall into the hands of the enemy who is fully motorized. Even the mobile troops are so closely involved in the battle that only elements will be able to disengage from the enemy . . . The shortage of fuel will not allow of a withdrawal to any great distance. There is only one road available and the Army, as it passes along it, will almost certainly be attacked day and night by the enemy air force.
>
> In these circumstances we must therefore expect the gradual destruction of the Army in spite of the heroic resistance and exceptionally high morale of the troops.[2]

Did the message mean Rommel *was* withdrawing; was asking permission to withdraw; or standing fast? Not until the early hours of 3 November did Rommel's next report reach OKW, in which he retrospectively announced his orders for the retreat of the Axis infantry, to begin at 10 p.m. on 2 November.

These two messages were decoded at Bletchley Park in England, and were in Brooke's hands by lunchtime on 3 November, as Brooke recorded in his diary:

---

[1] *The Rommel Papers*, op. cit.
[2] I. S. O. Playfair (British Official History of the Second World War), *The Mediterranean and the Middle East*, Vol. IV, London 1966.

Whilst at lunch I was called up by DMI and informed of the two recent intercepts of Rommel's messages to GHQ and Hitler in which he practically stated that his army was faced with a desperate defeat from which he could only extricate remnants![1]

In his *Notes on My Life* Brooke wrote: 'It can be imagined what the receipt of this message . . . meant to me. I dared not yet allow myself to attach too much importance to it, but even so felt as if I were treading on air the rest of that day.'[2] Even Bernard Montgomery's own staff were agreeably surprised. 'This Ultra message reached us extremely quickly,' Charles Richardson recalled. 'Being somewhat sceptical of the Army Commander's optimistic view of events, I shall never forget the elation of myself and of Bill Williams.'[3]

Hitler was flabbergasted. The second report, announcing Rommel's order to retreat, only reached him at 9 a.m. on 3 November, and immediately he countermanded it: 'In your present situation nothing else can be thought of but to hold on, not to yield a step, and to throw every weapon and every fighting man who can still be freed into the battle . . . You can show your troops no other road than to victory or death.'[4]

In his *Memoirs*, Rommel claimed that, without Hitler's countermand, he could have saved his Army:

Looking back, I am conscious of only one mistake – that I did not circumvent the 'Victory or Death' order twenty-four hours earlier. Then the army would in all probability have been saved, with all its infantry, in at least a semi-battleworthy condition.[5]

This was moonshine, for Hitler's countermand was only decoded at Rommel's HQ at 1.30 p.m. on 3 November, by which time the retreating Axis infantry had been on the march for more than fifteen hours, and could not be stopped, let alone be put back into line. Moreover the attack south-westwards by the infantry of the British 30 Corps had presaged a night assault by Lumsden's 10 Corps which, although poorly executed, so threatened the Italian-German line in the north that Rommel was forced to throw in his entire motorised and armoured reserves in order to prevent a rout. How, in these circumstances, he could have saved a 'semi-battleworthy' army is a mystery, for the fact of his infantry withdrawal was noted in Montgomery's diary at 8 a.m. on 3 November, and it was only the resolute

---

[1] Alanbrooke Diary, loc. cit.
[2] A. Bryant, *The Turn of the Tide*, op. cit.
[3] General Sir Charles Richardson to author, 24.9.80.
[4] I. S. O. Playfair (British Official History of the Second World War), *The Mediterranean and the Middle East*, Vol. IV, London 1966.
[5] *The Rommel Papers*, op. cit.

defence of the northern sector by the Afrika Korps, and the Italian Ariete Division – stiffened at 1.30 p.m. by Hitler's order calling for 'death or victory' – which postponed the disintegration of the once proud Panzer Army of Africa. Already a whole regiment of British armoured cars were causing havoc as far west as Daba, the RAF were mercilessly bombing the retreating infantry columns, and in order to speed up Lumsden's still-stalled break-out Bernard asked Leese at 9 a.m. on 3 November to undertake yet another infantry attack 'in order finally to push out the armour', as Leese recalled.[1] Bernard himself issued a Special Order of the Day:

> The present battle has now lasted 12 days, during which the troops have fought so magnificently that the enemy is being worn down. He has just reached the breaking point, and he is trying to get his army away. The RAF is taking a heavy toll of his columns moving west on the main coast road. I call on all troops to keep up the pressure and not relax for one moment. We have the chance of putting the whole Panzer Army in the bag, and we will do so. I congratulate all troops on what has been achieved. Complete victory is almost in sight. On your behalf, I have sent a separate message to the RAF thanking them for their quite magnificent support.

That day the Desert Air Force in fact flew no less than 1094 sorties, with a further 125 by the USAAF.

As the armour duelled across the Rahman track around Tell el Aqqaqir, Leese set up his last, decisive infantry attacks. He decided to make three separate assaults, beginning late that afternoon: 'The first attack was carried out by the 1st Gordons supported by a battalion of tanks, in the evening, west of Tell el Aqqaquir.'[2]

However, once again, Lumsden's 10 Corps headquarters fouled up the operation, as 'three or four hours before the attack was due to go in, 10 Corps informed us that their armour was 2000 yards beyond the Sidi Rahman track and were therefore in possession of our objective'. Accordingly Leese cancelled the artillery barrage ahead of his attack, making do with smoke.

> Just before zero hour the armour informed us that in actual fact they were still 2000 yards *short* of the Sidi Rahman track. It was too late to do anything; the attack went in unsupported and failed,

Leese wrote.[3] Major-General Wimberley, the 51st Highland Division Commander, had pleaded with Leese to clear the 10 Corps tanks, 'if

[1] Sir Oliver Leese, unpublished memoirs, loc. cit.
[2] Ibid.
[3] Ibid.

there were any there, and let my attack go in properly under a Barrage', but Lumsden had insisted his tanks were already on the Rahman track and the infantry had only to join them. 'The position was, as we had reported, strongly held, not a sign of our tanks was to be seen, but plenty of enemy ones . . . The Gordons made little progress, and lost a lot of men; I felt it had been sheer waste of life and was sick at heart,' Wimberley recalled later. Moreover he added: 'Worst of all, thinking that it was an advance rather an attack, the Gordons put a number of their Jocks on the top of the tanks, to be carried on them forward to the objective. I saw the tanks, later, coming out of action, and they were covered with the dead bodies of our Highlanders. It was an unpleasant sight and bad for morale.'[1]

I had learnt a lesson never again to cancel an artillery programme. Armour can always be moved quickly off any area at will by R/T. An artillery programme once decided on must be allowed to run,

Leese later reflected.[2] Bernard too drew the lesson; and though historians scoffed at later artillery programmes which proved unnecessary – as during the first Allied landings on the mainland of Europe at Reggio the following year – Bernard himself remained unrepentant. An infantryman's courage depended on his loyalty to his commander: and no good commander should abuse that loyalty simply to save shells. Wimberley was in fact so upset that when Leese explained the armour was still unable to gain the Tell el Aqqaqir feature, and that a further Highland infantry attack would be necessary to take it for Lumsden, Wimberley nearly broke down. 'I was so sick at heart at being overruled regarding not firing my barrage for the Gordon attack that I must have shown it over the phone, unmistakably. I remember Oliver [Leese] said over the phone, 'Surely now you, Douglas, of all people are not going to lose heart.'[3]

Argyll and Sutherland Highlanders and an infantry Brigade from 4th Indian Division, under command, were ordered to pave the final path for Lumsden's armour. At 2.30 a.m. on Wednesday, 4 November 1942, by the light of the waning moon Brigadier 'Pasha' Russell's 5th Indian Brigade advanced behind a creeping barrage, with medium artillery pounding known centres of resistance, and clearing a path for 10 Corps some five miles deep; and at 6.15 a.m. a battalion of Argyll and Sutherland Highlanders, in a separate attack, raced for its objective: Point 44, at the heart of the Tell el Aqqaqir feature.

[1] Unpublished memoir by Major-General Douglas Wimberley, communicated to Sir Denis Hamilton, 5.10.80.
[2] Sir Oliver Leese, unpublished memoirs, loc. cit.
[3] Unpublished memoir by Major-General Douglas Wimberley, loc. cit.

By dawn on 4 November, therefore, Bernard Montgomery knew he had finally won the battle of Alamein. At 6.30 a.m. he recorded in his diary:

The armour went through as the dawn was breaking; it got clear away and out into the open, 1 and 7 Armd Divs leading. We had at last passed our armoured formations into the enemy rear areas, and into country clear of minefields, and into country where they could manoeuvre.

The armoured cars raced away to the West, and were directed on FUKA and BUQQUSH.

I ordered the 2 NZ Div, with 4 Light Armd Bde under command, to move out SW, get on to the FUKA track and move with all speed to secure the FUKA bottleneck.

A wave of exhilaration went through the whole of 8th Army. After thirteen nights and twelve days of battle, Rommel's army was beaten. It was the first major offensive battle won by the Allies against a German-led army in the war, and the fact that it had been won by perseverance and dogged determination made it all the more moving a victory. As de Guingand wrote shortly before his death in 1980:

El Alamein was the proving ground of British military renascence in the Second World War. Without it one frankly cannot imagine the feats which were subsequently achieved. Behind us stretched a pathetic catalogue of bungled efforts and ultimate failures: the defence of Belgium, Dunkirk, Norway, Greece, Crete, Dieppe, and the loss of North Africa to the very gates of Cairo. Democracy had shown itself a poor opponent on the field of battle, when one must be willing to lay down one's life.[1]

Towards the end of his life Bernard Montgomery revisited the battle-field; but when asked if he wished to see the German and Italian cemeteries he shook his head. 'I think,' he said, having seen the serried rows of British crosses, white and rigid beneath the Egyptian sun, 'I've been responsible for enough deaths without seeing those too.'[2] Moreover the passage of the years made him feel less negative about the performance of the British armour in the battle. The self-sacrificing courage of Brigadier Currie's 9th Armoured Brigade at Tell el Aqqaqir 'paid in blood any debt they owed the infantry,' he declared.[3]

Churchill wept when Alexander's telegram came in. He had

[1] De Guingand, *From Brass Hat to Bowler Hat*, op. cit.
[2] To C. D. Hamilton, Editor of *The Sunday Times*, May 1967.
[3] *The Times*, 11 May 1967.

already seen, at breakfast, the Ultra-decrypt of Hitler's telegram to Rommel, ordering his soldiers to choose death or victory; Alexander's cable began: 'After 12 days of heavy and violent fighting the 8th Army has inflicted a severe defeat on the German and Italian forces under Rommel's command. The enemy's front has broken, and British armoured formations in strength have passed through and are operating in the enemy's rear areas. Such portions of the enemy's forces as can get away are in full retreat . . .'[1]

While Hitler was now urged to relent over his victory or death order, Churchill dictated the messages he had dreamed of. 'I send you my heartfelt congratulations on the splendid feat of arms achieved by the Eighth Army under the command of your brilliant lieutenant, Montgomery, in the Battle of Egypt . . .' he cabled to Alexander.[2]

Shortly after mid-day the Commander of the Afrika Korps was captured, carrying out Hitler's order to the letter, and standing unbowed amidst a raging tank battle, while his Chief-of-Staff, Bayerlein, ran away on foot as fast as his legs would carry him. David Irving, in his biography of Rommel, branded von Thoma a traitor, but Major Oswald, the G2 in charge of Montgomery's Tactical Headquarters, later well remembered the circumstances of von Thoma's capture, and his soldierly bearing when brought before the 8th Army Commander that afternoon.

A traitor? Nonsense, of course he wasn't. I've heard it said that he was pretty suicidal. But he was a very experienced officer. He'd commanded the Afrika Korps throughout the battle, had commanded the Condor Legion in the Spanish Civil War and was probably one of Germany's leading experts on the use of armour. He was rather a fine-looking chap. I thought he preserved a very soldier-like demeanour – after all his truck had been shot from under him in the heart of the battle, he'd had a pretty good dusting, and had been brought straight before the Army Commander.[3]

Bernard Montgomery, wearing a light-coloured pullover without insignia of rank, over a desert shirt and trousers, greeted his adversary's salute by staring intently into his gaunt, haggard eyes. Irving later attempted to characterise Montgomery's exhortations, prior to the battle, to 'kill Germans' as a distasteful blood-lust in stark contrast to Rommel's gentlemanly approach to war. Yet to anyone who served under Montgomery this was wholly to misunderstand the attitude of the 8th Army Commander. To defeat the Panzer Army

[1] Telegrams relating to operations July–December 1942, Prime Minister's file (PREM 3–310/6), PRO.
[2] Ibid.
[3] Major-General M. St. J. Oswald, loc. cit.

796

in battle would, Montgomery had been clear, entail a quality of courage and determination to kill or be killed not evidenced in the war so far. One of his first acts on 4 November, with victory assured, was to go straight to the headquarters of the 9th Australian Division to thank General Morshead whose troops had done so much to redeem the failure of the British armour between 25 October and Operation 'Super-charge' on 2 November. The 9th Australian Division alone sustained as many casualties at Alamein as the entire forces of 10 Corps.[1] That the infantry of this Commonwealth country, not directly threatened by German, should have been willing to lay down their lives in such an exemplary manner was to Bernard Montgomery the deepest proof that the Allies would go on to win the war.

Studying von Thoma's face that afternoon he saw the bearing not of a politically-motivated individual, nor of a traitor, but that of a fellow soldier, a fellow professional. Disregarding the possible publicity or even political consequences, Bernard told the Commander of the Afrika Korps he wished him to dine in his headquarters mess that evening, before going into captivity. In his diary Bernard noted:

> 2000 General VON THOMA, the Commander Africa Corps, was a prisoner at my HQ and he dined with me in my mess. He is a very nice chap and was quite willing to talk about past events. We discussed the battle in Sept. when ROMMEL attacked me, and we discussed this present battle.
>
> I doubt if many Generals have had the luck to be able to discuss with their opponent the battle that has just been fought.

More than any other episode during the battle, this image of the 8th Army Commander on the evening of possibly the most historic British victory of World War Two is perhaps the most revealing. While Churchill sought Brooke's approval for ringing the church bells of Britain and frantically despatched telegram after telegram to the heads of state of the Allied Nations – to Roosevelt, Stalin, Fraser, Curtin and others – Lt-General Bernard Montgomery sat beneath the camouflaged canvas of his mess-tent and, as soon as the meal was over, had the table cleared and a map of the Egyptian desert produced.

'Now, tonight my forces are approaching Fuka – what do you think about that? Come on, what would *you* do, von Thoma?'

[1] Allied casualties amounted to 13,560. Of these 8875 were sustained by 30 Corps (9th Australian Division 2827; 51st Highland Division 2495; 2nd New Zealand Division 2388; 1st South African Division 922; other units 223), while 10 Corps suffered a total of 2886 casualties. The file CAB 106/792 (notebooks of the official War Historian) relating to 4 November 1942, PRO et sequ.

Bernard harangued his 'luckless opponent, who'd had a pretty harassing afternoon', as General Oswald recalled.[1] But von Thoma would give nothing away.

He said: '*Sehr kritisch, wirklich sehr kritisch* –'
Monty was leading him on a bit, I'm afraid, for we weren't half as far forward as that, we hadn't even got to Galal, but anyway . . .[2]

Four days later, when informed that three Italian generals would be joining him in captivity, von Thoma 'asked that they should not be put in his compound, and if they were, a barbed wire fence to be put between them', Alexander cabled with amusement to Churchill;[3] but, for the 8th Army Commander who had dined him on the night of 4 November, von Thoma maintained a lasting admiration. 'I thought he was very cautious considering his immensely superior strength,' he declared after the war was over, 'but he is the only Field-Marshal in this war who won all his battles.

'In modern mobile warfare, the tactics are not the main thing. The decisive factor is the organisation of one's resources – to maintain momentum.'[4] Montgomery had done just that, despite all the vicissitudes of battle.

At 9.30 p.m. on 4 November 1942 Bernard retired to his caravan. There were still many thousands of miles of campaigning to go before he would be made a Field-Marshal, but he had won his first major offensive battle as an Army Commander and given the peoples of the Allied world the victory they had longed for.

[1] Ibid.
[2] Ibid.
[3] Telegrams, Cabinet Papers (CAB 105–19), PRO.
[4] Barton Maughan, *Tobruk and El Alamein*, 1966.

Sources and Bibliography

The Montgomery Papers

Since this biography is founded on the Private Papers of Field-Marshal Viscount Montgomery of Alamein, which are the property of the Thomson Organisation, a brief background to their acquisition and content may be of interest to the reader.

When Field-Marshal Montgomery was in hospital in the autumn of 1962 he summoned his friend and literary adviser, Denis Hamilton (then Editor of the *Sunday Times* and Editorial Director of Thomson Newspapers), to King Edward VII Hospital for Officers in London. Although not seriously ill, Montgomery insisted that the moment had come to appoint someone who would take responsibility for all his wartime and post-war papers. When Montgomery returned from hospital to his home in Hampshire he set out his proposal in characteristically clear wording:

Private

Isington Mill
ALTON
Hants
8 September 1962

My dear C.D.

You will remember that when in hospital I raised with you the question that Thomson Newspapers should acquire the diaries and private papers of my military life.

These begin on the day I arrived in Cairo to take command of the Eighth Army (12 August 1942), and continue up to September 1958 when I withdrew from active employment in the British Army. They are in definite sections.

1. Campaign from Alamein to Tunis.
2. Campaign in Sicily.
3. Campaign in Italy.
4. Preparations and planning for the campaign in North-West Europe.
5. Campaign in North-West Europe.
6. Post-war diaries beginning on 1 May 1946 and up to September 1958. These include my time as CIGS, as Chairman of the Western Union Defence set-up, and as Deputy Supreme Allied Commander in Europe. In all – 44 volumes.

The diaries tell the whole inside story of what went on in the conduct of the war, and give my personal correspondence with Alanbrooke – copies of my letters to him, and his letters to me all in his own handwriting.

What went on in Whitehall after the war, and in the Western Union, and in

NATO, is almost unbelievable. It is all recorded in the post-war 44 volumes.

In addition to the diaries themselves, there is a great deal of personal correspondence with various high personalities.

I imagine that when I am dead, somebody will want to write the full story of my military life in high command. It would be impossible to do this without possession of my diaries and private papers.

I offer them to you in complete confidence that all will be well.

I would have to have absolute right of veto on anything published in my lifetime. After that, you could do as you liked. There would have to be a legal document setting this out, and recording the sale.

I suggest you should come here and examine what I have to offer. You could get a very good idea fairly quickly, sufficient for you to decide if you want to acquire the diaries and papers. I think you would need a day, and a night – by yourself in my top flat.

Would you care to suggest a date when you could come?

Yours ever
Montgomery of Alamein

In the autumn of 1962 Field-Marshal Montgomery continued to press his friend; and finally on 6 December 1952 an agreement was made, whereby the existence of the papers would be kept secret during Montgomery's lifetime, and only afterwards be used as the basis of an official biography.

In the following years Field-Marshal Montgomery continued to send additions to the private papers. In particular he bound up and annotated all his surviving letters to his mother and father during World War One; he also collected much pre-1942 material, including training notes from the time of his command of 9th Infantry Brigade and 3rd Division – including his handwritten diary of the Dunkirk campaign.

These papers are of historic importance and will ultimately be preserved in one of the major national archives, together with the tape-recorded interviews and research material relating to this biography. Further collections of letters have been acquired for the archive as well as photographs. Copyright is reserved and remains with the Thomson Organisation at the personal discretion of Sir Denis Hamilton. The copyright of all writings by Field-Marshal Montgomery *outside* the Private Papers rests with his son David, the second Viscount Montgomery of Alamein.

Further unpublished sources

Although this biography is based primarily upon the Private Papers of Field-Marshal Montgomery, I have been privileged to be given access to many other private and public collections of unpublished documents. Copyright in anything written by Field-Marshal Montgomery among these papers lies with the present Viscount Montgomery; permission to see the material rests naturally with the respective owners, to whom I am most grateful.

The private collections I have used are as follows:

The papers of Lt-Colonel and Mrs John Carver (including Montgomery correspondence, letters of Betty Montgomery, etc.); of Colonel Richard Carver (including Montgomery correspondence); of Lt-Colonel C. P. ('Kit')

Dawnay (including Montgomery correspondence from 1940); of the late Major-General Sir Francis de Guingand (including Montgomery correspondence from 1934, now deposited with the Montgomery Papers); of Lt-General Sir Ian Jacob (including his diary account of Churchill's visit to Egypt in August 1942); the private papers of General Sir Oliver Leese, in the possession of Mrs Frances Denby (Montgomery correspondence, Sir Oliver Leese's unpublished memoirs, etc.); of Lady Winsome Michelmore (Montgomery correspondence and scrapbooks); of Major-General M. St. J. Oswald (including his diary of 8th Army desert campaign 1942–43); of the late Major Tom Reynolds (including Montgomery correspondence with his father and mother from 1942, now deposited with the Montgomery Papers); of General Sir Frank ('Simbo') Simpson (including Montgomery correspondence from 1942); of Brigadier H. R. W. Vernon (including his handwritten diary of the planning for Alamein, and a day-by-day account of the battle); of Major-General Douglas Wimberley (accounts of his association with Montgomery and a personal chronicle of the battle of Alamein).

The institutional collections I have used are:

The Imperial War Museum, Lambeth: The Percival Papers (by permission of Lt-Colonel A. J. MacG. Percival); the papers of Sir Peter Strickland; the German War Diaries.

Ministry of Defence: Personal files of Field-Marshal Montgomery, including medical records, correspondence regarding promotion, etc.

The Public Record Office, Kew: Unit war diaries, War Cabinet Papers, and other Government papers.

The Royal Military Academy, Sandhurst: Admission and passing-out records, log-books, etc.

The Royal Warwickshire Regimental Museum, Warwick: Regimental war diaries, regimental records and journal the *Antelope*, Montgomery correspondence, etc.

The Staff College, Camberley.

Published Sources

ALEXANDER, H., *The Alexander Memoirs*, (London 1962)
AMBROSE, S. E., *The Supreme Commander*, (New York 1970)

BARNETT, C., *The Swordbearers*, (London 1963)
— *The Desert Generals*, (London 1960)
— *El Alamein: Decision in the Desert*, (New York 1964)
BARRY, T., *Guerilla Days in Ireland*, (Dublin 1949 and Tralee 1962)
BELCHEM, R. F. K., *All in the Day's March*, (London 1978)
BLUMENSON, M., *The Patton Papers*, (Boston 1972)
BOND, B. (ED.), *Chief-of-Staff*, (London 1972)
— *Liddell-Hart: A Study of his Military Thought*, (London 1977)
— *British Military Policy Between The Two World Wars*, (London 1980)
BRERETON, L. H., *The Brereton Diaries*, (New York 1946)
BRYANT, A., *The Turn of the Tide*, (London 1957)
BUTLER, E., *Barry's Flying Column*, (London 1971)

CARVER, R. M. P., *Harding of Petherton*, (London 1978)
— *Second to None*, (Glasgow 1954)
— *El Alamein*, (London 1962)

CASEY, R., *Personal Experience: 1939–46*, (London 1962)
CHALFONT, A., *Montgomery of Alamein*, (London 1976)
CHANDLER, A. D. (ED.), *The Papers of Dwight David Eisenhower*, (Baltimore 1970)
CHURCHILL, W. S., *The Hinge of Fate*, (London 1951)
— *Their Finest Hour*, (London 1949)
CLARK, R. W., *Montgomery of Alamein*, (London 1960)
COLLIER, B., *The Defence of the United Kingdom*, (London 1957)
COLLINS, R. J., *Lord Wavell*, (London 1947)
COLVILLE, J. R., *Man of Valour*, (London 1972)
CONNELL, J., *Auchinleck*, (London 1959)
— *Wavell*, (London 1964)
COWLES, V., *The Phantom Major*, (London 1958)
CRIMP, R. L., *The Diary of a Desert Rat*, (London 1971)
CRUICKSHANK, C., *Deception in World War II*, (London 1979)
CUNLIFFE, M., *The Royal Warwickshire Regiment 1919–1955*, (London 1956)

DEIGHTON, L., *Blitzkrieg*, (London 1979)
DOUGLAS, K., *Alamein to Zem Zem*, (London 1946 and 1979)

EDMONDS, J. E. (ED.), *Military Operations in France and Belgium: 1914, 1915, 1916, 1917, 1918 (Official History of the First World War)*, (London 1928–1950)
ELLIS, L. F., *The War in France and Flanders*, (London 1953)
ENSER, A. G. S., *A subject bibliography of the Second World War, Books in English 1939–1974*, (London 1977)

FARRAR, R., *The Life of Frederic William Farrar*, (London 1904)
FARRAR-HOCKLEY, A., *The War in the Desert*, (London 1969)
FLEMING, P., *Invasion 1940*, (London 1957)

GALLAGHER, F., *The Anglo-Irish Treaty*, (London 1965)
GRIGG, P. J., *Prejudice and Judgment*, (London 1948)
GUINGAND, F. DE, *Operation Victory*, (London 1947)
— *Generals at War*, (London 1964)
— *From Brass Hat to Bowler Hat*, (London 1979)

HACHEY, T. E., *Britain and Irish separatism*, (Chicago 1977)
HARMAN, N., *Dunkirk, The Necessary Myth*, (London 1980)
HILLSON, N., *Alexander of Tunis*, (London 1952)
HINSLEY, F. H., *British Intelligence in the Second World War*, Vol. 2, (London 1981)
HOPKINS, H. L., *The White House Papers*, (London 1949)
HORNE, A., *To Lose a Battle*, (London 1969)
HORROCKS, B., *A Full Life*, (London 1960)
— *Corps Commander*, (London 1977)
HOUGH, R., *Mountbatten: Hero of our Time*, (London 1980)
HUNT, D., *A Don at War*, (London 1966)

IRVING, D., *Hitler's War*, (London 1977)
— *The Trail of the Fox*, (London 1977)
ISMAY, H. L., *Memoirs*, (London 1960)

JACKSON, W. G. F., *The Battle for North Africa 1940–43*, (London 1975)
— *Alexander of Tunis as Military Commander*, (London 1971)
JEWELL, D. (ED.), *Alamein and the Desert War*, (London 1967)
JOLY, C., *Take these Men*, (London 1955)

KEE, R., *The Green Flag*, (London 1972)
KEEGAN, J., *Encyclopaedia of World War II*, (London 1977)
KENNEDY, J., *The Business of War*, (London 1957)
KESSELRING, *The Memoirs of Field-Marshal Kesselring*, (London 1953)
KINGSFORD, C. L., *The Story of the Royal Warwickshire Regiment*, (London 1921)
KIPPENBERGER, H., *Infantry Brigadier*, (London 1949)
KÜHN, V., *Mit Rommel in der Wüste*, (Stuttgart 1977)
— *German Paratroops in World War II*, (London 1978)

LEWIN, R.,
— *Montgomery as Military Commander*, (London 1971)
— *Slim: The Standardbearer*, (London 1976)
— *The Life and Death of the Afrika Korps*, (London 1977)
— *Ultra goes to War*, (London 1978)
— *The Chief*, (London 1980)
LIDDELL HART, B. H., *The Tanks*, (London 1959)
— *History of the Second World War*, (London 1970)
— *History of the First World War*, (London 1970)
— *Memoirs*, (London 1965)
— *The Other Side of the Hill*, (London 1973)
— (ED.), *The Rommel Papers*, (London 1953)
LOVAT, *March Past*, (London 1978)

MACKSEY, K., *Kesselring: The Making of the Luftwaffe*, (New York 1978)
— *Armoured Crusader*, (London 1967)
MACLEOD, R. AND KELLY, D., *The Ironside Diaries*, (London 1972)
MCNISH, R., *Iron Division: The History of the 3rd Division*, (London 1978)
MAJDALANY, F., *The Battle of El Alamein*, (London 1965)
MARTEL, G., *An Outspoken Soldier*, (London 1949)
MAUGHAN, R., *Tobruk and El Alamein*, (Canberra, Australia 1966)
MAYER, S. L. AND KOENIG, W. J., *The Two World Wars*, (London 1976)
  (A guide to manuscript collections in the UK)
MELLENTHIN, W. VON, *Panzer Battles 1939–1945*, (London 1955)
MONTGOMERY, B., *A Field-Marshal in the Family*, (London 1973)
MONTGOMERY, B. L., *The Memoirs of Field-Marshal the Viscount Montgomery of Alamein*, (London 1958)
— *El Alamein to the River Sangro*, (London 1948)
— *A History of Warfare*, (London 1968)
— *The Path to Leadership*, (London 1961)
MONTGOMERY, H., *A Generation of Montgomerys*, (Privately published 1892)
MONTGOMERY, M., *I Remember, I Remember*, (Belfast 1945)
— *Bishop Montgomery*, (London 1933)
MOOREHEAD, A., *Montgomery*, (London 1946)
— *A Year of Battle*, (London 1943)
MORAN, *Winston Churchill: The Struggle for Survival*, (London 1966)
MORDAL, J., *Dieppe: The Dawn of Decision*, (London 1963)
MORGAN, F., *Peace and War*, (London 1961)

MUSGRAVE, V., *Montgomery in Pictures*, (London 1947)

NEESON, E., *The Civil War in Ireland*, (Cork, Ireland 1966)
NICOLSON, N., *Alex*, (London 1973)

O'CONNOR, U., *A Terrible Beauty is Born: The Irish Troubles 1912–1922*, (London 1975)
OWEN, R., *The Desert Air Force*, (London 1948)

PARKINSON, R., *The Auk, Victor at Alamein*, (London 1977)
— *Blood, Toil, Tears and Sweat*, (London 1973)
PEACOCK, LADY, *Field-Marshal Viscount Montgomery: His Life*, (London 1951)
PENIAKOFF, V., *Private Army*, (London 1950)
PHILLIPS, C. E. L., *Alamein*, (London 1962)
PILE, F., *Ack-ack*, (London 1949)
PLAYFAIR, I. S. O., *The Mediterranean and Middle East, Vol. III*, (London 1960)
PLAYFAIR, I. S. O. AND MOLONY, C. J. G., *The Mediterranean and Middle East, Vol. IV*, (London 1966)
PUBLIC RECORD OFFICE, *The Second World War: A Guide to Documents in the Public Record Office*, (London 1972)
PYMAN, H., *Call to Arms*, (London 1971)

REES, G., *A Bundle of Sensations*, (London 1960)
ROMMEL, E., *Attacks*, (Vienna, Virginia, USA 1979)

SCHMIDT, H. W., *With Rommel in the Desert*, (London 1951)
SCHOENFELD, M. P., *The War Ministry of Winston Churchill*, (Ames, Iowa, USA 1972)
SCOULLAR, J. L., *Battle for Egypt*, (Wellington, NZ and London 1955)
SEARS, S. W., *Desert War in North Africa*, (New York 1967)
SIXSMITH, E., *British Generalship in the 20th Century*, (London 1970)
— *Eisenhower as Military Commander*, (London 1973)
SLIM, W., *Defeat into Victory*, (London 1956)
STACEY, C. P., *Six Years of War*, (Ottawa, Canada 1955)

TAYLOR, A. J. P., *English History 1914–1945*, (London 1965)
TEDDER, A., *With Prejudice*, (London 1966)
TERRAINE, J., *The Western Front 1914–1918*, (London 1964)
— *To Win a War, 1918*, (London 1978)
— *The Life and Times of Lord Mountbatten*, (London 1968)
THOMPSON, R. W., *The Montgomery Legend*, (London 1967)
— *Dieppe at Dawn*, (London 1956)
TOBLER, D. H., *Intelligence in the Desert*, (Victoria, Canada 1978)
TOWNSHEND, C., *The British Campaign in Ireland 1919–1921*, (London 1975)
TUKER, F., *Approach to Battle*, (London 1963)
TURNBULL, P., *Dunkirk, Anatomy of Disaster*, (London 1978)

WALKER, R., *Alam Halfa and Alamein*, (Wellington, NZ 1967)
WESTPHAL, S., *The German Army in the West*, (London 1951)
WHEELER-BENNETT, J. (ED.), *Action this Day*, (London 1969)
WILLIAMSON, H., *The Fourth Division 1939 to 1945*, (London 1951)

Willkie, W., *One World*, (London 1943)
Winterbotham, F. W., *The Ultra Secret*, (London 1974)

Young, D., *Rommel*, (London 1950)
Younger, C., *Ireland's Civil War*, (London 1968)

List of Abbreviations

AA	Assistant Adjutant
ADC	Aide-de-Camp
AFV	Armoured Fighting Vehicle
ALG	Advanced Landing Ground
AOC	Air Officer Commanding
ASC	Air Support Control
AT	Anti-Tank
ATS	Auxiliary Territorial Service
Bde	Brigade
BEF	British Expeditionary Force
BGS	Brigadier General Staff
BM	Brigade-Major
BRA	Brigadier, Royal Artillery
CB	Companion of the Order of the Bath
CCRA	Commander Corps Royal Artillery
CE	Chief Engineer
CGS	Chief of the General Staff
CIGS	Chief of the Imperial General Staff
C-in-C	Commander-in-Chief
CO	Commanding Officer
COS	Chiefs-of-Staff
CRA	Commander, Royal Artillery
CRASC	Commander, Royal Army Service Corps
CRE	Commander, Royal Engineers
CSO	Chief Signals Officer
DAQMG	Deputy Adjutant & Quartermaster-General
DAK	Deutsche Afrika Korps
DCGS	Deputy Chief of the General Staff
DCOS	Deputy Chief-of-Staff
DDST	Deputy Director Staff & Training
DF	Direction Finding
DFM	Distinguished Flying Medal
DMI	Director of Military Intelligence
DMO	Director of Military Operations
DR	Despatch Rider
DSO	Distinguished Service Order

FDL	Forward Defence Locality
FOO	Forward Observation Officer
GHQ	General Headquarters
GOC	General Officer Commanding
GOC-in-C	General Officer Commanding-in-Chief
GS	General Staff
GSO 1, *etc.*	General Staff Officer, First Grade, *etc.*
HE	High Explosive
I	Intelligence
i/c	In command
ICS	Indian Civil Service
IRA	Irish Republican Army
KCMG	Knight Commander of St Michael and St George
KOSB	King's Own Scottish Borderers
LG	Lewis Gun
MA	Military Attaché
MC	Military Cross
MG	Machine-Gun
MMG	Medium Machine-Gun
MS	Military Secretary
MT (*also* MET)	Motor Transport
Mx	Middlesex
NCO	Non-Commissioned Officer
OC	Officer Commanding
OKW	Oberkommando der Wehrmacht (German Armed Forces High Command)
OP	Observation Post
OR	Other Rank
OTC	Officers' Training Corps
QMG	Quartermaster-General
RA	Royal Artillery
RAC	Royal Armoured Corps
RAF	Royal Air Force
RAMC	Royal Army Medical Corps
RAP	Regimental Aid Post
RASC	Royal Army Service Corps
RE	Royal Engineers
RFC	Royal Flying Corps
RHA	Royal Horse Artillery
RMA	Royal Military Academy
RSM	Regimental Sergeant-Major
R/T	Radio Telephone

RTC	Royal Tank Corps
SA	South African *or* Small Arms
SAS	Special Air Service
SHAEF	Supreme Headquarters Allied Expeditionary Force
SO	Signals Officer
SOS	Emergency Call for Help
SPG	Society for the Propagation of the Gospel
TA	Territorial Army
USAAF	United States of America Air Force
VC	Victoria Cross
VCIGS	Vice Chief of the Imperial General Staff
VTM	Vehicles per Mile
WO	War Office; *also* Warrant Officer
W/T	Wireless Telegraphy
Y service	Monitoring of Enemy Radio Signals

Index

811

819

820

825